ASPECTS OF TOURISM 16
Series Editors: Chris Cooper (*University of Queensland, Australia*),
C. Michael Hall (*University of Otago, New Zealand*)
and Dallen Timothy (*Arizona State University, USA*)

Strategic Management for Tourism Communities
Bridging the Gaps

Peter E. Murphy and Ann E. Murphy

CHANNEL VIEW PUBLICATIONS
Clevedon • Buffalo • Toronto

We wish to dedicate this book to
Susan and Margaret Murphy,
the two family members
working hard behind the scenes

Library of Congress Cataloging in Publication Data
Murphy, Peter E.
Strategic Management for Tourism Communities: Bridging the Gaps
Peter E. Murphy and Ann E. Murphy.
Aspects of Tourism: 16
Includes bibliographical references
1. Tourism–Management. 2. Strategic planning. I. Murphy, Ann E. II. Title. III. Series.
G155.A1M859 2004
910'.68'4–dc22   2004002644

British Library Cataloguing in Publication Data
A catalogue entry for this book is available from the British Library.

ISBN 1-873150-84-9 (hbk)
ISBN 1-873150-83-0 (pbk)

Channel View Publications
An imprint of Multilingual Matters Ltd

UK: Frankfurt Lodge, Clevedon Hall, Victoria Road, Clevedon BS21 7HH.
USA: 2250 Military Road, Tonawanda, NY 14150, USA.
Canada: 5201 Dufferin Street, North York, Ontario, Canada M3H 5T8.

Typeset by Archetype-IT Ltd (http://www.archetype-it.com).
Printed and bound in Great Britain by the Cromwell Press.

Contents

Acknowledgements

This book has taken several years to come to fruition and along the way there has been a collection of special people who have helped us put our facts and ideas together. We would like to acknowledge the growing and thoughtful literature provided by our peers in a variety of disciplines and the assistance of Ms Yan Zhang in accessing that material. We would like to thank our partners in the development of the four cases – Paul Miller, Wayne Kayler-Thomson, Theresa Szymanis and Robin Saunders. Their contributions have provided the real examples to flesh out our skeleton of ideas and observations.

In our various travels and work experiences we have been fortunate to come across many industry and government contributors committed to making tourism work for the industry and the host community. Among those who have been particularly helpful and inspirational are Rick Lemon, John Parker, Melissa McLean and Lorne Whyte in British Columbia. On the Florida Keys, particular thanks are due to the Monroe County Marathon City Council, Frank Greenman, the Board of County Commissioners, Shirley Freeman, and dedicated community advocates, especially Betty Vale. In Victoria, Australia, the helpful ideas and comments from Nicholas Hunt, Kathryn MacKenzie, David Riley and Tom O'Toole are appreciated.

Last, and by no means least, we wish to thank Glennis Derrick and the reviewers of the draft text. Glennis has been a wonderful person to work with in the preparation of this manuscript, transforming our scrawl and continuous changes into the document it is today. The two reviewers of the original draft provided much encouragement and some invaluable references. Plus we would like to thank the authors who have allowed us to reproduce their work and illustrations as cited individually.

With this significant academic and practitioner input it is hoped we have created a thoughtful and useful work. If there are any mistakes of fact or misinterpretations they remain the responsibility of the authors alone.

Part 1

Prologue

Setting the Scene

Many communities are entering the global tourism market in a naive and dangerous manner. One danger is to misread the market and the community's true competitive position within that market, leading to disappointing development results and financial losses. Another danger occurs when communities are successful with their development plans, and become a recognised destination but fail to appreciate the changes that tourism can bring. These changes can result in a form of community that may not have been foreseen or even wanted by local residents. While much has been made of tourism problems, little has been written about practical and widely applicable techniques that communities can use to develop tourism offerings that meet the needs of both tourists and residents.

This book takes a business and community approach to assessing and offering guidance on strategic tourism management. This dual approach is based on assessing the economic feasibility of pursuing tourism options that further community goals and objectives. Tourism is a business that requires extensive planning, marketing and investment in products and services. At the same time tourism relies on the host communities in which it occurs. The attitudes of local people, the quality of the environment and the availability of desired products and services are all factors in whether tourism will be a success. Without a solid understanding of the business and community aspects of tourism, resources can be squandered on inappropriate tourism developments that fail to meet the expectations of either the host community or the tourists.

Background

'Those who ignore history are doomed to repeat it,' is the message from researchers who warn of the negative impacts of tourism. In his book *Devil's Bargains* Rothman (1998) relates the disappointment experienced by many small and rural communities in the western reaches of the United States during the twentieth century. He notes that tourism often turned into a 'devil's bargain' for many of the regions and communities that embraced the industry as an economic boon. The tourism problems arose from the 'irrevocable changes' that occurred in 'unanticipated and uncontrollable ways' (Rothman, 1998: 10). He notes that 'community leaders make

3

imperfect choices based on insufficient information without recognising the consequences . . . The economist's fallacious dream of rational choice based on perfect information collapses as unanticipated consequences overwhelm expectations in tourist communities' (Rothman, 1998: 17). Like many before him Rothman finds tourism lacking, especially with regard to its promise of economic salvation, yet offers no solutions.

Tourism development 'solutions' in terms of practical advice derived from real world situations are what can help communities to decide what type of development works best for them. Tourism, like other resource industries, alters the landscape and social fabric of destination areas, while much of its development pace and direction are guided by broader global forces. Tourism, with its high visibility, is often seen as the primary cause of change rather than as one of many agents. However, the tourism industry is just a small part of larger global forces that are transforming the world's economic, environmental and societal relations. The combined impacts of the growth in the influence of international economic unions and multimedia organisations, changes in population patterns, environmental degradation, shifting political allegiances, terrorism and evolving cultural practices are all agents of profound global change.

As Brown (1998: 49) observes, 'unless we are prepared to sit back and literally do nothing, we have to expect that everything we do will have some effect on the environment'. The ability to guide the development of tourism in a manner that meets communities' needs is dependent upon understanding the factors intrinsically tied to this industry and then directing tourism development in a manner that promotes desired end-states, while mitigating less desirable impacts. Communities that are prepared to learn from the history and experiences of the tourism industry are better suited to adopt management plans that meet their needs.

On the whole tourism has been a successful growth industry since the end of World War II and holds much promise for the future. The key to successful and sustainable tourism development is to engage in this activity with as much careful analysis and planning as possible. Due diligence is also required in terms of monitoring industry progress and making appropriate adjustments to ensure that it is managed in a manner that meets stakeholder requirements.

Tourism Expectations

So much has been expected of tourism that it has often fallen short of the mark. Part of the problem has been its exaggerated role as an economic and social panacea with associated unrealistic expectations in many communities. Community enthusiasm or desperation can override economic realities when considering an area's tourism potential. Business issues relating to tourism supply and demand, accessibility and financing options all need to be considered in combination with community needs and available resources.

Another factor is that tourism is a more complex industry than many appreciate, since it crosses the traditional divisions of primary through to quaternary industries. Tourism's natural attractions can be equated with other primary industries in that they all are dependant on natural resources. Tourism's resort development and associated infrastructure are developed along the manufacturing lines of secondary industries. As a major service industry, tourism depends on varied customer segments each with their specific experience expectations. Tourism's global scale and need for detailed destination and travel information has resulted in its gaining a prominent place on the Internet and in other quaternary information businesses.

Part of the problem in developing realistic tourism expectations has been the limited focus of past research. Tourism researchers have restricted themselves in the main to engaging in critical analysis of the industry and its impacts rather than taking the next progressive step to prescriptive recommendations. In this regard the comments of Buck (1977) and Brown (1998) are very germane. Buck, an anthropologist, was critical of fellow social scientists for simply criticising the industry's efforts to represent culture rather than showing it how to produce more authentic and educational experiences. Brown, the past editor of *Tourism Management*, rightly states that, 'the proponents of alternative tourism have been better at highlighting the negative side of tourism than at providing cures' (Brown, 1998: 100).

Purpose

The purpose of this book is to provide strategic management guidance from a wide range of researchers and practitioners to assist communities in meeting their tourism expectations. Source material is drawn from the fields of social science, planning, business studies and environmental management. The book should be viewed as a sequel to Peter Murphy's book, *Tourism: A Community Approach*. That first book, which was published in 1985, has been described by some as a seminal work (Wheeler, 1994). This book builds on the multi-dimensional aspects promoted in the first book, while providing more of a business-oriented framework. It also builds on the community involvement principles that were presented in the first book. Collaborative decision-making processes are presented as an integral and practical way to ensure that stakeholders guide and evaluate the tourism plans and strategies to ensure their goals and objectives as well as those of the larger community are met. This new focus reflects the experiences of the authors since the original book was published. We believe that communities are better positioned to take the prescribed 'community approach' to tourism if they allow their actions to be guided by key business management principles and adopt a strategic management focus.

Professor Peter Murphy has over 25 years' experience as a tourism researcher, professor and consultant. He has served on several tourism boards, including Tourism Victoria in BC, Canada and Bendigo Tourism in Victoria, Australia, and been involved in a range of practical tourism studies, most notably the Visitor Surveys conducted via Tourism Victoria from 1989 to 1997. Professor Murphy has received many distinguished awards including the following: Association of American Geographers; Roy Wolfe Award for contributions to Tourism Research (1992); elected to the International Academy for the Study of Tourism (1995); and granted the Rino and Diana Grollo Endowed Chair on Tourism and Hospitality at La Trobe University (1997) in Melbourne.

In 1990, Professor Peter Murphy transferred from his long-standing association with Geography to a Faculty of Business to continue his research and teaching in tourism management. There he found many business principles and techniques relevant to resident and social science aspirations for community participation in tourism. As a result of his increased work with business entrepreneurs and tourism organisations he has found a willingness by these groups to work with the broader community, to achieve the type of community and quality of life that can be enjoyed by all.

In addition to representing an extension of academic thought, this book benefits from the views and experiences of an additional author – Ann Murphy, AICP. During Ann's career as a professional planner, she has worked for public and private firms in Canada, the US and Australia. Most of her tourism planning work has been conducted in British Columbia, Canada and the Florida Keys, in the United States. While working in the Florida Keys she initiated and oversaw the first ever Keys-wide survey of resident attitudes towards tourism. She is currently working on a PhD in Law at the University of Melbourne that explores ways in which Alternative Dispute Resolution techniques can be used to create solutions for community land use planning issues. She is committed to finding ways in which communities can survive and prosper as social units while engaging in a range of commercial endeavours, such as tourism, that enable them to meet their goals and objectives.

In this book, tourism is viewed from a business perspective and within that framework advocates a community development and strategic management approach. To achieve this objective it examines the multidimensional nature of tourism and its significant economic, social and environmental impacts, while emphasising certain features over others. These features start from the premise that tourism is a business, and to properly understand a community's tourism prospects, impacts and responsibilities the whole activity must be analysed in a business context.

To do this we will examine how broad business principles can be, and in some cases have been, applied to the development and management of tourism. The ways that modern business science overlaps with the social science's interest in tourism and its development issues will be demonstrated in the process.

To make the best of the situation where more communities are becoming involved with tourism, either willingly or unwillingly, requires a particular type of tourism development and planning. With respect to the emerging tourism community, it reflects a strong sense of belonging together and wanting to preserve and enhance the home territory. Such feelings are synonymous with smaller sized communities and could be equated with localised destination areas. The tourism within these communities is likely to include a combination of international tourists, domestic tourists and excursionists. Ideally an area's tourism industry is a mixture of direct, indirect and induced businesses, with the actual combination determined by the size, resources and aspirations of the host community and its travel markets.

Hence this book defines strategic tourism management at the community level as follows:

> Tourism activity that engages local community interests in a meaningful partnership with the tourism industry to construct a destination product that is appropriate from a local business, societal and environmental perspective.

This definition recognises that if a community is to become a successful destination within the competitive global marketplace it needs to enter a business partnership with the industry. Therefore each party brings to the table their own assets and priorities to see if there is a mutual and sustainable business opportunity. If it is felt that such an opportunity exists then the community and local industry could proceed together along established business lines muted with societal and environmental awareness and obligations. Community tourism is moving toward the positions of mutually beneficial partnerships and balanced tourism development. The outlook for these positions is shown to be promising in emerging research and practices. However, these sources also reveal that it will take a great deal of understanding, resources and cooperative efforts to build and sustain robust community tourism initiatives. To assist in this process the book starts with an assessment of present-day community tourism analysis and its relationship to general business management principles.

The primary audience for this book is serious students of tourism strategic planning. This would include senior undergraduate and postgraduate students taking topics related to strategic tourism management and community tourism. It is anticipated that professionals working in tourism planning, government agencies and community activists will also find this book a useful reference tool for understanding and managing tourism impacts.

Structure

Part 1

The opening part of the book sets the scene for the later more prescriptive emphasis found in subsequent sections. The Prologue introduces the concept of community tourism and the need to develop and adhere to prescriptive management strategies to realise its potential. Chapter 1 examines key definitions and theories used in community tourism and illustrates their relevance to developing broad-based tourism development. The second chapter of this part, Chapter 2, outlines the four basic functions of business management and their relevance to the study and development of strategic tourism management in host communities.

Part 2

The second part is structured around the four functions of business management: planning, organising, leadership and controlling. Chapter 3 examines the need for planning and how communities can benefit from adopting a business and community approach to developing mutual goals and objectives for their development aspirations. Such a process will encourage community residents to come together and express their particular interests and should provide an early indication as to whether local tourism development can be a part of such objectives. Chapter 4 describes how business sets about organising its resources to produce its product and suggests similar techniques are needed in strategic tourism planning. Strategic community tourism will need to consider organising multiple interests, resources and factions to deliver products that are acceptable to markets and residents alike.

Chapter 5 examines the important element of leadership in business management and tourism development. Business research has found leadership to be a vital catalyst to success and describes the qualities and context that encourage its formation. Leadership has become a major issue in community tourism, given the need to coordinate different stakeholder aspirations within a fragmented and complex industry. As with business in general, many tourism success stories can be attributed to the presence of a local leader and often exhibit themselves in the concept of entrepreneurship. So this chapter goes on to examine the qualities of entrepreneurship and how they can assist in moving from ideas to realities. Chapter 6, completes the review of business principles with an examination of the need to control business processes and outputs in order to meet organisational goals. For strategic community tourism management this requires a blending of business control principles with the administrative responsibilities regarding the management of public resources, so the two are mutually supportive.

Part 3

The third part examines how major stakeholder groups can be expected to play their roles with respect to the four business functions. The term 'stakeholders' refers to individuals, groups or organisations with a shared interest in an issue or problem. Few communities are homogeneous in their membership or aspirations, so a key feature of strategic community tourism management is how to access and integrate these varying perspectives into a community plan. The traditional division of community stakeholder groups is supply driven, in that it includes the host community's constituents of residents, industry and government. The principal focus from a business perspective is meeting the expectations and demands of the customer. To realise the tourism potential and development appropriate for a community it is essential to look at both the demand and supply side of the equation in terms of affected parties and developmental practices. Hence this book offers information and observations on the following four stakeholder groups: customers, industry, residents and government.

Chapter 7 examines customers' perspective on community tourism based on the four business functions. The choice of the title 'customer' rather than 'tourist' is deliberate in that it involves an analysis of both tourist and resident demands. This involves reviewing traditional marketing mix information and the evolving post-modernism research implications of increased market segmentation and micromarketing. Chapter 8 turns the spotlight on the industry and starts by examining the general relevance of a select number of business strategies and techniques to community tourism. As small and medium-sized businesses make up 80–90% of the industry, attention is focused on small business development and the crucial role of the entrepreneur in this process.

Chapter 9 investigates the roles of residents and the contributions they can make to this community industry. It examines what is meant by 'meaningful participation', the type of person who is willing and able to participate in joint ventures and how such participation can be facilitated. Chapter 10 describes how government and non-government organisations (NGOs) influence and are influenced by the previously identified business principles. It discusses the growing roles of partnership and facilitation.

Part 4

The final part proposes a community tourism strategic management framework that combines business principles with the needs and views of the four stakeholder groups. Chapter 11 examines aspects of group decision-making from a conflict resolution perspective. This chapter details issues of conflict, challenges with traditional decision-making processes and ways that Alternative Dispute Resolution methods, including collaborative decision making, can be used in a tourism planning context. Chapter 12 examines the applicability of gap analysis methods to tourism planning and pulls together the concepts and practices discussed earlier in the book to present a new model – bridging community tourism gaps.

Summary

The contribution of this book to the field of tourism study is the integration of established business practices and principles with current community tourism needs and processes. To date much of the research on tourism has focused on highlighting shortcomings and problems with the industry, with a handful of best practice cases. This book offers widely applicable prescriptive measures for managing tourism within its primary setting, the destination community. It is intended as a tool to empower people to make the strategic tourism management decisions that are right for them and their communities.

Chapter 1

Definitions, Theory and Practice

Tourism Definitions and Data

Tourism as the world's largest business is a complex system of integrated parts, and each dimension receives attention at different times and locations, depending on the specific purpose and interest of the study at hand. In a recent review of tourism development in Australia, Richardson (1999: 144) states 'somewhere along the way travel and tourism (have) become the world's biggest business'. He cites a World Tourism Organisation publication as an authority on the subject:

> Tourism is now the largest industry in the world by virtually any economic measure, including gross output, value added, employment, capital investment and tax contributions. (Wheatcroft, 1994)

Others have made increasing reference to the calculations and estimates emerging from the World Travel and Tourism Council (WTTC). This influential body came into existence in 1990 with membership open to chief executive officers of companies from all sectors of tourism and tourism related businesses. Its chief goal is to demonstrate the overall significance of this disparate collection of businesses to national and world economic development. Consequently it has hired consulting companies and researchers to develop estimates of the 'industry's' overall size and contribution. It estimated that 'in 2000 travel and tourism would generate, directly and indirectly, across the global economy US$4.2 trillion of economic activity and 7.8% of total employment' (World Travel and Tourism Council, 2002).

To collect the data to make estimates of tourism's impacts requires a definition of terms that have universal application. While considerable progress has been made in this direction over the past 10 years or so the situation is still clouded by inconsistencies. Reviews of these definitional problems can be encountered in good introductory texts such as French *et al.* (1999) and Goeldner *et al.* (2000). Therefore, this book focuses on the issues involved with using tourism definitions and data for the purpose of community analysis and planning. The structure suggested by Smith (1995) in his excellent survey of tourism data analysis is adapted. Namely, we need to define the principal customer (tourist), describe that person, define their trip, define the tourism businesses that serve the tourist and help to make the trips successful, and finally describe the principal components of the resulting 'tourist industry'.

The tourist

As with all sound business practice, community strategic tourism management should start with the definition of its principal customer – the tourist, but as will be discussed at a later stage another important customer is the local clientele. According to the World Tourism Organisation a tourist is a visitor who travels either internationally, by crossing an international border, or domestically by travelling within her/his own country. In both cases the visitor travels to a place other than her/his usual (home) environment, is away from home for at least one night and the purpose of the visit is not paid for by the place visited. Tourists that stay for a few hours but not overnight are called excursionists (World Tourism Organisation, 1991).

Distances travelled

Even this most recent definition of a tourist is not completely satisfactory, especially from an analytical and planning perspective. For example, there is no consistency regarding what area constitutes a usual (home) environment, because different countries and jurisdictional levels possess different scale needs. Therefore, to provide a technical-spatial description of the distance a person must travel from home before they become classified as a tourist varies from one country to another. In the United States the distance is 160 kms (100 miles), in Canada 80 kms (50 miles), and in Australia 40 kms (25 miles). Within these national classifications there is nothing to prevent state and local jurisdictions from further revising the actual cut-off distances to suit local scale conditions, so it is not uncommon to find a range of values from 30–50 kms being used to classify a traveller as a tourist. Furthermore, the remuneration clause can cause difficulties for occasions like Australia's recent and successful Olympic Games. In some cases the athletes and officials had their expenses covered by the Sydney Organising Committee of the Olympic Games, yet most would classify them as tourists to Sydney and Australia.

Masberg (1998) has explored the definition of a tourist from an interesting perspective – that of a user. She notes how the various official definitions of a tourist vary around the world and from publication to publication, so she asked managers of convention and visitors bureaux how they defined their customers. Most selected to do it by distance, a distance that 'fluctuates between 20 and 150 miles', but a considerable proportion also used 'purpose of trip', 'residence of the traveller' and 'length of stay' (Masberg, 1998: 68).

The trip

Having defined the tourist, it is also important to define the trip, which is the essence of the tourist experience. A trip can be considered to occur each time an individual or group leave their place of residence, travel a specified distance, and return home. It can involve one or more destinations, or be a circuit with no single destination. As such a trip is so intertwined with the tourist that the British Tourist Authority has long preferred to use tourist trips rather than tourist numbers as its guide to industry size and growth.

The tourism business

If there are still some difficulties associated with the definition of a tourist there is even more difficulty in defining the range of industries that serve and supply the tourist. Since the *tourism business* has grown into such a broad range of activities and penetrated every corner of the globe everyone is agreed that defining the business is a major and complex undertaking. Leiper (1979: 400) considers '(t)he tourist industry consists of all those firms, organizations, and facilities which are intended to serve the specific needs and wants of tourists'. Goeldner *et al.* (2000: 26) have developed an integrated systems model to capture the essential elements of what they call 'the tourism phenomenon'. In addition to the regular industry sectors of tourism, such as transport and accommodation, they included government and quasi-government agencies, the built environment, the natural environment and its resources, as well as activities such as research and stewardship.

As Smith (1995: 34–9) has indicated, such definitions of tourism businesses have two common features. They are supply-side oriented in that they focus on the production or supply of commodities for the tourist and not the demand for such products. These definitions also have a common weakness in terms of defining the tourism industry, in that they are so comprehensive they include ubiquitous businesses that serve local residents as well as tourists. This latter point is a major challenge to the World Travel and Tourism Council (WTTC) and any others who wish to differentiate the tourism component of businesses such as bakeries, petrol stations and restaurants that are used by both tourists and locals.

Tourism tiers of business

To solve the problem of over-counting tourism's share from such businesses and to indicate some businesses are core to the tourism industry while others are peripheral requires a more accurate and systematic description of the tourism industry and its component parts. A solution proffered to tackle this problem by the (Canadian) National Task Force on Tourism Data (1985) divides the tourist industry into two tiers of businesses, as detailed below.

- *Tier 1* tourism businesses are those that cannot exist if there were no tourism activity. Examples of these include airlines, travel agents and hotels.
- *Tier 2* tourism businesses are those that exist even in the absence of tourism, though at a lower capacity. Examples of such businesses include restaurants, taxis, and most shops. The actual division will be influenced by local conditions, with some shops and taxi businesses in small resort destinations being more reliant on the tourist trade than local customers, and hence in danger of closing if the tourist business disappeared.

To operate such a division of tourist businesses requires a classification system, so the (Canadian) National Task Force on Tourism Data based their division on the percentage of revenue expected to be generated from tourism. Utilising past empirical evidence they determined that businesses earning 91–100% of their revenue from tourists should be considered as Tier 1 tourism businesses. Those earning 10–90% of their revenue from tourists would be classed as Tier 2 tourism businesses. Like all classification systems of social activity there can be some discussion over the true breakpoints, but the task force attempted to act in a conservative manner to avoid any suggestion of inflating the industry's significance.

Smith (1995) considers that this system offers several important advantages. First, it is consistent with other industry definitions, in that it emphasises the commodities they produce. Second, it permits relatively easy measurement of the magnitude of the tourism activity, based on established Standard Industrial Classification (SIC) codes from industrial census studies and empirical surveys of individual firms. Third, the description recognises the WTO's distinction between tourists and excursionists. Tourists travelling long distance and staying overnight are served by Tier 1 businesses almost exclusively, while Tier 2 businesses serve both the tourists and excursionists. However, some would say there is a need for a still more elaborate classification system in order to reflect the total impact of this large and diverse industry.

One possibility is to emulate the economists' distinctions in their economic multiplier. For the direct expenditure, we could offer the task force's Tier 1 classification of tourist related facilities. For the indirect expenditure, we could offer the Tier 2 industries, but with a more conservative revenue generation classification of 25–90%. For the induced expenditure, we could include those professional firms which have become more involved in the operation of tourism businesses, yet have generally not been associated with tourism in past assessments. These include the growing number of service providers, such as lawyers, accountants, consultants and financial institutions. For such firms 10–24% would probably be a sufficient magnitude score, but some sectors, such as the consultants, can often exceed such levels of tourism-related business. One of the key areas where this type of classification is becoming important is with satellite accounting.

Satellite accounts

In several countries governments have developed tourism satellite accounts to obtain a clearer picture of tourism's size and contribution to the economy. As Campbell and Lapierre (1991: 7) state 'because tourism does not fit into the traditional industry structure established in most countries to measure economic activity, it has not enjoyed an acceptable level of "credibility" amongst other economic measures'. Consequently, Canada and other OECD countries have created statistics on the industry by 'mining' existing data sources and encouraging more standardised categorisation and survey definitions. An important part of this process has been to determine those industries that can be declared tourism industries or support activities, and to provide more rigour to the current tourist definition that includes the phrase 'away from the home environment'. Such accounting practices have helped to rationalise tourism definitions and data collection, but the cynics amongst us also realise they contributed to the development of the Goods and Service Tax (GST) and the Value Added Tax (VAT) taxes on the industry.

Meis (2001: 18–19) in a summary of Canada's experience with tourism satellite accounts (TSA) and a comparison with four other national TSA systems (Mexico, New Zealand, Norway and USA) finds the results 'from five very different and diverse countries indicate that tourism translates into significant and amazingly consistent levels of output, value added and employment'. For example, in terms of tourism's total output as a portion of the national Gross Domestic Product (GDP) for a year, Mexico's tourism was 6.5%, Canada 5%, Norway 4.3%, New Zealand 3.4% and the USA 2%. The slight difference between these figures is explained by the relative strength and diversity of the various national economies.

Community Definitions

The ability of community members to pull together and improve their quality of life is an oft-repeated story in religion, philosophy, history and everyday events. The following quote from Matthew Fox, a theologian cited by Anita Roddick, sums up some of the grandeur and promise of communities:

> Community comes from the word communion, to share a common task together. And it's in the sharing of that task that people do bigger things than they knew they were capable of. Then there is really something to celebrate. (Roddick, 2000: 55)

Two of the most remarkable aspects of communities can be their strength and their ability to get things done. The following paragraphs try to bring some structure and clarity as to what is meant by the term 'community'.

Paraphrasing Barkham's (1973: 218) description of carrying capacity the term 'community' is 'delightful in its simplicity, complex in its meaning, and difficult to define'. The simplicity of community lies in a word that has common usage, so everyone has a general idea as to what it refers. But its complexity starts to emerge when one turns to a dictionary, and finds a multiple definition. A good example of this is found in the *Macquarie Dictionary* (Delbridge & Bernard, 1988: 185) which defines community as 'a social group of any size whose members reside in a specific locality, share government and have a cultural and historical heritage'. Such multiple function definitions lead to a discussion of which aspects are more important, a question that is generally settled by the focus and intent of the inquirer.

A more recent discussion of community in terms of tourism supports many of these earlier notions and adds some new considerations. Joppe (1996: 475) claims that community is a self-defining term 'based on a sense of shared purpose and common goals'. Community can grow from mutual interests, such as caring for the environment. A community can also reflect geographic features and spatial relationships, such as natural boundaries that define a tourist region. However, a review of its definitions and uses would indicate that community has three general dimensions: social functions, spatial area and external recognition.

Social functions

The social function of people working together to create a place of their own, such as a neighbourhood, is a continuous feature of community research and planning. These social functions can be described as follows:

> Interest in community is based on the practical grounds that people increasingly are coming together to identify their needs and through cooperative action improve their social and physical environment. (Dalton & Dalton, 1975: Introduction)

This 'coming together' is viewed as a process of community building, whereby previously independent individuals or household units find they have common interests and choose to take some responsibility for what is happening to their lives. This social cohesion can take on a community development approach 'which encourages citizen participation, with or without government assistance, in efforts to improve the economic, social and cultural conditions of the locality, with emphasis on self-help' (Dalton & Dalton, 1975 : 1).

Gill (1997) feels one sociological definition of community is particularly relevant to community tourism. She focuses on Warren's definition of 'community' as:

> . . . an aggregation of people competing for space. The shape of the community, as well as its activities are characterized by differential use of space and by various processes according to which one type of people and / or type of social function succeeds another in the ebb and flow of structural change in a competitive situation. (Warren, 1977: 208)

The relevance of this definition to community tourism is derived from its being based on 'ecological principles that conceptualise change as an outcome of competition' (Gill, 1997: 56).

Gill has studied mountain resort communities and feels there are two crucial steps to understanding community tourism in those settings. The first is to recognise that residents have to compete with tourists for basic community resources such as space (on the road, on the ski slopes and in the restaurants) and facilities (such as decent and affordable housing, community centres, and public transit). The second is to recognise the number of stakeholder sub-groups that can exist within the usual classifications, resulting in very different views on what makes a good community. For example, in ski resort communities residents' views can be distinctively different along the lines of whether they are permanent residents, transient residents or second-home owners. A key discriminator between temporary residents, who are often the casual employees of the industry, and permanent residents would be the importance of property values. Temporary residents in the rental market would like to see property values kept low, whereas permanent residents would prefer to see them increase. The importance of stakeholder differences and the search for common ground will be discussed at length in Part 3 of this book.

Growth machine perspective

The link between community and development has been applied most strongly in the areas of social planning and economic development. In social planning communities can be viewed as locations of political and economic change (Gilbert, 1982). With the emphasis on change this often overlaps into struggles regarding the impact and direction of community development. Within this framework Molotch and others have developed a 'growth machine perspective' that suggests communities can become self-defined on the basis of their attitude to resource competition and future land use decisions (Logan & Molotch, 1987; Molotch, 1976).

Molotch found that three groups often emerge within a community over land development issues and that the future of the community often depends on the outcome of their power struggle. These *interest groups* can be divided into three categories.

- *Advocates* of change: Stand to benefit directly from
                             economic and land development
                             (e.g. land owners, speculators and
                             investors).
- *Statesman* of the growth   Facilitators of change (e.g. Realtors
  machine: and bankers).
- *Local residents*:   React to the development proposals,
                             often creating local (nested)
                             communities of interest.

In their examination of tourism development on the Hawaiian island of Molokai, Canan and Hennessy (1989) find the growth machine hypothesis explains much about the community tensions and development patterns that had occurred there. They point out that the growth machine perspective fits the political and economic competition over Molokai's land. Over a 15-year period its tourism development primarily benefited a small exploitative coalition (of advocates and statesmen). An anti-growth coalition of primarily native Hawaiians and environmental groups appeared because of the narrow spread of tourism's benefits and its perceived negative impact on the general population's quality of life.

Although tourism development has been successful in many areas, due to its highly visible nature it is often the negative experiences that receive most exposure. In both the media and academia it is the bad news and problems that have received the majority of attention. This is only natural since bad news sells papers and research is drawn to problem areas by funding priorities and an interest in helping to ameliorate problems. But these negative inclinations can provide a distorted picture of tourism's true record.

Tourism trepidations

Anti-growth sentiments can become focused on tourism due to its highly visible nature within communities (Mormont, 1987). 'It is easy to exaggerate impacts arising from tourism' according to Jenkins (1997: 58), because it is concentrated in a few areas and it emphasises conspicuous consumption. Anti-tourism sentiments of residents can be expressed in relatively benign ways, such as taunting bumper stickers, T-shirts (Figure 1.1) and critical letters in editorial pages. Such sentiments can inspire local residents to new endeavours, as in the case of one Floridian news columnist – Carl Hiaasen. His wonderfully humorous novels, starting with *Tourist Season* (Hiaasen, 1986), often draw upon irresponsible tourism practices and development in Florida as source material. More direct action against tourists includes vandalising and removing local access and tourism promotion signs, or confronting tourists to inform them that they are not welcome.

Figure 1.1 Anti-tourism sentiment on a holiday destination T-shirt

As an emerging service based industry, the range and magnitude of tourism's positive impacts, including the opportunities associated with tourism employment are not widely known. Tourism has helped to restore the cultural vitality of many indigenous groups and helped to justify the preservation of the natural, cultural and historical heritage in many countries. Tourism's labour intensive character and array of entry level positions make it an ideal long-term employer of the typically under-employed and unemployed sectors of the labour force, including women, youth, recent immigrants and Aboriginals (Gershuny & Miles, 1983). However, by employing those who do not typically have a strong economic or political voice, many of the voices of those who benefit most directly from tourism opportunities are not heard.

Benefits that Aboriginal groups can gain from tourism have been shown to go beyond job creation and income generation, to bringing new meaning to their cultural identity and a resurgence of traditional values and practices (Grinder, 1992). Tourism's potential benefits to Aboriginal people were summed at a recent Aboriginal achievement awards presentation in Canada by the following comments. 'Thanks to the visitors' high regard for traditional First Nations' culture, young Anishinable have become conscious of their own values, which is the greatest achievement of this project' (Mann, 2000: 29).

One of the few to address this bias issue against tourism is Brown, who notes the increasingly negative tone of research into tourism impacts, yet finds few critics have taken into account the context in which tourism takes place. 'Tourism impacts are difficult to isolate, invariably interrelated and conditioned also by phenomena external to tourism' (Brown, 1998: 91). The spread of Western culture, technological advances, the growth of multinational companies and the encroachment of development into previously remote areas are evident in many of the same areas as tourism growth (Mann, 2000). However, the spread of people from foreign lands can make more of an immediate and tangible impression than the spread of ideas.

Spatial context

It is frequently difficult to isolate the social function of community from its spatial context, because the two are often synonymous. That is when a group of people are linked together by a common condition of life, be it socio-economic status or a leisure activity such as golf, they often choose to live close together. Such proximity aids the development and continuity of the common condition and in the process gives a physical and symbolic context to the sentiment. This is the philosophy behind the evolution of neighbourhoods and the social planners' attempts to either retain natural neighbourhood clusters because of their self-support and self-reliance features, or to create neighbourhoods in the hope of facilitating such features. Schwilgin (1973: 63) has described such areas as being where:

> the residents commonly recognise some association with each other based on similarities of socio-economic status, or their desires in general for the future of the area; and its shape forms an intelligibly identifiable functional unit.

One way to define a community is to assess whether or not it practices communal decision-making (Mann, 2000). The level of communal decision-making is often a reflection of the size and structure of the group. In a business sense, well organised groups whose members have strong ties to each other and who share a history of cooperation and trust often practise communal decision-making (Roddick, 2000). Therefore, smaller groups can be better positioned to practise communal decision-making than larger groups.

Appropriate planning scale

Neighbourhoods occur in numerous forms and sizes. Planners generally attempt to identify neighbourhoods in a manner that retains the social characteristics and dynamics of a community. Essential characteristics to consider, as identified by Schwilgin and others, include neighbourhoods having sufficient size and capability to become a functional planning unit. In this regard (Suttles, 1970) suggests a need to balance the social function and the spatial planning scale. He offers within his continuum a four-tier hierarchy. This hierarchy ranges from a highly compact and socially comprehensive unit the size of a city block to an expanded community feeling that could extend over a whole city or region. Of these four levels, Suttles recommends his 'community of limited liability' as being suited particularly to community planning.

> The term 'limited liability' is given to this neighbourhood level because participation in the community is a voluntary choice. Most people of the area will participate in organisations and political interest groups, but some will not be activated unless their particular face-block or territory is threatened. (Suttles, 1970: 59)

The limited liability neighbourhood is expected to be the spatial unit to which most people will have some form of commitment. This commitment can take many forms and is often not very visible, such as informal coffee meetings or social group gatherings, but it can suddenly become very obvious if there is a perceived threat to the *status quo*. Incidents such as new land use proposals or changing school districts can galvanise quiet areas into demonstrable action. 'NIMBY' (Not in My Back Yard) and 'NOTE' (Not Over There Either) are just two of the terms commonly used to describe community groups that have developed primarily to stop a particular development they find undesirable. Such reactions are not uncommon when major tourism developments and road changes are proposed in tourist destinations.

Community activists

Community activist groups have their roots in the planning advocacy process that grew out of the political activism of the 1960s (Langlois, 1979). The early community advocacy groups helped to bring more democracy to the planning process by providing an avenue for community input. However, present-day anti-growth groups have been criticised for making the planning process less democratic, especially when their successful complaint campaigns merely shift the 'problem' development to neighbourhoods that are not so well organised, or advantaged (Barbalace, 2000). Therefore, the resources that could have been spent finding a widely accepted solution to a community planning dilemma, such as affordable housing or airport expansion, can be sapped away as opposing sides fight it out.

Core and boundary issues

Just as the concept of community has proved complex, so has the task of describing and locating it on a map. If a community or neighbourhood sentiment exists it is generally evident in the urban landscape, providing signs such as focal points for shopping and recreation within a relatively compact and walkable area. These locations often identify themselves with the neighbourhood sentiment, adopting its name in their business signs or park and recreation centre names. The difficulty emerges not so much with identifying a community or neighbourhood core, as with the mapping of its boundaries. Where does one area of community sentiment and responsibilities end and another begin? In reality those living in the border area are either ambivalent about which neighbourhood they belong to, or they use both neighbourhoods.

Likewise, the spatial description of regions is fraught with difficulties. Tosun and Jenkins (1996) have suggested regions need a 'sense of purpose' for tourism planning or any form of development to take place. But unfortunately such functional regions will vary in size according to the purpose. So we have the situation where any community can be placed in series of overlapping and different regions. This is the case of many small rural communities that are located in the larger Australian shires. They can easily be in one school district, an entirely different political district, sharing a marketed tourist region with other communities and all encompassed within a much larger water catchment region.

Lack of clear boundaries and jurisdictional control can lead to the unrestricted exploitation and conflicting uses of tourism resources. One example is the 'tragedy of the commons' (Hardin, 1969) as it applies to coral reefs, which often stretch across existing jurisdictional boundaries, resulting in a lack of cohesive management and a degradation of the resource. By creating new boundaries to encompass a physiological phenomenon jurisdictions are able to introduce protection and conservation measures that assist tourism and other activities such as fishing. This has been achieved with the Bonaire Marine Park in the Dutch Antilles which in 1992 existed in name only. By exercising sovereignty over the whole area as a park the government has been able to control uses within the park and generate substantial revenue for the island (*The Economist*, 2000a: 106).

Political and economic realities are forcing planners and governments to be more precise in drawing lines between communities for administrative purposes, such as policing or garbage collection. In the United States the rise of the 'incorporation movement', whereby larger political units are broken up into smaller and often exclusive incorporated areas, leads to much debate about where the boundaries for these communities should lie (Husock, 1998). In Florida, as in many other states in the US, there has been a surge in incorporations, resulting in vexatious debates over the boundaries for these 'new communities'. Issues of segregation and social equity are tied to the incorporation movement because the new boundaries for these areas carry with them dramatic taxation, servicing and self-determination implications. In some cases the boundary question has led to so much argument that the final decision has been left to the courts, such as in the Village of Islamorada, in the Florida Keys.

The relevance of a community's spatial context in tourism is very important because as a major and sometimes disruptive commercial activity it takes up space that often intrudes upon existing neighbourhoods, especially those close to a city core. One of the principal social impacts topics studied by tourism researchers has been the visitor–resident interface and the setting for such interaction has often been the neighbourhood. Several studies have found that the distance residents live from the focus of tourism activity often has a bearing on their attitude to local tourism. Generally, those living on top of or next to the tourism activity, with its congestion and noise, develop a negative attitude to the business (Murphy & Andressen, 1988; Sheldon & Var, 1984), especially when it overspills into residential areas.

Examples of this neighbourhood effect occur everywhere. In many towns there is tension between those households in residential areas that operate a bed and breakfast business, their neighbours who put up with the comings and goings of visitors, and the municipality which handles a greater load on its residential services. Another neighbourhood effect can be the loss of local convenience food shops, like a butcher or greengrocer, to souvenir shops as a shopping district changes from its traditional residential base to a more tourism and higher revenue market.

External recognition

The third dimension of community, especially from a planning and development perspective, is the existence of external recognition. Although a group can band together and create a strong sense of belonging, even with an internally recognised spatial context, it is of limited utility unless these two dimensions have been recognised and acknowledged by some external agency. Porteous (1973) gave a graphic example of this in his study of a teenage gang and its turf, as viewed through a cognitive mapping of its members' concept of their 'neighbourhood'. The gang knew their 'turf' but only received a modest acknowledgment of its existence from the local authorities, in part because of the transient nature of the group but mainly because of their lack of political relevance. Such a tenuous external recognition was insufficient to legitimise their existence and territorial claims.

If a community wishes to preserve its way of life and the character of its geographical location it needs to have its existence and right to self-determination acknowledged by others. Just as new nation states and national governments seek the recognition and support from the world's community of nations, so too do neighbourhoods, cities and regions seek the acknowledgment and approval of higher levels of government. Only if their existence has been validated can they expect to receive official jurisdictional status and support. Acknowledging these political entities can include recognising their rights and privileges along with their territorial boundaries. Community planning, whether it pertains to a neighbourhood or complete town, needs to be undertaken 'in parallel with (higher order) development objectives' (Tosun & Jenkins, 1996: 520), especially if it involves seeking some form of public funding.

External recognition of the history and rights of certain groups as communities can in turn empower these communities. Many of the world's indigenous groups are now recognised by non-Aboriginals as legitimate ongoing ethnic communities that deserve to be treated as such. The successful bid of the Canadian Cree to stop the construction of a major dam on their traditional hunting and fishing grounds is an example of how external recognition of a community can empower a group to bring about social justice. The Cree were unable to find a groundswell of support to stop the dam in their home province of Quebec. However, by reaching out to other levels of government and connecting with other communities, most notably environmental groups, the Cree gained substantial recognition and support for their cause (Susskind & Field, 1996). In Australia the growing public recognition and support for Aboriginal communities, as expressed in mass demonstrations across the county involving hundreds of thousands of people, is bringing pressure on the federal government to enter into treaty negotiations with Aboriginal Australians (*The Age*, 2000).

Suttles (1970) included an element of external recognition in the description of his 'community of limited liability', a community scale that he views as fulfilling both the social and planning needs of a community. Suttles (1970: 59) says this should be 'a neighbourhood that is not only recognised and defended internally but also receives outside recognition and sanction, leading to an "official" and more permanent identity'. When a community has such external recognition it can expect to be consulted about potential changes and to be able to seek its share of development funding.

Community empowerment

Another form of external recognition, equally relevant to the treatise of this book, is the rising importance of community empowerment on the world stage. One of those who have commented on the movement away from centralisation to decentralisation is the futurist John Naisbitt. He considers 'the real political power – that is the ability to get things done – has shifted away from Congress and the presidency to the states, cities, towns and neighbourhoods' (Naisbitt, 1984: 108). A part of this process is the growing importance of 'personal geography' – where you live – which is working hand-in-hand with the decentralisation process to enable people 'to tackle problems and create change at the local level' (Naisbitt, 1984: 141).

Someone who would agree with Naisbitt is planning critic and theorist Jane Jacobs. In her book, *The Death and Life of Great American Cities*, Jane Jacobs (1962) promoted the worthiness of maintaining and developing active residential neighbourhoods in central cities. Jacobs considered 'a city's very wholeness in bringing together people with communities of interest is one of its greatest assets, possibly the greatest' (1962: 119). But in order to function properly a city needs to operate at several levels and she recommends there be street and district neighbourhoods to act as functional building blocks to overall city life. To Jacobs these would provide the metropolitan areas with local caretakers, people who would look after the general security of property and safety of people because it was their home territory.

In her later work Jacobs (1984) championed the cause of small communities that in the global economy have become dependent on the metropolitan juggernauts of the modern economy. She suggests many communities can foster greater self-reliance and local employment by substituting more locally produced goods and services for their traditional imports from these distant suppliers. She illustrates how economies of scale advantages in the metropolitan production centres have now been eroded by customised demands and rising transport costs in a growing number of cases. Hence, small communities should check their existing trade relations with larger centres and see whether the economics of traditional trade patterns still hold true.

Social capital

Jacobs and others who have investigated community action and its contribution to a variety of activities have introduced the term 'social capital'. The origins of the term have been attributed to L.J. Hanifan who, as a supervisor of rural schools in West Virginia in 1916, advocated community involvement for the development of successful schools by using 'local social capital . . . the goodwill, fellowship, sympathy and social intercourse among the individuals and families who make up a social unit' (as cited in Putman, 2000: 19). Since then the concept of social capital has been extended to other community oriented topics, including its economic and social development contributions, but not without some debate (De Filippis, 2001; Putman, 1993). While it involves local knowledge and commitment that would be helpful to tourism development social capital cannot replace the fundamental advantages of possessing sufficient financial capital and skilled labour. However, its principles of teamwork and networking (Anderson & Jack, 2002) fit in well with the additional business strength that can be gained from agglomeration and clustering processes, as discussed later in this book.

Community Tourism Definitions

In 1980 as the result of a symposium on tourism development in Canada and his experience with tourism expansion around the world, Murphy described tourism as: 'An industry which uses the community as a resource, sells it as a product, and, in the process, affects the lives of everyone.' (1980a: 1)

This statement, which has been quoted extensively since it first appeared, clearly links the two terms discussed above, but in the process the concept of community tourism becomes bigger than the sum of its parts. The community under consideration is no longer just a home with a communal sense of belonging, it has become an actual or potential profit-making commodity in the global tourism market. If the community enters that market it will need to adjust and change in order to compete and to survive. The community will be promoted as a type of destination product that is expected to attract visitors but this may not appeal to all residents. These same residents will be involved in the successful delivery of the promoted product, whether they work for the industry or not, because they are part of the community that is now on show.

The interest in community tourism has been building over the past two decades. Pearce and Moscardo (1999) refer to its growing status in research and planning agendas. They demonstrate this through reference to:

> the World Tourism Leaders' Meeting on the Social Impacts of Tourism suggests that countries should, as a first priority, 'support greater in-volvement of communities in the planning, implementation, monitoring and evaluation processes of tourism policies, programmes and projects'. Similarly, the Asia Pacific Ministers' Conference on Tourism and the Environment suggested that tourism should foster lo-cal community involvement and integrated tourism planning for sustainability. (Pearce & Moscardo, 1999: 31–2)

In their review of past analysis Pearce and Moscardo note that while there has been much and varied research into community tourism there has been a tendency to focus on individual variables rather than many attempts to link the various facets into a theoretical framework.

More recently community tourism has been defined by the US based Ecotourism Society as: 'tourism that involves and benefits local communi-ties' (Mann, 2000: 26). This definition places the involvement of local people and how they are affected by tourism at the centre of discussion, rather than including them as a mere addition to the economic components of the industry, or worse yet – as an afterthought. Such definitions bring together the previously mentioned autonomous terms 'community' and 'tourism' into a strong and intertwined partnership.

Responsibilities

There has been a general increase in the attention paid to community tourism, both from an academic and pragmatic point of view. In the academic arena much of the concern has been over the impacts of tourism on the local residents and environment. The true impacts of tourism on host communities are often a matter of perspective that can be biased by personal impacts and reveal themselves in unexpected ways (Mathieson & Wall, 1982). Power structures of traditional societies can be threatened when those who benefit directly from tourism employment, such as young guides who earn more money than their elders, can threaten the authority and prestige of traditional leaders (Mann, 2000).

Tourism researchers with a social science background or emphasis have analysed resident–tourists interactions around the world. Apart from a relatively few tense situations, where there is open conflict between tourism developments and community aspirations, these studies generally reveal more support than opposition to the development of local tourism – an aspect to be discussed further in the 'residents' chapter. However, even where there is support for tourism it is generally not boundless, in the sense that residents don't exhibit excessive or irrational enthusiasm for the industry. Rather, residential support for tourism tends to be tempered and balanced as it draws on their first hand tourism experiences and learning about other destinations.

Increasingly a pragmatic approach to community tourism is being developed and adopted. One of the early leaders in this was the extension service of the University of Missouri-Columbia, who's College of Public and Community Services produced a guidebook for community tourism development (Weaver, 1986). The purpose of the book is 'to assist local communities in assessing and developing their tourism potential as a component of their economic development plan' (Weaver, 1986: iii). As part of the general guidelines the contributors identify three essential components of the industry which are listed below.

(1) *The community*
    This supplies the local public services and infrastructure, plus the personnel and volunteer labour for the local destination organisation, and the leadership needed to direct the local industry's product and marketing development.
(2) *Attractions and special events*
    This sector interacts with both the community and the tourist market. It plans and manages the tourist attractions and promotes them and the community to the outside tourism market.
(3) *The tourist market*
    This is the segment(s) willing to buy what the community is selling. To serve this market properly and create satisfied customers the commu-

nity must have the appropriate facilities and service standards for the targeted segments.

If we use Weaver's approach as a guide we can see evidence that all three elements – the host community, the tourists and the industry are beginning to play a combined role in striving for a form of community tourism that is attainable and acceptable to all.

Communal interests

While in the words of Tonge and Myott (1993: 7) 'confusion still reigns supreme' in how to best handle local tourism development, there are signs of progress in this area. Increasingly awareness of the need for tourism management is leading many communities to empower themselves in developing successful tourism products that reflect and promote their goals and values. This empowerment is fuelled by local commitment to tourism management, that involves planning for tourism development and drawing upon available resources to implement the plan. These resources include the following: knowledge, expertise and funding of tourism from the host community; data collection and analysis from local institutions of tertiary education; plan creation and implementation assistance from experienced government officials and consultants; and partnership opportunities with governments and businesses.

Examples of host communities taking a more proactive role include the African communities that are being given more control over the wildlife safaris and parks operating in their homeland. Baker (1997: 275) observes 'the concept of community-based conservation evolved in the 1980s to bolster support for both consumptive and non-consumptive uses of wildlife resources. The concept recognises that wildlife conservation is not just about animals but also people'. She notes that while a communal approach could lead to a 'tragedy of the commons' there is now sufficient knowledge and incentive to avoid this historic trap. After reviewing several national programmes in Africa she identifies five 'optimum conditions' for community-based natural resource management in that part of the world, which are listed below.

(1) Resources need a *focused value* to determine whether the benefit of managing a resource exceeds its cost.
(2) Those *bearing* the *higher cost* of living with the resource must benefit more than those who do not bear this cost.
(3) There must be a *positive correlation* between the quality of management and magnitude of derived benefits.
(4) Proprietorship (*ownership*) should match the unit of production, management and benefit.
(5) Proprietorship (*ownership*) should be as *small* as practicable, within ecological and socio-political constraints. (Baker, 1997: 282–3)

The application of such principles would be a better representation of eco-logical process, and a reduction of the leakage to middlemen and central governments.

More 'self-help' tourism development guidebooks for small communi-ties are being produced to assist these communities in establishing viable tourism ventures and obtaining maximum long-term benefit from the industry. Two recent Australian examples are *Developing Ecotourism: A Community Based Approach,* by Wearing and McLean (1998), and *Protecting Local Heritage Places: A Guide for Communities* (Australian Heritage Com-mission, 1999). The latter states 'this guide contains information to help individuals and groups working locally to identify, conserve and protect heritage places' (Australian Heritage Commission, 1999: 2).

Critical appraisal

Despite this growing development of community tourism interest and action there has been criticism of this approach to research and planning. Taylor (1995: 489) queries whether 'in the end, (community tourism) is different from any other kind of tourism development'. In coming to this conclusion he basically criticises the dual role seen for residents, in that they are expected to be outsiders and at the same time part of the local tourism product. He doubts whether they share the benefits along with the substantiated costs. Furthermore he also doubts whether a community approach to tourism can turn back the clock and allow communities to reverse the destination lifecycle, although we know of no one who has made such a claim.

Such views seem to miss essential points of the community approach to tourism. Community tourism is an attempt to integrate the interests of all community stakeholders, including the residents as an important group, in its analysis and development proposals. A dual or multi-functional role for individuals is not uncommon in modern society and if the tourism–host expectations are appropriate and properly communicated they should not form an impossible burden. The issue of balancing benefits and costs for the community at large and its residents lies at the heart of Murphy's (1983) ecological model that highlights the need for balance. It is true that the benefits, like the costs, will not always be tangible on an individual basis, but they do occur and need to be assessed by all involved. It is even possible with this approach to slow down or stop development, so while it may not be able to reverse a destination's lifecycle, it could help to mitigate its evolu-tionary progress. Thus a community tourism approach could place the host community at a stage it feels is more compatible with its aspirations.

In a response to Taylor's article Baum (1996) reports how community tourism has become a major research and planning focus in Canada and how an important ingredient is an education process for local residents. Such educational components within a community tourism perspective have been 'initiated at government level, in destinations such as Hawaii and Hong Kong (which) illustrate how this process can operate' (Baum, 1996: 149). However, Baum demonstrates such educational programmes need to be undertaken with care. Others, like Madrigal (1995) and Murphy (1991) now emphasise the need for more internal marketing by the industry, so that it demonstrates convincingly what net gains the industry can bring to the community.

Burr (1991) cited in Pearce *et al.* (1996: 27–8) gives some indication of the struggle ahead by observing 'the concept of what constitutes a community (in community tourism) has not been considered carefully by researchers'. In a review of 25 empirical studies on tourism impacts and communities Burr found a disappointing lack of clarity concerning definition and approach. In fact he argued that there are four possible theoretical approaches to the study of community in tourism impacts analysis. These are listed below.

- The *human ecology* approach emphasises the community living together and adapting to the setting.
- The *social systems* approach stresses the roles and institutions that govern society.
- The *interactional* approach that sees community as the sum of individual social interactions.
- The *critical* approach emphasises the power of key groups in the decision-making process.

Burr is quoted as favouring a combination of the interactional and critical approaches, as this 'focuses attention on the dynamic processes that create and alter community structure' (Pearce *et al.* 1996: 28). Such is the focus of this book, as it extends beyond the human ecology approach of *Tourism: A Community Approach*, to examine the interaction of business principles and stakeholder aspirations that leads to conflict resolution and collaborative decision-making processes.

Regardless of the definitions used and theoretical approach taken, few deny the need to concentrate more on the development of theory in the area of community tourism. If the growing academic and practical interest in community tourism is to take on a more solid form it needs the structure of a theoretical framework. If it is to take its place in the lexicon of tourism research it also needs to be positioned within the developing general theory of tourism.

Tourism Theoretical Developments

Like all relatively young academic fields of enquiry, tourism research has been building slowly toward a level of understanding that can lead to the prediction of behaviour and outcomes. In this process the inductive approach has been dominant. So far most research has concentrated on descriptive empirical analysis of particular case studies that lead, either directly or indirectly, to the proposal of a theory. Many of the tourism theories to date have focused on the challenges that can arise from a lack of management or mismanagement of tourism resources. Since tourism is such a broad and multi-dimensional subject many of these theories have their roots in other disciplines.

As inductive research activity has developed and matured there is now more evidence of a deductive approach, where the research and analysis is guided by a priori hypotheses based on earlier literature in both tourism and related fields.

Two outstanding examples of how the inductive approach can lead to theory and prediction are Doxey's (1975) 'irridex' model and Butler's (1980) destination area cycle of evolution. Doxey noted from his experience as a consultant in several Caribbean and Canadian communities that local residents' tolerance of tourism changes with its growing size and dominance. Consequently in his 'irridex' model of resident reaction to tourism he charts a continuum ranging from euphoric acceptance of the industry to open antagonism. Butler describes the development characteristics of a selection of well-known tourist destinations. He then demonstrates how they follow a lifecycle that moves from an exploration stage to a stagnation stage resulting in either rejuvenation or decline. Marketing research has proposed a similar product lifecycle model where the stages pass from introduction to decline (Figure 1.2). Both of these theoretical concepts are based on critical observation of actual experiences and have suggested a pattern of behaviour that can apparently explain many of the differences. It is interesting that such strong parallels exist in two separate academic fields, yet not so surprising since both are linked by a business emphasis. It should be apparent also that Butler and Doxey are describing the same phenomenon but from different perspectives. Butler is focusing on the industry and its development, while Doxey is recording the changing reactions of the host populations to this development (Figure 1.2).

Examples of the deductive approach are appearing more regularly now in tourism research, where the authors develop a theory of behaviour or outcomes based on either past research findings or their own intuition. They develop a series of hypotheses based on these theories and test them with respect to a particular case study. A good example of this can be seen in Palmer's (1998) evaluation of marketing groups' governance style. After reviewing the literature on collaborative tourism destination marketing he puts forward the following hypotheses.

H1: Local tourism marketing associations are more effective where they are associated with a 'tight' governance style.

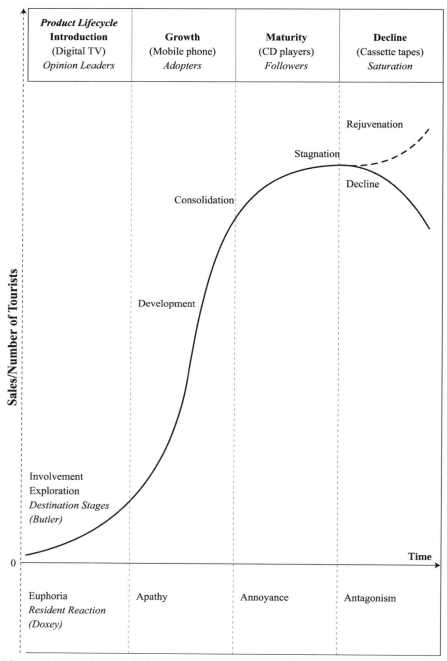

Figure 1.2 Product and destination lifecycles with potential resident reactions

H2: The effectiveness of local tourism marketing associations is greatest where there is a high level of compatibility among members.

These deductive statements were put to the test by developing an appropriate measurement scale and applying a statistical analysis. 'The results of the quantitative analysis strongly supported the hypothesis (H1) of a link between tight governance style and perceived effectiveness' (Palmer, 1998: 196). However, 'the hypothesis (H2) of a relationship between high levels of compatibility and effectiveness is not accepted' (Palmer, 1998: 197). This is because the statistical analysis indicated the actual relationship went in the opposite direction to that predicted in H2. Hence such studies take tourism research a small step forward by ratifying some concepts and raising doubts about others.

In addition to developing various approaches to the development of theory, tourism research demonstrates a growing sense of direction and responsibility. Jafari (1990) identifies four different themes in tourism research over time, that he calls tourism's platforms in the sense that they represent stepping stones. These platforms are described below.

(1) *Advocacy*
    The advocacy platform appeared during the economic reconstruction following World War II. This type of research emphasises the benefits associated with tourism, with a strong focus on economic benefits and is dominated by government reports.

(2) *Cautionary*
    The cautionary platform developed in the 1970s along with growing academic interest in the field of tourism research. This platform challenges the overly enthusiastic stance of the advocacy platform by highlighting the evidence of growing negative impacts.

(3) *Adaptancy*
    The adaptancy platform emerged during the late 1980s and focuses on alternative forms of tourism, that can avoid the principal problems of mass tourism by emphasising a more harmonious scale and functionality.

(4) *Knowledge-based*
    The knowledge-based platform is the fourth and present platform. It attempts to build on the previous work, using a multi-disciplinary approach to guide the development of tourism on a more harmonious scale. This 'new platform aims at positioning itself on scientific foundations' (Jafari, 1990: 35). It will hopefully combine the best of the previous platforms, which still exist in various forms, with modern multi-disciplinary scientific research.

It is this multi-disciplinary and scientific approach to theory building that Tribe (1997) embraces and embellishes in his critical analysis of tourism as an academic discipline and his proffered model regarding the creation of tourism knowledge. He presents tourism knowledge as a band of concentric rings. Proceeding from the outer rim to the core are a series of circles that represent the principal components of tourism knowledge, detailed as below.

- The *outer circle* represents the multitude of disciplines that have some bearing on and interest in the development of tourism knowledge and theory.
- The thin *inner circle*, called 'band k' is where these disciplines interact with each other and contribute to the field of tourism knowledge. This middle circle represents the field of tourism study, which Tribe has broken into two parts – TF1 (business related topics) and TF2 (non-business related topics such as social impacts). TF1 is 'the business world of tourism, pushing out at the expense of other parts of the diagram' (Tribe, 1997: 654), because it has a unifying theme that makes it dominant both in an academic and pragmatic sense. Tribe has trouble labelling TF2, beyond describing it as 'non-business' related. This is due in part to an apparent lack of a unifying thematic approach between the social and other sciences to tourism.
- The *core* of his model is referred to as 'mode 2', and represents the ultimate goal of tourism knowledge production – its own distinctive contribution to knowledge. Tribe describes this core as 'extra-disciplinarity' and quotes Gibbons *et al.* (1994: 168) in support of this view:

> Knowledge which emerges from a particular context of application with its own distinct theoretical structures, research methods, and modes of practice but which may not be locatable on the prevailing disciplinary map.

Important points to note according to Tribe are that mode 2 knowledge production occurs outside of higher education and that it is developing its own epistemology. Its success is judged 'by its ability to solve a particular problem, its cost effectiveness, and its ability to establish competitive advantage. Its results are highly contextualized for a specific project' (Tribe, 1997: 652).

We concur that tourism knowledge and theory should be viewed in such a multi-disciplinary or trans-disciplinary fashion because of its extensive variety of forms and impacts. Therefore, we offer strategic community tourism management as a way of filling some of the gaps in Tribe's model. For instance we suggest the 'community setting' for *TF2*. Host community resources attract the business of tourism in the first place while the community must live with the consequences of such engagements. The physical, social and cultural settings of a location are given form and substance to its host community and create the foundation for tourism development. Such a proposition fits with Tribe's core – mode 2, as his tourism knowledge production point is highly contextualised according to his own words. This recognises the folly in separating any tourism activity and analysis from its setting. Since destinations are the principal setting for tourism activity a host community approach to tourism theory building seems most appropriate.

The development of theory for strategic community management tourism will involve joint consideration of the tourism activity and its setting. Thus it will build on the TF1 and TF2 distinctions outlined by Tribe and in the process combine the tourism business interests with those of the physical and social sciences. In this way such research and development will combine the perspectives of several interest groups and help to create the 'extradisiplinary' approach Tribe thinks tourism study should be generating.

Community–business combination

As early as 1979 Rosenow and Pulsipher (1979: 43) produced a book with the wonderful and apt title – *Tourism: The Good, The Bad, and The Ugly*. In this book they recommended a *personality planning process* that attempts to identify those elements which make a community unique and brings this tourism appeal into a meaningful package for both residents and the tourism industry. A key aspect of this type of tourism is to emphasise a destination's sense of place.

In the view of Rosenow and Pulsipher (1979: 43) 'almost every area in the United States has certain elements of its setting and heritage that are unique'. It is this uniqueness that contributes to tourist interest, especially as tourism becomes more associated with the need to escape the routine experiences of daily life and the tourist market has shattered into many special interest segments. Consequently, more tourists are seeking something different or something that is a new example of their special interest. So this unique setting and heritage of individual places, that geographers call its 'sense of place' (Johnston et al. 1988: 425), becomes an important tourism resource.

While local residents may or may not perceive the significance of their unique qualities to tourism they are both important and fragile community elements that need to be protected in the face of progress and growth. Rosenow and Pulsipher (1979: 63) claim this can be a clear starting point for community action, by quoting from William K. Reilly's book – *In the Wake of the Tourist*:

> The principal advantage of having, or believing that you have, a place that is special is that planning can begin from an agreed-upon point of reference. Consensus, always elusive in land-use planning, is more attainable when special qualities have been commonly recognized.

So they proposed a 'personality planning process' that builds on any area's sense of place. They suggest a simple 'community planning process' that identifies those elements that constitute the local sense of place and assist in formulating policies to enhance its uniqueness. It basically consists of the following four steps.

(1) Delineate distinctive *features*.
(2) Plot critical *zones*.
(3) Establish use *objectives*.
(4) Formulate specific *action* programmes.

This recognition of the importance of a community's sense of place and the need to include and safeguard these features in the general business planning process is a major step toward the development of a strategic community tourism management approach.

Researchers have developed a range of strategic tourism planning models as a way of explaining the developmental potential of tourism destinations in various situations. These models have been tested around the world as a means of better understanding the impacts of tourism on communities and to develop appropriate strategies for managing tourism developments. The tourism models reviewed in this section include the following:

- Ecological tourism planning model,
- Harmonised travel model; and
- Planning modes.

Ecological tourism planning model

Murphy (1983) attempted to present community tourism in a theoretical context by developing an ecological model of community tourism planning that had five essential components (Figure 1.3).

Ecological process The first was to equate tourism planning and development with an ecological process, where a tourism destination could be treated as a living ecosystem. An ecosystem is seen as 'any area of nature that includes living organisms and non-living substances interacting to produce an exchange of materials between the living and non-living parts' (Odum, 1970: 262). Thus, tourism can be viewed as an exchange of materials between the living (human) and non-living (cultural and physical environment) substances of a community.

Community focus Within this ecological setting the model attempts to highlight some fundamental processes. The second component was the recognition that the model would need to involve the consideration of several dimensions of community life if it was to be as comprehensive as the

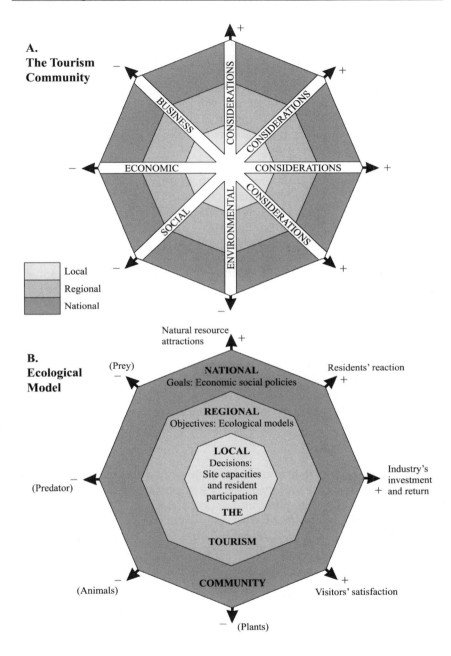

Figure 1.3 Ecological model of tourism planning
Source: Murphy (1985: 168)

term 'community' merited. In this respect Murphy suggested community tourism research and planning needed to focus on the following considerations: environmental, social, economic and business. While resident and visitor surveys are two widely used techniques for providing insight into local considerations associated with tourism, they often only provide a small 'quantitative' part of the picture and can leave out personal and private insights (Hughes, 1995). To obtain a full assessment of what tourism can mean to a community requires more extensive surveys and the inclusion of other stakeholder groups.

Stakeholders The third component was to identify principal actors associated with these four considerations in community tourism and in keeping with an ecological emphasis points out similarities with the features of natural environments. Accordingly, Murphy proposed that environmental and social considerations should focus on the natural attractions and the social/residential response of a tourism destination. These were equated with the native plants and animals of natural environments, that combine to create its overall ecosystem and attraction to potential visitors. The business consideration was equated with tourists, who come to experience the attractions and interact with the residents. In the natural setting the tourists are viewed as the prey, which come to feed on the natural environment and intermingle with the residents but in the process expose themselves to the tourism industry. The economic considerations were represented by the industry, which serves the tourist and provides the travel experience, which in the natural environment is viewed as the predator that feeds off the tourist as its prey. In this case, of course, the goal is not to consume the visitors, but to satisfy them and send them home as repeat visitors or goodwill ambassadors for the destination and its people.

Connectivity The fourth acknowledged component is that this ecological community can exist at a variety of levels. Murphy identifies three such levels of community: local, regional and national. Each level has its own goals and priorities which should be harmonised for maximum effectiveness. Local and regional levels in a community planning context hold particular relevance for destinations. It is these levels that represent the 'coalface' of the industry, where the tourists and the environment and its inhabitants will intermingle.

Interestingly, several prominent tourism writers have advocated more research and planning at the regional and local levels. Krippendorf (1982) has recommended that the most appropriate scale for the development and marketing of tourism would be a combination of local and regional levels. Getz (1983) has recommended more attention be given to planning and initiatives from the bottom up, meaning from and by the people directly affected rather than from higher levels of government, such as state or national legislators. Gunn (1997) has long been championing a corridor and node approach that brings together individual attractions of small communities into regional packages for modern mobile tourists with specific special interests.

Balance The fifth and most important component of the suggested model was that all these considerations, actors and scales had to be brought into balance if the ecosystem is to continue and prosper. This was illustrated by showing all the considerations had both positive and negative poles, and that a central point of balance starting at the local levels was the most desirable outcome. In this sense the model was championing the concept of sustainable development that came to the fore with the Brundtland report in 1987. Goodall and Stabler (2000) make a case for combining the top-down and bottom-up planning approaches to achieve a more balanced and appropriate environmental management on both local and global scales.

Application Murphy recognised that the above model was both a simplification of a complex entity and untested. Therefore, he put his ecological tourism community concept to the test in several empirical case studies and practical situations around the province of British Columbia, Canada over several years. The findings from these experiences were presented in a paper entitled 'Community driven tourism planning' (Murphy, 1988). The evidence from the four cases, involving communities ranging from small rural communities to the provincial capital, revealed some consistent patterns of behaviour. First, it showed the public were well aware of tourism and its potential impacts, so residents could hold their own in debate and discussions. Second, within the case study communities it was often small groups of people who became involved with tourism planning and 'in some cases it may be one determined person' (Murphy, 1988: 98). Third, there was evidence of goodwill in that the industry, local government officials and active residents often had more interests in common than many had suspected, and that given an early chance to express these interests led to a more community oriented perspective in the planning suggestions.

Independent calls for more community participation in the tourism planning process have come from a number of researchers including Krippendorf (1987) and Haywood (1988).

Harmonised travel model
Krippendorf (1987) utilising his extensive European, and particularly Swiss, experiences has suggested that if tourism is to survive and prosper it needs to humanise travel and bring about *greater harmony between hosts and visitors*. He advocates a 'soft and humane tourism' so those who are tourists and those who depend upon them can develop common goals. These goals are to bring 'the greatest possible benefit to all the participants – travellers,

the host population and the tourist business, without causing intolerable ecological and social damage' (Krippendorf, 1987: 106).

Tourism Truisms As part of the process to achieve this goal he reminds us to remember some truisms about tourism. First, for many people tourism is the last bastion of freedom, so regulations should not be overly burdensome. There can be a great feeling of release when you are able to act without those who know you being aware of your actions. However, taken to the extreme a tourist's release of inhibitions can lead to behaviour that is degrading to tourists and their hosts. Therefore, limits need to be set and conditions formulated so that tourism leads to more and not less consideration of others. Second, most people wish to relax on their holiday, so we must acknowledge this as a driving and unifying force for most tourists. Third, tourism is highly seasonal so institutional efforts by governments and education authorities must be made to break down the old Victorian and industrial based calendars. Fourth, we must ensure that there are fair economic transactions, with the advantages and disadvantages being equally distributed between hosts and guests.

Balanced tourist development To bring about the humanisation of travel and greater harmony between the hosts and guests Krippendorf proposed a concept of balanced tourism development. This was to be achieved by focusing on the needs and interests of the tourists and locals, and by coordinating them. The first step was to ascertain the interests and priorities of each group; if there was a reasonable match then planning and development could proceed, with the following provisos: 'One of the most important factors in a balanced development is the principle of local sovereignty in matters concerning the use of land' (Krippendorf, 1987: 119). Planned investment is best when both the industry and local interests are involved; in other words they have some form of community partnership. The local workforce should be used wherever possible to maximise individual benefits and to give locals an incentive to improve service. Last, but certainly not least, is the recommendation to 'emphasize and cultivate what is typically local' (Krippendorf, 1987: 123).

Planning modes

Haywood (1988) notes the growing interest in encouraging greater public participation in the general planning process, and he feels the community destination would make an ideal scale and forum for such a process in tourism planning. He considers:

> Tourism and tourists are consumers and users of community resources (which) implies that the community is a commodity ... Whenever communities become venues of and for consumption, 'social sensitivity'

comes to the fore and a call goes out – often unheeded – to incorporate democracy into the planning process . . . Well developed and stronger tourism planning at the community level is vital if any region or country wishes to deliver exciting and novel tourist experiences in which there is an emphasis on quality and high value-added components at the destination points. (Haywood, 1988: 106).

However, Haywood considers that given the diversity of planning situations around the world it would be better to seek *varied planning modes* rather than a particular type of planning model.

Planning perspectives Accordingly, Haywood (1988: 110) calls for a more applied situational approach, based on local planning realities and situational difficulties, in encouraging real community participation. Within this process he hopes to see five basic perspectives of the planning process enhanced, with the particular mix being guided by local conditions. He sees planning as a process for the following:

- designing the future;
- innovation;
- learning;
- influencing; and
- managing

Since management is the focus of this book it is germane to look in some detail at Haywood's suggestions in this area.

Haywood notes that at the community level tourism is more than a purely economic phenomenon. Therefore, tourism planners should reformulate a more sensitive and viable role for this activity within destination communities. He offers a schema to illustrate how the various interest groups within such communities could share their hopes for the future, their learning, their innovative ideas and attempts to influence others in a general process of management. One outcome of such a planning process would be 'a legitimacy strategy'; defined as:

A clear delineation of the role of tourism within a community. This will permit the establishment of guidelines outlining what needs to be done to make tourism more socially, ecologically and economically responsive and responsible. (Haywood, 1988: 115)

Such external recognition of the community and its planning process is one of the key elements of community planning referred to earlier. Haywood cites an example of such a planning process happening in Canada's Northwest Territories (NWT). There the territory government has attempted to legitimise community based tourism by promoting tourism as 'an industry which reflects the interests and aspirations of the communities in which it is located' (Ahmed, 1986, cited in Haywood, 1988: 115). This is achieved by encouraging the type of tourism activity that stimulates NWT purchases and profits for NWT residents, employs NWT residents in jobs compatible with traditional lifestyles, is environmentally sensitive, and offers tourists a variety of quality offerings at a fair price.

Like many discussants of tourism management Haywood declines to define this term, but he does indicate the actual planning process is only one step. '(T)he focus in community tourism is not merely on the formulation of strategy as a problem solving process, but on the problem of implementation and control' (Haywood, 1988: 115). In his concluding paragraph he recognises that for community tourism to be effective it must enhance the operating effectiveness of all parties. To ensure mutual effectiveness requires a more comprehensive management that incorporates elements of monitoring, such as visitor surveys and environmental audits, and controls, such as land use zoning. We will be returning to these management approaches in Part II of this book.

Agent of change

Despite the growing interest in community tourism most researchers and writers have tended to focus their discussions on particular aspects of the topic. For example, many have focused on the impacts of tourism on host populations in destination communities. Within those impact studies the major topic is either socioeconomic or sociocultural in its emphasis. Such a breakdown is natural given the need to concentrate on a specific question or issue in much modern research and that the research is seldom value free, meaning that social scientists will gravitate to social issues and physical scientists to environmental concerns. But the net effect has been to divide into segments that which needs to be managed as a whole.

To illustrate this point, one needs only to examine the multitude of social impact studies that have attempted to analyse the perceptions and attitudes of residents in a variety of tourism destination communities. In an article on host perceptions of sociocultural impacts Brunt and Courtney (1999) have constructed summary impact tables from the tourism literature. While not everyone would use the same classification structure, a condensation of their findings indicates that the social impact will be felt in several ways, differing with respect to diverse aspects of the tourism industry and the quality of the interactions. From their listing one theme emerges strongly, and that is tourism will be an agent of social change in destination communities. However, whether tourism initiates or is simply a facet of ongoing change is a subject of debate. As Brunt and Courtney (1999: 497) observe:

Because the (tourism) industry is highly visual it has often become the scapegoat for sociocultural change. The dynamic character of all societies and cultures should thus not be overlooked and the potential (global) influences must be considered against this background.

In their personal study, Brunt and Courtney found local residents referred frequently to many of the key impacts that their literature review had identified. This caused them to conclude 'while there are some specific differences, the general analyses of the sociocultural impacts of tourism can be applied to the perceptions of residents of a small British coastal tourist (resort)' (Brunt and Courtney, 1999: 511).

While individual research studies of this kind are useful in building up a general knowledge base of what is happening when residents and tourists meet in a tourist destination community, we need to pull such empirical strands together and develop theories that help to explain and predict these interactions. This was the thinking of John Ap, when he introduced social exchange theory as a possible theoretical base for understanding residents' perceptions of local tourism. Ap (1992: 667) states 'the advantages of using social exchange theory are that it can accommodate explanation of both positive and negative perceptions, and can examine relationships at the individual or collective level'.

Social exchange theory

An exchange process is a unique temporal relationship, where each transaction is linked to a history and future for the involved actors, emphasising a more or less durable social relationship between the two actors that is modifiable over time (Ap, 1992: 677–8). The basic components of any exchange process are seen as 'need satisfaction', in that exchanges are engaged in if they satisfy the needs of the involved parties. Linking these components is a set of processes that are presented as flows. These are (1) initiation of the exchange; (2) a positive exchange formation or; (2a) no exchange takes place; (3) an exchange transaction evaluation; (4) a positive evaluation of the exchange consequences or; (4a) a negative evaluation of the exchange consequences and a withdrawal from the process.

Need satisfaction In terms of community tourism Ap suggests several motives within the area of need satisfaction. These motives could include key community actors who may like to encourage tourism depending on local circumstances, such as civic officials, local business people, or residents wishing to improve economic conditions; on the other hand there may be similar groupings opposed to further tourism growth, because of perceived problems with congestion. This identified need satisfaction initiates the actual exchange process, which consists of antecedents and an actual form.

Antecendents The antecedents are those opportunities perceived by one of the actors in the exchange process, whereby they determine 'what's in it for me'. Such returns can cover a wide range of motives. They could be the rational choices of economics, such as increasing income. They could represent satisfying behaviour, where a merely satisfying outcome like a successful festival is regarded as a sufficient return. They could be a perceived win-win situation for both or more parties, such as when the tourism industry provides tangible benefits to residents as well as tourists. The returns could also be viewed as a form of justice, such as the recognition of native land title.

Actual form The actual exchange has two potential forms, in that it can be balanced or unbalanced regarding the sharing of benefits and costs. The actual outcome at this point is highly dependent on the respective powers of each actor. As the description of social exchange indicated, such powers can change over time. For instance, Ap and others consider that when a community embraces tourism it is placing itself at an exchange disadvantage with respect to the industry, because it is clearly signalling its desire to see growth. However, once the industry is established with a considerable equity investment in place the industry becomes more dependent on the cooperation of the host community, and the power relationships of the exchange process become more balanced.

Consequences When the exchange has been completed its consequences are evaluated. This can occur at several levels. The outputs refer to the physical, social or symbolic creations, such as increased income or amenities. Action refers to the behaviour of the two actors involved. Ap (1999: 685) states that:

> The extension of hospitality, courtesy, and friendliness toward tourists, or opposition to newly proposed tourism development are actions that residents may exhibit as a result of favourable and unfavourable encounters with tourists and the industry.

Outcomes refer to how the actors feel about the exchange. If the actors' needs have been satisfied the exchange reinforces the behaviour and encourages continued engagement.

Such a theoretical perspective would appear to hold considerable promise, in treating community tourism as a system of individual exchanges that combine to form a collective assessment which can change over time as circumstances change. It is one which is anchored in sociological theory (Emerson, 1972; Levi-Strauss, 1969), that is 'concerned with understanding the exchange of resources between individuals and groups in an interaction situation' (Ap, 1999: 668). That is certainly the situation in tourism, where the travel business has been described as a series of 'moments of truth' between the traveller and an industry representative (Carlzon, 1987). Furthermore, the community has been described as a commodity in a sales exchange (Haywood, 1988). So it seems perfectly reasonable to place the whole process into a social exchange paradigm. However, there have been few empirical studies that have tried to implement all or part of the social exchange theory and there is some criticism of its true utility.

Application One study that has put social exchange theory to the test is a survey of residents living in five counties surrounding the Mt Rogers National Recreation Area of southwest Virginia (Jurowski *et al.*, 1997). Their social impact survey attempts to refine and clarify previous direct social impact assessment studies by incorporating elements of the social exchange theory. They develop a path analysis to explain the screening process that residents use to weigh and balance factors that could influence their support for nature based tourism in the area. The analysis reveals that the three traditional tourism impact assessments of economic, social and environmental impacts could be influenced by exogenous (screening) variables.

Residents who see a potential for economic gain develop a stronger level of support than those who have an 'ecocentric' attitude (environmentalists) regarding their impact assessments. Those who use the same local resources as the tourist are relatively neutral in their support. Those who have a strong attachment to the region, as measured by their 'attitudinal feelings for the area', are relatively positive about the economic and social returns from local nature based tourism but are negative about its environmental impacts. Consequently, Jurowski *et al.* (1997: 9) consider 'the findings confirmed the interactive nature of the(ir) four exchange elements (economic gain, resource use, community attachment, and ecocentric attitude) and three types of perceptions (economic-, social -, and environmental impacts)'

Pearce *et al.* (1996: 20–7) have three major problems with Ap's support of social exchange theory. First, they feel that the social exchange theory is too simplistic. The proposal that individuals balance the costs and benefits of tourism to guide their support for the industry fails to give adequate acknowledgment to the complex nature of tourism and its relationship with the host community. Second, they doubt that the equity condition and social justice principle occur very frequently. Third, they find Ap offers no techniques with which to ascertain how an individual balances personal conditions with community costs and benefits.

The question of how individuals calculate personal and community costs and benefits of tourism is still largely unanswered. This is a major conundrum with respect to resident reactions to local tourism impacts, where many empirical studies have shown the majority of their samples are positive about tourism even though they receive no apparent personal benefits. Rather than simply offer a criticism of a refreshing attempt to introduce a theoretical framework by which to examine resident reactions to tourism, Pearce *et al.* proffer a social science theory of their own.

Social representations theory

They recommend that researchers and practitioners consider social representations theory (Moscovici, 1984) with respect to tourism – community relationships. This theory 'focuses on both the content of social knowledge and the way that this knowledge is created and shared by people in various groups, societies or communities' (Pearce *et al.* 1996: 31). Social knowledge is a combination of individual and societal values, ideas and practices that individuals use to describe and react to a stimulus. This knowledge becomes their social representations or public evaluation of that stimulus. Pearce *et al.* (1996: 38–40) claim Moscovici sees two key functions operating within these social representations. First, they establish an order by which individuals orientate themselves to the world – their 'orb'. Second, these representations enable an individual to communicate with other members of a community, by providing them with a code for identifying and classifying 'unambiguously' the various aspects of their world. Further, they claim social representations are 'particularly valuable' for explaining social conflict and individual reactions to issues, because it is conflict that brings social representations out into the open and in the process social representations help to turn the unfamiliar into the more familiar.

Social representations theory is seen as being more than personal attitude creation. It emphasises more of the social influences and interactions of community and society than simply relying on personal interpretations of events. The theory contains two major components that could be particularly useful to community tourism research and development – its objectification and anchoring processes.

Objectification process First, there is an 'objectification process' where abstract concepts or ideas are turned into more ordinary reference points to create a personal and understandable image of the concept. Thus, when a tourism development proposal includes references to economic multipliers and impacts, local residents will consider these terms as individuals and groups and give them a more personal and local meaning.

Anchoring process The objectification process leads to an 'anchoring process', which enables individuals to identify and classify an event or proposal by comparing it with what is known already. As such it involves comparisons with previously identified categories and draws upon existing social and cultural knowledge held by the individual and the group. This enables people to gauge the significance of concepts and proposals.

These two components could be equated to the cognitive and evaluative functions of attitude formation (Fishbein & Raven, 1967), but in a more socially determined context, and have been incorporated into the individual's orb. Objectification can be seen as the initial stage of individual reaction, as the person attempts to place the new concept within their own and group experiences. Having interpreted the concept in more personal and meaningful terms the individual categorised it as beneficial or not, based on their own interpretation and that of the social group to which they belong.

Application In their summary of the social representations theory Pearce *et al.* (1996: 56) emphasise the theory is opposed to either a completely individual or social deterministic approach to understanding social knowledge, but prefer to stress its 'emic' approach. This is where study 'draws upon the actor's interpretations and local inside knowledge of the meaning of the behaviour under study' (Pearce *et al.*, 1996: 4). This mutual individual and group assessment and response to situations is well illustrated in their summary of the theory's key features, and is illustrated in their selection of community tourism examples. Some of these features include the use of images, supplemented by the use of metaphors and analogies.

They offer two sets of examples. International cases, based essentially on secondary data, whereby they translate and reinterpret the cases in light of social representation theory; and Australian cases where the authors have been more directly involved with the research and have applied aspects of the theory. Examples of the Australian social representations research include the empirical studies of resident views in two different types of Queensland destination.

Australian social representations cases Port Douglas, a fast-growing resort, serving the growing market for visits to the Great Barrier Reef as well as providing its own tropical experiences, demonstrates a threefold grouping of resident sentiments. Based on responses to questions regarding general tourism impacts along with personal and community service impacts the analysis reveals three social representation groupings could be identified as positive, low negative and high negative groups. The low negative group consists of those who have broad concerns about the environment and economy, yet within this group many are moderately positive about items such as job opportunities and the scenic beauty associated with the tourism industry. When these three groups are compared with various development options significant differences are noted.

Townsville, a coastal destination that has experienced slow and steady growth, presents a different picture. There, questions relating to the type of visitor and industry desired by the local community along with the usual tourism impact and development questions failed to uncover any distinctive groupings. Rather the homogeneity of responses indicated its 'social representation could be characterised as "tourism for the community" since a dominant emphasis on the developments and facilities which were seen as desirable for tourism also served local citizen needs' (Pearce *et al.* 1996: 177–8).

The utility of the social representation theory is that its combination of individual and community assessments provides clearer directions for planning and development. The results from the Australian studies and the other empirical studies according to Pearce *et al.*:

> Direct attention away from the dominant concern with the impacts of tourism and how these are seen by the community to how hosts understand, define and evaluate the future of tourism. This concern with providing planning-relevant information, rather than assuming that a study of impacts per se provides planning-relevant material, is an important evolutionary step which the study of community attitudes needs to take. (1996: 178)

This is certainly the approach and purpose that has been taken by Beeton (2000) in her study of community response to film-induced tourism at Barwon Heads in southern Australia.

Beeton (2000) has examined the residents' reactions to the filming of a successful television series, *Sea Change*, on a small village of 800 households using the social representation theory framework. She utilises the three-staged approach advocated by Pearce *et al.* (1996) by first looking for a consensus among the residents concerning their views on the local tourism situation. This was followed by an examination of the links between the stated tourism impacts and residents' related ideas; the final stage being to cluster the core of images which portrayed residents' social representation of this feature in their lives. This methodology produces seven social representation clusters that were linked to three major factors – average length of residency, ex-city dweller, and the consideration of tourism as a preferred industry. These results indicate to Beeton (2000: 135) that differing attitudes towards economic development, costs of living and crowding have 'the potential to divide and destroy a community as it is today'. Social representations could become a useful planning tool for future community planning in that the theory helps to identify disenfranchised clusters and points to potential uniting strategies.

Summary

The above review indicates that tourism data definition and research are evolving and that certain academic fields are being tapped for inspiration and guidance. The data issues are being addressed by a combination of government and academic interests. These interests are primarily economic and taxation based but in the process we are developing a clearer picture of tourism's size and complexity.

Most of the analysed models and theories draw their inspiration from a single or small range of social science disciplines, primarily sociology and economics, and in some cases the broader fields of geography and ecology. However, to date there has been little evident use of the growing field of business management. This is surprising, given that tourism is a business and if any community is to succeed in this industry and to be sustainable in an economic sense it needs to incorporate business principles into its portfolio of management techniques.

Chapter 2

Key Business Management Functions

While we find many tourism studies referring to and extolling the virtues of management, we seldom find explicit definitions of this term or descriptions of the principles and functions they involve. Even though tourism is recognised as a business very few authors of tourism papers and texts have attempted to incorporate business principles into their research. On the other hand, many authors refer in one way or another to the concept of management that sometimes includes a passing reference to tourism's business perspective. It is the purpose of this chapter to indicate there are indeed some highly relevant business management principles that can have a major bearing on how community tourism operates and to show how similar they are to many of the concepts espoused by non-business authors, such as social scientists.

If tourism is to develop and fulfil its potential it will require careful and detailed management, as many authors have indicated. The need for such management is particularly relevant to community tourism, which will need to involve a wide variety of interests and opinions. However, because most authors have failed to define what they mean by the term 'management', including those who place it in their titles, we are forced to interpret their evidence and advice in terms of traditional dictionary definitions. Most dictionaries define management as the process of managing, where the verb 'to manage' is defined as to guide the running of an activity like a business or household. While such a definition may cover the general purpose and intent of most past uses by academics and government officials, it is no longer satisfactory as a guide to the complex business and environmental management needed for many aspects of tourism development.

Strategic community tourism management will involve a host community deciding which elements of its local 'sense of place' resources to sell as a community product to tourists and the tourism industry. Such a process needs to include a variety of stakeholders with a common under-standing of what is meant by management if they are to operate in successful collaboration. Given that tourism is a business, and the principal motivation for community tourism is to determine how to enter this business so as to achieve the best return for the community at large, one of the logical places to start this process is with the concept of business management.

Business Management

The field of business management is relatively young by academic standards and has come to the fore in the post-war reconstruction era, when businesses like tourism have become more complex and global, and the business environment more competitive than ever. Like all new academic fields of inquiry it has struggled to identify and distinguish itself from other academic disciplines and fields, and like most other academic areas it is now composed of a variety of sub-fields. One of business management's key differentiators has been to develop a scientific business management approach that leads to general principles of behaviour and outcomes. Within this approach the sub-field of organisation theory has focused on the total organisation of a business rather than individual worker–manager relations, leading to the current differentiation between organisational behaviour and human resource management studies. This interest in the total organisation has identified four principal functions of management that can be applied to an extensive range of situations, including areas like community tourism, that wish to combine business returns with other objectives.

One of the clearest descriptions of classical business management is offered by Daft *et al.* (1992: 5), who consider:

> Management is the attainment of organizational goals in an effective and efficient manner through planning, organizing, leading and controlling organizational resources.

This definition stresses the need to start with organisational goals, which will be both the signposts to later decision-making and the yardsticks by which to measure the success of subsequent actions. It identifies four basic functional steps in the process: planning, organising, leadership and controlling. These management principles are often used as the structure for many business texts and courses because of their general validity. All of which is encompassed in the pragmatic perspective of being effective and efficient, rather than presenting unattainable utopian systems.

A visual representation of the definition is presented in Figure 2.1. It shows how any organisation, be it a destination or single business, needs a vision of the future and its place within it. This vision needs to be converted into general goals and specific objectives through a *planning* process. To attain these objectives requires *organising* one's resources and assigning responsibility for different tasks and functions. An important task in any management process is *leading* staff through motivation and mentorship. Finally, there is a continuous need for *controlling* the efforts and outputs of

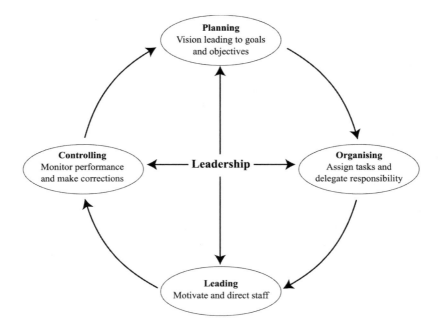

Figure 2.1 The process of management

the organisation, to ensure they are on track with respect to the original objectives and changing conditions.

This description is a compartmentalisation of continuous process, as indicated by the circular flow of the diagram, and as such is an artificial aid to highlight the individual importance of all four functions. One could argue about the placing and number of functions, and we have highlighted the need for *leadership* in all areas by placing it at the centre. This has been done because in the modern business world the only constant is change. It will require leadership to envision the new obstacles and opportunities, to assign tasks in a flexible and effective manner, and to select the appropriate forms of monitoring, as well as continue to motivate and retain key staff in a turbulent and competitive environment.

Four business management functions

Planning

The first management function of planning is needed to select which of the considered goals are more realistic and the possible ways to attain them. Such a process of selection should be guided at this stage and throughout by the need to be effective and efficient; effectiveness being viewed as the degree to which the organisation can achieve its stated objectives, and efficiency as indicated by the minimal use of resources to produced the desired outcomes (Daft, *et al.* 1992: 10–11). So the selection of which goals to pursue involves being realistic about potential returns rather than being overly optimistic about what one has to offer. Consequently, for community tourism this stage requires analysis that is both demand and supply driven. This stage also necessitates an objective assessment of their competitive position and not simply a reiteration of community pride. It is essential at this juncture to review and incorporate input from a range of stakeholders, especially those familiar with budgeting, marketing and community resources.

Organising

The second management function is organising. It is needed to assign specific task responsibilities to different departments, groups or individuals and to allocate sufficient resources to enable them to accomplish the selected planning goals. This should involve the matching of interests and capabilities with the assigned tasks. Increasingly in business, as well as tourism, the final delivery of the product or service requires a multitude of groups or individuals to combine their talents and skills. Similarly, in these competitive times everyone is being asked to 'do more with less', so the issue of resource allocation is a major one in all types of business.

Leadership

The third management function is leadership, which involves the motivation of people to achieve an organisation's objectives. Although Daft *et al.* have isolated leadership and identified it as the third function, this aspect of management is one which should and does pervade every function. It involves innovation and risk-taking and the ability to communicate ideas and enthusiasm.

For some this has become the most important element of modern management. *Time Magazine* reports:

> Once, the CEO had to run the business and watch the bottom line. Now he or she has to be a strategic visionary, an operations hawk and the chief salesman meanwhile keeping Wall Street investors happy. (Kelly, 2000: 58)

Such high expectations are now mirrored in the large salaries and benefit packages being paid to Chief Executive Officers (CEOs) of major companies and institutions, but they 'are also paying with their job for any big strategic failure' (Kelly, 2000: 58). Leadership is finally beginning to be recognised as an important element in tourism, and an example of this is presented in the case study at the end of this part of the book.

Controlling

The fourth function is controlling, which involves the monitoring of an organisation's activities to ensure they are on track with respect to the stated goals. Where deviations are detected, due to internal conditions or external factors, corrections are made as needed. Internal conditions needing correction in tourism could involve problems of communication and coordination between the different sectors, or unforeseen environmental and social impacts. External factors, like economic business cycles, currency fluctuations, and terrorism that cannot be predicted but can have significant ramifications on tourist destinations, require quick corrective responses on behalf of those destinations.

The tourism oriented terrorist attack in Bali required quick corrective responses from several parties and directions. The Australian government felt impelled to issue travel alert warnings to its citizens, advising them to avoid Bali and Indonesia in case of further incidents. Faced with a dramatic decline in business, the Balinese tourism industry developed a promotion campaign and adjusted prices to counter declining business. The airlines connecting Australia and Bali quickly reduced the number of flights until the shock and fear waned and travel numbers began to recover.

Tourism application

An example of these four functions at work in a community tourism situation can be seen in the Laws and Le Pelley (2000) article on managing tourism in the walled city of Canterbury, England (Figure 2.2). Although the authors do not specifically mention or advocate a complete business management approach involving the four functions, their review of the situation and current planning processes indicates these functions are present and being implemented to varying extents. Laws and Le Pelley (2000: 232) observe that the management challenges of a historic walled city are extreme, given that the different patterns of space usage by residents and visitors in such a confined area result in regular congestion and conflict. Consequently, the city of Canterbury has embarked on a series of initiatives that incorporate the four functions of business management.

They report that Canterbury's heritage tourism product was 'beginning to show signs of stagnation and decline' and that 'Canterbury can be considered to be approaching the zenith of its tourism life cycle, as the pressures of visitors is beginning to drive local people away'. Consequently, the city's *planning goal* is to reverse its decline as a tourist destination and sub-regional shopping centre by revising its visitor management strategies (Laws and Le Pelley, 2000: 234). To achieve this goal the city has *organised* a special legal entity, called the Canterbury City Centre Initiative (CCCI). This organisation is designed to 'develop a sustainable management strategy for tourists and shoppers that complement the

Figure 2.2 Canterbury's walled city catering to residents and visitors

qualities of life of Canterbury's residents by involving the tourist trade and residents in its evolution' (Laws and Le Pelley, 2000: 236).

Within the management structure of the CCCI Laws and Le Pelley identified a *leadership role*, and one which changes over time. They claim:

> the city visitor manager is the key individual who draws the partners together and administers the partnership and projects. In Phase 1, the manager was a quiet consolidator who built trust between the partners. In Phase 2, the new manager is a more outgoing personality who will 'sell' Canterbury's management initiatives and the benefits of the partnership. (Laws & Le Pelley, 2000: 236)

Such leadership changes are not uncommon in business or community ventures. The development of Victoria, Canada's successful 1994 Commonwealth Games, went through three different leadership needs and leaders. The first initiated the idea of hosting the Games and put together a team that eventually won the bid over Cardiff and New Delhi. Once the right to hold the Games had been won a different sort of leader was required, one who could coordinate the various municipalities and agencies to build the range of facilities that were needed to host this major event. The third and last leader was one who marketed the event to both domestic and international markets; especially to the challenging adjacent and lucrative United States market which has a limited understanding or appreciation of this major sporting event.

Control over the CCCI initiatives involves a comprehensive monitoring of its progress by an independent researcher based in a local college. This has resulted already in a revision to the original plans with 'the evolution of coach park management arrangements in conjunction with the users of the coach park' (Laws & Le Pelley, 2000: 241). In terms of results Laws and Le Pelley report most stakeholder groups are pleased with the current outcome of this management initiative, as shown in Table 2.1. Such evidence they feel 'demonstrates the value of partnership working, supported by a full-time manager and a sense of common purpose, in empowering a destination to manage its tourism industry in an environmentally and culturally sustainable manner' (Laws & Le Pelley, 2000: 243).

Environmental Scanning

As the above example indicates, any community tourism management will need to integrate tourism business needs with the host community's environmental setting and its tourism character. But that is true of any business, for all businesses are part of an open system. Business management regularly takes place within an open environmental situation that requires constant scanning if the business is to maximise its opportunities to succeed. Consequently the four functions of management cannot be

Table 2.1 Impacts of Canterbury's stakeholders

Stakeholders	Indicative tourism problems	Responses	Observed impacts
Residents	Congestion	Attract tourists into less visited areas	Group visit pressure dispersed on to four alternative pedestrian routes. Decrease in complaints from residents living on original route. Initial complaints from residents living on new routes have now decreased.
Tourists	Congestion Limited range of attractions	New walks Signing Maps Pedestrianisation New attractions	Increased tourist pressure in High Street as Cathedral management measures imposed. Tourists attract pedlars and buskers – complaints from shop keepers. Maps and signing effective in dispersing tourists.
Coach operators	Restricted and undeveloped parking	New coach park Visitor Shepherds	Complaints about length of walk to town centre and price of parking from some operators. Behaviour of tourists and congestion in town is modified by Visitor Shepherds welcoming tourists.
Cathedral	Crowds detract from experiences of visitors and worshippers	Shepherding scheme Entrance charges Burning incense	Ambience of Cathedral much improved. Visitor pressure is deflected into the town centre.
Environment	Air pollution Litter Inappropriate changes to historic buildings Wear and tear	Air quality monitoring at selected sites Park and ride to reduce cars in city New location for coach park Special planning controls	Air quality in town centre improves with increased pedestrianisation. Increased air pollution at new coach park. Drivers asked not to run engines whilst passengers away from coach. Special planning controls effective in maintaining historic ambience. Sheer volume of tourists overspills and widens paths provided.

Source: Laws and Le Pelley (2000: 242)

developed in isolation from the immediate setting of the host community or the wider context of our global economy, and must be viewed from the perspective of a business' overall organisational environment.

An organisational environment includes all the environmental elements that have the potential to affect an organisation. It is commonly drawn up into three major spheres of environmental influence, that also have particular relevance to tourism.

Internal environment

The internal environment is the area within the organisation's boundaries where it conducts its business. It is the corporate entity that manages its own affairs. It represents the opportunity to operate the four functions of management directly, but since no organisation operates in isolation, which is certainly true of tourism, it is influenced in its management options by the surrounding task and general environments.

Task environment

The task environment is the setting surrounding the actual organisation and consists of the sectors that 'conduct day-to-day transactions with the organisation and directly influence its basic operations and performance' (Daft *et al.* 1992: 68). In terms of community tourism this would be the host community setting, with its local labour pool, its supportive businesses, and visitors. In a community setting there are likely to be competitive businesses such as other attractions and hotels, but interestingly these competitors are sometimes collaborators.

Collaboration occurs in the development of partnership marketing, where individual and sometimes competitive businesses combine some of their marketing resources to attract visitors to their community destination. In the northwest corner of the United States the city of Seattle has periodically attempted to boost its attractiveness to distant urban markets in the rest of the country by linking with Victoria and Vancouver, British Columbia, to form a 'Discovery Triangle'. The strategy is that three different yet close destinations could present a combined product that would tempt Americans to travel the thousands of miles needed to reach Seattle and the Pacific Northwest.

General environment

The general environment is the outer layer representing the indirect affects of national policies and major global market and societal trends. In tourism such 'external' factors have long been recognised as major determinants of industry success, as demonstrated by Wahab's (1975: 94) assessment that 'tourism demand is highly sensitive to socio-political conditions and to changes in travel fashion'. For example, national policies regarding tourism marketing, currency exchange levels, and infrastructure such as international airports can have a major bearing on visitor volumes.

In the global and political arenas tourism has been shown to be susceptible to the insecurity generated by political instability and terrorism. Tourism in Fiji has suffered considerably from its series of political coups, and in Egypt terrorists have purposely targeted tourists in order to pressure their government into change. The 11 September terrorism in New York was aimed at corporate America, but it used a major tourism business – air travel, to destroy its targets.

Approach comparisons

As in all classifications of human behaviour the above definition of management with its four functional categories and the related environmental scanning factors should be viewed as simplified photographic snapshots of an ongoing and fluid process. Once planning goals have been selected and the management process put into operation it will take time to monitor the results and decide if corrective measures are needed. 'In this complex and dynamic environment, managers must continually adjust to changing conditions' (Stoner *et al.*, 1995: 18). In the past such a process traditionally was given a five-year period in which to unfold. But with the acceleration of the global business tempo and almost instantaneous communication of the modern media and Internet it is often no longer possible to stick to set time periods of any size. Tourism Victoria in Australia recently completed a standard five-year strategic plan for the state's tourism industry, that is discussed in more detail as a case study. Included in the five-year plan is a call for an annual review process:

> to evaluate the performance of strategies so that appropriate action can be taken if required. It may be necessary to change strategic directions within the plan in reaction to unforeseen events, or shifts in the global environment. (Tourism Victoria, 2002: 8)

This need to be flexible and to consider a series of decisions has led to strategic applications of the management processes discussed above. Henry Mintzberg (1979: 60–1), a major theorist in organisational structure, describes strategy as involving a stream of decisions that incorporates 'a complex multistage process' involving several elements, including 'a change in the environment'. So it is not surprising to see a strong link between our chosen definition of management and its associated need for environmental scanning with strategic management.

Strategic Management

The four business functions have much in common with the concept of strategic management, which is a business management process that has significant utility to the communal decision-making of community tourism. Mintzberg's view of strategy as 'a pattern in a stream of decisions' has two implications that have particular application to tourism, with its many sectors and exposure to significant external factors. First, this vision of strategic management consists of a series of decisions with some consistency between them based on pursuing the organisation's goals. Second, it means the organisation must consider decision alternatives, for 'strategy may be viewed as the rationale that governs the organisation's choices among its alternatives' (Stahl & Grigsby, 1992: 5).

Deliberate and emergent strategies

Mintzberg differentiates between deliberate strategy and emergent strategy, because changing business conditions are especially relevant given the fluid nature of our global economy. When strategies are the result of the management planning function they are a *deliberate strategy,* designed to achieve the organisation's goals. However, there are occasions when businesses do not intentionally set a specific strategy, but may simply fall into one as a reaction to outside forces or as the result of internal control procedures, which is the *emergent* approach.

If Athiyaman's (1995) assessment of tourism's use of strategic management is still valid then it would appear that many tourism businesses and destinations are in the emergent category. His study of tourism and hospitality research publications reveals few are concerned with strategy implications and he considers that this is due either to a reluctance to publish sensitive business information or a lack of activity in this area of management. He notes, however, that previous research did indicate 'tourism businesses lag behind manufacturing firms in strategic planning and the research necessary to support strategic planning' (Athiyaman, 1995: 452). This would indicate it is an area of weakness in many tourism businesses – including destinations.

Decision steps

A strategic management process according to Stahl and Grigsby (1992: 5–6) involves the entire range of decisions that an organisation makes to fulfil its purposes. It consists of the following three *procedural steps*:

- *Strategy formulation,* where a set of decisions determines the organisation's mission and establishes its specific objectives, strategies and policies.
- *Strategy implementation* that refers to decisions creating either a new strategy or reinforcing an existing one.
- *Evaluation and control.* These are the activities that keep the strategy on track and provide an information feedback loop to the first step.

Tourism Strategic Management

The tourism industry focuses on meeting the needs and expectations of visitors. To do this it needs to follow the four functions of management internally, and to undertake such procedures strategically in light of its task and general environments as well as its internal circumstances. In setting its goals the industry needs to work with the host community because it is selling the community as a commodity. In organising to welcome and accommodate the visitor the industry needs to include resident and community priorities and to look for leadership within the community as well as the industry. Finally, it needs to monitor the situation via visitor and resident surveys, environmental and financial audits, to ensure the stated industry and community goals are being achieved. While these essentially internal and task environment features are being considered and acted upon, both the industry and community need to be aware of the more general and external forces that can influence their management strategies. Features such as economic cycles or government policies need to be anticipated, and surprises, such as the Asian financial crisis of 1997 or the more recent terrorist attacks in New York and Bali, require contingency plans.

To operate tourism management strategies along business lines at the community level requires a strategic approach operating within an open system that can incorporate as many considerations as possible with input from different stakeholder groups. Such management cannot be highly detailed and specific, for it needs to be flexible enough to consider the evolving wishes of the community and tourism market, plus leaving itself enough room to meet changing outside forces. However, at all times it should be able to present clear community tourism objectives, outline a series of strategic steps to achieve those objectives, and be measurable so as to be accountable.

An example of this is seen in a South Australian award-winning strategic tourism plan (Tonge & Myott, 1993: 45–6). The Eyre Peninsula Tourism Association developed a simple *seven point plan* as outlined below:

(1) Establish a *structure* with multiple stakeholder representation.
(2) Establish an effective *communication* network.
(3) Create high *visibility*.
(4) Focus on *product development*.
(5) Establish/maintain necessary *funding* base.
(6) Ensure that there are *courses* to train industry participants.
(7) *Advertise* and promote.

The key to their success is that they have built the foundation for the presentation and operation of their tourism resources in a logical and practical manner.

Social responsibility

Clearly this form of community tourism management will be a major challenge, but it is not one that is unique nor is it that unusual in today's global economy. Many businesses have adopted the functional strategic management perspective outlined above and in the process have developed techniques and perspectives that can be of assistance to the goal of strategic community tourism management. Gordon *et al.* (1990: 90) refer to a trend toward 'social responsibility' where business executives 'see themselves as legitimate servants of a variety of constituencies'. This involves being more responsible to society at large and developing stronger and clearer ethical standards. Their motivations are not entirely altruistic as Klein (2000) points out in her book *No Logo*, for companies are under increasing pressure to act responsibly as their failures and shortcomings are noted and acted upon by knowledgeable consumers.

In the process of serving more constituents and acting ethically three particular business ideas have considerable applicability to the goal of strategic community tourism management. One is the concept of stakeholder analysis, whereby the interests and views of those affected by an organisation's activities are analysed and taken into account. This includes those outside of the organisation's internal environment, and is particularly germane to those living and working in the task environment which can be considered the equivalent of the host community. Another is the technique of portfolio analysis and strategy that brings together a variety of individual and business considerations to guide strategic planning. The other is the concept of corporate culture that reflects the shared values, beliefs and habits of an organisation that interact to produce behavioural norms and expectations.

Stakeholder analysis

As business has become more complex and now serves a multitude of interests, it is no longer sufficient to consider only those within an organisation. Now managers must not only consider profit margins and shareholder returns, but working with local communities and contributing in some way to the betterment of society. This need to think 'outside the box' stems from both pressures to include outside groups in decision-making and opportunities that arise when a broader perspective is taken. Community activism is assisted by the easier spread of information through modern technologies and legal precedents supporting community participation in local initiatives (American Planning Association, 1999).

Companies that observe and adapt to emerging global trends can position themselves appropriately and reap the benefits, as AT&T did when it transformed itself into a global communications company (Callenbach *et al.* 1993).

Gordon *et al.* (1990: 87–8) reflect this thinking in their *'primary roles of business'*, which they identify as consisting of three levels.

- *Level 1* 'represents the traditional economic functions of business'. It is where the business produces needed goods and services that in the process provides employment, contributes to economic growth and earns a profit for shareholders.
- *Level 2* represents the social responsibilities of business, to its workers in the sense of a safe working environment and to the surrounding community in terms of minimising the negative impacts of its operation, such as using resources carefully and reducing pollution.
- *Level 3* is concerned with business' 'responsibility for assisting society in achieving such broad goals as the elimination of poverty and urban decay through a partnership of business, government agencies, and other private institutions' (Gordon *et al.*, 1990: 88).

The parallels between the primary roles as identified above and environmental scanning's three zones are clear, and very relevant to the tourism business. The primary objective in each situation is to establish a healthy business that produces employment and profit within the organisation. But this is no longer the only role for business. It must now operate in a socially acceptable way and contribute to the general welfare of the task and general environments of society.

Proactive business practices

In many respects these broader social and environmental responsibilities have been placed on business by legislation, but some business scholars are demonstrating how a more proactive stance by business with regard to the Level 2 and Level 3 roles can lead to more harmonious relations between stakeholders. Howatson (1990) cites a study by the consulting firm of Arthur D. Little Inc. that in a survey of environmental management practices among United States' corporations found three *stages of development*.

- *Stage 1* represents those businesses that respond to problems only as they arise; in other words possess a 'reactive management' philosophy.
- *Stage 2* occurs when businesses establish systems and programmes to comply with legislation and regulations, which is compliance management.
- *Stage 3* occurs when businesses attempt 'to foresee hazards and regulations and, therefore, work systematically to minimise the effects of their operations on the environment, the health and safety of their workers, and the local community' (Howatson, 1990: vii).

The number of businesses at Stage 1 were thankfully small. Most businesses in the survey were classified as being at Stage 2, but a growing number of 'progressive firms' were moving into Stage 3 – 'beyond compliance'. Howatson considers this last stage is preferable from a business point of view, because they can be proactive, that is 'actively managing, rather than letting events force them to respond' (Howatson, 1990: viii).

From an environmental perspective there is a call to move beyond compliance, because this can be seen as 'shallow environmentalism' that focuses merely on meeting current environmental regulations and standards. 'Deep ecology', which strives to adopt a more progressive and holistic approach to management, is held up as the new ideal. These principles of deep ecology have found expression in the business community with firms such as The Body Shop and the Pantagonia Clothing Company (Callenbach *et al.*, 1993).

With these broader roles and responsibilities business has to consult and work with a larger group of stakeholders. Such stakeholders will vary from situation to situation, but in general terms researchers and practitioners have identified a manageable number of key groups. In Howatson's (1990: 11) review of Canadian businesses he identified four *stakeholder groups*. These included the following:

- *regulators* and *policy makers* in governments at all levels;
- *employees, investors* and *local communities* whose economic fortunes are tied to the corporation's well-being;
- *firms' customers* and *suppliers*; and
- *general public*, who watch 'The Journal' (the Canadian equivalent to 'Sixty Minutes' or 'Panorama'), support environmental groups and vote.

In one of the few tourism papers on the subject, Robson and Robson (1996) provided two examples in the tourism industry. In their schematic for a tour operator they identified 12 possible stakeholder groups, but it is possible to locate all of them within Howatson's broader framework. For example, we would place stakeholders in the following categories:

- central government bodies, national tourist organisations, regional tourist board;
- employees, local government tourism marketer;
- end users, transport providers, hoteliers, local and national attractions, travel agents; and
- Pressure groups and media.

Obviously in the modern world where individuals have multiple functions and responsibilities there can be some overlap between such groups. To a large extent this depends on which hat some stakeholders put on for the issue under examination. For example, in Robson and Robson's tour operator example the media could be functioning as an advertising forum or as the 'fourth estate', protecting the public's interest with its news stories.

Conflict issues

Regardless of the exact number of stakeholder groups identified in any particular analysis there is also the question of how they are to participate in any corporate decision-making. This has become a major issue in business management and general planning, for 'whenever people work together in groups, some conflict is inevitable' (Daft, *et al.* 1992: 529). Consequently, we are starting to see more research and experimentation with conflict resolution and facilitation processes.

Conflict types

In business increased attention is now paid to conflict causes, negotiation, and resolution. Conflict has been defined as 'antagonism or opposition between or among persons' (Gordon *et al.*, 1990: 532). It can take two forms. 'Substantive conflict' occurs in fundamental disagreements over goals and the means to accomplish them. 'Emotional conflict' involves interpersonal difficulties involving feelings of anger, dislike or resentment, and is commonly referred to as a 'clash of personalities' (Schermerhorn *et al.*, 1995: 203).

A key feature of modern business management is to manage both forms of conflict, so that the best possible outcome is achieved. Five potential conflict management approaches have been identified by Schermerhorn *et al.* (1995: 207) in Figure 2.3. The ideal outcome is the central box, when all parties view the decision as a 'win-win' situation. However, this may not always be obtainable, especially under the increasing circumstances of zero-sum situations, where the demands for more resources by one group can only be met by reducing another group's resources by a similar amount.

Negotiation

In the process of resolving such conflicts it is common to invoke a negotiation process. Negotiation 'is the process of making joint decisions when the parties involved have different preferences' (Schermerhorn *et al.*, 1995: 208), and two key goals are at stake in any negotiation. Most often attention is given to the *substance goals* that are concerned with the outcome relative to the content issues at hand, such as wage agreements or land use decisions. However, equally important are the *relationship goals* that indicate how well the parties will work together in the future, to make the negotiated settlement work. If the process of negotiation has been acrimonious it is unlikely that the final decision will be truly supported by all

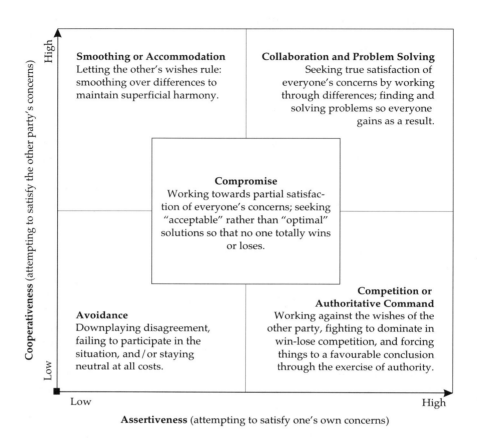

Figure 2.3 The conflict management grid with five conflict management styles
Source: Schermerhorn *et al.* (1995: 206)

parties, and in community tourism such an outcome will be reflected in sub-par products and service.

Participatory power

In planning, attention has been placed on securing real participation from various groups. Sherry Arnstein's (1969) now famous ladder of participation reveals how easy it is to dupe oneself and others into thinking there has been participation and not tokenism involved in a decision-making process. So planning agencies are now attempting to develop more open and effective processes by which to encourage participation and negotiation. One process that has been used effectively in land use planning situations and is being advocated for tourism is the nominal group technique (Ritchie, 1994). This technique facilitates the expression of individual views in a non-hostile situation, leading to the development of group priorities via a process of consensus building. More discussion of this technique and others will occur later in the book.

Portfolio analysis and strategy

A technique that has been developed in business management to provide information on a variety of dimensions that can guide strategic decision-making for a number of business units is portfolio analysis and strategy. Luehrman (1998) demonstrates how portfolio analysis is a common feature of general life as well as business life. Like anyone planning for the future when 'executives create strategy, they project themselves and their organisations into the future, creating a path from where they are today to where they want to be some years down the road' (Luehrman, 1998: 89). Such strategies become a series of options, and one of the most common facing everyone involves whether to take action or not. Action may be needed immediately, or deferred so as to benefit from circumstances as they evolve, or redundant because the opportunity has truly passed. These represent 'portfolios of real options' and can apply in everyday situations, as well as in business.

In business, the technique focuses on key dimensions such as market criteria or relative competitiveness, and applies those dimensions as criteria by which to judge the performance of various business units within a corporation. With that information strategic decisions regarding the best mix of business units can be made with respect to the corporation's goals and competitive advantage. In terms of community tourism the community can be considered the corporate entity and the business units its respective tourism businesses.

Boston Consulting Group matrix

One of the best known examples of this form of analysis and strategy is the Boston Consulting Group (BCG) matrix (Haspeslagh, 1982). It organises business units along the dimensions of market share and industry growth rate, and offers four distinct cells. Those business units that have a high market share in an industry with a high growth rate are called 'stars'. They will be attractive investments because they are already significant, maybe dominant, in the market and that market is growing. In the 1990s this description would have fit the cruise ship and gaming companies of the tourism industry. At the other extreme are the businesses in the low growth industries and which have a low market share of this stagnant or declining industry. These are the 'dogs' that have no bright future and if not currently profitable should be discarded, because their prospects are dim. Despite tourism being a significant growth industry over the past 50 years, there are some areas that could fall into this category. These would include some old-fashioned seaside resorts, with their piers and pinball arcades that have been forsaken for the sunnier climates and brighter lights of new destinations around the Mediterranean and Caribbean seas (Butler, 1980; *The Economist*, 2000b). However, it should not be forgotten that certain 'dogs' in tourism have rebounded by marketing their kitsch appeal as in the case of New Jersey's 'Jersey shore' or reinventing themselves such as Times Square in New York.

General Electric screen

A more sophisticated portfolio matrix has been developed by General Electric; this is their nine-cell GE screen (Daft *et al.*, 1992). This screen is based also on two composite dimensions – industry attractiveness and business strength – and offers the three options of low, medium and high scores. Industry attractiveness is a composite variable made up of factors such as market size and growth rate, plus industry profit margins, seasonality, and economies of scale. The business strength variable is composed from relative market share, profit margins and technological capacity. Such a screen in a tourism context could provide a more detailed assessment of individual business and destination prospects by equating a destination's position with industry attractiveness and a business' position with business strength.

Organisational strategy typology

Miles and Snow's (1978) organisational strategy typology indicates how business managers can formulate general strategies that are congruent with their organisational structure and external environment. It is significant in that it suggests strategies that combine the internal characteristics of a business with the external environment, and thus tries to pull together the three elements identified earlier in the environmental scanning process of this chapter. Their typology, as presented by Daft *et al.* (1992: 190), proposes four strategic positions and how they best relate to organisational characteristics and the task and general environments. These include a *prospector* strategy of innovation to create new markets; a *defender* strategy to protect existing markets; an *analyser* strategy to maintain current markets while encouraging moderate innovation; and a *reactor* strategy that simply reacts to changing conditions. Such strategies are particularly relevant to destinations entering the stagnation and beyond stages of Butler's tourist area evolution cycle, because they indicate possible options for businesses and the host community at that critical juncture.

Competitive strategy

Another portfolio typology that has received extensive interest, including from tourism writers, is Porter's (1980) competitive strategy.

Porter contends there are three ways to make a business competitive in this intensely competitive global environment. These are to emphasise its differentiation, overall cost leadership, and focus. The resulting competitive strategy has several components:

Differentiation

Differentiation is necessary to distinguish a business' products and service from those of its competitors. In tourism there is very little that a business or destination can offer that is truly unique, and hence one of a kind. Consequently many businesses and destinations have attempted to differentiate themselves from the competition by emphasising specific images and qualities. However, there is a growing appreciation that each destination does have something unique to offer – its sense of place. This is the essence of Rosenow and Pulsipher's (1979) place personality planning process.

A sense of place is the character and lifestyle that has evolved in each community and is the sum of local people interacting with the local environment and their history of this association. This has led to local building styles, traditional costumes, and local customs. If these traditional links with the past can be maintained in the face of increased global homogenisation then a destination has something 'unique' to offer the tourism market.

Cost leadership

Cost leadership is important in a free market situation, where the market determines prices and businesses can only influence their profit margins through the cost control of their operations. Cost control should be considered in real terms, which is the level of productivity associated with the costs involved, so it does not necessarily equate with minimising wages.

In a labour intensive industry such as tourism this is an important consideration. But rather than thinking simply of monetary costs tourism should consider real labour costs. These are the costs to be compared with the level of sales and service achieved, that in turn can be linked to the professional skills of the workforce. If cost considerations incorporate the skill levels of employees the chances of meeting or exceeding tourist expectations are increased, and tourists will return home satisfied and happy customers. Such happy customers become the goodwill ambassadors for a business and a destination, and spread the good news by word of mouth to their friends and relatives.

Investing in training and rewarding employees with higher wages or bonus systems have been shown to increase the levels of productivity and service quality in tourism. Some studies comparing German and British tourism workers have found the Germans, who received more training and higher salaries, are more productive and provide better service than their British counterparts (Scottish Tourism Research Unit, 1998 cited in

Nickson, 2000). The Butchart Gardens is one of Victoria, Canada's most successful tourist attractions and has a worldwide reputation for quality. One of the reasons for its success is the training it provides its young front-line staff. This not only produces knowledgeable and enthusiastic employees but also contributes to a low staff turnover rate from season to season, thereby reducing future staffing costs.

Focus

Although the first two dimensions of Porter's portfolio strategy are key to competitiveness they cannot be expected to work to the same degree on every market. A destination's 'sense of place' product, for example, will appeal to only a certain segment of the tourism market. The type of tourism developed in a destination will influence the expectations and hence the cost factors of the operations. So the expectations and costs involved in operating a heritage attraction like Colonial Williamsburg in the United States will differ significantly from operating a seaside resort, where the principal attraction is the public beach and not restored buildings and antiquities with first person interpretation.

Hence Porter's third dimension is to focus on a specific regional market, product line or buyer group. This involves matching the product with a market segment that will bring sufficient business to make the exercise worthwhile. An up-market product and price would appeal to certain special interest segments; whereas a more generic and low priced product would appeal to a mass market. This process equates to the common seg-mentation strategy of modern marketing, in that 'a market segment consists of consumers who respond in a similar way to a given set of marketing stimuli' (Kotler & Armstrong, 1989: 42).

To focus on a segment or several segments it needs to be possible for des-tinations to identify the following four segmentation characteristics.

(1) They should be *measurable,* in the sense one can determine their size and purchasing power.
(2) They should be *accessible,* in terms of being reached by any promotion and able to visit the destination.
(3) They should be *sustainable,* in that they are a long-term proposition and not a short-term fad or 'one-day wonder'.
(4) Finally, they should be *actionable,* in the sense that effective marketing programmes can be designed to attract and serve the targeted seg-ments.

While all of the above business techniques and management strategies have been discussed in isolation, it should be appreciated that they often operate in conjunction. In addition, these decisions not only influence the form and direction of a business; in turn they are influenced by the values and beliefs of the business operators themselves. Hence, any strategic management must consider the corporate culture of the organisation involved if it is to be implemented rather than left on a shelf.

Corporate and Community Culture

A corporate culture is 'the set of key values, beliefs, understandings, and norms that members of an organisation share' (Daft *et al.*, 1992: 540), and is frequently cited as a major factor in the success or otherwise of many businesses. The reason is that most businesses and certainly all communities are made up of a variety of people performing different tasks, and how they view events and proposals is strongly determined by the history and norms of their organisation.

Certain corporations, such as The Body Shop, are gaining profits and respect through the development of caring cultures to guide their businesses. Anita Roddick (2000: 58), founder of The Body Shop sees:

> The old views of business as a jungle where only the vicious survive will, I hope, soon be giving way to a new view of business as a community where only the responsible will lead. If your values are heralded and if your heart is in the right place, if your feelings are recognized and your spirit at play I believe there will be footprints out there for all of us.

Thus, once again we have a close parallel between business management and community tourism aspirations, in that both need to consider the background and feelings of their constituents.

Schein (1992) has suggested that there are three levels of culture in most organisations. The invisible yet basic building blocks of a corporate culture are its *fundamental underlying assumptions*. These are the unconscious and often taken-for-granted beliefs, perceptions, thoughts and feelings of those working in the organisation. They become the corporate body's source of values and interpretations and they influence how people will react to events or proposals. As such it leads to the sort of social representation that Pearce *et al.* (1996) identified as being important to community reaction to tourism.

The underlying assumptions of the organisation's personnel lead to their *espoused values*, or the reasons given for doing things the way they are done. Stoner *et al.* (1995: 185) relate how DuPont stresses the value of safety, based on its original business of making gunpowder; and in the cited words of a past chairman 'Either you make gunpowder safely, or you don't make it for very long'. Peters and Waterman (1984) in their book and video on company excellence reveal that the driving force for the Disney organisation is to make people happy, and this is the principal stated value for their theme parks.

Both of the preceding levels create the *artefacts* of a corporate culture, which are the visible forms of products, services, and the behaviour patterns of organisation members. These represent the external image of the organisation and its products and services. As such they indicate to consumers what the organisation publicly values and is willing to bring to the marketplace. It may be as mundane as a dress code or a company uniform, but it is part of the corporate culture that delivers the final product. For example, McDonald's is in the fast food business, but many weekend sports coaches know it also welcomes children and has clean toilets. In terms of community tourism a host destinations' artefacts, such as well-maintained facilities, good service and a friendly atmosphere, will signify visitors are welcome. Perhaps the prime example of this is Hawaii's famous 'Aloha' spirit.

Corporate game culture

Corporate culture has been described by some business analysts as a game (Gerber, 1995) and their description of the process makes it particularly relevant to the mood of tourism businesses. Businesses are considered to function well when their organisation produces the product and service as a game, and the corporate culture becomes one of creating fun and enjoyment. This enthusiasm and loyalty to the corporate culture has been nurtured and developed in some prominent tourism companies, such as Disney, Club Med, and McDonald's. From such evidence Gerber (1995: 204–6) identifies eight rules to create a *successful corporate game culture*. These are:

(1) Start with a *game strategy* (be prepared).
(2) *Know* and *play* the *game* yourself (be a team player).
(3) *Create ways* for *winning* without ending the game (create a reward system).
(4) Periodically *change the tactics* of the game, but not the strategy (be flexible but always stick to your ethics and beliefs).
(5) Keep the *game going* (remind staff of goals, roles and rewards).
(6) The game has to *make sense* (keep it interesting, effective, and simple).
(7) Keep it *fun* (fun as defined by the team).
(8) If you *can't think* of a *good game, steal one* (copy the corporate culture of a benchmark company in your industry).

With the many challenges tourism presents, like demanding work schedules and numerous community impacts, it is important that those involved create a corporate culture that strengthens their business and community. Achieving the 'right' corporate culture takes hard work to establish and requires a sensitivity and responsiveness to customer-, staff- and environment needs. Since an important component of tourism is fun, it makes sense for individual tourism businesses to incorporate an element of fun into their corporate culture.

Multicultural dimensions

Another feature of corporate culture that is emerging, as the workforce changes due to demographic trends and legislation, is *multiculturalism*. This recognises there are now 'many different cultural backgrounds and factors that are important in organisations, and that people from different backgrounds can coexist and flourish within an organisation' (Stoner *et al.* 1995: 191). The multicultural factors that have come to the fore include consideration of ethnicity, race, age, gender, physical ability and sexual orientation. While much of the public and press attention in this area has focused on organisations like the armed forces, the police and firefighters, it is particularly germane to tourism.

Tourism is a global industry that has a world market, which means customers come to a destination from a variety of ethnic and racial backgrounds, and they don't all speak or read English. If a community is to engage in tourism it must not only be prepared to serve such a varied market; it should be excited by the prospect. One of the best ways to meet the expectations of international visitors is to have staff from similar backgrounds or trained to speak and understand the different languages and cultures they will meet. Another rising market is the seniors' market, where personal needs can change dramatically over a 20- to 30-year period of retirement. But it is not only the global market that is changing and growing; in many parts of the world the sources of labour are changing. Many of the front-line positions in tourism are filled traditionally by young people, but as populations in the Western economies age the pool of such suitable labour has shrunk. This has encouraged some companies (the fast food sector in particular) to turn to other groups; and has seen the rise of part-time work for seniors. The tourism industry is only just beginning to adjust to such changing conditions and to recent legislation encouraging the hiring of minority groups, but if it wishes to survive and serve it needs to take on a more multicultural perspective.

Implementation

The four-function definition of business management along with the application of a strategic management approach holds great promise for the combination of community aspirations with the business interests of tourism. This book is not alone with such an assessment, for Swarbrooke (1999) in his recent book, *Sustainable Tourism Management*, has come to a similar conclusion. He notes that use of the term management has been rather casual and incomplete in the past and he too advocates a more complete model of strategic management that incorporates monitoring, evaluation and control mechanisms.

To date there has, perhaps, been too much emphasis placed on strategy generation rather than strategy implementation. Yet unless it can be implemented there is no point in having a strategy . . . Most existing strategies tend to be public-sector led destination strategies or rather academic, generic strategies for the tourism industry as a whole. (Swarbrooke, 1999: 355)

For any strategy to be implemented on a community basis it needs to address many of the business management principles and techniques outlined above. One of the best ways to illustrate the points of this argument is to conclude with an actual case study.

The selected case is of a small business in Victoria, British Columbia, Canada. The business – Victoria Harbour Ferry – has faced many of the issues discussed above and illustrates the close connection that can develop between a tourism business and its host community. It exemplifies the majority of tourism businesses in that it is an owner operated small business, it is dependent on the appeal of its host community, and it is seasonal in nature.

Case Study: Victoria Harbour Ferry

(Paul Miller, Victoria Harbour Ferry)

The Victoria Harbour Ferry Company operates a small water-bus system with a tourism rather than transport emphasis in and around the harbours of Victoria, which is the provincial capital of British Columbia on Vancouver Island and receives over four million visitors a year (Figure 2.4). It was started by Paul Miller in 1990 and by 2002 consisted of 10 small boats, a staff of 32, which handled around 150,000 passengers a year. In the years of its existence Paul has won several plaudits, including the GEM (Going that Extra Mile) Award from the Victoria Hospitality Society and becoming the President of Tourism Victoria (the destination tourism association) in 1999. The internal environment of the company exemplifies the *four functions of business management*, as outlined above. This case study is gleaned from several class presentations by Paul Miller and subsequent conversations. The interpretation of the facts is the sole responsibility of the authors.

Planning

In the *planning* stage Paul's initial goal was to provide a water-bus transport system around the three interlinked harbour areas of Victoria. Like most small business operators he was not in a position to undertake a detailed market analysis, but he did use his eyes and his head.

My market really consisted of a study of the way the system in Vancouver worked and in the isolation of differences and similarities with my proposed market (in Victoria). I thought at the time that what was required was a large mass of people in one place and an attraction or

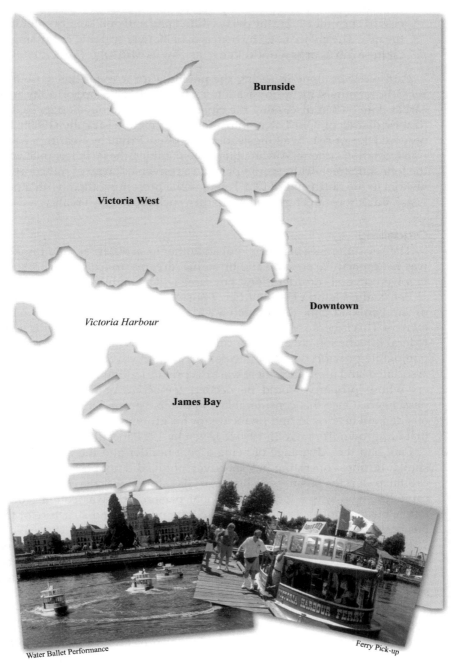

Figure 2.4 The Victoria Harbour Ferry operations

attractions in another place or places, across a body of water not in excess of one mile . . . Traffic delays didn't and still don't really enter into
the mix. The choice to go by boat is usually over walking or bussing or
taking a cab . . . or as we now know, just for its own sake. (Miller, 1998)

Paul was not alone in seeing the potential for a water-bus system in
Victoria, for others, including academics, had spotted the opportunity at an
earlier date. When discussing the city's aspirations to develop its central
historic district of 'Old Town' into a tourist attraction Murphy (1980b: 71)
observed the tourists' walking needs could be cut in half by creating a water
transportation system. 'A water bus system linking the ferry terminal with
the Johnson Street Bridge could provide a convenient way of transporting
visitors to the north end of Old Town, while presenting them with a new
vista'. But it took an entrepreneur to turn such ideas into a reality.

Organising

The key difference between Paul and other local observers and thinkers
was his capacity *to organise* and bring his 'dreams' to fruition. This stage
involved several considerations, but three will be highlighted here.

Before the Victoria Harbour Ferry business could become more than a
dream Paul had to negotiate with a wide range of jurisdictions and landowners. This is because a ferry system links land and water elements, with
federal jurisdiction covering the rules and regulations of sea transportation, while provincial and municipal jurisdiction cover the shoreline and
associated land uses. Then there were the private landowners and developers whose property would be needed for access and as a source of
passengers. Once this considerable and diverse group had been brought
onside Paul needed to find financing for his growing fleet of boats: a fleet
that has grown from two in 1990 to seven by 1994 and 10 in 2002.

Paul had the advantage of being a boat builder and the example of a
similar business operating in Vancouver, but he did not possess sufficient
capital to start the business on his own. His solution was finding a venture
capitalist, who was a local professional person, and was convinced by
Paul's business plan. This plan outlined the purpose and structure of the
business, along with realistic financial projections.

Finally, Paul insists a key to this stage of business formation was the
support he received from his wife who is an accountant. In all his presentations to students Paul emphasises what a blessing it has been to have such
support and such important skills at home.

Leadership

Paul demonstrated *leadership* in starting the project and building it into a
successful business. An example of this is his recruiting and compensation
procedures. Like all tourism businesses he relies heavily on the quality and

enthusiasm of his staff, for it is the single employee in charge of each boat – the 'skipper', who presents the company's face to the public. Skippers needed to be skilled people who possessed, or were willing to achieve, the appropriate master's certification needed to pilot his boats. They needed to be customer- and service-oriented, who knew and loved their local community. They needed to be available for seasonal employment, generally extending from April to October. What he found were retired airline pilots, retired navy officers and business people who were happy to work on the water during Victoria's warmer months and to take up to five months' vacation over the winter months. In recognition of his staff's contribution to the success of the business Paul instituted a profit-sharing system in addition to a regular salary. This system encourages each skipper to treat his boat as his personal contribution to the business and has helped the business develop a staff retention rate of 80%, which by industry standards is excellent.

Control

Paul's *control* over the business is demonstrated by his participation as one of the skippers in the early years, as a continuous observer of the operation, and as an auditor of its progress. As a skipper he was able to see how the business operates on the frontline, and as an external observer from points around the harbour he can see how well the transport system and schedule is working. It was based on these experiences that Paul changed the entire marketing direction of the business after its first few years of operation, as will be discussed in the next section. By auditing the business' progress Paul could determine when he needed to change from a partnership arrangement with the venture capitalist into a sole proprietorship. Which is also discussed in the next section under strategic management.

Strategic management

Strategic management, as exemplified by strategy formation, implementation, evaluation and control, can be seen in the evolution of Victoria Harbour Ferry. At its formation the initial goal of the business was to be a transport company, with an expected 50:50 split between locals and visitors using the service. However, by the end of the third season, an evaluation of the company's experience and observations from Paul and other skippers suggested transportation was not the company's main business. It became apparent that the major customers were tourists and these people had a thousand questions about what they were seeing.

As a result of this evaluation it was decided to change the focus of the business from transport to tourism. Paul and his skippers developed talks that provided a tour guide to the harbour waters and surrounding points of interest. Unlike the Disney example cited in Peters and Waterman (1984), where a set drama and script is composed for the boat guides in the 'Jungle River Cruise', 'each skipper lends his own style, personality and experience to his unique tour' (Miller, 1998). It is this paradigm shift in presentation, from a transport focus to a tour business, that Paul credits with much of his subsequent success.

Success also caused Paul to make a strategic change to the business' ownership. A key issue in working with silent partners, like the venture capitalist, is to know when to cut the umbilical cord and buy them out. Paul maintains that if he had not bought out his partner's share of the business when he did, after four years of operation, he would never have been able to afford to own his company outright. The reason was that as the business grew older and more successful it became more valuable, and to buy back the percentage owned by the venture capitalist would eventually have become too onerous. So a key element in the strategic relationships with external stakeholders is timing – knowing when to enter and exit such partnerships.

Stakeholder analysis

Besides concerning himself with internal stakeholders such as his staff and partner, Paul had to be aware of the interests of *external stakeholders* such as his customers and community partners. As a result of changing the business focus to tourism and listening to his customers Paul has extended the initial route structure to incorporate some additional tourism attractions. One of the longest runs now takes his small boats to the inner reaches of the harbour, where a renovated pioneer home – Point Elice House, which now nestles among the industrial uses of a 'working harbour', has become a local tourist attraction.

In tourism individual businesses do not operate in a vacuum. They are part of a destination (task environment), where the approach should be 'sell the destination first and your business second' if a business wishes to attract sufficient customers. To do this Paul networked extensively with existing tourism businesses and the destination association of 'Tourism Victoria'. In fact, one of the authors first met Paul on a Tourism Victoria committee that was attempting to boost interest in local events and festivals. However, such networking is not all business related. This community orientation revealed itself in several ways; including the rescuing of some competitor vessels and shuttling convention delegates from their hotel to a conference function at the provincial museum when an interconnecting road bridge was put out of commission. It was for acts like these that Paul won the GEM award.

Portfolio analysis

As part of his strategic planning Paul is a great advocate for one particular form of portfolio analysis, that being Covey's (1989) time management matrix. In this case the two dimensions under consideration are whether an activity should be classified as important or urgent. The resulting four-cell matrix indicates different time management priorities. Those in Quadrant 1 are both important and urgent so have been termed crises and require immediate attention. Those in Quadrant 2 are important but not urgent. As such they allow deliberation and the search for best solutions. Quadrant 3 activities are not important but urgent. We could add the insistent presence of e-mail to this category, in the sense that most e-mail messages are not vital but they carry the expectation of a quick response. In Quadrant 4 the activities can be classified as neither important nor urgent, thus allowing them to be postponed and attended to at convenient times. 'Effective people stay out of Quadrants 3 and 4 because, urgent or not, they aren't important. They also shrink Quadrant 1 down to size by spending more time in Quadrant 2' (Covey, 1989: 153).

For business and Paul it is in the 'important and not urgent' Quadrant 2, where a manager places emphasis on the long-term issues and require-ments that are essential to the health and prosperity of the company. Although tourism businesses are open to the influence of external factors over which they have little control, Paul believes that preparation can help to mitigate their negative effects and to enhance their positive ones. Hence he supports Covey's management emphasis on focusing on matters that are 'important and not urgent'. In this regard he uses the business' down-time to service and refurbish his boats to minimise any mechanical problems during the season. Paul always has a spare boat or two to cover for any internal or external emergency that should arise. Since the tourist season is determined to a large extent by the weather Paul has developed a flexible scheduling system that enables him to have a soft start or ending to the season.

Corporate to community culture

To guide his company's strategic management and make it stand out in a crowded marketplace Paul decided to create a strong and definite mission statement. When he started the ferry business in 1990 his original mission statement was 'To become the best loved business in town'. Which meant it had to be noticed and appreciated, not just by its customers but also the host community.

Given the above evidence it is apparent that the Victoria Harbour Ferry has taken a very proactive role in its community relations, but none that compare to the returns received from one generous gesture. At one of the Tourism Victoria meetings discussing events and festivals Paul volun-teered to have his 'fleet of five boats' open the spring boating festival with a water ballet. This meant he had to choreograph the performance and provide loudspeaker music to the inner harbour where the ballet was to be performed in the prime tourist district 15 minutes before the start of his regular schedule.

This offer was accepted with alacrity and seeing these small boats bob and weave to the strains of the 'Blue Danube Waltz' proved to be the hit of the festival. It was such a hit that it has been retained and is repeated each Sunday morning from mid-June to mid-September, before the start of that day's schedule. For this goodwill gesture Paul considers he has been repaid tenfold. As an example he cites a travelogue put together by a Seattle television station to demonstrate Victoria's potential as a weekend 'get-away' holiday destination. In their short two-minute presentation they refer to and show Paul's funky ferry boat water ballet six times. No small business could afford to purchase such advertising, but in this case it came for free.

Summary

This chapter notes that use of the term management by tourism researchers and writers has been rather casual in the past, and despite tourism being the largest industry in the world there has been a disappointing level of discussion of business management principles in the literature for this industry. Hence, this chapter attempts to demonstrate the relevance of many business functions and concepts to tourism in general and to strategic community tourism management in particular. Starting with the four basic functions of business and proceeding to strategic management with its portfolio analysis and other techniques, it is possible to show the direct applicability of many business concepts and techniques to tourism. This has been illustrated further by concluding with a detailed case study of one small tourism business that has been community oriented and successful.

Part 2

Key Business Management Functions in Tourism

Management Functions

A key feature of modern tourism and this book is to view tourism as a business providing value for its host community as well as its owner. To understand how we can arrive at such a symbiotic state between a business and its context requires a preliminary overview of management theory and tourism's place within this evolving discipline.

Management theory is an academic discipline of the twentieth century and it has evolved into several established specialisation sub-fields over time. According to (Stoner *et al.*, 1995) its early stirrings were associated with the need to increase productivity and efficiency which led to the development of the Scientific Management School. This in turn evolved into the Classical Organisational Theory School as the emphasis focused on large corporations. From these beginnings sprang the Behavioural School and Management Science sub-fields, as large corporations became global organisations requiring their own forms of technical and human management. As business functions became more complex and interrelated the Systems Approach was advocated as a way to direct the various component parts, and the Contingency or Situational Approach became necessary with the cross-cultural influence of international business. Finally, Stoner *et al.* identify the current era of management theory as one of Dynamic Engagement, where circumstances 'are forcing management to rethink traditional approaches in the face of constant, rapid change' (Stoner *et al.*, 1995: 49).

One who would agree with that last assessment is Normann (1991), who has championed the new era of service management. He maintains that management of services is different from the predominantly manufacturing management concepts because there are some basic differences between the two types of business. The ways service differs from manufacturing include:

- the service is tangible;
- the service product/experience cannot be resold;
- the service product/experience cannot be pre-demonstrated because it does not exist until the actual purchase;
- the service product cannot be stored;

- production and consumption generally coincide, and always coincide with a tourism experience;
- production, consumption and often even selling are spatially united;
- the service product cannot be transported;
- the buyer/client takes part directly in the production/experience;
- in most cases direct contact is necessary;
- the service cannot normally be exported, but the service delivery system can.

(Normann, 1991: 15)

To incorporate these distinctive service components into management theory Normann advocates a service management system that incorporates a new service culture combining a market segment with an image and delivery system that emphasises service. As such this is a perfect description of the modern tourism business.

Tourism is a service industry that sells travel experiences. It is made up of numerous components to provide the complete experience, and an important part of the travel experience is often the economists' 'free/public goods' – the landscape, amenities like beaches, parks and toilets, and access via roads or hiking trails. The economists are referring to goods that do not need to be purchased by an individual because they are provided as a public service by the host community, but these goods and services are not free. They cost host communities and local residents many dollars through their taxes. This makes tourism a distinctive service industry, for to function it not only requires a partnership between host and guest, it often depends on a symbiotic arrangement between the public and private sectors.

Another distinctive feature of tourism, and one that distinguishes it from much of the past management theories and literature, is that it is the realm of small business and not large corporations. Although it is the multinational companies that first come to mind it is really the small to medium-size enterprises (SMEs) that form the bulk of this industry; and they are maintaining their dominance as the market fragments into a myriad of special interest segments. Hence, one of the new 'dynamic engagement' areas of management has particular relevance to tourism, and that is the growing sub-field of entrepreneurship.

Tourism needs to be viewed as a multi-disciplinary subject that incorporates management principles with environmental, social and political considerations and this is the approach taken and explored in this part of the book. Its development should involve management – 'the process of getting things done through the efforts of other people' (Gordon *et al.*, 1990: 4) in a business and community sense. The management principles that are considered to be particularly relevant in this case are those general requirements that need to be considered by business and organisations of all sizes, namely the four generic functions of planning, organising, leading and controlling.

Part Outline

The four functions of business are an artificial division of what should be a continuous management process, but have been isolated and discussed in the following order to demonstrate their individual importance. The order generally represents a chronological sequence of management events, but the placement of leadership is somewhat arbitrary. One could argue that leadership is needed at all stages and at the planning stage in particular. Therefore, some authors feel all ambitious management processes should begin with leadership.

This part gets underway with a discussion of the planning function in Chapter 3. It examines how planning is used in a business context before moving on to how it has been applied in a community tourist context. Chapter 4 demonstrates the importance of organisation to put plans into operation and the increased difficulty of this step in community situations where there are so many different interests and opinions. What helps in situations where there is a wide variety of opinions is leadership, and this is discussed in Chapter 5. Although leadership is a fundamental function of management it has proved to be difficult to categorise and explain. However, there can be little doubt about its significance to tourism as the examples in this and other chapters so clearly illustrate. Chapter 6 discusses the importance of control, both in a business and tourism sense. The chapter demonstrates how controlling has moved from an emphasis on the operational and environmental features in tourism to a more comprehensive concern over matching consumer and community interests.

To demonstrate the effectiveness and interaction of the four business functions to strategic tourism management the part ends with a case study. The case is drawn from a recent strategic tourism plan in Australia. It highlights not only the business functions but the growing use of IT and the government's role as an important facilitator for the strategic management of this industry.

Chapter 3

Planning

The first step in any management process is planning. Although the first step is always crucial, in management the planning stage is only the beginning of a decision-making sequence. While this chapter will examine planning as a separate entity it should be appreciated that it is linked with the other three functions of management in a continuous exchange of information and ideas. This is particularly true when a business organisation's or community's participation in a global industry needs to be planned and integrated with various levels of government planning initiatives.

In a business sense, the increasingly global and competitive tourism market means the planning options and techniques outlined below should be viewed as general guidelines that can be customised to suit local environmental and market conditions. Given this competitive market and tourism's susceptibility to external forces, the ideal planning structure needs to be flexible and dynamic rather than rigid and sacrosanct. An important part of this flexibility and openness to change will be determined by planning's links to the information flowing back from the other three functions of organisation, leadership and control. In this way individual businesses and destinations can hope to adjust to changing market and social conditions in both a responsive and responsible manner.

As we are examining strategic planning options for a community tourism industry they will need to incorporate more than business concerns. Since the tourism industry will be selling a community the planning phase should be more oriented to the external task environment and more consensual in nature than normal business planning. This responsiveness involves consideration of land use and social planning principles in conjunction with the standard business objectives. Hence, as in the subsequent chapters of this part, this review will focus on concepts and techniques that have broad applicability and will attempt to blend business and societal planning principles that will provide for a solid strategic community tourism management approach.

Business Planning Process

The standard business approach to the planning process is to complete five steps that set the direction for the subsequent functions, realising that those functions in turn can and will impact on the planning phase. Although planning is an internal business function it needs to respond to and anticipate those forces in the task and general environments that can influence the organisation. Thus it is a dynamic process that should be continuously evaluated and adapted to conform to the unfolding situation faced by an organisation.

The first step is to determine the organisation's *vision* of the future and its place within it. A company's vision involves looking to the future, attempting to assess what is needed and the best ways to supply those needs. Visions are often the result of a documented consultation process, primarily consisting of market research and competitive analysis that are used to pull together the views of various people in an organisation regarding future prospects and alternative actions.

The second step is to establish a *mission* for the organisation. This represents its continuing purpose or reason for being. At its core a mission statement describes in a general sense a type of organisation and why it is needed. Published mission statements generally relate to the service of customers and a desire to be a benchmark company, that is one that sets the standards for its particular industry. The unpublished and assumed mission is to make a profit for shareholders and in order to survive. But according to some, corporate missions need to encompass a number of constituent groups besides the shareholders. These include:

Employees should be assured of continuing, profitable employment under conditions conducive to good health and personal growth. And the right of society to have good corporate citizens – who obey the laws, produce economic output efficiently, and sustain the environment must not be neglected. (Gordon *et al.*, 1990: 109)

In business the mission need not be published or promoted outside of an organisation but it needs internal promotion to be clearly understood by managers and staff at all levels. Small businesses and those run entirely by their founders are less likely to have a formal mission statement, or even a loosely defined long-term plan, but the more focused they are on a specific approach or plan the easier it will be to make all subsequent decisions.

The third step is to create *goals*. Goals are the very purpose(s) that an organisation strives to achieve, and they are either identified directly within a mission statement or are implied. While the mission statement represents the overarching ambitions of the company, goals provide a sense of direction. They are put in place to guide plans and decisions and help in focusing efforts and evaluating progress.

The fourth step in the business planning process is to establish objectives. These are the desired results. There are three types of objectives that are relevant to both individual businesses and to a community development situation. These are:

(1) *Economic objectives*, concerned with survival, profit and growth. These represent the engine of any business organisation that has to compete in an open market.
(2) *Service objectives* relate to the creation of benefits for society. These reflect the external relationships of the organisation and particularly its contribution to the wellbeing of the task environment of its host community.
(3) *Personal objectives* that are the objectives of individuals and groups within the organisation. These acknowledge the importance of teamwork and the importance of recognising individual contributions to the organisation's success.

Hence, this typology of objectives reveals the profit motivation is not the only consideration in business planning, many managers also recognise their obligation to society and the need to consider the personal aspirations of individual units and people within their organisation.

Good objectives possess the following *four basic characteristics* (Gordon *et al.*, 1990):

(1) They should be expressed *in writing*, so there can be no doubt as to what is proposed.
(2) They should be *measurable*, so it is possible to determine whether they have been achieved.
(3) They should be *time specific*, so it is known by when the objective should be accomplished.
(4) They should be *challenging but attainable*, so that some effort is needed to achieve the stated objective.

Such objectives should be set by top management and should be consistent with the overall mission of the organisation.

The fifth and final step in the business planning process is the actual act of *planning*, or stating how the objectives are to be accomplished. Three levels of planning are commonly recognised in business management. These are strategic planning, tactical planning and contingency planning.

Strategic planning

Strategic planning from a business perspective is concerned with developing practices that can attain the stated objectives over a period of time. 'One characteristic that strategic planning shares with budgeting/control and long-range planning management systems is that it is largely based on a periodic planning system, usually an annual (or even longer) system' (Aaker, 1992: 11). While annual planning periods suit most tourism businesses due to the regular seasonal nature of the business, there are times when more extensive planning or faster responses are needed.

Certain business practitioners and researchers would like to replace the term planning with all its time period and cycles ramifications with the broader term of management. Aaker (1992: 11) maintains that:

> Strategic management is motivated by the assumption that the planning cycle is inadequate to deal with the rapid rate of change that can occur in the environment facing the firm. To cope with strategic surprises and fast-developing threats and opportunities, strategic decisions need to be precipitated and made outside the (regular) planning cycle.

Consequently, Aaker suggests a continuous real-time process of decision-making to complement the structured periodic analysis of strategic planning. Thereby companies can still be counted on for their mandatory reviews, while having the flexibility to conduct further reviews and modifications as unforeseen circumstances arise. This is the process advocated in this book for all tourism businesses and destinations.

Strategic planning or management is often recommended, but given the complexity of modern business and the daily demands on managers' time it often receives only lip-service. However, in a study by Yip (1985), cited in Aaker (1992), of the strategic development of 13 companies, he found that strategic planning approaches had particular relevance for those businesses that are dependent or involved in the following:

- *multi-functional strategies*;
- *synergy* among multiple markets;
- *coordination* of strategies for *multiple brands*; and
- complex markets with multiple distribution channels, regional variation and multiple elements in the marketing mix.

What better description could one have of a tourist destination? Such places need to satisfy the strategic objectives of many sectors, plus the aspirations of the host community. A tourist destination needs to accommodate the various tourism and resident markets. It needs to coordinate the activities of its constituent parts into a corporate destination image and product with which they can all collaborate. Finally, a tourist destination needs to present this corporate destination image and product to a global and highly competitive marketplace.

Tactical plans

Part of this call for more flexible planning and management in business makes use of the other two planning approaches – tactical planning and contingency planning. Tactical plans are the more detailed plans designed to implement the strategic plans of top management. They often relate to specific functional areas, such as sales or personnel, and encompass a shorter time span than strategic plans. In tourism tactical plans often occur with the seasonal hiring, where in preparation for the upcoming 'high season', businesses hire and train the additional casual labour needed to handle the anticipated increase in business.

Contingency plans

Contingency plans need to be in place to be ready for a surprise break in the pattern of events. Certain changes, such as the slow season and a need to adjust staffing and service provisions, accordingly can be more easily anticipated and planned for than others. For example, Paul Miller's Victoria Harbour Ferry operation has nominal opening and closing dates for its season, but in reality these dates are determined by the weather and its customers' associated interest in taking a water trip. In tourism with its exposure to external forces over which it has no control some form of contingency planning is essential. With the Asian currency crisis of 1997, Australia's tourism industry faced a dramatic decline in some of its principal overseas markets. Fortunately, many companies and government agencies were able to implement contingency plans that shifted marketing and packaging toward the still buoyant North American market, and thus ameliorated the downturn of their Asian markets.

Policy

Those plans that are intended to have some permanency often develop policy statements on how objectives are to be accomplished. Policies are used to provide direction to the decision-making process, and can be referred to for guidance when dealing with new situations. 'As such, policies should be based on a thorough analysis of corporate objectives. Separate policies cover the important areas of a firm such as personnel, marketing, research and development, production and finance' (Gordon *et al.*, 1990: 117).

Several general principles associated with appropriate policy design are recommended:

(1) They should be based on *factual information*.
(2) They should *support* the organisation's *objectives*.
(3) Where different divisions or departments are involved they should be *coordinated*.
(4) They should be *definite*, understandable and preferably in writing.
(5) Given the dynamic nature of modern business they should be *flexible and stable*. This is not an oxymoron according to Gordon *et al.* (1990: 117) because 'stable policies change only in response to fundamental and basic changes in conditions'.
(6) Policies should be as *comprehensive* as possible in their scope, so as to maximise their utility to the decision-making process.

Challenges

While planning is widely recognised as a crucial component of management, understanding and committing to this process can be problematic. As we have seen, even this initial step in the management process involves several interrelated components that require clear delineation and development if the final planning phase is to be effective. Differences in interpretation and difficulties in arriving at consensus can challenge the process. Such difficulties need to be appreciated and avoided, where possible, if the planning process is to present the guidance value that is intended.

Three problems can be encountered in setting objectives within an organisation (Gordon *et al.*, 1990: 114–15), and these can be magnified within a community setting given the wider range of stakeholders and responsibilities. First, the real objectives may differ from the stated objectives, as a result of internal tension or as a response to external forces. To determine the real objectives one needs to look beyond the words of a document to the actual resource distribution and specific actions taken. Second, it is common for organisations to have multiple objectives, and given the limited resources available some priority needs to be established, which again will indicate the true objectives. Third, those objectives that are easier to quantify will receive the greater attention and pressure for completion. So when the forest industry and the tourism industry argue over the value of a tree, the forestry industry's 'hard data' regarding its market value in board feet always carries more weight with the politicians than the tourism industry's 'estimated' scenic value.

Aaker (1992) has identified several problems associated with business planning that have extensive relevance to the planning phase of tourism management. These include a financial or spreadsheet dominance that has a tendency to turn strategic plans into annual financial forecasts. These forecasts, in turn, become dependent on the projections of past performance rather than on visions for the future. The dominance of short-term financial returns to satisfy stockholders and banks can lead to a milking of the business and under-investing in its future. Plans can become too rigid and take on a life of their own, and in the process stifle innovation. Plans that are too vague or have little practical relevance to an organisation will not be utilised, but end up on the shelf.

Rather than fighting against the natural inclination of businesses to focus on monetary flows and short-term performances, a planning process can be responsive to these priorities. By incorporating planning processes into budgeting, a business is both recognising the importance of planning and responding to the consequences of its actions. Two budgeting styles that have particular relevance to business planning are performance budgeting and zero based budgeting. Both can raise the profile and effectiveness of planning. *Performance budgeting*, also referred to as management budgeting, sets performance goals and objectives and then uses performance measures to asses the extent to which these goals and objectives are achieved (Bertsch, 1999). The focus of this approach is on evaluating and ranking the options by ranking measurements that are based on economic and non-economic factors including technical feasibility, legal requirements, intangible benefits and opportunity costs. *Zero base budgeting* draws on goals and objectives to build a results-orientated, priority-setting budget within existing resources. Zero base budgeting involves the identification, ranking and commitment to alternative packages of actions as they reflect the priorities of the organisation. Each decision package is reviewed in terms of the intent of the package: what will be done, how much it will cost, how it meets the goals and objectives of the organisation and the cost of not adopting the package. The final rankings and approvals of decision packages, which are tied to long-range plan objectives, are contingent upon available funds.

Performance budgeting and zero based budgeting offer planning advantages to a business. While these budgeting techniques have a strong monetary focus, their ultimate success lies in their acting as a measure of how well the company is meeting its overall goals and objectives. Both of these planning techniques are usually conducted on an annual basis; however, this yearly review can act as a longitudinal monitor of organisation progress towards achieving its long-term goals and objectives. These two budgeting techniques are responsive to changes in the external and internal business climate of an organisation, and as such can be a practical and effective way to combine planning with monetary policy.

Community Tourism Planning Process

While the planning processes for community tourism follow similar steps to the business planning processes, differences can be found in terms of priorities and processes. The main priorities for a business are often straightforward and easily quantifiable, involve a limited number of stakeholders and are flexible in application and implementation. In contrast the priorities for a community can be complex, difficult to quantify, involve multiple stakeholders and can be onerous to prepare and implement. The desire to generate profits over the long term is one shared by business and community tourism planning organisations, as is the need to consider multiple stakeholders and external factors. Community tourism planning, as with business planning, looks at missions, goals and objectives. The primary difference between the two is one of scope. Community tourism planning is accountable to a wider range of stakeholders and as such additional factors need to be reviewed and included in their planning processes.

The motivating factors behind creating a community tourism plan can vary widely, from responding to a sudden influx or decrease in tourists to taking advantage of available funds and expertise for such planning exercises. Generally, one can identify two types of planning effort that relate to when the planning process starts:

- Retroactive
- Proactive

Retroactive

Certain tourist areas allow their tourism potential to evolve in an organic and unstructured way until a particular turning point is reached. This turning point could involve substantial damage to tourism resources or a substantial drop in tourism revenues. Typically an area that develops a tourism plan in a retroactive fashion is responding to tourism development that started on a small scale and evolved into a major industry. Once locals recognise the scope of the industry they begin to seek ways of controlling and guiding it, such as partnering with tour providers and retroactively integrating tourism planning into their community plans. Mann (2000: 24) refers to this type of tourism planning as 'demand led', since local tourism is driven by consumer demand. It is the type of tourism planning commonly associated with Butler's (1980) destination evolution model.

Proactive

Certain areas are identified as strong potential sites for tourism growth by outside interest groups. Such groups can primarily have a business perspective and profit generating motivation, such as hotel and resort chains, or they can primarily have a developmental, environmental or social perspective, or even an altruistic motivation, such as national developmental agencies and non-government organisations. Proactive community plans lay down the groundwork for tourism development, such as providing the necessary infrastructure and designating areas for concentrated tourism growth, before the development takes place. Proactive tourism planning can be referred to as 'supply led', since the 'supply' of tourism services and products are in place before the 'demand' comes from tourists (Mann, 2000: 24).

Determining the vision, goals, objectives and strategies for a community tourism planning process involves a great deal of organisation, commitment and resources. Public meetings and discussion groups need to be arranged and widely attended. Extensive amounts of background material that provide context to the impending planning decisions need to be gathered and shared with community members. Stakeholders need to be identified and able to contribute in a meaningful manner. Finally an organisational structure needs to draft, adopt, implement, monitor and adjust the resulting plan. A general framework for this process is presented in Figure 3.1. It shows the planning phase's individual components, operating

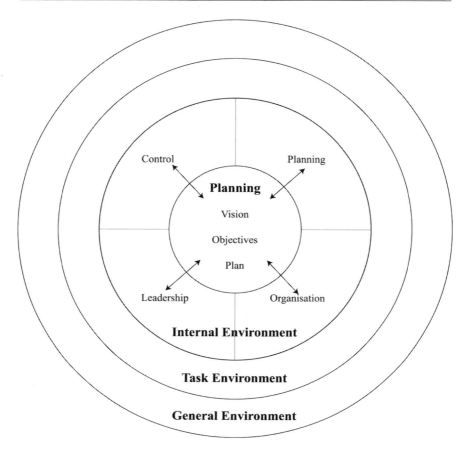

Figure 3.1 Planning tasks and environment for community tourism

within the four management functions and within the internal environment of local government. This internal environment has to be responsible to the task environment of its community and responsive to outside pressures from the general environment of its state government and world events.

To illustrate the steps of the planning process we offer examples of possible visions, mission, objectives goals and strategies for the fictitious community of Appleton and actual tourism examples in the following paragraphs.

Visioning

Visioning is a projection of what is desired that is unhindered by the constraints of reality (Becker, 1999). While businesses are often able to proceed with a largely personal and guarded vision of their future, community visions by their very nature are based on communal interests and aspirations for the future. As such, community visioning processes often involve community workshops and facilitated meetings at which the public can share their hopes and concerns for the future, and from this great diversity an inclusive and responsive future vision for the community is formed.

The visioning process is widely used in community planning. According to Bosselman *et al.* (1999: 26):

> When a community is considering ways to manage its tourism development and the use of its shared resources, it needs to create a process for meaningful participation by disparate parties with different objectives. In modern planning parlance, this is often referred to as a 'shared vision' theory of planning or even, to the disgust of language purists, as 'visioning'.

While the term visioning may strike some as being too whimsical, the practice of visioning can be a powerful tool for bringing diverse sections of a community together. Visioning can be especially useful in laying the foundations for an inclusive and supportive planning environment, as all participants are invited to share their views in a relaxed and non-binding manner. Visioning does not require an extensive gathering or review of data detailing current conditions; however, a certain awareness of such conditions is necessary to ensure that the visions for the future are not so far-fetched that they could never be realised (Becker, 1999). (See Box 3.1). A recent paper by Smith (2003a) examines how a visioning process has been used to refocus Canada's tourism industry and help it to become more competitive in a global market.

The increased use of the term 'vision' is associated with a growing concern over the future and in particular our environmental impacts on this globe. In suggesting their Tourism Opportunity Spectrum as a more long-term management tool for tourism and environmental planning Butler and

---

Box 3.1   Vision Statements:
- Appleton will be the premier tourist destination for the entire region.
- Residents of Appleton will enjoy a wide range of rewarding and sustainable economic opportunities.
- The Appleton Tourism Association will be an umbrella organisation that works with government, businesses and community groups to promote, protect and enhance the area's tourism resources for the enjoyment of visitors and residents.

Waldbrook (1991) recommend moving away from the traditional and rather static master planning approach to one that seeks to implement a process of continual reassessment within community-defined social and environmental carrying capacities. Others have gone further and called for an 'integrative vision' of long-term care for the natural environment that must flow through all environmental management and tourism-related activities (Coccossis, 1996; Hansen & Walker, 1997). Examples of tourism planning developing such visioning exercises and documents are presented below.

The Ministry of Tourism in the province of British Columbia developed a vision statement in 1992 because it considered it had reached a crossroads. After consulting with numerous bodies and businesses the Ministry felt it needed to ensure future economic success so it had to 'identify our options and clearly define our priorities and strategies' (Ministry of Tourism, 1992: 11). To do this it proposed general goals that encourage sustainability, improve the product, increase competitiveness, increase revenue generation and the sharing of benefits, encourage greater cooperation and communication. This vision is to guide subsequent business plans and forms the basis of the province's tourism growth management strategy (Tourism British Columbia, 1995).

Telfer (2000) reports on the visioning activities of a regional tourism activity in another part of Canada. Telfer talks about the successful alliance that has been created between the agricultural sector of the Niagara peninsula and the food processors, distributors, hotels, restaurants, wineries and chefs of the area, under the heading 'Tastes of Niagara: A Quality Food Alliance'. This programme 'started in 1993 and evolved out of the Agri-Hospitality Committee of Vision Niagara Planning and Development Inc., a non-profit, volunteer organisation' (Telfer, 2000: 76), a vision of various groups to enhance the image and productivity of this rural region close to major metropolitan markets like Toronto, Ontario and Buffalo, New York, that could tap into those market's desires for rural experiences and products.

Jamal and Getz (1997) have reviewed the vision-based experiences of four different community types: Jackson Hole (Wyoming) and Aspen (Colorado) as resort destinations, Calgary (Alberta) as an urban tourist destination, and Revelstoke (British Columbia) as an emerging tourist destination. They reviewed the visioning exercises of these four communities from both a process and content perspective. In terms of the visioning process, they found it was customised to suit local needs and resources, and not surprisingly the community concerns mentioned in the resulting vision statements varied in specificity with respect to the community's characteristics, values and aspirations. Of the resulting vision statements Aspen, as the most developed resort community, produced the most detailed and comprehensive vision statements. For Calgary the emphasis was economic and tourism viewed as an important supplement to a varied urban economy and lifestyle. While neither Revelstoke nor Jackson Hole 'made direct reference to the role of tourism in their community's future' Revelstoke was interested in opening up more opportunities for visitors (Jamal & Getz, 1997: 211).

Based on their review of these experiences Jamal and Getz (1997: 215–16) present three propositions:

(1) A well-articulated, community-based vision statement offers effective direction to the public and private sector for managing a community's tourism-related resources over the long term.
(2) The success of a community-based vision statement in achieving community consensus on destination planning and development is directly related to the level of community involvement in the vision formulation process.
(3) The effectiveness of a community visioning exercise to aid public and private planners will be enhanced by the existence of an ongoing representative body or bodies, to ensure implementation, monitoring and revision of the vision and / or of the strategic outcomes of the visioning exercise.

If such propositions can be achieved they feel a community visioning process would be invaluable in bringing together the various destination stakeholder groups and 'crafting' a joint direction for their community's future.

The third proposition that the visioning process will be aided by the presence of a representative body – has been confirmed by King *et al.* (2000), who have also demonstrated that such a process can operate in less developed countries. Their study of a new approach to tourism planning and development in Niue, an island in the South Pacific, revealed that consultants must now work closely with local residents and industry stakeholders. They must do this to ensure 'the tourism "product" reflects domestic social and cultural concerns and not simply the needs and aspirations of international tourists' (King *et al.*, 2000: 409–10). An important and constant element in this planning process is the Program Steering Committee made up of public servants, industry and community representatives. 'All proposals need endorsement by the steering committee prior to ratification by the Cabinet' (King *et al.*, 2000: 413), which means this body is central to the planning and implementation of future community tourism developments on the island.

Probably the most complete visioning exercise in the field of tourism is the one recently completed by the late Professor Bill Faulkner in the Gold Coast on behalf of the Australian Cooperative Research Centre for Sustainable Tourism. Key findings of this research process are that most residents have a positive perception of tourism; while the majority of tourists are domestic it is the international markets that will provide the highest growth rates; and there are several hinterlands to the main beach focus of the region. Given this information, the resort destination developed a vision for the next 20 years that incorporates:

- strengthen the Gold Coast as Australia's most preferred holiday destination;
- increase its knowledge, stewardship and development of its unique tourism advantages;
- develop Australia's most successful, concentrated tourism industry cluster;
- increase yield;
- provide ethical and sustainable tourism practices;
- develop greater dialogue, cooperation and partnerships between the public and private sectors.

Evidence of this last vision is exemplified in the vision and drive of Bill Faulkner and was acknowledged by the Chair of the Gold Coast Tourism Visioning project. In that visioning exercise Bill Faulkner states 'We cannot create a future unless we first imagine it' and the project was designed to enable a wide range of stakeholders to share their image and vision of the destination's future.

Mission

Missions, goals and visions are relatively new concepts in tourism planning. Much of tourism planning is based on the senior administration's and experts' interpretation of community mission and goals, and these interpretations have moulded subsequent objectives. Therefore, with tourism planning, as with other forms of community planning, one can see an evolution from plan formation being the domain of 'experts' and elected officials to that of the general public (Susskind & Field, 1996).

The mission step is vital to tourism management for it sets the scene and indicates what sort of destination a community wants to be. It requires an assessment of the community's tourism resources and potential, plus an analysis of stakeholder opinions. It is this type of auditing that will indicate whether a community is potentially competitive and whether the necessary industry and public support is present. If there is insufficient competitive advantage or public support for the changes a tourism development policy would bring, then it would be better to invest a community' time and resources elsewhere.

If you equate visioning with dreaming of the type of place you would like to be, then a mission statement is the actual destination that you plan on reaching. A mission statement which is a statement of purpose, can be seen as a declaration of self-determination. Without a mission statement businesses and communities can have difficulties prioritising their actions and can find themselves constantly reacting to events, rather than progressing towards their desired end state.

In terms of community tourism development use of the term mission is not very common, as yet, but we can find reference to its component parts. An illustration of this appears in Goeldner *et al.* (2000: 455), where they state:

> Although a 'tourism philosophy' sets out the overall nature of tourism in a destination, it is the *destination vision* (their emphasis) that provides the more functional and more 'inspirational portrait of the ideal future' that the destination hopes to bring about in some defined future (usually 5, 10, 20 or 50 years) . . . Visions can take many different forms. Some are very concise (the equivalent of a corporate 'mission statement'); others are much more extensive and idealistic.

They do not go into any detail regarding how such visioning is to be accomplished beyond the fact that 'the "crafting" of a destination vision is a stimulating, intellectual process that often attracts and involves the relevant stakeholders of a destination' (Goeldner *et al.*, 2000: 457). Nor do they indicate how visions become a mission statement.

The literature review of the business experience with mission statements indicates community tourism planning should reflect the priorities, resources and capabilities of the host community along with the expectations of the types of tourist that they hope to attract. Mission statements for community tourism planning can build upon existing community visions, or new visioning processes can be undertaken with the intent of creating a foundation for a community tourism plan. A mission statement should be succinct, realistic and ambitious. The mission statement for a community tourism plan should act as a mantra and a reference point to ensure that planning efforts stay on track (see Box 3.2.)

Box 3.2   Mission Statement:

The Appleton Tourism Association is the destination's umbrella tourism marketing organisation that will work with government, businesses and community groups to promote, enhance and protect the area's tourism resources for the enjoyment of visitors and residents.

Goals

A community tourism mission statement needs to be supported by goals, objectives and strategies in order for a community to realise its ambitions for the future. Goals are the broad statements of intent that underlie a mission statement. Goals, which are more specific than the mission statement, stake out the territory that will be covered by the organisation. Setting community goals can be difficult given that goals reflect values, aspirations and concerns and such feelings often differ widely among various people and groups. As such, developing attainable and acceptable goals for a community tourism plan that reflect the sentiments and resources of that community and its tourists can be especially challenging.

While developing community visioning and a mission statement is often conducted via a series of large public meetings, developing specific goals, objectives and strategies is often best accomplished using a smaller group that is representative of the wider circle of interests and expertise (Susskind, 2001). The stakeholders involved in developing community tourism goals need to be informed of the current context in order to develop realistic goals. Existing sources of information, such as tourism patterns and revenue, census data and existing plans for the area, should be utilised where available and appropriate. (See Box 3.3.)

Box 3.3 Goals:

(1) Increase Appleton's community awareness and support for tourism.
(2) Increase visitation yield.
(3) Effectively manage tourism impacts.

Although the business term 'mission' is not commonly used in tourism planning its associated components of goals and visions are becoming more accepted and commonplace. Bosselman *et al.* (1999: 10–11) talk of goals, claiming:

> the goal of any sensible community should be to maximise the benefits and minimise the risks of tourism ... the goals of each destination is the same: to secure those benefits that the community most desires; to avoid those impacts that the community deems harmful; to share the benefits and burdens in an equitable way; and to be resilient enough to adapt the chosen strategy to future changes.

The thrust of this goal has remarkable similarity to the broader constituent description of business goals provided earlier by Gordon *et al.* (1990). Both see a goal as a trade-off, maximising the positives such as employment and personal growth, while minimising the dangers of poor health and safety. Each emphasises the long-term goal of sustainable development.

The link between community goals and business goals can be seen very clearly in many tourism development plans. This is illustrated in Goeldner *et al.*'s (2000: 20) review of tourism development goals, where their five destination goals can be linked to regular business goals. (1) Providing a framework to facilitate the economic benefits of tourism is the same as a business organising itself to offer a product and service. (2) Developing an infrastructure is identical to a business creating its facility to appeal to tourists and residents alike. (3) Ensuring the appropriate type of development is the matching of customer expectations with what the destination and its individual businesses are prepared to offer. (4) Establishing a development programme that is consistent with the culture and history of the host area suits the sense of place emphasis of tourism business. (5) Optimising visitor satisfaction is in the interests of individual businesses and the host area at large, for it ensures repeat business and strong recommendations.

Objectives

Objectives are derived from and support the goals of a community tourism plan and should be clear and specific desires. Objectives represent real commitments and as such they usually have a quantitative component, relating to what exactly needs to be accomplished and when (Tonge & Myott, 1993). Developing community tourism goals and strategies can be stressful, since they involve the allocation of communal resources across a wide range of values and aspirations, plus the fact that opportunities and constraints created for other activities need to be considered.

Using a facilitator can be especially helpful in drawing out ideas, setting priorities and reaching consensus for establishing objectives. Such roles are becoming more in demand and generally are being filled by lawyers or professional facilitators. However, in the authors' experience, these early visioning exercises leading to specific objectives provide local universities with an excellent opportunity to link 'town and gown'. Murphy *et al.* (1985) have outlined one example of this approach when he and several graduate students took a large number of tourism and community interest groups through a workshop to identify local tourism priorities.

In community tourism management the objectives of a wide cross-section need to be considered and matched wherever possible. The various sectors and individual businesses within a destination must feel they are receiving equal attention and have an equitable opportunity to make a profit. Various areas of a community or region must feel they have the opportunity to participate in the tourism market, to the extent and style that they desire. It is not uncommon, therefore, to find tourism destination associations attempting to spread local tourism activity to a variety of businesses and areas. (See Box 3.4.)

Box 3.4 Objectives:

1.1 Create community oriented workshops and committees.

1.2 Survey and publish industry results.

2.1 Increase annual occupancy rates in local accommodation to an average of 75% over the next five years.

2.2 Increase revenue yield per visitor by 20% over the next five years.

3.1 Reduce taxi waiting times at Appleton International Airport by 50% over the next two years.

3.2 Reduce noise and light pollution around Appleton's waterfront centre.

3.3 Enter 'Tidy-Town' competition.

In terms of traditional land use planning the use of objectives, rather than goals, has been a common starting point. Inskeep (1991: 51) observes:

> As typically used by planners, goals refer to the more general aims of development and objectives to the more specific ones. Because the distinction between goals and objectives can be confusing to many users of planning studies, the approach used in this book (and in many actual planning studies) is to refer only to development objectives and not use the term goals.

In one respect there is no difference between the business and technical planning approach to the planning process in that both require clear and concise objectives to guide their subsequent actions. To achieve this state objectives should be SMART according to McDonnell *et al.* (1999: 61) in their book on festival and event management. *SMART* is the acronym for the following features of good objectives:

- *Specific,* carefully focused on the mission.
- *Measurable,* expressed in a concise and quantifiable form so they can be assessed after the event/plan is concluded.
- *Achievable,* the objectives can be realised given the resources available.
- *Relevant,* applicable to the current environment in which the tourism planning takes place.
- *Time specific,* to be achieved by a designated time.

Without such principles objectives run the danger of becoming 'immeasurable vague hopes and desires, without benchmarks for success' (McDonnell *et al.,* 1999: 62). An example of developing tourism objectives can be seen in the Canadian government's initiatives for the 1990s. After conducting a nation-wide discussion of the challenges facing Canada's tourism industry at the end of the 1980s, the government, in conjunction with industry and public sector representatives, drew up a strategy to help it grow and prosper through the next decade. This consultation exercise confirmed for the government that Canada's tourism stood at a crossroads, facing a number of significant challenges that included increasing international competition, shifting markets, new technologies, an ageing infrastructure and fragile environments in some key tourist destinations. To meet these challenges the Canadian government (Canada, 1990) identified eight tourism areas that needed attention if the country was to remain competitive. Among the objectives were the creation of the 'right products', 'sustainable development' and the 'development of new markets': concepts that have universal relevance to tourism planning at any level.

In tourism, as in any business, one needs products that the customer wants – the right products, and as we have seen, tastes change and products have an associated lifecycle. Hence a major objective of the Canadian tourism study was to develop products that would be in demand during the 1990s and beyond. To do this the government proposed priorities that included building on existing facilities and attractions, and assisting visitors by creating packages. It then listed specific activities to be undertaken, such as increased collaboration within the industry to build competitive packages, increased collaboration between government departments and agencies to assist the development of tourism, and closer working relationships with the provinces in order to spread the economic benefits of tourism.

Sustainable development is regarded in some circles as an oxymoron and in others as a dream, but with the above mentioned example we see an attempt to integrate this concept into specific planning objectives. The priorities to achieve this objective are striking the appropriate balance between business opportunity and community responsibilities. The industry is given the opportunity to self-regulate, but if that is not forthcoming or is inadequate there is the promise and threat of government regulations. Activities to support a community tourism planning objective and its priorities include the following:

- disseminating the action plan and recommendations at major conferences and other venues with a wide audience;
- support of jointly developed 'environmental' and 'conduct' codes; and
- dissemination of information from best cases and benchmark communities.

Planning

Strategic planning is the foundation of later management functions, without which the objectives, goals, missions and visions of a community tourism plan would not come to fruition. Strategies are the actions necessary to implement objectives, and as such are used to identify and resolve more immediate issues than long-term goals. 'Strategic planning (in tourism) is more oriented to rapidly changing future situations and how to cope with changes organizationally' according to Inskeep (1994: 9), who differentiates between this form of planning and long-range comprehensive planning that projects future development patterns 10 to 20 years ahead. (See Box 3.5.)

Box 3.5 Strategic Planning:

(1.1.1) Provide Appleton residents with discounts at government owned and operated tourist attractions, since they support these facilities already through their taxes.

(1.1.2) Create a 'be a tourist in your own town' promotional day, whereby residents can visit local tourist attractions for a minimal cost on a set day during the slow season. The purpose being to increase their awareness of what the community has to offer, and hoping they will recommend attractions to visitors or bring along their visiting friends and relatives.

(2.1.1) Partner with regional tour operators to encourage a steady flow of tourists throughout the year.

(2.1.2) Schedule conferences and other special events for off-peak tourist times.

(3.1.1) Issue more taxi licences and restructure taxi parking and flow at Appleton International Airport.

(3.1.2) Prohibit tour buses from certain congested parts of the downtown core and residential areas.

(3.1.3) Create attractive walkways and pedestrian only streets linking accommodation to attractions and shopping districts.

(3.1.4) Establish a 'Tidy-Town' committee and place more rubbish bins in popular areas, with a daily collection policy

---

Most of the published planning reports in tourism have been of a strategic planning nature, because these represent the culmination of a lengthy decision-making process that often requires public reporting. It is less common to see tactical and contingency plans in a published form because these are often internal documents that are to be used either by sub-units in the operational process or in response to crises. However, they are meant to be supporting the policies outlined in the strategic document.

Tourism planning has become more prevalent as the industry has grown and its impact problems have become more apparent. Although champions of more comprehensive tourism planning like Gunn (1994) and Inskeep (1991) have demonstrated the benefits that systematic planning can bring to destination areas it is still in its infancy as a specialisation. There are few planning departments with a tourism specialist but more community administrations are hiring tourism development officers to act as a liaison with the industry and to advise planning departments and councils. As a consequence, more communities are starting to include tourism considerations as part of their comprehensive economic and land use planning.

Despite its relatively short history, strategic tourism planning has been identified as passing through several phases. Getz (1987), as cited in Hall (1998) identified four approaches to tourism that could be placed in a rough chronological order. The earliest approach was 'boosterism', with its blind faith in any activity that brings visitors and their money to a community. This was followed by an economic/industry-oriented approach, which emphasises land use zoning and site considerations: a physical-spatial approach, which attempts to either concentrate tourism activity to minimise its disruption of local lifestyles or to spread its activity to peripheral areas with tourism potential of their own, or a combination of these two strategies. A community-oriented approach, which places more emphasis on the role the host community does and could play in the successful delivery of a tourism experience. Although Getz (1987: 5) points out these four approaches 'are not mutually exclusive, nor are they necessarily sequential' it has not stopped others, such as Hall and Kotler, engaging in similar classification exercises.

Hall (1998) has adopted Getz's typology of tourism planning approaches and added a fifth phase – that of sustainable tourism planning. Given the increasing concern over what is happening to our environment and tourism's dependency on a healthy and attractive environment Hall indicates that the issue of sustainability is now receiving more attention. Sustainable tourism planning is seen as 'an integrative form which seeks to provide lasting and secure livelihoods with minimal resource depletion, environmental degradation, cultural disruption and social instability' (Hall, 1998: 12).

Examples of this fifth and integrative strategic planning approach can be seen in the growth of various environment-oriented management strategies.

The Tourism Opportunity Spectrum (TOS) developed by Butler and Walbrook (1991) provides a framework within which information and data can be examined with respect to the tourism activities that should be allowed or prohibited, and the kind of facilities which should be developed. This has been augmented by the Ecotourism Opportunity Spectrum (ECOS) with respect to the growing ecotourism market and its ramifications for host communities, particularly the smaller and more isolated communities (Boyd & Butler, 1996).

Boyd and Butler's concept of the ECOS can be applied to the resource opportunities of a potential destination. Their template views eight factors as being worthy of consideration by communities. These are:

(1) Accessibility to major markets.
(2) Relationship between ecotourism and other resource users, such as forestry.
(3) Attractions in a region, their type and number.
(4) Presence of existing tourism infrastructure, such as roads and accommodation.
(5) Level of user skill and knowledge required, indicating whether it is a difficult or easy ecotourism product to undertake.
(6) Level of social interaction expected between visitors and the host community (ies).
(7) Degree of acceptance by local community of the impacts and controls associated with ecotourism products.
(8) Type of management needed to ensure the viability of areas on a long-term basis.

Such factors can and should be applied to a variety of tourism development opportunities.

To overcome the technical issues of calculating carrying capacity Stankey *et al.* (1985) have developed the Limits of Acceptable Change (LAC) approach, which allows community decisions to be made on a more general and perceptual basis. In the national parks of North America, which face the challenging dual mandate dilemma of conservation and recreation, two separate yet similar strategic approaches have been taken. The Visitor Activity Management Process (VAMP) of Canada (Graham *et al.*, 1988) and Visitor Impact Management Process (VIMP) of the United States (Loomis & Graefe, 1992) have been developed to establish a balance between these two contradictory, at times, objectives.

Kotler *et al.* (1993) have identified similar phases within strategic marketing, which is the broader type of management approach recommended earlier by Aaker. In terms of the strategic marketing of places they see three phases. The first is 'smokestack chasing', which is similar to the 'boosterism' and economic-industry phases in that the emphasis is on luring facilities to the area. The focus is on creating a friendly environment for business that could include government subsidies. One of this book's authors well remembers a welcoming sign on one of the freeway entrances to Ohio in the 1960s that read: 'Profit is not a dirty word in Ohio'. The second phase is 'target marketing', where planning and management moved to a multiplicity of goals – retention, start-ups, tourism, export promotion and foreign investment – during the 1970s and 1980s. The third, and current emphasis, views places as moving to product development and competitive niche marketing. Locations are seeking to define themselves as special places, with specific competitive advantages for their target industries.

The result of this evolution is that tourism is now one of those target industries for many communities and they are planning how to integrate this function into their overall comprehensive plans. The traditional process is to incorporate tourism issues into the objectives, survey, analysis and synthesis, policy and plan formulation, recommendations, implementation and monitoring, as outlined in Inskeep's comprehensive tourism development planning process (1988: 364). But this book is closer to the views of Kotler *et al.* (1993: 79), who claim 'places must begin to do what business organizations have been doing for years, namely strategic market planning'. Such a strategic market planning process puts tourism planning squarely in a business context, but from both an industry and host community perspective. According to Kotler *et al.* (1993: 81) it should consist of five stages to answer the following questions:

(1) *Place audit* – What is the community like today? What are its major strengths/weaknesses, opportunities/threats? What are its competitive advantages?
(2) *Vision and goals* – What do residents want the community to be or become?
(3) *Strategy formulation* – What broad strategies will help the community reach its goals?
(4) *Action plan* – What specific actions must the community undertake to carry out its strategic objectives?
(5) *Implementation and control* – What must the community do to ensure successful implementation?

We would suggest one modification to the Kotler process and that is to include policy statements as part of the strategy formulation, thereby providing clear guidelines as to what constitutes each community's tourism approach.

Policy

Policy creation is the most detailed and exacting component of the overall planning process. Whereas, the general plan and strategies lay out what needs to be done, the policies are the final step in the overall process. While the content for community tourism policies will be dependent largely on the circumstances particular to the community in which they will be adopted, there are some useful guidelines for policy formation.

Netter (1981) offers some guidelines for policy language and formation, that are provided below:

- comprehensive;
- precise;
- clearly stated;
- responsive to community needs as outlined in the vision, missions, goals and objectives of the plan;
- based on sound research and technical studies; and
- consistently applied.

Policy involves the establishment of local regulations, guidelines, development and promotion incentives that provide a framework to guide individual and collective decisions in the fulfilment of the overall strategy. 'In effect, tourism policy seeks to provide high-quality visitor experiences that are profitable to destination stakeholders while ensuring that the destination is not compromised in terms of its environmental, social, and cultural integrity' (Goeldner *et al.*, 2000: 445). With a ubiquitous industry like tourism, policy needs to be interrelated with other industry development plans and with community infrastructure priorities.

Challenges

The biggest issue with developing visions, missions and goals within community tourism will be creating an appropriate and real consultation process within the host community. As has been indicated, this will be a more challenging step for communities than for business, but given the growing trend to more inclusive planning and development it should not be insurmountable. Woodley (1992) in her study of tourism development in the isolated community of Baker Lake in the Canadian Northwest Territories noted that the concept of community planning existed in the region but had not spread to the visioning stage for tourism planning. She cited several barriers to a local visioning and goal setting process for this Inuit community, some of which will have broader relevance.

First, 'residents must have a basic level of awareness of the potential benefits and costs of tourism and of what is required to develop a successful tourism industry. . . . In Baker Lake, the concept of tourism is not well understood'. Second, a 'lack of trained tourism planners within peripheral communities has resulted in planners of a different cultural background being brought in to lead the process'. Third, language differences as well as cultural differences also mean 'that standard participation techniques are not effective'. Fourth, 'in most peripheral communities financing for tourism development is not available and must come from outside interests' (Woodley, 1992: 143–45). This not only reduces local ownership and control but leads back to the first point of lack of knowledge.

In community tourism there will be many stakeholder groups with different objectives and there will inevitably be power struggles leading to hidden agendas and a possible difference between stated and real objectives. One can expect some resistance to change from the established power groups, as Jackson (2002) has illustrated with respect to the difficulties in developing golf tourism within the Scottish countryside.

Although various government papers and acts have promoted the concept of rural recreation that has a benign impact on the countryside, golf has had a struggle to participate in such visions. Part of the cited problem is that 'the planning system remains better equipped for yesterday's problems of rural depopulation and urban sprawl than for the complex problems of what has been called the "contested countryside" in the 1990s' (Cabinet Office, 1999, paragraph 4.24 cited in Jackson, 2002: 190). Hence, visions to build on the status of St Andrews, as the home of golf and to spread golfing opportunities throughout its surrounding countryside, have created tensions. The countryside has become contested between those who wish to preserve their current built and natural environments and those who wish to develop a new economic and employment base in the countryside.

Planning in tourism is criticised sometimes for promising more than it delivers. While there will always be an element of scepticism concerning strategic planning effectiveness, 'during three decades of empirical research, strategic planning has been proven to be an essential prerequisite in successful organizations' (Phillips & Moutinho, 2000: 370). Such research, however, indicates the effectiveness of strategic planning should not be taken for granted.

In their study of hotel organisations using strategic planning Phillips and Moutinho (2000) found there were six key attributes that made this form of planning effective. First and foremost, a plan has to be implemented rather than left on the shelf, and to implement it a team should be drawn from all levels and departments. Strategic planning also needs to be focused on performance, necessitating extensive use of financial and other data. The exchange of information between parties is essential to effective planning, so the greater the functional integration of information and needs the better. The setting of specific and measurable goals via benchmarking or investment appraisal techniques helps to indicate levels of success and whether the plan is on track. To succeed, planning needs adequate resources and support from senior management, so that middle and line managers can devote the necessary time to this function.

While this study relates to the hotel industry there are many features that can relate to strategic planning for communities, especially when one considers that running a large hotel is very much like managing a small community. Based on their research Phillips & Moutinho (2000: 376) recommend the following steps to enhance strategic planning effectiveness:

- setting explicit goals;
- assigning clear responsibilities for implementation;

- obtaining a high level of commitment to the strategic plan;
- involving all levels of management;
- obtaining adequate functional coverage;
- using modern analytical techniques;
- obtaining a suitable level of staff planning assistance.

All of these are pertinent to the planning for community tourism, and should be kept in mind in order to make such strategic planning efforts more effective.

The community tourism planning process outlined above is a structured and detailed planning template for tourism management. However, in real world applications it is not always necessary or advantageous to follow all of the steps outlined above. The list of steps for strategic community tourism planning and management outlined in this section should be viewed more as a 'best practice' model from which elements can be chosen to suit the needs of the community, business or organisation that will be using them. The main reason for this is that many of the steps can be condensed, or folded into each other, such as combining the creation of community visions, missions and goals into one step. The desire to condense the steps makes practical sense given that many of the terms are used interchangeably, and it can be argued that some of the differences between these steps are based more on semantics than process.

It should not be assumed that the creation of community tourism plans and their subsequent application will be a straightforward or easy task. As detailed throughout this book community tourism planning involves the establishment of consensus among a wide range of stakeholders, and change will always be perceived as a threat to some.

Combining Approaches

The planning process in tourism has evolved with the industry's changing business needs and with changing emphases within the planning fields. Initially the focus was on growth and how to develop the industry and the destination areas. This was the era of centralised planning and master plans, and was dominant in both national and international spheres (Tisdell & Roy, 1998). With the growing scale and competitiveness of the industry, business interests changed to competitive strategies and destinations started to focus on minimising tourism's negative impacts (Gunn, 1997; Inskeep, 1991). Now the emphasis is on sustainable development and the integration of tourism planning into the overall planning objectives of host communities (Wahab & Pigram, 1997).

Throughout this evolution the business approach and host community approach to planning have generally run parallel courses, but given the growing convergence of a more societal orientation by business and a more fiscally creative approach from government administration the opportunities for a working partnership between the two have increased immensely. Consequently we are seeing an increasing use of business planning terms and approaches in the overall planning of this industry, from the higher order central planning agencies to the local planning processes of host communities.

Business planning has long been criticised for being too profit focused (MacArthur, 1999). However, community tourism planning initiatives also need to be concerned about profit generation for they need financial resources to meet the needs and expectations of residents and visitors. Lack of a business focus can be seen as one of the major pitfalls of community planning. Much can be gained, though, from combining the strengths of a business approach – economic viability and flexibility – with the strengths of a community planning approach – heightened concerns for social and environmental impacts and inclusive decision making processes. By adopting economic self-sufficiency, fiscal planning and market responsiveness from business, community tourism planning is in a stronger position for fostering a more equitable distribution of tourism's benefits and costs to a community.

Summary

This chapter examines the planning process as it is used in business management and applies it to the present research and practitioner perspectives of community tourism planning. It reveals that the initial steps of visioning and the creation of mission statements have been practised less frequently in tourism, in a formal sense. However, with the growing realisation that tourism has significant community impacts and in response to the growing demand for broader community input, the concept of community visioning is starting to become more evident. As such, the community tourism planning phase is beginning to replicate the management planning function even more closely than in the past.

There will always be one major difference between the business and community planning functions and that is the number of stakeholders and the need to seek broader consensus in the community setting than in the boardroom. However, these questions of scale and complexity do not negate the procedural steps outlined in the business management approach to planning, because the need for a logical and clear process becomes even more paramount in a community setting. Hence the need for visioning exercises that bring the community together, from which will emerge consensual goals, that in turn can be formulated into clear and measurable objectives, are all essential building blocks to a solid strategic plan.

Although the final step of the planning function is to create a plan, it is noticeable that more writers, in both business and tourism, prefer to use the term management because it symbolises increased flexibility and responsiveness. Given the increased pace of change, especially in a business context, managers are seeking plans and guidelines that permit contingency planning and rapid response. This is still a proactive procedure in that it attempts to anticipate change through the establishment of objectives and courses of action by which to best manage the organisation and its mission. The move from a planning mindset to a management one is germane also to the complexities of ecosystem management, where the interrelated nature of the system requires constant vigilance and adjustment. Such an approach is required not just of ecotourism but for all tourism that sells a community as a commodity.

It should be appreciated that in terms of management the strategic plan is only the first step, so even when considering the planning function the next step and other management functions must be borne in mind. The stakeholders who develop the strategies for their community plans must ensure that the appropriate organisational structures are available and are able to implement the plans, otherwise all will be wasted.

Chapter 4

Organising

To implement a strategic plan requires the allocation of resources and effort, which will involve many people. These people and their individual tasks need to be coordinated – and that involves organisation. 'A key aspect of implementing strategy is the need to institutionalize that strategy so that it permeates daily decisions and actions in a manner consistent with long-term strategic success' (Chon & Olsen, 1990: 213).

This chapter will start by examining some of the principal concepts in business organisation and then proceed to analyse their applicability and use within the strategic community tourism management context. It will focus on organisational structures that have developed to assist in the implementation of organisational goals and plans, and how they are changing in face of the growing complexity and dynamism of the business environment. It will review how the activities, responsibilities and interrelationships must be organised in a manner consistent with the chosen strategy, and how that in turn helps to mould the organisational culture. Finally, it will discuss the importance and role of leadership in this process.

Business Organisation Processes

In business the principal task is to fulfil the mission of developing a product and service that meets the needs of customers and provides a profit for the organisation and its shareholders in the process. Hence the first organisational task is to structure the business' people and resources in the best way possible to support that principal objective and any other ancillary planning objectives developed through its mission statement. Consequently an organisational chart outlining the different responsibilities and contributions of various individuals and departments to the overall planned outcome is an essential step.

Organisational structure

The traditional view of organisational management is that authority and responsibility flow from top management downward in a clear and unbroken line, following what is known as the *scalar principle* of management organisation. Within this system the ideas and responsibilities flow from the top, and it is senior management who not only contribute to the strategic plan but take principal responsibility in securing its implementation. This forms the basis of traditional organisational management and responsibility within both business and government. It explains why in the past a chairman or government minister felt obliged to tender his or her resignation if something went awry in their company or department – even if they were not personally aware or involved. However, like many traditions this philosophy of overall responsibility is no longer so sacrosanct.

Although the responsibility and accountability components of the scalar principle may be weakening, its effect on organisational structure is still very evident. It has produced the *line organisations*, those with 'direct and vertical relationships between different levels within the firm (that) include only line departments' (Gordon *et al.*, 1990: 251). This produces the standard pyramid organisational chart with the president or Chief Executive Officer (CEO) on top, supported by a few senior department managers, who in turn are supported by a larger number of department heads.

In recent times this standard structure has been criticised as being more appropriate to internal order and efficiency than in meeting the chief objective of many organisations – serving the needs of its customers. Consequently, instead of placing the president at the top some businesses, especially those in the service sector, are now inverting the pyramid and placing the customer on top, supported by the departments that bring the product or service directly to them, and placing the president or CEO at the bottom. Figure 4.1 offers a general inverted pyramid of a line organisation for a resort. The chain of command and directional control of senior management is not diminished by this inversion, for they still have the responsibility to implement the plan and meet customers' wishes.

As some businesses have become more complex and have started to serve a wider range of customers they have developed a *matrix organisational structure*. This uses teams of specialists from different functional areas within an organisation to work with specific product or project managers. Such structures imply the product or project managers have roughly the same power and authority as line managers of such key departments as finance and human resources. It can lead to special arrangements like the creation of 'skunk works', where certain individuals are given free reign over a certain period to develop a new idea or product, without the usual reporting responsibilities. Such arrangements can create 'the possibility of conflict and frustration, but the opportunity for prompt, efficient accomplishment is great' (Gordon *et al.*, 1990: 258).

An even more flexible form of organisational structure is the *open-systems* approach which facilitates interorganisational links to achieve planning objectives (Benson, 1975; Hall *et al.*, 1977). This concept is based on two major approaches to creating a more efficient organisational structure for these changing times. These involve taking advantage of exchange

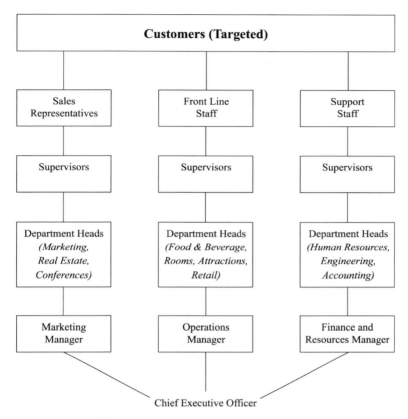

Figure 4.1 Inverted line organisation for a resort

theory or stressing power-dependency relations. Organisational exchange is 'any voluntary activity between two organisations which has conse-quences, actual or anticipated, for the realization of their respective goals or objectives' (Levine & White, 1961: 588), and forms the basis of many business partnerships. Power and dependency involve the issues of money and authority, and are closely linked to an organisation's concerns over domain and market share (Benson, 1975). Open-systems, therefore, encourage organisations to look beyond their own resource base to fulfil their objectives, and to look for partners to help meet the needs of their stakeholders and customers.

Organisational culture

While a structure and organisational chart outline the approach to be taken in implementing the strategic plan, it says little about the actual process and commitment. How individuals and departments react to their assigned *responsibilities* in the organisational chart structure will dictate the likelihood of success in implementing the plan. Certain people will have the authority to make decisions and to direct others to achieve the planning objectives. At times they can assign responsibilities to others through delegating work internally or out-sourcing certain responsibilities to outside specialists, such as accountants or advertising agencies. Their beliefs, values and expectations regarding the plan will influence their effort and will be reflected in the organisation's culture and commitment.

Along with responsibility goes *accountability*, which is where the individual or department becomes responsible for the way in which they operate and the success of their particular contribution to the organisation's objectives and mission. A commitment to the tasks at hand will be reflected in more enthusiastic and responsive effort in meeting the needs of the plan. With everything else being equal such an approach should lead to the successful implementation of the plan and positive business results.

Organisational leadership

Leadership has little to do with charisma or other so-called 'leadership qualities', according to Drucker, who is one of the most respected writers on business management. Rather, according to him, it 'is mundane, unromantic and boring. Its essence is performance' (Drucker, 1993: 119). Performance definitely is needed to turn the 'dreams' of a strategic plan into a reality, and Drucker outlines some key characteristics that need to be present to achieve such leadership performance.

The first and foremost requirement is a work ethic. 'The leader sets the goals, sets the priorities, and sets and maintains the standards' (Drucker, 1993: 121). An example of this was provided to the authors by a family member who attended a school with a renowned principal. When asked what made this principal so special, she responded 'he is everywhere', and one could certainly see the results in the quality and enthusiasm of the staff, the clean facilities and tidy grounds, and the strong after-school activities.

The second requirement according to Drucker (1993: 121) is 'that the leader sees leadership as responsibility rather than rank and privilege'. One CEO of a major tourist attraction once related how when he was first hired his jobs were to clean the toilets and pick up the cigarette butts. He still picks up the cigarette butts if he spots any on his regular tours of the facility. It means that leaders should be willing to 'pitch in', to make the tough decisions and to take the blame if things go wrong. Knowing that a team effort helps the organisation to be successful and helps the leaders to cope as an individual, effective leaders need strong associates who can share the burdens of management and carry on with the tasks in their absence

The third and final requirement identified by Drucker is to earn trust. 'Otherwise there won't be any followers – and the only definition of a leader is someone who has followers' (Drucker, 1993: 122). People within an organisation need to have confidence in their leaders as well as the plan, and a key element in this confidence building is consistency between words and actions. Leaders do not have to be liked, or even agreed with, but their word has to be trusted.

Drucker (1993: 123) concludes with the observation that many see these qualities of leadership as being synonymous with the requirements for an effective manager. To which he replies – 'Precisely'.

In order to create a structure and system to implement a strategic plan requires *champions* for the cause. That is people who believe in the plan and will use their energy and influence to ensure it is accomplished. Such people become the 'battlefield' leaders in the sense that they steer the necessary changes through the various committees and decision-making steps, plus take on the responsibility for ensuring that the required resources and staff are in place.

Leadership is expected to come from the top, but it need not be confined to senior management. If there is opportunity for junior members of an organisation to present ideas on implementation based on their more immediate knowledge of the market or suppliers then this should be incorporated within the overall implementation scheme. In the service industries in particular, with their thousands of daily 'moments of truth' between the customer and the company, the emphasis is on finding ways to *empower* line staff to take the initiative where necessary to ensure customers' needs are met.

Challenges

The choice of organisational structure should be determined by the objectives and tasks at hand, but in real life the choice is also strongly influenced by the resources available and any structure that is already in place. Responding to new planning directions and objectives often requires additional resources and sometimes requires new skills. To finance such adjustments means securing additional funding or transferring funds from existing programmes. In today's business and administrative world it is generally the latter, and this naturally causes resistance or opposition regardless of the merits of the proposed strategic plans. It is a rare situation where an organisation has a clean slate with respect to fulfilling its strategic plans, so in most situations the organisational structure to implement new planning objectives must be grafted onto existing systems and integrated with ongoing obligations. Consequently any organisational restructuring must take into account the power of inertia and existing commitments.

While a series of organisational structures has been discussed above they should not be viewed as being mutually exclusive. Given the increasing number and variety of objectives that large organisations, in particular, face there is often a combination of structures in place. While the move to matrix and open-system structures is a direct response to the growing market complexities, the traditional philosophy of management responsibility ensures that line-management systems still apply.

The presence of a suitable organisational structure to implement strategic plans represents only the skeleton of the organisation and its chances of overall success. The heart of the organisation and what will bring the structure to life is the organisation's corporate culture. This culture will determine the level of effort and degree of flexibility staff and management will apply to the new objectives, which reaffirms their involvement in the initial planning stages. However, such consultation needs to continue within the organisation phase, because department managers and line staff can contribute insights based on their closer experiences of serving the customer.

Throughout the whole process of implementing new strategic plans there has to be leadership. Leadership is crucial at all levels if strategic planning objectives are to be met, and this is strongly influenced by the corporate culture that exists within the organisation. Stimulating and facilitating leadership is one of the major challenges for business today and is becoming a more significant topic of research and teaching within business studies. As such we will explore this topic in more detail in the next chapter.

Community Tourism Organisation Processes

When it comes to implementing a strategic tourism plan within a community all of the above business concerns and methods will be at work, but on a more complex and comprehensive scale. To implement the plan will require the support and involvement of three major interest groups – the government, the tourism industry and the broader community. Within these three groups there will be specific interests and priorities that will need to be considered and integrated into the actual organisational delivery.

While the dominant government sector for community tourism will be the local level of government, because it has the responsibility for land use zoning and facility licensing, the direct and indirect interests of state and national governments cannot be ignored. These higher forms of government are directly involved when they offer various development inducements or assistance with grants and expertise, and through the promotional efforts of the National Tourist Offices and their state equivalents. Their indirect involvement with any implementation largely comes about through their influence over infrastructure developments, such as the location and state of the local road system and airport or ferry connections.

The tourism industry should be represented by a local destination association, where the various sectors of the industry have come together to form a united front of interest groups. The prime motivation for such associations is acceptance of the principle that any tourism business, regardless of its size and sector, must sell the destination first and its own business second. This means the individual competitors must collaborate in order to entice visitors to their destination, so the principal function of these associations becomes partnership marketing. However, as they take on the responsibility of marketing a community as a destination their tasks and responsibilities broaden accordingly. Unfortunately, due to the competitive and fragmented nature of the tourism business and relative newness of the industry in some locations not all communities have a destination association to represent the industry.

No tourism plan can be implemented successfully within a community without the support of the other business interests in the community and its citizens. Consequently an important step of the visioning and goal creation of the planning stage is to develop objectives that coincide with and, wherever possible, support other existing or latent economic activities within the community. The implementation of the tourism plans will be that much easier if it can be demonstrated that the proposed objectives have only a benign impact on existing businesses in other areas, such as on fisheries, agriculture, forestry or manufacturing. Or better still that it will have a supportive role for these industries, such as producing an increased demand for their products. It is this overall assessment of the benefits and costs that the residents will consider in terms of their endorsement, as suggested by Ap's social exchange theory.

To integrate these different yet related interests into a coordinated community tourism strategy will require the development of an organisational structure. Such a structure should build on what has worked in other areas of tourism and business, but should be modified to reflect the broader stakeholder framework of community tourism.

Organisational structure

Despite the significance of organisation as a major business management function little has been written on this subject in the tourism literature, and where it has occurred it is often related to the senior levels of tourism organisation – the National Tourist Offices (NTOs). In terms of textbooks Pearce's (1992) coverage is the most comprehensive, with an emphasis on national and regional destination organisations (defined as being between the national and local bodies) in the USA, Western Europe, and New Zealand. This work has been supported by chapters on tourism organisations in other texts, such as Middleton (1988) and Mill and Morrison (1992), and more recently by Morrison *et al.*'s (1995) study of overseas NTOs operating in North America.

The major conclusion from these studies is that a range of functions has emerged in these NTOs, such as marketing, development, planning, and research; but the dominant function by far is to promote the national product to overseas markets. The standard NTO brief is to promote national destinations *per se*, that is as places in their own right (Pearce, 1992: 7), without obvious favour to any particular region or product since it is taxpayer funds which essentially support this expensive process. The end result is broadly appealing images that are designed to attract international visitors to the country, supported by branch offices in the country's prime tourist generating markets. Good current examples of this are the New Zealand promotions, built around the success of the 'Lord of the Rings' films and the natural beauty of the country.

Middleton (1988) has identified two steps within this international destination marketing. These are *destination promotion*, whereby a primary level of awareness is created by the NTO promotions. This can be leveraged through *market facilitation* that enables regions and private companies to promote their own product, via processes like joint marketing or packaging. Once the international visitors arrive they become the responsibility of regional and local destination organisations, which must tempt them to their specific areas and products.

In addition to these prime marketing responsibilities NTOs have developed other functions. In the developing world they are often used to encourage and facilitate product development, acting as a conduit for government grants and subsidies designed to increase the nation's offerings and competitiveness. In some countries the NTO's close link to government, its knowledge of international markets, and all embracing coverage of the national product has encouraged some involvement in the actual planning of tourism development. 'Here again, united action is required to draw together the different operators and agents of development within a given destination, a role appropriate for a destination organization' (Pearce, 1992: 12). Another function that has developed in some NTOs is research. Most frequently this research arm is associated with market research, but in some cases it includes impact studies.

An often unstated yet very real function, for NTOs and all tourism organisations, is political lobbying. Tourism organisations need the acquiescence and support of government for their existence, and this does not come about without constant reminders of how much tourism is contributing to the local economy and quality of life. Too often legislators are blinded by the very ubiquity of tourism and the difficulty of measuring its direct impacts, so a regular function of tourism organisations is to maintain the awareness of the industry in the minds of politicians and administrators.

Some of the functions and characteristics associated with NTOs do spill over to organisations operating at the community level of individual destinations, as can be seen in the more recent research into the principal destination associations operating at this level. Morrison *et al.* (1998) have examined the structural profiles of Convention and Visitor Bureaus (CVBs) in the USA and have found several parallels with the NTOs. 'Strong local destination marketing organizations, typically known as convention and visitor bureaus in the USA, have emerged with the mandate of promoting their communities by bringing in more meeting and pleasure travellers' (Morrison *et al.*, 1998: 15). While their primary function is to promote the local destination, 'more of their attention is now being given to acting as a catalyst for development, facilitator, and supporter' (Morrison *et al.* 1998: 15).

In Europe destination associations have been called City Tourist Offices (CTOs) and surveyed by Wober (1997). In his analysis of 61 such associations he detects the same marketing and promotional emphasis as elsewhere. In addition to direct advertising most CTOs invite travel editors, writer and agents on 'familiarisation tours', because 'these groups are multipliers and it is of prime importance to stimulate their interest in selling the city' (Wober, 1997: 7). But marketing is no longer the only function of these CTOs. Many (76%), have become involved in product development, and a good number (41%) have become involved in the actual planning of tourist attractions. Several CTOs operate various tourism enterprises, such as guided walking tours (69%), bus tours (57%), and sell concert and theatre tickets (55%), but 'only 18 per cent maintain or manage tourist attractions' (Wober, 1997: 8).

Most of the organisational structures discussed in the tourism literature have been the traditional line organisations, responsible for the promotion of a single destination through a single umbrella organisation. There is usually a president or CEO, supported by line (department) managers responsible for finance, marketing, product development, and sometimes research. The organisation answers to an elected board that represents the cross-sectoral interests of the industry and usually has a few local politicians to liaise with city hall.

As the business of tourism management has become more complex and intertwined with community life some tourism associations have taken on a more matrix form of organisational structure. This occurs when the destination association attempts to be more than an umbrella organisation for the local industry by taking responsibility to contribute to the well-being of the whole community. An example of this is can be seen in Canada's Tourism Victoria (1995: 4) business plan priorities (goals), one of which reads:

To enhance member and community services for Greater Victoria.

This will be achieved by providing quality membership services to businesses and professionals in the tourism industry . . . Enhancing services for Greater Victoria communities will be achieved by increasing community awareness and support of tourism through improved communications and active grassroots involvement in the community by all facets of the local tourism industry.

What this organisation has done has been to create 'additional to the norm' working committees that are as concerned with the general community environment as with local tourism issues. Hence, thanks to the initiative and pressure of its 'Environment Committee', Tourism Victoria became the only business group in the city to support and commit to the expense of upgrading the local sewage treatment system. It also led to some of its prominent board members joining protests against the continual use of clear-cut logging elsewhere on Vancouver Island. In addition, the organisation has committed to an annual spring clean-up of the city centre and has hired a professional organiser to assist local community groups in operating their events and festivals.

None of this is completely altruistic. The tourism industry will gain from a more wholesome environment and from more professionally operated local events. But the drive for such initiatives has often come from the non-tourism members of this broad based community organisation and then been endorsed by the local industry.

Examples of open systems are beginning to emerge as various destinations see the advantages of collaboration that alliances and partnerships have brought to different industry sectors and firms within those sectors. A strategic alliance allows parties to invest their resources into mutually beneficial pursuits (Johanson *et al.* (1991). Consequently more organisations, including destination associations, are taking up the challenges of developing the synergistic opportunities that exist in mutually serving the tourist and enhancing their travel experiences and company revenues in the process (Crotts *et al.*, 2000).

However, research shows that interorganisational partnerships are not always easy to achieve. Selin and Beason (1991b: 641) point out two alternative theories have been used to explain interorganisational relations. One views organisations as voluntarily interacting to achieve mutual synergistic goals, and is commonly called an exchange theory. The other sees a dominant organisation inducing the interaction of various organisations, which is called the resource dependency theory. In their study of a potential exchange theory partnership, between the United States Forest Service and local tourism associations in an area of Arkansas, they found this type of relationship was impeded by several barriers. These included differing ideologies between the resource managers and the tourism associations, and a lack of awareness of each other's issues, but they felt that these difficulties could be overcome.

Palmer and Bejou (1995) have compared the effectiveness of marketing alliances between the private and public sectors in the UK and USA. They examined the coverage of such alliances, in terms of their functional competencies and geographic coverage; the *form* of the alliance, whether it was a joint promotion or a joint venture; the *mode* of the alliance, whether it was the responsibility of senior or junior staff; the *motives* for the alliance, whether it included the possibility of an exchange or dependency relationship. Their results from a survey of 67 visitor and convention bureaus in the USA and 24 tourism development companies in the UK reveal that the U.K. alliances have 'a greater domain coverage which included more strategic marketing activity, compared to the operational and promotion-focused domain of US collaboratives' (Palmer & Bejou, 1995: 627). They noted also that the alliances reflected the stakeholders' work environment, with the small business operators in the USA exhibiting a stronger 'self-centred entrepreneurship' compared with their UK counterparts who had more trust in their government agencies. Consequently they feel 'the most important generalizable conclusion from this research is that no one unique approach for creating marketing collaboratives is applicable in all business environments' (Palmer & Bejou, 1995: 628).

Selin and Myers (1998) explore one tourism marketing alliance in depth. Their case study of the Coalition for United Recreation in the Eastern Sierra (CURES) of California examines those factors that contribute to an effective interorganisational alliance or constrain such an alliances. Contributing factors include improved communication, strong leadership, trust, and personal investment. Constraining factors include turf protection, restrictive personnel and accounting procedures, the lack of a formal agreement, and a loss of momentum. An analysis of 45 coalition members' sense of effectiveness and satisfaction reveal some significant correlations. The highly correlated variables with members' 'effectiveness rating' are the level of administrative support, sense of belonging, personal benefit and level of trust. When it came to the members' level of 'satisfaction' all of those variables remain highly correlated to satisfaction, but are joined by such variables as leadership, give and take, inclusion and issue importance.

Several members provided some significant observations in this study, based on their interorganisational experience with CURES. One reported 'In this day and age, the only way to get anything funded or done is to have partners'. While another observed that barriers are always going to be there, but 'the real challenge is keeping the initial enthusiasm alive and producing beneficial results so people stay involved' (Selin & Myers, 1998: 93).

Organisational culture

As indicated in the business literature and confirmed in the above tourism studies the success of organisational structures depends to a large extent on the culture that is developed within and between organisations. Where there is encouragement and openness the various contributors feel more comfortable with the implementation process. Selin and Myers' (1998) study of tourism marketing alliances shows that the significance of administrative organisational support, give and take, a sense of belonging, feeling of interdependence, and level of trust are important variables.

These are all elements of a corporate culture and confirm the importance of common bonds.

Effective organisations are those that encourage innovative and responsive behaviour on the part of their staff, leading to levels of performance beyond the standard requirements needed to accomplish organisational functions. These include cooperative and collaborative acts, expressing ideas for improvement and promoting a positive organisational climate. Organ (1988: 4) has called such cooperative acts 'organizational citizenship behaviours' (OCBs) and defined them as 'individual behaviour(s) that (are) discretionary, not directly or explicitly recognized by the formal reward system, and that in aggregate promote the effective functioning of the organization'. Organ theorised there are five forms of organisational citizenship behaviour, these being altruism, conscientiousness, courtesy, sportsmanship, and civic virtue.

Walz and Niehoff (2000) have recently examined the relevance of Organ's five forms of OCB to corporate culture and organisational effectiveness in terms of the restaurant industry. Their findings 'clearly support the idea that aggregated OCBs are related to organizational effectiveness indicators. Specifically, as employees exhibited helping behaviours, food cost percentages were lower, and revenue to full-time equivalent employees, operating efficiency, customer satisfaction, and perceived company quality were higher' (Walz and Niehoff, 2000: 314). Furthermore, sportsmanship and civic virtue were associated with fewer customer complaints.

Based on this admittedly small and sector specific study Walz and Niehoff (2000) feel encouraged to recommend that managers consider what they can do to foster the OCBs and the associated positive corporate culture. They recommend that managers:

- clarify personal and organisational expectations during interviews and orientation, and periodically throughout the period of employment;
- remember and keep promises that are made to employees – document if necessary;
- provide needed resources so that employees can carry out their job responsibilities;
- make sure procedures used to allocate important organisational rewards are perceived as fair and equitable;
- be supportive of employees' well-being and considerate of their needs;
- provide an appropriate model for employees to follow;
- empower employees;
- foster the acceptance of group goals.

Such guidelines have wide applicability and can certainly assist in the effective implementation of strategic plans by the varied staff of any authorised organisation or inter-organisational association.

Organisational leadership

As we have seen above, many studies of organisational effectiveness in delivering strategic planning objectives come down to the type and quality of leadership. Selin and Myers (1998: 89) in their study of the CURES organisational experience claim 'several CURES members noted the importance of "strong leaders" and "the contributions of outstanding folks" in explaining the success of CURES efforts'. These are becoming common sentiments in tourism and will be explored briefly here and in more detail in the next chapter.

One example of leadership in developing an interorganisational structure in tourism has occurred with the development of the French ecomuseum concept. This approach to community tourism involves presenting the best of the past with the best of the present, so that the host community's future is assisted by the consideration of its heritage. An example of this approach occurred in the Cowichan and Chemainus Valleys Ecomuseum, located on Vancouver Island, Canada, with an area of 1000 square kilometres and a population of 57,000 in 1991.

Under the leadership of Wilma Wood the existing 12 museums, other heritage sites, the tourism industry, government, local industry and businesses, unions, cultural groups and organisations were brought together to form an 'ecomuseum' (Wood, 1993): a museum without walls that would develop a new heritage/cultural tourism industry for the region. The theme uniting all these groups was the 'forest legacy' of the two valleys. The past was remembered with individual museums and heritage sites, such as the Duncan Forestry Museum and the Native Heritage Centre. The present was portrayed by the forest management display projects throughout the region, outlining the sequence of clear-cut followed by replanting, thinning and re-harvesting. The future was represented by the forest research station which is developing faster growing and disease resistant trees, along with the championing of a community forest, where small local logging enterprises could maintain specialised forestry production. To bring all these elements together became the responsibility of the ecomuseum director – Wilma Wood. She liked to refer to the whole project as a living museum, 'to initiate an improvement in the quality of life at the request of and with the participation of its community members' (Wood, 1991: 449).

Challenges

Organisational structures do not always work smoothly because combining the work of many individuals and in some cases different and independent organisations can be a real challenge. There have been a few tourism studies that have reported on such difficulties and disappointments. Holder (1993: 219) reports on the frustratingly slow progress of the Caribbean Tourism Organisation in meeting the goals given to its predecessor the Caribbean Tourism Association some 40 years earlier 'to market the Caribbean as a region, as opposed to individual countries'. She lays the blame for this on the dominance of island over regional cultures, even though most outsiders view the Caribbean area as a whole. This in turn led to a lack of sufficient human and financial resources needed for the task.

Sometimes the problem is the reverse, with the higher order organisation assuming that what is beneficial for it would also benefit lower order organisations and meet their needs. Mutch (1996) reports on the demise of the English Tourist Network Automation (ETNA) project. Only 17% of the 500 English Tourist Information Centres went on-line within the start-up phase, so the original concept was 'shelved (and) replaced by the use of two private sector software houses' (Mutch, 1996: 604). Among the reasons given for this failure was that the regional tourist boards served several stakeholders and that the thrust of ETNA only satisfied some of these. At the local level tourist information centres are designed to serve local residents with information on local council services as well as the tourists. Plus, there is a powerful disincentive to invest heavily in a computer reservation system that handles not only local tourists but at times sells them products in other regions.

These difficulties in implementing strategic plans indicate that the second function of management – organisation – requires careful consideration and operation if it is to fulfil its function. Pearce (1992) has indicated all tourist organisations will face a number of constraints to their effective implementation of tourism plans. The biggest of these is that 'tourist organisations generally exercise only limited control over the product' (Pearce, 1992: 12). He feels that most organisations lack an adequate legislative base and apart from their leadership role in promotion and marketing they are relatively powerless to influence the direction and form of this fragmented and competitive industry. Indeed, Pearce feels (1992: 12) 'in general it is easier to plan to prevent something from happening than to ensure that something does take place'.

Not everyone would agree with Pearce's rather dismal assessment of the potential effectiveness of tourism organisations. As indicated in his use of the words 'control' and 'power' much will depend on local circumstances and the legitimacy of the organisation. As we have seen in the Palmer and Bejou study, tourist organisations will reflect their home environment and local needs, so in some areas all that is expected of these organisations is to coordinate destination promotion. Even if the situation envisaged by Pearce is correct, it signifies that at a minimum tourist organisations can be expected to coordinate the promotion and to police the image and product that has been selected for the destination – very important functions for community tourism.

However, in order for tourism organisations to become effective, even at the minimal and basic capacity outlined by Pearce, they need to possess the legitimacy to act. Legitimacy has been defined by Suchman (1994: 574) as 'a generalised perception or assumption that the actions of an entity are desirable, proper or appropriate within some socially constructed system of norms, values, beliefs, and definitions'. According to Lawrence *et al.* (1997) firms and organisations within tourism need to be perceived as legitimate by key stakeholders in order to access critical resources and the authority to fulfil their mandate.

> From a managerial perspective, the process of legitimacy management is the process of managing stakeholder perceptions of corporate and industry activity, managing the evaluative frameworks – the expectations – that stakeholders bring to bear on the firm or organization, and managing issues as they arise to ensure that they do not damage the carefully tended image of the firm or of the industry. (Lawrence *et al.*, 1997: 311)

Thus, if a tourist destination association is to implement a strategic plan its legitimacy to do so must be recognised as the first step, to be followed by the appropriate resources and authority needed to carry out the tasks. In some locations this legitimacy may be limited to promotional activities, while in others it may be more comprehensive, including the leadership and control functions discussed in later chapters.

Continuing in this vein is the work of Palmer (1998) on the governance of destination organisations. He has studied the effectiveness of destination marketing in terms of the various levels of control that the organisation has been able to use in pursuing its promotional objectives. He suggests the literature indicates that governance systems can be placed along a continuum which runs from loose and informal authority and control through to tight and formal. 'The results of the quantitative analysis (of his study) strongly supported the hypothesis of a link between tight governance style and perceived effectiveness' (Palmer, 1998: 196). Consequently Palmer recommends the development of a tight governance style that is more likely to emerge with the legitimacy needed to implement the marketing and other requirements of a strategic plan.

Throughout the discussion of organisations in general and in tourism in particular is the significance of recognising and responding to a growing number of stakeholder groups. Among the list of stakeholders that need to be considered in any organisational structure involving community tourism are the volunteer and non-profit groups, who in pursuing their individual or group interests contribute to the individual character of a destination's product offerings.

According to Drucker (1993: 213–21) volunteers have some specific demands they will make of non-profit or other organisations in which they devote their time and energy. 'Their first and most important demand is that the non-profit have a clear mission, one that drives everything the organization does', so they know their concerns are compatible with the organisation's objectives. The 'second thing this new breed requires, indeed demands, is training, training, and more training', so they can really contribute to the cause. 'Supporting all this activity is accountability', both on the part of the organisation and their own contribution.

The growing involvement of volunteers in tourism organisations is due to the attraction of unpaid staff and the rising numbers of retiring professionals who are seeking some interesting and useful part-time activity. However, as Deery and Jago (2001: 58) report 'the issue of service quality and reliability of volunteer attendance has become a concern'. They note the use of volunteers in visitor information centres requires special consideration, given that volunteers are not present at all times and may not be included in regular communication processes; that their roles need to be differentiated from, yet integrated into, those of the regular staff; and that their contribution needs to be appreciated and noted. Based on their research they propose several ways to improve the organisational management of volunteers. These include:

- developing clear job descriptions for both paid staff and volunteers;
- maintaining regular induction programmes:
- providing clear communication channels between management and staff/volunteers and between the staff and volunteers;
- managing the balance of power between paid staff and volunteers;
- training the workforce in understanding the needs of both paid staff and volunteers;
- training the volunteers in areas such as computing skills and cultural differences. (Deery & Jago, 2001: 66)

All of this leads to a type of organisation and board that is broader and more varied than found within a regular corporation, as illustrated by the structure of many tourist destination associations. But it requires a special structure and culture to tap the energy deriving from such volunteer activity. Drucker (1993: 209) acknowledges this in the following observation:

Precisely because the non-profit (as are most destination associations) is so committed and active, its relationship with the CEO tends to be highly contentious and full of potential for friction. Non-profit CEOs complain their board 'meddles'. The directors, in turn, complain that management 'usurps' the board's function.

All of these feelings have been experienced or witnessed by the authors and have been referred to at times in the tourism literature. But insufficient attention has been paid to its ramifications on developing a more effective implementation of community tourism objectives.

Summary

Organisation can be seen as the structure required to put the original vision, objectives and plans into operation. As such it needs to bring together various elements and stakeholders in a united effort to deliver the plan's promise. This can become a complicated process in large organisations and in terms of communities, where large numbers of stakeholders can have conflicting interests.

Although a tourism organisation will vary in size and scope according to its location and situation the evidence suggests there are several key components to consider. The structure of most organisations is one of line departments, undertaking the various primary functions of the organisation's purpose and plan. These in turn report to department managers who are coordinated by a CEO, who reports to a board of directors. In the service industries more organisations are inverting their structure to place the customer on top.

Another feature of tourism organisations is the growing awareness of the need to collaborate, both internally and externally. To compete on the global stage a destination association needs to coordinate the various elements of its tourism industry, to produce a united image and product. In order to be competitive smaller destinations need to seek external alliances to build up their critical mass of attractions and activities, to make their regions more appealing.

Such adjustments to the traditional and insular organisational structures are responses to changing market conditions, but it requires leadership to recognise this and to implement the changes. Leadership will be examined in more detail in the next chapter.

Chapter 5

Leadership

In business and in tourism it takes many people, and sometimes many separate units or sectors, to provide the customer product or experience. This necessitates a team environment and those teams look for leadership to help them fulfil their individual contributions to the overall plan and success of the organisation. Leadership is required at all levels and is now recognised as being a significant feature in helping organisations to develop their full potential and to become successful in competitive markets. For example, professional sports teams pay huge sums to their managers for their overall leadership of the team's structure, preparation and game tactics; but leadership is needed also on the field of play as the game unfolds and this becomes the formal responsibility of the team captain(s). Within the team and game situation there are generally some players who stand out by contributing above the average, and these 'stars' are the individual leaders who regularly stand out in their area of the game, whether it be on attack or defence.

So it is in a service industry like tourism where the CEOs of individual firms may develop the strategic plans for their businesses, but if they wish to see them implemented effectively, they need to involve their managers and key line staff during strategy formulation. In this way leadership will involve communication and motivation along with the hard work recognised by Drucker, to bring about a greater commitment to the new strategy. In the process it may well change the corporate values and culture of the organisation.

One particular type of leadership that is very important to the tourism industry is entrepreneurship, because so many of its individual components are small businesses owned and/or operated by an individual. The definition of business size differs from country to country, but generally micro businesses employ under ten people, small businesses employ fewer than 50 people (Page *et al.* 1999) and medium sized businesses employ less than 200 full-time employees (National Office for the Information Economy, 2000). In this regard it comes as no surprise that 80% or more of tourism business around the world can be classified as small to medium enterprises (SMEs). Indeed, in the United States Edgell (1993: 13) has claimed '98 percent of (travel related business) can be classified as small business'.

To make these small businesses successful the skills and leadership qualities of the owner/operator become vital, for they often have no one else to turn to for assistance within their own organisations. To lead these small businesses the qualities of entrepreneurship would be extremely helpful in today's competitive markets, 'but to be entrepreneurial, an enterprise has to have special characteristics over and above being new and small' (Drucker, 1985: 22). According to Drucker these characteristics involve creating something new, something different that changes the organisation's values. Drucker (1985: 26) goes on to declare 'entrepreneurship is behaviour rather than personality trait. And its foundation lies in concept and theory rather than in intuition'.

While leadership has become important in a business sense it becomes far more complex and vital in a community sense, because in that setting it involves many organisations and different groups with different priorities. Very often those communities seeking tourism as a means to replace dying industries or to broaden their economic base require leadership to set them on the path. Examples of this can be seen in Chemainus, British Columbia; where one man – Karl Shutz – helped to raise a community out of the economic and psychological depression associated with the closure of its one remaining wood processing plant. He achieved this by encouraging the town to recall its past forestry heritage and industrial glory by depicting them through murals that could, and did, attract thousands of tourists (Beyer & Bunbury, 1993: 10) Figure 5.1.

Likewise, the growth of New Zealand's tourism industry has been linked to a few pioneers, whose leadership helped to transform this agricultural and isolated nation into a broader-based economy, where tourism plays a growing role. Watkins (1987) has identified the efforts and achievements of several New Zealand in-bound tour operators and travel agencies, including Ron Guthrey of Guthrey's NZ Tours which developed into one of the country's leading in-bound tour operators. Guthrey started his business after World War II with his war gratuity of £500 and built it into a multi-million dollar business that has offices around the Pacific Rim selling coach tours, self-drive holidays, adventure tourism, farm stays, and educational and special interest tours around New Zealand.

Business Leadership

Leadership definitions

Leadership has proved to be both an important and elusive concept in business management. Organisational theory and behaviour studies and human resource practices and research have explored the subject and come

Figure 5.1 Murals of Chemainus

up with a variety of definitions. Among those that are germane to the purpose of this book are:

> Leadership is the behaviour of an individual when he (or she) is directing the activities of a group toward a shared goal. (Hemphill & Coons, 1957: 7)

> Leadership is the interpersonal influence, exercised in a situation, and directed, through the communication process, toward the attainment of a specified goal or goals. (Tannenbaum *et al.*, 1961: 24)

> Leadership is an interaction between persons in which one presents information of a sort and in such a manner that the other(s) becomes convinced that his (or her) outcomes (benefits and costs) will be improved if he (or she) behaves in the manner suggested or desired. (Jacobs, 1970: 232)

> Leadership is influencing others to do what the leader wants them to do. (Gordon *et al.* 1990: 553)

> Leadership is the process in which an individual influences other group members toward the attainment of group or organisational goals. (Shackelton, 1995: 2)

> Leadership is about harnessing people's energy towards achieving organisational goals. (Van der Wagen & Davies, 1998: 37)

From such definitions it is evident that much of the variation in leadership concepts and models can be accounted for 'by differences in who exerts influence, the nature of that influence, the purpose for the exercise of influence and its outcomes' (Leithwood *et al.*, 1999: 6).

Research and instruction in business management has generally focused on four aspects of leadership, moving from the most basic description of observable features to more complex interactional theories. Throughout these studies it has become apparent that there are strong similarities between management and leadership, since both involve getting tasks done through the efforts of others. The main distinction between the two is that leadership concentrates on human interactions, while management is more concerned with procedures and results. Kotter (1990) goes so far as to maintain leadership and management are two distinctive and complementary systems, which are both necessary for success. However, the general consensus is that 'no one leadership style is the most effective' (Gordon *et al.*, 1990: 577).

Leadership traits

One of the earliest approaches to studying leadership was to search for those physical and psychological characteristics or traits that identified leadership potential. A common, yet often unstated, assumption of much trait research has been that leaders are born, not made. Consequently, research has attempted to demonstrate correlations between leaders and their physical or psychological traits, producing appearance models and personality tests to indicate leadership potential based on these correlations. However, more recent research has demonstrated such simple correlations are not necessarily foolproof in that different leaders have different traits, both in their appearance and psychological make-up (Clancy & Webber, 1995). For example, while the image-makers would have us believe that leaders need to be tall and good-looking males, real life has provided a more varied profile via the likes of Napoleon, Ghandi and Margaret Thatcher to balance the likes of Ronald Reagan and John F. Kennedy.

Despite the difficulty in creating definite links between certain characteristics and leadership 'the trait approach to the study of leadership is not dead' according to Gordon *et al.* (1990: 556–7), who offer the evidence of Ghiselli's (1971) research. They identify six of Ghiselli's most significant traits related to effective leadership, which can be applied to most management situations, including tourism development. These are:

(1) *Supervisory ability*. The ability to perform the basic functions of management, which includes planning, organising, influencing and controlling the work of others. In other words the four management functions being discussed in this book.
(2) *Need for occupational achievement*. The desire for success and willingness to work toward such a goal and to seek the responsibility associated with it.
(3) *Intelligence*. Creative and verbal ability that includes a capacity for judgement, reasoning and thinking.
(4) *Decisiveness*. The ability to make decisions and solve problems capably and competently.
(5) *Self-assurance*. The extent to which individuals view their capability to cope with problems and their degree of comfort with such responsibilities.
(6) *Initiative*. The ability to act independently and develop courses of action not readily apparent to other people.

Evidence that trait research is still being pursued and championed can be seen in the publication of Goleman's work in the *Harvard Business Review*. Goleman (1998: 94) maintains 'effective leaders are alike in one crucial way: they all have a high degree of emotional intelligence'. The five components of his 'emotional intelligence' are self-awareness, self-regulation, motivation, empathy and social skill. These have considerable overlap with the six traits identified by Ghiselli.

Leadership styles and behaviours

Another of the descriptive models of leadership is based on leadership styles and behaviours, where four fundamental styles have been identified and recognised. One is *autocratic leadership*, where senior management instructs subordinate staff what to do and expects to be obeyed without question, as in the military. Another is *participative leadership*, where the leader involves subordinates in decision-making, but retains the final authority and responsibility for any decisions, as in government cabinets. One is *democratic leadership*, where the leader does what the majority of subordinate's desire, as in the case of committee chairs. Lastly, *laissez-faire leadership* occurs when someone not involved in the regular operations is brought in to offer expert advice, as in the case of outside consultants. However, such advice does not have to be acted upon.

Leadership involves communication and motivation, so a key concern has been to study leaders' behaviour in directing the effort of others toward organisational goals. One focus has been on two separate and distinctive dimensions of leadership behaviour, namely the: *initiating structure (task oriented)* – the extent to which leaders establish clear goals and structure their roles and those of their subordinates to achieve those goals; and *consideration (employee oriented)*– the leaders' relationships with subordinates as characterised by their consideration of employees' ideas and feelings and the development of mutual trust and respect.

Using these two dimensions it is possible to develop a leadership grid that indicates four potentially effective leadership styles (Stoner *et al.* 1995: 476–7). For example, those leaders who rank high on initiating but low on consideration could be identified as 'authoritarian' types, while those low on initiating and high on consideration could be labelled 'democratic' style leaders.

This model does not purport to provide the most effective leadership style for all situations, because the significance and magnitude of influence along its two dimensions will change with varying situations. For example, if an organisation expects and wants authoritarian leadership behaviour, it is more likely to be satisfied with that type of leadership, as exemplified by the 'high structure and low consideration' box. If an organisation is highly dependent on volunteers then it will need to emphasise the consideration dimension and, depending on the stage of development and experience within the organisation, will be in either the high or low structure box; the high structure and high consideration approach to leadership being more appropriate to those community festival groups that have considerable experience with past festivals and events. This is one reason why the management of international hallmark events is based on a professional and experienced core, who move from one event to another to help the host community put on a successful Olympic or Commonwealth Games.

A frequently cited behavioural leadership style theory along the same lines is Blake and Mouton's (1985) 'Managerial Grid'. This grid involves two basic dimensions of leadership in management, namely a concern for production and a concern for people. These dimensions are assessed along nine point scales from low to high concern, producing a 9 × 9 grid. Within the grid five cluster types of leadership style have been identified. These are:

(1.1) *Impoverished Management* – where the manager has little concern for either people or production matters.

(9.1) *Authority-Obedience* – where the manager stresses operating efficiency and controls above all else. Where the people element has little consideration and even less input.

(1.9) *Country Club Management* – where the manager is people oriented and has little concern for output.

(9.9) *Team Management* – where the manager seeks high output through working closely with and listening to his/her subordinates, developing mutual trust and respect in the process.

(5.5) *Organization Man Management* – where the manager attempts to balance and trade-off concern for output in exchange for a satisfactory level of staff morale.

According to Blake and Mouton the most effective leadership style is '9.9 Team Management', in that it will result in improved performance, lower employee turnover and absenteeism, and greater employee satisfaction. This is certainly a laudable objective and many organisations strive to achieve it, but its attainment can be difficult, especially when the two considerations are in opposition. For example, a common problem in tourism is that staff need to be at work and on peak form during public holidays like Christmas and New Year, when their hearts and minds may be elsewhere with family and friends.

Situational theories

Situational theories of leadership emphasise that different styles of leadership will be needed for different situations and with different people, so they attempt to move beyond the normative nature of the trait models. An example of these is Hersey and Blanchard's (1974) situational leadership theory, which has been outlined by Gordon *et al.* (1990: 571–4). This builds on the Ohio State work and the Managerial Grid by arguing 'an effective leader is one who can diagnose the demands of the situation and the level of readiness of the followers and use a leadership style that is appropriate' (Gordon, *et al.*, 1990: 571). This theory recognises that *work tasks* and priorities will change over time, much as we have described with the product and destination lifecycles. That in organisations with a high reliance on skilled and motivated staff the *task-relevance readiness of followers* will change with the stage of development, the targeted market segments and the seasons.

That a leader has to be cognisant of these variations and adjust his/her *task behaviour* style accordingly.

A simplified version of the Hersey and Blanchard situational model in Figure 5.2 shows how this flexible form of leadership style can be equated to the regular product lifecycle pattern of a tourism product or destination.

Stage 1

In the *early stage of development (S1)* when everything is new there will be a high task load, with many tasks needing to be done with much uncertainty regarding the best approach. At this stage the relevant task preparedness of staff will be low with respect to the organisation's specific needs. Under these conditions the leader will need to *tell staff* what to do and how to do it, in order to reach the organisation's goals and objectives.

Stage 2

At the *second stage (S2)* the leadership style must still deal with a high task load as the business and destination enter the rapid growth phase and new products or facilities are created. Now some staff have more experience and training so they have higher task relevance preparedness and can be used to supervise new or casual employees. At this stage the leader should be *selling* and embellishing the business goals to all staff by encouraging them to utilise their training and to increase their personal potential returns from the evolving business opportunities through career development.

Stage 3

In the *third stage (S3)* the staff continue to build on their training and high task preparedness, becoming more experienced and skilled in the process. Hence the level of task relevance remains high and becomes more diverse. The number of new tasks diminishes as the business and destination reaches maturity allowing leaders to focus more on selective quality product delivery and selecting staff for supervisory roles. Thus a more *participatory leadership* role should emerge at this stage.

Stage 4

In the fourth and *final stage (S4)* there are very few new tasks and little need for new staff, as the business or destination enters the stagnation and possibly declining stage of its product lifecycle evolution. The skill level of most staff should be at its highest level, therefore there is little need for new training and skill development. Hence there is a low relevant task readiness once again, but in this case it is because the staff are generally well prepared and not because of inexperience as in the S1 situation. Due to this high level of experience and skill the most appropriate leadership style at this stage would be to *delegate* more responsibilities to staff, to build on their

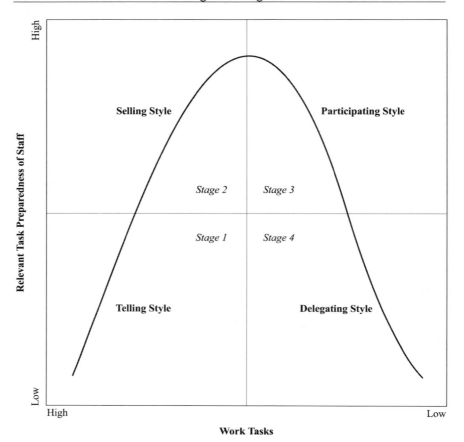

Figure 5.2 Changing leadership behaviour style
Source: After Hersey and Blanchard (1974)

individual expertise and provide them with the satisfaction of career development to middle or senior management.

As with the original product lifecycle theory this situational leadership theory appears logical and simple, but it is difficult to operationalise. For example, it is not always possible to identify when the stages of development and their associated leadership changes take place. Nor is it necessarily true that all businesses and employees proceed through the evolutionary cycle in a regular and unbroken sequence. This is especially true in tourism where the strong seasonal patterns often disrupt the steady progress of skill development for many staff. Tourism also struggles with staff turnover, which makes it difficult to build up the task and supervisory skill levels anticipated in this model. Furthermore, the logical and objective assessment process associated with the situation model has been challenged by some who feel it does not provide enough credence to the personal nature of leadership. One of these alternative theories is the attributional theory.

The *attributional theory* of leadership suggests that leadership exists only in a person's individual perception and assessment of a situation, rather than as an objective and measurable fact (Bartunek, 1981). This approach is linked with the phenomenological approach to research in the sense that what is true is only that which is perceived and accepted by the individual. Hence in this theory a leader's judgement about tasks needing to be done and who to assign to such tasks is influenced by their personal assessment of follower's attributes and behaviour. While championing individual perceptions and assessment of leadership, it is only natural to find followers attributing certain causality to the leader's behaviour. 'Subordinates tend to view leaders as the cause of group behaviour and, depending on members' attitudes to group behaviour, they develop either positive or negative attitudes about and reactions to the leader' (Gordon *et al.* 1990: 575).

New leadership theories

The term 'New Leadership' has been used to categorise a number of leadership styles that emerged in the 1980s and 1990s when business was experiencing major changes in structure and emphasis, especially in the US. According to Clegg *et al.* (1997) writers used a variety of terms to describe these new types of leadership, including 'transformational leadership', 'charismatic leadership', and 'visionary leadership'. The overall perception of these leaders or industry was

> as someone who defines organisational reality through the articulation of a vision which is a reflection of how he or she defines an organisation's mission and the value which will support it. Thus, the New Leadership approach is underpinned by a depiction of leaders as managers of meaning rather than in terms of an influence process. (Clegg *et al.*, 1997: 280)

The impact of these new leadership approaches was a dramatic rise to 'stardom' as stock markets rose and stock options increased, but come the bubble burst there has been a major reassessment of its desirability. Some have become concerned over the focus on heroic leaders, the preoccupation with leadership at the highest levels, and the focus on individuals rather than teams (Clegg *et al.*, 1997). Now there is a return to leaders being coaches, by building commitment and confidence, removing obstacles and creating opportunities for the whole team.

With this range of theories associated with leadership, business texts regularly conclude that there is no single leadership style that is the best or most effective. Four basic leadership styles have been identified in the literature, and all work effectively at certain times and for certain individuals. The trait approach has evolved from an emphasis on physical and psychological characteristics to a search for how leaders should behave, as exemplified by the Ohio State leadership studies and the Managerial Grid. Situational theories assert no single leadership style is sufficient, for leadership needs will change with the evolution of the business. Attributional theory runs counter to the normative nature of the other theories in promoting the significance of the individual to concepts about leadership, and shows how both leader and follower perceptions and assessments of situations can influence attitudes to leadership. This individualisation of leadership styles has led in the recent past to a business and media fixation on 'successful' leaders who participated in the recent stock market boom. However, many of them failed to see the big picture and others seemed to have exaggerated their business acumen through questionable accounting procedures.

Consequently, we find business texts recommend managers choose a technique and style that best suits the needs of the organisation and their own personality. One particular type of leadership that is beginning to emerge as a significant factor in both business and tourism is that of entrepreneurship.

Entrepreneurial Leadership

In both developed and under-developed countries the powerhouse of national economies has been the small to medium enterprises (SMEs). These have grown substantially over the past few decades. In part this trend is due to push factors such as a response to the downsizing of some of the major international corporations or to local high unemployment. In part it is due to the pull factors of seeking individual opportunity or new lifestyles, to introduce innovative ideas that permit enterprises to be more flexible in their responsiveness to changing global markets and business situations. In either case, to achieve the levels of success recorded around the world has required leadership and very often that leadership has come from the individuals who have started these SMEs.

Entrepreneurship definitions

In this chapter we will examine entrepreneurship as an aspect of leadership, a behavioural concept that is capable of being analysed and integrated into the business management process. 'The concept of entrepreneurship can best be understood by deconstructing it into three main overlapping components' (Shaw & Williams, 1998: 236). These are innovation, risk taking, and managerial capabilities. *Innovation* can be seen as a way to 'change the yield of resources' which is the basis of entrepreneurship, according to J.B. Say who originated the term (Drucker, 1985: 33). *Risk* is involved in any business venture, but especially in those that are new and innovative. Accordingly, Vesper (1996: 234) advises 'a business plan should be designed with maximum realism, and in real life risk is a part of the picture'. *Managerial capabilities* are needed to capitalise on the preceding components, and the classical process is operationalisation of the four business functions that form the structure of this book.

Entrepreneurship is synonymous with leadership, especially within the setting of small business enterprises (SBEs) where many are owner operated with a small staff. Early recognition of this came from the renowned Joseph Shumpeter, who described entrepreneurship as:

> Consist(ing) of doing things that are not generally done in the ordinary course of business routine; it is essentially a phenomenon that comes under the wider aspect of leadership. (Schumpeter, 1951: 255)

Similar expressions of the linkage between entrepreneurship and leadership can be seen in the following definitions:

> In . . . entrepreneurship there is agreement that we are talking about a kind of behaviour that includes: (1) initiative taking, (2) the organizing or reorganizing of social economic mechanisms to turn resources and situations to practical account, and (3) the acceptance of risk of failure. (Shapero, 1975: 187)

> Entrepreneurship is the ability to create and build a vision from practically nothing: fundamentally it is a human, creative act. It is the application of energy to initiating and building an enterprise or organization, rather than just watching or analyzing. This vision requires a willingness to take calculated risks – both personal and financial – and then to do everything possible to reduce the chances of failure. Entrepreneurship also includes the ability to build an entrepreneurial or venture team to complement your own skills and talents. (Timmons, 1994: 5–6)

> The entrepreneur is the aggressive catalyst for change in the world of business. He or she is an independent thinker who dares to be different in a background of common events. (Kuratko & Hodgetts, 1995: 4)

Such definitions include many of the leadership trait characteristics identified by Ghiselli and others, plus they reinforce the strong links to the other three functions of business management – namely planning, organising and controlling.

Entrepreneurial traits

Timmons (1994) has included leadership among the desirable attributes for entrepreneurs who reveal its importance to this form of business activity and its strong links with the other attributes. He has clustered various indicators of entrepreneurial activity into six dominant themes, which he calls 'desirable and acquirable' attributes. The second of these is leadership qualities, but if one considers the previous business definitions and studies of leadership one can see considerable overlap with his other themes, such as commitment, creativity and risk. Such a listing of attributes should be viewed as a critical mass of characteristics that can combine into different forms of entrepreneur and leadership, for 'effective entrepreneurs come in very different combinations of qualities which work for them in a particular context' (Morrison *et al.*, 1999: 42).

Morrison *et al.* (1999) also make the point that entrepreneurial leadership can be very different from the leadership characteristics and qualities outlined for corporate situations. While differences in organisational size and complexity can explain some of these leadership differences, they feel that the common autocratic and commanding style of entrepreneurial leadership is more closely linked with the psychological nature of the entrepreneurs themselves. 'One major reason for this is rooted back in the entrepreneurial personality and traits such as need for achievement, strong internal locus of control, and a driving ambition. They expect others to work at the same level and pace as themselves' (Morrison *et al.*, 1999: 137). Indeed, this may be one of the factors that make it so difficult for many small entrepreneurial businesses to grow into successful multi-unit and corporate structures. To make such an adjustment requires a change of leadership styles along with the evolution of the company, as indicated in the Hersey and Blanchard (1974) situational model of leadership. For a large number of small business entrepreneurs this proves to be a major challenge.

Role in small businesses

It should be appreciated, however, that entrepreneurial activity is only one of three key factors in managing small businesses, according to Longenecker *et al.*'s (1994) book on *Small Business Management*. Citing previous studies in the field, they consider the three important dimensions to small business management are:

(1) *Entrepreneurial values* – including intuition, risk-taking, creativity and flexibility.
(2) *Managerial skills* – including the selection of a niche strategy, effective cash flow and budget management, organisational structure and education.
(3) *Interpersonal skills* – including good relationship with one's banker, good customer and employee relations. (Longenecker *et al.*, 1994: 18).

Others agree that entrepreneurship plays an important role in small business development, and some feel it is the crucial element to success. One of these is Gerber (1995). He feels that people going into business should possess three characteristics: the best features of being an entrepreneur, a manager and a technician. According to Gerber (1995: 24) the entrepreneur within us is 'the innovator, the grand strategist, the creator of new methods for penetrating or creating new markets' and represents our 'creative personality'. But to be successful the creativity and leadership of the entrepreneurial spirit needs to be coupled with 'pragmatic' management and the technical ability to deliver the ideas. Gerber contends that many small businesses fail because the owner is more a technician than an entrepreneur, and too busy working at the job s(he) has created for themselves, rather than working to create a business.

The *Harvard Business Review on Entrepreneurship* supports the need for entrepreneurship that encompasses multiple skills. In the introductory paper Bhide (1999: 24) states that entrepreneurs must balance their bias for action with concern over the management issues of goals and strategies, and their resource capabilities to deliver the product. This is supported later in the same volume by Rock, who examines entrepreneurship from the viewpoint of a venture capitalist. He feels that 'good ideas and products are a dime a dozen. Good execution and good management – in a word, good *people* – are rare' (author's emphasis – Rock, 1999: 137). So he focuses on the quality of the business plan and the management skill ability of the entrepreneur to carry out their ideas. In some cases this may include the out-sourcing of particular functions, due to the lack of particular technical skills on the part of the entrepreneur or due to a realistic time management assessment on their behalf.

Regardless of the style and character of leadership in business and entrepreneurial settings, its significance and impact remain unchallenged in this era of intense global competition. Its role within the four-function model of business management extends beyond its individual functional box to influence the other three functions in terms of priorities and style. Nowhere is this more evident than in some of the management trends that have been noted by business analysts. Peters and Austin (1985) in their book *A Passion for Excellence* consider the concept of leadership is so crucial they recommended discarding words like 'managing' and 'management', with their associated images of controlling and arranging in favour of 'leadership' because it connotes unleashing energy, flexibility, building and growing. In a review of innovative business practices in Australia it was determined that 'sustained success with innovation is the product of consistent, concentrated efforts by people in enterprises around five key factors: customers, supply, leadership, resources and systems for innovation' (Carnegie & Butlin, 1993: xxxvii). All of these factors will be examined in terms of tourism and community tourism.

Tourism Leadership

Leadership within entrepreneurship and SMEs is a relatively new area of research interest within business management studies so there are few tourism specific studies as of this date. However, certain entrepreneurial and SME management studies would appear to have particular relevance to the tourism situation and we are beginning to see the extension of such research into the field of tourism. So we will examine those which appear to have particular relevance to the development of community tourism.

After a slow start the significance of leadership is beginning to be appreciated and starting to appear in the tourism literature, especially with respect to one area of tourism – entrepreneurship. This has occurred with the growing interest in business management studies links to tourism research and theory, as described by Tribe (1997) earlier in this book, and to a rise in interest in these topics within the field of business management. Their importance has also been demonstrated by various biographies of successful entrepreneurs in tourism related businesses and case studies into tourism development. These have acknowledged the important role played by individuals and the influence of entrepreneurs in developing the opportunities presented by the appearance of new consumer interests and destinations.

Examples of the impact of pioneers in tourism can be seen in the studies or biographies of some famous entrepreneurs who changed the face of the industry in various ways. Walt Disney (Capodagli & Jackson, 1999) created the modern theme park concept out of the traditional fairground milieu. Ray Kroc developed the modern fast-food industry with his McDonald's franchises (Love, 1995). Sir Richard Branson (Branson, 1998) created a new type of airline based on increased customer service.

There are equally important pioneers also at the other end of the tourism business spectrum, where individuals give birth to successful SMEs. A good example of this is Walsh-Martin's (1998) book on how 25 rural women have turned ideas into small owner-operated businesses. Included in that book are accounts of how these women developed a variety of SMEs, some of them tourism related, for a variety of reasons. For example, Lynne Bullen planted a maze on her country property, and 'provided an environment where everyone can indulge in the simple pleasures of life – eating, music, nature, literature, art, horticulture and socialising – in a friendly, comfortable, and exciting atmosphere' (Walsh-Martin, 1998: 41). In another example, Jeanette Basset-Pearse and her husband developed host farming in order to 'diversify just to bring in the extra income so we could remain on the farm' (Walsh-Martin, 1998: 171).

The linking of leadership with entrepreneurship and SMEs has occurred because so many of the leadership characteristics outlined above have been observed in tourism entrepreneurial behaviour, and as many of the SMEs in tourism are owner-operated they reflect the characteristics and priorities of their leaders. The dominance of the owner-operator is revealed in the work of Goffee and Scase 1983, cited by Shaw and Williams (1994: 134), who identified four types of SME firm characteristics of which three are owner-operated. Their organisational categories are 'self-employed', 'small employer', 'owner-controllers', and 'owner-directors' where there is a separation of ownership and management.

In their book on *Entrepreneurship in the Hospitality, Tourism and Leisure Industries*, Morrison *et al.* (1999: 44) state that leadership in these industries ranges from authoritarian to participative in style, but that all leaders require the same skills. 'These include the ability to select appropriate team members, communication, mediation, negotiation and persuasion skills.' These skills are generally developed over time and with experience rather than through formal education channels, either because such information sources are lacking or because individuals have entered into tourism entrepreneurship primarily for non-economic reasons.

Echtner (1995) maintains that tourism development has been held back in developing countries, and one could add in the peripheral regions of developed economies, by a lack of appropriate tourism education and training. Part of her proposed three-pronged model for such education and training is 'the development of entrepreneurship or the initiative to *work for oneself*' (author's emphasis – Echtner, 1995: 121). In addition, she maintains education should focus on professional management education and vocational skills. Such a model for education and training can prepare more people for the realities of entrepreneurship, and would be beneficial even if it convinced students such risk taking and hard work was not for them. For it will not be an easy process in developing countries or regions, that face 'issues such as inadequate financial assistance for new ventures, complex bureaucracies, and traditional barriers (that) may inhibit small scale entrepreneurship' (Echtner, 1995: 128).

Prime non-economic motives for becoming an entrepreneur in tourism are lifestyle and location. In the developed economies, where redundancy packages and retirement planning are providing more people with a lump sum to invest, more people are considering a small business in their retirement or semi-retirement, and want to live in an attractive part of the world. Such motivation often explains the choice of small bed and breakfast operations. They are often uneconomic business propositions in themselves, but provide the owners with some activity and interpersonal relationships during their retirement and may help to justify the expense of a larger home in an attractive destination than they could otherwise afford. Shaw and Williams (1998: 248) confirm both of these trends in their summary of studies on small-scale tourism entrepreneurs. Based on their own work and the work of others in various seaside resorts throughout England, Shaw and Williams (1998) show there is often little formal training undertaken to prepare for this type of activity and that a strong incentive is to live in such surroundings.

Leadership and entrepreneurship occur in various forms and settings within an industry as diverse as tourism. In a review of innovations and entrepreneurial activity within sustainable tourism, which was represented by nature tourism, Hjalager (1997) identified entrepreneurial enterprises in terms of nature tourism products, equipment sectors, professional tours and supplementary products. In fact she notes that many 'innovations in tourism and leisure are predominantly linked to innovations in the other sectors supplying it with products and services' (Hjalager, 1997: 40), revealing the strong links between tourism's entrepreneurial leadership and that of other business sectors. Such links can be seen also in cultural and urban tourism like festival and event management, where a plea can be made for more consideration of leadership in the management of festivals and events that depend so heavily on volunteer assistance. These 'volunteers are not just unpaid labour but people with needs, who probably present a greater leadership challenge than paid employees, since the rewards they seek are intangible and intrinsic to the job itself; they do not seek the extrinsic reward of salary' (McDonnell *et al.*, 1999: 83). The effectiveness of appropriate leadership and concern can be seen in the success of the Sydney Olympics, which depended on thousands of volunteers drawn from all over Australia.

Most of the leadership and entrepreneurship studies in business and tourism have been retrospective accounts of setting up a small business and developing it into a success. Such analytical approaches have revealed some broad generalisations regarding the characteristics of business founders (leaders), but as Davidsson (2000) has pointed out such post-event analysis could be tainted by selective memory. Consequently he has recently completed a study of nascent entrepreneurs in Sweden to test among other things if the generalisations hold true. Since nascent entrepreneurs will be at the creativity and innovative stage of leadership his findings are of particular interest to this book.

The general characteristics that have been associated with entrepreneurs, according to Davidsson (2000: 3–5), include:

(1) Parental occupations – a large proportion of self-employed people have parents who were themselves self-employed.
(2) Gender – self-employment is a male-dominated career choice.
(3) Ethnicity / race – some ethnic groups have demonstrated a higher propensity to self-employment, such as the Indian, Pakistani and Bangladeshi communities in the UK and the Jewish and Asian communities in the USA. The main explanation being that groups like these have access to critical resources such as financial and human capital (education and networks) before they enter a new country or new sector.
(4) Education and work experience – the level of education has a positive impact on self-employment, especially with regard to knowledge-intensive businesses, and previously self-employed individuals or un-

employed individuals are two occupational groups over-represented among business founders. The first category could be considered as pull motivation and the second as a push motivation to self-employment.

(5) Psychological profile – the individual's value system and cognitive mechanisms conditioned by their social context helps to explain the career choice of self-employment.

A sample comparison between nascent entrepreneurs, determined by whether they had undertaken one business gestation activity such as doing market research or saving money to start a business, and a control group produced the following results.

The importance of a parental role model is confirmed by the significant positive impact of 'having self-employed parents and a positive impression through observation of self-employed family members and friends'. The effects of education and experience are confirmed as well, with '41.2% having a university degree or at least some university education, compared to 26.4% for the control group'.

Males are over-represented among the nascent entrepreneur group, as are those already self-employed. There are some surprises, however. 'Interestingly, the unemployed did not show a higher probability of being nascent entrepreneurs.' In contrast to previous generalisations this study did 'not find a very strong over-representation of immigrants among the nascent entrepreneurs' (Davidsson, 2000: 12–14). Based on this evidence Davidsson (2000: 14) concluded 'the results imply that previous, retrospective studies have not been grossly misinterpreted, which increases their value'. Consequently, we can feel more secure that the characteristic indicators identified above are likely to be relevant generally, including to tourism and its SME leadership.

Community tourism applications

The rise of local leaders and their link with entrepreneurial activity in tourism has been seen as a positive factor in terms of community tourism. Koh (2000: 164) observes that 'touristic enterprises do not just sprout up from the earth but are creations of people . . . We call these touristic enterprise creators tourism entrepreneurs, and in their collectivity, they shape a community's touristscape, scale and impacts (economic, sociocultural, and physical)'. By responding to market opportunities or creating innovative concepts and products these entrepreneurs become as much tourism's agents of change as the tourists themselves, and thereby significant influencers of a community's future.

Two authors who feel that entrepreneurial leadership and community have a special relationship are Russell and Faulkner (1999). They make the point that those entrepreneurs who can be described as 'movers and shakers', or as leaders in our terms, can have a phenomenal impact on the local community. They note that the 'butterfly effect' of chaos theory, so dramatically demonstrated in Stephen Spielberg's movie 'Jurassic Park', can apply equally well to the activities and impacts of mover and shaker entrepreneurs. This happens 'in terms of (the) leverage entrepreneurs achieve from small advantages through their ability to identify opportunities and create the organisations and alliances required to maximise the benefits derived from these opportunities' (Russell & Faulkner, 1999: 417).

To illustrate their point Russell and Faulkner examine changes in Queensland's Gold Coast, which is Australia's largest resort destination by size and visitor number. They feel 'the sequence of changes that the Gold Coast has experienced can be interpreted in terms of the tension between the entrepreneurs (the chaos makers) and the planners and regulators (the dampeners), whose actions are generally focused on moderating and controlling change' (Russell & Faulkner, 1999: 411). They indicate that the innovative and risk-taking entrepreneur will constantly be battling the bureaucracy because an administration's mandate and style is different from that of the SME leader. However, when conditions are conducive, as they were in Queensland during the 1980s, when the state government 'was particularly accommodating to free enterprise and favourably disposed towards the Coast's development' (Russell & Faulkner, 1999: 420) substantial changes and development could and did occur. They offer the life experiences of two major 'movers and shakers' from the Gold Coast's developmental period – Bernard Elsey and Keith Williams, to illustrate how these men, as chaos makers, challenged the system. In the process they brought about a sequence of changes that transformed this area and created an international destination with its own worldwide image.

A key issue at the community level is the origin of local tourism entrepreneurs and their impact on the community's economy and lifestyles. 'The balance between external and local entrepreneurs is at the heart of the debate over ownership and control of the tourism economy and, in turn, which benefits from such economic growth' (Shaw & Williams, 1998: 238). On the whole it is considered that if entrepreneurs are local people then their impacts are likely to be more beneficial than harmful, due to the small scale of the enterprises, their dependence on local resources and labour, and their sociocultural links to the community. Dahles (2000: 156) reports:

> Liberal market theorists believe that prosperity is the outcome of successful individual entrepreneurship. Local ownership implies that economic success for the entrepreneur results in benefits to the local economy. Tourist developments based on local entrepreneurship are much more likely to rely on local sources of supplies and labour and are much less likely to produce negative socio-cultural effects associated with foreign ownership.

In contrast, a reliance on outside entrepreneurs, especially big business from distant metropolitan centres or foreign countries, often is seen as an initial economic booster that has little beneficial long-term effects on the local economy because of the leakage and dependency created in such relationships. Relying on external capital and entrepreneurship naturally weakens the local returns and control, as dividends flow back to the capital's source and expatriate management follows the transnational organisation's practices and corporate culture (Britton, 1982; de Kadt, 1979; Pearce, 1989).

A key issue in this debate is balance, and along with that the question of timing. Based on fieldwork and observations in the Caribbean, Lundgren (1973) has demonstrated that the arrival of a transnational business in a community does not necessarily have to mean a total leakage and loss of control. Using a transnational resort hotel as an example, Lundgren has developed a model that shows different community relationships can develop over time (Figure 5.3). In the initial stage of development the hotel will be dependent on overseas suppliers for most fittings, food and beverage supplies, and management. By the intermediate stage local wholesalers will have started to replace overseas sources with produce and supplies from local producers who can match the quality and quantity needs of the hotel. Certainly the hotel would welcome this, because it would save on the transport costs for such items and provide them with the greater flexibility and reliability associated with JIT supplies delivery. At the advanced stage the hotel will have a regular source of local suppliers, some operating directly with the hotel, and its dependence on overseas supplies will be limited to those which still retain a cost advantage or are linked to the parent company image. By this stage there should also be associated local businesses that complement the hotel's offerings, like local tours, and more local staff should be at the management level. Thus over time an outside entrepreneurial activity can act as a stimulus to local entrepreneurship, demonstrating the potential of an area and encouraging local participation.

In a similar vein the early dominance of local entrepreneurs does not guarantee long-term community success and harmony. Rothman's (1998) historical account of the growth of ski resorts in the American West indicates several examples where local business people first saw the skiing opportunity and developed small-scale resorts, only to be bought out by major corporations which could turn regional resorts into national or even international destinations.

> The increased importance of skiing changed the structure in which both local elites and communities functioned. Bill Janss (local developer of Snowmass in Sun Valley, Colorado) served as a precursor. His developments, the improved transportation to resorts, the growing

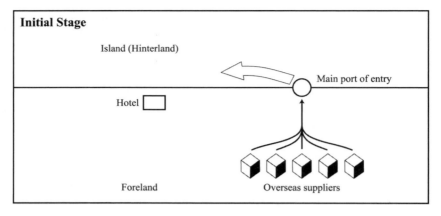

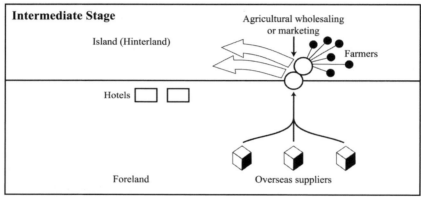

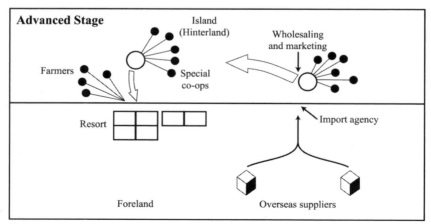

Figure 5.3 Lundgren's model of entrepreneurial development and hotel linkages

Source: After Lundgren (1974)

profits that could be realized, and other cultural factors attracted the interest of emerging multinational corporations. When CEOs noted that between the 1967–1968 and the 1970–1971 ski seasons, average pre-tax profits at ski resorts grew from 1.2 percent to 10.5 percent, they sought to join the expansion. As in other forms of tourism, the rise of skiing made the sport too lucrative to be left to locals or idiosyncratic private entrepreneurs. Ski resorts could become part of a corporation's image, a way to meld assets with a high-status capstone that served as a magnet for consumers. (Rothman, 1998: 254)

Thus we can see a reverse flow to the picture outlined by Lundgren, which only goes to emphasise the importance of timing and balance if a community wishes to exert some control over its tourism development. However, the degree of local control under these circumstances will be dictated by how open the host community is to the influences of the free market and local laws concerning property rights. Some communities have attempted to prevent the intrusion of major transnational corporations, at either end of the time spectrum, and have had mixed success.

Another factor to consider when discussing entrepreneurship at the community level is the presence of more than one economic system, especially in developing countries. In her investigation of small tourism enterprises and community development in Indonesia, Dahles identified a dual economy at work. Some entrepreneurs, like owners of guesthouses, restaurants and transport businesses, operate in the formal economy and rely on private property resources and work closely with government planning. Others, like street vendors or brokers of services to tourists, operate mainly in the informal sector and depend on personal networks and tolerant local officials to provide their services. Both types of entrepreneur are 'extremely flexible in using changing consumer preferences and government regulations to their advantage', but both need to 'be supported and to a certain extent controlled by the state' according to Dahles (2000: 166).

The issue of state control raises the possible contribution of government to the entrepreneurial process. A number of governments around the world have espoused the idea of encouraging free enterprise to stimulate their economies, but how to do this without the heavy hand of government legislation distorting or destroying the freedom and flexibility of entrepreneurship and SME development has proven difficult. It is notable that a leader in this approach, the Thatcher government of Britain, faced a philosophical dilemma when it attempted to stimulate free enterprise activity while committing to less government interference in the economy. It is apparent also that 'the costs of intervention have to be carefully assessed and the benefits estimated. To date there has been no such cost-benefit analysis in the UK' (Morrison *et al.*, 1999: 77). So it is doubtful how effective such government intervention can be.

Many writers now think governments should focus on encouraging entrepreneurial leadership and activity indirectly, by creating a supportive environment for its development. For example, Michael Porter (1980, 1998) who is the champion of developing a competitive advantage is now advocating a supportive, yet non-direct, government presence in his cluster theory. The type of policies considered helpful in this direction includes:

- Macro policies that dictate general conditions, like lower interest rates and taxation or education policies that facilitate entrepreneurship.
- Legislative deregulation and simplification that cuts the bureaucratic red tape or exempts small business from certain legislative requirements.
- Sector-specific legislation that tackles the problems associated with a particular industry, such as licensing and smoking laws for bars and restaurants.
- Financial assistance, such as start-up funds or loan guarantees.
- General assistance, such as information and incubator facilities.

In addition to these political measures a supportive environment needs to include sociocultural conditions that encourage individual enterprise and a free market approach to producing goods and services. Furthermore, these contributory factors need to be effective at all stages of the entrepreneurial process: at the formative stage when entrepreneurs are considering their ideas and the potential for success; at the mobilisation stage when they first attempt to seek financial help and premises or equipment; at the operational stage when they seek to establish themselves in the market place and attempt to operate in the business world of rules and regulations, including the burden of becoming a government tax agent with the spreading adoption of the VAT/GST tax systems.

One model to guide government and individual decision-makers in developing community tourism entrepreneurship has attempted to map the entrepreneurial process and identify the types of community assistance that would be helpful at each stage. Koh (2000: 207) feels entrepreneurism at a community level is dependent on two interactive factors – 'the differences in supply of tourism entrepreneurs and the perceived attractiveness of the investment climate for launching tourism enterprises'.

These factors thereby combine the individual nature of entrepreneurship and the environmental setting in which it must take place. According to Koh's conceptualisation the interaction of two factors, a P-factor that represents a community's propensity to enterprise, and a Q-factor that indicates the community's investment climate as perceived by nascent tourism entrepreneurs, can produce four basic types of community-entrepreneurial activity.

The four cell matrix indicates where community tourism entrepreneurship is likely to be successful or unsuccessful. In Quadrant 1 both resident and external entrepreneurs will be attracted by the record and culture of entrepreneurial activity along with the supportive investment environment created by the community. In Quadrant 3 the low record of individual enterprise and lack of community encouragement will deter much entreprenuerial activity.

To put this model to the test Koh examined the record of two comparable rural Texas communities (Athens and Mount Pleasant) along his two dimensions or factors and traced their enterprise record over a five-year period which was then compared to the state average. His measure of the P-factor was residents' attitudes to entrepreneurship and his Q-factor was measured by assessing the views of local tourism entrepreneurs. The analysis of this information placed the two communities in Quadrant 2 – high on the propensity to enterprise but low on creating a supportive environment. This should have placed these communities around the mid-point of the state's annual tourism enterprise birth rates for the five-year period, which 'ranged from 1.48 percent to 2.47 percent with a mean birth rate of 1.93 percent' (Koh, 2000: 212). Which is what happened, with Athens recording a mean enterprise birth rate of 1.87% and Mount Pleasant a mean of 1.6%. Consequently, Koh (2000: 214) felt 'the results of this study seemed to offer some empirical support for the model' and seem to support the notion that leadership in entrepreneurship at the community level is going to depend on a combination of individual initiative and community encouragement.

One example of leadership, entrepreneurship and government support at work, in a different country and at a different scale, is the experience of the London borough of Southwark. The local government of this dockland area had been struggling with declining business and employment for many years, but generally ignored tourism as a potential saviour because of its past commitment to an industrial way of life. It was not until the arrival of Jeremy Fraser as the Chairman of Southwark's Development Committee that 'tourism found a champion within the Council, not for tourism's own sake but as a means to economic regeneration' (Tyler, 1998: 57). In the 1990s Southwark began to emphasise its tourism potential, hired a tourism officer and joined other boroughs and agencies to promote the south-east area of London. The council developed a five-point strategy to guide its tourism development, of which a key area was education and training because of the change from industrial to service employment. 'Training has been given a top priority, as creating jobs that are not taken up by local people is of little benefit to a borough that at the last census point in 1991 had a male unemployment rate of 21.3% compared with 13.5% for the whole of London and 11.2% nationally' (Tyler, 1998: 60). The actions of Fraser and the teams he put together helped to transform Southwark from an inward-looking area concerned with hanging onto an industrial way of life into a more diverse and vibrant community where tourism became one of the platforms for its resurrection. According to Tyler (1998: 62), 'in 1991 a newly emerging leadership with a willingness to widen the vision and appreciation of the nature of economic decline and regeneration led to tourism being accepted as part of the post-Fordist service economy of London, which Southwark could not ignore'.

Summary

Tourism is an extremely competitive business and to attract tourists to a community needs not just people to plan and serve but people who will be innovative and develop new or better attractions. Such people will be leaders.

This chapter reveals that leadership types and styles will be diverse and variable. Research has moved from simple descriptive models of individuals to contextual situations where the stage of development and market forces will also be strong determinants of ideal leadership for a particular place or time. Leadership has been studied in the form of entrepreneurship because in tourism 80–90% of businesses are SMEs where owner operators make the key decisions that affect not only their own businesses but can impact the future of the host community.

Entrepreneurial leadership is an important agent of change for a community. The elements of innovation and risk taking embedded within entrepreneurs will have dramatic impacts on the host community. With the prospect of major change it becomes important to monitor events and impacts in order to control and direct change as much as possible. This issue of control becomes the focus of the next chapter.

Chapter 6

Controlling

In many tourism settings the establishment of a strategy and its associated operational conditions has been enough to exhaust the initiative and energy of those involved. Even if all the elements for a successful endeavour are in place, without the vigilance of regular monitoring and the willingness to adjust to changes and emerging weaknesses, such an endeavour can fall apart. In planning texts and diagrams there is often reference to monitoring a plan's progress and the provision of a feedback loop in the systems diagram. But how often is there detailed coverage of this planning stage so that the reader can appreciate its importance to the overall success of the endeavour? This chapter attempts to redress this imbalance, by emphasising that the fourth function of 'control' is necessary to ensure the planning, organisation and leadership that have gone before are all on track and providing the type of outcome initially envisioned in a community's tourism goals.

'Controlling' is a business term relating to how an organisation goes about establishing its standards or expectations, how it evaluates its actual performance, and how it takes corrective action where needed. It is a necessary step in any business to ensure its objectives are clear enough to be appreciated by the customer and its product or service able to meet their expectations. It should regularly monitor its performance not just in terms of the balance sheet but with respect to customer satisfaction. If its performance is proving disappointing in some respects and if the market expectations are beginning to change then it needs to consider ways to respond to these issues.

While tourism involves many sectors and different players this same controlling function is required, especially within destinations that are attempting to present a united image and product. Within a voluntary alliance the need for a controlling function will remain the same, but its actual form and delivery will have to take into account the commercial and political realities of the destination's situation. In community tourism it will need to consider a range of stakeholders and how their combined standards and performance are to be evaluated. If deficiencies are noted and it becomes necessary to take corrective action it should not always be left to government and legislative bodies to initiate corrective action because they are often too tardy and blunt an instrument of change.

Controlling in Business

In business management the control function is applied at all three phases of the manufacturing or service process – the input, processing, and output stages. At the input stage the main control concerns are the quality of materials and staff. In the processing phase attention turns to the most efficient and effective way to deliver the promised good or service. At the output stage an organisation needs to ensure the customer is satisfied with the quality of the product or service, and will either become a repeat customer or an invaluable advocate of the business. In the tourism industry a good example of this process would be the international airlines.

In terms of inputs international airlines put heavy emphasis on their materials and personnel. The chief material is the modern passenger plane that costs millions of dollars to buy or lease and must be kept flying as much as possible if it is to provide a good return on the investment. One airline – Singapore Airlines – has made a branding statement in this regard by claiming to have the youngest and most modern fleet of aircraft in the world. Another important element in their inputs is the quality of staff. International airlines have some of the highest selection standards in the world for their personnel and they spend millions of dollars on training and re-training them.

In tourism the actual travel component is an important part of the total experience and this part is the core business of international airlines, but as with many tourism businesses they can only deliver their service in conjunction with partners. The operation of a modern airline business is a complex process that required early and extensive use of IT to link the myriad of systems needed to deliver passengers to their destinations. These systems include the computer reservation systems, the scheduling of aircraft maintenance and delivery, the varying dietary needs of passengers, luggage handling, and frequent flier accounts. Besides ensuring that internal processes are in place to deliver passengers safely and comfortably to their destination, airlines need to work with others to make the whole operation possible. Governments are responsible for the quality of infrastructure that links each airport to the world, they control the permitted hours of operation and are responsible for traffic control. Airport authorities are responsible for the design and operation of the airport, including the provision of parking and location of facilities. Other important components of a trip that seem to be very difficult to control are the truly exogenous variables, such as the weather, to which some would add taxi drivers and customs-immigration officials.

Control of the outputs for international airlines extends beyond providing a satisfactory flight experience for individual passengers, to include maximum financial return and loyalty. The airlines have pioneered two important management techniques in these areas that have been adopted extensively by other sectors of the industry. To maximise their financial returns in a very time sensitive business, they introduced 'yield management'. This is a technique for maximising the sales revenue from time-perishable assets like a seat on a particular flight. To encourage loyalty in a very competitive business they introduced a rewards system of frequent flier points. This system builds on satisfactory performance by making an airline the first choice in future travel plans, and has now been extended to alliance partners and associated businesses in accommodation, transport and resorts.

An important element in business controlling is where to introduce such measures so they are effective but non-intrusive in the manufacturing or service process. According to Gordon *et al.* (1990: 314) critical control points must possess a number of characteristics:

- relate to key operations or events in the process that will have a bearing on other parts of the process;
- permit early identification of problems before serious damage or difficulties occur;
- indicate clearly the level of performance over a broad spectrum of key events;
- emphasise efficiency and utility in the amount of information collected;
- permit a balanced assessment of all three phases.

In the tourism industry this approach to control has become a regular feature of hospitality management, particularly with respect to food preparation and delivery. In this sector a Hazard Analysis Critical Control Point (HACCP) system has been developed to monitor and control contamination risks within facilities (Spears, 1995). Within this process a HACCP/Servsafe method is used to identify points at which contamination or the growth of micro-organisms can occur and indicates the control procedure required to eliminate such a hazard. For example, critical control points have been established where temperatures are taken during the cooking and storage phases to ensure food is cooked safely and handled appropriately.

Within the financial and operational literature of business studies are several control techniques that have relevance to tourism. Some basic budgetary and financial control techniques that need to be considered by businesses include the following. A cash flow analysis, to ensure the business is receiving enough revenue to pay its own bills. This can be a problem when major accounts take a month or more to process and pay an invoice, and to overcome this difficulty more small businesses are turning to factoring, which is explained in more detail in Chapter 8. Activity ratios, such as 'profitability ratios', that measure the operating efficiency and overall financial return of an organisation can be useful indicators for developing greater control over daily operations. Key ones in this regard include 'return on total assets' and 'earnings per share'. In terms of operational efficiency concepts like inventory control, using techniques like 'just in time' (JIT) delivery have been introduced to reduce asset costs and warehouse space. Likewise, 'critical path analysis' which displays the network of interactions needed to produce a product or service can be used to highlight crucial steps in the process or even to simplify it.

An important aspect of controls in today's competitive business world has been the rise of quality controls, which are designed to ensure a promised standard of excellence is delivered by an organisation. An example of this type of control is Total Quality Management (TQM), which is a proactive management approach designed to bring about continuous quality improvement. It has 10 main principles (Flood, 1993: 48), and these are as follows:

(1) There must be agreed requirements, for both internal and external customers.
(2) Customers' requirements must be met first time, every time.
(3) Quality improvement will reduce waste and total costs.
(4) There must be a focus on the prevention of problems, rather than an acceptance to cope in a fire-fighting manner.
(5) Quality improvement can only result from planned management action.
(6) Every job must add value.
(7) Everybody must be involved, from all levels and across all functions.
(8) There must be an emphasis on measurement to help to assess and to meet requirements and objectives.
(9) A culture of continuous improvement must be established.
(10) An emphasis should be placed on promoting creativity.

The central element of this concept is the achievement of 'quality' goods and service, with 'total' referring to a necessary wholeness for the process to be effective, and 'management' indicating the need to have everyone responsible for managing their own contribution to the overall quality goal.

The success of this approach has encouraged the development of several accreditation systems. One of the most recognised is the International Organisation for Standards, with its check marks/ticks logo. The ISO 9000 series of certification for various industries provide a series of standards for various aspects of an organisation's operation. Under the 'management responsibility' are four main areas of concern (Flood, 1993: 58), which all indicate the relevance of a controlling function. These are:

(1) Control and maintenance of the quality system
(2) Control functions to eradicate quality deficiencies.
(3) Feedback to ensure effective operation of both controls is being achieved.
(4) Review of the declared quality system to ensure that it reflects policy.

Such certification systems have their origin in manufacturing but have been extended to the service sector with varying degrees of success. This is due to the complexity of providing experiences to accompany products and the variability of priorities and expectations that a customer brings to any interactive service process, like a tourism experience.

However, there has been one outstanding tourism success with respect to a standards system that has generated a lot of interest and some action. In 1992 the Ritz Carlton Hotel Company won the prestigious Malcolm Baldridge National Quality Award that is offered annually to a recognised leader in quality achievement in US business. The Baldridge award tests companies on seven categories (Hart & Bogan, 1992). These include:

- leadership;
- information and analysis;
- strategic quality planning;
- human resources utilisation;
- management of process quality;
- quality and operational results;
- customer satisfaction.

The Ritz Carlton approach to these seven categories or standards demonstrates that a tourism-oriented company can indeed benefit from a quality management approach.

Controlling in Tourism

In her inaugural lecture as Professor of Tourism at Erasmus University in Rotterdam Myriam Jansen-Verbeke (1994) provided a reflective address on the development of tourism. She considered that tourism had reached a critical stage where it had to move from 'business as usual' into a form of 'crisis management'. The cause for the crisis is found in tourism's phenomenal success and growth, that now places many areas of natural beauty and some societies under stress. Noting that tourism has become a two-edged sword Jansen-Verbeke advocates tourism businesses must start to change from pure developers to become controllers, if tourism is to sustain itself and contribute to global sustainable development.

Jansen-Verbeke (1994: 15) maintains there are two global trends that tourism now needs to consider if it is to manage the current crisis of overdevelopment or inappropriate development. These are the growing

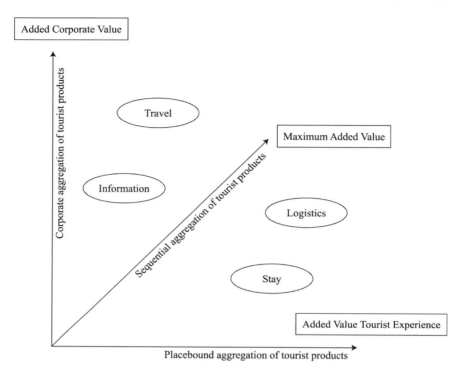

Figure 6.1 Strategic alliances and quality circles in the tourism sector
Source: Adapted from Jansen-Verbeke (1994)

concern for environmental quality and the growing demand for quality products. In both cases it requires a move from the old business management styles of independent growth strategies to one which involves more collaboration and a greater emphasis on controls to provide the quality experiences modern tourists are seeking in an environmentally benign way.

To move in this direction of sustainable quality experiences, Jansen-Verbeke (1994: 15–16) recommends a focus on eco-management, which aims at 'reducing the negative and damaging environmental impact of the various tourist activities . . . and requires more specific guidelines (controls) than the ideological concepts now to hand'. To provide the quality experience she recommends collaboration through 'strategies for assuring that all tourist products are geared to one another and hence improving the quality of the (total) tourist experience' (Jansen-Verbeke, 1994: 18). To do this she suggests greater use of strategic alliances and the use of 'quality circles' from the TQM techniques (Figure 6.1). The figure shows how corporate and community concerns, as the axis, need to be incorporated in the development of value. To bring these two groups together the quality circle concept from TQM could be used with respect to specific issues, such as 'stay' that would include consideration of local attractions, accommodation and culture, or 'travel' that would involve consideration of road and air links, connectivity to local airport and attractions, and the service quality of local transport and taxi operations. This allows 'research into the quality of tourist products by all actors involved in the entire chain of 'conceptualisation-production and commercialisation', which implies an understanding and responsibility concerning the entire process as targeted and managed' according to Michaud *et al.* (1991) as quoted by Jansen-Verbeke (1994: 25). As such it is a cry for greater control to serve the needs not only of the tourist but also of the host community and global environment.

Environmental controls

A large part of meeting customer expectations and providing satisfaction is related to the quality of the destination environment. Consequently the tourism industry is becoming more concerned with monitoring the state of the natural and cultural environments that attract the visitor, and should be attempting to integrate a control process into the overall goal of sustainable development. In the recent past environmental impact assessments have been required for proposed and new tourism developments, but little has been said or done about the more numerous existing facilities and the need for 'continued monitoring and revision of possible (environmental) objectives and operational procedures' according to Ding and Pigram (1995: 4).

Environmental impact assessments (EIAs) are carried out to ascertain the likely environmental effects of a new project proposal. EIAs are a legislated requirement of the preliminary planning process for major developments in many countries. However, the techniques involved are still in their infancy and clouded by the human element. Humans become involved as a direct feature of the impact process when they are tourists, with their own perceptions of when environmental stress is occurring that may not always match the scientific views. They are also the assessors of the presented environmental data, which means objectivity is sometimes difficult to guarantee. Inskeep's (1991) review of several large-scale EIAs provides an illustration of the mixture of scientific and human assessments involved. His example of an EIA matrix indicates clearly the scientific measures along the rows, as revealed in measures of air quality and road traffic; but the assessment of these measures is purely human and therefore more vague, as indicated by the 'minor', 'moderate' or 'serious' impact columns.

Environmental scientists have been attempting to devise a range of scientific measurements that can be used to assess environmental impact, so that the matrix approach is now only one of several available techniques. Williams (1994: 427–31) has demonstrated that EIA functions can be divided into three groups based on their primary (human) purpose. A key control purpose is to *identify and describe* what is happening in the environment, by monitoring changes in its condition. There are three major techniques in this category:

- Checklists that describe the presence and size of a particular feature via physical measurement where possible.
- Matrices that are two-dimensional checklists, with an evaluation of the potential impacts added to the physical measurement.
- Networks examine the secondary and tertiary effects associated with a project, such as following a sequence of outcomes up the food chain.

The second category involves *predictive* methodologies that are designed to forecast the probable outcomes of an activity or project. They often involve laboratory simulations like wave machines on different forms of coastline or river bank. The third category is *evaluative* methodologies that attempt to demonstrate the net result of a project development. This can be an assessment of trade-offs between various forms of development or group interests, or through a benefit–cost analysis. Despite this range of options however, most of the control work to date has been limited to the identification and monitoring category.

Due to the past emphasis on EIAs for major planned projects Ding and Pigram (1995) have recommended that greater attention should be paid to existing facilities that may be either at risk themselves or contributing to general destination wide environmental stress. They advocate a continuous application of environmental auditing that should involve:

- an ongoing process of self-monitoring;
- the collection and documentation of data that are relevant evidence of the environmental condition;
- a focus on environmental performance and direction;
- a comparison with predicted environmental performance and impacts.

This is starting to happen in a number of settings as businesses recognise the self-serving need for some form of environmental control and as destination authorities appreciate the need to consider environmental carrying capacities and their place on the product lifecycle. The WTO Environment Committee has assisted in this direction with the development of local and destination environmental indicators that include a consideration of the time factor (WTO, 1993). They have developed a matrix that considers different types of environmental indicator and assesses them in terms of a short-term list of existing data, leading to a medium-term set of indicators and finally to a long-term and ideal set of indicators.

Quality Controls

Such a call for more emphasis on quality controls has been gathering momentum as the tourism market became more complex and competitive. In service areas like tourism there is growing awareness that as customers become more experienced they become more value conscious and demanding. The senior author of this book, by age, still remembers his first family vacation just after World War II involved a quick trip to the English seaside, travelling in the back of a van with our own bedding and food supplies because rationing was still in force. Our rented seaside cottage overlooked a beach, but we had to be careful where we went because only part of the beach had been cleared of landmines. In the evening the entertainment consisted of board games and listening to the radio. The holiday was a great success because of the pentup demand and novelty of getting away for a few days. Today the family would not be so impressed, because since then we have experienced such a range of beautiful places and wonderful experiences that we have established far higher expectations.

What today's customer looks for is value, which is a combination of quality and price, and is central to the service profit chain concept developed by Heskett *et al.* (1997). Their concept maintains there is a strong relationship between the quality of goods and services presented and the customer's satisfaction and loyalty, with the two linked by the customer's sense of value received. In tourism, customer value assessment would therefore revolve around a combination of quality and price considerations. For example, budget travellers are only able or prepared to pay a certain amount for their trip experience, but still expect to receive a standard of facilities and service appropriate to basic travel – in that they are clean, safe and friendly as well as inexpensive. Luxury travellers are willing and able to pay far more for their travel experience, but they expect to receive premium products and service in return. The quality process is therefore directly related to value, and controls need to be in place to guarantee that the appropriate levels of value regarding the product and its relevant target market segment are in place.

The concept of value in a tourist experience can be either explicit or implicit, and is often a combination of both. Explicit value is visible and easily defined so it can be measured and controlled readily, such as with the assessment of a hotel room's qualities and associated cost or in the case of coach trip between two points in terms of its comfort, time and cost. Implicit value is related to the customer's perceived image of a product or service and its performance. An example of this would be how different tourists react to the explanations of a tour guide; is the guide 'knowledgeable' and is s(he) presenting the material at an appropriate level? It is a matter of individual taste and preference. Even in the two easily measured and controlled explicit examples provided above there is an implicit element of customer perception. The in-house experts and relevant external accreditation agencies may have agreed on the appropriate price and quality combinations, but if the tourist had a personal preference for a certain standard of lighting or access to a toilet that did not coincide with the norm then they would not be satisfied. Comfort is a nebulous concept, especially when it involves sharing with others, as on a coach trip.

At the customer service coalface, there has been growing dissatisfaction with the treatment of customers and clients in banking, transportation, and health-care services according to Ho (1995). We do not want to see tourism added to this growing list of customer disaffection, because unlike those listed services it is a discretionary activity and not an unavoidable activity. Hence, it needs to fulfil customer expectations and dreams if it wants to have tourists return or to act as goodwill ambassadors. 'There is an old saying in service industries that if customers like the service they will tell 3 people. If they don't like the service they will tell 11 people' (Augustyn and Ho, 1998: 73). So it is imperative to create satisfied customers.

It requires controls to ensure that tourism businesses are offering the quality and value that is expected. Gap analysis is one method for measuring service value whereby gaps between the expectations of customers and service providers are examined and identified. Gaps between the expectations of what groups want and their perceptions of the actual service received have been used to assess tourists' and community members' satisfaction with tourism. The concepts and premises of gap analysis and the applicability of this service quality measuring method to tourism are reviewed in detail in Chapter 12 of this book.

Dual controls

In tourism both the quality of the environment and the tourist experience need to be considered, hence the industry needs to monitor and control both at once. This is a major challenge as there are many variables, both endogenous (internal) and exogenous (external), that need to be considered. But efforts have been undertaken in select environments to try to develop techniques that will manage the visitor experience in such a way as to satisfy their particular needs and to conserve the environmental setting of the experience. Foremost among these are the Visitor Impact Management (VIM) schemes developed by a variety of researchers and well summarised in Glasson *et al.* (1995).

Most of the VIMs have originated from the concept of carrying capacity and the assumption that any tourism development will inevitably lead to some degree of change on the host environment. The traditional concept of carrying capacity is that each ecosystem has a threshold capacity for development and use, and that if a critical threshold level of development or use is breached there would be progressive deterioration in the environment, leading eventually to its destruction. In this respect it is very similar to the economic concept of an equilibrium point of production, beyond which the marginal costs of each additional unit of production (additional visitor) begin to exceed the marginal revenue to the company or destination.

There are several problems associated with the carrying capacity approach to tourism. These include:

(1) The search for a numeric threshold value is akin to searching for the 'holy grail', because to calculate the biophysical carrying capacity of an area or site requires meticulous scientific measurement and knowledge.

(2) Furthermore, the conditions in any area or site are always changing with the seasons and the different demands placed upon it. Hence there can be no inherent use level or maximum absolute capacity.

(3) A measurement without purpose offers no direction to management. This is because a carrying capacity measurement without the prior determinations of goals and objectives leaves it difficult to assess and incorporate into management strategies.

(4) There is no firm evidence in the tourism literature that lowering or raising business volumes around a calculated carrying capacity actually affects a destination's ability to absorb tourism's impacts.

(5) In tourism the critical variable in calculating carrying capacity often has been visitor numbers, but visitors are not constants. They do not behave the same way or have the same impacts on the environment, and therefore form an unreliable indicator of changing use.

(6) In tourism it is the visitor experience that is critical, but too often in carrying capacity calculations the views of the visitor have been ignored. For example, the visitor expectations and priorities of an allocentric type of tourist will be vastly different from those of a psychocentric tourist (Plog, 1973, 1978). Consequently, their personal views of crowds, environmental conditions and stress will vary considerably as will their impacts on the environment.

(7) Finally, the goal of tourism is to provide a satisfactory experience, yet traditional carrying capacity measurement makes no attempt to assess a customer's satisfaction. This is particularly germane in tourism when a customer may be restricted in what s(he) can do due to conservation goals, and need an appropriate communication to explain the situation.

As a result of such difficulties with the traditional concept of carrying capacity Glasson *et al.* (1995: 52) have suggested a modification of the concept and its measurement. Building on the prior work of Williams and

Dimensions   **Perspectives**

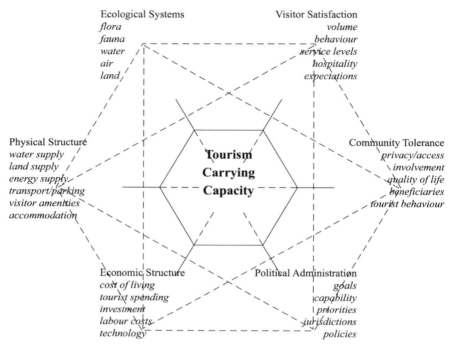

Figure 6.2 Tourism capacity networks
Source: Glasson *et al.* (1995: 52)

Gill (1991) they suggest tourism carrying capacity should be viewed more as a network of factors rather than as a simple direct relationship between usage levels and negative impact. The network involves linking the physical characteristics of the site with visitor satisfaction, community interests and political goals (Figure 6.2). It is this view that sets the scene for the more recent VIM measures.

VIM measures accept the assumption that tourism is likely to create change, but its direction and magnitude are determined by two separate elements: the physical and the human. The physical represents a descriptive component of what is happening to the environment and the human an evaluative component of how visitors and residents are assessing that change. An early exponent of this view is the Limits of Acceptable Change (LAC) methodology introduced by Stankey *et al.* (1985). The LAC technique examines the physical and social conditions in an area and seeks

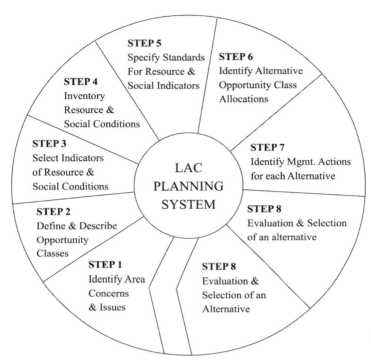

Figure 6.3 The Limits of Acceptable Change (LAC) planning system
Source: Stankey *et al.* (1985: 3)

to determine the degree of change local people, as stewards of the environment, are willing to accept in their community. It consists of nine steps that combine the previously missing managerial context with physical measurement and assessments of visitor and resident views (Figure 6.3).

An extension of the LAC approach is the more recent VIM methodologies, which focus more on human impacts and interactions in the change process. 'It is argued that, first, we need to better understand the nature of impacts and the factors related to their occurrence, and only then can we apply this to management strategies in an attempt to reduce (negative) tourism impacts' (Glasson *et al.* 1995: 57). VIM is also a sequential process that aims to reduce or control the negative impacts of visitor interactions with the environment that may threaten the quality of the destination and tourist experience. Its similarities to LAC may be seen in Figure 6.3, along with the greater emphasis on the tourists' role and responsibilities in Step 6. Graefe *et al.* (1990) have suggested that visitor management (Step 7) may be either direct, in that it regulates visitor activity and behaviour, or indirect when it attempts to influence visitor behaviour through various communications. In many cases it is a combination of both approaches.

Examples of the VIM approach are most common in park environments, where the threat to sensitive wildlife and fragile plant-life from over-visitation is real and evident; but the concept and technique has been extended to urban areas, particularly where heritage attractions have come under stress. National park systems around the world have introduced their own versions of VIM and use the type of impact indicators identified by the WTO. Parks Canada has introduced a Visitor Activity Management Process (VAMP) which, in conjunction with the usual park zoning, attempts to direct and manage visitor experiences and encourage their understanding of the parks' twin mandate (Graham *et al.* 1988). The United States National Park Service has introduced Visitor Experience and Resource Protection (VERP) to create desired ecological and social conditions rather than worry about specific numbers of visitors and measures of maximum sustainable use (Hof *et al.*, 1994). In Australia the various park systems are working on a best practice benchmarking system that incorporates better use of visitor related data in management decisions. 'The purpose of establishing best practice criteria was to assist in the design of a comprehensive Visitor Data Management System' (Archer *et al.*, 2001: 6), one that can link park data with state and national tourism data as well as with park environmental needs.

In the urban arena we are starting to see the introduction of VIM techniques and approach in Venice, Italy. Canestrelli and Costa (1991) have introduced a fuzzy linear programming model that calculates the socio-economic carrying capacity of the centre of Venice, based on the desire of residents and visitors to use the same facilities. According to their impact model Venice could bear about 25,000 visitors a day, which was exceeded on 156 days in 1987 and predicted to be exceeded on 216 days by the new millennium (Glasson *et al.*, 1995: 115). However, a separate resident survey conducted by Glasson and his students in 1993 showed local residents were less concerned about numbers than the experts. For many residents 'the decreasing quality of life in the city is perceived to be more a function of the poor management of the Municipality, than of the excess tourism demand' (Glasson *et al.*, 1995: 114). Hence, it is no surprise that Venice is still struggling with a specific VIM programme to balance its tourist interests with local needs and concerns for the physical condition of this world famous heritage attraction.

Despite the more balanced management controls of the VIM techniques that blend scientific measurement, behavioural modification and business goals to support a management strategy, the world's major attractions still face significant challenges, especially from exogenous factors that are beyond immediate control. A good example of this is the dilemmas facing Yellowstone National Park in the USA. In 1986 Alston Chase wrote a book called *Playing God in Yellowstone*, that as the title suggests and *Newsweek* interpreted 'portrays the Park Service as tourist-minded and scientifically inept' (*Newsweek*, 1986: 52). The basis of this judgement was that this national park, like all others, had placed artificial constraints and boundaries over a natural and much larger ecosystem. This produced a system that favoured the sensitivities of tourists over the natural order of the wilderness. One of Chase's major concerns was the elimination of wolves and cougars to protect animals like the elk, because this had led to severe overgrazing when the predators were removed. However, conscious that the park should represent a natural landscape for visitors, the park authorities did apply some hands-off and natural management approaches. But even that type of strategy can have its problems.

One such problem was the fires of 1988, which affected about 900,000 acres or 40% of the park's total land area in a patchwork of blazes that left some forest areas decimated and others untouched (*The Economist*, 1988: 34). These fires were started by lightning strikes and as such could be viewed both as exogenous variables and part of the regular process that forms the park's natural landscape. Consequently the Park Service initially left the fires alone to burn out naturally. Unfortunately several factors worked against this strategy, namely a long drought and the build up of forest debris and waste over the years meant the fires spread much more than usual. In the end 10,000 fire-fighters were called in to save the park and its icons, like the Yellowstone Lodge close to the 'Old Faithful' geyser. It being somewhat ironic that the historic lodge was saved thanks to prior tourist minded planning – 'protected not so much by the (fire-fighters') water as by the quarter-mile-wide paved parking lot that surrounds it' (*Newsweek*, 1988: 18).

However, one should not get carried away by the emotion of the events and should always treat immediate figures and estimates with some caution. Despite the 'inflammatory' titles of the news-stories at the time of the Yellowstone fires later and more objective assessments showed the situation was not as bad as first thought. 'A January 1990 analysis and mapping of burned areas in Yellowstone shows that the total acreage affected by the fire was 793,880. Of that 323,290 acres were 'canopy burn', which means that the trees lost all needles and were blackened. Of the remainder, 281,098 was 'surface burn' – only the forest understorey (the lower layer of the forest) was affected, sparing most of the trees. The rest was sage and grassland burn' (Randhawa, 1990: 7). Not surprisingly Yellowstone recovered much of its former glory with the arrival of the winter and spring rains, due to the fact that mineral nutrients in the ash acted as a fertiliser to promote new growth, and the return of the animals to feed on the new lushness. 'All tourist facilities were fully operational as of spring 1989 and, if anything, tourists were intrigued by the dramatic look of Yellowstone after the fires. A record number of 2.06 million visited the park during 1989' (Randhawa, 1990: 7). This demonstrates once again that there is life after most natural disasters, as Murphy and Bayley (1989) relate in their assessment of disaster recovery at the site of the St Helens volcanic eruption.

What these Yellowstone experiences demonstrate is the difficulty of implementing controls in open tourism environments. In addition to the normal business difficulties of obtaining timely information on relevant issues in the production and marketing areas, tourism organisations will need to be aware of changing public sentiments and expert opinions as they develop and refine their management priorities and control systems. One way more organisations are trying to set the stage for more acceptable priorities and controls is through the development of codes of conduct.

Codes of conduct

Like many industries facing internal competition and external legislative interest, the tourism industry has been developing a series of codes of conduct to guide its operational practices and hopefully forestall the arrival of outside pressures on how and where it conducts its business. Often the early codes were established by various organisations to encourage a more professional and long-term approach to the industry. They offer guidance to members with respect to 'best practice' and societal responsibilities. They often incorporate some ethical statements and are at times subdivided into codes for operators and customers.

Codes of conduct also have become more commonplace in certain areas of the industry that are deemed to be operating in highly sensitive locations. This is particularly germane to the ecotourism sector, with its intense interactive experiential product. It is often taking visitors into sensitive ecological areas and attempting to offer a high quality educative tourism experience, but the visitors must play their part and be as sensitive and unobtrusive as possible with their surroundings. Hence the ecotourism sector sees the need to ensure all operators act appropriately with respect to the environment and the experiences offered to their customers, with the customers primed as to what to expect and how to behave. To achieve such objectives the Canadian Environmental Advisory Council proposed a detailed code of ethics (Scace *et al.*, 1992). It attempts to set general ethical goals, then indicates the relative contribution that is expected from both the industry and the customers. The Tourism Industry Association of Canada has responded to such a call to action with their own code of conduct for tourists and the industry. Among the objectives for tourists are:

> Experience the friendliness of our people and the welcoming spirit of our communities. Help us to preserve these attributes by respecting our traditions, customs, and local regulations

and for the industry:

Strive to achieve tourism development in a manner which harmonizes economic objectives with the protection and enhancement of our natural, cultural and aesthetic heritage. (Hawkes & Williams, 1993: 87, 88)

When the quality of tourism development is enhanced by local cultural and political factors it is good practice to set certain ground-rules before the tourism business develops too far to ensure all party interests are respected, including those of the residents. This is what has happened in the Haida Gwai (Queen Charlotte) Islands off the coast of British Columbia, where wilderness and wildlife have been attracting increasing numbers of tourists to this world heritage site and home of the Haida people. The commercial tour operators have developed a code of conduct for their operations in this area, that includes statements regarding etiquette, wildlife observation, treatment of archaeological and cultural sites, and how to handle garbage (Falconer, 1991: 21–6).

All of the above codes of conduct are voluntary and depend on self-policing by members of the umbrella organisation or association that has initiated them. While such monitoring is generally effective because of the political and financial influence of the body concerned they do lack legal authority and what is worse they do not guarantee a standard of performance for the customer. Consequently we are starting to see the development of more formal codes of conduct that incorporate set standards of practice for the environment and the customer in the form of a commercially developed and promoted certification.

These certification processes set out the rules and expectations for operating a business that ensure a customer will receive the promised product quality and associated level of experience. To guarantee this there is regular inspection of the business and assessment of its practices. If the business can maintain the expected standards it is allowed to promote itself as having achieved a certain quality of business, with the expectation that over time the customer will come to associate that particular business with a certain standard of operational quality. This is the basis of most hotel and restaurant classifications but it is starting to expand into more general tourism fields with the introduction of Green Globe Awards by the WTTC. The Green Globe approach offers three levels of accreditation in its benchmarking process, designed to enhance a business' environmental sustainability and its customer appeal. The highest of these is certified status, that involves a developed environmental management system that has been audited and approved by an independent assessor.

However, even these attempts to bring more effective environmental certification into the industry have their problems. Font (2002: 203) considers:

there are too many ecolabels (and codes) with different meanings, criteria, geographical scope, confusing messages, limited expertise and expensive systems, only partly meeting the requirements of the process of compliance assessment.

He feels the future lies in further international accreditation and certification that will provide the tourist with recognised brands and levels of expectation. But even here such systems 'will have to negotiate the difficulties of site-specific and sub-sector requirements, different legislations and levels of support . . . that are likely to (lead) to very generic and vague standards and criteria' (Font, 2002: 204).

A case in point

Robbie Burns' warning that the best laid plans of mice and men can go astray reflects the importance of controlling and illustrates the problems that an American mouse had in France (Burns, 1996). In the mid-eighties, flush with popular support and financial success, the Walt Disney Corporation was very interested in opening a large-scale theme park somewhere in Europe. After narrowing the search to France and Spain, and then seeking the best deal, Disney committed to building 'Euro Disney' in Marne-la-Valee, a rural community in north-west France, about an hour outside of Paris.

Disney had a recognised product and name brand that was already enticing considerable numbers of Europeans into transatlantic flights to Disney World. The Disney theme parks were already widely popular in California, Florida and Japan and the public's love of everything Disney was showing no signs of slowing down. The Disney research and strategic planning followed past successful procedures which placed the new theme park 25 kilometres from central Paris, within a major hub for millions of travellers each year and within three and a half hours drive of 70 million people (Eisner with Schwartz, 1998: 265). Disney had the financing. The Walt Disney Corporation, French banks and multitudes of stock market players invested great sums in the proposed development. Disney had the infrastructure. The French government agreed to major infrastructure improvements including extending express train and subway (metro) service to the front gates of Euro Disney and to improve the freeway that ran near the site. Disney had a good measure of public support. There were only minor and isolated instances of public concern over the new theme park – mainly from the tenant farmers of the area who suddenly found that their 'life-long' government leases had been sold to this international company.

Everything that the Disney Corporation had done to prepare for this major initiative seemed to be appropriate and successful. Euro Disney opened on schedule in the spring of 1992, offering visitors the Magic

Kingdom theme park, a separate restaurant, nightclub and entertainment complex, six massive hotels, a full service campsite and an 18-hole golf course (Eisner with Schwartz, 1998: 282). Its stock opened at US $13 a share, closed at US $16 a share later that day and at its height reached US $30 a share (Eisner with Schwartz, 1998: 269). This Disney venture had so many advantages and was following an established and successful planning strategy that the company and its backers were confident it would be a great success. However, in its first year Euro Disney lost $900 million and there was soon widespread concern over the very survival of the park (*Newsweek*, 1994: 43).

The troubles of Euro Disney can be linked to several issues, but a key one was the lack of controls. This has been admitted by Michael Eisner, the CEO at the time, who states in his autobiography that, 'our primary goal was to control our financial exposure . . . and ensure a substantial share of the profits and management control' (Eisner with Schwartz, 1998: 266). But one can see that a lack of control over these and other factors precipitated the theme-park's woes. There were major cost overruns at Euro Disney, amounting to over $300 million before the opening day (Eisner with Schwartz, 1998: 267). There was insufficient control of known external cultural factors such as those relating to European preferences, like drinking alcohol with meals. There was an under appreciation of Europe's lower discretionary income which led to more economical approaches to travel such as choosing day trips or staying at lower cost accommodation. Furthermore, controlling for unpredictable aspects of the external environment, such as the poor winter weather and contingency plans for a downturn in the economy, were shown to be inadequate. While reports on the quality of the experience were high, Disney could have demonstrated more self-control in its media relations. Confidence slipped into arrogance as Disney officials were quoted as saying 'we are the best' and 'we're building something immortal, like the pharaohs built the pyramids' (Eisner with Schwartz, 1998: 281). Once Disney started having problems the press gleefully reminded the public of these gems.

Disney was able to turn around the situation at its French theme park after making careful adjustments to its control procedures. Disney started to control its costs by restructuring its debt load, adjusting its hotel room supply, laying-off some staff, and putting further development plans on hold. Disney became more responsive to its market by allowing alcohol to be served in the park and making minor changes to the services offered in the park, such as expanding facilities for sit-down meals (Eisner with Schwartz, 1998: 283). Disney responded to the downturn in the economy by lowering prices, cutting back its overhead, and refocusing its marketing. The cultural clash between the Europeans and Americans is demonstrated yet again in renaming the park 'Paris Disney'. American Disney officials felt the term 'Euro' was glamorous and exciting. However, market research showed the Europeans associated the term 'euro' with the slow moving new European currency and bureaucratic red-tape. Paris Disney is now more successful and the plans for expansion more realistic.

Controlling in Community Tourism

At the community level the monitoring and control of tourism becomes everyone's business but seldom anyone's responsibility. It becomes everyone's business because within a destination every individual and area is affected by tourism, not just the businesses engaged in the activity. Local residents not engaged in the industry must put up with the increased congestion and changed lifestyle that comes with thousands of visitors. Areas adjacent to tourist facilities will feel the pressure of business marked by traffic and noise, and if the destination is successful there will be a general increase in land and housing prices as the industry grows and visitors become second home owners or retirees to the destination. But who is to monitor these trends and who has the responsibility to control or legislate this industry?

The simple answer is government, but in free market economies government is generally not keen to become enmeshed in the detailed management control of industries because of the cost and poor track record of central planning. In terms of tourism with its diverse products and settings this would be even more challenging. However, there is always one exception that proves the rule and that has occurred in the Falkland Islands, where political considerations have led to close government control 'to maintain balance between the interests of growth and the environment' (Riley, 1995: 471). The official Falkland Islands Development Corporation has the 'status as the sole agent for change' on the islands and in terms of tourism has applied an absolute ceiling of 500 land-based tourists a year. Thanks to the islands' isolation and the political situation such a restraint had not been put to the test by the mid-nineties according to Riley.

The evidence suggests that control at the community level comes when both the industry and local population see it as a net benefit to all concerned. It is also evident that in this area of tourism management most progress has been made by small communities, often in a mountain resort or coastal setting.

Bosselman *et al.* (1999) refer to the monitoring efforts of several small communities around the world with respect to enforcing various performance and environmental standards in addition to the normal building codes and zoning regulations. Among these was the town of Chepstowe that monitored its tourism performance over a five-year period in order to increase the economic benefits it brought to the community. But the community to catch the imagination of the authors was the success story of

Whistler, British Columbia. To them 'The municipality (of Whistler) has for over twenty years had an active and evolving public community participation process that has resulted in a carefully crafted, and continually monitored, growth management strategy that responds to community needs and goals' (Bosselman *et al.*, 1999: 12).

One of those who observed the evolution of Whistler into an international ski resort with a four-season market appeal and contributed to its monitoring process and community participation has been Alison Gill. Gill (1997: 55) maintains 'few tourism communities have resolved the problems of how to successfully control and manage the balance between tourists and residents in a resort setting', but she feels the chances of success are dramatically increased through a community oriented approach to management and monitoring. She notes that in 1988 Whistler introduced a growth management approach to its tourism development through a comprehensive development plan that shifted the growth emphasis to a more balanced appraisal of resident and tourist needs. 'Community involvement lies at the heart of the growth management approach that underlies the development policy in Whistler' (Gill, 1997: 62), including such features as resident surveys and small group 'living room meetings' between various subgroups of the community and the tourism industry. 'Notably a commitment was made to a comprehensive community and resort monitoring system' (Gill, 1997: 63), that covered aspects of land use and development, and market demand as outlined in Table 6.1.

The type of monitoring system developed at Whistler is designed to provide information to guide both the industry and the community in their development decisions. It is facilitated through the input of primary and secondary data, assembled and assessed by arms-length and objective individuals. In the case of Whistler a nearby university (Simon Fraser University) has assisted the process, and there have been examples of similar successful approaches elsewhere, such as in the Austrian Alps.

In the 1970s the pressure of development on small ski villages in the Austrian Alps was reaching the critical point of threatening 'the ecological integrity and long-run socio-economic stability of the area' (Moser & Peterson, 1981: 68). A test-case of one village – Obergurgl in the Tyrolean Alps, was undertaken by the Alpine Research Institute of the University of Innsbruck as part of UNESCO's Man and the Biosphere (MAB) Project 6 to study the impact of human activity on the mountain environment. 'The MAB–6 Obergurgl Project lasted for about 12 years and has left a definitive mark on the village and on many of the scientists who participated.' Furthermore, 'Obergurgl's experience has been studied by many other communities, and the wider region around the village has been declared by the provincial government a zone of limited development – a move that was strongly supported by Obergurglers' according to Moser and Moser (1986: 102–3).

Table 6.1 Elements of monitoring systems, Resort Municipality of Whistler, 1994

Category	Indicator
Land Use/ Development	inventory of residential/commerical development
	construction activity
	hotel accommodation
	resort-related development and other land use changes in Highway 99 corridor
Environment	water system quality
	wastewater effluent quality
	air quality
	vegetation cover
	lakes and river quality
Commercial/ Social	population
	school enrolment
	health unit statistics
	unemployment
	crime, traffic violations
	community satisfaction survey
	selected community/recreational facility usage
Infrastructure/ Transportation	water system – remaining capacity
	sewer system – remaining capacity
	Highway 99 volumes
	transit system ridership
	BC Rail passenger volumes
Market	hotel occupancy, hotel rates
	skier volumes
	conference delegate volumes
	golf-green fees
	visitor satisfaction surveys
	residential sales prices

Source: RMOW, Planning Department

Working in conjunction with local residents, some of whom operated local ski facilities and hotels, the scientists developed a four-dimensional monitor model. The four dimensions considered were:

(1) *Recreational demand* – which examined the actual and potential tourist demands for the area.

(2) *Population and economic development* – which examined tourism's relative economic contribution to the local economy.
(3) *Farming and ecological change* – which measures the impact on the principal resource and activity in the area, its farmland and farming productivity.
(4) *Land use and development control* – which assessed the needs of all groups and industries in terms of their resource base and utility demands.

This process led to the identification of eight major problem areas for Obergurgl according to Moser and Moser (1986: 104). These were:

- Different villager attitudes to land ownership, emigration and economic development.
- Different perceptions of environmental quality between the villagers and tourists.
- Determining the effect of ski development on soil erosion.
- Determining the productivity of alpine pastures with respect to domestic and wild animals.
- Projecting future recreational demands with respect to changing public attitudes and transport options.
- Continual analysis of alternative development schemes.
- Experimental ecological studies involving the manipulation of grazing patterns and trekking routes.
- Economic impact assessment in terms of employment structure and savings patterns.

After examining these issues the scientists and villagers suggested various strategies to improve or alleviate the problems. For example, in the area of recreational demand some hotels reduced the number of guest beds as a quality improvement measure and natural history tours were introduced, guided by specially trained local residents. In terms of population and economic development there was an expansion of the youth education programme, a substantial revegetation of the ski runs, and better management of the summer visitor impacts. In the area of farming and ecological change there was the establishment of quiet zones and nature protection areas. Included among these was a calculation of vegetation resistance to the 'stamping damage' of hikers. In terms of land use and development control the village added a new biological sewage treatment plant to reduce local water pollution and applied restrictions on traffic in the village.

The success of such collaborative efforts has been duplicated elsewhere in Austria. Kariel (1989: 64) reports on the general 'acculturation to tourism and the desire to control growth' that spread through the alpine regions of Austria and he follows the experience of four other mountain communities.

He notes that most villages did not want 'to be totally given over to tourism to become another St. Moritz or Zermatt' (Kariel, 1989: 65), but that in order to control their own destiny they needed to take the responsibility for their development options away from the central government. For the changes they wanted to see 'are more likely to occur when there is local development and control, with suitable guidance from experts' (Kariel, 1989: 68).

Summary

This chapter emphasises the importance of including control measures in the development of tourism, because as an industry with some undeniable negative impacts it is imperative to minimise these effects if the industry is to succeed. It is noted that control measures have become a regular element of business management, and with the shift to a service economy and growing consumer sophistication there has been a change of emphasis from simple physical controls to one emphasising customer satisfaction.

In tourism past discussion of controls and monitoring has either been of a general nature or with a heavy emphasis on environmental issues. However, with the growing awareness of different consumer perceptions and priorities, and examples of successful quality control in the accommodation and transport sectors there is now emerging a broader interpretation of management control. Major companies have embraced the principles of total quality management and yield management, which involve consideration of different stakeholders and overall productivity. This has spread to certain destinations, where there are attempts to involve more stakeholders in the creation of a quality experience and efforts to vary the product and price through the seasons.

To illustrate the relevance of the four functions of business to modern tourism management the recent planning efforts of a state government will be examined. The strategic tourism management plan for the State of Victoria, Australia, is presented in the following case study. This major undertaking has been analysed in terms of the four business functions and with respect to its overall direction.

Case Study: State of Victoria's Strategic Tourism Plan

Tourism has become an important industry to the Australian state of Victoria over the years and it is becoming more important. It is important to the capital city of Melbourne's ambitions to become a world class city and to country Victoria's desire to diversify, as its traditional industries can no longer support previous population bases and amenity levels. Tourism in the state is comparable to the agricultural and communications industries, contributing A$8.5 billion to the Victoria economy and accounting for 150,000 jobs according to the Minister for Tourism (Tourism Victoria, 2002:

1). To build on this strong base the theme of the plan is to 'Advantage Victoria' by building on its economic, social and environmental advantages (Tourism Victoria, 2002: 4). This case reviews the plan according to the role of the four business functions outlined in this part. The data and quotes are taken from Victoria's Tourism Industry Strategic Plan, 2002–2006 (Tourism Victoria, 2002), but the interpretation is the responsibility of the authors.

Planning

Planning philosophy and statements naturally dominate such a document but certain trends and emphases are apparent. The first is that a state plan has to be as comprehensive and inclusive as possible. To achieve this the plan adopts the triple bottom line approach of considering environmental and social implications in addition to the more obvious economic drivers. It addresses the issue of exclusivity by promoting Melbourne as a gateway to the country and state, and enhancing its position as a world sport event and convention centre. It shifts its promotion of Victoria's rural regions from a general product emphasis to a more specific marketing of primary motivations for travel. Its new emphasis will be on certain 'destinations and attractions, desired experiences, special interest themes, products and touring routes' (Tourism Victoria, 2002: 66).

While marketing remains the dominant interest of the state its management has matured and so marketing is not the only planning interest. In its discussion of strategic marketing the plan considers trends in international and domestic tourism (Figure 6.4), along with branding and psychographic segmentation opportunities. It links these consumer interests to particular products in its section on product development, where it is particularly optimistic about Victoria's food and wine possibilities as well as the more common alpine, nature based and heritage themes of the past.

Organising

For the plan to work Victoria needs to ensure there is sufficient communication and organisational structure in place, for as the Minister for Tourism observes the plan needs to be 'underpinned' by stakeholder and government support (Tourism Victoria, 2002: 1). The plan notes 'there are about 24 tourism industry sector organisations in Victoria . . . There are also about 100 local and regional tourism associations . . . and numerous municipal tourism boards' (Tourism Victoria, 2002: 16), so one of its priorities is to encourage the development of one umbrella organisation to represent the industry. An appropriate body – the Victorian Tourism Industry Council – was created in 2001 and the state government hopes it can interact with this council to promote the plan's objectives.

One important consideration in the organising of Victoria's tourism is to ensure that the relevant information reaches potential customers. To achieve this the state plans to create an information distribution chain to

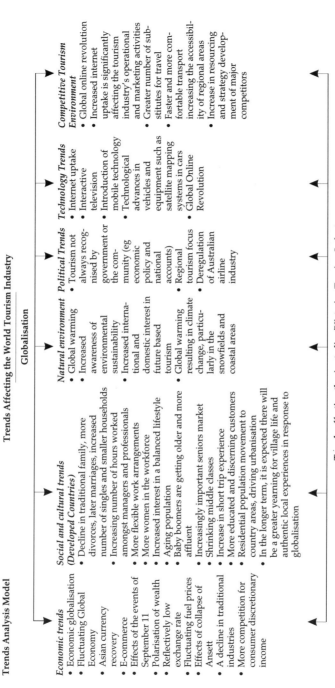

Figure 6.4 Trends analysis of international and domestic tourism   *Source:* Victoria (2000: 2)

link all products and regions with potential customers (Figure 6.5). The rising importance of 'electronic/online distribution channels' is evident, as more travel consumers are prepared to move from simply obtaining information via the web to making actual bookings.

The web and IT have become major sources of information in the development and distribution of this strategic plan. IT was a vital component in the extensive consultation and build-up of the plan, as the state sought input from a wide variety of industry and industry-related interest groups, including a small group of academics. The final version of the plan is available on Tourism Victoria's corporate website (www.tourismvictoria. com.au/strategicplan) for the first time, which ensures the widest possible dissemination to the industry and students of tourism.

Leadership

The very presence of a strategic plan epitomises leadership, for it indicates a willingness by the state government to coordinate and guide future tourism development for the benefit of as many as possible. But within this commitment to lead there are some significant innovations proposed for the state's tourism. One is the commitment to Agenda 21 and making tourism a positive contribution to a healthier planet by emphasising sustainable development. Another is the recognition that Tourism Victoria should 'take a leadership role in the tourism industry and encourage professional standards and the development of cooperative arrangements, which maximise industry effectiveness (according to the triple bottom line audit)' (Tourism Victoria, 2002: 15).

The determination that this industry needs to 'raise its game' in the area of professionalism and standards is one that bears repeating and emphasising on a continual basis. The plan recognises the difficulty in recruiting and retaining quality staff and presents several strategies to overcome these difficulties. Among them are the promotion of tourism's attractiveness and dynamics as a career, initiating a tripartite forum of industry, government and education to develop relevant training and education, and supporting the case for professional development courses in this industry. In terms of standards the plan seeks to use accreditation to ensure 'the delivery of an experience in a sustained and reliable manner consistent with promoted expectations' (Tourism Victoria, 2002: 109).

Controlling

The plan recognises the relevance of controlling and monitoring through a discussion of performance indicators and targets, but in addition to this auditing role it also provides insight into other ways the government can and will control the direction of Victoria's tourism. For example, since 'thirty percent of land within the state is Crown Land' the government will explore ways to facilitate the appropriate development of tourism on or

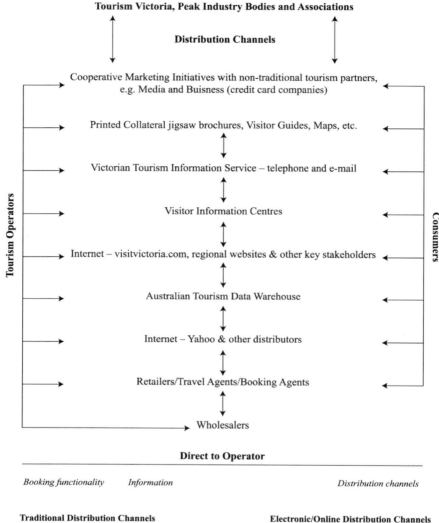

Tourism Victoria, Peak Industry Bodies and Associations

Distribution Channels

Cooperative Marketing Initiatives with non-traditional tourism partners, e.g. Media and Buisness (credit card companies)

Printed Collateral jigsaw brochures, Visitor Guides, Maps, etc.

Victorian Tourism Information Service – telephone and e-mail

Visitor Information Centres

Internet – visitvictoria.com, regional websites & other key stakeholders

Australian Tourism Data Warehouse

Internet – Yahoo & other distributors

Retailers/Travel Agents/Booking Agents

Wholesalers

Tourism Operators

Consumers

Direct to Operator

Booking functionality   *Information*   *Distribution channels*

Traditional Distribution Channels
- Wholesale Airlines
- Retail Travel Agents
- Visitor Information Centres
- Printed Collateral – Brochures, Guides, etc.
- Business and Madia partnerships

Electronic/Online Distribution Channels
- Internet (visitvictoria.com, australia.com)
- e-mail
- Visitor Information Centres
- Emerging technologies – Interactive
- Television, telephone message, web services

- **Direct Marketing**
- Telephone call centres

Figure 6.5 Tourism distribution chain
Source: Tourism Victoria (2000: 84)

adjacent to such high value national assets (Tourism Victoria, 2002: 116). The plan also recognises its controlling influence in relation to air transport links and development. Consequently the government commits to 'play a leadership role in Commonwealth (federal) regulatory matters affecting aviation, including input to bilateral negotiations . . . expanded or new air services . . . increasing the competitiveness of the Melbourne sector (airport) to foreign and Australian carriers' (Tourism Victoria, 2002: 129). It is only through such controlled transport development that the state can hope to raise the industry's yield factor and to control the spatial distribution of its important international and interstate tourists.

Summary

Only part of a very extensive strategic plan has been covered in this short review, but within these few pages it is evident that the state government of Victoria has considered and used all of the four business functions within its plan. In many cases these functional elements have been declared structural elements of the plan, in some areas they have been interwoven into other objectives as in the case of the leadership and controlling attributes. But throughout the plan there is a business emphasis which recognises the future of Victoria's tourism must be based on sound business principles, with a focus on serving and satisfying the customers' expectations.

Part 3

Tourism Community Stakeholders

Stakeholders

Widespread support for tourism initiatives will be necessary to success-fully integrate the four business management functions outlined in Part 2 into strategic community tourism management. Communities are made up of many individuals, each with their own interests and priorities. Since this book will be examining individuals' interests and priorities in their community's tourism development, we will use the term 'stakeholders' to describe the grouping of these individuals. The term 'stakeholder' in the business management literature has been defined as: 'Those groups or individuals who are directly or indirectly affected by an organization's pursuit of its goals' (Stoner *et al.*, 1995: 63). Such a definition reflects the concept of managing through organisation and recognising impacts will be more than simply economic when assessing tourism's impacts on a host community.

Stakeholders can have different types of relationship with a business in that they may be *internal stakeholders*, such as owners and employees, or *external stakeholders* such as customers, suppliers or special interest groups. Both of these have been described as 'direct action' stakeholders (Stoner *et al.*, 1995). But in the open system of a global economy with tourism busi-nesses' external environmental impacts affecting communities down-stream or overseas, the existence of an 'indirect-action environment' beyond the immediate community should be acknowledged also. This is where people and places well removed from an actual business site can be affected by that business organisation's actions and thus become indirect stakeholders.

Many stakeholder groups find they have to fight to be included in deci-sion-making processes. However, just because a group is included in a discussion does not automatically mean they will have a chance to partici-pate in an effective and efficient manner in management decisions. The strategy, whether intentional or incidental, of wearing down dissenters with tedious meeting agendas and schedules that fail to produce results can alienate stakeholders from group decision-making processes. Such proce-dural attrition might seem acceptable in the short term as they can clear the way for those remaining to make decisions. However, if important community decisions are made in such a manner they are likely to alienate public opinion and damage goodwill towards the participation process.

Decisions made with only limited community participation and support tend to survive only in the short term, as many underlying issues and opportunities will have been neglected due to the lack of full and vigorous participation by all stakeholder groups. Given the importance of stakeholder involvement in any successful community visioning exercise and the development of a truly communal tourism strategy it is remarkable that so little research attention has been placed on this aspect of tourism activity to date.

Those living in a community with a significant tourism activity will often find they have multiple roles and views regarding the industry. No categorisation of community stakeholders can be mutually exclusive due to the interlinked nature of community living and this industry. There are those who are employed directly in tourism or have a family member who is involved in a core or peripheral component of this extensive industry, as described in Chapter 9. Such people are likely to have a different perspective from those who are simply residents of the same community. This has certainly proven to be the case with many studies of resident attitudes and opinions demonstrating such differences of opinion (Lankford, 1994; Milman & Pizam, 1988; Murphy, 1983; Williams & Lawson, 2001).

In many communities residents with no apparent link to the industry could in effect be indirect shareholders, since so many of their local governments invest in tourism-related facilities such as piers, parks and parades. One example of this indirect shareholder relationship is the growing practice of offering residents a price discount when they enter local museums or a reserved camp ground space because they have contributed to these facilities already through their rates or property taxes.

The occurrence of multiple roles and perspectives is common in stakeholder analysis. Stoner *et al.* (1995: 74) describe the situation as 'multiple stakeholder relationships', where:

> Individuals may need to balance conflicting roles and values when they work for an organization, use its products, perhaps own stock in the company, and live and raise their families nearby. Such multiple stakeholder relationships are not uncommon.

To ensure the survival of a tourist organisation or business, along with the continued prosperity and appeal of the host community requires maintaining a balance among multiple key stakeholder groups and relationships.

To illustrate this point Stoner *et al.* (1995) refer to the McDonald's restaurants attempt to satisfy several stakeholder groups when it introduced its more environmentally friendly packaging. It had to satisfy its customers and provide the sort of convenient packaging to which they had become accustomed. It needed to increase the recycled component of its packaging to show greater environmental responsibility. It had to undertake such change with fiscal responsibility to maintain its market share and shareholder loyalty. Since then McDonald's has entered another key phase in its development by expanding into accommodation, and is experimenting with McDonald's hotels in certain European locations. Once again this will call for the balancing of various stakeholder group interests, including customers, local residents, employees and shareholders.

Like the key decision moments for McDonald's, pivotal questions for many tourism destinations with regards to stakeholders will include the following:

- Who are this community's various stakeholder groups in regards to a proposal?
- What sort of process should be established to incorporate the input of stakeholders into the proposal?
- How will stakeholders participate – will they provide only their separate opinions, or will they be encouraged to develop mutually acceptable options?
- Who will represent these stakeholders?
- What is the optimum number of stakeholder representatives to include in the process to ensure that they are manageable in number with respect to analysis and strategy formation?
- What level of ownership will the stakeholders have in the formation, adoption, monitoring and adjustments of implementation strategies relating to the proposal?

While tourism research has yet to address many of these questions some attempt has been made to identify the groups referred to in the first question. However, even this simple first step has proven challenging and illustrates the difficulty in ensuring all stakeholders receive adequate attention.

Researchers have identified a consistent handful of stakeholder group candidates, but not always the same groups. Wheeler (1994: 648) split tourism interests into three sectors: the commercial providers, the tourists and the host population, not including the providers. Wearing and Neil (1999: 74) divide community ecotourism stakeholders into four groups: the tourism industry, the government, the community, and non-government organisations. Cock and Pfueller (2000) have divided their ecotourism community stakeholders into the four groups of environmentalist, the tourism industry, the host communities and the visitors. Ritchie (2001: 64) has divided her tourism community into four stakeholder groups: the residents, the industry, the visitor, and local government.

Some authors have suggested a more detailed representation is needed than is found among the broad categories of stakeholders outlined above. Jamal and Getz (1995: 187) in their thoughtful paper on 'Collaboration theory and community tourism planning', argue that 'a domain-level (local) focus in community tourism planning is critical due to the interdependencies among multiple stakeholders in a community tourism destination'. They raise the issue of legitimacy and cite Gray (1985) in claiming a legitimate stakeholder is one who has the right and capacity to participate in any decision-making process. Blank (1989) notes that any community should be reasonably reassured that the stakeholders assembled are capable of representing their interests. In light of these and other considerations Jamal and Getz (1995: 198) propose:

> Collaboration for tourism destination planning will depend on encompassing the following stakeholder groups: local government plus other public organizations having a direct bearing on resource allocation; tourism industry associations and sectors such as Chamber of Commerce, Convention and Visitor Bureau, and regional Tourist authority; resident organizations (community groups); social agencies (e.g., school boards, hospitals); and special interest groups.

When the Canadians tried to develop a strategic vision along these lines for their 'global tourism icon of Banff National Park' they attempted to involve all legitimate 'interest sectors' in the process (Ritchie, 1999). The result was a round table composed of 14 interest sectors, each of which were to 'represent the interests of its constituents within the process designed to plan the future of the Banff-Bow Valley region' (Ritchie, 1999: 276).

The discussion paper for a new Australian 10-year strategic plan invites all stakeholders to respond to the challenge and attempts to stimulate a response by asking over 200 questions (Australia, 2002). Stakeholders in this context are identified as 'participants in the tourism, transport, construction, finance and other tourism-related industries, the education and research sector, government agencies and members of the general community' (Australia, 2002: 2). In other words – anyone, so as to be all inclusive at the first stage of this planning process.

When the division into stakeholder groups is undertaken there is no guarantee that the views of each group will have internal consistency. Within each group there will be some variation of feeling toward tourism based on personal values, experiences and opinions. Choy's (1995) study of employment within Hawaii's mature and varied tourism industry indicated some differences between its airline, hotel and restaurant/bar sectors that resulted in different perceptions of job satisfaction and presumably attitude toward the industry. But it should be noted that in this destination, where tourism is the major single industry, 'the quality of tourism employment is much better than that usually perceived by those outside the industry' (Choy, 1995: 137). Similar differences of opinion have emerged in studies of residents living in tourist destinations.

Several segmentation studies of resident attitudes and opinions toward the local tourism industry have revealed a series of internal variations within this single yet general stakeholder group. Davis *et al.* (1988) using cluster analysis segmentation of a sample of Florida residents discovered five segments within this category. These are:

- *Lovers* (20% of the sample) who have no negative opinions of tourism.
- *Haters* (16%) who have extremely negative opinions regarding tourism and tourists.
- *Cautious romantics* (21%) who although being positive toward tourism also agree with some negative features.
- *In-betweens* (18%) who hold moderate opinions, agreeing with statements to a lesser degree than lovers or haters.
- *Love 'em for a reason* (26%) that are pro-tourism but less strongly than lovers.

Ryan and Montgomery (1994) used a similar process in Bakewell, England. They identify three clusters:

- *Enthusiasts* (22%) who support tourism, 'but not excessively so'.
- *Somewhat irritated* (23.5%) who have negative opinions about tourism's impacts and are sceptical about its benefits.
- *Middle-of-the-roaders* (54.3%) who generally score between the other two clusters.

Williams and Lawson (2001) have produced a more recent and thorough analysis of resident clusters, using a sample of 1062 residents from 10 New Zealand towns. Within that large data set they identify four clusters:

- *Lovers* (44%) who approve of tourism the most and believe the benefits are distributed fairly throughout the community.
- *Cynics* (10%) who approve the least, and think tourism has changed their town for the worst.
- *Taxpayers* (25%) who do not feel very strongly about anything to do with tourism except how it has a bearing on their taxes, both good and bad.
- *Innocents* (20%) who seem to be missing both the benefits and problems of tourism because of their lack of direct contact with the industry.

Thus, we can see in this quick global coverage that resident stakeholders can be expected to have a variety of views regarding tourism development in their community and that once again it will require explanation and balance to develop a consensus from this or any group.

Part Outline

Different stakeholder groups all influence each other whether they like it or not. Understanding the positions, motivations, needs and resources of these groups is, therefore, invaluable in developing tourism plans and strategies. This part will try to set the scene for future tourism research and management by applying some basic elements of stakeholder analysis from the business management literature to several key groups in the community decision-making process. It has been subdivided into four chapters representing four different stakeholder groups, but as this introduction has demonstrated there is nothing sacrosanct about this division. It merely represents an attempt to be both comprehensive and compact.

In this part each stakeholder group's general objectives are described in an attempt to isolate their key interests and concerns. This is followed by an examination of the group's needs using the four key business management functions to emphasise the pertinence and potential effectiveness of this management link to tourism businesses' strategic planning at the community level. The involvement of all stakeholder groups might seem like an invitation to agony by some who would rather bypass or minimise the involvement of groups, who they feel have either little to contribute or are outright troublemakers. However, since broad-based community support is necessary for long-term and successful tourism developments it is prudent to invite all affected stakeholders to participate in the process in order to understand their views. Involving stakeholders in a meaningful way allows them to develop a greater understanding of their own group with its internal differences, and the views of other stakeholders. Once such an understanding is reached these groups can discuss the issues and develop strategies that offer a greater opportunity to the whole community.

The customer is examined first because tourism is intended to be a service industry, one which is established to serve the needs and expectations of customers from all walks of life and origins. This is followed by an examination of the industry, which due to its diversity also needs to be examined in terms of various sub-groups. Then comes an examination of the residents who are not directly related to the industry, but who need to be 'on-side' if the efforts of the industry are to be rewarded with a receptive environment. Finally, we will examine the multiple roles and expectations of government and its agencies, which can instigate or facilitate the process of tourism development at the community level.

Chapter 7

Customers

Customers are often referred to as the foundation of business success. While many companies are quick to say they 'put the customer first', what are they really doing to understand and respond to their customers? It has been suggested that despite the big push to develop more customer focused business practices, 'only a relatively small percentage, perhaps 30%, practice what they preach' (Christopher *et al.*, 1991: i). Most businesses are still selling what they produce rather than what the customer wants, so are supply driven rather than market driven.

Since tourism is about selling travel experiences it involves the combined efforts of several organisations and businesses to satisfy the expectations of its customers. This makes the tourism experience exchange more complex than a simple product exchange and causes it to involve more than price considerations. As Kotler (2001: 140) notes 'if customers only bought products and didn't care about services and surrounding benefits, and all products in the category were the same, all markets would be price markets'. This is certainly not the case in tourism where customers value not only the product, but the service with which it is presented, the setting in which the exchange takes place and the knowledge base of the host regarding the destination as well as the product. These become a significant aspect of the total experience and the customers' interaction with these components is an important part of the experience success.

Under the circumstances of a service experience involving customer-tourism industry interactions, the traditional 4P marketing mix has become insufficient in the management and marketing of tourism experiences. As Berry and Parasuraman (1991: 4–5) state the four Ps of marketing are missing an important ingredient for service industries, namely the quality of the exchange. They claim 'service quality is the foundation for services marketing because the core product being marketed is a performance', and in tourism that experiential performance involves the interaction between customer and supplier. Jan Carlzon (1987) astutely calls it tourism's 'moments of truth' and tourism marketing texts have found it necessary to expand the marketing mix to include factors such as packaging, people and partnerships to indicate this more interactive nature of the tourism product (Morrison, 1989: 210–13).

With tourism often operating in public places its sales and operations also need to consider non-profit situations and the impacts on the destination. Non-profit organisations such as governments, non-government organisations like arts and culture organisations, and even universities have become more involved with marketing as the need for customers and a clear message has become more acute. The major contribution of marketing to the customers of non-profit organisations has been to help position them in an ever-growing and competitive market. 'Marketing competition (among such non-profit organisations), at its best, creates a pattern of varied institutions, each clear as to its mission, market coverage, need specialisation, and service portfolio' (Kotler *et al.*, 1987: 13).

This has certainly been the case for cities, which now actively market themselves as ideal and distinctive homes for various businesses, including tourism. Place marketing has been identified and described by Kotler *et al.* (1993: 18), as embracing four activities:

- Designing the right mix of community features and services
- Setting attractive incentives for the current and potential buyers and users of its goods and services.
- Delivering a place's products and services in an efficient, accessible way.
- Promoting the place's values and image so that potential users are fully aware of the place's distinctive advantages

Such activities describe how a destination should structure its tourism marketing, producing a clear and differentiated image of its products and service strengths. Overlooking the marketing and operation of this industry should be the destination, with its formal and informal obligation to ensure customers' expectations are met within the capabilities and aspirations of the destination.

Objectives

The prime concern of the customer is a *satisfactory experience*, one where expectations have been met and possibly exceeded. For this to happen customers will need to receive sufficient value from the experience to make up for the time, money, and energy committed to the exercise. Under such circumstances the customer can be expected to become loyal, not only in terms of repeat patronage but as an ambassador/lobbyist for the business(es) and destination(s) visited.

To achieve this desirable state customers will benefit from:
- research that has identified their interests and needs;
- clear destination images that indicate the prime tourism product(s) and life style of the host community;

- relevant information to targeted consumers whose interests would match the destination image and offerings;
- sufficient facilities and service to match their expectations and to provide a satisfactory experience.

The issues that will arise in meeting customer objectives can be met through the application of the four business functions. First and foremost the customer wants to be understood and appreciated. This requires market research and planning within the planning phase. Business and destination organisation will be responsible primarily for determining what corporate and community image to develop, and how to position their business and this image to relevant target markets. This will require collaboration between many groups and is one of the biggest challenges facing destination marketing associations. The effort to create the right match between expectations and offered facilities and service will be determined largely through individual business and community leadership. Reaching the appropriate customers with the appropriate messages will require a large degree of control over selecting the most effective distribution channels, monitoring the response to current offerings and identifying possible alternate options. For both individual businesses and destination communities this necessitates an ongoing examination of their offerings, and should be linked with consumer research into new markets and opportunities. As such it completes the circle with the market research of the planning phase.

Planning

Consumer choice process

Customer research should be an integral part of the strategic planning process because knowing the needs and desires of customers enables communities to better judge whether they can meet such expectations and how to go about blending consumer wishes with commercial objectives.

A generalised model of a tourist's consumer decision-making process is presented in Figure 7.1. It is based on previous consumer and marketing research, where particular features have been shown to influence travel decisions. The internal factors are those personal traits and situations that affect an individual's propensity to travel. The external factors are those outside forces that impact on everyone's ability to travel such as global economic and political conditions, plus those that have a specific impact on the individual such as the effectiveness of destination marketing. Both have been shown to influence the cognitive processes (thinking and decision-making) that individuals are likely to consider.

The model starts with the various *stimuli* that can create an interest in travel. In this era of consumerism all of us are bombarded with external factors like *general marketing* information, most of it unsolicited in the form

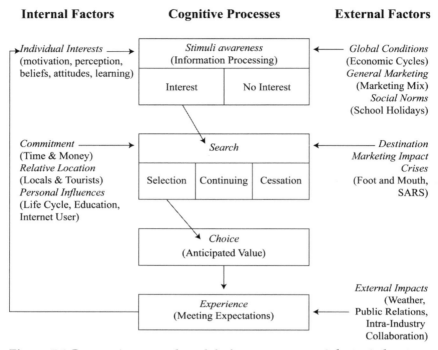

Figure 7.1 Composite general model of consumer travel choice behaviour

of billboards, media advertisements, junk mail and 'internet spam'. Despite our best efforts some of this bombardment penetrates and starts us thinking about a product or service, how it may fit our needs, and how we can obtain it. The success of such penetration often depends on the 4 Ps of the marketing mix – promotion, product, price and place (Kotler, 1997: 92–4). It also depends on general *global conditions*. For example, the terrorist acts in New York (2001) and Bali (2002), plus the SARS outbreak and Iraq War (2003) all caused temporary declines in the stock market and to the growth of international travel. Cultural factors such as national holidays and customs can have a strong influence on the timing and location of many holiday choices.

Whether and how a consumer responds to such marketing stimuli is conditioned a great deal by internal psychological factors – motivation, perception, learning and beliefs and attitudes that influence *individual interests* (Kotler & Armstrong, 1989: 130–6). Motivation drives a person to satisfy a need and can be initiated by physiological, social or personal forces, as outlined in the Maslow and Freudian theories. In terms of travel, which often involves advanced purchases based on incomplete knowledge, individual perception of potential destinations and their offerings is an important component of the decision-making process. To help broaden their knowledge base most travel consumers attempt to learn more about their intended purchase, especially when it involves a major cash and time commitment. All of these psychological factors are influenced by the beliefs and attitudes acquired by the customer over time. Some of these beliefs and attitudes will be formed through personal experience, but others will be moulded by societal stereotypes.

The importance of individual interests has been recognised in the growing area of psychographic research. Such research attempts to explain why people from the same demographic groups can make very different vacation choices based on their individual interests. One of the early commercial forays into this area of research was the Values and Life Style (VALS) methodology developed by SRI International. Based on US surveys of people's general attitudes and demographic profiles it was considered possible to identify nine lifestyle groups. At the time these were said to include survivors (4%), sustainers (7%), belongers (35%), emulators (9%), achievers (22%), I-am-me's (5%), experiential (7%), societally conscious (9%), and integrated (2%). Another has been the Roy Morgan Value Segments http://www/roymorgan.com.au/papers/1999/1999my1.html) that have been used widely in Australia. Tourism Victoria has identified Roy Morgan's 'Socially Aware', 'Visible Achievement', 'Traditional Family Life' and 'Young Optimism' psychographic groups as core market segments for Victoria's regional market (Tourism Victoria, 2002: 71).

If the above stimuli have created an interest in travel the consumer will enter and *search* a global marketplace, for many countries and their destinations will be vying for the customer's attention and business. Major external factors at this stage include the extensive national and individual destination marketing and promotions activity. Millions of dollars are spent annually on attracting the attention of potential tourists and this has become a principal expenditure item for destinations and individual businesses alike. However, even the best prepared marketing plans and searches can be disrupted by external crises. We have only to look at how the foot and mouth epidemic in Britain changed rural holiday plans, and the Severe Acute Respiratory Syndrome (SARS) deeply affected travel to and within South East Asia. The search process is expected to be a continual process leading to three possible outcomes. One is a selection process that leads to immediate action and a choice. Another is a continuing process that indicates the consumer is still undecided, but is still a prospective tourist. The final outcome is a temporary cessation of search due to an unsuccessful search or a change of circumstances.

The degree of search will depend to a large extent on the consumer's anticipated expenditure of time and money, which is represented in the model as their degree of *commitment*. If the trip under consideration is a 'weekend getaway' it is assumed that this is likely to a regional trip to areas that are well known or referenced through family and friends. It would be a relatively inexpensive option in terms of time and cash, requiring little search and preplanning and could be classified as a minor commitment. On the other hand, if the trip is a 'once in a lifetime' overseas trip it would justify a far greater search for information because such distant places are less known and require much more time to structure into a personal trip. This would be indicative of a major commitment.

While not commonly associated with the tourist decision-making process we have introduced a *relative location* factor into the model at this point. Local residents do not qualify as tourists in terms of distance travelled or overnight stops away from home, but these people are important customers nevertheless, especially in the slower months. Their level of commitment, in terms of the search process, is far less than distant decision-makers, but local people still undergo a selection process and are influenced by the same or similar factors. As such they should not be over-looked and should be included through internal marketing within the destination community. If local people are included in the overall marketing perspective, they not only become more loyal customers, they interact with visitors and can positively influence visitors' overall tourism experiences through their recommendations. Victoria, BC, has recognised this and encourages resident use of tourism businesses and facilities by hosting a 'Be a Tourist in your Own Town' function once a year and offering favourable resident host ticketing deals.

Although the level of commitment dictates the degree of analysis and planning involved in decision-making, the search process will be influenced by both personal and external destination influences. The personal inputs are discussed in some detail here, but the destination inputs are left to the next chapter on the industry, for that is where and how communities can best influence the customer's decision-making process.

Personal influences include the impact of personal circumstances and immediate family and friends on vacation travel decisions. One factor that influences the amount of discretionary time and cash available is the customer's position in the lifecycle. One of life's ironies is that when one is young there is plenty of time to travel but few funds, and when one is older more people find themselves 'cash rich and time poor'. That said, it is no coincidence that two prime long-distance travel segments are the youth and the seniors markets, both with the respective amounts of time and income to pursue their travel interests. When most people make travel decisions these days they are make them in consultation with others. At the household and family stages of the lifecycle it is the partner and children who need to be consulted, because a successful vacation will depend on group consultation and participation.

A growing personal influence in travel decisions is the ability to use the Internet. This relatively new and rapidly expanding form of information technology has revolutionised customer access to the global market of tourism and has been equated with the jet engine as having the most significant impact on modern tourism by Buhalis (2000). By the end of the last millennium large numbers of consumers had access to and were using the Internet. Taylor (1999) cited in Buhalis (2000: 166–7) claimed Norway is the largest Internet user nation (34% of its population) followed by the US (27%), Australia (23%), UK (14%) and Germany (9%). However, these figures represent a snapshot of a rapidly evolving situation, for the number of computers and their Internet sophistication has grown remarkably since then. Furthermore, use of this feature is strongly linked to other personal influences like being well-educated professionals with higher disposable income which are key contributors to travel interest (Smith & Jenner, 1998).

After searching the alternatives and taking into account the solicited and unsolicited advice from family and friends, via personal research and potential destinations' marketing efforts, the travel customer makes their *choice*. It is not clear in tourism or other areas of consumer behaviour whether this choice process is a rational or emotional one. It can be highly rational in the sense that some customers calculate the opportunity costs of one choice over another, and select the best value with an emphasis on its financial aspects. For some it is an emotional response to a personal crisis or success, and the need for a break or to celebrate. However, given the large number of influential variables and the frequent group decision-making involved more attention is being given to the role of satisfying personal and group interests. So rather than striving for the perfect vacation, whatever that may be, the majority of travel customers are looking for a satisfactory return on their time and money investment and something that will satisfy all members of the travel party. They are selecting based on perceived value.

In tourism, unlike most other businesses, there can be a substantial lagtime between making the trip decision, including a commitment of money, and actually experiencing the product. But it is the *experience* which determines the success or otherwise of the whole process and impacts later judgements and decisions. Once again the tourism industry is not in complete control of its own destiny. While its emphasis on quality and service will contribute significantly to a satisfactory experience there is little it can do about the weather. However, it can work to collaborate with associated or peripheral activities, such as the agricultural or forestry industries, and it can place more emphasis on internal marketing to host communities to foster good community relations.

A good experience is one where expectations are met or exceeded, and will create a loyal and possibly a repeat customer in tourism. The repeat customers are of great value to tourism destinations as they spread positive word of mouth advertising and often return to spend more money and stay longer (Alford, 1998; Ross, 1993). Destinations and tourism businesses can expect much higher returns for their advertising dollars when they target repeat as opposed to new customers (Christopher, *et al.*, 1991). However, loyalty does not necessarily transform into repeat visits, for in some situations like that 'once in a lifetime' overseas trip it would be unrealistic to expect much repeat travel. In fact for many the long-haul trips are generally separate excursions to different parts of the globe, to take in as much of this earth's diversity of landscape and customs as possible. But a good experience will always create a loyal ambassador, who will take up their role as a consultant to family and friends with the same vigour as they received when making their decisions.

The above model is presented as a general simplification of a very complex decision-making process. It is necessary for destination communities to consider models like this in order to guide their research into customer needs, and to adopt a customer oriented marketing and development approach to this industry. Having analysed their prospective market a destination needs to organise how it will approach its potential customers. One immediate adjustment that a destination should make is to optimise the model's potential through organising its marketing resources and efforts into a focus on specific target markets.

However, a note of caution is necessary with respect to the model in Figure 7.1 and all other 'grand models' of consumer behaviour, according to Hudson (2000). He notes that they are not predictive, but only general guides. They cannot predict specific customer choice because they are broad generalisations, and they do not include a time-line. Therefore they cannot indicate when and how to intervene in the process so as to actually influence the decision. What they are intended to do is to highlight the relevant areas for market research regarding types of activity and types of destination.

Organising

Segmenting tourist types

No business or destination community can be all things to all people, and it should not try to be. Rather the destination should segment its potential market into more or less homogenous subgroups, or tourist market segments, based on certain common characteristics and/or behavioural patterns, that they can serve and satisfy. The underlying reason for market segmentation is efficiency (Court & Lupton, 1997) and it takes organisation to match the product with the most appropriate market segment.

Tourists tend to be segmented according to their socio-demographic, psychographic or behavioural characteristics or some combination of these categories, as a way of predicting their travel interests and spending patterns. Any target market must be:

(1) *Measurable* – marketing objectives should be set in numerical terms so the results can be measured and the value of the investment assessed.
(2) *Substantial* – the target market should be large enough to warrant the investment.
(3) *Accessible* – it should be possible to identify and to reach the intended target market through specific channels.
(4) *Defensible* – the target market should be sufficiently different in character to justify its individual attention.
(5) *Durable* – it should be a long-term market segment, not necessarily the same people, that is worthy of the attention and investment.
(6) *Competitive* – if the first five criteria can be met, a destination must ascertain whether it can offer something distinct or unique to attract these targeted customers.

Segmentation methods

The most common form of market segmentation is to examine actual and potential visitors' *socio-demographic* characteristics, such as their gender, age, home location, income, education, occupation, marital status and stated travel purpose. This is because it is both an effective differentiator of tourist choices and it is easily accessible. A study of tourists' decision-making processes conducted in Belgium grouped travellers by the following socio-demographic categories: singles, couples, families with children and friend groups (Decrop, 1999). Each market segment was found to have its own set of priorities, personality traits and product experiences. For example, singles wanted to interact with other singles during their vacations and families with children were more concerned with safety than other groups. It has been noted that wealthier and more educated travellers tend to be more mobile (Hanson & Hanson, 1981), while older travellers and travellers with children tend to be the least mobile (Driver & Tocher, 1979).

Much of the socio-demographic information can be obtained from regular government publications such as the census and annual reports, from government-industry national surveys, and from the regularity of past survey results. Such information is easy to understand and lends itself readily to comparisons of groups that are segmented according to clear and quantifiable characteristics. Unfortunately, when a destination comes to use such material it will often find that the information is not broken down to the level of their particular area or township, or is out of date, or does not ask the exact right question for its market situation. Consequently, many destinations will need to conduct their own surveys to supplement this important aspect of market segmentation.

The main drawback with using socio-demographic data to track and predict tourist's actions is that this data only tells us about who the tourists are, not what they want and why they want it and what factors make them buy. Certain market researchers, like Cameron (1992) feel the key to under-standing how to attract visitors is by 'examining their values and linking both values and attitudes with actual and intended behaviour' Cameron (1992: 155). This approach supports the examination of *psychographic characteristics*, whereby actual and potential visitors are grouped according to their beliefs, attitudes, and values. A study in the UK conducted by Schul and Crompton (1983) used psychographic information as a way to analyse and segment the search behaviour of vacationers who used the Internet. A factor analysis revealed six composite psychographic dimensions, including 'cultural interest', 'convenience' and 'knowledge seeker' along which these travellers were described and evaluated. Analysis of the results led to the creation of two different psychographic profiles in the tourist consumer choice process: active and passive planners.

Perhaps one of the most commonly cited psychographic techniques is that developed by Plog (1998). Utilising the concept that all societies have a central tendency toward certain beliefs and behaviours Plog examined travellers in terms of how closely they fitted their society's psychological norm for any behaviour. As a result of his studies Plog developed a pattern of psychographic segments that had a normal distribution surrounding the mid-centric norm. Moving away from the central mid-centrics Plog (1998: 254–6) identifies an *allocentric* group who are more venturesome and self-assured individuals who seek out more novel and unique destinations.

At the other extreme are the *psychocentric* group, who are self-inhibited and anxious personality types seeking dependability in all that they do. These individuals are very conservative about travel, either selecting to stay close to home or if they try international travel, preferring to travel in the safe environmental bubble of a tour group that maximises the use of home language and facilities. However, this classification is a snapshot and individual categories can and do change over time. It is noticeable that the early American tourist ventures into Europe after World War II were dominated by tours – leading to the 'If it's Tuesday it must be Belgium' film topic. But with experience and survival many of these earlier psychocentric tourists became free independent travellers (FIT market) and moved to the mid-centric or allocentric areas of Plog's continuum.

The main benefit of using psychographic information for tracking and predicting tourist actions is that such information can be used to create a context for understanding traveller motivations. Understanding the moti-vations of travel market segments and preparing tourism offerings to satisfy them is the most direct route to pleasing customers and turning them into a loyal client. The main drawback with using psychographic data to track and predict tourist's actions is that while this data helps to better understand what tourists want, it is incomplete. This is because it only addresses the 'individual interests' section of Figure 7.1. There is not always a direct or obvious correlation between personal attitudes and actual behaviour, as various psychology studies have indicated (Mayo & Jarvis, 1981; Ross, 1994).

Another problem some destinations have experienced is translating the factor or cluster analysis groupings into meaningful and reachable subgroups. For example, how helpful are identified groups with catchy titles, if you do not know how stable these groups are or how best to reach them through the media. In addition, the commercial emphasis and proprietorship of some of the key psychographic techniques has prevented independent scholarly assessment of their validity and reliability (Ross, 1994). To overcome such limitations psychographic segmentation is now closely linked to other techniques, such as behavioural segmentation.

Behavioural segmentation focuses on past actions as a way of predicting future actions. 'Behavioural segmentation divides customers by their usage rates, usage status and potential, brand loyalty, use occasions, and benefits sought' (Morrison, 1989: 150). Woodside and Carr (1988) have used past behaviours as a way of segmenting markets according to their established 'decision styles', which they define as the ways in which people make their travel decisions. One problem with behavioural segmentation is that past actions will not always serve as a good predictor of future intentions, especially when personal conditions, needs and associated circumstances change over time. Hence, once again the best form of market segmentation is a combination of techniques.

Market positioning

To achieve a competitive edge in market segmentation will require businesses and destinations to position their product. *Positioning* is the 'development of a service and marketing mix to occupy a specific place in the minds of customers within target markets' (Morrison, 1989: 175). As such it is a prime way to differentiate the local product and to set it firmly in the mindset of the targeted market. Judd (1995) notes how US cities have been forced to promote and position themselves for the tourism market with the reductions in federal urban renewal funding in the early 1980s. This was one way they could raise their profile in the eyes of potential visitors and investors, and revitalise certain districts in their central areas.

According to Morrison (1989: 191) effective positioning requires five 'D' steps. These are:

(1) *Documenting* – identifying the benefits that are most important to your customers.
(2) *Deciding* – selecting the image that you want your customers to have within your chosen target markets.
(3) *Differentiating* – identifying the competitors from which you want to appear different and the things that will make you different.

(4) *Designing* – providing product or service differences and communicating these in positioning statements and via the marketing mix.
(5) *Delivering* – making good on your promises.

Part of preparing for customers is organising tourism offerings, to gain and maintain a distinctive position in the marketplace for a product, service or destination (Lovelock, 1992). If this process is successful and people come to associate a product, service or place with its marketed image, such as equating Florida with sunshine, then the commodity is referred to as 'branded'. That is it has common recognition and acceptance. As such it has a distinct advantage when customers come to consider their options.

Kotler (2001: 55) has linked positioning and branding as a two-phase process in his steps to develop a strong brand. His first phase is to develop a 'value' position by:

- choosing a *broad positioning* for the product;
- choosing a *specific positioning* for the product;
- choosing a *value positioning* for the product;
- developing a *total value proposition* for the product.

This then leads to the brand development by:

- choosing a *brand name*;
- developing *rich associations and promises* for the brand name;
- managing all the customers' *brand contacts* so that they meet or exceed the customers' expectations associated with the brand.

It has been demonstrated that when there is a clear recognition of a brand and its position (offerings) in the market it is possible to develop a loyal market following, as in the case of Wal-Mart. This worldwide chain has grown from a single store in Arkansas to 4600 stores across 10 countries on the basis of low prices and a wide range of products (Saporito, 2003). At the destination level the Mt Buller resort in Australia believes 'companies with a strong brand perform better. Their customers are more loyal and the brand is top of mind for the market when they go to make their purchasing decision' (Hamilton, 2002). Consequently its brand name 'Mt Buller My Mountain' attempts to build on its strong ski club history, its easy access to Melbourne, its leadership in tourism education and the warm hospitality of its village.

Destinations need to position themselves appropriately with their preferred customers to ensure they maximise their return on tourism investments. Procedures for a general positioning strategy include detailed analysis of the following elements:

Market

All businesses need to understand their customers in order to better meet their needs, but with the intangible service experiences of tourism and the collective nature of a destination visit who is going to find out this information and how? In many instances it has become a responsibility of the local destination-marketing organisation, which has various options open to it. To search for the appropriate market segments it can utilise state and national surveys that reveal market trends and interests. To identify potential visitors it can join the regular consumer omnibus surveys that use established panels of consumers or those annoying telephone surveys. A destination can purchase several questions in those consumer surveys relating to their potential appeal as part of general consumer and marketing questions. To determine how well it is serving its current customers a good method is an 'exit survey' of visitors, as they are leaving the area and their memories are sharp.

Determining a destination's market potential should start by examining the current travellers to the area. Visitor surveys, as well as interviews with tourism providers and focus group discussions with tourism stakeholders in the community can provide data to understand what attracts the tourists and how satisfied they are with the current product. Surveys can both confirm conventional local wisdom and reveal some unexpected nuggets of information.

Competition

All businesses and destinations should be aware they are not operating alone in the tourism market and should know who their competition is and what they are offering. Many businesses hire 'secret shoppers' to scout out what rivals are offering and doing to attract their customers. In business being copied is not viewed as the highest form of compliment but as one of the greatest threats to long-term success. To minimise this risk they must focus on an aspect that will differentiate them and would be difficult to emulate.

For most destinations the competition is local, with nearby communities offering similar landscape and heritage products. But it does not have to be that way. Tourism, like certain retail establishments can build upon the drawing power of agglomeration and the provision of a critical mass to entice tourists to visit a destination area (Jones & Simmons, 1987). Just as the retail sector has found it advantageous to place similar outlets together at times to facilitate comparison shopping, as with fashion and car sales, tourist destinations can benefit from aligning themselves with other destinations in a region. This could provide sufficient combined attractiveness to draw visitors and to hold them overnight somewhere in the region, especially for those visitors travelling a long distance.

Internal operations

To operationalise the above market research and develop a competitive image requires the organisation of resources and development of a marketing strategy. Community and industry cohesion over issues of tourism development can be challenging due to the large number of affected stakeholders and the uncertainties that surround tourism growth. The information gained in assessing an area's market potential and principal competitors needs to be organised and assessed within the context of what's best for the industry and the community. Consultative meetings with stakeholders can assist in developing appropriate tourism strategies and plans, which in turn will direct the marketing position of the destination.

The importance of organisational structure and collaboration has become more evident as the tourism industry has become increasingly competitive and the need for collaboration more evident. Pearce (1992) has outlined the growth and complexity of various levels of tourism organisation that have evolved over the past decades. Selin and Beason (1991a: 208) have been pioneers in examining ways to enhance collaboration between tourism organisations and note that 'while the tourism industry has become increasingly competitive, there are strong incentives for tourism organisations to collaborate under certain conditions'. These conditions include the benefits of combining forces to draw visitors to a region.

Top of mind awareness

Even if a destination has what tourists desire, they are unlikely to visit unless the destination is one of their top destination choices. It has been documented that many people considering a vacation will consider approximately four destinations prior to making their holiday plans (Bronner & de Hoog, 1985; Thompson & Cooper, 1979). 'First brand awareness', which is also referred to as 'top of mind awareness (TOMA)' has shown itself to be a strong predictor of consumer purchasing in general (Axelrod, 1968: Woodside & Wilson, 1985).

Woodside and Carr (1988) conducted a study to assess the awareness of foreign travel destinations by US vacation travellers, as a means of determining the relationship between TOMA and travel choices. They asked respondents which countries outside of the US first came to mind when they thought about taking a vacation. The top four countries that came to mind for the survey participants were the UK (27%), France (10%), China (9%) and Australia (8%). Upon comparing this data with actual international travel choices by US tourists, they found a strong correspondence between a high awareness of a destination and high visitation rates for the top two destinations. However, countries that were not even mentioned, including Canada and Mexico, received far greater US tourist numbers than either China or Australia. One needs to realise that while certain places will stand out in people's minds, even in a very positive way, other factors such as time, distance, cost, and a lack of information regarding distant destinations can keep dreams of visiting such places from becoming reality. This is represented as the search cessation in Figure 7.1.

Positioning involves three interrelated customer focused components: image, market segmentation and priority promotional features (Aaker & Shansby, 1982). Given the importance of image, it is not surprising that a considerable amount of attention has been paid to this specific aspect of destination development.

Image

An important aspect of positioning is the image a destination wishes to develop and portray of itself. Deciding on what image to develop and designing the relevant promotional material generally has been left to industry or government experts, with little input from local residents who have to live with the outcome. At times this can lead to some unfortunate and unpopular choices that can create embarrassment all around. As Metelka (1977: 4) observed in an old, but still relevant, paper 'past and present marketing practices reflect the fact that destination area residents are overwhelmingly unaware of how their homeland is described in promotional material'. At other times the experts have hit the right button for residents as well as visitors. For example, British Columbia in Canada has long positioned itself as the 'SuperNatural' province; that describes its scenic wonders concisely and fits with its residents' views of their homeland. Likewise, the state of Victoria in Australia has positioned its variety and heritage very well with its 'Jigsaw' campaign, that invites visitors and locals alike to explore every piece of the state.

The more that destinations and individual service providers understand the image their target markets have of them then the better suited they will be to meet visitor needs and fulfil or exceed their expectations. Visitors have been found to prefer destinations that have strong, salient and benign images (Hunt, 1975: Woodside & Lysonski, 1989). Providing a strong, clear image that resonates with selected target markets in a positioning strategy helps potential visitors to establish a 'mental fix' on tourism offerings. The intangibility of the vacation experience makes this type of explicit positioning strategy necessary, as it provides both a means of differentiating tourism offerings from one another and an incentive to purchase.

Within the general positioning strategies tourist destinations have payed particular attention to the development of an appropriate and competitive image to assist the customer's search process. Gunn (1997: 37–8) describes images of tourist destinations as either being *organic*, in that they are formed from one's previous information, such as news coverage and books, or as being *induced*, in that they are formed as a direct result of marketing and promotion. Before setting out on a vacation customers'

image of a potential holiday destination will likely include some precon-
ceived ideas of what they can expect, supplemented by promotional
materials and travel advice from others.

The attention to image is increasingly combining research into customer
expectations, their reactions to the proffered images, and how these images
compare to their real experiences and assessments. Customers tend to look
for clues about a provider's capabilities and qualities prior to making
purchases (Berry & Clark, 1986; Shostack, 1977). This tendency increases
with the cost and uncertainty of the commodity in question. In regard to
tourism, these clues play an important role in forming destination images
(Pearce, 1982). Since taking a holiday can be costly in terms of time, money
and energy people explore their options to help them make the right
holiday choices (Schul & Crompton, 1983).

Once the choice has been made the tourist-customer will experience the
realities of the destination environment and will judge how well they
support the promoted image. Bitner (1992) used the term 'servicescape' to
describe the ability of a working environment to affect customers. She
found that servicescapes can either assist with or detract from the organisational and marketing goals of a service provider, including the promoted
image. Bitner found that the physical design of service industries assisted
with their positioning and segmentation strategies and enhanced certain
marketing objectives, including customer satisfaction and attraction.
Servicescape elements that can influence customer behaviours include the
following:

- *ambient conditions* – such as lighting, noise, and smells;
- *spatial layout and general functionality* – the appearance of the physical
  setting and how well the elements work together; and
- *signs* – these can include written signs as well as more subtle indicators of values and appropriate codes of behaviour.

A good example of this process at work on a micro-scale is McDonald's
interior design work, developed to create an attractive, friendly and clean
environment that is welcoming to their families target market. On a larger
plant scale there is the example of the Disney theme parks. Their attention
to access and parking, convenient transfers to the park gate, theme areas
within the park, and a queue management process that converts an
unpleasant activity into a bearable experience has helped to make these
attractions world leaders in their field. The benchmark examples set by
these successful companies have been noted and copied by a variety of
tourist destinations, and have worked even when the destination did not
possess the full control of a private company. York, England, has turned an
archaeological find into a major tourism attraction using Disney principles
at its Jorvik Centre. Williamsburg, Virginia, has restored and recreated a

pioneer settlement in the midst of a modern city. Kyongju, in South Korea, has surrounded its tomb mounds of Shilla dynasty kings with beautiful gardens and restored artefacts and attractions (Figure 7.2).

As has been noted elsewhere, customers of the tourism industry will include employees and local residents, so the servicescape should also consider their needs. It has been found that the environments of service organisations affect employees as well as the customers they serve. Work environments that meet employees' needs have been found to increase their motivation, satisfaction and productivity (Bitner, 1992; Davis, 1984). Furthermore, it stands to reason that an attractive tourism environment in their community can affect residents' support for local tourism. Resident surveys that will be reported more fully in a later chapter indicate strong support for tourism where it has contributed to the appearance and amenities of the community.

Bramwell and Rawding (1996) have presented a clear delineation of the importance of imagery and how different perspectives influence its assessment. Geographers emphasise the importance of local 'landscape, history and traditions, cultural patterns, community values and power relations, and these come together in a unique way within the locality' (Bramwell & Rawding, 1996: 203), creating its 'sense of place'. Shaw and Williams (1994) recommend that places need to project their distinctive local and 'unique' place images in order to enhance their tourism appeal. This would respond to Urry's (1990) argument that modern tourists are seeking cultural and landscape features that draw them out of their everyday lives through their 'tourist gaze'.

Marketers emphasise the issue of place/destination substitution and advocate images that build on the unique benefits of a destination, be they natural or artificial, to enhance its competitive advantage. By integrating place images into a planned brand identity approach to positioning, it is expected to build visitor and investor confidence in the area by its contribution to a planned cohesive marketing strategy. An example of this approach is provided by Rouse's festival marketplaces and harbour redevelopment projects throughout the US (Kotler *et al.* 1993: 125–6). Gilbert (1990) has recommended that places use images to position themselves as status areas rather than as commodity areas. A status area is one that promotes its special attributes that cannot be found elsewhere and thus appeals to up-market visitors who wish to be associated with such status. It is the difference between a resort that emphasises its villas, exclusive casinos and yacht clubs, and one that promotes its beaches and inexpensive accommodation and entertainment.

Critical sociologists contend that as tourism becomes more global the pressures to differentiate through image increase, and as mass tourism loses its appeal the marketing emphasis is shifting more to individual consumption (Urry, 1990). However, at the same time the challenge is to stand

Figure 7.2 Kyongju, old capital of the Shilla dynasty in South Korea

out in an increasingly homogenised global economy while respecting the needs and desires of local residents (Britton, 1991; Harvey, 1989). As one can see from recent World Trade Organisation meetings around the world on advancing the global economy, some people feel the threat to local economies and ways of life is too high a price to pay for such progress and have demonstrated against such globalisation.

In their analysis of the tourist images created for five old industrial English cities Bramwell and Rawding (1996: 217) conclude 'tourism marketing images have a wider significance than initially may be apparent'. They note there will be both 'winners' and 'losers' in the development of community tourism images. Consequently, they call for a broader multidisciplinary approach that analyses images in relation to their distribution of benefits among residents as well as with respect to regular business accountability.

At the community level one of the biggest challenges is to coordinate the numerous individual business and personal interests into a united message that will promote the community in the tourism marketplace. To achieve this more communities are organising themselves into destination-marketing associations that have the mandate to create a corporate community image and positioning strategy to present to the world. These are just one of the elements in the general organisation of the travel trade, which has the role of connecting tourism products with prospective customers through a variety of distribution channels.

When Gunn (1979: 145) noted that 'one of the weakest links in all tourism is that of imparting information', his words spoke of the need to analyse and improve the performance of the tourism industry with particular regard to consumer awareness and response. To create such improved industry performance in this area will require leadership.

Leadership

New and emerging theories of customer behaviour and marketing are starting to re-shape the ways tourism operators and destinations view their target markets. The growing sophistication and individual demands of increasingly knowledgeable and experienced travellers is forcing the industry to not only segment the market into sub-groups but at times down to specific individuals, or a market of one. The Internet is providing new ways to reach customers and for them to book directly. Finally, destination-marketing organisations are taking on a greater leadership role in that they are becoming the focal point for tourism research, analysis, marketing and planning for the industry in their area. This leadership, taking place across the many spectrums of tourism development, provides a guide to improve the functioning of the tourism industry.

Marketing leadership

The intense level of competition for modern consumers has led to some marketing innovations that destinations need to consider. According to *The Economist* (2001b: 9) 'only happy customers will be loyal ones – and loyalty is something companies desperately need if they are to survive in today's difficult climate'. It goes on to say 'The right approach to retaining customers starts with trying to understand more about them, and then to work out what to do with the knowledge'. This advice and some recent marketing trends have particular relevance to tourism destinations.

Relationship marketing is one relevant strategy because it addresses 'the twin concerns (of) getting and keeping customers' (Christopher *et al.*, 1991: vii). It is a strategy of building long-term satisfying relations with key parties such as customers and business partners (Kotler, 1997) and involves the development of quality products, customer service and marketing into a combined and total approach to customer relations. In tourism it is a process of detecting prospective customers, turning them into first-time visitors, then into repeat visitors who become 'clients' and advocates for the destination – in effect partners in its success. As such relationship marketing is based on the premise that important customers and associates require continuous and focused attention.

Some people consider that if relationship marketing is taken to its full extent it becomes the *marketing of one*, focusing on each customer as an individual with their own needs and expectations to be fulfilled. The power of individual consumers, with their own wishes and schedule, has become an important factor and meeting such needs is one important way to differentiate a destination. However, one should always remember the 80:20 rule adopted from Pareto, that says it is best to concentrate on those customers (the 80%) you can please rather than spend too many resources on customers (the remaining 20%) who will be difficult if not impossible to satisfy.

Catering to one or a few individuals is an expensive personal service and not every community can afford such a strategy. Butler (1990) was one of the first to point this out as a major pitfall to the alternative or green tourism market ideal and the experiences in many parts of the world have borne him out. Consequently, many destinations need to find ways in which to appeal to individual or small group interests, but in such numbers as provide sufficient returns on the investments made by the host community. One possible solution is the concept of *mass customisation* that 'involves the selling of highly individual products but on a mass scale' (*The Economist*, 2001c: 63).

Mass customerisation can be seen as an extension of the 'built-to-order' process in manufacturing. Where companies such as 'Dell Computer and Renault already make extensive use of BTO systems, shortening delivery times and trimming work-in-progress ... that means turning a production-push industry into a demand-pull one' (*The Economist*, 2001c: 63). In tourism this can be and is being, achieved by developing guest profiles to ensure their needs are anticipated and by variable packaging that enables more customised products for the visitor. This move to mass customerisation is a real boon to small businesses with local contacts, for they can adjust schedules and improvise more easily than large corporations that are often locked into long-term contractual arrangements.

Since such long-term and customer oriented marketing strategies would undoubtedly have significant impacts on the type of image and product developed by a destination, they can be seen as worthy of *macro-marketing* analysis. 'Macro-marketing refers to the study of (1) marketing systems, (2) the impact and consequences of marketing systems on society, and (3) the impact and consequences of society on marketing systems' (Meade II and Nason, 1991: 73). In such a context the marketing strategies of a destination would be assessed in terms of a two-way interaction, between the customer and the destination. This would recognise two customers – the visitor and the host, and could help to minimise some of the false expectations that have been created in the past for both parties.

As indicated in the above marketing relationships, to reach and satisfy today's demanding customer will require more effort and partners. Day, who is an advocate of using marketing to create value, has identified three positioning themes to help make customer-oriented marketing more successful. For him a business should strive to be:

- *Better* – through the provision of superior quality and service.
- *Faster* – by being able to sense and meet shifting customer requirements quicker than its competitors.
- *Closer* – with the creation of desirable linkages, relationships, and even partnerships which channel members and customers. (Day, 1990: 173)

Responding to customer wishes is still the main route to success, but in terms of modern marketing it now involves a combination of individual customisation with the higher total returns of less noticeable mass production, all within the setting of destination accountability.

Technology

One of the first to highlight the significance of technological development and leadership to tourism was Poon (1993). She noted 'By far the most important area of impact of technology will be in the areas of marketing, distribution and sales' (Poon, 1993: 176), and went on to demonstrate what significant strides in efficiency and productivity had been achieved with the introduction of computer reservation systems (CRS). However, most of her examples relate to major corporations and destinations, where the high cost of CRS development and IT infrastructure in the 1980s encouraged strategic corporate linkages and a significant delay to the return on investment. What has occurred since Poon's important work is the rise of the Internet and the marketing power this is placing in the hands of the small operator and less well-known destinations to reach their targeted customers.

The Internet's interactive capabilities have assisted in the delivery of quality products and service by creating opportunities to monitor what aspects of a tourism product, service or destination appeal to customers (Tierney, 2000). The raw interest or appeal can be measured through 'hits per site', which is the number of times a site is viewed by customers browsing the Web. Such basic information can be enhanced by including interactive elements in website designs to measure specific customer interests. This can be achieved by providing options for the down-loading of particular features or attractions, as well as offering direct purchase and booking services.

There is an opportunity to combine information and sales with customer surveys over the Web that has the potential to produce more customer intelligence for individual operations and destinations in an efficient and relatively low cost manner. However, some methodological weaknesses have been found with such surveys; such as response and non-response bias, and multiple and unwanted entries (Schonland & Williams, 1996). In his study of the research effectiveness of tourism websites Tierney (2000) suggests that while the Internet can provide more frequent and targeted contact with customers, the greatest challenge with the tourism surveys on the Web is low response rates. He suggests these could be bolstered by providing incentives, such as prize drawings, to attract people to complete the survey. However, care should be taken to ensure the prize is not too grand, which may tempt people more interested in the prize than the topic to enter more than once.

One point that Poon makes is that destinations will be dealing with 'new tourists' and will have to market accordingly. These new tourists are 'consumers who are flexible, independent and experienced travellers, whose values and lifestyles are different from those of the mass tourists' (Poon, 1993: 114). These new tourists have the following key attributes that require different focuses and approaches.

- More experienced – their travel experiences have made them more aware of quality and more demanding, they now seek more variety and wish to fulfil their special interests.
- Changing values – they are more educated and have a greater appreciation of global differences, they search for authentic experiences, are sensitive to the environment, and wish to become involved.
- Changing lifestyles – they are healthier, have more flexible hours, more income, and view travel as a way of life.

- Products of changing demographics – the aging population of Western countries, fewer children, longer retirements with sufficient funds for travel.
- More flexible – they are better informed and freer of constraints so they can be spontaneous, flexible and unpredictable leading to hybrid consumption patterns.
- More independent-minded – they want to be 'in charge', are more willing to take risks, and to break out of the mould. (Poon, 1993: 114–15).

Examples of some of these new tourists and their relevance to destination marketing are presented below.

Adventure tourists

Adventure tourists are those who seek some excitement in their activity, including a sense of danger for some. This segment ranges from 'soft' adventures such as bird or whale watching activities, to 'hard' adventures such as overnight wilderness hikes or sea kayaking, scuba diving and ski sports. Such tourism opportunities can be provided in a variety of destinations and can involve a range of business types and scales. One issue which is impacting this sector, however, is the growing number of insurance claims and court cases that are causing liability insurance rates to skyrocket and generating the need for strong risk management.

Backpackers

Backpackers are young travellers, who prefer budget accommodation, long and informal independent vacation experiences (Ross, 1993). Such travel takes them beyond the major cities and tourist icons to the regional areas of overseas destinations; as they seek to learn more about the country and its people or casual work, often both. This market has become a major international tourism segment for Australia, and is one segment that is holding up well despite the world terrorism of the past two years.

Ecotourists

Ecotourists are tourists who visit natural areas and engage in some form of education-based field excursion (Wight, 1996). This special interest group does open up many new areas to tourism, including the Arctic and Antarctica, and provides business opportunities to small businesses and communities. However, Butler (1990) has cautioned industry enthusiasts about the need to maintain small-scale development for this market segment, and Price (2003) has noted that the education component needs far more development.

Education market

The biggest element of the large 'Meetings, Incentives, Conferences and Events' (MICE) sector are the small corporate or local association meetings. These are designed to bring together members on a regular basis, but outside of their normal work environment, so they can interact and learn without interruption. Accordingly, resort businesses and destinations that are different yet convenient make ideal locations for such business. This provides significant opportunity to resorts and destinations which surround major urban centres to provide business meeting getaways that can supplement their regular tourism business and help even out the seasonality of pleasure travel.

Seniors

Today's seniors are significantly healthier, better educated and financially more secure than in the past, plus many can expect 10 years or more of active retirement. Thus, they are becoming an important tourist segment. Many are travelling as FITs, to visit with global friends and relatives or to catch up with long-awaited vacation dreams. Some are settling down with their favourite sport (such as golf) or moving to their favourite climate and holiday spot (Florida, Queensland, Mediterranean), while others are increasing their knowledge through group tours and university level instruction (Elder Hostel and Odyssey Travel). Therefore, this market is proving to be as diverse in its interests as the fragmenting mass market, making many different destinations and tourism activities attractive to the seniors.

Controlling

To understand how well a business and destination are satisfying their customers requires regular monitoring of customer experiences and the outcomes of current marketing and operational strategies. Both the individual businesses and the destination community need to develop indicators of achievement with which to measure their programmes and products. These should be applied in such a way as to minimise customer inconvenience and conducted on a regular basis to provide a realistic profile of customer experiences and reactions.

A good place to start is with the image and positioning strategy, to see if the customer is aware of the business or destination message in a very crowded marketplace. To determine whether current advertising practices are meeting performance objectives will require a marketing audit. 'A marketing audit is a comprehensive, systematic, independent, and periodic examination of a company's environment, objectives, strategies, and activities to determine problem areas and opportunities and to recommend a plan of action to improve the company's marketing performance' (Kotler & Armstrong, 1989: 540). Among these broad objectives is the 'marketing functions audit' that includes an assessment of advertising and sales, and the effectiveness of the distribution system (Kotler, 2001: 197).

Conversion studies

A logical method to assess the effectiveness of advertising is to determine the level of enquiries, patronage or sales generated by a specific advertising campaign, which is called its conversion rate. Unfortunately, conversion studies have generally been internal operations so there are relatively few in the public domain, and those that have been published reveal it is a challenging task to link customer behaviour with specific marketing campaigns. In fact conversion studies can become misleading to the uninitiated.

Burke and Gitelson (1990) have written a cautionary tale about the pitfalls of conversion studies. They note that in the past some rather questionable claims have been made of 60–80% conversion rates and returns on advertising investment ratios of $23–100:$1. Such results often occur due to a lack of rigorous research standards, so Burke and Gitelson's article points out potential research design pitfalls and ways to bring more rigour and objectivity to these measures. They advocate the following 10 steps for developing better conversion rate studies.

(1) Understand the travel decision process is an information search that is influenced by a host of variables and not just advertising. As shown in Figure 7.1 at the beginning of this chapter.

(2) Recognise the limitations of conversion studies, to minimise their misuse and misinterpretation.

(3) Understand that accomplishing the goal of increased 'return business' will reduce the 'net' conversion rate from advertising.

(4) Select proportionally representative and randomly selected research samples.

(5) Determine an acceptable sampling precision for the study.

(6) Address non-response bias by determining if respondents are representative of all enquirers.

(7) Differentiate between those who were influenced by an advertising campaign to visit ('net' conversion) and those who had already decided to visit.

(8) Define the destination area in detail so that actual visitor numbers and spending are attributed correctly.

(9) Identify the portion of a tourist's spending that produces economic benefits for the destination.

(10) Include all costs (not just advertising, production and placement) in

determining the return on investment of a promotional campaign. (Based on Burke & Gitelson, 1990: 50)

It is challenging to accomplish all the steps, but simply striving for such goals will improve the quality of a conversion study and the accuracy of its findings.

A specific conversion return study of a British Columbia 'Spring Visit campaign' aimed at the California market reveals the utility of this audit approach. The study by Pritchard and Swanson (1993) sampled 1205 Californians who had responded to advertisements placed in their state by using a toll-free telephone number supplied by Tourism BC. Pritchard and Swanson's postal survey of the California residents revealed a 23% conversion of those callers who made specific enquiries. They estimated that each Californian traveller to BC that season spent an average C$1005.32, resulting in a total revenue of C$2,200,977 from the campaign. This compares favourably with a C$303,199 expenditure on various Californian media outlets used in the campaign, representing a sevenfold return without taking into account the cost of assembling and designing the advertising campaign. However, examination of the return from the various distribution channels reveals the return on investment varied significantly across the different media outlets (Table 7.1). Even though the major city newspaper was the most expensive media outlet used, it presented one of the better returns due to its prestige and circulation. But the best return came from the city magazine and the worst from radio advertising.

Satisfaction audits

Once customers are at the place of business or destination it is important to determine how well the travel experience is matching their expectations and how satisfied they are with their experience. To find out how happy

Table 7.1 Return on investment

Media	ROI ($CN)
Big City Newspaper	$11.06
Community Newspapers	$4.37
Big City Magazine	$11.11
Bus Sides/Other	$9.93
Radio	$4.09
Direct Mail	$7.91
Total	$7.26

Source: Pritchard and Swanson (1993), BC Tourism 1993 Advertising Effectiveness Study, Victoria BC, Tourism BC and School of Business, University of Victoria, 10

customers are, operators need only to use their eyes and ears. They should study their customers by 'walking the talk' and working alongside their staff at times. They should place themselves in the position of a customer and see how the approach to their business will be viewed by a stranger and what sort of welcome they receive when they come through the door. A lot of this is 'common sense', but it is remarkable how rare this intuition has become.

A common problem is adequate and appropriate signage, but fieldtrip experiences with tourism students has revealed some amazing experiences. These include:

- wrong instructions on a directional sign;
- a blank wall separating a tourist attraction from the major highway link;
- lack of things to do or buy at transport terminals;
- lack of product knowledge;
- lack of instruction and care with certain adventure tourism activities.

If the business operator wishes to investigate beyond surface levels s(he) will need to interrupt the service experience with some form of survey. This could be a casual enquiry through striking up a conversation with customers that includes some questions regarding their experiences with the business and destination, or through simple survey questionnaires as are found in many restaurants and hotels. Either way this form of information gathering should not become intrusive, to the extent that it interferes with the experience.

The importance of marketing audits to destinations has been emphasised in Mazanec's (1997) book on city tourism. Within this review of organisational needs and processes in Europe, Wober (1997: 26–38) noted the need for local destination marketing associations to gather data on accommodation usage, visitor activities spending patterns and origins, that should be coordinated with published national and state statistics. By combining local primary data with published secondary data a destination can develop a long-term profile of its visitors and industry performance. This type of information can be used to identify shortcomings and to guide future promotion and development. This has certainly been the case within the city of Victoria in British Columbia, Canada.

Victoria's destination marketing association – Tourism Victoria – has been collecting data on its visitors since 1989. It has been aided in this by the support it has received from its constituent members, especially the transport sector that has assisted with its visitor exit surveys and the hotels and motels that have participated in the regular occupancy – charges surveys conducted by a local accountancy company. Victoria is particularly fortunate in having an ideal situation for exit surveys, because it is on an island and most visitors need to wait for a certain period of time for their ferry or airline connection to the mainland. Under these circumstances a short survey of their recent travel experiences is a welcome diversion, so excellent response rates have been the norm.

Data from the visitor exit surveys have revealed both problems and potential opportunities for future development. An early problem was disappointing visitor responses to the question regarding 'value for money'. This is a major issue for an industry that depends on tourists incurring the extra travel costs to reach Vancouver Island while mainland destinations like Vancouver and Seattle were becoming more aggressive and competitive for the tourism business. Tourism Victoria shared this information with its members and encouraged them to focus on changing the situation. It was gratifying to see a steady rise in the evaluation of Victoria's value for money over the years, to the point where the clear majority of tourists now feel they receive good value for money. Potential future developments have arisen from questions regarding 'what is missing' or what type of attractions 'would attract tourist back' to the city. An early identified 'missing' element was the opportunity to view the local whales and seals. This has now been rectified with the development of several whale/ wildlife watching tours. Another was the popularity of the British Columbia Provincial Museum's early 'block-buster' exhibits. These generated such a favourable response that they have become a regular feature, giving locals and visitors a reason to return to this outstanding attraction.

Risk management

An important aspect of delivering the promised and anticipated level of experience is an appropriate 'duty of care'. If businesses or destinations fail to deliver reasonable care and attention in their operations they can expect to be sued for unsatisfactory experiences, injury or death in this litigious age. 'Between 1998 and 2000, the number of public liability claims Australia-wide rose by 60% to 88,000; total payments rose by 52% to A$724 million' (Feizkhah, 2002: 46). The cost of protecting themselves against lawsuits is causing many businesses, community groups and destinations to limit activities like adventure tourism and festivals. It has become so bad that a _Time Magazine_ article on the subject cites the following experience. 'Can I sue' asked one wit in a letter to the Sydney _Morning Herald_ "if I walk into a warning sign if there is no warning sign warning me of the warning?' (Feizkhah, 2002: 46). Consequently, another relevant audit for today's customer is the risk management audit.

There is an element of risk in almost every undertaking or decision people engage in, but the key in law is that business operators must demonstrate they provided 'reasonable care' for 'foreseeable acts or situations' with respect to their customers. Consequently, tourism businesses and destinations need to show they have established a reasonable duty of care toward the safe enjoyment of their products and experiences, and the best way to achieve that is to manage the risk. This is accomplished by identifying potential risks involved with the tourism business. Measure the frequency and magnitude of loss due to those risks, using established records or own data, to determine their degree of seriousness. Develop systems (physical or human) to either reduce or eliminate the risks. Determine, when there is an incident, whether to absorb the costs through direct compensation or to call upon insurance companies, to whom the risk has been transferred through an insurance policy and premiums.

In his book on risk management in adventure tourism, Cloutier (2000: 104–5) cites some advice from Will Leverette that has wide applicability. Leverette recommends six easy risk management steps for tourism operators:

(1) Develop a means to prove that guests were adequately warned and informed.
(2) Any guarantee of safety made in a business' literature, or marketing materials is an open invitation to be sued.
(3) All field staff must have current training in basic first aid.
(4) The business should develop a written emergency / evacuation plan for all areas and activities to be used.
(5) One good witness statement will shut down a frivolous lawsuit faster, more cheaply and less painfully than will anything else.
(6) The business must use a properly drafted liability release form.

He goes on to make the point that such management should be motivated by the desire to ensure a tourist has the best possible experience. The fact that this same planning will reduce the chance of a frivolous lawsuit is simply a bonus.

Summary

It is essential in this competitive business world that businesses put the customer first.

Their needs and priorities will need to be considered and wherever possible met, if individual tourism businesses and destinations are to draw sufficient numbers and revenue to survive and prosper. An important planning step in reaching that goal is to understand how customers choose their options and how individual businesses and destinations can identify those segments they feel best able to satisfy.

The organising component of this chapter provides an in-depth look at how the marketing positioning of destination influences the likelihood that desired tourists will visit these places. Destination awareness and preferences are strong factors in predicting what types of tourists and how many of these tourists a destination can hope to attract. The value of emerging theories and technologies in marketing and organising, and their relevance to community tourism, are a focus of the leadership component of this chapter. Finally, the control component in this chapter looks at the scope and scale and impact of tourism advertising. Particular attention is paid to the challenges inherent in taking the appropriate care of tourists once they arrive, to ensure their visit is both enjoyable and safe.

Questions that destinations need to ask themselves are which customers are likely to be attracted to us, which of these customers do we want and how can we better attract our desired markets? Once these questions have been answered then the questions to explore include which customers are actually visiting us, how satisfied are they with their experiences and finally what are the appropriate changes to be made to the travel destinations products, services and marketing in order to remain competitive. The following chapter explores the role that industry can play in the development of community oriented tourism destinations.

Chapter 8

Industry

The popularity of the phrase 'tourism industry' in both scholarly and industry publications implies there really is such an industry. However, this is 'not the case' claims Smith (2003b: 1). Because the 'tourism industry' cannot be captured statistically by a system of national accounts and census definitions Smith would rather consider tourism as an 'economic constellation – a grouping of numerous industries in the transportation, accommodation, food service, recreation and entertainment, and travel trade sectors that creates a picture of something more than the simple collection of the parts' (Smith, 2003b: 1). Consequently Smith would prefer to speak of 'tourism industries'.

While the current facts support Smith's perspective, the shape of modern industry and spirit of innovation would not. Most of the standard industrial classification (SIC) systems developed around the world have their origin in the Victorian era when the emphasis was on primary and secondary manufacturing processes, not on service. Consequently, if we examine one of the SICs used by Smith in his paper to determine the scale and structure of Canada's tourism we find under the classification 'Education Service Industries' only one entry – Museums and Archives. Although these represent a tangible achievement of the Victorian era and we have all benefited from this legacy, it is no longer an adequate description of this important tourism sector. Where are the Visitor Information Centres, the tertiary education departments that specialise in tourism, or the myriad of consultants? All of these groups earn a living by contributing to the knowledge base of tourists and providers.

This one example of the inadequacy of official statistical classifications for the tourism industry is repeated in every SIC because tourism is a modern service industry that has witnessed innovations in service and products that were unheard of in Victorian times. Developments such as sub-orbital space flights and tram / trolley dining are difficult to place in any of the current transport or dining categories. The growing interest in space tourism, where the tourist expenditures can make the critical difference between launch or no launch, is probably still classified as scientific research rather than transportation, and certainly not as tourism.

The spirit of tourism activity has been innovation but one of the major shortcomings in its operators has been a tardiness to come together and work as one industry with one voice. This has not been helped by government bureaucratic statistics and the suspicions of established industries to the newcomer on the block, nor by the small business orientation of most operators and the ubiquitous nature of tourism activity. But if one is to look at various definitions of industry there is hope and direction as to how this situation may be changed. The *Macquarie Dictionary* (Delbridge and Bernard, 1988: 490) defines industry as 'any large-scale business activity: the tourist industry' as well as the more traditional definition of 'a particular branch of trade or manufacture'. The *Webster New World Dictionary* (1962) also offers the origin of the term industry as 'intelligent work, skill, cleverness and the application' and it is these features that will be crucial to the success of the industry.

This chapter will focus on these foundation attributes of industry and treat tourism as a conglomerate industry that focuses on serving a common customer – the tourist: one that will require lots of personal intelligence, hard work and skill to meet the various demands of the customer while meeting individual business objectives and community priorities; and one that requires intensive collaboration between its component parts in order to supply the expected travel experience.

Australia's new tourism strategic plan intends to consider tourism as an industry, although it recognises its constellation qualities. It has chosen to treat the tourism industry in the sense of managing its supply and demand factors.

> Unlike many industry sectors, tourism is unable to be defined simply as a group of businesses that produce particular, similar products. Rather, the 'tourism industry' embraces a diverse range of providers and users of a variety of goods and services, and overlaps with other sectors of the economy.

> However, the elements of tourism may be described in the conventional terms of 'supply' and 'demand'. 'Supply' involves the companies which deliver tourism products and services, including tour operators and travel agents, and companies for which tourism is not the main focus of business . . .

> Tourism 'demand' is usually measured in terms of the number of tourists, the number of nights they stay in hotels or other types of accommodation and the money they spend. (Australia, 2002: 4)

This generic and official use of the term 'tourism industry' is adopted in this book.

Objectives

To succeed and survive all businesses must develop sufficient business volume and yield to produce a profit. In addition for tourism industries, they will need to demonstrate external benefits, especially the more they are reliant on public resources. This certainly applies to the non-government organisations that have developed to serve and coordinate the industry.

To achieve the above state of success businesses and destinations need to *target* the appropriate market segments, those segments whose needs and interests they can meet. This will take careful research and planning, ensuring the destination community's image and development coincide with customer expectations and desires.

To satisfy those customers who visit and turn them into loyal supporters will require the basic fundamental of business – provide a product and service of *value*. Porter's theories of competitive advantage are based on finding ways to produce value, whether it be by cost leadership, differentiation or niche marketing. Others emphasise quality as a path to value differentiation. To provide any of these features of value for the customer will involve considerable internal organisation and management, and in tourism much of this depends on the entrepreneurial skills of the small business owners.

As noted in the introduction, the tourism industry involves a range of businesses to produce a tourism experience, therefore an essential ingredient to customer satisfaction and value will be the level of *external coordination* that individual businesses and destination can develop. This will involve a broader and more collegial form of organisation of the sort advocated by Porter (1998) in his cluster model of industrial development. It is in this area that tourism leadership particularly comes to the forefront, and it is notable how many successful small business operators are contributing to the general appeal of their destination.

Since tourism can be identified as a community industry that makes extensive use of public resources it should be contributing to the host community's quality of life as well as ensuring it is on track to corporate success and sustainability. To assess how well the industry is meeting its own business goals of satisfying the customer and its *broader obligations to the host community* requires some form of monitoring. Control measures will be needed, therefore, for both internal operations and external impacts.

Planning

The range of attractions for tourists is extensive and incorporates both natural and created artefacts. Major attractions include marvels of the natural world and the intriguing aspects of human culture. Many tourist attractions were not created for tourism purposes; rather they were originally used or built for other purposes and were later adapted for tourism. As fashions and tastes change tourism products and services need to adapt to meet new market conditions. Accordingly we find a variety of industry classifications that represent the variations in the industry by location and over time.

One aspect which helps this industry to stand out is that it is a service industry that depends on developing the appropriate service skills in its labour-intensive delivery. The ultimate product – the service experience, involves an interaction between the tourist customer and a staff provider. The provider needs to be knowledgeable, efficient and friendly, which means people make a big difference to the success of tourism regardless of what form and structure the industry takes.

Industry structure

Tourism products and services can be categorised into sectors within the tourism industry, yet there is no agreement on how this categorisation should be done. The created divisions often reflect local interests within the more regular divisions. We offer two examples of this.

The six interconnecting sectors of the tourism industry, as described by Funnel and Ainsworth (1996: 248) are as follows:

- transport;
- property and business service;
- personal and household goods;
- accommodation;
- food and retail;
- recreation service,

This division of the industry reflects a business and suppliers emphasis and could be associated with big city tourism.

The Pacific Rim Institute of Tourism (PRIT) in Canada, which was a non-government organisation designed to facilitate the linkage between industry and education in British Columbia, operated on an eightfold division of the industry. These were:

- accommodation;
- food and beverage;
- transportation;
- attractions;
- ecotourism;
- conferences and events;
- travel trade;
- travel services.

The accommodation and food and beverage sectors in PRIT's classification equate to the 'hospitality' side of the industry, which in most countries represents the largest component by employment and revenue. The last two sectors represent the importance of information channels to this industry and reflect the information mission of PRIT. This aspect of the industry was divided into a private sector delivery via travel agencies, travel writers and tour wholesalers (travel trade) and public sector delivery via government departments and visitor information centres (travel services). Another feature of local significance in the PRIT interpretation of the industry was the inclusion of an ecotourism sector. This represents a major area of business in a province that promotes itself as 'SuperNatural BC'.

The above descriptive divisions of the industry represent just two ways to divide this expansive and interrelated business of tourism. Sectors of the tourism industry can be further described according to broad categories of ownership, including public, private, public-private partnerships and voluntary organisations. The important thing to note is that to plan this industry it is beneficial to divide it into component parts, and these components should make sense in both a business and local context.

People power

What keeps businesses focused on the customer and working together is people. Tourism is a people industry that needs to go beyond regular service if it is to understand its customers and deliver on their expectations. To provide for this growing industry and its need for professional service management there has been an explosion of college and university courses over the past 20 years. However, there has been little emphasis in this training and education on the engine-room of the industry, its dominant SMEs and their leaders – the entrepreneurs.

Entrepreneurship consists of three distinct yet interacting elements: creativity, risk-taking and business capabilities (Echtner, 1995: 122, cited in Shaw & Williams, 1998). Entrepreneurs tend to be seen as those who shake up the *status quo* by pushing ahead with their dreams, sometimes in unconventional ways, and they are growing in number as the tourism market fragments into a myriad of special interests and large corporations are cutting back on middle management personnel. In a review of why more people do not engage in entrepreneurial activities, the following three perceptual barriers to entrepreneurial behaviour have been identified by Mitchell (1997):

(1) Starting and running one's own business is too risky.
(2) Someone must be a 'born' entrepreneur to succeed in self-started ventures.
(3) Engaging in a single economic relationship, such as when one's

employed, is easier and preferable to multiple economic relationships, such as with suppliers, employees and customers.

However, Mitchell considers that all of these perceptions are flawed and stresses that in today's uncertain economic and employment environments, venturing out on one's own could become synonymous with personal economic security and job satisfaction, while at the same time promoting overall economic growth and prosperity for society.

The driving desires to be self-employed include independence, lifestyle change and the opportunity for greater financial rewards. But that does not mean everyone wishes to become another Conrad Hilton, Walt Disney or Richard Branson. Webster (1998: 207) drawing upon statistics from the US shows the majority of new businesses started by entrepreneurs are 'lifestyle' or 'marginal small firms' and that 'lifestyle firms are those which are privately held and usually achieve modest growth owing to the nature of the business'. Growth potential does not rank that highly for many small firms. Harkim (cited in Webster, 1998: 208) found in her research that 55% of small businesses did not want to grow while 35% aspired to modest growth.

Due to their propensity to break or change the rules, entrepreneurs often thrive in areas that are just beginning to realise their development potential and are therefore not highly regulated. The Gold Coast in Australia went through a boom period that lasted from the 1960s through to the 1980s, when a procession of remarkable individuals transformed this tropical beach area into a centre of night life, theme parks, high rise buildings and resort development (Russell & Faulkner, 1999). While the economy has thrived in the Gold Coast, the changes to the cultural and natural environments have been substantial and for some unacceptable. The spectacular successes and failures of local entrepreneurs, their strong personalities and abilities to transform communities can leave many observers to view entrepreneurs with either a combination of admiration and awe, or of ridicule and contempt. Entrepreneurs can be the bane of planners and regulators who seek to moderate and control change, but their energy and ideas can invigorate a destination.

Tourism entrepreneurs can be seen as 'brokers' between tourists and host communities in that they immerse themselves in the business side of tourism, while maintaining their ties with the host community (Jafari, cited in Shaw & Williams, 1998). While this ability to see tourism opportunities through the eyes of a business and of a citizen should enable entrepreneurs to respond more appropriately and decisively to issues and priorities arising from the business and community aspect of tourism, their performance results on these matters are mixed. Too often in the past many small owner-operated businesses have failed due to insufficient business acumen regarding the basic principles of management.

This is certainly the view of Gerber (1995) and his *E-Myth,* and is the *raison d'être* for many university business programmes that emphasise entrepreneurship. Gerber (1995: 19) considered that 'everybody who goes into business is actually three people-in-one: the entrepreneur, the manager and the technician'. Many people have a technical skill and some feel they can turn it into a successful business. A prime example of this in tourism is the professional or amateur chef who feels they could operate such a successful restaurant that people would be lining up to get in. They may well be first-rate technicians but do they have the entrepreneurial flair to deliver their product in a special way, and the management skills to pick the best location, hire the right staff, control costs, and listen to their customers? Unfortunately, the survival record of independent restaurants would suggest the answer is often, no!

To help the tourism industry plan for its future, both large and small businesses, and for them to develop the symbiotic relationships with the host communities that can assist their survival and success, several planning theories have been developed.

Planning Theories

One aspect of business development that has received some attention in management planning is that of product lifecycles (PLC). The PLC theory argues that products and the industries associated with them undergo an aging process, passing through several stages and leading to an eventual decline (Gordon *et al.*, 1990: 159–69). Typically many new products are 'introduced' to the market, but only a few take-off and 'grow' because that stage requires the support of opinion leaders (Figure 1.2, p. 32). After the product gains wider acceptance its sales 'mature', but growth starts to slow as it saturates its market. Its production either 'declines' to a replacement rate or terminates altogether as new or better products emerge to take its place. Examples of this process are legion, but some of the more recent include the disappearance of vinyl records, eight-track cassettes, and typewriters.

Destination lifecycle and adjustments

The most well-known 'stage' or 'step' model in tourism research is Butler's Destination Life-Cycle Model (DLC) (1980). This model sees destinations as passing through a number of stages of tourism development, whereby the number of tourists increases with time until a point is reached when either the destination renews itself or starts to deteriorate. Butler's model predicts that destinations will be drawn through a series of set stages in a predictable manner, with the ultimate fate of the destination being decided by local management practices.

Debate has arisen over the application and utility of this model. It has been argued that while the idea behind the model is intuitively appealing and frequently substantiated, it is hard to apply to any specific tourist situation. This is because it is difficult to assemble the required data (number of visitors) over an extensive period (30–50 years) to provide the necessary time frame for the evolution profile to occur (Foster and Murphy, 1991; Haywood, 1986). It is also difficult to determine the exact turning point between the various stages on the S-shaped evolution curve (Douglas, 1997; Grabler, 1997). In addition the model has been criticised for being descriptive rather than prescriptive, which limits its strategic planning relevance.

In one recent empirical test of the model Lundtorp and Wanhill (2001) examined the development of two resorts that they believed had the uniformity and replication necessary to empirically test its propositions. Their data were drawn from the case study areas of the Isle of Man in the UK from 1912–67 and the Danish island of Bornholm that spanned 1912–67, but excluded the duration of World War II. They found in the early years the case study areas followed the model quite well; however, over time so many other external factors influenced the evolution of tourism in these destinations that clear linkages to the DLC were no longer evident.

In most cases the DLC model is applied in a more general manner to destinations drawing heavily on limited data, anecdotal evidence and researcher observation. Given the difficulties in applying the DLC model using quantitative analysis, this model may be best suited as a general paradigm within which to view destinations, rather than as an empirical research method (Haywood, 1986; Lundtorp & Wanhill, 2001).

The value of attaching management styles and motivations to stage models like the DLC as one way of making them more relevant to management is an approach being undertaken by some. Churchill and Lewis (1983) apply management implications to each development stage for organisation. Their first stage 'existence' has an owner managing the firm with little need for an organisational structure, while their final stage 'resource maturity' predicates that a well-developed management structure should be in place to enable the firm to maximise its profits. Other researchers dispute the relevance of a linear stage model that progresses in a regular fashion from inception to maturity. Gray (1993), cited in Webster (1998: 210), notes that such models are too static and unrealistic given the small size and modest growth expectations of most new businesses. He also raises concerns that management's attitudes towards growth largely dictate the extent to which a company will develop and also need to be included in development models. Adopting a more inclusive and flexible view of business development incorporating personal motivations and external factors that allow for businesses to move up and down the development scale without necessarily going through a set number of stages is probably the most practical way of utilising stage and step models.

Schumpeter's theory

The importance of personal motivations as drivers in the development of tourist businesses and destinations is reflected in several theories and models. Schumpeter's theory of entrepreneurship highlights the essential role that innovation plays in business cycles. Given that radical innovations can open up new markets as well as disrupt existing business practices then businesses must respond to these changes (Schumpeter, 1934). The individual who is well placed to respond to such changes is the individual who is free of the incumbrances of large organisations and is willing to innovate. The tourism entrepreneur can be seen as agents of this 'creative destruction' in that their innovative efforts can transform existing conditions and can propel business and destinations in their development.

Chaos/complexity theory

A key aspect of chaos/complexity theory is that relationships are highly complex and unstable, which enables small factors to trigger substantial changes if the timing is right. This theory is now used widely as a way of explaining weather patterns since they are highly complex and interrelated. Consequently, unstable and dramatic changes can be triggered by numerous small factors, such as changes in moisture, temperature and wind flow. This theory can also be seen as relevant to tourism in that the factors affecting the industry are highly complex and often unstable and dramatic changes in the industry can be triggered by any number of factors, such as hurricanes, terrorist attacks or the fall of the Berlin Wall.

Russell and Faulkner (1999) have combined the principles of entrepreneurship and chaos/complexity theory with Butler's destination lifecycle as a way of providing an alternative framework within which to assess the dynamics of tourism development. In their study of the development of Queensland's Gold Coast, they found that entrepreneurs played a vital role in moving this destination along the development curve of its tourism industry, especially in its formative and rejuvenation stages. They propose that during the 'involvement stage' (stage 2), local entrepreneurs act as triggers to take destinations to the next level of intensification, while during the 'development stage' (stage 3) migrant entrepreneurs play a larger role. The entrepreneurs are seen to be attracted to opportunities that only present themselves when areas are ripe for change, such as either coming out of a difficult economic period, or when councils are seen to be pro-growth with the powers of regulators held in check. The role of entrepreneurs as 'triggers' enabling destinations to progress onwards from one stage to another is also supported by the research of Shaw and Williams (1998).

Russell and Faulkner (1999) consider an important explanation of the entrepreneurs' role in the development of a destination is their tendency to thrive in periods of change, or periods of chaos in the minds of regulators.

They demonstrate the contrasting decision-making styles of entrepreneurs as 'chaos makers', compared with government administrators as 'regulators'. These decision-making differences lead to the dual notions of 'edge of chaos' and 'phase shifts' in the development of a community. A situation reaches the edge of chaos when the existing community equilibrium state is on the verge of collapse and facing rapid change. When that happens the relative stability of the equilibrium phase can be jolted into a burst of activity by entrepreneurial or innovative actions, leading to an evolutionary change or phase shift. In this way entrepreneurs can be viewed as significant agents of the evolutionary shifts from stage to stage as predicted in tourism's destination lifecycle.

Value chain and beyond

All businesses, whether they are local SMEs operated by entrepreneurs or multi-national corporations, need to offer customers value if they are to succeed. It is value which drives the exchange process involved with any form of business, and if customers cannot see any value to them in the exchange they will move on to other alternatives and opportunities.

Porter 1990 has emphasised the importance of understanding each business' value chain in order to identify the 'add-on' opportunities that lie at each step of a manufacturing or service process. His 'generic value chain' consists of a business' primary activities such as assembling inbound materials, processing them and the outbound distribution of goods and services. Other front line primary activities that assist this process are the marketing and service departments. Also recognised are the important contributions of the behind-the-scenes support activities of the business' infrastructure, its purchasing department, the human resource department and the growing importance of the technology area. All of these activities make individual contributions to the overall value and profit margin. The generic model is shown in Figure 8.1A and hypothetical tourism example is offered in Figure 8.1B.

One of the strengths of this model is its applicability to service industries and its flexibility to take into account changing circumstances. For example, a travel agency's inbound materials will be information on the selected destinations, packages and companies the business has chosen to promote. Travel agency information operations are linked closely with marketing and service, in order to create the outbound product of satisfied customers. Behind the scenes, key areas include the human resource function of selecting the best travel consultants, those who have the required knowledge, personal and sales skills to service a customer and close a sale. In travel agencies it is important to keep up with technological advances such as the Internet and Web, and individual businesses will undoubtedly benefit from infrastructure arrangements such as association and franchise networks.

Figure 8.1 Modified value chain
Source: After Porter (1990) and Moore (1992)

Its flexibility can be seen in Moore's (1992) modifications to the basic model in Figure 8.1A. These reveal how the value chain can incorporate customer concerns over the origin of inbound materials, as has become important in terms of the 'sweat shop' origins for many tourism souvenirs or low-cost overseas trip options. At the other end of the chain there is growing concern over the disposal of packaging and old products like rusting cars and discarded fridges in the manufacturing sector, while in tourism there are increased expectations regarding visible community benefits from visitor expenditures. In terms of the travel agency example these are represented by the input reputation of the destinations and packages the agency wishes to promote and with which to be associated. At the end of the process will be the test of the customers' experiences and whether they will use the same travel agency again or recommend it to their friends.

As the modified value chain indicates businesses have to be aware of external factors and changing conditions, and Porter (1990) suggests five competitive forces always need to be considered in today's business environment. These he identifies as:

- *The threat of new entrants.* In the free market system of global tourism new entrants are appearing regularly.
- *The threat of substitute products and services.* New variations and models are a constant in consumer industries like tourism; witness the rise of snow boarding in 'ski' resorts.
- *The bargaining power of suppliers.* As tourism has grown, big multinational corporations have developed and now have considerable clout in negotiating volume and price.
- *The bargaining power of buyers.* In tourism this has increased as a result of growing customer experience and raised expectations.
- *Rivalry among existing competitors.* This occurs in tourism as with other industries, but more businesses are approaching it as collaborative competition within their own destinations. This recognises that businesses must collaborate to first draw tourists to their destination and then compete to attract them to their particular business

But external conditions do not always represent threats, for under certain circumstances the presence of local competitors and rival interests can be turned into a locational advantage.

Cluster theory

Porter's (1998) cluster theory attempts to explain why certain industrial concentrations have maintained their dominance while their initial locational advantages have eroded with time. His answer is that during their existence they have built institutional advantages which more than make up for the competitive advantages of new firms and locations. The essential institutional advantage is the power of clusters, which take advantage of local collaboration, a growing international reputation, and government assistance. Clusters can be viewed as an extension of the economic and spatial features of industrial districts to incorporate organisational and social features such as business administration and leadership (Jackson & Murphy, 2002).

The changing nature of competition has been recognised by Porter (1998). He has shown how his earlier diamond model of competition can be modified to include the advantages of collaboration and clusters. Within the premises of this model tourism businesses can be expected to meet *demand* by working with government to streamline visa and other entry or access requirements. In terms of *inputs* they will work together to gather market information and provide attractive packages. They will work with local service providers to develop the appropriate human resource skills and management techniques, and will form local associations to limit their insurance liability exposure and to leverage their marketing funds. As indicated in this new approach to business operation the individual businesses' *strategic planning* and relationship to rival and *supporting industries* will change. It will consist of a combination of collaboration and competition. Tourism businesses will collaborate to bring the tourist to their destination and then compete to become the business of choice within that destination.

Clusters have become significant forces in tourism development, particularly where they have gelled into active destination associations. The main function of these associations is to market the local area and to provide cooperative marketing opportunities for their members, that will in effect give them greater market exposure and reach than would be possible within their individual marketing budgets. This is often aided by government encouragement in the form of partnership marketing, whereby the government provides matching marketing dollars. But many destination associations have moved beyond marketing to include research, training, services and product development under their umbrella.

A good example of an umbrella destination association is 'Tourism Victoria' in Victoria, BC Canada. This organisation grew out of a more focused visitor information centre to produce a broader and more open task structure, yet its principal focus remains on the marketing of Victoria (Figure 8.2). Its structure is open-ended to permit the entry of any

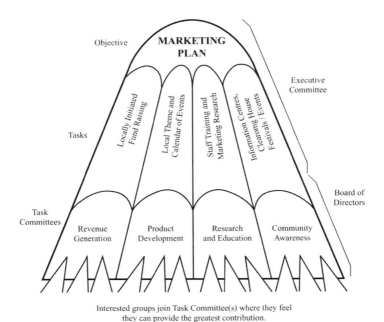

Figure 8.2 Original task model for 'Tourism Victoria'
Source: Murphy (1985: 278)

interested parties to a variety of tasks, and the chairs of these task committees serve on the executive board. The local university and college serve the
area of research and education, while a broad cross-section of the
community serve on its product development and environment
committees.

Such broad-based involvement in the marketing and improvement of a
destination is being repeated around the world. In Victoria, Australia, the
'gold rush' town of Bendigo exemplifies the community cluster approach
to marketing their city and region. In addition to its gold rush heritage
Bendigo wants to remind visitors of its agricultural delights, and through a
word play on being the central piece of the state's 'Jigsaw Campaign' and
the well-known desert red centre of Australia, it promotes its excellent red
wines (Figure 8.3). To put these and other ideas in front of the tourist and
public the Bendigo Tourism Board has called upon a wide range of
community members to assist its professional staff. These members include
not only industry representatives, but council appointees that includes
local citizens and the odd professor (Figure 8.4).

Organisation

Competition and limited resources are forcing all businesses to organise
their internal operations and to explore any external collaboration that can
help them become more efficient and effective in meeting their goals and
objectives. The need for improved organisation is important everywhere,
but is especially acute for businesses and communities beyond the major
urban and resort destinations. In the UK it has been shown that many small
coastal resorts are suffering since their attractions are too small to act as
major destination draws and this lack of business is feeding a downward
cycle of decreased investment in products, services and marketing (Shaw &
Williams, 1997). Where internal operations lack the economies of scale or
critical mass to operate efficiently and effectively external collaboration can
assist survival and sustainability.

It has been suggested that external collaboration can take on three
different forms (Jacobs & de Man cited in Vanhaverbeke, 2001: 99):

(1) Regional (i.e. geographical concentration of successful and related
    firms).
(2) Vertical relations (i.e. networking between companies).
(3) Aggregations of connected sectors (i.e. concentrations of complemen-
    tary and mutually supportive businesses).

These organisational groups can be viewed as based primarily on place or
on some form of strategic relationship. International examples of the
former include the Pacific Asia Travel Association (PATA) which promotes
travel and professionalism within the Asia-Pacific region. Examples of the

Figure 8.3 Bendigo's food and wine product with an emphasis on its red wine reputation

Figure 8.4 "Bendigo Toursim" Board 2003, representing a diversity of interests

Figure 8.4 'Bendigo Tourism' Board of 2003, representing a diversity of interests

latter include the World Travel and Tourism Council (WTTC) which is an international lobby group for the industry, and strategic airline alliances like 'One World' or 'Star Alliance' that permit individual airlines to offer global coverage via code-sharing and other business arrangements.

Given the focus of this book on tourism businesses of all sizes and their particular strategic management challenges in operating within destination communities, this section will focus on national and regional organisational structures.

Place based organisations

Convention and Visitor Bureaus (CVB) represent some of the oldest, most pervasive and best funded destination tourism organisations. Detroit, Michigan, is credited with being the birthplace of the first Convention and Visitor Bureau (CVB) in 1896 (Morrison *et al.*, 1998: 2). The International Association of Convention and Visitor Bureaus (IACVB), has grown from an initial 28 member cities in 1920 to over 900 members in the US alone. CVBs can represent towns, cities, regions and are the most common form of destination association.

While the traditional focus of CVBs was marketing their destination, increasingly they are becoming involved in product development, research, facilitation and tourism planning, as illustrated in the earlier discussion of 'Tourism Victoria' in Victoria, BC, Canada. CVBs are seen to represent four publics: members, local citizens, visitors and elected officials. In North America most CVBs fit into one of the following four categories (Morrison *et al.*, 1998: 3):

- independent (non-profit associations/business leagues);
- Chambers of Commerce (non-profit associations, or independent subsidiaries);
- local government agencies, department or public authority; or
- Special legal entity/authority.

Regardless of which category CVBs fit into, those CVBs that engage in active public–private partnerships outperform their counterparts, according to Morrison *et al.*, (1998).

Most of the IACVB members are independents (60%), the second single largest membership category is that of Chambers of Commerce (15%), and the remaining members are split between the last two categories and can be described as being 'public agencies' (25%) (IACVB cited in Morrison *et al.*, 1998: 3). Funding for CVBs can be extraordinary, sometimes exceeding the funds for government tourism offices at the state, national and international level. The budget for the CVB of Las Vegas continuously exceeded that of the past US Travel and Tourism Administration (Morrison *et al.*, 1998).

Common forms of funding for CVBs include bed or room taxes (often accounting for more than half of a CVB's budget), bonds, general tax dollars, membership dues, user fees and charges for information and other services. Of these the less argumentative are user fees for they are usually seen as legitimate service charges to both customers and local providers. But raising funds through a bed or room tax is far more contentious. This is because only one group, the accommodation sector, is targeted for funds that are used to assist every tourism sector in the local destination. While in most instances the accommodation sector is prepared to become the fund raiser for a common good it becomes problematic when this 'small' local tax is added to existing federal and state taxes, making the destination less competitive. For example, it is not unknown for some major destinations to be adding 20–25% of taxes to room rates, which makes them a very expensive option.

The benefits of combining resources at key locations, particularly expertise and skills from a cross-section of industries and sectors were demonstrated in the Local Enterprise and Development (LEAD) in tourism programme as initiated by the Wales Tourist Board. The LEAD concept is based on growth pole theory, in that is provides government grants and a supporting tourism framework for the development of 'lead' businesses in 'growth pole' areas, so that these areas can attract additional investments and generate sustainable tourism growth (Wanhill, 1996). LEAD areas were identified based on those areas with tourism proposals that were judged to be the most achievable, cost effective and offer the greatest package of well-rounded benefits. The LEAD approach draws upon extensive utilisation of available local knowledge regarding tourism opportunities and constraints, so that the return on tourism investments can be maximised. In the Wales example the LEAD approach was seen to provide 'an integrated approach to tourism development, stimulating local authority investment and offering a tourism framework for the allocation of resources' (Wanhill, 1996: 42).

Value constellations

The concept of 'value constellations' as developed by Normann and Ramirez (1993) builds upon the benefits of constructing strong ties between key businesses as a way to effectively stimulate economic development in specific sectors. This concept was developed in response to criticisms that the 'value chain' concept limits value to something that is accumulated as one moves along an internal chain of production, without due regard to the importance external relationships play in building value. 'Within the value constellation concept companies do not just add value but they reinvent it by means of a system. Within this logic, networking and inter-organizational relationships become central pieces of corporate strategy design' (Vanhaverbeke, 2001: 98).

According to Vanhaverbeke value constellations are seen as a useful way to view tourism services for three main reasons:

(1) Since value is created by relationships between companies and customers, cooperation between companies is necessary to ensure they provide the most attractive package of offerings to customers.
(2) As tourism offerings become more multi-dimensional, strategies that address the growing complexities of providing these offerings to consumers are needed.
(3) True competitive advantage can be realised by developing and implementing value-creating systems.

Since the tourism industry involves multiple sectors and interacts with a variety of other industries, such as resource development and manufacturing, it can be challenging to develop and implement value-creating systems that incorporate the needs, potential and constraints that affect many different sectors and industries.

One way to foster value constellations is to form strategic alliances. Strategic alliances have been defined as: 'voluntary arrangements between firms involving, sharing, or co-development of products, technologies or services. They can occur as a result of a wide range of motives and goals, take on a variety of forms, and occur across vertical and horizontal boundaries' (Gulati cited in Telfer, 2001: 21–2).

At their core all strategic alliances have a form of collaborative arrangement; and the businesses, organisations and individuals who are part of the alliance agree to share or divide managerial control (Starke & Sexty, cited in Telfer, 2001). Benefits of such alliances relate to power, in that group members can pool their resources and benefit from the expertise and skills of others in the association, while in turn the association can develop strategies to effectively address complex issues. An additional benefit is that working together as part of an alliance can reduce competitive rivalries between members.

This transformation from competitors to partners can be particularly striking in rural and regional areas when limited understanding of market conditions and marketing impacts can lead to misconceptions as to who the 'real competitors' for tourist dollars are and how to respond appropriately to out-perform these competitors. A recent study found that the performance of companies that were part of a strategic alliance out-performed their peers between 1983 and 1992 (Chan *et al.*, 1997). Strategic alliances can take a formal approach, by invoking codes of conduct and quality standards, or an informal approach, by providing networking opportunities, or a combination of these approaches. Strategic alliances can either function as vertical organisations, by forming a hierarchy of organisation within a particular sector; or as horizontal organisations by creating ties between sectors, as happens in destination marketing associations; or a combination of these organisational orientations as occurs with national lobby groups.

Roles

Developing a destination image requires a collective effort, as a broad array of public and private sector organisations are responsible for the goods, services, atmosphere and marketing of destinations. The interdependency of these organisations often leads to the creation of collaborative destination or industry associations. Many of these organisations revolve around marketing a destination, for through a pooling of resources a greater audience for the destination can be reached and a more comprehensive and compelling image of the destination can be created and sold to tourists. While there appear to be natural advantages to forming such organisations, the effectiveness of these organisations can vary markedly. Much of this variation depends on the effectiveness with which an association's multiple roles are conducted.

To help identify the multiple roles that need to be considered, Pearce *et al.* (1998: 351–2) have compiled a list of the top 10 roles for tourism organisations:

(1) *Pursuing standards.* Within destination (place) organisations this involves meeting customer expectations by demanding an acceptable base level of service and quality and building up from these to offer an accredited range of facilities that provide customers with a maximum choice.

(2) *Promoting training.* Within sector and destination organisations this places an emphasis on service quality, by providing the necessary staff training. A base level training system called 'Superhost' was developed by Tourism British Columbia in preparation for the Vancouver Exhibition in 1986. It proved so popular and successful it has since been franchised and sold around the world. In Australia it trades under the name 'Aussie Host'.

(3) *Developing codes.* One of the ways to ensure a quality product and travel experience is to operate in an environmentally sensitive manner. Increasingly more destinations and sectors are introducing some form of self-regulation codes of behaviour to ensure they do not overburden the physical and social environments of a destination. Examples of this are offered later under the heading of 'control'.

(4) *Professional organisation management.* To handle the complexity of modern business more organisations are turning to professional business managers. This team of educated and experienced managers generally operate key functional areas under the supervision of a CEO, and work alongside the numerous volunteer or appointed board members representing the industry and the community.

(5) *Supporting research.* To manage an organisation requires information and while some of this comes from government or industry sources these often do not address local issues because of their generic and large scale nature. Consequently, more organisations are striving to complement published data sources with their own surveys of members and customers. It is in this area that university links can be very helpful, by ensuring objective and professional analysis.

(6) *Partnerships with government groups.* Whether the organisation is a sector or destination association it will need to work with different levels of government and different government departments. Sector organisations find it useful to work with government before legislation is introduced on topics such as health and safety standards. Destination associations find such working relationships equally helpful, as they rely on government goodwill and the occasional government operating and infrastructure grants.

(7) *Enhanced networking.* No single organisation is solely responsible for local tourism activities given the ubiquitous nature of the industry and the mobility of its customers. Consequently, networking with other organisations is an essential ingredient to drawing visitors to a destination and ensuring they have plenty to do and see while they are there. Specific examples of this in tourism include packaging, where individual businesses and destinations combine to present tourists with an appealing combination of activities.

(8) *Expanding the view of tourism.* Despite tourism's size and significance its very ubiquitous nature makes it invisible to many. This means it is often an under-appreciated economic activity and that its potential to collaborate with other sectors goes unrecognised. To make people more aware of the industry and its benefits a prime function for organisation CEOs and presidents is to promote the industry and handle media relations.

This point was emphasised in Tourism Victoria's (Australia) Industry Strategic Plan for 2002–2006. Its first 'challenge' was recorded as being: 'Low community and government (specifically other departments) awareness of the value of tourism. There is a need to clearly articulate the economic, social and environmental benefits of tourism' (Tourism Victoria, 2002: 9).

(9) *Signature events.* One popular way to put tourism on the map for locals as well as tourists is to promote local events. Many communities have developed local festivals and events over time to celebrate and remember significant occurrences. Some of these have evolved naturally into signature tourism events, such as Munich's 'Oktoberfest', and New Orleans' 'Mardi Gras'. Others have required more artificial stimulation and management such as Melbourne's Grand Prix and the annual American Super Bowl.

(10) *Operation by delegation.* Given the size and complexity of the task of organising tourism at a destination level or via a sector, it is normal to witness a great deal of responsibility delegation. Destination associations in particular are dependent on the collaboration of many independent operators and at their visitor information centres and special events they rely heavily on volunteers. A growing trend around the world is the appearance of 'local ambassadors' at key destinations. These are generally volunteers who are trained to meet and greet visitors, assisting them with enquiries and directions. It is at this personal and informal coalface that all the destination management and planning is being presented to the customer – truly operation by delegation.

Collaboration

A common thread to all organisations is the collaboration between members. It is the willingness to assist others for a common good that enables a group's output to exceed the sum of individual enterprise efforts. In recognition of this fact there is growing research into what elements can assist the collaboration process. Among the literature on this topic, with respect to tourism organisations, is research into management styles, the integration of volunteers, and the responsiveness to community interests.

The governance patterns of local tourism associations vary considerably, depending on the size of the community and relative importance of tourism to the local community. Palmer's (1998) examination of the governance styles in tourism marketing associations found that key factors in the success of such tourism organisations is a formal governance style, decisive leadership and strong administrative support. Formal or 'tight' governance of these organisations is typified by following set rules and procedures, as well as having formalised role functions and codes of conduct for dealing with inter- and intra-organisational issues. He found that 'incompatibility among members results in a more effective local association' (Palmer, 1998: 197), demonstrating that those destination associations with a broad membership base can be expected to be more successful in reaching their objectives.

One area which destination associations need to embrace and integrate into their organisation is the active support of local volunteers. The multiple functions of tourism, especially local festivals and events, depend on volunteers; but there is also a need for regular professional assistance from the ranks of bankers, lawyers and accountants, and the enthusiasm of special interest factions concerned with the environment and heritage. Bringing these volunteers together helps to make the industry more aware of community resources and potential, while allowing citizens to help plan the level and type of future tourism development for their community.

Responding to community needs will be an important goal and function for tourism organisations, but there is always a danger of becoming too inward looking and failing to appreciate the full ramifications of tourism as an open system. Tourism involves customers who are mobile and this means any destination is only one of several options for their time and expenditure. Consequently all tourism organisations should look beyond their boundaries and extend collaboration to surrounding destinations and regions. This is particularly relevant to those smaller destinations that may not have sufficient attractions to hold tourists overnight, when the majority of tourist spending occurs. In some focus group research certain regional tourism boards have been criticised for being too insular. Berry and Ladkin (1997: 437) report how participants wanted to see a more regional focus with an 'integrated, hierarchical marketing structured with clear lines of responsibility and terms of reference'.

'Manager strength can influence the existence of competitive advantage by developing appropriate organisational competencies' (Dimmock, 1999: 323). Researchers suggest that developing positive interpersonal styles in organising, coordinating and controlling can make a firm more successful as such a style can improve productivity effectiveness and teamwork building (Blake & Mouton; Tomer cited in Dimmock, 1999). What works for individual businesses becomes a vital ingredient for an organisation representing a sector or destination, with all its various interests. Hence, leadership is becoming an essential factor in the successful development of individual businesses and destinations alike.

Leadership

As discussed in the earlier chapter on leadership this feature of management has taken on greater significance as business has become more competitive and uncertain. But since leadership involves a combination of technical and personal skills plus timing, it has proved difficult to isolate, analyse and prescribe the elements that create an effective leader. This is even more so in the area of tourism where so much depends on the collaboration of others and the political environment, as indicated in Russell and Faulkner's (1999) assessment of the Gold Coast's development.

Since there is little tourism-related leadership research that has led to specific hypotheses and guidelines we offer three examples of successful tourism leadership drawn from secondary sources and personal observation. These three cases represent three scales of operation, international/national, regional and local leadership with a focus on the leadership lessons that can be learned from each.

On the *international and national scale* is the example of Walt Disney and his personal drive to establish a theme park concept that has been emulated around the world. Disney's theme park concept was so innovative that despite his success as a film maker he struggled to raise the capital to open Disneyland. 'Walt raised the money through a variety of channels, of which the most frequently referred to are borrowing on his life insurance policies and forming a liaison with television' (Bryman, 1995: 12). In the end his concept of a fun, safe and clean fairground based on the theme of his movie characters proved to be so popular that it has spread around the world, and it helped the Disney company purchase its television 'banker' in 1995, to form one of the world's major entertainment conglomerates.

Among the entrepreneurship lessons that have emerged from Walt Disney's early theme park decisions and the company's later strategies one key factor has been the purchase of sufficient land. Mark Twain once recommended: 'Buy land, they're not making it anymore', and the Disney Company needs a lot of land for its theme parks. Walt Disney's early financial difficulties were caused in part by the large amount of land needed for his concept; and upon opening his theme park he wished he could have purchased more, as he saw other businesses feeding off his customers and turning the surrounding area into a strip development of hotels and restaurants. Walt Disney learned his lesson, and when he assembled the site for his second theme park near Orlando, Florida, he purchased 27,400 acres (11,088 hectares) – far more than was needed for one or two theme parks. The other land was to be developed for the financially beneficial accommodation sector; to provide other attractions such as golf courses and water parks to create a resort environment so there is little need for customers to leave the property; and to act as a buffer to the inevitable parasitical businesses drawn to the business opportunities presented by this major attraction.

Associated with the expense incurred with such large rural land purchases is the need to receive government assistance in its development. Walt Disney started negotiations with the State of Florida before committing to the Orlando site, and among the agreements he secured was the right to create his own local government jurisdiction. This enabled Disney to build according to his own high standards and to raise capital as a government authority, which translates into lower interest rates. Such political negotiations over the final purchase of land were continued in France when the Disney Company set up Euro Disneyland, which is now called Paris Disneyland.

In Europe the 'Disney company was able to assemble such a large amount of land (2,000 hectares) thanks to the assistance of the French government, which owned the land and had been leasing it to local farmers but was eager to see economic development in this part of rural France' (Murphy, 1997: 228). To entice Disney the French government offered the land at 1971 agricultural prices and guaranteed those prices for 20 years (Flower, 1991: 208). In addition it linked the site of the new theme park to Paris via a freeway and extension of the Metro subway system. Plus, it linked the theme park to the high speed rail system, which with the opening of the Channel Tunnel places Paris Disney within three and a half hours of London.

While one of the early reasons for such extensive land assembly was to protect the Disney investments from surrounding businesses, the presence of undeveloped land next to a successful and attractive resort has presented the opportunity to create greenfield residential complexes. This process has started in Disney World with the construction of Celebration, a state of the art residential community (Diski, 2000). It will continue in Europe, where the opportunity to build a satellite town both for Paris and within Europe's golden triangle of development makes a perfect complement to the clean air industry of a theme park resort.

As a consequence Disney's entrepreneurial experience has shown the importance of buying sufficient land for a tourism venture that is land intensive in its own right and can benefit from the control of adjacent land, either to protect the original investment or to create attractive spin-off investments. It also reveals the importance of negotiating from a position of strength, especially when tourism is bringing economic activity and amenity development to rural and depressed regions. However, land acquisition and negotiation is not a simple process, as the Disney experience in Virginia illustrates. This is discussed elsewhere in the book.

At the *regional scale* is the enterprise of Tim Smit, who is the visionary behind the Eden Project in Cornwall, England. The Eden Project is a living theatre of plants and people designed to link people with their global environment and is located in rural southwest England. It is situated in an old clay quarry near St Austell with two giant greenhouse biomes presenting a humid tropical environment and a warm temperate Mediterranean climatic zone (Figure 8.5). The rest of the 15 hectare site is in its early planting and development phase and will eventually contain native Cornish flora. This facility opened in March 2001 after a seven year capitalisation of £86 million (A$235 million), with half the funding coming from the UK's millennium lottery grant. Since its opening it has exceeded projected visitor numbers, and now attracts around one million visitors a year.

The entrepreneur who put this project together was a successful Dutch-born record producer in London who moved to Cornwall for a change of lifestyle in 1987. Once there Smit's energy and drive drew him to his first horticultural project, the revival of the 'Lost Gardens of Heligan' which has become 'Britain's most visited private garden, attracting over 300,000 visitors a year' (*The Weekend Australian*, 2001: R5). Then his thoughts turned to the potential of this discarded quarry in the Cornish countryside.

Smit's vision was to create 'a futuristic botanical institute exploring the relationship between man and plants' that would combine education, research, conservation and entertainment (*Western Morning News*, 2001: 2 and 5). It was expected to become a major inland tourist attraction that would balance the coastal magnets of Devon and Cornwall, and bring a boost to the declining rural economy. His main task was to garner sufficient support and funding to turn this vision into action. He achieved this via his 'Tinkerbell theory':

> ... if you believe in a great idea then it will exist. Also, if you don't go away you will irritate people so much that after a while they will give you whatever you want. Put those two things together, you've got a pretty immovable force. (*Western Morning News*, 2001: 5)

But there is obviously more to it than that. First, this entrepreneur had a good track record in business and horticulture-tourism. Second, he was able to see the big picture of Cornwall's inland potential and the prospects of combining research, education and entertainment into a tourist attraction. Third, he could convince various governments that his tourism vision could bring employment and investment to a rural backwater and he was able to secure their funding support as an investment in the future of this region.

The Eden Project has become a success in the short time it has been open and continues to exhibit innovative management. Not only has it exceeded its visitor projections, some days it has been overwhelmed with visitors – especially on wet days when holiday makers have fled inland in search of a wet weather attraction. 'Now, the project has taken out advertisements asking people to choose more carefully when they come – and not to visit at all on wet days' (McGinnes, 2001: 4). This 'de-marketing' may be viewed as an 'unusual step', but it really reflects good management. In attempting to control the flow of visitors the project is trying to provide an optimal experience and develop satisfied customers.

At the *local scale* is the baker, Tom O'Toole, who has converted his business into a multi-million dollar tourist attraction that has helped to convert Beechworth in rural northeast Victoria, Australia into a burgeoning regional tourism venue. The small town of Beechworth, with a current population of just over 3000, was a significant regional centre in the nineteenth century, but since then has been bypassed by economic and political developments. Over time it has become a small and sleepy rural community, blessed with significant history and heritage buildings, but steadily losing its few remaining public sector institutions as modernisation and economies of scale overtook them. Consequently, it has become a town that needed to reinvent itself and one of the leaders in this process was the local baker – Tom O'Toole.

O'Toole is a believer in 'the power of positive thinking' and on purchasing the small bakery in Beechworth converted it into a multi-million dollar business that depended on the growing tourism business as well as locals. His strategy was:

Figure 8.5 Eden Project in Cornwall, England

I worked really hard and the bakery became successful. I did some creative marketing which really helped. I started getting wacky promotional ideas. And most important of all, I started to blend the bakery into the Beechworth local community through sponsorships and general community support. Then my business started to really grow. (O'Toole with Tarling, 2000: 161)

In the process he converted a peripheral tourism business into a major local attraction that worked with the community in developing its heritage tourism potential (Figure 8.6).

O'Toole created his successful tourism business by implementing and personalising some basic management concepts. Many of these are included in his book. *Breadwinner: A Fresh Approach to Rising to the Top* and are introduced as 'The Gospel of Thomas'. Among our favourites are:

- *Entrepreneurship*
  'Get out of your comfort zone! Take a risk – smile! Shock people! Enjoy your work! Have goals! Get famous! Beware of the dream-takers!' (The bankers who assess your business plan from an actuarial perspective only.)
- *Teamwork*
  'None of us is as strong as all of us. I know when we all work together, we all win together'.
- *Continuous Learning*
  'The more you learn, the more you earn'.
- *Recruitment*
  'Without good people, you're ratshit . . . My staff is my biggest asset, because without them I don't have a business. My staff are my biggest investors – they invest their time, their energy and their imagination . . . you can buy your milk and bread anywhere, why buy it from my place? It's because of them'.
- *Marketing*
  'If I can get them (customers) to Beechworth I've got a chance of getting a dollar out of their pockets – but first I've got to get them to Beechworth'.
- *Training*
  'I spend a lot of money training my staff. Some think I'm investing too much in my people and they say to me: "Tom, what if you train them and they leave?" To which I usually reply: "What if I don't train them and they stay".'
- *Personal Motivation*
  'Choose to be happy. The power of choice is incredible. We can choose to think great thoughts, we can choose enthusiasm, we can choose to bunge jump right out of our comfort zones'.

Figure 8.6 Beechworth Bakery
Source: Beechworth Bakery

- *Personal Philosophy*
  'It's got to be simple . . . all the customers want you to do is, look at them, greet them, talk to them, and thank them'.

It is not that simple of course, and none of this comes about without hard work, for to paraphrase Edison 'success is 1 percent inspiration and 99 percent perspiration', and entrepreneurs such as these put body and soul into their businesses.

Controlling

The need to ensure that private company and corporate destination objectives are being achieved and are appropriate for long-term sustainable relationships requires consideration of control measures. While this management function is widely recognised it is seldom operated to its fullest extent in tourism for a variety of reasons. First, the reliance on collaboration and the support of others means individual businesses and destinations are not in complete control of their own destiny. These external relationships make monitoring and measurement more challenging than normal, and leave corrective responses dependent in part on outside cooperation. Second, the seasonality of many tourism businesses and destination means there is a back-breaking and mind-numbing period of intense activity when it is difficult to stand back and assess how well the organisation is satisfying its customers and meeting its objectives. Third, given the dependence of tourism on a healthy social and physical environment it is frustrating how few dependable and simple impact indicators have been developed.

All three control issues for businesses and destinations are clearly illustrated in Lennon's (2001) report on Scotland's 'Visitor Attraction Monitor'. Like a growing number of monitoring procedures the Scottish Tourist Board has linked up with a university, in this case Glasgow Caledonian University, to monitor an aspect of the industry. This centrally funded collaborative research provides the type of data central agencies and individual businesses need in order to measure their own performance. The seasonality of the attractions, that can range from 'free entry' museums and galleries to entry fee castles and zoos, is concentrated in the high season of July to September, with a strong shoulder season between April and June. During these busy time periods most attractions can register the basic information relating to their number of visitors, but some (13%) depend on periodic samples or visitor books and 'honesty / donation' boxes.

Collaboration

A 'distribution channel is the path products take as they move from the producer to the ultimate consumer' (Richardson, 1996: 76). The producer is generally a separate business that operates within a destination community and the ultimate consumer can be a local resident, a domestic tourist or an international tourist from another country. In many destinations, especially where most of the businesses are small, the majority of sales are direct, with entry or bed nights sold directly to the passing customer. However, to reach more distant and targeted markets many tourism businesses utilise a variety of distribution channels to build inbound travel. These distribution channels in effect become control mechanisms for much of the tourism business because to use such marketing devices requires accreditation, monitoring and collaboration.

The first and least expensive distribution channel for most businesses is the local destination-marketing organisation. Membership in these organisations permits businesses to place their brochures at information centres, to be included in generic destination advertising and trade shows, and to participate in local booking services. Many businesses, especially those in the hospitality sector, link up with motoring organisations to be included in their travel directories. In addition, some businesses will use wholesale tour package operators to combine their product into packages that are of interest to distant target markets, while others will use additional distribution channel operators like high street travel agents. A good description of these distribution channel networks can be found in Heath and Wall (1992).

The distribution channels and associated businesses are facing a turbulent future. The Internet and e-commerce are providing customers with more information and purchasing options than ever before, but just as importantly they are providing individual businesses with more direct access to customers, near and far. This provides smaller businesses with the opportunity to match traditional distribution channels and to sell directly to customers, with the associated savings in commission and flexibility of pricing and individual control.

Financing

The financial health of any organisation determines its survival, although some airlines and other national institutions seem to be able to delay the inevitable result of continual losses through government subsidy. However, for the majority of businesses and organisations the crucial control factor is their financial position. While some lifestyle tourism businesses will feel this factor is not so crucial for them because 'the business' is simply supporting their chosen lifestyle and location, they will still find that financial concerns can undermine their management practices and personal relationships.

For small businesses in tourism a primary source of capital has been personal or family savings, and as a result two important control points can be missed. Many who rely on self-funding fail to prepare a disciplined and detailed business plan. Among the many calculation omissions this can lead to is a failure to assign a reasonable salary to the operator(s). Thus many end up paying themselves nothing and fail to consider forsaken opportunity costs.

Boer (cited in Thomas, 1998: 9) has identified several sources of small business failure that can contribute to a poor financial situation. These include 'poor operational management, high gearing, poor senior management and a weak local economy'. Taking these in reverse order, it is important for tourism entrepreneurs to enquire about the economic health of their local region and its tourism industry, rather than be guided by its tourism delights. The importance of an objective business plan from senior management cannot be over-emphasised, and such a cold and analytical document can be a sobering experience for the entrepreneur as well as the banker. An overenthusiastic assessment of business opportunities and a rush to get started can lead to an overcommitment.

Kuratko and Hodgetts (1998: 430–1) describe five common fund-raising dilemmas, and offer some sensible advice which has been paraphrased below:

(1) *What do you plan to do with the money?*
    If you can compartmentalise the business, seek funding support for the low-risk and therefore more secure components.
(2) *How much do you need?*
    Determine the exact amount you need for each component and prioritise those components. See if you can plan and expand the business in stages.
(3) *When do you need it?*
    Do not approach a banker without a business plan, and one that includes time-lines regarding loan(s) and repayments.
(4) *How long will you need it?*
    The shorter the requested loan period the better, as this indicates the business is likely to be in a profit-making position quickly and the banker's funds will not be committed for too long.
(5) *How will you repay the loan?*
    'This is the most important question', and can be answered with conviction if there are other sources of income or forms of collateral.

A common problem in terms of operational management is the question of cash flow, which can become crucial in seasonal businesses like tourism. One answer to this problem which is gaining in popularity in the UK is factoring. Factoring is a process whereby businesses send their invoices to a company that pays them most of their money upon receipt of the invoices and then collects the debt for the company, all for a small fee. This sort of debt-collection service can be of great benefit to small companies that regularly have to wait for one or more months for full payment of services from their clients. The UK has experienced a boom in factoring, fuelled by the growing number of small businesses. Most business owners are put in touch with factors by banks. Factoring has been found to be primarily bene-ficial to companies with an annual turnover of more than £100,000 (A$300,000). The owner of one chauffeuring company in the UK credits factoring with enabling him to expand his business from six cars and six employees to a company valued over £1 million with 34 employees (*Daily Express*, 2000: 56).

Customer expectations

To achieve financial success businesses must meet their customer expectations, and if possible exceed them within their operational and financial constraints. One problem is that the quality expectations of customers are rising as they have experienced an ever-increasing array of quality tourism options. It has been found in recreational research that aggregate levels of visitor satisfaction tend to rise, and that it can be inde-pendent of changes in the types or amount of use (Lindberg *et al.*, 1997). This phenomenon can be a reflection of 'succession and displacement' process. This occurs when one group is first attracted to an area for certain qualities, but as their satisfaction wanes due to the area becoming more crowded the new and larger groups who visit the now 'accessible' and popular recreational spots express increased satisfaction. The findings of Lindberg *et al.* suggest concerns about customer satisfaction and quality can be handled by managing the demand for tourism products and services, such as targeting different markets, rather than managing the supply of actual products or services. However, once a tourist destination becomes degraded in the eyes of some, the market potential for its associ-ated product and services can decline as negative word of mouth spreads and the competition looks more attractive. Furthermore, once a service or product is viewed as sub-standard it can no longer charge top prices, which will create a downward spiral or reduced prices, profits, invest-ment and demand.

The above customer expectation model has obvious parallels to the product lifecycle model and Butler's associated destination evolution model.

Ethics

Ethics refers to a system of morality. In practice ethics can refer to ensuring that one's actions are just, fair and honourable. The extent to which tourism businesses have a responsibility to act in an ethical manner, beyond obeying the law, is debatable.

As is well know, Friedman argues that ethics are not the province of business, while Davis insists that business must embrace social respon-sibility, not merely profitability. (Walle, 1995: 263)

Milton Friedman (cited in Walle, 1995) stresses that the only legitimate role for businesses is to pursue profits, while dwelling on ethical considerations for any reason other than generating profits is unsupportable. Others, including Davis, believe that businesses have an obligation to society to act ethically due to their profound and pervasive influence on society. Friedman and those who support him believe that businesses should act in an ethical way if it is part of their strategy, such as building goodwill or diversifying their product to improve their profits. Walle (1995: 264) suggests that there is a continuum of ethical behaviour, which is outlined below:

- *Social obligation.* Businesses are only required to obey the law (Friedman's approach).
- *Social responsibility.* Businesses are required to act in ethical and socially responsible ways (Davis' approach).
- *Social responsiveness.* Businesses build on their ethical role of 'social responsibility', with the added requirement to anticipate and respond in an ethical manner to potential future challenges.

The tourism industry has some key characteristics that need to be considered when determining its ethical responsibilities. First of all, progress in terms of appropriate development, investments and marketing can be a divisive issue in tourism as different stakeholders have different views of 'progress'; therefore, a careful balance needs to be achieved between what customers want, what other stakeholders want and what is profitable. Secondly, the industry can effectively destroy that which it relies upon, so even from just a profitability viewpoint, businesses need to be highly aware of the potential impact of their actions and help to ensure that 'their money makers' are preserved. Third, the needs of all stakeholders need to be identified and appropriately addressed in the interest of widespread support for the industry and its prolonged profitability, as well as its moral responsibilities to affected people and environments. Therefore, the domain of ethical behaviour for tourism businesses can be addressed from either a pragmatic perspective, based on pursuing actions that improve the bottom line, or on more philosophical lines, based on pursuing actions that are 'right', 'just' and 'for the betterment of society'. It is our contention that those perspectives are not necessarily mutually exclusive.

Stakeholder-community ethics

Engaging in ethical behaviour that meet stakeholders' needs can be good for business as indicated by Mitchell's (1997: 21) assertion: 'the ability to identify, prioritize, and respond to stakeholders is the ability to recognise opportunity'. In the interest of increasing their return on investments, businesses are discovering a range of potential benefits from taking a 'green approach'. This includes 'cost savings, increased efficiencies, early identification of potential environment liabilities, improved corporate image, marketing and sales benefits, enhanced visitor and regulatory confidence, and improved staff motivation' (Goodall, cited in McBoyle, 1996: 255). But others have pointed out the unethical approach of some companies, which brand their product as eco-sensitive or green, without any substantial effort to apply sustainable practices. To overcome this dilemma more tourism businesses are being encouraged to join an independently accreditation system, like the WTTC's Green Globe programme.

Even if a corporation endeavours to be ethical and responsible in its actions, imposing its ethics and practices on a community can cause problems, especially if these ethics and practices are not in keeping with those of the local community in which it operates. This situation can be exacerbated in isolated and underdeveloped communities, where there is a history of colonial activities that have threatened the culture and rights of local citizens. Baldacchino (1997) describes a situation that he refers to as 'small-scale labour syndrome', whereby incompatibilities arise between small island communities and multi-national operations that establish businesses in these communities. He found that a small-scale labour syndrome worked on the following levels:

- large corporations sending expatriates to exercise 'gunboat diplomacy', by imposing the corporate line on the locals; and
- local communities subverting the corporate rules and regulations in a manner that reflected their own culture, experience and values.

Baldacchino (1997: 176) sees this syndrome as representing 'a foray into forms of worker resistance to the global threat . . . [that shapes] the contested terrain of labour-management relations'. Examples of small-scale labour syndrome are found with regard to the acceptability of hiring friends and relatives, issues of confidentiality and responsibilities to the company. Baldacchino advocates that corporations recognise and plan for the small-scale labour syndrome. This planning involves achieving the right balance between creating strategies, procedures and policies that uphold corporate objectives and ensuring that the organisation is also responsible to local cultural conditions and requirements.

Others have suggested that the association between multi-national corporations and host communities, especially in developing countries, has been in favour of corporate values. Britton, S.C. (1982) and Lundgren (1972) have emphasised the dominance of core economies over the pleasure periphery nations, but over time these host nations have learned to be more demanding negotiators. It is now more common to find clauses in development agreements relating to the hiring of locals within the management ranks and the use of local suppliers, but the balance still remains in favour of the multi-national corporations which have more options than the individual communities or developing nations.

Now the emphasis is on community partnerships, so that as many stakeholders as possible can benefit from tourism development. The community approach has emphasised the ethical and business benefits to be obtained through an industry-community business partnership. This can be seen at several levels of development. With international 'hallmark events' the industry can benefit not only from hosting the event, but thanks to the international exposure can expect subsequent years of higher international visitation. The community can benefit from an increased supply of infrastructure, amenities and in some cases housing. Some claim that this has hardly moved us beyond the Roman era of cake and circuses and that many of the infrastructure and amenity developments would have come eventually (Hall, 1992; Murphy, 1991); but it takes a community spirit to bring these things together in an event and it is that collaboration that is often a springboard to further community development. At the other extreme are the local museums and festivals that increasingly depend on tourist revenue to survive. Economic studies of community festivals continually reveal the importance of tourist revenue to the event and community at large (Carmichael & Murphy, 1996; Getz, 1991).

Codes of behaviour

Perhaps the most evident sign of the growth of ethics and a community approach in tourism is the rise in codes of behaviour. These codes have been introduced by different tourism organisations as pre-emptive management strategies to help ensure the industry remains in harmony with local environments and therefore sustainable. The most evident are those relating to the environment, as is the case of the 'Code of Conduct for Commercial Tour Operations in Gwaii Haanas/South Moresby' in British Columbia referred to elsewhere in this book. But there are less visible codes that are also changing the industry. The Australian Federation of Travel Agents has created a binding code of conduct for all of its members, which was developed to protect customer interest (Pearce *et al.*, 1998). A Global Code of Ethics for Tourism was prepared by the World Tourism Organisation (WTO) to recognise the role of tourism in the world and to outline the responsibilities of the industry to the people of the world (WTO, 1999).

Summary

This chapter outlines the wide variety of components within the industry and discusses the issue of its definition. It suggests the industry be viewed as a conglomerate industry with a service focus on its customers. It reveals there is a range of tourism products and industry types that can be expected to change in importance and emphasis depending on local resources and priorities, and over time.

To plan for this industry various management theories are explored and applied. The organising components examine various organisational types and their inter- and intrarelations. The leadership component of this chapter focuses on innovators and the importance of training and inspiring industry workers: the control component looks at the dynamics of product and service mix and how important it is for small businesses as well as large organisations to monitor and improve performance. The chapter closes with an overview of the growing importance of ethics and offers some guiding principles and examples for the tourism industry.

As an industry tourism holds much promise for the future, but like all industries this promise can only be realised through careful planning of inputs and outputs. Tourism, more than most industries, is acutely reliant on the goodwill of residents in that part of the product it sells is the community itself. It has been noted that successful communities involve a broad cross-section of residents in determining and planning for the future and this is certainly the case in tourism. The following chapter explores the needs, types and actions of residents as they relate to community tourism initiatives.

Chapter 9

Residents

The amount of research concerned with tourist destination residents has been extensive, especially with respect to the social science perspectives on resident–visitor relationships. Such research has revealed some consistent patterns concerning resident attitudes and opinions of local tourism. These appear to be related to factors such as the residents' proximity to and involvement in the industry, the volume of and type of tourism experience and the level of similarity between the visitor origin and destination cultures.

With the growth of tourism as a global industry and its more evident impacts on local communities planning for this activity has received more attention. Initially such planning research and practice focused on the physical and spatial issues, but more recently there has been a shift to incorporate the human and political dimensions. Included in this area of investigation has been the need to find processes that will facilitate the involvement of a wide range of stakeholders, including differing resident reactions.

What has been missing in much of the previous resident research and tourism management has been an exploration of resident involvement in the delivery and management of local tourism. This is beginning to change with some research exploring prospective models of resident-tourism industry collaboration and in certain destinations that are beginning to involve residents more proactively in the development and delivery of the local tourism product.

Objectives

Even though communities are made up of different individuals and group interests there are some common objectives that can be expected among local resident stakeholders. On an individual basis it is a very human trait to desire to 'have one's cake and to eat it too'. In terms of tourism this translates into wanting to live in a beautiful location, to have significant cultural icons and amenities, and to have the revenue to support a comfortable lifestyle that permits a person to enjoy the above. Then we want to keep all this to ourselves! In today's global village that is not likely; for modern communication and media attention will ensure that news about such communities spreads and the global tourism industry will endeavour to bring visitors to the residents' door.

Once tourists arrive at the community's door there are three general objectives that most residents will consider. First and foremost they will view tourism as a business and want to see a return to individuals and the community. The economic return can be in several forms. For many it will be employment, for some business revenue, and for all a substantial tax base – for tourism is one of the most taxed businesses in the world now that VAT and GST have become widespread. In most cases tourism will make an ideal supplementary community industry, because many tourists come to see a living community and its sense of place. They like to see people going to work, being prosperous and happy. If tourism is the only or major local industry a community will lose its variety and some vitality, which becomes very evident with the regular seasonal downturns of tourism or the aftermath of a terrorist act.

Many residents will be aware of the environmental resources and attractions in their local community and will be among the first detectors of stress and damage. They will appreciate the taxes that are used to support local parks, beaches and amenities such as toilets, parking and interpretation facilities. But they will become concerned if they cannot access these themselves or see them overrun to the extent that the site and recreation experience begin to deteriorate. It will often be the tourists who are blamed for such difficulties because they are highly visible, but they are only a portion of the users and their tax dollars will have contributed to the environment's care and protection.

The importance of human perception is paramount at the social level of host–tourist interaction. Residents have the right and expectation to go about their own business in their own home community, but this relationship will be seriously challenged by the arrival of tourists who have a different agenda and timetable. The management of these human expectations and flows within a community will be crucial to the success of tourism's local operations and image. Some of this management will involve physical planning to separate conflicting group interests, such as separating local traffic from tourist traffic wherever possible. Some will involve behavioural management. One of our favourite examples of this are the small signs at Cape Canaveral, Florida, which tell you to stick to the path because of snakes. No one wandered off the path while we were there. Who would risk it?

These three dimensions of resident objectives can be managed and brought into a sustainable development context through Elkington's 'triple bottom line'. His concept is:

> Sustainable development involves the simultaneous pursuit of economic prosperity, environmental quality, and social equity.

Companies aiming for sustainability need to perform not against a single, financial bottom line but against the triple bottom line. (Elkington, 1999: 397)

Since its introduction this concept has received increased attention and is beginning to appear in more government tourism planning, such as the Tourism Victoria (Australia) Industry Strategic Plan of 2002–2006 (Tourism Victoria, 2002). Its appeal is particularly strong for communities seeking a new direction as their traditional industries decline, and they desire to develop public–private sector partnerships to tap all remaining community resources and redefine their future. Rogers (2001: 136–139) in talking about this situation for Australia's country towns feels that using the triple bottom line audit along with community-based indicators and local leadership can lead such communities to more sustainable futures. This would involve a more proactive stance from local residents and planning methods to integrate these stakeholders more effectively into the decision-making process on the future of their communities.

Planning

The relationship between 'host' resident and 'guest' tourist has been examined in a variety of contexts and locations. A leader in this area is Valene Smith (Smith, 1989; Smith & Brent, 2001) who has explored the social and anthropological relationships between visitors and host populations in a variety of settings. Another concern of anthropologists is the effect of globalisation on established concepts such as 'culture' and 'society' (McGibbon, 2000), that in many cases will take the form of tourism and increase its capacity to change host environments. The imagery of a borderless world 'suggests states (and all communities) have been rendered impotent in the face of overwhelming global forces and that there is little they can do except adjust to the imperatives of the global market' argues Richardson (1997: 55). Yet it is remarkable how resilient communities have been in the past to economic and military imperialism. From such studies have emerged certain theories and stratagems that indicate possible ways to integrate resident concerns and viewpoints into a general strategic plan for community tourism.

One of the earliest theories of resident–tourist interrelationships was Doxey's 'irridex', which has been embellished into more comprehensive and practical models. As the title of Doxey's (1975) model indicates, he saw the relationship as undirectional and inevitably apocalyptic, with increased exposure to tourism leading to increased negative reactions from residents. He envisioned community–visitor relationships steadily progressing downward, from a state of euphoria to one of apathy, to annoyance and eventually antagonism. He provided evidence of such a pattern from his consultancy work and since then there have been incidents which unfortunately confirm rising tourist numbers are still an influential factor. However, this correlation is simplistic and begs the introduction of management techniques such as physical planning or behavioural management to reduce the impact of increasing numbers.

One of the earliest modifications to Doxey's approach was the recognition that not all residents would develop the same negative reactions, and that their attitudes to local tourism would be influenced by a variety of factors. Lankford and Howard (1994) in their development of a tourism impact attitudinal scale identify from the literature ten variables that could influence a resident's opinion about local tourism. These are presented below with our elaborations:

- *Length of residency*
  The longer people had lived in the community the more negative they are likely to become towards tourism because of the changes it brings. It appears that the perceived negative changes are often more noticeable than the positive changes.
- *Economic dependency on tourism*
  Residents who depend on tourism-based employment (directly or indirectly) have been found to be more favourable toward tourism and tourists.
- *Distance of tourism (activity) centre from resident's home*
  In general the 'out-of-sight out-of-mind' syndrome seems to work in tourism cases. Those living far from the industry have been found to be in favour of its development because they are not personally bothered by the associated congestion and other nuisances. Of course a resident's home location does not necessarily correlate with their exposure, especially when their place of work is close to the major tourism areas.
- *Resident involvement in tourism decision-making*
  When residents are involved with various local development decisions they appear to be more favourable to community change and this includes tourism.
- *Birthplace*
  Residents' origins appear to have an influence on their views. We have observed in various locations that newly arriving retirees from big cities sometimes wish to 'pull up the drawbridge' and see their retirement haven remain the quiet and beautiful retreat they had perceived it to be.
- *Level of knowledge*
  The general level of knowledge about tourism and its significance to the local economy has been shown to influence local attitudes regarding its development and tourists.

- *Level of contact with tourists*
  Although obviously related to the earlier employment and resident location factors it has been found that personal contact with tourists has an influence on residents' attitudes, both positive and negative.
- *Demographic characteristics*
  Related to many of the above factors is the influence of age and gender. A resident's personal profile will have an impact on how they perceive tourism's influence. While we have noted some negativity from certain retirees tourism is generally popular with local youth because of its employment and excitement prospects.
- *Perceived impacts on local outdoor recreation opportunities*
  When local residents have difficulty in accessing their favourite outdoor recreation activities because tourists got there first, the desire for further tourism development understandably weakens.
- *Rate of community growth*
  The rate of community growth or decline appears to influence residents' interest regarding further tourism development. When a community is losing its traditional industries some 'boosters' point to tourism as a potential saviour without due consideration of its implications. Such enthusiasts often fail to recognise that tourism is a very competitive industry; that it takes quality products with a critical mass of attractions to draw tourists overnight; and it depends on quality service to build up its reputation for value and excellence.

With this wide range of potential influences on resident attitudes to tourism and signs of correlation or overlap between some of the variables, Lankford and Howard (1994) conducted a factor analysis of these variables in data gathered from several small Oregon communities. They found two significant factors associated with resident attitudes in these towns. These were a 'concern for local tourism development' and the perceived 'personal and community benefits', which combine several of the listed variables into significant attitude motivations for these communities.

Given this multi-dimensional nature of resident attitudes toward local tourism, there have been several attempts to broaden the Doxey causation model. One early adjustment was Bjorklund and Philbrick's portfolio approach that took into consideration residents' involvement with the industry and the degree of similarity between host and tourist cultures (cited in Butler, 1975). From such a two-dimensional approach it is possible to incorporate Doxey's original observation into a broader context than one simply based on tourist numbers.

This multi-dimensional approach to modelling resident reactions to tourism and finding ways to incorporate them into the planning process has been developed as part of the Australian Cooperative Research Centre's Gold Coast Revisioning Project. Faulkner and Tideswell (1997)

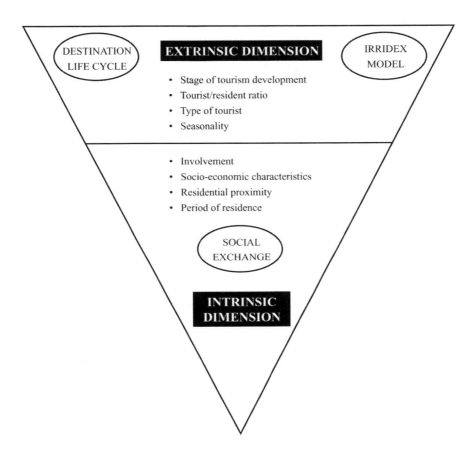

Figure 9.1 A framework for analysing the social impacts of tourism
Source: Faulkner and Tideswell (1997: 6)

have proposed a multi-dimensional model for analysing the community impacts of tourism (Figure 9.1). This model identifies extrinsic forces that include the tourist–resident ratio from the Doxey model and the stage of development from the Butler model of destination development. In addition they identify the potential impact of the type of tourist attracted and the influence of seasonality. These extrinsic forces represent the external influences of tourism impacting on a community, while the intrinsic forces are how residents of the community react to these external forces and attempt to integrate tourism into their general life. The major way residents are expected to respond to local tourism is through the sequence of social exchange, as outlined in Chapter 1. But they recognise individuals' intrinsic assessment of their personal trade-off between costs and benefits will be influenced by personal variables such as their level of involvement with the industry, their socio-economic standing, and their period of residence.

Faulkner and Tideswell (1997) examined the significance of the identified extrinsic and intrinsic variables in a survey of Gold Coast residents. The Gold Coast is a mature beach resort destination and a factor analysis of resident responses revealed the classical 'juxtaposition of an appreciation of the benefits of tourism (Factor 1) on the one hand and an acknowledgement of its costs on the other (Factor 2)' (Faulkner & Tideswell, 1997: 14).

On the whole, Gold Coast residents viewed tourism in a positive light, and the specific contribution of individual extrinsic and intrinsic forces varied relatively little from the predicted patterns. Such evidence led Faulkner and Tideswell (1997: 26) to conclude:

> The positive view of tourism among Gold Coast residents overall, and the marginal variation in opinion irrespective of such background variables as period of residence, place of residence and involvement, suggests that the altruistic surplus factor may apply to tourism.

This and other empirical studies support the existence of a complex yet stable pattern of relationships between resident perceptions of local tourism and their attitude toward its development. Jurowski *et al.* (1997) surveyed residents from the Mt Rogers National Recreation Area in Virginia to determine the interplay of factors that impact on residents' views of tourism. They use a path analysis model to track the link between what residents perceive to be tourism's economic, social and environmental impacts and their personal values, listed below:

- *Economic gain* – the potential for personal and community economic benefit from tourism.
- *Resource use* – the importance residents place on their use of tourism resources like parks and beaches.
- *Community attachment* – resident sentiments toward their town and surrounding region.
- *Ecocentric attitude* – ecological perspective of residents, particularly with respect to maintaining a balanced ecosystem.

They found the model helps to explain ambiguities in residents' views of tourism by demonstrating how residents' values and experiences shaped their perceptions of tourism impacts. Community attachment and potential economic gain were the strongest positive variables in shaping the residents' views of tourism's impacts, whereas resource use and an ecocentric attitude were negatively related. However, within these general relationships were certain sub-groupings that demonstrated it is not a simple linear relationship for any of the studied values. For example,

within the generally positive economic gain variable its most positive relationship for the residents occurred with social impacts, while it had little
effect on their environmental assessments. Similarly, while the resource
users were reticent to support development in natural settings they were
more positive elsewhere.

Gursoy *et al.* (2002) find support for local tourism is influenced primarily
by the state of the local economy, which in turn influences residents' perceptions of tourism's benefits and costs, thus confirming 'the usefulness of
exchange theory in explaining residents' attitudes toward tourism'
(Gursoy *et al.* 2002: 100). However, the authors point out that their study
like 'most research on residents' reactions toward tourism has been
confined to rural and small town populations' (Gursoy *et al.*, 2002: 100) and
needs to be extended to larger urban areas.

Following social exchange theory, one can see how residents' support
for tourism initiatives intended to benefit them will be influenced by their
values. Williams and Lawson (2001) found that differences between
residents grouped according to 'community interests' were more statistically significant than those grouped according to socio-demographic
factors. These researchers go on to suggest that 'value' measures of
residents can be a more accurate way of understanding residents' views of
tourism. Once the key values of stakeholder groups are understood then
decision-makers are in a better position for developing proposals on how
tourism generated funds and public funds raised to further tourism should
be spent.

In New Zealand, Horn and Simmons (2002) examine two very different
destinations. Rotorua in the North Island is a bustling rural regional centre
where tourism is based on their hot springs and Maori attractions and
accounts for 18% of local employment. Kaikoura in the South Island is a
small coastal town, where the key tourist attractions are the beach and local
fishing, especially crayfish. In this small town tourism accounts for 30% of
local employment. Their research shows the following five factors affect
local perceptions of tourism in Rotorua and Kaikoura.

- the relative economic importance of tourism;
- the visibility of tourists;
- the actions of the two local councils;
- the sense of control residents felt they had over local tourism development;
- the meaning of tourism in relation to local conditions and history.

They conclude that Rotorua residents view tourism as a source of stability,
supplementing other local economic activities and that they have control
over it, while Kaikoura residents associate tourism with rapid change and
feel they are reacting to change, not directing it.

These community perceptions and various models indicate that while a general pattern of explanatory variables links resident reactions to tourism, we can expect to see local variations and nuances. These local variations are to be expected as local conditions and opportunities vary from place to place. After all, variety and something different are principle tourism motivators! But throughout these studies there is an overwhelming pattern of residents wishing to have more input into local tourism development decisions.

Organising

Butler's model of destination evolution indicates that the early stages of tourism development are likely to be spontaneous responses to the demands of small numbers of inquisitive tourists. As tourist numbers grow, destinations need to develop more formal and commercial relationships to handle increased volumes and benefit from them. This calls for organisation on behalf of the community, as well as for the industry.

McGibbon's (2000) anthropological study of tourism development in the village of St Anton in the Tirolean Alps of Austria demonstrates many of the community issues facing smaller destinations around the world. She considers:

> the development of tourism in St Anton is neither 'a blessing nor a blight', but rather a complex process with diverse and uneven effects. While a few residents have been able to build up small local empires in the context of tourism, others struggle with the pressures of high debts . . . Local struggles focus on how much tourism (development) communities should permit, how the industry should be organised, and the nature of future tourism developments. (McGibbon, 2000: 218)

The organisation and regulation of tourism in St Anton involves the local council (*Gemeinderat*), the local tourist association that is run as a public corporation, where each business pays a 1% turnover tax on its tourism component, and a range of voluntary organisations that contribute to community life and local tourism activities.

Lewis (1998) developed a *Rural Tourism Development Model* as a way of explaining the stages of tourism development that he observed in four small rural communities in the US. Unlike Doxey's causation model, Lewis' model was developed as an organisational process to manage tourism at a slower and more manageable pace. The four stages of Lewis' model and the intervening transitionary stages are listed below.

- **Evolution:** Beginning stage of development; tourism growth is organic; home-grown tourism services and goods are provided; no planning or advertising, resources and word-of-mouth attract visitors.

> Transition No. 1: Beginnings of tourism infrastructure, businesses and organisations

- **Formation**: Second stage of development; establishment of tourism infrastructure, businesses and organizations; provisional tourism planning.

> Transition No. 2: Beginnings of tourism events, attractions, programmes and marketing

- **Development**: Third stage of development; establishment of special tourism events and attractions; increased promotion for individual businesses and events as well as the destination; beginning of scheduling conflicts.

> Transition No. 3: Beginnings of tourist taxes, increased coordination of tourism providers and packaging of destination

- **Centralisation**: Final stage of development; establishment of Convention and Visitors Committees; implementation of tourist taxes; coordinated tourism planning, promotion and advertising at the local, regional and national levels.

Lewis states that the ability of local residents to increase their control over the tourism process is one of the main features that differentiates his model from other models, such as those of Butler (1980) and Doxey (1975). In addition to a strong local desire to keep control of tourism development, perhaps the success that locals have in controlling the impacts of tourism in the rural case study areas of Indiana, used by Lewis, can be attributed also to limited development demands in these areas. One can postulate that the limited appeal of certain areas to tourists also limits the potential profits, and therefore the appeal of these areas to either outside tourism investors, or local entrepreneurs, would be limited. If this is so, Lewis' model holds more promise for rural communities being able to develop tourism at a modest pace, where they can maintain a larger degree of control over the industry.

One tourist destination that has attracted a great deal of interest from both internal and external investors is Australia's Gold Coast. This major coastal resort has been a popular urban destination for many years and has become both a popular international-national destination and retirement area. In the process its residents have seen a tremendous growth in population and the waxing and waning of individual businesses within the general record of tourism growth. Within this context Weaver (2000) has asked whether the stages of stagnation and decline within the Butler model are inevitable or whether some form of regulation and organisation can delay or prevent such deterioration.

Management model

Weaver (2000) proposes that regulation, which includes planning and organisation, can divert the inevitable decline of the Butler destination evolution model. His proposed model consists of four potential outcomes for destination tourism, conditioned by the volume of tourism business and degree of regulation or organisation (Figure 9.2A):

- *Circumstantial Alternative Tourism* (CAT)   This represents a non-regulated, small-scale tourism sector that resembles alternative tourism or early stages of the Butler model.
- *Unsustainable Mass Tourism* (UMT)   This represents the end result of the Butler model, where unchecked development has led to decline as a destination's tourism resources have become overwhelmed in the absence of restrictive regulation and appropriate organisation.
- *Deliberate Alternative Tourism* (DAT)   This outcome occurs when a destination deliberately caps its development at the small-scale development levels of CAT. Weaver provides examples of this happening in a growing number of locations around the world. But it is noticeable they are either located in distant developing countries or are well removed from the urban centres of developed economies, permitting the creation of exclusive up-market nature-based or culture-based attractions. This would support our previous comments regarding the suitability of the Lewis model to smaller and rural communities.
- *Sustainable Mass Tourism* (SMT)   This represents the coexistence of large volumes of visitors and a large-scale tourism sector operating within local carrying capacities and sustainable limits.

Given the acceptance of Butler's model and its predecessor the product lifecycle, some would consider this STM objective to be an oxymoron, an impossibility. But it does not have to be so, for regulation in the form of planning and organising can set parameters and development directions that ensure the two sides of the sustainable development coin can be

A. Destination Possibilities

B. Gold Coast Destination Development Scenarios

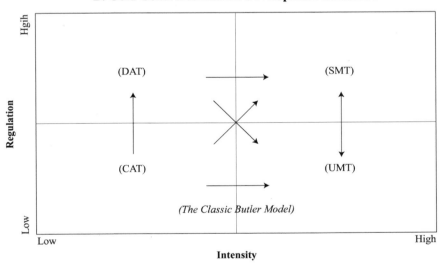

Figure 9.2 Potential influence of regulation and development intensity on destination evolution

Source: Weaver (2000: 218, 219)

achieved. Examples generally involve carefully planned resort destinations like Cancun in Mexico or Disney World in Florida. In the latter a marginal agricultural area was transformed into a global destination through water management, business planning and organisational control: a destination that now attracts millions of visitors to a site that includes a wilderness sanctuary which has restored the central Florida wetlands to something approaching their original state – a sanctuary that is easier to protect because it is in private ownership and thus does not face the public access pressures of national parks.

Weaver applied his model to Australia's Gold Coast resort and reported that all four outcomes were either apparent or emerging due to the size and different circumstances within the region (Figure 9.2B). Along the developed coastline he considers tourism is moving from its UMT to a SMT state due to the move toward more extensive planning and organising and the presence of high threshold sites such as the developed shoreline and beach environment. In comparison, the rural and tropical rain forest areas of the hinterland have smaller numbers of tourists and can be converted from their present CAT situation to a DAT status with the appropriate policy directives.

Moving from the theoretical approach to community organisation of tourism to real-life examples reveals residents are ready and willing to participate in the development of this community industry. Many community responses spring up around a particular issue, which is a feature of neighbourhood organisations. These grassroots groups tend to be spontaneous in their establishment, focus on a single or limited range of issues, are informal in practice, and have relatively short life-spans. More lasting and interactive with the industry are those groups that have been assigned to establish planning and advisory roles by government or the industry. These residents are selected or volunteer as representatives of community interests and participate in local tourism associations and planning as sounding boards. Between the dichotomy of grassroots and government/ industry appointments on local boards, there are a number of organisations that combine the features of both.

Examples of communities responding in an *ad-hoc* organisational style to tourism can be drawn from the sudden and unexpected influx of tourists when their location has been selected as the site for a popular television or film location. As Beeton (2000: 129) reports:

> An influx of visitors is not always welcome or advantageous, with many town unsuited to supporting the concomitant (film-induced) tourism growth because of limited infrastructure, facilities and services. In most cases the local community did not seek to be the site for the filming, yet they are left to cope with the consequences of increased traffic, crowding and pollution.

This situation has been experienced around the world, but especially in those small rural communities that exemplify the tranquil scenic atmosphere that some films and television programmes are trying to relate in their stories. Examples include the *Ballykissangel* television series based on the village of Avoca in Ireland (O'Connor & Flanagan, 2002) as illustrated in Figure 9.3; the English series *Heartbeat* based on the town of Goathland (Demetriadi, 1996); the Hollywood film *Roxanne* shot on location in Fort Nelson, British Columbia, Canada; and the television series *Sea Change* based on the fishing village of Barwon Heads in southern Australia (Beeton, 2000).

In Victoria, Canada, where a coal baron's 'castle' located in a prime residential area became a tourist attraction, because of its architectural and heritage appeal, tensions rose between its new commercial users and its residential neighbours. Local residents banded together around their concerns over the manner and magnitude of tourism development in their neighbourhood. These residents collectively opposed the development of bus-coach access and parking on its grounds because of the increased noise, pollution and perceived danger to local inhabitants, especially children and the elderly. So now coach tourists have to disembark a few blocks away on a major street and walk the remainder of the way to the castle. The residents surrounding the castle have no objection to walking tourists, because that style of visitation fits in with a quiet residential neighbourhood. They are also prepared to live with the increased car traffic associated with the castle and its FIT market. It is the intrusion and perceived danger of bus-coaches that caused the neighbourhood to protest and pressure city hall.

In Melbourne, Australia, an example of grassroots residential advocacy arose with the introduction of the Formula One Grand Prix. This international event with global television coverage was a coup for this event-oriented city and tourist destination, but its establishment in a public park within a wealthy suburb drew a great deal of opposition. The Albert Park Action Group was formed as a reaction to the anticipated negative impacts in terms of noise, safety, interruption of daily activities and a general threat to the overall quality of life. The actions of this group, which included large-scale protests and civil disobedience, received extensive media coverage. Although the group was able to persuade the state government to make some minor changes to their policies relating to the event and venue, they felt they were prevented from having a meaningful say in the running of this annual event. The state government passed special legislation – the F1 Act – that gave extra powers to the government and Grand Prix promoters to proceed with the event while curtailing opportunities for the public to prevent or otherwise impair the abilities for the mega-event to proceed as planned.

The more formal organising of resident input into tourism development

Figure 9.3 'Ballykissangel' image for the village of Avoca

has occurred mainly in established tourism destinations. An example of this is the Florida Keys, where residents have a formal role as advisers to district branches of the Tourism Development Council, an umbrella organisation that advises elected officials and markets the Keys as a destination from a bed tax funding source. Residents can also express their tourism views by contributing to the Comprehensive Plans that guide development in the Keys. They do this by voting for elected officials based on public stances on tourism development issues and attending public meetings to influence the creation and implementation of tourism-related policies and actions. Despite these established processes many residents felt their views were not being heard and were taking an increasingly pessimistic view towards tourists and tourism.

The Tourism Development Council (TDC) and the Board of County Commissioners (BOCC) – two organisations with a keen interest in tourism in the Keys – decided they needed to have a better understanding of residents' views on tourism so that they could incorporate these into their plans and policies (see case study at the end of Chapter 10). Their survey results indicated that the residents were at odds with the tourism industry and the organisations in place to guide its development on a range of important issues. Particular concerns were that they did not have enough of a direct say over tourism management and the allocations and priorities for spending tourism-generated funds. In response to the survey results and the public's views expressed at associated meetings, inclusive tourism planning was given a higher priority and more tourist dollars have been redirected to public works and infrastructure (Monroe County, Florida, 1999). More information on this example is provided in the case study at the end of this part of the book, pp. 328–335.

Leadership

A number of factors can impact on whether or not leaders in tourism development will emerge from communities. Community leaders can certainly stand out in all sorts of communities, as the earlier examples in this book of Tom O'Toole in Beechworth, Australia and Paul Miller, in Victoria, Canada, have shown. Community cohesion can encourage the formation of staunch support bases from which leaders can draw strength and resources. Governments also play an important role in creating environments that either encourage or stifle innovations, and encouraging the leaders responsible for the conceptions and spread of these innovations.

Leadership and resident relationships can be complex and multifunctional in nature, because while many leaders are also residents their success depends on the response from other residents including those who hold important local government roles. To simplify this natural mix of motives and behaviours we have focused on the individual business and government leaders as being a proactive force within the community. Local residents, with their own priorities and interests, are viewed largely as reactive agents to innovation. Local government is treated as an interpreter and facilitator, helping residents and voters appreciate the broader community implications and opportunities. However, it should be appreciated that individual roles and behaviours will not necessarily follow these artificially imposed categorisations.

Motivation

The motivation for taking on a leadership role tends to come from personal and community interests. These motivating factors can include beliefs, values, interests, abilities, resources, support, and relationships. However, Madrigal (1995: 87) points out that those motivations for taking on a leadership role in community politics can be far from altruistic.

> The political organisation of many communities is often dominated by individuals benefiting either directly from a specific development alternative (property owners, investors, speculators) or indirectly as a result of overall growth (realtors, bankers, owners of industries servicing the direct beneficiaries).

Although personal self-interest, either direct or indirect, may explain motivation as the driving force for many leaders, interest in a 'greater good' with respect to improving the community can also be a strong motivator. Furthermore, once leaders have started a crusade around a narrowly defined set of interests, they often grow to understand and advocate for a wider range of interests. Bono has used his rock star status as lead singer for the group U2 to advocate for a growing number of humanitarian issues. Bono's dedication to human rights has expanded from giving benefit concerts to meeting with top ranking political, religious and business representatives as he advocates for debt relief (Tyrangiel & Nugent, 2002). Government interest in addressing the issue of global debt relief created the opening needed to convert the dedication that individuals were showing to this cause by developing the policies necessary to put these ideas into action.

Many tourism leaders, who started out by promoting their enterprise, similarly go on to promote the destination and finally align themselves with quality of life issues for their communities. These community ambitions can be more easily realised if they are aligned with the aspirations that local governments have for their communities. In Bali, several of the top local surfers during the 1970s and who are now successful businessmen, have followed this pattern. While they initially focused on promoting their surfing businesses in the early 1980s, they went on to promote Bali as a destination and are now heavily involved in environmental issues aimed at preserving the spectacular natural resources of their island home (Australian Broadcasting Corporation, 2002).

Resident response

Community size can be a factor in how people respond to tourism and the ability for leaders to direct tourism's development. Mason and Cheyne (2000) studied residents' views regarding a cafe/bar development for use by tourists and locals in a small New Zealand village with minimal tourist visitations. They found that residents were concerned over the potential impacts of the bar/cafe on their community, even though they supported the development and 58% stated they would use it. This research confirms earlier findings that small communities are likely to express more concern over tourism developments and that the high visibility of such developments leads to heightened concerns (Capenerhurst, 1994).

Tourism leaders promoting public participation in tourism planning in small communities need to be aware of the challenges and opportunities such communities present. Small communities, such as rural areas or neighbourhoods within cities, tend to lack sufficient specialists or retired locals who can be identified as relevant stakeholders and active volunteers for community planning projects. However, even when communities are small a wide range of differing attitudes can be expressed regarding tourism developments (Allen *et al,*. 1988, Perdue *et al.,* 1990). Therefore, tourism leaders need to anticipate and respond appropriately to a range of opinions and values that exist even in small communities which in many other respects appear quite cohesive. Furthermore, a lack of adequate resources, especially funds, expertise, legislation and experience can make it harder for leaders in small communities to put into practice their ideas for change. This forces some to do a great number of additional tasks themselves, as well as bringing in necessary resources from outside the community. Community members' preference for local control may outweigh some or all of the benefits of outsourcing, which can hinder tourism leaders' options for developing and otherwise changing destinations.

The attitudes of elected representatives towards economic development, quality of life issues and tourism's desired role in their communities can make a big difference in how tourism develops and how the residents participate in its development. Elected officials and the government structures that support them often 'take the lead' in tourism development, in that their decisions create the legislative and functional context for tourism growth and controls. Richins (1997/98) assessed elected officials' attitudes towards various tourism development scenarios as a way to understand the direction in which they would lead tourism development in their communities. In Richins' study, 789 local government councillors in Queensland and New South Wales, Australia, were presented with 10 characteristics to describe a range of potential development scenarios. These are shown in Figure 9.4, and the councillors were asked to rate the scenarios in terms of what they would choose.

The councillors were then presented with the following five potential

Range of characteristics of various scenarios

Characteristic category for comparison

Expansionist extreme   ↔   Contractionist extreme

1. Encouragement of tourism development – *Level of encouragement and development rate expected*

Maximum development encouragement   ↔   Minimal development encouragement
and very high rate expected   and low or reduced rate expected

2. Restrictions on tourism development – *Level and enforcement of barriers and restrictions*

Little or no barriers and restrictions nor   ↔   Comprehensive controls/restrictions
enforcement   which are strenuously enforced

3. Orientation of tourism development – *Focus regarding residential vs. tourism development*

Peripheral residential with substantial   ↔   Residential orientation to the community
tourism and shopping development   with minimal tourism development

4. Degree and source of development – *Scale of tourism development and origin of investors*

Large-scale tourism development with   ↔   Small scale, if any development with
multi-national investors   only local investors

5. Impact motivation for decision-making – *Economic, socio-cultural, environmental motivation*

Economic motivation in decision-making   ↔   Sociocultural and environmental
motivation

6. Growth of population – *Visitor population vs. residential growth rate*

Very high visitor population growth rate   ↔   Decreased visitor growth rate, moderate–
compared to residential   low residential growth rate

7. Promotion of tourism from local government/community – *Encouragement level and funds available*

Very high visitor population growth rate   ↔   Decreased visitor growth rate, moderate–
compared to residential   low residential growth rate

8. Visitor target market encouraged – *International, capital city, regional, local*

International and capital city visitor   ↔   Visitors not encouraged, but may have
market   some local/regional and VFRs

9. Visitor facilities encouraged – *Priority of accommodation, attractions, activities encouraged*

Higher end accommodation, attractions   ↔   Visitors not encouraged, but may have
activities encouraged   some local/regional and VFRs

10. Council priority regarding provision of services and facilities – *Visitor or resident focus of Council*

Primary visitor focus with lower resident   ↔   Local residents as priority, visitors low
priority   priority

Figure 9.4 Continuum of tourism development in communities
Source: Richins (1997/98: 32)

development scenarios based on the continuum characteristics of Figure 9.4, and their associated political platforms (Richins, 1997/98).

- Expansionist   'Develop at any cost'
- Tempered Expansionist 'Develop but control it'
- Moderationist   'Be cautious regarding development'
- Preservationist   'Keep things as they are within the community'
- Contractionist   'Reduce development in the community'

The most desired scenario was that of the moderationist, followed by preservationist and tempered expansionist. These results indicated that many elected officials might be predisposed to be cautious in regards to supporting tourism development. It is important to note that the moderationist approach to tourism can also be a strong reflection of the middle-of-the road or centrist approach; whereby politicians opt for the safety of satisfying as many voters as possible by pursuing policies that offend as few people as possible. The obvious drawback of such a guarded approach is that rather than leading their constituents forward with development and conservation options, a moderationist approach can result in conventional, lack-lustre policies that fail to achieve remarkable results. As noted by Richins, the community tourism scenarios could serve as an excellent way to gauge political support for tourism development. Once the positions that elected officials take on tourism development are better understood, then stakeholder groups are in a better position to more effectively lobby their elected representatives on tourism issues. Therefore, once a community better understands its elected leaders' views of tourism, its non-elected leaders can more efficiently prepare their own tourism strategies.

On a larger scale, Honolulu in Hawaii, USA has benefited from the actions and ideas of a number of notable leaders. A recent example of a leader at this level is Jeremy Harris, who is currently the Mayor of the City and County of Honolulu and previously served as its managing director (City and County of Honolulu, 2002). The mayor was awarded the American Planning Associations' 2002 award for distinguished leadership by an elected public official in recognition of his substantial contributions to planning (APA, 2002). His notable achievements included the '21st Century Oahu: A Shared Vision for the Future'. This community based planning initiative involved thousands of members of the general public and stakeholder representatives in determining quality of life issues in a tourism dependent community. The mayor has devoted US$38 million in capital improvement funds to support this initiative, helping ensure that residents' ambitions for their communities are realised (APA, 2002: 17).

Tourism leaders promoting tourism development in large communities also need to be aware of the challenges and opportunities such communities present. Large communities, such as major cities or regional growth cores, tend to have sizeable populations in which a variety of stakeholder groups and other members of the public may exist and need to be included in community planning initiatives. Tourism leaders need to anticipate and respond appropriately to the wide range of opinions and values that exist in large and often disjointed communities, where people can be separated not only by socio-demographic, attitudinal and behavioural factors, but also by great distances. In large communities people can be isolated from other community members to such an extent that they may feel they have little if anything in common. Larger communities often, but not always, tend to have extensive resources in terms of funds, expertise, legislation and experience that tourism leaders can draw on when pursuing their goals. While these resources may be more plentiful in large communities, tourism leaders may find the competition with other community members for these resources is so fierce that a significant portion of their time is devoted to differentiating their proposals from other resource competitors.

Controlling

Understanding the range of tourism impacts requires careful analysis because of the many interrelationships and dimensions involved. To manage those impacts effectively, so the negative factors are ameliorated and the benefits are enhanced, requires community willpower and consensus. One advantage for tourism in this regard is that most people have been tourists at one time or another so they have first-hand experience with the industry, but associated with that is a mistaken belief that they know all about the industry. So to examine residents' participation in the control of tourism we start with an examination of their knowledge and education, before turning to questions regarding their involvement and authority.

Education

One of the key ingredients to enhancing resident input into the control over local tourism is to improve their knowledge of the industry through education. A knowledgeable resident will be in a far better position to understand the nuances of the industry and the necessary trade-offs that will need to take place if this industry is to complement other activities and contribute to the general quality of life. But few residents can develop such knowledge without some form of education and this is one area where tourism, an industry built on information and marketing, has so often fallen short. What business refers to as 'internal marketing', informing an organisation's employees what is happening and why, becomes essential when you are selling community resources and depending on local goodwill. Yet evidence of such internal marketing in community tourism is sparse.

Many studies show that with increased understanding of the tourism industry, residents demonstrate increased levels of support for the industry. However, opportunities to educate residents can digress into efforts to 'sell' residents on tourism development that does not meet their needs. Residents have expressed concern that the tourism information made available to them is often insufficient. They tend to question the sources of the pro-tourism educational information. Since this information usually comes from groups with a blatant tourism bias, such as local tourism marketing and promotional bodies, the reasons for their concern are understandable. Residents also have concerns about the depth and relevance of the data they receive in terms of understanding what the typical expenditure patterns of tourists are and how much they contribute in taxes and job creation compared to the costs incurred while servicing their needs. Simmons (1994: 103) found residents were unimpressed with the tourism information provided to them, as one-third rated it as either 'poor' or 'very poor'. These residents also ranked tourism, marketing and promotion as the lowest rated information source, indicating their dissatisfaction with the industry's ability to provide them with the information they wanted.

Psychology and experience tells us how we are more likely to take in and respond to messages in a positive manner if they are in keeping with our world view. Depending on how far removed pro-tourism messages are from a resident's perception of the industry, these messages will either be cynically received or rejected. Messages that are dramatically different from a person's existing beliefs can even cause a shift in attitude that is opposite to what was intended (Eagly & Chiken, cited in Lindberg & Johnson, 1997). If a tourism message presented to residents is seen to be a lie, then angered residents might become less hospitable to tourists and can turn on the industry. Tourism insiders and those with anti-tourism feelings will be more resistant to messages that overstate the benefits of tourism.

In their review of ways to increase the effectiveness of educating residents on tourism impacts, Lindberg and Johnson (1997) put forward several suggestions that are summarised below.

- Balanced: The message needs the right balance of scale (the attitude continuum from highly negative to highly positive) and weight (impact on residents' attitudes).

- Clear and unencumbered: The message needs to be easily
                             understandable, succinct and
                             disentangled from other issues.
                             Linking tourism with a decline in other
                             industries in the message can carry the
                             impression that tourism is the cause of
                             such declines.
- Fit 'world view':   The message needs to be in keeping
                             with the world view of the community.
                             If there is already a widely held
                             negative perception of tourism then a
                             message needs to address these
                             concerns.
- Credible source: The message will be more readily
                             accepted if it comes from a source that
                             is either already trusted, or is seen to
                             be impartial. In many cases an
                             assessment from an outside source,
                             such as a university, will be seen as
                             less biased.

Destinations should not shy away from painting a realistic picture of tourism impacts to residents in their educational efforts. While the tourism industry may hope to minimise information on tourism's negative impacts, these impacts are generally well known (King *et al.*, cited in Lindberg & Johnson, 1997). In his article on tourism decision-making groups Murphy (1991a: 12) suggested that:

> ... an annual independent audit of the taxes paid and people employed by the tourism industry, published locally, would demonstrate to the public the industry's contribution to the local economy.

Knowing who pays for tourism research and analysis and who will be privy to the results can have a large impact on how well such information is received. Ideally such research should be funded and directed by more than just pro-tourism factions. If such partnerships are not possible then a great deal of transparency and impartiality needs to be demonstrated throughout the process. Part of this transparency should include providing reports that clearly layout in data tables, charts and graphs the numerous impacts of tourism. Providing stakeholder groups with complicated and unsorted data is as unacceptable as only providing them with one page 'good-news' fact sheets that try to make tourism seem as shiny as the glossy paper they are printed on. Only when governments, industry and businesses speak to residents in a language that they understand and in a manner that is convincing will their tourism educational messages achieve their desired effects.

Involvement

The potential for investing tourism dollars in initiatives that are roundly supported by the community can be realised only if the public has an opportunity to participate in tourism planning and management. Public participation in deciding tourism matters needs to involve the following (adapted from Sewell & Phillips, cited in Simmons, 1994):

(1) Decision-maker support.
(2) Extensive citizen involvement.
(3) Equity in participation.
(4) Efficiency in participation.
(5) Implementable results.

It is important to realise that a measure of flexibility is required when following these guidelines. Depending on decision maker support (factor 1), which can relate to available budget, time, professional assistance or delegated power, certain trade-offs between factors 2 to 4 will be necessary. Therefore, in the interests of hearing and then incorporating a wide range of opinions on a matter (factor 3), the efficiency of the process (factor 4) would likely be impaired. In practice public participation in tourism planning tends to include one or more of the following techniques: public meetings, special committees, workshops, interviews, surveys and focus group discussions.

Simmons (1994) utilised informal interviews, a postal survey and focus groups to create and evaluate a public participation programme for an area that had not undergone extensive tourism development – Huron County, Ontario. Simmons was interested in determining the extent to which integrating field and survey methods would help with understanding tourism planning issues and improve the validity of collected data. He found that this combined approach identified key issues and objectives (through the interviews), provided hard data to access broad public sentiment about the issues and objectives (through the surveys) and then enabled citizens to develop appropriate strategies to guide tourism development (through the focus groups). The outcome of the public participation initiative in the case study area was a commitment by the county to develop advisory committees to allow for further public input into tourism planning. The success of the overall process builds upon the outputs of each of the three steps. Simmons notes that 'meaningful participation' in tourism planning will be dependent on residents' abilities to contribute to the process as well as their perceptions of influence over final and related decisions. The abilities of residents to contribute in a meaningful manner to tourism planning are determined by their own commitment to the process as well as the support, guidance, resources and data that are made available to them.

Lankford and Howard (1994) developed a multiple item tourism impact attitude scale as a way of providing a standardised measure of residents' attitudes towards tourism and assessing the effects of independent variables on these attitudes. Using multiple regressions they found that the 'ability to influence tourism decision making' had the most significant impact on the category of 'perceived personal and community benefits of tourism' compared to the other independent variables presented in the analysis. They found their results supported earlier studies that demonstrated a strong connection between positive attitudes towards tourism and the residents' perceived abilities to participate in the tourism decision-making process. Lankford and Howard (1994: 135) go on to provide the following advice:

> If people feel they (a) have access to the planning/public review process *and* (b) that their concerns are being considered, they are inclined to support tourism. Local governments and tourism promoters should pay particular attention to these pre-conditions for public support.

One of the most visible and enduring impacts of tourism can be increased public investment in amenities like parks, museums, promenades and piazzas. The public's support of such investment can again be linked to the social exchange theory, in that if residents see a personal or community net gain from such investment they are more likely to support them. Many resident surveys show that the public is aware of the improvements to the appearance and functioning of their town that tourism can bring (Brunt & Courtney, 1999; Oakes, 1997). Thus, their support of the industry and its tax contribution can enable a community to enhance its infrastructure and amenity base.

Just as having guests over to your house can motivate you to make your house look its best, tourists can motivate communities to 'look and act their best'. In the Brunt and Courtney (1999) study, the influx of visitors is seen to help justify investments in the town centre of an old seaside resort, and overall tourism development is supported. Many resident surveys have shown support for new developments that will be used by locals and residents. Lindberg and Johnson (1997) found that while residents rank the economic benefits of tourism most highly, those that increase the number and variety of local facilities are also valued. Perdue *et al.* (1990: 597) found that more residents support the statement 'tourism development increases the number of recreational opportunities for local residents', than the statement 'tourism reduces the quality of outdoor recreation'.

The research of Mason and Cheyne (2000) confirms earlier findings that small communities are more likely to express concerns over tourism developments and that the high visibility of such developments leads to heightened concerns. Many residents prefer small-scale tourism developments (Prentice, 1993; Ritchie, 1988). Such residents are less likely to support sport stadiums and conference centres, even if these facilities would be used by locals and residents. Limited financial resources and concerns over rapid change generally encourage smaller and less intrusive investments. Simmons (1994: 104) found in his focus group discussions with rural residents in New Zealand that preferences for small and medium scale developments are linked to residents' 'fear of "loss of control" over their rural way of life, visual landscape and environment'.

Tourism-generated funds should be invested in community amenity enhancements that benefit tourists and residents. However, when tourist dollars are to be spent 'for the good of the public', it is essential that the public be consulted on how and where they want these funds spent. If such consultation is lacking then statements that tourism dollars are being spent to better the community can produce results that are disappointing to the community. Community consultation needs to reach as wide a range of stakeholders as possible to ensure that tourism's investments in a community are effective in meeting broadly supported community goals. Murphy (1983a) found in one study that a major point of contention between different stakeholder groups is facility development, with business representatives enthusiastically supporting additional leisure facilities, while other groups are more sceptical of such developments. To address divided opinions on appropriate tourism investments intended to benefit residents Murphy (1991a: 12) suggests that: '. . . facilities requiring public funds become truly multipurpose, designed and operated for local residents as well as visitors'.

A good example of this is the Royal British Columbia Museum's 'Futures Project', where widespread consultation revealed 'we needed to become more accessible, relevant and responsive to our public' (Barkley, 1997: 154), the public being both the residents of Victoria, the province of British Columbia, and the tourist industry, because the provincial museum is one of Victoria, BC's major attractions.

Power

To provide all residents a chance to control the development of tourism within their community requires an open system that permits real and effective participation. Some would consider this as either idealistic or impractical, but there is plenty of evidence to suggest it is feasible when there is trust and collaboration on all sides. In democratic societies it is not idealistic when all residents have the vote and exercise their rights freely. It is not impractical because experience has shown it is only a few opinion leaders who have the conviction and patience to become involved.

When residents believe they have the ability to personally influence tourism impacts in their area they are likely to have much more positive views of tourism than if they feel their views are not heard (Madrigal, cited in Lindberg & Johnson, 1997). More favourable attitudes towards tourism have been closely linked with high levels of community members' perceived control over tourism planning and development (Lankford & Howard, 1994). Low levels of perceived resident control of tourism have been linked to negative attitudes towards tourism, tourists' dissatisfaction with their vacation experience and the eventual decline of tourist destinations (Hernandez *et al.*, 1996; Potts & Harrill, 1998). Host communities often express strong preferences for local ownership (Simmons, 1994). A factor in this support can be that local residents feel they can understand and trust local people and their ideas to a greater extent than 'foreign people and ideas'. Local ownership can enable residents to keep tourism development in check with their priorities and set within a familiar context.

The abilities of destinations to control tourism development vary according to a range of factors noted by France (1998) who depicts the levels of public participation in tourism in the West Indies islands utilising Pretty's earlier model. The West Indies model of participation in tourism starts with the low level involvement of residents during the plantation era and progresses on to higher levels of local control demonstrated in the 'self-mobilisation' era. During the earlier stages the money earning tourism ventures are owned and controlled by individuals and companies with ties to traditional elites and overseas capital. The purpose of these ventures is to provide profits for the owners and little consideration is given to the impacts of these ventures on the local community or the means by which they could contribute beyond menial labour. As tourism ventures expand and endeavour to secure loans and other forms of financial backing the opportunities for public participation tend to increase.

The roles of local/residents builds slowly as the tourism industry expands, in that increasingly locals are asked to contribute ideas, resources and a wider range of services to the tourism sector (France, 1998). It is only in the final two stages of France's seven stage model that the public are seen to exercise real control over tourism development in terms of guiding planning, being in control of local decisions and being able to proceed successfully with independent initiatives. The author notes that the control local residents are able to demonstrate in the final stages of this model are tied strongly to their improved economic situation, stating that 'local people who have amassed capital from tourism strengthen and extend their activities and also use this capital to move into a wider range of economic activities' (France, 1998: 225). One can also extrapolate from this model that the locals' increased sophistication in dealing with tourism, coupled with their increased personal and community income, contributes greatly to their empowered position.

Summary

This chapter outlines the role of residents in community tourism. The chapter opens with an overview of residents' needs and ways of measuring these needs as a means of guiding tourism plans. Close attention is paid to the Irridex model and its relevance to resident perceptions and reactions to tourism in their communities; different types and functions of resident groups are reviewed in the organising component of the chapter; the value of community involvement in tourism planning initiatives and ensuring that tourism expenditures benefit visitors and locals are a focus of the leadership component; and finally, the control component looks at the scope and scale of tourist–resident benefits.

Residents bring life, vitality, history and services to their communities. Tourists are attracted to the types of places where residents want to live – areas that are beautiful, vibrant, prosperous, well serviced by infrastructure, accessible and shine as something special. Residents can have great enthusiasm, ideas and in many cases reservations about tourism development; however, without a proper conduit they can find that their contributions are largely ignored, or marginalised. The following chapter explores the roles that governments serve in creating mechanisms to realise the ambitions of their constituents. The growing importance of non-government agencies in providing a voice and a means by which community groups can share their views and help shape their communities are also explored throughout the next chapter.

Chapter 10

Government

Government involvement in tourism takes place to varying degrees at different levels as per a government's scope of powers, commitment to tourism management and available resources. Government involvement in tourism can include local councils, regional government, state, national and international bodies. Aboriginal government involvement in tourism also ranges from the local through to the international level and can help to reorientate the way Aboriginal and non-Aboriginal people regard and interact with tourism destinations. All levels of government in tourism typically focus on the economic aspects of tourism, with a strong focus on tourism promotion. Priorities for the types, locations and the magnitude of public sector financial support of tourism developments are established through a range of government policies; and this chapter will focus on the situation in countries with developed economies and democratic institutions.

Governments aim to serve the people they represent in a just and effective manner. A government's ability to make and enforce laws, including those relating to land uses and taxation, can enable it to wield great influence over tourism developments and subsequent management. In democratic societies government's extensive powers tend to be held in check by the 'separation of powers' approach to governing. This approach reserves law making authority for the executive, while the legislature administers these laws and the judiciary interprets them (Beazer, 1998). While democratic systems of government are primarily accountable to their constituents, their actions are directed largely by commitments made to other entities as well as regulations and requirements from other levels, or types of governments. Therefore, while a community might call on its local and state governments to invest in a tourism attraction, such as setting aside land for a new park, the local government might not be able to afford having this area taken off its tax rolls and paying for maintenance. Other factors that could work against a park designation could include state government commitments to other uses, or federal environmental regulations that severely limit the development of essential infrastructure, such as roads, necessary to open up the area's tourism potential. These various and sometimes conflicting commitments can make it difficult for governments to make the 'right' decisions in terms of deciding how and to what extent they will support and regulate tourism.

Tourism's complexities and heterogeneous nature challenge elected officials and policy makers alike, as they struggle to understand and manage the industry. Most countries in the world recognise tourism as a way to diversify their economies and create corresponding tourism programmes and strategies to support the industry. Tourism can provide a multitude of economic benefits for governments, including attracting outside investors, creating jobs and earning foreign currency to help with a country's trade balance. As a service industry tourism has become a principal source of employment and tax revenue. Governments also benefit when tourism enhances an area's international, national and regional reputation, which in turn can attract additional investment while fostering a sense of pride of place, culture and history among their citizenry.

Typical tourism challenges that governments face include determining the appropriate physical areas for tourism development, the types of tourism products and services that they will support, the level of funding for these tourism initiatives and how to integrate them with other government priorities. Since tourism is a relatively new industry and one that is dominated by small businesses, it can be especially difficult for governments to predict the potential impacts of their tourism efforts.

An underlying factor in the long-term success of tourism in any destination is the perceived legitimacy of the industry by the general public, which is related to its overall costs and benefits and the extent to which they are distributed. Another factor of legitimacy that governments must address is whether or not their investments in tourism and other industries are perceived to be in the best interests of the community. Governments can control tourists directly by limiting who is allowed to travel and where they are allowed to travel. Governments can also limit lengths of stay for tourists and the types of uses and visitation numbers to specified areas through visa controls and other associated measures.

This chapter outlines the pivotal role that governments play as facilitators in creating situations that are either conducive or inauspicious for tourism. The planning component of the chapter examines the roles of different levels of government, including Aboriginal groups, in tourism developments. The change in orientation of governments as they move from a welfare or social responsibility approach to take on more of an entrepreneurial or business approach is also discussed in detail. The organising component of the chapter looks at tourism infrastructure and financing. The issue of financing is discussed at length with particular regard given to raising funds to support tourism-related expenditures and ways to realise revenue from tourists and the tourism industry. The leadership component of the chapter focuses on how governments are re-evaluating and transforming their roles as 'leaders' as they embark on a number of different approaches in their efforts to fulfil their mandates. The increasing leadership shown by non-government organisations (NGOs) in terms of delivering community services and watching out for the interests of stakeholder groups is also discussed. The control component of the chapter focuses on how government actions shape community growth and development through legislation, policies and politics. The courts in turn play an important role in interpreting the tourism-related laws created by government and ensuring that the intent and purpose of such laws are upheld.

Objectives

In order for governments to act in the best interest of the people they serve they need to meet several prime objectives, the first of which is to identify and appropriately respond to the potential that tourism has for meeting stakeholder requirements. Governments need to be aware of their legal obligations when considering what these groups want and how these things can be provided to them. For example, there are often restrictions on what revenues from 'tourist taxes', such as bed taxes, can be spent on, which in turn limits governments' options for financing tourism proposals. Another objective for governments is to create a balanced approach to the development of resources and provision of services and other deliverables to their communities. This involves going beyond the 'highest and best use' criteria based on short-term economic return, such as zoning land for high density commercial uses, to look at potential social, environmental and 'spin-off economic returns'. This can occur when devoting land to passive recreation increases the property values and subsequent taxes for surrounding properties. Governments need to be cognisant of stakeholder priorities and resources to find the right balance, given that complex negotiations and detailed problem solving can be required to satisfy the demands of their constituents and the other stakeholders. Such a balance needs to be considered when deciding on allocating resources to worthy tourism proposals, while honouring existing financial commitments.

An additional objective of government is to ensure that a balanced approach is actually implemented and maintained. While investing in discretionary developments, such as conference centres, can bring many benefits to communities, there are many other essential services, such as education, that must be adequately resourced. Governments need to find the right mix between investing in projects that have the potential to stimulate further economic development and community enhancement, while ensuring that they devote enough resources to provide the core services upon which both residents and tourists depend.

Policy needs to be guided by information so an important objective of any government should be to gather the best intelligence possible about the tourism industry. To use an accounting dictum, something 'never measured is never managed'. Therefore, there has been more effort put into obtaining more tourism data, either directly through primary research or indirectly through satellite accounts. There is great potential for more efficient and economical information gathering through partnering. For example, Canada, Mexico and the US have funded a series of reports on the characteristics of potential overseas travel from specific travel markets around the world (Coopers & Lybrand Consulting, 1995, 1996). The highly detailed data bases created from this research were then made available to major universities from these countries, which allowed for even more refined information searches, such as looking at the characteristics of potential Japanese and German travellers to rural destinations in Canada (Murphy & Williams, 1999).

Finding the right balance between investing in tourism and adequately addressing other government commitments and priorities requires integrity, expertise and information. The use of triple bottom line assessments where the environmental, social and economic impacts of proposals are all considered is an important starting point for finding this balance. The potential impacts of tourism options must be effectively appraised and audited so that the appropriate community balance for tourism can be achieved. The effectiveness of such assessment will be dependent largely on the following factors:

- political context (time, money and support for the processes);
- who conducts these assessments (in-house, or impartial outside observers);
- assessment criteria (most important factors and their weighting);
- feedback loop (necessary adjustments need to be highlighted and then implemented).

Government priorities and their corresponding regulations and policies impact greatly on the success of tourism industries at different locations. Establishing community tourism goals and objectives can be an emotionally charged and openly challenged act. In many ways the final decisions on tourism planning are political decisions.

Planning

Tourism depends heavily on scarce and finite physical resources, ranging from pristine and uncrowded wildernesses to primate cities with the world's best cultural and sporting attractions. Such exceptional places represent an inherently unequal distribution of resources and keeping these places exceptional is a result of largely political decisions. These decisions are political in that governments consistently favour particular stakeholder interests over those of other groups when making decisions in the 'public's interests'. Huffman (1994) notes that competing groups, such as environmentalists and land developers, will often claim that they are acting in the best interests of the public as they assert their views. Environmentalists' desire for a healthy environment that is preserved for the world's inhabitants belies the fact that it is primarily the world's elites who have the resources to visit environmental reserves and partake in ecotourism activities. At the same time the desire of developers to ensure that a strong and diversified economy is maintained must also be seen in the context of the personal financial risks and gains facing individuals associated with such developments.

If governments shared their tourism resources equally among all their constituent groups and areas, they could effectively water-down the attractiveness of any single location and the tourist drawing potential of their overall area since the nexus of a 'must see destination' would be lost. Governments select certain areas where they will concentrate their tourism activities and which public interests they will favour over others. Around the world we see governments strongly market and invest in their main cities as destinations and gateways for tourists, who are subsequently encouraged to explore beyond those centres and enjoy regional areas.

The attempts of governments to attract and then dispense visitors can be seen in operation globally. In Australia, Victoria is an example of how a state government focuses on its main city, Melbourne, to draw people in and once they have arrived tries to tempt them to take short trips out into regional areas (Tourism Victoria, 2002: 30–1). Regional areas in Victoria, Australia still have reason to be concerned about their secondary tourism status, especially given that many of their targeted 'hero' destinations (primary regional tourist areas) identified in the strategic plan are only a few hours drive from Melbourne.

Making large cities the base for rural tourism excursions does not necessarily encourage the types of extended or overnight stays, which bring in the maximum financial returns. However, in some cases there are insufficient attractions to hold tourists overnight and the hero strategy provides a start in raising the profile of local tourism. Likewise, the international icon of London, England, is very successful at drawing international visitors but less so in dispensing them to the tourist attractions of its suburbs or home counties (Murphy, 1982). Victoria, as the capital city of British Columbia in Canada, dominates the tourist market of Vancouver Island and continues to do so despite marketing and transport developments to facilitate its growth elsewhere on the island (Keller & Murphy, 1990). In China, the tourism dominance of its coastal provinces is encouraging the central government to select certain inland growth centres to encourage more international visitors to explore its eastern and highland provinces (Zhang, 2001).

Government roles are largely shaped by the level at which they occur. These levels can be divided into the following categories:

- national;
- state;
- regional/local.

As the impacts, both positive and negative of tourism, become better understood and the competition for tourists increases, so too many governments are creating tourism strategies and plans to direct the manner and direction of tourism growth in their communities. Different levels of government have different levels of resources as well as different primary goals and objectives, all of which impact on their tourism regulations and spending. At the various government levels tourism planning policies address issues of product development, security and protection of natural, historic and cultural resources along with tourism marketing, promotion and related economic incentives.

National

While tourism is being integrated increasingly into national policies (Edgell, 1993, cited in Butler, 1999; Gunn, 1997), the main focus in many of these policies is marketing, as opposed to tourism education and product development. In the United States the *National Tourism Policy Act (1981)* built upon the *US International Travel Act (1961)*, and promoted increased visitation as well as reducing barriers to tourism and increasing awareness of the tourism industry. The *United States Travel and Tourism Administration* (USTTA) was established under the 1981 Act to take on the role of a national office for tourism. The USTTA's established policies were to promote travel to and within the US and reduce the country's travel deficit. The USTTA was replaced by *US National Tourism Organisation* (USNTO) in 1996 which had a much more restrained mission, focusing on international promotion and budget matters (Goeldner *et al.*, 2000). The United States also has a *Tourism Industries Office*, a *Tourism Policy Council* and a *Rural Tourism Development Foundation* that are responsible for creating and implementing plans that will increase travel and tourism revenues by attracting foreign markets (US Code, 2001a,b). The chaotic aftermath of September 11 promoted a flurry of new bills, such as the *Travel America Act (2001)* that provides tax and other travel incentives to support the travel and tourism industry (US Senate, 2001). In light of the lack of consistent, adequately funded tourism management guidance at the national level, Goeldner *et al.* (2000: 109) consider 'the United States (policy making) is an example of how not to develop tourism'.

There are some better examples of national tourism management from the UK and Australia. The English Tourism Council (ETC) is committed to partnering with industry and other stakeholders in implementing *Tomorrow's Tourism*, a comprehensive document that provides 'leadership and direction to England's fragmented tourism industry in the implementation of the government's strategy' (ETC, 2002: 1). The national *Tomorrow's Tourism* strategy aims to exceed a 12% growth rate for British tourism by the end of 2010 (Tourism Forum [UK], ND: 1).

The 15 action points that make up the core of this strategy include the following: a blueprint for sustainable tourism, incentives to increase access, increased funds for promotion, new information and reservation technologies. In the wake of September 11 and the outbreaks of foot and mouth disease, the Scottish Tourism Board (STB) developed a *Tourism Framework for Action: 2002–2005* (STB, ND). This action plan is built around partnerships, as it provides detailed recommendations and assigns responsibilities for these actions to different tourism stakeholder groups. This collaborative approach is working, according to Eccles from the Monarch of the Glen Project (STB, ND: 18):

> Led by the private sector and with the support of all the public agencies, the success of the Monarch Country initiative has been twofold. The availability of the same advertising material to all businesses throughout the Strath has increased visitor awareness and drawn us all together in an area which has suffered from in-fighting for many years.

The Australian Tourist Commission (ATC) was established in 1967 to attract overseas visitors to Australia and continues to work towards this aim in partnership with the tourism industry and other agencies (ATC, 2003). The ATC receives approximately $123 million a year in funding from the Australian government and the tourist industry to help it achieve its objectives. The result has been some very successful promotional campaigns involving Paul Hogan, Elle McPherson, Ian Thorpe and others, and a steady increase in international visitor arrivals.

Nations that fully access their tourism potential, develop comprehensive tourism plans with realistic targets, and provide the funds to implement these plans create a solid foundation upon which many other tourist initiatives can develop.

National parks and World Heritage Sites

National parks serve the needs of numerous stakeholders and it is the domain of national governments to manage the parks to meet various stakeholder requirements. National park customers are those who visit the parks for reasons as diverse as relaxation, recreation, education, spirituality and sightseeing. However, tourism is not the only stakeholder in national parks. Different industry groups from mining, forestry and farming lobby the government for different usage and access rights to national parks.

In most national parks people are not allowed to live within park boundaries; however, there are some notable exceptions. Aboriginal people can have special rights to reside in national parks that were traditionally their lands, as is the case with the Smoky Mountains National Park in the US. In Canada's Banff National Park people reside permanently within the boundaries of the national parks in designated areas, such as the Banff township that grew up with the early railway development and the Banff Springs Hotel. In the UK the crowded nature of the countryside meant that areas of outstanding beauty and cultural significance had to be preserved by superimposing park status on living communities, creating national parks that allow the coexistence of the past with the economic and cultural structures of the present.

Residential and tourist communities within parks tend to be highly regulated with strict caps on the number of units and maximum occupancy of these units, plus they are constrained by specific architectural and development guidelines. Even with these restrictions it can be difficult to contain the pressures to live in or adjacent to such desirable areas. The strict development restrictions on national parks tend to encourage robust development just outside the park boundaries, as is evident with the rapid growth of Canmore, just outside of Banff National Park in Canada, and Gatlinburg, which serves as a gateway community to the Great Smoky Mountains National Park in the US.

Various federal laws protect the natural, cultural and agricultural resources in national parks. In the US there are detailed federal laws that prohibit possessing or damaging living or dead wildlife, plants, geological features and other aspects of these environments (US Code, 2001, c). Similar laws can be found in many countries; however, it can be exceedingly difficult for developing countries to enforce these requirements if they are beleaguered with inadequate funds, corruption and other factors contributing to negligence in management.

The lack of a strong legal system that balances environmental, commercial and community rights is just one of the substantial challenges to sustainable tourism management in the developing world. According to (Tosun 2000: 626) there are many obstacles to collaborative planning in developing countries which lead to:

> political instability, patron–client relationships, low level of literacy, unfair and unequal distribution of income, severe macro-economic problems, lack of services of the welfare state, lack of democratic institutions, lack of democratic understanding among state elites, unwillingness of the elite to share the fruits of development with the majority in society in the developing world.

The tourism challenges facing developing countries need to be addressed in a manner appropriate to the economic and political development of these countries. Problems of tourism mismanagement in developing countries can be exacerbated when it goes against cultural practices to challenge established decision-makers. In countries where traditionally power is placed in the hands of a few and challenging their rights of leadership is seen as an affront to unity, citizens may not be prepared to hold their governments accountable for their actions (Timothy, 1999). Rather than grafting tourism planning ideas onto other countries Tosun and Jenkins (1998: 111) suggested that:

> perhaps the most appropriate way to address these needs is to train and develop indigenous planning expertise. This is already happening in a number of developing countries where tourism is an important sector in the economy.

Once governments are aware of their tourism opportunities and constraints they can direct their tourism growth in a manner that they feel is appropriate.

International recognition and planning has transformed some sites into major world destinations. World Heritage Site status has been a boon for conserving areas of exceptional beauty and cultural significance around the world for projects as diverse as colonial slave trading complexes in Africa, ancient cities in Asia and wilderness reserves in the Americas (UNESCO, 1993). The historic city of Sukhothai in Thailand has benefited from its world heritage designation through aid in developing a Master Plan, funds of over US$500,000 for implementation of the plan and an associated campaign to raise awareness and enable significant restoration works (UNESCO, 1993: 17). Africa's wildlife parks represent an effective partnership between international agencies and national governments that has conserved the distinctive flora and fauna of this region of the world and turned them into world-class tourist attractions. By 2002 there were 730 world heritage sites and 'nations lobby hard to get their glorious buildings, wilderness, and historic ruins on the list, a stamp of approval that brings prestige, tourist income, public awareness, and, most important, a commitment to save the irreplaceable' (O'Neill, 2002: 60).

Indigenous

Indigenous people around the world are asserting their rights to control their culture, lands and economic development. Indigenous people are recognised in certain countries, such as Canada and the US, as sovereign people who have rights attributed to their state within a state. In certain African and European countries, the rights of indigenous people relate primarily to the lands and other resources that they own or traditionally use, rather than being recognised rights to establish and maintain their own system of laws.

In Kenya wildlife tourism is one of the country's most profitable industries, yet until recently the Massai, the indigenous people, have not had a significant role in its tourism management, or benefits (Berger, 1996). The Massai are now bringing their skills to park management, as well as leasing their land to tourism operators by establishing some of their own tourism businesses and attractions (Berger, 1996).

Wildlife tourism is also of great importance in Zimbabwe, yet the successes of tourism there have brought many hardships to indigenous people in terms of denying them access to their traditional resources. The Zimbabwe government developed the CAMPFIRE programme that encourages local decision-making through consensus and directs tourism proceeds towards community development, as a way of sharing tourism management and its benefits with local people (Potts *et al.*, 1996).

The Sampi are indigenous people who are now primarily found in the northern part of Norway, in an area commonly referred to as Lapland. The rights of the Sampi, such as free access to the countryside, have been largely usurped by Norway's citizens and through default by the tourists (Pedersen & Viken, 1996).

> This has resulted in a race for the best fishing areas and hunting grounds, and pressure on, or even suppression of, the old Sampi rights to harvest according to kin-group (siida) agreements. Sampi protests against this encroachment of their old rights were not heard, and as a minority, they had no power to defend their old common rights. (Pavel, 1979 cited in Pedersen & Viken, 1996: 80)

This marginalisation of the role of indigenous people and the threats that increased tourist visitations bring to their environment and traditional ways of life is found around the world. The best way to ensure that the rights of indigenous people are protected is to enshrine these rights in law, with sovereign rights providing the highest level of indigenous independence and opportunities.

Extensive sovereign rights of the Inuit people of Northern Canada were recognised in 1993 with the creation of Nunavut – a territory three times the size of France – as a semi-autonomous nation (Smith, 1996). These land, resource and governing rights combine to provide the Inuit people with unique tourism development opportunities. The primary attractions to this area are its pristine environment and cultural resources, yet its tourism potential remains underdeveloped. It has been suggested that the indigenous people in Nunavut take a self-assessment of their tourism potential, using the four H's of tourism (Smith, 1996: 42):

- *Habitat*: access options, costs, distinguishing features, partnering opportunities.
- *Heritage*: what aspects are appropriate to share and how, monitoring, social issues, such as whether or not to allow alcohol.

- *History*: what events occurred, landmarks, who will be involved and how.
- *Handicrafts*: distinctive, availability, distribution, special events and marketing.

Applying the 'Four H's' to indigenous tourism ventures can be particularly useful given its focus on traditional values and attributes. With each of these steps the potential impacts of the proposals on the indigenous community are examined by its members, which allows for greater self-determination in tourism management.

In the US indigenous people are working towards managing the tourism resources of their own land, within the confines of limited sovereign rights recognised by the federal government. In the US the *1934 Indian Reorganisation Act (1934)* restored what remained of Indian lands to tribal ownership and established a process that enabled tribes to organise for the purposes of self-government under the supervision of the federal government (Minnesota Indian Gaming Association (MGA), 2002). The classification of 'what remained of Indian lands' in 1934 was controversial then and is even more so now.

Hawaii was officially recognised as a sovereign nation by the US as early as 1826, however, the nation's government was overthrown and subsequently annexed by the US in 1893 (Masten, 2002: 2). Native Hawaiians are petitioning the federal government *(see bills S. 2899 and H.R. 4904)* to formally apologise for the overthrow of the Hawaiian government and to recognise the sovereignty of Native Hawaiians. These measures are seen by many people to be essential to protecting Hawaiian culture and lands. The culture and natural resources of Hawaii are the foundations of the rich tourism industry that has flourished there for over half a century and if they are degraded the appeal of Hawaii will diminish greatly. Therefore, the potential ramifications of Native Hawaiian sovereign rights on the tourism industry are immense.

Another landmark statute relating to indigenous sovereignty in the US that has particular relevance to tourism is the *Indian Gaming Regulatory Act (1988)* (MIGA, 2002: 1). This Act allows sovereign governments to choose to allow gaming on their lands. The Act recognises that gaming and gambling on Indian lands can assist with the economic development and self-determination of indigenous people. Since areas recognised as Native American lands tend to be isolated, stripped of natural resources, poorly served by infrastructure and community services, economically depressed and battling immense social problems, gambling and gaming represent one of the few viable options for economic development on Native Indian reservations in the US. In a recent review of developments Thompson (2003) notes the money generated by gaming has been used to benefit social capital and other enterprises on many reservations, but it also exposes the indigenous people to exploitation and criminal activity. But he also comments that some tribes are using gaming revenue for lobbying and campaign funds as they recognise the importance of influencing policy makers.

The limitations of gambling and gaming as a means of economic development and its potential negative social consequences have been recognised by indigenous and non-indigenous people around the world. In fact most indigenous nations in the US do not engage in gaming and where gaming does occur on native reservations it makes up less than 10% of the entire gaming industries in the US (MIGA, 2002). However, the development of these islands of gambling in areas where it is illegal to operate casinos outside of the reservations/reserves has created local tensions (Carmichael *et al.* 1996). Hsu (2003: 229) argues the 'debate continues about the costs and benefits of Native American gaming within tribes, and about the legitimacy of gambling as a Native American enterprise'.

In the US a number of indigenous groups have come together as 'tribal nations' to promote their tourism products. Comprehensive tourism development policies have been developed by the Pueblos at Taos, New Mexico, the Navajos of Arizona and the Cherokees of North Carolina (Smith, cited in Gunn, 1997: 15). The residents of the Acoma pueblo, which is close to Alburquerque, New Mexico, and well serviced by freeways, established their own tourism policies to preserve and promote their native heritage and have developed into a major tourist destination that includes a casino. The *Alliance of Tribal Tourism Advocates* (ATTA), which was established in 1993 by a number of tribes in the South Dakota region of the US, is an example of a tourism association created and run by Aboriginal people (ATTA, 2002). The goals of this organisation are to enhance tourism development opportunities for tribes by bringing economic and employment benefits to Indian communities. The beliefs and priorities of this indigenous tourism organisation include the following (ATTA, 2002):

- Support cultural integrity and traditional values in the development of tribal tourism.
- Acknowledge the sovereignty of tribes.
- Preserve the sanctity of sites, artefacts, rituals and ceremonies considered sacred by tribes.
- Protect the natural environment of tribal homelands.
- Assist in tourism code and policy development.
- Publish and distribute intertribal tourism material.
- Host tribal tourism workshops and training.
- Provide technical assistance to members in developing publicity materials and tour packages.

- Sponsor national and international marketing efforts and trade missions.
- Develop inter-tribal tour packages.
- Broker the sale of tours for ATTA members.

In Australia the _Native Title Act of_ 1993 enshrines in law the rights and interests of Aboriginal and Torres Strait Islander peoples to lands over which their title is recognised (National Native Title Tribunal, 2003). Unfortunately, it is exceedingly difficult under this legislation to establish native title, which greatly curtails the powers of Aboriginal and Torres Strait Islanders peoples to control their traditional lands. Ayers Rock, now known as Uluru, in Uluru-Kata Tjuta National Park is now managed under the guidance of the Uluru-Kata Tjuta Board of Management. This board consists of six indigenous people, the Director of National Parks and Wildlife, a scientist and representative from the Ministry of Environment and the Ministry for Tourism (Parks Australia, 2000). At the state level there are some promising developments, such as the _South Australia's Department of Environment and Planning_'s 1987 management framework that incorporates indigenous skills and knowledge in the management of its parks (ParksWeb, 2003).

State

At the national level, legislation can be too broad and complex to influence key factors for tourism's success, while at a local level the resources necessary for preparing and enforcing effective tourism management policies can be lacking. Therefore, the state level can be a practical and effective way of influencing the development and management of tourism, as it benefits from a larger share of financial, technical and professional resources than local government, while being close enough to the issues to properly understand and respond to them. The _Alaska Community Tourism Handbook_ offers expert guidance on assessing the potential impacts of tourism on communities and how to invest resources so they will have their desired impacts (State of Alaska, ND). State agencies can use handbooks and other information sources to highlight key issues that destinations should consider in developing their own approaches to tourism management.

In many countries each state is responsible for preparing an official state plan to guide development that in turn serves as a set of standards that all local governments must adhere to in preparing their own official plans. In regard to land use or town planning, state plans set general goals and objectives that municipal governments must support in their detailed planning goals and objectives and related land development regulations. Land use or town planning can have as great an impact on the development and management of tourism enterprises as tourism specific legislation. Land use or town planning requirements are the primary means by which governments establish and maintain standards for developing and managing resources in developed areas. A state planning directive to increase the use of coastal resources by residents and visitors could be supported by a municipal planning objective to encourage the development of marinas and by specific land use regulations, such as those relating to zoning that allow for the development of these marinas.

Specific tourism planning legislation is still a rarity and often serves more as a marketing flourish than as a detailed guide of what is required by the industry and how it is to be achieved. However, a good example of comprehensive state guidance in tourism planning can be drawn from the state of Queensland in Australia, which has created a 'whole-of-government strategy' to integrate and coordinate tourism policies throughout State legislation and general government practices (Tourism Queensland, 2002). Under the state's goal to 'increase Queensland's visitor market share while ensuring its sustainability in the long term' the state has committed to 'initiating cooperative research on yield management issues' (Tourism Queensland, 2000). An example of the state of Victoria's approach to tourism management is offered elsewhere in this book as a case study.

State resource management and service requirements can be relied upon to a lesser or greater degree by local governments depending on their motivations and capabilities to guide their tourism development. When departing from state standards the onus is on local governments to show that such departures will still enable to them to meet state goals and objectives. If a local government does not have the resources to develop its own tourism strategies, it can draw on those of the state, thereby ensuring a consistent base-line standard in developmental and environmental practices relating to tourism. However, local government provides one of the best opportunities for residents to directly participate in tourism decision-making within developed and democratic countries.

Local

Local government areas with well-established tourism industries tend to have detailed plans and strategies to guide their tourism development. The *1992 General Plan for the City and County of Honolulu* shows a strong commitment to combining local quality of life issues with tourism development. Throughout this document the needs of visitors are discussed alongside those of residents creating an almost seamless approach to managing the natural, physical and cultural environments of Honolulu for current and future inhabitants of this area. A main objective of this plan is, 'to maintain the viability of Oahu's visitor industry' (City and County of Honolulu, 1992: 15), for the resort area of Waikiki comes under the county jurisdiction. Policies supporting this objective include the following:

- designating Waikiki as Oahu's main resort destination and directing public expenditures to this area to support this role;
- placing caps on accommodation units and densities;
- managing the development of new resort areas to minimise adverse impacts on the environment and the cost of providing public services to these areas.

The *1992 General Plan for the City and County of Honolulu* encourages extensive public participation in the planning process, as evident from the following extract (City and County of Honolulu, 1992: 9–10):

> To provide the residents of the City and County of Honolulu with the opportunity to democratically and meaningfully participate in the determination of the direction and quality of future growth of Oahu, a citizen participation process which focuses on citizen advisory boards as called for in the City Charter has been established. . . . Members of the advisory boards can provide valuable assistance by soliciting the input of other neighbourhood groups and residents and identifying the concerns of the areas they represent. By monitoring conditions they can also help to make sure the policies of the General Plan are implemented.

The commitment of the City and County of Honolulu to public participation in tourism planning is further evident in their community visioning programmes, special areas plans and sustainable community plans (City and County of Honolulu, DPP, 2002).

The need to integrate tourism with other economic and social activities becomes paramount at the local level (Butler, 1999). The growing interest in heritage and cultural tourism attractions means that more tourists wish to learn about the past and present workings of the host community – its sense of place. This has resulted not only in a growing link with museums and festivals but a tourism interest in 'industrial tourism', where visitors learn about current industrial practices (Frew & Shaw, 1998). To facilitate such an interface more local jurisdictions are engaging in planning and management policies that will permit the leisure interests of tourists to operate alongside the commercial interests of various industrial sectors. An example of this can be seen in the earlier description of Canterbury's planning for its historic shopping district (Laws & Le Pelley, 2000).

Entrepreneurial approaches

The characteristics of governments and governing, especially at the local level, are widely viewed as going through an evolutionary change. One of the most notable changes is that many governments are moving from a welfare state orientation to a business or entrepreneurial orientation. The welfare state approach focuses on issues regarding the re-distribution of available resources, 'from each according to his ability to each according to his need', whereby the larger society is seen as being responsible for the well-being of all its citizens. In contrast, taking a business approach to government operations involves a number of entrepreneurial characteristics such as innovation, profit focus, risk-taking and promotion (Hall & Hubbard, 1998). The objectives of entrepreneurial governments are intrinsically tied to growth and minimal regulation of the 'free market' environment. These objectives include the following:

- job creation;
- expanded tax base;
- support for small firm development;
- attract new investment;
- simpler tax regulations;
- streamline development process;
- privatisation of utilities and transport sectors.

Increasing global competition fuels the need to take an entrepreneurial approach, as those governments that are not perceived as being innovative and business focused risk a net drain of resources. As noted by Hall and Hubbard (1998: 6):

> The idea of the internationalisation of economic activity, the increased geographic mobility of production and investment and the rising power of transnational corporations appears to have instilled an edgy insecurity at all levels of the urban hierarchy.

Unlike many other industries, tourism is less threatened by the unbridled competitive impacts of globalisation in that it has never been a tariff protected industry and the sense of place qualities intrinsic to a destination, can make it 'unique' and still desirable. However, investing in 'mega projects' that appeal to mass tourism and global markets as well as residents, such as sport stadiums, waterfront activity areas and entertainment districts is more susceptible to global competition and investment pressures, and can lead to a sense of 'placenesses'. The proliferation of colourful banners, royal palms, neo-classical architecture and transnational chain establishments in the retail, food and beverage and entertainment sectors can blur the differences between destinations. Environments can increasingly be replicated through artificial means. The large bio-domes in Cornwall, England, enable visitors to feel like they have had a 'tropical experience' while the indoor ski facilities in Japan enable users to enjoy outdoor recreation experiences, without travelling far or facing the elements.

Taking an entrepreneurial approach translates into engaging in proactive strategies to create partnerships with the private sector to provide services and to stimulate overall economic development. While an entrepreneurial approach is seen to raise the standards of what a destination has to offer, these offerings tend to be championed by elite groups and to largely serve their interests. New sports stadiums and arts performance centres can draw heavily on public funds, while the admission charges for these venues can be beyond the means of many members of the public. The potential trickle-down effect of spending public funds on improving the look and level of discretionary services offered by a jurisdiction are often used to justify diverting public funds from basic public services. Spending on 'big ticket' entrepreneurial projects, however, can divert public funds from less glamorous, but highly necessary areas of public investment in schooling, transport, housing and medical care.

A successful example of the entrepreneurial approach is the 'Glasgow's Miles Better' campaign with its prominent placement of Mr. Happy from the Mr. Men cartoon, exuding a sense of fun, optimism and opportunity at a time when Glasgow was suffering from numerous economic and social challenges (Ward, 1998). A campaign of related policies to invest in the city's cultural and service assets is credited with encouraging local businesses and entrepreneurial activity as well as attracting investment to Glasgow. The increase in civic pride from a successful promotion and investment in a city can invigorate local economies and encourage residents, tourists and outside backers to invest their time and money in these special places. Another example of this was Vancouver's successful international *Expo'86* which helped to raise international awareness of this Pacific Rim city and left behind tourist infrastructure like its new cruise ship terminal, that has been an important part of the 'Inside Passage' to Alaska cruise market growth (Figure 10.1).

Organising

Government processes and procedures relating to financing and infrastructure have particular relevance to the ability of government to set into motion the goals and objectives established through the planning process. It needs to balance the priorities of its residents and voters with those of specific interest groups, such as the tourism industry. It does this by organising its powers and resources according to its administrative philosophy. Government organisation can involve minimal assistance through the development of a basic infrastructure or take a more proactive approach via the creation of government departments and an investment in major attractions and events. An important part of governments' approach to tourism is how they organise their financial and taxation structure with respect to this industry.

Figure 10.1 Vancouver's cruise ship terminal and cruise ship

Financing

Governments can put in place regulations and incentives to bolster tourism development given they have sufficient funds to support these efforts. However, governments may be reluctant to make the necessary financial commitment to tourism given the complexities of the industry, varying levels of public support for the industry and limited available funds and funding options for tourism. The financial management of governments is under increased scrutiny, as evident by the number of external audits of government departments that are being demanded by the public and various interest groups. The financial management of governments is also increasingly restricted due to balanced budget laws that require governments and their departments to achieve a balanced budget each financial year and to caps placed on the taxation burden that governments can levy on their citizens. As governments try to 'do more with less', they are utilising different forms of financial analysis to help them determine how best to spend their money.

All methods of financial analysis involve varying degrees of forecasting, in that they all try to predict the future using imperfect information. However, they are still required to give a strong indication of appropriate budgeting and auditing practices. Given that tourism is a service based industry made up primarily of small businesses, it can be very difficult to track the return on tourism investments and to make future predictions. An over-reliance on such forms of analysis can favour investments that are more conventional and easy to track, which can disadvantage tourism. Of all the available financial analysis options, cost–benefit analysis, shift–share analysis and input–output modelling are among the most applicable for predicting the impacts of tourism investments.

Cost–benefit analysis endeavours to assign numerical values to all potential costs and benefits associated with a proposed project, and rates proposals with a ratio higher than one as providing more benefits than costs (Davis, 1993). Applying this form of analysis to potential tourism expenditures takes into account many of the factors, such as those relating to quality of life, that are missed by less inclusive forms of analysis. Shift–share analysis is useful for understanding how well an area, or region is doing in terms of tourism development compared to the nation. This form of analysis can be useful for studying competitive advantage between regions and nations, and for determining growth potential in regard to larger trends, such as with a national tourism industry that is either expanding or retracting. Input–output modelling addresses secondary impacts and is adept at showing how changes in different industry sectors create impacts that reverberate throughout the economy (Davis, 1993). Given that tourism is highly interdependent on the rest of the economy, this form of modelling provides a more comprehensive picture of how changes in tourism will impact on the economy, as well as how changes in non-tourism sectors will impact on tourism.

Funding options
When properly managed, tourism can improve the quality of life for communities; however, when mismanaged the reverse can occur. Governments address tourism costs through a variety of methods. These include making developers and users pay fees and charges aimed at capturing the direct and indirect costs of development and use. Governments also fund tourism programmes and pay for tourism costs through dedicated funds, tourist related taxes, sales taxes, lottery funds, grants, loans, tax exempt bonds and loan guarantees.

Typically, governments attempt to place the financial costs of tourism development, including the cost of development and use of infrastructure and services, on developers. These developers, in turn, pass the costs along to business owners who pass the costs along to their customers. The actual costs of tourism growth and development can be difficult to calculate in a proactive manner, especially given that many tourism impacts indirectly affect communities and that it can take years for signs of its impacts to become evident. Therefore, calculating the costs of growth for communities and sorting out who currently pays for this growth and who should pay is difficult.

Development and impact fees Tourism developers and business owners pay for tourism growth through a system of development charges and impact fees. These sources of government revenue can include permitting fees, infrastructure costs, utilities levies, real estate transfer taxes and contributions to government programmes for community enhancement, such as affordable housing and parks programmes. These 'contributions' can raise difficult issues for governments if they are seen to be 'exaction', whereby cost burdens are inappropriately placed on individuals or businesses. In the US while the issue of 'exactions' is dealt with differently by different states, the main responsibility of governments is to show that all their development charges and fees are warranted and that funds collected by these fees are not spent in unrelated areas. The scope of governments' abilities to fund projects and services linked to tourism, such as subsidising affordable housing to offset increased prices spurred on by tourism, or investing in road improvements and buying new lands for preservation, can be hampered by legal and government restrictions relating to 'exactions'.

Dedicated funds Capital Improvement Funds, transfer taxes and bonds can be useful sources of funding for projects that serve the interests of both residents and visitors. The bike trail linking Ohio's major cities, recreation areas and parks has received widespread government support and $2 million of the state's Capital Improvement Funds (Thompson, 2001: 6). A transfer tax on the sale of properties in Vail, Colorado, that was approved by referendum in 1980 generates over $2 million a year for open space acquisitions that are used for natural, park and recreation areas (Howe *et al.*, 1997: 76). In America a series of bills that would provide between $20 to $70 billion dollars in tax-exempt bonds and loan guarantees have been proposed to help save Amtrak (Eisenberg *et al.*, 2001: 69). In Canada there is a long history of the government providing funds to assist communities in developing tourism plans. In Alberta a partnership programme between the public and private sector provides funds for the development of community tourism action plans that includes goal setting, identification of local priority projects and programmes to support tourism development (Gunn, 1997).

Tourist taxes Tourists' taxes are commonly imposed as a minor tax on accommodation to help offset some of the costs of tourism – particularly marketing. Such taxes are quite popular amongst residents as the people who vote for these taxes do not have to pay for them. However, industry groups are concerned that tourists should not be over-taxed, and argue that when prices are raised by increasing taxes tourism businesses have to reduce their costs to compensate for the price increase to stay competitive with other destinations. The tourist industry is also opposed to tourists taxes, such as those on accommodation, airports, parks, transportation and other facilities and utilities being used to fund items that are not related to tourism, as can be the case if these monies go towards general government funds.

A 'tourist impact tax' was approved by Florida Keys voters in 1988 to help to offset some of the costs of providing services to tourists and to improve the area (Howe *et al.*, 1997: 78). Half of the funds raised by the 1% tax on hotels and motels goes towards the county's general fund, while the rest is used to pay for the acquisition of lands for purposes that include land preservation and affordable housing. A 2% bed tax has been in existence in Victoria, BC, for a decade or more. Half of the money raised, generally over C$4 million a year, goes to supporting the city's conference centre. The rest supports the marketing and community efforts of Tourism Victoria, the local destination's marketing association.

Public support

It is politically astute to fund projects that are seen to serve the greater public good, strike the right balance between public and private sector funding and do not jeopardise funding for other community priorities. Funding for parks, historical restorations and highway improvements can be viewed as more equitable uses of the public coffers than offering tax breaks, reducing user fees and subsidising land prices for tourism businesses. An example of public spending that was seen by some to go beyond acceptable levels is the £331 million that the Birmingham City Council invested in its 'city-centre prestige projects'. These included a convention centre, indoor arena, hotel complex and aquarium, between 1986/87 and 1991/92, and were clearly oriented toward increasing tourism (Loftman & Nevin, 1998: 137–9). While many residents were supportive initially of the improvements, over time the real cost associated with these projects, in terms of drastic cuts in spending on health, education and housing were seen to be too high. Another point of contention was that more than half of the total cost for these capital improvements was subsidised by the local council while the council also underwrote private sector funds, which in effect was a double contribution if things went wrong. Therefore, the use of 'public-private partnerships' to finance these improvements became viewed by many as over-dependent on government funds. The pro-growth council was replaced by a new council with 'back to basics' priorities and led to dramatic changes in budgeting.

More recently, Manchester served as the host city for the *2002 Commonwealth Games* and attracted worldwide praise for its excellent facilities, vibrant urban centre and friendly and welcoming citizens. The Manchester example underlies the impact that local government's successive fiscal policies can have on the overall social, economic and physical environment of destinations. But it is a continuous struggle between competing interests and views as to how best address these community needs, and in turn their impact on the attractiveness of a city to residents and tourists.

Infrastructure

The potential monetary gains from tourism can only be realised if infrastructure that meets the needs of both tourists and residents is available and in good condition. This physical manifestation of organisation becomes an essential building block for tourism business. The infrastructure for tourists goes beyond the provision of airports, roads and other facilities and includes tourist services and needs like safe food and water, sewerage systems, hospitals and policing. In the Great Ocean Road region of Victoria, Australia, which is home to the world famous Bells Beach surfing area, the local council estimates that is has spent close to a million dollars on building and maintaining basic tourist infrastructure, such as toilet and changing room facilities over a 10-year period (DOI, 2001: 8). This is a significant expense for a small community. As the state and local governments work on preparing a comprehensive management plan for the region they recognise that 'funding the necessary infrastructure to support tourism growth will be a major challenge' (DOI, 2001: 8).

Transportation

Transportation is a key component of tourism, as it can either facilitate or hinder the safe, efficient and cost-effective means of access for visitors and goods. The dominant forms of transportation that are regulated and funded by federal and state governments are airlines, trains and roads. The problem with most forms of travel infrastructure is that they are very expensive to build and maintain, while the public baulks at paying the full price for using the infrastructure. The high costs are tied to the technical expertise, expensive materials and high number of employees needed to build and maintain transportation infrastructure. Health and safety concerns, especially with regard to the potential for disruption of services, injury and death, greatly increase both the liabilities of governments and the associated funds that governments must pour into the infrastructure to make it as safe and reliable as possible.

One common problem for all infrastructure is its periodic use. Whether it be roads, water or electricity systems each has its peak periods, which means the system is under pressure for certain limited time periods, but in excess of requirements for much of the time. This peaking inefficiency can be exacerbated by tourism seasons. When a community's roads that are designed for the permanent population are put under pressure by the inflow of thousands of tourists, special management is required. Some of the government organisation that takes place under these circumstances includes temporary adjustments such as additional traffic lanes and parking spaces, or park and ride schemes. At times tourism business has to be diverted elsewhere because the community is full to capacity, as has happened occasionally in Venice.

Airports and airlines

Many nations of the world have established their own airlines, also referred to as 'national flag-carriers', as a way of providing a network of internal flights as well as transportation to international destinations. The prestige factor of having a national airline, the economic opportunities associated with a well integrated national airline service, the high employment potential of these airlines, and the internal dependency on air service to regional and out-of-the way destinations all contribute to nations supporting flag-carriers. Unfortunately, many of these flag-carriers have struggled to stay out of debt, both as public and private sector businesses. Deregulation has been blamed for increased flight delays and overcrowding as privatised airlines struggle to make profits in a highly competitive environment. In a study of the 31 busiest airports in the US the *Federal Aviation Administration* (FAA) found there were eight airports with significant passenger delays: New York La Guardia, Newark, New York Kennedy, Chicago O'Hare, San Francisco, Philadelphia, Atlanta and Boston (FAA, 2001: 2). It is also predicted that the first six of these airports along with Los Angeles will continue to have significant delays over the next 10 years. As these airports are all major national hubs and several are world hubs, significant delays at these airports cause service problems on a much larger scale, as delayed flights can lead to missed connections and loss of bookings for other tourism services.

The costs associated with offering a range of services on all flights and travelling to marginal destinations, along with high employee costs have left many national airlines struggling to make a profit. The last few years have seen the loss of a number of major airlines including Canadian (Canada), Ansett (Australia), Swiss Air (Switzerland) and Sabena (Belgium), with many others in desperate situations. Sabena airlines made a profit only twice during the 75 years it was in operation (*The Economist*, 2001d). The second largest airline in the US, United Airlines has recently sought the protection of Chapter 11 status. Chapter 11 is a 'time out' lifeline that allows companies on the verge of insolvency to restructure and get their business in order, to hopefully avoid a complete and irreversible declaration of bankruptcy. At the same time that many major airlines are struggling, discount carriers, such as Ryanair, Easy Jet and Virgin, are making profits by cutting costs, and customising their service. They provide minimal on-flight services, limit flights to popular destinations, use less expensive second tier airports wherever possible, vary prices according to time of day, and provide inclusive packages and other traveller incentives to tempt passengers.

The loss of national carriers can be devastating for tourist destinations more than a few hours from international airports. Many smaller regional areas are unable to attract a high and continual flow of tourists and therefore are primarily ignored by airlines that do not have a mandate to serve these areas, as is usually only the case with national carriers. Some regional centres have been able to adjust by working with the discount carriers, who are able to offer a point-to-point service using smaller planes.

Rail

Railways hold an important tourism role in some nations, while in others they are sliding into obscurity. India's rail service has the highest capacity of any in the world and dominates the movement of people and goods in that country. Romantic notions of touring the continent or more practical considerations can draw tourists to riding the rails as part of their experience of India. However, India's rail system suffers from one of the world's worst safety records, so tourists need to take that into account. The UK is famous for its train travel, its magnificent old stations and the grand expanses of countryside that can be viewed while riding the rails. The pleasantries of the rail experience in the UK have become corroded, however, by chronic under-investment that has contributed to endless train delays and a number of tragic accidents (*The Economist*, 2001d).

Public transportation around the world, particularly passenger railways, receives substantial government subsidies, as it represents not only an essential government service but also an emotionally charged indication of political power. A well-run railway network is in a nation's interest as it allows for the effective and efficient movement of goods and people and generates a sense of pride. It is noticeable that some publicly operated passenger systems which have received substantial public investment, as in France and Japan, can offer a service that rivals domestic airlines for speed and efficiency. America's national rail system, Amtrack, however is chronically under-funded. In America passenger trains receive US$0.5 million in federal subsidies compared with the US$13 billion received by airports, while highways receive annual federal subsidies of over US$30 billion a year (Eisenberg *et al.*, 2001: 68). America dedicates federal funding to airlines and highways, through gasoline and ticket taxes, while rail services have no such source of federal funding.

Highways and roads

Road and highway services are important to tourism, as they tend to be the least expensive and most convenient way of 'touring'; so it comes as no surprise that tourist surveys often indicate 80% of tourists use car or bus travel to get around. In the developed world most countries have elaborate highway systems that connect regional areas with hub cities. A recent study of the Newell Highway in Australia, which links Melbourne and Brisbane, revealed the creation of a route promotions committee to take advantage of such linear regional travel. Their communal brochure promoted 478 local tourism operators, 53 towns and 31 local governments over its 1100 kilometre length, and 35% of surveyed highway travellers were using the brochure (Houghton *et al.*, 2002).

The joint levels of funding and responsibilities for a nation's highways are well demonstrated by the creation of the interstate highway system in the US. In 1944 the *Federal-Aid Highway Act* authorised the designation of a 65,000 mile 'National System of Interstate Highways' that was to be a cooperative effort between national and state highway departments (Public Roads On Line, 1996: 4). In 1952 the *Federal-Aid Highway Act* authorised only US$25 million for this system on a 50:50 matching funds basis; however, by the mid-1950s it was estimated that state and national investments in the highway system would require over a hundred billion dollars (Public Roads on Line, 1996: 11). The highway system was financed subsequently through dedicated funds, bonds, gas taxes and various highway user charges. The current annual budget for America's Federal Highways Administration exceeds US$30 billion (FHA, 2001: 1). In Australia, during the late 1990s the federal government provided A$750 million to upgrade the Pacific Highway, which assisted several coastal tourism destinations and provided a more efficient transportation for Australia's east coast economy (Houghton *et al.*, 2002).

There can be mixed results with regard to the impacts of major highway improvements for tourism. One of the most famous highways in the US is

'Route 66', which for a time served as the primary means of connecting the northeast and southwest corners of the country. The Chicago-to-Los Angeles route connected the main streets of many rural and urban communities and brought these areas the benefits of access to a major national east-west artery from the 1930s to the 1960s (NHR66F, 1995: 2–6). A number of tourist innovations came to life along Route 66, including motels, service stations and fast food outlets. Most of the original sections of Route 66 were replaced by a four-lane highway in the 1970s, which has left many of the towns along this once bustling trade route struggling to survive. When super highways with limited access, via select entry/exit points, are installed the resulting impact is that towns without access lose business, as people bypass these areas in their quest to arrive at their destinations quickly. However, there are tourism advantages to be gained when the loss of highway traffic is treated as an opportunity to make towns less car focused by creating environments where travellers want to walk around, shop and enjoy a quieter ambience. The tourism success of small rural towns that have been bypassed by major highway, such as Ross Village in Tasmania and West Bury in Victoria, Australia, is testament to how some communities can weather the storms of organisational change that government infrastructure priorities can create (Kelly & Spark, 2001).

Leadership

The very nature of the tourism industry makes it a challenge for governments to understand and manage in that tourism is service based, dominated by small businesses and difficult to separate from larger community services. The diversity of tourism industry membership can create real difficulties in producing a united vision and then effectively conveying this vision through leaders. Most lobby groups for tourism are neither as well organised, nor as powerful as entrenched interest groups, which can lead to them being overlooked by government agencies. When governments make a firm commitment to tourism they can help unite this diverse industry and motivate others to work towards a clear tourism vision, but this requires leadership.

Leadership in government on behalf of tourism can take many forms. It can come directly from elected officials, as part of their mandate. It can emerge from the initiative and tenacity of senior government service personnel. It can arise from the efforts of NGOs which often depend on government funding and support in order to be effective. It can emerge from the efforts of individuals in the private sector who have caught the imagination of government and have been facilitated in the pursuit of their dreams.

An example of the first has occurred in Tasmania, where unlike the normal situation of tourism being the responsibility of a junior minister the past Premier, the Right Honourable Jim Bacon, took responsibility for this portfolio. This fortunate combination brought strong leadership and much appreciated political commitment and resources to tourism development in Tasmania. Further leadership is provided through *Tourism Tasmania Corporate*, a statutory agency established in 1997 and guided by a diverse group of high-level tourism experts, including the co-founder of Lonely Planet (Tourism Tasmania, 2002: 1). Tourism Tasmania Corporate organises its business across four key areas: tourism marketing, retail, wholesale and tourism development. This business approach enables it to function as a leader to the industry across many diverse sectors. Part of this organisation's leadership comes from its active Market Research Unit that engages in extensive data collection and the sharing of numerous surveys to its tourism stakeholders.

Even when elected politicians take on the responsibility for tourism they often have other responsibilities, and tourism is usually incorporated as part of a joint ministry. Consequently these busy ministers become heavily dependent on the advice and vision of their senior bureaucrats. The authors have lived in a variety of locations around the world and have been impressed with the knowledge, commitment and initiative of these individuals. They genuinely want to see the industry succeed but have a tough assignment obtaining the funding they require and the unified support of a very disparate industry. But overall they are slowly gaining the respect and support of other government departments and senior politicians.

In a growing number of cases the leadership from government has come indirectly through NGOs or partnerships with private individuals. Unfortunately, the poor performance of many governments as leaders in tourism development has led certain researchers to believe that the public sector is not the best leader for directing tourism development, given governments' strong role as regulators and limited experience and success in creating new and viable opportunities for community development. While a government's role as regulator is valuable for setting standards of acceptable conduct, its limitations are noted by Howe *et al.* (1997: 71) who state that:

> By themselves, however, regulations will not bring out the best in a community or protect what people value most about their town. Because they focus on prevention regulations cannot offer a positive vision of how things should be. Without other approaches, communities might well experience indistinguishable look-alike development that simply follows the letter of the law.

The 'other approaches' as advocated by Howe *et al.* (1997) and Ritchie (2001), can include a shift in focus from a primary role as a regulator towards that of being a 'facilitator'. Governments can act as 'facilitators' in helping communities find and nurture their own leaders and in turn develop appropriate tourism plans and environments to encourage individual innovations. Governments can also help communities see their local issues in broader governing, economic, social, environmental and legal contexts.

Godschalk *et al.* (1994) note that as governments are being forced to do more with less, in terms of answering to a wider range of interest groups with less direct taxation dollars, they have to change their ways of doing business. Decreases in government funds are tied to the public reluctance for increases in taxes, especially in the US, along with their scepticism that the public sector can provide quality goods and services on budget and on time. Changing government priorities and decreasing levels of government funding are spurring governments to re-think their roles and form new relationships with private industry, different levels of government and interest groups, to receive the financial and moral support to move forward with proposed projects. The rise in the power and prominence of NGOs can be attributed directly to the changing, and in many cases weakening, role of governments.

The traditional government approach is a top-down approach whereby the leaders are seen to both know what is best and have the means to ensure that their decrees are followed. Haywood (1994) details a number of approaches to community development of leisure and recreation opportunities that can be applied also to tourism development. Several of these approaches are outlined below, sorted under the categories of *Top-Down, Client Led* and *Partnerships.*

Top-down

Direct provision

Governments can prescribe certain actions if they have the authority to do so and believe their requirements are in the best interests of those they represent. An example of direct provisions for tourism-related issues is the 'concurrency' requirements in Chapter 9J–5 of Florida's Administrative Code (Florida Dept. of State, 2002). The state of Florida mandates all of its local jurisdictions ensure that an 'acceptable' level of service standards is provided before allowing additional development to occur. This concurrency provision helps to ensure that the booming development that typifies this large tourist drawing state does not exceed the abilities of local jurisdictions to provide an adequate level of public facilities such as roads, potable water and parks. Given the unrelenting pressures to build new tourist facilities, including resorts, hotels, restaurants and amusement parks in Florida, this legislation has helped to slow down and in some cases prevent developments that would otherwise overwhelm local communities.

Facilitating approach

Governments can be seen to apply facilitating approaches when they provide resources to a different governing body or non-government organisation as a means of furthering a goal that involved parties mutually support. One of the most common forms of government assistance in this manner is the government grant. It is interesting to note that many NGOs that are referred to as 'grass roots' organisations, owe much of their existence and power to government funding making them the offspring of 'top-down' support. Tourism-oriented government grants are evident in downtown revitalisation schemes, heritage restoration works, upgrading existing parks and purchasing public recreational lands. Government assistance that follows the facilitating approach is also evident in tourist-related investments, such as the provision of affordable housing. Such housing is often needed for an industry located in desirable and high price locations, and where many of its positions are front-line service positions paying low or minimum wages. In regard to affordable housing in the US, the agency of *Housing and Urban Development* (HUD) sets the definition of categories of affordability throughout the US each year. These categories then serve as parameters to guide the standards for evaluating and funding affordable housing initiatives by the various levels of government, as well as the NGOs that work in the affordable housing field.

Outreach work

The outreach approach is a way of expanding opportunities for groups and individuals who are in need of government assistance yet have difficulty accessing available services. A great deal of outreach work is accomplished by new arms of government services and by NGOs, since the outreach effort is necessitated by an inability of traditional government services to reach certain people. *The Community Futures Development Corporations* is a government-funded organisation that has offices throughout regional Canada. The mission statement of one of these offices in Alberta is as follows (West Central Community Futures Development Corporation, 2002: 1):

> To assist individuals within the West Central Community Futures region with their business goals and objectives, thereby significantly improving local employment, sustainable development, and the economic well-being of communities.

The *Community Futures* office in Cowichan, BC, Canada, has been involved in re-training unemployed forestry workers for work in the service industry, with much of this work relating to tourism enterprises in this scenic rural region. Through the innovative use of government funds, organisations such as *Community Futures* can establish and run business assistance centres in rural regional centres. These centres provide a 'one stop shopping' approach to support small business and local economies in communities that might otherwise miss out on these opportunities as they are outside of major metropolitan areas.

Client led

Community development groups

Community development groups can be described as those groups that form in a spontaneous manner due to a shared sense of purpose. These groups tend to have medium- to long-term goals and as such their pace of action can be relatively moderate. Tourism examples can include 'friends of' groups, such as the *1000 Friends of Florida* who work to improve the quality of life in their community. These groups tend to show a great deal of creativity in drawing upon local resources including their members to achieve most of their aims (One Thousand Friends, 2002). NGOs that promote festivals, environmental protection or any of the many enriching aspects of community life can be seen to fit into this sub-category.

Community action groups

Community action groups tend to form around a particular cause that is pursued in the short to medium term. They tend to be more focused than community development groups and can be typified by bursts of intense activity in output as they strive to achieve their goals. Following the loss of the World Trade Centre due to terrorist activities, there was a spontaneous and unstoppable public outpouring of offers by citizens to help in any way they could. One of the top priorities for many people was to be involved in charting the course for how the World Trade Centre site should be redeveloped. Under this cause a number of organisations formed, including *New Visions: Coalition for the Rebuilding of Lower Manhattan* and *The Civic Alliance*, each of which consists of hundreds of volunteers who are forming committees and working groups to put together ideas on how to rebuild after this tragedy (Langdon, 2001).

Social groups

Social groups tend to form primarily for the purpose of social interaction and have an orientation that includes the short term through to the long term. The benefits to the larger community can be subtle in terms of adding to the overall colour and flavour of an area, or they can be readily apparent. Many tourists are drawn to visiting 'artists' quarters', be they along the River Seine in Paris or in Soho in Manhattan, or artist communities in rural areas, where they hope to soak up the atmosphere and buy some pieces. The rising prominence of noted 'gay areas' such as the 'Boys Town' neighbourhood in Chicago and the West End of Vancouver present spectacles and social attitudes that have a widening appeal. Certain cities, such as Key West, Florida, are now well known for their gay culture and draw huge crowds of gays and straights to public art exhibits, drag shows and gay pride parade days. The fashion and trend sensibilities of gay culture has led to gay groups often being in the forefront of identifying, visiting and enriching 'must see' destinations, such as South Beach, Florida, and San Francisco, California.

Partnerships

Tourism's low integration with other areas of government can leave it at cross-purposes with other government departments and agencies. This need for greater integration, especially when there are multitudes of involved stakeholder and decision-making groups, spurs on the creation of partnerships. A principle objective of the recent *Strategic Tourism Plan* in the State of Victoria, Australia, is to raise the awareness of tourism's importance to other government departments (Tourism Victoria, 2002). This objective recognises that a high level of understanding and cooperation between government bodies is necessary to achieve efficiency and effectiveness in the creation and implementation of all government policies, not just in the tourism area. For example, tourism development impacts areas like roads and transport, major industries like forestry, fishing and agriculture, and is having a growing influence on a variety of revenue and finance issues.

The planning process associated with the Great Ocean Road Region in Victoria, Australia, cuts across five local council areas and contains numerous national parks and other conservation areas, yet this region relies heavily on tourism as well as traditional resource extraction industries and farming for its economic well-being. The Great Ocean Road Region receives more visitors than any other area of Victoria, outside of Melbourne, attracting 2.7 million overnight visitors and 5.4 million day-trip visitors, which places great developmental pressure on this region (Department of Infrastructure, 2001: 7). The state's Department of Infrastructure is taking the lead in coordinating this planning process as it endeavours to work in partnership with the local councils, the Department of Natural Resources and Environment, VicRoads, Tourism Victoria and the Victorian Coastal Council, along with numerous community and development groups and infrastructure authorities (DOI, 2001: 5). The consultation process has included a number of stakeholder/community workshops to examine issues and concepts. The draft strategy has been widely available for public comment, which included allowing for written public submissions, as well as feedback provided on line. It is intended to be an inclusive planning process that permits tourism to work with other industries and the various communities within the region.

Just as NGOs can benefit from the financial, technical and political support of governments, governments can benefit from their associations with NGOs. A strong advantage to partnering is that it allows for a level of experimentation and risk in exploring new tourism options that government agencies would be unwilling to explore by themselves, due to concerns of incurring long-term financial obligations that carry with them some unpredictable outcomes. Another advantage of partnering is that it is seen by the wider community as bringing more democracy to the running of public affairs, in that a cross-section of community stakeholder groups and individuals are provided with an opportunity to guide and possibly conceive community initiatives. The advantages of partnerships encourage governments to shift from direct providers to 'enablers' of tourism products and services.

Close connections between the public and private sector can help highlight areas where either the public or the private sector is more appropriate to take the lead. The *Alberta Tourism Partnership Corporation* was founded in 1996 as a way of transferring marketing responsibilities from the state to the business sector (Gunn, 1997). In British Columbia, Canada, tourism marketing and research has been separated out from the provincial ministries. These services are now undertaken by *Tourism BC*, which was recast as a crown corporation with a strong businesses focus and its own budget and money earning capabilities.

The *Cooperative Research Centre* (CRC) initiative in Australia is an example of a government supported body acting as a facilitator of industry led tourism research and development strategies. The CRC for Sustainable Tourism was started in 1997 and was renewed in 2002 with an A\$26.7 million grant from the federal government for its second iteration (CRC, 2002). A variety of CRCs have been created in Australia to bring industry and universities together through central funding to tackle identified issues and opportunities in their respective fields. While there is only one tourism CRC there are 13 related to agriculture, but they all leverage the initial federal contribution with either in-kind or additional funding support from their respective industry and university partners.

Transborder tourism partnerships may be required in order to manage tourism in a sustainable manner. In a study of managing parks along the US-Canada border it was found that making progress on joint management issues can be both costly and time-consuming (Timothy, 2000). Despite the inefficiencies and frustrations that can accompany cross-boundary management these partnering endeavours are often the only way of ensuring that joint tourism resources are properly managed and promoted.

Cross-border partnerships can benefit from treaty agreements, where the roles and responsibilities of each party to the agreement are clearly stated. Not all transboundary agreements need to be legally binding or to address joint management issues, as is evident from the numerous regional tourism promotion partnerships that have formed between different levels of government and various stakeholder groups. Timothy (1998) reports on how the New England states have formed a cooperative marketing policy to promote themselves as part of a tourism region.

Tourism partnerships ebb and flow as they progress from early to advanced stages of development. Different levels of activity, end-products and motivation can be expected from tourism partnerships as they pass through what Caffyn (2000) refers to as the 'tourism partnership lifecycle'. The tourism partnership lifecycle draws upon Butler's (1980) tourist area lifecycle to illustrate the various challenges and opportunities that arise as tourism partnerships mature. This lifecycle is useful for breaking down the steps of tourism partnerships into discrete and easily understood components. Arduous tasks relating to the prepartnership, take-off and growth phases must be completed as pre-requisites to tourism partnerships before they can reach their peak level of utility. Caffyn (2000) finds the primary factors to successful tourism partnerships are adequate financial and social capital, with the skills of project managers featuring strongly. The fact that many tourism umbrella organisations and other forms of tourism partnerships go through frequent shuffles of top level management, can be seen as a reflection of the different skills, such as consensus building or revenue raising, required by project managers at each partnering phase.

Controlling

Control for government is achieved through regulation, persuasion and education. Governments have a responsibility to regulate on behalf of the common good, to ensure health and safety standards are met and that development proceeds within legal and statutorial limits. This role is present in all areas of public responsibility and for many is the *raison d'être* for governments. However, with tourism's ubiquitous and interrelated nature it is often difficult for government to determine exact causes and impacts, or to monitor every transaction and transgression. Therefore it is difficult to comprehend let alone 'prove' tourism's impact which raises difficult issues for governments as they struggle to monitor tourism and make the necessary changes to keep the industry on track. While the available data can serve as useful reference points in setting limits on prices and access, the numbers cannot speak for themselves. This opens up great room for debate about what the numbers mean and interpretation of their meaning can vary according to which stakeholder group one belongs to and the interests that one represents.

Tourism standards

Standards for tourism development can only be assured if they are formalised and enforced. Standards that are firmly established in law, through legislation and associated policies and then upheld through legal challenges, are robust. Tourism standards developed under less rigorous conditions can falter more easily. It shows real political commitment to create a comprehensive legislative and policy framework for tourism development at the national, state and local level. Examples of state legislation affecting tourism development can be drawn from *Environmental*

Impact Assessments (EIAs) or *Statements* (EISs) that are required for medium to large-scale developments around much of the world. In their study of the impacts of EIAs on coastal tourism developments in Australia, Warnken and Buckley (1996) found that while EIAs placed additional restrictions on development proposals they were not actually barriers to tourism development.

Court findings can greatly impact on the extent to which governments can uphold the standards they establish through the political process. Lake Tahoe, a popular US tourist destination, has been embroiled in law-suit over government's rights to control development that has made it all the way to the US Supreme Court. The case of *Tahoe-Sierra Preservation Council Inc. v. Tahoe Regional Planning Agency* looked at the question of whether or not temporary development moratoriums are legal (Lucero & Soule, 2002). The court upheld the government's rights to create temporary development moratoriums, literally stopping the development clock, if such moratoriums are used to provide communities with time to work on preparing citizen-based plans for their communities. While the land rights of private citizens in the US are particularly strong, this court case highlights legal and political challenges that government agencies around the world are faced with as they try to provide a balanced system for development in their communities.

It can be very difficult for governments to find the time, resources and political support necessary to consult with and explore the needs of all stakeholders so they can develop appropriate and popular tourism plans and strategies. Threats of legal challenge heighten the perceived risks that governments take when trying to be progressive in their planning. However, inaction is not a real alternative given that governments are also legally required to meet numerous regulations, such as those relating to environmental integrity and service provision, as well as facing the wrath of their constituents if they fail to prepare for the future.

Even when tourism development standards, such as those relating to environmental impacts, public consultation and allowable uses are established in law, the ability of governments to pass amending or new legislation can alter the playing field of what is allowable. Queensland initiated fast track legislation, such as the *Sanctuary Cove Development Act 1985* and the *Integrated Resort Development Act 1987* that exempted a number of large resorts from formal EIA procedures, effectively removing the public's consultation rights, while putting in place other requirements, as a means of encouraging tourism growth (Warnken & Buckley, 1996: 242). Therefore tourism standards need to be backed by ongoing political and industry support, as well as community vigilance to ensure that these standards are not only put in place, but are able to work effectively over the long term.

Tourism's low level of integration with other areas of government is problematic when it is kept out of important discussions on resource use and other government policies that are profoundly interrelated with a healthy tourism sector. The lack of communication between various government departments can not only cause tourism to lose opportunities, it can also lead to a less than optimal return on government investment and policy. An excellent example of where government has recognised the importance of developing an inclusive and coordinated approach to managing its tourism industry comes from the US. The *Tourism Policy Council* (TPC) was established in 1996 to 'ensure that the United States' national interest in tourism is fully considered in Federal decision making' (US Code, 2001b). The members of this senior council include the following:

(1) The Secretary of Commerce, who serves as the Chair.
(2) The Under-Secretary of Commerce for International Trade.
(3) The Director of the Office of Management and Budget.
(4) The Secretary of State.
(5) The Secretary of the Interior.
(6) The Secretary of Labour.
(7) The Secretary of Transportation
(8) The Commissioner of the United States Customs Service.
(9) The President of the United States National Tourism Organisation.
(10) The Commissioner of the Immigration and Naturalisation Service.
(11) Representatives of other Federal agencies which have affected interests at each meeting, as deemed appropriate and invited by the Chairman.

The members of this council meet at least twice a year in order to discuss and coordinate the activities of their respective agencies in regard to tourism impacts and other national interests. 'The council shall coordinate national policies and programmes relating to international travel and tourism, recreation, and national heritage resources which involve federal agencies' (US Code, 2001b: 1–2). The council also works with private sector interests and other levels of government to further the coordination of interests and actions.

At the other end of the spectrum state and local governments set and apply basic health and safety standards. For many small tourism businesses their most common interaction with government control comes in the form of health inspectors and other local government compliance officials. These are important ways for government to ensure standards are being met and to gauge the effectiveness of current policy as society and technology changes. Perhaps one of the biggest changes to occur at this level around the world has been the growing legislation banning smoking in public places. This has certainly affected leisure behaviour and has been resisted by certain businesses like pubs and casinos, but in general the predicted business catastrophes have not occurred and everyone can breathe easier.

Regulating tourist flows

Nations can engage in various practices to either encourage or restrict the travel patterns of tourists. Countries restrict the number and type of tourists that visit them through their customs and immigration procedures. Countries can require visas for some or all international visitors as a way of conducting cursory background checks on potential visitors and as a way of controlling the number of visitors by limiting the numbers of visas granted. Visa quotas can be set for certain countries, while routinely denied for others. Some borders are quite open and allow for drive-through custom checks, as is the case between Canada and the US, while crossing other borders can be a long and complicated procedure. Trade blocks, such as NAFTA and the EU, encourage much freer movement of people and goods between member countries, which saves costs and encourages travel.

While most citizens of Western countries are allowed to travel freely around the world, there are still controls on travel. It is still illegal for most Americans to travel to Cuba, although they still slip in via flights from countries outside the US and by boat. Nations also post travel advisories to warn their citizens of those countries they consider risky to visit, which unfortunately has been the fate for many African countries and became an issue in South East Asia after the Bali bombings. Health concerns, such as SARS, have led to the issuance of a WHO travel warning advising tourists not to travel to Beijing and Toronto, which has greatly hurt their tourism trade and convention business (*The Economist*, 2003b). Certain Islamic countries, such as Iran, Egypt and Saudi Arabia, restrict the ability of women to freely travel within and outside their borders (Beyer, 2001). Nations can also 'recall' tourists and foreign nationals at times of pending crisis, as has happened in Indonesia repeatedly over the past 10 years, with the East Timor drive to independence and more recently with the Bali bombings of 2002. In addition to government policies relating to freedom of movement within and between countries, foreign exchange policies and restrictions to the amount and types of goods that can be brought back into a country impact on tourism growth and patterns.

Education

Governments endeavour to educate residents and visitors in tourism matters as a means to accomplishing various ends. In Wales tourism education has been aimed at both residents and travellers as a way of building and strengthening positive images of the country. Tourism's educative role in this process is to 'promote and protect Welsh culture, to consciously and deliberately craft its messages about Wales that are sent through the medium of tourism' (Berger (1980) cited in Morgan & Pritchard, 1998: 154). Despite the long historic efforts of the English to assimilate the Welsh, since the 1990s Wales has made great strides in promoting its unique 'Welshness', by using a number of strategies including those relating to tourism promotion and education. Another example of tourism education aimed primarily at residents is Indonesia's national 'Seven Charms' programme (Timothy, 1999). This programme uses advertisements in print and the electronic media to increase national pride and encourage actions that will increase safety, beauty, environmental protection and hospitable behaviours.

Dispersing tourism impacts

Governments often try to spread the impacts of tourism around their jurisdictional areas in an attempt to prevent patchy tourism development that presents a pattern of 'tourism haves and have-nots'. The tourism development offices of the government of British Columbia have been working for years to spread tourism development around the province beyond the Victoria-Vancouver-Whistler areas that are known as the 'golden triangle' of tourism in BC. Regional tourism development policies pursued by the provincial government in BC include the following:

- increased advertising for attractions in outlying areas;
- staging large events in these areas;
- encouraging package tours that include city and rural tourism experiences;
- providing better access to these areas;
- improving the infrastructure in outlying areas and investing in the development of tourism products and services outside of major tourism centres.

A recent study by Zhang (2001) of regional tourism development for the international tourist market shows the concern for spreading tourism's positive aspects is global. In a comparison of Australian and Chinese experiences she notes how the state of Victoria has tried to encourage international visitors to travel beyond Melbourne and explore the delights of country Australia. Likewise, China has attempted to spread international visitors from its eastern provinces into the more rural regions of the mountainous western provinces. To achieve this China has identified certain tourism growth poles and it is focusing on those with the development of quality attractions and good transport links to major regional airports.

Given that the economies of most developing countries are neither as diverse, nor as robust, as those in developed countries, the impacts of either transnational companies or national government decisions in developing countries can be monolithic. Brohman (1996: 54) notes that 'if provisions are not made to increase local economic participation, this greatly increases the likelihood of the domination of Third World tourism sectors by transnational capitals from the metropolitan core'. In developing countries uneven tourism development can be exasperated by centralised political decisions, as demonstrated in Oakes' (1997) study of tourism development in rural China.

Oakes finds that tourism opportunities in the rural communities of Gaozeng and Zhaoxing in the province of Guizhou are greatly impacted by government policy and funding decisions. Gaozeng was designated as historically important by the government in 1982 which made it eligible for a number of government grants for repairing and enhancing the cultural heritage features of the village (Oakes, 1997: 58). By 1988 a large number of tourists, including 20 tour groups a year, were visiting Gaozeng and the economic and social benefits of tourism were widely shared throughout the village. Unfortunately, when a fire destroyed much of the village later that year, the government withdrew its special historical status along with all related funds and did not provide funds to restore the village as it was felt restored features would 'have no value as traditional antiques' (Oakes, 1997: 58). Government focus and funds then shifted to the village of Zhaoxing, which is now seen by government officials and tourism operators as the principal cultural heritage tourism destination in the region.

Gaozeng has seen its tourism opportunities dry up as tourism entrepreneurs either leave the village or focus their efforts in other areas and remaining policies supporting tourism growth and protecting cultural heritage have been revoked as the tourism potential of the village was seen to be 'ruined' (Oakes, 1997: 59). This example shows that government decisions in terms of granting or withdrawing support for tourism development can have a profound impact on the development of tourism in developing countries.

Conflicting roles and interests

Government needs to balance not only different regional opportunities but different interests if it is to control tourism for the public benefit. However, it is important to note that substantial power imbalances between parties can leave certain groups and local administrations largely out of the loop when it comes to determining tourism policies. Mitchell and Reid (2001) observe that the well-balanced and integrated nature of community based tourism in the Taquile islands of Peru has been threatened by a change in national policies. The federal government of Peru passed a series of anti-monopolisation laws that challenged the traditional ways local people operate their tourism ventures and share the benefits. Under the new legislation outsiders won the right to use docking and other tourism facilities that had previously been the sole domain of the islanders. Mitchell and Reid caution that the new federal laws bring in outsiders who not only compete based on the price of their services, but also bring different values with them that threaten the traditional communal ways of the islanders.

In free market economies it is challenging for governments to control tourism for the benefit of the community, when they are philosophically committed to free enterprise. The dilemma becomes one of setting standards and numbers that will ensure a sustainable industry while denying certain business interests and citizens from participating in the industry. A common example of this dilemma and the balancing act it requires occurs with the issue of taxi licences. The number and cost of such licences is generally based on anticipated demand and the estimated revenue needed to keep the vehicle in good order and to provide a reasonable living. Once this 'imperfect' calculation has been made and all the licences issued no further licences are available until a major change in the supply–demand equation occurs. As such it favours the first mover and established businesses, which in places has encouraged illegal operations and fringe operators.

The same dilemma and balancing act is now required with sustainable nature tourism strategies. In some locations governments are being pressured to add to the early first mover whale watcher or ecolodge operator because of increased demand, but they do not know what the exact carrying capacity is in terms of the environment or economic sustainability. Under these circumstances it is safest to act with caution and to expand slowly, if at all. This of course exposes government to accusations of favouritism, but it also rewards the first mover – the original risk taker.

The diversity of tourism industry membership can create real difficulties in producing a united vision and then effectively conveying this vision to governments. Therefore, governments can find themselves trying to forge effective tourism policies with the cooperation of warring interest groups. In her study of community-based tourism planning in Squamish, BC, Canada, Reed (1997) found a great deal of dissension among and between stakeholders led to the development of an unsatisfactory planning strategy, and that in the end was not implemented. The public participation process was prompted by the provincial government's refusal to approve a major resort in the area unless the municipal government could show that the proposal had the support of the people of Squamish. A tourism coordinating committee was established by the municipality to make tourism planning recommendations to the municipal council. There were concerns that the committee was not representative of all stakeholders groups, that the scope of the planning was too closely tied to the proposed ski resort and that the recommendations were made without due regard to available funding sources. These concerns and associated divergent views split the committee and led to the creation of a rival committee that also put forward recommendations and added to the confusion and concerns about the validity of the process.

Best practice

Factors and processes that enhance a destination's ability to adequately access and then change elements of the tourism industry so that its goals and objectives are met are worthy of study. Howe *et al.* (1997) looked at a number of areas throughout the US, many of which are prime tourist destinations, to determine the 'secrets of successful communities'. They found that most of the successful communities had engaged in several of the following controlling activities (1997: 47):

- develop a widely shared vision;
- create an inventory of local resources;
- build on local assets;
- minimise the need for regulations;
- meet the needs of both landowner and community;
- team up with public land managers;
- recognize the role of non-governmental organisations;
- provide opportunities for leaders to step forward;
- pay attention to the aesthetics.

The benefit of creating a shared vision is that such a vision is much more likely to be supported than one that is perceived to meet only the needs of certain groups. Howe *et al.* (1997) recommend that inventories of local resources should include extensive public participation and result in the creation of maps of ownership, historical land use, current land use, current and pending zoning and potential future uses. In terms of building on assets, it is advisable that communities look to those characteristics that make them unique and attractive to tourists. The unique features could relate to environmental conditions, local history and culture, price competitiveness or convenient access. Since regulations are used to restrict options, often with the intent of achieving a greater good, they can have the less desirable effect of stifling creativity, innovation and fun.

Governments need to be careful that in their efforts to regulate they do not 'dull down' their communities. Increased stakeholder involvement in creating regulations allows for a greater understanding of divergent needs and views along with the flexibility to accommodate these differences. Governments should not only work diligently on establishing overall development plans for their communities, but they should also 'court reputable developers who are willing to do more than what's mandated by law and who work closely with the entire community, not just elected officials, throughout the development process (Howe *et al.* 1997: 83). Teaming up with managers of public lands, such as parks and wildlife reserves, as well as representatives of NGOs and other community leaders can allow for the sharing of resources and ideas in terms of joint planning, management and marketing initiatives. Developments that are aesthetically pleasing as well as functional help to make destination areas more enjoyable places in which to live and work.

Summary

Tourism's complexities and heterogeneous nature challenge elected officials and policy makers alike as they struggle to understand and manage the industry. Most countries in the world recognise tourism as a way to diversify their economies and create corresponding tourism programmes and strategies to support the industry. Tourism can provide a multitude of economic benefits for governments, including attracting outside investors, creating jobs and earning foreign currency to help with a country's trade balance. Governments also benefit when tourism enhances an area's international, national and regional reputation, which in turn can attract additional investment while fostering a sense of pride of place, culture and history amongst their citizenry. Some of the biggest tourism challenges that governments face is determining the appropriate physical areas, types of products and services and levels of funding for tourism. Given that tourism is a relatively new industry and one that is dominated by small businesses, governments can find themselves perplexed if not dumbfounded in terms of understanding the potential impacts of their policies and spending on tourism development.

The processes outlined in this section will never be straightforward and easy to implement in the real world of tourism strategic planning. To demonstrate this point we have included an appraisal of the efforts undertaken in one of the world's most treasured locations – the Florida Keys. The case study by Theresa Szymanis, an experienced regional and town planner who has worked in the Keys, illustrates that many of the processes advocated in this book are underway. But in the real world of personal greed, political expediency, uncertain data and analysis, appropriate and acceptable management will require considerable goodwill to be achieved.

Case Study: Tourism Management in the Florida Keys, USA

(Theresa A. Szymanis, AICP)

Ensuring that a high quality tourism product remains viable for future generations is a challenge which local governments in the Florida Keys are addressing. Connected by Highway US 1 to the Florida mainland south of Miami and Everglades National Park, this fragile chain of 46 bridged keys

Figure 10.2 The Florida Keys

(coral islands), situated on the third largest barrier reef ecosystem in the world, curves 170 kilometres from Key Largo to its southernmost point, Key West (Figure 10.2). The scenic Overseas Highway, in addition to scheduled airlines and a growing cruise ship industry, transport more than three million visitors to the Keys annually (Leeworthy & Wiley, 1996: 7). Visits are concentrated during the cooler months of December to April, and then subside as hurricane season accelerates to an October tourism low (English *et al.*, 1996: 3). On peak season nights up to 65,800 visitors, close in number to the Keys 80,000 permanent population, are estimated to sleep over (Leeworthy & Wiley, 1996: 8). The whole region falls under the jurisdiction of Monroe County, with the county seat being located in the central town/key of Marathon.

Tourism, the main employment industry in the Keys, in 1995/96 directly and indirectly engaged 21,848 local 'Conchs' in daily economic activities and generated $506.01 million, or 45% of official reported income (English *et al.*, 1996: 6). In spite of this success, in a 1999 Monroe County Tourist Development Council (TDC) survey to which 24.2% of Monroe County registered voters responded, 52.3% agreed that the negative impacts of tourism outweighed the positive economic benefits when it came to community needs and quality of life issues. Furthermore, 51.7% felt that the county should attract fewer visitors, 80.3% identified traffic as the major disadvantage of tourism, followed by environmental degradation (57.2%) and overcrowding (52.6%) (Shivlani, 2000: 13–17). This pivotal survey garnered much media attention, as the results challenged the common philosophy that economic growth is beneficial at any cost, and called for a reorganisation of available resources to counterbalance the perceived negative effects of tourism, to make the industry more locally acceptable.

Planning

While the 1999 TDC tourism survey gathered and collated qualitative data regarding voters' perceptions and reactions to tourism, *planning studies* conducted by state and county governments in the Keys confirmed that improvements to community quality of life, the foundation on which tourism is based, are indeed necessitated. Notably, issues of concern include: overtaxed infrastructure (highways; water supply; wastewater treatment; stormwater treatment; and hurricane evacuation) with capacity stretched to or exceeding acceptable limits (Monroe County, 1998–2002; URS Greiner, 1999–2002; Miller Consulting, Inc., 2001); planning policies and land development regulations which deter real estate investment, resulting in urban blight and decay; and resident dissatisfaction with service delivery from Monroe County resulting from disproportionate spending directed towards the county seat in Key West (Florida Legislative Committee on Intergovernmental Relations, 2001: 40). Remedies fall within the non-market realm and require changes to public policy and capital expenditures, which can be brought about through effective regional planning.

Organising

In combination, these and other concerns helped shape resident attitudes towards tourism and also towards the responsible government bodies, prompting a grassroots movement of citizens groups to lead the *re-organization* of the political structure from a county-wide government with a five-member Board of County Commissioners (BOCC) into more cohesive local government units. Incorporation into smaller communities allows citizens better access to decision-making processes and representation to senior governments, plus more fiscal control over local affairs. With an emphasis on citizen input for the planning and prioritising of budgetary items, solutions can be tailor-made for each community reflecting the specific values and goals of its residents and property owners.

Between 1997 and 2000, four separate municipal incorporation votes were held for small groupings of keys oriented around local commercial centres within Monroe County. Two of the votes were successful resulting in the incorporation of Islamorada, Village of Islands on 31 December 1997, and of the City of Marathon on 30 November 1999. Votes to incorporate Key Largo in November 1999 and to amalgamate Paradise Islands, Village of the Lower Keys in November 2000 failed. The new political structure of the Florida Keys is shown in Table 10.1. Citizen representation is increased dramatically through new Advisory Committees and Task Forces on local development issues, with 47 representatives in Islamorada and 26 in Marathon alone. This community autonomy is a far cry from the previous BOCC with its jurisdiction previously covering the 106 mile chain, except Key West, Layton and Key Colony Beach.

Community planning

The break away municipalities launched immediately into the task of drafting Comprehensive Plans to guide their redevelopment, required by Florida Statute to be adopted within three years of municipal incorporation. Comprehensive Plans consolidate data for analysis, used to formulate government policy, programmes and strategies addressing: future land use; transportation; housing; public infrastructure; coastal management; conservation; recreation and open space; intergovernmental coordination; and capital improvements, projected 20 years into the future. Simultaneously, in 1999 the Monroe County Planning Department initiated the Liveable CommuniKeys Master Plan Programme, with community planning focused on Big Pine / No Name Keys and Key Largo, where incorporation votes failed.

Award winning growth management rules from the Monroe County

Table 10.1 New political structure of the Florida Keys

Jurisdiction	Location by mile marker on US 1	Permanent population projection (2000)
City of Key West (Inc. 8 Jan. 1828)	MM 0–6	26,102
City of Marathon (Inc. 30 Nov. 1999)	MM 47 to 60	11,272
City of Key Colony Beach (Inc. 24 Sept. 1957)	MM 55	1,101
City of Layton (Inc. 18 Sept. 1963)	MM 68	208
Islamorada, Village of Islands (Inc. 31 Dec. 1997)	MM 72.5 to 91	7,665
Monroe County (Est. 2 July 1823)	Remaining Keys	39,274
Total		85,622

Data source: Monroe County Public Facilities Capacity Analysis, 2002

Year 2010 Comprehensive Plan (1992), approved by the Florida Department of Community Affairs (DCA) under Area of Critical State Concern legislation in 1997, provide a starting point for new planning efforts. Through the 2010 Plan policy the county slowed the real estate boom to the maximum extent of the law, protecting both the rare native ecology and private property rights. However, with a strong focus on conservation, this plan failed to adequately address the built environment, community character and citizen quality of life (Monroe County, 1999: 4). Now in the Keys, *community planning* with and for residents and property owners has ascended as a priority, with many secondary benefits arising from local improvements to accrue to the tourism industry. Revised Land Development Regulations are being drafted by both new municipalities and Monroe County to guide land developers in synchronisation with Comprehensive Plan policy and government investment.

In addition to plan-making the new governments embarked upon fulfilment of election promises, projects for which consensus was immediately clear. Budgets were allocated for a dream field of community enhancements including: public land acquisition; wastewater and stormwater planning; development of parks, Olympic swimming pools and recreation complexes; redevelopment of beaches and harbours; streetscape and highway beautification; construction of a linked cyclist/pedestrian network paralleling US 1; support for a Keys-wide Monroe-Dade Express bus service; and ecological rehabilitation. Using extensive community visioning and consultation, local identities are being defined and further improvements prioritised. Re-allocated Tourist Development Council bed tax dollars have been channelled through its five District Advisory

Committees (DACs) for many of these projects, but bank loans, intergovernmental transfers, fund balance transfers from Monroe County, grants and private-public partnerships are all in vogue to creatively address the latent demand for quality of life improvements.

Leadership

While local enhancement projects improve the liveability and attractiveness of Keys communities, such projects only partly mitigate the quandaries identified by the 1999 TDC tourism survey. By magnifying the attractiveness of the Keys as a prized destination, the larger growth management issues of population and tourism pressures on infrastructure and the environment may be exacerbated.

In the search for solutions, the fragmentation of Monroe County into multiple jurisdictions presents a new challenge – how to organise all of these disparate political units now that the independent municipalities are asserting their differences? At present, there is no agency, group or mechanism in place to resolve disputes over issues that transcend local boundaries, arising from articulated visions and clashing development policies. In a 2001 presentation to the Florida Legislature, the Legislative Committee on Intergovernmental Relations (LCIR) warned that there is increasing concern about such matters:

> The DCA continues to have conflicting jurisdictional issues arise, and the many *programs* for which it is responsible are not always easy to integrate. Communities in the Keys have not been strong adherents to intergovernmental coordination, thus leaving the area at risk to potentially serious problems concerning emergency management [hurricane evacuation, etc.] and water related matters. (Florida Legislative Committee on Intergovernmental Relations, 2001: 41)

Consider the pressing question, 'How many more residents and tourists can the Florida Keys reasonably manage?'; given the impacts to the marine environment from inadequate wastewater and stormwater treatment facilities, a finite supply of piped-in potable water being shared by all Keys jurisdictions, and the US 1 artery already bursting on peak season days. Acknowledging the impacts of new development, Islamorada's Comprehensive Plan (2001) caps growth at 14 residential units and 1340 sq. ft. of commercial space annually, with strict conditions limiting new tourist facilities. The new City of Marathon, on the other hand, encourages redevelopment through its draft Comprehensive Plan by allowing developers to build out to the maximum densities and intensities possible (City of Marathon, 2002: 1). Any traffic increase associated with new development downstream of Islamorada will exert pressure for a generally unwanted highway widening from three to five lanes throughout the Village (Miller Consulting, Inc., 2001) with impacts most severe in the Village Centre where the displacement of business parking, access and some commercial buildings is likely (Islamorada, Village of Islands, 2001: 2–7). With no mandated dispute resolution body in place, all jurisdictions independently push onward with their individual plan implementation, regardless of regional implications.

Florida Keys Carrying Capacity Study

It is hoped that the Florida Keys Carrying Capacity Study (FKCCS), ordered in 1996 by the Florida Administration Commission and the Governor, under the *leadership* of the US Army Corps of Engineers (USACE) and Florida DCA, will address these broader growth management concerns. The purpose of the $6 million dollar study and computer model is to ' . . . determine the ability of the Florida Keys ecosystem and infrastructure to withstand all impacts of additional land development activities and associated population growth' (US Army Corps of Engineers, 2002). Outcomes of the study will be used to modify the growth management policies within the separate Comprehensive Plans consistent with the study findings, thus promoting compatibility between the development goals of the county and municipalities.

However, when presented with the study and resulting draft Carrying Capacity Analysis Model (CCAM) for peer review, the National Academy of Sciences National Research Council (NRC) March 2002 report found that the fundamental problems remain. According to the NRC, the computer model does not adequately account for the impact of tourism on the islands; makes unrealistic assumptions about hurricane evacuation; fails to evaluate how shifts in population would affect the Keys; and does not address the effects of growth and tourism on water quality and the coastal marine environment (National Academy of Sciences, 2002: 1–4). Further modifications are now being made to revise the computer model to enable it to resolve crucial questions facing growth managers in the Florida Keys. A second independent peer review has been completed.

Control

The Monroe County Board of County Commissioners and Tourist Development Council took a step forward with the 1999 tourism survey, for the first time linking tourism planning with growth management concerns. These agencies heeded public opinion to guide their actions resulting in re-allocated funding and a higher quality tourism product throughout the Keys, enjoyed by local residents and tourists alike. While residents may feel that some of the problems associated with tourism in the late 1990s are now less critical due to the many new community facilities and enhancements, the real issues remain unresolved, and will be amplified as more visitors are attracted to the region.

Resolution of growth management issues has driven planning in the

Florida Keys since designation by the Florida government as an Area of Critical State Concern in 1974. The Department of Community Affairs, once responsible for consistency review and oversight of all plans and ordinances for Monroe County and Key West only, is now inundated with jurisdictional files, without a regional template to guide their decisions. Being economically reliant on tourism, there is a pressing need to strike the right balance between the number of people living in and attracted to the Florida Keys, in line with the ability of the Keys' infrastructure to accommodate their needs, and the fragile environmental resources to absorb their impacts. The carrying capacity model offers promise as a tool to help grasp changes to public policy and the capital expenditures needed to achieve this balance. More important than having the tool, however, is how the tool is to be used. Currently, the political will to initiate stakeholder discussion about conflicting regional issues is lacking. Still in the early stages of establishing a balanced tourism and growth management approach, Florida's Keys communities have accomplished much with independence, but have yet to discover the full benefits of a region melded together under ONE shared vision of sustainable development.

Part 4

A New Paradigm

New Approach

Up to this point we have analysed the major components of business management and stakeholder groups within a community tourism framework. To do so we have separated and dissected what is, in reality, a continual and fluid process of management. It is hoped that the discourse has demonstrated the need to link tourism management with the four functions of business and how these relate to the interests of all stakeholder groups.

It is necessary to combine management principles with community decision-making to develop local tourism that is in harmony with community aspirations and business realities. In tourism destinations there is considerable common interest and potential synergy between various stakeholder groups. Yet the identified business functions and groups tend to operate in a rather haphazard manner, and generally in response to crisis rather than as a result of deliberate forethought and planning.

What is needed is some way to pull the functions and stakeholders involved in community tourism together, to offer a process that will permit the relevant factors and players to come together. It requires a framework that will channel all pertinent elements and viewpoints along a realistic course. To be effective it will need to consider how to facilitate discussion that leads to constructive outcomes. These are challenging goals in themselves, but there is plenty of evidence in the previous pages that there is both a means and will in many communities to achieve a more strategic tourism management approach.

Part Outline

This part demonstrates methods to assist in decision-making and offers a model to ensure all relevant functions and stakeholders become involved. Chapter 11 reviews some of the components of conflict and how various individuals and organisations have developed techniques to harness the positive aspects of conflict. Chapter 12 describes a conceptual model that can help to ensure all relevant components and stakeholders are considered by presenting them as a bridge between tourism's potential and its reality. The bridge analogy is particularly relevant as a physical and widely recognised way of bringing essential tourism elements together.

Chapter 11

Working Together

Strategic community tourism management grows out of stakeholder cooperation. Tourism is an area where the public has a good grasp of basic facts
and needs based on their own travel encounters. Tourism stakeholders
have the knowledge and experiences necessary for providing a well-
rounded view of issues. These groups are also empowered by increased
access to information and favourable changes to legal and governance
systems. The options for collaborative decision-making outlined in this
chapter focus on non-emergency situations in a developed and democratic
country where there is both the opportunity and the necessity to work with
tourism stakeholders over a sustained period.

While collaborative decision-making processes have many merits, they
are not appropriate for all situations. If there is an emergency or if essential
elements of fruitful collaborative efforts are absent, then more centralised
decision-making, such as through a state or national tourism body, might
be the best way of ensuring that tourism will be sustainable. An emergency
situation is an isolated occurrence for which abrupt, highly controlled and
centralised measures are necessary. This can translate to an area responding to a sudden and dramatic plummet in visitor numbers, or an
environmental catastrophe.

Objectives

This chapter looks briefly at some examples of challenges to collaborative planning in developing areas dealing with emergency situations and
endemic under-resourcing. Collaborative tourism planning efforts are
highly appropriate when there are long-standing disagreements in communities over how tourism resources should be managed and resources
are available to support alternative proposals. As tourism impacts become
more apparent and more options open up in relation to how tourism
growth can be managed, stakeholders push for a larger role in directing the
growth of the industry. The collaborative decision-making options
outlined in this chapter focus in the main on non-emergency situations,
where there are sufficient financial, environmental and social resources to
enable stakeholders to work together over a sustained period.

The chapter examines ways to bring stakeholder groups together to create fair, effective and efficient tourism development decisions using the four business management functions approach of earlier chapters. It opens with an examination of conflict and problems using traditional methods of decision-making. Planning issues and options are then explored from the vantage points of the various levels of citizen participation. In the organising portion of the chapter appropriate levels of public participation based on particular circumstances are detailed. Promising leadership options for tourism management arise from emerging collaborative decision-making methods, which draw upon principled negotiation techniques. Ways of controlling group-decision-making processes so they can fulfil their potential are then explored. Particular attention is given to ensuring that all stakeholders can participate in tourism decision-making processes in a manner that strengthens their individual power as well as enhancing the decision-making capabilities of the larger group.

Tourism conflicts

Tourism development in any community is bound to generate some conflict given that it modifies landscapes and changes community dynamics. Tourism conflicts are costly in terms of loss of trust, legal fees, financial overruns, project delays and lost opportunities. As the Urban Land Institute (1994: 15) notes, 'whether the result of greater racial, ethnic or economic diversity or an altered landscape, change generates tremendous uncertainty, that may lead to greater community conflict and political instability'. Conflict is described as a 'process that begins when one party perceives that the other has frustrated, or is about to frustrate, some concern of [theirs]' (Gordon, *et al.*, 1990: 532). These definitions can be expanded to include disagreements between individuals and within stakeholder groups and communities.

Once a community or a significant segment of it sours on tourism, reactions against tourists can damage its image and economic prospects. Public reaction against tourism activities can be as pointed as direct legal action, picketing, boycotting, blocking proposals for further development or removing from power those who are tied to the controversial matters. The terrorist attacks on tourists to Egypt led to a drop of 21.9% in the number of tourists and a 42.5% decline in tourism receipts between 1992 and 1993 (Aziz, 1995: 92). More recently, 'the tragic events of September 11 affected tourism in every region of the world' (WTO, 2002: 1). Certain groups are exploiting the fact that tourism is a soft and effective target for terrorist action, as shown with the Bali bombings of 2002. As these acts of terrorism show, the results of political concerns fuelled by anger can be devastating.

Anger

Anger is primarily a reaction against a real or perceived threat that gives rise to conflict. Susskind and Field (1996: 16) in their book *Dealing with an*

Angry Public: The Mutual Gains Approach to Resolving Disputes list three circumstances when anger is likely to flare up:

- people have been hurt;
- they feel threatened by risks not of their own making; or
- they believe that their fundamental beliefs are being challenged.

Susskind and Field (1996) found anger can be magnified by any number of related factors, most of which are tied to issues of power. These factors include people feeling weak against a much stronger adversary, such as when a group has limited financial and technical resources and is fighting a well-funded corporation or government agency. The anger of resident groups can become ferocious if they believe their views are not being taken seriously. Another anger factor is when people feel they have been treated unfairly, or with disrespect. Anger and conflict can create hostile tourism environments that make things unpleasant if not unbearable for all concerned, but it can lead also to benefits.

Anger in a tourism context can be fuelled by any number of injustices and imbalances in power relationships. Tensions between visitors and residents can arise if a destination is treated as a mere 'playground' for privileged outsiders who act disparagingly towards the people and environments they visit. The anger and disappointment expressed by locals towards tourists can stem from deep social issues, such as those arising from developing colonies being 'recolonised' by tourism firms and visitors who transform these countries into something that meets their needs, rather than those of the country's sovereign people. Morgan and Pritchard (1998: 242) are greatly concerned with the power imbalances that can be reflected in and propagated by tourism, as they note:

> This misrepresentation of historical relationships [between former colonies and the new colonisers] is just one facet of a much more complex, multi-dimensional power reality in which powerful white worlds dominate and define black worlds; in which male dominates female; and a dynamic First World contrasts itself with a static, timeless and unchanging Third World. This is not power confined to international politics and global players – this is the power and politics of everyday life.

Tourism management carries with it a moral responsibility to recognise inherent power imbalances and to develop practical and just ways to work with tourism stakeholders in pursuing more sustainable and equitable options.

Conflict can create both negative and positive outcomes for destinations, as 'within organisations, conflict can prevent stagnation, encourage the search for new solutions and developments and foster better understanding'

(Montgomery, 1986). This is certainly the view of Sumner Redstone, an American media magnate, who says 'It may sound strange but I invite confrontation, confrontation leads to truth' (*The Economist*, 2003a: 59). Potential negative and positive impacts of conflict from a business perspective are detailed below (Gordon *et al.* 1990: 537):

Negative

(1) Participants feel demeaned or defeated.
(2) Creates distance and hostility amongst participants.
(3) Creates a climate of mistrust.
(4) Participants focus on furthering their own best interests.
(5) Teamwork is eroded and resistance rises.
(6) Turnover of staff and customers increase.

Positive

(1) Creates better ideas.
(2) Identify and resolve long standing-issues.
(3) Clarify individual views.
(4) Raise interest and creativity.
(5) Explore new approaches.

Due to the high probability for conflict with many tourism issues, viewing conflict as an inevitable yet manageable occurrence and planning for it is the most sensible course of action. Organisational ways of addressing conflict include legal advisers, human resources advice, ombudspersons and other systems designed to deal with these conflicts. Organisations lacking a formal system for managing conflicts and disputes are likely to have informal ones. These informal systems are more *ad hoc* and dependent on the actions of key individuals as well as organisation norms and the pervading culture's ways of resolving issues (Stitt, 1998). When a conflict becomes so large that it includes multiple organisations as well as many different factions of stakeholder groups, a more elaborate technique for dealing with the conflict is required.

Problems with traditional methods

As stated earlier, tourism development is often an agent of change. Local governments are widely perceived as not being able to adequately address the threats that change brings to communities (Urban Land Institute, 1994). Concerns over local government's inabilities to manage factors of great community importance are expressed widely in Australia's country towns (Collits, 2001). Reasons for questioning the abilities of established decision-makers to make the right decisions are explored by Susskind and Cruikshank in their book *Breaking the Impasse: Consensual Approaches to Resolving Public Disputes* (1987). They identify a series of problems with traditional public dispute resolution methods that prevent effective deci-sion-making on major public issues. These findings are summarised below and presented in a tourism context.

- *Tyranny of the Majority*
  When the option that is most acceptable to the largest group is the measure by which a decision is judged, innovative ideas can be ignored. Under these circumstances, a watered-down proposal not requiring extensive discussion or revision can be chosen rather than working through issues surrounding new ideas. Since tourism desti-nations need to offer something 'special' that will help differentiate them from their competitors, communities that will commit only to conservative measures, may find their return on tourism investments to be disappointing or even negligible.
- *Lack of long-term commitment*
  Pressures to perform well in the short term can override concerns and responsibilities for the long-term implications of actions. This is espe-cially true for politicians with limited terms of office. Heads of busi-nesses must give priority to their financial backers, be it their shareholders or bankers. Often destinations and tourism businesses are assessed on the basis of 'last season's results', rather than in terms of general trends and the results from similar businesses and destina-tions.
- *Limitations of voting*
  Voting does not encourage a building of options – it limits them. Voting tends to cause a polarisation of 'us' and 'them' views rather than a cross-fertilisation of ideas and motivations. When questions are put to a vote, such as referendums on tourist taxes, they should be simple and straightforward, so that people are clear on what options they are being asked to consider.
- *Complexity*
  There can be a range of technical issues and scientific uncertainties re-garding the impacts of proposed options. Lack of clarity makes it dif-ficult, if not impossible, to make the most appropriate decision. Therefore, when considering tourism development options, it is im-portant to realise that to a certain degree the outcome will be unpre-dictable. As such, a degree of flexibility and responsiveness to change needs to be built into implementing these options.
- *Pre-disposition to win/lose conclusions*
  When there are identified 'losers' then the public interest has not been served. The losers may not only be the developers, but also larger seg-ments of the community that could have benefited from the economic opportunities and job creation that a development could have cre-ated. If those opposed to a proposal work with its supporters, to-

gether they can develop options that may mitigate negative impacts. By working together they might agree upon certain flaws in the initial proposal and then move forward, creating opportunities for mutual gain.

More people are questioning the abilities and rights of established decision-makers to decide on their own what is best for communities. While past actions may be valiant, automatically deferring to the 'way things have always been done', can be symptomatic of rigidity, laziness and fear of the unknown (Montgomery, 1986). Studies show that public trust in government and organisations has plummeted, as the shortcomings of the people and policies associated with these groups are exposed and acted against (Klein, 2000; Roddick, 2000).

Prior to the political activism of the 1960s many Western societies were seen to be more cohesive. However, such cohesiveness masked a range of social, economic and environmental problems that were perpetuated by exclusionary practices. Diversity is becoming a more recognised component of today's society. This recognition is based on changing public perceptions and court interpretations of civil rights, resource allocations and government's role in society. Paradoxically, just as the public is increasingly questioning the abilities of elected officials to make the right decisions, many people in power have little confidence or trust in the public's abilities to understand and appropriately respond to pressing issues (Renn & Levine, 1990, cited in Dienel & Renn, 1995).

One of the best ways of dealing with conflict is to ensure that issues are dealt with as soon as possible. Conflict prevention can include educational measures, such as cultural awareness training, and the establishment of procedures to appropriately address issues before they progress into conflict. Partnering is a conflict prevention process used widely in the construction industry (Stitt, 1998). Before a construction project begins, all of the operators working on the job agree on how disputes will be resolved if they arise, with the underlying premise that dispute resolution will not stop construction activities (Stitt, 1998). This approach brings operators together as 'partners', creating an environment of understanding and mutual responsibility and reward. Destinations, like major construction operations, rely on many different parties to provide quality products. Therefore, it is advisable for tourism management strategies to include conflict prevention measures similar to partnering, that enable stakeholders to create strategies for dealing with issues before they mutate into problems.

Planning

Early planning can go a long way towards preventing, or at least mitigating, tourism conflicts. The public's ability to block tourism proposals should not be underestimated. The public has become more capable of stopping developments believed to be wrong. Advocates for citizen and environmental rights have helped to transform the way much of the world now looks at these issues. Dotson *et al.* (1989: A–6) list the following factors as contributing to increased public concern and action over contemporary planning issues:

- more active interest groups;
- greater legal scrutiny of public actions;
- increased scarcity of government resources;
- higher public awareness of planning impacts;
- more complex planning problems.

Governments endeavour to incorporate degrees of public participation in their decision-making processes. However, in their attempts to include public participation in their deliberations elected officials are often criticised for pandering to the most vocal interest groups, at the expense of the greater public good and for producing insipid appeasement packages.

Each stage of the tourism planning process is ripe for controversy and conflict. A brief description of these stages, drawing from Dotson *et al.* (1989), is provided below:

(1) Identifying goals and objectives, which involves gathering a wide range of opinions from effected stakeholders.
(2) Policy formation, which involves working with stakeholders' representatives to develop potential regulations that are responsive to the needs and objectives of the entire community.
(3) Plan preparation and adoption, which involves working with stakeholders to debate and formulate a specific strategy.
(4) Plan and programme implementation, which involves community debate at public hearings that can involve enabling language, budgets and council approval.
(5) Regulatory administration, which tends to involve stakeholders battling over the approval of specific private development projects.

At each of these stages differences and misunderstandings between stakeholders can intensify tensions and erode options. Different tourism stakeholders are bound to have different ideas and different levels of power in regards to determining what is best for them and the community. While a great deal of power is invested in the elites of society, operating from a top-down perspective, power also circulates through society at various levels like a web (Foucault, 1990, cited in Morgan & Pritchard, 1998). Therefore, certain stakeholders, such as charismatic and well-known environmental leaders, can have more power than other stakeholders.

Regardless of their positions and attributes, many stakeholders may be unsure of tourism's full impacts and potential for their community.

Government can assist in bringing members of stakeholder groups together to share their views and develop options in a manner that is sensitive and responsive to their differences. Providing adequate information on tourism's effects builds trust and empowers stakeholder groups to make informed suggestions. Planning departments are well positioned to assist destinations in developing tourism plans due to their experience and expertise in creating plans that account for a diverse range of impacts on an area's economic, social and environmental elements. While traditional decision-makers, such as elected officials and tourism boards, have the ultimate authority in most tourism decisions, there are various levels of public participation that can influence these decisions.

Levels of participation

The level of stakeholder participation in tourism issues can vary considerably, ranging from outside agitators to actual decision-makers. The eight steps of Sherry Arnstein's classic *A ladder of citizen participation* (1969) and our views of how these steps can apply to tourism stakeholders involved with a resort development proposal, are outlined below.

(1) *Manipulation* – Non-participatory
   - 'Decide-announce-defend' approach, where the public cannot change what has been pre-determined.
   - Educate the public as to what will be done, often through a set presentation to local government and through supportive stories in the media.

   Sell the public a finished package for a proposed resort development.

(2) *Therapy* – Very low level of participation
   - Provide an opportunity for the public to share its frustrations and concerns, often through a 'special meeting' at the local government level.
   - Focus on identifying and managing 'problem people' or types.

   Present a resort development's supposed benefits to members of the public and provide them with an opportunity to 'have their say' on the issue, without providing feedback mechanisms for modifying the proposal.

(3) *Informing* – Low level of participation
   - First legitimate step in participation.
   - Public concern over a pending decision can lead to minor alterations to the decision, the scope of these changes is limited.

Inform members of the public of a resort development concept and provide limited opportunities for them to suggest small changes, such as those relating to the appearance of the resort.

(4) *Consultation* – Minor level of participation
- Special forums for the public to share its views through mechanisms, such as surveys and workshops, designed to draw out the public's goals, ideas and concerns in relation to the pending decision.

Control the extent of public discussion on tourism and use these discussions as a means of assessing community support for the proposed resort and other pending tourism decisions. While some changes to the proposal will be considered in response to the public's expressed views, whether it should be built will not be questioned.

(5) *Placation* – Moderate level of participation
- Public influences the decision in a broad-based manner, while certain individuals or groups have the opportunity to more closely advise the decision-making body(ies).
- Create taskforces, committees or other groups that are seen to represent the broader interests of the community and these groups advise the decision-making body(ies).

A public advisory group with members hand-picked by elected representatives could be created to make recommendations for significant changes to the resort proposal. However, depending on the level of legitimacy that the decision-making body(ies) give to this group only politically palatable recommendations will be adopted, while more radical recommendations are deferred for 'further study'.

(6) *Partnership* – High level of participation
- Actual decision-making shared with members of the public.
- Redistribution of power through negotiations between the established decision-making body(ies) and members of the public through the establishment of joint committees.

A joint committee made up of members from established decision-making body(ies) and the public reviews issues and makes recommendations that the decision-making body(ies) adopt, as long as these recommendations are supported by all committee members.

(7) *Delegated power* –Very high level of participation
- High level of participation in terms of actual decision-making being led by members of the public.

- The balance of power is weighted in favour of members of the public through the establishment of joint committees.

  A joint committee made up of members from established decision-making body(ies) and the public, where members of the public are in the majority, review the issues and make recommendations that the decision-making body(ies) will adopt as long as these recommendations are supported by a majority of the committee members.

(8) *Citizen control* – Top level of participation
  - Highest level of public participation, in the sense that the general public holds all decision-making power.
  - Create cooperatives that are responsible for planning, policies and decisions that affect community members.

  Certain ecotourism groups establish cooperative tourism boards, to plan and operate local tourism ventures, including resorts. The political success of such a process will be determined by the extent to which the public's representatives in this process are seen to legitimately represent their community and be in a position to make the best possible decisions for their community.

Power

It can be argued that much of the public's involvement in tourism decision-making processes ranges from 'manipulation' to 'placation' (Hall, 1995). Governments typically ask citizens to share their views on issues once the relevant decisions on these issues have already been made (Webler, 1995). Reasons given for minimising the role and importance of public participation in deciding community issues include concerns over the effectiveness of such participation and its costs. Concerns about diminishing returns, in terms of the overall value of increasing public participation are understandable. What is needed are practical ways of providing the right level of public participation for a given situation to produce practical, effective and fair decisions.

While elected representatives and heads of organisations are accountable for their actions and are subject to either elections or some form of vote of confidence, the general public has no such accountability (Dienel & Renn, 1995). This lack of accountability combined with limited expertise can lead to citizens advocating options that are not politically, financially or physically possible, especially over the long term. Furthermore, removing entrenched decision-making abilities from traditional decision-makers can be illegal, unconstitutional or otherwise unacceptable. If elected representatives or the heads of organisations are to respond to the 'public's general will' when making decisions they need to enter into a form of public discourse to understand how the public views the issues at hand, so they can respond appropriately (Webler, 1995). Therefore, the rights and responsibilities of appointed decision-makers need to be balanced with those of the public.

The level of participation that the public obtains is a direct reflection of local power dynamics. Power in decision-making processes can be defined as 'the potential or actual ability to influence others in a desired direction' (Gordon *et al.*, 1990: 589). Power begets power, in that if a particular stakeholder group shows itself to be powerful before, during and after negotiations, they are in a much stronger position to ensure that their contributions are meaningful. Power is a reflection of resources, including money, intellect, experiences, negotiation and leadership skills, as well as the ability to inspire. Those without substantial resources can increase their power by making strategic alliances, rallying support for their views and conducting themselves well in the collaborative decision-making process (Susskind & Field, 1996). Laws, institutions, cultural norms and language all profoundly influence power situations, thereby largely determining the extent to which the views of various stakeholder groups will be incorporated into tourism management strategies and approaches.

The final steps in Arnstein's model may be unachievable for political and economic reasons. Yet there are still strong arguments for the earlier steps, such as partnership, as a way of complementing existing systems (Webler, 1995). Tourism advisory groups, such as boards or committees, with representatives from industry, government and residents are a common way to include the public in tourism management decisions. These advisory groups are often used as a reference base for decision-making, but they can also serve on the boards that make the actual decisions. *Tourism Victoria*, the destination marketing association of Victoria, BC in Canada, has a general membership and executive made up of local citizens as well as industry and government representatives. Therefore, residents have an opportunity to influence the actions of this organisation in an advisory capacity, by serving as general members, or as decision-maker on its executive board. The abilities of citizens to influence tourism advisory groups are a function of their proportional representation in the general membership and executive of these groups, as well as the extent to which the other stakeholders support their views and are willing to work with them.

Processes

There are a number of processes for increasing the public's role in tourism management strategies. Public meetings, taskforces, small group workshops and shuttle diplomacy are all described in the control component of this chapter. Three processes that can be particularly useful in the planning stage of destination management are focus groups, the

Delphi technique and the nominal group technique. These techniques allow for a high level of analysis, the results of which can be used to enrich subsequent discussions and decision-making.

Focus groups tend to consist of eight to 10 participants who are brought together to discuss a narrow range of topics with guidance from a third party (La Page, 1994). These participants are chosen according to their abilities to provide insight into the views of particular stakeholder groups, or segments of these groups. Benefits of focus groups are that their members can explore issues and develop options together. The group dynamic of this approach can strengthen the relationships between stakeholder groups and lead to more comprehensive findings. The propensity for strong personalities to dominate these groups and problems with representativeness – especially given the low number of participants – are drawbacks to using focus groups.

The Delphi technique synthesises expert opinions on current issues and events to gain greater insight into likely future outcomes (Moeller & Shafer, 1994). This technique involves providing participants with rounds of questionnaires, the results of which are tabulated and fed back to participants for their consideration and refinement. The median responses drawn from these questionnaires are interpreted as the most likely future outcomes. Benefits of this approach are that group dynamics do not need to be managed, nor do schedules have to be coordinated, as the individual participants work in isolation and in fact usually remain anonymous. Also experts tend to be highly aware of opportunities and constraints in their field, which enhances the accuracy of their predictions. Challenges with this approach include missed opportunities for improving understanding between stakeholders and that the directors of these processes can easily influence process outcomes, due to their pervasive role in directing the process.

The nominal group technique (NGT) 'provides two specific types of output: first, it provides a list of ideas relevant to the topic in question; and second, the technique provides qualified individual and aggregate measures of the relative desirability of the ideas raised in the session' (Ritchie, 1994: 494). This highly structured technique uses a third party facilitator to guide the groups of experts through the processes. NGT starts with initial statements or topics being put to group participants who then reflect on them individually and share their views with the group. Options are expressed in written form, such as on a flip chart, and reviewed and ranked by all present. The facilitator compiles the results using voting preferences to indicate group priorities. The main benefit of using this approach is that it brings various stakeholder groups together in a constructive forum, where facilitators ensure negative views are subsumed by positive consensus. The largest challenge with NGT is to convert the declared priorities into action.

Peter Murphy used a particular NGT technique – the Delbecq technique (Delbecq *et al.*, 1975; Runyan, 1977) to pull together the ideas and opinions of 54 groups in Victoria, BC, Canada, regarding local tourism development and directions. He developed a three-stage workshop. At the opening session all representatives expressed their concerns about local tourism; these views were written on flip charts and then posted around the large assembly room. The second stage was a simulation exercise, where individuals were placed in unfamiliar roles and asked to locate a high rise commercial development in a sensitive environmental area of a 'sim-city'. The objective of this exercise was to encourage stakeholders to think of other viewpoints and to be prepared to make compromises. They needed to do that to construct the partnerships necessary to 'win the game' and achieve their preferred development option. The third and crucial last stage was to use the Delbecq technique (Murphy *et al.*, 1985).

The Delbecq technique necessitates the division of the whole group into several small mixed interest groups that separate to think about ways to solve the problems and concerns identified in the first session. With the help of a facilitator each small group thinks of 'solutions' individually and in silence. Then they share their thoughts, without any group comment allowed, which are placed on a flip chart. Once all thoughts are on the board the small group is allowed to comment on the preferred solutions, but *only* in a positive and constructive manner. For example, certain similarities may be observed with respect to some of the proffered solutions, enabling the construction of a joint solution. The final step at this stage is for the small group to rank their solutions. The top three to five small group ideas are then brought before the total assembly by the facilitator, with no reference to whose ideas they were. The total group is then invited to discuss the proposed solutions, again in a positive and constructive manner only, before voting on their individual favourites. In a variety of settings this approach has produced one to three dominant suggestions, which can be used to direct future community decision-making.

A key challenge is to move from the 'group-hug' atmosphere of the workshop to actual action. In the case of the Victoria, BC workshop a 'blue-ribbon' committee was created to develop an action plan to implement the leading and dominant recommendation. In this case it was to create a structure that would coordinate all the industry and community energy that was evident throughout the workshop. This committee, under the chair of a neutral representative – Professor Peter Murphy – reported back to the total group within the specified time period and presented a proposed umbrella organisation to guide the city's future tourism development. The proposal was accepted and *Tourism Victoria* was born as the capital region's destination marketing association.

Organising

Organising requires an understanding of what is needed to get the job done. Group decision-making can require significant resources (Tiegerman-Farber & Radziewicz, 1998). When putting a plan into action there should be a good fit between the matters of concern and the level of public participation necessary to solve them. It is also advisable to provide pertinent background information to participants before meetings and to brief them on issues on an 'as needed basis' (Dotson *et al.*, 1989). These processes are aided by structuring meetings in a prudent fashion and establishing ambitious, yet realistic deadlines for a deliverable outcome from the collaborative group.

Scale and scope

When organising resources to manage tourism development, the likely levels of potential conflict and corresponding public interest need to be anticipated. Dotson *et al.* (1989: A11) identify three types of conflict – issues, disputes and impasses – that they rank according to their level of intensity. Drawing upon Dotson *et al.*'s (1989) work, these conflict types are illustrated within the context of a proposal to develop a marina in an isolated location, as discussed below.

(1) **Issues**
- *Conflict level*   Low to moderate and contained level of disagreement.

   The marina proposal is of a modest scale, it would be owned and run by local people and would not be in an environmentally sensitive area.

- *Negotiation required*   Informal discussions by affected stakeholders.

   People interested in the proposal have the opportunity to meet and discuss the matter with its proponents in an *ad hoc* manner.

- *Third party involvement*   Not usually required, often resolved at the staff level.

   The small number of people interested in the proposal and their low level of concern negate the need for outside assistance. The proponents with the possible assistance of affected government agencies are able to manage consultative processes to the general satisfaction of those involved.

- *Participation techniques*   Public meetings to frame issues, examine alternatives, and help build consensus.

The general public can participate in the decision-making process by attending regularly scheduled meetings, such as those of local councils. At these meetings potential modifications to the proposal can be discussed.

(2) **Disputes**

- *Conflict level*   High and more public displays of concern.

  The proposal is for a large-scale marina, owned by outside investors, operated by local people and would not be in an environmentally sensitive area.

- *Negotiation required*   Formal discussions by affected stakeholders.

  More people are interested in the proposal than would have the opportunity individually and informally to discuss the matter with either its proponents or governing agencies. Therefore, particular forums, such as open houses and workshops, need to be set up so that information can be shared with a large number of people within a relatively short period of time.

- *Third party involvement*   Usually required, in the form of direct negotiations or the mediation of stakeholders' interests through a neutral third party.

  The range of people directly involved in the proposal and a growing and diverse range of people interested in the proposal and its impacts make negotiations with stakeholders more difficult. Therefore, outside assistance in establishing and running a consultation process is advisable.

- *Participation techniques*   Disputes involving only a few parties are well suited for direct negotiation, while others will likely need to hold a series of facilitated group meetings.

  An advisory group consisting of the parties involved with the proposal (local government representatives, developers, management company) as well as representatives from other interested parties (local residents, environmentalists, business and tourist associations) should hold a series of meetings that are open to the public. Input from other forums, such as council meetings and open houses, should be used to inform the discussions of the advisory council seeking viable options.

(3) **Impasses**

- *Conflict level*   Extreme and entrenched positions on areas of contention.

  The marina proposal is of a large scale, owned and operated by people from outside the community and is in an environmentally sensitive area.

- *Negotiation required*   Formal, often judicial.

  The complexities of finding a solution acceptable to all parties and an inability of the negotiation options to meet the needs of stakeholders, can lead parties to initiate legal proceedings. Alternatively potential environmental impacts or public outcry might be so great as to trigger formal review mechanisms, such as an environmental impact assessment (EIS), or a special government commission to review the issues.

- *Third party involvement*   Arbitration or litigation.

  Arbitration or mediation prior to, or in place of, court proceedings would be advisable.

- *Participation techniques*   Typically adversarial, though there are still opportunities to examine alternatives and help build consensus.

  Formal court and governmental hearings to decide on the fate of a proposal provide a more limited range of options for public participation. Stakeholder groups can become a party to these proceedings, which can include hiring legal representation and expert witnesses. Stakeholders can also submit petitions, reports and other forms of written responses as a way of conveying their views. If affected and interested parties are able to work together to find areas of agreement that they present to court or government hearings, these efforts will likely be viewed favourably and influence the final decision on the matter.

The marina example illustrates how contributing factors to increased tension and the corresponding process demands related to increasing the scale of the development, the degree of outside ownership and anticipated environmental impacts. This escalation of interests, costs and uncertainty could also be caused if public anger is triggered by concerns that the public is being deceived, cheated or otherwise excluded from having its rightful say. This example highlights the importance of planning a public participation process based on the level of need for increased public participation.

While some tourism development processes only require minimal resources for public participation, the greater the potential for conflict the more important it becomes to plan and invest in a negotiation process so that it can function as intended.

Assessment techniques

Once the decision has been made to work together with various stakeholders on a tourism project, the challenges of identifying and including the appropriate representatives from these groups must be confronted. Gray (1985), a renowned author in the area of collaborative decision-making, sees 'legitimate stakeholders' as having the ability and right to engage in the decision-making process. Their ability to participate is tied to available resources, including time, skills and a belief in the joint decision-making process. Their right to participate is tied to their being impacted by the outcome of the decision-making process and their capacity to accurately convey the views of both their interest group and the negotiation group.

Questions of legitimacy are often raised in determining who will represent tourism stakeholder groups (Blank, 1989) and ensuring that these decision-making processes are inclusive and effective (Haywood, 1988). As resources are not equitably distributed throughout societies, there can be great discrepancies at a negotiation table between the different members of a collaborative decision-making process. Given the interrelatedness of economic, social and environmental actions, we are all somewhat affected by these actions. Therefore, someone's right to participate in a decision-making process is usually related to perceptions of level of impact. Those living next to a proposed development can be seen as having a right to participate, as can the larger community to a lesser degree. As noted by Webler (1995) those with more at stake or more power may have a greater ability to undermine the decision-making process, either during implementation or through subsequent revisions if they feel they are not properly represented in the process.

Determining early in the process the level of potential public interest and conflict that a tourism proposal is likely to raise is highly advisable. However, sometimes it can be unclear as to the level of public interest in a tourism matter and the correspondingly appropriate planning response. Factors indicative of a highly contentious tourism proposal include, but are not limited to, the following situations:

- *Stakeholders* Large numbers, diverse, disjointed, uncertainties relating to representation and legitimacy or hostile relations between parties.
- *Proposal* Large scale, reliant on substantial government assistance,

does not fit in with current standards or could be a threat to other businesses.

- *Community* Potentially significant environmental, social and economic impacts.

If the potential for conflict is great it can be highly advantageous to engage in some exploratory assessment of issues in the preplanning stage of a tourism proposal. One method to consider is the *Conflict Assessment Technique* that has been used constructively many times in various countries as a way of identifying the potential to use mediation in resolving conflicts (Susskind, 2001). The basis of this technique is to identify a range of stakeholders and the issues underlying the conflict. While this technique might be too elaborate and resource intensive for most tourist destinations, it contains excellent ideas that could be adapted to suit an area's specific needs and capabilities.

The *Conflict Assessment Technique* begins with an assessment team approaching obvious 'players' concerned about a certain issue and interviewing them. These interviews are confidential as the views participants share are not attributed to them, but rather are noted in relation to general concerns and ideas relating to the issue. The first group of interviewees is asked to recommend additional people to contact in regards to the issue in question. The second group of potential stakeholders is interviewed in the same manner. Pending negotiations on the pressing issue are then announced publicly and more interviews are conducted of those parties that respond to the announcement.

The assessment team maps out the issues and sends this map back to all participants to see if they feel their input has been accurately represented. After making the necessary adjustments and responding to feedback from the survey participants, the assessment team makes a list of potential stakeholders to invite to the process and a potential negotiating procedure. The next steps involve drafting a 'suggested' agenda, budget for the process, allocation of fiscal responsibilities and ground rules for the mediation process. The assessment team then reports back to the lead agency with its opinion as to whether or not key stakeholders will participate in process and if such a process has the potential of being a viable means of resolving the issues.

The *Conflict Assessment Technique* advocates the use of an impartial third party to conduct this process. However, based on resources and the level of conflict this entire process or parts of it could be done in-house. Government is particularly well positioned for approaching other stakeholder groups and in cases act as an acceptable mediator given its mandate of protecting community interests. Government can act as a leader in moving forward the possibilities for different stakeholder groups to work as allies in tourism management.

Leadership

Leadership in tourism management can be by the few or it can be by the many. Conventional problem solving looks to the leadership of the few, where individuals make decisions with little input from outside sources. If 'a problem is easily defined, money is not an issue, the level of public concern is low, conventional problem solving works well' (Urban Land Institute, 1994: 16). When this is not the case, as is often true with tourism issues, the ranks of leaders need to be expanded and the cooperation between leaders and stakeholders must increase. A more inclusive approach to leadership should be considered under the following circumstances:

- complex issue;
- high level of public concern;
- wide range of affected stakeholders;
- emergency action is not required;
- long-term issue;
- no one agency has sole jurisdiction;
- the issues are negotiable and the parties are willing to negotiate.

Of all the above listed circumstances 'willing to negotiate' can be the key factor in whether a more collective leadership approach to tourism management will succeed.

There are different types of negotiation whose applicability and effectiveness can vary according to situational factors. Lewicki and Litterer (1985) divide negotiation processes into two types: distributive and integrative. Distributive bargaining revolves around trying to get the best possible personal outcome without regard to the other parties, while integrative bargaining revolves around creating a solution that is beneficial and acceptable to all of the negotiating parties. When there is little trust between parties and the willingness to working together is low then distributive negotiations might be the only option that parties are willing to pursue. When relations between groups are not openly hostile and there is a belief that by working together a better outcome can be achieved then integrative bargaining can be promising.

Principled negotiations

Leading with integrity is essential to ensuring that negotiations fulfil their higher potential, and those involved need to commit to a process of fair and effective negotiations. Fisher *et al.* (1991) developed a four-step process for *Principled Negotiations* that is highly effective in leading negotiations. These principles create an environment of trust and productivity and can result in innovative, widely supported and timely outcomes. Fisher *et al.* (1991: 15–81) principles are presented below with tourism examples added for the purposes of this book.

(1) *Separate the people from the problem*

Personal differences and tensions can cloud issues being negotiated. Therefore, it takes vigilance to be aware of when concerns are drifting over to personal issues and away from those being negotiated and to ensure that these are acknowledged and dealt with separately. A tourism example could involve members at the negotiation table who have clashed publicly and who are inclined to carry past grievances and personal problems with each other into the current negotiations. If a ground rule is made to forbid personal attacks, then participants who break this rule are quickly identified and effectively dealt with as per the rules of the process.

(2) *Focus on interests not positions*

When a hard line approach is taken on a position, then a tug-of-war between positions can ensue. Basic human interests relate to one's physical, emotional and economic well-being, which can include issues of protection, recognition, self-destiny and social connections. Positions, which are adopted stances, tend to complicate and undermine group negotiations. Positions represent set ways of doing things and are a form of prejudice in that they are believed to be the best and often only way of meeting one's interests. During tourism management meetings many interests are shared and they are a good starting place for discussion. Many tourism stakeholders' interests are similar, such as maintaining a high quality of life, while their positions meeting these interests can be manifestly divergent. Once shared interests are identified and documented then all negotiators can see they are working together towards certain common goals.

(3) *Invent options for mutual gain*

This step involves working together to generate ideas, analyse these ideas and then determine which ones will work best for the group. People need to feel comfortable in putting forward their ideas and collaborating with others, to create something that is better for the larger group. Unfortunately, this step does not often come naturally to a group made up of diverse participants. The role of a well-trained third party is to guide such groups through the negotiating process especially in regard to developing new ways of addressing lingering problems. It is essential that negotiation members treat each other respectfully to ensure that each person shares their input and does not stifle their ideas or bottle up complaints. If a tourism negotiation team is looking for ways to increase tourism revenues while not damaging the overall community well-being, they will need a well-rounded understanding of the issues and the possibilities for workable solutions. Economic realities play a substantial role in determining the feasibility of options, as do the availability of the organisational structures and qualified people to put proposed actions in motion.

(4) *Insist on using objective criteria*

Objective criteria only work if all of those negotiating feel comfortable that they are in fact 'objective'. Such criteria can be drawn from existing sources of information and the input of experts, when they are acceptable to all parties. If they are not acceptable to all parties, then practices of joint fact finding and the hiring of impartial experts chosen by the group can create new and broadly acceptable information. Tourism impact surveys and studies, designed and endorsed by a negotiation team is seen as relevant to the negotiators and the larger stakeholder groups that they represent.

These principles help to create an environment that is conducive to problem solving. Collective decisions are decided by either arguing, bargaining, voting or a combination of these techniques (Elster, 1998); and ground rules for behaviour coupled with a commitment to approach a problem based on principled negotiations are highly advisable. Ground rules, such as not allowing personal attacks, interruptions, or other signs of disrespect, let negotiating parties know what is expected of them and of others. Even if the relationships between the parties are poor, such principles and ground rules can discipline and enhance the actions and interactions of the negotiating parties.

Aspects of Fisher *et al.*'s 'Principled Negotiations' were incorporated into the Banff-Bow Valley Study that took a consensus building approach towards developing a tourism management strategy. 'Interest Based Negotiations' (the second principle) serves as the founding principle for this study that was directed by a Task Force of the Canadian government (Ritchie, 2000). The Task Force recommended that stakeholders should drive the process within the format of Round Table discussions of 14 interest sectors facilitated by a technical expert. The facilitator helped the different sectors reach consensus on a series of statements that they developed by moving beyond their initial positions to sharing their interests and looking for common ground. The study was deemed a well-rounded success in terms of participant satisfaction, the development and implementation of recommendations with broad-based support, greater understanding and cooperation between stakeholders, and improved management practices in the study area. The success of this study was aided by its generous budget ($2.4 million), time-frame (two years), and process support by the main stakeholder groups (Ritchie, 2000: 46).

Control

Even under the guidance of processes that have been designed to include stakeholders in a fair and effective manner there is still a need to monitor and control the system to achieve the desired results. Many local elites are predisposed to strongly promote economic growth, which can bias discussions on appropriate development strategies and initiatives for these communities (Little & Krannich, 1982: Reed, 1997). As noted by Jamal and Getz (1995) a collaborative decision-making process for tourism issues can be complicated by the need to attract outside assistance in terms of financiers, entrepreneurs and developers to help a community reach its tourism objectives. To convince outside investors of the viability of tourism proposals requires regular monitoring and controlled decision-making.

The challenges inherent in creating more equitable environments and processes for the collaborative decision-making process can be immense. Larissa Behrendt, an Aboriginal solicitor who obtained her doctorate at Harvard University, details the entrenched barriers to the just treatment of Aboriginal people in land disputes and proposes radical changes to address these injustices. Behrendt (1995) developed a conceptual model for dispute resolution within Aboriginal and Torres Strait Islander communities. This model encourages public participation by having a group of elders, with decision-making authority, preside over a series of public meetings, which take place in an informal way within the affected community. Such an approach could counteract biases against indigenous people in traditional tourism negotiations, as non-indigenous groups, such as major hoteliers, would be required to conform and operate within an indigenous way of doing things. This work with indigenous communities shows how culture plays a large role in determining appropriate ways of incorporating community views into community leadership.

Collaborative decision-making

Collaborative decision-making can be viewed as a mutual gains approach, where the ideas generated by a diverse range of people create more effective and inclusive decisions than those formulated from a single point of view. Taking a collaborative approach to tourism management strengthens the abilities of diverse people to work together and to create something greater than they can produce on their own. A collaborative approach can also motivate destinations to take a comprehensive look at the diverse factors that impact on their tourism developments and proposals, thereby enabling them to make better management decisions. Collaborative-decision making can only take place if it supported by established decision-makers as well as key stakeholder groups. Decisions that arise from collaborative processes supplement, rather than supplant those of established decision-makers, such as local councils and heads of industry.

Collaborative decision-making is an interactive process that empowers stakeholders to create innovative solutions for problems that are mutually defined by the participants in the process. Tiegerman-Farber and Radziewicz (1998), who have studied the application of collaborative decision-making in the educational system, find 'sharing' as the key to successful collaboration. They see mutual goals and shared participation, resources, respect and accountabilities as the foundation of an effective collaborative decision-making process.

Mediation and facilitation

Mediation and facilitation are two methods widely used to help with collaborative decision-making. Mediation refers to negotiations between parties that are assisted by a neutral third party who helps the parties arrive at solutions themselves (Boulle, 1996). Facilitation is similar to mediation in that it also refers to negotiations between parties that are assisted by a neutral third party. However, the role of the third party in running the process and finding solutions is much more active in facilitation (Stitt, 1998). A trained facilitator can be viewed like an excellent host who makes everyone feel comfortable, provides everyone with an opportunity to speak, keeps conversations moving in a constructive fashion and helps ensure that the event is viewed as worthwhile by all who attend. Facilitation can be the preferred option for multi-party disputes, especially when there are problems with power imbalances, communication difficulties, issue identification and cultural differences. Mediation and facilitation need not be seen as threats, but rather as methods of getting better results than by using traditional methods, such as political representation and legal challenges.

Skilled mediators and facilitators guide negotiations through the difficult periods of collaborative decision-making processes. When engaged in a conflict people are predisposed to believe their views and actions are 'right', while those that do not correspond to their views are 'wrong'. Facilitators and mediators can keep such feelings in check by drawing attention to actions or views that spring forth from misguided perspectives. This can be as simple as asking pointed questions as to why a meeting participant responded in a particular manner, or talking the group through the likely impacts of different proposals. Other methods include having participants engage in a series of role-playing exercises so that they understand other's values more clearly and are less judgemental and more empathetic when dealing with differences.

Consensus

It can be impractical to hold out for an agreement that all tourism stakeholder groups 'whole heartedly support'. An essential part of negotiation, facilitation and mediation processes is predetermining what level of consensus will be acceptable to all parties. Susskind (2001) categorises levels of consensus that move from the highest level of support (level 1) to the lowest level of mutual support acceptable to the group (level 3):

(1) Participants strongly support the solution.
(2) Participants can 'live with' the solution.
(3) Some participants do not support the solution, but they agree not to veto it.

These levels of support can be seen as degrees of enthusiasm for proposed options. It is advisable to strive for the solutions that stakeholder groups can 'live with' rather than holding onto an idealised outcome (Susskind, 2001). If the group accepts the lowest level of consensus at the beginning of the process, even those stakeholders who are upset with the settlement will not have the power to kill it.

Providing a voting mechanism within group negotiations can hold groups hostage to unreasonable demands. Disproportionate bargaining power can be provided to individual parties if their single vote has the power to swing the vote. This power is often used in the interests of the single party rather than larger group. Susskind strives to identify, activate and meet the needs of the 'constructive middle', rather than meeting the demands of the outer extremes that are often in the minority. Once the group collectively agrees on key issues and a good effort has been made to address any concerns that group members have of the proposal, then consensus is reached by 'overwhelming agreement', rather than by unanimous decision (Susskind, 2001).

Forums

There are various ways to build consensus over tourism issues in response to a destination's needs and resources (Creighton, 1980: Smith & Hester, 1982) several of which are discussed briefly below.

Public meetings

- Public meetings tend to be low cost ventures that provide good opportunities for providing information to the public and receiving a cross-section of opinions. However, they are not conducive to developing new options and assertive and organised groups can literally drown out other stakeholders.

Task forces

- Task forces are established on a temporary basis to carry out a specific function within a set period of time. Task forces tend to be well structured and run in an efficient manner. However, their disadvantages include a lack of representation of all stakeholder groups and a tightly constrained scope of action.

Small group workshops

- Small group workshops tend to consist of less than 50 participants and have an assigned task to be completed during one or more workshops. Although these groups can benefit from their diversity of opinions in generating options and the ability to build productive and lasting relationship, they can have limited participation and once again strong personalities can dominate the group.

Shuttle diplomacy

- If relations between stakeholder groups are openly hostile then shuttle diplomacy is worth considering. In this process a neutral third party sends messages between stakeholder groups, so that ideas can be considered without the added complexities of caustic personal relations. Shuttle diplomacy carries the disadvantage of being somewhat covert and more susceptible to manipulation by powerful stakeholders. While these techniques are primarily used by government agencies, they can also be utilised by the business sector and other tourism entities.

The appropriate form of consensus building will be determined largely by community support for the process and the nature of the issue. It is essential that affected stakeholders believe they have a key role in the decision-making process. Listening to stakeholders as early as possible and using their input as a way of setting up the decision-making process, lays the foundation for a solid and lasting agreement between diverse interest groups.

Tourism applications

Different forms and levels of collaboration in tourism management are achieved through a variety of processes. Three distinct examples of public participation in tourism initiatives are provided to highlight how these methods are used, as well as their strengths and limitations. The first example outlines collaborative tourism planning requirements that were developed by Canadian researchers. The last two examples, one from America and the other from Australia, are illustrations of what can go wrong when appropriate levels of public participation are not incorporated into the planning and development of tourism proposals.

Jamal and Getz (1995: 188) define collaboration for community-based tourism planning as 'a process of joint decision-making among autonomous, key stakeholders of an inter-organizational, community tourism domain to resolve planning problems of the domain and/or to manage issues related to the planning and development of the domain'. Upon reviewing theories and applications of collaborative decision-making in a tourism context, Jamal and Getz (1995: 195–200) developed six propositions for the application of collaborative tourism planning, which are summarised below.

(1) Recognise the high level of interdependence in planning and managing tourism products and services.
(2) Recognise the individual benefits as well as joint benefits derived from the collaborative process.
(3) Produce results that are implementable, otherwise participation in the process will be stymied and the process can lose its validity and effectiveness.
(4) Include representatives from the following key stakeholder groups: local government, tourism industry associations, resident groups, regional tourism organisations, social agencies and special interest groups.
(5) A mediator or facilitator who is experienced and acceptable to all parties is required to initiate and run the community based decision-making process.
(6) The following elements are necessary for collaborative strategic tourism planning: a vision statement for tourism development; jointly developed goals and objectives; self-regulation of the industry through the establishment of a collaborative organisation, or an oversight committee to monitor and make the necessary adjustment to the tourism plan's implementation.

Tourism is dependent upon continually meeting the expectations of residents and host communities in order to create and maintain environments that support the industry. Understanding the opportunities and costs of a potential tourism proposal involves an appreciation of market, political, economic, environmental and social conditions. Integrating public participation into tourism planning can be an essential step in understanding these conditions. However, as the following two examples show, there are a number of areas where public participation in tourism planning can become derailed. The first example looks at the proposal to build a historical theme park in Virginia, USA, while the second example looks at a proposal to build a Club Med Resort in Byron Bay, Australia.

Disney's America (Manassas, Virginia, USA)

In 1993 the Walt Disney Company unexpectedly announced its intention to open a historic theme park, 'Disney's America', in northern Virginia on 3000 acres of rural countryside (Zenzen, 1998: 166–7). Disney acquired the land and planned the Disney's America theme park in secrecy, which prevented the company from including local politicians and other stakeholders in the planning process. This lack of local participation during the early stages led to a loss of legitimacy for the theme park and is seen as one of the 'key mistakes' in the proposal (Eisner with Schwartz, 1998: 323). The Disney site in Virginia had the advantages of being easily accessible via Interstate 66 to Washington DC's large population and its 19 million annual visitors, many of whom are interested in the nation's history (Eisner with Schwartz, 1998: 320).

Although the chosen site was not designated as historically significant, it was within five miles of a Civil War battlefield in Manassas, which concerned a number of locals and historians (Zenzen, 1989: 166–7). There were concerns about scrutinising the ways of the South and making painful historical events 'entertaining'. There were also concerns that traditional ways of life would be challenged and potentially lost if there was the usual surge in developmental activity triggered by the theme park. Associated environmental concerns also were raised relating to the potential impacts of increased development on this largely undeveloped, rural corner of Virginia.

Disney's America was intending to highlight a cross-section of American history in an accurate, yet entertaining way, with a strong focus on the Civil War. Disney was 'committed to bringing history alive by telling emotionally compelling stories in dramatic ways' (Eisner with Schwartz, 1998: 325). The proposal's potential benefits included $680 million in tax revenue over 30 years, 2700 new jobs, a boom in visitation to historic sites in the area and a strengthened economy. These were all attractive to a county that had listed job creation and economic development as its top goals (Zenzen, 1998: 169–70).

After being widely criticised for excluding stakeholders from the early planning stages of the proposal, Disney showed itself willing to work with stakeholders by meeting with a range of community members, historians and government agencies. Disney offered to invest in local improvements, set aside extensive green space, promote surrounding historical sites and sell local products as part of its theme park proposal. In February 1994, several independently conducted polls indicated that Virginians supported the Disney proposal by margins averaging 3 to 1 (Eisner with Schwartz, 1998: 327). Despite well-financed opposition from prominent Southern families, including the Duponts and the owners of the *Washington Post*, Disney's America was fully approved at the state level. However, the theme park was shelved after extensive national media coverage ridiculed the proposal and due to the continual resistance from some local powerbrokers. Losing this ambitious development caused substantial losses for the community in terms of jobs, economic opportunities and a forum to openly debate the legacy and future of the South.

Club Med Resort (Byron Bay, NSW, Australia)

Please note that the details on this case are drawn from Roger Brooks's (2000) article 'The collaborative approach to resolving tourist related conflict', in the *Australian Planner,* unless sourced otherwise.

Byron Bay is well loved for its tropical beauty, colourful locals and relaxed way of life. It has become a popular surfing destination, and has attracted many retirees (Figure 11.1). Byron Shire, which is 800 km north of Sydney and 180 km south of Brisbane, has a population of close to 30,000 and attracts approximately 1.7 million tourists a year (Byron Shire Council, 2003: 1). 'Byron has a reputation for fierce vigilantism against development' (Kinninment, 2003: 13). This reputation was earned from fighting large development proposals, with the battle over Club Med being one of the most notable examples.

The proposed Club Med resort was to consist of bungalow style units with a capacity for 641 beds, four restaurants and assorted conference and recreational facilities (bulletin cited in Brooks, 2000: 189). In response to the submissions, Club Med made some minor design and siting amendments and the proposal was approved subject to a substantial number of conditions. There was fierce opposition to the proposal, as evident by an anti-development petition with over 7000 signatures and a legal challenge to the proposal (*Echo,* cited in Brooks, 2000: 189). Residents rallied against the proposal with '"No Club Med" T-shirts, stickers and banners, and even TV advertisements' (Kinninment, 2003: 13). In response to this opposition Club Med scaled down its original proposal by half in terms of size and two-thirds in terms of its capacity.

The supporters of the proposal felt the resort would greatly boost tourism, provide a large market for local goods and services, infuse $16 million a year into the local economy and provide 200 jobs (*Australian Tourism Monitor,* cited in Brooks, 2000: 189). Opponents felt the potential negative impacts of the resort would exceed any economic benefits. There were also concerns that it would set a precedent for large-scale resorts and draw in multi-national companies – threatening the local environment and way of life. The Byron Shire Council tried to address community concerns by providing public meetings, group discussions and an extended display period to review the proposal. The developer initiated dialogue with community groups, modified the proposal and offered to enter into a community contract to resolve community concerns.

Club Med used an out-of-town consulting firm to run its community negotiations. These collaboration endeavours opened up dialogue between stakeholder groups and led to some compromises. However, process participants were critical of Club Med for not fulfilling its promise to invite all stakeholders to participate in the negotiation process and to enter into a 'community contract' to address key issues. Since Club Med hired the leaders of the negotiation team many residents felt that Club Med

Figure 11.1 Byron Bay, Australia

was primarily promoting its views, rather than listening and responding to what they said. The processes established by council and the developer were seen to lack legitimacy and fairness by a number of stakeholder groups. Club Med's inability to resolve key issues with stakeholders resulted in prolonged community opposition to the proposal and to legal actions. The *Land and Environment Court* overturned council approval to build the resort in 1996 and three years later Club Med pulled out of the area (Kinninment, 2003).

Analysis

If Disney and Club Med had included more meaningful input from stakeholder groups along the lines advanced in the first example, they could possibly have realised their ambitions as well as many of those of other affected parties. Perhaps a more collaborative approach was not taken in part because these companies did not want to let their competition know what was planned. However, a clandestine approach can be counter-productive when you need the support of a wide range of stakeholders, including at times your competition, to successfully complete a development.

Large development proposals create opportunities to work with developers to gain advantages for the community, such as increasing green space or investing in local priorities. These concessions to a community can be formalised with local governments in terms of community contracts, memorandums of understanding, or in certain cases development approvals. When large developments are consistently blocked they are often superseded by patchwork development whose impacts are harder to control. In Byron Bay it has been noted that 'the incremental creep has probably had as much effect as a couple of Club Meds ... it's been a war of attrition' (Kinninment, 2003: 13). Due to the substantial positive and negative impacts that large developments can wield, approval for such proposals can be removed from local authorities and made the preserve of state or federal entities. In New South Wales the state government has usurped the right to make decisions on major coastal developments, as part of its new coastal protection regulations (Patterson, 2003).

Summary

Working together creates a larger pool of resources in terms of experiences, skills, funds and ideas. As individuals and communities become more empowered through education, sharing of information, organisation and the legal system they are in a stronger position to influence issues that affect them. Emerging ways to deal with conflict, such as mediation and facilitation, offer great promise for addressing community tourism issues. Tourism proposals that include meaningful public participation from the start are in a better position to build a climate of trust and cooperation. By working with broader community interests in a cost appropriate manner elected officials, government agencies and businesses can create innovative, responsive and effective tourism proposals. While not all stakeholders will embrace collaborative decision-making processes, as long as concerted efforts are made to address their interests and they can live with the final outcomes, then these processes can be considered a success. Despite the inherent challenges associated with collaborative tourism processes, they bring more legitimacy to decision-making processes. Broad-based community support for tourism initiatives can be both established and maintained in communities through the use of collaborative tourism processes.

Chapter 12

Bridging Tourism Gaps Through Strategic Management

Closing the distance between what stakeholders want and expect with what they experience increases their satisfaction. Tourist destinations need efficient and effective tools to help evaluate the levels of satisfaction that they achieve with various stakeholder groups, on both the demand and supply sides. Assessing satisfaction with services can be perplexing since the components of a 'service experience' can be difficult to isolate and measure. However, gap analysis has become a widely used technique for measuring service quality, and has strong potential for use in tourism management (Murphy, A., 2003).

Gap analysis can be used as a tool to draw attention to 'services and/or functions that have been accidentally left out, deliberately eliminated, or are yet to be developed or procured' (Open Group, 2002: 1). Gap analysis can be an impetus for ensuring data on the 'moments of truth' for various tourism stakeholder groups is relevant, disciplined and up-to-date. However, it is a indicator, not a management template. Gap analysis does not provide answers regarding why a gap occurs, whether or not the gap should be addressed, and if it is to be addressed the best way for doing so. These answers can only be found by considering the key business management functions and stakeholders' views through a collaborative decision-making approach. The *Bridging Tourism Gaps Model* presented in this chapter presents a framework for comprehensive tourism management that combines the indicative features of gap analysis with a business focused collaborative decision-making process.

Objectives

Understanding the needs and expectations of tourism stakeholders creates the opportunity for sound tourism management. The inability of many destinations to realise their tourism potential can be tied to a lack of any of the following:

- Adequate information, which can be drawn from an inventory of tourism resources, competitors' tourism offerings and stakeholder groups.
- Awareness of key variables, with particular regards to the core requirements of the stakeholder groups, compatibility of tourism with other sectors of the destination's economy and global economic, social and environmental trends.
- Ability to successfully act on available information, which relies on a tourism plan, funding, management tools and the political, financial and personal commitments necessary for ensuring that the goals and objectives of the tourism plan are achieved.

Tourist destinations must engage in realistic assessments of their abilities to meet the needs and expectations of tourism stakeholders and then act on these assessments so their goals and objectives can be achieved. While moving towards the successful implementation of a tourism plan, destinations can falter in a number of areas, often without realising the extent to which they are slipping, or that they are slipping at all. These tourism errors or omissions can be seen as gaps between what is required and what is achieved. The *Bridging Tourism Gaps Model* is intended to keep destinations focused on the most important factors in developing and maintaining tourism as a beneficial and vital part of their communities.

Planning

Difficulties in understanding what stakeholders want from tourism are exacerbated by the fact that the initial stages of tourism development are rarely informed by a community vision for the industry (Mitchell & Reid, 2001). As outlined earlier, the impetus for tourism development tends to be entrepreneurs. However, the personal motivations of entrepreneurs may not necessarily reflect what is best for the overall community. Tourism planning should take place before stakeholders become entrenched in positions and community commitments are made (McIntyre, 1993). Tourism development in communities can evolve quickly, in a manner that is relatively un-answerable to community views of appropriate tourism development. The drawback of the 'wait and see' approach is that it allows problems between stakeholders to grow and can turn into a 'wait for a crisis and react' approach. Identifying and working to enhance those factors that underpin the success or otherwise of tourism destinations during the planning stages, helps to ensure that development retains the right focus.

Tourism success stories are built on service quality, as we have illustrated throughout this book. While planning for quality products and services might seem like an obvious priority, understanding what quality means to different stakeholder groups and planning for its appropriate level can be perplexing. Quality is an important component of value, which many consider to be the key choice determinant in a competitive marketplace. Value itself is consistently cited as a prime impetus for tourism demand (Murphy & Pritchard, 1997; Nagel, 1987). Quality is generally tied to notions of 'goodness' and 'luxury' (Takeuchi & Quelch, 1983). Quality can be defined as 'the ability of a service or product to perform its specified tasks' (Ennew *et al.*, 1993: 59) and should be at the core of all tourism management strategies.

Stakeholders' expectations as well as the performance of service providers guide their evaluations of quality and overall satisfaction. LeBlanc (1992) found that potential tourists strongly associated perceptions of 'quality services' with their level of satisfaction for the travel agency services they received. Customer satisfaction is also related to providing extra options or better values as well as the absence of deficiencies (Juran, cited in Flynn *et al.*, 1994). A tour company that offers an array of day trip options can be judged as being of higher quality than one who's tours are of the same excellent standard, yet does not provide as extensive a range of tours as its competition. However, a negative experience, such as a service-delivery failure, can overshadow otherwise positive views and lower customer perceptions of quality. The personal side of quality perceptions underlies how important it is for stakeholders to form realistic expectations of their tourism options.

'Service quality is the foundation for services marketing because the core product being marketed is a performance', according to Berry and Parasuraman (1991: 5), and performance permeates tourism. Parasuraman *et al.* (1985) suggest there are 10 criteria that consumers use regularly in developing their service perceptions. These factors are worth considering when planning for tourism development and management due to their impact on user satisfaction. Parasuraman *et al.*'s (1985) original service quality characteristics are listed below and placed in the context of quality elements for which Disney's theme parks are famous:

Service quality characteristics

(1) *Tangibles*   Ensuring all public areas of the theme park, from rides, to walkways and rest facilities, are attractive, safe and clean.
(2) *Reliability*   Maintaining an enticing, family-friendly and fun atmosphere at all times and at all Disney facilities.
(3) *Responsiveness*   Catering to customer service demands, such as providing alcohol in the European theme park and training street cleaners to be on-the-spot guides and counsellors.
(4) *Communication*   Providing information in various languages and formats, and informing customers how much longer they need to wait before reaching the end of a queue.

(5) *Credibility* Taking a conservative and measured approach that builds on Disney's legacy.

(6) *Security* Offering exciting but safe experiences for guests, while ensuring that they are not subjected to unruly behaviour or other threats

(7) *Competence* Training for all levels of staff is provided on site and through Disney University.

(8) *Courtesy* Careful staff selection and training of staff by Disney before they meet the public.

(9) *Understanding* Extensive customer research is conducted by and for Disney.

(10) *Access* Accessibility of the more modern Disney facilities is enhanced by freeway and railway agreements with local governments, while park and ride operations within all Disney theme parks allow guests to leave their cars and hop onto monorails, carriages and trams

Although knowing what stakeholders want is an indispensable part of the planning process, the resulting information is only valuable to the extent that it informs decisions on priority issues. Tourism plans need to consider where to invest resources and why. Another 80:20 rule of business is when 80% of business sales can be attributed to 20% of customers, with some industries, such as airlines and retail, consistently relying on a minority of their customers to provide them with most of their profits (Eckhouse, 2002: 2). Applying this rule to tourism suggests that trying to attract and satisfy a wide range of tourists and interests dilutes the impacts of these investments. Many destinations segment tourists based on their area of origin, demographic profile, length of stay, the amount they spend, and repeat visitations. Segmenting tourist markets according to their value and then focusing investments on attracting and satisfying these 'desired tourists' can result in greater potential returns or yield.

Determining which tourists are desirable to a destination is a reflection of a destination's tourism resources as well as the views and capabilities of its other tourism stakeholders. Up-to-date data on industry, residents and government should be collected, stored and analysed. This data needs to go beyond basic inventories of existing tourism businesses and tourism employment, so that an accurate picture of these stakeholder groups and the ways in which they interact with each other can be understood. A deeper level of understanding of all stakeholder groups helps to gain a realistic understanding of how tourism priorities can be achieved.

Process design

The processes established to enable collaborative decision-making are very powerful in directing likely outcomes. Even when a particular tourism management model has been selected as a means of addressing a tourism issue, a detailed process must be established that meets local conditions and stakeholder requirements. The process involves many aspects that may seem mundane, such as setting ground rules for how stakeholders will treat each other in negotiations, yet all these procedural items shape the environment within which decisions will be made. For example, the Canmore Growth Management Committee was established as part of a community round table tourism planning process. The committee consisted of 40 interest group representatives from the community of Canmore, just outside of Banff National Park, in Alberta Canada (Jamal & Getz, 2000).

Key process design features were seen to encourage consensus but often at the expense of the less powerful members of the group, who felt pressured to conform. In particular the 'shotgun rule', by which if any representative left the table then the process would collapse, was seen by several participants to be a coercive measure. One of the participants noted that:

> there were on numerous occasions groups who said I can't buy into this, whatever point was being made. And the: _rest of the group, they became a single force, telling this group they couldn't leave_ . . . and so we literally had to debate _issues until we got everybody to a position_ where it wasn't a deal breaker issue anymore. Lots of deal breakers. That was a very, very fundamentally important point without which we would never have succeeded. (Business-participant interview cited in Jamal & Getz, 2000: 172 – their emphases)

By the very nature of group decision-making extreme opinions are discouraged as they deviate from the opinions of the majority and therefore do not represent viable options to the group. Through discussion within the framework of the process design, the group works to treat each member respectfully as an individual, while working towards a decision that each group member can support for the good of the group. The level of group pressure in consensus decision-making is a product of process design as well as power imbalances, the intensity of the conflict, the issues and the available resources. Therefore, the process needs to be defined to fit the context.

Another contextual item influencing process design is the varying amounts of time that specific stakeholders will be prepared to devote to the process. The Costa Dourada collaborative tourism planning process in Alagoas Brazil involved a broad range of stakeholders, yet there were disparities in representation (de Araujo and Bramwell, 2000). Government officials and workers were over-represented, while industry leaders NGOs and community organisations were seen by many to be under-represented. The inequality in stakeholder representation was caused in part by cultural and historical factors, given that emerging from a dictatorship the participants were used to government having unchecked power. Process issues in this case related also to concerns that involvement in the process would be too time consuming and would not produce worthwhile results. Some stakeholders indicated they felt it would be better to wait and see how the process evolved before becoming involved, especially since the time spent on such processes would translate into time away from their jobs and other pressing responsibilities.

Our own experiences with public participation planning processes in developed countries show similar trends in stakeholder participation. Government workers, whose attendance at these meetings is often part of their job, tend to be over-represented at these meetings. Those who are working full time in the private sector usually cannot afford to take much time off from work to attend daytime or early evening meetings, that tend to be set up by and for the convenience of the public sector. Industry leaders can contribute greatly to developing plans that appeal to the private sector. However, their time can be so valuable that they cannot justify participating in lengthy tourism planning processes. Therefore, with the exception of development proponents, industry tends to be chronically under-represented at these processes. Some of the ways processes can be designed to better accommodate varying stakeholder needs include the following:

- clear goals and objectives;
- adequate resourcing;
- concise time frame;
- clear component parts to the process;
- meetings scheduled at various times – preferably evenings;
- options for participation – written submissions, attend open, houses, public meetings, interview, questionnaires and web applications.

A well-designed process enables various stakeholders to make informed decisions regarding the amount of their time and effort they will need to devote to a process to reach a successful outcome.

Organising

Putting a tourism plan into action requires a comprehensive, straightforward and adaptable approach. Finding the right approach can be difficult given the complexities of the tourism industry and that the organisational options for destinations are confined by limited budgets, staff and political support. Weiermair (1997) supports the use of the gap model for managing tourism's service quality based on two propositions: (1) that service quality is of great importance to tourism due to the highly competitive nature of the industry; and that (2) quality control systems need to be sufficiently detailed to be effective. Strengths and weaknesses in the provision of tourism services can inform decisions on the allocation of resources and assignment of tasks.

Parasuraman *et al.* (1985) developed *Gap Analysis* as a way to conceptualise service quality requirements. It compares how service performance measures up to customer expectations. Gap analysis used in relation to their concurrent *Gap Model* (Parasuraman, *et al.*, 1990) measures both tangible and intangible service elements. If there is a discrepancy between what is expected and what is provided, this represents a 'gap'.

Gap analysis can serve as a highly flexible and broadly applied assessment tool, as is evident from its application to the health care, education, environmental and tourism and hospitality sectors. Gap analysis is widely used as 'a scientific method for identifying the degree to which native animal species and natural communities are represented in our present-day mix of conservation lands' (Iowa Gap, 1997: 1). Some organisations specialise in preparing gap analysis processes designed to meet the particular needs of individual companies and governments (Alamo, 2002); however, the main focus of these ready-made gap processes tends to be accounting and inventory issues. Gap analysis has been used to measure perceived service quality in several tourism sectors, including airlines, hotels, restaurants and ski resorts (Fick & Ritchie 1991; Weiermair, 1997) and as a tourism planning tool (Murphy, 2003).

Gap model

Parasuraman *et al.* (1985) introduced the gap analysis model as a way to conceptualise service quality in terms of meeting customer expectations. This model moves the analysis of service provision from the overall picture of whether or not customers were satisfied with their service experience to one that breaks down the customer–business interaction into its individual components. It enables us to ask where and how businesses are not meeting customer expectations.

Five key service interfaces between customers and businesses have been identified. At these points gaps can occur between what is provided and what is expected. Such gaps can result in service failure and loss of business (Parasuraman *et al.*, 1985, 1990). Using the gap model as a base we illustrate this process using the example of a small rural community trying to attract stopover visits through the provision of basic services, like public toilets. While toilets may seem mundane they have considerable appeal to the motoring public, which is often the principal source of visitors to rural destinations (Strong, 2002; van Tiggelen, 2001).

The tourist on a motoring tour through the countryside expects to find a certain level of amenities, including toilets, at each potential stop. The community destination is aware of this expectation on behalf of the tourist, as well as of its own residents, so it constructs a public toilet facility in the centre of town close to the shops and other attractions of the main street.

Gap 1 can occur when the destination misunderstands what the tourists' specific needs are with respect to a toilet facility. Over and above the general desire for a clean facility they require adequate signage, because they may be unfamiliar with the destination, and convenient parking, because they are driving.

Gap 2 can occur when the destination's perception of the tourists' toilet expectations are not met by the service specifications for the facility. For example, failing to provide sufficient cleaning and maintenance through-out the day can turn a modern facility into a disaster area.

Gap 3 can occur when the local authority has the correct specifications to keep the toilet block clean and well stocked, but is unable to deliver to the necessary standard. For example, scheduling regular maintenance but lacking the staff or will to fulfil this requirement.

Gap 4 can arise when the destination fails to adequately inform the tourists of the toilet facility. In this case appropriate information in travel maps and brochures will alert tourists to the presence of such an amenity. Once in the town, visual cues such as signage and an attractive building will encourage people to stop.

Gap 5 occurs when there is a discrepancy between what the tourists expect and what they receive at the toilet block.

In this tourism gap example if the toilet block is easy to access, is clean and stocked with the appropriate supplies, tourists will have their expectations met and may well extend their stop to look around the town. If tourists' expectations are not met, their impression of the town will be tainted and they may need to continue onto the next opportunity immediately. However, as in all business situations there has to be a balance between what the tourists can reasonably expect and the community's ability and willingness to invest in a corresponding facility.

There are various ways of measuring service quality gaps when conducting a gap analysis. Parasuraman *et al.* (1988) developed the SERVQUAL scale to measure precisely ratings of service expectations and perceptions for service quality characteristics. This method can be described as a two-column technique, in that gaps are measured by subtracting rankings of service quality characteristics from those of service expectations. In the field there have been difficulties associated with using the SERVQUAL scale with regards to its consistency and the validity of results (Grapentine, 1994; Teas, 1993: Yoon and Ekinci, 2001). Literature review and research showed that the generic use of service quality characteristics (please refer back to the Disney example in the planning section of this chapter) and the use of 'ideals' as a standard of assessment were major limitations of SERVQUAL.

A more basic and conceptual approach to gap analysis shows much promise in tourism and hospitality. Instead of using 10 or five service quality dimensions as recommended by Parasuraman *et al.* (1988, 1991), service quality in tourism can be attributable to just a few key characteristics. Mei *et al.* (1999) cite three service quality characteristics – the behaviour of employees, tangibles and reliability – as the best predictors of service quality evaluations in the hospitality industry. These researchers also found that a simplified one-column survey provided a valid, reliable and user-friendly survey. The one-column approach ranks services from one to seven, with one representing total failure in meeting service expectations and seven representing greatly exceeded expectations (Mei *et al.*, 1999: 138).

Ennew *et al.* (1993) recommend creating 'an index of service quality' in which respondents' rank service characteristics as per their importance and then these rankings are compared with their quality perceptions. Oppermann (1995) used a gap analysis to explore the relationship between guests and operators of rural bed and breakfast (B&Bs) in Germany. The minimal gaps in the perceptions and expectations of these groups reflected the high level of understanding between the groups, which in turn is attributable to their shared culture, preferences and language, and the generally close and congenial contact between the B&B hosts and guests. Drawing from these findings destinations that wish to minimise gaps and corresponding disappointments between the expectations of their tourism stakeholders need to create opportunities for these groups to get to know each other.

Augustyn and Ho's (1998) application of the *Gap Model* to travel agencies revealed a number of service gaps which are summarised below.

Gap 1: Management does not know what customers expect
Travel agencies hardly ever conduct research on their customers, yet they presume to know their customers' expectations and design vacation packages based on their presumptions of what their customers want.

Gap 2: Service specifications work against fulfilling customers' expectations
Management's inaccurate perceptions of customers' service expectations become ingrained in the running of the business. Travel agencies generally pitch their efforts to profiles of what they believe to be typical customers and design their service delivery systems accordingly. This approach neglects differences in travel abilities and preferences and leaves large gaps between what is needed and the systems developed to address these needs. Service standards that consist of sweeping statements, such as 'the customer is always right', that fail to provide clear and easy steps for implementation are not helpful.

Gap 3: Management service specifications are on target, but staff cannot meet them
In travel agencies there is often a discrepancy between the level of professionalism and knowledge that management wants to provide and the
capabilities of their staff. Agencies that function as general travel consultants rather than specialising, such as focusing on particular countries or
activities, are especially prone to this gap.

Gap 4: Management promises too much
Types and quality of services advertised for travel agencies do not match
what is available to customers. Many customers expect all-inclusive service
from their travel agencies and are annoyed when they find that many of the
responsibilities, such as arranging ground transportation, are left for them
to sort out. The growing array of travel options can make it difficult for
travel agents to know what is available while the widespread use of the
Internet can serve to raise unrealistic expectations of travel services and
vacation bargains. A lack of two-way communication between travel
agencies and customers can exacerbate this gap.

Gap 5: Customers believe their service expectations have not been met
Gaps one to four all contribute to customers' perceptions of services, so
problems with gaps at these earlier stages will feed into the final gap
between customers' expectations of travel agencies and the way they
perceive these businesses. There are also a number of personal factors, such
as customers' world views, and external factors, such as the friendliness of
hosts, that impact on customers' overall evaluation of whether a travel
agency did a good job.

In stressful tourism environments, such as travel agencies and popular
destinations, customer expectations are high. Yet often management does
not truly understand its customers and front-line staff lack the resources
and guidance necessary to close gaps between expectations and reality.
These same challenges constrict the abilities of stakeholder groups to
understand each other and to find solutions. However, these challenges
should not be interpreted as 'fatal flaws'. Rather, they point to the value in
identifying where differences in opinions and capabilities lie and the extent
of these differences so that appropriate actions can be taken. True leadership is necessary to ensure that destinations take a hard look at what they
have to offer, what their stakeholders want and then use this information to
guide their development.

Leadership

Realising the tourism potential of destinations requires adept and
responsive leadership. Leadership is capable of inspiring widespread

support when it is seen to further the aspirations of the larger group in a way that people can relate to and actively support. Models are a useful way of conceptualising the steps communities need to take to achieve their tourism aspirations and lead communities in the right direction. Numerous models of tourism development have been created as a way to help guide communities, as discussed in earlier chapters, but they all have limitations.

Limitations of existing models

Models are helpful in drawing attention to many of the potential dimensions and impacts of tourism, yet their applicability as management tools for communities has been limited. Butler's evolutionary cycle of tourism development (1980) uses a bell curve to illustrate tourism's rising and then falling fortunes, yet offers little in the way of practical advice on how communities can avoid tourism's pitfalls. Murphy's community approach model to tourism development has been criticised as not recognising fundamental power inequalities that undermine the democratic principles and for not having more fully developed theoretical underpinnings (Reed, 1997). Some factors that limit the applicability of tourism models to real world situations are summarised below:

Economic

- difficult to quantify the benefits and costs of tourism;
- strong social science approach that neglects to consider proven business practices.

Social

- limited awareness of tourism impacts and low political commitment;
- difficult to find broadly acceptable solutions, given the conflicting needs and priorities of stakeholder groups.

Environmental

- undervalue the role of the environment in destination attractiveness;
- difficult to measure carrying capacities and stress levels;
- neglect political, social and economic factors that ultimately determine the extent to which sustainable environmental practices can be developed and maintained.

A new model and framework is necessary to address the limitations of earlier models. The proposed model is offered as a practical alternative, as it is based on demonstrated business techniques and is responsive to the interplay of elements that affect the fortunes of tourist destinations. Flexibility in tourism planning is essential. The endless array of variables that define a particular destination make the implementation of blanket and rigid requirements unworkable. Guidance on this matter is provided by Martin *et al.* (1998: 50) who found that:

- models that embrace and include differences may be more effective than models that attempt to achieve unanimity.

Tourism models need to go beyond advocating a collaborative approach to provide the comprehensive guidance necessary for turning tourism ambitions into reality (Reed, 2000). Structural and procedural elements, that include understanding power dynamics, business principles, stakeholder requirements, available resources and legislative and legal aspects all set the context within which workable tourism proposals can be forged.

While researchers strive to make their findings helpful to tourism practitioners, some feel 'a major gap still exists between the users and the procedures of research' Taylor *et al.* (1994: 9). Such gaps lead to unacceptable inefficiencies within the industry and the authors suggest some key elements to 'bridge' the research gap between industry and researchers. Among their suggestions are:

- develop a meaningful dialogue between tourism researchers and the industry;
- glean as much information from existing data sources as possible;
- develop regular and customised customer and operator surveys to supplement published data;
- provide big picture trend analysis as well as small picture and business specific information.

These suggestions are incorporated in the following model.

Other useful suggestions for tourism development approaches come from MacEochaidh (1994), who draws on planning experience in disadvantaged areas of rural Ireland. MacEochaidh suggests the following steps are essential for successful tourism development where the resources for change are limited (1994: 186):

- tourist agencies gain local support for tourism development on a range of tourism development issues, including financing;
- educate and train locals so they can make informed tourism decisions;
- support locals so they can identify their own tourism opportunities;
- establish networks and encourage partnerships so tourism information and resources can be shared – especially for marketing and product development;
- help communities develop comprehensive strategies for the long term.

These suggestions are incorporated in the following model.

Bridging tourism gaps model

The challenges that prevent tourism from meeting its potential can seem insurmountable at times. In tourism management, as in life, a bridge can be used to take you from where you are to where you want to be. The *Bridging tourism gaps model* shows how destinations can bridge the gap between tourism's promise and its reality by uniting the four business functions and major stakeholder groups into a community focused strategic management process (Figure 12.1). This model uses the analogy of a bridge to explain the necessary components and linkages of tourism management. Its structure is as follows:

- Business management functions: Footings
- Stakeholders: Pilings
- Collaboration: Cross-beams
- Gap analysis Surface

If we view the *business management functions* as the footings for the bridge and the *stakeholders* as bridge pilings, it is evident that additional elements are necessary to realise a community's overarching tourism objectives and goals. *Collaboration* functions as cross-beams for strength and connectivity, while *Gap analysis* functions as the bridge road surface and responds to changing conditions. All of these elements in the model come together, creating a bridge between what is envisioned and what is achievable for a tourist destination.

Business management functions: Footings

Tourism strategies, like bridges, need firm footings in their environments. A sound business foundation is the reliable base from which sustainable tourism developments grow. The business management functions can act as cornerstones for successful tourism ventures. In this case we start with the need for leadership.

Leadership Visualising the building of an actual bridge, one can see leadership as the starting point in construction. Leadership, rather than planning, often is the first step in developing a tourism management system, as it can take the push of strong leader to kick-start these processes. Leadership is also an important element in each of the other three business management functions. Leaders need to understand and make the most out of local conditions. An understanding of the current situation combined with a vision for what is possible and the ability to motivate others to adopt and move towards this vision are hallmarks of an effective leader. Local environmental, social and economic factors and the way that these factors interact with external elements create unique situations that need to be understood and incorporated into management plans. Customers, industry, residents and

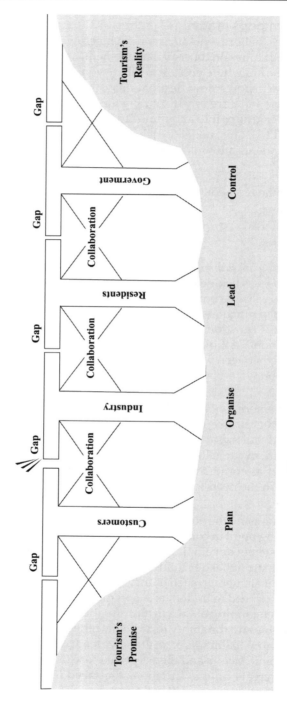

Figure 12.1 Bridging tourism gaps model

customers all impact upon the fortunes of tourism development, so adept leadership will acknowledge and work with these groups in developing tourism strategies.

Planning Planning, like the foundation stone of a bridge, is a logical and necessary starting point from which the actual development can occur. Planning grounds tourism's potential within the context of community goals and objectives. Planning explores the aspirations and abilities of tourism stakeholder groups, which are then incorporated into the larger vision of destination management. A community destination's tourism planning involves four steps:

Step 1:
Clarify or otherwise establish a community's general tourism goals and objectives.
Step 2:
Collect information on stakeholders, resources and other factors that serve as opportunities or constraints to tourism development.
Step 3:
Create forums in which community members can discuss tourism goals and objectives drawing on available information.
Step 4:
Assess the extent to which tourism can help or hinder a community's efforts to achieve its general and wider goals and objectives. Tourism strategies should be created and supported to the extent that they further tourism and overall community goals.

Organising Organising for strategic community tourism management means putting a process in place so that a community can achieve its goals and objectives. Tasks need to be assigned and resources allocated so that responsible parties, such as government departments and destination associations, can administer and respond to the impacts of their programmes in a timely and effectual manner. This does not have to be an excessively bureaucratic process for, as Porter's (1998) cluster theory advocates, simply creating a positive and entrepreneurial environment may be the best facilitation process any government can provide.

Controlling Control for community tourism development is concerned with the implementation, monitoring and adjustment of tourism initiatives that support community tourism goals and objectives. Just as the foundations of a bridge construction are soon overshadowed by the structure that arises from them, subsequent stages of tourism management can become the focus of attention while the importance of control is undervalued. Even though control is one of the more tedious aspects of tourism management, its role in understanding and responding to tourism's impacts needs to be recognised and resourced accordingly.

Stakeholder groups: Pilings

Stakeholders can be conceptualised as bridge pilings supported by the four business management functions foundation. Stakeholders, like bridge pilings, rise up with the promise of what is possible. Different stakeholder groups might not appear to complement each other, or even serve any useful purpose on their own. However, they are the elements upon which tourism management rests.

Strategic tourism management examines the strengths and weaknesses of its stakeholder groups, in terms of their abilities to help a destination realise its tourism vision. A destination's primary stakeholders are indicative of and responsive to local conditions. Bringing in outside tourism experts, focusing on desirable, yet hard to reach markets and adopting proposals that have worked under very different conditions carry with them great expense and often disappointing results. Communities should focus on the needs and abilities of their established customer bases and industries, while working within the guidelines of what is acceptable to their residents and proven funding sources. Imported ideas and new markets can make a valuable contribution to an area's tourism potential if the resources devoted to bringing them in are proportion to their net benefits.

Collaboration: Cross-beams

The pilings of a bridge, like stakeholder groups, are isolated, so additional resources are needed to bind them together to support tourism's potential. Collaborative decision-making processes can be seen as cross-beams that bring together the four stakeholder pillars. A combined strategic management approach that draws upon the opinions and views of all four stakeholder groups creates strong and durable decisions. Whereas, an approach that neglects any of the major stakeholder groups will be unbalanced and less likely to hold up over time.

At regular intervals tourism issues should be discussed in public forums, such as local council meetings. These forums provide a quick and relatively low cost way of gauging the community's tourism opinions and options. Quantitative tourism research, such as phone or postal surveys, can provide more detailed information on stakeholders' views and provide a more representative picture of stakeholders' opinions and likely actions. Once tourism issues have been identified, advisory groups can work on addressing these issues. Advisory groups should have representatives from the tourism industry, resident groups, administrators and elected officials. Advisory groups need adequate financial, political, administrative and technical support to working collaboratively in developing

tourism management recommendations that meet stakeholders' requirements (Lynn & Kartez, 1995).

Gap analysis: Surface

Just as laying down cross-beams makes it possible to sustain a bridge
surface, collaborative processes pave the way for making informed
decisions on how a community should invest its tourism resources. A
bridge's surface contains a number of gaps that provide the necessary flexibility in responding to changing conditions, such as freeze-thaw cycles in
colder climates, and load conditions. If these gaps are for the most part
small, then they allow for the safe, reliable, timely, smooth and inexpensive
transportation of goods and people. Larger gaps can be expected and
planned for at certain key junctures, such as where the bridge surface
transfers from land to the bridge supports. Gaps in a bridge's surface may
be too large to allow for a pleasant and easy crossing by all vehicles, which
can deter or prevent certain people from using the bridge. If the expected
traffic volumes are high the surface and its underlying components need to
be strengthened in readiness for heavy (mass) use.

Similarly, a tourism management strategy should recognise and incorporate gaps between tourism stakeholders' expectations and what a
destination provides. Accommodating such gaps allows a destination to be
flexible in the face of changing conditions. These changes can be in relation
to stakeholders' preferences as well as the tourism resources of a destination. If these gaps are kept small then the range of people who will be
satisfied with a tourism destination is large. If differences between what is
desired and what a destination can deliver are too incongruent then certain
stakeholder groups will be unwilling or unable to enjoy a destination. A
destination may want to attract high spending overnight visitors who
travel as singles or couples. However, if a destination does not offer what
these market segments expect, such as gourmet dining and areas of exceptional cultural significance, then it may have to focus on budget tourists.

Gap analysis results can be part of a clear-headed assessment of tourism
development options, ranging from the structural plan through to the
availability of resource. The extent to which stakeholders' tourism expectations are being met can be assessed using gap analysis. Potential questions
to explore using gap analysis include the following:

- Residents' expectations for tourism in their community /
  Residents perceptions of tourism's impacts on their community.
- Residents' expectations for tourism in their community /
  Desirable markets' tourism expectations.
- Desirable markets' tourism expectations /
  Abilities of a destination to meet these expectations.

The discrepancies between different groups that are revealed by these questions need to be evaluated within the context of a destination's general and tourism specific goals and objectives.

Controlling

The *Bridging tourism gaps model* can only function as a relevant and adaptive strategic management tool if appropriate control mechanisms are established and maintained. The tourism potential of a destination evolves as the cumulative effects of the industry become more apparent over time and limitations to development are addressed. Control mechanisms should be involved in this process. They should be both straightforward and adaptive so they can be applied by tourism's various stakeholders in different and changing environments.

Model limitations

There are a number of limits on citizen participation and collaboration in tourism planning, especially in destinations that are struggling to develop and maintain their tourism industry as a way of improving the overall quality of life for their constituents. Potential limitations to the applicability of the *Bridging tourism gaps model* can occur due to operational, structural and cultural factors. For example, Tosun's (2000: 613–33) study of tourism processes in developing nations identifies the following challenges to community participation in tourism management:

Operational

- centralised tourism administration;
- poor coordination within and between industry and government;
- insufficient information on industry resources, trends and impacts.

Structural

- professionals undervalue the contributions of the public;
- low levels of expertise among 'professionals';
- elites largely control tourism and enjoy its benefits;
- insufficient legal support in regards to legislation, case law and appeal processes;
- poor training of industry workers;
- potentially high cost of public participation;
- insufficient financial resources;

Cultural

- poor people struggling to meet basic needs have a limited capacity to participate;
- low levels of public awareness and interest

All of these factors identified by Tosun can be seen to be at work in developed countries also to varying degrees, especially in disadvantaged areas in the rural hinterlands of predominently wealthy countries. The balance point between the benefits of taking an inclusive planning approach, such as that advocated by the *Bridging Tourism Gaps Model*, and taking a more traditional tourism management approach hinges on the availability of resources to a community. Communities with a robust enabling environment (ample and sustained political, social, legal, economic and environmental resources) are in a strong position to empower their citizens' participation in the guidance of tourism development. Therefore, destinations need to undergo a thorough assessment of the enabling environment so they can adapt the *Bridging Tourism Gaps Model* to meet their particular circumstances.

As noted by a government official in Indonesia 'if a neighbourhood is being improved physically for tourism, it is unnecessary to involve the local people' (Timothy, 1999: 384). While this statement contradicts emerging Western ways of viewing citizen power, it speaks to the importance of not sacrificing desired end states (improved quality of life for residents) for the sake of well-meaning processes. This model can be a valuable tool to help communities; however the destinations need resources to utilise this model to the best of its abilities. Communities that are in an emergency situation, such as responding to sudden and debilitating losses in tourism revenues, or are severely under-resourced, might find traditional methods of centralised decision-making are their only viable options, at least in the short term. However, such circumstances can be prepared for to some extent under the controlling function, with regular reviews of progress and the inclusion of a crisis management component.

The impact of an enabling environment on a tourist destination's abilities to successfully take a collaborative approach to tourism planning is illustrated by comparing two destinations facing similar challenges. In the 1990s the Florida Keys and Bonaire, two Caribbean tourist destinations, were investigating ways to sustain their tourism industries in the face of mounting environmental damage and citizen discontent. Of particular concern for both areas was the damage being caused to their waters and coral reefs by the lack of a central sewerage system and the corresponding threat to tourism revenues caused by a degraded environment.

Both of these destinations engaged in collaborative tourism planning endeavours involving various levels of government, industry and resident groups. In Bonaire, these processes were *ad hoc,* lacked financial support and drew primarily upon existing networks and partnerships between industry, government and other established organisations (Parker, 2000). In Bonaire the limits noted by Tosun (2000) all eroded the abilities of this area to come to a successful solution using collaborative efforts (Parker, 2000). A bizarre situation arose where in order to keep Bonaire's stakeholders working together planning discussions centred around unrealistic 'best case' scenarios despite the area's limited resources and options. Even with 50% of their 1000 rooms unoccupied it was projected that by greatly increasing room numbers Bonaire would attract more flights (Parker, 2000: 91). This was expected to bring more tourists and then allow the cost of a sewerage system to be more manageable by spreading the funding over a greater number of rooms. Unfortunately, by the late 1990s tourist numbers to Bonaire failed to meet projected growth and 'no coordinated progress has been made on hotel construction, the treatment plant or the question of airline capacity since 1997' (Parker, 2000: 94). Bonaire can be seen as an example where an under-resourced planning environment thwarted local aspirations for a successful collaborative approach to tourism management.

In contrast, at this time the Florida Keys made great strides in its collaborative tourism efforts. The Florida Keys drew upon its wealth of economic, political and social resources in ensuring that these processes were formalised, well-financed and included extensive community outreach programmes to supplement the contributions of existing networks (please see earlier discussions on planning processes in the Keys). The Florida Keys obtained millions of dollars of financial assistance from various levels of government to address its sewerage problems. These funds were obtained through the hard work, dedication and political skills of elected officials as well as members of industry, environmental and resident groups. Although tourism development in general and waste-water projects in particular are highly contentious (see www.Florida.Keynoter.com), efforts to take a collaborative approach have been fruitful. The Florida Keys can be seen as an example where a non-emergency situation and an enabling planning environment created a situation where collaborative approaches to tourism development, such as those advanced by the *Bridging Tourism Gaps Model,* can aid in the development of a sustainable tourism destination.

Appropriate scale

Some problems in operating the *Bridging Tourism Gaps Model* can be overcome by adjusting the scale and scope of operations to suit local conditions and resources and starting with small and manageable tasks. Applying the model to a discrete and well-defined aspect of a destination's tourism offerings, will allow communities to learn how to use the model and evaluate its effectiveness as a tourism management tool. Timothy's

(1999) exploration of participatory planning in rural Indonesia can be seen as an example of how the model can be applied at a small scale. Rural residents' recognition of the tourism potential of their region's unique fruit and their grassroots approach to developing its tourism potential incorporate the main features of this model namely: business management, stakeholders, collaboration and gap analysis. The four business management principles are all evident in the community developing its own tourism goals and strategies.

Timothy notes that leaders in the community presented the fruit promotion idea to the local council, which supported the idea and successfully petitioned other levels of government and industry to support this local tourism initiative. Stakeholder involvement started with residents, who devised the idea. Government supported the idea through actions that included hiring private consultants to study its tourism potential. Industry involvement included promotion, while domestic, Japanese and Dutch travellers were targeted as customers.

Collaborative efforts were evident in residents, government and industry working together to develop the area's tourism potential, which culminated in a fruit agrotourism project which commenced in 1992 (Timothy, 1999: 380). Elements of gap analysis can be observed when looking at the strategy to develop the area's tourism potential. Specific tourism products and services were developed, in relation to fruit production, leaving other tourism needs such as accommodation to other suppliers. Half-day tours were developed linking the area to more established tourist destinations to allow for the specialisation of local tourism offerings, according to the needs and capabilities of the host destination. Communities can therefore start small, by looking at a particular tourism product they want to develop and progress through the stages of the model, building on what they learn.

Measuring performance

It is essential that the relevant data inform the planning and implementation of the *Bridging Tourism Gaps Model,* from its inception through its implementation and maintenance. Since the quality of decisions depends heavily on the quality of available information, gathering information in an efficient and effective manner is important to the fortunes of tourist destinations.

Enthusiasm for knowing as much as possible about a situation can run high as typified by this quote from a management consulting firm that sells its gap analysis services to other companies, 'In God, we trust . . . All others bring data' (Adams Six Sigma, 2002). The relevance of data is a function of its usefulness, cost, quality, timeliness and focus. The high cost of collecting, storing and updating databases is a reflection of the reluctance of many organisations to commit substantial resources to this matter. But for tourism operators and destinations data collection and management can be made less onerous if they work with state governments and local tertiary education institutions on these matters.

Since the expectations of customers can be measured with reasonable accuracy and are relatively stable over time (Clow & Vorhies, 1993), customers' satisfaction and views on quality can help inform community tourism planning. Berry (1995: 34–5) and Eckhouse (2002: 4–6) suggest that to understand customers the following guidelines would be helpful:

(1) Randomly check on customers at regular intervals and where possible include these check-ups as part of the regular service delivery.
(2) Use a website as a two-way communication device (provide a comment section and customer surveys), and track what items on the website are the most popular.
(3) Provide comment cards at customer interfaces.
(4) Conduct representative surveys of stakeholder groups and where practical hire outside firms or tertiary education institutions to conduct these surveys.
(5) Coordinate and regularly update all data sources. This can be aided by linking with national and state data banks and drawing from other sources of published data.

While it seems natural that service industries should collect and use data on service quality, research in this area has produced surprising results. A recent study of 150 business-technology professionals found that most of their companies did not regularly track customer satisfaction and the customer data they had was neither readily available nor effectively used to guide management decisions (Eckhouse, 2002: 3–4). These results are surprising and disappointing, given that service firms are so dependent on customer satisfaction as a way of differentiating themselves from the competition and ensuring that they stay in business.

There are numerous government and non-government organisations that provide excellent data on broad tourism trends, such as numbers of visitors, top visitor activities and attractions, and the revenue and jobs generated by tourism. These sources are an excellent first stop for information. Researchers at Oklahoma State University have been exploring ways that communities can use existing databases to assist them in conducting gap analysis as a tool for community economic development. Barta and Woods (2002) recommended that communities use data from the state's tax commission data, which is reported according to Standard Industrial Classification (SIC) codes, along with data from the Bureau of the Census on local and county population and per capita income to identify gaps in retail sales. Gap analysis of retail sales identifies the supply and demand of retail items in relation to local and non-local customers, which in turn can provide an indication of the importance of tourist spending in an area.

More specific tourism information may require detailed searches and a measure of original primary research. Government and industry grants are sources of potential funding for tourism research. Since many universities include tourism and hospitality in their curriculum there are excellent opportunities to work with these universities on tourism research. Such partnering efforts can greatly lower costs, as well as providing a cross-fertilisation of ideas between academics, students and practitioners. This is the fundamental philosophy behind Australia's successful Cooperative Research Centre for Sustainable Tourism.

Prior to engaging in new research it is important to check on how related data has been collected and stored and to replicate these conditions where possible. This can involve asking the same questions in the same manner and using the same statistical methods to analyse the data. Another useful data management approach is to keep copies of raw data. This allows data to be segmented and re-analysed according to different needs, while a comprehensive set of the overall results remains intact. If such precautions are not taken then research opportunities are restricted. For example, researchers at the Chugach (Alaska) National Forest could not compare findings across different study periods due to significant changes in data collection and computation methods within the parks database (Brooks & Haynes, 2001).

An ongoing concern with customer surveys is when they are only developed for tourists, neglecting the views of other stakeholders – industry, resident and government. The ability to compare the views of stakeholder groups can be hampered by inconsistencies between different types of data, and the methods used to collect and store data. Since community tourism involves local stakeholders it is important to extend data collection beyond customer considerations. Strategic community tourism management should incorporate regular assessments of community impacts and reactions. Ideally this could be incorporated into the stakeholder involvement processes outlined above. If tourism is to be treated as a community industry, destinations should also produce an annual tourism progress report along the lines of corporate annual reports.

Summary

Bridging tourism gaps pulls together elements essential to identifying and making the most of tourism opportunities. This approach is responsive to the requirements and resources of tourism stakeholders and the community at large. The *Bridging Tourism Gaps Model* unites many of the assessment and management approaches that are currently being used in business, community and tourism settings. The model brings these approaches together to create a coherent and manageable context for understanding and directing tourism developments.

To illustrate the type of comprehensive management process the proposed model would provide, we offer a final case study. The case has used several of the techniques and approaches recommended in this book, but it was not set up as a complete bridging exercise. This case is provided because it reveals the importance of stakeholder consultation, the relevance of the four business functions, and the benefits of combining these two aspects, rather than because of its outcome.

The outcome was to resist development. Since that decision was made many feel, with the advantage of hindsight, that it was the correct one; given that the Australian ski resorts have been struggling with declining snowfalls and interest over the past few years. Some feel the collaborative decision-making process was wasteful because of the time and money spent on simply maintaining the *status quo* (Michael & Plowman, 2002). However, it is the ability of the process to produce effective and inclusive decisions that matters most. This example reveals how different stakeholder groups analyse a situation collectively to create a community response.

Case Study: Bridging the Gaps at Mt Stirling

(Robin Saunders, Principal, Robin Saunders Environmental Solutions Pty Ltd)

Overview

The processes and issues that surrounded the proposal to develop downhill skiing at a largely undeveloped area in Australian Alps show how the components of the *Bridging Tourism Gaps Model* can come together to provide clearer guidance on the appropriate course of action. This case study draws upon the tourism planning process surrounding a major development proposal for Mount Stirling in Victoria, Australia.

Background

Tasmania, Victoria and New South Wales are the only states in Australia with conditions conducive to snow skiing and snowboarding. Mt Stirling, with its peak elevation of 1746m, is one of Victoria's six designated alpine resorts. Mt Stirling is about a three-hour drive from Melbourne, which at four million people is Australia's second largest city and a state capital. Mt Stirling is located next to Victoria's most popular ski resort, Mt Buller (Figure 12.2). Mt Buller is the closest and most accessible alpine resort to Melbourne with reliable snow, and attracts a variety of downhill skiers and day-trippers, with an annual visitation of approximately 500,000 persons during the period 1982 to 1995 (Saunders & Stephens, 1998: 10). The neighbouring Mt Stirling snowfields have poor road access, and are used for cross-country skiing in the winter months.

In 1979 the Land Conservation Council, which was appointed by the

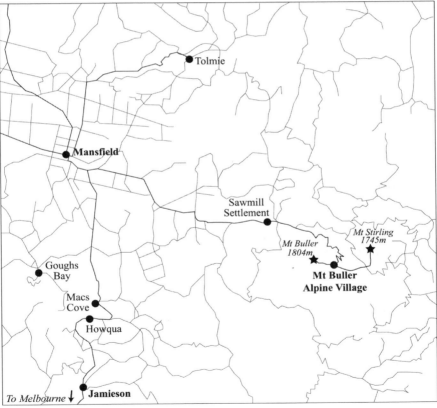

Figure 12.2 Mt Buller and Mt Stirling

state government to advise on the use of public lands, recommended that Mt Stirling be developed for downhill and cross-country skiing to address the anticipated boom in demand for such facilities (Saunders & Stephens, 1998: 4). In 1983 the Forests Commission prepared plans for developing the downhill skiing potential of Mt Stirling; however, lacking private sector interests these plans languished. In 1989 the Alpine Resorts Commission prepared a draft strategy for developing a resort facility to service both Mt Buller and Mt Stirling. This ambitious proposal included a high-speed gondola that would link the two mountains to a new base station as well as building 14 ski lifts with a capacity for 12,500 skiers on Mt. Stirling (Saunders & Stephens, 1998: 4). This proposal was so controversial that the government of the day decided not to endorse it. A change in government and renewed private sector interest in Mt Stirling prompted the Minster for Natural Resources to announce new plans to offer a lease to Buller Ski Lifts Ltd that upon acceptance would act as a trigger for an Environmental Impact Statement (EIS), which would carry with it opportunities for public input. The reaction to this proposal was swift and volatile, leading to a Supreme Court injunction blocking the proposal on procedural grounds.

In response, the government required the preparation of an EIS to investigate a range of possible developments for Mt Stirling. As there was little confidence in the independence of the Alpine Resorts Commission, and it was subsequently dissolved, in April 1994 the government required the Environment Assessment Branch within the Department of Planning and Development to manage and prepare the EIS. This branch had the responsibility of managing the EIS legislation in Victoria, and providing advice on the Environment Effects Act (1978) to the Minister for Planning. In the following analysis, the Environment Assessment Branch will be referred to as the proponent of the EIS for the future planning for Mt Stirling. The analysis will apply the *Bridging Tourism Gaps Model* to the decision-making process that took place with Mt Stirling's tourism management.

Business management functions

The widespread public interest in how Mt Stirling should be developed, the uncertainty over the potential impacts of different uses on the mountain, and the high level of public mistrust over the general handling of previous development proposals, put pressure on the government to address the issue in a more open and comprehensive way. Given that Mt Stirling is on public land there is an extra level of responsibility on government to show that it is acting in the public's best interests when deciding on how these lands should be managed. There were also concerns that development of this primarily undeveloped mountain would rely too much on the public purse in terms of establishing the necessary infrastructure. In view of the controversy surrounding the Buller Ski Lifts Ltd proposal, the government was compelled to look at ways to open up the planning process to greater public involvement. In reviewing the processes that were established to determine appropriate uses of Mt Stirling, one can see how the four key business management functions all played important roles in this major community land use decision.

Leadership

The *1978 Environment Effects Act* provided the then Minister of Planning with the authority to administer this Act with a great deal of discretion over assessment processes, including the determination of whether an EIS would be required on a case-by-case basis, and direction of the proponent on the scope of the EIS, the alternatives considered, and the degree of public consultation. The practice of the Minister appointing a Consultative Committee, with all major stakeholders and the community represented, to guide the preparation of the EIS, was established in the later 1980s. The Minister showed leadership in requiring an EIS, and appointing such a committee for the EIS, inviting the participation of interest groups both favouring and opposed to downhill ski development at Mt Stirling. The members appointed to the Consultative Committee included the following: '5 government agencies; the local council; various tourism operators; and community groups representing downhill skiing, nordic [cross-country] skiing, the local community and environmental interests' (Saunders & Stephens, 1998: 7).

The proponent met with representatives of the major interest groups involved, and assured them of the commitment to an open, consultative process. The EIS was then managed in a manner that kept faith with the assurances given, building the commitment of the stakeholders to the process.

Planning

Principal steps in developing and assessing the EIS are listed below in point form:

- Appointment of the Consultative Committee.
- Developing a consensus within the Committee to the objectives of the study.
- Preparing a study brief that detailed the issues that needed to be addressed and the alternatives to be considered.
- Engaging a consulting firm to undertake the work of preparing the EIS.
- Seeking public submissions on the EIS.
- Referring the EIS and the submissions to an independent Inquiry Panel for a report.
- The panel make recommendations to the Minister, the Minister mak-

ing an assessment of the EIS, as required by the Act, and providing it to the decision maker (government) as advice. Government to make a subsequent decision.

The community goals and objectives for developing Mt Stirling related to issues of equity, fairness, accountability and sound financial as well as economic management. Early in the study process the Minister made two important rulings. The first was that for the purpose of the study, earlier government policy decisions on the future of Mt Stirling were to be disregarded. The second was that the EIS would not include a preferred option, so that all alternatives would be considered equally on their merits during the exhibition period. Often when a proponent designates a preferred option, other options attract little consideration in public submissions.

Had the Buller Ski Lifts Ltd agreement been completed, the EIS would have focused on their proposal, while other options might not even have been considered. Stakeholder groups are often predisposed to fight against those decisions that they had no role in formulating, and where their only role is to offer their opinions on whether to accept or reject proposals. The mechanisms for the public to express their view on the development of Mt Stirling included serving on (or being represented on) the consultative committee, responding to invitations to respond to the initial study scope, attending forums and displays during the preparation of the EIS, making written submissions after the EIS was put on public display, and making a presentation to the independent inquiry panel that would make recommendations to government on the EIS.

Organising

The organising principles for the Mt Stirling decision-making processes were expressed in the objectives developed for the study, the assessment criteria developed for evaluating the alternatives, and the management of time and the limited money available to the proponent. The scoping process assisted in focusing on the key environmental, social and economic parameters that needed study, and developing alternatives that ranged from virtually a 'do nothing' alternative, through low-scale recreation and cross-country skiing alternatives, to full downhill skiing development.

The consultant brief was drafted by the proponent, and was subject to exhaustive discussion at the Consultative Committee, over several committee meetings. In the end it was amended to meet the reasonable expectations of all members of the committee. The rigour with which the brief was vetted proved a key factor in managing the consultant process, and controlling costs. Late in the study process it became apparent that a further alternative would be useful in drawing out the implications of a variation of one of the existing alternatives. Additional funds were sought therefore to expand the study brief to include the additional alternative.

Preparing the Mt Stirling EIS involved th

- Identifying current and potential future uses
- Developing a range of options for the mountain.
- Assessing the potential social, environmental and econ of the options.
- Evaluating the options based on EIS criteria established at the be ning of the process.

The assessment criteria looked at potential environmental, social and economic impacts from both quantitative and qualitative perspectives. Environmental criteria included the potential impacts of global warming and issues relating to water quality and soil stability. Social criteria included considering the impacts development would have on Aboriginal and European heritage, and impacts development would have on residents in nearby towns and current and potential users of the mountain. The economic criteria looked at the potential financial impacts of the options and how they impacted on the viability of these options.

The established procedures for the preparation and assessment of an EIS reflect the political, administrative and economic realities that underlie available options as a state government endeavours to identify and support proposals that will help the state achieve its overall goals and objectives, as well as those that it specifically sets for tourism related initiatives. The elected government retains the legal responsibility and right to decide how best to manage public funds and lands in relation to a tourism and recreation development proposal, while creating opportunities for public review and participation in the process.

Control

Control for the Mt Stirling proposal related to ensuring that effective and fair decision-making processes would be implemented, monitored and adjusted to support overall state goals and objectives. The consultative committee played an important role in holding the government and other involved stakeholder groups accountable for their review processes and recommendations. Enabling other interested groups to participate in the process by acting as observers, commentators and presenters to the committee furthered this accountability. The level of transparency that was provided through the open consultative meetings and the ready access to the materials that they drew upon and produced helped to build confidence in the process. Furthermore, by providing the consultative committee with the responsibility for reviewing key issues that would need to be addressed, the range of potential alternatives and the criteria that would be used to assess them, a large measure of control was delegated. Thus the stakeholders who represented a diversity of ideas and views

,ed had a strong degree of
n this created an atmosphere
decision-makers to make the

. the management of Mt Stirling rep-
e used to either facilitate or block
.sources included monetary funds, as
.unity contacts and an understanding of
. perspectives. The stakeholder groups
osal can be divided into the categories of
.nd government used in this book, and their
conu..   opment included the following:

Customers

- Knowledge of how they would like to use the area, what they currently value about the area, and what they would like to see happen.
- Knowledge about the environmental and social attributes of the mountain and its environs.
- Networking with local and regional contacts to raise awareness about the process and the issues.

Industry

- Detailed knowledge of the industry and its requirements was provided by the Mt Buller Committee of Management.
- Knowledge, ideas and critical comments were provided by other groups using the mountain, such as the cross-country ski industry and nature-based and educational tourism operators.

Residents

- Environmental groups with a particular interest in nature conservation ensured that natural values were appropriately addressed.
- Residents in the immediate vicinity of Mt Stirling, and beyond, contributed their knowledge of potential social impacts, and concern about regional impacts on water quality and accessibility.

Government

- The Alpine Resorts Commission championed the downhill ski development, and subsequently was an advocate for this alternative.
- The Environment Assessment Branch, Department of Planning and

Development acted as the proponent for the EIS, and managed the EIS process.

- The Mansfield Shire Council provided local government knowledge to the Consultative Committee.
- State Government Departments responsible for nature conservation, water resources, tourism, heritage protection and pollution control contributed to the development of the EIS.
- The Minister of Planning initiated the EIS, appointed the Independent Inquiry Panel, and made the final assessment of the EIS (as a recommendation to government).

Collaboration

As detailed earlier in the paper, the approach taken to the preparation of the EIS was a collaborative one, where all stakeholders were involved in the shaping of the study, and wide opportunities for public input and comment were provided during the EIS preparation.

In addition to the public's opportunities to participate in earlier stages of the decision-making processes, the completion of the EIR opened up the process for even wider public review and comment. The EIS was exhibited to the public from the end of June until the end of August in 1996 (Saunders & Stephens, 1998: 10). Information on the EIS findings relating to Mt Stirling was displayed at over 30 locations in urban and rural areas throughout Victoria. More than 600 submissions were received during the public exhibition period of the EIS and over 60 stakeholder groups and individuals made presentations to the planning panel charged with making recommendations on the management of Mt Stirling to the Minister of Planning (Saunders & Stephens, 1998: 11).

After completing the public hearings the panel put forth its recommendations to the Minister, which the Minister accepted. The panel had found that the overall economic and environment costs associated with developing downhill skiing at Mt Stirling could not be offset by the potential benefits that such as development could bring to the state. The Victorian government promptly announced that Mt Stirling was to be retained as 'an all season, nature-based recreational and educational destination' (ibid: 11) and ruled out the development of downhill skiing facilities. Saunders and Stephens note that the reactions of stakeholder groups to the government's announcement were overwhelmingly positive as environmental groups, nature based tourism groups and even the public sector proponent for downhill skiing publicly supported the government's handling of the issues and final decision.

The continual involvement of the public from the early stages of proposing options and setting the criteria, against which their options would be evaluated, to the final stages of widespread public exhibition and feedback on the options, enabled the government to make a wise decision. The consultative committee and the public interest groups that observed and communicated their views to the committee during the important preliminary stages of the EIS consisted of a cross-section of affected stakeholders. The stakeholder group representatives were drawn from various segments of the tourism industry, residents, environmental groups and administrators. The key stakeholders publicly supported the EIS process and outcome.

The Victorian National Parks Association (an environmental group) described the Mount Stirling EIS as an 'exemplary process' and 'a major watershed in the alpine resort development debate . . .. It is by far the most comprehensive planning study ever conducted into a proposed alpine resort development in Victoria and has important implications for future alpine development and planning'.

The Mount Stirling Development Task Force (a community group supporting nature-based tourism) stated; 'There can be no doubt that this process succeeded for its impartiality in that no one was excluded and all were given the fullest of opportunities to be heard'.

Buller Ski Lifts Ltd (which initially favoured downhill skiing development on Mount Stirling) welcomed the government decision and said: 'We are looking forward to working with the government and the community to ensure Mount Stirling is well looked after and preserved for future generations of Australians' (Saunders & Stephens, 1998: 11).

Although the public was not able to have the final say on how Mt Stirling should be developed, their pervasive and formalised involvement in the process ensured that the right questions were asked throughout the process, which in turn clearly illuminated for government the right decision. Indeed the openness of all stages of the process, and the strong conclusions of the Inquiry Panel, would have made any other decision by Government open to public scorn.

Gap analysis

The key budgeting issue was to ensure that the limited funds available for the study (some A$250,000) were allocated to the investigation of critical gaps in information and analysis. At the beginning of the study, all available baseline data was assembled, and key issues were highlighted through the public scoping phase. The study brief reflected areas where further data needed to be collected, and listed the key issues. The brief required six alternatives to be prepared and analysed, but left it up to the consultants to frame each of these alternatives.

Independent consultants who were acceptable to both the Department of Planning and Development and the consultative committee representatives conducted the EIS. The consultants drew upon their professional expertise when evaluating the alternatives, using the committee's assessment criteria. The consultants presented the likely impacts of each alternative without ranking the options, so as not to be seen as favouring one option over another. Saunders and Stephens (1998: 9) note that the following revelations arose from the EIS:

- Earlier studies had not adequately addressed the potential of the mountain for education and nature based tourism.
- Skiing was not growing as expected in Victoria, or worldwide, as the baby-boomers became too old to ski and their children decided to spend their money on other types of activities and vacations.
- Mt Stirling had significant native vegetation and rare species that could be adversely affected by the development of downhill skiing facilities.
- The greenhouse effect could have particularly dire consequences for ski resorts in Australia given the low altitudes of the country's mountain ranges.
- Developing downhill skiing facilities at Mt Stirling would not be commercially viable, due to the extensive infrastructure costs that would be incurred as a direct result of developing the facility and the limited demand for more skiing facilities in Victoria.

While a formal gap analysis was not a part of the Mt Stirling EIS process, elements of a gap analysis approach are apparent. Foremost among these was the gathering of a wide range of applicable data relating to stakeholders' expectations and resources and then looking at the costs and benefits of developing the mountain under the different scenarios. This comparison of what is desired to what is required to meet these desires is also a key principle of budgeting, as one considers how to best allocate resources. These resources can be financial, such as the costs of building new roads, as well as nature based, such as the potential impacts that road development would have on the integrity of an area's ecosystem. When all the relevant resources, expectations, costs and benefits for the six options were considered it became evident that developing downhill skiing facilities on the mountain raised significant concerns, while other options held more promise.

Management implications

The processes involved in deciding how to develop and manage Mt Stirling in the best interests of stakeholder groups and the general public went beyond a typical Environmental Impact Statement or Analysis to include a greater range of opinions and resources. These processes were still streamlined and carried out in a prompt and effective manner without costing the government or other stakeholders groups an unacceptable amount of money, or time. Had a private sector proponent implemented the original concept for a downhill ski resort, the costs documented in the EIS included likely financial failure of the resort through lack of suitable snow conditions, high impacts on the fragile ecosystem of the mountain, and significant public funds required for road infrastructure upgrading. These costs can be compared to the very considerable benefits of supporting low-impact tourist and recreational uses on the mountain.

Epilogue

The purpose of this book is to advocate strategic business management as a practical way to convert a community's interest in tourism into the most appropriate and competitive position for today's tough global tourism market. It is based on the premise that tourism at the community level should be viewed as a business first and foremost, that should incorporate the host community as a major stakeholder. The book uses the expanding business management literature, that is built on the four functions of management, and has demonstrated how business can be more socially responsible, and its tenets applied to small business and entrepreneurial situations. It makes extensive use of the tourism literature that has been moving toward Jafari's (1990) knowledge platform, in advocating a multi-disciplinary approach to tourism management that will embrace the findings of many disciplines to address the broad and complex task of developing the most appropriate tourism product for a host community.

In drawing these management and tourism threads together the book takes a prescriptive role, to guide the tourism development process for a wide range of community sizes and types. It focuses on communities as living organisms, where tourism is but one economic activity that needs to be considered along with other activities and options. Communities are the coalface of this industry, where tourists come to gaze and 'the production of many services is *context* dependent, they depend for their successful production upon aspects of the social and physical setting within which they occur' (Urry, 1990: 72). Such communities as destination settings, providers of attractions and labour, and political support are fundamental to the success of this industry.

After setting the scene for community tourism management the book has divided the complex and continuous strategic management process for tourism communities into three major sections, to facilitate its comprehension. The first is to emphasise how well the four basic functions of business management fit the community's need for an objective assessment of tourism's local potential, and how to plan and organise for its development. These functions also emphasise the need to monitor and control this industry, so that it does not bolt and drag the community into undesirable directions and consequences. While much of the management literature defers to corporate situations there is a growing appreciation of its relevance, with appropriate modifications, to the small business environment and entrepreneurship. Last, but certainly not least, the management function of leadership becomes vital to small business within tourism when it is viewed as a community industry. To pull the various industry and community components together to form an approved and competitive community tourism product will be fundamental to the success of a destination, and this whole process calls for leadership to come from some quarter. As we have shown, such leadership can come from a variety of stakeholders.

The second emphasis has been on understanding the views of major stakeholder groups with respect to tourism development in the destination community. We have chosen to analyse four major groups that cover the total spectrum, but the actual division is not sacrosanct and should vary according to local circumstances. One group we feel should always be identified and analysed is the customer, for this industry and its community investment is nothing if it cannot attract tourists. Tourists are now experienced and demanding, compared to the early post-World War II era, and have split into a multitude of special travel interests. This variety of interests provides many communities with a tourism development opportunity, but given the sophistication of modern tourists and the global competition for their business an aspiring community must develop a quality product and experience.

The final section attempts to show a way in which the business functions and interests of stakeholders can and should be linked. It offers a bridging model that shows the importance of collaborative decision-making and the significance of identifying gaps that may exist between the anticipated and actual experiences with this industry. Using the growing literature on conflict resolution we recommend some tried and tested techniques that can or have been used in tourism management, and we relate these to the service industry's interest in gap analysis. While this type of analysis has focused on potential gaps between providers' and customers' perceptions it has equal relevance to the different perspectives of various stakeholders. The various collaborative decision-making models in planning offer the chance for many of these perceptual gaps to be explored and minimised.

Conclusion

The *Bridging Tourism Gaps Model* is offered as a framework for communities to consider in the management of their tourism products and experience. Its main purpose is to ensure that communities consider all the pertinent facts and players, but from a pro-active business perspective. Such an approach will encourage a more complete assessment of development opportunities and current business activities, and as illustrated in the final case study, can produce a development freeze as well as a new product and image. Either way, if a community has applied the four functions of management, consulted the relevant stakeholders, and done so in an open partnership process, it will be in a better position to develop its tourism potential and take its place in the global marketplace.

Appendix

Strategic Tourism Planning Resources

International Organisations

World Tourism Organization
http://www.world-tourism.org/
This site is full of excellent quantitative measures of the global tourism industry. Analyses of tourism impacts are provided at multiple-levels, from international to national.
From this main page try the following links:

- Facts and figures and statistics and economic measures of tourism
- Sustainable development of tourism – links to Code of Ethics
- Regional activities

Accessed on 14/11/03

World Travel and Tourism Council
http://www.wttc.org/
This industry lobby group site provides an overview of global tourism trends and issues. The website emphasises the positive economic and employment impacts of tourism drawing on quantitative research.
From this main page try the following links:

- TSA Research
- Regional Initiatives
- Media & Resource Centre

Accessed on 16/11/03

Regional Organisations

European Travel Commission
http://www.etc-corporate.org/
The European Travel Commission is made up of the 33 National Tourism Organisations of Europe. There are two websites for the ETC – one with a corporate focus and the other with a traveller focus. This site provides a myriad of information on the impacts and potential of tourism in Europe. The site is a rich resource of tourism date.

From this main page try the following links:

- Statistics
- European Tourism News
- New Media Review

Accessed on 16/11/03

Pacific Asia Travel Association

http://www.pata.org

This website focuses on the activities of the Pacific Asia Travel Association and its members. The website has many interesting links and features, including annual reports that abound with tourism data. The website also has a members only component containing information and data searches that are free to PATA members.

From this main page try the following links:

- Events
- Publications
- Destinations – direct links to government tourism offices and other travel-related services throughout Asia and the Pacific.

Accessed on 16/11/03

National Organisations

Office of Travel and Tourism Industries (USA)

http://tinet.ita.doc.gov/

This site provides quantitative information on the tourism industry in the USA.

From this main page try the following links:

- About OTTI – links to tourism development and tourism policy
- Research Programmes – links to basic and monthly statistics
- Latest statistics/outreach – links to inbound and outbound figures
- TI News – summary of impacts, forecasts for arrivals and updates on tourism policy

Accessed on 14/11/03

ATC Online – tourism industry essential (Australia)

http://www.atc.net.au/

This site provides a wide array of information on the status of Australia's tourism industry. There are numerous links presented as overviews and in more detailed forms.

From this main page try the following links:

- Daily News Service
- Latest Statistics/outreach – links to visitor arrivals and tourist profiles
- Quick Find – annual report, FAQ, marketing advice and visitor arrivals

Accessed on 14/11/03

Scottish Tourism Organisation

http://www.world-tourism.org/
This site is tailored to travellers and is an excellent example of the how a website can convey the 'must see' aspects of a destination. The site is accessible in a number of languages and is customised for the needs of different international travellers. There is also a newsletter service that can be subscribed to along with numerous value and special interest packages.
　　From this main page try the following links:

- Short Breaks
- Festive Breaks
- Customised international links

Accessed on 17/11/03

Japan Travel Bureau

http://www.jtb.co.jp/eng/
This site is aimed primarily at travellers with a wide array of information on opportunities for exploring and enjoying Japan. There are useful links to tourism service providers, with the connections to train service proving especially helpful.
　　From this main page try the following links:

- Japan Now
- Location Focus
- In-depth Guide to the Regions

Accessed on 17/11/03

Switzerland Tourism

http://www.myswitzerland.com/
This site provides a comprehensive overview of tourism opportunities fro travellers in several different languages. There are useful links to tourism service providers, with plenty of maps and web cams to give a real feel for the country. The website customises its information to the area from which a request is made.
　　From this main page try the following links:

- Services
- Experiences
- Swiss Travel System

Accessed on 17/11/03

Indigenous Organisations

Alliance of Tribal Tourism

http://www.attatribal.com/attatribal/

The alliance of Tribal Tourism Advocates is an association of Tribes, Indians, and Non-Indian individuals, agencies and organisations that are concerned about responsible tourism development on the reservation and in off-reservation communities. This is an important site for tourism planners and others interested in sustainability issues, especially with respect to cultural issues.

From this main page try the following links:

- Mission
- Board
- Goals

Accessed on 17/11/03

Centre for World Indigenous Studies

http://www.cwis.org/

This site provides extensive information on indigenous issues around the world. While not tourism specific, it does provide background on many facets of indigenous life that need to be considered in regard to tourism's potential and limitations. From this main page try searching for 'tourism' to see relevant documents.

Accessed on 16/11/03

State and Local Organisations

Welcome to Victoria (Australia)

This site, which is aimed at travellers, offers many interesting links and has sites specifically created for visitors from key target markets.

From this main page try the following links:

- Experience Victoria – see Travel Planner
- Special Interest
- Related Links – customised fro specific target markets

Accessed on 16/11/03

Tourism BC (Canada)

This site is the official travel and accommodation site for British Columbia and advertises the 1800HELLOBC travel information hotline. While this site is aimed at travellers, it has useful links to tourism data as well.

From this main page try the following links:

- Travel Articles
- Tourism BC Corporate Website – see tourism research, plans and reports

Accessed on 16/11/03

The City and County of Honolulu, Hawaii

http://www.co.Honolulu.hi.us/

While this site is not tourism specific, searching by 'tourism' provides excellent quantitative measures of the tourism industry. Honolulu has integrated tourism into its strategic planning, thereby linking the well-being of tourism to that of the city.

From this main page try search by the keyword tourism for access to the following:

- Hawaii Tourism Authority County Product Enrichment Program
- Economic development opportunities relating to tourism
- Tourism education and training
- Council bills and resolutions relating to tourism

Accessed on 18/11/03

Florida Keys

http://www.co.Monroe.fl.us/
http://www.fla-keys.com

While The Monroe County site is not tourism specific, tourism is a cornerstone of the planning, development and management of the Keys. The website offers translation options, and a direct link to the Tourism Development Council, which is primarily a marketing body, is provided.

From this main page it is also useful to look at the following government websites of the other municipalities of the Florida Keys:

- Marathon
- Islamorada
- Key Colony Beach
- Key West

Accessed on 18/11/03

Bibliography

Aaker, D.A. (1992) *Developing Business Strategies* (3rd edn). New York: John Wiley.

Aaker, D.A. and Shansby, J. (1982) Positioning your product. *Business Horizons* (May–June), 56–62.

Abbot, J. (1995) Community participation and its relationship to community development. *Community Development Journal* 30 (2), 164.

Adams Six Sigma (2002) Gap analysis through data analysis turns data into information. *Adams Six Sigma.* http://www.adamsixsigma.com/Newsletters/data_analysis.htm. Accessed on 19 December 2002.

Alamo (2002) Gap analysis. *Alamo Learning Systems.* http://www.alamols.com/consulting/gap.htm. Accessed on 19 December 2002.

Alberta Tourism (1988) *Community Tourism Action Plan Manual.* Edmonton, Alberta: Alberta Tourism.

Alford, P. (1998) Positioning the destination product – can regional tourist boards learn from private sector practice? *Journal of Travel and Tourism Marketing* 7 (2), 53–68.

Allen, L.R., Long, P.T., Perdue, R.R. and Kieselbach, S. (1988) The impact of tourism development on residents' perceptions of community life. *Journal of Travel Research* 27 (1), 16–21.

Alliance of Tribal Tourism Advocates (ATTA) (2002) *ATTA.* http://atta.indian.com. Accessed on 15 January 2002.

American Planning Association (1999) *Study Guide for the Comprehensive AICP Exam.* Memphis, TN: University of Memphis.

American Planning Association (2000) Development moratoria, not a property taking. *APA Public Information: For the Press.* www.planning.org. Accessed on 5 December 2001.

American Planning Association (2001) Land-use planners cautious about Supreme Court decision rejecting taking claim but expanding future claim standards. *APA Public Information: For the Press.* www.planning.org. Accessed on 5 December 2001.

American Planning Association (2002) Leaders. *APA Planning: Special Awards Issue* 68 (3), 16–18.

Anderson, A.R. and Jack, S.L. (2002) The articulation of social capital in entrepreneurial networks: A glue or a lubricant? *Entrepreneurship and Regional Development* 14 (3), 193–210.

Ap, J. (1992) Residents' perceptions of tourism impacts. *Annals of Tourism Research* 19 (4), 665–90.

Archer, D., Griffin, T. and Hayes, A-L. (2001) Managing people by understanding people: A review of current visitor monitoring practices by Australian parks agencies. In C. Pforr and B. Janeczko (eds) *Capitalising on Research.* Proceedings of the Council of Australian University Tourism and Hospitality Education (CAUTHE) Conference, Canberra, 1–16.

413

Arnstein, S. (1969) A ladder of citizen participation. *Journal of the American Planning Association* 35 (4), 216–24.

Athiyaman, A. (1995) The interface of tourism and strategy research: An analysis. *Tourism Management* 16 (6), 447–53.

Augustyn, M. and Ho, S.K. (1998) Service quality and tourism. *Journal of Travel Research* 37 (1), 71–5.

Australia (2002) *The 10 Year Plan for Tourism: A Discussion Paper.* Canberra: Industry Tourism Resources.

Australian Broadcasting Corporation (ABC-TV) (2002) *True Stories: A* Balinese *Adventure.* Directed and produced by Bill Leimbach. Thursday, 21 February 2002 (10:00–11:00 p.m.).

Australian Heritage Commission (1999) *Protecting Local Heritage Places: A Guide for Communities.* Canberra, ACT: Commonwealth of Australia.

Australian Tourist Commission (2003) About the ATC. *ATC Online.* http://www.atc.australia.com/. Accessed on 28 January 2003.

Axelrod, J. (1968) Attitude measures that predict purchase. *Journal of Advertising Research* 8, 3–17.

Ayala, H. (1995) From quality product to eco-product: Will Fiji set a precedent? *Tourism Management* 16 (1), 39–47.

Aziz, H. (1995) Understanding attacks on tourists in Egypt. *Tourism Management* 16 (2), 91–5.

Bacrach, S. and Lawler, E. (1981) *Bargaining: Power, Tactics and Outcomes.* San Franciso: Jossey-Bass Publishers.

Badger, A., Barnett, P., Corbyn, L. and Keefe, J. (1996) *Trading Places: Tourism as Trade.* London: Tourism Concern.

Baker, J.E. (1997) Development of a model system for touristic hunting revenue collection and allocation. *Tourism Management* 18 (5), 273–86.

Baldacchino, G. (1997) *Global Tourism and Informal Labour Relations: The Small-Scale Syndrome at Work.* London: Mansell.

Barbalace, R. (2000) Environmental justice and the NIMBY principle. http://EnvironmentalChemistry.com. Accessed on 17 November 2000.

Barkham, J.P. (1973) Recreational carrying capacity: A problem of perception. *Area* 5, 218–22.

Barkley, B. (1997) An institution in transition: The Royal British Columbia Museum's Futures Project. In P.E. Murphy (ed.) *Quality Management in Urban Tourism* (pp. 149–56). Chichester: Wiley.

Barta, S.D. and Woods, M.D. (2002) Gap analysis as a tool for community economic development. *Oklahoma State University (OSU) Extension Facts.* (WF–917). www.agweb.okstate.edu. Accessed on 19 December 2002.

Bartunek, J.M. (1981) Why did you do that? Attribution theory in organizations. *Business Horizons* 24 (Sept.–Oct.), 66–71.

Baum, T. (1996) Tourism and the host community: A cautionary tale. *Tourism Management* 17 (2), 149–50.

BC Ferries (2002) *Inside Passage and Queen Charlotte Islands Schedules.* http://www.bcferries.bc.ca. Accessed on 31 December 2002.

Beazer, M. (1998) *Access and Justice: Legal Studies for Units 1 and 2* (3rd edn). Sale, Victoria: Beazer Publishing Co.

Becker, B. (1999) Visioning. In *Study Guide for the Comprehensive AICP Exam* (p. 66). Memphis, TN: University of Memphis.

Beeton, S. (2000) 'It's a wrap'. But what happens after the film crew leaves? An examination of community responses to film-induced tourism. In *Lights, Camera, Action:*

Spotlight on Tourism in the New Millennium (pp. 127–36). 31st Annual Proceedings of the Travel and Tourism Research Association, San Fernando Valley, California.

Behrendt, L. (1995) *Aboriginal Dispute Resolution.* Sydney: Federation Press.

Bellamy, D. (1992) The grand tour: A force for good or evil? *Traveller* 22 (3), 46–7.

Benson, J.K. (1975) The interorganizational network as political economy. *Administrative Science Quarterly* 20 (2), 229–49.

Berger, D.J. (1996) The challenge of integrating Maasai tradition with tourism. In M.F. Price (ed.) *People and Tourism in Fragile Environments* (pp. 175–98). Chichester, UK: John Wiley and Sons.

Berry, L.L. (1995) *On Great Service: A Framework for Action.* New York: Free Press.

Berry, L.L. and Clark, T. (1986) Four ways to make services more tangible. *Business.* (October–December), 53–4.

Berry, L.L. and Parasuraman, A. (1991) *Marketing Services: Competing Through Quality.* New York: Free Press.

Berry, S. and Ladkin, A. (1997) Sustainable tourism: A regional perspective. *Tourism Management* 18 (7), 433–40.

Bertsch (1999) Budgeting. In *Study Guide for the Comprehensive AICP Exam* (pp. 199–205). Memphis, TN: University of Memphis.

Beyer, H. and Bunbury, C.M. (1993) *The Chemainus Murals.* Chemainus, BC: Chemainus Festival of Murals Society.

Beyer, L. (2001) The women of Islam. *Time International: Special Report.* 3 December, 50–5.

Bhide, A. (1999) The questions every entrepreneur must answer. In the *Harvard Business Review on Entrepreneurship.* Boston, MA: Harvard Business School Press, 1–28.

Bitner, M.J. (1992) Servicescapes: The impact of physical surroundings on customers and employees. *Journal of Marketing* 56 (2), 57–71.

Blake, R.R. and Mouton, J.S. (1985) *The New Managerial Grid.* Houston: Gulf Publishing.

Blank, U. (1989) *The Community Tourism Imperative: The Necessity, the Opportunities, its Potential.* State College, PA: Venture Publishing.

Boothroyd, P. and Davis, C.H. (1993) Community economic development. *Journal of Planning Education and Research* 12 (3), 230–9.

Bosselman, F.P., Peterson, C.A. and McCarthy, C. (1999) *Managing Tourism Growth: Issues and Applications.* Washington, DC: Island Press.

Boulle, L. (1996) *Mediation: Principles, Process, Practice.* Sydney: Butterworths.

Boyd, S.W. and Butler, R.W. (1996) Managing ecotourism: An opportunity spectrum approach. *Tourism Management* 17 (8), 557–66.

Bramwell, B. (1994) Rural tourism and sustainable rural tourism. In B. Bramwell and B. Lane (eds) *Rural Tourism and Sustainable Rural Development* (pp. 1–6). Proceedings of the 2nd International School on Rural Development, 28 June–9 July 1993, University College Galway, Ireland 2 (1&2).

Bramwell, B. and Rawding, L. (1996) Tourism marketing images of industrial cities. *Annals of Tourism Research* 23 (1), 201–21.

Branson, R. (1998) *Losing my Virginity.* London: Virgin Publishing.

Britton, R.A. (1979) The image of the third world in tourism marketing. *Annals of Tourism Research* 6 (3), 318–29.

Britton, S.C. (1982) The political economy of tourism in the Third World. *Annals of Tourism Research* 9 (3), 331–58.

Britton, S. (1991) Tourism, capital and place: Towards a critical geography of tourism. *Environment and Planning, Society and Space* 9, 451–78.

Britton, S. and Clarke, W.C. (1987) *Ambiguous Alternative: Tourism in Small Developing Countries*, Suva, Fiji: University of Fiji.

Brohman, J. (1996) New directions in tourism for third world development. *Annals of Tourism Research* 23 (1), 48–70.

Bronner, F. and de Hoog, R. (1985) A recipe for mixing decision ingredients. *European Research* 13, 109–15.

Brook, R. (2000) The collaborative approach to resolving tourist related conflict. *Australian Planner* 37 (4), 186–94.

Brooks, D.J. and Haynes, R.W. (2001) *Recreation Tourism in South-Central Alaska: Synthesis of Recent Trends and Prospects*. United States Forest Service.

Brougham, J.E. and Butler, R.W. (1981) A segmentation analysis of resident attitudes to the social impact of tourism. *Annals of Tourism Research* 8 (4) 569–90.

Brown, F. (1998) *Tourism Reassessed: Blight or Blessing?* Oxford: Butterworth-Heinemann.

Brundtland, G.H. (1987) The Brundtland Report – *Our Common Future*. World Commission on Environment and Development. Oxford: Oxford University Press.

Brunt, P. and Courtney, P. (1999) Host perceptions of sociocultural impacts. *Annals of Tourism Research* 26 (3), 493–515.

Bryman, A. (1995) *Disney and his Worlds*. London: Routledge.

Buck, R.C. (1977) Making good business better: a second look at staged tourist attractions. *Journal of Travel Research* 15 (3), 30–2.

Buhalis, D. (2000) Tourism in an era of information technology. In B. Faulkner, G. Moscardo and E. Laws (eds) *Tourism in the 21st Century: Lessons from Experience* (pp. 163–80). London: Continuum.

Burke, J.F. and Gitelson, R. (1990) Conversion studies: assumptions, applications, accuracy and abuse. *Journal of Travel Research* 26 (3), 46–51.

Burnett, P. (1980) Spatial constraints-oriented approaches to movement, micro-economic theory and urban policy. *Urban Geography* 1, 53–67.

Burns, R. (1996) *Robert Burns Selected Poems*. London, England: Penguin Books.

Burr, S.W. (1991) Review and evaluation of the theoretical approaches to community as employed in travel and tourism impact research on rural community organisation and change. In A.J. Veal , P. Johnson and G. Cushman (eds) *Leisure and Tourism: Social and Environmental Changes* (pp. 540–53). Proceedings of the World Leisure and Recreation Association Congress, Sydney, Australia.

Butler, R.W. (1975) Tourism as an agent of social change. *Tourism as a Factor in National and Regional Development* (pp. 85–90). Occasional Paper 4, Peterborough, Ontario: Department of Geography, Trent University.

Butler, R.W. (1980) The concept of a tourist area cycle of evolution: implications for management of resources. *The Canadian Geographer* 24 (1), 5–12.

Butler, R.W. (1990) Alternative tourism: Pious hope or Trojan horse? *Journal of Travel Research* 28 (3): 40–6.

Butler, R.W. (1999) Problems and issues of integrating tourism development. In D.G. Pearce and R.W. Butler (eds) *Contemporary Issues in Tourism Development* (pp. 46–80). London and New York: Routledge.

Butler, R.W. and Walbrook, L.A. (1991) A new planning tool: The tourism opportunity spectrum. *The Journal of Tourism Studies* 2 (1), 2–14.

Byron Shire Council (2003) *Byron Bay Council – Concepts*. www.byron.nsw.gov.au. Accessed on 19 January 2003.

Cabinet Office (1999) *Rural Economics: A Performance and Innovation Unit Report*. London: Cabinet Office.

Caffyn, A. (2000) Is there a tourism partnership life cycle? In B. Bramwell and B. Lane (eds) *Tourism Collaboration and Partnerships: Politics, Practice and Sustainability* (pp. 200–29). Clevedon, UK: Channel View Publications.

Calantone, R.J. and Mazanec, J.A. (1991) Marketing management and tourism. *Annals of Tourism Research* 18 (1), 101–19.

Callenbach, E., Capra, F., Goldman, L., Lutz, R. and Marburg, S. (1993) *EcoManagement*. San Francisco: Berrett-Koehler.

Cameron, B. (1992) Creative destinations: Marketing and packaging: Who wants what and why? An overview of the Canadian Pleasure Market Study. In *Tourism Partnerships and Strategies: Merging Vision with New Realities* (pp. 154–67). TTRA 23rd Annual Conference Proceedings. June, Minneapolis.

Campbell, K. and Lapierre, J. (1991) Developing a satellite account for tourism and information system for tourism. In *Tourism Building Credibility for a Credible Industry* (pp. 7–17). Proceedings of the 22nd Annual Conference of the Travel and Tourism Research Association, Long Beach, California.

Campfens, H. (1997) International review of community development. In H. Campfens (ed.) *Community Development Around the World: Practice, Theory, Research, Training* (pp. 13–46). Toronto: University of Toronto Press.

Canada (1990) *Tourism on the Threshold*. Ottawa: Industry, Science and Technology Canada.

Canan, P. and Hennessy, M. (1989) The growth machine, tourism, and the selling of culture. *Sociological Perspectives* 22 (2), 227–43.

Canestrelli, E. and Costa, P. (1991) Tourist carrying capacity: a fuzzy approach. *Annals of Tourism Research* 18 (2), 295–311.

Capenerhurst, J. (1994) Community tourism. In L. Haywood (ed.) *Community, Leisure and Recreation* (pp. 144–71). Oxford: Butterworth-Heinemann.

Capodagli, B. and Jackson, L. (1999) *The Disney Way*. New York: McGraw-Hill.

Carlzon, J. (1987) *Moments of Truth: New Strategies for Today's Customer-Driven Economy*. New York: Harper & Row.

Carmichael, B. and Murphy, P.E. (1996) Tourism economic impact of a rotating sports event: The case of the British Columbia Games. *Festival Management and Event Tourism* 4, 127–38.

Carmichael, B.A., Peppard, D. and Boudreau, F. (1996) Mega resort on my doorstep: Local resident attitudes towards Foxwoods Casino and casino gambling on nearby Indian Reservation land. *Journal of Travel Research* 34 (3), 9–16.

Carnegie, R. and Butlin, M. (1993) *Managing the Innovating Enterprise: Australian Companies Competing with the World's Best*. Canberra: Business Council of Australia.

Carpenter, S.L. (1990) *Solving Community Problems by Consensus*. Washington, DC. Program for Community Problem Solving.

Chacko, H. (1996) Personal communications with authors, June 10. Cited in Pizam *et al.* (1997) Making tourists feel safe: whose responsibility is it? *Journal of Travel Research* 36 (1), 23–8.

Chan, S.H., Kensinger, J.W., Keown, A.J. and Martin, J.D. (1997) Do strategic alliances create value? *Journal of Financial Economics* 46, 199–221.

Chon, K-S. and Olsen, M.D. (1990) Applying the strategic management process in the management of tourism organizations. *Tourism Management* 11 (3), 206–13.

Choy, D.J.L. (1995) The quality of tourism employment. *Tourism Management* 16 (2), 129–37.

Christopher, M., Payne, A. and Ballantyne, D. (1991) *Relationship Marketing: Bringing Quality, Customer Service and Marketing Together*. Oxford, UK: Butterworth-Heinemann.

Church, N. (1989) Promoting rural tourist regions in Canada and the United States: Characteristics of successful regional marketing campaigns. In F. Dykeman (ed.) *Rural Tourism Opportunity Recognition: Insightful Marketing and Development Concepts* (pp. 1–13). Rural and Small Town Research and Studies Programme. New Brunswick: Mount Allison University.

Churchill, N. and Lewis, V. (1983) The five stages of business growth. *Harvard Business Review.* May/June, 30–50.

City and County of Honolulu (1992) *General Plan: Objectives and Policies.* Honolulu: City and County of Honolulu, Department of General Planning.

City and County of Honolulu, Department of Planning and Permitting (DPP) (2002) *Planning Information.* www.co.honoluludpp.org/Planning/. Accessed on 31 December 2002.

City and County of Honolulu (2002) *Biography of Mayor Jeremy Harris.* www.co.honolulu.hi.us/mayor/major.htm. Accessed on 31 December 2002.

City of Marathon, Florida (2002). *City of Marathon Comprehensive Plan Draft Elements,* Marathon, FL.

Clancy, D. and Webber, R. (1995) *Roses and Rust: Redefining the Essence of Leadership in a New Age.* Sydney: Business and Professional Publishing.

Clegg, S.R., Hardy, C. and Nord, W.R. (eds) (1997) *Handbook of Organisation Studies.* London: Sage Publications.

Cloutier, K.R. (2000) *Legal Liability and Risk Management for Adventure Businesses.* Kamloops, BC: Bhudak Consultants Ltd.

Clow, K.E. and Vorhies, D.W. (1993) Building a competitive advantage for service firms. *Journal of Services Marketing* 7 (1), 22–33.

Coccossis, H. (1996) Tourism and sustainability: Perspectives and implications. In G. Priestly, J.A. Edwards and H. Coccossis (eds) *Sustainable Tourism? European Experiences.* Oxford: CAB International.

Cock, P.H. and Pfueller, S. (2000) *Australian Ecotourism: Contributing to Ecological and Community Sustainability.* Monash Publications in Geography and Environmental Science Number 54, Melbourne: Monash University.

Cohen, E. (1988) Authenticity and commoditization. *Annals of Tourism Research* 15 (3), 371–86.

Collits, P. (2001) Small town decline and survival: Trends, causes and policy issues. In R. Rogers and Y. Collins (eds) *The Future of Australia's Country Towns* (pp. 32–56). Centre for Sustainable Regional Communities, La Trobe University, Bendigo, Victoria: Australia.

Coopers and Lybrand Consulting (1995) *The Canadian Tourism Commission, US Tourism Industries/International Trade Administration and the Secretarial de Tursimo (Mexico) Pleasure Travel Markets to North America: Japan Travel Trade Report.* Toronto, Ont.: Canadian Tourism Commission.

Coopers and Lybrand Consulting (1996) *The Canadian Tourism Commission, US Tourism Industries/International Trade Administration and the Secretarial de Tursimo (Mexico) Pleasure Travel Markets to North America: German Travel Trade Report.* Toronto, Ont.: Canadian Tourism Commission.

Court, B. and Lupton, R. (1997) Customer portfolio development: Modeling destination adopters, inactives, and rejecters. *Journal of Travel Research* 36 (1), 35–43.

Covey, S.R. (1989) *The Seven Habits of Highly Effective People.* Melbourne: Business Library.

CRC (2002) Media Release: Record Funding for Cooperative Research Centres. The Honourable Peter McGauran, Minister for Science, 10 December.

Creighton, J.L. (1980) *Public Involvement Manual.* Washington, DC: US Department of the Interior.

Cressy, R. and Cowling, M. (1996) Small business finance. In M. Warner (ed.) *International Encyclopaedia of Business and Management*. London: Routledge.

Crompton, J. (1979) An assessment of image of Mexico as a vacation destination and the influence of geographical location upon that image. *Journal of Travel Research* 17 (Spring), 18–23.

Crotts, J.C., Buhalis, D. and March, R. (2000) Global alliances in tourism and hospitality management. *International Journal of Hospitality and Tourism Administration* 1 (1), 1–10.

Daft, R.L., Fitzgerald, P.A. and Rock, M.E. (1992) *Management* (First Canadian Edition). Toronto: Dryden Canada.

Dahles, H. (2000) Tourism, small enterprises and community development. In G. Richards and D. Hall (eds) *Tourism and Sustainable Community Development* (pp. 154–69). London: Routledge.

Daily Express (2000) Payment upfront put me on the road to success. *Enterprise Express-Daily Express*, 11 September 2000, 56.

Dallen, J.T. and White, K. (1999) Community-based ecotourism development on the periphery of Belize. *Current Issues in Tourism* 2 (2&3), 226–42.

Dalton and Dalton (1975) *Community and its Relevance to Australian Society*. Canberra: Department of Tourism and Recreation.

D'Amore, L.J. (1983) Guidelines to planning in harmony with the host community. In P.E. Murphy (ed.) *Tourism in Canada: Selected Issues and Options* (pp. 135–59). *Western Geographical Series* 21, Victoria: University of Victoria.

Davidson, T.L. (1985) Strategic planning: a competitive necessity. *The Battle for Market Share: Strategies in Research and Marketing* (pp. 103–8). Travel and Tourism Research Association, Salt Lake City: Graduate School of Business, University of Utah.

Davidsson, P. (2000) Where do they come from? Prevalence and characteristics of nascent entrepreneurs. *Entrepreneurship and Regional Development* 12 (1), 1–23.

Davies, J. (1994) Less Mickey Mouse, more Dirty Harry: Property, policing and the modern metropolis. *Polemic* 5 (2), 63–9.

Davis, C.H. (1993) *Regional Economic Impact Analysis and Project Evaluation*. Vancouver, BC: UBC Press.

Davis, D., Allen, J. and Cosenza, R.M. (1988) Segmenting local residents by their attitudes, interests and opinions toward tourism. *Journal of Travel Research* 27 (2), 2–8.

Davis, T.R.V. (1984) The influence of the physical environment in offices. *Academy of Management Review* 9 (2), 271–83.

Day, G.S. (1981) The product life cycle: Analysis and applications issues. *Journal of Marketing* 45 (4), 60–7.

Day, G.C. (1990) *Market Driven Strategy: Processes for Creating Value*. New York: Free Press.

de Araujo, L.M and Bramwell, B. (2000) Stakeholder assessment and collaborative tourism planning: The case of Brazil's Costa Dourada project. In B. Bramwell and B. Lane (eds) *Tourism Collaboration and Partnerships: Politics, Practice and Sustainability* (pp. 272–74). Clevedon, UK: Channel View Publications.

Decrop, A. (1999) Personal aspects of vacationers' decision making processes: An interpretivist approach. *Journal of Travel and Tourism Marketing* 8 (4), 59–68.

De Filippis, J. (2001) The myth of social capital in community development. *Housing Policy Debate* 12 (4), 781–806.

Deery, M. and Jago, L. (2001) Paid staff or volunteers? The dilemma facing tourism organisations. In C. Pforr and B. Janecko (eds) *Capitalising on Research* (pp. 57–68). Proceedings of the Council of Australian Tourism and Hospitality Education (CAUTHE) Conference Canberra.

De Kadt, E. (ed.) (1979) *Tourism: Passport to Development?* Oxford: Oxford University Press.

Delbecq, A.L., Van de Ven, A.H. and Gustafson, D.H. (1975) *Group Techniques for Program Planning.* Glenview, IL: Scott, Foresmen & Co.

Delbridge, A. and Bernard, J.R.L. (eds) (1988) *The Macquarie Concise Dictionary* (2nd edn). New South Wales: Macquarie University.

Demetriadi, J. (1996) The tele-tourists. *Hospitality*, October/November: 14–15.

Department of Infrastructure & Sinclair Knight Merz (1996). *Mount Stirling Environment Effects Statement.* Melbourne: Victoria Government.

Department of Infrastructure (DOI) (2001) *Great Ocean Road: Towards a Vision for the Future (Discussion Paper).* Melbourne: DOI.

Department of Infrastructure (DOI) (2002) *Planning Panel Reports and Hearings.* www.doi.vic.gov.au/doi. Accessed on 31 December 2002.

Dienel, P.C. and Renn, O. (1995) Planning cells: A gate to 'fractal' mediation. In O. Renn, T. Webler and P. Wiedemann (eds) *Fairness and Competence in Citizen Participation: Evaluating Models for Environmental Discourse* (pp. 117–40). The Netherlands: Kluwer Academic Press.

Dietvorst, A. (1993) Planning for tourism and recreation: A market-oriented approach. In H.N. van Lier and P.D. Taylor (eds) *New Challenges in Recreation and Tourism Planning* (pp. 87–124). Amsterdam/London: Elsevier.

Digance, J. (1997) Life cycle model. *Annals of Tourism Research* 24 (2), 452–5.

Dimmock, K. (1999) Management style and competitive strategies among tourism firms in the Northern Rivers. *Tourism Management* 20 (3), 323–39.

Ding, P. and Pigram, J. (1995) Environmental audits: An emerging concept in sustainable tourism development. *Journal of Tourism Studies* 6 (2), 2–10.

Diski, J. (2000) What a Mickey Mouse Scheme. *The Scotsman.* 26 August S2 Weekend, 1–5.

Dotson, B.A., Godschalk, D. and Kaufman, J. (1989) *The Planner as Dispute Resolver: Concepts and Teaching Materials.* NIDR Teaching Material Series. National Institute for Dispute Resolution (NIDR).

Douglas, N. (1997) Applying the life cycle model to Melanesia. *Annals of Tourism Research* 24 (1), 1–22.

Doxey, G.V. (1975) A causation theory of visitor-resident irritants: methodology and research inferences. In *The Impact of Tourism* (pp. 195–98). Sixth Annual Conference Proceedings of the Travel Research Association, San Diego, California.

Driver, B. and Tocher, S.R. (1979) Towards a behavioral interpretation of recreational engagements with implications for planning. In C.S. Van Doren, G.B. Priddle and J.E. Lewis (eds) *Land and Leisure: Concepts and Methods in Outdoor Recreation* (pp. 86–104). London: Methuen.

Drucker, P.F. (1985) *Innovation and Entrepreneurship.* New York: Harper Business.

Drucker, P.F. (1993) *Managing for the Future.* New York: Plume/Penguin Books.

Drucker, P.F. (1994) The age of social transformation. *The Atlantic Monthly* 294 (5), 53–71.

Dunn, K.D. and Brooks, D.E. (1990) Profit analysis: Beyond yield management. *Cornell Hotel and Restaurant Administration Quarterly* 31 (3), 80–91.

Echtner, C.M. (1995) Entrepreneurial training in developing countries. *Annals of Tourism Research* 22 (1),119–34.

Eckhouse, J. (2002) Customer strategy: Think your customers are just names in a database? Think again – your survival may depend on a more human touch. In Gap Analysis. *Optimize: Ideas. Action. Results.* (February). http://optimizemag.com/issue/oo4/pr_gap.fhtml. 1–12. Accessed on 19 December 2002.

Edgell, D.L. (1993) *World Tourism at the Millennium*. Washington, DC: US Travel and Tourism Administration.

Eisenberg, D., Coady, E., Kher, U. and Ressner, J. (2001) Is this any way to run a railroad? *Time International: Special Report* (pp. 68–9). 3 December.

Eisner, M. with Schwartz, T. (1998) *Work in Progress*. London: Penguin Books.

Elkington, J. (1999) *Cannibals with Forks: The Triple Bottom Line of 21st Century Business*, Oxford: Capstone Publishing.

Elster, J. (1998) Introduction. In J. Elster (ed.) *Deliberative Democracy* (pp. 1–18). Cambridge: Cambridge University Press.

Emerson, R. (1972) Exchange theory. Part 1: A psychological basis for social exchange. In J. Berger, M. Zelditch and B. Anderson (eds) *Sociological Theories in Progress* (pp. 38–87). New York: Houghton-Mifflin.

English Tourism Board (ND) *Tomorrow's Tourism: A Growth Industry for the New Millennium*. Department for Culture, Media and Sport.

English Tourism Council (ETC) (2002) Building partnerships. ETC. www.englishtourism.org.uk/default.asp?id-2226. Accessed on 28 January 2002.

English, D.B.K., Kriesel, W., Leeworthy, V.R. and Wiley, P.C. (1996) *Economic Contribution of Recreating Visitors to the Florida Keys. Key West: Consulting Report*.

Ennew, C.T., Reed, G.V. and Binks, M.R. (1993) Importance-performance analysis and the measurement of service quality. *European Journal of Marketing* 27 (2), 59–70.

Falconer, B. (1991) Tourism and sustainability: The dream realised. In L.J. Reid (ed.) *Tourism – Environment – Sustainability Development: An Agenda for Research* (pp. 21–6). Conference Proceedings of the Travel and Tourism Association of Canada.

Faulkner, B. and Tideswell, C. (1997) A framework for monitoring community impacts of tourism. *Journal of Sustainable Tourism* 5 (1), 3–28.

Federal Aviation Administration (FAA) (2001) *Airport Benchmark Report: Executive Summary*. FAA. www.faa.gov/events/benchmarks/download.htm. Accessed on 3 December 2001.

Federal Highways Administration (FHA). (2001) *Funding for Highways and Disposition of Highway User Revenues, All Units of Government*. FHA. www.fhw.dot.gov/ohim/hs00/hf1.htm. Accessed on 5 December 2001.

Feizkhah, E. (2002) She's not right mate: A big damages award for a surf accident adds to concerns about the future of the Aussie lifestyle. *Time International* 27 (May 46).

Fick, G.R. and Ritchie, J.R.B. (1991) Measuring service quality in the travel and tourism industry. *Journal of Travel Research* 30 (2), 2–9.

Fishbein, M. and Raven, B.H. (1967) The AB scales: An operational definition of belief and attitude. In Fishbein, M. (ed.) *Readings in Attitude Theory and Measurement* (pp. 183–9). New York: John Wiley.

Fisher, R. and Ury, W. (1981) *Getting to Yes: Negotiating Agreement Without Giving In*. Boston: Houghton Mifflin.

Fisher, R., Ury, W. and Patton, B. (eds) (1991) *Getting to Yes: Negotiating Agreement Without Giving In* (2nd edn). New York: Penguin Group.

Fleischer, A. and Felsenstein, D. (2000) Support for rural tourism: Does it make a difference? *Annals of Tourism Research* 27 (4), 1007–24.

Flood, R.L. (1993) *Beyond TQM*. Chichester: John Wiley.

Florida Department of State, Division of Elections (2002) *Florida Administrative Code*. http://fac.dos.state.fl.us/fac. Accessed on 31 January 2002.

Florida Statute. Chapter 163.3164. Local Government and Comprehensive Planning and Land Development Regulation Act.

Florida Statute. Chapter 380. Land and Water Management.

Flower, J. (1991) *Prince of the Magic Kingdom: Michael Eisner and the Re-Making of Disney*. New York: John Wiley.

Flynn, B.B., Schroeder, R.G. and Sakakibara, S. (1994) A framework for quality management research and an associated measurement instrument. *Journal of Operations Management* 11 (4), 339–66.

Foley, M. (1994) Managing the tourist gaze: Visitor services at Edinburgh Castle. In A.V. Seaton (ed.) *Tourism: The State of the Art* (pp. 792–98). Chichester: John Wiley.

Font, X. (2002) Environmental certification in tourism and hospitality: Progress, process and prospects. *Tourism Management* 23 (3), 197–205.

Foster, D. and Murphy, P.E. (1991) The resort cycle and retirement: A reappraisal of the Butler model. *Annals of Tourism Research* 18 (4), 553–67.

France, L. (1998) Local participation in tourism in the West Indian Islands. In E. Laws, B. Faulkner and G. Moscardo (eds) *Embracing and Managing Change in Tourism: International Case Studies* (pp. 222–34). London: Routledge.

French, C.N., Craig-Smith, S.J. and Collier, A. (1999) *Principles of Tourism*. Melbourne: Addison Wesley Longman Australia.

Frew, E.A. and Shaw, R.N. (1998) An empirical study of industrial tourism attractions. In B.J. Gray and K.R. Deans (eds) *Marketing Connections: Proceedings of the Australian New Zealand Marketing Academy Conference* (pp. 772–85), Dunedin, NZ.

Funnel, B. and Ainsworth, P. (1996) The nature of the tourism market as an occupational field and the place of small businesses and training within it. In J. Stevenson (ed.) *Learning in the Workplace: Tourism and Hospitality* (pp. 245–89). Centre for Learning and Work Research, Griffith University, Queensland.

Gee, C.Y. (1996) *Resort Development and Management* (2nd edn). East Lansing, Michigan: Educational Institute of the American Hotel and Motel Association.

Gerber, M.E. (1995) *The E-Myth Revisited*. New York: Harper Business.

Gershuny, J. and Miles, I. (1983) *The New Service Economy: The Transformation of Employment in Industrial Societies*. London: Frances Printer.

Getz, D. (1983) A research agenda for municipal and community-based tourism in Canada. Paper presented at the Fourteenth Annual Conference of the Travel and Tourism Research Association, Banff, Alberta.

Getz, D. (1987) Tourism planning and research: Traditions, models and futures. Paper presented at The Australian Travel Research Workshop, Bunbury, Western Australia, 5–6 November.

Getz, D. (1991) *Festivals, Special Events and Tourism*. New York: Van Nostrand Reinhold.

Ghiselli, E. (1971) *Explorations in Managerial Talent*. Pacific Palisades, California: Goodyear.

Gibbons, M., Limoges, C., Nowotny, H., Schwartzman, S., Scott, P. and Trow, M. (1994) *The New Production of Knowledge*. London: Sage.

Gilbert, J. (1982) Rural theory: the ground of rural sociology. *Rural Sociology* 47 (4), 609–33.

Gilbert, D. (1990) Strategic marketing planning for national tourism. *The Tourist Review* 1, 18–27.

Gill, A.M. (1997) Competition and the resort community: Towards an understanding of residents' needs. In P.E. Murphy (ed.) *Quality Management in Urban Tourism* (pp. 55–65). Chichester: John Wiley.

Glasson, J., Godfrey, K. and Goodey, B. (1995) *Towards Visitor Impact Management*. Avebury: Ashgate Publishing.

Godschalk, D., Parham, D., Porter, D., Potapchuk, W., Schukraft, S. (1994) *Pulling Together: A Planning Development Consensus-Building Manual*. Washington, DC: Urban Land Institute.

Goeldner, C.R., Ritchie, J.R.B. and McIntosh, R.W. (2000) *Tourism: Principles, Practices, Philosophies* (8th edn). New York: John Wiley.

Goleman, D. (1998) What makes a leader? *Harvard Business Review* 76 (6), 93–102.

Goodall, B. and Stabler, M. (2000) Environmental standards and performance measurement in tourism destination development. In G. Prichard and D. Hall (eds) *Tourism and Sustainable Community Development* (pp. 63–82). London: Routledge.

Google.com. (2002) http://www.google.com/search?q=Gap+Analysis. Accessed on 19 December 2002.

Gordon, J.R., Mondy, R.W., Sharplin, A. and Premeaux, S.R. (1990) *Management and Organizational Behavior*. Boston: Allyn & Bacon.

Grabler, K. (1997) Cities and the destination life cycle. In A.J. Mazanec (ed.) *International City Tourism*. London: Pinter.

Graefe, A.R., Kuss, F.R. and Vaske, J.J. (1990) *Visitor Impact Management: The Planning Framework*. Washington, DC: National Parks and Conservation Asssociation.

Graham, R., Nilsen, P. and Payne, R.J. (1988) Visitor management in Canadian National Parks. *Tourism Management* 9 (1), 44–62.

Grapentine, T. (1994) Problematic scales. *Marketing Research* 6 (4), 8–21.

Gray, B. (1985) Conditions facilitating interorganizational collaboration. *Human Relations* 38 (10), 911–37.

Griffen, D.W. and Ross, L. (1991) Subjective construal, social interference, and human misunderstanding. *Advances in Experimental Social Psychology* 23, 319–59.

Grinder, B. (1992) Dance carries on traditions. *Windspeaker* 10 (6), 10–14.

Gunn, C. (1972) *Vacationscape*. TX: University of Texas Press.

Gunn, C.A. (1979) *Tourism Planning*. New York: Crane Russak.

Gunn, C.A. (1994) *Tourism Planning* (3rd edn). Washington, DC: Taylor & Francis.

Gunn, C.A. (1997) *Vacationscape: Developing Tourist Areas* (3rd edn). Washington, DC: Taylor & Francis.

Gursoy, D., Jurowski, C. and Uysal, M. (2002) Residents attitudes: A structural modelling approach. *Annals of Tourism Research* 29 (1), 79–105.

Hall, C.M. (1992) *Hallmark Tourist Events*. London: Belhaven Press.

Hall, C.M. (1995) *Introduction to Tourism in Australia: Impacts, Planning and Development*. Melbourne, Australia: Longman.

Hall, C.M. (1998) The politics of decision-making and top-down planning: Darling Harbour, Sydney. In D. Tyler, Y. Guerrier and M. Robertson (eds) *Managing Tourism in Cities* (pp. 9–24). Chichester: John Wiley.

Hall, R.H., Clark, J.P., Giordano, P.C., Johnson, P.V. and Roekel, M. (1977) Patterns of interorganizational relationships. *Administrative Science Quarterly* 22 (3), 457–72.

Hamilton, S. (2002) Marketing Mt Buller Ski Resort. Workshop Presentation, La Trobe University Campus, Mt Buller.

Hansen, D.J. and Walker, R.H. (1997) *Ecologically Based Macro-Marketing and Management of Tasmania as a Tourism Destination*. Working Paper Series 97–05. Hobart: Department of Management, University of Tasmania.

Hanson, S. and Hanson, P. (1981) The travel-activity patterns of urban residents: dimensions and relationships to socio-demographic characteristics. *Economic Geography* 57 (4), 332–47.

Hardin, G. (1969) The tragedy of the commons. *Science* 162, 1243–8.

Hart, C. and Bogan, C. (1992) *The Baldridge*. New York: McGraw-Hill.

Harvey, D. (1989) From managerialism to entrepreneurialism: The transformation in urban governance in late capitalism. *Geografisk Annaler* 71, 3–17.

Haspeslagh, P. (1982) Portfolio planning; uses and limits. *Harvard Business Review*, 60 (1), 58–73.

Hawkes, S. and Williams, P. (eds) (1993) *The Greening of Tourism*. Centre for Tourism Policy and Research, Simon Fraser University, Vancouver, Canada.

Hawkins, G. and Backman, K.F. (1998) An exploration of sense of place as a possible explanatory concept in nature-based traveler conflict. *Tourism Analysis* 3, 89–102.

Haywood, K.M. (1986) Can the tourist-area life cycle be made operational? *Tourism Management* 7 (3), 154–67.

Haywood, K.M. (1988) Responsible and responsive tourism planning in the community. *Tourism Management* 9 (2), 105–18.

Haywood, K.M. (1990) Revising and implementing the marketing concept as it is applied to tourism. *Tourism Management* 11 (3), 195–205.

Haywood, K.M. (1997) Creating value for visitors to urban destinations. In P.E. Murphy (ed.) *Quality Management in Urban Tourism* (pp. 169–82). Chichester: John Wiley.

Haywood, L. (ed.) (1994) *Community Leisure and Recreation: Theory and Practice*. Oxford: Butterworth-Heinemann.

Heath, E. and Wall, G. (1992) *Marketing Tourism Destinations*. New York: John Wiley.

Hemphill, J.K. and Coons, A.E. (1957) Development of the leader behavior description questionnaire. In R.M. Stogdill and E.A. Coons (eds) *Leader Behavior: Its Description and Measurement*. Columbus, OH: Ohio State University, Bureau of Business Research.

Hernandez, S.A., Cohen, J. and Garcia, H.L. (1996) Resident attitudes towards an instant enclave resort. *Annals of Tourism Research* 23 (4), 755–9.

Hersey, P. and Blanchard, K. (1974) So you want to know your leadership style? *Training and Development Journal* (February), 22–32.

Heskett, J.L., Sasser, Jr W.E., Schlesinger, L.A. (1997) *The Service Profit Chain*. New York: Free Press.

Heung, V.C.S. and Leung, K.P. (1998) Co-operative approach to marketing: Implications for hotel and tourism industry in Indo China. *Journal of Travel and Tourism Marketing* 7 (2), 105–18.

Hiaasen, C. (1986) *Tourist Season*. New York: Warner Books.

Hjalager, A-M. (1997) Innovation patterns in sustainable tourism. *Tourism Management* 18 (1), 35–41.

Ho, S.K. (1995) *TQM: An Integrated Approach – Implementation through Japanese 5-S and ISO 9000*. London: Kogan Page.

Hof, M., Hammett, J., Rees, M., Beinap, J., Poe, N., Lime, D. and Manning, B. (1994) Getting a handle on visitor carrying capacity – a pilot project at Arches National Park. *Park Science*, Winter, 11–13.

Holder, J.S. (1993) The Caribbean Tourism Organization's role in Caribbean tourism development towards the year 2000. In D.J. Gayle and J.N. Goodrich (eds) *Tourism Marketing and Management in the Caribbean* (pp. 205–19). London: Routledge.

Horn, C. and Simmons, D. (2002) Community adaption to tourism: Comparisons between Rotorua and Kaikoura, New Zealand. *Tourism Management* 23 (2), 133–43.

Houghton, M., Jackson, J. and Ritchie, M. (2002) The long road to . . . a study of Newell Highway visiting patterns. Unpublished paper, School of Tourism and Hospitality, La Trobe University, Melbourne, Australia.

Hovinen, G.R. (1995) Heritage issues in urban tourism: An assessment of new trends in Lancaster County. *Tourism Management* 16 (5), 381–8.

Howatson, A.C. (1990) *Toward Proactive Environmental Management: Lessons from Canadian Corporate Experience*. Ottawa: The Conference Board of Canada.

Howe, J., McMahon, E. and Propst, L. (1997) *Balancing Nature and Commerce in Gateway Communities*. Washington, DC: Island Press.

Hsu, C.H.C. (2003) Social impacts of Native American Casino Gaming. In C.H.C. Hsu (ed.) *Legalised Casino Gaming in the United States* (pp. 221–32). New York: Haworth Hospitality Press.

Hubbard, P. and Hall, T. (1998) The Entrepreneurial City and the 'New Urban Politics'. In T. Hall and P. Hubbard (eds) *The Entrepreneurial City: Geographies of Politics, Regime and Representation* (pp. 1–23). New York, NY: John Wiley.

Hudson, S. (2000) Consumer behaviour related to tourism. In A. Pizam and Y. Mansfeld (eds) *Consumer Behaviour in Travel and Tourism* (pp. 7–32). Binghampton, NY: The Haworth Hospitality Press.

Huffman, J.L. (1994) The inevitability of private rights in public lands. *University of Colorado Law Review* 65, 241–77.

Hughes, G. (1995) The cultural construction of sustainable tourism. *Tourism Management* 16 (1), 49–59.

Hunt, J.D. (1975) Image as a factor in tourist development. *Journal of Travel Research*. 13 (Winter) 1–7.

Husock, H. (1998) Let's break up the big cities. *City Journal* 8 (1), 71–87.

Hutchison, J. (1997) *Tourism: Getting it Right for the Millennium*. Sydney: Sydney Convention and Visitors Bureau.

Inskeep, E. (1988) Tourism planning: An emerging specialization. *American Planning Association Journal* 54 (3), 360–72.

Inskeep, E. (1991) *Tourism Planning: An Integrated and Sustainable Development Approach*. New York: Van Nostrand Reinhold.

Inskeep, E. (1994) *National and Regional Tourism Planning*. A World Tourism Organisation Publication. London: Routledge.

Iowa Gap (1997) What is Gap Analysis? *Iowa Gap*. http://www.ag.iastate/edu/ denters/cfwru/iowagap/whatisit. Accessed on 18 December 2002.

Islamorada, Village of Islands (2001) Islamorada, Village of Islands Comprehensive Plan: Reclaiming the Keys. Florida: Islamorada Municipality.

Jackson, T. (2002) Major sporting and leisure investments in the 'contested countryside': golf tourism and sustainable rural development in Scotland. In N. Andrews, F. Convery, S. Flanagan and J. Ruddy (eds) *Tourism and the Environment: Developing Sustainable Tourism* (pp. 189–208). Dublin: Dublin Institute of Technology.

Jackson, J. and Murphy, P.E. (2002) Tourism destinations as clusters: Analytical experiences from the New World. *Tourism and Hospitality Research* 4 (1), 36–52.

Jacobs, J. (1962) *The Death and Life of Great American Cities*. London: Jonathan Cape.

Jacobs, J. (1984). *Cities and the Wealth of Nations: Principles of Economic Life*. New York: Random House.

Jacobs, T.O. (1970) *Leadership and Exchange in Formal Organizations*. Alexandria, VA: Human Resources Research Organization.

Jafari, J. (1990) Research and scholarship: The basis of tourism education. *Journal of Tourism Studies* 1 (1), 33–41.

Jamal, T.B. and Getz, D. (1995) Collaboration theory and community tourism planning. *Annals of Tourism Research* 22 (1), 186–204.

Jamal, T.B. and Getz, D. (1997) Visioning for sustainable tourism development community-based collaborations. In P.E. Murphy (ed.) *Quality Management in Urban Tourism* (pp. 199–220). Chichester: John Wiley.

Jamal, T. and Getz, D. (2000) Community roundtables for tourism-related conflicts: The dialectics of consensus and process structures. In B. Bramwell and B. Lane (eds) *Tourism Collaboration and Partnerships* (pp. 159–82). Clevedon, UK: Channel View Publications.

Jansen-Verbeke, M. (1994) *Tourism: Quo Vadis? From Business as Usual to Crisis Management.* Rotterdam: Centre for Tourism Management, Erasmus University.

Jenkins, C.L. (1997) Impacts of the development of international tourism in the Asian region. In F.M. Go and C.L. Jenkins (eds) *Tourism and Economic Development in Asia and Australasia* (pp. 48–64). London: Pinter.

Jenshel, L. (1994) Of mice and men: There's turmoil in Disney's Magic Kingdom. Can America's fantasy maker find a happy ending? *Newsweek* 41–7.

Johanson, J., Lars, H. and Nazeem, S.M. (1991) Interfirm adaptation in business relationships. *Journal of Marketing* 55 (2), 29–37.

Johnston, R.J., Gregory, D. and Smith, D.M. (1988) *The Dictionary of Human Geography* (2nd edn). Oxford: Blackwell Reference.

Jones, K. and Simmons, J. (1987) *Location, Location, Location: Analyzing the Retail Environment.* Toronto: Methuen.

Joppe, M. (1996) Sustainable community tourism development revisited. *Tourism Management* 17 (7), 475–9.

Judd, D.R. (1995) Promoting tourism in US cities. *Tourism Management* 16 (3) 175–87.

Jurowski, C., Uysal, M. and Williams, D.R. (1997) A theoretical analysis of host community resident reactions to tourism. *Journal of Travel Research* 36 (2), 3–11.

Kariel, H.G. (1989) Socio-cultural impacts of tourism in the Austrian Alps. *Mountain Research and Development* 9 (1), 59–70.

Kaufman, D. (2000) Running on empty: Building the online economy. *The Age* Tuesday, 7 November I.T.2.

Keller, P. and Murphy, P. (1990) Destination travel patterns: An examination and modelling of tourist patterns on Vancouver Island, British Columbia. *Leisure Sciences* 12 (1), 49–65.

Kelly, K. (2000) Blood in the boardroom. *Time International* 6 November, 58.

Kelly, I. and Spark, M. (2001) Tourism as a strategy for bypassed towns. Paper presented at the Council for Australian University Tourism and Hospitality Education (CAUTHE) Conference, Canberra, February.

Kent, N. (1977) A new kind of sugar. In B.R. Finney and K.A. Watson (eds) *A New Kind of Sugar: Tourism in the Pacific* (pp. 169–98). Santa Cruz, California: Center for South Pacific Studies, University of California, Santa Cruz.

King, B., McVey, M. and Simmons, D. (2000) A societal marketing approach to national tourism planning: evidence from the South Pacific. *Tourism Management* 21 (4), 407–16.

King, J. (2001) The Vision. *Welcome to Eden* 1 (1), 4–5.

Kinninment, M. (2003) Stopping paradise from being lost. *The Age* (Melbourne): Perspective. Wednesday 15 January 2003, 13.

Klein, N. (2000) *No Logo, No Space, No Choice, No Jobs: Taking Aim at the Brand Bullies.* London: Flamingo.

Klemm, M. (1996) Langeudoc Roussillon: adapting the strategy. *Tourism Management* 17 (2), 133–9.

Koh, K.Y. (2000) Understanding community tourism entrepreneurism. In G. Richard and D. Hall (eds) *Tourism and Sustainable Community Development* (pp. 205–17). London: Routledge.

Koh, K.Y. and Combs, C.S. (2000) The tourism entrepreneurial process: A qualitative study. In *Lights, Camera, Action: Spotlight on Tourism in the New Millennium* (pp. 164–72). 31st Annual Conference Proceedings of the Travel and Tourism Research Association, San Fernando Valley, California, June.

Korca, P. (1996) Resident attitudes toward tourism impacts. *Annals of Tourism Research* 23 (3), 695–726.

Kotler, P. (1997) *Marketing Management* (9th edn). Upper Saddle River, NJ: Prentice-Hall.

Kotler, P. (2001) *Kotler on Marketing: How to Create, Win and Dominate Markets*. London: Simon & Schuster.

Kotler, P. and Armstrong, G. (1989) *Principles of Marketing* (4th edn). Englewood Cliffs, NJ: Prentice-Hall.

Kotler, P., Fennell, O.C. and Lamb, C. (1987) *Strategic Marketing for Non-profit Organisations* (3rd edn). Englewood Cliffs, NJ: Prentice-Hall.

Kotler, P., Haider, D.H. and Rein, I. (1993) *Marketing Places*. New York: Free Press.

Kotter, J.P. (1990) What leaders really do. *Harvard Business Review on Leadership* (pp. 37–60). Boston, MA: Harvard Business Review Press.

Krippendorf, J. (1982) Towards new tourism policies. *Tourism Management* 3, 135–48.

Krippendorf, J. (1987) *The Holiday Makers*. London: Heinemann.

Kuratko, D.F. and Hodgetts, R.M. (1995) *Entrepreneurship: A Contemporary Approach* (3rd edn). Fort Worth, TX: Dryden Press.

Kuratko, D.F. and Hodgetts, R.M. (1998) *Entrepreneurship: A Contemporary Approach* (4th edn). Fort Worth, TX: Dryden Press.

Land Use Coordination Office (LUCO) (2001) About LUCO: Background. http://www.luco.gov.bc.ca/lucoinfo

La Page, W.F. (1994) Using panels for travel and tourism research. In B. Ritchie and C.R. Goeldner (eds) *Travel, Tourism, and Hospitality Research: A Handbook for Managers and Researchers* (2nd edn) (pp. 481–92). Toronto: John Wiley.

Langdon, P. (December, 2001) The long road to rebuilding Lower Manhattan. *Planning – American Planning Association* 67 (12), 12–15.

Langlois, T. (1979) The practice of local government planning. In American Planning Association (APA) (1999) *Study Guide for the Comprehensive AICP Exam* (pp. 132–9). Memphis, TN: University of Memphis.

Lankford, S.V. (1994) Attitudes and perceptions toward tourism and rural regional development. *Journal of Travel Research* 32 (3), 35–43.

Lankford, S.V. and Howard, D.R. (1994) Developing a tourism impact scale. *Annals of Tourism Research* 21 (1), 121–39.

Lawrence, T.B., Wickens, D. and Phillips, N. (1997) Managing legitimacy in ecotourism. *Tourism Management* 18 (5), 307–16.

Laws, E. and Le Pelley, B. (2000) Managing complexity and change in tourism: The case of a historic city. *International Journal of Tourism Research* 2 (4), 229–46.

Laycock, G. (1991) 'Good times' are killing the Keys. *Audubon*. Sept/Oct, 38–49.

Le Blanc, G. (1992) Factors affecting customer evaluations of service quality in travel agencies: An investigation of customer perceptions. *Journal of Travel Research* 30 (4), 11–16.

Leeworthy, V.R. and Wiley P.C. (1996) Visitor profiles: Florida Keys. Key West: Consulting Report.

Legislative Committee on Intergovernmental Relations, Florida Legislature, February 2001. Overview of Municipal Incorporations in Florida, Tallahassee, FL.

Leheny, D. (1995) A political economy of Asian sex tourism. *Annals of Tourism Research* 22 (2), 367–84.

Leiper, N. (1979) The framework of tourism: towards a definition of tourism and the tourist industry. *Annals of Tourism Research* 6 (4), 380–407.

Leithwood, K., Jantzi, D. and Steinbach, R. (1999) *Changing Leadership for Changing Times*. Buckingham/Philadelphia: Open University Press.

Lennon, J.J. (2001) Towards a better understanding of visitor attractions in Scotland: The case of the Scottish Visitor Attraction Monitor. In J.J. Lennon (ed.) _Tourism Statistics: International Perspectives and Current Issues_ (pp. 142–59). London: Continuum.

Levi-Strauss, C. (1969) _The Elementary Structures of Kinship_. Boston: Beacon Press.

Levine, S. and White, P.E. (1961) Exchange as a conceptual framework for the study of interorganizational relations. _Administrative Science Quarterly_ 5, 583–601.

Lewicki, R. and Litterer, J. (1985) _Negotiation_. Homewood, IL: Richard D. Irwin, Inc.

Lewis, J.B. (1998) A rural tourism development model. _Tourism Analysis_ 2, 91–105.

Lewis, M. (2000) The soul of St. Louis. The community's gathering place. Our regional backyard. _Planning_ (American Planning Association). April, 10–11.

Lindberg, K. and Johnson, R.L. (1997) Modeling resident attitudes towards tourism. _Annals of Tourism Research_ 24 (2), 402–24.

Lindberg, K., McCool, S. and Stankey, G. (1997) Rethinking carrying capacity. _Annals of Tourism Research_ 24 (2), 461–65.

Little, R.L. and Krannich, R.D. (1982) Organizing for local control in rapid growth communities. In B.A. Weber and R.E. Howell (eds) _Coping with Rapid Growth in Rural Communities_ (pp. 73–81). Boulder, CO: Westview Press.

Logan, J. and Molotch, H.L. (1987) _Urban Fortunes: The Political Economy of Place_. Berkley: University of California Press.

Loftman, P. and Nevin, B. (1998) Pro-growth local economic development strategies: Civic promotion and local needs in Britain's second city. In T. Hall and P. Hubbard (eds) _The Entrepreneurial City: Geographies of Politics, Regime and Representation_ (pp. 129–48). Chichester, UK: John Wiley.

Longenecker, J.G., Moore, C.W. and Petty, J.W. (1994) _Small Business Management: An Entrepreneurial Emphasis_ (9th edn). Cincinnati, OH: South Western Publishing.

Loomis, L. and Graefe, A.R. (1992) Overview of NPCA's visitor impact management process. Paper presented at the IVth World Congress on Parks and Protected Areas, Caracas, Venezuela.

Love, J.F. (1995) _McDonald's: Behind the Arches_. New York: Bantam Books.

Lovelock, C.H. (1992) The search for synergy: What marketers need to know about service operations. In C.H. Lovelock (ed.) _Managing Services_ (2nd edn) (pp. 392–408). Englewood Cliffs, NJ: Prentice Hall.

Lucero, L. and Soule, J. (2002) A win for Lake Tahoe: The Supreme Court validates moratoriums in a path-breaking decision. _Planning – American Planning Association_ 68 (6), 4–7.

Luehrman, T.A. (1998) Strategy as a portfolio of real options. _Harvard Business Review_ 76 (5), 89–99.

Lundgren, J.O. (1972) The development of tourist travel systems – a metropolitan economic hegemony par excellence. _Jarbuch für Fredenverkehr_, 20, 86–120.

Lundgren, J.O. (1973) Agricultural marketing and distribution arrangements with respect to the resort hotel in the Caribbean. In _Proceedings of the Sixth West Indian Agricultural Economics Conference_, University of the West Indies.

Lundtorp, S. and Wanhill, S. (2001) The resort lifecycle theory: Generating processes and estimation. _Annals of Tourism Research_ 28 (4), 947–64.

Lynn, F.M. and Kartez, J.D. (1995) The redemption of citizen advisory committees: A perspective from critical theory. In O. Renn, T. Webler and P. Wiedemann (eds) _Fairness and Competence in Citizen Participation: Evaluating Models for Environmental Discourse_ (pp. 87–101). The Netherlands: Kluwer Academic Press.

MacArthur, B. (1999) _Twentieth Century Protest_. London: Penguin Books.

MacCannell, D. (1973) Staged authenticity: arrangements of social space in tourist settings. *American Journal of Sociology* 79, 583–603.

MacEochaidh, G. (1994) Tourism development at the community level in disadvantaged areas. In U. Kockel (ed.) *Travel, Culture, Tourism and Development: The Case of Ireland* (pp. 183–8). Liverpool: Liverpool University Press.

MacIntyre, D. (2000) This is only the beginning of the tourism revolution. *THESCOTSMAN.CO.UK..*scotsman.com. Accessed on 12 January 2000.

McBoyle, G. (1996) Green tourism and Scottish distilleries. *Tourism Management* 17 (4), 255–63.

McCarthy, E.J. and Perreault, W.D. (1984) *Basic Marketing* (8th edn). Homewood, IL: Irwin.

McDonnell, I., Allen, J. and O'Toole, W. (1999) *Festival and Special Event Management.* Milton, Queensland: Jacaranda Wiley.

McGibbon, J. (2000) *The Business of Alpine Tourism in a Globalising World* (p. 203). Rosenheim, Germany: Vetterling Druick.

McGinnes, J. (2001) Eden asks visitors to choose their days as popularity soars. *Western Morning News*, 28 July, 4.

McGinnes, S. (2000) Symphony spectacle. *Times Colonist.* Victoria, British Columbia, 8 August: A1–2.

McIntyre, G. (1993) *Sustainable Tourism Development: Guide for Local Planners.* Madrid: World Tourism Organization.

Madrigal, R. (1995) Residents' perceptions and the role of government. *Annals of Tourism Research* 22 (1), 86–102.

Mann, M. (2000) *The Community Tourism Guide: Exciting Holidays for Responsible Travellers.* London: Earthscan Publications Ltd.

Mazanec, J.A. (ed.) (1997) *International City Tourism.* London: Pinter.

Martin, B., McGuire, F. and Allen, L. (1998) Retirees' attitudes towards tourism: Implications for sustainable development. *Tourism Analysis* 3, 43–51.

Masberg, B. (1998) Defining the tourist: Is it possible? A view from the convention and visitors bureau. *Journal of Travel Research* 37 (1), 67–70.

Mason, P. and Cheyne, J. (2000) Residents' attitudes to proposed tourism development. *Annals of Tourism Research* 27 (2), 391–411.

Masten, S. (2000) *Testimony on S. 2899 and H.R. 4909 Native Hawaiian Recognition Before the Senate Committee on Indian Affairs and House Committee on Resources.* www.ncai.org/main/pages/issu . . . sues/documents/presmastestS2889.htm: Accessed on 30 August 2000.

Masters, J., Buris, T., Hollon, S. and Rimm, D. (1987) *Behavior Therapy: Techniques and Empirical Findings* (3rd edn). Toronto: Harcourt Brace Jovanovich College Publishers.

Mathieson, A. and Wall, G. (1982) *Tourism Economic, Physical and Social Impacts.* London: Longman.

Mayo, E.J. and Jarvis, L.P. (1981) *The Psychology of Leisure Travel.* Boston, MA: CBI.

Meade II, W.K. and Nason, R.W. (1991) Toward a unified theory of macromarketing: A systems theoretic approach. *Journal of Macromarketing* Fall, 72–82.

Mei, A., Dean, A. and Whit, C. (1999) Analysing service quality in the hospitality industry. *Managing Service Quality* 9 (2), 136–43.

Meis, S. (2001) Towards comparative studies in tourism satellite accounts. In J.J. Lennon (ed.) *Tourism Statistics* (pp. 14–23). London: Continuum.

Meisch, L. (1995) Gringas and Otavalenos: changing tourist relations. *Annals of Tourism Research* 22 (2), 441–62.

Metelka, C.J. (1977) Tourism and development: With friends like these who needs enemies? Paper presented at the Fifth Pacific Regional Science Conference, Vancouver, August.

Michael, E. and Plowman, G. (2002) Mount Stirling: The politics of process failure. *Journal of Sustainable Tourism* 10 (2),154–69.

Michaud, J.L. *et al.* (1991) Tourisme qualitatif – ses conditions et ses chances futures sur le plan economique, social et ecologique. *Tourisme Qualitatif*, AIEST Publication, 33, 63–78.

Middleton, V.T.C. (1988) *Marketing in Travel and Tourism.* Oxford: Butterworth-Heinemann.

Midwest Treaty Network (1997) *Midwest Treaty Network Calls for Governor to Drop Gaming Threat.* December. www.alphacdc.com/treaty/gaming.html Accessed on 30 August 2000.

Miles, R.E. and Snow, C.C. (1978) *Organizational Strategy, Structure, and Process.* New York: McGraw-Hill.

Mill, R.C. and Morrison, A.M. (1992) *The Tourism System: An Introductory Text* (2nd edn). Englewood Cliffs, NJ: Prentice-Hall.

Miller Consulting, Inc. (2001) Florida Keys Hurricane Evacuation Study: Final Report. Contract No. C7391. Tallahassee, FL: Florida Department of Transportation.

Miller, P. (1998) Email from Paul Miller to Peter Murphy, 9/9/98.

Milman, A. and Pizam, A. (1988) Social impacts of tourism on Central Florida. *Annals of Tourism Research* 15 (2), 191–204.

Ministry of Tourism (1992) *A Vision for Tourism.* Victoria, British Columbia: Ministry of Tourism.

Minnesota Indian Gaming Association (MIGA) (2002) *The Principle of Indian Sovereignty.* www.minnesotagaming.com/migasix.html.: Accessed on 12 December 2002.

Mintzberg, H. (1979) *The Structuring of Organizations.* Englewood Cliffs, NJ: Prentice-Hall.

Mitchell, R.E. (1997) Entrepreneurship and economic security: Enemies or allies. Unpublished paper. Faculty of Business, University of Victoria, Canada.

Mitchell, R.E. and Reid, D.G. (2001) Community integration: island tourism in Peru. *Annals of Tourism Research* 28 (1), 113–39.

Moeller, G.H. and Shafer, E.L. (1994) The Delphi technique: A tool for long-range travel and tourism planning. In B. Ritchie and C.R. Goeldner (eds) *Travel, Tourism, and Hospitality Research: A Handbook for Managers and Researchers* (2nd edn) (pp. 473–80). Toronto: John Wiley.

Molotch, H.L. (1976) The city as a growth machine: toward a political economy of place. *American Journal of Sociology* 82 (2), 309–22.

Monroe County Growth Management Division (1992) Monroe County Year 2010 Comprehensive Plan. Marathon, FL: Monroe County.

Monroe County Growth Management Division (1992) Ordinance No. 16 – 1992 – Rate of Growth Ordinance. Marathon, FL: Monroe County.

Monroe County Growth Management Division (1998–2002). Monroe County Public Facilities Capacity Assessments. Marathon, FL: Monroe County.

Monroe County, Florida (1999) *1999 Annual Report.* Key West, FL: Office of Management and Budget Staff.

Monroe County Growth Management Division (1999) Liveable Community Keys Work Program: An Initiative of the Monroe County Planning Department. Marathon, FL: Monroe County.

Monroe County Board of County Commissioners (MCBOCC) (2002) *Fiscal Year 2002 Adopted Annual Operating and Capital Budget*. Key West, FL: Office of Management and Budget Staff.

Monroe County. Monroe County Code of Ordinances. Chapter 9.5 Land Development Regulations.

Montgomery, B. (1986) *Working Together: A Practical Guide to Collaborative Decision Making*. Melbourne: Nelson.

Moore, K. (1992) Greening corporate strategy – extending the firm's value chain. Paper presented at the Administrative Sciences Association of Canada, Quebec City.

Morgan, N. and Pritchard, A. (1998) *Tourism Promotion and Power: Creating Images, Creating Identities*. Chichester, NY: Wiley.

Mormont, M. (1987) Tourism and rural change: the symbolic impact. In M. Bouquet and M. Winter (eds) *Who from their Labours Rest? Conflict and Practice in Rural Tourism* (pp. 35–43). Aldershot: Avebury.

Morrison, A.M. (1989) *Hospitality and Travel Marketing*. Albany, NY: Delmar.

Morrison, A.M., Braunlich, C.G., Kamaruddin, N. and Cai, L.A. (1995) National tourist offices in North America: An analysis. *Tourism Management* 16 (8), 605–17.

Morrison, A.M., Bruen, S.M. and Anderson, D.J. (1998) Convention and visitor bureaus in the U.S.A.: A profile of bureaus, bureau executives, and budgets. *Journal of Travel and Tourism Marketing* 7 (1), 1–19.

Morrison, A., Rimmington, M. and Williams, C. (1999) *Entrepreneurship in the Hospitality, Tourism and Leisure Industries*. Oxford: Butterworth-Heinemann.

Moser, P. and Moser, W. (1986) Reflections on the MAB–6 Obergurgl project and tourism in an alpine environment. *Mountain Research and Development* 6 (2), 101–18.

Moser, W. and Peterson, J. (1981) Limits to Obergurgl's growth. *Ambio*, 10 (2–3): 68–72).

Moscovici, S. (1984) The phenomenon of social representations. In R.M. Farr and S. Moscovici (eds) *Social Representations* (pp. 3–69). Cambridge: University of Cambridge Press.

Moutinho. L. (1999) Segmentation, targeting, positioning and strategic marketing. In L. Moutinho (ed.) *Strategic Management in Tourism* (pp. 121–66). Wallingford, Oxon: CABI Publishing.

Murphy, A.E. (2003) Illustrating the utility of a modified gap analysis as a regional tourism planning tool: Case study of potential Japanese and German travellers to the Cowichan Region. *Journal of Travel Research* 41 (4), 400–9.

Murphy, A.E. and Williams, P.W. (1999) Attracting Japanese tourists into the rural hinterland: implications for rural development and planning. *Tourism Management* 20, 487–99.

Murphy, P.E. (1980a) Tourism management in host communities. *The Canadian Geographer* 24 (1), 1–2.

Murphy, P.E. (1980b) Tourism management using land use planning and landscape design: the Victoria experience. *The Canadian Geographer* 24 (1), 60–71.

Murphy, P.E. (1982) Tourism planning in London: An exercise in spatial and seasonal management. *The Tourist Review* 1, 19–23.

Murphy, P.E. (1983a) Perceptions and attitudes of decision-making groups in tourism centers. *Journal of Travel Research* 21 (3), 8–12.

Murphy, P.E. (1983b) Tourism as a community industry – an ecological model of tourism. *Tourism Management* 4 (3), 180–93.

Murphy, P.E. (1985) *Tourism: A Community Approach*. London: Methuen.

Murphy, P.E. (1988) Community driven tourism planning. *Tourism Management* 9 (2) 96–104.

Murphy, P.E. (1991a) Community partnerships: The need for mutual education. In R.D. Bratton, F.M. Go and J.R.B. Ritchie (eds) *New Horizons in Tourism and Hospitality Education, Training and Research* (pp. 7–16). Conference Proceedings, Calgary, Alberta: University of Calgary.

Murphy, P.E. (1991b) Getting the most from hallmark events. In P.E. Murphy (ed.) *Tourism Research: Meeting the Needs of Industry* (pp. 85–90). Annual Conference Proceedings of the Travel and Tourism Research Association (Canada), Victoria, BC, Canada.

Murphy, P.E. (1997) Attraction land use management in Disney theme parks. In P.E. Murphy (ed.) *Quality Management in Urban Tourism* (pp. 221–33). Chichester: John Wiley.

Murphy, P.E. and Andressen, B. (1988) Tourism development on Vancouver Island. *Professional Geographer* 40 (1), 32–42.

Murphy, P.E. and Bayley, R. (1989) Tourism and disaster planning. *Geographical Review* 79 (1), 34–42.

Murphy, P.E. and Pritchard, M. (1997) Destination price-value perceptions: An examination of origin and seasonal influences. *Journal of Travel Research* 35 (3), 16–22.

Murphy, P.E., Pritchard, M. and Smith, B. (2000) The destination product and its impact on traveller perceptions. *Tourism Management* 21 (1), 43–52.

Murphy, P.E., Andressen, B., Duffus, D., Hays, W., Newcomb, J., Nowell, D. and Searle, R. (1985) Geographers as assistants in a community decision-making process. *The Operational Geographer* 8, 55–7.

Mutch, A. (1996) The English tourist network automation project: A case study in interorganizational system failure. *Tourism Management* 17 (8), 603–9.

Nagel, T. (1987) *The Strategy and Tactics of Pricing*. Englewood Cliffs: Prentice-Hall.

Naisbitt, J. (1984) *Megatrends: Ten New Directions Transforming our Lives*. New York: Warner Books.

National Academy of Sciences, Oceans Study Board, Water Science and Technology Board, Division on Earth and Life Studies (2002). A Review of the Florida Keys Carrying Capacity Study. Washington, DC: National Academy Press.

National Native Title Tribunal (2003) Home Page. *NNTT. www.nntt.gov.au/* Accessed on 29 January 2003.

National Office for the Information Economy (2000) *Take the Plunge 2000: Sink or Swim?* Canberra, Australia: National Office for the Information Economy.

National Task Force on Tourism Data (1985) *Final Joint Report of the Working Groups on User Needs and Current Data Issues*. Ottawa: Statistics Canada.

Netter, E. (ed.) (1981) Land use law issues for the eighties. *Land Use Law and Zoning Digest*. Washington, DC: Planners Press, American Planning Association.

New Oregon Meridian (2001) *We Have Met the Enemy and he is us*. www. planneronline.homestead.com/files/pororeport.htm. Accessed on 5 December 2001.

Newsweek (1986) The fall of the wild. *Newsweek* 28 July, 52–4.

Newsweek (1988) Fighting for Yellowstone. *Newsweek*, 19 September, 18–20.

Newsweek (1994) Of mice and men. *Newsweek*, 5 September, 41–7.

Nickson, D. (2000) Human resource issues in travel and tourism. In Moutinho, L. (ed). *Strategic Management in Tourism* (pp. 169–85). Wallingford, Oxon: CABI Publishing.

Normann, R. (1991) *Service Management*. Chichester: John Wiley.

Normann, R. and Ramirez, R. (1993) From value chain to value constellation: designing interactive strategy. *Harvard Business Review* 71, 65–77.

Nozick, M. (1993) Five principles of sustainable community development. In E. Shragge (ed.) *Community Economic Development: In Search of Empowerment and Alternatives* (pp. 18–43). Montreal: Black Rose Books.

Oakes, T.S. (1997) Ethnic tourism in rural Guizhou: Sense of place and the commerce of authenticity. In M. Picard and R.E. Wood (eds) *Tourism, Ethnicity, and the State in Asian and Pacific Societies* (pp. 35–70). Honolulu: University of Hawaii Press.

O'Connor, N. and Flanagan, S. (2002) The sociological impacts of *Ballykissangel* on the village of Avoca, County Wicklow. In N. Andrews, F. Convery, S. Flanagan and J. Ruddy (eds) *Tourism and the Environment: Sustainability in Tourism Development* (pp. 255–65). Dublin: Dublin Institute of Technology.

Odum, E.P. (1970) The strategy of ecosystem development, *Science* 164, 262–70.

One Thousand Friends of Florida (2002) Building better communities. *1000 Friends of Florida.* http://www.1000fof.org/. Accessed on 18 December 2002.

Open Group (2002) Conduct a gap analysis. *Open Group.* http://www.opengroup.org/togaf/p2/ta/ta_gapan.htm. Accessed on 19 December 2002.

Oppermann, M. (1995) Holidays on the farm: A case study of German hosts and guests. *Journal of Travel Research* 34 (1), 63–72.

Organ, D.W. (1988) *Organizational Citizenship Behavior: The Good Soldier Syndrome.* Lexington, MA: Lexington Books.

O'Neill, T. (2002) Saving places. *National Geographic* 202 (4), 58–73.

O'Toole, T. with Tarling, L. (2000) *Bread Winner: A Fresh Approach to Rising to the Top.* Melbourne, Victoria: Information Australia.

Page, S.J., Farer, P. and Lawton, G.R. (1999) Small business development and tourism: *terra incognita? Tourism Management* 20 (4), 435–59.

Palmer, A. (1998) Evaluating the governance style of marketing groups. *Annals of Tourism Research* 25 (1) 185–201.

Palmer, A. and Bejou, D. (1995) Tourism destination marketing alliances. *Annals of Tourism Research* 22 (3), 616–29.

Parasuraman, A., Zeithaml, V.A. and Berry, L.L. (1985) A conceptual model of service quality and implications for future research. *Journal of Marketing* 49 (Fall), 41–50.

Parasuraman, A., Zeithaml, V.A. and Berry, L.L. (1988) SERVQUAL: A multiple item scale for measuring consumer perceptions of service quality. *Journal of Retailing* 64 (1),12–40.

Parasuraman, A., Zeithaml, V.A. and Berry, L.L. (1990) *Delivering Quality Service.* New York: Free Press.

Parasuraman, A., Zeithaml, V.A. and Berry, L.L. (1991) Refinement and reassessment of the SERVQUAL scale. *Journal of Retailing* 67 (4), 420–50.

Parker, S. (2000) Collaboration on tourism policy making: Environmental and commercial sustainability on Bonarie, NA. In B. Bramwell and B. Lane (eds) *Tourism Collaboration and Partnerships: Politics, Practice and Sustainability* (pp. 78–97). Clevedon, UK: Channel View Publications.

Patterson, L. (2003) State planning authority stumbles at first hurdle. *Echo* (Byron Shire). Thursday, 14 January, 17 (33), 1–2.

Pearce, D. (1989) *Tourist Development* (2nd edn). Harlow, UK: Longman.

Pearce, D. (1992) *Tourist Organizations.* Harlow, UK: Longman.

Pearce, P.L. (1982) *The Social Psychology of Tourist Behaviour.* Oxford: Pergamon.

Pearce, P.L. and Stringer, P.F. (1991) Psychology and tourism. *Annals of Tourism Research* 18 (1), 136–54.

Pearce, P.L., Moscardo, G. and Ross, G.F. (1996) *Tourism Community Relationships*. Oxford: Pergamon – Elsevier Science.

Pearce, P.L., Morrison, A.M. and Rutledge, J.L. (1998) *Tourism: Bridges Across Continents*. Sydney: McGraw-Hill.

Pearce, P.L. and Moscardo, G. (1999) Tourism community analysis: asking the right questions. In D.G. Pearce and R.W. Butler (eds) *Contemporary Issues in Tourism Development* (pp. 31–51). London and New York: Routledge.

Pedersen, K. and Viken, A. (1996) From Sami nomadism to global tourism. In M.F. Price (ed.) *People and Tourism in Fragile Environments* (pp. 69–88). Chichester, UK: John Wiley.

Perdue, R., Long, P. and Allen, L. (1987) Rural resident tourism perceptions and attitudes. *Annals of Tourism Research* 14 (3), 420–9.

Perdue, R., Long, P. and Allen, L. (1990) Resident support for tourism development. *Annals of Tourism Research* 17 (4), 586–99.

Peters, T.J. and Austin, N. (1985) *A Passion for Excellence*. New York: Random House.

Peters, T.J. and Waterman, R.H. (1984). *In Search of Excellence*. New York: Warner Books.

Peterson, D. (2002) *Florida Keys Carrying Capacity Study*. Department of the Army, Jacksonville District, 6 September 2002. Personal communication.

Phillips, P.A. and Moutinho, L. (2000) The strategic planning index: a tool for measuring strategic planning effectiveness. *Journal of Travel Research* 38 (4), 369–79.

Pine II, J.B. and Gilmore, J.H. (1999) *The Experience Economy*. Boston: MA: Harvard Business School Press.

Pizam, A., Tarlow, P.E. and Bloom, J. (1997) Making tourists feel safe: whose responsibility is it? *Journal of Travel Research* 36 (1), 23–8.

Plog, S.C. (1973) Why destination areas rise and fall in popularity. *Cornell Hotel and Restaurant Administration Quarterly*, November, 13–16.

Plog, S.C. (1998) Why destination preservation makes economic sense. In W.F. Theobald (ed.) *Global Tourism* (2nd edn) (pp. 251–66). Oxford: Butterworth-Heinemann.

Poon, A. (1993) *Tourism, Technology and Competitive Strategies*. Wallingford, Oxon: CAB International.

Porteous, J.D. (1973) The Burnside gang: territoriality, social space, and community planning. In C.N. Forward (ed.) *Residential and Neighbourhood Studies in Victoria* (pp. 130–48). Western Geographical Series, Vol. 5. Victoria, BC: University of Victoria.

Porter, M.E. (1980) *Competitive Strategy*. New York: Free Press.

Porter, M.E. (1990) *The Competitive Advantage of Nations*, New York: Free Press.

Porter, M.E. (1998) *On Competition*. Cambridge, MA: Harvard University Press.

Potts, F.C., Goodwin, H. and Walpole, M.J. (1996) People, wildlife and tourism in and around Hwange National Park, Zimbabwe. In M.F. Price (ed.) *People and Tourism in Fragile Environments* (pp. 199–220). Chichester, UK: John Wiley.

Potts, T.D. and Harrill, R. (1998) Enhancing communities for sustainability: A travel ecology approach. *Tourism Analysis* 3, 133–42.

Prentice, R. (1993) Community-driven tourism planning and residents' preferences. *Tourism Management* 14 (3), 218–27.

Price, G.C. (2003) Ecotourism and environmental learning: Opportunities and obstacles in the Australian milieu. Paper presented at Annual Council of Australian University Tourism and Hospitality Education (CAUTHE) Conference, Coffs Harbour, NSW, Australia.

Pritchard, M. and Swanson, W. (1993) *B.C. Tourism: 1993 Advertising Effectiveness Study*. Victoria, BC: Faculty of Business, University of Victoria.

Public Roads On-Line (Summer 1996) *Creating the Interstate System.* www.tfhrc. gov/pubrds/summer96/p96su10.htm. Accessed on 3 June 2001.

Putnam, R.D. (1993) *Making Democracy Work: Civic Traditions in Modern Italy*, Princeton, NJ: Princeton University Press.

Putnam, R.D. (2000) *Bowling Alone: The Collapse and Revival of American Community.* New York: Simon & Schuster.

Queen Charlotte Islands Information (2002) Welcome to the Queen Charlotte Islands/Haida Gwaii. *General Island Information.* www.qcinfo.com. Accessed on 1 January 2002.

Raiffa, H. (1982) *The Art and Science of Negotiation.* Cambridge, MA: Harvard University Press.

Randhawa, H. (1990) Out of the ashes: Rediscovering Yellowstone National Park. *Westworld*, September: 7–8.

Reed, M.G. (1996) Co-operative management of environmental resources: A case study from Northern Ontario, Canada. *Economic Geography*, 71, 132–49.

Reed, M.G. (1997) Power relations and community-based tourism planning. *Annals of Tourism Research* 24 (3), 556–91.

Reed, M.G. (2000) Collaborative tourism planning an adaptive experiment in emergent tourism settings, In B. Bramwell and B. Lane (eds) *Tourism Collaboration and Partnerships: Politics, Practice and Sustainability* (pp. 247–71). Clevedon, UK: Channel View Publications.

Richardson, J.T. (1996) *Marketing Australian Travel and Tourism*, Melbourne: Hospitality Press.

Richardson, J.L. (1997) Economics: Hegemonic Discourse, *Quadrant*, March, 52–60.

Richardson, J.L. (1999) *A History of Australian Travel and Tourism*. Melbourne: Hospitality Press.

Richins, H. (1997/98) Community tourism development scenarios and their use in tourism research. *Asia Pacific Journal of Tourism Research* 2 (1), 31–42.

Riley, M. (1995) Tourism development under close control: The case of the Falkland Islands. *Tourism Management* 16 (6), 471–74.

Ritchie, J.R.B. (1988) Consensus policy formation in tourism. Measuring resident views via survey research. *Tourism Management* 9, 199–212.

Ritchie, J.R.B. (1994) The nominal group technique – applications in tourism research. In J.R.B. Ritchie and C.R. Goeldner (eds) *Travel, Tourism, and Hospitality Research* (2nd edn) (pp. 493–501). New York: John Wiley.

Ritchie, J.R.B. (1999) Crafting a value-driven vision for a national tourism treasure. *Tourism Management* 20 (3), 273–82.

Ritchie, J.R.B. (2000) Interest based formulation of tourism policy for environmentally sensitive destinations. In B. Bramwell and B. Lane (eds) *Tourism Collaboration and Partnerships: Politics, Practice and Sustainability* (pp. 44–77). Clevedon, UK: Channel View Publications.

Ritchie, M. (2001) An assessment of the role and effectiveness of local government in tourism destination development: Case study of Nillumbik. Unpublished MA thesis. La Trobe University, Melbourne, Australia.

Robson, J. and Robson, I. (1996) From shareholders to stakeholders: Critical issues for tourism marketers. *Tourism Management* 17 (7), 533–40.

Rock, A. (1999) Strategy vs. tactics from a venture capitalist. In the *Harvard Business Review on Entrepreneurship*. Boston, MA: Harvard Business School Press, 135–47.

Roddick, A. (2000) *Business as Unusual.* London: Thorsons.

Roehl, W.S., Ditton, R.B. and Fesenmaier, D.R. (1989) Community-tourism ties. *Annals of Tourism Research* 16 (4), 504–13.

Rogers, M. (2001) Triple bottom line audit: A framework for community based action. In M.F. Rogers and Y.M.J. Collins (eds) *The Future of Australia's Country Towns* (pp. 135–45). Centre for Sustainable Regional Communities, La Trobe University, Bendigo, Victoria, Australia.

Rosenow, J.E. and Pulsipher, G.L. (1979) *Tourism: The Good, The Bad, and The Ugly.* Lincoln, NE: Century Three Press.

Ross, G.F. (1993) Ideal and actual images of backpacker visitors in northern Australia. *Journal of Travel Research.* Fall, 32 (2), 54–7.

Ross, G.F. (1994) *The Psychology of Tourism.* Melbourne: Hospitality Press.

Rothman, H.K. (1998) *Devil's Bargains.* Lawrence, KS: University Press of Kansas.

Runyan, D. (1977) Tools for community managed impact assessment. *AIP Journal – American Institute of Planners* 43 (2), 125–35.

Russell, R. and Faulkner, B. (1999) Movers and shakers: chaos makers in tourism development. *Tourism Management* 20 (4), 411–23.

Ryan, C. and Montgomery D. (1994) The attitudes of Bakewell residents to tourism and numbers in community responsive tourism. *Tourism Management* 15 (5), 358–69.

Sakal, M., Brown, J. and Mak, J. (2000) Population aging and Japanese international travel in the 21st century. *Journal of Travel Research* 38 (3), 212–30.

Saunders, R. (1995) *Conflict Resolution through Environmental Impact Assessment.* International Association of Impact Assessment Conference, Durban, South Africa. A version of this paper was also presented to the Environmental Defender's Office Conference on Commonwealth EIA in Sydney, October 1995, and was reprinted in 'Significant Environmental Speeches' Summer 1995/96.

Saunders, R. and Stephens, A. (1998). *Mount Stirling: political and environmental convergence for sustainable development.* Conference Paper, University of Manchester, October 1998 (subsequently reprinted with some editing in *Environmental Impact Assessment Review* 19 (3), 319–32.

Saporito, B. (2003) Can Wal-Mart get any bigger? *Time International,* 13 January 40–5.

Scace, R.C., Grifone, E. and Usher, R. (1992) *Ecotourism in Canada.* Canadian Environmental Advisory Council. Ottawa: Environment Canada.

Schein, E. (1992) *Organisational Culture and Leadership* (2nd edn). San Francisco: Jossey-Bass.

Schermerhorn, Jr, J.R., Hunt, J.G. and Osborn, R.N. (1995) *Basic Organizational Behavior.* New York: John Wiley.

Schonland, A. and Williams, P.W. (1996) Using the internet for travel and tourism survey research: experiences from the net traveller survey. *Journal of Travel Research* 35 (2), 81–7.

Schul, P. and Crompton, J.L. (1983) Search behaviour of international vacationers: travel-specific lifestyles and sociodemographic variables. *Journal of Travel Research* 22 (2), 25–30.

Schumpeter, J. (1934) *The Theory of Economic Development.* Cambridge, MA: Harvard University Press.

Schumpeter, J.A. (1951) Change and the entrepreneur. In R.V. Clemence (ed.) *Essays of J.A. Schumpeter.* Reading, MA: Addison-Wesley.

Schwilgin, F.A. (1973) *Town Planning Guidelines.* Ottawa: Department of Public Works.

Scottish Tourism Board (ND) *Tourism Framework for Action 2002–2005.* Scottish Executive.

Selin, S.W. (1993) Collaborative alliances: new interorganizational forms in tourism. *Journal of Travel and Tourism Marketing* 2 (2), 217–27.

Selin, S.W. and Beason, K. (1991a) Conditions facilitating collaborative tourism planning: a qualitative perspective. *Tourism: Building Credibility for a Credible Industry* (pp. 203–9). Proceedings of the Twenty Second Travel and Tourism Research Association, Long Beach, California.

Selin, S.W. and Beason, K. (1991b) Interorganizational relations in tourism. *Annals of Tourism Research* 18 (4), 639–52.

Selin, S.W. and Myers, N.A. (1998) Tourism marketing alliances: Member satisfaction and effectiveness attributes of a regional initiative. *Journal of Travel and Tourism Marketing* 7 (3), 79–94.

Service General Technical Report INT–176, Intermountain Forest and Range Experiment Station, Ogden, UT.

Shackelton, V. (1995) *Business Leadership*. London: Routledge.

Shapero, A. (1975) *Entrepreneurship and Economic Development*. Project ISEED, Ltd. Milwaukee, WI: Center for Venture Management.

Sharpley, R. and Sharpley, J. (1997) *Rural Tourism: An Introduction*. Oxford: Alden Press (International Thomson Business Press).

Shaw, G. and Williams, A.M. (1994) Tourism and entrepreneurship. In G. Shaw and A.M. Williams, *Critical Issues in Tourism: A Geographical Perspective* (pp. 120–37). Oxford: Blackwell.

Shaw, G. and Williams, A.M. (1994) *Critical Issues in Tourism: A Geographical Perspective*. Oxford: Blackwell.

Shaw, G. and Williams, A.M. (1997) The private sector: tourism entrepreneurship – a constraint or resource? In G. Shaw and A. Williams (eds) *The Rise and Fall of British Coastal Resorts: Cultural and Economic Perspectives*. London: Mansell.

Shaw, G. and Williams, A.M. (1998) Entrepreneurship, small business culture and tourism development. In D. Ioannides and K.G. Debbage (eds) *The Economic Geography of the Tourist Industry* (pp. 235–55). London: Routledge.

Sheldon, P.J. and Var, T. (1984) Resident attitudes to tourism in North Wales. *Tourism Management* 5 (1), 40–7.

Shivlani, M. (2000) *Monroe County's Registered Voters' Views on Tourism and Related Issues*. Marathon, FL: Growth Management Division, Monroe County.

Shostack, G.L. (1977) Breaking free for product marketing. *Journal of Marketing*, 41 (April), 73–8.

Simmons, D.G. (1994) Community participation in tourism planning. *Tourism Management* 15 (2), 98–108.

Smith, C. and Jenner, P. (1998) Tourism and the internet. *Travel and Tourism Analyst* 1, 62–81.

Smith, F.J. and Hester, R.T. (1982) *Community Goal Setting*. Stroudsburg, PA: Hutchinson Press.

Smith, S.L.J. (1995) *Tourism Analysis: A Handbook* (2nd edn). Harlow, Essex: Longman.

Smith, S.L.J. (2003a) A vision for the Canadian tourism industry. *Tourism Management* 24 (2), 123–34.

Smith, S.L.J. (2003b) The geographical structure of Canadian tourism. In J. Aramberri and R. Butler (eds) *Tourism Development: Issues for a Vulnerable Industry*. Clevedon, UK: Channel View Publications (forthcoming).

Smith, V.L. (ed.) (1989) *Hosts and Guests: The Anthropology of Tourism* (2nd edn). Philadelphia: University of Pennsylvania Press.

Smith, V.L. (1996) The Inuit as hosts: Heritage and wilderness tourism in Nunavut. In M.F. Price (ed.) *People and Tourism in Fragile Environments* (pp. 33–50). Chichester, UK: John Wiley.

Smith, V.L. and Brent, M. (eds) (2001) *Hosts and Guests Revisited: Tourism Issues of the 21st Century*. New York: Cognizant Communication Corp.

Spears, M.C. (1995) *Foodservice Organisations: A Managerial and Systems Approach* (3rd edn). Columbus, OH: Merrill.

Special Hilo/East Hawaii Tourism Group (1998) *Opportunities at Hand*. Hilo, HI: Office of the Governor.

Stahl, M.J. and Grigsby, D.W. (1992) *Strategic Management for Decision Making*. Boston: PWS-Kent.

Stankey, G.H., Cole, D.N., Lucas, R.C., Peterson, M.E., and Frissell, S.S. (1985) *The Limits of Acceptable Change (LAC) System for Wilderness Planning*. USDA Forest.

State of Alaska Division of Community and Economic Development (ND). *Alaska Community Tourism Handbook: How to Develop Tourism in Your Community*. Department of Community and Economic Development.

Stitt, A.J. (1998) *Alternative Dispute Resolution For Organizations: How to design a system for effective conflict resolution*. Toronto: John Wiley and Sons, Canada Ltd.

Stoner, J.A.F., Freeman, R.E. and Gilbert, Jr, D.R. (1995) *Management* (6th edn). Englewood Cliffs, NJ: Prentice-Hall.

Storey, D.J. (1994) *Understanding the Small Business Sector*. Routledge: London.

Strong, G. (2002) Struggling country towns use the toilet to make tourists spend a penny. *The Age* (Melbourne), 23 September, 6.

Suchman, M.C. (1994) Managing legitimacy: Strategic and institutional approaches. *Academy of Management Review* 20 (3), 571–610.

Sullivan, T. (1984) *Resolving Development Disputes Through Negotiation*. New York: Plenum Press.

Susskind, L. (2001) *Mediating Public Disputes Seminar*. RMIT University, Melbourne, Australia. Thursday, 15 March.

Susskind, L. and Cruikshank, J. (1987) *Breaking the Impasse: Consensual Approaches to Resolving Public Disputes*. New York: Basic Books.

Susskind, L. and Field, P. (1996) *Dealing with An Angry Public: The Mutual Gains Approach to Resolving Disputes*. New York: The Free Press.

Susskind, L., Amundsen, O., Matsuura, M., Kaplan, M. and Lampe, D. (1999) *Using Assisted Negotiation to Settle Land Use Disputes: A Guidebook for Public Officials Public Disputes*. Cambridge, MA: Lincoln Institute of Land Policy.

Susskind, L., McKearnan, S. and Thomas-Larmer, J. (1999) *The Consensus Building Handbook: A Comprehensive Guide to Reaching Agreement*. Thousand Oaks, CA: Sage Publications.

Suttles, G.D. (1970) *The Social Construction of Communities*. Chicago: University of Chicago Press.

Swarbrooke, J. (1999) *Sustainable Tourism Management*. New York: CABI Publishers.

Takeuchi, H. and Quelch, J. (1983) Quality is more than making a good product. *Harvard Business Review*, 61 (July-August), 139–45.

Tannenbaum, R., Weschler, L.R. and Massarik, F. (1961) *Leadership and Organization*. New York: McGraw-Hill.

Task Force on Regional Development (TFRD) (1993) *Developing Australia: A Regional Perspective*. Canberra: Australian Government Printing Office.

Taylor, G. (1995) The community approach: Does it really work? *Tourism Management* 16 (7), 487–9.

Taylor, G., Rogers, J. and Stanton, B. (1994) Bridging the research gap between industry and researchers. *Journal of Travel Research* 32 (4), 9–11.

Taylor, P. (1999) Business urged to get a connection as web turns out to be more than a fad. *The Financial Times*, 6 July, 14.

Teas, K. (1993) Expectations, performance evaluation and consumer perceptions of quality. *Journal of Marketing* 57 (4), 18–34.

Telfer, D.J. (2000) Tastes of Niagara: building strategic alliances between tourism and agriculture. *International Journal of Hospitality and Tourism Administration* 1 (1), 71–88.

Telfer, D.J. (2001) Strategic alliances along the Niagara Wine Route. *Tourism Management* 22 (1), 21–30.

The Age (2000) Reconciliation report urges treaty talks. *The Age* 7 December, 1.

The Economist (1988) National parks: Live and let die. *The Economist* 17 September, 34.

The Economist (1999) The Florida Keys: Death in the Afternoon. *The Economist* 11 September, 35–6.

The Economist (2000a) What price coral? *The Economist* 4–10 November, 103–6.

The Economist (2000b) Blackpool as Las Vegas. *The Economist* 26 August–1 September, 50.

The Economist (2000c) Tourism in South Africa: Image problem. *The Economist* 16–22 December, 75.

The Economist (2001a) Survey the Young: The kids are all right. *The Economist* 23–5 December, 4–6.

The Economist (2001b) Keeping the customer satisfied. *The Economist* 14 July, 9.

The Economist (2001c) A long march: Special report on mass customisation. *The Economist* 14 July, 63–5.

The Economist (2001d) Airlines: Flying blind. *The Economist* 13 October, 16–7.

The Economist (2001e) When Hawaii's loss is Tokyo's gain. *The Economist* 22 December, 79.

The Economist (2003a) Fear and management: When to terrorise the talent. *The Economist* 22 February, 59–60.

The Economist (2003b) SARS: A plague on all our businesses. *The Economist* 19 April, 51.

The Weekend Australian (2001) The green dream. *The Weekend Australian* August 18–19, R4-R5.

Thomas, R. (1998) Introduction. In R. Thomas (ed.) *The Management of Small Tourism and Hospitality Firms* (pp. 1–16). London: Cassell.

Thomas, R. (2000) Small firms in the tourism industry: Some conceptual issues. *International Journal of Tourism Research* 2 (5), 307–82.

Thompson, J.R. and Cooper, R.D. (1979) Additional evidence on the limited size of evoked and inept sets of travel destinations. *Journal of Travel Research* 18, 23–5.

Thompson, L. (2001) The long good buy: How to plan, fund, and complete a multijurisdictional recreation corridor. *Planning – American Planning Association* 67 (5), 4–9.

Thompson, W.N. (2003) History, development and legislation of Native American Casino Gaming. In C.H.C. Hsu (ed.) *Legalized Casino Gaming in the United States* (pp. 41–61). New York: Haworth Hospitality Press.

Tiegerman-Farber, E. and Radziewicz, C. (1998) *Collaborative Decision-making: The Pathway to Inclusion*. Upper Saddle River, NJ: Prentice-Hall.

Tierney, P. (2000) Internet based evaluation of tourism web site effectiveness: methodological issues and survey results. *Journal of Travel Research* 39 (2) 212–19.

Timmons, J. (1994) *New Venture Creation*. Boston, MA: Irwin.

Timothy, D.J. (1998) Cooperative tourism planning in a developing destination. *Journal of Sustainable Tourism* 6 (1), 52–68.

Timothy, D.J. (1999) Participatory planning: A view of tourism in Indonesia. *Annals of Tourism Research* 26 (2), 371–91.

Timothy, D.J. (2000) Cross-border partnership in tourism resource management: International parks along the U.S. Canada border. In B. Bramwell and B. Lane (eds) *Tourism Collaboration and Partnerships: Politics, Practice and Sustainability* (pp. 20–43). Clevedon, UK: Channel View Publications.

Tisdell, C.A. and Roy, K.C. (eds) (1998) *Tourism and Development: Economic, Social, Political and Environmental Issues.* Commack, New York: Nova Science Publishers.

Tonge, R. and Myott, D. (1993) *How to Plan, Develop and Market Local and Regional Tourism.* Coolum Beach, Queensland: Gull Publishing Pty Ltd.

Tosun, C. (2000) Limits to community participation in the tourism development process in developing countries. *Tourism Management* 21 (6), 613–33.

Tosun, C. and Jenkins, C.L. (1996) Regional planning approaches to tourism development: The case of Turkey. *Tourism Management* 17 (7), 519–31.

Tosun, C. and Jenkins, C.L. (1998) The evolution of tourism planning in third-world countries: A critique. *Progress in Tourism and Hospitality Research* 4, 101–14.

Tourism British Columbia (1995) *Towards a Tourism Growth Management Strategy.* Victoria, British Columbia: Ministry of Small Business, Tourism and Culture.

Tourism Concern (2000) *The Community Tourism Guide.* London: Earthscan.

Tourist Development Council (1999) *Approved Resident Survey.* Marathon, FL: Monroe County.

Tourism Forum (UK) ND. *Tomorrow's Tourism: A Growth Industry for the New Millennium.* Department for Culture, Media and Sport.

Tourism Queensland (2000) *Tourism Queensland 2000–2001 Annual Report.* Brisbane, Queensland: Tourism Queensland.

Tourism Tasmania (2002) Tourism Tasmania Board of Directors. *Tourism Tasmania Corporate.* http://www.tourismtasmania.com.au/org/board/index.html. Accessed on 18 December 2002.

Tourism Victoria (2002) *Victoria's Tourism Industry Strategic Plan, 2002–2006*, Melbourne, Australia: Tourism Victoria.

Tourism Victoria (1995) *Five Year Business Plan (1996–2000).* Victoria, British Columbia, Canada: Tourism Victoria.

Tribe, J. (1997) The indiscipline of tourism. *Annals of Tourism Research* 24 (3), 638–57.

Trist, E.L. (1977) Collaboration in work settings: A personal perspective. *The Journal of Applied Behavioral Sciences* 13, 268–78.

Trist, E.L. (1988) Referent organizations and the development of interorganizational domains. *Human Relations* 36, 247–68.

Tyler, D. (1998) Getting tourism on the agenda: policy development in the London borough of Southwark. In Tyler, D., Guerrier, Y. and Robertson, M. (eds) *Managing Tourism in Cities* (pp. 45–64). Chichester: John Wiley.

Tyrangiel, J. and Nugent, B. (2002) 'Bono: The world's biggest rock star is also Africa's biggest advocate. But Bono knows he has to make the case for aid with his head, not his heart.' *Time International.* 4 March, 54–60.

UNESCO (1993). *World Heritage Newsletter.* No. 2. http://whc.unesco.org/news/2newsen.htm. Accessed on 15 November 2002.

US Army Corps of Engineers Jacksonville District. Florida Keys Carrying Capacity Study. [Online], Available: http://www.saj.usace.army.mil/projects/proj4.htm [August, 2002].

US Code (2001a) Title 22, Foreign Relations and Intercourse, Chapter 31, International Travel, Subchapter III, Administration, Section 2.124. Tourism Policy Council. *U.S. Code Online via GPO Access.* [cite: 22USC2124] www.wais.access.gpo.gov. Accessed on 25 September 2002.

US Code (2001b) Title 22, Foreign Relations and Intercourse, Chapter 31, International Travel, Subchapter III, Administration, Section 2.124c. Rural Tourism Development Foundation. *U.S. Code Online via GPO Access*. [cite: 22USC2124] www.wais.access.gpo.gov. Accessed on 25 September 2002.

US Code (2001c) Title 36, Parks, Forests and Public Property, Chapter 1, National Park Service Department of the Interior, Part 2, Resource Protection, Public Use and Recreation. *U.S. Code Online via GPO Access*. [cite: 36CFR2] www.wais. access.gpo.gov. Accessed on 25 September 2002.

US Senate (2001) *Travel America Now Act of 2001*. 107th Congress, 1st Session [cite: S1500IS] www.//thomas.loc.gov/cgi-bin/query . . . Accessed January 2002.

Urban Land Institute with Program for Community Problem Solving (1994). *Planning and Development Consensus – Building Manual*. Washington, DC: ULI.

Ury, W.L. and Smoke, R. (1985). Anatomy of a crisis. *Negotiation Journal* 1, 1.

Urry, J. (1990) *The Tourist Gaze*, London: Sage.

URS Greiner, Inc., 1999–2002. US 1 Travel Time and Delay Studies for Monroe County. Marathon, FL: Monroe County.

Van der Wagen, L. and Davies, C. (1998) *Supervision and Leadership*. Melbourne: Hospitality Press.

Vanhaverbeke, W. (2001) Realizing new regional core competencies: establishing a customer-oriented SME network. *Entrepreneurship and Regional Development* 13 (2), 97–116.

Van Tiggelen, J. (2001) Beyond the Big Koala: Teaching small towns how to cheat death (Lesson One: Turn the toilet block into a tourist attraction). *The Age – Good Weekend Magazine* (Melbourne). 5 May, 18–23.

Vesper, K.H. (1996) *New Venture Experience*. Seattle: Vector Books.

Waddock, S.A. and Bannister, B.D. (1991) Correlates of effectiveness and partner satisfaction in social partnerships. *Journal of Organizational Change Management* 4 (2), 74–89.

Wahab, S. (1975) *Tourism Management*. London: Tourism International Press.

Wahab, S. and Pigram, J.J. (eds) (1997) *Tourism, Development and Growth: The Challenge of Sustainability*. London: Routledge.

Wall, G. (1996) Perspectives on tourism in selected Balinese villages. *Annals of Tourism Research* 23 (1), 123–37.

Wall, G. and Dibnah, S. (1992) The changing status of tourism in Bali, Indonesia. *Progress in Tourism, Recreation and Hospitality Management* 4, 120–30.

Walle, A.H. (1995) Business ethics and tourism: from micro to macro perspectives. *Tourism Management* 16 (4), 263–8.

Walsh-Martin, M. (1998) *Making it Happen*. Melbourne: Scribe Publications.

Walz, S.M. and Niehoff, B.P. (2000) Organizational citizenship behaviors: their relationship to organizational effectiveness. *Journal of Hospitality and Tourism Research* 24 (3), 301–19.

Wanhill, S.R.C. (1996) Local enterprise development in tourism. *Tourism Management* 17 (1), 35–42.

Ward, S. (1998) Place marketing: A historical comparison of Britain and North America. In T. Hall and P. Hubbard (eds) *The Entrepreneurial City: Geographies of Politics, Regime and Representation* (pp. 31–53). New York, NY: John Wiley.

Warnken, J. and Buckley, R. (1996) Coastal tourism development as a test-bed for EIA triggers: Outcomes under mandatory and discretionary EIA frameworks. *Environment and Planning Law Journal* 13 (4), 239–45.

Warren, R.L. (1977) *Social Change and Human Purpose*. Chicago: Rand McNally.

Watkins, L. (1987) *Billion Dollar Miracle*. Auckland: Traveldigest.

Wearing, S. and McLean, J. (1998) *Developing Ecotourism: A Community Based Approach*. Williamstown, Victoria: HM Leisure Planning.

Wearing, S. and Neil, J. (1999) *Ecotourism: Impacts, Potentials and Possibilities*. Oxford: Butterworth-Heinemann.

Weaver, D.B. (2000) A broad context model of destination development scenarios. *Tourism Management* 21 (3), 217–24.

Weaver, D. and Opperman, M. (2000) *Tourism Management*. Milton Keys, Essex: John Wiley.

Weaver, G.D. (1986) *Tourism USA: Guidelines for Tourism Development*. Columbia, Missouri: University of Missouri-Columbia, Department of Recreation and Park Administration/Washington, DC: United States Travel and Tourism Administration.

Webler, T. (1995) Right discourse in citizen participation: An evaluative yardstick. In O. Renn, T. Webler and P. Wiedemann (eds) *Fairness and Competence in Citizen Participation: Evaluating Models for Environmental Discourse* (pp. 35–86). The Netherlands: Kluwer Academic Press.

Webster, M. (1998) Strategies for growth. In R. Thomas (ed.) *The Management of Small Tourism and Hospitality Firms* (pp. 208–18). London: Cassell.

Weiermair K. (1997) Service quality and its management in tourism enterprises. (Calidad de servicios y su gestion en las empresas turisticas). In Papers de Turisme, Fundacion de Cavanilles de Altos Estudios Turisticos (pp. 54–68). University of Alicante, Spain. No. 20.

West Central Community Futures Development Corporation (WCCFDC) (2002) *West Coast Community Futures Development Corporation* (pp. 1–2). www.agt.net/public/westcent. Accessed on 1 February.

Western Morning News (2001) *Welcome to Eden*. Plymouth: Western Morning News Company.

Wheatcroft, S. (1994) *Aviation and Tourism Policies: Balancing the Benefits: A World Tourism Organisation Publication*. London & New York: Routledge.

Wheeler, B. (1994) Egotourism, sustainable tourism and the environment – a symbiotic, symbolic or shambolic relationship. In A.V. Seaton (ed.) *Tourism: The State of the Art* (pp. 647–54). Chichester: John Wiley.

Wight, P. (1996) North American ecotourism markets: motivations, preferences and destinations. *Journal of Travel Research* 35 (1), 3–10.

Williams, A.M., Shaw, G. and Greenwood, J. (1989) From tourist to tourism entrepreneur, from consumption to production: evidence from Cornwall, England. *Environment and Planning A* 21, 1639–53.

Williams, J. and Lawson, R. (2001) Community issues and resident opinions of tourism. *Annals of Tourism Research* 28 (2), 269–90.

Williams, P.W. (1994) Frameworks for assessing tourism's environmental impacts. In J.R.B. Ritchie and C.R. Goeldner (eds) *Travel, Tourism, and Hospitality Research* (2nd edn) (pp. 425–36). New York: John Wiley.

Williams, P.W. and Gill, A. (1991) *Carrying Capacity Management in Tourism Settings: A Tourism Growth Management Process*, Centre for Tourism Policy and Research, Simon Fraser University, Vancouver, BC, Canada.

Williams, P.W. and Gill, A. (1998) Tourism carrying capacity management issues. In W. Theobald (ed.) *Global Tourism: The Next Decade* (2nd edn) (pp. 231–46). Oxford: Butterworth-Heinemann.

Winkle, G., Olson, R., Wheeler, F. and Cohen, M. (1976) *The Museum Visitor and Orientation Media: An Experimental Comparison of Different Approaches in the Smithsonian Institute and National Museum of History and Technology*. New York: City University of New York, Center for Environment and Behavior.

Wober, K. (1997) Local tourism organizations in European cities. In J.A. Mazanec (ed.) *International City Tourism* (pp. 3–12). London: Pinter.

Wober, K. (1997) Introducing a harmonization procedure for European City tourism statistics. In J.A. Mazanec (ed.) *International City Tourism* (pp. 26–38). London: Pinter.

Wood, W.A. (1991) Partnership in action – the Cowichan and Chemainus Valleys ecomuseum heritage region project. In R.S. Tabata, J. Yamashiro and G. Cherem (eds) *Joining Hands for Quality Tourism* (pp. 447–50). Proceedings of the Heritage Interpretation International Third Global Congress, Honolulu, Hawaii.

Wood, W. (1993) *The Making of a Heritage Region Ecomuseum.* Duncan, BC: The Cowichan and Chemainus Valleys Ecomuseum Society.

Woodley, A. (1992) Tourism and sustainable development: The community perspective. In J.G. Nelson, R. Butler and G. Wall (eds) *Tourism and Sustainable Development: Monitoring, Planning and Managing* (pp. 135–47). Waterloo, Ontario: Heritage Resources Centre, University of Waterloo.

Woodside, A.G. and Wilson, E.J. (1985) Effects of consumer awareness of brand advertising on preference. *Journal of Advertising Research,* 25, 44–53.

Woodside, A.G. and Carr, J.A. (1988) Consumer decision making and competitive marketing strategies: applications for tourism planning. *Journal of Travel Research* 26 (3) 2–7.

Woodside, A.G. and Lysonski, S. (1989) A general model of traveler destination choice. *Journal of Travel Research* 17 (Spring) 8–14.

World Tourism Organisation (1991) *Resolutions of International Conference on Travel and Tourism* (Recommendation No. 29). Ottawa, Canada.

World Tourism Organisation (1993) *Indicators for the Sustainable Management of Tourism.* Winnipeg: International Institute for Sustainable Development.

World Tourism Organisation (1999) *Global Code of Ethics for Tourism.* www.world-tourism.org/projects/ethics/ethics.htm. Accessed on 23 April 2003.

World Tourism Organisation (2002) Tourism stalls in 2001. *News Releases. www.world-tourism.org/market_research/recovery/background.htm.* Accessed on 8 August 2002.

World Travel and Tourism Council (1999) www.wttc.org/economic_research/keystats.htm. Accessed on 31 July 2000.

Yip, G.S. (1985) Who needs strategic planning? *The Journal of Business Strategy* 6 (Fall) 30–41.

Yoon, T. and Ekinci, Y. (2001) An examination of the SERVQUAL scale using the Guttman scaling procedure. In *2001 – A Tourism Odyssey: 32nd Annual Conference Proceedings Travel and Tourism Research Association Annual* (pp. 399–406). 10–13 June 2001, Fort Myers, FL.

Zeithaml, V., Parasuraman, A. and Berry, L.L. (1990) *Delivering Quality Service: Balancing Customer Perceptions and Expectations.* New York: Free Press.

Zenzen, J.M. (1998) *Battling for Manassas: The Fifty-Year Preservation Struggle at Manassas National Battlefield Park.* University Park Pennsylvania: The Pennsylvania State University Press.

Zhang, Y. (2001) A comparative examination of the diffusion of international tourism in Yunnan (PRC) and Victoria (Australia). Unpublished MA thesis, School of Tourism and Hospitality, La Trobe University, Australia.

Index

We dedicate this book to the leaders of the past from whom we have learned, the leaders of today whose behaviors and actions shape our ever-changing world, and the leaders of tomorrow who will hopefully benefit from the lessons of this book as they face the challenges of globalization in an increasingly interconnected world.

About the Authors

Rich Hughes is a Senior Enterprise Associate at the Center for Creative Leadership, an international organization devoted to behavioral science research and leadership education. He works primarily with senior executives in the areas of strategic leadership and organizational culture change. He joined the Center in 1995 after having served for the previous decade as Head of the Department of Behavioral Sciences and Leadership at the U.S. Air Force Academy. He is a clinical psychologist, and a graduate of the U.S. Air Force Academy. He has an MA from the University of Texas and a PhD from the University of Wyoming.

Robert Ginnett is a Senior Fellow at the Center for Creative Leadership. Besides his ongoing research concerning the leadership of high-performance teams and organizations, Robert is a lead instructor in the Leadership at the Peak course for CEOs and Presidents, ranked no. 1 in executive education by *Bricker's* as reported in *The Wall Street Journal.* He has worked with hundreds of organizations including General Motors, Novartis, FMC, Prudential, Masterfoods, GlaxoSmithKlein, Daimler Benz, NASA, the Central Intelligence Agency, United Airlines, and Delta Airlines. Prior to joining the Center for Creative Leadership, Robert was a tenured professor at the U.S. Air Force Academy and served as the director of leadership and counseling. He also served in numerous line and staff positions in the Air Force, including leadership of an 875-man combat force during the Vietnam War. Robert is an organizational psychologist whose education includes master of business administration, master of arts, and master of philosophy degrees, and a PhD from Yale University.

Gordy Curphy is the President of C3, a human resource consulting firm that helps public and private sector clients achieve better results through people. Gordy has over 25 years of leadership and technical expertise in job analysis and competency modeling; hourly staffing systems; multirater feedback systems; performance management design and implementation; leadership development design, delivery, and evaluation; survey construction, administration, and analysis; assessment center methodology; executive coaching, training, and team building; succession planning; team and organizational effectiveness; and strategic and business planning. Prior to forming his own consulting firm, Gordy spent 10 years as a Vice President of Institutional Leadership at The Blandin Foundation and as a VicePresident and General Manager at Personnel Decisions International. He is an industrial/organizational psychologist and a graduate of the U.S. Air Force Academy. He has an MA from the University of St. Mary's and a PhD in industrial/organizational psychology from the University of Minnesota.

Foreword

Often the only difference between chaos and a smoothly functioning operation is leadership; this book is about that difference.

The authors are psychologists; therefore the book has a distinctly psychological tone. You, as a reader, are going to be asked to think about leadership the way psychologists do. There is much here about psychological tests and surveys, about studies done in psychological laboratories, and about psychological analyses of good (and poor) leadership. You will often run across common psychological concepts in these pages, such as personality, values, attitudes, perceptions, and self-esteem, plus some not-so-common "jargon-y" phrases like double-loop learning, expectancy theory, and perceived inequity. This is not the same kind of book that would be written by coaches, sales managers, economists, political scientists, or generals.

Be not dismayed. Because these authors are also teachers with a good eye and ear for what students find interesting, they write clearly and cleanly, and they have also included a host of entertaining, stimulating snapshots on leadership: cartoons, quotes, anecdotal highlights, and personal glimpses from a wide range of intriguing people, each offered as an illustration of some scholarly point.

Also, because the authors are, or have been at one time or another, together or singly, not only psychologists and teachers but also children, students, Boy Scouts, parents, professors (at the U.S. Air Force Academy), Air Force officers, pilots, church members, athletes, administrators, insatiable readers, and convivial raconteurs, their stories and examples are drawn from a wide range of personal sources, and their anecdotes ring true.

As psychologists and scholars, they have reviewed here a wide range of psychological studies, other scientific inquiries, personal reflections of leaders, and philosophic writings on the topic of leadership. In distilling this material, they have drawn many practical conclusions useful for current and potential leaders. There are suggestions here for goal setting, for running meetings, for negotiating, for managing conflict within groups, and for handling your own personal stress, to mention just a few.

All leaders, no matter what their age and station, can find some useful tips here, ranging over subjects such as body language, keeping a journal, and how to relax under tension.

In several ways the authors have tried to help you, the reader, feel what it would be like "to be in charge." For example, they have posed quandaries such as the following: You are in a leadership position with a budget provided by an outside funding source. You believe strongly in, say, Topic A, and have taken a strong, visible public stance on that topic. The head of your funding source takes you aside and says, "We disagree with your stance on Topic A. Please tone down your public statements, or we will have to take another look at your budget for next year."

What would you do? Quit? Speak up and lose your budget? Tone down your public statements and feel dishonest? There's no easy answer, and it's not an unusual situation for a leader to be in. Sooner or later, all leaders have to confront just how much outside interference they will tolerate in order to be able to carry out programs they believe in.

The authors emphasize the value of experience in leadership development, a conclusion I thoroughly agree with. Virtually every leader who makes it to the top of whatever pyramid he or she happens to be climbing does so by building on earlier experiences. The successful leaders are those who learn from these earlier experiences, by reflecting on and analyzing them to help solve larger future challenges.

In this vein, let me make a suggestion. Actually, let me assign you some homework. (I know, I know, this is a peculiar approach in a book foreword but stay with me, I have a point.)

YOUR ASSIGNMENT: To gain some useful leadership experience, persuade eight people to do some notable activity together for at least two hours that they would not otherwise do without your intervention. Your only restriction is that you cannot tell them why you are doing this.

It can be any eight people: friends, family, teammates, club members, neighbors, students, working colleagues. It can be any activity, except that it should be something more substantial than watching television, eating, going to a movie, or just sitting around talking. It could be a roller-skating party, an organized debate, a songfest, a long hike, a visit to a museum, or volunteer work such as picking up litter or visiting a nursing home.

If you will take it upon yourself to make something happen in the world that would not have otherwise happened without you, you will be engaging in an act of leadership with all of its attendant barriers, burdens, and pleasures, and you will quickly learn the relevance of many of the topics that the authors discuss in this book. If you try the eight-person-two-hour experience first and read this book later, you will have a much better understanding of how complicated an act of leadership can be. You will learn about the difficulties of developing a vision ("Now that we are together, what are we going to do?"), of motivating others, of setting agendas and timetables, of securing resources, of the need for follow-through. You may even learn about "loneliness at the top." However, if you are successful, you will also experience the thrill that comes from successful leadership. One person *can* make a difference by enriching the lives of others, if only for a few hours. And for all of the frustrations and complexities of leadership, the tingling satisfaction that comes from success can become almost addictive. The capacity for making things happen can become its own motivation. With an early success, even if it is only with eight people for two hours, you may well be on your way to a leadership future.

The authors believe that leadership development involves reflecting on one's own experiences. Reading this book in the context of your own leadership experience can aid in that process. Their book is comprehensive, scholarly, stimulating, entertaining, and relevant for anyone who wishes to better understand the dynamics of leadership, and to improve her or his own personal performance.

David P. Campbell

Preface

The fifth edition contains two broad categories of changes that we believe will further enhance the text's usefulness. There were improvements in this edition that cut across chapters, as well as continuing refinements to each chapter. Let us describe the key aspects of both of those kinds of changes.

An entirely new feature in the fifth edition involves end-of-chapter minicases that examine current leadership situations in organizational settings. Some of the companies profiled in these minicases include UPS, McDonalds, and Disney. All of the minicases include summary situations and questions for the students to answer. Suggested solutions can be found in the Instructor's Manual. There also has been rather substantial changes to the Highlights features in every chapter, including elimination of the more dated material as well as the addition of new material.

The "Three Leaders" feature has been retained as a textual vehicle to facilitate exploration of how the unique perspectives from different chapters can be applied to develop progressively richer portraits of three particular leaders who are "followed" throughout the book. Two new leaders, however, have been added to this feature: Peter Jackson, the producer and director of the Academy Award-winning film trilogy, *The Lord of the Rings;* and Aung San Suu Kyi, one of the heroic civil rights leaders in the world today. Colin Powell will continue from the last edition as the third featured leader throughout the chapters.

There have been changes within every chapter in the book, but three chapters underwent fairly substantial revision. Chapter 6 ("Leadership and Values") was significantly revised. The fourth edition's treatment of the moral development of leaders has been eliminated entirely, and the chapter has been rewritten to focus more on how values impact the leadership process in general. In addition, the chapter's entire treatment of gender roles and leadership has been moved to Chapter 2 ("Leadership Involves an Interaction between the Leaders, the Followers, and the Situation").

Chapter 9, "Motivation, Satisfaction, and Performance," also underwent significant revision. The section on ProMES, a cognitive approach to motivation, was eliminated. There is greater emphasis on job satisfaction, including material on the Gallup survey approach, and its impact on organizational outcomes, as well as movement of the existing treatment of Herzberg's work to this part of the chapter. There's a new section dealing with the part that role ambiguity and values play in job dissatisfaction. And there is an expanded treatment of organizational justice.

The other chapter that was significantly changed from previous editions was Chapter 10, "Groups, Teams and Their Leadership." Two major changes were made, both in response to reviewer suggestions. First, the section differentiating groups and teams was moved to the early part of the chapter. Secondly, the description and diagrams of the Team Effectiveness Leadership Model were simplified while still retaining the model's practicality and utility. The popular diagnostic portion of the model remains intact.

The Leadership Skills section in Part V remains essentially unchanged, although there has been an updating of the section "Building Blocks of Team Building."

There are a number of individuals we wish to thank for their significant contributions to this edition. We deeply appreciate the enthusiastic encouragement, guidance, and support of our friends and colleagues at McGraw-Hill/Irwin, including Andy Winston, Kelly Lowery, Amy Luck, Meg Beamer, and Kirsten Guidero.

We are also indebted to a number of individuals whose evaluations and constructive suggestions about the previous edition provided the foundations for our revisions. We are grateful for the scholarly and insightful comments from all of our reviewers:

Kevin Banning
Auburn University

Jeffrey Bauer
University of Cincinatti–Claremont

Rhonda Davis
Isothermal Community College

James Johnson
Purdue University–Calumet

Jeffrey C. Kohles
California State University–San Marcos

A. Cybelle Lyon
Portland State University

Charles Millick
Jesuit University

Melanie Minarik
University of Nevada–Reno

William Murry
Duquesne University

Rhonda Palladi
Georgia State University

W. Robert Sampson
University of Wisconsin–Eau Claire

David Swanz
Couly-Sawyer College

David Thrope
Clark University

Susan Verhulst
Des Moines Community College

Richard Williams
Nashville State Technical Community College

Steven Wolff
Marist College

Robert Young
Lorraine Community College

Finally, the authors wish to express their deep gratitude to Kate Beatty for having no input whatsoever to this edition.

Richard L. Hughes
Robert C. Ginnett
Gordon J. Curphy

Brief Contents

Contents

Part 1

Leadership Is a Process, Not a Position

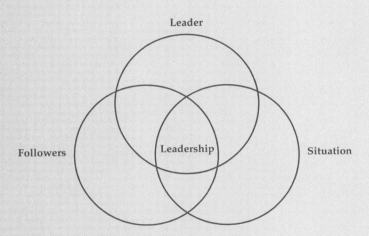

If any single idea is central to this book, it is that leadership is a process, not a position. The entire first part of the book explores that idea. One is not a leader—except perhaps in name only—merely because one holds a title or position. Leadership involves something happening as a result of the interaction between a leader and followers.

In Chapter 1 we define leadership and explore its relationship to concepts such as management and followership. We also suggest that better leadership is something for which everyone shares responsibility. In Chapter 2 we discuss how leadership involves complex interactions between the leader, the followers, and the situation they are in. We also present an interactional framework for conceptualizing leadership which becomes an integrating theme throughout the rest of the book. Chapter 3 looks at how we can become better leaders by profiting more fully from our experiences, which is not to say that either the study or the practice of leadership is simple. Part I concludes with a chapter examining basic concepts and methods used in the scientific study of leaders and leadership.

1

Leadership Is Everyone's Business

Introduction

In the spring of 1972, an airplane flew across the Andes mountains carrying its crew and 40 passengers. Most of the passengers were members of an amateur Uruguayan rugby team en route to a game in Chile. The plane never arrived. It crashed in snow-covered mountains, breaking into several pieces on impact. The main part of the fuselage slid like a toboggan down a steep valley, finally coming to rest in waist-deep snow. Although a number of people died immediately or within a day of the impact, the picture for the 28 survivors was not much better. The fuselage initially offered little protection from the extreme cold, food supplies were scant, and a number of passengers had serious injuries from the crash. Over the next few days, several of the passengers became psychotic and several others died from their injuries. Those passengers who were relatively uninjured set out to do what they could to improve their chances of survival.

Several worked on "weatherproofing" the wreckage, others found ways to get water, and those with medical training took care of the injured. Although shaken from the crash, the survivors initially were confident they would be found. These feelings gradually gave way to despair, as search and rescue teams failed to find the wreckage. With the passing of several weeks and no sign of rescue in sight, the remaining passengers decided to mount several expeditions to determine the best way to escape. The most physically fit were chosen to go on the expeditions, as the thin mountain air and the deep snow made the trips extremely taxing. The results of the trips were both frustrating and demoralizing; the expeditionaries determined they were in the middle of the Andes mountains, and walking out to find help was believed to be impossible. Just when the survivors thought nothing worse could possibly happen, an avalanche hit the wreckage and killed several more of them.

The remaining survivors concluded they would not be rescued and their only hope was for someone to leave the wreckage and find help. Three of the fittest passengers were chosen for the final expedition, and everyone else's work was

3

directed toward improving the expedition's chances of success. The three expeditionaries were given more food and were exempted from routine survival activities; the rest spent most of their energies securing supplies for the trip. Two months after the plane crash, the expeditionaries set out on their final attempt to find help. After hiking for 10 days through some of the most rugged terrain in the world, the expeditionaries stumbled across a group of Chilean peasants tending cattle. One of the expeditionaries stated, "I come from a plane that fell in the mountains. I am Uruguayan . . ." Eventually, 14 other survivors were rescued.

When the full account of their survival became known, it was not without controversy. It had required extreme and unsettling measures; the survivors had lived only by eating the flesh of their deceased comrades. Nonetheless, their story is one of the most moving survival dramas of all time, magnificently told by Piers Paul Read in *Alive* (1974). It is a story of tragedy and courage, and it is a story of leadership.

Perhaps a story of survival in the Andes is so far removed from everyday experience that it does not seem to hold any relevant lessons about leadership for you personally. But consider for a moment some of the basic issues the Andes survivors faced: tension between individual and group goals, dealing with the different needs and personalities of group members, and keeping hope alive in the face of adversity. These issues are not so very different from those facing many groups we're a part of. We can also look at the Andes experience for examples of the emergence of informal leaders in groups. Before the flight, a boy named Parrado was awkward and shy, a "second-stringer" both athletically and socially. Nonetheless, this unlikely hero became the best loved and most respected among the survivors for his courage, optimism, fairness, and emotional support. Persuasiveness in group decision making also was an important part of leadership among the Andes survivors. During the difficult discussions preceding the agonizing decision to survive on the flesh of their deceased comrades, one of the rugby players made his reasoning clear: "I know that if my dead body could help you stay alive, then I would want you to use it. In fact, if I do die and you don't eat me, then I'll come back from wherever I am and give you a good kick in the ass" (Read, 1974, p. 77).

The Purpose of This Book

Lives of great men all remind us
We can make our lives sublime
And, departing, leave behind us
Footprints on the sands of time.
Henry Wadsworth Longfellow

Few of us will ever be confronted with a leadership challenge as dramatic as that faced by the Andes survivors. We may frequently face, however, opportunities for leadership that involve group dynamics which are just as complex. The purpose of this book is to help you be more effective in leadership situations by helping you better understand the complex challenges of leadership.

More specifically, we hope this book will serve as a sort of guide for interpreting leadership theory and research. The book describes and critically evaluates a number of leadership theories and research articles, and also offers practical advice on how to be a better leader. This book is designed to fill the gap between books that provide excellent summaries of leadership research but little practical advice on how to be a better leader and those that are not based on theory or research but primarily offer just one person's views on how to be a better leader (e.g., "how to" books, memoirs).

Three Leaders

One way we will bridge that gap between leadership research and more personalized accounts of leadership will be through personal glimpses of individual leaders. Dozens of different leaders are mentioned illustratively throughout the text, but three particular individuals will be a continuing focus across many chapters. They are Colin Powell, Peter Jackson, and Aung San Suu Kyi. Let us introduce you to them now.

Colin Powell

Until 2005, Colin Powell has been the United States secretary of state. No African American has ever held a higher position in the U.S. government. He is also a former chairman of the Joint Chiefs of Staff, the highest-ranking officer in the U.S. armed forces. He has commanded soldiers, advised presidents, and led a national volunteer movement to improve the future for disadvantaged youth. He is one of the most respected individuals inside or outside of government.

We might wonder whether his leadership of a national volunteer movement or the State Department differs in any way from his leadership of his country's military forces. We might also wonder what there is about him that inspired so many to hope he would run for elective office himself. And we might wonder, was he always a great leader, or did even Colin Powell need to learn a few things along the way? These are some of the questions we will consider ahead. One thing, however, is virtually certain: Colin Powell will continue to exert strong leadership *whatever* his role.

Peter Jackson

When Peter Jackson read *The Lord of the Rings* trilogy at the age of 18, he couldn't wait until it was made into a movie; 20 years later he made it himself. In 2004 *The Lord of the Rings: The Return of the King* took home 11 Academy Awards, winning the Oscar in every category for which it was nominated. This tied the record for the most Oscars ever earned by one motion picture.

Such an achievement might seem unlikely for a producer/director whose film debut was titled *Bad Taste,* which it and subsequent works exemplified in spades. Peter Jackson made horror movies so grisly and revolting that his fans nicknamed him the "Sultan of Splatter." Nonetheless, his talent was evident to discerning eyes—at least among horror film aficionados. *Bad Taste* was hailed as a cult classic at the Cannes Film Festival, and horror fans tabbed Jackson as a talent to follow.

When screenwriter Costa Botes heard that *The Lord of the Rings* would be made into a live action film, he thought those responsible were crazy. Prevailing wisdom was that the fantastic and complex trilogy simply could not be believably translated onto the screen. But he also believed that "there was no other director on earth who could do it justice" (Botes, 2004). And do it justice he obviously did. What was it about the "Sultan of Splatter's" leadership that gave others such confidence in his ability to make one

> *The halls of fame are open wide and they are always full. Some go in by the door called "push" and some by the door called "pull."*
>
> Stanley Baldwin,
> British prime minister in 1930s

of the biggest and best movies of all time? What gave *him* the confidence to even try it? And what made others want to *share* in his vision? We'll see.

Aung San Suu Kyi

In 1991 Suu Kyi already had spent two years under house arrest in Burma for "endangering the state." That same year she won the Nobel Prize for Peace. Like Nelson Mandela, Suu Kyi stands as an international symbol of heroic and peaceful resistance to government oppression.

Until the age of 43, Suu Kyi led a relatively quiet existence in England as a professional working mother. Her life changed dramatically in 1988 when she returned to her native country of Burma to visit her sick mother. That visit occurred during a time of considerable political unrest in Burma. Riot police had recently shot to death hundreds of demonstrators in the capital city of Rangoon (the demonstrators had been protesting government repression!). Over the next several months, police killed nearly 3,000 people who had been protesting government policies.

When hundreds of thousands of pro-democracy demonstrators staged a protest rally at a prominent pagoda in Rangoon, Suu Kyi spoke to the crowd. Overnight she became the leading voice for freedom and democracy in Burma. Today she is the most popular and influential leader in her country even though she's never held political office. What prepared this woman whose life was once relatively simple and contented to risk her life by challenging an oppressive government? What made her such a magnet for popular support? We'll examine those and other questions in the chapters ahead.

What Is Leadership?

The Andes story and the lives of the three leaders we just introduced provide numerous examples of leadership. But just what *is* leadership? People who do research on leadership actually disagree more than you might think about what leadership really is. Most of this disagreement stems from the fact that **leadership** is a complex phenomenon involving the leader, the followers, and the situation. Some leadership researchers have focused on the personality, physical traits, or behaviors of the leader; others have studied the relationships between leaders and followers; still others have studied how aspects of the situation affect the ways leaders act. Some have extended the latter viewpoint so far as to suggest there is no such thing as leadership; they argue that organizational successes and failures often get falsely attributed to the leader, but the situation may have a much greater impact on how the organization functions than does any individual, including the leader (Meindl & Ehrlich, 1987).

Remember the difference between a boss and a leader: a boss says, "Go!"—a leader says, "Let's go!"

E. M. Kelly

Perhaps the best way for you to begin to understand the complexities of leadership is to see some of the ways leadership has been defined. Leadership researchers have defined leadership in many different ways:

- The process by which an agent induces a subordinate to behave in a desired manner (Bennis, 1959).
- Directing and coordinating the work of group members (Fiedler, 1967).
- An interpersonal relation in which others comply because they want to, not because they have to (Merton, 1969).
- Transforming followers, creating visions of the goals that may be attained, and articulating for the followers the ways to attain those goals (Bass, 1985; Tichy & Devanna, 1986).
- The process of influencing an organized group toward accomplishing its goals (Roach & Behling, 1984).
- Actions that focus resources to create desirable opportunities (Campbell, 1991).
- The leader's job is to create conditions for the team to be effective (Ginnett, 1996).
- The *ends* of leadership involve getting results through others, and the *means* of leadership involve the ability to build cohesive, goal-oriented teams. Good leaders are those who build teams to get results across a variety of situations (Hogan, Curphy, & Hogan, 1994).

As you can see, these definitions differ in many ways, and these differences have resulted in various researchers exploring very different aspects of leadership. For example, if we were to apply these definitions to the Andes survival scenario described earlier, researchers adopting Munson's definition would focus on the behaviors Parrado used to keep up the morale of the survivors. Researchers using Roach and Behling's definition would examine how Parrado managed to convince the group to stage and support the final expedition. One's definition of leadership might also influence just *who* is considered an appropriate leader for study. For example, researchers who adopted Merton's definition might not be interested in studying Colin Powell's leadership as an army general. They might reason that the enormous hierarchical power and authority of an army general makes every order or decision a "have to" response from subordinates. Thus, each group of researchers might focus on a different aspect of leadership, and each would tell a different story regarding the leader, the followers, and the situation.

Although such a large number of leadership definitions may seem confusing, it is important to understand that there is no single correct definition. The various definitions can help us appreciate the multitude of factors that affect leadership, as well as different perspectives from which to view it. For example, in Bennis's definition, the word *subordinate* seems to confine leadership to downward influence in hierarchical relationships; it seems to exclude informal leadership. Fiedler's definition emphasizes the directing and controlling aspects of leadership, and thereby may deemphasize emotional aspects of leadership. The emphasis Merton placed on subordinates' "wanting to" comply with a leader's wishes seems to exclude coercion of any kind as a leadership tool. Further, it becomes problematic to identify ways in which a leader's actions are really leadership if subordinates voluntarily comply when a leader with considerable potential coercive power merely asks others to do something without explicitly threatening them. Similarly, Campbell used the phrase *desirable opportunities* precisely to distinguish between leadership and tyranny.

All considered, we believe the definition provided by Roach and Behling (1984) to be a fairly comprehensive and helpful one. Therefore, this book also defines leadership as "the process of influencing an organized group toward accomplishing its goals." There are several implications of this definition which are worth further examination.

Leadership Is Both a Science and an Art

Saying leadership is both a science and an art emphasizes the subject of leadership as a field of scholarly inquiry, as well as certain aspects of the practice of leadership. The scope of the science of leadership is reflected in the number of studies—approximately 8,000—cited in an authoritative reference work, *Bass & Stogdill's Handbook of Leadership: Theory, Research, & Managerial Applications* (Bass, 1990). However, being an expert on leadership research is neither a necessary nor a sufficient condition for being a good leader. Some managers may be effective leaders without ever having taken a course or training program in leadership, and some scholars in the field of leadership may be relatively poor leaders themselves.

Any fool can keep a rule. God gave him a brain to know when to break the rule.

General Willard W. Scott

This is not to say that knowing something about leadership research is irrelevant to leadership effectiveness. Scholarship may not be a prerequisite for leadership effectiveness, but understanding some of the major research findings can help individuals better analyze situations using a variety of perspectives. That, in turn, can give leaders insight about how to be more effective. Even so, because the skill in analyzing and responding to situations varies greatly across leaders, leadership will always remain partly an art as well as a science.

Leadership Is Both Rational and Emotional

Leadership involves both the rational and emotional sides of human experience. Leadership includes actions and influences based on reason and logic as well as those based on inspiration and passion. We do not want to cultivate leaders like Commander Data of *Star Trek: The Next Generation,* who always responds with logical predictability. Because people differ in their thoughts and feelings, hopes and dreams, needs and fears, goals and ambitions, and strengths and weaknesses, leadership situations can be very complex. Because people are both rational and emotional, leaders can use rational techniques and/or emotional appeals in order to influence followers, but they must also weigh the rational and emotional consequences of their actions.

A democracy cannot follow a leader unless he is dramatized. A man to be a hero must not content himself with heroic virtues and anonymous action. He must talk and explain as he acts—drama.

William Allen White,
American writer and editor,
Emporia Gazette

A full appreciation of leadership involves looking at both these sides of human nature. Good leadership is more than just calculation and planning, or following a "checklist," even though rational analysis can enhance good leadership. Good leadership also involves touching others' feelings; emotions play an important role in leadership too. Just one example of this is the civil rights movement of the 1960s. It was a movement based on emotions as well as on principles. Dr. Martin Luther King, Jr., *inspired* many people to action; he touched people's hearts as well as their heads.

Aroused feelings, however, can be used either positively or negatively, constructively or destructively. Some leaders have been able to inspire others to deeds of great purpose and courage. On the other hand, as images of Adolf Hitler's mass rallies or present-day angry mobs attest, group frenzy can readily become group mindlessness. As another example, emotional appeals by the Reverend Jim Jones resulted in approximately 800 of his followers volitionally committing suicide.

The mere presence of a group (even without heightened emotional levels) can also cause people to act differently than when they are alone. For example, in airline cockpit crews, there are clear lines of authority from the captain down to the first officer (second in command) and so on. So strong are the norms surrounding the authority of the captain that some first officers will not take control of the airplane from the captain even in the event of impending disaster. Foushee (1984) reported a study wherein airline captains in simulator training intentionally feigned incapacitation so that the response of the rest of the crew could be observed. The feigned incapacitations occurred at a predetermined point during the plane's final approach in landing, and the simulation involved conditions of poor weather and visibility. Approximately 25 percent of the first officers in these simulated flights allowed the plane to crash. For some reason, the first officers did not take control even when it was clear the captain was allowing the aircraft to deviate from the parameters of a safe approach. This example demonstrates how group dynamics can influence the behavior of group members even when emotional levels are *not* high. (Believe it or not, airline crews are so well trained, this is *not* an emotional situation.) In sum, it should be apparent that leadership involves followers' feelings and nonrational behavior as well as rational behavior. Leaders need to consider *both* the rational and the emotional consequences of their actions.

If you want some ham, you gotta go into the smokehouse.

Huey Long,
Governor of Louisiana

Leadership and Management

In trying to answer "What is leadership?" it is natural to look at the relationship between leadership and management. To many, the word **management** suggests words like *efficiency, planning, paperwork, procedures, regulations, control,* and *consistency.* Leadership is often more associated with words like *risk taking, dynamic, creativity, change,* and *vision.* Some say leadership is fundamentally a value-choosing, and thus a value-laden, activity, whereas management is not. Leaders are thought to *do the right things,* whereas managers are thought to *do things right* (Bennis, 1985; Zaleznik, 1983). Here are some other distinctions between managers and leaders (Bennis, 1989):

- Managers administer; leaders innovate.
- Managers maintain; leaders develop.
- Managers control; leaders inspire.

- Managers have a short-term view; leaders, a long-term view.
- Managers ask how and when; leaders ask what and why.
- Managers imitate; leaders originate.
- Managers accept the status quo; leaders challenge it.

Stow this talk. Care killed a cat. Fetch ahead for the doubloons.

Long John Silver,
in Robert Louis Stevenson's
Treasure Island

Zaleznik (1974, 1983) goes so far as to say these differences reflect fundamentally different personality types, that leaders and managers are basically different kinds of people. He says some people are managers *by nature;* other people are leaders *by nature.* This is not at all to say one is better than the other, only that they are different. Their differences, in fact, can be quite useful, since organizations typically need both functions performed well in order to be successful. For example, consider again the civil rights movement in the 1960s. Dr. Martin Luther King, Jr., gave life and direction to the civil rights movement in America. He gave dignity and hope of freer participation in our national life to people who before had little reason to expect it. He inspired the world with his vision and eloquence, and changed the way we live together. America is a different nation today because of him. Was Dr. Martin Luther King, Jr., a leader? Of course. Was he a manager? Somehow that does not seem to fit, and the civil rights movement might have failed if it had not been for the managerial talents of his supporting staff. Leadership and management complement each other, and both are vital to organizational success.

Never try to teach a pig to sing; it wastes your time and it annoys the pig.

Paul Dickson,
Baseball writer

With regard to the issue of leadership versus management, we take a middle-of-the-road position. We think of leadership and management as closely related but distinguishable functions. Our view of the relationship is depicted in Figure 1.1. It shows leadership and management as two over-lapping functions. Although some of the functions performed by leaders and managers may be unique, there is also an area of overlap.

Leadership and Followership

One aspect of our text's definition of leadership is particularly worth noting: Leadership is a social influence process shared among *all* members of a group. Leadership is not restricted to the influence exerted by someone in a particular

FIGURE 1.1
Leadership and
management
overlap.

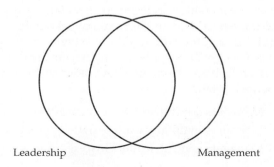

Leadership   Management

FIGURE 1.2
The leadership/ followership Möbius strip.

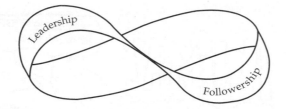

position or role; followers are part of the leadership process, too. In recent years, both practitioners and scholars have emphasized the relatedness of leadership and **followership.** As Burns (1978) observed, the idea of "one-man leadership" is a contradiction in terms.

Thus, the question *What is leadership?* cannot be separated from the question *What is followership?* There is no simple line dividing them; they merge. The relationship between leadership and followership can be represented by borrowing a concept from topographical mathematics: the Möbius strip. You are probably familiar with the curious properties of the Möbius strip: When a strip of paper is twisted and connected in the manner depicted in Figure 1.2, it proves to have only one side. You can prove this to yourself by putting a pencil to any point on the strip and tracing continuously. Your pencil will cover the entire strip (i.e., both "sides"), eventually returning to the point at which you started. In order to demonstrate the relevance of this curiosity to leadership, cut a strip of paper. On one side write *leadership,* and on the other side write *followership.* Then twist the strip and connect the two ends in the manner of the figure. You will have created a leadership/followership Möbius strip wherein the two concepts merge one into the other, just as leadership and followership can become indistinguishable in organizations (adapted from Macrorie, 1984).

> *He who would eat the fruit must climb the tree.*
>
> Scottish proverb

This does not mean leadership and followership are the same thing. When top-level executives were asked to list qualities they most look for and admire in leaders and followers, the lists were similar but not identical (Kouzes & Posner, 1987). Ideal leaders were characterized as honest, competent, forward looking, and inspiring; ideal followers were described as honest, competent, independent, and cooperative. The differences could become critical in certain situations, as when a forward-looking and inspiring subordinate perceives a significant conflict between his own goals or ethics and those of his superiors. Such a situation could become a crisis for the individual and the organization, demanding choice between leading and following.

Leadership on Stages Large and Small

Great leaders sometimes seem larger than life. Charles de Gaulle, a leader of France during and after World War II, was such a figure (see Highlight 1.1). Not all good leaders are famous or powerful, however, and we believe leadership can be best understood if we study a broad range of leaders, some famous and some not so famous. Most leaders, after all, are not known outside their own particular sphere or activity, nor should they be. Here are a few examples of leadership on

The Stateliness of Charles de Gaulle

Highlight 1.1

Certain men have, one might almost say from birth, the quality of exuding authority, as though it were a liquid, though it is impossible to say precisely of what it consists. In his fascinating book *Leaders,* former president Richard Nixon described the French president Charles de Gaulle as one of the great leaders he had met. Following are several aspects of de Gaulle's leadership based on Nixon's observations.

- *He conveyed stately dignity.* De Gaulle had a resolute bearing that conveyed distance and superiority to others. He was at ease with other heads of state but never informal with anyone, even close friends. His tall stature and imperious manner conveyed the message he was not a common man.

- *He was a masterful public speaker.* He had a deep, serene voice and a calm, self-assured manner. He used the French language grandly and eloquently. According to Nixon, "He spoke so articulately and with such precision that his message seemed to resonate apart from his words" (p. 59).

- *He played the part.* De Gaulle understood the role of theater in politics, and his meetings with the press (a thousand at a time!) were like audiences with royalty. He staged them in great and ornate halls, and he deftly crafted public statements that would be understood differently by different groups. In one sense, perhaps, this could be seen as a sort of falseness, but that may be too narrow a view. Nixon reflected on this aspect of de Gaulle's leadership: "General de Gaulle was a facade, but not a false one. Behind it was a man of incandescent intellect and a phenomenal discipline. The facade was like the ornamentation on a great cathedral, rather than the flimsy pretense of a Hollywood prop with nothing behind it" (p. 60).

Source: R. Nixon, *Leaders* (New York: Warner Books, 1982).

the small stage, where individuals influenced and helped their respective groups attain their goals.

- An elderly woman led an entire community's effort to organize an advocacy and support group for parents of mentally ill adult children and provide sheltered living arrangements for these people. She helped these families while also serving an invaluable role in educating state legislators and social agencies about the needs of this neglected constituency. There had been numerous parents with mentally ill children in this community before, but none had had the idea or took the initiative to organize among themselves. As a result of this woman's leadership, many adults live and work in more humane conditions than they did before.

- A seasoned air force sergeant took two young, "green" enlistees under her wing after they both coincidentally reported for duty on the same day. She taught them the ropes at work and took pride as they matured. One of them performed so well that he went on to be commissioned as an officer. Unfortunately, the sergeant discovered the other pilfering cash from the unit gift fund. Though it pained her to do so, the sergeant took action for the enlistee to be discharged from the service. Leadership involves significant intrinsic rewards such as seeing others blossom under your tutelage, but with its rewards also goes the responsibility to enforce standards of conduct.

- The office manager for a large advertising agency directed its entire administrative staff, most of whom worked in the reception area. His engaging personality and concern for others made everyone feel important. Morale in the office was high, and many important customers credit their positive "first impression" of the whole agency to the congeniality and positive climate among the office staff. Leaders set the tone for the organization, and followers often model the behaviors displayed by the leader. This leader helped create an office mood of optimism and supportiveness that reached outward to everyone who visited.

These examples are representative of the opportunities every one of us has to be a leader. To paraphrase John Fitzgerald Kennedy, we all can make a difference and each of us should try. However, this book is more than an exhortation for each of us to play a more active leadership role on the various stages of our lives. It is a review of what is known about leadership from available research, a review we hope is presented in a way that will foster leadership development. We are all more likely to make the kind of difference we want if we understand what leadership is and what it is not, how you get it, and what improves it (see Highlight 1.2 for a contrasting view of how much of a difference leaders really make). Toward that end, we will look at leaders on both the large and the small stages of life throughout the book. We will look at leaders on the world stage like Powell, Jackson, and Suu Kyi; and we will look at leaders on those smaller stages closer to home like principals, coaches, and managers at the local store. You also might want to see Highlight 1.3 for a listing of women leaders throughout history from many different stages.

The Romance of Leadership

Highlight 1.2

This text is predicated on the idea that leaders can make a difference. Interestingly, though, while people in the business world generally agree, not all scholars do.

People in the business world attribute much of a company's success or failure to its leadership. One study counted the number of articles appearing in *The Wall Street Journal* that dealt with leadership and found nearly 10 percent of the articles about representative target companies addressed that company's leadership. Furthermore, there was a significant positive relationship between company performance and the number of articles about its leadership; the more a company's leadership was emphasized in *The Wall Street Journal,* the better the company was doing. This might mean the more a company takes leadership seriously (as reflected by the emphasis in *The Wall Street Journal*), the better it does.

However, the authors were skeptical about the real utility of leadership as a concept. They suggested leadership is merely a romanticized notion, an obsession people want and need to believe in. Belief in the potency of leadership may be a sort of cultural myth, which has utility primarily insofar as it affects how people create meaning about causal events in complex social systems. The behavior of leaders, the authors contend, does not account for very much of the variance in an organization's performance. Nonetheless, people seem strongly committed to a sort of basic faith that individual leaders shape organizational destiny for good or ill.

Source: J. R. Meindl, S. B. Ehrlich, and J. M. Dukerich, "The Romance of Leadership." *Administrative Science Quarterly* 30 (1985), pp. 78–102.

Women and Leadership: A Few Women Leaders throughout History

Highlight 1.3

1429 Joan of Arc is finally granted an audience with Charles the Dauphin of France and subsequently captains the army at the siege of Orleans.

1492 Queen Isabella of Spain finances Columbus's voyage to the New World.

1638 Religious dissident Anne Hutchinson leads schismatic group from Massachusetts Bay Colony into wilderness and establishes Rhode Island.

1803–1806 Sacajawea leads the Lewis and Clark expedition.

1837 Educator Mary Lyons founds Mount Holyoke Female Seminary (later Mount Holyoke College), the first American college exclusively for women.

1843 Dorothea Dix reports to Massachusetts legislature on treatment of criminally insane, resulting in a significant reform of American mental institutions.

1849 Harriet Tubman escapes from slavery and becomes one of the most successful "conductors" on the Underground Railroad. She helps more than 300 slaves to freedom.

1854 Florence Nightingale, the founder of modern nursing, organizes a unit of women nurses to serve in the Crimean War.

1869 Susan B. Anthony is elected president of the National American Woman Suffrage Association.

1900 Carry Nation gains fame destroying saloons as head of the American Temperance Movement.

1919 Mary Pickford becomes the first top-level female executive of a major film studio.

1940 Margaret Chase Smith is the first woman elected to Congress.

1966 National Organization of Women (NOW) is founded by Betty Friedan.

1969 Golda Meir is elected prime minister of Israel.

1979 Mother Teresa receives Nobel Prize for her three decades of work leading the Congregation of Missions of Charity in Calcutta, India.

1979 Margaret Thatcher becomes the United Kingdom's first female prime minister.

1981 Sandra Day O'Connor is first woman appointed to the U.S. Supreme Court.

1988 Benazir Bhutto is elected first female prime minister of Pakistan.

1991 Aung San Suu Kyi wins Nobel Prize for Peace.

1994 Christine Todd Whitman becomes governor of New Jersey, later appointed to cabinet by President Bush in 2001.

1996 Madeleine Albright is appointed U.S. secretary of state.

Source: Originally adapted from the *Colorado Education Association Journal,* February–March 1991. Based on original work by the Arts and Entertainment Network.

Myths That Hinder Leadership Development

Few things pose a greater obstacle to leadership development than certain unsubstantiated and self-limiting beliefs about leadership. Therefore, before we begin examining what leadership and leadership development are in more detail, we will consider what they are not. We will examine several beliefs (we call them myths) that stand in the way of fully understanding and developing leadership.

Myth: Good Leadership Is All Common Sense

At face value, this myth says one needs only common sense to be a good leader. It also implies, however, that most if not all of the studies of leadership reported in scholarly journals and books only confirm what anyone with common sense already knows.

The problem, of course, is with the ambiguous term *common sense.* It implies a common body of practical knowledge about life that virtually any reasonable person with moderate experience has acquired. A simple experiment, however, may convince you that common sense may be less common than you think. Ask a few friends or acquaintances whether the old folk wisdom "Absence makes the heart grow fonder" is true or false. Most will say it is true. After that ask a different group whether the old folk wisdom "Out of sight, out of mind" is true or false. Most of that group will answer true as well, even though the two proverbs are contradictory.

A similar thing sometimes happens when people hear about the results of studies concerning human behavior. On hearing the results, people may say, "Who needed a study to learn that? I knew it all the time." However, several experiments by Slovic and Fischoff (1977) and Wood (1979) showed that events were much more surprising when subjects had to guess the outcome of an experiment than when subjects were told the outcome. What seems obvious after you know the results and what you (or anyone else) would have predicted beforehand are not the same thing. Hindsight is always 20/20.

> *Never reveal all of yourself to other people; hold back something in reserve so that people are never quite sure if they really know you.*
>
> Michael Korda,
> Author, editor

The point might become clearer with a specific example you may now try. Read the following paragraph:

> After World War II, the U.S. Army spent enormous sums of money on studies only to reach conclusions that, many believed, should have been apparent at the outset. One, for example, was that southern soldiers were better able to stand the climate in the hot South Sea islands than northern soldiers were.

This sounds reasonable, but there is just one problem; the statement above is exactly contrary to the actual findings. Southerners were no better than northerners in adapting to tropical climates (Lazarsfeld, 1949). Common sense can often play tricks on us.

Put a little differently, one of the challenges of understanding leadership may well be to know when common sense applies and when it does not. Do leaders need to act confidently? Of course. But they also need to be humble enough to recognize that others' views are useful, too. Do leaders need to persevere when times get tough? Yes. But they also need to recognize when times change and a new direction is called for. If leadership were nothing more than common sense, then there should be few, if any, problems in the workplace. However, we venture to guess you have noticed more than a few problems between leaders and followers. Effective leadership must be something more than just common sense.

Myth: Leaders Are Born, Not Made

Some people believe being a leader is either in one's genes or not; others believe that life experiences mold the individual, that no one is born a leader. Which view is right? In a sense, both and neither. Both views are right in the sense that innate factors as well as formative experiences influence many sorts of behavior, including leadership. Yet both views are wrong to the extent they imply leadership is *ei-*

ther innate *or* acquired; what matters more is how these factors *interact*. It does not seem useful, we believe, to think of the world as composed of two mutually exclusive types of people, leaders and nonleaders. It is more useful to address the ways in which each person can make the most of leadership opportunities he or she faces.

If you miss seven balls out of ten, you're batting three hundred and that's good enough for the Hall of Fame. You can't score if you keep the bat on your shoulder.

Walter B. Wriston,
Chairman of Citicorp,
1970–1984

It may be easier to see the pointlessness of asking whether leaders are born or made by looking at an alternative question of far less popular interest: Are *college professors* born or made? Conceptually, the issues are the same, and here, too, the answer is that every college professor is both born *and* made. It seems clear enough that college professors are partly "born" since (among other factors) there is a genetic component to intelligence, and intelligence surely plays some part in becoming a college professor (well, at least a *minor* part!). But every college professor is also partly "made." One obvious way is that college professors must have advanced education in specialized fields; even with the right genes one could not become a college professor without certain requisite experiences. Becoming a college professor depends partly on what one is "born with" and partly on how that inheritance is shaped through experience. The same is true of leadership.

More specifically, research indicates that many cognitive abilities and personality traits are at least partly innate (McGue & Bouchard, 1990; Tellegen, Lykken, Bouchard, Wilcox, Segal, & Rich, 1988; McCrae & Foster, 1995). Thus, natural talents or characteristics may offer certain advantages or disadvantages to a leader. Take physical characteristics: A man's above-average height may increase others' tendency to think of him as a leader; it may also boost his own self-confidence. But it doesn't "make" him a leader. The same holds true for psychological characteristics which seem related to leadership. The very stability of certain characteristics over long periods of time (e.g., at school reunions people seem to have kept the same personalities we remember them as having years earlier) may reinforce the impression that our basic natures are fixed, but different environments nonetheless may nurture or suppress different leadership qualities.

Myth: The Only School You Learn Leadership from Is the School of Hard Knocks

Some people skeptically question whether leadership can develop through formal study, believing instead it can only be acquired through actual experience. It is a mistake, however, to think of formal study and learning from experience as mutually exclusive or antagonistic. In fact, they complement each other. Rather than ask whether leadership develops from formal study or from real-life experience, it is better to ask what kind of study will help students learn to discern critical lessons about leadership from their own experience. Approaching the issue in such a way

Progress always involves risks. You can't steal second base and keep your foot on first.

Frederick B. Wilcox

recognizes the critical role of experience in leadership development, but it also admits that certain kinds of study and training can improve a person's ability to discern critical lessons about leadership from experience. It can, in other words, help accelerate the process of learning from experience.

We would argue that one of the advantages of formally studying leadership is that formal study provides students with a variety of ways of examining a particular leadership situation. By studying the different ways researchers have defined and examined leadership, students can use these definitions and theories to better understand what is going on in any leadership situation. For example, earlier in this chapter we used three different leadership definitions as a framework for describing or analyzing the situation facing Parrado and the remaining survivors of the plane crash, and each definition focused on a different aspect of leadership. These frameworks can similarly be applied to better understand the experiences one has as both a leader and a follower. We think it is very difficult for leaders, particularly novice leaders, to examine leadership situations from multiple perspectives, but we also believe developing this skill can help you become a better leader. Being able to analyze your experiences from multiple perspectives may be the greatest single contribution a formal course in leadership can give you.

An Overview of This Book

In order to fill the gaps between leadership research and practice, this book will critically review the major theories of leadership as well as provide practical advice about improving leadership. As our first steps in that journey, the next three chapters of the book describe how: (*a*) leadership is an interaction between the leader, the followers, and the situation; (*b*) leadership develops through experience; and (*c*) leadership can be assessed and studied. The remainder of the book uses the leader–follower-situation interaction model described in Chapter 2 as a framework for organizing and discussing various theories and research findings related to leadership. The chapters in Part II focus on the leader, beginning with an examination of the issues of power and influence, then of ethics, values, and attitudes. Other chapters look at theories and research concerning the leader: how good and bad leaders differ in personality, intelligence, creativity, and behavior. Part II concludes by looking at charismatic leadership. Part III primarily focuses on the followers; it summarizes the research and provides practical advice on such topics as motivating subordinates and using delegation. Part IV examines how the situation affects the leadership process. Part V looks at several dozen specific leadership skills, including practical advice about handling specific leadership challenges. While Part V represents in one sense the "end" of the book, you may want to start reading about and practicing some of the skills right now.

Nurture your mind with great thoughts. To believe in the heroic makes heroes.

Benjamin Distaeli,
British prime minister, 1874–1880

Summary   Although many definitions of leadership exist, we define leadership as the process of influencing others toward achieving group goals. The chapter also looks at the idea that leadership is both a science and an art. Because leadership is an immature science, researchers are still struggling to find out what the important questions in leadership are; we are far from finding conclusive answers to them. Even those individuals with extensive knowledge of the leadership research may be poor leaders. Knowing what to do is not the same as knowing when, where, and how to do it. The art of leadership concerns the skill of understanding leadership situations and influencing others to accomplish group goals. Formal leadership education may give individuals the skills to better understand leadership situations, and mentorships and experience may give individuals the skills to better influence others. Leaders must also weigh both rational and emotional considerations when attempting to influence others. Leadership sometimes can be accomplished through relatively rational, explicit, rule-based methods of assessing situations and determining actions. Nevertheless, there is also an emotional side of human nature that must be acknowledged. Leaders are often most effective when they affect people at both the emotional level and the rational level. The idea of leadership as a whole-person process can also be applied to the distinction often made between leaders and managers. Although leadership and management can be distinguished as separate functions, a more comprehensive picture of supervisory positions could be made by examining the overlapping functions of leaders and managers. Leadership does not occur without followers, and followership is an easily neglected component of the leadership process. Leadership is everyone's business and everyone's responsibility. Finally, learning certain conceptual frameworks for thinking about leadership can be helpful in making your own on-the-job experiences a particularly valuable part of your leadership development. Thinking about leadership can help you become a better leader than you are right now.

Key Terms   leadership, *6*   management, *9*   followership, *12*

Questions   1. We say leadership involves influencing organized groups toward goals. Do you see any disadvantages to restricting the definition to organized groups?

2. How would you define *leadership*?

3. Are some people the "leader type" and others not the "leader type"? If so, what in your judgment distinguishes them?

4. Identify several "commonsense" notions about leadership that, to you, are patently self-evident.

5. Does every successful leader have a valid theory of leadership?

6. Would you consider it a greater compliment for someone to call you a good manager or a good leader? Why? Do you believe you can be both?

7. Do you believe leadership can be studied scientifically? Why or why not?

8. To the extent leadership is an art, what methods come to mind for improving one's "art of leadership"?

Activity   Describe the best leader you have personally known, or a favorite leader from history, a novel, or a movie.

Minicase

"Richard Branson Shoots for the Moon"

The Virgin Group is the umbrella for a variety of business ventures ranging from air travel to entertainment. With close to 200 companies in over 30 countries, it is one of the largest companies in the world. At the head of this huge organization is Richard Branson. Branson founded Virgin over 30 years ago and has built the organization from a small student magazine to the multibillion-dollar enterprise it is today.

Branson is not your typical CEO. Branson's dyslexia made school a struggle and sabotaged his performance on standard IQ tests. His teachers and tests had no way of measuring his greatest strengths—his uncanny knack for uncovering lucrative business ideas and his ability to energize the ambitions of others so that they, like he, could rise to the level of their dreams.

Richard Branson's true talents began to show themselves in his late teens. While a student at Stowe School in England in 1968, Branson decided to start his own magazine, *Student*. Branson was inspired by the student activism on his campus in the sixties and decided to try something different. *Student* differed from most college newspapers or magazines; it focused on the students and their interests. Branson sold advertising to major corporations to support his magazine. He included articles by Ministers of Parliament, rock stars, intellectuals, and celebrities. *Student* grew to become a commercial success.

In 1970 Branson saw an opportunity for *Student* to offer records cheaply by running ads for mail-order delivery. The subscribers to *Student* flooded the magazine with so many orders that his spin-off discount music venture proved more lucrative than the magazine subscriptions. Branson recruited the staff of *Student* for his discount music business. He built a small recording studio and signed his first artist. Mike Oldfield recorded "Tubular Bells" at Virgin in 1973—the album sold 5 million copies. Virgin records and the Virgin brand name were born. Branson has gone on to start his own airline (Virgin Atlantic Airlines was launched in 1984), build hotels (Virgin Hotels started in 1988), get into the personal finance business (Virgin Direct Personal Finance Services was launched in 1995), and even enter the cola wars (Virgin Cola was introduced in 1994). And those are just a few of the highlights of the Virgin Group—all this while Branson has attempted to break world speed records for crossing the Atlantic Ocean by boat and by hot air balloon.

As you might guess, Branson's approach is nontraditional—he has no giant corporate office or staff and few if any board meetings. Instead, he keeps each enterprise small and relies on his skills of empowering people's ideas to fuel success. When a flight attendant from Virgin Airlines approached him with her vision of a wedding business, Richard told her to go do it. He even put on a wedding dress himself to help launch the publicity. Virgin Brides was born. Branson relies heavily on the creativity of his staff—he is more a supporter of new ideas than a creator of them. He encourages searches for new business ideas everywhere he goes and even has a spot on the Virgin Website called "Got a Big Idea?"

In December 1999, Richard Branson was awarded a knighthood in the Queen's Millennium New Year's Honours List for "services to entrepreneurship." What's next on Branson's list? He recently announced that Virgin was investing money in "trying to make sure that, in the not too distant future, people from around the world will be able to go into space." Not everyone is convinced that space tourism can become a fully fledged part of the travel industry, but with Branson behind the idea it just may fly.

1. Would you classify Richard Branson as a manager or a leader? What qualities distinguish him as one over the other?
2. As mentioned earlier in this chapter, followers are part of the leadership process. Describe the relationship between Branson and his followers.
3. Identify the myths of leadership development that Richard Branson's success helps to disprove.

Sources: http://www.johnshepler.com/articles/branson.html; http://www.wma.com/richard_branson/summary/; http://www.virgin.com/aboutvirgin/allaboutvirgin/thewholestory/; http://www.virgin.com/aboutvirgin/allaboutvirgin/whosrichardbranson/; http://www.qksrv.net/click-310374-35140; http://www.guardian.co.uk/space/article/0,14493,1235926,00.html

2

Leadership Involves an Interaction between the Leader, the Followers, and the Situation

Introduction

In Chapter 1, we defined leadership as the process of influencing an organized group toward accomplishing its goals. In this chapter, we will expand on this definition by introducing and describing a three-factor framework of the leadership process. We find this framework to be a useful heuristic both for analyzing various leadership situations and for organizing various leadership theories and supporting research. Therefore, the remainder of this chapter is devoted to providing an overview of the framework, and many of the remaining chapters of this book are devoted to describing the components of the framework in more detail.

Looking at Leadership through Several Lenses

In attempting to understand leadership, scholars understandably have spent much of their energy studying successful and unsuccessful leaders in government, business, athletics, and the military. Sometimes scholars have done this systematically by studying good leaders as a group (see Bennis & Nanus, 1985; Astin & Leland, 1991), and sometimes they have done this more subjectively, drawing lessons about leadership from the behavior or character of an individual leader such as Martin Luther King, Jr., Bill Gates, or Hillary Clinton. The latter approach is similar to drawing conclusions about leadership from observing individuals in one's own life, whether it be a high school coach, a mother or father, or one's boss. It may seem that studying the characteristics of effective leaders is the best way to learn about leadership, but such an approach tells only part of the story.

Consider an example. Suppose a senior minister was told by one of his church's wealthiest and consistently most generous members that he should not preach any more prochoice sermons on abortion. The wealthy man's contributions were a big reason a special mission project for the city's disadvantaged youth had been funded, and we might wonder whether the minister would be influenced by this outside pressure. Would he be a bad leader if he succumbed to this pressure and did not advocate what his conscience dictated? Would the minister be a bad leader if his contin-

A leader is best
When people barely know that he exists
Not so good when people obey and acclaim him,
Worst of all when they despise him.
"Fail to honor people,
They fail to honor you;"
But of a good leader, who talks little,
When his work is done, his aim fulfilled,
They will all say, "We did this ourselves."

Lao-tzu

ued public stand on abortion caused the wealthy man to leave the church and withdraw support for the youth program?

Although we can learn much about leadership by looking at leaders themselves, the preceding example suggests that studying only leaders provides just a partial view of the leadership process. Would we really know all we wanted to about the preceding example if we knew everything possible about the minister himself? His personality, his intelligence, his interpersonal skills, his theological training, his motivation? Is it not also relevant to understand a bit more, for example, about the community, his parishioners, the businessman, and so on? This points out how leadership depends on several factors, including the situation and the followers, not just the leader's qualities or characteristics. Leadership is more than just the kind of person the leader is or the things the leader does. Leadership is the process of influencing others toward the achievement of group goals; it is not just a person or a position.

If we use only leaders as the lens for understanding leadership, then we get a very limited view of the leadership process. We can expand our view of the leadership process by adding two other complementary lenses: the followers and the situation. However, using only the followers or the situation as a lens also would give us an equally limited view of the leadership process. In other words, the clearest picture of the leadership process occurs only when we use all three lenses to understand it.

The Interactional Framework for Analyzing Leadership

Perhaps the first researcher formally to recognize the importance of the leader, follower, and situation in the leadership process was Fred Fiedler (1967). Fiedler used these three components to develop his contingency model of leadership, a theory of leadership that will be discussed in more detail in Chapter 12. Although we recognize Fiedler's contributions, we owe perhaps even more to Hollander's (1978) transactional approach to leadership. We call our approach the **interactional framework.**

FIGURE 2.1

An interactional framework for analyzing leadership.

Source: Adapted from E. P. Hollander, *Leadership Dynamics* (New York: Free Press, 1978).

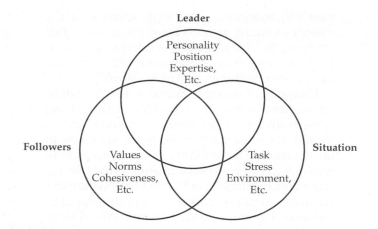

The crowd will follow a leader who marches twenty steps in advance; but if he is a thousand steps in front of them, they do not see and do not follow him.

Georg Brandes

There are several aspects of this derivative of Hollander's (1978) approach that are worthy of additional comment. First, as seen in Figure 2.1, the framework depicts leadership as a function of three elements—the **leader,** the **followers,** and the **situation.** Second, a particular leadership scenario can be examined using each level of analysis separately. Although this is a useful way to understand the leadership process, we can have an even better understanding of the process if we also examine the interactions among the three elements, or lenses, represented by the overlapping areas in the figure. For example, we can better understand the leadership process if we not only look at the leaders and the followers but also examine how leaders and followers affect each other in the leadership process. Similarly, we can examine the leader and the situation separately, but we can gain even further understanding of the leadership process by looking at how the situation can constrain or facilitate a leader's actions and how the leader can change different aspects of the situation in order to be more effective. Thus, a final important aspect of the framework is that leadership is the result of a complex set of interactions among the leader, the followers, and the situation. These complex interactions may be why broad generalizations about leadership are problematic; there are many factors that influence the leadership process (see Highlight 2.1).

An example of one such complex interaction between leaders and followers is evident in what has been called in-groups and out-groups. Sometimes there is a high degree of mutual influence and attraction between the leader and a few subordinates. These subordinates belong to the **in-group** and can be distinguished by their high degree of loyalty, commitment, and trust felt toward the leader. Other subordinates belong to the **out-group.** Leaders have considerably more influence with in-group followers than with out-group followers. However, this greater degree of influence also has a price. If leaders rely primarily on their formal authority to influence their followers (especially if they punish them), then leaders risk losing the high levels of loyalty and commitment followers feel toward them.

Followership Styles

Highlight 2.1

The concept of different styles of leadership is reasonably familiar, but the idea of different styles of followership is relatively new. The very word *follower* has a negative connotation to many, evoking ideas of people who behave like sheep and need to be told what to do. Robert Kelley (1992), however, believes that followers, rather than representing the antithesis of leadership, are best viewed as collaborators with leaders in the work of organizations.

Kelley believes that different types of followers can be described in terms of two broad dimensions. One of them ranges from **independent, critical thinking** at one end to **dependent, uncritical thinking** on the other end. According to Kelley, the best followers think for themselves and offer constructive advice or even creative solutions. The worst followers need to be told what to do. Kelley's other dimension ranges from whether people are **active followers** or **passive followers** in the extent to which they are engaged in work. According to Kelley, the best followers are self-starters who take initiative for themselves, whereas the worst followers are passive, may even dodge responsibility, and need constant supervision.

Using these two dimensions, Kelley has suggested five basic styles of followership:

1. *Alienated followers* habitually point out all the negative aspects of the organization to others. While alienated followers may see themselves as mavericks who have a healthy skepticism of the organization, leaders often see them as cynical, negative, and adversarial.

2. *Conformist followers* are the "yes people" of organizations. While very active at doing the organization's work, they can be dangerous if their orders contradict societal standards of behavior or organizational policy. Often this style is the result of either the demanding and authoritarian style of the leader or the overly rigid structure of the organization.

3. *Pragmatist followers* are rarely committed to their group's work goals, but they have learned not to make waves. Because they do not like to stick out, pragmatists tend to be mediocre performers who can clog the arteries of many organizations. Because it can be difficult to discern just where they stand on issues, they present an ambiguous image with both positive and negative characteristics. In organizational settings, pragmatists may become experts in mastering the bureaucratic rules which can be used to protect them.

4. *Passive followers* display none of the characteristics of the exemplary follower (discussed next). They rely on the leader to do all the thinking. Furthermore, their work lacks enthusiasm. Lacking initiative and a sense of responsibility, passive followers require constant direction. Leaders may see them as lazy, incompetent, or even stupid. Sometimes, however, passive followers adopt this style to help them cope with a leader who expects followers to behave that way.

5. *Exemplary followers* present a consistent picture to both leaders and coworkers of being independent, innovative, and willing to stand up to superiors. They apply their talents for the benefit of the organization even when confronted with bureaucratic stumbling blocks or passive or pragmatist coworkers. Effective leaders appreciate the value of exemplary followers. When one of the authors was serving in a follower role in a staff position, he was introduced by his leader to a conference as "my favorite subordinate because he's a loyal 'No-Man.'"

Exemplary followers—high on both critical dimensions of followership—are essential to organizational success. Leaders, therefore, would be well advised to select people who have these characteristics and, perhaps even more importantly, *create the conditions that encourage these behaviors.*

There is even a theory of leadership called **Leader-Member Exchange Theory** that describes these two kinds of relationships and how they affect the types of power and influence tactics leaders use (Graen & Cashman, 1975).

We will now examine each of the three main elements of the interactional framework in turn.

The Leader

This element primarily examines what the leader brings *as an individual* to the leadership equation. This can include unique personal history, interests, character traits, and motivation. Peter Jackson's effectiveness as a leader has been due in large part to a unique combination of personal qualities and talents. One associate, for example, called him "one of the smartest people I know," as well as a maverick willing to buck the establishment. Jackson is also a tireless worker whose early successes were due in no small part to the combination of his ambition and dogged perseverance (Botes, 2004).

Source: The "Bizarro" cartoon by Dan Piraro is reprinted courtesy Chronicle Features, San Francisco, California. All rights reserved.

I'll be blunt, coach. I'm having a problem with this 'take a lap' thing of yours . . .''

Leaders are *not* all alike, but they do tend to share many common characteristics. Research has shown that leaders differ from their followers, and effective leaders differ from ineffective leaders, on various personality traits, cognitive abilities, skills, and values (Stogdill, 1948, 1974; Hogan, Curphy, & Hogan, 1994; Lord, De-Vader, & Allinger, 1986; Kanter, 1983; Baltzell, 1980). Another way personality can affect leadership is through temperament, by which we mean whether the leader is generally calm or is instead prone to emotional outbursts. Leaders who have calm dispositions and do not attack or belittle others for bringing bad news are more likely to get complete and timely information from subordinates than are bosses who have explosive tempers and a reputation for killing the messenger.

Another important aspect of the leader is how he or she achieved leader status. Leaders who are appointed by superiors may have less credibility with subordinates and get less loyalty from them than leaders who are elected or emerge by consensus from the ranks of followers. Often, emergent or elected officials are better able to influence a group toward goal achievement because of the power conferred on them by their followers. However, both elected and emergent leaders need to be sensitive to their constituencies if they wish to remain in power.

More generally, a leader's experience or history in a particular organization is usually important to her or his effectiveness. For example, leaders promoted from within an organization, by virtue of being familiar with its culture and policies, may be ready to "hit the job running." In addition, leaders selected from within an organization are typically better known by others in the organization than are leaders selected from the outside. That is likely to affect, for better or worse, the latitude others in the organization are willing to give the leader; if the leader is widely respected for a history of accomplishment, then she may be given more latitude than a newcomer whose track record is less well known. On the other hand, many people tend to give new leaders a fair chance to succeed, and newcomers to an organization often take time to learn the organization's informal rules, norms, and "ropes" before they make any radical or potentially controversial decisions.

A leader's legitimacy also may be affected by the extent to which followers participated in the leader's selection. When followers have had a say in the selection or election of a leader they tend to have a heightened sense of psychological identification with her, but they also may have higher expectations and make more demands on her (Hollander & Offermann, 1990). We also might wonder what kind of support a leader has from his own boss. If followers sense their boss has a lot of influence with the higher-ups, then subordinates may be reluctant to take their complaints to higher levels. On the other hand, if the boss has little influence with higher-ups, subordinates may be more likely to make complaints to these levels.

The foregoing examples highlight the sorts of insights one can gain about leadership by focusing on the individual leader as a level of analysis. Even if we were to examine the individual leader completely, however, our understanding of the leadership process would be incomplete.

The Followers

Followers are a critical part of the leadership equation, but their role has not always been appreciated. For example, one can look at history and be struck by the contributions of extraordinary individual leaders. Does the relative inattention to their followers mean the latter made no contributions themselves to the leadership process? Wasn't Mr. Spock's logic an important counterbalance to Captain Kirk's intuition on Star Trek? Wasn't the Lone Ranger daring partly because he knew he could count on Tonto to rescue him from impossible situations (Jones, 2003).

Even the major reviews of the leadership literature show that researchers have paid relatively little attention to the roles followers play in the leadership process (see Bass, 1981, 1990; Stogdill, 1974). However, we know that the followers' expectations, personality traits, maturity levels, levels of competence, and motivation affect the leadership process too (Sutton & Woodman, 1989; Burke, 1965; Moore, 1976; Scandura, Graen, & Novak, 1986; Sales, Levanoni, & Saleh, 1984).

Impressive as Aung San Suu Kyi is as a populist leader, it is impossible to understand her effectiveness purely in terms of her own personal characteristics. It is impossible to understand it independent of her followers—the people of Burma. Her rapid rise to prominence as the leading voice for democracy and freedom in Burma must be understood in terms of the living link she represented to the country's greatest modern hero—her father. He was something of a George Washington figure in that he founded the Burmese Army in 1941 and later made a successful transition from military leadership to political leadership. At the height of his influence, when he was the universal choice to be Burma's first president, he was assassinated. Suu Kyi was two years old. Stories about his life and principles indelibly shaped Suu Kyi's own life, but his life and memory also created a readiness among Suu Kyi's countrymen for her to take up his mantle of leadership.

The nature of followers' motivation to do their work is also important. Workers who share a leader's goals and values, and who feel intrinsically rewarded for performing a job well, might be more likely to work extra hours on a time-critical project than those whose motivation is solely monetary.

Even the number of followers reporting to a leader can have significant implications. For example, a store manager having three clerks working for him can spend more time with each of them (or on other things) than can a manager responsible for eight clerks and a separate delivery service; chairing a task force with five members is a different leadership activity than chairing a task force with eighteen members. Still other relevant variables include followers' trust in the leader and their confidence (or not) that he or she is interested in their well-being.

Changing Roles for Followers

The preceding examples illustrate just a few ways in which followers compose an important and complementary level of analysis for understanding leadership. Such examples should point out how leadership must be understood in the context of a particular group of followers as well as in terms of an individual leader. Now, more than ever before, understanding followers is central to understanding leadership. That is because the leader–follower relationship is in a period of dynamic change (Lippitt, 1982; Block, 1992; Hollander, 1994). One reason for this changing relationship is an increasing pressure on all kinds of organizations to function with reduced resources. Reduced resources and company downsizing have reduced the number of managers and increased their span of control, which in turn leaves followers to pick up many of the functions traditionally performed by leaders. Another reason is a trend toward greater power sharing and decentralized authority in organizations, which in turn creates greater interdependence among organizational subunits and increased need

If you act like an ass, don't get insulted if people ride you.

Yiddish proverb

for collaboration among them. Furthermore, the nature of problems faced by many organizations is becoming so complex and the changes are becoming so rapid that more and more people are required to solve them.

These trends suggest several different ways in which followers can take on new leadership roles and responsibilities in the future. For one thing, followers can become much more proactive in their stance toward organizational problems. When facing the discrepancy between the way things are in an organization and the way they could or should be, followers can play an active and constructive role collaborating with leaders in solving problems. In general, making organizations better is a task that needs to be "owned" by followers as well as by leaders. With these changing roles for followers, it should not be surprising to find that qualities of good followership are statistically correlated with qualities typically associated with good leadership. One recent study found positive correlations between the followership qualities of active engagement and independent thinking and the leadership qualities of dominance, sociability, achievement orientation, and steadiness (Tanoff & Barlow, 2002).

In addition to helping solve organizational problems, followers can better contribute to the leadership process by becoming better skilled at "influencing upward." Because followers are often at the level where many organizational problems occur, they can provide leaders with relevant information so that good solutions are implemented. Although it is true that some leaders need to become better listeners, it is also true that many followers need training in expressing ideas to superiors more clearly and positively. Still another way followers can assume a greater share of the leadership challenge in the future is by staying flexible and open to opportunities. The future portends more change, not less, and followers who face change with positive anticipation and an openness to self-development will be particularly valued and rewarded (Senge, 1990).

Thus, to an ever increasing degree, leadership must be understood in terms of both leader variables and follower variables, as well as the interactions among them. But even that is not enough. In addition to understanding the leader and the followers, we must also understand the particular situations in which leaders and followers find themselves.

The Situation

The situation is the third critical part of the leadership equation. Even if we knew all we could know about a given leader and a given set of followers, leadership makes sense only in the context of how the leader and followers interact in a given situation (see Highlight 2.2).

The situation may be the most ambiguous aspect of the leadership framework since it can refer to anything from the specific task a group is engaged in all the way to broad situational contexts such as the remote predicament of the Andes survivors.

Berkeley in the 1960s

Highlight 2.2

The 1960s were a period of dissent and conflict, and perhaps even today no place epitomizes the decade more than Berkeley, California. But Berkeley did not always have a radical reputation.

The Berkeley campus of the huge University of California system had not always been a center of student protest and large-scale demonstrations. For a long time, it had been relatively sedate and conservative, even if also quite large; more than 20,000 students attended Berkeley in 1960. Campus leaders were clean-cut students who belonged to fraternities and sororities. Berkeley changed, however, in the fall of 1964 when a relatively small number of students launched what became known as the Free Speech Movement. Subsequent protests at other campuses across the country, and later globally, are traceable to the Free Speech Movement at Berkeley. One of its leaders was Mario Savio.

The sources of conflict and radicalism at Berkeley were many, including civil rights and the Vietnam War. But protest in Berkeley first erupted over the issue of whether students could solicit donations and distribute political materials near campus. Whether students could solicit donations or distribute materials on campus had been settled earlier; they could not. In response to having been ordered off campus, however, some student groups set up card tables just off campus, between the university's impressive Sproul Plaza and Berkeley's Telegraph Avenue, with its exciting and bohemian milieu of bookstores and coffeehouses.

Perhaps because their appearance so near the campus offended university officials—the student workers were rarely dressed or groomed in the clean-cut image favored by conservative administrators—even this activity eventually was prohibited. Outraged, a few students defiantly set up tables back in Sproul Plaza, right in the heart of the campus. Disturbed at this open rebuke to its authority, the university directed police to arrest one of the disobedient students. It was October 1, 1964, the birth of the Free Speech Movement.

Presumably, university officials believed this show of force on their part would dishearten the band of student protesters and break them up. As the arrested

student got into the waiting police car, however, someone shouted, "Sit down!" and hundreds of other students immediately did just that. They sat down on the plaza right where they were, effectively blocking the car's movement. The police and administration had never before confronted such massive defiance, and for 32 hours the car stayed put (with the "prisoner," Jack Weinberg, inside) while demonstrators used its roof as a podium from which to speak to the crowd. One who climbed up to speak several times, and who clearly had a gift for energizing the crowd, was Mario Savio. In many ways, the Free Speech Movement, which pitted a rigid university bureaucracy against increasing numbers of alienated students, became a confrontation between just two people: Mario Savio and the university's brilliant but aloof president, Clark Kerr. It was not, however, a fair fight.

As W. J. Rorabaugh has observed, Kerr didn't stand a chance. The student activists were prepared for war, and Kerr wasn't. He was out of touch with the sentiments of increasing numbers of students, sentiments that in part were a direct result of the university's continuing neglect of undergraduate education at the expense of graduate study and government-sponsored research.

The students, on the other hand, had a clear objective—the freedom to be politically active on campus (i.e., free speech). Furthermore, many were politically experienced, seasoned by their participation in civil rights marches in the South. They understood the politics of protest, crowd psychology, the importance of the media, and how to maintain spirit and discipline in their own ranks. Thus, many ingredients for a successful social movement were present. All that was needed was a spark to ignite them and a leader to channel them.

Mario Savio was not a typical undergraduate. His commitment to social reform already was deep, and his experiences were broad. Raised in a devout Catholic family, he had worked in rural Mexico for a church relief organization and had taught in a school for black children in Mississippi. He was proud, cocky, and defiant. It was his ability to articulate his rage,

(continued)

Berkeley in the 1960s *(continued)*

however, that set Savio apart. He could give words and reason to the frustration and anger others were only feeling. Interestingly, Savio was a very different person in private than in public. In private, he seemed cold, hesitant, and self-doubting, but in front of a crowd he could be inspiring.

He may have been at his best at a protest rally in December 1964. Here is what it was like to be in Berkeley in the 60s, listening to a new kind of student leader, one giving voice to the sense of powerlessness and frustration with modern life, which would be a common theme in student revolts throughout the rest of the decade:

> There is a time when the operation of the machine becomes so odious, makes you so sick at heart, that

you can't take part; you can't even passively take part, and you've got to put your bodies upon the gears and upon the wheels, upon the levers, upon all the apparatus and you've got to make it stop. And you've got to indicate to the people who run it, to the people that own it, that unless you're free, the machines will be prevented from working at all (Rorabaugh, p. 31).

Earlier that year, Savio had written, "I'm tired of reading history. Now I want to make it." He did. Try to analyze the emergence of Mario Savio in terms of the interactional framework.

Source: W. J. Rorabaugh, *Berkeley at War* (New York: Oxford University Press, 1989).

Colin Powell

We can also understand the interactional framework better by looking more closely at Colin Powell's situation (Powell, 1995). In November of 1992, Bill Clinton had been elected president but had not yet assumed office. He asked to see Colin Powell, then chairman of the Joint Chiefs of Staff. Powell's political affiliation and preferences at that time were unknown, but he had served faithfully under Presidents Reagan and Bush and had successfully orchestrated a wartime victory for President Bush in Operation Desert Storm.

The president-elect began by complimenting Powell about a speech he had made, and inquired about a few matters of national defense. Clinton particularly asked for Powell's thoughts about a possible nominee to secretary of defense; in other words, about the general's potential next boss. Clinton was inclined to name Congressman Les Aspin, pointedly complimenting Aspin's intelligence. Despite Clinton's evident intent to name Aspin, however, Powell said he had reservations about the nomination. He, too, complimented Aspin's intelligence but expressed concern that Aspin's disorganized management style would be inappropriate for a person having responsibility for such a large bureaucracy. The two went on to discuss other issues for over an hour, but when Powell rose to leave there was one more thing he needed to say. He felt he needed to address a political promise Clinton had made during the presidential campaign: a promise to end the ban on gays in the military. He said the senior military leadership didn't want it lifted, military people in general didn't want it lifted, and most in Congress didn't want it lifted. The concern, Powell stressed, was privacy. He wondered how the ban could be made to work in the close circumstances of living in army barracks or on naval ships. He asked the president-elect not to make this issue the first priority of the new administration.

You've got to give loyalty down, if you want loyalty up.

Donald T. Regan,
Former CEO and White House
chief of staff

Despite Powell's counsel, however, it did become so, and a highly controversial one at that. Through both private negotiation and public media questioning, both Powell and Clinton remained committed to their respective positions. Eventually, a compromise policy, popularly known as "don't ask, don't tell," was instituted that is still considered hopelessly flawed by many on both sides. But now let us look at this situation from the perspective of the interactional framework.

First of all, note how much more complex the situation of their meeting was than a mere first meeting between two successful men. One of them was the top military leader in the world at that time, the other would soon be his commander in chief by virtue of free election in a constitutional government which subordinates the military to civilian authority (just to be clear, this is *not* the case for most countries throughout history). In their first face-to-face meeting, which would set the tone for their future working relationship, Powell disagreed with several proposals favored by Clinton (frank and open disagreement, of course, is often the sign of a *constructive* relationship, and that is most likely the way the counsel was both given and received). Perhaps more significantly, both felt obligated to different courses of action and to different groups of stakeholders. Clinton, as a politician and new world leader, must also have been concerned about how the controversy would affect national and international perceptions of his leadership and credibility.

So just what was the situation here? It was the constitutionally mandated nature of their authority relationship. It was the interpersonal context of one person giving unpopular feedback or advice to someone else. It was the very real pressure being exerted on each man independently by different constituencies having different agendas. It was all these things, and more. Leadership, here as everywhere, involves the leader, the followers, and the complex situation they're a part of.

Are Good Women Leaders Hard to Find?

One important case in point of the complex interactions among leaders, followers, and the situation involves women in leadership roles. In this section we'll examine the extent to which women are taking on greater leadership responsibility than ever before, whether there are differences in the effectiveness of men and women in leadership roles, and what explanations have been offered to explain differences between men and women in being selected for and succeeding in positions of leadership. This is an area of considerable academic research and popular polemics, as evident in many recent articles in the popular press that claim a distinct advantage for women in leadership roles (e.g., Conlin, 2003).

Aung San Suu Kyi also has quite strong opinions herself on this subject. She said, "It is the woman who has to manage the household and I cannot accept the fact that a woman leader can't be given the leadership position in a country. That's why I am of the opinion that if a woman rules Burma, there will be progress in all sectors of the country."

It is clear that women are taking on leadership roles in greater numbers than ever before. That's certainly true in government. In the U.S. Senate, for example, 42 percent of the women who have ever served there were holding office in 2003 (White House Project, 2002). Around the world, 43 of the 59 women ever to serve as presidents or prime ministers came into office since 1990 (Adler, 1999; de Zarate, 2003). The increasing proportion of women in leadership is evident outside of government as well. In 1972 women held 18 percent of managerial and administrative positions in the United States, but by 2002 the figure had risen to 46 percent (U.S. Bureau of Labor Statistics, 1982, 2002).

While these statistics are important and promising, however, the fact is that problems still exist which constrain the opportunity for capable women to rise to the highest leadership roles in organizations (see Highlight 2.3). Many studies have been done considering this problem, a few of which we'll examine here.

In a classic study of sex roles, Schein (1973, 1975) demonstrated how bias in sex role stereotypes created problems for women moving up through these managerial roles. Schein asked male ($n = 300$) and female ($n = 167$) middle managers to complete a survey on which they rated various items on a five-point scale in terms of how characteristic they were of (*a*) men in general, (*b*) women in general, or (*c*) successful managers. Schein found a high correlation between the ways both male and female respondents perceived "males" and "managers," but no correlation between the ways the respondents perceived "females" and "managers." It was as though being a manager was defined by attributes thought of as masculine. Furthermore, it does not appear that the situation has changed much over the past two decades. In 1990, management students in the United States, Germany, and Great Britain, for example, still perceived successful middle managers in terms of characteristics more commonly ascribed to men than to women (Schein & Mueller, 1990). One area where

Insights of a Woman Who Broke the Glass Ceiling

Highlight 2.3

Kim Campbell distinguished herself in many ways. She was Canada's first female prime minister, and she now chairs the Council of Women World Leaders. In 2002 she was interviewed about the challenges and opportunities for women rising into senior leadership positions in organizations, and here are two brief excerpts of what she said:

You've held many positions that are traditionally filled by men. What's the greatest obstacle you've encountered?

There is a deeply rooted belief that women are not competent and can't lead. That's because there's an overlap in people's minds between the qualities that we associate with leadership and the qualities that we associate with masculinity—decisiveness, aggressiveness, competence. There is

much less overlap between leadership qualities and those we associate with being feminine—an inclination toward consensus-building, to be communal, expressive, nurturing. That's why for many people it was rather disturbing that I was prime minister. A woman wasn't supposed to be prime minister. I wasn't entitled to be there.

You've said that having women in leadership is more important now than ever. Why now?

We're living in a time when we see the frightening limitations of masculine cultures. Cultures that are totally masculine can give rise to fundamentalisms—they can be intolerant, narrow, violent, corrupt, antidemocratic. That's at a state level. At a corporate level, a macho culture made Enron possible.

Source: Excerpted from *Harvard Business Review,* 2002, pp. 20–21.

views *do* seem to have changed over time involves women's perceptions of their own roles. In contrast to the earlier studies, women today see as much similarity between "female" and "manager" as between "male" and "manager" (Brenner, Tomkiewicz, & Schein, 1989). To women, at least, being a woman and being a manager are not a contradiction in terms.

There also have been many other studies of the role of women in management. In one of these, *Breaking the Glass Ceiling* (Morrison, White, & Van Velsor, 1987), researchers documented the lives and careers of 78 of the highest-level women in corporate America. A few years later the researchers followed up with a small sample of those women to discuss any changes that had taken place in their leadership paths. The researchers were struck by the fact that the women were much like the senior men they had worked with in other studies. Qualitatively, they had the same fears: They wanted the best for themselves and for their families. They wanted their company to succeed. And, not surprisingly, they still had a drive to succeed. In some cases (also true for the men) they were beginning to ask questions about life balance—was all the sacrifice and hard work worth it? Were 60-hour workweeks worth the cost to family and self?

Looking more quantitatively, however, the researchers expected to find significant differences between the women who had broken the glass ceiling and the men who were already there. After all, the popular literature and some social scientific literature had conditioned them to expect that there is a feminine versus a masculine style of leadership, the feminine style being an outgrowth of a consensus/team-oriented leadership approach. Women, in this view, are depicted as leaders who, when compared to men, are better listeners, more empathic, less analytical, more people oriented, and less aggressive in pursuit of goals.

In examining women in leadership positions, the researchers collected behavioral data, including ratings by both self and others, assessment center data (gathered from leadership development programs at the Center for Creative Leadership), and their scores on the California Psychological Inventory. Contrary to the stereotypes and popular views, however, there were no statistically significant differences between men's and women's leadership styles. Women and men were equally analytical, people oriented, forceful, goal oriented, empathic, and skilled at listening. There were other differences between the men and women, however, beyond the question of leadership styles. The researchers did find (and these results must be interpreted cautiously because of the relatively small numbers involved) that women had significantly lower well-being scores, their commitment to the organizations they worked for was more guarded than that of their male counterparts, and the women were much more likely to be willing to take career risks associated with going to new or unfamiliar areas of the company where women had not been before.

Continued work with women in corporate leadership positions has both reinforced and somewhat clarified these findings. For example, the lower scores for women with regard to their ratings of general well-being may reflect the inadequacy of their support system for dealing with day-to-day issues of living. This is tied to the reality for many women that in addition to having roles in their companies they remain chief caretakers for their families. Further, there may be additional pressures of being visibly identified as proof that the organization has women at the top.

Other types of differences—particularly those around "people issues"—are still not evident. In fact, the hypothesis is that such supposed differences may hinder the opportunities for leadership development of women in the future. For example, turning around a business that is in trouble or starting a new business are two of the most exciting opportunities a developing leader has to test her leadership abilities. If we apply the "women are different" hypothesis, then the type of leadership skills needed for successful completion of either of these assignments may well leave women off the list of candidates. However, if we accept the hypothesis that women and men are more alike as leaders than they are different, then women will be found in equal numbers on the candidate list.

Neither shall you allege the example of the many as an excuse for doing wrong.

Exodus 23.2

Research on second-generation managerial women suggest many of them appear to be succeeding *because of* characteristics heretofore considered too feminine for effective leadership (Rosener, 1990). Rosener's survey research identified several differences in how men and women described their leadership experiences. Men tended to describe themselves in somewhat transactional terms, viewing leadership as an exchange with subordinates for services rendered. They influenced others primarily through their organizational position and authority. The women, on the other hand, tended to describe themselves in transformational terms. They helped subordinates develop commitment for broader goals than their own self-interest, and described their influence more in terms of personal characteristics like charisma and interpersonal skill than mere organizational position.

According to Rosener such women leaders encouraged participation and shared power and information, but went far beyond what is commonly thought of as participative management. She called it **interactive leadership.** Their leadership self-descriptions reflected an approach based on enhancing others' self-worth and believing that the best performance results when people are excited about their work and feel good about themselves.

How did this interactive leadership style develop? Rosener concluded it was due to these women's socialization experiences and career paths. As we indicated above, the social role expected of women has emphasized they be cooperative, supportive, understanding, gentle, and service-oriented. As they entered the business world, they still found themselves in roles emphasizing these same behaviors. They found themselves in staff, rather than line, positions, and in roles lacking formal authority over others such that they had to accomplish their work without reliance on formal power. What they had to do, in other words, was employ their socially acceptable behavioral repertoire in order to survive organizationally.

> What came easily to women turned out to be a survival tactic. Although leaders often begin their careers doing what comes naturally and what fits within the constraints of the job, they also develop their skills and styles over time. The women's use of interactive leadership has its roots in socialization, and the women interviewees firmly believe that it benefits their organizations. Through the course of their careers, they have gained conviction that their style is effective. In fact, for some it was their own success that caused them to formulate their philosophies about what motivates people, how to make good decisions, and what it takes to maximize business performance. (p. 124)

"That's what they all say, honey."

Rosener called for organizations to expand their definitions of effective leadership—to create a *wider* band of acceptable behavior so that both men and women will be freer to lead in ways which take advantage of their true talents. The extent of the problem is suggested by data from a study looking at how CEOs, almost all male, and senior female executives explained the paucity of women in corporate leadership roles. Figure 2.2 compares the percentages of CEOs versus female executives who endorsed various possible explanations of the situation. It is clear that the CEOs attributed it primarily to inadequacies in the quantity and quality of experience of potential women candidates for the top spots, while the females themselves attributed it to various forms of stereotyping and bias.

A recent study sheds additional light on factors that impact the rise of women in leadership positions (Eagly & Carli, 2003). It identifies four general factors that explain the shift toward more women leaders.

The first of these is that *women themselves have changed.* That's evident in the ways women's aspirations and attitudes have become more similar to those of men over time. That's illustrated in findings about the career aspirations of female university students (Astin, Parrott, Korn & Sax, 1997), women's self-reports of traits

FIGURE 2.2

What prevents women from advancing to corporate leadership?

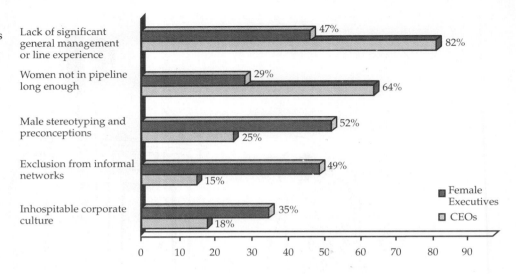

such as assertiveness, dominance and masculinity (Twenge, 1997, 2001), and the value that women place on characteristics of work such as freedom, challenge, leadership, prestige, and power (Konrad, Ritchie, Lieb, & Corrigal, 2000). The second factor is that *leadership roles have changed,* particularly with regard to a trend toward less stereotypically masculine characterizations of leadership. Third, *organizational practices* have changed. A large part of this can be attributed to legislation prohibiting gender-based discrimination at work, as well as changes in organizational norms that put a higher priority on results than an "old boy" network. Finally, the *culture has changed.* This is evident, for example, in the symbolic message often intended by appointment of women to important leadership positions, one representing a departure from past practices and signaling commitment to progressive change.

Leadership and Management Revisited

In Chapter 1 we looked at the relationship between leadership and management, and between leaders and managers. While these terms are not mutually exclusive, they do refer to a person's distinctive *style* and *approach.* Even in a particular role, two people may approach it differently; one more like a leader, the other more like a manager. The governor of one state, for example, may function more as a leader, whereas the governor of another state may function more as a manager (and not because there's anything different about the two states). It will be helpful to revisit those concepts in the context of the interactional framework.

Let's begin by reviewing some of the distinctions Bennis makes between leaders and managers.

Leaders	**Managers**
Innovate	Administer
Develop	Maintain
Inspire	Control
Long-term view	Short-term view
Ask what and why	Ask how and when
Originate	Initiate
Challenge the status quo	Accept the status quo
Do the right things	Do things right

Bennis is hardly alone in contrasting leaders and managers. Numerous other scholars echo the idea of a basic distinction between leadership and management. Kotter (1990), for example, described management in terms of coping with complexity, and leadership in terms of coping with change. Kotter noted how managerial practices and procedures can be traced to the 20th-century phenomenon of large organizations and the need to bring order and consistency to their functioning. Renewed interest in leadership, on the other hand, springs from the challenge of maintaining organizational success in an increasingly dynamic world. He said most U.S. corporations today, for example, are overmanaged and underled; but that "strong leadership with weak management is no better" (p. 103). Fairholm (1991) emphasized still other differences between leadership and management when he wrote that

> leadership and management are different in purpose, knowledge base, required skills, and goals. We distinguish leaders as more personal in their orientation to group members than managers. They are more global in their thinking. Leaders, we suggest, focus on values, expectations, and context. Managers, on the other hand, focus on control and results. Leaders impact followers and constituent groups in a way that allows volitional activity of followers, not through formal authority mechanisms . . . Managers give clear direction, make solitary assignments, and work hard for cooperation. The leader communicates indirectly, gives overlapping and ambiguous assignments, and sometimes sets employees up for internecine strife—to test loyalty and the leader's personal strength. Leaders value cooperation, not just coordination. They foster ideas of unity, equality, justice, and fairness in addition to efficiency and effectiveness, the bastions of management value. (p. 40)

Such differences are just what our framework is all about—**interactions.** In other words, the differences between leaders and managers, or between leadership and management, involve more than just differences between types of individuals. The differences extend to how such individuals *interact with* their followers and the situations they confront. Let's explore how these distinctions affect the other two elements of the framework.

Leader-Follower-Situation Interactions

Leaders create environments within which followers' innovations and creative contributions are welcome. Followers feel a stake in *shaping* something new, not just maintaining a status quo. Leaders also encourage growth and development in their followers in ways broader than what we might call mere job training (e.g., encouraging a follower to take on something really new, something that would stretch the follower but may involve failure on the task; or taking on a developmental experience not directly tied to the follower's present job requirements). Leaders generally are more interested in the big picture of followers' work, and tend to assess their followers' performance less formally and less in terms of specific criteria than managers, and more in terms of holistic, personal, idiosyncratic, or intuitive criteria. Leaders motivate followers more personally and through more personal and intangible factors (e.g., through inspiration, or the reward of just being able to work with the leader, or on a particular project). Leaders redefine the parameters of tasks and responsibilities, both for individual followers and for the entire group. In that sense, leaders actively *change* the situations they're in rather than just optimize their group's adaptation to it. They are forever "moving outside the constraints of structure" (Fairholm, p. 39). Such redefinitions also may occur through taking a long-term rather than a short-term perspective, through accentuating critical values or ends, or by marshaling energy to cope with some new threat.

Manager-Follower-Situation Interactions

Managers are more likely to emphasize routinization and control of followers' behavior. This might be expressed in terms of greater emphasis on making sure followers conform to policies or procedures ("doing it the way we've always done it") or in a tendency to assign narrower rather than broader tasks for followers to perform. It might be expressed in lesser degrees of decision-making discretion or autonomy given to followers, as in a manager's tendency to review *details* of work for them. Managers tend to assess their followers' performance in terms of explicit, fairly specific job descriptions. Managers motivate followers more with extrinsic, even contractual consequences, both positive and negative. Managers tend to accept the definitions of situations presented to them. They might be unlikely, for example, to reorient a group's task or mission in a whole new direction; or to change the whole culture of an organization. When managers do change things, they would be more likely to effect change officially, through control tactics such as developing new policies or procedures.

All men have some weak points and the more vigorous and brilliant a person may be, the more strongly these weak points stand out. It is highly desirable, even essential, therefore, for the more influential members of a general's staff not to be too much like the general.

Major General Hugo Baron von Freytag-Loringhoven, Anti-Hitler conspirator

In reading the preceding paragraphs, it may seem to you that it's better to be a leader than a manager (or, perhaps, vice versa). But such a conclusion would ignore important characteristics of the followers. In some situations leaders are successful and managers are not, but in other situations the opposite is true. Consider, for example, one of Bennis's prototypical leaders: an inspiring individual having a vision of major institutional change that can be achieved only through the energy and creativity of committed followers. Such an inspiring individual may be thwarted, nonetheless, unless her followers share her value-based vision. If they are motivated primarily by economic incentives and are satisfied with their present lot, then the leader may fail to achieve her vision. The whole idea of *interaction* is that the effectiveness of any particular leader approach can be understood only in the context of certain follower and situational conditions. To return to Bennis's distinctions, managers emphasize *stability* whereas leaders emphasize *change*. Managers emphasize consistency and predictability in follower behavior (doing what's expected, doing things right), whereas leaders emphasize *changing* followers. That may mean transforming them or getting them to do more than they thought they could or thought they would. We'll see a similar distinction in Chapter 13 when we contrast transactional and transformational leadership (Bass, 1985).

Leadership, Management, and the Disney Brothers

Walt Disney is surely one of the most familiar names in the world. Roy Disney is not. Roy was Walt's brother, and he played a vital but different role in the success of the Disney enterprises. In many ways you can think of the differences between them in terms of the distinctions we've been making between leadership and management. In many ways Walt was the creative leader, Roy the manager or "financial guy." The success of the Disney enterprises was due to their *complementary* contributions, and their story provides an interesting illustration of how leaders interact with their followers and situations differently than managers do (Snyder, Dowd, & Houghton, 1994).

One of Walt's distinctive qualities was his drive to experiment and find new ways to improve motion picture quality. He was an innovator himself, but even more importantly he encouraged his staff to be innovative. His studio was always "on the move." He wanted it to be on the technological cutting edge of animation art and never fall prey to a cut-and-dried way of doing things. From the early days, Walt handled the creative side of Disney productions whereas Roy handled the job of securing financing for their cartoons. Walt was never interested in making money as an end in itself, but rather as a means to producing ever-better films. He would not compromise his sense of film quality to increase profit. In fact, he was a gambler willing to risk all for an idea he believed in. Walt's enthusiasm for the creative process was infectious and spread to his staff, who themselves were more dedicated to their art than to the bottom line. Walt's staff believed they were pioneers who were changing the very nature of mass media. He created an energetic and informal environment; he resisted rigid procedures and bureaucracy, yet his staff believed he ran the best studio in the world. One way Walt inspired such commitment among his followers was through his own commitment to *their* development and creative involvement in the studio's work. He brought out the best in them, a quality of work beyond what they believed themselves capable of. He wanted all the people working for him to feel they were making indispensable contributions to the overall project. He encouraged his staff to use their *own* skills to devise original solutions to challenges rather than merely find out what he wanted them to do.

An interesting case in point of the difference between a leader's and manager's orientation may be in the disagreement Walt and Roy Disney had over Walt's idea of a new amusement park. What we now know as Disneyland, and may incorrectly assume looked like a surefire success as soon as Walt proposed it, was initially opposed by Roy. Roy thought it was just another one of Walt's crazy ideas, and was only willing to risk $10,000 of studio money on what he thought was a harebrained project. Trusting his own vision more than his brother's risk-averse conservatism, Walt scraped together the money needed to finance Disneyland—in part by borrowing on his own life insurance. Even after Walt's death the differences between him and his brother illustrate what's different between leadership and management. Without Walt's creative leadership, the studio fell under the management of

"Roy men" who produced moderately successful but uninspired formula pieces for two decades. Only under Michael Eisner, a "Walt man" who understands popular culture, did the studio regain a leading place in American business.

A Final Word

Fairholm (1991) argued that organizations may need *two different kinds of people at the helm:* good leaders *and* good managers. He wrote, "We need competent, dedicated managers to provide continuity of process, to insure program productivity, and to control and schedule the materials needed for production or service delivery. We also need people who can infuse the organization with common values that define the organization, determine its character, link it to the larger society, and ensure its long-term survival" (p. 41). This view is certainly consistent with the success the two Disney brothers had bringing distinctive but complementary sets of competencies and values to their studio. But do examples like this prove that leaders and managers represent inherently different sorts of talents and interests? We think Kotter (1990) is on solid ground when he advises organizations preparing people for executive jobs to "ignore the recent literature that says people cannot manage and lead" (p. 104). He said they should try to develop leader-managers. In other words, it may be useful to distinguish between the functions of leadership and management but still *develop* those complementary functions in the same individuals.

This point may be particularly important with regard to developing the talents of *younger* leader-managers. It would seem inappropriately narrow and limiting for a young person to define himself or herself as "the manager type" or "the leader type." Premature self-definitions of being a leader *or* manager present such *reductio ad absurdum* eventualities as foreclosing real developmental opportunities (e.g., "I guess I shouldn't seek that student body position since it's a leadership role, and I'm really more the management type") or as inappropriate reactions to the sorts of job responsibilities typical for a person early in her career (e.g., "Boss, you've been giving me too many management-type tasks, and I see myself more as a leader around here"). It seems prudent to note the commonalities—as shown in Figure 1.1—between leadership and management and not focus exclusively on the differences between them, *especially in the early stages of a person's professional development.*

There Is No Simple Recipe for Effective Leadership

As noted previously, it is important to understand how the three domains of leadership interact—how the leader, the followers, and the situation are all part of the leadership process. Understanding their interaction is necessary before you can draw valid conclusions from the leadership you observe around you. When you see a leader's behavior (even when it may appear obviously effective or ineffective to you), you should not automatically conclude something good or bad about the leader, or what is the right way or wrong way leaders should act. You need to think about the effectiveness of that behavior in *that* context with *those* followers.

As obvious as the above sounds, we often ignore it. Too frequently, we just look at the leader's behavior and conclude that he or she is a good leader or a bad leader apart from the context. For example, suppose you observe a leader soliciting advice from subordinates. Obviously, it seems unreasonable to conclude that good leaders always ask for advice or that leaders who do not frequently ask for advice are not such good leaders. The appropriateness of seeking input from subordinates depends on many factors, such as the nature of the problem or the subordinates' familiarity with the problem. It may be that the subordinates have a lot more experience with this particular problem, and soliciting their input is the correct action to take in this situation.

Little things affect little minds.
Benjamin Disraeli

Consider another example. Suppose you hear that a leader disapproved a subordinate's request to take time off to attend to family matters. Was this bad leadership because the leader did not appear to be "taking care of her people"? Was it good leadership because she did not let personal matters interfere with the mission? Again, you cannot make an intelligent decision about the leader's actions by just looking at the behavior itself. You must always assess leadership in the context of the leader, the followers, and the situation.

The following statements about leaders, followers, and the situation make the above points a bit more systematically.

- A leader may need to respond to various followers differently in the same situation.
- A leader may need to respond to the same follower differently in different situations.
- Followers may respond to various leaders quite differently.
- Followers may respond to each other differently with different leaders.
- Two leaders may have different perceptions of the same followers or situations.

Conclusion: Drawing Lessons from Experience

All of the above leads to one conclusion: The right behavior in one situation is not necessarily the right behavior in another situation. It does *not* follow, however, that any behavior is appropriate in any situation. Although we may not be able to agree on the one best behavior in a given situation, we often can agree on some clearly inappropriate behaviors. Saying that the right behavior for a leader depends on the situation is not the same thing as saying it does not matter what the leader does. It merely recognizes the complexity among leaders, followers, and situations. This recognition is a helpful first step in drawing meaningful lessons about leadership from experience.

Summary

Leadership is a process in which leaders and followers interact dynamically in a particular situation or environment. Leadership is a broader concept than that of leaders, and the study of leadership must involve more than just the study of leaders as individuals. The study of leadership must also include two other areas: the followers and the situation. In addition, the interactive nature of these three domains has become increasingly important in recent years and can help us to better understand the changing nature of leader–follower relationships and the increasingly greater complexity of situations leaders and followers face. Because of this complexity, now, more than ever before, effective leadership cannot be boiled down to a simple and constant recipe. It is still true, however, that good leadership makes a difference, and it can be enhanced through greater awareness of the important factors influencing the leadership process.

Key Terms

interactional framework, 23	out-group, 24	passive followers, 25
leader, 24	independent, critical thinking, 25	Leader-Member Exchange Theory, 26
followers, 24	dependent, uncritical thinking, 25	interactive leadership, 36
situation, 24	active followers, 25	interactions, 39
in-group, 24		

Questions

1. According to the interactional framework, effective leader behavior depends on many variables. It follows there is no simple prescription for effective leader behavior. Does this mean effective leadership is merely a matter of opinion or subjective preference?

2. Generally, leaders get most of the credit for a group's or an organization's success. Do you believe this is warranted or fair?

3. What are some of the other characteristics of leaders, followers, and situations you could add to those listed in Figure 2.1?

Skills

Leadership skills relevant to this chapter include:

- Building effective relationships with superiors.
- Building effective relationships with peers.

Activity

In this activity you will explore connotations to the words *leadership* and *management*. Divide yourselves into small groups and have each group brainstorm different word associations to the terms *leader* and *leadership* or *manager* and *management*. In addition, each group should discuss whether they would prefer to work for a manager or for a leader, and why. Then the whole group should discuss similarities and differences among the respective perceptions and feelings about the two concepts.

Minicase

"Can Disney Save Disney?"

The Disney name identifies an institution whose $22 billion in annual sales make it the world's largest media company. It was Walt Disney's creative leadership that established the Disney company as one of the leaders in American business. Walt

Disney and his brother Roy started Disney Brothers Studio in Hollywood in 1923. Artistically, the 1930s were Disney's best years. Walt Disney embraced new advances in color and sound, and pushed his team of enthusiastic young artists to pursue the most sophisticated techniques of the day. Disney risked everything on his first feature film, *Snow White and the Seven Dwarfs,* released in 1937. Audiences loved it. His focus on the positive and the life-affirming themes he incorporated into all his work provided much-needed smiles and laughter for audiences during the depths of the Great Depression.

Roy Disney became chairman after Walt died of lung cancer in 1966. In 1971 Roy died and his son, Roy E. Disney, became the company's principal individual shareholder. In 1984 new CEO Michael Eisner and president Frank Wells ushered in an era of innovation and prosperity. They instituted marathon meetings for generating creative ideas, forcing everyone to work grueling hours. The approach worked and for the first 10 years of his tenure, Eisner was considered a genius. He revived Disney's historic animation unit, invested in the theme parks, led the expansion into Europe, and breathed new life into the company by partnering with cutting-edge companies like Pixar and Miramax. Eisner built Disney into a formidable media powerhouse, boosting its profits sixfold and sending its share price soaring almost 6,000 percent.

But more recent years have been challenging for Eisner and the Disney company. Eisner's initial magical effect has lost its shine and his more recent actions and decisions have had less-than-desirable effects on the company. Roy Disney, the last of the founding family to work at the company, quit the board in 2003 and began a campaign to try and oust Eisner. In his letter of resignation Disney asserted that Eisner has become an ineffective leader, claiming that Eisner consistently "micro-manages" everyone resulting in loss of morale. He saw Eisner's cost-conscience decisions to shut down an Orlando animation studio and cut costs at theme parks as resulting in "creative brain drain" and creating the perception that the company is looking for "quick buck" solutions rather than long-term value. Disney also cited Eisner's inability to maintain successful relationships with creative partners like Pixar and Miramax (both contracts with these studios were not renewed) and his lack of a succession plan as dangerous to the future of the company.

Disney has found a lot of support in his plan to "SAVE DISNEY." In the spring of 2004 stockholders supported Disney by voting against Eisner's re-election as president. Eisner still maintains his position as CEO and has expressed his intention to hold on to that position until his contract expires in 2006.

1. Consider Walt Disney's effectiveness in terms of the three domains of leadership—the leader, the followers, and the situation. For each domain name factors that contributed to Disney's success.

2. Now think about Michael Eisner's leadership effectiveness. Name factors within the three domains of leadership that might be responsible for controversy now surrounding Disney.

Sources: R. Grover, *The Disney Touch* (Burr Ridge: Irwin, 1997); BBC News Online business reporter Friday, 13 February, 2004, 08:03 GMT; http://www.usatoday.com/money/media/2004-01-19-disneyoutlook_x.htm; http://www.savedisney.com; http://www.usatoday.com/money/media/2004-01-19-disneyoutlook_x.htm

3

Leadership Is Developed through Education and Experience

Introduction

In Chapter 1, we discussed the importance of using multiple perspectives to analyze various leadership situations. Moreover, we argued that it is relatively difficult for leaders to develop this method of analysis on their own and that formal education is one of the best ways to develop multiple perspectives on leadership. Given the importance of formal education and experience in leadership development, this chapter reviews some of the ways you can better learn about leadership. As an overview, we begin this chapter by presenting a general model that describes

Leadership and learning are indispensable to each other.

John F. Kennedy

how we learn from experience. Next, we describe how perceptions can affect a leader's interpretation of, and actions in response to, a particular leadership situation and why reflection is important to leadership development. In addition, this chapter reveals how the people you work with and the task itself can help you become a better leader, and reviews some of the typical content and pedagogy found in many formal leadership education programs. Fi-

nally, we discuss how to evaluate and choose between the many different kinds of leadership programs available. A fitting place to begin the chapter might be to look at Highlight 3.1, which identifies the most critical skills leaders will need to be successful in the years ahead.

The Action-Observation-Reflection Model

Consider for a moment what a young person might learn from spending a year working in two very different environments: as a staff assistant in the U.S. Congress or as a carpenter on a house construction crew. Each activity has a rich store of leadership lessons there for the taking. Working in Congress, for example, would pro-

What Skills Will the Successful Leader Need in 2010?

Highlight 3.1

The Conference Board is a not-for-profit organization that conducts research, assesses trends, and makes forecasts about management to help businesses strengthen their performance and better serve society. In 2002 it identified critical skills leaders will need to be successful in the year 2010. Here's its list:

- Cognitive ability—both raw "intellectual horse-power" and mental agility.
- Strategic thinking, especially with regard to global competition.
- Analytical ability, especially the ability to sort through diverse sources of information and sort out what's most important.

- The ability to make sound decisions in an environment of ambiguity and uncertainty.
- Personal and organizational communication skills.
- The ability to be influential and persuasive with different groups.
- The ability to manage in an environment of diversity—managing people from different cultures, genders, generations, etc.
- The ability to delegate effectively.
- The ability to identify, attract, develop, and retain talented people.
- The ability to learn from experience.

Source: Barrett, A. and Beeson, J. Developing Business Leaders for 2010. *The Conference Board,* New York (2002).

vide opportunities to observe political leaders both onstage in the public eye and backstage in more private moments. It would provide opportunities to see members of Congress interacting with different constituencies, to see them in political defeat and political victory, and to see a range of leadership styles. A young person could also learn a lot by working on a building crew as it turned plans and materials into the reality of a finished house: watching the coordination with subcontractors, watching skilled craftsmen train younger ones, watching the leader's reactions to problems and delays, watching the leader set standards and assure quality work. At the same time, a person could work in either environment and *not* grow much if he or she is not disposed to. Making the most of experience is key to developing one's leadership ability. In other words, leadership development depends not just on the kinds of experiences one has but also on how one uses them to foster growth. A study of successful executives found that one key quality that characterized them was an "extraordinary tenacity in extracting something worthwhile from their experience and in seeking experiences rich in opportunities for growth" (McCall, Lombardo, & Morrison, 1988, p. 122).

But how does one do that? Is someone really more likely to get the lessons of experience by looking for them? Why is it not enough just to be there? Experiential learning theorists, such as Kolb (1983), believe people learn more from their experiences when they spend time thinking about them. These ideas are extended to leadership in the **action-observation-reflection** (A-O-R) **model,** depicted in Figure 3.1, which shows that leadership development is enhanced when the experience involves three different processes: action, observation, and reflection. If a person acts but does not observe the consequences of her actions or reflect on their significance and meaning, then it makes little sense to say she has

FIGURE 3.1
The spiral of
experience.

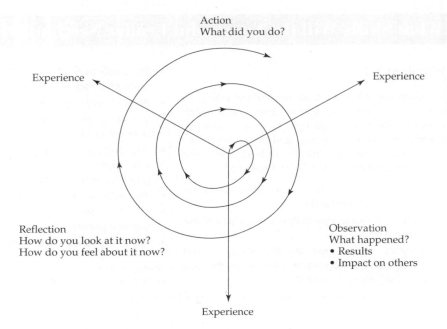

Action
What did you do?

Experience

Experience

Reflection
How do you look at it now?
How do you feel about it now?

Observation
What happened?
• Results
• Impact on others

Experience

*We shall not cease from exploration
And the end of all our exploring
Will be to arrive where we started
And know the place for the first
time.*

T. S. Eliot

learned from an experience. Because some people neither observe the consequences of their actions nor reflect on how they could change their actions to become better leaders, leadership development through experience may be better understood as the growth resulting from repeated movements through all three phases rather than merely in terms of some objective dimension like time (e.g., how long one has been on the job). We believe the most productive way to develop as a leader is to travel along the **spiral of experience** depicted in Figure 3.1.

Perhaps an example from Colin Powell's life will clarify how the spiral of experience pertains to leadership development. In 1963, Powell was a 26-year-old officer who had just returned to the United States from a combat tour in Vietnam. His next assignment would be to attend a month-long advanced airborne Ranger course. Near the end of the course, he was to parachute with other troops from a helicopter. As the senior officer on the helicopter, Powell had responsibility for assuring it went well. Early in the flight he hollered for everyone to make sure their static lines were secure, the cables which automatically pulled the chutes open when you jump. Nearing the jump site, he yelled for the men to check their hookups one more time. Here are his words describing what happened next:

> Then, like a fussy old woman, I started checking each line myself, pushing my way through the crowded bodies, running my hand along the cable and up to each man's chute. To my alarm, one hook belonging to a sergeant was loose. I shoved the dangling line in his face, and he gasped . . . This man would have stepped out of the door of the helo and dropped like a rock. (Powell, 1995, p. 109)

So what did Powell learn from this experience? Again, in his own words:

> Moments of stress, confusion, and fatigue are exactly when mistakes happen. And when everyone else's mind is dulled or distracted the leader must be doubly vigilant. "Always check small things" was becoming another one of my rules. (p. 109)

Let us now examine this incident in light of the A-O-R model. *Action* refers to Powell's multiple calls for the parachutists to check their lines. We might speculate from his self-description ("like a fussy old woman") that Powell might have felt slightly uncomfortable with such repeated emphasis on checking the lines, even though he persisted in the behavior. Perhaps you, too, sometimes have acted in a certain manner (or were forced to by your parents!) despite feeling a little embarrassed about it; and then, if it was successful, felt more comfortable the next time acting the same way. That seems to be just what happened with Powell here. The *observation* phase refers to Powell's shocked realization of the potentially fatal accident that would have occurred had he *not* double-checked the static lines. And the *reflection* phase refers to the lesson Powell drew from the experience: "Always check the small things." Even though it was obviously not a totally new insight, its importance was strongly reinforced by this experience. In a very real sense, Powell was "spiraling" through a lesson he'd learned from other experiences too, but embracing it even more this time, making it part of his style.

We also should note how Powell himself described his learning in a manner consistent with our interactional framework. He emphasized the situational importance of the leader's attention to detail, especially during moments of stress, confusion, and fatigue, when mistakes may be most likely to happen. Finally, it's worth noting that throughout Powell's autobiography he discusses many lessons he learned from experience. One of the keys to his success was his ability to keep learning throughout his career.

The Key Role of Perception in the Spiral of Experience

Experience is not just a matter of what events happen to you; it also depends on how you perceive those events. Perception affects all three phases of the action-observation-reflection model and thus plays a very important role in what anyone will extract from a leadership course or from any leadership situation. Human beings are not passive recorders of experiences that happen to them; rather, people actively shape and construct their experiences. In order to better understand how perception affects experience, we will examine its role in each part of the action-observation-reflection model. We will begin with the stage that seems to correspond most directly with perception—the observation phase.

Perception and Observation

Observation and perception both deal with attending to events around us. Both seem to take place spontaneously and effortlessly, so it is easy to regard them as passive processes. Our common mental images of the perceptual process reflect this implicit view. For example, it is a common misconception that the eye operates essentially like the film in a continuously running camera. The fallacy of this passive view of perception is that it assumes we attend to all aspects of a situation equally. However, we do not see everything that happens in a particular leadership situation, nor do we hear everything. Instead, we are selective in what we attend to and what we, in turn, perceive. One phenomenon that demonstrates this selectivity is called **perceptual set.** Perceptual sets can influence any of our senses, and they are the tendency or bias to perceive one thing and not another. Many factors can trigger a perceptual set, such as feelings, needs, prior experience, and expectations. Its role in distorting what one hears proved a costly lesson when a sympathetic airline pilot told his depressed co-pilot, "Cheer up!" The copilot thought the pilot had said, "Gear up," and raised the wheels while the plane was still on the ground (Reason & Mycielska, 1982). Try your own ability to overcome perceptual set with the following exercise. Read through the narrative passage below several times:

FINISHED FILES ARE THE RESULT
OF YEARS OF SCIENTIFIC STUDY
COMBINED WITH THE
EXPERIENCE OF MANY YEARS.

Make sure you have read it to yourself several times *before going any further.* Now, go back to the text and count the number of times the letter *F* appears.

It's not what we don't know that hurts, it's what we know that ain't so.
Will Rogers

How many did you count? Three? Four? Five? Six? Most people do not get the correct answer (six) the first time. The most frequent count is three; perhaps that was how many you saw. If you did not find six, go back and try it again. The most common error in this seemingly trivial task is overlooking the three times the word *of* appears. People easily overlook it because the word *of* has a *v* sound, not an *f* sound. Most people unconsciously make the task an auditory search task and listen for the sound of *F* rather than look for the shape of *F*; hence, they find three *F*s rather than six. Listening for the sound constitutes a counterproductive perceptual set for this task, and having read the passage through several times before counting the *F*s only exaggerates this tendency. Another reason people overlook the word *of* in this passage is that the first task was to *read* the passage several times. Because most of us are fairly accomplished readers, we tend to ignore little words like *of.* It disappears from our perceptual set. Then, when we are asked to count the number of *F*s, we have already defined the passage as a reading task, so the word *of* is really not there for us to count.

There are strong parallels between the example of perceptual set above and the perceptual sets that come into play when we are enrolled in a leadership course or observe a leadership situation. For example, your instructor for this class may dress unstylishly, and you may be prejudiced in thinking that poor dressers generally do not make good leaders. Because of your biases, you may discount or not attend to some things your instructor has to say about leadership. This is unfortunate, as your instructor's taste in clothes has little to do with his or her ability to teach (which is, after all, a kind of leadership).

A similar phenomenon takes place when one expects to find mostly negative things about another person (e.g., a problem employee). Such an expectation becomes a perceptual set to look for the negative and look past the positive things in the process. Stereotypes about gender, race, etc., represent powerful impediments to learning since they function as filters which distort one's observational abilities. For example, if you do not believe women and/or minorities are as successful as white males in influencing others, then you may be biased to identify or remember only those instances where a woman or minority leader failed, and discount or forget those instances where women or minority members succeeded as leaders. Unfortunately, we all have similar biases, although we are usually unaware of them. Often, we only become aware of our perceptual sets when we spend time reflecting about the content of a leadership training program or a particular leadership situation. Still another factor affecting the role observation plays in our ability to learn from experience is described in Highlight 3.2.

Perception and Reflection

Perceptual sets influence what we attend to or do not attend to, what we observe or do not observe. In addition, perception also influences the next stage of the spiral of experience—reflection—since reflection deals with how we interpret our observations. Perception is inherently an interpretive, or a meaning-making, activity. One important aspect of this deals with a process called **attribution.**

Attributions are the explanations we develop for the behaviors or actions we attend to. For example, if you see Julie fail in an attempt to get others to form a study group, you are likely to attribute the cause of the failure to dispositional factors within Julie. In other words, you are likely to attribute the failure to form a study group to Julie's intelligence, personality, physical appearance, or some other factor even though factors beyond her control could have played a major part. This tendency to overestimate the dispositional causes of behavior and underestimate the environmental causes when others fail is called the **fundamental attribution error** (Nisbett & Ross, 1980). People prefer to explain others' behavior on the basis of personal attributions, even when obvious situational factors may fully account for the behavior.

On Being Observant, Lucky, and Learning from Experience

Highlight 3.2

It's often said that some people have all the luck. Do you think that's true—are some people luckier than others? Richard Wiseman, a professor at the University of Hertfordshire, has written a book about just that question (2003), and his findings are very relevant to the role observation plays in our spiral of experience.

In one of his experiments, Wiseman placed advertisements in national newspapers asking for people to contact him who either felt consistently lucky or consistently unlucky. In one experiment, he gave both self-described lucky and unlucky people a newspaper to read, and asked them to look it over and tell him how many photographs were inside. Halfway through the paper he'd put a half-page message with two-inch lettering saying, "Tell the experimenter you have seen this and win $250."

The advertisement was staring everyone in the face, but the unlucky people tended to miss it whereas the lucky people tended to notice it. One reason may be related to the fact that Wiseman claims unlucky people are somewhat more anxious than lucky people, and that might disrupt their ability to notice things that are unexpected.

"Just don't make any personal appearances until after the election."

Source: Reprinted from *The Saturday Evening Post* © 1964.

Common sense is the collection of prejudices acquired by age 18.

Albert Einstein

On the other hand, if *you* attempted to get others to form a study group and failed, you would be more likely to blame factors in the situation for the failure (e.g., there was not enough time, or the others were not interested, or they would not be good to study with). This reflects a **self-serving bias** (Miller & Ross, 1975), the tendency to make external attributions (i.e., blame the situation) for one's own failures, yet make internal attributions (i.e., take credit) for one's successes. A third factor which affects the attribution process is called the **actor/observer difference** (Jones & Nisbett, 1972). It refers to the fact that people who are observing an action are much more likely than the actor to make the fundamental attribution error. Consider, for example, a student who gets a bad score on an exam. The person sitting *next* to her (i.e., an observer) would tend to attribute the bad score to *internal* characteristics (e.g., not very bright, weak in this subject) whereas the student herself would be more likely to attribute the bad score to *external* factors (e.g., the professor graded unfairly). Putting all these factors together, each of us tends to see our own success as due to our intelligence, personality, or physical abilities, but others' success as more attributable to situational factors or to luck.

We hasten to note in concluding this section that reflection also involves higher functions like evaluation and judgment, not just perception and attribution. We will address these broader aspects of reflection, which are crucial to learning from experience, just ahead.

Perception and Action

We have seen ways perception influences both the observation and reflection stages in the spiral of experience. It also affects the actions we take. For example, Mitchell and his associates (Green & Mitchell, 1979; Mitchell, Green, & Wood, 1981; Mitchell & Wood, 1980) have examined how perceptions and biases affect supervisors' actions in response to poorly performing subordinates. In general, these researchers found that supervisors were biased toward making dispositional attributions about a subordinate's substandard performance and, as a result of these attributions, often recommended that punishment be used to remedy the performance deficit.

Another perceptual variable that can affect our actions is the **self-fulfilling prophecy.** The self-fulfilling prophecy occurs when our expectations or predictions play a causal role in bringing about the events we predict. It is not difficult to see how certain large-scale social phenomena may be affected this way. For example, economists' predictions of an economic downturn may, via the consequent decreased investor confidence, precipitate an economic crisis. But the self-fulfilling prophecy occurs at the interpersonal level, too. A person's expectations about another may influence how he acts toward her, and in reaction to his behavior she may act in a way that confirms his expectations (Jones, 1986). One typical interaction sequence is shown in Figure 3.2.

Some of the best evidence to support the effects of the self-fulfilling prophecy on leadership training was collected by Eden and Shani (1982). Eden and Shani conducted a field experiment where they told leadership instructors their students had either unknown, regular, or high command potential. However, the students' actual command potential was never assessed, and unbeknownst to the instructors, the students were actually randomly assigned to the unknown, regular, or high command potential conditions. Nevertheless, students in the high-potential condition had significantly better objective test scores and attitudes than the students in the unknown- or regular-potential conditions, even though instructors simultaneously taught all three types of students. Somehow the students

FIGURE 3.2

The role of expectations in social interaction.

Source: Abstracted with permission from E. E. Jones, "Interpreting Interpersonal Behavior: The Effects of Expectancies, *Science* 234, no. 3 (October 1986), p. 43. Copyright 1986, American Association for the Advancement of Science.

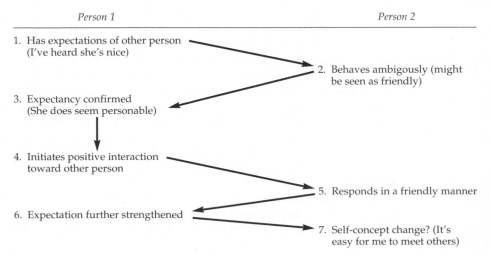

picked up on their instructor's expectations and responded accordingly. Thus, just having expectations (positive or negative) about others can subtly influence our actions, and these actions can, in turn, affect the way others behave.

Reflection and Leadership Development

Perhaps the most important yet most neglected component of the action-observation-reflection model is reflection. Reflection is important because it can provide leaders with a variety of insights into how to frame problems differently, look at situations from multiple perspectives, or better understand subordinates. However, most managers spend relatively little time on this activity, even though the time spent reflecting about leadership can be quite fruitful.

One reason the reflection component is often neglected may be time pressure at work. Leaders are usually very busy people working in pressure-filled situations and often do not have time to ponder all the possible consequences of their actions or reflect on how they could have accomplished a particular action better. Sometimes it takes an out-of-the-ordinary experience to focus one's attention on developmental challenges (see Highlight 3.3). In addition, some leaders may not be aware of the value of reflection in leadership development. Intentional reflection might even prompt one to see potential benefits in experience not initially considered relevant to leadership in organizational settings (see Highlight 3.4). Hopefully, this section will clarify the value of reflection, and in so doing can complement the emphasis, throughout the remainder of the book, on looking at leadership from different perspectives.

Single- and Double-Loop Learning

It is difficult for leaders to fundamentally change their leadership style without engaging in some kind of reflection. Along these lines, Argyris (1976) described an intensive effort with a group of highly successful chief executive officers who became even better leaders through increased self-awareness. Argyris's model for conceptualizing this growth is applicable to any level of leader and is worth considering in more detail.

Argyris (1976) said that most people interact with others and the environment on the basis of a belief system geared to manipulate or control others, and to minimize one's own emotionality and the negative feelings elicited from others. This belief system also tends to create defensive interpersonal relationships and limits risk taking. People "programmed" with this view of life (as most of us are, according to Argyris) produce group and organizational dynamics characterized by avoidance of conflict, mistrust, conformity, intergroup rivalry, misperceptions and miscommunications with others, ineffective problem solving, and poor decision making. Most important for our purposes here, it generates a certain kind of learning that Argyris called **single-loop learning.**

Single-loop learning describes a kind of learning between the individual and the environment in which learners seek relatively little feedback that may significantly confront their fundamental ideas or actions. There is relatively little public testing

Leadership Development Dilemmas for Women

Highlight 3.3

The Women's Leadership Program, offered by The Center for Creative Leadership (CCL), emphasizes receiving feedback, improving self-awareness, and setting leadership and life goals. Members of the CCL staff conducted a series of interviews with 60 executive women who had attended the program, and identified several salient issues these women were struggling with (Ohlott, 1999). Four particular themes stood out:

WHOLENESS AND AUTHENTICITY

These executive women desired to have a whole and full life. They felt job demands had forced their lives to become one-dimensional. Often they felt they had given up an important part of themselves: a creative self, friendly self, musical self, athletic self, and so forth. Sometimes they felt their organizations required them to ignore or suppress some part of their true selves in order to succeed.

CLARITY

After the program, many women developed great clarity about their own strengths, weaknesses, values, needs, priorities, and goals as leaders.

CONNECTION

Many women expressed concerns that they did not have the degree of interpersonal connectedness with others they would have preferred. They expressed a desire for closer friendships and family ties. Many said they felt isolated in their organizations, with few confidants of either gender.

CONTROL

One of the strongest themes identified in the interviews was the need to feel more in control. This need was manifested in a number of different ways, including the need to feel more comfortable exercising authority and a need to deal differently with organizational situations that made them feel helpless. Many women also expressed a desire to become more politically sophisticated.

To reflect upon the overall findings of the study, it is encouraging that virtually all of these executive women believed they were continuing to grow both personally and professionally. The experiences of this group of executive women certainly support the view that development persists throughout life.

of ideas against valid information. Consequently, an actor's belief system becomes self-sealing and self-fulfilling, and little time is spent reflecting about the beliefs. Argyris used the term *single-loop learning* because it operates somewhat like a thermostat; individuals learn only about subjects within the "comfort zone" of their belief systems. They might, for example, learn how well they are achieving a designated goal. They are far less likely, however, to question the validity of the goal or the values implicit in the situation, just as a thermostat does not question its temperature setting. That kind of self-confrontation would involve **double-loop learning.**

Double-loop learning involves a willingness to confront one's own views and an invitation to others to do so, too. It springs from an appreciation that openness to information and power sharing with others can lead to better recognition and definition of problems, improved communication, and increased decision-making effectiveness. Mastering double-loop learning can be thought of as learning how to learn. With considerable collective work, including the difficult task of working through personal blind spots, Argyris's group of leaders did move to this stage. In other words, through reflection they learned how to change their leadership styles by questioning their assumptions about others, their roles in the organization, and their underlying assumptions about the importance of their own goals and those of the organization.

The Relevance of Women's Personal Experiences to Their Leadership Effectiveness

Highlight 3.4

Record numbers of women are active in the managerial workforce. Not surprisingly, a widespread perception has arisen that the relationship between work and nonwork domains of women's lives is almost inherently one of conflict. Managerial women are described as constantly torn between the demands of their managerial and personal roles. Less attention has been paid to the question of possible benefits of combining employment and personal roles.

Psychologists at *The Center for Creative Leadership* studied how the roles women play in their personal lives can impact their effectiveness at work (Ruderman, Ohlott, Panzer, & King, 2002). In telephone interviews with women managers, they asked this question (among others): *Are there any dimensions or aspects of your personal life that enhance your professional life?* Six themes characterized the women's responses:

- *Opportunities to enrich interpersonal skills* like motivating, respecting, and developing others—honed at home in raising children—are transferable to motivating, developing, and directing employees.
- *Psychological benefits* from overcoming obstacles, taking risks, and succeeding in personal arenas bolster esteem, self-confidence, energy, and courage.
- *Emotional support and advice* from friends and family who act as sounding boards and motivators, and allow one to vent feelings in a safe environment.
- *Handling multiple tasks* such as planning and juggling a busy family's schedules develop administrative skills such as prioritizing and planning.
- *Personal interests and background* provide skills and helpful perspectives for understanding and connecting with people at work.
- *Leadership opportunities* in volunteer, community organizations, or family settings provide leadership lessons and increase comfort in authority roles.

Thinking Frames and Multiple Perspectives

Another way to conceptualize reflection in leadership development involves **thinking frames,** which refer to the tactics and strategies people use to organize their thinking and to construe the meaning of events (Perkins, 1986). Thinking frames are our mental tools, and they may or may not be useful, just as a hammer or saw may or may not be useful depending on the task at hand. In addition, just as a child with a hammer perceives that the whole world needs hammering, our thinking frames can also represent limits on the ways we can (conceptually) operate on our environment. Leadership development can be thought of as the process of developing more complex and differentiated frames for organizing one's thinking (and hence action) about leadership. Moreover, because some thinking frames are relatively subtle, their development may be better assisted through structured educational experiences. For example, most people would not have thought of the action-observation-reflection model on their own. The development of multiple frames, or perspectives, may be one of the greatest contributions a formal course in leadership can make to a leader's development. The overarching idea in discussing the different definitions and theories of leadership in this text is to help you to develop different frames or perspectives for interpreting leadership situations, which in turn may help you to better influence others to achieve organizational goals. Perhaps one key to leadership success is having a variety of tools to choose from and knowing when and where to use them. We hope the theories and concepts described in this text will give you the tools, and by reflecting about your experiences as a leader, you should begin to gain some insight on when and where to use them.

Leadership Development through Experience

Although using the action-observation-reflection model will help you make the most of your leadership experiences and mature into a better leader, it is also important to realize that some situations are developmentally richer than others. In many ways, these developmentally rich situations can be thought of as "crucibles" of experience, re-

Good flutists learn from experience; unfortunately, so do bad flutists.

Anonymous

calling the vessels that were used by medieval alchemists in trying to turn base metals into gold (Bennis & Thomas, 2002).

In this section, we will review two developmental factors that make any given experience potent in fostering managerial growth: the people you work with and the characteristics of the task itself (Kouzes & Posner, 1987; Lombardo & Eichinger, 1989). These factors are important because they provide opportunities for a leader or a leader-to-be to apply the action-observation-reflection model and reflect on how to be a better leader. Let's begin by looking at how one of our three leaders, Peter Jackson, approached learning.

In the early stages of Peter Jackson's development, his learning was focused primarily on mastering his chosen craft of filmmaking. As a young man, Jackson learned his craft primarily by trial and error, but also by studying any instructional materials he could get his hands on, whether they pertained to film editing, creating special effects, or anything else. Through these early years, Jackson's talent grew, and his genius with the camera was apparent from the outset. In making *The Lord of the Rings* trilogy, however, Jackson needed to call upon far more skills than "just" with a camera. By the time he was about 30, in fact, Jackson had learned that he needed to improve his skill in screenwriting to progress to the next plateau. It was with just that objective in mind that in 1990 one of the most powerful experiences shaping his effectiveness as a filmmaker occurred—when a Hollywood expert on story structure delivered a seminar in New Zealand. Over three days, this expert offered a series of principles and practical tools that had, as one colleague describes it, a "seismic" impact on Jackson (Botes, 2004). Since one of the Academy Awards Jackson received at the Oscars was for screenwriting, he must have learned his lessons well.

Jackson's story underscores an important point about leadership development. People who become leaders in any field tend to first stand out by virtue of their technical proficiency. Typically, leaders emerge or are selected for initial supervisory, managerial, or leadership roles on the basis of their competence or proficiency in their primary role requirements. For example, if you got an engineering degree in college, then your success in your first job—if you were lucky enough to get a job in your chosen field—is very likely to depend upon your expertise as an engineer. If and when you are promoted to a role of managing other engineers, however, what becomes more important for your success (and your organization's) is not so much your individual proficiency as an engineer (or chemist, accountant, salesman, or football player) but rather your effectiveness in getting the best out of other engineers (or chemists, accountants, salesmen, football players, etc.). This is depicted in Figure 3.3, and it seems to accurately reflect Peter Jackson's development as a filmmaker and leader. His initial success was driven largely by his budding genius in making films on a low budget and with virtually no other staff. In reading others' comments who worked with him on the *LOTR* project, however, it's clear that his leadership continued to develop over the years, too. It was Jackson's ability to communicate a shared vision and inspire such extraordinary work out of the incredibly large staff that made *LOTR* so spectacularly successful.

The People You Work With

The people you associate with can stimulate development in many ways. Kouzes and Posner (1987) noted the diverse ways others nurture our growth:

> Other people have always been essential sources of guidance. We all remember the parent we looked to for advice and support; the special teacher who filled us with curiosity for our favorite subject; the neighbor who always let us watch, even take part in, the tinkering in the garage; the coach who believed that we had promise and inspired us to give our best; the counselor who gave us valuable feedback about our behavior and its impact; the master artisan who instructed us in the fundamentals of a craft; or the first boss who taught us the ropes to skip and the hoops to jump. (p. 286)

Others play an especially important role in personal and professional development at work, so we will focus attention there.

A boss, especially a very good or very bad one, can be a powerful catalyst for growth. Exceptional bosses are vivid examples of how to (or how not to) put values into action. However, bosses are not the only people who contribute to growth

FIGURE 3.3
Changing
requirements
for success.

Source: Adapted
from *Preventing
Derailment: What to
do Before It's Too Late*
by Michael M.
Lombardo and
Robert W. Eichinger.
© 1989 Center for
Creative Leadership.

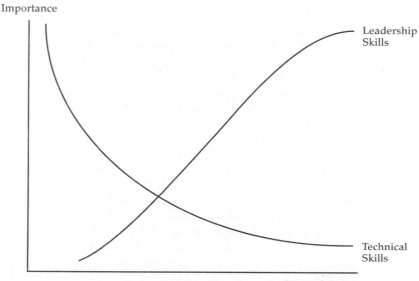

and development at work. Working with others who have different backgrounds, perspectives, or agendas can often be a growth experience. Working with problem subordinates can stimulate managerial growth, but so can the need to influence others over whom you have no direct authority or control. You may work on a project and report to a superior other than your own boss, or you may head a team of peers; such situations are particularly helpful in developing negotiation and other informal influence skills. Finally, different management skills are called on when you must make major changes to a group or project such as downsizing it, restructuring it, or starting it from scratch (Lombardo & Eichinger, 1989).

You can learn about effective and ineffective leadership by paying attention to the positive and negative models around you beyond your immediate boss. Watching others in leadership roles may suggest what to do as well as what not to do. Peers, especially, can be a great resource for developing one's effectiveness as a leader. In one program of peer coaching, school principals observed each other interacting in feedback conferences with their respective teachers and then met together afterward to share ideas about how well the conferences went (Gibble & Lawrence, 1987). Such principal-to-principal interaction is especially valuable in that it is rare for any supervisor to get feedback on his or her skill in providing feedback to subordinates. The principals praised their peer coaching as an extremely effective mechanism for enhancing their effectiveness as supervisors.

In an organization, you also can gain valuable perspectives and insights through close association with an experienced person willing to take you under his wing. Such an individual is often called a **mentor,** after the character in Greek mythology whom Odysseus trusted to run his household and see to his son's education when Odysseus went off to fight the Trojans. Now, 3,000 years later, Mentor's name is used to describe the process by which an older and more experienced person helps to socialize and encourage younger organizational colleagues (Wilson & Elman, 1990).

Generally, mentors are highly placed, powerful individuals who develop relatively long-lasting relationships with younger colleagues whose professional careers are influenced and furthered as a result (Hunt & Michael, 1983; Uecker & Dilla, 1985). Typically, the mentoring relationship is informal, though its value has encouraged some to recommend its use formally and systematically in organizations (Clutterbuck, 1982). In terms of value, both mentors and mentorees benefit from having this relationship. Mentors benefit by the greater influence they accrue by having former mentorees in various positions across the organization. Mentors also benefit by having a younger replacement ready to fill their position if they are promoted (Bass, 1990). The mentoree benefits from this relationship by gaining an influential ally and by learning through the mentor's tutoring about the subtler aspects of organizational ethics, influence, and leadership. Having a mentor can also result in more career opportunities for the mentoree (Whitely, Dougherty, & Dreher, 1988; Zey, 1984), and the lack of mentors for women has been cited as one reason there are relatively few women in executive positions (Astin & Leland, 1991). Although some may advocate systematizing mentorship programs to improve the career opportunities for all employees, it remains to be seen whether a formalized program would preserve the essence and qualities of more informal, self-selected mentoring relationships (Rosenbach, 1989).

An idea somewhat related to mentoring is that of **executive coaching.** Increasingly, executive coaching is seen as a general responsibility of all executives toward managers who report to them. The failure to coach managers in their professional development makes as little sense as a football team composed of the best recruited players going through an entire season without a practice session or coach (Witherspoon & White, 1996). More simply, good coaching is nothing more than good management. It is investment that can help change counterproductive behavior, often interpersonal, that threatens to derail an otherwise valued manager (Waldroop and Butler, 1996).

The Task Itself

In addition to the various sorts of relationships with other people, certain kinds of work-related tasks can also be particularly developmental. Developmental tasks are often more complex and ambiguous than those one has faced before. In addition, leadership development can be enhanced if the environment one works in is changing, dynamic, uncontrollable, and unpredictable. The nature of the task may require new and creative solutions; old answers may not work anymore. Projects involving strategic planning and projections into an uncertain future can be quite challenging intellectually and can contribute to a leader's development (Lombardo & Eichinger, 1989).

I took a great deal o' pains with his education, sir; let him run the streets when he was very young, and shift for his-self. It's the only way to make a boy sharp, sir.

Charles Dickens,
Pickwick Papers

Although we have emphasized the importance of applying the action-observation-reflection model to enhance one's learning from experience, the developmental value of the challenging tasks themselves cannot be denied. The best developmental opportunities are those that stretch individuals and allow them to test themselves against new and difficult tasks (Kouzes & Posner, 1987). Of course, the difficulty level of tasks and how much one will be stretched by doing them is meaningful mostly in the context of a given individual's maturity and experience. The following are the words of one college student who was in charge of the flag section of her school's marching band:

I have 30 people under me broken into four sections. I am responsible for conducting our rehearsals, teaching flag routines, taking care of any problems, recruiting new members, and motivating my people. I do some of this through my four section leaders, so I have to make sure they are doing their jobs properly. The biggest challenge of all this is keeping motivation high and making sure that everyone learns what they are supposed to and performs it well. It is really giving me a lot of experience in interacting with people.

Another student described his own best leadership experience in terms of his unique background as an instructor on his collegiate parachute team:

During this period I learned a lot about what it takes to teach a person to jump out of an airplane successfully and injury free. The foremost concern and responsibility is the welfare of the student, so I had to be certain that they learned the procedures correctly, and be thoroughly convinced that they would be safe once out the door no matter what situation may arise. I was responsible for someone else's life. I had to be very patient and understanding many times when they would not grasp an idea or a procedure properly, spending a lot of time in certain areas until they were proficient. Other times I had to be stern and strict to emphasize certain emergency procedures and safety hazards in order to be sure they were aware of the seriousness of the situation. During this period I experienced everything that goes into leadership. I had to work with many people. Many of them were my peers, which makes things more difficult in some cases.

Feeling responsible for someone else's life certainly increases one's personal pressure, and it was partly this pressure that made this student-instructor's role such a valuable leadership experience. Whether or not a particular task is perceived as developmentally challenging and generates a high level of personal pressure depends on several factors. The most commonly cited developmental challenge mentioned by managers was a task where both success and failure were possible and would be obvious to others. The risk of possible failure is a strong incentive for managers to learn. Managers also mentioned deadlines, travel requirements, and longer hours as factors that, while adding to personal pressure, also contributed to professional growth (Lombardo & Eichinger, 1989).

One last aspect of leadership-developing tasks should be mentioned. Just as mentoring relationships fail to develop for all members, organizations may not provide the same developmental opportunities for all their members. In particular, there is a striking difference between large and small organizations in the opportunities they offer. This is apparent, for example, in the chances of having a significant responsibility in the school play in schools with either large or small student bodies. In small schools, virtually anyone who wants to have a significant part in putting on the play will be able to do so. In large schools, though, the number of students far exceeds the number of important functions; many motivated students will miss out on the chance to participate and grow from the experience. As John Gardner (1990) has pointed out, the sheer size and impersonalness of some of our organizations does not provide the soil in which a young person's leadership can grow.

Making the Most of Your Leadership Experiences: Learning to Learn from Experience

This section builds on the ideas previously introduced in this chapter by providing leadership practitioners with a few suggestions to enhance learning from experience (see Highlight 3.5 for a description of some executives who apparently did not learn enough from experience). For well over a decade, researchers at the Center for Creative Leadership have been studying the role of learning from experience as an important developmental behavior for people in executive positions. While this research has contributed a great deal to *what* people need to learn to be successful (see Highlight 3.6 for a comparison of lessons men and women managers learn from experience), less is known about the process of learning or *how* we learn to be successful. Bunker and Webb (1992) asked successful executives to list adjectives describing how they felt while working through powerful learning events

What would a man be wise; let him drink of the river
That bears on its bosom the record of time;
A message to him every wave can deliver.
To teach him to creep till he knows how to climb.

John Boyle O'Reilly

Executive Derailment: Knocking Yourself off the Track to Success

Highlight 3.5

Some executives on an apparently clear track to the top never make it. They become derailed. For more than a decade, researchers at the Center for Creative Leadership have studied executives who had fallen short of the levels of success predicted of them earlier in their careers. Typically, their derailments were the result of several factors, though insensitivity to others was the most frequent problem. Sometimes styles that served them well earlier became liabilities in new circumstances, and sometimes long-standing liabilities, previously outweighed by other aspects, eventually took their career toll. A 1996 study expanded the work and included samples of European as well as North American executives. In general, the derailment themes in Europe and North America were consistent:

Characteristics of Successful Leaders

Ability to develop or adapt.

Ability to establish collaborative relations.

Ability to build and lead a team.

Nonauthoritarian.

Consistent exceptional performance.

Ambitious.

Characteristics of Derailed Leaders

Inability to develop or adapt.

Poor working relations.

Inability to build and lead a team.

Authoritarian.

Poor performance.

Too ambitious.

How would you interpret these executives' derailments in terms of the action-observation-reflection model? Do you think the problem was in their actions? Their observation or awareness of the consequences of their actions? Or something else?

Source: Adapted from J. B. Leslie and E. Van Velsor, *A Look at Derailment Today: North America and Europe* (Greensboro, NC: Center for Creative Leadership, 1996).

and potent developmental experiences. Their typical responses were a combination of both positive and negative feelings.

Negatives	Positives
Pained	Challenged
Fearful	Successful
Frustrated	Proud
Stressed	Capable
Anxious	Growing
Overwhelmed	Exhilarated
Uncertain	Talented
Angry	Resourceful
Hurt	Learning

This pattern strongly supports the long-hypothesized notion of a meaningful link between stress and learning (Janis, 1971). The learning events and developmental experiences that punctuate one's life are usually, perhaps always, stressful

What Do Men and Women Managers Learn from Experience?

Highlight 3.6

For a quarter century or so, significant numbers of women have been represented in the management ranks of companies. During that period companies have promoted large pools of high-potential women, but relatively few of them have achieved truly top-level positions. Several factors probably account for this, but one possibility is that men and women learn differently from their work experiences. Researchers at the Center for Creative Leadership have studied how male and female executives describe the important lessons they've learned from their career experiences, and there are some interesting differences between the genders as well as significant overlap.

Most Frequent Lessons for Men and Women

Directing and motivating employees.

Self-confidence.

Basic management values.

How to work with executives.

Understanding other people's perspective.

Dealing with people over whom you have no authority.

Handling political situations.

For Men Only

Technical/professional skills.

All about the business.

Coping with ambiguous situations.

Shouldering full responsibility.

Persevering through adversity.

For Women Only

Personal limits and blind spots.

Taking charge of career.

Recognizing and seizing opportunities.

Coping with situations beyond your control.

Knowing what excites you.

Why would there be any learning differences between the genders? One hypothesis is that men and women managers tend to have somewhat different career patterns. For example, there is some evidence that women receive fewer truly challenging developmental opportunities.

Source: Adapted from E. Van Velsor, and M. W. Hughes, *Gender Differences in the Development of Managers: How Women Managers Learn from Experience* (Technical Report No. 145), Greensboro, NC: Center for Creative Leadership, 1990.

(Grey & Gordon, 1978; Hambrick, 1981; Jennings, 1971; Schein, 1978).

Bunker and Webb (1992) note that executives try to be successful without experiencing stress. They are most comfortable when they can draw upon a proven repertoire of operating skills to tackle a challenge they have conquered in the past. Combined with the organizational pressure to have "proven performers" in important positions, there is a tremendous initial pressure to "continue to do what we've always done." In stressful situations, this tendency may become even more powerful. What results is one of the great Catch-22s of adult development: The times when people most need to break out of the mold created by past learning patterns are the times when they are most unwilling to do so. Being able to *go against the grain* of one's personal historical success requires an unwavering commitment to learning and a relentless willingness to let go of the fear of failure and the unknown.

Teach a highly educated person that it is not a disgrace to fail and that he must analyze every failure to find its cause. He must learn how to fail intelligently, for failing is one of the greatest arts in the world.

Charles F. Kettering, Inventor, automotive pioneer, and corporate leader

FIGURE 3.4
Anatomy
of a learning
experience.

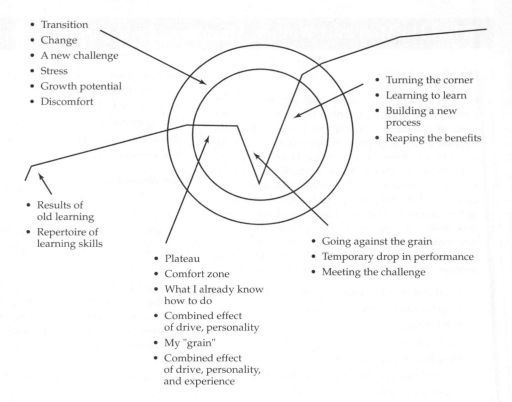

- Transition
- Change
- A new challenge
- Stress
- Growth potential
- Discomfort

- Turning the corner
- Learning to learn
- Building a new
  process
- Reaping the benefits

- Results of
  old learning
- Repertoire of
  learning skills

- Going against the grain
- Temporary drop in performance
- Meeting the challenge

- Plateau
- Comfort zone
- What I already know
  how to do
- Combined effect
  of drive, personality
- My "grain"
- Combined effect
  of drive, personality,
  and experience

*Anyone who stops learning is old,
whether at 20 or 80. Anyone who
keeps learning stays young. The
greatest thing in life is to keep your
mind young.*

Henry Ford

Figure 3.4 depicts the Center for Creative Leadership's work on the process of "learning to learn from experience." Bunker and Webb (1992) describe the figure as a segment of life containing a series of learning opportunities. The circled segment represents a stressful episode of life—a potentially dramatic learning-to-learn event. The left side of the curve represents the growth and development that was stimulated by prior learning experiences. Also represented is a flattening out of learned skill value that often occurs; over time, new skills often become mere routinized habits. People operating in this stabilizing period, called the comfort zone, must overcome the caution generated by ongoing success and the fear of challenging what they already know how to do. The smaller concentric circle represents the tension created by the appearance of a new learning challenge—often arising out of a transition or a stressful experience that requires a response. The sharp dip in success depicts the performance regression that generally accompanies attempts at learning a new set of responses and strategies. One gets through this period (and thus performs at a higher level with broader skills) by coping with the stress or letting go of short-term expectations in favor of more long-term learning. Of course, if one is not willing to go against the grain and tolerate a small dip in performance, then the learning curve becomes flat—no learning.

To be successful, learning must continue throughout life, beyond the completion of one's formal education.

> The end of extrinsically applied education should be the start of an education that is motivated intrinsically. At that point the goal of studying is no longer to make the grade, earn a diploma, and find a good job. Rather, it is to understand what is happening around one, to develop a personally meaningful sense of what one's experience is all about. (Csikszentmihalyi, 1990, p. 142)

And that applies to the specific challenge of *becoming* and *remaining* an effective leader, too. People who lead in modern organizations need to be engaged in a never-ending learning process (Hogan & Warrenfeltz, 2003).

Leadership Development through Education and Training

Although we believe experience plays a large role in leadership development, we believe formal education can play an important role, too. For example, Bray, Campbell, and Grant (1974), Howard (1986), and Wakabayashi and Graen (1984) all found that education level or academic performance in college was positively related to future managerial success. Furthermore, in a major review of the effectiveness of managerial training programs, Burke and Day (1986) found that educational programs generally had a positive effect on leadership development. Thus, formal education and training programs can help one become a better leader. However, it is important to note that these programs vary substantially in both content and pedagogy, and not all programs are appropriate for all leaders. The content of different leadership programs varies considerably, depending on the target audience; university-level courses generally provide a survey of the major leadership findings, programs for first-level supervisors often focus on how to train subordinates and give them feedback about their progress, and programs for senior executives often focus on strategic planning and public relations. In this regard, Brungardt (1996) helpfully distinguished between leadership development and leadership education, the latter being a component of the former. Programs also vary in the extent to which they are based on well-established and professionally accepted practices and standards. Some leadership training programs represent little more than fads or popularized pseudoscience. In the following pages, we will review some of the more common educational and training techniques used to teach and develop leadership.

University Courses in Leadership

Spitzberg (1987) estimated that over 500 colleges or universities offer some type of leadership training program. Often these programs consist of extracurricular leadership activities run out of the student development office or are courses much like the one for which you are using this book. The extracurricular activities can vary greatly, but the leadership courses often have a high degree of overlap in both content and pedagogy. In terms of content, the topics covered in most leadership courses are similar to the subjects addressed in this book and include

An educated man can experience more in a day than an uneducated man in a lifetime.

Seneca, Roman statesman, 1st century A.D.

how personality traits, cognitive abilities, values, behaviors, motivation, group dynamics, communication, situational factors, and different theories of leadership can all be used to describe the leadership process. In addition, many universities offer specialized courses that focus primarily on historical, business, minority, or female leaders.

The techniques, or pedagogy, used to impart these different leadership concepts to students can vary greatly. Many courses use the standard lecture method, and Burke and Day (1986) found this method to be an effective way of imparting knowledge about leadership. Some courses also provide **individualized feedback** to students in the form of personality, intelligence, values, or interests test scores or leadership behavior ratings. A relatively new twist to individualized feedback is to have subjects compare the results of their personality or behavior self-ratings with those given to them by their peers (Curphy, 1991). **Case studies** consist of descriptions of various leadership situations and are used as a vehicle for leadership discussions. **Role playing** is also a popular methodology. In role playing, participants are assigned parts to play (e.g., a supervisor and an unmotivated subordinate) in a job-related scenario. Role playing has the advantage of letting trainees actually practice relevant skills and thus has greater transferability to the workplace than do didactic lectures or abstract discussions about leadership. **Simulations** and **games** are other methods of training. These are relatively structured activities designed to mirror some of the challenges or decisions commonly faced in the work environment. One of the better-known leadership simulations is the Center for Creative Leadership's "Looking Glass" (McCall & Lombardo, 1982), in which participants play different leadership roles in a glass manufacturing plant. A newer approach to leadership development puts participants in relatively unfamiliar territory (e.g., outdoors rather than offices) and presents them physical, emotionally arousing, and often team-oriented challenges.

Leadership Training Programs

There are numerous leadership training programs aimed particularly toward leaders and supervisors in industry or public service. In many ways, these have strong parallels to both the content and techniques used in university-level courses on leadership. However, these programs are usually much shorter (typically less than a week), and the content tends to be more focused than that of a university course. The content of these programs also depends on the organizational level of the recipients; programs for first-level supervisors focus on developing supervisory skills such as training, monitoring, giving feedback, and conducting performance reviews with subordinates. Generally, these programs use lectures, case studies, and role-playing exercises to improve leadership skills.

All rising to a great place is by a winding stair.

Francis Bacon,
Philosopher

The programs for midlevel managers often focus on improving interpersonal, oral-communication, and written-communication skills, as well as giving tips on time management, planning, and goal setting. These programs rely more heavily on individualized feedback, case studies, presentations, role playing, simulations, **in-basket exercises,** and **leaderless group discussions** as techniques to help leaders develop. In in-basket exercises, participants are given a limited amount of time to prioritize and respond to a number of notes, letters, and phone messages from a fictitious manager's in-basket. This technique is particularly useful in assessing and improving a manager's planning and time management skills. In leaderless group discussions, facilitators and observers rate participants on the degree of persuasiveness, leadership, followership, or conflict each member manifests in a group that has no appointed leader. These ratings are used to provide managers with feedback about their interpersonal and oral-communication skills.

Tell me and I'll forget; show me and I may remember; involve me and I'll understand.

Chinese proverb

In reviewing the general field of leadership development and training, Conger (1996) offered this assessment: "Leadership programs can work, and work well, if they use a multi-tiered approach. Effective training depends on the combined use of four different teaching methods which I call personal growth, skill building, feedback, and conceptual awareness" (p. 52). Some programs seek to stimulate leadership development by means of oftentimes emotionally intense personal growth experiences such as river rafting, wilderness survival, and so forth. Leadership development through skill building involves structured activities focusing upon the sorts of leadership skills featured in the final section of this book. Some approaches to leadership development emphasize individualized feedback about each person's strengths and weaknesses, typically based upon standardized assessment methods. Feedback-based approaches can help identify "blind spots" an individual may be unaware of, as well as help prioritize which aspects of leadership development represent the highest priorities for development focus. Still other sorts of programs develop leadership by emphasizing its conceptual or intellectual components. An example of this approach would be an emphasis on theory and the use of case studies, common in many MBA programs. There are merits in each of these approaches, but Conger was on solid ground when he emphasized the value of combining elements of each.

In a related vein, Nevins and Stumpf (1999) emphasized that leadership development in the 21st century must occur in more lifelike situations and contexts. Toward that end, they advocated creating better practice fields for leadership development analogous to the practice fields whereon skills in competitive sports are honed, or practice sessions analogous to those in music training wherein those skills are sharpened. Increasingly, leadership development is occurring in the context of work itself (Hernez-Broome & Hughes, 2004).

Leadership programs for senior executives and CEOs tend to focus on strategic planning, public relations, and interpersonal skills. Many times, the entire senior leadership of a company will go through a leadership program at the same time. One goal of such a group might be to learn how to develop a strategic plan for their organization. In order to improve public relations skills, some programs have CEOs undergo simulated, unannounced interviews with television reporters and receive feedback on how they could have done better.

Here's one final thought about *choosing* a program of leadership training. Although a number of leadership training programs are based on sound theory and research, some other programs have no basis in science and should be considered speculative at best. Still others are based on unwarranted and simplistic extensions of scientific findings. Perhaps the best way to guarantee that a leadership program will be useful to you or your organization is to adopt a systematic approach to leadership training. There is value in being an informed consumer, and this is just as true in investing one's time, energy, and money in leadership programs as it is in other products and services.

Building Your Leadership Self-Image

This chapter has explored how leadership develops through experience and formal education. Before concluding, however, we should acknowledge that not everyone wants to be a leader or believes he can be. John Gardner (1965) has argued that many of our best and brightest young people actually have been immunized against, and dissuaded from, seeking leadership opportunities and responsibilities. Other young people, even if they want to be leaders, may not believe they have what it takes. Both groups, we believe, are selling themselves short.

For those who merely want to avoid the responsibilities of leadership, we encourage an openness of mind about leadership's importance and pervasiveness. We hope this book offers ways of thinking about leadership that make it at once more immediate, more relevant, and more interesting than it may have seemed before. For others, we encourage flexibility in self-image. Do not stay out of the leadership arena based on some global and self-defeating generalization such as "I am not the leader type." Experiment and take a few risks with different leadership roles. This will help you appreciate new facets of yourself as well as broaden your leadership self-image.

Summary

This chapter reviews several major points regarding how leadership can be developed through both formal education and experience. One way to get more out of your leadership courses and experiences is through the application of the action-observation-reflection model. This model provides a framework for better understanding of leadership situations. In addition, being aware of the role perception plays in leadership development is also important, as it affects what you observe, how you interpret your observations, and what actions you take as a leader. Finally, it is important to remember that both education and experience can contribute to your development as a leader by enhancing your ability to reflect on and analyze leadership situations. Exposure to formal leadership education programs can help you to develop thinking frames or multiple perspectives to analyze leadership situations, and the people you work with and the task itself can also provide you with insights on how to be a better leader. However, what you gain from any leadership program or experience is a function of what you make of it. Successful leaders are those who have "an extraordinary tenacity in extracting something worthwhile from their experience and in seeking experiences rich in opportunities for growth" (McCall, Lombardo, & Morrison, 1988, p. 122). If you want to become a better leader, then you must seek challenges and try to get all you can from any leadership situation or opportunity.

Key Terms

action-observation-reflection model, *47*
spiral of experience, *48*
perceptual set, *50*
attribution, *51*
fundamental attribution error, *51*
self-serving bias, *52*
actor/observer difference, *52*

self-fulfilling prophecy, *53*
single-loop learning, *54*
double-loop learning, *55*
thinking frames, *56*
mentor, *59*
executive coaching, *60*
individualized feedback, *66*
case studies, *66*
role playing, *66*

simulations, *66*
games, *66*
in-basket exercises, *66*
leaderless group discussions, *66*

Questions

1. Not all effective leaders seem to be reflective by nature. How do you reconcile that with the concept of the spiral of experience and its role in leadership development?

2. Explain how you can use knowledge about each of the following to enrich the benefits of your own present leadership experiences:

   a. The action-observation-reflection model.

   b. The people you interact and work with.

   c. The activities you're involved in.

3. Using the role of teacher as a specific instance of leadership, discuss how a teacher's perceptual set, expectations of students, and attributions may affect student motivation and performance. Do you think some teachers could become more effective by becoming more aware of these processes? Would that be true for leaders in general?

4. If you were to design the perfect leadership development experience for yourself, how would you do so and what would it include? How would you know it was effective?

5. Do you think people have a need for growth and development?

6. One important aspect of learning from experience is observing the consequences of one's actions. Sometimes, however, the most significant consequences of a leader's actions do not occur for several years (e.g., the ultimate impact of certain personnel decisions or a strategic decision to change a product line). If that is so, then is there any way individuals can learn from the consequences of those actions in a way to modify their behavior? If consequences are so delayed, is there a danger they might draw the wrong lessons from their experiences?

Skills

Leadership skills relevant to this chapter include:

- Learning from experience
- Communication
- Listening
- Building technical competence
- Building effective relationships with superiors

- Building effective relationships with peers
- Problem solving
- Improving creativity
- Diagnosing performance problems in individuals, teams and organizations

Activity

Divide yourselves into groups and in each group contrast what attributions you might make about the leadership style of two different individuals. All you know about either of them is the following:

	Person A	Person B
Favorite TV show	*60 Minutes*	*Survivor*
Car	Ford Mustang	Volkswagen Beetle
Favorite sport	American football	Mountain biking
Political affiliation	Republican	Democrat
Favorite music	Country & western	New Age

Minicase

"Developing Leaders at UPS"

UPS is the nation's fourth largest employer with 357,000 employees worldwide and operations in more than 200 countries. UPS is consistently recognized as a "top companies to work for" and was recently recognized by *Fortune* as one of the 50 best companies for minorities. A major reason for UPS's success is the company's commitment to its employees. UPS understands the importance of providing both education and experience for its next generation of leaders—spending $300 million dollars annually on education programs for employees and encouraging promotion from within. All employees are offered equal opportunities to build the skills and knowledge they need to succeed. A perfect example of this is Jovita Carranza.

Jovita Carranza joined UPS in 1976 as a part-time clerk in Los Angeles. Carranza demonstrated a strong work ethic and a commitment to UPS and UPS rewarded her with opportunities—opportunities Carranza was not shy about taking advantage of. By 1985 Carranza was the workforce planning manager in Metro LA. By 1987 she was district human resources manager based in Central Texas. By 1990 she had accepted a move to district human resources manager in Illinois. She received her first operations assignment, as division manager for hub, package, and feeder operations, in Illinois in 1991. Two years later, she said yes to becoming district operations manager in Miami. In 1996 she accepted the same role in Wisconsin. By 1999 Carranza's progressive successes led UPS to promote her to president of the Americas Region. From there she moved into her current position as Vice President of UPS Air Operations, based in Louisville, Kentucky.

The $1.1 billion air hub she currently oversees sprawls across the equivalent of more than 80 football fields. It can handle 304,000 packages an hour, its computers process nearly 1 million transactions a minute, and it serves as the lynchpin for the $33 billion business that has become the world's largest package-delivery company.

Carranza attributes much of her success to her eagerness to take on new challenges: "The one error that people make early on in their careers is that they're very selective about opportunities so they avoid some, prefer others," she says. "I always accepted all opportunities that presented themselves because from each one you can learn something, and they serve as a platform for future endeavors."

It has also been important, she says, to surround herself with capable, skilled employees who are loyal to the company and committed to results. After nearly 30 years with UPS, it is teamwork, interaction, and staff development that Carranza says is one of the achievements of which she is proudest: "Because that takes focus, determination, and sincerity to perpetuate the UPS culture and enhance it through people."

Carranza's corporate achievements, determination, drive, innovation, and leadership in business have earned her the distinction of being named *Hispanic Business Magazine*'s Woman of the Year. She credits her parents, both of Mexican descent, with teaching her "the importance of being committed, of working hard, and doing so with a positive outlook," principles she says that continue to guide her personal and professional life. The principles mirror those of the company whose corporate ladder she has climbed nonstop, an organization she says that values diversity, encourages quality, integrity, commitment, fairness, loyalty, and social responsibility, among other values.

Among Carranza's words of wisdom: ". . . sit back and listen and observe," she says. "You learn more by not speaking. Intelligent people learn from their own experiences; with wisdom, you learn from other people's mistakes. I'm very methodical about that."

1. What are the major skills Jovita Carranza has demonstrated in her career at UPS that have made her a successful leader?
2. Consider the spiral of experience that Jovita Carranza has traveled. How has her experience affected her ability as a leader?
3. Take a look at the characteristics of successful leaders in Highlight 3.5. How many of these are demonstrated by Jovita Carranza?

Sources: Http://www.ups.com; http://www.hispaniconline.com/vista/febhisp.htm; http://www.hispanicbusiness.com/news/newsbyid.asp?id=15535&page=3; http://www.socialfunds.com/csr/profile.cgi/1841.html

4

Assessing Leadership and Measuring Its Effects

Introduction

On a practical level, leadership is a topic that almost everyone is interested in at one time or another. For political scientists this interest manifests itself in the question "Who shall rule?" Psychologists take a different slant on the question and ask, "Who should rule?" People do have a vested interest in who is running their government, schools, company, or church; and because of this interest thousands of books and articles have been written about the topic of leadership. Curphy (2004a) and Hogan and Curphy (2004) believe these manuscripts can be divided into two major camps. The **academic tradition** consists of articles that use data and statistical techniques to make inferences about effective leadership. Although the academic tradition is research based, for the most part these findings are written more for other leadership researchers than leadership *practitioners*. As such, leadership practitioners are often unfamiliar with the research findings of the academic tradition. One notable exception here is the book *Good to Great* (Collins, 2001), where the author and his research team systematically reviewed those companies that significantly outperformed the stock market over a 15-year period. Many practitioners have read Collins's book and are attempting to adopt his lessons on leadership, staffing, and change.

Only 8 percent of Fortune 1000 executive directors rate their leadership capacity as excellent, while 47 percent rated their leadership capacity as fair to poor.

The Conference Board

The second camp of leadership literature is the **troubadour tradition.** These books and articles often consist of nothing more than the opinions or score-settling reminiscences of former leaders. Books in the troubadour tradition, such as *Who Moved My Cheese?* (Johnson, 1999), *What the CEO Wants You to Know* (Charan, 2001), *Awakening the Leader Within* (Cashman & Forem, 2003), and *Jack: Straight from the Gut* (Welch & Byrne, 2001) are wildly popular, but it is difficult to separate fact from fiction or determine whether these opinions translate to other settings. People who are unfamiliar with the findings of the academic tradition and the limitations of the troubadour tradition find it extremely difficult to differentiate research findings from opinion. There are numerous examples where the conventional wisdom about leadership proved to be wrong once it was properly investigated. For example, only

70 years ago it was assumed that people who were taller and more athletic were better leaders. As a result, a number of books and articles were written about the importance of these attributes to leadership success. Not until the 1940s did leadership researchers systematically investigate these two attributes and show that the conventional wisdom was wrong (Stogdill, 1948).

Although the example above is fairly dated, there are more recent examples where the research findings ran contrary to the conventional wisdom about leadership. For a long time many people thought smarter people made better leaders; people who were not as smart were believed to be less effective leaders. On the surface this seems to make sense, because if given a choice most people would rather work for a smart than a dull leader. But research by Fiedler and his colleagues showed that in some situations smarter leaders consistently performed less well than those who were less smart. This was the case when smart, inexperienced leaders were asked to perform in highly ambiguous and stressful situations. Leaders who were less smart but more experienced often performed at a much higher level than their more gifted counterparts because they had already learned how to operate effectively under high levels of stress.

> *One-fifth of large American companies will lose at least 48 percent of their top talent to retirement between 2000 and 2005.*
>
> Development
> Dimensions International

Perhaps the biggest challenge to improving the practice of leadership is to provide practitioners with timely, easily digestible, research-grounded advice on how to effectively lead others. Leadership practitioners often want fast answers about how to be more effective or successful. Paradoxically, another challenge is that high-quality leadership research is difficult, expensive, and time consuming to conduct. For example, it often takes five years or more for a leadership study to be conducted and published (Fiedler, 1995). Obviously, leadership practitioners cannot wait this long for answers (see Highlight 4.1 and Table 4.1).

This tension between discovering the "truth" about a leadership question and being able to apply what is learned is what we call the **practice-research gap.** Leadership practitioners often seek information about how to improve their leadership skills, but typically find little help in the work of leadership researchers whose studies may seem untimely or of little practical value (Curphy, 2003a, b; 2004a, e; Hogan & Curphy, 2004; Rynes, Bartunek, & Daft, 2001). Hogan, Curphy, and Hogan (1994) pointed out that the knowledge accumulated from 80 years of leadership research is of tremendous value, yet scientists have paid little attention to the ultimate consumers of their work—leaders and leaders to be. As a result, "real" leaders understandably turn to popular books and articles that *appear* to provide timely answers to their practical concerns. Unfortunately, however, the claims in the popular or "trade" literature are rarely based on sound research; they oversimplify the complexities of the leadership process; and many times they actually offer bad advice. Relatively little weight is given to well-researched leadership studies, primarily because the arcane requirements of publishing articles in scholarly journals make their content virtually unreadable (and certainly uninteresting) to actual leadership practitioners.

The Ten Things We Really Know about Leadership

Highlight 4.1

The sheer volume of material written in the academic and troubadour traditions of leadership research make it very difficult to separate myth from fact when it comes to leading others. Curphy and Hogan (2004b) have reviewed both bodies of leadership research and concluded that there are ten basic things people and organizations can do to improve leadership effectiveness. What is interesting about these ten findings is that they usually cost very little to implement, but many organizations seem hesitant to put these recommendations into practice. These ten findings, why they are ignored, and possible solutions are listed in Table 4.1. It is important to note that all of the possible solutions can be found in this and other chapters in this textbook.

It may be worthwhile to briefly describe why some of these key findings are ignored. One reason is that many organizations suffer from the **"we are different" syndrome.** These organizations wrongly believe that they use different methods for getting results through others and building high performing teams, and thus they need leaders with unique skills. Consultants and Human Resource professionals often fuel this myth, as doing so allows them to make more money or build empires. In reality, the skills needed to build teams and get results through others are remarkably similar within leadership levels (see Highlight 4.2). Certainly the technical and functional knowledge needed by leaders can be unique, but the skills needed to get results through others are remarkably similar across organizations.

Another reason is that many hiring managers suffer from **judgment of character bias**—they falsely believe they are excellent judges of character and do not need to use more rigorous assessment techniques to hire or promote leaders. Yet many of these same hiring managers have also experienced a divorce or a painful breakup with a significant other. If hiring managers have difficulties selecting intimate partners, then why would they be any better at selecting employees? A third reason is that many leaders do not set clear goals or provide team members with the feedback they need to be successful. Some managers seem to lack the necessary skills to take these actions, but more often than not this is more likely due to laziness or a lack of focus. Many persons in leadership positions seem to take more pleasure in their titles than in setting strong accountability standards or achieving results. And the lack of clear goals, performance expectations, and feedback are among the key factors contributing to a base rate of managerial incompetence that is close to 50 percent.

Source: Curphy, G. J. & Hogan, R. T. "What We Really Know about Leadership (But Seem Unwilling to Implement)," working paper, 2004b.

One key objective of this book is to make the results of leadership research more usable to leaders and leaders to be. This chapter is specifically designed to help readers better understand how leadership research is conducted, gain an appreciation for some of the practical applications of this research, and sharpen critical thinking skills about leadership and leadership research. However, it is also worth noting that this entire book is dedicated to bridging the practice-research gap. This book reviews what researchers know about various leadership topics, translates these findings into useful advice for practitioners, describes how practitioners might apply these findings in the work setting, and predicts what results practitioners should see if they apply this information at work.

At the same time, however, we stress that this book is *not* intended to be a guide for conducting leadership research; rather, it is a guide to help leadership students and budding practitioners *be* better leaders by helping them understand the complex relationships among many factors affecting leadership. This book provides

TABLE 4.1
Top Ten
Leadership
Findings

Finding	Why Ignored?	Possible Solutions
1. A leader is a leader	"We are different" syndrome	Formally assess key individual differences
2. Individual differences	Judgment of character bias	Good assessment practices matter
3. Leader incompetence	Poor expectations Lack of accountability Poor selection Poor development	SMART goals ± feedback Assessment ` Critical components of development
4. Integrated talent practices	"We are different" syndrome Lack of skill Lack of alignment	Common leadership competency model
5. Leadership strengths and weaknesses are context specific	Bad popular advice on strengths and weaknesses	Focus on behaviors to keep, start, and stop doing
6. Clear goals	Lack of managerial skill or will	SMART goals
7. Feedback	Lack of managerial skill or will	Positive and constructive feedback
8. Building teams	Lack of framework	Rocket model
9. Developing leadership skills	Lack of knowledge of behavioral change	Critical components of leadership development
10. Optimism bias	Wishful thinking Narcissism	Critical thinking assessment

multiple frameworks for conceptualizing leadership in order to help practitioners maximize what they learn from experience. As an overview, this chapter uses several practical examples to review the major techniques leadership researchers have used to assess or measure leadership. When assessing leadership, researchers are looking at the ways that leaders are different from followers or how successful leaders differ from unsuccessful leaders in terms of variables such as their values, personality traits, intelligence, job knowledge, experience, or behavior. Next, the chapter continues with these practical examples to discuss the major indicators used to measure leadership effectiveness. After that, we look at several methodologies that are used to study leadership. This section explores the empirical foundations of studying the *relationship* between leadership and other variables. In other words, this section looks at different ways to study the relationship between leadership (e.g., what leaders do) and its effects (e.g., what happens as a result).

Assessing Leadership

Because this chapter is about assessing leadership, it seems appropriate to begin with an example from research. The research in this case deals with leadership in commercial airline crews. Many airline crews consist of two positions with very distinct responsibilities. The aircraft captain is the final authority for all decisions regarding the aircraft and is ultimately responsible for the safety of the passengers and crew. The copilot helps the captain fly the aircraft and is also responsible for the aircraft's preflight inspections and operation of systems (e.g., electrical, hydraulic, fuel, communication). Since airline crews must work together as a coordinated team to successfully complete a flight, one of the authors of this text studied factors affecting crew coordination (Ginnett, 1988). As a part of this project, he flew with a number of different airline crews and recorded conversations between crew members. The following is an excerpt of an interview between a copilot and the researcher:

Researcher: Are all the captains you fly with pretty much the same?

Aircrew member: Oh, no. Some guys are the greatest guys in the world to fly with. I mean they may not have the greatest hands in the world but that doesn't matter. When you fly with them, you feel like you can work together to get the job done. You really want to do a good job for them. Some other captains are just the opposite . . . you just can't stand to work with them. That doesn't mean you'll do anything that's unsafe or dangerous but you won't go out of your way to keep him or her out of trouble either. So you'll just sit back and do what you have to and just hope he or she screws up.

Researcher: How can you tell which kind of captain you're working with?

Aircrew member: Oh, you can tell.

Researcher: How?

Aircrew member: I don't know how you tell but it doesn't take very long. Just a couple of minutes and you'll know.

By and large, executives make poor promotion and staffing decisions. By all accounts, their batting average is no better than .333. At most, one-third of such decisions turn out right; one-third are minimally effective; and one-third are outright failures. In no other area would we put up with such miserable performance; indeed, we need not and should not. Managers making people decisions will never be perfect, of course, but they should come pretty close to batting 1.000.

Peter Drucker

The above conversation details some of the difficulties in assessing leadership. Although it was the airline pilot's personal opinion that it was relatively easy to recognize good captains, personal opinions about leadership effectiveness can vary substantially across individuals. Thus the copilot may feel that the captain may not be a good leader, but the flight attendants and ground crews might think this captain is very effective. Who is right or whose opinion carries more weight in this situation? Moreover, the copilot thought he could tell good from bad leaders once they were on the job, but many organizations want to know this information *before* they make a hiring decision. As the high profile cases with Enron, Parmalat, Worldcom, Vivendi, Health South, and Tyco have pointed out, putting the wrong people into key leadership positions can literally cost stockholders billions of dollars and lead to organizational ruin (Leib, 1998). There are a number of ways to improve the odds of making good leadership hiring decisions, and some hiring techniques are much more effective than others in predicting leadership success. How do we know this? We know this because researchers have systematically determined which leadership assessment techniques yield more valid and accurate predictions than other techniques. Because the identification of leadership talent is so important to organizations these days, many of them have capitalized on these research findings to create practical tools and processes for assessing the leadership capabilities of potential first-line supervisors through CEOs (Bunker, Kram & Ting, 2002; Conger & Fulmer, 2003; Curphy, 2004a, e; Lewis, Robie, Nilsen, & Curphy, 2001; Swan & Mills, 2004; Schlesinger, 2002).

Another practical example might help to illuminate the various techniques organizations use to assess leadership. Suppose the president of your college left to head up a large university, and you were asked to head up the search committee that was responsible for picking your next college president. The former president left the school in tough shape—the school's budget is a mess because of reductions in state funding and alumni donations over the past two years. The janitorial and administrative staffs are threatening a boycott over low wages, and many of the college's best professors have been recruited away by other universities. Because of budget cuts and the hemorrhaging of talent, faculty morale is poor. Students are unhappy with the quality of the teaching assistants and steep tuition increases over the past three years. Finally, the athletic department has just been penalized for several NCAA recruiting violations and the basketball team will be ineligible for postseason play for the next two years. You advertised nationally, and over 50 people have formally applied for the position by the application cutoff date. So what would you do to pick the best candidate from this pool of 50 applicants?

When doctors make a poor diagnosis, their patients die and they don't have to deal with it anymore. When lawyers fail to present a good case, their clients go to jail and they don't have to deal with it anymore. But when hiring managers make a mistake, they have to say "good morning" to it every day.

Pete Ramstad, Personnel Decisions International

If you didn't know anything about hiring college presidents, then you would probably do what most other organizations do when hiring new leaders. You would begin the process of hiring a college president by reviewing the resumes of the 50 candidates. You would use the results of this resume screening to identify who you believe are the top 5 to 10 candidates. You would bring this narrower pool of candidates in for one or more interviews and perhaps narrow the pool down to the top two candidates. At this point you would probably call the references of the top two candidates and make a final hiring decision based on the candidate who seemed to have the best "chemistry" or "job fit." Although this hiring process appears to make perfect sense, it is very unlikely that you would pick a college president who will be able to successfully achieve a balanced budget, recruit and retain top faculty, and keep students and staff happy. It may be that the odds of picking a good college president through this process are not much better than picking one of the 50 applicants at random. But how do we know this? As seen in Table 4.2, we know this because leadership research shows that application blanks, unstructured interviews, and

TABLE 4.2

Typical Correlations between Different Assessment Techniques and Job Performance in the United States

Assessment Technique	Correlation	U.S. Companies Using This Technique (percent)
Work sample/skill test	.54	1–20%
Assessment center/job simulation	.50	1–20
Job knowledge test	.48	20–30
Personality test	.48	1–20
Job tryout .	44	1–20
Biographical questionnaire	.40	1–20
Structured interview*	.40	unknown
Mental abilities test	.24	1–20
Unstructured interview	.20	90+
Reference check	.14	80+
Application blank	.10	90+

*Although interviews are among the most popular assessment techniques, it is uncertain how many are structured versus unstructured interviews.

Sources: K. Pearlman, "Validity Generalization: From Theory to Application" (paper presented at the Center for Human Resources Programs, Institute of Industrial Relations, University of California–Berkeley, 1985); T. A. Judge, "The Impact of I/O Psychology," *The Industrial and Organizational Psychologist* 35 (1997), pp. 108–110; A. M. Ryan, L. McFarland, H. Baron, and R. Page, "An International Look at Selection Practices: Nation and Culture as Explanations for Variability in Practices," *Personnel Psychology* 52, no. 2 (1999), pp. 359–92; American Management Association, *Job Skill Testing and Psychological Measurement*, June 2000; T. A. Judge, A. E. Colbert, & R. Ilies. "Intelligence and Leadership: A Quantitative Review and Test of Theoretical Propositions," *Journal of Applied Psychology*, 89 no. 3, pp. 542–552.

reference checks are very poor predictors of leadership effectiveness. Yet these techniques are among the most frequently used by organizations making leadership hiring decisions. That the most frequently used leadership hiring techniques are also the least valid shows how wide the practice-research gap truly is (see Highlights 4.2 and 4.3 for more information about the negative consequences of using poor leadership assessment techniques).

Best Practices in Assessing Leadership Potential

So what should you do if you want to improve the odds of hiring the right college president? Research has shown that the best place to start is to clearly define what you are looking for in a prospective college president. To do this, you would first need to determine the **leadership level** of the position. Leaders at different hierarchical levels in an organization have different responsibilities, and as such the challenges for each leadership level also vary. For example, a front-line supervisor at a fast-food restaurant has very different leadership responsibilities and challenges than a CEO. Both types of leaders need to get results through others and build cohesive teams, but differences in their followers and the situations they face have a profound impact on how these two groups of leaders get results through others. Some of the major responsibilities for the six primary leadership levels can be found in Highlight 4.4. In all likelihood the college president would be at the CEO level, in that he or she would need to: (a) develop a long-term vision for the college; (b) develop strategies to successfully compete with other colleges and universities; (c) determine which educational departments to emphasize, maintain, or shut down; (d) balance financial, student, faculty, staff, alumni, and legislative

The Base Rate of Managerial Incompetence

Highlight 4.2

Perhaps the best way to understand the notion of managerial incompetence is to count the number of leaders you have ever worked or played for. Of these leaders, how many would you work for again? Chances are you only need a single hand to count the number of leaders who could pass this test. Hogan and Curphy (2004) and Curphy and Hogan (2004b) maintain that less than 50 percent of the people in leadership positions can consistently build the teams necessary to get results through others. The five major reasons for this high level of incompetence are: (a) unclear goals and performance expectations for leaders; (b) leaders spending large amounts of time

doing activities below their leadership level; (c) an inability or unwillingness of organizations to actually hold leaders accountable to company standards and results; (d) poor leadership selection and promotion systems; and (e) poor leadership development systems. The base rate of managerial incompetence will remain high as long as organizations continue to adopt leadership selection, development, and promotion systems that are not in line with what we really know about leadership.

Sources: Curphy, G. J. & R. T. Hogan. "Managerial Incompetence: Is There a Dead Skunk on the Table?" working paper, 2004a. Hogan, R. T. & G. J. Curphy. "Leadership Matters: Values and Dysfunctional Dispositions," working paper, 2004.

needs; (e) hire and develop department chairs; and (f) build and maintain relationships with key internal and external constituencies.

The second step would be to build a **competency model** for the college president position. A competency model is the set of skills, knowledge, abilities, or other attributes that are relevant to successful performance in a particular job. In this situation the competency model for a college president might consist of the following: problem-solving and decision-making skills, visioning skills, planning and coordinating skills, fundraising skills, budgeting skills, delegation skills, organizational change skills, coaching skills, performance management skills, the ability to create high-performing teams, conflict management skills, the ability to build relationships with and earn the trust of key internal and external stakeholders, communication skills, the ability to motivate others, honesty and integrity, the ability to cope with high levels of stress, and in-depth knowledge of the higher education system and various educational techniques. The best candidate would be the person who possessed most if not all of these skills and attributes. How would you go about determining how many of these skills and attributes each of the 50 applicants possessed? And wouldn't it be even more important to know how well developed these skills and attributes are in each

If you don't know where you are going, you'll probably end up somewhere else.

David Campbell, The Center for Creative Leadership

The best predictor of future leadership behavior is past leadership behavior in similar circumstances.

Personnel Decisions International

Leadership Levels

Highlight 4.3

What leaders need to do to build cohesive, goal-oriented teams and get results through others varies by leadership level. Examples of the six primary leadership levels and what leaders need to do to get work done through others can be found below. It is worth noting that leaders who spend significant amounts of time doing work at lower leadership levels than is dictated by their position will have difficulties building teams and getting results through others. For example, if a business unit leader was constantly making decisions that should be made by Front-Line Leaders (such as scheduling work, monitoring worker output, or dealing with employee grievances), then all the Front-Line Leaders, Mid-Level Leaders, and Functional Leaders will basically be disempowered and reduced to doing the work normally associated with Individual Contributors. Many leaders have difficulties letting go of those activities they enjoyed doing at lower leadership levels, and run the risk of being perceived as incompetent. The six primary leadership levels are as follows:

- **Individual Contributors (Hourly Employees):** Focus on solving technical problems, building technical expertise, and getting tasks done. The best individual contributors manage their own time and resources wisely, take pride in their technical proficiency, and perform high quality work.

- **Front-Line Leaders (Sales Managers, Department or Shift Supervisors, etc.):** Focus on getting work done through others. The best first-line leaders hire the right people, clearly define performance expectations for others, provide coaching and feedback, and set priorities for their people. They also spend time gathering information from employees, communicating work assignments, and developing hourly employees into front-line leaders.

- **Mid-Level Leaders (District Managers, Store Managers, etc.):** Keep track of work unit performance, set priorities for the work unit, allocate resources to achieve optimal work unit results, get work done through front-line leaders, and manage issues and relationships with other mid-level leaders. The best MLLs focus on hiring the best FLLs, developing FLL bench strength, and building effective teams of FLLs.

- **Functional Leaders (VP of Sales, Human Resources, IT, etc.):** Have responsibility for an overall function within an organization, such as sales or IT. These leaders need to understand how their function contributes to organizational performance and often lead teams of subfunctional MLLs (i.e., VPs of Human Resources lead directors of Compensation and Benefits, Recruiting, Training, and Organizational Effectiveness).

- **Business Unit Leaders (Business Unit Presidents):** Have responsibility for a particular business unit within an organization. BULs take a more strategic approach to work by keeping abreast of industry and market trends, developing strategies and services to counter competitive threats, and allocating functional and operational resources to maximize profits and achieve business unit results. The best BULs focus on hiring the best functional leaders and building effective staffs.

- **Chief Executive Officers (CEOs):** These top executives lead teams of business unit leaders. CEOs decide what businesses their companies will pursue, the overall strategies for these businesses, how much to invest in the businesses, when to sell or acquire new businesses, etc. The best CEOs focus on maximizing shareholder value; determining business portfolios; determining what strategic investments to make in each business; hiring, developing, and retaining BULs; and developing a pool of successors for the CEO position.

Sources: Charan, R., S. Drotter & J. Noel. *The Leadership Pipeline.* San Francisco: Jossey-Bass, 2001; Curphy, G. J. "Leadership Transitions and Teams," presentation given at the Hogan Assessment Systems International Users Conference, Istanbul, September 2003b; Curphy, G. J. "What We Really Know About Leadership (But Seem Unwilling to Implement)," presentation given at the Minnesota Professionals for Psychology and Applied Work, Minneapolis, MN, January, 2004a; Curphy G. J. *Team Leader Program,* St. Paul, MN: Curphy, 2004b.

The Glass Ceiling Effect

Highlight 4.4

Research has shown that significantly fewer women than men make it to the top leadership positions in corporate America. For example, women make up more than 40 percent of the workforce, but only 10 percent of the executive positions in Fortune 500 companies are held by women. Moreover, only 2 percent of women hold one of the top five jobs in these organizations; about 100 of the Fortune 500 companies have no women at all in top positions. The percentage of women in top leadership positions is no better in Japan, where only 9 percent of midlevel managers are women. However, research has shown that there are few developmental differences between male and female executives, and at least at midmanagement level there seem to be few practical differences in performance between men and women. This underrepresentation at the executive level is also known as the **glass ceiling effect.** So, if there are few performance and developmental differ-

ences between men and women at the midmanagement level, then why aren't a higher percentage of underrepresented groups filling executive positions? It may well be that top executives hire people in their own image, and if that image is one of a white male, then it is likely white males will be chosen to become their successors. Perhaps the first step in breaking this cycle is to adopt best-practice leadership assessment systems. In all likelihood these systems will reveal few practical performance differences between gender groups. If there are few performance differences at the midmanagement level, and if executive successors are coming primarily from midmanagement ranks, then over time a higher percentage of women should reach the executive level.

Sources: J. R. Renshaw, *Kimono in the Boardroom: The Invisible Revolution of Japanese Women Managers* (New York, Oxford University Press, 1999); S. Gebelein, "As Leaders, Women Rule," *Business Week,* November 24, 2000, p. 74; E. A. Powell, "Women Hit a 'Glass Wall,'" *Denver Post,* November 12, 1999, p. C-1.

candidate? Fortunately, researchers have collected a wealth of data that provide answers to these two questions (see Figure 4.1 for an example of a mid-level leader competency model.)

Once the competency model for college presidents had been finalized, research shows that a **multiple hurdles approach** would be the most cost-effective and valid way to identify the best candidate from the applicant talent pool (Saal & Knight, 1988; Curphy, 2000, 2001; Lewis, Nilsen, Robie, & Curphy, 2001). In a multiple hurdles approach, applicants are put through a series of leadership assessment techniques and only the applicants who "pass" one assessment are allowed to move on to the next, and so forth. Typically the most inexpensive leadership assessment techniques are used first, with the most expensive (and often most valid) techniques used as the last hurdles in the hiring process (see Figure 4.2).

We would begin the multiple hurdle approach for our candidates by having the pool of 50 applicants take various **Internet or paper-and-pencil measures** of leadership effectiveness (Curphy 2003a, b; 2004a, e; Naglieri, Drasgow, Schmitt, Handler, Prifitera, Margolis, Velasquez, 2004). As shown in Table 4.2, researchers have indicated that biographical questionnaires, personality inventories, mental abilities tests, and interest inventories can do a very good job predicting future leadership effectiveness. Moreover, these measures are inexpensive and relatively easy to administer. In the case of identifying the right college president, we would begin the hiring process by having all 50 candidates fill out a biographical questionnaire

FIGURE 4.1
Example of a
mid-level
leader
competency
model.

Source: Louiselle, K.,
S. Bridges & G. J.
Curphy. "Talent
Assessment
Overview," working
paper, 2003.

Leading the Business
- Analyzing Problems and Making Decisions
- Thinking Strategically
- Financial and Technical Savvy
- Planning and Organizing
- Managing Execution

Leading People
- Inspiring Shared Purpose
- Driving Change
- Building the Talent Base
- Fostering Teamwork

Building and Sustaining Relationships
- Creating Open Communications
- Building Relationships
- Customer Focus
- Credibility

Adaptive Capacity
- Personal Drive
- Adaptability
- Learning Approach

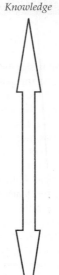

*Intelligence/
Knowledge*

*Easier to
Teach/Change*

*Personality/
Values*

*More
Difficult to
Change*

FIGURE 4.2
Multiple
hurdles
approach.

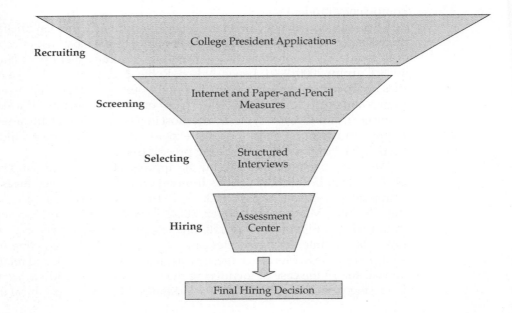

Recruiting — College President Applications

Screening — Internet and Paper-and-Pencil Measures

Selecting — Structured Interviews

Hiring — Assessment Center

Final Hiring Decision

(McElreath & Bass, 1999; Oswald, Schmitt, Kim, Ramsay, & Gillespie, 2004). This questionnaire would ask candidates to identify what they had done in the past that was related to the college president competencies, such as solving problems, making decisions, managing budgets, raising funds, and so forth. The responses to the questionnaire would be scored and only the top 10 scoring candidates would be allowed to proceed to the next hurdle.

The next step in the multiple hurdles approach would be to interview the remaining talent pool. In **structured interviews,** the interviewer asks the leader a predetermined set of questions; in **unstructured interviews** the interviewer does not follow a predetermined set of questions (Campion, Palmer, & Campion, 1997; Ganzach, Kluger, & Klayman, 2000; Van der Zee, Bakker & Bakker, 2002; Posthuma, Morgeson, Campion, 2002; Poundstone, 2003). In an unstructured format, the interviewer has the latitude to allow the interview to proceed in whatever direction seems appropriate. The conversation between the researcher and aircrew member earlier in this chapter is an excerpt from an unstructured interview. Although unstructured interviews can provide interesting insights into the leadership process, it is difficult to compare the results of interviews from different leaders. Structured interviews, with their common set of questions and rating scales, usually make it much easier to compare different leaders' attributes and skills. To use structured interviews for hiring a new college president, you would begin by asking each candidate the same set of questions. These questions would ask participants to describe situations in the past where they had to exhibit the skills and attributes identified in the college president competency model. The answers to the questions would then be evaluated using common rating scales. Examples of some structured and unstructured interview questions and examples of what not to do in an interview can be found in Highlight 4.5. Selection practices in different countries are summarized in Table 4.3.

The last step in the multiple hurdles approach would be to put the top three candidates through a college president assessment center. **Assessment centers** probably represent the most sophisticated and expensive method for assessing leadership potential. The historical underpinnings of assessment centers lie in Europe where they were used in the 1920s to select officers for the German military (Simoneit, 1944) and civil servants and foreign service officers for the British government (Garforth, 1945). In the United States, assessment centers were first used to select special agents and spies for the Office of Strategic Services, now known as the Central Intelligence Agency (Murray & MacKinnon, 1946). The purpose of modern-day assessment centers is to assess, identify, and develop leadership potential, and well over 200 institutions utilize this process (Jansen & Stoop, 2001; Highhouse, 2002; Byham, Smith, & Pease, 2002; Sorcher & Brant, 2002; Arthur, Day, McNelly, & Edens, 2003; Spychalski, Quinones, Gaugler, & Pohley, 1997; Personnel Decisions International, 2001).

The three candidates attending an assessment center would go through a "virtual reality" experience specifically designed for college presidents. They would begin the process by completing personality inventories and mental abilities tests while attending the assessment center. They would also spend one to two days in a simulated college setting where they would be put in a number of difficult, complex situations and their behaviors recorded by highly trained observers. Some of the

Interviewing: The Good, the Bad, and the Ugly

Highlight 4.5

THE GOOD: STRUCTURED INTERVIEWS

Managers make much better hiring decisions if they use structured interviews. Structured interviews use the same set of questions to ask prospective candidates about situations where they have had to demonstrate targeted skills and behaviors in the recent past.

Some of the questions for a college president applicant might include:

1. Driving Change: Describe the biggest, most complex change you had to make at a college or university. What were the circumstances surrounding the need to change, what did you specifically do to make the change happen, and what were the outcomes?

2. Labor Relations: What have been the most difficult labor relations issues you have had to deal with? What was the situation, what did you do, and how did the negotiations turn out?

3. Talent Management: Specifically describe what you have done to recruit, develop, and retain top faculty. What happened as a result of these efforts?

You can see that these questions are very job related, ask about specific behavior and outcomes, and make it much easier to compare candidates.

THE BAD: UNSTRUCTURED INTERVIEWS

In unstructured interviews candidates are asked whatever questions the interviewer deems necessary. Although this is probably the most popular leadership selection technique, it is also one of the least valid ways to hire effective leaders. At best, many of the questions in unstructured job interviews lack job relevance; at worst they are just plain offensive, illegal, or easy to fake. Many hiring managers use this tech-

nique because they suffer from judgment of character bias or are unfamiliar with the research surrounding structured versus unstructured interviews. Typical unstructured interview questions for a college president applicant might include:

1. How well do you get along with others?
2. If you could go out to dinner with anyone, who would it be and why?
3. Do you plan on having any more children?

THE UGLY: EXAMPLES OF STUPID INTERVIEWING TRICKS

One would think that most candidates would be motivated to paint the rosiest picture possible during an interview. But as the examples below all too amply demonstrate, some candidates apparently never learned this lesson:

1. The candidate interrupted the interview so that he could phone his therapist for advice on answering the questions.

2. During the interview the took off his right shoe and sock and sprinkled medicated foot powder on his foot. While he was putting his shoe back on, he mentioned that he had to use foot powder four times a day, and this was one of those times.

3. She wore a Walkman and said she could listen to me and the music at the same time.

Sources: T. Janz, L. W. Hellervik, and D. C. Gilmore, *Behavior Description Interviewing.* (Boston: Allyn and Bacon, 1986); V. Arnold, "Management and Executive Assessment" (paper presented at Personnel Decisions International, Denver, September 1997); B. Byham, *Landing the Job You Want: How to Have the Best Job Interview of Your Life* (Pittsburgh: DDI Press, 1997); L. Littlewood, "First Impression: Honesty, Attitude Turn Interviews into Jobs," *Denver Post,* May 24, 1998, p. E-3.

simulations used in an assessment center include in-basket exercises and role plays. An **in-basket exercise** is a work simulation that requires candidates to read an overview of a fictitious college, and its budgets, enrollments, departments, and organizational charts. The candidates are then given two hours to indicate how they would handle various articles, e-mails, letters, voice mails, and memos in a typical college president's in-basket. Candidates would then participate in a series of **role-play simulations,** of work, some of which might include a 30-minute meeting with a department head who is having performance problems, a mock interview with a

TABLE 4.3   Selection Practices in Europe, Africa, Asia, and Australia

Americans alone cannot be blamed for making poor leadership selection decisions. People all over the world seem to make many of the same leadership selection mistakes. For example, consider the popularity of the assessment techniques used by the following countries:

Assessment Technique	Percent Usage							
	Australia	China	France	Germany	Hong Kong	Japan	South Africa	Sweden
Work sample/skill test	>5%	?	>5%	>5%	>5%	0%	>5%	>5%
Mental abilities test	20–50	?	20–50	1–20	1–20	0	50–80	20–50
Assessment center/ job simulation	1–20	2%	1–20	1–20	1–20	0	20–50	1–20
Personality test	20–50	72%	50–80	1–20	20–50	0	50–80	50–80
Job tryout	1–20	?	20–50	1–20	1–20	0	20–50	1–20
Biographical form	1–20	?	1–20	20–50	1–20	1–20	1–20	1–20
One-on-one interviews	50–80	95%	80–100	80–100	50–80	50–80	80–100	80–100
Reference check	80–100	16	50–80	20–50	50–80	50–80	80–100	80–100
Application blank	50–80	68	80–100	50–80	80–100	80–100	80–100	1–20
Graphology (Handwriting analysis)	>5	?	50–80	>5	>5	0	1–20	1–20
Foreign language test	>5	?	20–50	1–20	20–50	0	1–20	20–50

This table provides a nice overview of the process a person would likely go through if hired for a leadership position in another country; those of you with poor handwriting may not want to apply for a leadership position in France. Although French companies seem to believe that graphology can be used to accurately predict leadership potential, there has yet to be a single shred of evidence to support this notion.

Sources: A. M. Ryan, L. McFarland, H. Baron, and R. Page, "An International Look at Selection Practices: Nation and Culture as Explanations for Variability in Practices," *Personnel Psychology* 52, no. 2 (1999), pp. 359–92; S Ju, Y. & M. Liang, The Application of Modern Human Resources Assessment Techniques in the Chinese Enterprises. Retrieved July 6 from http://www.pecc.net/HRD/SUYonghva.doc.

TV reporter, a meeting with a group of angry janitorial and administrative staff, and a presentation to the Board of Trustees on budget issues. The actors in the role-play simulations are trained assessors who observe and rate the performance of each candidate on the competencies embedded in each simulation. The assessors would then look across all of the instruments and simulations to create overall competency scores for each candidate, which would then be summarized in a written report. You and the rest of the search committee would then review the report and make a final hiring decision.

Assessing leadership is like using a micrometer to measure jello.

Rex Blake,
Independent consultant

It is to be hoped that the process makes sense: first defining what you want in a leader, using job-relevant paper-and-pencil measures as an initial screen for leadership candidates, and then using structured interviews and high-fidelity work simulations to identify those candidates with the most potential for a leadership position. The first step in improving the bench strength of the leaders within an organization is to hire or promote the right people to begin with, and this process provides a road map for doing just that. Not only will organizations see an increase in their leadership bench strength, but also they will see improved organizational performance by using these leadership assessment processes (Heine, 2000; Hogan & Hogan, 2000; Curphy, 2000, 2003a, 2004e; Lewis, Nilsen, Robie, & Curphy, 2001; Byham, Smith, & Pease, 2002). This does not mean that organizations need to adopt all of these steps in the multiple-hurdles process to hire and promote people with leadership potential. Many times having a clearly defined competency model, a biographical form, and structured interview questions linked to the model will do a fairly good job of improving the odds of hiring good leaders. This is particularly true when hiring lower-level leaders. However, research has shown that adding mental abilities tests and personality inventories can substantially improve the odds of hiring effective front-line leaders to CEOs. These assessments often get at abilities and behavioral tendencies that can be difficult to assess using biographical questionnaires and structured interviews alone (Curphy, 2003a, 2004a, e; Louiselle, Bridges, & Curphy, 2003). With respect to work simulations, we know they do a good job predicting leadership performance if used by themselves, but still do not know if in-basket exercises or role plays help to predict leadership performance over and above biographical questionnaires, mental ability tests, personality inventories, and structured interviews. In other words, once we assess candidates using these cheaper, easier to administer methods, we do not know whether the benefits of putting candidates through in-basket and role-play simulations outweigh the costs. And work simulations are quite expensive. Many paper-and-pencil measures cost less than $50 per assessment, whereas assessment centers can cost between $2,000–10,000 per candidate. It is clear that the work simulations do provide good developmental feedback for candidates, however.

Although there are important organizational benefits to hiring the right leaders, perhaps the most important point to be made about the preceding section is that there would be little to write about if it weren't for the efforts of leadership and organizational researchers. Research is the only way we know which assessment techniques are the most valid for which leadership positions. Researchers have conducted thousands of studies to determine how well various assessment techniques work for predicting future leadership effectiveness. Not only has this research helped companies to hire the right leaders, it has also leveled the playing field for candidates by creating fairer hiring processes. Unfortunately, Tables 4.2 and 4.3 show that most of this research continues to be ignored by the people making leadership hiring decisions. Organizations will continue to experience a short-fall in leadership talent as long as they continue to use assessment techniques that essentially result in little more than random selection (see Highlight 4.6).

Measuring the Effects of Leadership

After investment of time, energy, and money to hire the right candidate, the next key question is whether the new college president has truly had any positive impact on the organization. After one year on the job, have the relationships between the college president and department heads and the administrative and janitorial staff improved? Has the president been able to achieve a balanced budget by cutting costs and/or securing more funding? Have the skills of teaching assistants improved, and

The Impact of Best Practice Leadership Selection Techniques

Highlight 4.6

Recently a very large manufacturer acquired two other large manufacturing firms. The top leaders of the combined organization were faced with several key leadership dilemmas. The first was to determine which individuals would fill the top leadership positions in the combined company, as there was no particularly good information about the leadership talent in any of the three organizations. The second was to create a new culture for the combined organization that emphasized financial acumen, customer service, global perspective, attracting and developing talent, and a new business strategy that focused on services rather than production. Working against this new culture was the frequent emphasis of the three heritage organizations on technical excellence to the exclusion of profitability and customer service. The third was that many of the top 300 leaders in all three organizations were due to retire in the next three years and top leadership was uncertain how it could start to identify and build its leadership talent to fill these gaps.

To address these three needs, the combined organization started by having the top 250 executives go through a two-day customized assessment center. The results of the center were used to place people in key leadership positions, identify strengths and weaknesses of individual leaders and leadership teams, and help executives understand the demands, challenges, and expectations of leaders in the new organizational culture. The next 750 leaders in the combined organization are currently going through another customized assessment center in order to identify and build replacement leaders for those executives who will soon be retiring. The results of the assessment center process on some of the key unit performance indices of the company have been nothing short of remarkable. In the year after the assessment center was used to identify and deploy the top 250 executives in the company:

- Sales increased from $35 to $38 billion.
- Earnings improved from −$277 million to $1.902 billion.
- On-time deliveries improved from 48 percent to 100 percent.
- Stock price increased 27 percent.

Sources: D. Heine, "Using I/O Psychology to Turn Around a Business," in G. J. Curphy (chair), *The Role of I/O Psychology in Executive Assessment and Development* (symposium at the 15th Annual Conference of the Society for Industrial and Organizational Psychology, New Orleans, 2000).

are students happier with their college experiences? Has the president been able to recruit and retain key faculty? What information would you need to collect in order to evaluate the performance of the college president on these issues? And if there are any changes in these performance indicators, are they the direct result of, in spite of, or completely independent of the efforts of the new college president? Similarly, how would you evaluate the performance of Colin Powell as secretary of state? Would you look at the level of morale in the State Department, the number of peace treaties or trade negotiations signed, the number of coalition partners recruited and retained for the war against terrorism, the number of resolutions passed in the United Nations, and so on? Just as various techniques are used to assess leaders, there also are various ways to measure their *effects* on subordinates, organizations, or in the case of our secretary of state, the world. But what do we mean by "effects on subordinates"? A useful way to think about this is in terms of the ways that we typically define leadership success. We usually do not differentiate between successful and unsuccessful leaders by the behaviors they exhibit or the attributes they possess; rather, we are more likely to consider whether their followers are productive or satisfied. For example, we could make judgments about the success of a leader by looking at the college president's ability to raise funds, a coach's win-loss record, a college professor's end-of-course student ratings, or the production or quality rates for a production manager's work unit. Although the leader's behavior or personality traits will probably play a key role in these indices, when making judgments about the relative success of a leader we are examining the *consequences* or *impact* of these behaviors and not the behaviors per se. The material in this section describes how researchers typically measure leadership impact and their respective strengths and limitations.

Common Measures of Successful and Unsuccessful Leadership

Half of the CEOs in the world are below average.

David Campbell, The Center for Creative Leadership

In reality, there are a vast number of measures available to judge successful and unsuccessful leaders (see, for example, Table 4.4). Some of the more commonly used measures include a superior's effectiveness or promotion ratings, subordinates' ratings of their job satisfaction and morale or of their leader's effectiveness, and various work-unit performance indices. We will use the college president example to discuss each of these in further detail below.

Superiors' Effectiveness and Performance Ratings

One way to judge Colin Powell or any leader's success is in terms of his or her performance appraisal ratings. Most **superiors' performance ratings** are arrived at by a leader's superior and include ratings of performance on several relevant dimensions, as well as a recommendation (or not) for promotion. For example, Bass and Yammarino (1988) used superiors' overall performance ratings and promotion recommendations as criteria for judging the leadership effectiveness of navy surface fleet officers.

Because almost all organizations use some type of performance appraisal system, it may be worthwhile to briefly describe a typical performance appraisal form. The better performance appraisal forms typically include several features. First, superiors use some type of scale to rate how well a target leader accomplished several key objectives. Superiors also rate the leader on several key dimensions the organization believes are important, such as integrity, leadership, administrative skills, communication impact, and so forth. Finally, superiors then rate the overall performance and/or the promotability of the leader (Arvey & Murphy, 1998; Marentette, 2000). In

TABLE 4.4
Common Measures of Successful and Unsuccessful Leadership

Measure	Advantages	Disadvantages
Superiors' ratings	Frequently used	Superiors' biases
		Raters unaware of true performance
		Raters' unwillingness to provide tough feedback
Subordinates' ratings	Subject of leaders' behaviors	Unmotivated subordinates
		Subordinates' biases
	Multiple raters	May be no links between ratings and unit performance
Unit performance indices	Actual results	Results due to factors beyond leaders' control

our college president example, you would rate the college president on *what* he or she actually accomplished over the past year. In other words, how successful was the college president in balancing the budget, resolving staff conflict, building relationships with faculty and alumni, increasing student satisfaction, or making decisions about new economic programs? You would also rate *how* the college president went about accomplishing these objectives. This usually involves rating each of the college president competencies, such as the ability to solve problems and make decisions, meet budgets, coach others, create high-performing teams, manage conflict, and build relationships with and earn the trust of key internal and external stakeholders. These what and how ratings would then be combined to provide an overall rating of the college president's performance over the past year.

If you were on the college's Board of Trustees, you would probably want to complete a performance appraisal on the college president. However, you should also know that many times performance appraisal ratings might not be an accurate reflection of the college president's true impact on his or her followers or the organization. Sometimes superiors simply do not take the time to provide accurate and comprehensive performance appraisal ratings; at other times superiors may be largely unaware or unfamiliar with a target leader's performance. This latter phenomenon is becoming more prevalent as organizations move toward virtual teams or increase the number of people any one superior may supervise. Some superiors have difficulty dealing with conflict and would rather give average ratings than consider the emotions and distress associated with unflattering ratings. In addition, friendships, perceptual sets, and attribution errors can bias superiors' ratings of a leader's true performance. Some performance appraisal systems do such a poor job measuring a leader's true impact that superiors find them to be virtually useless when making promotion or compensation decisions.

Subordinates' Ratings of Satisfaction, Organizational Climate, Morale, Motivation, and Leadership Effectiveness

If leadership is defined partly in the eyes of followers, then perhaps a better way to judge the college president's success is through **subordinates' ratings of effectiveness.** In this method subordinates are asked to rate their level of satisfaction or the effectiveness of the president. Subordinates may be relatively satisfied or dissatisfied, may be motivated or unmotivated, may feel relatively committed or uncommitted to the organization, or may believe their leader is relatively effective or ineffective. Fostering a sense of motivation, cohesiveness, cooperation, and morale among unit members is a goal toward which most leaders will strive, yet several cautions may be in order when using subordinates' motivation or cohesiveness ratings to judge a leader's effectiveness. For one thing, some subordinates may be relatively unmotivated toward work no matter what the leader does. For example, it may be relatively difficult for the college president to motivate a highly unionized janitorial or administrative staff, or a group of tenured professors. For another, success in instilling a strong sense of motivation and cohesiveness in subordinates does not guarantee effective performance. It often is also necessary, for example, to ensure that subordinates are adequately trained and have the necessary equipment and resources to do the job. Without training and equipment, subordinates' performance still might be relatively low even if the subordinates are motivated. In addition, subordinates may be performing at a low level yet rate their leader as being relatively effective because he or she does not make them work very hard. Conversely, some subordinates may rate the leader as relatively ineffective if he or she does make them work hard. Thus, the links between subordinates' ratings and the performance of the college president may be unclear or affected by various factors beyond the president's control (Ittner & Larcker, 2003).

Despite these cautions, there are two reasons why followers' ratings may be a more accurate reflection of a leader's impact than superiors' ratings of performance. First, followers are often in a better position to make these judgments. They usually are the direct recipients of their boss's day-to-day leadership behaviors. Second, although subordinates' ratings can also suffer from distortion or bias, such effects tend to cancel each other out when multiple raters are used (Greguras, Robie, Schleicher and Goff, 2003). In our example, you could collect this information by asking direct reports to rate the college president on the college president competencies. These ratings would be averaged and used as another source of information for evaluating the performance of the college president.

Unit Performance Indices

Rather than use ratings to judge a leader's effectiveness, we could use **unit performance indices** to examine what impact leaders have on the "bottom lines" of their organizations. In other words, we could make judgments about leadership success by examining store sales, profit margins, the number of defective products returned, the number of on-time deliveries, crime rates, high school graduation rates, the dollar amount of charitable contributions collected, win-loss records, or days lost due to accidents. Like the two other sets of measures described earlier, none of these measures are perfect. The biggest qualification to remember in using them as measures of leadership is that these measures are often affected by factors beyond a leader's control. For example, many different factors can affect the college budget. These can include economic conditions, alumni fund-raising efforts, school scandals, state legislative efforts, drops in student enrollment, changing demographics, and so on. Conceivably, the college president could do "all the right things," yet still not balance the budget from one year to the next, primarily due to circumstances beyond his or her control. Conversely, the president may make a number of mistakes but may work in a city that sees an economic uptick due to the arrival of several new companies. These companies could provide hundreds of new jobs, which in turn would increase tax revenues and student enrollments. Leadership practitioners need to remember that unit performance indices are often affected by several factors, some of which have more impact than anything a leader might do (Phelps & Addonizio, 2002). It is important to estimate how much a leader's behavior might affect a particular unit performance index before using that index to judge the leader's effectiveness.

Best Practices in Measuring Leadership Success

Right about now you may be wondering if it is even possible to develop accurate measures of leadership success. Ratings by superiors and subordinates have their inherent problems, as do unit performance indices. Despite such problems, these measures generally yield useful information about a leader's effectiveness. Moreover, these measures get at different aspects of effectiveness. It is entirely possible for a leader to get strong ratings from his or her superiors but poor ratings from subordinates. This may be the case if a leader was brought in to turn

If you can't measure it, then you can't manage it.

Peter Drucker

around a poorly performing college or if a leader has spent a considerable amount of time engaging in "strategic sucking up" with the Board of Trustees. On the other hand, leaders could have poor relationships with their boss and great relationships with their subordinates, and such relationships would be reflected in the ratings they get from these two groups. Practitioners need to understand the advantages and problems associated with the different measures, and that multiple measures often yield the best information about leadership success (Greguras, Robie, Schleicher, & Goff, 2003).

Practitioners also need to think critically about how their behavior affects the measures used to judge leadership success. Leaders may perform relatively poorly on several unit performance indices yet also realize that performance on these indices is both relatively insensitive to their behavior and largely a function of, say, local economic conditions or inadequate resources. Leaders instead may choose to focus on improving their effectiveness in terms of criteria more sensitive to their actions, such as improving subordinates' perceptions of motivation, climate, or satisfaction (see Highlights 4.7 and 4.8).

Another concern for leadership practitioners might be the degree to which leadership success measures are biased. A study of over a million performance appraisals from the British National Health Service revealed that women received significantly lower performance appraisal evaluations than men (Alimo-Metcalfe, 1994). Females receive less pay for the same job as their male counterparts in both the United Kingdom and the United States (Alimo-Metcalfe, 1994; Jackson, 1996), and minority female managers make only 57 percent of the earnings of their white male counterparts in the United States (*Denver Post,* October 23, 1997). These results imply that females receive lower performance appraisal ratings across most jobs in these two countries. Because males make up the majority of managers in both countries, it may be some time before both genders receive the same level of effectiveness and performance ratings from their superiors (see Highlight 4.4). It is important to remember, however, that not all male managers automatically give all female subordinates lower performance appraisal ratings. The research cited above represents overall trends; individual male managers may or may not give female subordinates lower performance or effectiveness ratings.

Methodologies Used to Study Leadership

So far we have discussed the techniques used to assess a leader's personality traits or behaviors. We have also gone over the measures commonly used to evaluate a leader's success. What we have not discussed is how researchers determine whether there is a *relationship* between a leader's personality traits, behaviors, or values and their win-loss records, sales results, percentage of on-time takeoffs, subordinates' level of satisfaction, and so forth. Do leaders who are more outgoing, better problem

The War for Talent

Highlight 4.7

Many organizations believe that they suffer from a chronic shortage of leadership talent. Top leaders have very little confidence that they will have the leaders with the right skills in the right positions to achieve organizational outcomes over the next five years. This has led to a **War for Talent**—where organizations are actively recruiting some of the best and brightest leaders away from other companies or putting forth considerable effort to identify and develop top internal talent. Perhaps one of the most visible examples of the War for Talent can be found in the television series, *The Apprentice.* In this show contestants participate in a series of leadership challenges and the person who comes closest to demonstrating what Donald Trump is looking for in leadership talent is eventually chosen to join the Trump organization. Many companies, such as General Electric, The Home Depot, Best Buy, The Limited, and Coors also believe that leadership talent is a critically important competitive advantage, and they put a tremendous amount of emphasis on identifying (i.e., assessing), developing, promoting, and retaining the right leaders. One of the reasons why so many General Electric managers and executives are recruited by other companies is because of GE's emphasis on leadership talent management.

But what do we mean by leadership talent management? Essentially, this means reviewing where the organization wants to go over the next 5–10 years and then identifying the key leadership positions and competencies needed to help the organization achieve its goals. Once the key positions and competencies are identified, organizations then use many of the assessment techniques described in this chapter to determine who currently has these critical leadership skills, who can develop these skills, and who may not be able to develop talent gaps. Each year teams of superiors at General Electric differentiate all its leaders using a three-letter system:

- **A players** make up the top 10 percent of the management population and are the superstars of the company. Leadership talent management often focuses on the development and retention of these leaders.

- **B players** make up the middle 70 percent of the management population and are the solid performers in the company. Leadership talent management programs are designed to help develop B players into A players.

- **C players** are the bottom 20 percent of the management population and are usually managed out of the organization.

Gladwell (2002) correctly points out that many organizations do a poor job categorizing leaders—they tend to overemphasize financial skills (i.e., MBAs) and pay little attention to the skills needed to get results through others. As a result, many of the A players are often promoted so quickly that they do not learn the important lessons at each leadership level and are not in jobs long enough to see the real impact of their leadership skills (or lack thereof). These A players eventually get promoted into positions of managerial incompetence—their positions are large enough that they can no longer rely solely on their own technical and financial skills to get the job done, and they lack those skills needed to build cohesive, goal-oriented teams and get results through others. Because many organizations are loathe to remove failing A players, many high performing followers who could replace the failing leader choose to leave rather than continue to work for an incompetent leader. In these cases poor talent management processes cost organizations both former A player leaders and followers.

Sources: Bunker, K. A., K. E. Kram, & S. Ting. "The Young and the Clueless." *Harvard Business Review,* December 2002, pp. 80–88; Byham, B. C., A. B. Smith, & M. J. Pease. *Grow Your Own Leaders: How to Identify, Develop, and Retain Leadership Talent.* New York, Financial Times/Prentice Hall, 2002; Conger, J. A, & R. M. Fulmer. "Developing Your Leadership Pipeline." *Harvard Business Review,* December 2003, pp. 76–85; Curphy, G. J. and R. T. Hogan. "Managerial Incompetence: Is There a Dead Skunk on the Table?" working paper, 2004a; Gladwell, M. "The Talent Myth: Are Smart People Overrated?" *The New Yorker,* July 22, 2002, pp. 28–33; Michaels, E., H. Handfield-Jones, & B. Axelrod. *The War for Talent.* Boston, MA: Harvard University Press, 2001.

Succession Planning and Failure at the Top

Highlight 4.8

For better or worse, investors hold Chief Executive Officers (CEOs) responsible for company performance. CEOs have big, complex jobs—those leading *Fortune* 500 companies often head up organizations having tens of thousands of employees that generate billions of dollars of revenue every year. These top executives decide what businesses their companies will pursue, the overall strategies for these businesses, how much to invest in the businesses, when to sell or acquire new businesses, etc. They are also among the best compensated individuals in the world, often making $1,000,000 to $200,000,000 in salary and stock options each year. Given the scope, responsibilities, and the rewards associated with the CEO position, it seems natural that these individuals should be held accountable for company performance.

Each year over the past 10 years somewhere between 20–33 percent of the CEOs in North American, European, and Asian Pacific firms are asked to leave for poor performance. And the high visibility scandals at Enron, Worldcom, Parmalat, Xerox, Adelphia, Royal Dutch Shell, Arthur Andersen, and Boeing indicates that Boards of Directors and shareholders may be even less likely to tolerate mediocre or poor performing CEOs than they have in the past. But when CEOs are finally asked to leave, their companies are often teetering on the brink of bankruptcy. (Nevertheless, dismissed CEOs are almost always given multimillion dollar severance packages as a reward for their less

than stellar performance, which probably says more about Boards of Directors' judgment and intestinal fortitude than it does about CEO incompetence.)

But should the successor for the CEO position come from inside or outside the company? Many companies on the brink of disaster look for an external charismatic leader to return the organization to financial health. But research by Khurana (2002) indicates that outside CEOs do no better than internal successors. And because outside CEOs lack organizational and industry specific knowledge and tend to want to change everything about those organizations they are leading, these leaders often create even more problems than their predecessors. Being an insider was once an important factor in CEO succession: back in 1980 only 7 percent of the CEOs came from outside the company. Now approximately 50 percent of new CEOs come from the outside. This shift in the percentage of CEOs coming from the outside indicates that many organizations may be losing the War for Talent, in that their leadership talent management processes have failed to produce the most important leaders for the organizations.

Sources: Biggs, E. L. "CEO Succession Planning: An Emerging Challenge for Boards of Directors." *Academy of Management Executive,* 2004, 18 (1), pp 105–110; Khurana, R. "The Curse of the Superstar CEO." *Harvard Business Review,* September, 2002, pp. 60–67; Sonnenfeld, J. A. & R Khurana. "Fishing for CEOs in Your Own Backyard." *The Wall Street Journal,* July 30, 2002, p. B2; Woodruff, D. "Europe Shows More CEOs the Door." *The Wall Street Journal,* July 31, 2002, p. A11.

solvers, or good listeners, or can handle stress well really have happier and more productive subordinates? The nature and strength of the relationships between various leadership attributes and performance or effectiveness measures is of primary importance to researchers and practitioners alike. If there is little or no relationship between a leader's personality traits or behaviors and subordinates' satisfaction levels, then organizations would be wasting their time and money to assess these values and traits as part of their hiring or promotion processes. However, a large body of research shows that certain leadership attributes can be reliably assessed and are related to a number of positive leadership outcomes. How do leadership

The color of leadership is bright orange. The color of leadership research is slate gray.

Jerry Hunt
Texas Tech University

researchers systematically determine whether there is a relationship? The techniques used by researchers to determine these relationships can generally be grouped into either qualitative or quantitative approaches.

The Qualitative Approach

The most common qualitative approach is the case study. **Case studies** are an in-depth analysis of a particular leader's activities and fall into the troubadour tradition described at the beginning of this chapter. A common form of the case study is the biography, such as *My American Journey* (Powell & Persico, 1995). Biographies usually provide detailed descriptions of the various situations facing the leader, the actions taken in response to these situations, and the results of the leader's actions. Case studies can provide leadership practitioners with valuable ideas on what to do in different leadership situations, particularly if the situations facing the practitioner are similar to those described in a biography. However, there is no objective way to determine whether the actions taken actually caused the results described in a case study. Often factors beyond the leader's actions have a greater role in determining outcomes. Because of these problems, caution should always be used when trying to apply lessons discerned from a case study or biography; they may not fit your particular leadership style or apply to your leadership situation. Nevertheless, case studies often provide interesting and valuable reading, and offer leadership practitioners alternative perspectives for analyzing leadership situations. Case studies can also provide researchers with hypotheses to test further using more precise quantitative methods (Conger, 1998).

Quantitative Approaches

The two major quantitative approaches include correlational studies and experiments, both of which fall into the academic tradition described earlier in this chapter. **Correlational studies** are used to determine the statistical relationship between leaders' traits, mental abilities, or behaviors and various measures of leadership effectiveness such as subordinates' satisfaction or climate ratings. An example of a correlational study would be to identify a group of leaders (e.g., police chiefs in 100 midsized cities), collect their scores on some type of paper-and-pencil test (a mental abilities test), and also collect satisfaction ratings from their respective subordinates. A **correlation coefficient** would then be calculated between the intelligence test scores and subordinates' satisfaction ratings. A correlation coefficient is a statistical index of the strength of the relationship between two variables and can range between -1.00 and $+1.00$. Correlation coefficients close to 1.00 would indicate a strong, positive relationship, those close to 0 would indicate no relationship, and those close to -1.00 would indicate a strong inverse relationship between mental ability scores and subordinates' satisfaction ratings. A good example of a correlation study was published by Dorfman, Howell, Hibino, Lee, Tate, and Bautista (1997). These authors found that leaders who exhibited higher levels of supportive, contingent reward, and charismatic behaviors had more satisfied and motivated subordinates in the United States, Mexico, Japan, South Korea, and Taiwan (all correlations were in the .3–.6 range).

Correlational studies are among the most common methods used to study leadership. Both the ease of data collection and the ability of correlational studies to illuminate relationships between leader characteristics and effectiveness measures are major advantages of these studies. However, they do have one major drawback. It is usually difficult (though it is often tempting) to make **causal inferences** based on correlational data. A causal inference occurs when leadership researchers can definitely say that certain leadership behaviors or attributes *cause* various kinds of leadership outcomes. Although correlational studies help researchers to determine the relationship between leadership attributes and outcomes, they cannot be used to make causal inferences. For example, in the study by Dorfman and his coauthors we cannot tell if a leader's supportive behaviors cause their subordinates to be more satisfied, or if more satisfied subordinates cause their leaders to exhibit more supportive leadership behaviors. Indeed, some of the most common erroneous reasoning from research results involves inferring causal relationships between variables when only a correlational relationship has been established (see Highlight 4.9).

Experiments allow researchers to make causal inferences about leadership, and experimental designs are often based on the results of earlier case and correlational studies. Experiments generally consist of both independent and dependent variables. The **independent variable** is what the researcher manipulates or varies to test the hypothesis; it causes change in the dependent variable. In leadership research, the independent variable is often some type of leadership behavior and the **dependent variable** is usually some measure of leadership effectiveness, such as work-unit performance or subordinates' satisfaction ratings.

A description of a "laboratory" experiment on leadership may help make the distinction between independent and dependent variables a bit clearer. Howell and Frost (1988) were interested in determining whether charismatic leaders caused subordinates to perform at a higher level than supportive or directive leaders. These researchers trained two actresses to manifest either charismatic, directive, or supportive leadership styles. Thus, the style of leadership exhibited by the actress-leader for different groups of subordinates was the independent variable in this experiment; with some groups the actress-leaders exhibited charismatic behaviors, with others they exhibited only supportive or directive behaviors. The dependent variable was subordinates' performance, which in this case was measured by the number of memos subordinates successfully completed during a 45-minute in-basket exercise. As you can see, the researchers manipulated or changed the independent variable (the actresses' leadership styles varied across different groups of subordinates), but they merely recorded the subordinates' performance on the dependent variable (the number of memos successfully completed) at the end of each 45-minute session. The researchers reported that subordinates' performance levels were highest when leaders exhibited charismatic behaviors and as a result concluded that these leadership behaviors caused subordinates to perform at the highest levels.

Although experiments allow us to make causal inferences about leadership, experiments have drawbacks of their own. One is that the effects obtained in many laboratory experiments are stronger than the effects obtained when the same experiments are conducted in organizations. This is primarily due to the tightly controlled conditions under which laboratory experiments are run, whereas experiments in organizations cannot be so tightly controlled. Extraneous influences often minimize or distort the effects of the independent variable on the dependent variable

Global Leadership

Highlight 4.9

There is no doubt about it, the world is getting smaller. Globalization has allowed goods and services to be manufactured, traded, and delivered in places no one thought possible just 10 or 20 years ago. World business leaders, such as Jeffery Immelt of General Electric, John Brown of British-Petroleum, and Steve Ballmer of Microsoft all believe these global trends are irreversible and gaining momentum. But what are the implications of globalization for leadership? It is clear that the ways in which leaders get results through others and build cohesive, goal-oriented teams will vary somewhat from one country to the next. For example, Malaysian culture inhibits assertive, confrontational behavior and puts a premium on maintaining harmony. Effective leaders are expected to show compassion while demonstrating more of an autocratic than participatory leadership style. German culture does not value compassion, and interpersonal relationships are rather straightforward and stern. Effective leaders in Germany generally value autonomy and participation, but have a low team orientation.

So how does one lead in a global economy? Certainly appreciating what different cultures value and how things get done in different countries is an important first step. But will the leaders of the future need to speak multiple languages or actually live in other countries in order to be effective? The answers to these questions will depend to some extent on the global orientation of the organization. Some organizations, such as Waste Management or ServiceMaster, primarily operate in Canada and the United States and probably will not need to have leaders who have lived in other countries or speak multiple languages. Other organizations, such as 3M, Hewlett-Packard, or Pfizer, have significant manufacturing, marketing, and sales operations in multiple countries. These organizations often use a global competency model to outline the expectations for leaders in all countries, and these models tend to vary more by leadership level than by country (see Figure 4.1 for an example of a competency model).

It seems likely that leaders who have spent time in other countries, have applied the Action-Observation-Reflection model to maximize the lessons learned from their expatriot experiences, and can speak multiple languages would be better able to lead international organizations. But currently this is conjecture, as more research is needed before we can definitively say whether international experience matters, how much and what kind of experience is needed, what are the key lessons to be learned from these experiences, and how do we select and develop leaders to successfully lead international organizations. The good news here is that a group of 150 social scientists working on the GLOBE (Global Leadership and Organizational Behavior Effectiveness) project are actively seeking the answers to these questions.

Sources: Green, S., F. Hassan, J. Immelt, M. Marks, & D. Meiland. "In Search of Global Leaders." *Harvard Business Review,* August 2003, pp 38–45; Kennedy, J. C. "Leadership in Malaysia: Traditional Values, International Outlook." *The Academy of Management Executive,* 2002, 16 (3), pp. 15–24; Brodbeck,. F., M. . Frese, M. Javidan, & F. G. Kroll. "Leadership Made in Germany: Low on Compassion, High in Performance." *The Academy of Management Executive,* 2002, 16 (1), pp. 16–30; GLOBE program: http://mgmt3.ucalgary.ca/web/globe.nsf/index

when the experiment is conducted in an organizational setting. Another problem concerns the subjects used in many laboratory experiments. Many times, college undergraduates are used as subjects in leadership experiments, and these individuals may have little leadership or followership experience. For such reasons it becomes legitimate to ask how much the results of any particular laboratory experiment can be generalized to actual organizations.

Literally thousands of qualitative and quantitative studies have looked at what leaders do and how their actions affect important team or organizational outcomes. Organizations that have capitalized on this accumulation of knowledge and successfully bridged the practice-research gap have been able to design better hiring,

How to Win the War for Talent

Highlight 4.10

So far we have seen that building teams and getting results through others gets increasingly complex as people move up leadership levels, and globalization and technology will likely make the role of a leader even more complex in the future. Although it may be impossible to estimate the exact percentage of incompetent managers, it is clearly much higher than it can or should be. The high level of leadership failure from Front-Line Leaders through CEOs indicates that most leadership talent management programs are missing the mark. So what can organizations do to improve their leadership talent management processes?

The best or most comprehensive way to improve leadership talent is to create an **integrated talent management process.** To do this, companies must take the following steps:

1. Create leadership competency models to identify what people need to do at different leadership levels.

2. Align human resource systems (recruiting, selection, development, succession planning, compensation and benefits, performance management, and retention) around the leadership competency models. This will help ensure that those leadership behaviors being developed are the same ones being rewarded and promoted.

3. Ensure selection, development, performance management, and succession planning systems have adopted best practice techniques. For example, the leadership selection and succession planning systems should utilize the best techniques found in Table 4.2. The performance management system should utilize all of the measures found in Table 4.4.

These three steps sound simple enough, yet it is rare to find companies that actually do all three steps well.

Many companies have ill-defined leadership competency models, others have misaligned human resource systems, and still others use ineffective selection or performance management techniques. A large part of the problem here is that the "owners" of these talent management processes (i.e., Human Resource professionals) are either unaware of these three steps or are unable to get their organizations to buy-in to the benefits of an integrated process. It seems likely that the base rate of managerial incompetence will remain higher than it should be as long as organizations fail to adopt an integrated talent management process.

Sources: Batt, R. "Managing Customer Service: Human Resource Practices, Quit Rates, and Sales Growth." *Academy of Management Journal,* 45 (3), 2002, pp. 587–598; Byham, B. C., A. B. Smith, & M. J. Pease. *Grow Your Own Leaders: How to Identify, Develop, and Retain Leadership Talent.* New York, Financial Times/Prentice Hall, 2002; Collins, C. J. & K. D. Clark. "Strategic Human Resource Practices, Top Management Team Social Networks, and Firm Performance: The Role of Human Resource Practices in Creating Organizational Competitive Advantage." *Academy of Management Journal,* 46 (6), 2003, pp. 740–751; Conger, J. A. & R. M. Fulmer. "Developing Your Leadership Pipeline." *Harvard Business Review,* December 2003, pp. 76–85; Curphy, G. J. "What We Really Know about Leadership (But Seem Unwilling to Implement)." Presentation given at the Minnesota Professionals for Psychology and Applied Work, Minneapolis, MN, January, 2004a; Curphy, G. J. & Hogan, R. T. "What We Really Know about Leadership (But Seem Unwilling to Implement)." Working paper, 2004b; Hogan, R. T., G. J. Curphy & R. A. Gregory. "Risk-Taking in the Energy Industry." *Well Connected,* 5 (6), 2003, pp. 5–7; Rynes, S. L., K. G. Brown, & A. E. Colbert. "Seven Common Misconceptions about Human Resource Practices: Research Findings versus Practitioner Beliefs." *Academy of Management Executive,* 16(3), 2002, pp. 92–99; Schlesinger, L. "Building a Family." Presentation given at The Limited Brands Leadership Meeting, Columbus, OH, May 20, 2002; Swan, M. & V. Mills. "Building Impact and Influence Through a Client-Centered Approach." Presentation given at the Society of Consulting Psychology Mid-Winter Conference, Pasedena, CA. February, 2004.

performance management, training and development, and succession planning systems for their leaders. These systems almost always result in stronger leadership bench strength and in turn better organizational performance (see Highlight 4.10). Nevertheless, there are a number of important leadership questions that still need to be answered. Gary Yukl, one of the world's premier leadership researchers,

TABLE 4.5
Some
Common and
Uncommon
Variations of
Leadership
Studies

Feature	Common	Uncommon
Research method	Surveys	Experiments
Time frame	Static	Longitudinal
Research objective	Replication	Explore new issues
Locus of leadership	Heroic individual	Shared/distributed
Causality	Unidirectional	Reciprocal
Data sources	Single	Multiple
Level of leader	Supervisor	Executive

Source: G. Yukl, *Reflections and Directions in Leadership Research* (presentation made at the 14th Annual Conference of the Society of Industrial and Organizational Psychologists, Atlanta, May 1999).

maintained that although there is much we still need to learn about leadership, a great deal of the leadership research being conducted these days misses the mark. Leadership researchers appear to be too obsessed with surveys, too ready to replicate previous research, think only of leadership as a one-way relationship, or use the same quantitative designs too frequently for this research to be of much use (see Table 4.5). Yukl (1999) maintained that the yield rate of current research is only 11 percent; this is the percentage of studies that actually add something over and above what we already know about leadership. And as stated earlier, much of this leadership research provides little if any useful advice to leadership practitioners. So if the leadership research is not adding to our body of scientific knowledge and practitioners cannot use any of the findings, then what is truly driving leadership research? Unfortunately, it appears that the requirements for tenure are resulting in leadership research that is of little use to anyone.

Maxims and Theories of Leadership

Everything you do at work counts.
Mike Watkins, Western Area
Power Administration

Most of what people read about leadership amounts to little more than someone else's opinion about it. Often, such material is both anecdotal and prescriptive: anecdotal in the sense it reflects just one leader's views, and prescriptive in advising others how to be more effective. For example, although Colin Powell is an outstanding leader whose rules make intuitive sense (see Highlight 4.11), it is nonetheless uncertain whether his maxims would apply equally well for very different leaders in very different situations. **Maxims** are personal opinions that can give leaders valuable advice about leadership. It is important to be mindful of the difference between this kind of literature about leadership and more scientific or empirical approaches to understanding it. The latter are represented by data-based studies and theories reported in this book. Although both approaches have legitimate purposes, it is vital to understand the differences between them.

The scientific alternative to leadership maxims is leadership theory. A leadership **theory** is a framework for conceptualizing relationships between variables and guiding research toward a fuller understanding of phenomena. With a theory a researcher makes public predictions about how certain leadership attributes or

Colin Powell's Rules

Highlight 4.11

1. It ain't as bad as you think. It will look better in the morning.
2. Get mad, then get over it.
3. Avoid having your ego so close to your position that when your position falls, your ego goes with it.
4. It can be done!
5. Be careful what you choose. You may get it.
6. Don't let adverse facts stand in the way of a good decision.
7. You can't make someone else's choices. You shouldn't let someone else make yours.
8. Check small things.
9. Share credit.
10. Remain calm. Be kind.
11. Have a vision. Be demanding.
12. Don't take counsel of your fears or naysayers.
13. Perpetual optimism is a force multiplier.

Source: C. Powell and J. E. Persico, *My American Journey* (New York: Random House, 1995).

behaviors will systematically impact certain leadership effectiveness measures. Then the researcher collects the leadership assessment and effectiveness data prescribed by the theory, and conducts statistical analyses to determine whether his or her predictions are supported or refuted. For example, suppose a researcher predicted that the personality traits of dominance (wanting to be in charge of others) and dependability (being a reliable, trustworthy, and hard-working employee) were positively related to sales results in the computer retail industry. The researcher could use a paper-and-pencil measure of personality to assess store managers' standings on the traits of dominance and dependability. The researcher could then collect annual sales results for each store and conduct a correlational study to determine the nature and strength of the relationships between these three variables. The researcher might then publish the results of his or her findings in a scientific journal so that other researchers can gather more information that would support or refute the original theory and findings.

The public predictions of how leadership variables are interrelated, the systematic gathering and analysis of data, and the peer review of results are what make theories so central to scientific research. Theories are often modified to take new findings into account as researchers collect, analyze, and publish their findings about the theory. For example, other researchers may find that store managers' intelligence levels also are related to store performance. The original theory would then need to be modified so that dominance, dependability, and intelligence could all be used to predict sales managers' success. These findings could in turn be used to develop a competency model and selection system for future store managers in the computer retail industry.

The essence of theories of leadership, then, is to provide a reasonably coherent conceptual structure of how critical variables interact, involving ideas that can be put to the test and revised as new data accumulate. Simply put, theories of leadership involve testable ideas, whereas prescriptive approaches to leadership involve no such intended testability. Although both leadership maxims and theories are useful for understanding leadership situations, in general only leadership theories

The Top Five Critical Thinking Questions Practitioners Should Ask When Reading about Leadership

Highlight 4.12

1. *Who is in the sample?*
   - How big is the sample?
   - Is the sample representative of most leaders?
   - How similar are the leaders to you?

2. *What is the situation?*
   - What challenges and opportunities do the leaders face?
   - If reading about an experiment, how generalizable are the conditions to the "real world"?
   - What situational factors could affect the results of the experiment?
   - Is the situation similar to the one you currently face?

3. *What leadership qualities, characteristics, or behaviors are being assessed?*
   - Are the right attributes being assessed?
   - Are the best assessment techniques being used?

4. *How is leadership success being determined?*
   - By means of superiors' ratings, subordinates' ratings, or unit performance indices?
   - Are the best measures being used, or would alternative measures paint a different picture?
   - How might these measures be affected by factors beyond the leader's control?

5. *How do the writers link leadership assessment to success?*
   - By means of case studies, correlational studies, or experiments?
   - Are the right conclusions being drawn?
   - Are there any other plausible alternative explanations?
   - Did the writers acknowledge these alternative explanations?

add to the body of knowledge concerning the science of leadership and help in the development of universal laws of leadership. It is also important to understand that theory building is hard, painstaking work. It is fairly easy to state one's opinions on how one should act as a leader; it is an entirely different matter to design a study, collect data, analyze, and finally publish the results.

Despite all of the advantages of conducting systematic research around the topic of leadership, there remains the question of why case studies and maxims carry so much weight among leadership practitioners. Academicians may be prompted to wonder why books such as *Who Moved My Cheese?* (Johnson, 1998), *Working with Emotional Intelligence* (Goleman, 1998), *Leading with Soul* (Bolman & Deal, 1995), and *Awakening the Leader Within* (Cashman & Forem, 2003) are so popular among practitioners. Perhaps the more central question, however, is why research-based articles in leadership and management journals are not more popular themselves. One reason is probably that the very format of research articles, with their emphasis on statistical results and so forth, is fairly dull and inaccessible to anyone but university professors and graduate students. However, we also suspect that leadership researchers themselves sometimes forget that other academicians should not be their only important audience. Leadership researchers need to do a better job of making the findings from their studies more relevant and accessible to practicing managers and leaders (see Highlight 4.12).

Summary   Although this chapter focused on leadership research, there are several reasons why it is relevant for leadership practitioners even though they are unlikely to actually conduct leadership research themselves. First, organizations can and do use a number of techniques to assess the values, personality, intelligence, and behaviors for any applicant pool. Although none of these techniques are perfect, they can help hiring managers make substantially better staffing decisions, and many organizations are using fairly sophisticated assessment techniques to improve the odds of hiring good leaders. In all likelihood most of the people applying for any type of management position will go through one or more of the assessment techniques described in this chapter.

Second, practitioners need to understand that there are multiple ways to measure success. Superiors' ratings, subordinates' ratings, and unit performance measures can many times paint different pictures about the relative success of a leader. Practitioners need to understand which of these measures are the most important to their long-term success, which are the most sensitive to their efforts, and which may be more strongly influenced by factors beyond their control.

Third, practitioners also should know that there are three methods commonly used to study the linkage between what leaders do with different success measures. Case studies have the advantage of helping practitioners better understand the context in which a leader acts. However, they usually only describe the actions of one leader in one situation, and the generalizability of their findings to the reader may be questionable. Correlational studies have the advantage of using larger sample sizes and describe the statistical relationships between the results of different assessment techniques and success measures. These studies cannot tell us much about cause and effect relationships, however. Leadership experiments do yield valuable information about the cause and effect relationships between independent and dependent variables. Thus, experiments can tell us how different leadership behaviors affect group performance, subordinates' satisfaction levels, and so forth. But experiments are hard to conduct in field settings, and most laboratory experiments of leadership use college students as subjects; the generalizability of the findings for the latter experiments is always questionable.

Finally, leadership practitioners should understand the difference between maxims and theories of leadership. Maxims may represent valid advice, but they are ultimately no more than personal opinion. Since they amount to little more than personal opinion, different maxims sometimes give conflicting advice, and by their very nature there is no systematic way to "test" maxims. Theories, on the other hand, are a collection of testable predictions about the relationships between certain variables. Theories are developed on the basis of observations, and their corresponding hypotheses are tested and refined by means of correlational and experimental studies. Theories are useful in that they guide research and make predictions about how different variables interact. Theories add to our collective leadership knowledge, whereas maxims do not. Because we will describe a number of different leadership theories throughout this book, practitioners need to be able to think critically about leadership theories and determine how these theories can help them be better leaders.

Key Terms   academic tradition, *72*   structured interviews, *83*   War for Talent, *92*
troubadour tradition, *72*   unstructured   case studies, *94*
practice-research gap, *73*   interviews, *83*   correlational studies, *94*
"we are different"   assessment centers, *83*   correlation coefficient, *94*
syndrome, *74*   in-basket exercise, *84*   causal inferences, *95*
judgment of character   role-play simulations, *84*   experiments, *95*
bias, *74*   superiors' performance   independent variable, *95*
leadership level, *78*   ratings, *88*   dependent variable, *95*
competency model, *79*   subordinates' ratings of   integrated talent
glass ceiling effect, *81*   effectiveness, *89*   management process, *97*
multiple hurdles   unit performance   maxims, *98*
approach, *81*   indices, *90*   theory, *98*
Internet or paper-and-
pencil measures, 81

Questions   1. How do you react to the phrase *assessing leadership*? What positive and negative connotations does it have for you?

2. Some organizations are using graphology, or handwriting analysis, to make selection decisions. What do you think about this technique?

3. What are some of the measures you could use to judge the performance of a
coach? A teacher? A student? What are the advantages and disadvantages with
each of these measures? How much impact would the leader's behaviors have
on each of these measures?

4. If you were to design an interview for hiring a restaurant manager, what questions would you include, and why?

5. How could you design a correlational study or an experiment to test one of
Colin Powell's Rules in Highlight 4.11?

6. What is the single best work you have ever read about leadership or being a
leader? What does this book or article say about assessing leadership, measuring leadership effectiveness, methods used to study leadership, or leadership
maxims and theories?

Skills   Leadership skills relevant to this chapter include:

- Communication
- Building Effective Relationships with Superiors
- Building Effective Relationships with Peers

Activity   1. Assign groups of students the task of identifying various criteria by which
any one of the following leaders (or any others) might be evaluated: an assistant coach, a teacher, a minister, an army general. Then each group should
try to achieve consensus about the prioritization of these different criteria.
The class as a whole can share views about each group's prioritization, as
well as the extent to which there are unique or similar criteria across the different roles or the extent to which the various criteria are measurable.

2. Assign groups of students the task of determining which measures of leadership they would use to evaluate the performance of Peter Jackson, Colin Powell, and Aung San Suu Kyi. Who would be the key groups to rate the effectiveness of these leaders, and would they provide different ratings? Which group would provide the "best" ratings of leadership effectiveness, and why? What would the appropriate unit performance indicators be for these three leaders?

3. Ask groups of students to determine the leadership levels of Peter Jackson, Colin Powell, and Aung San Suu Kyi. Then have the students develop a leadership competency model for leaders at this level. How are the three leaders similar and different in terms of leadership levels and competencies? Of these three leaders, who has the most difficult leadership role, and why?

Minicase

"McDonald's Strategies for Success"

McDonald's is one of the most well-known and valuable brands in the world. It is the world's leading food service retailer with more than 30,000 restaurants in 119 countries serving 47 million customers each day. With the biggest franchise system in the world and a cash flow that is the envy of just about any industry, the role of the CEO is a complex one—especially during times of change.

The changes at McDonald's began when Jim Cantalupo (a longtime executive of the company) came out of retirement in late 2003. McDonald's business was sagging and Cantalupo faced numerous challenges including market saturation, increased competition, and changing tastes in the U.S. fast-food market. Cantalupo recognized these problems and quickly instituted an ambitious three-year turnaround plan: the first phase involved putting money back into existing stores in the United States rather than opening new franchises—cleaning them up and speeding up service and getting back to the core concepts that McDonald's was built on. The second phase would be to revitalize foreign restaurants in much the same way.

Turning around a large global company plagued by years of mismanagement is an enormous challenge and generally takes years to accomplish, yet in less than a year McDonald's had made tremendous progress—profits and stock prices were up and the company appeared to have built real momentum. The first phase was paying off.

Then in the spring of 2004 Jim Cantalupo died suddenly of a heart attack. The McDonald's board had to act swiftly. They called on the company's Chief Operating Officer, Charlie Bell (another veteran of the McDonald's corporation) as Cantalupo's replacement. Franchisees, in the midst of the company's stunning turnaround, rallied behind Bell and the company didn't miss a beat. Bell took Cantalupo's turnaround plan and ran with it. Good news for employees and investors who saw continued growth. The succession was a success . . . the company would now begin the second phase of the turnaround plan—focusing on the international component of the company.

Sadly, within two weeks of his appointment, Bell disclosed that he had been diagnosed with colon cancer. With the death of Cantalupo and Bell's promotion to CEO, the position of Chief Operations Officer—typically number 2 in a succession plan—was left open. A new succession plan became imperative.

1. What are some measurable factors of the success of Jim Cantalupo's turnaround plane?
2. What are some of the critical components of a competency model for a new CEO for the McDonald's corporation?
3. Consider the profile of the current CEO, Charlie Bell:

Charlie Bell, the current CEO, previously served as president and chief operating officer, and was responsible for the company's more than 30,000 restaurants in 119 countries. He began his career at age 15 as a part-time crew member at the Kingsford restaurant in Sydney, Australia. Bell progressed quickly through the ranks, becoming Australia's youngest store manager at age 19. Bell's career included working for the McDonald's Europe development company in operations across Europe. He has held the positions of operations director and regional manager, vice president of marketing, and managing director, McDonald's Australia. Bell also served as president of McDonald's Europe, as well as president of Asia/Pacific, Middle East, and Africa Group.

What trends do you see in the career of this executive that has likely contributed to his success at the McDonalds' corporation?

Sources: http://www.chicagotribune.com/business/printedition/chi-0407160286jul16,1,7963282.column; http://www.fool.com/news/commentary/2003/commentary031017wt.htm?source=mppromo; http://www.phillyburbs.com/pb-dyn/news/24-05072004-296442.html; http://www.mcdonalds.com; *McDonald's keeps right on cookin', Fortune Magazine* May 17, 2004 p. 174.

Focus on the Leader

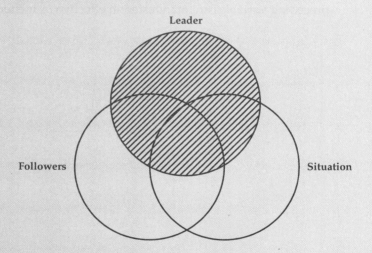

Part II focuses on the leader. The effectiveness of leadership, good or bad, is typically attributed to the leader much more than to the other elements of the framework. Sometimes the leader is the only element of leadership we even think of. One great leader's views were clear enough about the relative importance of leaders and followers:

Men are nothing; it is the man who is everything . . . It was not the Roman army that conquered Gaul, but Caesar; it was not the Carthaginian army that made Rome tremble in her gates, but Hannibal; it was not the Macedonian army that reached the Indus, but Alexander.

Napoleon

Because the leader plays such an important role in the leadership process, the next four chapters of this book review research related to the characteristics of leaders, and what makes leaders effective. Part II begins with a chapter on power and influence since those concepts provide the most fundamental way to understand the process of leadership. Chapter 6 then looks at the closely related issues of leadership and values. In Chapter 7 we consider what aspects of personality are related to leadership, and in Chapter 8 we examine how all these preceding variables are manifested in effective or ineffective leader behavior.

Chapter 5

Power and Influence

Introduction

We begin this part, called "Focus on the Leader," by examining the phenomenon of power. Some of history's earliest characterizations of leaders concerned their use of power. Shakespeare's plays were concerned with the acquisition and failing of power (Hill, 1985), and Machiavelli's *The Prince* has been described as the "classic handbook on power politics" (Donno, 1966). Current scholars have also emphasized the need to conceptualize leadership as a power phenomenon (Gardner, 1986; Hinkin & Schriesheim, 1989). Power may be the single most important concept in all the social sciences (Burns, 1978), though scholars today disagree on precisely how to define power or influence. But it's not just scholars who have different ideas about power. The concept of power is so pervasive and complex that each one of us probably thinks about it a little differently.

What comes to *your* mind when *you* think about power? Do you think of a person wielding enormous authority over others? Do you think of high office? Do you think of making others do things against their will? Is power ethically neutral, or is it inherently dangerous as Lord Acton said? ("Power corrupts, and absolute power corrupts absolutely.") Do you think a leader's real power is always obvious to others? What sorts of things might enhance or detract from a leader's power? What are the pros and cons of different ways of trying to influence people? These are the kinds of issues we will explore in this chapter.

Some Important Distinctions

Power has been defined as the capacity to produce effects on others (House, 1984), or the potential to influence others (Bass, 1990). While we usually think of power belonging to the leader, it is actually a function of the leader, the followers, and the situation. Leaders have the potential to influence their followers' behaviors and attitudes. However, followers also can affect the leader's behavior and attitudes. Even the situation itself can affect a leader's capacity to influence his followers (and vice versa). For example, leaders who can reward and punish followers may have a greater capacity to influence followers than those leaders who cannot use rewards or punishments. Similarly, follower or situational characteristics may diminish a leader's potential to influence followers, as when the latter belong to a strong, active union.

Several other aspects of power also are worth noting. Gardner (1986) made an important point about the exercise of power and its effects. He stated that "power does not need to be exercised in order to have its effect—as any hold-up man can tell you" (Gardner, 1986, p. 5). Thus, merely having the capacity to exert influence can often bring about intended effects, even though the leader may not take any action to influence his or her followers. For example, some months after the end of his term, Eisenhower was asked if leaving the White House had affected his golf game. "Yes," he replied, "a lot more people beat me now." Alternatively, power represents an inference or attribution made on the basis of an agent's observable acts of influence (Schriesheim & Hinkin, 1990). Power is never directly observed but rather attributed to others on the basis and frequency of influence tactics they use and on their outcomes.

Many people use the terms *power, influence,* and *influence tactics* synonymously (Bass, 1990), but it is useful to distinguish between them. **Influence** can be defined as the change in a target agent's attitudes, values, beliefs, or behaviors as the result of influence tactics. **Influence tactics** refer to one person's actual behaviors designed to change another person's attitudes, beliefs, values, or behaviors. Although these concepts are typically examined from the leader's perspective (e.g., how a leader influences followers), we should remember that followers can also wield power and influence over leaders as well as over each other. Leadership practitioners can improve their effectiveness by reflecting on the types of power they and their followers have and the types of influence tactics that they may use or that may be used *on* them.

Whereas power is the *capacity* to cause change, influence is the degree of actual change in a target person's attitudes, values, beliefs, or behaviors. Influence can be measured by the behaviors or attitudes manifested by followers as the result of a leader's *influence tactics*. For example, a leader may ask a follower to accomplish a particular task, and whether or not the task is accomplished is partly a function of the leader's request. (The follower's ability and skill as well as access to the necessary equipment and resources are also important factors.) Such things as subordinates' satisfaction or motivation, group cohesiveness and climate, or unit performance indices can be used to measure the effectiveness of leaders' influence attempts. The degree to which leaders can change the level of satisfaction, motivation, or cohesiveness among followers is a function of the amount of power available to both leaders and followers. On the one hand, leaders with relatively high amounts of power can cause fairly substantial changes in subordinates' attitudes and behaviors; for example, a new and respected leader who uses rewards and punishments judiciously may cause a dramatic change in followers' perceptions about organizational climate and the amount of time followers spend on work-related behaviors. On the other hand, the amount of power

The true leader must submerge himself in the fountain of the people.

V. I. Lenin

followers have in work situations can also vary dramatically, and in some situations particular followers may exert relatively more influence over the rest of the group than the leader does. For example, a follower with a high level of knowledge and experience may have more influence on the attitudes, opinions, and behaviors of the rest of the followers than a brand-new leader. Thus, the amount of change in the attitudes or behaviors of the targets of influence is a function of the agent's capacity to exert influence and the targets' capacity to resist this influence.

Leaders and followers typically use a variety of tactics to influence each other's attitudes or behaviors (see Highlight 5.1 for a description of some nonverbal power cues common to humans). Influence tactics are the overt behaviors exhibited by one person to influence another. They range from emotional appeals, to the exchange of favors, to threats. The particular tactic used in a leadership situation is probably a function of the power possessed by both parties. Individuals with a relatively large amount of power may successfully employ a wider variety of influence tactics than individuals with little power. For example, a well-respected leader could make an emotional appeal, a rational appeal, a personal appeal, a legitimate request, or a threat to try to modify a follower's behavior. The follower in this situation may only be able to use ingratiation or personal appeals in order to change the leader's attitude or behavior.

At the same time, because the formal leader is not always the person who possesses the most power in a leadership situation, followers often can use a wider variety of influence tactics than the leader to modify the attitudes and behaviors of others. This would be the case if a new leader were brought into an organization in which one of his or her subordinates was extremely well liked and respected. In this situation, the subordinate may be able to make personal appeals, emotional appeals, or even threats to change the attitudes or behaviors of the leader, whereas the new leader may be limited to making only legitimate requests to change the attitudes and behaviors of the followers.

Power and Leadership

We began this chapter by noting how an understanding of power has long been seen as an integral part of leadership. Several perspectives and theories have been developed to explain the acquisition and exercise of power. In this section we will first examine various *sources* of power. Then we will look at how individuals vary in their personal *need* for power.

Sources of Leader Power

Where does a leader's power come from? Do leaders *have* it, or do followers *give* it to them? As we shall see, the answer may be both . . . and more.

Something as seemingly trivial as the arrangement of furniture in an office can affect perceptions of another person's power. One vivid example comes from John Ehrlichman's (1982)

And when we think we lead, we are most led.

Lord Byron

Gestures of Power and Dominance

Highlight 5.1

We can often get clues about relative power just by paying attention to behaviors between two people. There are a number of nonverbal cues we might want to pay attention to.

The phrase **pecking order** refers to the status differential between members of a group. It reminds us that many aspects of human social organization have roots, or at least parallels, in the behavior of other species. The animal kingdom presents diverse and fascinating examples of stylized behaviors by which one member of a species shows its relative dominance or submissiveness to another. There is adaptive significance to such behavioral mechanisms since they tend to minimize actual physical struggle and maintain a stable social order. For example, lower-ranking baboons step aside to let a higher-status male pass; they become nervous if he stares at them. The highest-status male can choose where he wants to sleep and whom he wants to mate with. Baboons "know their place." As with humans, rank has its privileges.

Our own stylized power rituals are usually so second-nature we aren't conscious of them. Yet there is a "dance" of power relations among humans just as among other animals. The following are some of the ways power is expressed nonverbally in humans.

Staring. In American society, it is disrespectful for a person of lower status to stare at a superior, though superiors are not bound by a similar restriction. Children, for example, are taught not to stare at parents. And it's an interesting comment on the power relationship between sexes that women are more likely to avert their gaze from men than vice versa.

Pointing. Children are also taught it's not nice to point. However, adults rarely correct each other for pointing because more than mere etiquette, pointing seems to be a behavior that is acceptable for high-status figures or those attempting to assert dominance. An angry boss may point an index finger accusingly at an employee; few employees who wanted to keep their jobs would respond in kind. The same restrictions apply to frowning.

Touching. Invading another person's space by touching the person without invitation is acceptable when one is of superior status but not when one is of subordinate status. It's acceptable, for example, for bosses or teachers to put a hand on an employee's or a student's shoulder, but not vice versa. The disparity also applies to socioeconomic status; someone with higher socioeconomic status is more likely to touch a person of lower socioeconomic status than vice versa.

Interrupting. Virtually all of us have interrupted others, and we have all been interrupted ourselves. Again, however, the issue is who was interrupting whom? Higher-power or -status persons interrupt; lower-power or -status persons are interrupted. A vast difference in frequency of behaviors also exists between the sexes in American society. Men interrupt much more frequently than women do.

Source: D. A. Karp and W. C. Yoels, *Symbols, Selves, and Society* (New York: Lippincott, 1979).

book, *Witness to Power.* Ehrlichman described his first visit to J. Edgar Hoover's office at the Department of Justice. The legendary director of the FBI had long been one of the most powerful men in Washington, D.C., and as Ehrlichman's impressions reveal, Hoover took every opportunity to reinforce that image. Ehrlichman was first led through double doors into a room replete with plaques, citations, trophies, medals, and certificates jamming every wall. He was then led through a second room, similarly decorated, then into a third trophy room, and finally to a large but bare desk backed by several flags and still no J. Edgar Hoover. The guide opened a door behind the desk, and Ehrlichman went into a smaller office, which Hoover dominated from an impressive chair and desk that stood on a dais about six inches high. Erhlichman was instructed to take a seat on a lower couch, and Mr. Hoover peered down on Ehrlichman from his own loftier and intimidating place.

On a more mundane level, many people have experienced a time when they were called in to talk to a boss and left standing while the boss sat behind the desk. Probably few people in that situation misunderstand the power messages there. In addition to the factors just described, other aspects of office arrangements also can affect a leader's or follower's power. One factor is the shape of the table used for meetings. Individuals sitting at the ends of rectangular tables often wield more power, whereas circular tables facilitate communication and minimize status differentials. However, specific seating arrangements even at circular tables can affect participants' interactions; often individuals belonging to the same cliques and coalitions will sit next to each other. By sitting next to each other, members of the same coalition may exert more power as a collective group than they would sitting apart from each other. Also, having a private or more open office may not only *reflect* but also *affect* power differentials between people. Individuals with private offices can dictate to a greater degree when they want to interact with others by opening or closing their doors or by giving instructions about interruptions. Individuals with more open offices have much less power to control access to them. By being aware of dynamics like these, leaders can somewhat influence others' perceptions of their power relationship.

Prominently displaying symbols like diplomas, awards, and titles also can increase one's power. This was shown in an experiment in a college setting where a guest lecturer to several different classes was introduced in a different way to each. To one group he was introduced as a student; to other groups he was introduced as a lecturer, senior lecturer, or professor, respectively. After the presentation, when he was no longer in the room, the class estimated his height. Interestingly, the same man was perceived by different groups as increasingly taller with each increase in academic status. The "professor" was remembered as being several inches taller than the "student" (Wilson, 1968).

> *He who has great power should use it lightly.*
>
> Seneca

This finding demonstrates the generalized impact a seemingly minor matter like one's title can have on others. Another study points out more dramatically how dangerous it can be when followers are overly responsive to the *appearances* of title and authority. This study took place in a medical setting and arose from concern among medical staff that nurses were responding mechanically to doctors' orders. A researcher made telephone calls to nurses' stations in numerous different medical wards. In each, he identified himself as a hospital physician and directed the nurse answering the phone to prescribe a particular medication for a patient in that ward. Many nurses complied with the request despite the fact it was against hospital policy to transmit prescriptions by phone. Many did so despite never even having talked to the particular "physician" before the call—and despite the fact that the prescribed medication was dangerously excessive, not to mention unauthorized. In fact, 95 percent of the nurses complied with the request

The Milgram Studies

Highlight 5.2

One intriguing way to understand power, influence, and influence tactics is to read a synopsis of Stanley Milgram's classic work on obedience and to think about how this work relates to the concepts and theories discussed in the present chapter. Milgram's research explored how far people will go when directed by an authority figure to do something that might injure another person. More specifically, Milgram wanted to know what happens when the dictates of authority and the dictates of one's conscience seem incompatible.

The participants were men from the communities surrounding Yale University. They were led to believe they were helping in a study concerning the effect of punishment on learning; the study's legitimacy was certainly enhanced by being conducted on the Yale campus itself. Two subjects at a time participated in the study, one as a teacher and the other as learner. The roles apparently were assigned randomly. The teacher's task was to help the learner memorize a set of word pairs by providing electric shocks whenever the learner (who would be in an adjacent room) made a mistake.

A stern experimenter described procedures and showed participants the equipment for administering punishment. This "shock generator" looked ominous, with rows of switches, lights, and warnings labeled in 15-volt increments all the way to 450 volts. Various points along the array were marked with increasingly dire warnings such as *extreme intensity* and *danger: severe*. The switch at the highest level of shock simply was marked XXX. Every time the learner made a mistake, the teacher was ordered by the experimenter to administer the next-higher level of electric shock.

In actuality, there was only one true subject in the experiment—the teacher. The learner was really a confederate of the experimenter. The supposed random assignment of participants to teacher and learner conditions had been rigged in advance. The real purpose of the experiment was to assess how much electric shock the teachers would administer to the learners in the face of the latter's increasingly adamant protestations to stop. This included numerous realistic cries of agony and complaints of a heart condition, all standardized, predetermined, tape-recorded messages delivered via the intercom from the learner's to the teacher's room. If the subject (i.e., the teacher) refused to deliver any further shocks, the experimenter prodded him with comments such as "The experiment requires that you go on" and "You have no other choice; you must go on."

Before Milgram conducted his experiment, he asked mental health professionals what proportion of the subjects would administer apparently dangerous levels of shock. The consensus was that only a negligible percentage would do so, perhaps 1 or 2 percent of the population. Milgram's actual results were dramatically inconsistent with what any of the experts had predicted. Fully 70 percent of the subjects carried through with their orders, albeit sometimes with great personal anguish, and delivered the maximum shock possible—450 volts!

Source: S. Milgram, "Behavioral Study of Obedience;" *Journal of Abnormal and Social Psychology* 67 (1963), pp. 371–78.

made by the most easily falsifiable symbol of authority, a bare title (Cialdini, 1984). (Also see Highlight 5.2.)

Even choice of clothing can affect one's power and influence. Uniforms and other specialized clothing have long been associated with authority and status, including their use by the military, police, hospital staffs, clergy, and so on. In one experiment, people walking along a city sidewalk were stopped by someone dressed either in regular clothes or in the uniform of a security guard and told this: "You see that guy over there by the meter? He's overparked but doesn't have any change. Give him a dime!" Whereas fewer than half complied when the requestor was dressed in regular clothes, over 90 percent did when he was in uniform

(Bickman, 1974). This same rationale is given for having personnel in certain occupations (e.g., airline crew members) wear uniforms. Besides more easily identifying them to others, the uniforms increase the likelihood that in emergency situations their instructions will be followed. Similarly, even the presence of something as trivial as tattoos can affect the amount of power wielded in a group. One of the authors of this text had a friend named Del who was a manager in an international book-publishing company. Del was a former merchant marine whose forearms were adorned with tattoos. Del would often take off his suit coat and roll up his sleeves when meetings were not going his way, and he often exerted considerably more influence by merely exposing his tattoos to the rest of the group.

A final situational factor that can affect one's potential to influence others is the presence or absence of a crisis. Leaders usually can exert more power during a crisis than during periods of relative calm. Perhaps this is because during a crisis leaders are willing to draw on bases of power they normally forgo. For example, a leader who has developed close interpersonal relationships with followers generally uses her referent power to influence them. During crises or emergency situations, however, leaders may be more apt to draw on their legitimate and coercive bases of power to influence subordinates. That was precisely the finding in a study of bank managers' actions; the bank managers were more apt to use legitimate and coercive power during crises than during noncrisis situations (Mulder, de Jong, Koppelar, & Verhage, 1986). This same phenomenon is observable in many dramatizations. In the television series *Star Trek, the Next Generation,* for example, Captain Picard normally uses his referent and expert power to influence subordinates. During emergencies, however, he will often rely on his legitimate and coercive power. Another factor may be that during crises followers are more willing to accept greater direction, control, and structure from leaders, whatever power base may be involved.

A Taxonomy of Social Power

French and Raven (1959) identified five sources, or bases, of power by which an individual can potentially influence others. As seen in Figure 5.1, these five sources include one that is primarily a function of the leader; one that is a function of the relationship between leaders and followers; one that is primarily a function of the leader and the situation; one that is primarily a function of the situation; and finally, one that involves aspects of all three elements. Understanding these bases of power can give leadership practitioners greater insight about the predictable effects—positive or negative—of various sorts of influence attempts. Following is a more detailed discussion of French and Raven's (1959) five bases of social power.

Expert Power

Expert power is the power of knowledge. Some people are able to influence others through their relative expertise in particular areas. A surgeon may wield considerable influence in a hospital because others depend on her knowledge, skill, and judgment, even though she may not have any formal authority over them. A mechanic may be influential among his peers because he is widely recognized as the best in the city. A longtime employee may be influential because his corporate memory provides a useful historical perspective to newer personnel. Legislators

FIGURE 5.1
Sources of
leader power
in the leader-
follower-
situation
framework.

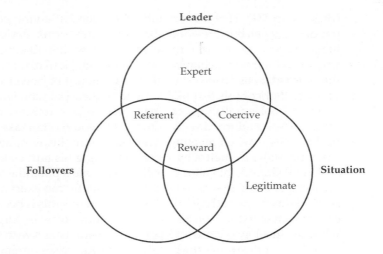

who are experts in the intricacies of parliamentary procedure, athletes who have played in championship games, and soldiers who have been in combat before are valued for the lessons learned and wisdom they can share with others.

Because expert power is a function of the amount of knowledge one possesses relative to the rest of the members of the group, it is possible for followers to have considerably more expert power than leaders in certain situations. For example, new leaders often possess less knowledge of the jobs and tasks performed in a particular work unit than the followers do, and in this case the followers can potentially wield considerable influence when decisions are made regarding work procedures, new equipment, or the hiring of additional workers. Probably the best advice for leaders in this situation is to ask a lot of questions and perhaps seek additional training to help fill this knowledge gap. So long as different followers have considerably greater amounts of expert power, it will be difficult for a leader to influence the work unit on the basis of expert power alone.

Peter Jackson has considerable expert power (as well as other forms), and judging by comments made about him by other members of *The Lord of the Rings* film team who also won Academy Awards, he respects the expert power of others too.

Referent Power

One way to counteract the problems stemming from a lack of expertise is to build strong interpersonal ties with subordinates. **Referent power** refers to the potential influence one has due to the strength of the relationship between the leader and the followers. When people admire a leader and see her as a role model, we say she has referent power. For example, students may respond positively to advice or requests from teachers who are well liked and respected, while the same students might be unresponsive to less-popular teachers. This relative degree of responsiveness is primarily a function of the strength of the relationship between the students and the different teachers. We knew one young lieutenant who had enormous referent power with the military security guards working for him due to his selfless concern for them, evident in such habits as bringing them hot chocolate and homemade cookies on their late-night shifts. The guards, sometimes taken for granted by other superiors, understood and valued the extra effort and sacrifice this young supervisor put forth for them. When Buddy Ryan was fired as head coach of the Philadelphia Eagles football team, many of the players expressed fierce loyalty to him. One said, "We'd do things for Buddy that we wouldn't do for another coach. I'd sell my body for Buddy" (Associated Press, January 9, 1991). That is referent power. Aung San Suu Kyi also has referent power. She is a symbol in her country and to the world of peaceful resistance in the face of oppression.

Another way to look at referent power is in terms of the role friendships play in making things happen. It is frequently said, for example, that many people get jobs based on who they know, not what they know. The fact is, there is some truth to that. But we think the best perspective on this issue was offered by David Campbell, who said, "It's not who you know that counts. It's what who you know *knows about you* that counts!" (personal communication).

Referent power often takes time to develop. Furthermore, it can have a downside in that a desire to *maintain* referent power may limit a leader's actions in particular situations. For example, a leader who has developed a strong relationship with a follower may be reluctant to discipline the follower for poor work or chronic tardiness, as these actions could disrupt the nature of the relationship between the leader and the follower. Thus, referent power is a two-way street; the stronger the relationship, the more influence leaders and followers exert over each other. Moreover, just as it is possible for leaders to develop strong relationships with followers and, in turn, acquire more referent power, it is also possible for followers to develop strong relationships with other followers and acquire more referent power. Followers with relatively more referent power than their peers are often the spokespersons for their work units and generally have more latitude to deviate from work-unit norms. Followers with little referent power have little opportunity to deviate from group norms. For example, in an episode of the television show *The Simpsons,* Homer Simpson was fired for wearing a pink shirt to work (everybody else at the Springfield nuclear power plant had always worn white shirts). Homer was fired partly because he "was not popular enough to be different."

> *Power in an organization is the capacity generated by relationships.*
> Margaret A. Wheatley, Futurist

Legitimate Power

Legitimate power depends on a person's organizational role. It can be thought of as one's formal or official authority. Some people make things happen because they have the power or authority to do so. The boss can assign projects; the coach can decide who plays; the colonel can order compliance with uniform standards; the teacher assigns the homework and awards the grades. Individuals with legitimate power exert influence through requests or demands deemed appropriate by virtue of their role and position. In other words, legitimate power means a leader has authority because he or she has been assigned a particular role in an organization (and the leader has this authority only as long as he or she occupies that position and operates within the proper bounds of that role).

It is important to note that legitimate authority and leadership are not the same thing. Holding a position and being a leader are not synonymous, despite the relatively common practice of calling position holders in bureaucracies the leaders. The head of an organization may be a true leader, but he also may not be. Effective leaders often intuitively realize they need more than legitimate power to be successful. Before he became president, Dwight Eisenhower commanded all Allied troops in Europe during World War II. In a meeting with his staff before the Normandy invasion, Eisenhower pulled a string across a table to make a point about leadership. He was demonstrating that just as you can pull a string, not push it, officers must lead soldiers and not push them from the rear.

It is also possible for followers to use their legitimate power to influence leaders. In these cases, followers can actively resist a leader's influence attempt by only doing work specifically prescribed in job descriptions, bureaucratic rules, or union policies. For example, many organizations have job descriptions that limit both the time spent at work and the types of tasks and activities performed. Similarly, bureaucratic rules and union policies can be invoked by followers to resist a leader's influence attempts. Often the leader will need to change the nature of his or her request or find another way to resolve the problem if these rules and policies are invoked by followers. If this is the case, then the followers will have successfully used legitimate power to influence their leader.

> *Unreviewable power is the most likely to self-indulge itself and the least likely to engage in dispassionate self-analysis.*
>
> Warren E. Burger,
> Chief Justice, U.S. Supreme
> Court, 1969–1986

Reward Power

Reward power involves the potential to influence others due to one's control over desired resources. This can include the power to give raises, bonuses, and promotions; to grant tenure; to select people for special assignments or desirable activities; to distribute desired resources like computers, offices, parking places, or travel money; to intercede positively on another's behalf; to recognize with awards and praise; and so on. Many corporations use rewards extensively to motivate employees. At McDonald's, for example, there is great status accorded the All-American Hamburger Maker, the cook who makes the fastest, highest-quality hamburgers in the country. At individual fast-food restaurants, managers may reward salespersons who handle the most customers during rush periods. Tupperware holds rallies for its salespeople. Almost everyone wins something, ranging from pins and badges to lucrative prizes for top performers (Peters & Waterman, 1982). Schools pick teachers of the year, and professional athletes are rewarded by selection to all-star teams for their superior performance.

The potential to influence others through the ability to administer rewards is a joint function of the leader, the followers, and the situation. Leaders vary considerably in the types and frequency in which they mete out rewards, but the position they fill also helps to determine the frequency and types of rewards administered. For example, employees of the month at Kentucky Fried Chicken are not given new cars; the managers of these franchises do not have the resources to offer such awards. Similarly, leaders in other organizations are limited to some extent in the types of and frequency with which they can administer awards. Nevertheless, leadership practitioners can enhance their reward power by spending some time reflecting on the followers and the situation. Often a number of alternative or innovative rewards can be created, and these rewards, along with ample doses of praise, can help a leader overcome the constraints his or her position puts on reward power.

Although using the power to administer rewards can be an effective way to change the attitudes and behaviors of others, there are several situations where a leader's use of reward power can be problematic. For example, the perception that a company's monetary bonus policy is handled equitably may be as important in motivating good work (or avoiding morale problems) as the amount of the bonus itself. Moreover, a superior may mistakenly assume that a particular reward is valued when it is not. This would be the case if a particular subordinate were publicly recognized for her good work when she actually dislikes public recognition. Leadership practitioners can avoid the latter problem by developing good relationships with subordinates and administering rewards that they, not the leader, value. Another potential problem with reward power is that it may produce compliance but not other desirable outcomes like commitment (Yukl, 1989). In other words, subordinates may perform only at the level necessary to receive a reward and may not be willing to put forth the extra effort needed to make the organization better. An overemphasis on rewards as payoff for performance may also lead to resentment and feelings by workers of being manipulated, especially if it occurs in the context of relatively cold and distant superior-subordinate relationships. Extrinsic rewards like praise, compensation, promotion, privileges, and time off may not have the same effects on behavior as intrinsic rewards such as feelings of accomplishment, personal growth, and development. There is evidence that under some conditions extrinsic rewards can decrease intrinsic motivation toward a task and make the desired behavior less likely to persist when extrinsic rewards are not available (Deci, 1972; Ryan, Mims, & Koestner, 1983). Overemphasis on extrinsic rewards may instill an essentially contractual or economic relationship between superiors and subordinates, diluting important aspects of the relationship like mutual loyalty or shared commitment to higher ideals (Wakin, 1981).

All these cautions about reward power should not cloud its usefulness and effectiveness, which is very real. As noted previously, top organizations make extensive use of both tangible and symbolic rewards in motivating their workers. Furthermore, some of the most important rewards are readily available to all leaders—sincere praise and thanks to others for their loyalty and work. The bottom line is that leadership practitioners can enhance their ability to influence others based on reward power if they (*a*) determine what rewards are available, (*b*) determine what rewards are valued by their subordinates, and (*c*) establish clear policies for the equitable and consistent administration of rewards for good performance.

Finally, because reward power is partly determined by one's position in the organization, some people may believe followers have little, if any, reward power. This may not be the case. If followers have control over scarce resources, then they may use the administration of these resources as a way of getting leaders to act in the manner they want. Moreover, followers may reward their leader by putting out a high level of effort when they feel their leader is doing a good job, and they may put forth less effort when they feel their leader is doing a poor job. By modifying

Reprinted with special permission of King Features Syndicate

their level of effort, followers may in turn modify a leader's attitudes and behaviors. And when followers compliment their leader (e.g., for running a constructive meeting), it is no less an example of reward power than when a leader compliments a follower. Thus, leadership practitioners should be aware that followers can also use reward power to influence leaders.

Coercive Power

Coercive power, the opposite of reward power, is the potential to influence others through the administration of negative sanctions or the removal of positive events. In other words, it is the ability to control others through the fear of punishment or the loss of valued outcomes. Like reward power, coercive power is partly a function of the leader, but the situation often limits the coercive actions a leader can take. Examples of coercive power include policemen giving tickets for speeding, the army court-martialing AWOL soldiers, a teacher detaining disruptive students after school, employers firing lazy workers, and parents spanking children (Klein, 1991). Even presidents resort to their coercive powers. Historian Arthur Schlesinger, Jr., for example, described Lyndon Johnson as having a "devastating instinct for the weaknesses of others." Lyndon Johnson was familiar and comfortable with the use of coercion; he once told a White House staff member, "Just you remember this. There's only two kinds at the White House. There's elephants and there's ants. And I'm the only elephant" (Barnes, 1989).

> *You do not lead by hitting people over the head—that's assault, not leadership.*
>
> Dwight D. Eisenhower

Coercive power, like reward power, can be used appropriately or inappropriately. It is carried to its extreme in harsh and repressive totalitarian societies. One of the most tragic instances of coercive power was in the cult led by Jim Jones, which tragically and unbelievably self-exterminated in an incident known as the Jonestown massacre (Conway & Siegelman, 1979). Virtually all of the 912 who died there drank, at Jones's direction, from large vats of a flavored drink containing cyanide. The submissiveness and suicidal obedience of Jones's followers during the massacre were due largely to the long history of rule by fear Jones had practiced. For example, teenagers caught holding hands were beaten, and adults judged slacking in their work were forced to box for hours in marathon public matches against as many as three or four bigger and stronger opponents. Jim Jones ruled by fear, and his followers became self-destructively compliant.

Perhaps the preceding example is so extreme that we can dismiss its relevance to our own lives and leadership activities. On the other hand, it does provide a dramatic reminder that reliance on coercive power has inherent limitations and drawbacks. This is not to say the willingness to use disciplinary sanctions is never necessary. Sometimes it is. Informal coercion, as opposed to the threat of formal punishment, can also be used to change the attitudes and behaviors of others. Informal coercion is usually expressed implicitly, and often nonverbally, rather than explicitly. It may be the pressure employees feel to donate to the boss's favorite charity, or it may be his glare when they bring up an unpopular idea. One of the most common forms of coercion is simply a superior's temperamental outbursts.

The intimidation caused by a leader's poorly controlled anger is usually, in its long-term effects, a dysfunctional style of behavior for leaders.

It is also possible for followers to use coercive power to influence their leader's behavior. For example, a leader may be hesitant to take disciplinary action against a large, emotionally unstable follower. Followers can threaten leaders with physical assaults, industrial sabotage, or work slowdowns and strikes, and these threats can serve to modify a leader's behavior. In all likelihood, followers will be more likely to use coercive power to change their leader's behavior if they have a relatively high amount of referent power with their fellow co-workers. This may be particularly true if threats of work slowdowns or strikes are used to influence a leader's behavior.

Concluding Thoughts about French and Raven's Power Taxonomy

On the basis of all this, can we reach any conclusions about what base of power is best for a leader to use? As you might have anticipated, we must say that's an unanswerable question without knowing more facts about a particular situation. For example, consider the single factor of whether or not a group is facing a crisis. This might affect the leader's exercise of power simply because leaders usually can exert *more* power during crises than during periods of relative calm. Perhaps this is because during a crisis leaders are willing to draw on bases of power they normally forgo. For example, a leader who has developed close interpersonal relationships with followers generally uses her referent power to influence them, but during crises or emergency situations leaders may be more apt to draw on their legitimate and coercive bases of power to influence subordinates. That was precisely the finding in a study of bank managers' actions; the bank managers were more apt to use legitimate and coercive power during crises than during noncrisis situations (Mulder, de Jong, Koppelar, & Verhage, 1986). Furthermore, it may be that during crises followers are more *eager* to receive direction and control from leaders.

But can't we make *any* generalizations about using various sources of power? Actually, there has been considerable research looking at French and Raven's ideas, and generally the findings indicate that leaders who relied primarily on referent and expert power had subordinates who were more motivated and satisfied, were absent less, and performed better (Yukl, 1981). However, Yukl (1981) and Podsakoff and Schriesheim (1985) have criticized these findings, and much of their criticism centers on the instrument used to assess a leader's bases of power. Hinkin and Schriesheim (1989) developed an instrument that overcomes many of the criticisms, and future research should more clearly delineate the relationship between the five bases of power and various leadership effectiveness criteria.

Even though much of the research to date about the five bases of power may be flawed, four generalizations about power and influence still seem warranted. First, effective leaders typically take advantage of *all* their sources of power. Effective leaders understand the relative advantages and disadvantages of different sources of power, and they selectively emphasize one or another depending on their particular objectives in a given situation. Second, whereas leaders in well-functioning organizations have strong influence over their subordinates, *they are also open to being influenced by them.* High degrees of reciprocal influence between leaders and followers characterize the most effective organizations (Yukl, 1989). Third, leaders vary in the extent to which they share power with subordinates. Some leaders seem to view their power as a fixed resource that, when shared with others (like cutting a pie into pieces), reduces their own portion. They see power in zero-sum terms. Other leaders see power as an expandable pie. They see the possibility of increasing a subordinate's power without reducing their own. Needless to say, which view a leader subscribes to can have a major impact on the leader's support for power-sharing activities like delegation and participative management. A leader's support for power-sharing activities (or, in today's popular language, *empowerment*) is also affected by the practice of holding leaders responsible for subordinates' decisions and actions as well as their own. It is, after all, the coach or manager who often gets fired when the team loses (Hollander & Offermann, 1990; Pfeffer, 1977). Fourth, effective leaders generally work to increase their various power bases (i.e., whether expert, referent, reward, or legitimate) or become more willing to use their coercive power.

Leader Motives

Thus far we have been looking at how different *sources* of power can affect others, but that's only one perspective. Another way of looking at the relationship between power and leadership involves focusing on the individual leader's personality. We will look most closely at the role personality plays in leadership in an upcoming chapter, but it will be nonetheless useful now to briefly examine how all people (including leaders) vary in their personal motivation to have or wield power.

People vary in their motivation to influence or control others. McClelland (1975) called this the **need for power,** and individuals with a high need for power derive psychological satisfaction from influencing others. They seek positions where they can influence others, and they are often involved concurrently in influencing people in many different organizations or decision-making bodies. In such activities they readily offer ideas, suggestions, and opinions, and also seek information they can use in influencing others. They are often astute at building trusting relationships and assessing power networks, though they can also be quite outspoken and forceful. They value the tangible signs of their authority and status as well as the more intangible indications of others' deference to them. Two different ways of expressing the need for power have been identified: **personalized power** and **socialized power.** Individuals who have a high need for personalized power are relatively selfish, impulsive, uninhibited, and lacking in self-control. These individuals exercise power for their own self-centered needs, not for the good of the group or the organization. Socialized power, on the other hand, implies a more emotionally mature expression of the motive. Socialized power is exercised in the service of higher goals to others or organizations and often involves self-sacrifice toward those ends. It often involves an empowering, rather than an autocratic, style of management and leadership.

Although the need for power has been measured using questionnaires and more traditional personality inventories, McClelland and his associates have used the Thematic Apperception Test (TAT) to assess need for power. The TAT is a **projective personality test** consisting of pictures such as a woman staring out a window or a boy holding a violin. Subjects are asked to make up a story about each picture, and the stories are then interpreted in terms of the strengths of various needs imputed to the characters, one of which is the need for power. Since the pictures are somewhat ambiguous, the sorts of needs projected onto the characters are presumed to reflect needs (perhaps at an unconscious level) of the storyteller. Stories concerned with influencing or controlling others would receive high scores for the need for power.

The need for power has been found to be positively related to various leadership effectiveness criteria. For example, McClelland and Boyatzis (1982) found the need for power to be positively related to success for nontechnical managers at AT&T, and Stahl (1983) found that the need for power was positively related to managers' performance ratings and promotion rates. In addition, Fodor (1987) reported that small groups of ROTC students were more likely to successfully solve a subarctic survival situation if their leader had a strong need for power. Although these findings appear promising, several cautions should be kept in mind. First, McClelland and Boyatzis (1982) also reported that the need for power was unrelated to the success of technical managers at AT&T. Apparently, the level of knowledge (i.e., expert power) played a more important role in the success of the technical managers versus the nontechnical managers. Second, McClelland (1985) concluded that although some need for power was necessary for leadership potential, successful leaders also have the ability to inhibit their manifestation of this need. Leaders who are relatively uninhibited in their need for power will act like a dictator; such individuals use power impulsively, to manipulate or control others, or to achieve at another's expense. Leaders with a high need for power but low activity inhibition may be successful in the short term, but their followers, as well as the remainder of the organization, may pay high costs for this success. Some of these costs may include perceptions by fellow members of the organization that they are untrustworthy, uncooperative, overly competitive, and looking out primarily for themselves. Finally, it may be worth pointing out that some followers have a high need for power too. This can lead to tension between leader and follower when a follower with a high need for power is directed to do something.

Individuals vary in their motivation to manage, just as in their need for power. Miner (1974) described **motivation to manage** in terms of six composites:

- Maintaining good relationships with authority figures.
- Wanting to compete for recognition and advancement.
- Being active and assertive.
- Wanting to exercise influence over subordinates.
- Being visibly different from followers.
- Being willing to do routine administrative tasks.

Like McClelland, Miner also used a projective test to measure a person's motivation to manage. Miner's Sentence Completion Scale (MSCS) consists of a series of incomplete sentences dealing with the six components described above (e.g., "My relationship with my boss . . ."). Respondents are asked to complete the sentences, which are then scored according to established criteria. The overall composite MSCS score (though not component scores) has consistently been found to predict leadership success in hierarchical or bureaucratic organizations (Miner, 1978). Thus, individuals who maintained respect for authority figures, wanted to be recognized, acted assertively, actively influenced subordinates, maintained "psychological distance" between themselves and their followers, and readily took on routine administrative tasks were more apt to be successful in bureaucratic organizations. However, Miner also claimed that different qualities were needed in flatter, nonbureaucratic organizations, and his (1978) review of the MSCS supports this view.

Findings concerning both the need for power and the motivation to manage have several implications for leadership practitioners. First, not all individuals like being leaders. One reason may be that some have a relatively low need for power or motivation to manage. Because these scores are relatively stable and fairly difficult to change, leaders who do not enjoy their role may want to seek positions where they have fewer supervisory responsibilities.

Second, a high need for power or motivation to manage does not guarantee leadership success. The situation can play a crucial role in determining whether the need for power or the motivation to manage is related to leadership success. For example, McClelland and Boyatzis (1982) found the need for power to be related to leadership success for nontechnical managers only, and Miner (1978) found motivation to manage was related to leadership success only in hierarchical or bureaucratic organizations.

Third, in order to be successful in the long term, leaders may have to have both a high need for socialized power and a high level of activity inhibition. Leaders who impulsively exercise power merely to satisfy their own selfish needs will probably be ineffective in the long term. Finally, it is important to remember that followers, as well as leaders, differ in the need for power, activity inhibition, and motivation to manage. Certain followers may have stronger needs or motives in this area. Leaders may need to behave differently toward these followers than they might toward followers having a low need for power or motivation to manage.

Influence Tactics

Whereas power is the capacity or potential to influence others, influence tactics are the actual behaviors used by an agent to change the attitudes, opinions, or behaviors of a target person. Kipnis and his associates accomplished much of the early work on the types of influence tactics one person uses to influence another (Kipnis & Schmidt, 1982). Various instruments have been developed to study influence tactics, but the Influence Behavior Questionnaire, or IBQ (Yukl, Lepsinger, & Lucia, 1992), seems to be the most promising. Here is a detailed discussion of the different influence tactics assessed by the IBQ.

Types of Influence Tactics

The IBQ is designed to assess nine types of influence tactics, and its scales provide us with a convenient overview of various methods of influencing others. **Rational persuasion** occurs when an agent uses logical arguments or factual evidence to influence others. An example of rational persuasion would be when a politician's advisor explains how demographic changes in the politician's district make it important for the politician to spend relatively more time in the district seeing constituents than she has needed to in the recent past. Agents make **inspirational appeals** when they make a request or proposal designed to arouse enthusiasm or emotions in targets. An example here might be when a minister makes an impassioned plea to members of his congregation about the good works which could be accomplished if a proposed addition to the church were built. **Consultation** occurs when agents ask targets to participate in planning an activity. An example of consultation would be if the minister in the preceding example established a committee of church members to help plan the layout and uses of that new church addition. In this case the consultative work might not only lead to a better building plan but also *strengthen member commitment* to the very idea of a new addition. **Ingratiation** occurs when the agent attempts to get you in a good mood before making a request. A familiar example here would be a salesperson's good-natured or flattering banter with you before you make a decision about purchasing a product. Agents use **personal appeals** when they ask another to do a favor out of friendship. A sentence that opens with, "Bill, we've known each other a long time and I've never asked anything of you before" represents the beginning of a personal appeal, whereas influencing a target through the exchange of favors is labeled **exchange.** If two politicians agree to vote for each other's pet legislation despite minor misgivings about each other's bills, that is exchange. **Coalition tactics** are different from consultation in that they are used when agents seek the aid or support of others to influence the target. A dramatic example of coalition tactics occurs when several key significant people in an alcoholic's life (e.g., spouse, children, employer, neighbor) agree to confront the alcoholic in unison about the many dimensions of his problem. Threats or persistent reminders used to influence targets are known as **pressure tactics.** A judge who gives a convicted prisoner a suspended sentence but tells him to consider the suspension a "sword hanging over your head" if he breaks the law again is using pressure tactics. Finally, **legitimizing tactics** occur when agents make requests based on their position or authority. A principal may ask a teacher to be on the school's curriculum committee, and the teacher may accede to the request despite reservations just because it is the principal's prerogative to appoint any teacher to that role. In practice, of course, actual tactics often reflect combinations of these different approaches. Rarely, for example, is an effective appeal purely inspirational, without any rational elements at all.

Influence Tactics and Power

As alluded to throughout this chapter, a strong relationship exists between the relative power of agents and targets and the types of influence tactics used. Because leaders with relatively high amounts of referent power have built up close relationships with followers, they may be more able to use a wide variety of influence tactics to modify the attitudes and behaviors of their followers. For example, leaders with a lot of referent power could use inspirational appeals, consultations, ingratiation, personal appeals, exchanges, and even coalition tactics to increase the amount of time a particular follower spends doing work-related activities. Note, however, that leaders with high referent power generally do not use legitimizing or pressure tactics to influence followers since by threatening followers, leaders risk some loss of referent power. Leaders who have only coercive or legitimate power may be able to use only coalition, legitimizing, or pressure tactics to influence followers.

Other factors also can affect the choice of influence tactics (Kipnis & Schmidt, 1985). People typically use hard tactics (i.e., legitimizing or pressure tactics) when an influencer has the upper hand, when she anticipates resistance, or when the other person's behavior violates important norms. People typically use soft tactics (e.g., ingratiation) when they are at a disadvantage, when they expect resistance, or when they will personally benefit if the attempt is successful. People typically use rational tactics (i.e., the exchange and rational appeal) when parties are relatively equal in power, when resistance is not anticipated, and when the benefits are organizational as well as personal.

Other studies, too, have shown that influence attempts based on factual, logical analyses are the most frequently reported method by which middle managers exert lateral influence (Keys, Case, Miller, Curran, & Jones, 1987) and upward influence (Case, Dosier, Murkison, & Keys, 1988). Other important components of successful influence of one's superiors include thoroughly preparing beforehand, involving others for support (i.e., coalition tactics), and persisting through a combination of approaches (Case, Dosier, Murkison, & Keys, 1988).

Findings about who uses different tactics, and when, provide interesting insights into the influence process. It is clear that one's influence tactic of choice depends on many factors, including intended outcomes and one's power relative to the target person. Whereas it may not be very surprising that people select influence tactics as a

> *Don't threaten. I know it's done by some of our people, but I don't go for it. If people are running scared, they're not going to make the right decisions. They'll make decisions to please the boss rather than recommend what has to be done.*
>
> Charles Pilliod

function of their power relationship with another person, it is striking that the relationship holds true so universally across different social domains. The relationship holds true for business executives, for parents and children, and for spouses. There is a strong tendency for people to resort to hard tactics whenever they have an advantage in clout if other tactics fail to get results (Kipnis & Schmidt, 1985). As the bank robber Willie Sutton once said, "A gun and a smile are more effective than a smile by itself." This sentiment is apparently familiar to bank managers, too. The latter reported greater satisfaction in handling subordinates' poor performance when they were relatively more punishing (Green, Fairhurst, & Snavely, 1986). Highlight 5.3 offers thoughts on how men and women managers sometimes use different techniques in "managing upward." It would be interesting to contrast the uses of power and influence of Suu Kyi and Colin Powell, not only because of their gender but also because of their differing bases of power.

Although hard tactics can be effective, relying on them can change the way we see others. This was demonstrated in an experiment wherein leaders' perceptions and evaluations of subordinates were assessed after they exercised different sorts of authority over the subordinates (Kipnis, 1984). Several hundred business students acted as managers of small work groups assembling model cars. Some of

Gender Differences in Managing Upward: How Male and Female Managers Get Their Way

Highlight 5.3

Both male and female managers in a Fortune 100 company were interviewed and completed surveys about how they influence upward—how they influence their own bosses. The results generally supported the idea that female managers' influence attempts showed greater concern for others, while male managers' influence attempts showed greater concern for self. Female managers were more likely to act with the organization's broad interests in mind, consider how others felt about the influence attempt, involve others in planning, and focus on both the task and interpersonal aspects of the situation. Male managers, on the other hand, were more likely to act out of self-interest, show less consideration for how others might feel about the influence attempt, work alone in developing their strategy, and focus primarily on the task alone.

One of the most surprising findings of the study was that, contrary to prediction, female managers were less likely than male managers to compromise or negotiate during their influence attempts. The female managers were actually more likely to persist in trying to persuade their superiors, even to the point of open opposition. At first this may seem inconsistent with the idea that the female managers' influ-

ence style involved greater concern for their relatedness to others. However, it does seem consistent with the higher value placed by the women managers on involvement. Perhaps female managers demonstrate more commitment to their issue, and greater self-confidence that they are doing the "right thing," precisely because they have interacted with others in the organization more already and know they have others' support.

While male and female managers emphasized different influence techniques, it is important to note neither group overall was more effective than the other. Nonetheless, there may be significant implications of the various techniques for a manager's career advancement. At increasingly higher management levels in an organization, effectiveness may be defined primarily by its fit with the organization's own norms and values. Managers whose style matches most closely that of their superior's may have an advantage in evaluations and promotion decisions. This may be a significant factor for women, given the highly skewed representation of males in the most senior executive ranks.

Source: K. E. Lauterbach and B. J. Weiner, "Dynamics of Upward Influence: How Male and Female Managers Get Their Way," *Leadership Quarterly 7*, no. 1 (1996), pp. 87–107.

It is not power that corrupts, but fear. Fear of losing power corrupts those who wield it and fear of the scourge of power corrupts those who are subject to it.

Aung San
Suu Kyi

the students were told to act in an authoritarian manner, exercising complete control over the group's work; others were told to act as democratic leaders, letting group members participate fully in decisions about the work. As expected, authoritarian leaders used more hard tactics, whereas democratic leaders influenced subordinates more through rational methods. More interesting was the finding that subordinates were evaluated by the two types of leaders in dramatically different ways even though the subordinates of both types did equally good work. Authoritarian leaders judged their subordinates as less motivated, less skilled, and less suited for promotion. Apparently, bosses who use hard tactics to control others' behavior tend not to attribute any resultant good performance to the subordinates themselves. Ironically, the act of using hard tactics leads to negative at-

To Be or Not to Be . . . a Porcupine

Highlight 5.4

We said before that there are no simple recipes for leadership. This is perfectly evident in the various ways power and influence are exercised in the halls of Congress. In *The Power Game,* author Hedrick Smith offers numerous examples of how Washington, D.C., actually works. For example, it is true that interpersonal relationships play a key part in one's effectiveness, but there are many paths to interpersonal power and influence in government, as the following anecdotes point out.

Barney Frank, a Democratic congressman from Massachusetts, likens success in the House of Representatives to high school. Nobody in the House can give any other member an order, not even the Speaker of the House. Neither can anyone be fired except by his or her own constituencies. That means, therefore, that those in Congress become influential by persuading people and having others respect but not resent them. In that sense it's like high school.

Sometimes, however, it may pay to be *unlikable,* at least in some situations. Former senator (and later secretary of state) Ed Muskie had a reputation for being a "porcupine," for being difficult in the conference committees where final versions of legislation were hammered out. A former staff member said Muskie was the best porcupine of them all because nobody wanted to tangle with him. Muskie will "be gross. He'll smoke a god-awful cigar. He'll just be difficult, cantankerous." One of the reasons Muskie was so successful as a legislator was precisely that he could be nearly impossible to deal with. People would rather ignore him, try to avoid fights or confrontations with his notorious temper. Muskie knew how to be a porcupine, and he used that behavior to advantage in authoring critical legislation.

Source: H. Smith, *The Power Game* (New York: Random House, 1988).

tributions about others, which, in turn, tend to corroborate the use of hard tactics in the first place.

Finally, we should remember that using influence tactics can be thought of as a social skill. Choosing the right tactic to use may not always be enough to ensure good results; the behavior must be *skillfully executed.* We are not encouraging deviousness or a manipulative attitude toward others, merely recognizing the obvious fact that clumsy attempts to influence do often come across as phoney. They may be counterproductive in the end. See Highlight 5.4 for some interesting ways skills are applied in the political arena.

A Concluding Thought about Influence Tactics

In the above discussion, an implicit lesson for leaders is the value of being conscious of what influence tactics one uses and what effects are typically associated with each tactic. Knowledge of such effects can help a leader make better decisions about her manner of influencing others. It might also be helpful for leaders to think more carefully about why they believe a particular influence tactic might be effective. Research indicates that some reasons for selecting among various possible influence tactics lead to successful outcomes more frequently

All forms of tampering with human beings, getting at them, shaping them against their will to your own pattern, all thought control and conditioning, is, therefore, a denial of that in men which makes them men and their values ultimate.

A. A. Berle, Jr.,
Writer on corporations

than others. More specifically, thinking an act would improve an employee's self-esteem or morale was frequently associated with successful influence attempts. On the other hand, choosing an influence tactic because it followed company policy and choosing one because it was a way to put a subordinate in his place were frequently mentioned as reasons for unsuccessful influence attempts (Dosier, Case, & Keys, 1988). In a nutshell, these results suggest that leaders should pay attention not only to the actual influence tactics they use—to *how* they are influencing others—but also to *why* they believe such methods are called for. It is perhaps an obvious but nonetheless important conclusion to reach from these results that influence efforts intended to build others up more frequently lead to positive outcomes than influence efforts intended to put others down.

Summary

This chapter has defined power as the capacity or potential to exert influence, influence tactics as the behaviors used by one person to modify the attitudes and behaviors of another, and influence as the degree of change in a person's attitudes, values, or behaviors as the result of another's influence tactic. Because power, influence, and influence tactics play such important roles in the leadership process, this chapter provides ideas to help leaders improve their effectiveness. By reflecting on their different bases of power, leaders may better understand how they can affect followers and even expand their power. The five bases of power also offer clues as to why subordinates are able to influence leaders and successfully resist leaders' influence attempts.

Leaders also may gain insight into why they may not enjoy certain aspects of their responsibilities by reflecting on their own need for power or motivation to manage; they may also better understand why some leaders exercise power selfishly by considering McClelland's concepts of personalized power and activity inhibition. Leaders can improve their effectiveness by finding ways to enhance their idiosyncratic credit and not permitting in-group and out-group rivalries to develop in the work unit.

Although power is an extremely important concept, having power is relatively meaningless unless a leader is willing to exercise it. The exercise of power occurs primarily through the influence tactics leaders and followers use to modify the attitudes and behaviors of each other. The type of influence tactics used seems to depend on the amount of different types of power possessed, the degree of resistance expected, and the rationale behind the different influence tactics. Because influence tactics designed to build up others are generally more successful than those that tear down others, leadership practitioners should always consider why they are using a particular influence attempt before they actually use it. By carefully considering the rationale behind the tactic, leaders may be able to avoid using pressure and legitimizing tactics and to find ways to influence followers that build them up rather than tear them down. Being able to use influence tactics that modify followers' attitudes and behaviors in the desired direction at the same time they build up followers' self-esteem and self-confidence should be a skill all leaders strive to master.

Key Terms

power, *107*
influence, *108*
influence tactics, *108*
pecking order, *110*
expert power, *113*
referent power, *114*
legitimate power, *115*
reward power, *116*

coercive power, *119*
need for power, *121*
personalized power, *121*
socialized power, *121*
projective personality
test, *121*
motivation to manage, *122*
rational persuasion, *123*

inspirational appeals, *124*
consultation, *124*
ingratiation, *124*
personal appeals, *124*
exchange, *124*
coalition tactics, *124*
pressure tactics, *124*
legitimizing tactics, *124*

Questions

1. The following questions all pertain to the Milgram studies (Highlight 5.2).

   a. What bases of power were available to the experimenter, and what bases of power were available to the subjects?

   b. Do you think subjects with a low need for power would act differently from those subjects with a high need for power? What about subjects with differing levels of the motivation to manage?

   c. What situational factors contributed to the experimenter's power?

   d. What influence tactics did the experimenter use to change the behavior of the subjects, and how were these tactics related to the experimenter's power base?

   e. What actually was influenced? In other words, if influence is the change in another's attitudes, values, or behaviors as the result of an influence tactic, then what changes occurred in the subject as the result of the experimenter's influence tactics?

   f. Many people have criticized the Milgram study on ethical grounds. Assuming that some socially useful information was gained from the studies, do you believe this experiment could or should be replicated today?

2. Some definitions of leadership exclude reliance on formal authority or coercion (i.e., certain actions by a person in authority may work but should not be considered leadership). What are the pros and cons of such a view?

3. Does power, as Lord Acton suggested, tend to "corrupt" the power holder? If so, what are some of the ways it happens? Is it also possible subordinates are corrupted by a superior's power? How? Or is it even possible that superiors can be corrupted by a subordinate's power?

4. Some people say it dilutes a leader's authority if subordinates are allowed to give feedback to the leader concerning their perceptions of the leader's performance. Do you agree?

5. Is leadership just another word for influence? Can you think of some examples of influence that you would *not* consider leadership?

6. Compare and contrast Colin Powell, Peter Jackson, and Aung San Suu Kyi in their respective sources of power.

Skills

Leadership skills relevant to this chapter include:

- Assertiveness
- Building technical competence
- Building effective relationships
- Punishment
- Negotiation

Activity

This activity will demonstrate how the five bases of power are manifest in behavior. Write the five bases of power on the blackboard or put them on an overhead. Break students into five groups, and give each group a 3 × 5 card that lists one of the five bases of power. Give the group 10 minutes to plan and practice a 1-minute skit which will be presented to the rest of the class. The skit should demonstrate the base of power listed on the 3 × 5 card. After the skit is presented, the remaining groups should guess which base of power is being used in the skit. As an alternative, you might choose a project for out-of-class work. Another variation is to assign the groups the task of finding a 3–4 minute segment from a movie or video and bring that in to the class.

Minicase

"The Prime Minister's Powerful Better Half"

Ho Ching's power has been recognized by many. As Chief Executive Officer of Temasek Holdings, she ranked number 18 on a list of Asia's Most Powerful Business People and number 24 on Forbes's list of the World's Most Powerful Women. How does a shy, Stanford-educated electrical engineer end up with this kind of power? Ho was a government scholar who started off in civil service and ended up working for the Defense Ministry in Singapore. There she met and married Lee Hsien Loong, Singapore's current Prime Minister and the son of Lee Kwan Yew—one of modern Singapore's founding fathers. Ho's experience, education, and connections led to her appointment as chief executive of Temasek where she oversees a portfolio worth over $50 billion and influences many of Singapore's leading companies.

Temasek Holdings was established in 1974 in an attempt by the Singapore government to drive industrialization. Through Temasek Holdings the Singapore government took stakes in a wide range of companies including the city-state's best-known companies: Singapore Airlines, Singapore Telecommunications, DBS Bank, Neptune Orient Lines, and Keppel Corp. The company's website describes Temasek's "humble roots during a turbulent and uncertain time" and its commitment "to building a vibrant future [for Singapore] through successful enterprise."

Ho's appointment to Temasek in May 2002 caused some controversy; as Prime Minister her husband has a supervisory role over the firm. Ho denies any conflict of interest:

> The issue of conflict does not arise because there are no vested interests. Our goal is to do what makes sense for Singapore, I don't always agree with him (Mr. Lee) and he doesn't always agree with me. We have a healthy debate on issues.

In her role as CEO, Ho is pushing for a more open policy and an aggressive drive into the Asian market. Under Ho's leadership Temasek has decided to publicly disclose its annual report with details of its performance—details that have formerly remained private and known only to Temasek executives.

Ho is concentrating on broadening Temasek's focus beyond Singapore, most recently opening an office in India. At a recent conference of top Indian companies, Ho appealed to investors to look to India for opportunities for Asian growth:

> Since the Asian Financial Crisis in 1997, the word *Asia* had lost a bit of its sparkle. But that sparkle is beginning to return. In the 60s and 70s, the Asia economic miracle referred to East Asia, specifically Japan. The 70s and 80s saw the emergence of the four Asian Tigers of Korea, Taiwan, Hongkong, and Singapore.
>
> Now is India's turn to stir, standing at an inflexion point, after 10 years of market liberalisation and corporate restructuring. Since 1997, Singapore's trade with India grew by 50 percent, or a respectable CAGR of about 7.5 percent. Confidence is brimming in India, and Indian companies began to reach out boldly to the world over the last five years.
>
> All these waves of development have shown that Asia, with a combined population of 3 billion, has been resilient. If Asia continues to work hard and work smart, honing her competitive strengths and leveraging on her complementary capabilities across borders, the outlook in the next decade or two looks very promising indeed.

1. We have described *power* as the capacity to cause change and *influence* as the degree of actual change in a target's behaviors. Ho Ching's power as a leader has been recognized by many, but would you describe Ho Ching as an influential leader? Why?

2. Based on the excerpt from Ho Ching's speech, what type of tactics does she use to influence the behavior of others?

3. Ho Ching has been named one of the most powerful leaders in Asia. What are her major sources of power?

Sources: http://www.fastcompany.com/online/13/womenofpr.html; http://www.forbes.com/finance/lists/11/2004/LIR.jhtml?passListId=11&passYear=2004&passListType=Person&uniqueId=OO5O&datatype=Person; http://www.businessweek.com/magazine/content/02_36/b3798161.htm; http://www.laksamana.net/vnews.cfm?ncat=31&news_id=5292; http://in.rediff.com/money/2004/apr/03spec.htm; http://www.theaustralian.news.com.au/common/story_page/0%2C5744%2C10427548%255E2703%2C00.html; http://in.news.yahoo.com/040812/137/2fgoc.html

6

Leadership and Values

Introduction

In the previous chapter, we examined many different facets of power and its use in leadership. The topics in this chapter go hand in hand with understanding the role of power in leadership. That is because leaders can use power for good or ill, and the leader's personal values may be one of the most important determinants of how power is exercised or constrained. For example, a political leader may be able to stir a group into a frenzy (and become even more popular) by identifying a scapegoat to blame for a community's or nation's problems, but would it be right? Is it *ever* right for a political leader to stir a populace into a frenzy? And what standards should govern the application of such power? Or, a person may be promoted to leadership positions of ever-greater responsibility and reward, but at a cost of broken relationships in his family life; would *you* choose that trade-off?

The mere possession of power, of any kind, leads inevitably to ethical questions about how that power should and should not be used. The challenge of leadership becomes even more complex when we consider how individuals of different backgrounds, cultures, and nationalities may hold quite different values yet be thrown into increasingly closer interaction with each other as our world becomes both smaller and more diverse. This chapter will explore these fascinating and important aspects of leadership.

Leadership and "Doing the Right Things"

In Chapter 1, we referred to a distinction between leaders and managers that says leaders do the right things whereas managers do things right (Bennis, 1985). But just what does the "right things" mean? Does it mean the "morally right" things? The "ethically right" things? The "right things" for the company to be successful? And who's to say what the "right things" are?

Leaders face dilemmas that require choices between competing sets of values and priorities, and the best leaders recognize and face them with a commitment to doing what is right, not just what is expedient. Of course, the phrase *doing what is right* sounds deceptively simple. Sometimes it will take great moral courage to do what is right, even when the right action seems clear. At other times, though, leaders face complex challenges that lack simple black-and-white answers. Whichever the case, leaders set a moral example to others that be-comes the model for an entire group or organiza-tion, for good or bad. Leaders who themselves do

> *Leadership cannot just go along to get along . . . Leadership must meet the moral challenge of the day.*
>
> Jesse Jackson

not honor truth do not inspire it in others. Leaders mostly concerned with their own advancement do not inspire selflessness in others. Leaders should internalize a strong set of **ethics,** principles of right conduct or a system of moral values.

Both Gardner (1990) and Burns (1978) have stressed the centrality and impor-tance of the moral dimension of leadership. Gardner said leaders ultimately must be judged on the basis of a framework of values, not just in terms of their effec-tiveness. He put the question of a leader's relations with his or her followers or constituents on the moral plane, arguing (with the philosopher Immanuel Kant) that leaders should always treat others as ends in themselves, not as objects or mere means to the leader's ends (which, however, does not necessarily imply that leaders need to be gentle in interpersonal demeanor or "democratic" in style). Burns (1978) took an even more extreme view regarding the moral dimension of leadership, maintaining that leaders who do not behave ethically do not demon-strate true leadership.

Whatever "true leadership" means, most people would agree that at a minimum it would be characterized by a high degree of trust between leader and followers. Bennis and Goldsmith (1997) describe four qualities of leadership that engender trust. These qualities are vision, empathy, consistency, and integrity. First, we tend to trust leaders who create a compelling *vision:* who pull people together on the ba-sis of shared beliefs and a common sense of organizational purpose and belonging. Second, we tend to trust leaders who demonstrate *empathy* with us—who show they understand the world as we see and experience it. Third, we trust leaders who are *consistent.* This does not mean that we only trust leaders whose positions never change, but that changes are understood as a process of evolution in light of rele-vant new evidence. Fourth, we tend to trust leaders whose *integrity* is strong, who demonstrate their commitment to higher principles through their actions.

Another important factor impacting the degree of trust between leaders and fol-lowers involves fundamental assumptions people make about human nature. Sev-eral decades ago, Douglas McGregor (1966) explained different styles of managerial behavior on the basis of their implicit attitudes about human nature, and his work remains quite influential today. McGregor identified two contrasting sets of as-sumptions people make about human nature, calling these **Theory X** and **Theory Y.**

In the simplest sense, Theory X reflects a more pessimistic view of others. Man-agers with this orientation rely heavily on coercive, external-control methods to motivate workers such as pay, disciplinary techniques, punishments, and threats. They assume people are not naturally industrious or motivated to work. Hence, it is the manager's job to minimize the harmful effects of workers' natural laziness and irresponsibility by closely overseeing their work and creating external incentives to do well and disincentives to avoid slacking off. Theory Y, on the other hand, reflects a view that most people are intrinsically motivated by their work. Rather than needing to be coaxed or coerced to work productively, such people value a sense of achievement, personal growth, pride in contributing to their organization, and respect for a job well done. Peter Jackson's leadership was clearly consistent with a Theory Y view of human nature. When asked, "How do you stand up to executives?" Jackson answered, "Well, I just find that most people appreciate honesty. I find that if you try not to have any pretensions and you tell the truth, you talk to them and you treat them as collaborators, I find that studio people are usually very supportive."

But are there practical advantages to holding a Theory X or Theory Y view? Evidently there are. There is evidence that success more frequently comes to leaders who share a positive view of human nature. Hall and Donnell (1979) reported findings of five separate studies involving over 12,000 managers that explored the relationship between managerial achievement and attitudes toward subordinates. Overall, they found that managers who strongly subscribed to Theory X beliefs were far more likely to be in their lower-achieving group.

One behavior common to many good leaders is that they tend to align the values of their followers with those of the organization or movement; they make the links between the two sets more explicit. But just what are values? How do values and ethical behavior develop? Is one person's set of standards better or higher than another's? These are the sorts of questions we will address in this section.

What Are Values?

Values are "constructs representing generalized behaviors or states of affairs that are considered by the individual to be important" (Gordon, 1975, p. 2). When Patrick Henry said, "Give me liberty, or give me death," he was expressing the value he placed upon political freedom. The opportunity to constantly study and learn may be the fundamental value or "state of affairs" leading a person to pursue a career in academia. Someone who values personal integrity may be forced to resign from an unethical company. Thus, values play a fairly central role in one's overall psychological makeup and can affect behavior in a variety of situations. In work settings, values can affect decisions about joining an organization, organizational commitment, relationships with co-workers, and decisions about leaving an organization (Boyatzis & Skelly, 1989). It is important for leaders to realize that individuals in the same work unit can have considerably different values, especially since we cannot see values directly. We can only make inferences about people's values based on their behavior.

Some of the major values that may be considered important by individuals in an organization are listed in Table 6.1. The instrumental values found in Table 6.1 refer to modes of behavior, and the terminal values refer to desired end states (Rokeach, 1973). For example, some individuals value equality, freedom, and having a comfortable life above all else; others may believe that family security and salvation are important goals to strive for. In terms of instrumental values, such individuals may think that it is important always to act in an ambitious, capable,

TABLE 6.1
People Vary in
the Relative
Importance
They Place on
Values Like
the Following

Source: Adapted
from M. Rokeach,
*The Nature of Human
Values* (New York:
Free Press, 1973).

Terminal Values	Instrumental Values
An exciting life	Being courageous
A sense of accomplishment	Being helpful
Family security	Being honest
Inner harmony	Being imaginative
Social recognition	Being logical
Friendship	Being responsible

and honest manner, whereas others may think it is important only to be ambitious and capable. We should add that the instrumental and terminal values in Table 6.1 are only a few of those Rokeach has identified.

How Do Values Develop?

According to Massey (1979), each person's values reflect the contributions of diverse inputs, including family, peers, the educational system, religion, the media, science and technology, geography, and current events (see Figure 6.1). Although one's values can change throughout one's life, they are relatively firmly established by young adulthood. Figure 6.2 represents the building blocks of leadership skills as a pyramid, and you can see that values are on the bottom of the pyramid (along with interests, motives, lifelong goals, personality traits and preferences, and intelligence). All of the attributes in that bottom row are relatively enduring and permanent; they serve as a foundation to other attributes of leadership that are less enduring and thus more modifiable. At the top of the pyramid are leadership skills and competencies that can be developed through practice.

Massey used the term **value programming** to highlight the extent to which forces outside the individual shape and mold personal values. He analyzed changes in the value-programming inputs that characterized each of the decades since the 1920s and related them to dominant and distinctive values held among people who were value-programmed during those respective periods.

FIGURE 6.1
Some
influences
on the
development
of personal
values.

Source: Adapted
from M. Massey, *The
People Puzzle*
(Reston, VA.: Reston
Publishing, 1979).

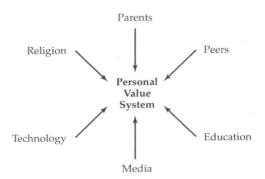

FIGURE 6.2
The building
blocks of
skills.

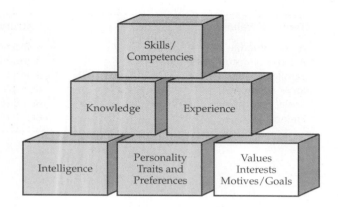

Boyatzis and Skelly (1989), Maccoby (1983), and Massey (1979) have all said that the pervasive influence of broad forces like these tend to create common value systems among people growing up at a particular time that distinguish them from people who grow up at different times. There are, of course, significant differences among individuals *within* any generational group, but these authors emphasized differences *between* groups. They attributed much of the misunderstanding between older leaders and younger followers to the fact that their basic value systems were formulated during quite different social and cultural conditions, and these analyses offer a helpful perspective for understanding how differences in values can add tension to the interaction between some leaders and followers.

One indication of the ways times continue to change, in fact, is that the phrase *older leaders and younger followers,* as used above, is no longer so universally applicable as it once seemed. There are increasing numbers of younger leaders who have older followers, which makes an appreciation of generational differences more important than ever. Zemke (2001) is another researcher who has looked at differences in values across generations, and how those value differences impact their approaches to work and leadership. Here is his delineation of four generations of workers, each one molded by distinctive experiences during their critical developmental periods:

The Veterans (1922–1943): Veterans came of age during the Great Depression and World War II, and represent a wealth of lore and wisdom. They've been a stabilizing force in organizations for decades, even if they are prone to digressions about "the good old days."

The Baby Boomers (1942–1960): These were the postwar babies who came of age during violent social protests, experimentation with new lifestyles, and pervasive questioning of establishment values. But they're graying now, and don't like to think of themselves as "the problem" in the workplace even though they frequently are. Boomers still have passion about bringing participation, spirit, heart, and humanity to the workplace and office. They're also concerned about creating a level playing field for all, but they hold far too many meetings for the typical Gen Xer.

The Gen Xers (1960–1980): Gen Xers grew up during the era of the Watergate scandal, the energy crisis, higher divorce rates, MTV, and corporate downsizing; many were latchkey kids. As a group they tend to be technologically savvy, independent, and skeptical of institutions and hierarchy. They are entrepreneurial and they embrace change (Baldwin & Trovas, 2002). Having seen so many of their parents work long and loyally for one company only to lose their job to downsizing, Xers don't believe much in job security; to an Xer, job security comes from having the kinds of skills that make you attractive to an organization (Foley & LeFevre, 2001). Hence, they tend to be more committed to their vocation than to any specific organization. In fact, the free-agency concept born in professional sports also applies to Xers, who are disposed to stay with an organization until a better offer comes along. Among the challenges they present at work is how to meet their need for feedback despite their dislike of close supervision. Xers also seek balance in their lives more than preceding generations; they work to live rather than live to work. (Also see Highlight 6.1)

The Nexters (1980+): This is *your* generation, so any generalizations we make here are particularly risky. In general, however, Nexters share an optimism born, perhaps, from having been raised by parents devoted to the task of bringing their generation to adulthood; they are the children of soccer moms and Little League dads. They doubt the wisdom of traditional racial and sexual categorizing, perhaps not unexpected from a generation rich with opportunities like having Internet pen pals in Asia whom they can interact with any time of the day or night.

Researchers at *The Center for Creative Leadership* have also been interested in Gen Xers and how their values impact the leadership process at work. One clear finding from this research involved the distinctively different view of authority held by Xers than previous generations. "While past generations might have at least acknowledged positional authority, this new generation has little respect for and less interest in leaders who are unable to demonstrate that they can personally produce. In other words, this generation doesn't define leading as sitting in meetings and making profound vision statements, but instead as eliminating obstacles and giving employees what they need to work well and comfortably" (Deal, Peterson, & Gailor-Loflin, 2001). Gen Xers expect managers to "earn their stripes," and not be rewarded with leadership responsibilities merely because of seniority. Often that attitude is interpreted as an indication of disrespect toward elders in general, and bosses in particular. It may be more accurate, however, to characterize the attitude as one of skepticism rather than disrespect. Such skepticism could have arisen from the fact that Generation X grew up during a time when there were relatively few heroes or leaders it could call its own. It also might have arisen from growing up in an environment of such pervasive marketing that anything smacking of "hype" is met with suspicion (Deal, Peterson, and Gailor-Loflin). That skepticism is also evident in the fact that 53 percent of them believe that the soap opera *General Hospital* will be around longer than Medicare, and that a majority of them are more likely to believe in UFOs than that Social Security will last until their retirement (Foley & LeFevre).

> *Question authority, but raise your hand first.*
>
> Bob Thaues

Lest we overemphasize the significance of intergenerational differences, however, we should consider the results of a scientific sampling of over 1,000 people living in the United States (Ladd, 1994) which found *little* evidence of a generation gap in basic values.

Main Events in the Lives of Gen Xers

Highlight 6.1

A number of historical events over the past three and a half decades have had significant impacts on the lives and worldviews of today's emerging leaders.

GENERAL

1968 Martin Luther King, Jr., assassinated

1969 U.S. lands on the moon

1973 Watergate scandal begins

1975 Vietnam war ends

1976 Energy crisis

1979 Iran hostage crisis

1981 Center for Disease Control's first published report on AIDS

1981 Reagan assassination attempt

1984 Ozone depletion detected

1984 Extensive corporate downsizing begins

1986 Space shuttle disaster

1986 Chernobyl disaster

1989 Berlin Wall falls

1990 Persian Gulf War

1991 USSR dissolves

2001 Terrorist attacks on World Trade Center

2003 Enron and other corporate scandals

TECHNOLOGICAL

1971 Intel's first chip developed

1972 First e-mail management program

1974 Videocassette recorder introduced on the consumer market

1975 Microsoft founded

1975 Personal computer introduced on the consumer market

1979 First commercial cellular telephone system

1980 CNN begins 24-hour broadcasting

1981 MTV launched

1983 C Shugs@holly.colostate.eduompact discs mass marketed

1991 World Wide Web launched

Source: Adapted from B. Baldwin and S. Trovas, *Leadership in Action*, 21 (6), January/February 2002, p. 17.

Indeed, the director of one of the largest polling organizations in the world called the results some of the most powerful he had seen in 30 years of public-opinion research. They showed, he said, "that even though young people buy different CDs and clothes, they do *not* buy into a set of values different from their elders" (Ladd, p. 50).

Thus, while it's true that experiences unique to particular generations help explain certain values characteristic of people in one generation, people from different generations still share many of the same values. But what might explain value differences *within* a given age group? Actually, they're the same factors depicted in Figure 6.1 which Massey used to explain value differences *across* generations. There may be significant differences in the value-programming experiences of teenagers from the same generation based on factors like their family's religious affiliation and involvement, the norms of the particular peer group they associate with, their formal education, and so on.

Given all of this research on work values and how values develop, there are several issues worth commenting on further. First, like the title of this book, values are the result of education and experience. Values develop fairly early in life; education and religious, family, societal, and peer experiences play key roles in the development of a leader's values. Second, once established, it is relatively difficult to change a leader's values. If a person valued money, helping others, or being the center of attention while growing up, then it is very likely that they will find these same activities to be personally motivating as an adult leader. (Third, because it is difficult to change people's underlying values, it's probably unrealistic to expect that university level ethics courses or char-

So near is a falsehood to truth that a wise man would do well not to trust himself on the narrow edge.

Cicero

acter development programs will change one's underlying values.) Perhaps the only way to get leaders and followers to adhere to standards that run counter to their values is to have well-established and enforced codes of conduct, where the benefits of compliance far outweigh the costs of noncompliance (Curphy, Gibson, Macomber, Calhoun, Wilbanks, & Burger, 1998). Unfortunately, as we have seen with the numerous scandals of Wall Street over the past several years, many corporations appear to have poorly established or nonenforced codes of conduct.

Values and Leadership

How Values Impact Leadership

Because values play such a central role in a person's psychological makeup, they have a profound effect on leadership. First and foremost, it is important to understand that values play a key role in the choices made by leaders (Curphy, 2003; England & Lee, 1974). Values are a primary determinant in what data are reviewed by leaders and

What Would You Do?

Highlight 6.2

Here are several situations in which values play a large part in determining your response. How would you act in each one, and by what principles or reasoning process do you reach each decision?

- Would you vote for a political candidate who was honest, competent, and agreed with you on most issues if you also knew that person was alcoholic, sexually promiscuous, and twice divorced?

- Assume that as a teenager you smoked marijuana once or twice, but that was years ago. Would you answer truthfully on an employment questionnaire if it asked whether you had ever used marijuana?

- Your military unit has been ambushed by enemy soldiers and suffered heavy casualties. Several of your soldiers have been captured, but you also captured one of the enemy soldiers. Would you torture the captured enemy soldier if that were the only way of saving the lives of your own soldiers?

- Terrorists have captured a planeload of tourists and threatened to kill them unless ransom demands are met. You believe that meeting the ransom demands is likely to lead to the safe release of those passengers, but also likely to inspire future terrorist acts. Would you meet the terrorists' demands (and probably save the hostages) or refuse to meet the terrorists' demands (and reduce the likelihood of future incidents)?

- If you were an elementary school principal, would you feel it was part of your school's responsibility to teach moral values, or only academic subject matter?

- Assume that you have been elected to your state's legislature, and that you are about to cast the deciding vote in determining whether abortions will be legally available to women in your state. What would you do if your own strong personal convictions on this issue were contrary to the views of the majority of the people you represent?

Source: Adapted from Stock (1991).

Ask Yourself These Questions

Highlight 6.3

An important foundation of behaving ethically at work is to become more self-conscious of one's own ethical standards and practices. The National Institute of Ethics uses the following questions in its Self-Evaluation to facilitate that kind of self-reflection:

- How do I decide ethical dilemmas?
- Do I have set ethical beliefs or standards?
- If so, do I live by these beliefs or standards?
- How often have I done something that I am ashamed of?
- How often have I done things that I am proud of?
- Do I admit my mistakes?
- What do I do to correct mistakes that I make?

- Do I often put the well-being of others ahead of mine?
- Do I follow the golden rule?
- Am I honest?
- Do people respect my integrity?
- List the three best things that have ever happened to me.
- What is the most dishonest thing I have ever done?
- Did I ever rectify the situation?
- What is the most honest thing that I have ever done?

Source: N. Trautman, *Integrity Leadership* (Longwood FL: National Institute of Ethics, 1998).

how they define problems. Leaders with strong Commercial values are likely to focus on financial results and shortcomings; those with strong Aesthetic values are more likely to review quality indicators. Values also affect the solutions generated and the decisions made about problems. For example, followers with strong Security values will offer solutions that help ensure a stable and predictable work environment. But if the leader had a strong Recognition value, she might be more likely to choose a riskier solution that would thrust her in the spotlight. In addition, values often influence a leader's perceptions of individual and organizational successes as well as the manner in which these successes are achieved. Leaders with strong Science values will define organizational success differently than those with strong Power values.

Values also help leaders choose right from wrong, and between ethical and unethical behavior. Along these lines, research has shown that leaders with strong Commercial values and weak Altruistic values are often seen as greedy and selfish (Hogan & Curphy, 2004; Hogan, 2003). Many of these leaders are so obsessed with wealth and material possessions that they think nothing of "cooking the books" in order to make money. Unfortunately, many of the high visibility examples from Enron, Arthur Andersen, Tyco, WorldCom, Charter Communications, Computer Associates, Parmalat, Ahold NV, Boeing, Royal Dutch Shell, and the investment banking and mutual fund industries seem to confirm the notion that many top level executives are willing to do whatever it takes in order to make money (see Highlight 6.4). Even those executives with strong Commercial and weak Altruistic values who do not engage in organizationally delinquent behaviors think nothing of cutting thousands of jobs in order to improve "shareholder value." These same executives, who also happen to own a considerable number of shares in their companies, often run their companies into the ground but personally make tens to hun-

Values, Greed, and Leadership

Highlight 6.4

Leaders with strong Commercial and weak Altruistic values are often characterized as being preoccupied with money. They can often be found just about anywhere in corporate America, but they seem to have the heaviest concentrations in the financial services industry. These leaders like to review financial information, look for opportunities to make more money, make decisions primarily driven by short-term or long-term financial gain, and enjoy the accumulation of wealth. Barbara Ley Toffler's book *Final Accounting: Ambition, Greed, and the Fall of Arthur Andersen* provides a detailed account of how a culture of greed can ruin an organization. Arthur Andersen started as a highly reputable accounting firm that focused on helping corporations reconcile their finances at the end of the year. Recognizing that more money could be made by providing consulting versus accounting services, Arthur Andersen began to vigorously pursue the consulting business. One of the consulting services offered was ethics consulting. Barbara Toffler was the head of the Ethics and Responsible Business Practices Group, where she was responsible for helping companies establish internal ethics programs. These programs helped to generate tremendous fees

for Arthur Andersen, some to the tune of $250,000 per month for specific clients. Toffler goes on to state that many of these programs were ill-designed, not needed, and had little impact. But the drive for fees overrode any need to service clients, and greed became the mantra of the day.

David Peterson, of Personnel Decisions International, maintains that many leaders do not really understand their underlying values. And because leaders do not really know what they stand for, they oftentimes make choices that are not aligned with their personal values. Like the consulting services offered by Toffler, many of these choices appear to have positive short-term benefits but can have devastating long-term effects. Peterson maintains that the better leaders understand their values and how they affect the choices they make, the less likely they will be to make decisions that are misaligned with their values.

Sources: B. Ley Toffler, *Final Accounting: Ambition, Greed, and the Fall of Arthur Andersen* (New York: Broadway Books, 2003); D. Peterson, "Character, Competence, and Context: Assessing and Improving Integrity Through Executive Coaching," in R. T. Hogan (chair), *Assessing Executive Failure: The Underside of Performance*, symposium presented at the 18th Annual Conference of the Society of Industrial and Organizational Psychology, Orlando, FL, 2003.

dreds of millions of dollars in the process (examples include the Qwest acquisition of US West or the AOL-Time Warner merger).

Values not only affect the choices leaders make about what is and what is not important, they also have an impact on the choices leaders make about direct reports. Leaders tend to like followers with similar values and dislike those with dissimilar values. If you knew nothing about a person except his or her values, and those values were similar to your own, then it would be very likely that you would like this individual. The opposite is also true. Because unstructured interviews are a very common selection technique (see Chapter 4), in most cases these are more valued than competence-based assessments. Although hiring direct reports with similar values will make the decision-making process much easier, in many cases groups with identical values can sometimes miss the forest for the trees. For example, one of the authors worked with the top nine leaders of a billion dollar health care system in the United Kingdom. The system was $50,000,000 in debt, and the nine leaders were likely to get sacked if they did not turn their financial problems around by the end of the year. None of the nine leaders had strong

Commercial or Power values, but they all had strong Affiliation and Altruistic values. Their meetings focused entirely on patient care and staff morale and they did little real work to address their budget shortfall. Consequently, many of these leaders were let go at the end of the year. The key point here is that it is important for leaders to surround themselves with followers who possess divergent values. This will likely cause more tension and conflict within the group, but this approach will also make it more likely that a broader variety of problems and solutions will be brought forward for discussion (Hogan & Curphy, 2004).

What values are most important to the leadership process? There is no definitive answer to that question; many different value schemas have been proposed, and many different instruments to measure values have been developed. For purposes of illustration we'll look at one of these, presented in Table 6.2.

In looking over the values in Table 6.2, it is important to note that there is nothing right or wrong, or good or bad, about any of these work values per se; some

TABLE 6.2
Key Work
Values

Source: Adapted
from J. Hogan and
R. T. Hogan,
*Motives, Values and
Preferences Inventory
Manual* (Tulsa, OK:
Hogan Assessment
Systems, 1996).

Recognition: Leaders with strong Recognition values, such as politicians, want to stand out and be the center of attention. They value fame, visibility, and publicity, and are motivated by public recognition and seek jobs where they will be noticed.

Power: Leaders with strong Power values enjoy competition, being seen as influential, and drive hard to make an impact. They value achievement and accomplishment and are motivated to work in jobs where they can achieve, get ahead, and succeed.

Hedonism: Leaders with strong Hedonism values like to have fun at work and entertain others. They are motivated by pleasure, variety, and excitement, and can often be found in the entertainment, hospitality, recreation, sports, sales, or travel industries.

Altruistic: Leaders with strong Altruism values, such as health care or educational leaders, believe in actively helping others who are less fortunate. They are motivated to help the needy and powerless, improve society, and believe in social justice.

Affiliation: Leaders with strong Affiliation values, such as sales leaders, find being around and working with others to be highly motivating. They value meeting new people, networking, working in team environments.

Tradition: Leaders with strong Tradition values, such as religious or military leaders, believe in family values and codes and conduct, and value moral rules and standards. These individuals are motivated to live a lifestyle that is in accordance to religious or institutional customs and standards of behavior.

Security: Leaders with strong Security values, such as bureaucratic leaders, are motivated to work in stable, predictable, and risk-free environments. They create structure and processes in order to minimize uncertainty and avoid criticism.

Commerce: Leaders with strong Commerce values, such as business leaders, are motivated by financial success. They are constantly on the lookout for new business opportunities and are concerned about wealth and material possessions.

Aesthetics: Leaders with strong Aesthetics values, such as film directors, musical conductors or marketing leaders, are motivated to work in environments that place a premium on experimentation, artistic expression, and creative problem solving. They place more importance on appearance or quality than on quantity.

Science: Leaders with strong Science values, such as research and development leaders, enjoy learning, digging deeply into problems, and keeping up to date on technology. They enjoy analyzing data to get at the truth.

leaders think making money is very important, other leaders believe that their most important responsibility is helping others, and other leaders may believe being in the limelight or living a life according to one's religious beliefs to be very important. Leaders are motivated to act in ways consistent with their values, and they typically spend most of their time engaged in activities that are consistent with their values. Similarly, as individuals, leaders and followers are not particularly motivated to work on activities that are inconsistent with their values.

In most cases leaders possess several key values. The example in Figure 6.3 shows the results of a formal values assessment for a Vice President of Product Development for a leadership consulting firm. This individual is responsible for a team that creates, markets, sells, and delivers various psychological assessment and development products for leaders. Figure 6.3 indicates that she believes that working in a team environment (Affiliation), making a difference and having an impact (Power), and doing creative, high quality work (Aesthetics) are extremely important. Conversely, having the opportunity to work in a stable and predictable environment (Security), make money (Commerce), or do research (Science) are not nearly as important or motivating for her.

Although our three leaders have not been subject to a formal values assessment, we can still speculate about which values each of them might consider most important. Peter Jackson appears to have strong Aesthetic and Power values. Colin Powell is likely to have strong Power, Recognition, and Tradition values. And Aung San Suu Kyi probably has strong Altruism and Tradition values. In other words, these three leaders—each successful—seems to have somewhat distinct values driving their behavior. Still another aspect of individual values is addressed in Highlight 6.5 on page 146.

FIGURE 6.3
Leadership
values profile.

Source: Adapted
from J. Hogan and
R. T. Hogan,
*Motives, Values and
Preferences Inventory*
(Tulsa, OK: Hogan
Assessment
Systems, 2002).

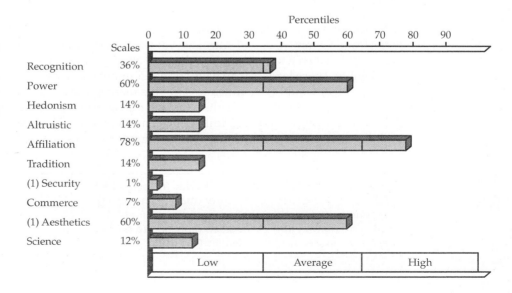

Leadership and Organizational Values

Just as individuals possess a set of personal values, so too do organizations possess a set of organizational values. Many times these values are featured prominently in the company's annual report, website, and posters. These values represent the principals by which employees are to get work done and treat other employees, customers, and vendors. Whether these stated values truly represent operating principals or so much "spin" for potential investors will depend on the degree of alignment between the organization's stated values and the collective values of top leadership (Hogan & Hogan, 1996; Hogan & Curphy, 2004). For example, many corporate value statements say very little about making money, but frankly this is the key organizational priority for most business leaders, and as such is a major factor in many company decisions. It is interesting to note, by the way, that there is often a significant gap between a company's stated values and the way it truly operates. Knowing the values of top leadership can sometimes tell you more about how an organization actually operates than the organization's stated values will.

In any organization, the top leadership's collective values play a significant role in determining organizational culture, just as an individual leader's values play a significant role in determining team climate. Related to the notion of culture and climate is employee "fit." Research has shown that employees with values similar to the organization or team are more satisfied and likely to stay; those with dissimilar values are more likely to leave (Hogan & Hogan, 1996; Hogan & Curphy, 2004). Thus, one reason why leaders fail is not due to a lack of competence, but rather due to a misalignment between personal and organizational values. This is unfortunate, as leaders with dissimilar values may be exactly what the company needs to drive change and become more effective (Hogan & Curphy, 2004).

Beware of the man who had no regard for his own reputation, since it is not likely he should have any for yours.

George Shelley

Finally, values are often a key factor in conflict. Many of the most difficult decisions made by leaders have to do with choices between two values. This is particularly true when the choices represent values in opposition (see Table 6.3). Leaders with strong Commercial and Altruistic values, for example, would probably struggle mightily when having to make a decision about cutting jobs in order to improve profitability. Those leaders who have strong Commercial and weak Altruistic values (or vice versa) would have much less trouble making the same decision. Likewise, some leaders would have difficulties making decisions when friendships may get in the way of making an impact (Affiliation versus Power), or when taking risks to gain visibility runs counter to stability (Recognition versus Security). It is important to

TABLE 6.3
Values in Opposition

Source: Adapted from G. J. Curphy, *Team Leader Program* (St. Paul, MN: Author, 2004).

Commercial (making money) vs. Altruistic (helping others)
Affiliation (having friends) vs. Power (making an impact)
Recognition (taking risks) vs. Security (minimizing risks)
Hedonism (having fun) vs. Tradition (adhering to norms)
Aesthetic (appearance) vs. Scientific (the truth)

note that values also play a key role in conflict between groups. The differences between Bill O'Reilly and Al Franken, the Israelis and Palestinians, the Shiite and Sunni Muslims in Iraq, the Muslims and Hindus in Kashmir, and Christians and Muslims in Kosovo all have to do with values. Because values develop early and are difficult to change, it will be extremely difficult to resolve the conflicts between these groups.

It's vital for a leader to set a personal example of values-based leadership, and it is also important for leaders—especially more senior ones—to make sure that clear values guide *everyone's* behavior in the organization. That's only likely to happen, of course, if the leader's behavior sets an example of desired behavior. You might think of it as a necessary but not sufficient condition for principled behavior throughout the organization. That's because if there is indifference or hypocrisy toward values at the highest levels, then it is fairly unlikely that principled behavior will be considered important by others throughout the organization. Bill O'Brien (1994), the former CEO of a major insurance company, likened an organization's poor ethical climate to a bad odor one gets used to:

> Organizations oriented to power, I realized, also have strong smells, and even if people are too inured to notice, that smell has implications. It affects performance, productivity, and innovation. The worst aspect of this environment is that it stunts the growth of personality and character of everyone who works there (p. 306).

Carried to an extreme, it can lead to the kinds of excesses all too frequently evident during the past decade:

> Who knew the swashbuckling economy of the 90's had produced so many buccaneers? You could laugh about the CEOs in handcuffs and the stock analysts who turned out to be fishier than storefront palm readers, but after a while the laughs became hard. Martha Stewart was dented and scuffed [and subsequently convicted]. Tyco was looted by its own executives. Enron and WorldCom turned out to be the twin towers of false promises. They fell. Their stockholders and employees went down with them. So did a large measure of faith in big corporations.
>
> *Time Magazine,* January 2, 2003

Others, too, are calling attention to the organizational dimensions of ethical behavior. It seems clear that ethical behavior within an organization (or *by* it) is not simply the sum of the collective moralities of its members. Covey (1990), for example, has developed and popularized an approach called **principle-centered leadership.** This approach postulates a fundamental interdependence

Subordinates cannot be left to speculate as to the values of the organization. Top leadership must give forth clear and explicit signals, lest any confusion or uncertainty exist over what is and is not permissible conduct. To do otherwise allows informal and potentially subversive "codes of conduct" to be transmitted with a wink and a nod, and encourages an inferior ethical system based on "going along to get along" or the notion that "everybody's doing it.

Richard Thornburgh, Former U.S. attorney general

It's important that people know what you stand for. It's equally important that they know what you won't stand for.

Mary Waldrop

The Average Self-Rating on "Ethical Behavior" Is Way above Average

Highlight 6.5

David Campbell, a senior fellow at *The Center for Creative Leadership,* is one of the most prolific reseachers in the world in the field of leadership. Among other things, he has authored numerous widely used surveys to assess various facets of leadership. The following story relates his efforts to develop an ethics scale for the Campbell Leadership Index (CLI).

In preliminary work on the CLI, it seemed obvious that "ethics" was central to the practice of good leadership and, therefore, should be one of the scales on the instrument (the CLI now includes 17 scales, including ambitious, enterprising, considerate, entertaining, organized, and productive). Consequently, in the early versions of the survey Campbell included adjectives such as *ethical, honest, trustworthy,* and

candid, and negative adjectives such as *deceptive* and *scheming.* As with other CLI scales, this one was normed so that the average person would receive a score of 50 on the ethics scale; obviously some would get higher scores and some lower scores.

During the CLI testing period, however, a major problem emerged because almost no one wanted to believe that he or she was merely "average" in ethical behavior, let alone "below average." To soften the impact of such feedback, Campbell changed the name of the scale to "trustworthy" in the hope that this would retain the meaning but lessen the adverse reaction. But that change helped little. Eventually Campbell changed the name of the scale to "credible," which is more acceptable and also better captures the reasons why some executives may get low ratings on the scale despite self-perceptions of scrupulous honesty.

between the personal, the interpersonal, the managerial, and the organizational levels of leadership. The unique role of each level may be thought of like this:

Personal: The first imperative is to be a trustworthy person, and that depends on both one's character *and* competence. Only if one is trustworthy can one have trusting relationships with others.

Interpersonal: Relationships that lack trust are characterized by self-protective efforts to control and verify each other's behavior.

Managerial: Only in the context of trusting relationships will a manager risk empowering others to make full use of their talents and energies. But even with an empowering style, leading a high-performing group depends on skills such as team building, delegation, communication, negotiation, and self-management.

Organizational: An organization will be most creative and productive when its structure, systems (e.g., training, communication, reward), strategy, and vision are aligned and mutually supportive. Put differently, certain organizational alignments are more likely to nurture and reinforce ethical behavior among its members than others.

Conflicts over values can arise even when an organization has clearly published values that are embraced by everyone. That can happen when employees and leaders have divergent perceptions of whether the leader's behavior embodies important corporate values. At one company, for example, employees concluded that their CEO's behavior had betrayed the very corporate values that he had been instrumental in establishing. As they perceived the CEO's behavior deviating more and more from those values, employees gradually concluded that he had "sold out," and they became disillusioned with his leadership.

That disillusionment was a far cry from the initial perceptions employees had of their CEO. Consider the situation at Maverick when the CEO, John Bryant (both fictionalized names), started the company:

> Bryant located Maverick's offices in an unassuming warehouse district and gave each member of his small staff a festive company shirt with a logo on the back and their name stitched over the front pocket, like shirts mechanics wear. He provided a companywide profit-sharing plan, above-market salaries, and perks like free lunch on Friday, and he encouraged people to head home by six o'clock. He recruited employees whose varied races, backgrounds, and lifestyles broadcast Maverick's commitment to diversity, and on the weekends he let a minority youth organization use the company's offices. He spoke passionately to everyone about Maverick's people-oriented values and promoted them in company posters, client materials, and the employee handbook.
>
> In short, Bryant did everything right. And by all accounts, Maverick in its early years was a great place to work—employees were motivated, loyal, hardworking, and enthusiastically committed to the company and the ideals Bryant promoted (Edmondson & Cha, 2002, p. 18).

Then the finger-pointing began. As the small, young company more than doubled in size during the 1990s, a remarkable shift occurred in how employees perceived the company and its leader. They came to see Bryant as a hypocrite, whose behavior violated everything he continued to proclaim the company stood for. As a consequence, employee commitment and creativity declined sharply.

What could account for such an unfortunate turnaround? That's not a simple question to answer, especially when the leader—Bryant himself—continued to see his own behavior in much more positive ways. Part of the answer to this enigma, it seems, involved a pivotal event in the company's history. In 1995 Bryant decided to double the size of the company's staff and operations. To him, this was a way to provide more professional growth and reward opportunities for staff. Employees, however, saw this as an act of greed on Bryant's part that would erode company values by disrupting the small, close-knit family the company had been. They also saw other decisions by him as similarly self-serving. When he decided to give long-term employees shares in the company as a reward for their hard work, for example, other employees perceived this as inconsistent with the company's commitment to equality. All the while this was happening, no one ever let Bryant himself know that perceptions of him had taken a 180-degree turn.

In doing a sort of organizational postmortem of what happened at Maverick, it became clear that over time employees had *implicitly and unconsciously* shaped their understanding of the company's values to correspond more closely with their own. For example, employees came to believe that hierarchies of position and power were inconsistent with Maverick's values. In fact, no one ever had said anything like that. Thus, Bryant's behavior *was* inconsistent with company values *as the employees had come to understand them,* even though it *wasn't* inconsistent with Bryant's understanding of the values on which he'd founded the company.

There's an important lesson for leaders in this story that's hinted at in Bryant's own lack of awareness of the growing negative perceptions of his behavior. It's unlikely that subordinate members of an organization will offer unsolicited negative perceptions to leaders when they think that the latter have violated the values. It's essential, then, for leaders themselves to proactively invite discussion by regularly asking people what they're thinking and feeling. You don't want to be caught blind-sided like John Bryant was (Edmondson & Cha).

When Good People Do Bad Things

An important aspect of ethical conduct involves the mental gymnastics by which people can dissociate their moral thinking from their moral acting. One's ability to reason about hypothetical moral issues, after all, does not assure that one will *act* morally. Furthermore, one's moral actions may not always be consistent with one's espoused values. Bandura (1986, 1990), in particular, has pointed out several ways people with firm moral principles nonetheless may behave badly without feeling guilt or remorse over their behavior. We should look at each of these.

Moral justification involves reinterpreting otherwise immoral behavior in terms of a higher purpose. This is most dramatically revealed in the behavior of combatants in war.

> Moral reconstrual of killing is dramatically illustrated by the case of Sergeant York, one of the phenomenal fighters in the history of modern warfare. Because of his deep religious convictions, Sergeant York registered as a conscientious objector, but his numerous appeals were denied. At camp, his battalion commander quoted chapter and verse from the Bible to persuade him that under appropriate conditions it was Christian to fight and kill. A marathon mountainside prayer finally convinced him that he could serve both God and country by becoming a dedicated fighter. (Bandura, 1990, p. 164)

Another way to dissociate behavior from one's espoused moral principles is through **euphemistic labeling.** This involves using "cosmetic" words to defuse or disguise the offensiveness of otherwise morally repugnant or distasteful behavior. Terrorists, for example, may call themselves "freedom fighters," and firing someone may be referred to as "letting him go." **Advantageous comparison** lets one avoid self-contempt for one's behavior by comparing it to even more heinous behavior by others ("If you think *we're* insensitive to subordinates' needs, you should see what it's like working for *Acme*"). Through **displacement of responsibility** people may violate personal moral standards by attributing responsibility to others. Nazi concentration camp guards, for example, attempted to avoid moral responsibility for their behavior by claiming they were merely "carrying out orders."

A related mechanism is **diffusion of responsibility,** whereby reprehensible behavior becomes easier to engage in and live with if others are behaving the same way. When everyone is responsible, it seems, no one is responsible. This way of minimizing individual moral responsibility for collective action can be one negative effect of group decision making. Through **disregard or distortion of consequences,** people minimize the harm caused by their behavior. This can be a problem in bureaucracies when decision-makers are relatively insulated by their position from directly observing the consequences of their decisions. **Dehumanization** is still another way of avoiding the moral consequences of one's behavior. It is easier to treat others badly when they are dehumanized, as evidenced in epithets like "gooks" or "satan-worshippers." Finally, people sometimes try to justify immoral behavior by claiming it was caused by someone else's actions. This is known as **attribution of blame.**

How widespread are such methods of minimizing personal moral responsibility? When people behave badly, Bandura (1977) said, it is *not* typically because of a basic character flaw; rather, it is because they use methods like these to construe their behavior in a self-protective way.

Darley (1994) suggested still another way people justify seemingly unethical conduct, and his observations illuminate certain common leadership practices. Darley said *ethical problems are almost inherent in systems designed to measure performance.*

> The more any quantitative performance measure is used to determine a group's or an individual's rewards and punishments, the more subject it will be to corruption pressures and the more apt it will be to distort and corrupt the action patterns and thoughts of the group or individual it is intended to monitor. . . The criterial control system unleashes enormous human ingenuity. People will maximize the criteria set. However, they may do so in ways that are not anticipated by the criterion setters, in ways that destroy the validity of the criteria. The people "make their numbers" but the numbers no longer mean what you thought they did. (Darley, 1994)

This has been called **Darley's law,** and it is exemplified in a story from Joseph Heller's novel *Catch-22.* You can read about it in Highlight 6.6, though Darley's law is not limited to fiction. Halberstam (1986) described another organization in which the "numbers game" had a corrupting effect. In this case, it was in the Ford Motor Company. In the eyes of those who worked in Ford plants around the country in the 1950s, Detroit "number crunchers" like Robert McNamara (later a secretary of defense during the Vietnam War) did not want to know the truth. McNamara and his people in Detroit were the ones who kept making liberal agreements with the unions and at the same time setting higher and higher levels of production while always demanding increased quality. They talked about quality, but they did not give the plant managers the means for quality; what they really wanted was production. So the plant managers were giving them what they wanted, numbers, while playing lip service to quality. Years later in Vietnam, some American officers, knowing McNamara's love of numbers, cleverly juggled the numbers and played games with body counts in order to make a stalemated war look more successful than it was. They did this not because they were dishonest, but because they thought if Washington really wanted the truth it would have sought the truth in an honest way. In doing so they were the spiritual descendants of the Ford factory managers of the 1950s (p. 220).

Only mediocrities rise to the top in a system that won't tolerate wave making.

Lawrence J. Peter,
Author of *The Peter Principle*

Darley described three general problems that can arise when performance measurement systems are put in place. A person might cheat on the measurement system by exploiting its weaknesses either in hopes of advancement or through fear of falling behind. Or, even with the best will in the world, a person might act in a way that optimizes his or her performance measurements without realizing that this outcome was not what the system really intended. Finally, a person may even have the best interests of the system in mind and yet manipulate the performance measurement system to allow continuation of the actions that best fulfill his or her reading of the system goals. One major disadvantage of this particular approach is that it "takes underground" constructive dialogue about system goals or modifications in system measurements.

What, ethically, should one do when one is part of a performance measurement system? Darley suggested "that the time for the individual to raise the moral issue is when he or she feels the pressure to substitute accountability for morality, to act wrongly, because that is what the system requires. And that intervention might then be directed at the system, by honorably protesting its design." For those who are governed by a performance measurement system, a constant moral vigilance is necessary—it is needed most of all by those in leadership positions.

Catch-22

Highlight 6.6

This story is about Yossarian, the central character of Joseph Heller's novel *Catch-22*. It demonstrates how a performance measurement system can create forces that morally corrupt the individuals functioning within that system.

During World War II, the allied high command needed some measure of when each bomber crew flying over Germany had "done enough." The answer they came up with was simply to count the number of bombing missions each crew had flown. It seemed to demand a commensurate risk among all concerned, and also seemed correlated with other primary objectives like the number of enemy factories destroyed. After flying a certain number of missions, crews expected to be rotated back to the states.

What was Yossarian's story? Terrified of flying the dangerous combat missions assigned to him, he flew his B-29 on different and infinitely safer routes over the open ocean. He simply dropped the plane's entire payload of bombs there over water. *From the point of view of the military indicator of missions flown, these were successful missions* which even earned Yossarian points toward a safe follow-on assignment. Driven by fear, Yossarian had corrupted the indicator from one that was correlated with organizational success to

one that was arguably negatively correlated with organizational success.

You might wonder whether this proves the indicator was inherently flawed. Wasn't the bomber command justified in designing the measurement system without consideration of this particular possibility? Was it not entitled to assume American soldiers would not commit acts of treasonous cowardice? The intriguing point of Heller's novel is that *Yossarian's act was a perfectly normal response to the particular dynamics in which it arose.* In Heller's novel, *Yossarian's commanders were cheating on the system themselves!* Some, for example, were trying to gain promotion by raising the number of missions required to go home while not flying any missions themselves. Other commanders let friends and favorites accumulate missions by flying "milk runs" in which little enemy opposition was experienced. Still other leaders tried to get credit for bombing missions even though, in fact, they had not flown any. The leadership itself, in other words, destroyed any possibility that pilots like Yossarian would see any moral barriers to cheating. *Corruption is contagious,* and Darley suggests that performance measurement systems inherently invite widespread corruption.

Source: Adapted from Darley (1994).

Leading across Cultures

A rather common problem for office managers in the United States is controlling the use of the office copier. Frequently, office managers publish policies and procedures to govern use of the machines, and hence control administrative costs. When a U.S. manager of a water resources project in Indonesia did the same thing, however, an action he considered routine, he was accused of insensitivity to Indonesian ways—in fact, accused not just of unfriendliness but of unethical behavior. After a series of similar incidents, he lost his job. Leading across cultures requires an appreciation of the sometimes profound differences in the value systems of other cultures.

What Is Culture?

A good starting place for understanding differences in cultural value systems is with the concept of culture itself. **Culture** refers to those learned behaviors characterizing the total way of life of members within any given society. Cultures differ from one another just as individuals differ from one another. To outsiders, the most salient aspect of any culture typically involves behavior—the distinctive actions, mannerisms, and gestures characteristic of that culture. Americans visiting Thailand, for example, may find it curious and even bothersome to see male Thais hold hands with each other in public. They may react negatively to such behavior since it is untypical to *them,* and laden with *North American* meaning (e.g., "It's okay for women to hold hands in public, but men just shouldn't do that!"). Salient as such behaviors are, however, they are also just the tip of the iceberg. The "mass" of culture is not so readily visible, just as most of an iceberg lies beneath the water. Hidden from view are the beliefs, values, and myths that provide context to manifest behaviors (Kohls, 1984). A clear implication for business leaders in the global context, therefore, is the need to become aware and respectful of cultural differences and cultural perspectives. Barnum (1992) pointed out the importance of being able to look at one's own culture through the eyes of another:

> Consciously or unconsciously they will be using their own beliefs as the yardsticks for judging you, so know how to compare those yardsticks by ferreting out their values and noting where they differ the least and most from yours. For example, if their belief in fatalism outweighs your belief in accountability, there will be conflicts down the road. This is a severe problem in the Middle East, for instance, and affects management styles in companies and even the ability to market life insurance, which is frowned upon in communities where Muslim observances are strong. (p. 153)

A Framework for Understanding Cultural Differences

Thus, it can be helpful to see one's own culture through the eyes of another; just as it also can be helpful to see other cultures through eyes unbiased (or at least less biased) by one's own filters. Hofstede (1980) described four dimensions of cultural values and beliefs: individualism versus collectivism, masculinity versus femininity, tolerance versus intolerance of uncertainty, and power distance versus power equalization. More recently, researchers at the Center for Creative Leadership have developed a conceptual framework for analyzing cultural differences based on seven fundamental dilemmas that people of all cultures face (Wilson, Hoppe, & Sayles, 1996). Let us look at each of these seven dilemmas in greater detail.

> *Source of Identity: Individual–Collective.* This deals with the degree to which individuals should pursue their own interests and goals or contribute to a larger group, whether extended family, ethnic group, or company.
>
> *Goals and Means of Achievement: Tough–Tender.* This deals with how success is defined in a culture. Is it defined by tangible rewards like financial success and material well-being or by intangible rewards such as good relationships with others or spiritual satisfaction?
>
> *Orientation to Authority: Equal–Unequal.* How should people of different status, authority, or power behave toward each other—as equals or unequals?
>
> *Response to Ambiguity: Dynamic–Stable.* To what extent is uncertainty accepted or tolerated? In running an organization, are tight controls and structure imposed to ensure certainty, or is greater tolerance for ambiguity and uncertainty evident via loose or nonexistent control systems?
>
> *Means of Knowledge Acquisition: Active–Reflective.* Is action or reflection more valued as a means of acquiring information and knowledge?
>
> *Perspective on Time: Scarce–Plentiful.* Is the sense or experience of time urgent or relaxed?
>
> *Outlook on Life: Doing–Being.* Which is preferred—mastery over nature or living in harmony with nature? Is the outcome of life more dependent upon human effort or on the expression of divine will?

You probably can see how misunderstandings and slights can occur when people from different cultures are working together, but let us look at two specific applications of this scheme. First, consider the historic U.S. emphasis on individualism (e.g., the focus on *self*-confidence, *self*-control, *self*-concept, *self*-expression, or the way rugged individualists are heroically portrayed in film, television, and literature) and how it might impact work. Given an individualist perspective, certain management practices and expectations seem self-evident, such as the idea of individual accountability for work. When individual accountability is valued, for example, decision-making authority tends to be delegated to individual managers. What's more, those same managers may be inclined to take personal credit when the job is well done. A different norm, however, applies in industrialized Japan. Decision making is often very time-consuming, to assure that everyone who will be impacted by a decision has input on it beforehand. Another "self-evident" principle to the U.S. mind is that individual career progress is desirable and "good." In some other cultures, however, managers resist competing with peers for rewards or promotions so as not to disturb the harmony of the group or appear self-interested.

Another example of potential conflict or misunderstanding can be seen in the case of orientation to authority, how people should handle power and authority relationships with others. The United States is a relatively young and mobile country, populated mostly by immigrants. Relative to other countries, there is little concern with family origin or class background. There is a belief that success should come through an individual's hard work and talent, not by birthright or class standing. This all leads to a relative informality at work, even among individuals of strikingly different position within a company. Subordinates expect their bosses to be accessible, even responsive in some

I do believe in the spiritual nature of human beings. To some it's a strange or outdated idea, but I believe there is such a thing as a human spirit. There is a spiritual dimension to man which should be nurtured.

Aung San Suu Kyi

ways to their subordinates. In some other cultures, however, higher status in a company confers nearly unchallengeable authority, and an expectation as well that most decisions will be referred *up* to them (as distinguished from delegated down to others). You can see even from these two examples that the seven dimensions of cultural values create quite an array of possible tensions between people from different cultures working together.

The Universality of Leadership Attributes

It is an interesting question whether the attributes of effective leaders are shared universally around the world, or whether different attributes of leadership are valued more in some cultures than in others. A very ambitious project known as the GLOBE research program is addressing that question. Its goal is to develop an empirically based theory of leadership to help predict the effectiveness of leader and organizational practices in different countries. The GLOBE program has been going on since 1993, collecting data from over 17,000 middle managers from 92 different countries. So far, the project has identified 21 specific attributes and behaviors that are viewed universally across cultures as contributing to leadership effectiveness (House et al., 1999). They are listed in Table 6.4. In addition, the project has identified eight characteristics that were universally viewed as impediments to leader effectiveness (see Table 6.5). And GLOBE has identified 35 leader characteristics that are viewed as positive in some cultures but negative in others (see Table 6.6).

TABLE 6.4
Leader Attributes and Behaviors Universally Viewed as Positive

Trustworthy	Positive	Intelligent
Just	Dynamic	Decisive
Honest	Motive arouser	Effective bargainer
Foresighted	Confidence builder	Win-win problem solver
Plans ahead	Motivational	Administratively skilled
Encouraging	Dependable	Communicative
Informed	Coordinator	Team builder
Excellence oriented		

Adapted from House et al., 1999, *Cultural Influences on Leadership and Organizations: Project Globe. Advances in Global Leadership*, Vol. 1, pp. 171–233. JAI Press Inc.

TABLE 6.5
Leader Attributes and Behaviors Universally Viewed as Negative

Loner	Nonexplicit
Asocial	Egocentric
Noncooperative	Ruthless
Irritable	Dictatorial

Adapted from House et al., 1999, *Cultural Influences on Leadership and Organizations: Project Globe. Advances in Global Leadership*, Vol. 1, pp. 171–233. JAI Press Inc.

TABLE 6.6
Examples of Leader Behaviors and Attributes That Are Culturally Contingent

Ambitious	Logical
Cautious	Orderly
Compassionate	Sincere
Domineering	Worldly
Independent	Formal
Individualistic	Sensitive

Adapted from House et al., 1999, *Cultural Influences on Leadership and Organizations: Project Globe. Advances in Global Leadership*, Vol. 1, pp. 171–233. JAI Press Inc.

Implications for Leadership Practitioners

The perspectives and findings presented in this chapter have significant implications for leadership practitioners. Perhaps most important, leadership practitioners should *expect* to face a variety of challenges to their own system of ethics, values, or attitudes during their careers. Additionally, values often are a source of interpersonal conflict. Although we sometimes say two people don't get along because of a personality conflict, often these conflicts are due to differences in value systems, not personality traits. Often, people on either side of an issue see *only* themselves and their own side as morally justifiable. Nonetheless, people holding seemingly antithetical values may still need to work together, and dealing with diverse and divergent values will be an increasingly common challenge for leaders. As noted earlier, interacting with individuals and groups holding divergent and conflicting values will be an inevitable fact of life for future leaders. This does not mean, however, that increased levels of interpersonal conflict are inevitable. Both leaders and followers might be well advised to minimize the conflict and tension often associated with value differences. Leaders in particular have a responsibility not to let their own personal values interfere with professional leader–subordinate relationships unless the conflicts pertain to issues clearly relevant to the work and the organization.

Summary

This chapter reviews evidence regarding the relationships between values and leadership. Values are constructs that represent general sets of behaviors or states of affairs that individuals consider to be important, and they are a central part of a leader's psychological makeup. Values impact leadership through a cultural context within which various attributes and behaviors are regarded differentially— positively or negatively.

Key Terms

ethics, *133*
Theory X, *133*
Theory Y, *133*
values, *134*
value programming, *135*
Veterans, *136*
Baby Boomers, *136*
GenXers, *136*
Nexters, *137*

principle-centered
leadership, *145*
moral justification, *148*
euphemistic labeling, *148*
advantageous
comparison, *148*
displacement of
responsibility, *148*

diffusion of
responsibility, *148*
distortion of
consequences, *148*
dehumanization, *149*
attribution of blame, *149*
Darley's law, *149*
culture, *151*

Questions

1. Do you think it always must be "lonely at the top" (or that if it is not, you are doing something wrong)?
2. How do you believe one's basic philosophy of human nature affects one's approach to leadership?
3. Identify several values you think might be the basis of conflict or misunderstanding between leaders and followers.
4. Can a leader's public and private morality be distinguished? Should they be?
5. Can a bad person be a good leader?
6. Are there any leadership roles men and women should not have equal opportunity to compete for?

Skills

Leadership skills relevant to this chapter include:

- Communication
- Listening
- Managing conflict
- Credibility

Activity

1. Each person should select his or her own 10 most important values from the following list, and then rank-order those 10 from most important (1) to least important (10). Then have an open discussion about how a person's approach to leadership might be influenced by having different "highest priority" values. The values are: Achievement, Activity (keeping busy), Advancement, Adventure, Aesthetics (appreciation of beauty), Affiliation, Affluence, Authority, Autonomy, Balance, Challenge, Change/Variety, Collaboration, Community, Competence, Competition, Courage, Creativity, Economic Security, Enjoyment, Fame, Family, Friendship, Happiness, Helping Others, Humor, Influence, Integrity, Justice, Knowledge, Location, Love, Loyalty, Order, Personal Development, Physical Fitness, Recognition, Reflection, Responsibility, Self-Respect, Spirituality, Status, Wisdom.

2. Explore how the experiences of different generations might have influenced the development of their values. Divide into several groups and assign each group the task of selecting representative popular music from a specific era. One group, for example, might have the 1950s, another the Vietnam War era, and another the 1990s. Using representative music from that era, highlight what seem to be dominant concerns, values, or views of life during that period.

Minicase

"Balancing Priorities at Clif Bar"

Gary Erickson is a man of integrity. In the spring of 2000 Erickson had an offer of more than $100 million from a major food corporation for his company Clif Bar, Inc. He had founded Clif Bar, Inc., in 1990 after a long bike ride. Erickson, an avid cyclist, had finished the 175-mile ride longing for an alternative to the tasteless energy bars he had brought along. "I couldn't make the last one go down, and that's when I had an epiphany—make a product that actually tasted good." He took a look at the list of ingredients on the package and decided he could do better. He called on his experience in his family's bakery and after a year in the kitchen, the Clif Bar—named for Erickson's father—was launched in 1992. Within five years sales had skyrocketed to $20 million. He considered the $100 million offer on the table and what it meant for his company and decided against the deal. He realized that the vision he had for the company would be compromised once he lost control, so he walked away from the $100 million deal.

He has stuck to his vision and values ever since. His commitment to environmental and social issues are evident in everything he does. On the environmental front, his company has a staff ecologist who is charged with working to reduce Clif Bar's ecological footprint on the planet. More than 70 percent of the ingredients in Clif Bars are organic. A change in packaging has saved the company (and the planet) 90,000 pounds of shrink-wrap a year. And the company funds a Sioux wind farm to offset the carbon dioxide emissions from its factories. On the social side, Erickson launched a project called the 2,080 program (2,080 is the total number of hours a full-time employee works in one year). Through the 2,080 program employees are encouraged to do volunteer work on company time. Recently Erickson agreed to support employees who wanted to volunteer in Third World countries with salaries and travel expenses.

Erickson is also committed to his team. He thinks about things like, "What should our company be like for the people who come to work each day?" He sees work as a living situation and strives to make Clif Bar, Inc.'s offices a fun place to be—there are plenty of bikes around; a gym and dance floor; personal trainers; massage and hair salon; a game room; an auditorium for meetings, movies, and music; dog days everyday; and great parties.

As the company grows, however, maintaining such values may not be easy. Clif Bar already has 130 employees, and revenue has been rising by more than 30 percent a year since 1998, according to Erickson. "We're at a point where we have to find a way to maintain this open culture while we may be getting bigger," says Shelley Martin, director of operations. "It's a balancing act."

1. Without knowing Gary Erickson's age, where would you guess he falls in the four generations of workers as delineated by Zemke?
2. Consider the key work values in Table 6.2. Recalling that leaders are motivated to act consistently with their values, what values appear to be most important to Gary Erickson? How does this compare to the leadership values profile for the Vice President of Product Development in Figure 6.3?

3. Clif Bar, Inc., possesses a definite set of organizational values. If you visit the company website (www.clifbar.com) you will see evidence of these values: "Fight Global Warming" and "Register to Vote" are just as prominent as information about the product. Knowing some of the values of Gary Erickson, how closely aligned do you think the organizational values are to the way the company actually operates?

Sources: http://www.fortune.com/fortune/smallbusiness/managing/articles/ 0,15114,487527,00.html; http://www.clipbar.com; July 2004, The Costco Connection, "Marathon Man," p. 19.

Chapter 7

Leadership Traits

Introduction

Powell's Rules for Picking People: Look for intelligence and judgment and, most critically, a capacity to anticipate, to see around corners. Also look for loyalty, integrity, a high energy drive, a balanced ego, and the drive to get things done.

Colin Powell

In Chapter 1 leadership was defined as "the process of influencing an organized group toward accomplishing its goals." Given this definition, one question that leadership researchers have tried to answer over the past 100 years is whether certain personal attributes or characteristics help or hinder the leadership process. In other words, does athletic ability, height, personality, intelligence, or creativity help a leader to influence a group? Put in the context of our three leaders, are Colin Powell, Aung San Suu Kyi, or Peter Jackson smarter, more creative, more ambitious, or more outgoing than their less successful counterparts? Do these three leaders act in fundamentally different ways than their followers, and are these differences in behavior due to differences in their innate intelligence, certain personality traits, or creative ability? If so, then could these same characteristics also be used to differentiate successful from unsuccessful leaders, executives from first-line supervisors, or leaders from individual contributors? It was questions like these that led to what was perhaps the earliest theory of leadership, the **Great Man theory** (Stogdill, 1974).

The roots of the Great Man theory can be traced back to the early 1900s, when many leadership researchers and the popular press maintained that leaders and followers were fundamentally different. This led to hundreds of research studies that looked at whether certain personality traits, physical attributes, intelligence, or personal values differentiated leaders from followers. Stogdill (1948) was the first leadership researcher to summarize the results of these studies, and he came to two major conclusions. First, leaders were not qualitatively different than followers; many followers were just as tall, smart, outgoing, and ambitious as the people who were leading them. Second, some characteristics, such as intelligence, initiative, stress tolerance, responsibility, friendliness, and dominance, were modestly related to leadership success. In other words, people who were smart, hardworking, conscientious, friendly, or willing to take charge were often more successful in influencing a group to accomplish its goals than people who were less smart, lazy, impulsive, grumpy, or did not like giving orders. Having "the right stuff" in and of itself was no guarantee of leadership success, but it did improve the odds of successfully influencing a group toward the accomplishment of its goals.

Subsequent reviews by Mann (1959) and Stogdill (1974) involving hundreds of more sophisticated studies came to the same two conclusions. Although these three reviews provided ample evidence that people with the right stuff were more likely to be successful as leaders, many leadership researchers focused solely on the point that leaders were not fundamentally different than followers. They erroneously concluded that personal characteristics could not be used to predict future leadership success; as a result most of the subsequent research shifted toward other leadership phenomena. It was not until the publication of seminal articles by Lord, DeVader, and Allinger (1986) and Hogan, Curphy, and Hogan (1994) that intelligence and personality regained popularity with leadership researchers. Because of these two articles and subsequent leadership research, we now know a lot about how intelligence and various personality traits help or hinder leaders in their efforts to influence others. This research also provided insight on the role that various situational and follower characteristics have in affecting how a leader's intelligence and personality play out in the workplace. The purpose of this chapter is to summarize what we currently know about personality, intelligence, and leadership. As an overview, this chapter defines personality, intelligence, creativity, and emotional intelligence, reviews some of the key research findings for these concepts, and discusses the implications of this research for leadership practitioners.

Personality Traits and Leadership

What Is Personality?

There is an optical illusion about every person we ever meet. In truth, they are all creatures of a given temperament, which will appear in a given character, whose boundaries they will never pass: but we look at them, they seem alive, and we presume there is impulse in them. In the moment, it seems like an impulse, in the year, in the lifetime, it turns out to be a certain uniform tune, which the revolving barrel of the music box must play.

Ralph Waldo Emerson

Despite its common usage, Robert Hogan (1991) noted that the term **personality** is fairly ambiguous, and has at least two quite different meanings. One meaning refers to the impression a person makes on others. This view of personality emphasizes a person's *social reputation* and reflects not only a description but also an evaluation of the person in the eyes of others. From the standpoint of leadership, this view of personality addresses two distinct issues: "What kind of leader or person is this?" and "Is this somebody I would like to work for or be associated with?" In a practical sense, this view of personality comes into play whenever you describe the person you work for to a roommate or friend. For example, you might describe him or her as pushy, honest, outgoing, impulsive, decisive, friendly, and independent. Furthermore, whatever impression this leader made on you, chances are others would use many of the same terms of description. In that same vein, many people would probably say that Colin Powell is self-confident, friendly, conventional, outgoing, and achievement-oriented, and that he handles pressure well.

The second meaning of personality emphasizes the underlying, unseen structures and processes inside a person that explain why we behave the way we do; why each person's behavior tends to be relatively *similar across different situations,* yet also *different from another person's behavior.* Over the years psychologists have developed many theories to explain how such unseen structures may cause individuals to act in their characteristic manner. For example, Sigmund Freud (1913) believed that the intrapsychic tensions among the id, ego, and superego caused one to behave in characteristic ways even if the real motives behind the behaviors were unknown (i.e., unconscious) to the person. Although useful insights about personality have come from many different theories, most of the research addressing the relationship between personality and leadership success has been based on the **trait approach,** and that emphasis is most appropriate here.

"**Traits** refer to recurring regularities or trends in a person's behavior" (R. Hogan, 1991, p. 875), and the trait approach to personality maintains that people behave the way they do because of the strengths of the traits they possess. Although traits cannot be seen, they can be inferred from consistent patterns of behavior and reliably measured by personality inventories. For example, the personality trait of dependability differentiates leaders who tend to be hardworking and rule abiding from those who do not like to work hard and are more prone to break rules. Leaders getting higher scores on the trait of dependability on a personality inventory would be more likely to come to work on time, do a thorough job in completing work assignments, and rarely leave work early. We would also infer that leaders getting lower scores on the trait of dependability would be late to work more often, make impulsive decisions, or fail to follow through with commitments.

Personality traits are useful concepts for explaining why people act fairly consistently from one situation to the next. This cross-situational consistency in behavior may be thought of as analogous to the seasonal weather patterns in different cities (Hogan, Hogan, & Roberts, 1996; Roberts, 1996). We know that it is extremely cold and dry in Minneapolis in January, and hot and humid in Hong Kong in August. Therefore, we can do a pretty good job predicting what the weather will generally be like in Minneapolis in January, even though our predictions for any particular day will not be perfect. Although the average temperature in Minneapolis hovers around 20°F, the temperature ranges from −30°F to 30°F on any single day in January. Similarly, knowing how two people differ on a particular personality trait can help us predict more accurately how they will tend to act in a variety of situations.

Just as various climate factors can affect the temperature on any single day, so can external factors affect a leader's behavior in any given situation. The trait approach maintains that a leader's behavior reflects an interaction between his or her personality traits and various situational factors (see, for example, Highlight 7.1.) Traits play a particularly important role in determining how people behave in unfamiliar, ambiguous, or what we might call **weak situations.** On the other hand, situations that are governed by clearly specified rules, demands, or organizational policies—**strong situations**—often minimize the effects traits have on behavior (Curphy, 1997a, c, 1996b; Hogan & Holland, 2003; Tett & Burnett, 2003).

The strength of the relationship between personality traits and leadership effectiveness relationship is often inversely related to the relative strength of the situation (i.e., personality traits are more closely related to leadership effectiveness in weak situations). Given the accelerated pace of change in most organizations today, it is likely that leaders will be facing even more unfamiliar and ambiguous situations in the future. Therefore, personality traits may play an increasingly important role in a leader's behavior. If organizations can accurately identify those personality traits and the individuals who possess them, then they should be able to do a better job promoting the right people into leadership positions. And if the right people are in leadership positions, the odds of achieving organizational success should be dramatically improved. The next section describes some of the

Personality and the Presidency

Highlight 7.1

Traits are unseen dispositions that can affect the way people act. Their existence can be inferred by a leader's consistent pattern of behaviors. One way of examining a leader's standing on the trait of achievement orientation is to examine one's achievements and accomplishments over the life span. Leaders with higher levels of achievement orientation tend to set high personal goals and are persistent in the pursuit of these goals. When considering the following leader's achievements and accomplishments, think about this person's standing on this personality trait, and try to guess who this person might be:

Age 23: lost a job.

Age 23: was defeated in bid for state legislature.

Age 24: failed in business venture.

Age 25: was elected to legislature.

Age 26: sweetheart died.

Age 27: experienced several emotional problems.

Age 27: was defeated in bid to be speaker of the house.

Age 34: was defeated for nomination to Congress.

Age 37: was elected to Congress.

Age 39: lost renomination to Congress.

Age 40: was defeated in bid for land office.

Age 45: was defeated in bid for U.S. Senate.

Age 47: was defeated for nomination to be vice president.

Age 49: was defeated in bid for Senate a second time.

Age 51: was elected president of the United States.

The person was Abraham Lincoln.

efforts researchers have taken to identify those personality traits related to leadership effectiveness.

The Five Factor Model of Personality: The Bright Side of Personality

Although personality traits provide a useful approach to describing distinctive, cross-situational behavioral patterns, one potential problem is the sheer number of traitlike terms available to describe another's stereotypical behaviors. As early as 1936 Allport and Odbert identified over 18,000 trait-related adjectives in a standard English dictionary. Despite this large number of adjectives, research has shown that most of the traitlike terms people use to describe others' behavioral patterns could be reliably categorized into five broad personality dimensions. Historically, this five-dimension model was first identified by Webb in 1915 (Deary, 1996) and independently verified by Thurstone (1934), but over the years a number of researchers using very diverse samples and assessment instruments have noted similar results (see Hogan, Curphy, & Hogan, 1994). Given the robustness of the findings, there appears to be a compelling body of evidence to support these five dimensions of personality. These dimensions are referred to in the personality literature as the **Five Factor Model (FFM) of personality,** and most modern personality researchers endorse some version of this model (Azar, 1995; Barrick & Mount, 1996; Curphy, 1998b; Hogan, 1991; Costo & McCrae, 1992, 1995; Hogan, Hogan, & Roberts, 1996; Barrick, 1999; Quirk & Fondt, 2000; Curphy, 2003c).

At its core, the FFM of personality is a categorization scheme. Most, if not all, of the personality traits that you would use to describe someone else could be reliably categorized into one of the FFM personality dimensions. A description of the model can be found in Table 7.1. The five major dimensions include surgency, dependability, agreeableness, adjustment, and intellectance. Perhaps the easiest way to understand this categorization scheme is to describe how our three world leaders would fall into each of the FFM categories.

Rule 13: When put into a position of command, take charge.
Norman Schwarzkopf

Surgency (also referred to as dominance, self-confidence, the need for power, or dynamic) involves patterns of behavior often exhibited in group settings and generally concerned with getting ahead in life (Michel & Hogan 1996; Hogan, 2000; Hogan & Holland, 2003; Curphy, 2003c). Such behavioral patterns often appear when someone is trying to influence or control others. Individuals higher in surgency are outgoing, competitive, decisive, impactful, and self-confident. Individuals lower in surgency prefer to work by themselves and have relatively little interest in influencing or competing with others.

Because leaders' decisiveness, competitiveness, and self-confidence can affect their ability to successfully influence a group, it is not surprising that leaders often have higher surgency scores than nonleaders (Barrick, 1999; Hurtz & Donovan, 2000; Judge, Bono, Ilies, & Gerhardt, 2002; Hogan & Holland, 2003; Salgado, 2003). Given the behaviors associated with surgency, it is likely that our three world leaders would have higher surgency scores than most other people. More specifically, all three leaders appear to be driven, resourceful, goal oriented, and like influencing others, and as such they would all receive high scores on the Ambition dimension of Surgency. For example, Peter Jackson's debut feature, *Bad Taste,* was an illustration of dogged perseverance. There was no budget for the

TABLE 7.1
The Five
Factor Model
of Personality

Five Factor Dimensions	Hogan Personality Inventory Dimensions	Behaviors/Items
Surgency	Ambition	I like having responsibility for others.
	Sociability	I have a large group of friends.
Agreeableness	Interpersonal sensitivity	I am a sympathetic person.
Dependability	Prudence	I usually make "to do" lists. I practice what I preach. I rarely get into trouble.
Adjustment	Adjustment	I remain calm in pressure situations. I take personal criticism well.
Openness to Experience	Inquisitive	I like traveling to foreign countries.
	Learning Approach	I like staying up to speed on certain topics.

film; he paid for it all himself from his salary as a photo engraver. He had no equipment with which to make the film, so he bought a camera and built the rest himself. He had no cast or crew, but his friends volunteered, for a laugh. But the Sociability scores for our three leaders would vary dramatically. Peter Jackson and Aung San Suu Kyi do not have a high need to be around others. They can speak out on issues when necessary, but tend to work behind the scenes and avoid the limelight. Colin Powell, on the other hand, likes crowds and enjoys being the center of attention. He would likely have a much higher Sociability score than our other two key leaders.

Another FFM personality dimension is **agreeableness** (also known as empathy, friendliness, interpersonal sensitivity, or the need for affiliation). This personality dimension concerns how one gets along with, as opposed to getting ahead of, others (Hogan, 2000; Hogan & Holland, 2003; Curphy, 2003c). Individuals high in agreeableness tend to be empathetic, approachable, and optimistic; those lower in agreeableness are more apt to appear insensitive, distant, and pessimistic.

> *If you need a friend in Washington, get a dog.*
>
> Harry Truman

Because teamwork and cooperation are important components of group functioning, it should not be surprising that leaders often have higher agreeableness scores than people in individual contributor roles (Barrick, 1999; Sandal, Endressen, Vaernes, & Ursin, 1999; W. H, Burke, Barrett, & Mount, 2002; Hogan & Holland, 2003; Salgado, 2003). Chances are that all three of our key leaders have fairly high agreeableness scores—all project warm, down-to-earth, and approachable images and appear to be genuinely concerned about others.

> *Rule 14: When put into a position of command, do what is right.*
>
> Norman Schwarzkopf

Level 5 Leadership

Highlight 7.2

Over the past 20 years, some private corporations, such as Coca-Cola, General Electric, British Petroleum, IBM, and Wal-Mart, have performed very well. People who invested $10,000 in these companies would have seen their investments increase four- to tenfold over this time. But there are some companies that outperformed even these high fliers. Jim Collins and his staff examined all the companies that appeared on the *Fortune* 500 list from 1965 to 1995 and found 11 companies that dramatically beat all the others in terms of returns. One critical component of this tremendous financial success was **Level 5 Leadership.** According to Collins, all of these companies were led by leaders who had a unique combination of humility and will. As Collins says, Abraham Lincoln never let his ego get in the way of his dream of building a great, enduring nation. Similarly, these corporate leaders did not let their egos get in the way of building great companies. These leaders avoided the spotlight (low Sociability scores), but they were very focused on creating a company that delivered outstanding results (high Ambition scores). They also possessed an unbreakable resolve that channeled all of their energy toward the success of their companies, as opposed to the pursuit of ever grander personal titles. All of these leaders were calm in crises,

were never boastful and took responsibility for failure (high Adjustment scores), and were courteous and polite (high Agreeableness). These leaders set the tone for their respective organizations and spent a considerable amount of time surrounding themselves with the right people and building high performing teams. As a result, these companies returned $471 for every dollar invested in 1965.

It is worth noting that Level 5 Leaders act quite differently from stereotypical corporate executives. Back in the late 1990s senior executives would do all they could to get on television, and many of these charismatic leaders seemed more interested in personal aggrandizement than company success (e.g., Dennis Kozlowski, John Rigas, Jeffrey Skilling, or Bernie Ebbers). Unfortunately, it appears that many Boards of Directors have not paid attention to the key lessons of Collins's book, as they continue to look for charismatic rather than Level 5 CEOs to run their organizations.

Sources: J. Collins, *Good to Great* (New York: Harper Collins, 2001); R. Khurana, "The Curse of the Superstar CEO," *Harvard Business Review,* September, 2002, pp. 60–67; J. A. Sonnenfeld and R. Khurana, "Fishing for CEOs in Your Own Backyard," *The Wall Street Journal,* July 30, 2002, p. B2; R. S. Peterson, D. B. Smith, P. V. Martorana, and P. D. Owens, "The Impact of Chief Executive Officer Personality on Top Management Team Dynamics: One Mechanism by Which Leadership Affects Organizational Performance," *Journal of Applied Psychology,* 88 (5), 2003, pp. 795–808.

Dependability (also known as conscientiousness or prudence) does not involve interacting with others but rather concerns those behavioral patterns related to one's approach to work. Leaders who are higher in dependability tend to be planful and hardworking, follow through with their commitments, and rarely get into trouble. Those who are lower in dependability tend to be more spontaneous, creative, and rule bending, and less concerned with following through with commitments. Like surgency and agreeableness, research shows that individuals with higher dependability scores are more likely to be effective leaders than those with lower scores (Judge, Bono, Ilies, & Gerhardt, 2002; Hogan & Holland, 2003; Salgado, 2003).

In many ways dependability may be more concerned with management than leadership tendencies. Although leaders with higher scores are planful, organized, goal oriented, and prefer structure, they also tend to be risk averse, uncreative, somewhat boring, and dislike change. Again, the situation will determine whether these tendencies can help or hinder a leader's ability to influence a group toward the accomplishment of its goals. For our three world leaders, Colin Powell would likely have the highest dependability scores; Peter Jackson and Aung San Suu Kyi might have somehat lower scores.

Adjustment (also known as emotional stability or self-control) is concerned with how people react to stress, failure, or personal criticism. Leaders higher in adjustment tend to be calm and tend not to take mistakes or failures personally, whereas those lower in adjustment may become tense, anxious, or exhibit emotional outbursts when stressed or criticized.

Followers often mimic a leader's emotions or behaviors under periods of high stress, so leaders who are calm under pressure and thick-skinned can often help a group stay on task and work through difficult issues. Unfortunately, the opposite is also true. With her calm demeanor and high stress tolerance, Aung San Suu Kyi would probably have the highest adjustment scores of our three world leaders. Colin Powell would also have fairly high scores. Peter Jackson is more emotionally expressive and would likely have lower than average adjustment scores.

Those behavioral patterns dealing with how one approaches problems, learns new information, and reacts to new experiences are related to the personality dimension of **openness to experience** (also known as intellectance, curiosity, inquisitiveness, and learning approach). Leaders higher in openness to experience tend to be imaginative, broad-minded, curious, and are more strategic, big-picture thinkers; they seek out new experiences through travel, the arts, movies, sports, reading, going to new restaurants, or learning about new cultures. Individuals lower in openness to experience tend to be more practical and have narrower interests; they like doing things the tried-and-true way rather than experimenting with new ways. It is important to note that openness to experience is not the same thing as intelligence—smart people are not necessarily intellectually curious. Our three world leaders all appear to be open to new experiences and intellectually curious. All are well traveled, have a broad set of interests, and are more strategic, big-picture thinkers; therefore, they would all have higher than average openness to experience scores.

Like the other FFM dimensions, research has shown that openness to experience is an important component of leadership effectiveness (Judge, Bono, Ilies, & Gerhardt, 2002; Hogan & Holland, 2003; Leivens, Harris, Van Keer, & Bisqueret, 2003; Salgado, 2003). Openness to experience seems particularly important at higher organizational levels or for overseas assignments. For example, people with higher openness to experience scores like to take a more strategic approach to solving problems. These higher scores help business unit leaders and CEOs to keep abreast of market trends, competitive threats, new products, and regulatory changes. And because people with higher openness to experience scores also like new and novel experiences, they often enjoy the challenges associated with living and leading in foreign countries.

Some people are just more excitable than others.

Kozmo Kramer, *Seinfeld*

I knew a college professor that was in the same job for 37 years. What do you think this guy's threshold for stimulation is?

David Campbell
The Center for Creative Leadership

Implications of the Five Factor Model

The trait approach and the FFM provide leadership researchers and practitioners with several useful tools and insights. For one, personality traits provide researchers and practitioners with an explanation for leaders' and followers' tendencies to act in consistent ways over time. They help us to understand why some leaders are dominant versus deferent, outspoken versus quiet, planful versus spontaneous, warm versus cold, and so forth. It is also important to note that the behavioral manifestations of personality traits are often exhibited automatically and without much conscious thought. People high in surgency, for example, will often maneuver to influence or lead whatever groups or teams they are a part of without even thinking about it. Although personality traits predispose us to act in certain ways, we can nonetheless learn to modify our behaviors through experience, feedback, and reflection.

As seen in Figure 7.1, personality traits are one of the key components of behavior and are relatively difficult to change. Moreover, because personality traits tend to be stable over the years and the behavioral manifestations of traits occur somewhat automatically, it is extremely important for leaders, and leaders to be, to have insight into their personalities. For example, consider a leader who is relatively low in the trait of adjustment, but also is deciding whether to accept a high-stress/high-visibility job. On the basis of his personality trait scores alone, we might predict that this leader could be especially sensitive to criticism, and could be moody and prone to emotional outbursts. If the leader understood that he may have issues dealing with stress and criticism, then he could choose not to take the position, modify the situation to reduce the level of stress, or learn techniques for effectively dealing with these issues. A leader who lacked this self-insight would probably make poorer choices and have more difficulties coping with the demands of this position (Curphy, 1996a).

The FFM has proved to be very useful in several different ways. It is fairly robust, and most personality researchers currently embrace some form of the Big Five model (Azar, 1995; Barrick, 1999; Mount, Barrick, & Strauss, 1994; Barrick & Mount, 1996; Curphy, 1998b; Hogan, Hogan, & Roberts, 1996; Howard & Howard, 1995; Hurtz & Donovan, 2000; Judge, Bono, Ilies, & Gerhardt, 2002; Hogan & Holland, 2003; Tett & Burnett, 2003; Salgado, 2003). Furthermore, the model has proved to be a very useful scheme for categorizing the findings of the personality-leadership performance research. Because of the results of this research, organiza-

FIGURE 7.1
The building blocks of skills.

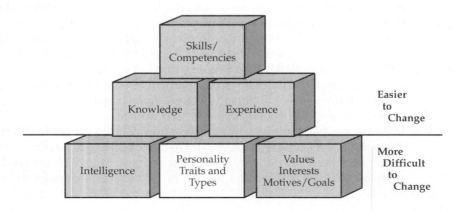

tions now use the results of FFM personality assessments for hiring new leaders, providing leaders with developmental feedback about various personality traits, and as a key component in succession planning processes to promote leaders.

Another advantage of the FFM is that it is a useful method for profiling leaders. For example, a business unit leader's results on a FFM personality assessment, the Hogan Personality Inventory (Hogan & Hogan, 2002) can be found in Figure 7.2. According to this profile, this leader will generally come across to others as optimistic, resilient, and calm under pressure (high Adjustment); self-confident, goal oriented, and competitive (high Ambition); outgoing, liking to be the center of attention, but also distractible and a poor listener (high Sociability); diplomatic and charming, but will have trouble dealing with performance problems (high Interpersonal Sensitivity); planful and rule abiding (high Prudence); a strategic, big-picture thinker (high Inquistive); but who prefers to learn using a just-in-time, hands-on approach as opposed to sitting in a classroom setting. Other leaders will have different behavioral tendencies, and knowing this type of information *before* someone gets hired or promoted into a leadership position can help improve the odds of organizational success.

When aggregated, these individual personality profiles can yield some interesting results. For example, Mumford, Zaccaro, Johnson, Diana, Gilbert, and Threlfall (2000) reported that a unique set of personality traits differentiated senior leaders in operational units compared with those in staff functions in the U.S. Army. Heckman and Roberts (1997) showed that engineers and accountants tended to be lower in the trait of surgency but higher in the trait of dependability. On the other hand, marketing and sales place a premium on creativity and on influencing others, and people in these occupations tended to be higher in surgency but lower in dependability. There is a compelling body of evidence showing that surgency, agreeableness, dependability, adjustment, and openness to experience are all positively correlated with leadership success—the higher the scores on these five FFM dimensions, the more likely an individual will be an effective leader (Curphy, 2001, 2003c, 2004e; Hogan, Curphy, & Hogan, 1994; Barrick, 1999; Quirk & Fandt, 2000;

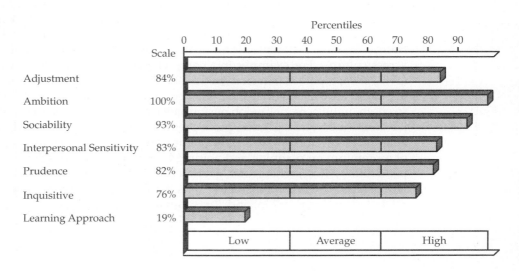

FIGURE 7.2

Leadership potential profile.

Source: Adapted with permission from Hogan Assessment Systems.

Hurtz & Donovan, 2000; Judge, Higgens, Thoresen, & Barrick, 1999; Judge, Bono, Ilies, & Gerhardt, 2002; Hogan & Holland, 2003; Tett & Burnett, 2003; Salgado, 2003). Some of this research also showed that surgency is the best predictor of a leadership job offer after an interview and successful completion of an overseas leadership assignment (Caldwell & Burger, 1998; Caliguiri, 2000). Agreeableness and openness to experience are also key factors in completing overseas leadership assignments and working in tightly confined team situations, such as submarine crews (Sandal, Endressen, Vaernes, & Ursin, 1999; Lievens, Harris, Van Keer & Bisqueret, 2003). Dependability is related to the amount of time people take to prepare for an interview and their overall job performance and satisfaction; lower scores increase their likelihood of engaging in counterproductive work behaviors (Barrick, 1999; Caldwell & Burger, 1998; Hurtz & Donovan, 2000; Sarchione, Cuttler, Muchinsky, & Nelson-Grey, 1998; Judge, Heller, & Mount, 2002; Barrick & Mount, 1996; Barrick, 1999). Higher adjustment scores also helped leaders to complete an overseas assignment, successfully cope with change, and report positive earnings per share after an initial public offering (Judge, Thoresen, Pucik, & Welbourne, 1999; Welbourne & Cyr, 1999). In a similar vein, Blake (1996) reported some interesting findings for military cadets who were higher in agreeableness and surgency. His research indicated that higher agreeableness was positively related to performance ratings during the freshman and sophomore years but that higher surgency was more strongly related to performance ratings over the last two years at the U.S. Coast Guard Academy. Apparently getting along with others and developing strong social supports are very important during the first two years of a military cadet's life, but getting ahead becomes more important over the last two years. It may be that it takes a couple of years to develop strong social networks and supports, and once they have been established, other personality traits, such as surgency, become more important.

Another advantage of the Five Factor Model is that it appears universally applicable across cultures (Curphy, 1997a, 1996b; Hogan, Hogan, & Roberts, 1996; Schmidt, Kihm, & Robie, 2000; Salgado, 1997, 2003c). People from Asian, Western European, Middle Eastern, Eastern European, or South American cultures seem to use the same five personality dimensions to categorize, profile, or describe others.

Not only do people from different cultures describe others using the same FFM framework, these dimensions all seem to predict job and leadership performance across cultures. For example, in a comprehensive review of the research, Salgado (1997, 2003) reported that all five of the FFM dimensions predicted blue collar, professional, and managerial performance in various European countries. But the strength of the personality-job performance relationship depends on the particular job. Some jobs, such as sales, put a premium on interpersonal skills and goal orientation (e.g., surgency and agreeableness); whereas manufacturing jobs put more of a premium on planning and abiding by safety and productivity rules (e.g., dependability). Researchers often get much stronger personality-job performance relationships when the personality traits being measured have some degree of job relatedness (Hogan & Holland, 2003; Tett & Burnett, 2003).

Can Offices and Bedrooms Be Used to Predict Personality Traits?

Highlight 7.3

As described in this chapter, personality traits are fairly well ingrained and their associated behaviors almost automatic. We usually make estimates of others' personality traits based on our interactions with them. But is it possible to make accurate predictions of others' personality traits based on the way in which they organize and decorate their personal space? Azar (2002) describes a study where seven to eight raters made predictions of others' FFM dimension scores based solely on inspections of their offices or bedrooms. Approximately 140 offices and bedrooms were inspected, and the occupants of these rooms also completed an FFM personality assessment. The researchers found that the inspectors were very good

at predicting occupants' dependability and openness to experience FFM dimension scores. Some offices and bedrooms were neat and tidy; others were messy (the dependability dimension). Some had collections of art from strange and exotic lands; others were strictly functional in nature (e.g., openness to experience dimension). But other FFM dimension scores, such as adjustment and surgency, were much more difficult to predict based on environmental scanning and seem to depend more on interpersonal interactions with others. So the next time you visit a professor's office, see if you can predict his or her dependability and openness to experience scores. Chances are you will be pretty close to getting it right.

Source: B. Azar, "Does Your Office Betray Your Personality?" *Monitor on Psychology,* March 2002, pp. 26–27.

In summary, there are several things we can say about the bright side of personality. First, people tend to describe others using traitlike terms, and personality traits can be reliably categorized into the five major dimensions of the FFM. Second, personality traits can be reliably assessed, and these assessments can be used to make predictions about how people will typically behave at work. Third, there is an overwhelming body of research that shows all five of the FFM dimensions are related to leadership success across different cultures. However, the strength of the personality-leadership performance relationships will depend on the particular demands of the situation and the job. Fourth, personality tends to be difficult to change—people are "hard wired" to exhibit those behaviors associated with their personality traits. Fifth, all behavior is under conscious control. We may more or less have an automatic response to stress based on our adjustment scores, but we can choose to act differently if we want to. But it does take conscious effort to exhibit nontrait behaviors. Sixth, having insight into one's personality traits can give people information about their potential leadership strengths and development needs and how much effort they will have to put forth to overcome these needs.

Why Do Some Leaders Fail?
The Dark Side of Personality

One of the more provocative ideas in the recent leadership literature concerns the base rate of **managerial incompetence.** Hogan and Hogan, (2001), Curphy (2003a, b; 2004 a, e), Curphy and Hogan (2004 a, b) and Hogan and Curphy (2004) maintain that approximately 50 percent of the

Managerial failure may be due more to having undesirable qualities than lacking desirable ones.

Bob and Joyce Hogan
Hogan Assessment
Systems

persons in leadership positions may be incompetent. This means that half of these individuals are unable to build the cohesive, goal-oriented teams needed to get long-term results through others. Some people in leadership positions seem able to get results without building a team, but these results are typically very short-term. Others seem more focused on playing the role of a cheerleader and are able to build cohesive teams, but these teams often do not get much accomplished.

Many of you might think that the base rate is actually closer to 5–7 percent—companies or organizations could not be successful with such a high level of incompetence among the management ranks. But a simple test of managerial incompetence might help shed some light on the matter. Count up the number of people you have ever worked for. These individuals might be former teachers, volunteer group leaders, coaches, supervisors, etc. Of these former bosses, how

---

I did not have sexual relations with that woman.

Bill Clinton

---

many of them would you work or play for again? If you are like many of the other people who have answered this question, then the chances are you need less than one hand to count the number of former bosses you would work for again. Curphy and Hogan (2004a) state there are several reasons for this high level of incompetence, some of which include invalid selection and succession planning systems (see Chapter 4), ill-defined performance expectations (see Chapter 9), and poorly designed leadership development programs (see Chapter 3). But **dark-side personality traits** are some of the other key reasons for the high failure rate of leaders. Dark-side personality traits are irritating, counterproductive behavioral tendencies that interfere with a leader's ability to build cohesive teams and cause followers to exert less effort toward goal accomplishment (Hogan & Hogan, 2001; Dotlich & Cairo, 2003). A listing of 11 common dark-side traits can be found in Table 7.2. Any of these 11 tendencies, if exhibited on a regular basis, will negatively affect the leader's ability to get results through others. And if you examined the reasons why those former bosses did not make your short list of leaders you would like to work for again, then it is very likely that these incompetent leaders possessed one or more of these 11 dark-side personality traits.

There are several aspects of dark-side personality traits that are worth noting. First, everyone has at least one dark-side personality trait. Figure 7.3 shows a graphic output from a typical dark-side personality measure, and indicates that this individual has strong leisurely and diligent tendencies and moderate cautious and dutiful tendencies (scores above the 90th percentile indicate a high risk and 70–89th percentile indicate a moderate risk of dark-side tendencies). Second, these dark-side traits have a bigger influence on performance for people in leadership versus followership roles. An individual contributor might have leisurely or cautious tendencies, but because they do not have to get work done through others these tendencies have less of an impact on their work units than if these same individuals were first-line supervisors or business unit leaders. Let there be no doubt that these individual contributors may not be fun to work with, but their counterproductive tendencies will not be as debilitating to their teams as they would if these people were leading their teams. Third, the dark-side traits are usually only apparent when leaders are not attending to their public image. In other words, people will not see the behaviors associated with dark-side traits when leaders are

TABLE 7.2
Dark-Side
Personality
Traits

Source: Hogan
Assessment
Systems, *The Hogan
Development Survey*
(Tulsa, OK. 2002).

Excitable	Leaders with these tendencies have difficulties building teams because of their dramatic mood swings, emotional outbursts, and inability to persist on projects.
Skeptical	Leaders with this dark-side trait have an unhealthy mistrust of others, are constantly questioning the motives and challenging the integrity of their followers, and are vigilant for signs of disloyalty.
Cautious	Because these leaders are so fearful of making "dumb" mistakes, they alienate their staffs by not making decisions or taking action on issues.
Reserved	During times of stress these leaders become extremely withdrawn, are uncommunicative, difficult to find, and unconcerned about the welfare of their staffs.
Leisurely	These passive-aggressive leaders will only exert effort in the pursuit of their own agendas and will procrastinate or not follow through with requests that are not in line with their agendas.
Bold	Because of their narcissistic tendencies, these leaders often get quite a bit done. But their feelings of entitlement, inability to share credit for success, tendency to blame their mistakes on others, and inability to learn from experience often results in trails of bruised followers.
Mischievous	These leaders tend to be quite charming but take pleasure in seeing if they can get away with breaking commitments, rules, policies, and laws. When caught, they also believe they can talk their way out of any problem.
Colorful	Leaders with this tendency believe they are "hot" and have an unhealthy need to be the center of attention. They are so preoccupied with being noticed that they are unable to share credit, maintain focus, or get much done.
Imaginative	Followers question the judgment of leaders with this tendency, as these leaders think in eccentric ways, often changing their minds, and make strange or odd decisions.
Diligent	Because of their perfectionistic tendencies, these leaders frustrate and disempower their staffs through micro-management, poor prioritization, and an inability to delegate.
Dutiful	These leaders deal with stress by sucking up to superiors. They lack spines, are unwilling to refuse unrealistic requests, won't stand up for their staffs, and burn them out as a result.

concerned with how they are coming across to others. These tendencies are much more likely to appear under times of stress, when multitasking or focusing on task accomplishment, during crises, or when leaders feel comfortable enough around others to "let their guard down" (Hogan & Hogan, 2001; Dotlich & Cairo, 2003; Curphy, 2003c; Hogan & Curphy, 2004). And given the high level of stress, challenge, and complexity associated with most leadership positions, the conditions are ripe for the appearance of dark-side traits.

Fourth, many dark-side traits co-vary with social skills and are difficult to detect in interviews, assessment centers, or with bright-side personality inventories (Hogan & Curphy, 2004; Curphy & Hogan, 2004a; Hogan & Hogan, 2001; Dotlich

FIGURE 7.3

Leadership
challenge
profile.

Source: Adapted
with permission
from Hogan
Assessment
Systems.

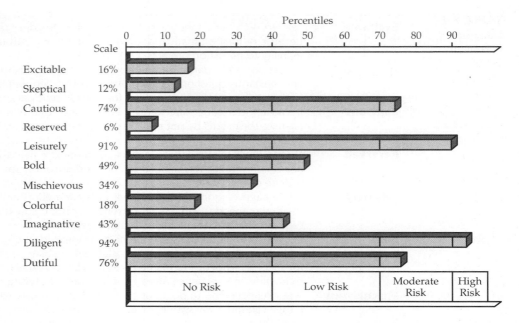

& Cairo, 2003; Brinkmeyer & Hogan, 1997; Brown, 1977; Curphy, 1997d; Curphy, Gibson, Asiu, Horn, & Macomber, 1994; Hogan, Curphy, & Hogan, 1994; McDaniel, 1999; Rybicki & Klippel, 1997). Fifth, the 11 dark-side personality traits are related to extreme FFM scores. For example, diligent is often associated with extremely high dependability scores, and excitable is associated with extremely low adjustment scores. However, just because a person has an extremely high or low FFM dimension score does not necessarily mean they also possess the corresponding dark-side personality traits. But there are strong relationships between the FFM and the dark-side personality traits (Hogan & Hogan, 2001; Curphy 2003c). Sixth, the behaviors associated with dark-side personality traits can occur at any leadership level, and many times organizations tolerate these behaviors because the leader is smart, experienced, or possesses unique skills (see Highlight 7.4). Along these lines, persons with bold tendencies are particularly adept at moving up in organizations. Nothing ever got launched without a healthy dose of narcissism, and leaders with bold tendencies are quick to volunteer for new assignments, take on seemingly impossible challenges, and consistently underestimate the amount of time, money, and effort it will take to get a job accomplished. In some cases these leaders pull out the seemingly impossible and get promoted because of their accomplishments. But when things go south (which they often do), these same leaders are quick to blame the situation or others for their failures, and as a result never learn from their mistakes (Hogan & Curphy, 2004; Curphy & Hogan, 2004a; Kramer, 2003; Lubit, 2002; Dotlich & Cairo, 2003; Hogan & Hogan, 2001).

So if virtually everyone has dark-side personality tendencies, what can he or she do about them? First and foremost, leaders and leaders to be need to identify their dark-side personality traits. This can be done by asking trusted others about how

An Example of Dark-Side Personality Traits

Highlight 7.4

The subject in this case is a CEO of a $2 billion book publishing company who was dismissed as part of a corporate buyout. The individual started his career with the company as a book salesman over 30 years ago and reigned as the CEO for over 15 years. His leadership credo was "business is conflict. . . You don't get excellence by saying yes. You get love, but you don't get excellence. This company has raised the hurdles of excellence every bloody day."

According to his staff, the subject ruled by intimidation and fear. His profane harangues were an industry legend. Scores of former employees tell of meetings at which he publicly threatened to lop off people's hands or private body parts or tear out their throats for failure to perform. Whenever something went wrong or a goal wasn't achieved, the subject always saw it as a personal matter rather than the result of the business situation. As a result, the subject always placed personal blame for failure and the staff quickly

learned not to come forward with problems. He rarely went through a single meeting without going after someone, and people saw his use of degradation and humiliation as a way of controlling his staff.

Many of his staff saw the buyout as the only way to get rid of the CEO. He had been in place for over 15 years and played a key role in making the company a multibillion-dollar organization. Nevertheless, after the buyout the parent organization faced the specter of mass resignations if the subject was allowed to remain as CEO. As a result of the discontent of his staff, the CEO was asked to resign. Unfortunately, even to this day the CEO has no idea why he was let go, and seems genuinely despondent over the decision. When confronted with stories of abuse and intimidation, he either denies that they ever took place or claims that they were blown all out of proportion.

Source: R. T. Hogan, G. J. Curphy, and J. Hogan, "What Do We Know about Leadership: Effectiveness and Personality," *American Psychologist* 49 (1994) pp. 493–504.

one acts under pressure or what behaviors interfere with their ability to build teams, or by completing a dark-side personality assessment. Once these counterproductive tendencies are identified, leaders then need to understand the situations or conditions in which these tendencies are likely to appear. Again, dark-side traits are most likely to appear during times of stress and heavy workload, so finding ways to better manage stress and workload will help reduce the likelihood of these dark-side tendencies. Just being aware of one's dark-side tendencies and understanding the circumstances in which they appear will go a long way toward controlling the manifestation of counterproductive leadership behaviors. Exercise and other stress reduction techniques, and having trusted followers who can tell leaders when they are exhibiting dark-side traits, can also help control these tendencies. Finally, having higher scores on the FFM dimension of adjustment also helps with some of these dimensions, as these leaders seem to be better able to cope with stress than those with low scores (Curphy, 2003a, c).

Intelligence and Leadership

What Is Intelligence?

The first formal linkage between intelligence and leadership was established around 1115 B.C. in China, where the dynasties used standardized tests to determine which citizens would play key leadership roles in the institutions they had

Personality Types and Leadership

Highlight 7.5

Bright and dark-side traits provide useful frameworks for describing leaders' behaviors, but they are not the only way to describe personality. An alternative way to describe how leaders and followers differ in their day-to-day behavior patterns is through **types,** or in terms of a **personality typology.** Unlike traits, which assume people fall somewhere along a continuum of low to high scores on any particular bright- or dark-side personality dimension, personality typology assumes that there are qualitatively different types of people and leaders. The signs of the Zodiac provide an unscientific but popular illustration of personality typology. For example, Leos are assumed to be fundamentally different than Pisces or Aquarians. The same holds true for the Chinese calendar; people born in the year of the Monkey are assumed to be qualitatively different than people born in the year of the Pig or Goat.

One group of personality researchers has expanded the notion of types to formal personality assessment. Myers (1976, 1977, 1980; Myers & Briggs, 1943/1962; Myers & McCaulley, 1985) extended the research of a famous psychologist, Carl Jung, and has created an instrument that categorizes people into one of 16 personality types. This instrument, the **Myers-Briggs Type Indicator (MBTI)** (Myers & Myers, 2001, 2003; Quenk & Kummerow, 2001), is perhaps the most popular psychological assessment and is taken by over 2 million people per year (Quast & Hansen, 1996; Thayer, 1988). The MBTI is used in 89 of the *Fortune* 100 companies and in college-level and adult leadership development courses, career and marriage counseling, child-rearing programs, coaching programs, and team-building interventions.

According to Myers and McCaulley (1985), people differ on four bipolar dimensions, which include **extraversion–introversion, sensing–intuition, thinking–feeling,** and **judging–perceiving.** Scores on each of the four dimensions results in one of the 16 personality types (e.g., extraversion, intuition, thinking, and judging type, or an introversion, sensing, thinking, and judging type, etc.). The test publishers have done extensive research on the MBTI, and overall it is a well-designed instrument that can help people understand differences and what they might need to do to be more effective. But the instrument does have some limitations. First, the MBTI has somewhat of a cultlike following, and many of its converts can only see the world through MBTI glasses (Curphy & Gibson, 1996). Personality types can become a perceptual filter by which we perceive others, as well as a rationalization for our own or others' behavior. Second, personality types are not stable—research indicates that types will change 50 percent of the time during a retest (McCarley & Carskadon, 1983; Myers & McCaulley, 1985). Because of the instability of types, it is difficult to see how the assessment could be used for selection or development purposes, as types are likely to change from one setting to the next. Despite these limitations, the MBTI is a very popular and useful instrument for understanding the nature of personality and how it plays out in day-to-day behaviors.

Sources: McCarley and Carskadon, 1983, p. 570; Myers, 1976, 1977, 1980, p. 572; Myers and Briggs, 1943/1965, p. 573; Myers and McCaulley, 1985, p. 573; P. B. Myers and K. D. Myers. *The Myers-Briggs Type Indicator Step II (Form Q) Profile* (Palo Alto, CA: Consulting Psychologists Press, 2001, 2003); Quast & Hansen, 1996, p. 577; N. L. Quenk and J. M. Kummerow. *The Myers-Briggs Type Indicator Step II (Form Q) Profile (Form B)* (Palo Alto, CA: Consulting Psychologists Press, 2001); Thayer, 1988, p. 584.

set up to run the country (DuBois, 1964). Using intelligence tests to identify potential leaders in the United States goes back to World War I, and to a large extent this use of intelligence testing continues today. Over 100 years of very comprehensive and systematic research provides overwhelming evidence to support the notion that general intelligence plays a substantial role in human affairs (Arvey et al., 1994; Humphreys, 1984; Neisser et al., 1996; Ree & Earles, 1992, 1993; Riggio, 2002; Schmidt & Hunter, 1992; Scarr, 1989; Sternberg, 1997, 2002, 2003a; Salgado, Anderson, Moscoso, Bertua, de Fruyt & Rolland, 2003). Still, intelligence and intelligence testing are among the most controversial topics in the social sciences today. There is contentious debate over questions like how heredity and the environment affect intelligence, whether intelligence tests should be used in public schools, and whether ethnic groups differ in average intelligence test scores. For the most part, however, we will bypass such controversies here. Our focus will be on the relationship between intelligence and leadership. (See Arvey et al., 1994; Azar, 1995; Brody, 1992; Cronbach, 1984; Humphreys, 1984; Linn, 1989; Neisser et al., 1996; and Sternberg, 1997, for reviews of these controversies.)

> *Perhaps no concept in the history of psychology has had or continues to have as great an impact on everyday life in the Western world as that of general intelligence.*
>
> Sandra Scarr

We define **intelligence** as a person's all-around effectiveness in activities directed by thought (Arvey et al., 1994; Cronbach, 1984). So what does this definition of intelligence have to do with leadership? Research has shown that more intelligent leaders are faster learners; make better assumptions, deductions, and inferences; are better at creating a compelling vision and developing strategies to make their vision a reality; can develop better solutions to problems; can see more of the primary and secondary implications of their decisions; and are quicker on their feet than leaders who are less intelligent (Herrnstein & Murray, 1994; Lord, DeVader, & Allinger, 1986; Ferris, Witt, & Hochwarter, 2001; Curphy, 2000, 2001, 2002, 2003b, 2004e; Sternberg, 1997, 2002, 2003a, b; Salgado et al., 2003; Nutt, 1999). To a large extent people get placed into leadership positions to solve problems, be they customer, financial, operational, interpersonal, performance, political, educational, or social in nature. Therefore, given the behaviors associated with higher intelligence, it is easy to see how a more intelligent leader will oftentimes be more successful in influencing a group to accomplish its goals than a less intelligent leader. Like personality traits, however, intelligence alone is not enough to guarantee leadership success. There are plenty of smart people who make poor leaders just as there are less intelligent people who are great leaders. Nevertheless, many leadership activities do seem to involve some degree of decision-making and problem-solving ability, which means that a leader's intelligence can affect the odds of leadership success in many situations.

> *To a large extent, leaders get paid to solve problems and get results.*
>
> Gordy Curphy

As seen in Figure 7.4, intelligence is relatively difficult to change. Like personality, it is also an unseen quality and can only be inferred by observing behavior. Moreover, intelligence does not affect behavior equally across all situations. Some activities, such as following simple routines, put less of a premium on intelligence than others (Salgado et al., 2003). Finally, we should point out that our definition of intelligence does not imply that intelligence is a fixed quantity. Although heredity plays a role, intelligence can be and is modified through education and experience (Arvey et al., 1994; Brody, 1997; Cronbach, 1984; Humphreys, 1989; Neisser et al., 1996; Rushton, 1997; Sternberg, 2002, 2003a, b).

FIGURE 7.4
The building
blocks of
skills.

Source: © Personnel
Decisions
International, 1997.

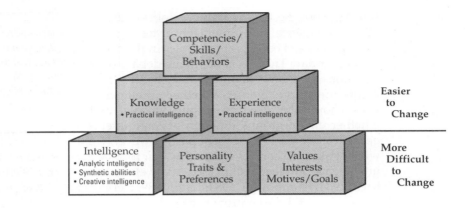

The Triarchic Theory of Intelligence

Although there is a strong, positive relationship between intelligence and leadership effectiveness, there is still an ongoing debate about the nature of intelligence. Many psychologists have tried to determine the structure of intelligence; is intelligence a unitary ability, or does it involve a collection of related mental abilities (Azar, 1995; Gardner, 1983; Herrnstein & Murray, 1994)? Other psychologists have said that the *process* by which people do complex mental work is much more important than determining the number of mental abilities (Sternberg, 1985, 1997). Perhaps the most comprehensive and compelling theory of intelligence developed and tested over the past 20 years is Sternberg's (1985, 1997, 2002, 2003a, b) **triarchic theory of intelligence.** It also offers some of the most significant implications for leadership. The triarchic theory focuses on what a leader *does* when solving complex mental problems, such as how information is combined and synthesized when solving problems, what assumptions and errors are made, and the like. According to this theory, there are three basic types of intelligence. **Analytic intelligence** is general problem-solving ability and can be assessed using standardized mental abilities tests. Leaders and followers with higher levels of analytic intelligence tend to be quick learners, do well in school, see connections between issues, and have the ability to make accurate deductions, assumptions, and inferences with relatively unfamiliar information.

There is still much, however, that analytic intelligence does not explain. There are a number of people who do well on standardized tests but not in life (Sternberg, Wagner, Williams, & Horvath, 1995; Ferris, Witt, & Hochwarter, 2001; Sternberg, 2002, 2003a, b). At the same time, some people do relatively poorly on standardized intelligence tests but often develop ingenious solutions to practical problems. For example, Sternberg and his associates described a situation where students in a school for the mentally retarded did very poorly on standardized tests yet consistently found ways to defeat the school's elaborate security system. In this situation the students possessed a relatively high level of **practical intelligence,** or "street smarts." People with street smarts know how to adapt to, shape, or select new situations in order to get their needs met better than people lacking street smarts

The first method for estimating the intelligence of a ruler is to look at the men he has around him.

Niccolò Machiavelli

Everyone is ignorant, only on different subjects.

Will Rogers

(e.g., think of a stereotypical computer nerd and an inner-city kid both lost in downtown New York). In other words, practical intelligence involves knowing how things get done and how to do them. For leaders, practical intelligence involves knowing what to do and how to do it when confronted with a particular leadership situation, such as dealing with a poorly performing subordinate, resolving a problem with a customer, or getting a team to work better together (Hedlund, Forsythe, Horvath, Williams, Snook, & Sternberg, 2003) (see Highlights 7.6 and 7.7).

Because of its potential importance to leadership effectiveness, there are several other aspects of practical intelligence worth noting. First, practical intelligence is much more concerned with knowledge and experience than analytic intelligence (see Figure 7.4). Leaders can build their practical intelligence by building their leadership knowledge and experience. Thus, textbooks such as this one can help you to build your practical intelligence. Getting a variety of leadership experiences, and perhaps more important, reflecting on these experiences, will also help you to build practical intelligence. Second, practical intelligence is *domain specific*. A leader who has a lot of knowledge and experience in leading a pharmaceutical research team may feel like a duck out of water when asked to lead a major fund-raising effort for a charitable institution. As another example, one of the authors worked with a highly successful retail company having over 100,000 employees. All of the key leaders had over 20 years of retail operations and merchandising experience, but they also did very poorly on standardized intelligence tests. The company had successfully expanded in the United States (which capitalized on their practical intelligence), but their attempt to expand to foreign markets was an abysmal failure. This failure was due in part

Real Examples of Analytic and Practical Intelligence (or Lack Thereof)

Highlight 7.6

Chuck Shepherd's newspaper article "News of the Weird" and Wendy Northcutt's book, *The Darwin Awards,* provide ample examples of the importance of analytic and practical intelligence. Here are some of the typical stories you can find in these manuscripts and at *www.DarwinAwards.com*:

1. AT&T fired President John Walter after only nine months, saying he lacked intellectual leadership. He received a $26 million dollar severance package for his efforts. Perhaps it is not Walter who is lacking intelligence . . .

2. Police in Los Angeles had good luck with a robbery suspect who just couldn't control himself during a lineup. When detectives asked each man in the lineup to repeat the words, "Give me all your money or I'll shoot," the man shouted, "That's not what I said!"

3. Some folks, new to boating, were having a problem. No matter how hard they tried, their brand new 22-foot power boat was very sluggish in almost every maneuver, no matter how much power was applied. After about an hour of trying to make it go, they putted to a nearby marina, thinking someone there could tell them what was wrong. A thorough topside check revealed everything in perfect working condition. The engine ran fine, the outboard drive went up and down, and the prop was the correct size and pitch. One of the marina guys then jumped into the water to check underneath and nearly choked from laughing so hard. He discovered that the trailer was still strapped securely in place under the boat.

The Triarchic Theory of Intelligence and Decision Making

Highlight 7.7

Leaders spend a significant amount of time solving problems, and the Triarchic Theory of Intelligence has some important implications for decision making. First, if practical intelligence is an important component of decision making (which it is), then it is equally important that the knowledge leaders possess accurate information about their organizations and the environments in which they operate. Although leaders see lots of data, they tend to only focus on the here and now and have difficulties seeing the forest from the trees. As a result, top leaders often have a distorted picture of their organizations and environments. For example, research by Mezias and Starbuck (2003) shows that business unit leaders and CEOs can be off by as much as 200 percent on industry growth estimates, business unit sales growth, quality indicators, etc. And this imprecise knowledge of the business, combined with an advocacy problem-solving process and a tendency for leaders to surround themselves with yea-sayers may be primary reasons why approximately half of all major organizational decisions turn out wrong (Nutt, 1999; Garvin & Roberto, 2001).

There are several things leaders can do to avoid making poor decisions based on imperfect data. Perhaps the most important step is to get leaders to look at the *same* data before making important organizational decisions. All too often leaders come to key decision-making meetings with very different ideas of what is happening with their organizations. And as described above, many of these ideas are simply wrong. By reviewing the same data, asking probing questions, and discussing how the data fit together can go a long way toward getting decision makers on the same page and developing better solutions to organizational problems.

Sources: G. J. Curphy, *The Blandin Health Care Leadership Program* (Grand Rapids, MN: The Blandin Foundation, 2004f); G. J. Curphy, *The Blandin Education Leadership Program* (Grand Rapids, MN: The Blandin Foundation, 2004g); D. A. Garvin and M. A. Roberto, "What You Don't Know about Making Decisions," *Harvard Business Review,* September 2001, pp. 108–14; P. T. Nutt, "Surprising but True: Half the Decisions in Organizations Fail," *Academy of Management Executive* 1999 (4), pp. 75–90; J. Magretta, "Why Business Models Matter," *Harvard Business Review,* May 2002, pp. 86–95; J. M. Mezias and W. H. Starbuck, "What Do Managers Know, Anyway?" *Harvard Business Review,* May 2003, pp. 16–17.

to the leaders' inability to learn, appreciate, or understand the intricacies of other cultures (analytic intelligence), their lack of knowledge and experience in foreign markets (practical intelligence), and in turn their development of inappropriate strategies for running the business in other countries (a combination of analytic and practical intelligence). Thus, practical intelligence is extremely useful when leading in familiar situations, but analytic intelligence may play a more important role when leaders are facing new or novel situations.

Third, this example points out the importance of having both types of intelligence. As seen in Highlight 7.7, organizations today are looking for leaders and followers who have the necessary knowledge and skills to succeed (practical intelligence) and the ability to learn (analytic intelligence) (Stamps, 1996; Sternberg 2002, 2003a, b; Connelly, Gilbert, Ziccaro, Threlfell, Marks, & Mumford, 2000; Cox, 2000). Fourth, it may be that high levels of practical intelligence may compensate for lower levels of analytic intelligence. Leaders having lower analytic abilities may still be able to solve complex work problems or make good decisions provided they have plenty of job-relevant knowledge or experience. But leaders with more analytic intelligence, all things being equal, may develop their street smarts more quickly than leaders with less analytic intelligence. Analytic intelligence may play a lesser role once a domain of knowledge is mastered, but a more important role when encountering new situations.

The third component of the triarchic theory of intelligence is **creative intelligence.** Creative intelligence is the ability to produce work that is both novel and useful (Sternberg, 1997, 2001; Sternberg & Oess, 2001; Kersting, 2003; Sternberg & Lubart, 1996). Using *both* criteria (novel and useful) as components of creative intelligence helps to eliminate many of the more outlandish solutions to a potential problem by ensuring that adopted solutions can be realistically implemented or have some type of practical payoff. Several examples might help to clarify the novel and practical components of creative intelligence. The inventor of Velcro got his idea while picking countless thistles out of his socks; he realized that the same principle that produced his frustration might be translated into a useful fastener. The inventor of 3M's Post-it notes was frustrated because bookmarks in his church hymnal were continually sliding out of place, and he saw a solution in a low-tack adhesive discovered by a fellow 3M scientist. The scientists who designed the *Spirit* and *Opportunity* missions to Mars were given a budget that was considerably smaller than that of the previous missions to Mars. Yet the scientists were challenged to develop two spacecraft that had more capabilities than the *Pathfinder* and the *Viking Lander.* Their efforts with *Spirit* and *Opportunity* were a resounding success, due in part to some of the novel solutions used both to land the spacecrafts (an inflatable balloon system) and to explore the surrounding area (both were mobile rovers).

> *The best way to have a good idea is to have a lot of ideas.*
>
> Dr. Linus Pauling

Two of the more-interesting questions surrounding creativity concern the role of intelligence and the assessment of creative ability. Research by Sternberg and Lubart (1996) shows that analytic intelligence correlates at about the .5 level with creative intelligence. Thus, the best research available indicates that analytic intelligence and creativity are related, but the relationship is far from perfect. Some level of analytic intelligence seems necessary for creativity, but having a high level of analytic intelligence is no guarantee that a leader will be creative. And like practical intelligence, creativity seems to be specific to certain fields and subfields: Most composers are not architects, and most writers are not mathematicians (Cronbach, 1984; Sternberg & Lubart, 1996; Sternberg & Oess, 2001; Sternberg 2002a, 2003a, b).

In addition, actually assessing creativity is no simple matter. Tests of creativity, or **divergent thinking,** are very different from tests that assess **convergent thinking.** Tests of convergent thinking usually have a single best answer; good examples here are most intelligence and aptitude tests. Conversely, tests of creativity or divergent thinking have many possible answers (Guilford, 1967). Although Sternberg and Lubart (1996), Sternberg and Oess (2001), and Sternberg (2001) all showed that it is possible to reliably judge the relative creativity of different responses, the fact remains that judging creativity is more difficult than scoring convergent tests. For example, there are no set answers or standards for determining whether a movie, a marketing ad, or a new manufacturing process is truly creative. Another difficulty in assessing creativity is that it may wax and wane over time; many of the most creative people seem to have occasional dry spells or writer's block. This is very different from analytic intelligence, where performance on mental abilities tests remains fairly constant over time.

The Components of Creative Intelligence

So far we have discussed creative intelligence as a unitary ability. However, as seen in Table 7.3, research suggests that creativity appears to be made up of seven components: *synthetic ability, analytic intelligence, practical intelligence, thinking style, personality factors, intrinsic motivation,* and *environmental factors* (Amabile, 2001; Amabile & Conti, 1995; Amabile, Schatzel, Moneta, & Kramer, 2004; Reiter-Palmon & Illies, 2004; Kersting, 2003; Kohn, 1987; Oldham & Cummings, 1996; Sternberg, 1985, 2001, 2003a, b; Sternberg & Grigorenko, 1997; Sternberg & Lubart, 1996). **Synthetic ability** is what we traditionally view as creativity; these skills help people see things in new ways or recognize novel patterns or connections. Analytic intelligence helps people to evaluate solutions, and practical intelligence provides the knowledge and experience base from which novel solutions are developed. According to Sternberg and Lubart (1996), and Sternberg, (2003a, b) these first three components are very important to the creative process, and leaders lacking in any one of them will be less creative than those possessing all three.

Most artists have to hack through a tangled thicket of negativity, logic, and procrastination on the way to creating anything. Peter seems to be supernaturally free of any such concerns. This is a guy with a big wide conduit running from the creative, imaginative part of his brain, straight to the place where most of us keep our willpower. That could be a recipe for a monstrously selfish ego. Again, Jackson's ability to chase goals doesn't come with that type of baggage. He's driven, and he's incredibly demanding, but he's always focused on results, never on himself.

Costa Botes
Screenwriter

Thinking style is somewhat related to synthetic ability. Thinking styles are not abilities per se, but rather are the preferred ways for using the abilities one has (Sternberg & Grigorenko, 1997). For example, some people seem to prefer improving or adapting already existing products or processes. A first-line supervisor in a manufacturing facility may be very adept at modifying existing production schedules or equipment in order to better meet customers' needs. Other people seem to prefer developing completely new products. A team leader tasked with developing a new ad campaign for a major brewer

TABLE 7.3
The Components of Creative Intelligence

Synthetic Ability: These skills help people see things in new ways or recognize novel connections between seemingly unrelated issues or concepts.
Analytic Intelligence: This helps to evaluate the usefulness of potential solutions to problems.
Practical Intelligence: Novel solutions to problems are usually based on relevant knowledge and experience.
Thinking Style: People either prefer to modify what already exists or completely start over with new solutions.
Personality Factors: Lower prudence, higher openness to experience, and higher surgency scores are related to creativity.
Intrinsic Motivation: People tend to generate more creative solutions when the problem at hand is personally interesting.
Environmental Factors: Supportive leadership, a lack of time pressure, team stability, and weaker social ties are all related to generating more creative solutions to problems.

might come up with a series of promotional ads using novel attention-getting devices, such as frogs or chameleons. According to Kirton (1987), these two examples illustrate the difference between **adaptive** and **innovative thinking styles.** Adaptors prefer to modify or change existing products or processes; innovators prefer to create entirely new processes or products. Adaptors and innovators may have the same level of synthetic ability, but they just seem to use this ability in different ways. It is important to note that U.S. companies seem particularly adept at developing new technology (i.e., innovation), whereas Japanese industries are very good at improving the technology and finding efficient ways to bring it to the marketplace (i.e., adaptation).

Several personality factors also seem to play a role in creativity. More specifically, people having higher levels of self-confidence, independence, and energy (syngery), risk-taking and impulsiveness (dependability), and natural curiosity (openness to experience) seem to be more creative than people who lack self-confidence, are more conforming, and are less open to new and novel experiences (Amabile, 2001; Amabile & Gryskiewicz, 1987; Hogan & Morrison, 1993; Oldham & Cummings, 1996; Sternberg & Lubart, 1996; Zhou, 2003; Curphy, 2003c). People will also be more creative when they are intrinsically motivated or feel challenged by the subject matter or problem itself (Amabile, 2001; Amabile & Hennessey, 1988; Sternberg, 2002; Amabile et al., 2004; Tierney & Farmer, 2002; Tierney, Farmer, & Graen, 1999). Creative people are more likely to focus attention on solving the problem at hand, not on the need to meet deadlines, make money, or impress others.

Finally, several situational or environmental factors appear related to creativity. People who have more complex or challenging jobs, who have supportive, non-controlling leaders and are given ample time seem to be more creative than people in uninteresting jobs who are under tight deadlines and also have highly controlling supervisors (Oldham & Cummings, 1996; Zhou, 2003; Shalley & Gilson, 2004; Amabile et al., 2004; Dingfelder, 2003; Basadur, 2004; Farson & Keyes, 2002; Farmer, Tierney, & Kung-McIntyre, 2003). Several aspects of work groups also seem to affect creativity. Although the size of the group did not seem to matter, teams that were given clear goals, stayed task focused, and provided mutual support and participation often developed more innovative solutions than teams lacking these qualities (West & Anderson, 1996).

Team stability also seems to play a role in creativity. Amabile and Conti (1995; 1997) studied companies before, during, and after going through a large downsizing, and reported that teams that remained relatively intact during this process were substantially more creative in terms of patent applications than teams that were broken up. These authors also reported that an organization's support for creativity, in terms of time and resources, was a key factor in the creativity of individual employees.

Another factor that affects creativity is team cohesiveness. You might think that teams with higher levels of cohesiveness would be more creative than teams that do not get along, but research shows that just the opposite is true. Because highly cohesive teams tend to share the same values, their team members often look at the world in similar ways. Teams having members with dissimilar values will likely have more conflict, but they are also more likely to look at problems from different perspectives. And looking at issues differently is critical to creative problem solving (Florida, Cushing, & Gates, 2002; Perry-Smith & Shalley, 2003).

The story of Chester Carlson provides a good example of how some of the seven components play important roles in developing a creative and useful solution to a problem. Chester Carlson invented the photocopy duplicating process, which revolutionized office work. Duplicating machines are relied on so much today that most people probably assume the invention was met with instant acceptance. That was not the case, however. Most people do not realize that it was 22 years from the time Carlson got the idea to the time his product became commercially available—or that refining and "selling" his concept was an uphill battle primarily because of the existence of carbon paper. (With carbon paper, people thought, why would you need anything else?) His solution for making copies of documents was certainly imaginative, but it was also derived from his considerable technical expertise. Moreover, his persistence in developing and persuading others of the potential of his process is a testament to the importance of intrinsic motivation in creativity.

> *The fastest way to succeed is to double the failure rate.*
>
> Thomas Watson, Sr.
> IBM

Creative thinking is not an entirely rational or conscious process. Many times we do our most imaginative thinking unconsciously; people often gain sudden insights to an old problem out of the blue. There are interesting anecdotal accounts of how different creative thinkers recognized and even harnessed these unconscious processes. Albert Einstein, for example, once remarked that he got his best ideas in the morning when he was shaving. The great inventor Thomas Edison reportedly developed a technique to awaken himself and capture the typically unusual imagery and mental activity occurring as one falls asleep. These thinkers recognized the mind's fertility during its resting periods. Einstein's and Edison's receptivity to ideas emerging from their nonlogical mental processes was surely an important part of their genius. They were able to harness their unconscious rather than censor it, as many of us may do by suppressing or discounting mental activity that seems purposeless, nonsensical, or threatening.

Implications of the Triarchic Theory of Intelligence

The three types of intelligence in Sternberg's theory correspond nicely with the three leaders identified in Chapter 1. Although the three leaders probably possess high levels of all three types of intelligence, Colin Powell has a highly developed level of practical intelligence for leading in the military. He has commanded a number of large and small military units and held line and staff positions during times of peace and war. And over the past four years he has been able to build his knowledge of foreign affairs in his role as secretary of state. Likewise, Aung San Suu Kyi has developed a highly evolved knowledge base of the Burmese political system and how to change it. Peter Jackson clearly has the highest level of creative intelligence; few people could match the professional awards and financial gains made by his *Lord of the Rings* films.

> *If I had to sum up in one word what makes a good manager, I'd say decisiveness. You can use the fanciest computers to gather the numbers, but in the end you have to set a timetable and act.*
>
> Lee Iacocca

Some 200 separate studies have examined the relationship between intelligence test scores and leadership effectiveness or emergence, and these studies have been the topic of major reviews by Stogdill (1948); Mann (1959); Ghiselli (1963); Stogdill (1974); Bray, Campbell, and Grant (1974); Cornwell (1983); Bray and Howard (1983); Lord, DeVader, and Allinger (1986); Bass (1990); and Fiedler (1992). These 10 reviews provided overwhelming support for the idea that leadership effectiveness or emergence is positively correlated with analytic intelligence. Nonetheless, it is important to recognize that the correlation between analytic intelligence and leadership success is far from perfect. Leadership situations that are relatively routine, unchanging, or require specific in-depth product or process knowledge may place more importance on practical intelligence than analytic intelligence. Having a high level of analytic intelligence seems more important when solving ambiguous, complex problems, such as those encountered by executives at the top levels of an organization. Here leaders must be able to detect themes and patterns in seemingly unrelated information, make accurate assumptions about market conditions, or make wise merger, acquisition, or divestiture decisions. Further evidence that higher levels of analytic intelligence are associated with top leaders can be found in Figure 7.5.

Although a high level of analytic intelligence is usually an asset to a leader, research also suggests that in some situations analytic intelligence may have a *curvilinear* relationship with leadership effectiveness (Ghiselli, 1963; Stogdill, 1974). When differences in analytic intelligence between leader and followers are too great, communication can be impaired; a leader's intelligence can become an impediment to being understood by subordinates (Bass, 1990; Ferris, Witt, & Hochwarter, 2001). An alternative explanation for the curvilinear relationship between analytic intelligence and leadership effectiveness may have to do with how stress affects leader–subordinate interactions. Fiedler (1992, 2002) and Gibson (1992) found that smart but inexperienced leaders were less effective in stressful

FIGURE 7.5
Average intelligence test scores by management level.

Source: N. Kuncel, "Personality and Cognitive Differences among Management Levels" (Unpublished manuscript, Personnel Decisions International, Minneapolis, 1996).

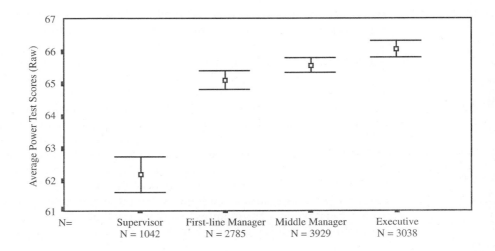

situations than less intelligent, experienced leaders. An example of this finding was clearly demonstrated in the movie *Platoon.* In one frantic scene, an American platoon is ambushed by the Vietcong, and an inexperienced, college-educated lieutenant calls for artillery support from friendly units. He calls in the wrong coordinates, however, and as a result artillery shells are dropped on his own platoon's position rather than the enemy's position. The situation comes under control only after an experienced sergeant sizes up the situation and tells the artillery units to cease firing. This example points out the importance of practical intelligence in stressful situations. Leaders revert to well-practiced behaviors under periods of high stress and change, and leaders with high levels of practical intelligence have a relatively broad set of coping and problem-solving behaviors to draw upon in these situations. Because of the level of stress and change associated with many leadership positions today, systematically improving practical leadership skills through education and experience is extremely important for leaders and leaders-to-be.

With respect to creative intelligence, perhaps the most important point leaders should remember is that their primary role is not so much to be creative themselves as to *build an environment where others can be creative.* This is not to say that leaders should be uncreative, but rather that most innovations have their roots in ideas developed by people closest to a problem or opportunity (i.e., the workers). Leaders can boost the creativity throughout their groups or organizations in many ways, but particularly through selecting creative people in the first place, and providing opportunities for others to develop their creativity, and through broader interventions like making sure the motivation or incentives for others are conducive to creativity and providing at least some guidance or vision about what the creative product or output should look like (Basadur, 2004; Reiter-Polman & Illies, 2004; Shalley & Gilson, 2004; Amabile et al., 2004; Mumford, Scott, Gaddis, & Strange, 2002; Zhou, 2003; Sternberg, Kaufman, & Pretz, 2003).

There are several things leaders can do to improve the group and organizational factors affecting creativity. Leaders should be mindful of the effect various sorts of incentives or rewards can have on creativity; certain types of motivation to work are more conducive to creativity than others. Research has shown that people tend to generate more creative solutions when they are told to focus on their intrinsic motivation for doing so (i.e., the pleasure of solving the task itself) rather than focusing on the extrinsic motivation (i.e., public recognition or pay) (Amabile, 1985, 2001; Amabile & Hennessey, 1988; Tierney, Farmer, & Graen, 1999). When they need to foster creativity, leaders may find it more effective to select followers who truly enjoy working on the task at hand (i.e., are intrinsically motivated) rather than relying on rewards (i.e., extrinsic motivation) to foster creativity.

It is also helpful to remember that synthetic abilities can also be hindered if people believe that their ideas will be evaluated. The experiments of Amabile (1983, 1987) and Zhou (1998) showed that students who were told their projects were to be judged by experts produced less creative projects than students who were not told their projects would be judged. A similar sort of phenomenon can occur in groups. Even when a group knows its work must ultimately be evaluated, there is a pronounced tendency for members to be evaluative and judgmental too early in

TABLE 7.4
Creativity
Killers: How
to Squelch the
Creativity of
Direct Reports

Source: T. M.
Amabile and J.
Zhou, in S. F.
Dingfelder,
"Creativity on the
Clock," *Monitor on
Psychology,*
November, 2003,
pp. 56–58.

The following is a list of things leaders can do if they wish to stifle the creativity of their followers:

Take Away All Discretion and Autonomy: People like to have some sense of control over their work. Micromanaging staff will help to either create yea-sayers or cause people to mentally disengage from work.

Create Fragmented Work Schedules: People need large chunks of uninterrupted time to work on novel solutions. Repeated interruptions or scheduling "novel solution generation time" in 15-minute increments around other meetings will disrupt people's ability to be innovative.

Provide Insufficient Resources: People need proper data, equipment, or money to be creative. Cut these off, and watch creativity go down the tubes.

Focus on Short-Term Goals: Asking a person to be creative at right this moment is like asking Chris Rock to be funny the first time you meet him. People can be creative and funny if given enough time, but focusing on only short-term outcomes will dampen creativity.

Create Tight Timelines: The tighter the deadlines, the more likely that innovation will be reduced.

Discourage Collaboration and Coordination: The best ideas often come from teams having members with very different work experiences and functional backgrounds. By discouraging cross-functional collaboration, leaders can help guarantee that team members will only offer up tried and true solutions to problems.

Keep People Happy: If you keep workers happy enough, then they will have little motivation to change the status quo.

the solution-generating process. This tends to reduce the number of creative solutions generated, perhaps because of a generally shared belief in the value of critical thinking (and in some groups the norm seems to be the more criticism the better) and of subjecting ideas to intense scrutiny and evaluation. When members of a group judge ideas as soon as they are offered, two dysfunctional things can happen. People in the group may censor themselves (i.e., not share all their ideas with the group), as even mild rejection or criticism has a significant dampening effect (Prince, 1972), or they may prematurely reject others' ideas through negativistic focus on an idea's flaws rather than its possibilities. Given these findings, leaders may want to hold off on evaluating new ideas until they are all on the table, and should also encourage their followers to do the same.

Finally, leaders who need to develop new products and services should try to minimize the level of turnover in their teams and provide them with clear goals. Teams having unclear goals may successfully develop new or novel products, but these products may have low marketability or usefulness. Two examples might help illustrate this point. In the 1980s Texas Instruments (TI) decided to delve into the personal computer business. TI had a reputation for technical excellence, and one of the best managers in the company was asked to head up the project. The manager did not have a clear sense of what customers wanted or what a personal computer should be able to do. This lack of clarity had some fairly dramatic effects. As more and more engineers were added to the project, more and more innovative hardware ideas were added to the computer design. These additions caused the project to take much longer and cost a lot more than planned, but the TI personal computer ended up winning a number of major engineering awards. Unfortunately, it was also a business disaster, as the product ultimately failed to meet customer needs. Although Compaq computers arose from the ashes of TI's failure, the TI project serves as a good example for a concept called **creeping elegance.** Leaders not having a clear vision of what a final project should look like may end up with something that fails to meet customer needs. Leaders need to provide enough room for creativity to flourish, but enough direction for effort to be focused (Shalley & Gilson, 2004; Farson & Keyes, 2002).

One industry that places a premium on creativity is the motion picture industry. Because creativity is so important to the commercial success of a movie, it is relatively easy for a movie to succumb to creeping elegance. But how do movie directors successfully avoid creeping elegance when dealing with highly creative people having huge egos? Part of the answer may be in the approach of two of Hollywood's most successful directors. Steven Speilberg and Ron Howard said that before they ever shot a scene they first had a very clear picture of it in their own minds. If they did not have a clear picture, then they sat down with the relevant parties and worked it out. Both situations point out the importance of having a clear vision when managing creativity.

Intelligence and Stress: Cognitive Resources Theory

In the preceding section we noted that intelligence may be a more important quality for leaders in some situations than others. You may be surprised to learn, however, that recent research actually suggests there are times when intelligence may be a disadvantage. A key variable affecting this paradoxical finding seems to be whether or not the leader is in a stressful situation. Recent research suggests that stress plays a key role in determining just how a leader's intelligence affects his or her effectiveness. While it is not surprising that stress affects behavior in various ways, Fiedler and Garcia (1987) developed the **cognitive resources theory (CRT)** to explain the interesting relationships between leader intelligence and experience levels, and group performance in stressful versus nonstressful conditions.

As first described in Chapter 4, CRT consists of several key concepts. Certainly one of these is intelligence. Fiedler and Garcia (1987) and Fiedler (1995, 2002) defined intelligence as we have earlier—it is one's all-around effectiveness in activities directed by thought and is typically measured using standardized intelligence tests (i.e., analytic intelligence). Another key concept is experience, which represents the habitual behavior patterns, overlearned knowledge, and skills acquired for effectively dealing with task-related problems (i.e., practical intelligence). Although experience is often gained under stressful and unpleasant conditions, experience also provides a "crash plan" to revert back to when under stress (Fiedler, 1992, 1995, 2002). As Fiedler observed, people often act differently when stressed, and the crash plan describes this change in behavior patterns. For most of the CRT studies, experience has been defined as time in the job or organization. A third key concept in CRT is stress. Stress is often defined as the result of conflicts with superiors or the apprehension associated with performance evaluation (Fiedler, 1995; Gibson, 1992). This interpersonal stress is believed to be emotionally disturbing and can divert attention from problem-solving activities (Sarason, 1986). In other words, people can get so concerned about how their performance is being evaluated that they may fail to perform at an optimal level. In sum, cognitive resources theory provides a conceptual scheme for explaining how leader behavior changes under stress levels to impact group performance.

Cognitive resources theory makes two major predictions with respect to intelligence, experience, stress, and group performance. First, because experienced leaders have a greater repertoire of behaviors to fall back on, leaders with greater experience but lower intelligence are hypothesized to have higher-performing groups under conditions of high stress. Experienced leaders have "been there before" and better know what to do and how to get it done when faced with high-stress situations. Leaders' experience levels can interfere with performance under low-stress conditions, however.

That leads to a second hypothesis. Because experience leads to habitual behavior patterns, leaders with high levels of experience will have a tendency to misapply old solutions to problems when creative solutions are called for (Fiedler, 1992, 1995, 2002). Experienced leaders overrely on the tried and true when faced with new problems, even when under relatively low periods of stress. Thus, leaders with higher levels of intelligence but less experience are not constrained by previously acquired behavior patterns and should have higher-performing groups under low-stress conditions. In other words, experience is helpful when one is under stress but is often a hindrance to performance in the absence of stress.

These two major predictions of CRT can be readily seen in everyday life. For the most part, it is not the most intelligent but the most experienced members of sporting teams, marching bands, acting troops, or volunteer organizations who are selected to be leaders. These leaders are often chosen because other members recognize their ability to perform well under the high levels of stress associated with sporting events and public performances. In addition, research with combat troops, firefighters, senior executives, and students has provided reasonably strong support for the two major tenets of CRT (Fiedler & Garcia, 1987; Fiedler, 1992, 1995, 2002; Gibson, 1992).

Despite this initial empirical support, one problem with CRT concerns the apparent dichotomy between intelligence and experience. Fiedler and Garcia's (1987) initial investigations of CRT did not examine the possibility that leaders could be *both* intelligent and experienced. Subsequent research by Gibson (1992) showed not only that many leaders were both intelligent and experienced, but also that these leaders would fall back on their experience in stressful situations and use their intelligence to solve group problems in less-stressful situations.

Another issue with CRT concerns the leader's ability to tolerate stress. As Schonpflug (1995) and Zaccaro (1995) correctly pointed out, some leaders may be better able to tolerate high levels of stress than others. Some leaders may have personalities characterized by high adjustment scores, and it may be that such leaders may do well in high-stress situations even when they lack experience because of their inherent ability to handle stress. Further research on this issue seems warranted.

In general, Fiedler and his colleagues have provided solid evidence to support the major tenets of CRT. Because of this research, CRT has several important implications for leaders. First, it may be that the best leaders are often smart *and* experienced. Although intelligence tests are good indicators of raw mental horsepower, it is just as important for leaders to broaden their leadership knowledge and experience if they want to be successful in high-stress situations. This latter point may be very important today, where the additional stress of organizational downsizing and "delayering" may cause the performance of leaders to be scrutinized even more closely than in the past. In fact, this additional scrutiny may well cause leaders who were previously successful to perform rather poorly in this high-stress environment.

Second, leaders may not be aware of the degree to which they are causing stress in their followers. If followers perceive that their performance is being closely watched, then they are likely to revert to their crash plans in order to perform. If the situation calls for new and novel solutions to problems, however, the leaders' behavior may be counterproductive. A key point here is that leaders may be unaware of their impact on followers. For example, they may want to review their followers' work more closely in order to be helpful, but followers may not perceive it this way.

Third, the level of stress inherent in the position needs to be understood before selection of leaders. Those doing the selection to fill high-stress leadership positions can either look for experienced leaders or reduce the stress in the situation so that more intelligent leaders can be more successful (Levy-Leboyer, 1995; Fielder, 2002). Another alternative could be to hire more intelligent leaders and put them through some type of stress management program so that the effects of stress are minimized (Fielder, 1995, 2002). It is also possible that experienced leaders may get bored if placed into low-stress positions (Ganzach, 1998).

Emotional Intelligence and Leadership

What Is Emotional Intelligence?

In terms of the building blocks of skills, Chapter 6 described the role values play in leadership. Similarly, this chapter has discussed how bright- and dark-side personality traits and analytic, practical, and creative intelligence are related to leadership effectiveness. But we have not discussed whether moods affect leaders' ability to build teams and get results through others. Moods and emotions are constantly at play at work, yet most people are hesitant to discuss moods with anybody other than close friends. It also appears that moods can be contagious, in that the moods of leaders often affect followers in both positive and negative ways. And charismatic or transformational leaders use emotions as the catalyst for achieving better than expected results (see Chapter 13). Given the importance and prevalence of emotions in the workplace, it would seem that there would be a wealth of research regarding mood and leadership effectiveness. But this is not the case. Researchers have really begun to seriously examine the role of emotions in leadership only over the past 15–20 years.

The relationships between a leader's emotions and their effects on teams and outcomes became popularized with the publication of a book, *Emotional Intelligence* (Goleman, 1995). But what is emotional intelligence (EQ), and how is it the same as or different from personality or the three types of intelligence described in this chapter?

Unfortunately, there appears to be at least four major definitions of **emotional intelligence.** The term *emotional intelligence* can be attributed to two psychologists, Peter Salovey and John Mayer, who studied why some bright people fail to be successful. Salovey and Mayer (1990) discovered that many of them ran into trouble because of their lack of interpersonal sensitivity and skills, and defined emotional intelligence as a group of mental abilities that help people to recognize their own feelings and those of others. Bar-On (1996) believed that emotional intelligence was another way of measuring human effectiveness and defined it as a set of 15 abilities necessary to cope with daily situations and get along in the world. Aberman (2000) defined emotional intelligence as the degree to which thoughts, feelings, and actions were aligned. According to Aberman, leaders are more effective and

There is no single entity called EQ (emotional intelligence quotient) as people have defined it. One sympathetic interpretation of what journalists were saying is that there were a dozen unrelated things, which collectively might predict more than intelligence, things like warmth, optimism, and empathy. But there was nothing new about that. Instead, the story became this fabulous new variable that is going to outpredict intelligence. There is no rational basis for saying that.

John Mayer

"in the zone" when their thoughts, feelings, and actions were perfectly aligned. Daniel Goleman, a science writer for the *New York Times,* substantially broadened these definitions and summarized some of this work in his books *Emotional Intelligence* (1995) and *Working with Emotional Intelligence* (1998). Goleman argued that success in life is based more on one's self-motivation, persistence in the face of frustration, mood management, ability to adapt, and ability to empathize and get along with others than on one's analytic intelligence or IQ. Table 7.5 provides a comparison between the Salovey and Mayer, Bar-On, and Goleman models of emotional intelligence.

Caruso, Mayer, and Salovey (2002) maintain that these four definitions of EQ can be broken down into two models: an ability model and a mixed model of emotional intelligence. The ability model focuses on how emotions affect how leaders think, decide, plan, and act. This model defines emotional intelligence as four separate but related abilities, which include: (a) the ability to accurately perceive one's own and others' emotions; (b) the ability to generate emotions to facilitate thought and action; (c) the ability to accurately understand the causes of emotions and the meanings they convey; and (d) the ability to regulate one's emotions. According to Caruso, Mayer, and Salovey (2002), some leaders might be very good at perceiving emotions and leveraging them to get results through others, but have difficulties regulating their own emotions. Or they could be very good at understanding the causes of emotions but not as good at perceiving others' emotions. The ability model is not intended to be an all-encompassing model of leadership, but rather supplements the FFM and Triarchic Theory of Intelligence. Just as leaders differ on adjustment or practical intelligence, so do they differ on their ability to perceive and regulate emotions. The ability model of EQ is helpful because it allows researchers to determine if EQ is in fact a separate ability and whether it can predict leadership effectiveness over and above the FFM and cognitive abilities.

The Goleman and Bar-On definitions of EQ fall into the mixed model category. These researchers believe emotional intelligence includes not only the abilities outlined in the previous paragraph but also includes a number of other attributes. As

TABLE 7.5
Ability and
Mixed Models
of Emotional
Intelligence

Sources: R. Bar-On,
*Emotional Quotient
Inventory* (North
Tonawanda, NY:
Multi Health
Systems, Inc. 2001);
D. Goleman,
*Working with
Emotional Intelligence*
(New York: Bantam
Doubleday Dell,
1998); D. R. Caruso,
J. R. Mayer, and P.
Salovey, "Emotional
Intelligence and
Emotional
Leadership," in R. E.
Riggio, S. E.
Murphy, and F. J.
Pirozzolo (Eds.),
*Multiple Intelligences
and Leadership*
(Mahwah, NJ:
Lawrence Erlbaum
Associates, 2002),
pp. 55–74;
On line source:
http://www.
eiconsortium.org.

Ability Model	Mixed Models	
Mayer, Salovey, and Caruso	**Goleman et al.**	**Bar-On**
Perceiving Emotions	Self-Awareness	Intrapersonal
	Emotional Awareness	Self-Regard
	Accurate Self-Assessment	Emotional Self-Awareness
	Self-Confidence	Assertiveness
		Independence
		Self-Actualization
Managing Emotions	Self-Regulation	Interpersonal
	Self-Control	Empathy
	Trustworthiness	Social Responsibility
	Conscientiousness	Interpersonal Relationship
	Adaptability	
	Innovation	
Using Emotions	Motivation	Adaptability
	Achievement	Reality Testing
	Commitment	Flexibility
	Initiative	Problem-Solving
	Optimism	
Understanding Emotions	Empathy	
	Understanding Others	Stress Management
	Developing Others	Stress Tolerance
	Service Orientation	Impulse Control
	Diversity	
	Political Awareness	General Mood
		Optimism
	Social Skills	Happiness
	Influence	
	Communication	
	Conflict Management	
	Leadership	
	Change Catalyst	
	Building Bonds	
	Collaboration/Cooperation	
	Team Capabilities	

such, the mixed model provides a much broader, more comprehensive definition of emotional intelligence. A quick review of Table 7.5 shows that the attributes of emotional intelligence are qualities that most leaders should have, and Goleman (1998) and Goleman, Boyatzis, and McKee (2001; 2002) maintain that leaders need more or less all of these attributes to be emotionally intelligent. Moreover, the mixed model of emotional intelligence has been much more popular with human resource professionals and in the corporate world than the ability model. But does the mixed model really tell us anything different from what we already know? More specifically, is the mixed model any different than the FFM of personality? The fact of the matter is that the mixed model is very, very similar to the FFM. Comprehensive research by Van Rooy and Viswesvaran (in press) showed that EQ predicts job performance no better than the FFM, and research by Caruso, Mayer, and Salovey (2002) that the mixed model does not predict important job outcomes over and above the FFM. Goleman and Bar-On should deservedly get credit for popularizing the notion that noncognitive abilities are important predictors of leadership success. But on the negative side, they also maintain that they have discovered something completely new and do not give enough credit to the 100 years of personality research that underlie many of the attributes in the mixed model.

Can Emotional Intelligence Be Measured and Developed?

The publication of *Emotional Intelligence* (Goleman, 1996) has sprouted a cottage industry of books, training programs, and assessments related to measurement and development of emotional intelligence. Mayer, Salovey, and Caruso Emotional Intelligence Test (MSCEIT) is a measure of the ability model of emotional intelligence and asks subjects to recognize the emotions depicted in pictures, what moods might be helpful in certain social situations, and so forth (Mayer, Salovey, and Caruso, 2001). Bar-On has self, self-other, youth, and organizational measures of emotional intelligence, such as the Bar-On Emotional Quotient—360 or EQi-S (Bar-On, 2002).

The Emotional Competence Inventory (ECI) was developed by Goleman and consists of 10 questionnaires. These questionnaires are completed by the individual and nine others; the responses are aggregated and given to the participant in a feedback report. Because these researchers have defined emotional intelligence differently and use a different process to assess EQ, it is not surprising that these instruments often provide leaders with conflicting results (Schwartz, 2000). Nevertheless, the Air Force Recruiting Service has used the EQi to screen potential recruiters; it found that candidates scoring higher on the attributes of assertiveness, empathy, happiness, self-awareness, and problem solving were much less likely to turn over prematurely in the position and had a 90 percent chance of meeting their recruiting quotas (Schwartz, 2000).

One issue that most EQ researchers do agree upon is that emotional intelligence can be developed. Goleman and Aberman have developed one- to five-day training programs to help leaders improve their emotional intelligence; Bar-On has developed 15 e-learning modules that are available at EQ University.com. One of the big adopters of EQ training has been the sales staff at American Express Financial Advisors (AEFA). Leaders at AEFA discovered that the company had a well-respected set of investment and insurance products for customers, but many sales staff were struggling with how to respond to the emotions exhibited by clients during sales calls. Moreover, the best salespeople seem to be better able to "read" their clients' emotions and respond in a more empathetic manner. Since 1993 more than 5,500 sales staff and 850 sales managers at AEFA have attended a five-day training program to better recognize and respond to the emotions exhibited by clients. AEFA found that sales staff attending this program increased annual sales by an average of 18.1 percent, whereas those who did not attend training only achieved a 16.1 percent increase. However, the sample was very small and the comparison somewhat unfair because the control group did not receive any kind of sales training in lieu of the EQ training (Schwartz, 2000). Therefore, it is uncertain whether the EQ training content actually adds value over and above five days of sales training.

Implications of Emotional Intelligence

Aberman (2000) maintained that people can be extremely ineffective when their thoughts, feelings, and actions are misaligned—for example, arguing with someone on your cellular phone when driving on the interstate highway. It seems likely that leaders who are thinking or feeling one thing and actually doing something else are probably less effective in their ability to influence groups toward the accomplishment of their goals. The EQ literature should also be credited with popularizing the idea that noncognitive abilities, such as stress tolerance, assertiveness, and empathy, can play important roles in leadership success. Today, many organizations are using *both* cognitive and noncognitive measures as part of the process of hiring or promoting leaders. Finally, the EQ literature has also helped to bring emotion back to the workplace. Human emotions are very important aspects of one-on-one interactions and teamwork (Druskat & Wolff, 2001), but too many leadership practitioners and researchers have chosen to ignore the role they play. When recognized and leveraged properly, emotions can be the motivational fuel that help individuals and groups to accomplish their goals. When ignored or discounted, emotions can significantly impede a leader's ability to influence a group. As discussed in the FFM section of this chapter, leaders who can empathize and get along with others are often more successful than those who cannot.

Some of the more recent research in emotional intelligence indicates what moderates employees' reactions to job insecurity and their ability to cope with stress when threatened with job loss. Employees with lower EQ reported more negative emotional reactions and used less effective coping strategies when dealing with downsizing than those with higher EQ (Jordan, Ashkanasy, & Hartel, 2002). Along these lines, Wong and Law (2002) report positive relationships between leaders' and followers' EQ scores, job performance, and job satisfaction. And Boyatzis, Stubbs, and Taylor (2002) accurately point out that most MBA programs are more focused on cognitive abilities and developing financial skills than on those abilities needed to successfully build teams and get results through others.

Despite these positive contributions, emotional intelligence has several limitations. First, some researchers, Goleman in particular, have maintained that EQ is more important than intelligence when it comes to leadership success. Unfortunately, none of the research bears this out. The simple fact of the matter is that leaders will not be successful if they have lots of EQ but little IQ; the most effective leaders have both of these qualities. Second, Goleman and his associates and Bar-On have not acknowledged the existence of personality, much less 100 years of personality–leadership effectiveness research. As seen in Table 7.6, Goleman's conceptualizations of EQ look very similar to the FFM found in Table 7.1. At least as conceptualized by these two authors, it is difficult to see how EQ is any different from personality. Third, if the EQ attributes are essentially personality traits, then it is difficult to see how they will change as a result of a training intervention. Personality traits are very difficult to change, and the likelihood of changing 20 to 40 years of day-to-day behavioral patterns as the result of some e-learning modules or a five-day training program seems highly suspect. As we will see in the next chapter, people can change their behavior, but it takes considerable effort and coaching over the long term to make it happen. Finally, an important question to ask is whether EQ is really something new, or simply a repackaging of old ideas and findings? If EQ is defined as an ability model, such as the one put forth by Mayer, Salovey, and Caruso, then emotional intelligence probably is a unique ability and worthy of additional research (see Figure 7.6). A leader's skills in accurately perceiving, regulating, and leveraging emotions seem vitally important in building cohesive, goal-oriented teams, and measures like the MSCEIT (Mayer, Salovey, & Caruso, 2001) could be used in conjunction with FFM and cognitive abilities measures to hire and develop better leaders. But if EQ is defined as a mixed model, then it is hard to see that Goleman and his associates and Bar-On are really telling us anything new.

TABLE 7.6
Comparison between the FFM and Goleman's Model of EQ

Goleman et al.	Likely FFM Correlates
Self-Awareness	
Emotional Awareness	Agreeableness
Accurate Self-Assessment	Adjustment
Self-Confidence	Surgency
Self-Regulation	
Self-Control	Adjustment, Dependability
Trustworthiness	Dependability
Conscientiousness	Dependablity
Adaptability	Adjustment, Dependability
Innovation	Openness to Experience, Dependability
Motivation	
Achievement	Surgency
Commitment	Surgency
Initiative	Surgency
Optimism	Adjustment
Empathy	
Understanding Others	Agreeableness
Developing Others	Openness to Experience
Service Orientation	Agreeableness
Diversity	Agreeableness
Political Awareness	Agreeableness
Social Skills	
Influence	Surgency, Agreeableness
Communication	Surgency
Conflict Management	Agreeableness
Leadership	Surgency
Change Catalyst	Surgency
Building Bonds	Agreeableness
Collaboration/Cooperation	Agreeableness
Team Capabilities	Surgency, Agreeableness

FIGURE 7.6
Emotional
intelligence
and the
building
blocks of
skills.

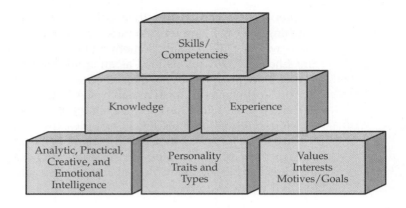

Summary This chapter examined the relationships between personality, intelligence, and emotional intelligence with leadership success. In general, all of these attributes can help a leader to influence a group toward the accomplishment of its goals, but in and of themselves they are no guarantee of leadership success. Oftentimes the situation will dictate which personality traits, components of intelligence, or emotional intelligence attributes will positively affect a leader's ability to influence a group.

Although the term *personality* has many different meanings, we use the term to describe one's typical or characteristic patterns of behavior. There are several different theories to describe why people act in characteristic ways, but the trait approach to personality has been the most thoroughly researched, and as such plays a key role in the chapter. The adoption of the Five Factor Model (FFM) of personality has helped to clarify the personality–leadership relationships, and researchers have noted that leadership success is positively correlated with the FFM personality dimensions of surgency, dependability, agreeableness, and adjustment.

The FFM comprises the bright side of personality, but there are a number of traits that also constitute the dark side of personality. Dark-side personality traits are irritating, counterproductive behaviors that are exhibited during times of stress and interfere with a leader's ability to build teams or get results through others. Virtually everyone has one or two dark-side traits; some of the keys to being a more successful leader is knowing which dark-side traits you possess, identifying the situations in which they appear, and developing strategies to manage them.

The most recent theory for understanding intelligence divides it into three related components: analytic intelligence, practical intelligence, and creative intelligence. All three components are interrelated. Most research shows that leaders possess higher levels of analytic intelligence than the general population, and that more intelligent leaders often make better leaders. Analytic intelligence appears to confer two primary benefits upon leaders. First, leaders who are smarter seem to be better problem solvers. Second, and perhaps more important, smarter leaders seem to profit more from experience.

The roles of practical and creative intelligence in leadership are receiving increasing attention. Practical intelligence, or one's relevant job knowledge or experience, is proving to be extremely important for leaders. Leaders with higher levels of practical intelligence seem to be better at solving problems under stress. Moreover, practical intelligence seems to be the easiest of the three components to change. This implies that leaders should use techniques such as the action-observation-reflection model, described in Chapter 3, to extract the most learning from their experiences.

Creative intelligence involves developing new and useful products and processes, and creativity is extremely important to the success of many businesses today. Creativity consists of seven components, including synthetic abilities, analytic intelligence, practical intelligence, thinking skills, relevant personality traits, intrinsic motivation, and several environmental factors. Understanding the seven components of creativity is important as the factors can give leaders ideas about how to improve their own and their followers' creativity. It is important that leaders learn how to successfully stimulate and manage creativity, even more than being creative themselves.

In some ways emotional intelligence is a relatively new concept, and there are at least four different definitions of emotional intelligence. Generally, emotional intelligence has to do with understanding and responding to one's own and others' emotions. Leaders who can better align their thoughts and feelings with their actions may be more effective than leaders who think and feel one way about something but then do something different about it. Although emotional intelligence has helped to point out the role emotions and noncognitive abilities play in leadership success, some of it seems to be nothing more than another label for personality. If this is the case, then emotional intelligence may be a leadership fad that will fade away over time.

Key Terms

Questions

1. What FFM and dark-side personality traits do you think would help professional sports players be more or less successful? Would successful coaches need the same or different personality traits and preferences? Would successful players and coaches need different traits for different sports?

2. Do you think personality is a helpful dimension for understanding the effectiveness of political leaders? Does this question necessarily imply that successful political leaders have good personalities, and unsuccessful ones bad personalities? (Hint: explore this issue by considering both the bright and the dark side of personality.)

3. Think of all the ineffective leaders you have ever worked or played for. What dark-side traits did these leaders possess that caused them to be ineffective?

4. Individuals may well be attracted to, selected for, or successful in leadership roles early in their lives and careers based on their analytic intelligence. But what happens over time and with experience? Do you think *wisdom*, for example, is just another word for intelligence, or is it something else?

5. What role would downsizing play in an organization's overall level of practical intelligence?

6. We usually think of creativity as a characteristic of individuals, but might some organizations be more creative than others? What factors do you think might affect an organization's level of creativity?

7. Can better leaders more accurately perceive and leverage emotions? How could you determine if this was so?

Skills

The leadership skills relevant to this chapter include:

- Learning from experience
- Problem solving
- Improving creativity
- Diagnosing performance problems in individuals, groups, and organizations

Activity

1. Your instructor has access to as on-line FFM and dark side personality assessments. Both instruments take about 40 minutes to complete and could be given as homework. Once the assessments are completed, you should review the feedback reports and discuss in class.

2. Your instructor could suspend a 30-foot rope approximately 2 feet off the ground. You and the rest of the class would get on one side of the rope. The rope represents an electrified fence, and your task is to get everyone successfully *over* the rope without touching it. You may not touch, lower, raise, or adjust the rope in any manner. You may not let any part of your skin or clothing touch the rope, nor can you drape anything over the rope to protect you from the current. There are two rules you must follow to successfully navigate the rope. First, before starting to cross the fence, everyone in the group must form a line parallel to the rope and hold hands with the people on either side. These links with the other people in the group cannot be broken. Second, a quality

error is committed if any group member touches the fence. If the group detects their own error, then only the person currently attempting to navigate the fence needs to start over. If the instructor catches the error but the group does not, then the instructor has the right to have the entire group start over. This is analogous to catching a bad product before it is delivered to a customer instead of delivering defecting products to customers. You will have about 25 minutes to plan and execute this exercise.

Minicase

"Lessons on Leadership from Ann Fudge"

How do you rescue one of the largest advertising and media services firms in the world from a downward spiral? That is the question Martin Sorrell faced when his London-based WPP Group acquired Young & Rubicam in 2000. After many years on top, Y&R was starting to lose momentum—and clients. Kentucky Fried Chicken, United Airlines, and Burger King had all decided to take their advertising dollars elsewhere. Sorrell needed to stop the exodus, but how? He decided a fresh face was needed and started a search for a new CEO for Y&R—he wanted a dynamic leader who could revitalize Y&R. He found such a leader in Ann Fudge.

Ann Fudge was formerly president of Kraft Foods. At Kraft she had been responsible for the success of the $5 billion division that included well-known brands such as Maxwell House, Grape Nuts, Shredded Wheat, and General Foods International Coffees. Fudge's reputation as a charismatic leader who listens was a major issue for Sorrell when he went looking for a new CEO for Y&R. Among the talents Fudge had to offer was an ability to interact effectively with all constituencies of a consumer business. Mattel Chairman and CEO Bob Eckert was Fudge's boss when he was president and CEO of Kraft. Of Fudge, Eckert says, "She is equally comfortable with consumers at the ballpark, factory workers on a production line, and executives in the boardroom. She could engage all three constituents in the same day and be comfortable. She is very comfortable with herself, and she's not pretending to be someone else. That's what makes her such an effective leader."

Her commitment to her work and the people she works with is evident in the lesson she offers to other leaders:

1. Be yourself, do not feign behavior that you think will make you "successful."
2. Always remember it's the people, not you. A leader cannot be a leader if he/she has no followers. Be honest with people. Give them feedback. Put the right people in the right jobs. Surround yourself with the smartest people you can find— people who will offer differing perspectives and diversity of experience, age, gender, race.
3. Touch your organization. It's easy to get stuck behind your desk. Fight the burden of paperwork and get out in the field. Don't be a remote leader. You cannot create a dynamic culture if people can't see, hear, touch you. Let them know you as a person.

4. Steer the wheel with a strategic focus, yet maintain a wide peripheral vision. Know when to stop, speed up, slow down, brake quickly, swerve, or even gun it!

Fudge had a difficult decision to make when she was approached by Sorrell about the position at Y&R. She was in the midst of a two-year break—after 24 years working for corporate America, Fudge decided to take some time for herself. She had left her position as president of Kraft Foods in 2001 based not on her dissatisfaction with her job, but on a desire to define herself by more than her career. "It was definitely not satisfaction, it was more about life," says Fudge about her sabbatical. During her two-year break she traveled, cycling around Sardinia and Corsica; she took up yoga; and she wrote a book: *The Artist's Way at Work,* a manual for improving creatively and innovation on the job.

Fudge took on the challenge and has not looked back. In her tenure at Y&R she has worked hard to get Y&R back on top. She has traveled the globe, visiting with Y&R employees around the world living rule number 3 of her own leadership rules. She frequently puts in 15-hour days pushing her strategy to focus on clients, encouraging teamwork, and improving creativity. A major undertaking for Fudge is to try and bring together the various business entities under the Y&R umbrella to better meet the needs of clients. She's also trying to institute a Six Sigma method for creativity—looking for ways to increase productivity so employees have more time to be creative.

Fudge's hard work is paying off. Y&R has recently added Microsoft and Toys R Us to their list of clients, and, if Fudge has her way, the list will continue to grow until Y&R is back on top.

1. How would Ann Fudge fall into each of the Five Factor Model (FFM) categories?
2. Consider the components of creative intelligence from Table 7.3. Identify the key components that have impacted Ann Fudge's success.
3. Ann Fudge decided to take a sabbatical to focus more on her personal life. Based on her experience, what are some of the benefits to such a break? What might be some of the drawbacks?

Sources: Diane Brady, "Act Two: Ann Fudge's two-year break from work changed her life. Will those lessons help her fix Young & Rubicam?", *Business Week* (3/29/04), p. 72; http://www.internet-marketing-branding.com/News/african_american.htm; http://www.brandweek.com/brandweek/search/article_display.jsp?vnu_content_id=1000506747; http://www.linkageinc.com/conferences/leadership/gild/

Chapter 8

Leadership Behavior

Introduction

> The leader sets the example. Whether in the Army or in civilian life, the other people in the organization take their cue from the leader—not from what the leader says, but what the leader does.
>
> *Colin Powell*

Throughout Chapters 4–7 we have been talking about different ways to assess leaders. But when all is said and done, how can we tell "good" leaders from "bad" leaders? One way to differentiate leaders is to look at results; some leaders have a track record of getting good results across a variety of situations whereas others seem to have difficulties getting work done through others. But another key way we distinguish between effective and ineffective leaders is to look at what they do on a day-to-day basis. Some leaders do a good job making decisions, providing direction, creating plans, giving regular feedback, and getting their followers the resources they need to be successful. Other leaders have difficulties making decisions, set vague or unclear goals, and ignore followers' requests for equipment. Although a leader's values, personality, and intelligence are important, variables like these only have an indirect relationship with leadership effectiveness. Their effect presumably comes from the impact they have on leader behavior, which appears to have a more direct relationship with the leader's ability to build teams and get results through others.

One advantage of looking at leaders in terms of behavior instead of, say, personality is that behavior is often easier to measure; leadership behaviors can be observed whereas personality traits, values, or intelligence must be inferred from behavior or measured with tests. Another advantage of looking at leader behavior is that many people are less defensive about, and feel in more control of, specific behaviors than they do about their personalities or intelligence. This point has significant implications for developing leadership skills, a topic we will take up in detail at the end of this book.

Leaders with certain traits, values, or attitudes may find it easier to effectively perform some leadership behaviors than others. For example, leaders with higher agreeableness scores (as defined in Chapter 7) may find it relatively easy to show concern and support for followers but may also find it difficult to discipline followers. Likewise, leaders with low recognition and affiliation values (Chapter 6) and who score low on the personality trait of sociability (Chapter 7) will be less comfortable giving public presentations. But because behavior is under conscious control, we can always choose to change our behavior as leaders if we want to. It is important to remember, however, that the ease in which we exhibit or can change behavior will partly be a function of our values, personality, and intelligence.

Followers and the situation are the two other major factors to keep in mind when evaluating leadership behavior. As described in Chapter 7, strong situational norms can play pervasive roles in leaders' behavior. Similarly, follower and situational factors can help determine whether a particular leadership behavior is "bad" or "good." Say a leader provided a group of followers with extremely detailed instructions on how to get a task accomplished. If the followers were new to the organization or had never done the task before, then this level of detail would probably help the leader get better results through others. But if the followers were very experienced, then this very same leader behavior would likely have detrimental effects. The same would be true if the company was in a financial crisis versus having a very successful year.

This chapter begins with a discussion on why it is important to study leadership behavior. We then review some of the early research on leader behavior, and discuss several ways to categorize or conceptualize different leadership behaviors. Next, we briefly summarize what is currently known about a common leadership behavior assessment technique, the 360-degree, or multirater, feedback questionnaire. The last section provides both a research perspective and some practical advice on behavioral change. It includes such topics as development planning, coaching, and mentoring.

Studies of Leadership Behavior

Why Study Leadership Behavior?

Thus far, we have reviewed research on a number of key variables affecting leadership behavior, but we have not directly examined fundamentally what leaders actually do to successfully influence a group. For example, what did Colin Powell do as a lieutenant to influence his platoon in Vietnam, and were the behaviors needed to be successful as the chief of the Joint Chiefs of Staff or secretary of state the same as or different from those needed in Vietnam? What exactly did Peter Jackson do to get a troupe of actors to commit to seven years of filming a trilogy that many said could not be done? Or to get New Line Productions to invest the $250,000,000 needed to create the movies? What did Aung San Suu Kyi do to win the Nobel Prize for Peace, and what does she continue to do that allows her to attract followers to the democracy movement in Burma? Because of these questions, it is appropriate to turn our attention to leader behavior itself, for if we could identify how successful leaders act compared with unsuccessful leaders, then we could design systems that would allow us to hire, develop, and promote the skills necessary for organizations to succeed in the future. Unfortunately, given the success of the Dilbert comic strip and the explosive growth of management consulting firms, it appears that there are a number of leaders (or persons in positions of leadership) who either do not know what to do and how to do it, or do not realize how their behavior is affecting the people who work for them (Curphy, 1996a; 1998a; 2002; 2003a, b, 2004a, e, h; Curphy & Hogan, 2004a, b; Hogan & Curphy, 2004; Chavan & Colvin; 1999).

> *For every person who's a manager and wants to know how to manage people, there are 10 people who are being managed and would like to figure out how to make it stop.*
>
> Scott Adams,
> the creator of "Dilbert"

Before we go into the different ways to categorize what leaders do to influence a group, it might be good to review what we know so far about leadership skills and behaviors. As seen in Figure 8.1, leadership behaviors (which include skills and competencies) are a function of intelligence, personality traits, emotional intelligence, values, attitudes, interests, knowledge, and experience. The factors in the bottom layer of blocks are relatively difficult to change, and they predispose a leader to act in distinctive ways. As described in Chapter 7, one's personality traits are pervasive and almost automatic, occurring typically without much conscious attention. The same could be said about how values, attitudes, and intelligence affect behaviors. Over time, however, it is hoped that leaders learn and discern which behaviors are more appropriate and effective than others. It is always useful to remember the pivotal roles individual difference and situational variables can play in a leader's actions (see Highlight 8.1).

The Early Studies

If you were asked how to study and identify the behaviors that best differentiated effective from ineffective leaders, how would you do it? Interviews, behavioral observation, and paper-and-pencil techniques (e.g., questionnaires) would seem

FIGURE 8.1
The building blocks of skills.

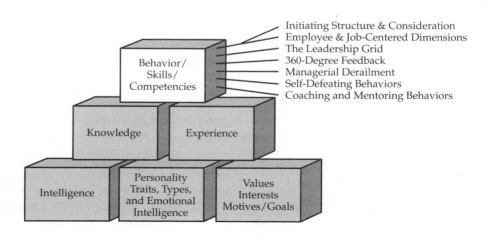

Initiating Structure & Consideration
Employee & Job-Centered Dimensions
The Leadership Grid
360-Degree Feedback
Managerial Derailment
Self-Defeating Behaviors
Coaching and Mentoring Behaviors

Behavior/ Skills/ Competencies

Knowledge   Experience

Intelligence   Personality Traits, Types, and Emotional Intelligence   Values Interests Motives/Goals

Behaviors versus Skills

Highlight 8.1

Leadership behaviors are somewhat different from leadership skills. A leadership behavior concerns a specific action, whereas a leadership skill consists of three components, which include a well-defined body of knowledge, a set of related behaviors, and clear criteria of competent performance. Perhaps leadership skills may be better understood by using an analogy from basketball. People differ considerably in their basketball skills; good basketball players know when to pass and when to shoot, and are adept at making layups, shots from the field, and free throws. Knowing when to pass and when to shoot is an example of the knowledge component, and hitting layups and free throws are examples of the behavioral component of skills. In addition, shooting percentages can be used as one criterion for evaluating basketball skills. Leadership skills, such as delegating, can be seen much the same way. Good leaders know when and to whom a particular task should be delegated (i.e., knowledge), they effectively communicate their expectations concerning a delegated task (i.e., behavior), and they check to see whether the task was accomplished in a satisfactory manner (i.e., criteria). Thus, a skill is knowing when to act, acting in a manner appropriate to the situation, and acting in such a way that it helps the leader accomplish team goals.

to be the most likely approaches. You could ask leaders what they do, follow the leaders around to see how they actually behave, or administer questionnaires to ask them and those they work with how often the leaders exhibited certain behaviors. These three approaches have been used extensively in past and present leadership research.

Much of the initial leader behavior research was conducted at Ohio State University and the University of Michigan. Collectively, the Ohio State University studies developed a series of questionnaires to measure different leader behaviors in work settings. Hemphill (1949) began this development effort by collecting over 1,800 questionnaire items that described different types of leadership behaviors. These items were collapsed into 150 statements, and these statements were then used to develop a questionnaire called the **Leader Behavior Description Questionnaire (LBDQ)** (Hemphill & Coons, 1957). In order to obtain information about a particular leader's behavior, subordinates were asked to rate the extent to which their leader performed behaviors like the following:

He lets subordinates know when they've done a good job.

He sets clear expectations about performance.

He shows concern for subordinates as individuals.

He makes subordinates feel at ease.

In analyzing the questionnaires from thousands of subordinates, the statistical pattern of responses to all the different items indicated leaders could be described in terms of two independent dimensions of behavior called consideration and initiating structure (Fleishman, 1973; Halpin & Winer, 1957). **Consideration** refers to how much a leader is friendly and supportive toward subordinates. Leaders high in consideration engage in many different behaviors that show supportiveness and concern, such as speaking up for subordinates' interests, caring about their personal situations, and showing appreciation for their work. **Initiating structure** refers to how much a leader emphasizes meeting work goals and accomplishing tasks. Leaders high in initiating structure engage in many different task-related behaviors, such as assigning deadlines, establishing performance standards, and monitoring performance levels.

The LBDQ was not the only leadership questionnaire developed by the Ohio State researchers. They also developed, for example, the Supervisory Descriptive Behavior Questionnaire (SBDQ), which measured the extent to which leaders in industrial settings exhibited consideration and initiating structure behaviors (Fleishman, 1972). The Leadership Opinion Questionnaire (LOQ) asked leaders to indicate the extent to which they believed different consideration and initiating behaviors were important to leadership success (Fleishman, 1989). The LBDQ-XII was developed to assess 10 other categories of leadership behaviors in addition to consideration and initiating structure (Stogdill, 1959). Some of the additional leadership behaviors assessed by the LBDQ-XII included acting as a representative for the group, being able to tolerate uncertainty, emphasizing production, and reconciling conflicting organizational demands.

Rather than trying to describe the variety of behaviors leaders exhibit in work settings, the researchers at the University of Michigan sought to identify leader behaviors that contributed to effective group performance (Likert, 1961). They concluded that four categories of leadership behaviors are related to effective group performance: leader support, interaction facilitation, goal emphasis, and work facilitation (Bowers & Seashore, 1966).

Both goal emphasis and work facilitation are **job-centered dimensions** of behavior similar to the initiating structure behaviors described earlier. **Goal emphasis** behaviors are concerned with motivating subordinates to accomplish the task at hand, and **work facilitation** behaviors are concerned with clarifying roles, acquiring and allocating resources, and reconciling organizational conflicts. Leader support and interaction facilitation are **employee-centered dimensions** of behavior similar to the consideration dimension of the various Ohio State questionnaires (see Table 8.1). **Leader support** includes behaviors where the leader shows concern for subordinates; **interaction facilitation** includes those behaviors where leaders act to smooth over and minimize conflicts among followers. Like the researchers at Ohio State, those at the University of Michigan also developed a questionnaire, the Survey of Organizations, to assess the degree to which leaders exhibit these four dimensions of leadership behaviors (Bowers & Seashore, 1966).

Although the behaviors composing the task-oriented and people-oriented leadership dimensions were similar across the two research programs, there was a fundamental difference in assumption underlying the work at the University of Michigan and that at Ohio State. Researchers at the University of Michigan considered job-centered and employee-centered behaviors to be at *opposite ends of a single continuum of leadership behavior.* Leaders could theoretically manifest either strong employee *or* job-centered behaviors, but not both. On the other hand, researchers at Ohio State believed that consideration and initiating structure were

TABLE 8.1

Ohio State Dimensions	University of Michigan Dimensions
Initiating Structure	Goal Emphasis & Work Facilitation
Consideration	Leader Support & Interaction Facilitation

independent continuums. Thus, leaders could be high in both initiating structure and consideration, low in both dimensions, or high in one and low in the other.

The key assumption underlying both research programs was that certain behaviors could be identified that are universally associated with a leader's ability to successfully influence a group toward the accomplishment of its goals. Here are the kinds of questions researchers were interested in:

> From the University of Michigan perspective, who tends to be more effective in helping a group to accomplish its goals, job- or employee-centered leaders?
>
> From the Ohio State perspective, are leaders who exhibit high levels of *both* task- and people-oriented behaviors more effective than those who exhibit *only* task or people behaviors?
>
> What role do situational factors play in leadership effectiveness? Are employee-centered leadership behaviors more important in nonprofit organizations or downsizing situations, whereas job-centered behaviors are more important in manufacturing organizations or start-up situations?

The answers to these questions have several practical implications. If leaders need to exhibit only job- or employee-centered behaviors, then selection and training systems need to focus only on these behaviors. But if situational factors play a role, then researchers need to identify which variables are the most important, and to train leaders how to modify their behavior accordingly.

As you might suspect, the answer to all of these questions is, "It depends." In general, researchers have reported that leaders exhibiting a high level of consideration or employee-centered behaviors had more satisfied subordinates. Leaders who set clear goals, explained what followers were to do and how to get tasks accomplished, and monitored results (i.e., initiating structure or job-centered) often had higher-performing work units if the group faced relatively ambiguous or ill-defined tasks (Bass, 1990; Judge, Piccolo, & Ilies, 2003; Eisenberger, Stinglhamber, Vandenberghe, Sucharski, & Rhoades, 2002). At the same time, however, leaders whose behavior was highly autocratic (an aspect of initiating structure) were more likely to have relatively dissatisfied subordinates (Bass, 1990). Findings like these suggest that *there is no universal set of leader behaviors always associated with leadership success.* Often the degree to which leaders need to exhibit task- or people-oriented behaviors depends upon the situation, and it is precisely this finding that prompted the research underlying the contingency theories of leadership described in Chapter 12. If you review these theories you will see strong links to the job- and employee-centered behaviors identified 40 years ago.

Alternative Conceptualizations of Leadership Behaviors

The Ohio State and University of Michigan studies were a good first step in describing what leaders actually do. Other researchers have extended these findings into more user-friendly formats or developed different schemes for categorizing

FIGURE 8.2
The Leadership Grid figure.

Source: Robert R. Blake and Anne Adams McCanse, *Leadership Dilemmas—Grid Solutions* (Houston: Gulf Publishing, 1991), p. 29. Copyright 1991, by Scientific Methods, Inc. Reproduced by permission of the owners.

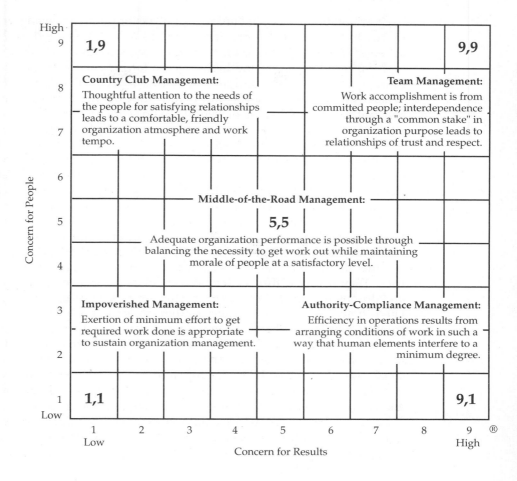

High
9 — **1,9** **9,9**

8 — **Country Club Management:** .... **Team Management:**
Thoughtful attention to the needs of the people for satisfying relationships leads to a comfortable, friendly organization atmosphere and work tempo. — Work accomplishment is from committed people; interdependence through a "common stake" in organization purpose leads to relationships of trust and respect.

7 —

6 —

Middle-of-the-Road Management:
5 — **5,5**
Adequate organization performance is possible through balancing the necessity to get work out while maintaining morale of people at a satisfactory level.
4 —

3 — **Impoverished Management:** .... **Authority-Compliance Management:**
Exertion of minimum effort to get required work done is appropriate to sustain organization management. — Efficiency in operations results from arranging conditions of work in such a way that human elements interfere to a minimum degree.
2 —

1 — **1,1** **9,1**
Low

Concern for People (vertical axis)

1   2   3   4   5   6   7   8   9   ®
Low   High
Concern for Results

leadership behaviors. Like the earlier research, these alternative conceptualizations are generally concerned with: (*a*) identifying key leadership behaviors, (*b*) determining whether these behaviors have positive relationships with leadership success, and (*c*) developing those behaviors related to leadership success. One popular conceptualization of leadership is really an extension of the findings reported by the University of Michigan and Ohio State leadership researchers. The **Leadership Grid**® profiles leader behavior on two dimensions: **concern for people** and **concern for production** (Blake & McCanse, 1991; Blake & Mouton, 1964). The word *concern* reflects how a leader's underlying assumptions about people at work and the importance of the bottom line affect leadership style. In that sense, then, the Leadership Grid deals with more than just behavior. Nonetheless, it is included in this chapter because it is such a direct descendant of earlier behavioral studies.

As Figure 8.2 shows, leaders can get scores ranging from 1 to 9 on both concern for people and concern for production depending on their responses to a leadership questionnaire. These two scores are then plotted on the Leadership Grid, and the two score combinations represent different leadership orientations.

Each orientation reflects a "unique set of assumptions for using power and authority to link people to production" (Blake & McCanse, 1991, p. 29). Amid the different leadership styles, the most effective leaders are claimed to have both high concern for people and high concern for production, and Leadership Grid training programs are designed to move leaders to a 9,9 leadership style. Whereas this objective seems intuitively appealing, where do you think Aung San Suu Kyi, Colin Powell, or Peter Jackson score on these two dimensions? Do all three of them show a high concern for production and people? Are there differences between the three leaders, or are all three 9,9 leaders?

Although the Leadership Grid can be useful for describing or categorizing different leaders, we should note that the evidence to support the assertion that 9,9 leaders are the most effective comes primarily from Blake, Mouton, and their associates. However, other more recent research might shed some light on whether 9,9 leaders are really the most effective. Robie, Johnson, Nilsen, and Hazucha (2001) conducted a study of 1,400 managers in the United States, Germany, Denmark, the United Kingdom, Italy, Spain, France, and Belgium to determine whether the same leadership behaviors were related to effectiveness across countries. They reported that leadership behaviors associated with problem solving and driving for results (initiating structure or 9,1 leadership) were consistently related to successfully influencing a group to accomplish its goals, regardless of country. Similar results about initiating structure and job performance were reported by Judge, Piccolo, and Ilies (2003). Using 800 managers in a U.S. high-tech firm, Goff (2000) reported that managers who spent more time building relationships (consideration or 1,9 leadership) also had more satisfied followers (i.e., they were less likely to leave the organization). Likewise, Judge, Piccolo, and Ilies (2003) and Eisenberger et al. (2002) reported strong support for the notion that higher consideration behavior can reduce employee turnover. These results seem to indicate that the most effective leadership style might just depend on the criteria used to judge effectiveness. The context and style of a leader's behavior are factors which affect impact (see Highlight 8.2).

So far in this section we have described several ways to categorize leaders or leadership behaviors, but what are the implications of this research for leadership practitioners? Believe it or not, you can see the practical application of this leadership behavior research in just about every Global 1000 company. As first discussed in Chapter 4, competency models describe the behaviors and skills managers need to exhibit if an organization is to be successful (King, Fowler, & Zeithaml, 2001). Just as leaders in different countries may need to exhibit behaviors uniquely appropriate to that setting to be successful, different businesses and industries within any one country often emphasize different leadership behaviors. Therefore, it is not unusual to see different organizations having distinct competency models depending upon the nature and size of the business, its level of globalization, or the role of technology or teams in the business (Peterson, 1998; Ulrich, Zenger & Smallwood, 1999). An example of a competency model for a major high-tech firm can be found in Figure 8.3. The inside wheel represents the general competencies, and the outside wheel represents the more specific skills managers in this company need to carry it successfully through the 21st century.

Does Humor Matter?

Highlight 8.2

Leaders exhibit many kinds of behavior. Some are focused on task accomplishment, whereas others are more related to supporting followers. Some leaders are naturally funny, and others seem stern and humorless. Does a leader's sense of humor affect his or her ability to influence a group toward the accomplishment of its goals? Several researchers examined this question and discovered the answer is not a simple yes or no. Laissez-faire leaders (1,1) who used humor reported having more satisfied followers, but did not have higher performing work groups. Task-focused leaders (9,1) who used humor actually had less satisfied and lower performing work units. Apparently their use of humor seemed out of sync with their constant focus on goal setting, productivity, and cost-cutting

initiatives. Transformational leaders (9,9), and those leaders with high levels of emotional intelligence who used humor seemed to have higher performing work groups. The key lesson from this research appears to be that the impact of a leader's humor will depend on the leader's style and the context in which it is delivered. Task-focused leaders should be keenly attuned to followers' needs when the company is facing an economic downturn or a difficult organizational dilemma, and also be aware that the use of humor in these situations will probably have just the opposite effect as intended.

Sources: B. J. Avolio, J. M. Howell, and J. J. Sosik, "A Funny Thing Happened on the Way to the Bottom Line: Humor as a Moderator of Leadership Style Effects," *Academy of Management Journal* 42, no. 2 (1999), pp. 219–27; F. Sala, "Laughing All the Way to the Bank," *Harvard Business Review,* September 2003, pp. 16–17.

Many of the best organizations now have competency models for different levels of management. For example, the behaviors and skills needed by department supervisors, store managers, district managers, regional vice presidents, and division presidents at The Home Depot vary considerably, and these differences are reflected in the competency models for each management group. These models help to clarify expectations of performance and describe the skills necessary for promotion. They also help human resource professionals to design selection, development, performance management, and succession planning programs so that organizations have a steady supply of leadership talent (Bracken, 1994; Curphy, 2001, 2002, 2003a, 2004a, e; Hogan & Warrenfelz, 2003; Louiselle, Bridges, & Curphy, 2003; Gebelein, 1994, 1996; Schippmann, Ash, Battista, Carr, Eyde, Hesketh, Kehoe, Pearlman, Prien, & Sanchez, 2000; Tett, Guterman, Bleier, & Murphy (in press).

According to Hogan and Warrenfelz (2003), the skills and behaviors found in virtually every organizational competency model fall into one of four major categories. **Intrapersonal skills** are those leadership competencies and behaviors having to do with adapting to stress, goal orientation, and adhering to rules and include the competencies found in Demonstrating Adaptability and Personal Values & Mastery in Figure 8.3. It is important to note that these skills and behaviors do not involve interacting with others, and they are among the most difficult to change. **Interpersonal skills** are those that involve direct interaction, such as communicating and building relationships with others. The competencies of Communication Skills and Aligning People & Processes in Figure 8.3 fall into this category, and these skills are somewhat easier to develop. The competencies of Sponsoring

FIGURE 8.3

An example of
a management
competency
model for a
Fortune 500
high-tech firm.

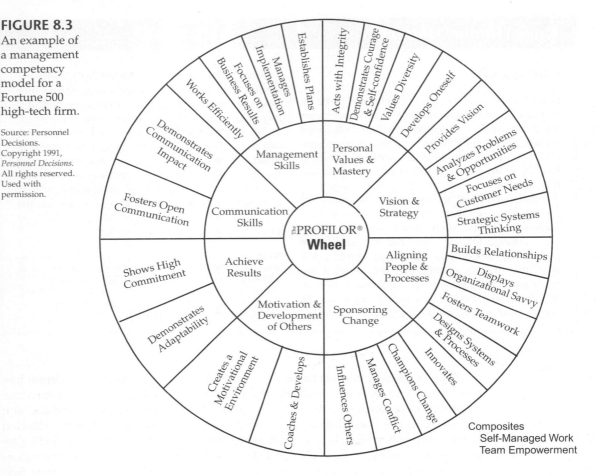

Change and Motivation & Development of Others in Figure 8.3 fall into the **Leadership skills** category. These are the skills and behaviors concerned with building teams and getting results through others, and these are more easily developed than the skills and behaviors associated with the first two categories. Finally, the competencies of Vision & Strategy and Management Skills fall into the **Business skills** category. These skills and competencies are often the focus of MBA programs and are the easiest to learn of the four categories. The Hogan and Warrenfelz (2003) domain model of leadership competencies is important as it allows people to see connections between seemingly different organizational competency models and makes predictions about how easy or difficult it will be to change various leadership behaviors and skills.

Although organizational competency models have played a pervasive role in selecting, developing, and promoting government and business leaders, they have not played much of any role in another common form of leadership, which is community leadership. **Community leadership** is the process of building a team of volunteers to accomplish some important community outcome (Krile, Lund, & Curphy, 2005), and represents an alternative conceptualization of leadership behavior. Examples of community leadership might include forming a group to raise funds for a new library, gathering volunteers for a blood drive, or organizing a campaign to stop the construction of a Wal-Mart. Thus, community leadership takes place whenever a group of volunteers gets together to make something happen (or not happen) in their local community.

But leading a group of volunteers is very different than being a leader in a publicly traded company, the military, or in a government agency. For one thing, community leaders do not have any position power; they cannot discipline followers who do not adhere to organizational norms, get tasks accomplished, or show up to meetings. They also tend to have fewer resources and rewards than most other leaders. And because there is no formal selection or promotion process, anyone can be a community leader. But whether they will be successful in their community change effort will depend on three highly interrelated competencies (see Figure 8.4). Just as you need the three ingredients of oxygen, fuel, and an igniter to start a fire, so will you need the three competencies of framing, building social capital, and mobilization to successfully drive community change efforts.

Framing is the leadership competency of helping a group or community recognize and define its opportunities and issues in ways that result in effective action. Framing helps the group or community decide *what* needs to be done, *why* it is important that it be done, and *how* it is to be done, and to communicate that in clear and compelling ways. Any community could take on a myriad of potential projects, but many of these projects never get off the ground because the person "in charge" never framed the project in such a way that others could understand: (*a*) the outcome; (*b*) how they would benefit by the outcome; or (*c*) what they would need to do to achieve the outcome.

Building social capital is the leadership competency of developing and maintaining relationships that allow people to work together in the community across their differences. Just as financial capital allows an individual to make choices

FIGURE 8.4
The components of community leadership.

Source: J. Krile, D. Lund & G. Curphy, *The Handbook of Community Leadership* (Grand Rapids, MN: The Blandin Foundation, 2005).

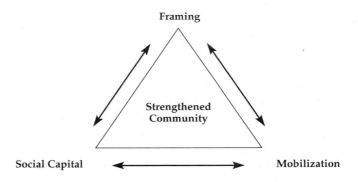

The Components of Community Leadership

about what they can purchase, such as buying a new television, car, or house, so too does social capital allow a community leader to make choices about which community change initiatives or projects are likely to be successful. If you have very little money, your options are severely limited. Likewise, leaders lacking social capital will have a very difficult time getting anything done in their communities, as they will not be able to mobilize the resources necessary to turn their vision into reality. Social capital is the power of relationships shared between individuals, an individual and a group, or between groups.

Engaging a critical mass to take action to achieve a specific outcome or set of outcomes is the leadership competency of **mobilization.** Community leaders will have achieved a critical mass when they have enough human and other resources to get done what they want to get done. People, money, equipment, and facilities are often needed to pass bond issues or attract new businesses to a community. Mobilization is about strategic, planned purposeful activity to achieve clearly defined outcomes. Almost anyone can get resources moving, but it takes leadership to get enough of the right resources moving toward the same target.

So how would the community leadership model come into play if you wanted to have a new student union built on your campus? First, you would need to frame the issue in such a way that other students understood what was in it for them and what they would need to do to make a new student union become reality. Second, you would need to reach out and build relationships with all of the current and potential users of the new student union. You would need to identify the formal and informal leaders of the different user groups and meet with them in order to gain and maintain their trust. Third, you would need these different user groups to take action in order to get the new student union built. Some of these actions might include raising funds, making phone calls, canvassing students to sign petitions, mounting a publicity campaign, and meeting with university and state officials who are the key decision makers about the issue.

It is worth noting that you need to do all three of the community leadership components well if you are to be successful. You might be able to succinctly frame the issue, but if you lacked social capital or could not get a critical mass mobilized, then you would probably not get very far on building the new student union. The same would be true if you had a broad and well-established network of students but did not frame the issue in such a way that followers could take action. It is likely that as many community change efforts fail as succeed, and the reasons for failure often have to do with inadequate framing, social capital, or mobilization.

Assessing Leadership Behaviors: Multirater Feedback Instruments

One way to improve leadership effectiveness is to provide leadership practitioners with feedback regarding the frequency and skill with which they perform various types of leadership behaviors. A $200-million industry has developed over the past two decades to meet this need. This is the **360-degree,** or **multirater feedback,** instrument industry, and it is difficult to overestimate the importance it has had on management development both in the United States and overseas. Jack Welch, the former CEO of General Electric, has stated that these tools have been critical to GE's success (Gebelein, 1994; Tichy & Cohen, 1997). Practically all of the Global 1000 companies are using some type of multirater feedback instrument for managers and key individual contributors (Edwards & Ewen, 1996; Campbell, Curphy, & Tuggle, 1995; Lepsinger & Lucia, 1997; Tornow & London, 1998; Collins, 1999; Morical, 1999; Bracken, Timmreck, & Church, 2000; Atkins & Wood, 2002; Curphy, 2002, 2003a, 2004a; Toegel & Conger, 2003). Multirater feedback instruments have been translated into 16 different languages, and well over five million managers have now received feedback on their leadership skills and behaviors from these instruments (Curphy, 2001). Because of the pervasiveness of multirater feedback in both the public and private sectors, it will be useful to examine some of the issues surrounding these instruments.

Every ten years or so a new management innovation comes along that generates much enthusiasm in organizations. Three hundred and sixty degree feedback has perhaps been the most notable management innovation of the 1990s.

LeeAnn Atwater
and David Waldman

Bracken, Timmreck and Church (2000) and Atkins and Wood (2002) pointed out that many managers and human resource professionals have assumed that a manager's self-appraisal was the most accurate source of information regarding leadership strengths and weaknesses. This view has changed, however, with the introduction of multirater feedback instruments. These tools show that direct reports, peers, and superiors can have very different perceptions about a target leader's behavior, and these perspectives can paint a more accurate picture of the strengths and development needs of the leader than self-appraisals alone (see Figure 8.5). A manager may think he or she gets along exceptionally well with others, but if 360-degree feedback ratings from peers and direct reports indicate that the manager is very difficult to work with, then the manager should gain new insights on what to do to improve his leadership effectiveness. Prior to the introduction of 360-degree instruments, it was difficult for managers to get accurate information about how others perceived their on-the-job behaviors since the feedback they received from others in face-to-face meetings tended to be adulterated or watered down (Campbell, Curphy, & Tuggle, 1995; Peiperl, 2001; Curphy 2002a, 2004a; Toegel & Conger, 2003; Jackman & Strober, 2003). Moreover the higher one goes in an organization, the less likely one is to ask for feedback which results in bigger discrepancies between self and other perceptions (Jackman & Strober, 2003; Sala, 2003). And, as described in Chapter 7, many of the most frequent behaviors exhibited by leaders are rooted in personality traits and occur almost automatically, and many leaders do not understand or appreciate their impact on others. As a result,

FIGURE 8.5
Sources for 360-degree feedback.

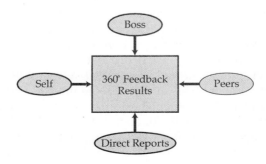

for a long time it was difficult for managers to determine how to leverage leadership strengths and overcome behavioral deficits. Today, most organizations use 360-degree tools for management development, as a part of a training or coaching program, in succession planning, or even as a part of the performance appraisal process (Lepsinger & Lucia, 1997; Ghorpede, 2000; DeNisi & Kluger, 2000; Bracken, Timmreck, & Church, 2000; Church & Waclawski, 2001; Curphy, 2002, 2004a; Pfau & Kay, 2002; Toegel & Conger, 2003).

Given the pervasive role 360-degree feedback plays in many organizations today, it is interesting to note that research is just starting to catch up with the use of these tools. Much of this research has explored whether 360-degree feedback even matters, whether self-observer perceptual gaps matter, whether leaders' ratings can improve over time, and whether there are meaningful culture/gender/race issues with 360-degree feedback ratings. With respect to the first issue, Atwater, Waldman, Atwater, and Cartier (2000) and Sala and Dwight (2002) reported that leaders who received 360-degree feedback had higher performing work units than leaders who did not receive this type of feedback. Church (1997, 2000) looked at independent measures of performance and reported that leaders receiving higher other (i.e., boss, peer, and direct report) ratings did get more accomplished than those who received lower ratings. These results indicate that 360-degree feedback ratings do matter (Ghorpade, 2000). But a study of 750 firms by Watson-Wyatt, a human resource consulting firm, reported that companies that used 360-degree feedback systems had a 10.6 percent decrease in shareholder value (Pfau & Kay, 2002). Although this research provides strong evidence that 360-degree feedback may not "work," it is important to note how these systems were being used in these firms. For the most part, Pfau and Kay (2002) examined firms using 360-degree feedback for performance appraisal, not development purposes. This distinction is important, as most 360-degree feedback systems are not designed to make comparisons *between* people. Instead, these systems are designed to tell leaders about their own relative strengths and development needs. But because 360-degree feedback are data based and provide good development feedback, many organizations decided to modify the process for performance appraisal purposes. This was a mistake, as with performance appraisals people are looking for favorable versus accurate feedback, and raters are induced to collude with each other if they know their pay or bonuses are going to be based on 360-degree feedback ratings (Toegel & Conger, 2003; Jackman & Strober, 2003; Greguras, Robie, Schleicher, & Goff III, 2003; Curphy, 2004g). When organizations use 360-degree feedback for performance appraisal purposes, they often get highly inflated ratings that do not provide good developmental feedback and make it difficult to make comparisons between leaders. The end result is a costly, time-intensive performance appraisal system that has little if any benefit to the individual or the boss and yields organizational results similar to those reported by Pfau and Kay (2002). The bottom line is that 360-degree feedback systems can add tremendous value, but only if they are used for development purposes (Toegel & Conger, 2003; Curphy & Hogan, 2004b).

> *Three hundred and sixty degree feedback results show that there are plenty of leaders who are leadership legends in their own minds but are also charismatically challenged in the eyes of others.*
>
> Gordy Curphy

As stated earlier, one of the advantages of 360-degree feedback is that it provides insight into self-perceptions and others' perceptions of leadership skills. But do self-observer gaps matter? Are leaders more effective if they have a high level of insight (i.e., rate their strengths and weaknesses as a leader the same as others do)? Some level of disagreement is to be expected, as bosses, peers, and direct reports may each have different expectations for a leader (Chueng, 1999; Hooijberg & Choi, 2000; Greguras & Robie, 1998; Mount, Judge, Scullen, Sytsma, & Hezlett, 1998). Nevertheless, insight does not seem to matter as far as leadership effectiveness is concerned. Even leaders with large self-observer gaps were effective as long as they had high observer ratings. On the other hand, the least effective leaders were those with high self and low others' ratings (Fleenor, McCauley, & Brutus, 1996; Church, 1997; Atwater, Ostroff, Yammarino, & Fleenor, 1998; Brett & Atwater 2001; Atkins & Wood, 2002; Sala & Dwight, 2002; Sala, 2003). The important lesson here is that leadership is in the eyes of others. And the key to high observer ratings is to develop a broad set of leadership skills that will help groups to accomplish their goals. Highlight 8.3 illustrates the responses of leaders who rejected their 360-degree feedback.

Another line of research has looked at whether 360-degree feedback ratings improve over time. In other words, is it possible to change others' perceptions of a leader's skills? One would hope that this would be the case, given the relationship between others' ratings and leadership effectiveness. Walker and Smither (1999) reported that managers who shared their 360-degree feedback results with their followers and worked on an action plan to improve their ratings had a dramatic improvement in others' ratings over a five-year period. Johnson and Johnson (2001)

> *In many cases the only person who is surprised by his or her 360-degree feedback results is the feedback recipient.*
>
> Gordy Curphy

Some of the Top Reasons for Rejecting Observer Feedback

Highlight 8.3

Being a leader is a tough job. Being a good leader is even tougher. Everyone you work with believes he or she is an expert on the subject of leadership, and it is difficult to keep everyone happy all of the time. Most leaders put forth considerable effort to be effective only to discover that they may be coming up short in the eyes of others. As a result, many leaders find 360-degree feedback to be a very valuable but somewhat unpleasant experience. The most effective leaders are those who accept unflattering feedback and do something about it. Less effective leaders are those who refuse to accept their 360-degree feedback results. The following are actual quotes of leaders who rejected their 360-degree feedback results:

- "My former boss told me to act this way. I'm actually nicer."
- "These ratings are biased because some of my observers are jealous of my promotion."
- "Human resources should have given this survey to more conscientious people."
- "The strengths are accurate, but the weaknesses are overstated."
- "I think my observers had the rating scale backwards when they completed the questionnaires."
- "These people aren't aware that I have changed those behaviors."

looked at 360-degree ratings over a two-year period and reported leadership productivity improvements of 9.5 percent for 515 managers in a manufacturing company. DeNisi and Kluger (2000), Church and Waclawski (2001), Curphy (2002), Waldman (2003), Smither, London, Flautt, Vargas & Kucine (2003), and Curphy & Hogan (2004a, b) aptly pointed out that 360-degree feedback alone is often not enough to improve leadership skills. Leaders must set development goals and commit to a development plan to improve skills if they want to see improvement in others' ratings (and, in turn, leadership effectiveness) over time.

The last line of research has explored whether there are important cultural, racial, or gender issues with 360-degree feedback. In terms of cultural issues, some countries, such as Japan, do not believe that peers or followers should provide leaders with feedback (Tornow & London, 1998). Other countries, such as Saudi Arabia, tend more to avoid conflict and provide only positive feedback to leaders (Curphy, 2001). The latter phenomenon is not limited to other countries, but appears also in the United States where researchers working in small organizations or in rural communities often report similar findings. People seem more hesitant to provide leaders with constructive feedback if they have to deal with the consequences of this feedback both on and off work (Curphy, 2001, 2002, 2003a, 2004a, g, h). The implication of these findings is that 360-degree feedback is not a management panacea; societal or organizational culture plays a key role in the accuracy and utility of the 360-degree feedback process.

With respect to racial differences, a comprehensive study by Mount, Sytsma, Hazucha, and Holt (1997) looked at the pattern of responses from bosses, peers, and subordinates for over 20,000 managers from a variety of U.S. companies. In general, these researchers reported that blacks tended to give higher ratings to other blacks, irrespective of whether they were asked to provide peer, subordinate, or boss ratings. However, the overall size of this effect was rather small. White peers and subordinates generally gave about the same level of ratings for both black and white peers and bosses. This was not the case for white bosses, however, who tended to give significantly higher ratings to whites who reported directly to them. These findings imply that black leaders are likely to advance at a slower pace than their white counterparts, as 80–90 percent of salary, bonus, and promotion decisions are made solely by bosses (Bernardin & Beatty, 1984). Later in this chapter Thomas (2001) will describe now these racial differences play out in mentoring programs.

With respect to gender issues, research indicates that there are some gender differences, though these differences tend to be slight. Female managers tend to get higher ratings on the majority of skills, yet their male counterparts are generally perceived as having higher advancement potential. There does not appear to be any same-sex bias in 360-degree feedback ratings, and female managers tend to be lower self-raters. Male managers tend to have less accurate self-insight and a higher number of blind spots when compared to their female counterparts (Personnel Decisions International, 1995).

So what should a leadership practitioner take away from all of this 360-degree feedback research? First, given the popularity of the technique, it is likely that you will receive 360-degree feedback sometime in your career. Second, 360-degree feedback should be built around an organization's competency model, which in turn describes the leadership behaviors needed to achieve organizational goals (Ulrich, Zenger, & Smallwood, 1999, Curphy 2004a; Curphy & Hogan, 2004a, b). Third, 360-degree feedback may be one of the best sources of "how" feedback for leadership practitioners. Leaders get plenty of "what" feedback—what progress they are making toward group goals, what level of customer service is being achieved, win–loss records, and so on, but they get very little feedback on "how" they should act to get better results. Multirater instruments provide this feedback. Fourth, effective leaders seem to have a broad set of well-developed leadership skills. Fifth, leaders need to create specific goals and development plans in order to improve leadership skills—360-degree feedback results give leaders ideas on what to improve but may not be enough in and of themselves to affect behavioral change. Sixth, leadership behavior can change over time, but it may take a year or two to acquire new skills and for the changes to be reflected in 360-degree feedback ratings. Finally, there are some cultural, racial, and gender issues associated with 360-degree feedback, and practitioners should be aware of these issues before implementing any 360-degree feedback process.

Managerial Derailment and Self-Defeating Behaviors

So far we have talked about what leaders can do in order to improve their effectiveness. The first lesson might be to determine which behaviors are most closely aligned with success, perhaps by identifying key behaviors by means of a competency model. Another lesson might be to get 360-degree feedback on these key behaviors. This feedback helps identify strengths and potential development needs. Not all leaders, however, truly learn such lessons. It might behoove us to look not just at how leaders succeed, but at the complementary question: why some leaders *fail*? We can learn valuable lessons about what *not* to do as a leader by studying them.

CEOs are three times more likely to get booted than a generation ago.

Ram Charan and
Geoffrey Colvin

There is a growing body of research that indicates that somewhere between 30 and 50 percent of managers and executives fail (Charan & Colvin, 1999; Hogan, Curphy, & Hogan, 1994; Sloane, Hezlett, Kuncel, & Sytsma, 1996; Dotlich & Cairo, 2001; Curphy, 2003a, 2004a; Curphy & Hogan, 2004a). These figures imply that up to half of the leaders in any organization are not going to be able to build cohesive teams or achieve business results, which unfortunately lends some weight to Scott Adams's quote at the beginning of the chapter. Initial research on **managerial derailment**—whereby individuals who at one time were on the fast track now had their careers derailed—was conducted in the early 1980s by researchers at the Center for Creative Leadership. The researchers went to the human resource departments in a number of Fortune 100 companies seeking lists of their "high-potential" managers. McCall and Lombardo (1983) defined high potentials as those individuals who had been identified as eventually becoming either the CEO/president or one of his or her direct reports sometime in the future. They waited for three years

We believe managerial failure is due more to having undesirable qualities than lacking desirable ones.

Robert and Joyce Hogan
Hogan Assessment Systems

and then returned to these organizations to ask what had happened to the people on the lists. They discovered that roughly a quarter of the high potentials had been promoted to one of the top two levels in the organization, and an equal percentage had not yet been promoted but would be as soon as a position became available. Another 25 percent had left the company; some had quit to form their own company and others were given a better offer somewhere else. Finally, about a quarter of the people on the list were no longer being considered for promotion. If they were still with the company, then they had been moved to a less influential and visible position. Many others had been asked to leave the company. These individuals represented cases of managerial derailment.

Several other researchers have investigated the managerial derailment phenomenon (Hazucha, 1992; Lombardo, Ruderman, & McCauley, 1987; Peterson, 1993a, 1993b; Van Velsor & Leslie, 1995; Dotlich & Cairo, 2001). This more recent research used much larger samples (Peterson examined over 600 derailed managers), European samples, and more sophisticated assessment tools (i.e., 360-degree feedback instruments). Moreover, a substantially higher percentage of women and minorities were represented in this more recent research, as the initial high-potential list was dominated by white males. As Van Veslor and Leslie (1995) pointed out, this research focused on identifying those factors which helped derailment candidates get initially identified as high potentials, as well as on those factors contributing to their ultimate professional demise. Although these studies varied in many ways, there are many consistent findings across them. Both groups were smart, ambitious, willing to do whatever it took to get the job done, and had considerable technical expertise. In other words, all of the high-potential candidates had impressive track records in their organizations.

On the other hand, the derailed candidates exhibited one or more behavioral patterns not evident in the high potentials who succeeded. The derailment themes can be found in Table 8.2 and are described in more detail below. It is important to note that four of the derailment themes included in Table 8.2 have been consistently reported in the research both in the United States and Europe, and that apparently a new theme is emerging and another is disappearing over time. The first derailment pattern has to do with an **inability to build relationships** with co-workers. The derailed managers exhibiting this pattern of behavior were very insensitive to the needs and plights of their followers and co-workers, and were often overly competitive, demanding, and domineering. They embraced the "my way or the highway" school of management. Many were also extremely arrogant and truly believed no one in their organizations was as good as they were, and they let their co-workers know it every chance they could. Some of these derailed managers also did whatever they felt necessary to get the job done, even if it meant stepping on a few toes in the process. Unfortunately, this is not one of the recommended techniques for winning friends and influencing people. It's better to remember the old adage that you should be careful whom you step on going up the ladder, because you may meet them again on your way down. Many of these managers left a trail of bruised people who were just waiting for the right opportunity

TABLE 8.2 Themes in Derailment Research

Four Enduring Themes	McCall & Lombardo (1983)	Morrison et al. (1987)	Lombardo & McCauley (1988)	United States (1993–94)	Europe (1993–94)
Problems with interpersonal relationships	Insensitive to others; cold, aloof, arrogant; overly ambitious	Poor relationships, too ambitious	Problems with interpersonal relationships, isolates self	Poor working relations	Poor working relations, organizational isolation, authoritarian, too ambitious
Failure to meet business objectives	Betrayal of trust; poor performance	Performance problems	Lack of follow-through	Too ambitious, lack of hard work	Too ambitious, poor performance
Inability to build and lead a team	Failing to staff effectively	Can't manage subordinates	Difficulty molding a staff	Inability to build and lead a team	Inability to build and lead a team
Inability to develop or adapt	Unable to adapt to a boss with a different style, unable to think strategically	Unable to adapt to a boss or culture, not strategic	Strategic differences with management, difficulty making strategic transitions	Unable to develop or adapt to conflict with upper management	Unable to develop or adapt
Emergent themes	—	Too narrow business experience	—	Not prepared for promotion, narrow functional orientation	Not prepared for promotion, narrow functional orientation
Disappearing themes	Overdependent on advocate or mentor	—	Over-dependence	—	—

Source: E. Van Velsor and J. B. Leslie, "Why Executives Derail: Perspectives across Time and Cultures," *Academy of Management Executive* 9, no. 4 (1995), pp. 62–71.

to bring these leaders down. Highlight 8.4 illustrates the case of a sales manager with derailment potential.

According to Van Velsor and Leslie (1995), approximately two-thirds of European and one-third of American derailment candidates fall into this pattern. For example, a female vice president of marketing and sales for a cellular phone company was fired from her $200,000 a year job for exhibiting many of the behaviors just listed. She was very bright, had an excellent technical background (an engineer by training), had already been the CEO for several smaller organizations,

An Example of a Derailed Leader

Highlight 8.4

The following is a story about a sales manager who seems to have derailment potential. See if you can pick out which derailment factors may be at play in this story. In addition, what advice would you give to the writer to "fix" the problem?

I've been working in a medium-sized manufacturing company for the past 20 years. I'm not in sales, but interact with salespeople on a daily basis. Over the past year or so, I have noticed the sales force has been frustrated. After numerous conversations not only with the sales force, but also with other people in all aspects of the company, I have realized that the poison is coming from one person: Mike, the sales manager. Mike has been with the company for over 10 years and has successfully maneuvered his way to the position of sales manager. All of his promotions were given to him because of his own self-promotion. He has an enormous ego. His tactics of bulldog management, double standards, and outright lying is driving his sales force out and is frustrating people all over the company. He is

disliked, even hated, by almost everyone in the company. Amazingly, Mike doesn't realize what people think of him. I believe the owners tolerate Mike's behavior because he has produced decent sales over the years. This year sales are substantially down. I believe the company is going to start to lose good salespeople because of Mike. Here's why: Nobody will confront him because if they do, he threatens them or makes them do some ridiculous assignment. All conversations with Mike are one-sided. If you bring up a concern that involves him, he will change the subject and dismiss you. It's like he is afraid of the truth. He is dishonest and essentially a loose cannon. I believe the owners know the truth about Mike but they continue to let him act this way. I believe Mike will never leave because he knows he could never get away with the things he does anywhere else. My concern is that if the owners don't fix the "Mike problem" they will start to lose good salespeople. Any advice?

Source: J. Lloyd, "Good Firms Work to Find Out Truth about Bad Managers," *Milwaukee Journal Sentinel,* August 20, 2000, p. 20.

and worked very long hours. Her in-depth managerial assessment results (Chapters 4 and 7) indicated that she also had a strong leaderlike personality, with higher scores in surgency and dependability and average scores in agreeableness and adjustment. This assessment also indicated she had extremely high bold scores, and at work this dark-side trait would manifest itself by her talking down to people, quickly identifying and capitalizing on others' faults, constantly commenting on their incompetence, running over her peers when she needed resources or support, promoting infighting among her peers and subordinates, and expecting to be pampered. Interestingly, she had no idea she was having such a debilitating effect on those she worked with until she received her 360-degree feedback. Had she received this feedback sooner, she might have been able to stop her career from derailing.

The devil that you know is better than the one you do not know.

Old folk saying

Charan and Colvin (1999) and Dotlich & Cairo (2001) stated that people problems are one of the primary reasons why CEOs fail. However, unlike derailed midlevel managers, most CEOs get along with others in the company. The problem with CEOs is that they get along with some of their direct reports too well and do not take timely action to address problem performers. More specifically, some CEOs fail because they place loyal subordinates into jobs they are incapable of handling, falsely believe they can help poorly performing subordinates to change ineffective behavior, do not want to offend Wall Street or the board by letting popular (but ineffective) executives go, or do not feel comfortable hiring outsiders to fill key executive positions.

Another derailment pattern identified in Table 8.2 is a **failure to meet business objectives.** Although both successful and derailed managers experience business downturns, the groups handled setbacks quite differently. Successful managers took personal responsibility for their mistakes and sought ways to solve the problem. Derailed managers tended to engage in finger-pointing and blaming others for the downturn. *But as long as things were going well,* it was difficult to differentiate these two groups on this factor. Some of these managers were also untrustworthy. They either blatantly lied about business results or failed to keep promises, commitments, or deadlines. The most common reason for CEO failure is the inability to meet earnings projections (Charan & Colvin, 1999; Dotlich & Cairo, 2001). However, this inability to meet financial projections is not the result of a poor business strategy, unwanted products and services, or inadequate distribution channels. Most CEOs have well-above-average analytic and practical intelligence, so they usually do not have a problem developing a vision or strategy for the company, nor do they make poor decisions concerning which markets to pursue and products to develop. In many cases, CEOs fail to get results because of their inability to execute according to the business strategy. They tend to get distracted and lose focus or do not hold their direct reports accountable for getting the results outlined in their business plans.

The third derailment pattern identified by Van Velsor and Leslie (1995) was an **inability to lead and build a team.** Some managers derailed because they hired staff who were just like themselves, which in turn only served to magnify their own strengths and weaknesses. Others wanted to stay in the limelight and hired staff less capable than they were. Still others micromanaged their staffs, even when not expert themselves in the tasks (not that it's ever recommended). These bosses wanted their followers to "check their brains at the door" before coming to work. One thing that often underlies this pattern is a lack of trust and high

> *When the dog is dead, the fleas are gone.*
>
> Puerto Rican folk saying

colorful and diligent scores (Chapter 7).

All of the dark-side traits listed in Chapter 7 can make it difficult for leaders to build cohesive, goal-oriented teams. But another key reason why leaders cannot build teams is when they spend too much time doing activities below their leadership level. The notion of leadership levels was first introduced in Chapter 4, which outlined the activities normally associated with individual contributor, front-line leaders, mid-level leaders, functional leaders, business unit leaders, and CEOs. Leaders who are at the functional leader level but spend too much time doing individual contributor or front-line leader tasks risk disempowering all the managers who work for them. Because these leaders are making all the decisions that their followers would normally make, followers become disengaged with work and team performance suffers as a result.

Another derailment profile has to do with a leader's **inability to adapt** to new bosses, businesses, cultures, or structures. As pointed out earlier in this chapter, many business situations require different leadership behaviors and skills, and some derailed managers could not adapt or adjust their styles to changing bosses, followers, and situations. They persisted in acting the same way, even when it was no longer appropriate to new circumstances. When solving problems, they often imposed past solutions that were no longer viable (i.e., high cautious scores from Chapter 7). For example, a first-line supervisor for an electronics firm that built video poker machines was having a very difficult time transitioning from his old job as a missile guidance repairman in the U.S. Air Force. He thought he should lead his subordinates the way he led others in the military: his staff should be willing to work long hours and over the weekends without being told, and to travel for extended periods of time with short notice. Their thoughts or opinions on ways to improve work processes did not matter to him, and he expected everyone to maintain cool and professional attitudes at work. After half of his staff quit as a direct result of his supervision, he was demoted and replaced by one of his subordinates.

In the past, organizations could afford to take their time in identifying and developing leadership talent. Many of the best organizations today have strong programs for systematically developing leadership bench strength (Charan, Drotter, & Noel, 2001; Tichy & Cohen, 1997; Curphy, 1998a, 2002, 2003c, 2004a, c; Curphy & Hogan, 2004a, b). However, more and more organizations today are under increasing pressure to find good leaders quickly, and they are increasingly asking their own high-potential but inexperienced leadership talent to step up to the plate and fill these key roles. Although these new leaders are bright and motivated, they often have narrow technical backgrounds and lack the leadership breadth and depth necessary for the new positions. These leaders often skip various leadership levels (see Chapter 4), and the unfortunate result is that many of these leaders leave the organization because of **inadequate preparation for promotion.**

For example, a relatively young woman attorney was promoted to be the vice president of human resources in a large telecommunications firm. Although she was extremely bright and ambitious, it soon became apparent that she lacked much of the necessary skill or knowledge. Although she tried very hard to be successful, she kept acting as a front-line leader instead of a functional leader and failed to earn the respect of her staff. After six months she was given a generous separation package and asked to leave the company. According to Van Velsor and Leslie (1995), this is a relatively new derailment theme. Given the contributing factors, it is also a theme that is likely to be more prevalent in the future.

Most derailed managers manifested several of these themes; the presence of only one of these behavioral patterns was usually not enough for derailment. The only exception to this rule was a failure to meet business objectives. Managers who did not follow through with commitments, broke promises, lied, were unethical, and did not get results did not stay on the high-potential list for long (i.e., high mischievous and bold scores from Chapter 7). Although this research has not identified any unique derailment patterns for minorities, some male-female differences have been noted. Females were more likely to derail because of their inability to deal with broader and more complex organizational issues or to lead people from different technical backgrounds than their own (practical intelligence). Males were more likely to derail because of their arrogance, inflexibility, or abrasive interper-

TABLE 8.3
Common Self-Defeating Behaviors

Source: M. R. Cudney and R. E. Hardy, *Self-Defeating Behaviors* (San Francisco: HarperCollins. 1993).

Procrastination	Suspiciousness
Defensiveness	Overcommitted
Worrying	Overly critical
Alienating	Rigidity
Hostility	Overcontrolling
Perfectionism	Inability to trust others

sonal style (bold, cautious, or excitable dark side traits).

One might think that most managers exhibiting derailment behavioral patterns would be aware of the negative impact they have on others. Unfortunately, this is not always so. Many managers on the path to derailment are simply unaware of the way they come across to others. Research on self-defeating behaviors may explain how these counterproductive behavior patterns develop and why some managers lack insight into their behavior. According to Cudney and Hardy (1993), a **self-defeating behavior** is an action or attitude that once helped an individual cope with a stressful experience but interferes with the individual's ability to cope in new situations.

A list of some of the more common self-defeating behaviors can be found in Table 8.3. You can also see that the behaviors in Table 8.3 are similar to the derailment themes and the dark-side personality traits previously identified in Chapter 7. Like the behaviors associated with dark-side personality traits, a big part of the problem with self-defeating behaviors is that they are highly practiced and often performed automatically, with little conscious thought. Furthermore, a person may rationalize the appropriateness of a self-defeating behavior by recalling some particular situation where the behavior *was* adaptive (or seemed so). But problems may occur when such behaviors get generalized from *unusual* circumstances to *most* circumstances. For example, everyone worries about some things sometimes (e.g., how an interview is going to go; whether your presentation made a good impression on the audience, whom to select for an important assignment, whether to major in this subject or that). Worrying becomes a problem, however, when it becomes habitual and consuming—when it keeps you from *doing* anything else or from actually *making* a decision. It may never be particularly helpful, but that's when it becomes truly self-defeating.

The first and paramount responsibility of anyone who purports to manage is to manage the self: one's own integrity, character, ethics, knowledge, wisdom, temperament, words, and acts. It is a complex, unending, incredibly difficult, oft-shunned task. We spend little time and rarely excel at self-management precisely because it is so much more difficult than prescribing and controlling the behavior of others. However, without management of self, people are not fit for authority no matter how much they acquire, for the more authority they acquire the more dangerous they become. It is management of the self that should occupy 50 percent of our time and the best of our ability. And when we do that, the ethical, moral, and spiritual elements of management are inescapable.

Dee Hock

How could such a seemingly irrational and counterproductive behavior ever become a habit for some people? Strange as it may seem, it can happen through reinforcement. The head of a management consulting firm was asked to open a new office in a large U.S. city. He worked an average of 70–80 hours a week identifying and building relationships with and delivering products and services to key clients. These efforts paid off, and in less than three years the office had grown from 1 to 15 people and from $50,000 to $2,500,000 in annual revenue. As staff and revenues grew, the head of the firm was reinforced through bonus and salary increases to continue to build relationships with, and deliver services to, clients. Unfortunately, this leader failed to acknowledge the importance of supporting, coaching, and developing his people—he was a classic task-focused, 9,1 leader. He also spent a vast majority of his time doing individual contributor versus mid-level leader work. Although this style of leadership was effective for opening the office, his overcommitment to task performance began to have a debilitating effect on the morale of the office. The leader in this case was fortunate enough to recognize the impact of his self-defeating behaviors, and was able to utilize some of the techniques in the next section to change these behaviors, improve morale, and continue to obtain good business results. Another example of the potential consequences of self-defeating behaviors is in Highlight 8.5.

The Invisible Barrier—What Precludes Black Managers from Advancement?

Highlight 8.5

Herdie Baisden, a black general manager and vice president of a management consulting firm, has investigated why black managers failed to advance in many organizations. Working with a variety of psychological assessment instruments as well as 360-degree feedback tools, Baisden noted that black managers tended to react differently to negative feedback than white managers. Baisden stated that blacks tended to dismiss this information as a product of racism rather than viewing it as a springboard for improvement. Blacks also tended to avoid feedback because they felt they needed to be exceptionally competent to succeed and wanted to project an image that "everything is under control and I don't need any help." When black managers did seek feedback from others, they often turned to others they could trust—other blacks. Blacks make up only 6 percent of management but they turned to blacks 22 percent of the time when soliciting feedback. These reactions often resulted in distorted 360-degree feedback ratings for black managers. These individuals tended to overrate their own performance and have bigger self-other gaps between their own ratings and their bosses' ratings of them when compared to white managers.

Baisden stated that some of these protective behaviors may be natural outgrowths of the work situations facing black managers. If a black manager perceives that a work environment is nonsupportive at best or hostile at worst, then these behaviors make sense. Unfortunately, these reactions ultimately become self-defeating behaviors, as they prevent black managers from getting the feedback they need in order to improve. Baisden maintains that blacks wishing to advance need to be receptive to feedback from others. This not only provides them with developmental ideas, it also tells the organization that the manager is willing to take risks and grow.

Source: H. Baisden, *PDI Indicator: The Rise of Black Managers* (Minneapolis: Personnel Decisions, 1993).

Changing Behavior

Why Change Behavior?

The material covered so far can help leadership practitioners better understand the key behaviors associated with success; how successful leadership behaviors may vary depending on the leadership level, country, culture, or business; what kind of behaviors could get them into trouble; and how to get feedback on these behaviors. But the fact of the matter is that knowing this information is not enough. Ultimately, some of the leader's behavior needs to *change*. But changing behavior, especially long-standing patterns of behavior, can be quite difficult.

> *Organizations don't change; people change. If you want your organization to do something differently, then you'll have to figure out how to get people to change their behavior.*
>
> David B. Peterson

How many times have you asked yourself how you could possibly change your own or another's behavior? Learning how to change your own and others' behaviors is a key leadership skill, given that situations, technology, organizational structure, followers, bosses, products, rules and regulations, and competitors seem to be in a constant state of flux. Moreover, think about the new behaviors and skills you will need to acquire as you move from individual contributor, front-line supervisor, mid-level manager to executive roles. Just as the head of the management consulting firm learned to add more supportive or employee-centered behaviors to his repertoire, so must you learn how to adapt your behavior to meet the changing demands of the role or situation (see Highlight 8.6). But learning how to change your own behavior is often not enough. Good leaders also know how to change and modify the behaviors of their followers so that they can be more effective team members and better achieve team goals. In the next section we discuss research surrounding three common methods of behavioral change: development planning, coaching, and mentoring. While this section is primarily research focused, practical tips on how to change behavior through development planning and coaching can be found in Part V of this book.

Development Planning

How many times have you made a resolution to change a habit, only to discover two months later that you are still exhibiting the same behaviors? This is often the fate of well-intentioned New Year's resolutions. Most people do not even make such resolutions since the failure rate is so high. Given this track record, you might wonder if it is even possible to change one's behavior, particularly if it has been reinforced over time and is exhibited almost automatically. Fortunately, however, it is possible to change behavior,

> *When you're in a new job where you're stretched, your focus should be on learning, not getting an A.*
>
> Mary Dee Hicks

even long-standing habits. For example, many people permanently quit smoking or drinking without going through any type of formal program (Miller & Rollnick, 1991; Polivy & Herman, 2002). Others may change after they gain insight into how their behavior affects others. Some will need support to maintain a behavioral change over time, while still others seem destined to never change.

Can People Really Change?

Highlight 8.6

When all is said and done, the terms *leadership* and *change* are almost synonymous. Effective leaders are those who are constantly changing their own and followers' behaviors in order to better adapt to the situations they face. Leaders and followers often have to exhibit new behaviors with the launch of new products and services, the introduction of new IT or financial systems, the acquisition or divestiture of companies, or the downsizing of staff. Although there is constant pressure to change, it is important to understand that many people naturally resist change. Some of this resistance stems from difficulty in dealing with ambiguity, some of it comes from a fear of no longer knowing the rules and what it will take to succeed, and some of it is out of competing agendas and a strong fear of failure. Successful leaders are those that can consistently overcome the resistance to change and get people to exhibit different behaviors in order to achieve team goals.

But how much can people really change? According to the book, *First, Break All the Rules* (Buckingham & Coffman, 1999), people change very little. These authors believe people are more or less "hard wired" as a result of their values, intelligence, and personality, so leaders would be better off trying to find jobs that leverage followers' natural strengths rather than try to change their behaviors. Although this book has proved wildly popular over the past five years, some

of the advice contained therein is simply wrong. First, there is in fact ample evidence to show that people can and do change. They may not change that much, but even subtle changes can have large payoffs for people in leadership positions. Second, many leaders simply do not have the luxury of changing jobs to fit their followers' strengths. For example, a typical route manager at Waste Management may supervise 25 drivers of garbage trucks. It would be nice to find 25 different jobs that leveraged each of the drivers' strengths, but at the end of the day the garbage still needs to get picked up. Third, and perhaps most importantly, what may at one time be seen as strengths can easily turn into fatal flaws. Someone who was very planful and detail oriented as an individual contributor could also be a micromanager as a mid-level manager. Leaders need to understand where and when to leverage their strengths and when these same behaviors can get them into trouble. On the positive side, Buckingham and Coffman are correct in pointing out that hiring the right people and putting them in the right jobs can go a long way towards achieving team goals.

Sources: M. Buckingham and C. Coffman, *First, Break All The Rules* (New York: Simon & Schuster, 1999); R. Kegan and L. Laskow Lahey, "The Real Reason People Won't Change," *Harvard Business Review,* November 2001, pp. 84–93; P. LaBarre, "Marcus Buckingham Thinks Your Boss Has an Attitude Problem," *Fast Company,* August 2001, pp. 88–98.

Managers seem to fall into the same categories; some managers change once they gain insight, others change with support, and others may not ever change. But do people just fall into one of these groups by accident? Is there any way to stack the odds in favor of driving behavioral change? Research by Hazucha, Hezlett, and Schneider (1993); McCauley, Ruderman, Ohlott, and Morrow (1994); Hezlett and Koonce (1995); Peterson and Hicks (1995, 1996); Dalton (1998); DeNisi and Kluger (2000); Behar, Arvidson, Omilusik, Ellsworth, and Morrow (2000); and Peterson (2001) provides several suggestions that leaders can take to accelerate the development of their own leadership skills. We can use the Development Pipeline described in Chapter 3 as a way to categorize these suggestions. As seen in Figure 8.6, the first step in changing behavior is knowing what to work on. Leaders need to have insight about their development needs, and 360-degree feedback can provide very useful information in this regard (Brett & Atwater, 2001; Curphy, 2002, 2003c,

FIGURE 8.6 The development pipeline.

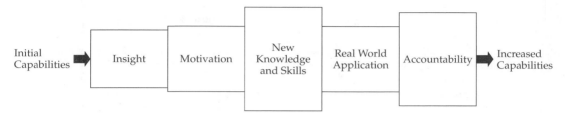

2004h). Other sources of information about development needs can come from the results of an assessment center, a performance appraisal, or direct feedback from others.

Nine out of 10 information technology workers said they would feel more loyal to their employer if they had an individual development plan, but only 30 percent reported having any kind of development plan.

Jeff Stoner

The next step in developing one's own leadership skills is working on development goals that matter. No leader has all of the knowledge and skills necessary to be successful; as a result most leaders have multiple development needs. Leaders need to determine which new skills will have the highest personal and organizational payoffs and build development plans that address these needs. The development plan should be focused on only one or two needs; plans addressing more than this tend to be overwhelming and unachievable. If leaders have more than two development needs, then they should first work to acquire one or two skills before moving on to the next set of development needs.

Figure 8.6 indicates that acquiring new knowledge and skills is the next step in the Development Pipeline. For leaders, this means creating a written **development plan** that capitalizes on available books, seminars, college courses, e-learning modules, and so forth, to acquire the knowledge underlying a particular development need (see Figure 8.7). For example, you can either learn how to delegate through the school of hard knocks or take a seminar to learn the best practices of delegation skills. As we will see, knowledge alone is not enough to develop a new skill, but relevant books and courses can accelerate the learning process (Arthur Jr., Bennett Jr., Edens & Bell, 2003). In addition, it is important not to underestimate the power of having a written development plan. Leaders (and followers) who have a written plan seem more likely to keep development on their radar screens and take the actions necessary to acquire new skills.

The more you crash, the more you learn.

David B. Peterson

Taking courses and reading books are good ways for leaders to acquire foundational knowledge, but new skills will only be acquired when they are practiced on the job. Just as surgeons can read about and watch a surgery but will only perfect a surgical technique through repeated practice, so too will leaders only acquire needed skills if they practice them on the job. Therefore, good development plans

FIGURE 8.7 Sample individual development plan.

Source: K. Louiselle, S. Bridges, and G. J. Curphy, "Talent Assessment Overview," working paper, 2003.

Name: Chris   **Date:** August, 2003

Sample _____

Career Objective: To get promoted to a director-level position.

Development Objective: Build a stronger team and better teamwork in my group.	Success Criteria: Consistently meet our quarterly team goals and increase ratings of "effective teamwork" by 20% on the employee survey.
Assets: Highly capable/skilled team members.	**Liabilities:** Lack agreement on and commitment to team goals. Lack clear accountability for results.

Action Steps	Measures of Progress/Results	Feedback or Other Resources Needed	Review/Completion Date
Convene team meeting to discuss and reach agreement on team goals.	Documented goals shared at department meeting.	Full team	9/15/03
Convene team meeting to begin establishing specific action plans for meeting team goals. Assign subgroups to develop plans for different goals.	Formal plans prepared and shared at department meeting. Plans specify individual accountability for steps and results.	Full team	1/15/03
Review and get bosses buy-in to team goals and action plans.	Boss's agreement and stated support.	Boss	10/15/03
Meet with individual team members to identify things I should stop, start, or continue doing in order to create a stronger sense of teamwork.	Create and share with full team a short list of high-priority things I am committed to doing in order to foster a stronger sense of teamwork.	Individual team members	10/15/03
Hold space on the agenda of each monthly meeting for team reporting on progress against team goals.	Minutes from each meeting reflect progress reports.	Admin. Asst. to circulate minutes.	Monthly
Solicit feedback from team at least quarterly to check my progress on the high-priority things I will commit to doing.	Team recognizes my progress (as reported informally in team meetings).	Full team	Quarterly beginning 12/1/04
	Annual employee survey results related to team effectiveness increase by 20% for my group and remain at that level.	Employee Survey	Summer 2004 and annually thereafter

capitalize upon on-the-job experiences to hone needed leadership skills. Peterson (2001) wrote that most leadership positions offer ample opportunities to develop new skills, provided that leaders leverage all of the experiences available to them. These on-the-job activities are so important to development that 70 to 80 percent of the action steps in a development plan should be job related.

The last step in acquiring new skills is accountability, and there are several ways to make this happen with a development plan. One way to build in accountability is to have different people provide ongoing feedback on the action steps taken to develop a skill. For example, leaders could ask for feedback from a peer or direct report on their listening skills immediately after staff meetings. Another way to build accountability is to periodically review progress on development plans with the boss. This way the boss can look for opportunities to help the leader further practice developing skills and determine when it is time to add new development needs to the plan.

It is important to realize that **development planning** is more than a plan—it is really a process (Peterson & Hicks, 1995). Good development plans are constantly being revised as new skills are learned or new opportunities to develop skills become available. Leaders who take the time to write out and execute best-practice development plans usually report the most improvement in later 360-degree feedback ratings. Development planning provides a methodology for leaders to improve their behavior, and much of this development can occur as they go about their daily work activities.

Coaching

Development plans tend to be self-focused; leaders and followers use them as a road map for changing their own behaviors. When trying to change the behavior of followers, however, leaders can often do more than review a follower's development plan, provide ongoing feedback, or review plans periodically with followers. The next step in followers' development often involves coaching. Coaching is a key leadership skill, as it can help leaders to improve the bench strength of the group, which in turn should help the group to accomplish its goals. Because of its role in development, coaching can also help to retain high-quality followers (Wenzel, 2000). Because of these outcomes, coaching is a popular topic these days, but it is also a frequently misunderstood one. It is hoped that the material in this section will help to clarify what coaching is, and identify some best-coaching practices.

> *Coaching is the quickest, most customized, and most powerful behavior change technique available to a leader.*
>
> David B. Peterson

Coaching is the "process of equipping people with the tools, knowledge, and opportunities they need to develop themselves and become more successful" (Peterson & Hicks, 1996, p. 14). In general, there are two types of coaching, informal and formal coaching. **Informal coaching** can occur anywhere in an organization, and occurs whenever a leader helps followers to change their behaviors. According to Peterson and Hicks (1996), the best informal coaching generally consists of five steps (see Table 8.4). In *forging a partnership,* leaders build a trusting relationship with their followers, identify followers' career goals and motivators, and learn how their followers view the organization and their situation. The key question to be answered in this first step of coaching is "development for what?" Where do the followers want to go with their careers? Why do they want to go there? The answers to these questions help to create a target or end goal as well as a personal payoff for development. Nevertheless, if a leader fails to build a relationship based on mutual trust with a follower, then chances are the follower will not heed the leader's guidance and advice. Therefore, it is important that coaches also *determine the level of mutual trust,* and then improve the relationship if necessary before targeting development needs or providing feedback and advice. Too many inexperienced coaches either fail to build trust, or take the relationship for granted, with the long-term end result being little, if any, behavioral change, and a frustrated leader and follower.

Once career goals have been identified and a solid, trusting relationship has been built, leaders then need to *inspire commitment.* In this step, leaders work closely with followers to gather and analyze data to determine development needs. A leader and a follower may review appraisals of past performance, feedback from peers or former bosses, project reports, 360-degree feedback reports, and any organizational standards that pertain to the follower's career goals. By reviewing this data, the leader and the follower should be able to identify and prioritize those development needs most closely aligned with career goals.

The next step in the coaching process involves *growing skills.* Followers use their prioritized development needs to create a development plan, and leaders in turn develop a **coaching plan** that spells out precisely what they will do to support the followers' development plan. Leaders and followers then review and discuss the development and coaching plans, make necessary adjustments, and execute the plans.

TABLE 8.4 The Five Steps of Informal Coaching		
Forge a Partnership	Coaching only works if there is a trusting relationship between the leader and his or her followers. In this step leaders also determine what drives their followers and where they want to go with their careers.
Inspire Commitment	In this step leaders help followers determine which skills or behaviors will have the biggest payoff if developed. Usually this step involves reviewing the results of performance appraisals, 360-degree feedback, values, and personality assessment reports, etc.
Grow Skills	Leaders work with followers to build development plans that capitalize on on-the-job experiences and create coaching plans to support their followers' development.
Promote Persistence	Leaders meet periodically with followers in order to provide feedback, help followers keep development on their radar screens, and provide followers with new tasks or projects to develop needed skills.
Shape the Environment	Leaders need to periodically review how they are role-modeling development and what they are doing to foster development in the workplace. Because most people want to be successful, doing this step well will help attract and retain followers to the work group.

Source: D. B. Peterson and M. D. Hicks, *Leader as Coach: Strategies for Coaching and Developing Others* (Minneapolis, MN: Personnel Decisions International, 1996).

Just because a plan is developed does not mean it will be executed flawlessly. Learning often is a series of fits and starts, and sometimes followers either get distracted by operational requirements or get into developmental ruts. In the step called *promote persistence,* leaders help followers to manage the mundane, day-to-day aspects of development. Leaders can help followers refocus on their development by capitalizing on opportunities to give followers relevant, on-the-spot feedback. Once the new behavior has been practiced a number of times and becomes part of the follower's behavioral repertoire, then leaders help followers to *transfer the skills to new environments* by applying the skills in new settings and revising their development plans. In this step, leaders need to also ask themselves how they are role-modeling development and whether they are creating an environment that fosters individual development.

There are several points about informal coaching worth additional comment. First, the five-step process identified by Peterson and Hicks (1996) can be used by leadership practitioners to diagnose why behavioral change is *not* occurring and what can be done about it. For example, followers may not be developing new skills because they do not trust their leader, the skills have not been clearly identified or are not important to them, or they do not have a plan in place to acquire these skills. Second, informal coaching can and does occur anywhere in the organization. Senior executives can use this model to develop their staffs, peers can use it to help each other, and so forth. Third, this process is just as effective for high-performing followers as it is for low-performing followers. Leadership practitioners have a tendency to forget to coach their solid or top followers, yet these individuals are often making the greatest contributions to team or organizational success. Moreover, research has shown that the top performers in a job often produce 20–50 percent more than the average performer, depending on the complexity of the job (Hunter, Schmidt, & Judiesch, 1990). So if leaders would focus on moving their solid performers into the highest-performing ranks and making their top performers even better, chances are their teams might be substantially more effective than if they only focused on coaching those doing most poorly (see Figure 8.8).

Fourth, both "remote" coaching of people and coaching of individuals from other cultures can be particularly difficult (Curphy, 1996a; Peterson & Hicks, 1996, 1997). It is more difficult for leaders to build trusting relationships with followers when they are physically separated by great distances. The same may be true with followers from other cultures—what may be important to, say, a Kenyan follower and how this person views the world may be very different from what his or her Dutch or Singaporean leader believes.

The kinds of behaviors that need to be developed can also vary considerably by culture. For example, one senior executive for a high-tech firm was coaching one of his Japanese direct reports on how to do better presentations to superiors. The follower's style was formal, stiff, and somewhat wooden, and the leader wanted the follower to add some humor and informality to his presentations. However, the follower said that by doing so he would lose the respect of his Japanese colleagues, so his commitment to this change was understandably low. What was agreed upon was that his style was very effective in Japan, but that it needed to change when he was giving presentations in the United States.

FIGURE 8.8
What were the
most useful
factors in the
coaching you
received?

Source: "The
Business Leader as
Development
Coach," *PDI
Portfolio*, Winter
1996, p. 6.

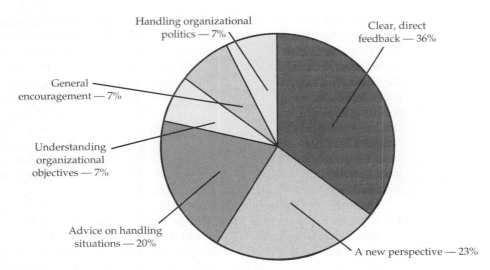

Handling organizational
politics — 7%

Clear, direct
feedback — 36%

General
encouragement — 7%

Understanding
organizational
objectives — 7%

Advice on handling
situations — 20%

A new perspective — 23%

Informal coaching can help groups to be successful as well as to reduce turnover among employees, but what does it take to be a good informal coach? Research by Wenzel (2000) showed that the most effective informal coaches had a unique combination of leadership traits and skills. Leaders with higher levels of intelligence, surgency, and agreeableness were often more effective as coaches than those with lower scores. These leadership traits were the foundation for the relationship building, listening, assertiveness, and feedback skills associated with effective informal coaches. Good informal coaches use these traits and skills to build trusting relationships with their followers, build best-practice coaching and development plans, and deliver tough and honest feedback when necessary. Suggestions on how to improve relationship building, listening, assertiveness, feedback, and informal coaching skills can be found in Part V of this book.

Most people are familiar with the idea of a personal fitness trainer, a person who helps design a fitness program tailored to a specific individual's needs and goals. **Formal coaching** programs provide a similar kind of service for executives and managers in leadership positions (Curphy, 1996a, 2002; Peterson, 1996, 1999; Witherspoon & White, 1996, 1997; Peterson & Hicks, 1998; Kampa-Kokesch & Anderson, 2001; Frisch 2001; Berglas, 2002; Cashman & Forem, 2003; Wasylyshyn, 2003; Waldman, 2003; Smither, London, Flautt, Vargas, & Kucine, 2003). Approximately 65 percent of the Global 1000 companies use some form of formal coaching (Peterson & Hicks, 1998). Formal coaching programs are quite individualized by their very nature, but several common features deserve mention. There is a one-on-one relationship between the manager and the coach (i.e., an internal or external consultant) which lasts from six months to more than a year. The process usually begins with the manager's completion of an extensive battery of personality, intelligence, interests, value, and 360-degree feedback instruments, as well as with interviews by the coach of other individuals in the manager's world of work. As the result of the assessment phase of this process, both the manager and the coach have a clear picture of development needs and how the different components of the building-block model interact and affect these needs. The coach and the manager meet regularly (roughly monthly) to review the results of the feedback instruments and work on building skills and practicing target behaviors. Role plays and videotape are used extensively during these sessions, and coaches provide immediate feedback to clients practicing new behaviors in realistic work situations. Another valuable outcome of coaching programs can involve clarification of managers' values, and identification of discrepancies between their espoused values and their actual behaviors and devising strategies to better align their behaviors with their values.

Approximately 6,000 managers and executives have been through one of the coaching programs designed by Peterson and his associates (Peterson, 1993a, 1993b, 1996; Peterson & Hicks, 1996, 1998). Some were derailment candidates, but many were not. Some were high potentials with a few rough edges, and others were successful managers and executives who needed leadership or skill training in one or two key areas. This large sample and PDI's commitment to research have produced some interesting findings (see Highlight 8.7).

A formal coaching program can cost more than $30,000 (Smith, 1993; Curphy, 1996a), and it is reasonable to ask, Is it worth it? The answer seems to be an unqualified yes. A solid body of research shows that well-designed and well-executed coaching programs do in fact change behavior (Waldman, 2003; Smither et al., 2003; Kampa-Kokesch & Anderson, 2001; Curphy, 2002, 2003c, 2004h). Figure 8.9 reveals that some of this research shows that coaching may be even more effective at changing behavior than more traditional learning and training approaches (Peterson, 1993a, 1993b, 1996; Witherspoon & White, 1997). Moreover, the behavioral changes appear to be in place one year after the termination of a coaching program, indicating permanent behavioral change (Peterson, 1999). Such changes can be particularly important if the person making them—that is, the leader being coached—is in a highly placed or very responsible position. Most coaching candidates have hundreds, if not thousands, of subordinates, and usually oversee multimillion- or multibillion-dollar budgets. Thus, the money spent on a coaching program can be relatively small in comparison to the budgets and resources the candidates control. Many organizations believe if a coaching program helps a leader better utilize resources or get higher productivity from workers, then it is likely that they will see a high return on investment from a coaching program.

Mentoring

Mentoring is a personal relationship in which a more experienced mentor (usually someone two to four levels higher in an organization) acts as a guide, role model, and sponsor of a less experienced protégé. Mentors provide protégés with knowledge, advice, challenge, counsel, and support about career opportunities, organizational strategy and policy, office politics, and so forth (Murray & Owen, 1991; Lall, 1999; Ragins & Cotton, 1999; Ragins, Cotton, & Miller, 2000; Thomas, 2001; Scandura & Lankau, 2002; De Janasz, Sullivan, & Whiting, 2003; Menttium, 2004; Allen, Eby, Poteet, Lentz, & Lima, 2004). Although mentoring has a strong developmental component, it is not

Parents are the first leadership trainers in life.

Bruce Avolio

Some Critical Lessons Learned from Formal Coaching

Highlight 8.7

1. **The person being coached has got to want to change.** It is very difficult to get someone to change their behavior unless they want to change. Coaches need to ensure that coachees clearly understand the benefits for changing their behavior and the consequences if they do not change. Oftentimes it is much easier to get people to change when coaches link the new behaviors to coachees' values and career goals.

2. **Assessments are important.** Formal assessments involving personality, values, mental abilities, and multi-rater feedback are essential to understanding what behaviors coachees' need to change, what is driving these needed changes, and how easy or difficult it will be to change targeted behaviors.

3. **Some behaviors cannot be changed.** Some behaviors are so ingrained or unethical that the best option may be termination. For example, one of the authors was asked to coach a married Vice President who got two of his executive assistants pregnant in less than a year. Given that the coach was not an expert in birth control or Lamaze, the coach turned down the engagement.

4. **Practice is critical.** Good coaches not only discuss what needs to change, but also make coachees practice targeted behaviors. Often the initial practice takes place during coaching sessions, where the coach may play the role of another party and provides the coachee with feedback and suggestions for improvement. These practices are then extended to work, where the coachee must use these newly acquired behaviors in real world situations.

5. **There is no substitute for accountability.** Superiors must be kept in the loop about coachees' progress, and must hold them accountable for on-the-job changes. If coaches are working with potential derailment candidates, then superiors must be willing to let coachees go if they do not make needed changes. Although fear or threats are not the best way to get people to change, some derailment candidates are in so much denial about their problems that it is only by fear of losing their high status jobs that they are motivated to change.

Sources: S. Berglas, "The Very Real Dangers of Executive Coaching," *Harvard Business Review*, June 2002, pp. 86–93; G. J. Curphy, "What Role Should I/O Psychologists Play in Executive Education?" presentation given in R. T. Hogan (Chair), *Models of Executive Education*, at the 17th Annual Society for Industrial and Organizational Psychology, Toronto, Canada, April 2002.

---

the same as coaching. One key difference is that mentoring may not target specific development needs. Protégés often meet with their mentors to get a different perspective of the organization or for advice on potential committee and task force assignments or promotion opportunities. Another difference is that this guidance is not coming from the protégé's immediate supervisor, but rather from someone several leadership levels higher in the organization. Protégés often do receive informal coaching from their boss, but may be more apt to seek career guidance and personal advice from their mentors. Another difference is that the mentor may not even be part of the organization. Some mentors may have retired from the organization, or may have been someone for whom the protégé worked a number of years earlier.

As in coaching, there are both formal and informal mentoring programs. *Informal mentoring* occurs when a protégé and mentor build a long-term relationship based on friendship, similar interests, and mutual respect. These relationships often begin with the protégé working in some part of the mentor's organization or on a high-visibility project for the mentor. *Formal mentoring* programs occur when

FIGURE 8.9

The power of coaching.

Source: D. B. Peterson, *Individual Coaching Services: Coaching That Makes a Difference* (Minneapolis, MN: Personnel Decisions International, 1999).

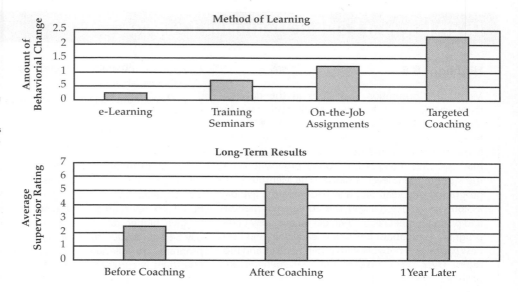

the organization assigns a relatively inexperienced but high-potential leader to one of the top executives in the company. The protégé and mentor get together on a regular basis so that the protégé can gain exposure and learn more about how decisions are made at the top of the organization. Oftentimes organizations implement formal mentoring programs to accelerate the development of female or minority protégés (Thomas, 2001; Ragins, Cotton, & Miller, 2000; Menttium, 2004; Allen et al., 2004).

Mentoring is quite prevalent in many organizations today. Steinberg and Foley (1999) reported that 74 percent of the noncommissioned officers and officers in the U.S. Army had mentors, and Lall (1999) reported that 67 percent of all U.S. Navy admirals had mentors sometime in their career. Moreover, many admirals reported having an average of 3.5 mentors by the time they retired. Scandura and Lankau (2002) reported positive relationships between mentoring, personal learning, career satisfaction, and retention. Looking across multiple mentoring-outcome studies, Allen and her colleagues (Allen et al., 2004) found strong relationships between mentoring and career satisfactory and retention. They also reported that mentoring was related to pay and promotions, although these relationships were not as strong. This was likely due to the fact that pay and promotions are affected by many variables above and beyond mentoring. But Ragins, Cotton, and Miller (2000) found formal mentoring programs, although well intended, were much less effective than informal mentoring for protégé compensation and promotion. The reason for this is that most formal mentoring programs have a difficult time replicating the strong emotional bonds found in informal programs. In addition, most formal mentoring programs only lasted a year, whereas many informal mentoring relationships can last a lifetime (see Highlight 8.8).

Overview of a Formal Mentoring Program

Highlight 8.8

Menttium Corporation specializes in the development and delivery of formal mentoring programs for high potential females in individual contributor to mid-level leadership roles. Most of the protégés have 6–20 years of professional experience and are matched with mentors from other organizations at the Vice President level or higher. The Menttium 100 program is one year long and begins with a five-day kickoff conference. During this conference mentors and protégés meet each other, get an overview of the program, learn about important leadership and business topics, and network with other mentors and protégés. Over the course of the year mentors and protégés meet at least once a month in one-on-one, face-to-face meetings. Protégés also attend a number of one-half-day business education and networking events during the year.

To date, end of program ratings from protégés indicate that:

- 75% said the program helped improve their leadership capabilities.
- 77% are more likely to stay with their parent companies.
- 80% believe their companies have benefited by their attending the program.

Although these results are promising, the jury is still out whether this formal mentoring program has any tangible benefits. The percentages above are based on self-ratings, and there is some pressure to give higher ratings when parent organizations pay $4,500–$7,000 per protégé to participate in the program. To alleviate these potential problems, Menttium is currently engaged in a more rigorous, long-term study to assess the overall impact of its program on both mentors and protégés.

Source: Menttium, *Menttium 100: Cross-Company Mentoring for High Potential Women* (Minneapolis, MN: The Menttium Corporation, 2004).

Thomas (2001) examined the role mentoring played in the careers of minority leaders. He reported that minority leaders who made it to the top of their organizations often had two key qualities. First, successful minority executives were concerned with getting the right experiences and developing the right foundation of leadership skills when they first joined the organization. Their focus was more on personal growth at each leadership level than with titles and rewards. Second, they had an extensive set of mentors and corporate sponsors who provided guidance and support over their careers. These mentors and sponsors helped the executives to develop the three Cs critical to advancement: confidence, competence, and credibility. Thomas (2001) also stated that the most successful white mentor–minority protégé relationships recognized that race was a potential barrier to advancement but were still able to bring up and work through touchy issues. Less successful white mentor–minority protégé relationships engaged in "protective hesitation," in which race or sensitive issues were avoided, ignored, or discounted.

Because of the benefits of informal mentoring, leadership practitioners should look for opportunities to build mentoring relationships with senior leaders whenever possible (de Janasz, Sullivan, & Whiting, 2003). However, Lall (1999) aptly pointed out that protégés cannot make these relationships happen by themselves. In many cases, mentors seek out protégés, or mentors and protégés seek out each other to build relationships. But leaders and leaders-to-be can do a couple of things to improve the odds of finding a mentor. The first step is to do one's current job extremely well. Mentors are always looking for talent, and they are very unlikely to take someone under their wing who appears unmotivated or incompetent. The second step is to look for opportunities to gain visibility and build social relationships with potential mentors. Working on a key task force, doing presentations for the executive committee, or signing up for community activities sponsored by a top executive are just a few of the pathways one could take to gain the attention of potential mentors.

Summary

Leaders can benefit from the leadership behavior research in several ways. First, the behavioral approach has served the important purpose of directing attention to identifying types of leadership behavior critical to success. Second, the behavioral approach allows leadership practitioners to focus on concrete and specific examples of leader behavior. Third, an outgrowth of the behavioral approach has been the development of competency models and 360-degree feedback instruments. The 360-degree feedback instruments can be used to provide valuable feedback to leadership practitioners and often play important roles in many training, coaching, and succession-planning programs.

Research has also helped to identify factors that can cause high-potential managers to fail. This research on managerial derailment has identified "fatal flaws," including such counterproductive leadership behaviors as arrogance, insensitivity, or untrustworthiness. Another body of research indicates that many of these derailment factors may be self-defeating behaviors, behaviors that developed as a way of coping with a stressful situation but are misapplied in other situations.

The chapter also examined the process of behavior change. Research shows that some managers seem to be able to change on their own after gaining insight on how their behavior affects others. This insight is often gained through reflection, in-depth assessments, or 360-degree feedback. Nevertheless, more managers will change if some formal system or process of behavioral change is put into place; these systems include development planning, informal and formal coaching programs, and mentorships. Development planning is the process of pinpointing development needs, creating development plans, implementing plans, and reflecting on and revising plans on a regular basis. Good development plans focus on one or two development needs, capitalize upon on-the-job experiences, and specify sources of feedback. Organizations with formal development systems are likely to realize greater behavioral changes from a greater number of managers than organizations having no system or only an informal one.

Leaders can create development plans for themselves, and they can also help their followers with behavioral change through coaching or mentoring programs. Informal coaching programs often consist of a series of steps designed to create permanent behavioral changes in followers, and both leaders and followers play active roles in informal coaching programs. Formal coaching persons utilize a formal assessment process and a senes of one-on-one coaching sessions over a six- to twelve-month period. These sessions target specific development needs and capitalize on practice and feedback to acquire needed skills. Mentoring programs have many of the same objectives as coaching programs but take place between an individual (the protégé) and a leader several levels higher in the organization (the mentor).

Key Terms

Leader Behavior Description Questionnare (LBDQ), *202*
consideration, *202*
initiating structure, *203*
job-centered dimensions, *203*
goal emphasis, *203*
work facilitation, *203*
employee-centered dimensions, *203*
leader support, *203*
interaction facilitation, *203*
Leadership Grid, *205*
concern for people, *205*
concern for production, *205*

intrapersonal skills, *207*
interpersonal skills, *207*
leadership skills, *208*
business skills, *208*
community leadership, *208*
framing, *209*
building social capital, *209*
mobilization, *210*
360-degree or multirater feedback, *210*
managerial derailment, *215*
inability to build relationships, *216*
failure to meet business objectives, *219*

inability to lead and build a team, *219*
inability to adapt, *219*
inadequate preparation for promotion, *220*
self-defeating behavior, *221*
development plan, *225*
development planning, *227*
coaching, *227*
informal coaching, *227*
coaching plan, *228*
formal coaching, *230*
mentoring, *231*

Questions

1. Could you create a competency model for college professors? For college students? If you used these competency models to create 360-degree feedback tools, who would be in the best position to give professors and students feedback?

2. Do you know anyone who has derailed from a leadership position? What did this person do? Use the leader-follower-situation model to better understand why this individual derailed.

3. Can you identify any self-defeating behaviors in yourself? In what situations are these behaviors likely to be exhibited? How could you ensure these behaviors are not misapplied?

4. What would a development plan for students look like? How could you capitalize on school experiences as part of a development plan?

5. What would a leadership coaching or mentoring program for students look like? How could you tell whether the program worked?

Skills

The leadership skills relevant to this chapter include:

- Providing constructive feedback
- Setting goals
- Development planning
- Coaching
- Empowerment

Activity

1. Read the Development Planning material in Part V of this book. Complete a GAPS analysis and create your own development plan. Share your development

plan with someone in class. Your partner should use the Development Planning Checklist found in the Coaching section of Part V to critique your plan. Check with your partner in two to four weeks to review progress on your plans.

2. Read the Coaching material in Part V of this book. Complete a GAPS analysis for someone you would like to coach. Use the results of the GAPS analysis to create development and coaching plans for this individual.

3. Given the model of community leadership described earlier in this chapter, analyze an on-going community change initiative. Has the leader framed the issue in such way to make it easy for others to take action? Have they strong bonds to other groups? Have they created a plan and mobilized a critical mass of people and resources to make the change become reality?

Minicase

"Paying Attention Pays Off for Andra Rush"

Paying attention has been the key for Andra Rush. As a nursing school graduate she was paying attention when other nurses complained about unfair treatment and decided she wanted to do something about it—so she enrolled in University of Michigan's MBA program so she could do something about how employees were treated. As she completed her business courses and continued to work as a nurse, she was paying attention when a patient described his experience in the transport business. The business sounded intriguing and so, with minimal experience and minimal resources, Rush took a risk and started her own trucking business. She scraped together the funds to buy three trucks by borrowing money from family and maxxing out her credit cards. She specialized in emergency shipping and accepted every job that came her way, even if it meant driving the trucks herself. She answered phones, balanced her books, and even repaired the trucks. She paid attention to her customers and made a point of exceeding their expectations regardless of the circumstances. When the terrorist attacks of September 11 shut down local bridges, Rush rented a barge to make sure a crucial shipment for DaimlerChrysler made it to its destination on time.

Rush continues to pay attention and credits her listening skills as a major reason for her success. Rush is distinct in the traditionally white male-dominated trucking industry—a woman and a minority (Rush is Native American) who credits her heritage and the "enormous strength" of her Mohawk grandmother for helping her prevail.

"It is entirely possible that my Native spirit, communicated to me by my grandmother and my immediate family, have enabled me to overcome the isolation, historical prejudice, and business environment viewed as a barrier to Native- and woman-owned businesses. The willingness to listen, to understand first and act directly and honestly with integrity is a lesson and code of conduct my elders have bequeathed to me. Being an entrepreneur has reinforced those lessons again and again."

Her Mohawk heritage is pervasive. Rush's company logo is a war staff with six feathers representing the Six Nations of the Iroquois: Mohawk, Onondaga, Oneida, Cayuga, Tuscarora, and Seneca. She believes in the power of a diverse workforce and as a result more than half of the 390 employees at Rush Trucking are women and half are minorities.

Rush keeps close tabs on her company and its employees. Though the company has grown from its humble three-truck beginning to a fleet of 1,700 trucks, Rush still takes time to ride along with drivers. She has provided educational programs like "The Readers' Edge," a literacy program, to improve the skills and lives of her employees. Rush is actively involved in several organizations that work to improve the position of minorities—she's on the boards of directors of the Michigan Minority Business Development Council, Minority Enterprise Development/ Minority Business Development Agency, Minority Business Roundtable, and has served as president of the Native American Business Alliance.

1. As we have discussed, competency models describe the behaviors and skills managers need to exhibit if an organization is to be successful. Consider the general competencies found in the Profilor Wheel (Figure 8.3) and apply these to Andra Rush, providing examples of why these competencies apply.

2. Mentoring has played a role in the careers of many successful minorities in leadership positions. Who could be identified as a coach or mentor for Andra Rush?

3. Consider some of the self-defeating behaviors outlined in this chapter that contribute to management derailment. What lessons has Andra Rush obviously learned from the failure of others?

Sources: http://www.inc.com/magazine/20040401/25rush.html; http://www.crainsdetroit.com/cgi-bin/page.pl?pageId=400; http://www.readfaster.com/pr20030912.pdf; http://www.turtle-tracks.org/issue41/i41_3.html; http://www.indiancountry.com/?2224

Part

3

Focus on the Followers

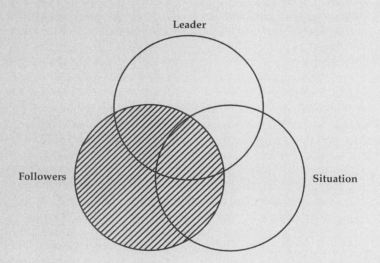

We began Part II with Napoleon's belief that the individual leader is the crucial element of leadership. We begin Part III by qualifying that sentiment. Although the importance of a good leader cannot be denied, followers also play an equally important, if often overlooked, role in the success of any group or organization. It was not, after all, Napoleon by himself who won or lost battles; his soldiers obviously played some part too. In Part III we look at the vital role played by followers in affecting the leadership process.

Chapter 9

Motivation, Satisfaction, and Performance

Introduction

> Polls estimate that if companies could get 3.7 percent more work out of each employee, the equivalent of 18 more minutes of work for each eight-hour shift, the gross domestic product in the U.S. would swell by $355 billion, twice the total GDP of Greece.
>
> *The Gallup Organization*

Why do followers join some teams but not others? How do you get followers to exhibit enough of those behaviors needed for the team to succeed? And why are some leaders capable of getting followers to go above and beyond "the call of duty"? Motivation is all about getting people to do things, and motivating others is a fundamental leadership skill. Researchers studying motivation try to determine why followers do certain things and how to make them start or stop exhibiting specific behaviors. The importance of follower motivation is suggested in findings that most people believe they could give as much as 15 percent or 20 percent more effort at work than they now do with no one, including their own bosses, recognizing any difference. Perhaps even more startling, these workers also believed they could give 15 percent or 20 percent *less* effort with no one noticing any difference (Kinlaw, 1991). Moreover, variation in work output varies significantly across leaders and followers. Hunter, Schmidt, and Judiesch (1990) estimated the top 15 percent of workers in any particular job produced from 20 to 50 percent more output than the average worker, depending on the complexity of the job. Put another way, the best computer programmers or salesclerks might write up to 50 percent more programs or process 50 percent more customer orders. Might better methods of motivating workers lead to higher productivity from *all* the workers? And are more motivated workers happier or more satisfied workers? What can leaders do to increase the motivation and satisfaction levels of their followers?

Creating highly motivated and satisfied followers depends, most of all, on understanding others. Therefore, whereas motivation is an essential part of leadership, it is appropriate to include it in this part of the book, which focuses on the followers. As an overview, this chapter will address three key areas. First, we will examine the links between leadership, satisfaction, motivation, and performance—four closely related concepts. Second, we will review the major theories and research for motivation and satisfaction. Last, and perhaps most important, we will discuss what leaders can do to enhance the motivation and satisfaction of their followers if they implement these different theories.

Defining Motivation, Satisfaction, and Performance

The real challenge [for leaders] is to manage human resources as effectively as possible in order to attain world-class performance.

Fred Luthans and
Alexander Stajkovic

Motivation, satisfaction, and performance seem clearly related. For example, Colin Powell probably could have pursued a number of different vocations, but was *motivated* to complete ROTC and join the army. He was also motivated to put in extra time, energy, and effort in his various positions in the army, and he was judged or rated by his superiors as being an exceptional performer. His outstanding *performance* as an officer was crucial to his promotion as the head of the Joint Chiefs of Staff during the Reagan and Bush administrations and his later appointment as secretary of state. We could also infer that he was happy or *satisfied* with military life, as he was a career officer in the army. Figure 9.1 provides an overview of the relationships between leadership, motivation, satisfaction, and performance. As we can see, some leadership behaviors, such as building relationships or consideration (Chapter 8), result in more satisfied followers. More satisfied followers are more likely to remain with the company and engage in activities that help others at work (i.e., organizational citizenship behaviors). Other leadership behaviors, such as setting goals, planning, providing feedback, and rewarding good performance (initiating structure from Chapter 8), appear to more directly influence followers to exert higher levels of effort toward the accomplishment of group goals. Research has shown that these follower behaviors result in higher levels of customer satisfaction and loyalty, which in turn leads to better team performance in retail, sales, or restaurant settings (Huselid, 1995; Sirota Consulting, 1998; Koys, 2001; Harter, Schmidt, & Hayes, 2002; Pugh, Dietz, Wiley, & Brooks, 2002; Koene, Vogelaar, & Soeters, 2002; Gelade, & Ivery, 2003; Carr, Schmidt, Ford, & DeShon, 2004; Smithey-Fulmer, Gerhart, & Scott, 2003). And teams with higher levels of performance often achieve more rewards, which further increases follower satisfaction and performance (Kiewitz, 2004; Schneider, Hanges, Smith, & Salvaggio, 2003). Thus, the leader's ability to motivate followers is vitally important to both the morale and the performance of the work group. However, it is important to understand that the leader's use of good motivational techniques is not the only factor affecting group performance. Selecting the right people for the team (Chapter 4), correctly using power and influence tactics (Chapter 5), being seen as ethical and credible (Chapter 6), possessing many of the bright-side and none of the dark-side personality

FIGURE 9.1 Relationships between leadership, job satisfaction, and performance.

Sources: M. A. Huselid, "The Impact of Human Resource Management Practices on Turnover, Productivity, and Corporate Financial Performance," *Academy of Management Journal* 38, no. 4 (1995), pp. 635–72; T. Butorac, *Recruitment and Retention: The Keys to Profitability at Carlson Companies*, presentation given at Personnel Decisions International, Minneapolis, MN, June 11, 2001; D. J. Koys, "The Effects of Employee Satisfaction, Organizational Citizenship Behavior, and Turnover on Organizational Effectiveness: A Unit Level, Longitudinal Study," *Personnel Psychology* 54, no. 1 (2001), pp. 101–14; J. Husserl, "Allied's Organizational Life Cycle," *Management Education & Development* 24, no. 3 (1998), p. 8; Sirota Consulting, *Establishing the Linkages between Employee Attitudes, Customer Attitudes, and Bottom-Line Results* (Chicago, IL: Author, 1998); Pugh, D. S., J. Dietz, J. W. Wiley, & S. M. Brooks "Driving Service Effectiveness through Employee–Customer Linkages," *Academy of Management Executive*, 16(4), 2002, pp. 73–84; Schneider B., P. J. Hanges, D. B. Smith, & A. N. Salvaggio, "Which Comes First: Employee Attitudes or Organizational, Financial and Market Performance?" *Journal of Applied Psychology*, 88(5), 2003, pp. 836–51.

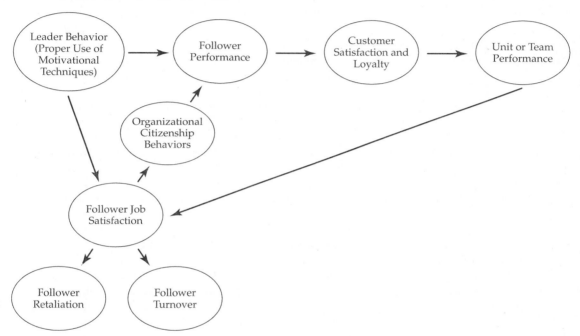

traits (Chapter 7), and acquiring the necessary resources and developing follower skills (Chapter 8) are other leadership factors affecting a group's ability to accomplish its goals.

Most people probably think of motivation as dealing with choices about what we do and how much effort we put into doing it. According to Kanfer (1990), **motivation** is anything that provides *direction, intensity,* and *persistence* to behavior. Another definition considers the term *motivation* a sort of shorthand to describe choosing an activity or task to engage in, establishing the level of effort to put forth on it, and determining the degree of persistence in it over time (Campbell & Pritchard, 1976). Other researchers define motivation as a behavior probability; it is the likelihood an individual will initiate and continue exhibiting certain behaviors (Miller & Rollnick, 1991). Like personality traits and types, motivation is not directly observable; it must be inferred from behavior. We would infer that one person would be highly motivated to do well in school if she spent a lot of time studying for exams. She could

There is no substitute for hard work. It will always outweigh brilliance over time.

Carly Fiorina
Hewlett-Packard

choose to spend her time and energy on socializing, intramurals, or volunteer work, but because she is spending time outlining readings and reviewing class notes we say she is motivated to do well in school. At work, if one person regularly assembles twice as many radios as any other person in his work group—assuming all have the same abilities, skills, and resources—then we likely would say this first person is more motivated than the others. We use the concept of motivation to explain differences we see among people in the energy and direction of their behavior. Thus, the energy and effort Peter Jackson expended creating the *Lord of the Rings* trilogy or Aung San Suu Kyi expends to keep the democratic movement alive in Burma would be examples of the direction, intensity, and persistence components of motivation.

Performance, on the other hand, concerns those behaviors directed toward the organization's mission or goals, or the products and services resulting from those behaviors. At work or school we can choose to perform a wide variety of behaviors, but performance would only include those behaviors related to the production of goods or services or obtaining good grades. Performance differs from **effectiveness,** which generally involves making judgments about the adequacy of behavior with respect to certain criteria such as work-group or organizational goals. Peter Jackson spent seven years creating the three movies in the *Lord of the Rings* series. The total revenues collected and Academy Awards won by the series would be indicators of his effectiveness as a movie director. However, it is important to understand that performance is affected by more than a follower's motivation. Factors such as intelligence, skill, and the availability of key resources can affect a follower's behavior in accomplishing organizational goals (i.e., performance) independently of that person's level of motivation. *Thus, an adequate level of motivation may be a necessary but insufficient condition of effective performance.*

Job satisfaction is not how *hard* one works or how *well* one works, but rather how much one *likes* a specific kind of job or work activity. Job satisfaction deals with one's attitudes or feelings about the job itself, pay, promotion or educational opportunities, supervision, co-workers, workload, and so on (Saal & Knight, 1988; Judge, Thoresen, Bono, & Patton, 2001; Smithey-Fulmer, Gerhart, & Scott, 2003). Various polls over the past half century have consistently shown the vast majority of men and women report liking their jobs (see Campbell & Hyne, 1995; Health, Education, & Welfare Task Force, 1973; Hoppock, 1935; Smith, Scott, & Hulin, 1977; or Staines & Quinn, 1979). Research has also shown that people who are more satisfied with their jobs are more likely to engage in **organizational citizenship behaviors**—behaviors not directly related to one's job that are helpful to others at work. Organizational citizenship behaviors make for a more supportive workplace. Examples might include volunteering to help another employee with a task or project, or filling in for another employee when asked (Organ & Ryan, 1995; Chen, Mui, & Sego, 1998; Bettercourt, Gwinner, & Meuter, 2001; Lee & Allen, 2002; LaPine, Erez & Johnson, 2002; Cropanzano,

Fifty-five percent of workers are unengaged; 19 percent are so uninterested and negative about their jobs that they poison the workplace to the point that companies might be better off if they called in sick.

The Gallup Organization

Source: Reprinted with special permission of King Features Syndicate.

Rupp, & Byrne, 2003; Bolino & Turnley, 2003; Tepper & Taylor, 2003; Tepper, Duffy, Hoobler, & Ensley, 2004). Happier workers tend to be more helpful workers.

Although people generally like the work they do, two related events have caused a downturn in job satisfaction levels among employees in the United States. Over the past 10 years, many organizations have downsized or substantially reduced the number of people on the company payroll. Examples of some of the companies that have substantially downsized can be read about in the Michael Moore book, *Downsize This* (Moore, 1997). These positions were eliminated to reduce costs and improve profitability, but they also dramatically increased the workload for the remaining workers (i.e., the same amount of work was being performed by fewer people), and severed the implicit contract between workers and employers (i.e., if workers performed at a high level, then employers guaranteed a job for life). The end result is that job dissatisfaction among workers is at an all-time high (see Highlight 9.1). Although people report being satisfied with what they do for a living, the forced overtime, increased workload, and erosion of trust between employers and employees has significantly lowered levels of job satisfaction (Howard, 1996; Curphy, 1998b; Mills, 1999; Quigley, 2001; Hales & Hales, 2001; Curphy & Hogan 2004a; Curphy 2004h). Although the slowdown in the economy from 2000–2004 helped to reduce the rate of turnover, dissatisfied employees will leave as soon as the economy starts to pick up. And when it does, it will be very difficult to maintain various indices of organizational effectiveness when many of the best and brightest employees are leaving the company. Job satisfaction may not have as direct an effect on the accomplishment of organizational goals as motivation or performance, but the indirect effects of reduced organizational citizenship behaviors or increased turnover are so important that leaders can ill afford to ignore them (McElroy, Morrow, & Rude, 2001; Krug, 2003).

> *People don't leave companies, they leave bad bosses.*
>
> Beverly Kaye

As a result of the economic downturn, many leaders today are facing the dual challenges of having to achieve increasingly difficult unit performance goals while having fewer followers available to do the work. The best leaders and organizations understand that one way to meet these challenges is to recruit, develop, and retain

Productivity and Satisfaction across the Globe

Highlight 9.1

Over the past few years American businesses have downsized considerably, but many have been able to maintain high customer satisfaction and revenue levels with fewer employees. In terms of the number of hours worked, the average U.S. employee works 137 hours per year more than the typical Japanese employee, 260 hours more per year as compared to the average British employee, and 499 hours more than the average French employee. In other words, over the course of a 40-year work career, U.S. employees will work the equivalent of 10 more years than the average French employee. Although American companies are noted for having some of the highest productivity in the world, might there also be a downside to these high levels of productivity? Research has

shown that some of the risks associated with longer workweeks include job dissatisfaction, poorer physical and mental health, and distressed family and social relationships. As long as the U.S. economy is not adding many jobs, many employees seem to prefer those consequences associated with longer work hours than those of being unemployed. But if the economy heats up and jobs become more readily available, leaders should not be surprised if many of these employees leave for greener pastures.

Sources: J. M. Brett and L. K. Stroh, "Working 61 Plus Hours a Week: Why Do Managers Do It?" *Journal of Applied Psychology,* 88 (1), 2003, pp. 67–78; G. J. Curphy, "What We Really Know about Leadership (But Seem Unwilling to Implement)," presentation given at the Minnesota Professionals for Psychology and Applied Work, Minneapolis, MN, January, 2004a.

top leadership and technical talent. Savvy companies that spend considerably more time and effort attracting, developing, and retaining the best people often report superior financial results (Butorac, 2001; Charan, Drotter, & Noel, 2001; Schneider, Hanges, Smith, & Salvaggio, 2003; Gelade & Ivery 2003; Smithey-Fulmer, Gerhart, & Scott, 2003; Pfau & Cohen, 2003; Curphy 2004a, e; Curphy & Hogan, 2004b). For example, many of the organizations appearing in *Fortune* magazine's "The 100 Best Companies to Work For" also do very well when compared to the S&P 500 Index. *The best leaders may well be those who can motivate workers to perform at a high level while maintaining an equally high level of job satisfaction.*

Executives owe it to their organization and fellow workers not to tolerate nonperforming people in important jobs.

Peter Drucker
Drucker Institute

Having now defined motivation, performance, and job satisfaction, we can explore their relationships a bit further. We have already noted how motivation does not always assure good performance. If followers lack the necessary skills or resources to accomplish a group task, then trying to "motivate them more" could be unproductive and even frustrating (Campbell, 1977; 1988). For example, no high school basketball team is likely to defeat the Los Angeles Lakers, however motivated the players may be. The players on the high school team simply lack the abilities and skills of the Lakers players. Higher motivation will usually only affect performance if followers already have the abilities, skills, and resources to get the job done. Motivating others is an important part of leadership, but not all of it; pep talks and rewards are not always enough.

The relationships between motivation and job satisfaction are a bit more straightforward—as a matter of fact, many theories of motivation are also theories of job satisfaction. The implicit link between satisfaction and motivation is that satisfaction increases when people accomplish a task, particularly when the task requires a lot of effort. It might also seem logical that *performance* must be higher among more satisfied workers, but actually this is not always so (Iaffaldano & Muchinsky, 1985; Podsakoff & Williams, 1986; Judge, Thoresen, Bono, & Patton, 2001). Although satisfaction and performance are correlated at the r = .3 level, it is just not true that happy workers are always the most productive ones, nor is it true that unhappy or dissatisfied workers are always the poorest performers. It is entirely possible, for example, for poorly performing workers to be fairly satisfied with their jobs (maybe because they are paid well yet do not have to work very hard, like Homer Simpson in the television show *The Simpsons*). It is also possible for dissatisfied workers to be relatively high performers (they may have a strong work ethic, or they may be trying to improve chances to get out of their current job). Despite the intuitive appeal of believing that satisfied workers usually perform better, it may be that satisfaction has only an indirect effect on performance (Locke & Latham, 1990). Nevertheless, having both satisfied *and* high-performance followers is a goal leaders should usually strive to achieve.

Understanding and Influencing Follower Motivation

So what do leaders do to "motivate" followers to accomplish group goals? Are all leaders and followers motivated the same way? Is there a universal theory of motivation? In other words, did Peter Jackson, Colin Powell, or Aung San Suu Kyi use the same or different techniques to motivate their followers? As seen in Highlight 9.2, organizations spend billions on motivating the troops, but do these interventions actually help to improve job satisfaction, retention, and performance? Research can provide the answers to these questions, and few topics of human behavior have been the subject of so much attention as that of motivation.

> *Some players you pat their butts, other players you kick their butts, and some players you leave alone.*
>
> Pete Rose

So much has been written about motivation that a comprehensive review of the subject is beyond the scope of this book. We will, however, survey several major approaches to understanding worker motivation, as well as address the implications of these approaches for follower satisfaction and performance. (See Kanfer, 1990; Campbell & Pritchard, 1976; and Personnel Decisions International, 2000 for more comprehensive reviews.) These motivational theories and approaches provide leadership practitioners with a number of suggestions to get followers to engage in and persist with different behaviors. It is important to understand that some motivational theories are particularly useful in certain situations but are not as applicable in others. Just as a carpenter can successfully build better wooden structures or furniture by having a larger set of tools, so can leadership practitioners solve a greater number of motivational problems among followers by becoming familiar with different motivational theories and approaches. People who have only hammers in their tool kits are more likely to see every problem as a nail needing hammering, and it is not unusual for less effective leaders to call on a very limited number of approaches to any motivational problem. *Leaders who are knowledgeable about different motivational theories are more likely to choose the right*

Organizations Spend Billions on Motivational Programs for Employees, and All They Get Are Burned Feet

Highlight 9.2

Organizations are constantly looking for quick fixes to their performance and effectiveness problems. The barriers to team or organizational performance often include a lack of resources and skills, unclear goals, poor performance or accountability standards, or dysfunctional work teams; in other words incompetent leadership plays a key role in many of these barriers. But many organizations would rather send employees to motivational speakers or white-water rafting, bungee jumping, or fire walking events than take a hard look at their leadership talent. For example, software consulting firm EMC has spent $625,000 to have 5,000 employees walk over burning coals. But do expensive speakers and extreme activities actually help to improve organizational performance? Unfortunately, exhaustive research has shown there is virtually no link between motivational spending and company revenues, profitability, or market share. Perhaps the biggest problem is that employees may find it difficult to see the link between walking over a bed of hot coals and making another 20 sales calls every week. Other than bankrolling the motivation industry, these programs do seem to have another benefit. Nine U.S. Air Force recruiters had to go to the emergency room after they received second- and third-degree burns on their feet after one of these "motivational" programs.

Sources: D. Jones, "Firms Spend Billions to Fire Up Workers—With Little Luck," *USA Today,* May 10, 2001, pp. 1–2A; P. G. Chronis, "9 Burn Feet in National Guard Recruiters' Fire Walk," *Denver Post,* December 28, 1998, pp. 1A, 17A; Curphy, G. J. & R. T. Hogan, "Managerial Incompetence: Is there a Dead Skunk on the Table?" Working Paper, 2004a.

theory for a particular follower and situation, and often have higher-performing and more satisfied employees as a result.

It is important to understand that most performance problems can be attributed to unclear expectations, skill deficits, resource/equipment shortages, or a lack of motivation. Of these underlying causes, leaders seem to have the most difficulty recognizing and rectifying motivation problems. An example might help to illustrate this point. A major airline was having serious problems with the customer service of its flight attendants. Passenger complaints were on the rise and airplane loading (the average number of people per flight) was decreasing. The perceived lack of customer service was beginning to cost the airline market share and revenues; to fix the problem they decided to have all 10,000 flight attendants go through a two-day customer service training program. Unfortunately, passenger complaints only got worse after the training. A thorough investigation of the underlying cause of the problem revealed that flight attendants knew what they were supposed to do, had all of the skills necessary to perform the behaviors, and usually had the resources and equipment necessary to serve customers. The root cause was a lack of motivation to "go the extra mile" for customers. When asked what they found to be the most motivating aspect of being a flight attendant, most stated "time off." In other words the flight attendants were most motivated when they were *not* at work. Given that a strong union represented the flight attendants, how would you go about solving this dilemma? The next section will give you some ideas on how to resolve this and other motivation problems that you may face as a leader.

In this section we will discuss the key aspects of 11 different approaches to understanding motivation in a work or leadership context. We have organized the approaches into four broad categories: need theories, individual-difference approaches, cognitive theories, and situational approaches. This categorization seems helpful for explanatory purposes, even though it is admittedly atheoretical. These theories and approaches are listed in Table 9.1. For illustrative purposes we will also discuss how leadership practitioners could apply these approaches to motivate two fictitious followers, Julie and Ling Ling. Julie is a 21-year-old ski lift operator in Banff, Alberta. Her primary job is to ensure that people get on and off her ski lift safely. She also does periodic equipment safety checks and maintains the lift lines and associated areas. Julie works from 7:30 A.M. to 5:00 P.M. five days a week, gets paid a salary, and has a pass that allows her to ski for free whenever she is off work. Ling Ling is a 35-year-old real estate agent in Hong Kong. She works for an agency that locates and rents apartments for people on one- to three-year business assignments for various multinational companies. She works many evenings and weekends showing apartments, and gets paid a salary plus a commission for every apartment she rents. How the 11 approaches could be used to motivate Julie and Ling Ling will be discussed periodically throughout this section.

Need Theories

Assume people all have basic needs, and leaders can motivate followers by helping them satisfy their needs. One way to get followers to engage and persist with the behaviors needed to accomplish group goals is to appeal to their needs. What underlying needs do flight attendants have, and would they exhibit higher levels

TABLE 9.1
Eleven
Motivational
Approaches

Category	Theory or Approach	Major Themes of Characteristics
Need	Maslow's hierarchy of needs	Satisfy needs to change behavior.
	Alderfer's ERG theory	Can satisfy multiple needs simultaneously.
Individual difference	Achievement orientation	Personality trait.
	Values	People are aligned with their personal values.
	Intrinsic motivation	People are more motivated to do some activities than others.
Cognitive	Goal setting	Set goals to change behavior.
	Expectancy theory	Motivate others by clarifying links between behaviors, performance, and rewards.
	Equity theory self-efficacy	People are motivated to reduce inequities between rewards and effort. One's beliefs about being able to successfully complete a task.
Situational	Operant approach	Change rewards and punishments to change behavior.
	Empowerment	Give people automony and latitude in order to increase their motivation for work.

of customer service behaviors if leaders satisfied these needs? The two major need theories include Maslow's (1954) hierarchy of needs and Alderfer's (1969) existence-relatedness-growth (ERG) theory. These theories assume that all people share a common set of basic needs; the theories primarily differ in the types of needs that supposedly underlie or drive people's behavior. **Needs** refer to internal states of tension or arousal, or uncomfortable states of deficiency people are motivated to change (Kanfer, 1990). Hunger would be a good example of a need, as people are motivated to eat when they get hungry. Other needs might include the need to live in a safe and secure place, to belong to a group with common interests or social ties, or to do interesting and challenging work. If these needs were not being met, then people would choose to engage in and persist with certain behaviors until they were satisfied. According to these motivational approaches, leadership practitioners can get followers to engage in and persist with certain behaviors by correctly identifying and appeasing their needs.

Maslow's Hierarchy of Needs

According to Maslow (1954), people are motivated by five basic sorts of needs. These include the need to survive physiologically, the need for security, the need for affiliation with other people (i.e., belongingness), the need for self-esteem, and the need for self-actualization. Maslow's conceptualization of needs is usually represented by a triangle with the five levels of needs arranged in a hierarchy (see Figure 9.2) called, not surprisingly, the **hierarchy of needs.** According to Maslow, any person's behavior can be understood primarily as the effort directed to satisfy one particular level of need in the hierarchy. Which level happens to be motivating a person's behavior at any time depends on whether or not lower needs in the hierarchy have been satisfied. According to Maslow, lower-level needs must be satisfied before the next-higher level becomes salient in motivating behavior.

FIGURE 9.2

Maslow's hierarchy of needs.

Maslow (1954) said higher-level needs like those for self-esteem or self-actualization would not become salient (even when unfulfilled) until lower needs were satisfied. Thus, a practical implication of his theory is that leaders may only be successful in motivating follower behavior by taking account of the follower's position on the needs hierarchy. Applying Maslow's hierarchy to Julie, it might be relatively inefficient to try to motivate our ski lift operator by appealing to how much pride she could take in a job well done (i.e., to her self-esteem) if she was underdressed for weather conditions. If her boss wanted Julie to do more, then she should first make sure that Julie's physiological (i.e., clothing) needs were met, that she worked and lived in a secure place, and that she had ample opportunities to socialize with other employees. Only after these lower needs have been met should the boss try to increase Julie's self-esteem. Thus, if leadership practitioners want to use Maslow's hierarchy of needs to motivate employees to work harder, then they need to determine where their followers fall on the needs hierarchy and ensure all lower-order needs are satisfied before appealing to their followers' self-esteem or self-actualization needs. Leadership practitioners should watch for "mismatches" between their motivational efforts and followers' *lowest* (on the hierarchy) unsatisfied needs.

ERG Theory

Alderfer's (1969) **existence-relatedness-growth (ERG) theory** is similar to Maslow's hierarchy of needs. In the terms of ERG theory, *existence* needs basically correspond to Maslow's physiological and security needs; *relatedness* needs are like Maslow's social and esteem needs; and *growth* needs are similar to the need for self-actualization. Beyond those similarities, however, are two important differences.

First, Alderfer (1969) reported that people sometimes try to satisfy *more than one need at a time.* For example, even though a follower's existence needs may not be entirely satisfied, she may still be motivated to grow as a person. Second, he claimed *frustration of a higher-level need can lead to efforts to satisfy a lower-level need.* In other words, a follower who is continually frustrated in achieving some need might regress and exert effort to satisfy a lower need that has already been satisfied. For example, if Ling Ling had strong relatedness needs but was unable to build friendships with her co-workers, she might regress to satisfying her existence needs. Some of these behaviors might include moving to an upscale neighborhood; buying a more expensive wardrobe, a new sportscar, or new stereo equipment; or demanding more pay. Alderfer called this the **frustration regression hypothesis.**

The practical implications for motivating followers using ERG theory are three-fold. First, leadership practitioners should identify the degree of need for existence, relatedness, and growth for their followers. Followers having relatively unmet existence or relatedness needs will focus their behaviors on satisfying these needs, and leadership practitioners may be able to help with these endeavors. Second, followers having relatively satisfied existence and relatedness needs are more apt to focus on growth needs. Leadership practitioners can get a lot of motivational "mileage" by helping followers satisfy their growth needs, as these followers are more willing to develop and master new skills, apply skills in new situations, look for more responsibility and independence, and strive to achieve greater personal and organizational challenges. Third, leadership practitioners should also be on the lookout for the frustration regression hypothesis among followers. If followers are repeatedly thwarted in satisfying a need, and have shifted their efforts to over-satisfying a lower-level need, then appealing to the need that was thwarted may be relatively fruitless. For instance, trying to motivate Ling Ling to work harder by stating the real estate agency is a team and needs to work together to get results will probably not result in substantial behavioral change for Ling Ling. Instead, the leader may need to work closely with Ling Ling to determine why she has been unable to satisfy her relatedness needs, and coach her on how to build relationships with others in the agency. Only after these relationships are established will the leader be able to motivate Ling Ling to work as a part of a team to get results.

Concluding Thoughts on Need Theories

According to the two need theories, leaders should start by determining if lower-level needs are being satisfied. In most cases it will be difficult for followers to exhibit the behaviors necessary for group success if these lower-level needs are not being met; therefore, leaders should do all they can to help followers meet these needs. Once the lower-level needs are satisfied, leaders can then work to satisfy higher-level needs, which in turn should improve the odds of group success. So how would you apply the need theories to improve the customer service of flight attendants? How would you go about determining the needs of flight attendants, and what kind of program would you implement to improve customer service? Although the two need theories do provide some useful ideas on how to improve customer service, it is important to note that they have several limitations. For one thing, none of the theories makes specific predictions about what an individual will do to satisfy a particular need (Betz, 1984; Kanfer, 1990). In the example, Ling Ling may exert considerable effort to establish new friendships at work, try to make friends outside work, or even spend a lot of money on a new car or stereo equipment (the frustration regression hypothesis). The theories' lack of specificity and predictive power severely limits their practical applicability in real-life settings. On the other hand, awareness of the general nature of the various sorts of basic human needs described in these theories seems fundamentally useful to leaders. Leaders will have a difficult time getting followers to maintain various work behaviors by emphasizing good relationships with co-workers or appealing to their sense of pride if the job pays only minimum wage and followers are having a difficult time making ends meet. A person may be reluctant to volunteer for a self-actualizing opportunity in support of a political campaign if such participation may risk that person's financial security. Perhaps the greatest insight provided by these two theories is that leadership practitioners may need to address some basic, fundamental areas before their attempts to get followers to expend more effort on work-related behaviors will be successful.

Individual Differences in Motivation

Assume people differ in key personality traits and values and the work they like to do. Leaders can motivate followers by hiring those with the right traits, values, and work interests. Is it possible that some people are naturally more "motivated" than others? Do some people automatically put forth a higher level of effort toward group goals simply because of who they are or because they enjoy what they do? Unlike the two need theories that claimed all people share some fundamental needs, the individual difference approach to motivation assumes that people vary substantially in their achievement orientation, values, or intrinsic motivation. This approach to motivation is rather simple. To improve group performance, leaders should select only those followers who possess both the right skills and have a higher level of achievement orientation, the right values, or find the work to be intrinsically motivating.

The body of every organization is made up of four kinds of bones. There are the wishbones, who spend all of their time wishing someone would do the work. Then there are the jawbones, who do all the talking, but little else. The knucklebones knock everything anybody else tries to do. Fortunately, in every organization there are also the backbones, who get under the load and do most of the work.

Leo Aikman,
On Bones

Achievement Orientation

Atkinson (1957) proposed that an individual's tendency to exert effort toward task accomplishment depended partly on the strength of his or her motive to achieve success, or, as Atkinson called it, **achievement orientation.** McClelland (1975) further developed Atkinson's ideas and said that individuals with a strong achievement orientation (or in McClelland's terms, a strong *need for achievement*) strived to accomplish socially acceptable endeavors and activities. These individuals also preferred tasks that provided immediate and ample feedback and were moderately difficult (i.e., tasks that required a considerable amount of effort but were accomplishable). Additionally, individuals with a strong need to achieve felt satisfied when they successfully solved work problems or accomplished job tasks (McClelland, 1975). Individuals with a relatively low need to achieve generally preferred easier tasks and did not feel satisfied by solving problems or accomplishing assigned tasks. McClelland (1975) maintained that differences in achievement orientation were a primary reason why people differed in the levels of effort they exerted to accomplish assignments, objectives, or goals. Thus, achievement orientation is a bit like "fire in the belly"; people with more achievement orientation are likely to set higher personal and work goals and are more likely to expend the effort needed to accomplish them. People with low levels of achievement motivation tend to set lower personal and work goals, and are less likely to accomplish them.

Achievement orientation is also a component of the Five Factor personality dimension of dependability (see Chapter 7). Like intelligence, dependability has been found to be positively related to performance across virtually all jobs (Barrick & Mount, 1991; Ones, Mount, Barrick, & Hunter, 1994; Tett, Jackson, & Rothstein, 1991; Tett, Jackson, Rothstein, & Reddon, 1994; Judge & Ilies, 2002; Curphy, 2003c). Achievement orientation has been found to predict success in school (Gough, 1987), in the military (Curphy & Osten, 1993; Hough, 1992), in blue-collar and retail workers (Hogan & Hogan, 1992; Paajanen, Hansen, & McLellan, 1993), and in managers (Nilsen, 1995; Curphy, 1998b, 2000, 2001, 2003c; Hewlett, 2002). All things being equal, people with higher levels of achievement orientation are likely to do better in school, pursue postgraduate degrees, get promoted more quickly, and get paid higher salaries and bonuses than their lower-scoring counterparts.

Can Women Have It All?

Highlight 9.3

Research has shown that it is very difficult for women to both have a high-powered career and a family. At midlife 30–50 percent of achievement-oriented women do not have children, and those who chose to do so often suffer numerous career setbacks. Because of the media hype of older women having children, many of these high-powered females falsely believe that they can wait until their late 30s and early 40s to start a family. But medical research shows that female fertility rates drop precipitously starting in the mid-30s. What is particularly unfortunate is that high-achieving men do not suffer these same problems; of the 79 percent who want children, 75 percent do in fact have them. And the more successful the male, the more likely they are to have a wife and kids.

Until United States laws provide more liberal support to working parents, women will need to be more deliberate about their career/family choices. But another potential solution to this dilemma is for women to develop better frameworks for success. Oftentimes high achieving women (and men, for that matter) only define success in terms of career outcomes. But by doing so, people can never get promoted quickly or high enough. As soon as a person gets promoted from manager to director, they immediately start doing what is necessary to become a Vice-President.

Over time, many of these people begin to feel that they are on a treadmill, and they get disillusioned and eventually burn out. Nash and Stevenson (2004) suggest it might be better to define success as having four components:

- Happiness: do I enjoy what I am doing?
- Achievement: am I accomplishing the goals I have set for myself?
- Significance: am I doing something important?
- Legacy: will my efforts and achievements endure over time?

People who use these four components to define success will likely avoid climbing the corporate ladder just for the sake of doing so. These individuals may max out the achievement component, but the happiness, significance, and legacy components of success are likely to suffer. By defining success more broadly, men and women should be able to make better choices about the kind of work they want to pursue, where they want to go with their careers, and if and when they want to start a family.

Sources: A. Fels, "Ambition, Gender, and Defining Success," *Harvard Business Review,* April 2004, pp. 50–61; L. Nash and H. Stevenson, "Success That Lasts," *Harvard Business Review,* February 2004, pp. 102–9; S. A. Hewlett, "Executive Women and the Myth of Having It All," *Harvard Business Review,* April 2002, pp. 66–67.

Given that individuals with higher achievement orientation scores set high personal goals and put in the time and effort necessary to achieve them, it is hardly surprising that achievement orientation is often a key success factor for people who advance to the highest levels of the organization. For example, achievement orientation appears to be a common success factor underlying the careers of Peter Jackson, Colin Powell, and Aung San Suu Kyi. Although achievement orientation is often associated with higher performance, it is important to note that high achievers can get extremely demoralized when faced with unclear or impossible tasks. Working with elite Army Ranger units, Britt (2003) found that these units almost always performed at very high levels and were often very successful. But when given unclear missions with few resources and impossible timelines, these same units could self-destruct. In these situations the units felt they were being set up to fail, and fail they did. This phenomenon is clearly depicted in the movie *Black Hawk Down,* where Army Ranger units were sent to Mogadishu, Somalia, to capture a Somalian war lord. The important lesson here is that leaders need to give high achievers clear goals and the resources they need to succeed.

So how could a leader apply this knowledge of achievement motivation to improve the performance of Julie, Ling Ling, and the flight attendants? Perhaps the first step would be to ensure the hiring process selected those individuals with higher levels of achievement orientation. Assuming they had higher scores, we would expect Ling Ling to work with her boss to set aggressive goals for renting apartments and then work as many nights and weekends as are needed to achieve them. We might also expect Ling Ling to obtain her MBA from Hong Kong University over the next few years. Julie could also be expected to set high personal and work goals, but she may find that her job limits her ability to pursue these goals. Unlike Ling Ling, who can control the number of nights and weekends she wants to work, Julie has no control over the number of people who ride on her lift. The job itself may limit Julie's ability to fulfill her high level of achievement orientation. As a result, she may pursue other activities, such as becoming an expert skier, joining the ski patrol, doing ski racing, looking for additional responsibilities or opportunities for advancement, or finding another job where she has the opportunity to achieve and get rewarded for her efforts. Because Julie will set and work toward high personal goals, a good boss would work closely with Julie to find work-related ways to capitalize on her achievement orientation. Thus, achievement orientation may be a dual-edged sword. Leadership practitioners may be able to hire a group of highly motivated followers, but they also need to set clear expectations, provide opportunities for followers to set and achieve work-related goals, and provide feedback on progress toward goals. Otherwise followers may find different ways to fulfill their high levels of achievement orientation.

> *People go to work to succeed.*
> Norman Schwarzkopf

Values

If motivation is all about choosing to engage and persist with particular behaviors, then appealing to followers' values can be a very powerful motivational strategy (Hogan & Curphy, 2004). As described in Chapter 6, values represent a person's most important and enduring beliefs and make up another set of individual difference variables that are related to motivation. In the world of work, some people believe creating high quality products to be very important, whereas others might believe that making money or helping others to be more important. A listing of 10 common work values and suggestions for what leaders can do to motivate followers with specific values can be found in Table 9.2.

It is important to realize that there are no right or wrong values per se, but followers will be motivated to do activities that are aligned with their personal values and unmotivated to work on those activities they do not believe to be important. Most followers possess two to four key work values, and leaders can motivate followers to engage and persist in certain activities by aligning these activities to followers' underlying values. Just as transformational or charismatic leaders appeal to followers' values as an important motivational strategy to drive change (see Chapter 13), so can other leaders align work activities to followers'

TABLE 9.2
Key Work
Values and
Motivational
Strategies

Sources: Adapted
from J. Hogan and
R. T. Hogan,
*Motives, Values and
Preferences Inventory
Manual* (Tulsa, OK:
Hogan Assessment
Systems, 1996) and
G. J. Curphy, *Hogan
Assessment Systems
Certification
Workshop Training
Manual* (Tulsa, OK:
Hogan Assessment
Systems, 2003c).

Recognition: Followers with strong Recognition values believe fame, visibility, and publicity are important. Leaders can get followers to engage in and persist with desired behaviors by giving them opportunities for public recognition.

Power: Followers with strong Power values enjoy competition, being seen as influential, and driving hard to make an impact. Leaders can motivate these followers by putting them in jobs where they can achieve, get ahead, and succeed.

Hedonism: Followers with strong Hedonism values are motivated by pleasure, variety, and excitement. Providing these followers with opportunities to take risks, entertain others, and have fun are ways leaders can motivate these individuals.

Altruistic: Leaders can motivate followers with strong Altruism values by giving them opportunities to improve society and help others who are less fortunate.

Affiliation: Followers with strong Affiliation values are motivated if their work allows them to meet new people or work in team environments.

Tradition: These individuals are most motivated when they work in organizations that have strong customs and standards of behavior.

Security: Followers with strong Security values can be motivated to engage in various activities if these activities help create stable, predictable, and risk-free environments.

Commerce: These followers are motivated by financial success. The more they are paid, the more they are motivated to work.

Aesthetics: These followers are most motivated when in environments that place a premium on experimentation, artistic expression, creative problem solving, and quality.

Science: These followers are most motivated when digging deeply into problems, and keeping up to date on technology. They enjoy analyzing data to get at the truth.

values in order to increase satisfaction and performance. The trick is accurately identifying and aligning work activities to followers' values.

Unfortunately, most leaders do not appear to be very good at accurately assessing followers' values. When followers are asked to list the things they believe to be most important at work, they describe many of the values found in Table 9.2. But when they are asked to describe what motivates others at work, 75 percent report that money is the best way to motivate others. As such, many leaders appear to suffer from **extrinsic motivational bias** and falsely believe followers are more motivated by money (i.e., Commercial values) rather than by job security, recognition, or helping others (Morse, 2003). Research has shown that most followers value doing important work (i.e., Power) and being recognized for good performance (i.e., Recognition) over making money, but many people falsely believe that paying followers more will result in higher performance (Curphy, 2003c). Extrinsic motivational bias is a variation of the fundamental attribution error described in Chapter 3, where people are biased to believe that their own success is due to their own efforts and others' success is due to external factors, such as pay.

So how could we apply what we have learned about values to motivate our flight attendants, Ling Ling, and Julie to perform at higher levels? Like achievement orientation, values develop early in life and are quite difficult to change. So leaders will need to accurately assess what these individuals value and then restructure work so that it is better aligned with their underlying beliefs. In the case of the flight attendants, it appears that these individuals may have stronger Altruism and Security values. So paying flight attendants more money will probably not help to improve customer service, but leaders might have success by emphasizing how good customer service would better help passengers and reduce the risk of downsizing if the planes were kept fully loaded with passengers. Because Ling Ling works in sales, she might be more motivated to work harder because part of her compensation is contingent upon performance. The more apartments she rents, the more commission she gets paid, and the harder she will work. Julie, on the other hand, appears to have stronger Hedonism, Affiliation, and Altruism scores. Her boss might be most successful in motivating Julie to work hard by giving her the opportunity to work with and help others and giving her time off so she can go skiing. These three examples all point out the importance of hiring followers that have values similar to those emphasized in a particular job or restructuring work so that it better fits with followers' values (see Table 9.2).

Intrinsic Motivation

Work behavior is motivated by both internal and external factors. In this section, we will focus on the former, although we also will examine how the two factors interact. We use the term **intrinsic motivation** to describe behavior seemingly motivated for its own sake, for the personal satisfaction and increased feelings of competence or control one gets from doing it. In other words, some people are motivated to persist in certain behaviors for the simple reason that they like to do them. As such, intrinsic motivation is closely related to personal values, in that people often enjoys doing those activities aligned with their personal values. But intrinsic motivation is more specific than personal values, as it relates to the specific activities that one enjoys doing. Someone might have strong altruism values and is intrinsically motivated to teach middle school students. They may not like to counsel families, draw blood, work in a homeless shelter, etc., although all of their activities are related to altruism. Getting back to our two characters, Julie or Ling Ling might spend a lot of time operating ski lifts or showing apartments simply because they enjoy these activities. What is intrinsically motivating for one person, however, may not be for someone else. Hobbies, for example, are almost by definition intrinsically motivating, yet they also reflect the diversity of human tastes for different activities. Stamp collecting may be intrinsically motivating to one person, yet exceedingly boring to many others. The key for leadership practitioners is to identify the activities their followers like to perform (within reason), and increase their job opportunities to do them.

Deci (1975); Dawes (1991); Boyatzis, McKee, and Goleman (2002); Levinson (2003); and Brett and Stroh (2003) observed that individuals often voluntarily put forth effort toward activities they enjoy doing. If an individual is already engaged in an intrinsically motivating activity, we might ask what would result if extrinsic rewards were added to the intrinsic reward of just performing the activity. It might seem at first as though the activity would be even further strengthened if external rewards were added to the internal rewards. Sometimes, though, that is not the case. Some research has shown that external rewards or incentives may backfire if they are given to people already intrinsically motivated to perform the tasks. That can result in a *decrease* in the person's intrinsic motivation toward the tasks (Calder

& Staw, 1975; Deci, 1972; Kohn, 1993). Further study of this **overjustification effect** has shown that external rewards can result in a decrease in intrinsic motivation when they are perceived to be "controlling"; however, rewards seen as providing "informational" value (e.g., letting a person know how well he or she is doing) or those that are consistent with societal norms concerning pay and benefits typically do not result in a decrease in intrinsic motivation for the task (Deci, 1975; Eisenberger & Cameron, 1996; Fisher, 1973; Lepper, Greene, & Nisbett, 1973). After reviewing the results of approximately 100 studies, Eisenberger and Cameron (1996) went on to say that the overjustification effect is more of a myth than reality; the number of situations where this occurs is so limited and so easily avoided that it rarely, if ever, happens in the real world. Despite this preponderance of evidence, however, many educators and leaders continue to believe in the notion that rewards reduce the intrinsic motivation of tasks.

So how would intrinsic motivation and the overjustification effect work with Julie and Ling Ling? In both cases, the leaders would need to spend time with both individuals to find out what they enjoy doing at work. Not only might the boss learn that Julie really likes to work outdoors; she might also like the social nature of interacting with the crowds waiting in lift lines. This might indicate Julie would particularly enjoy working in the largest and most crowded lifts, something other lift operators may not enjoy so much. Ling Ling might really like sales but hate the paperwork associated with closing leases. Her boss could assign the administrative aspects of Ling Ling's job to an administrative support person, or find other ways (such as using technology) to reduce her administrative workload. Although followers will almost always have to perform activities they may not like, the more a leader aligns her followers' intrinsic interests with their work activities, the more motivated her team is likely to be.

Concluding Thoughts on Individual Differences in Motivation

Because people vary in their achievement orientation, values, and in the tasks they find intrinsically motivating, one way to ensure that followers will exert the effort needed to accomplish their tasks is to select individuals already high in these motives. Although McClelland (1985) has reported successfully training people to be higher in achievement orientation, this can be a relatively expensive and inefficient process; putting more emphasis on selecting the right people for the job in the first place may be a preferable approach for leaders to take.

It is also important to remember that perhaps the most effective way to determine what followers find to be important or intrinsically motivating is to simply ask them what they like to do. However, many leaders either do not have particularly good relationships with their followers or assume they know what motivates them, so they often fail to ask this simple question. While it may not be possible to completely align tasks with followers' intrinsic interests, leaders may be able to reassign or periodically rotate tasks to increase the level of follower motivation. Leaders often assume that jobs and task assignments are static and unchangeable, but most organizations do not care who does the work as long as it gets done. Leaders may be able to get higher-quality work and have more satisfied employees by reassigning work according to values and intrinsic interests. As the head of customer service, how would you use this information about individual differences in motivation to improve the customer service levels of flight attendants?

Cognitive Theories

Assume people are motivated by having clear goals, when they see the connections between efforts and rewards, and believe they can accomplish tasks. Leaders can motivate followers by setting goals and bolstering their beliefs about task accomplishment.

Another way to get followers to engage and persist with the behaviors associated with group success is to persuade them to think differently about their efforts. Rather than appealing to needs or hiring individuals who are naturally more "motivated," the cognitive theories look at whether followers will exert more effort toward group goals

Goals drive behavior.

David B. Peterson,
Personnel Decisions
International

when the expectations for performance and the links between the level of effort and desirable outcomes are clear. Should leaders set goals for their teams or simply tell them to do their best? Similarly, should leaders explicitly point out what rewards a group will get if they achieve certain outcomes, or will followers exert more effort if rewards are vague and only loosely tied to performance? The research underlying the cognitive theories provides leadership practitioners with the answers to these two important questions.

Goal Setting

One of the most familiar and easiest formal systems of motivation to use with followers is **goal setting.** From the leader's perspective, it involves helping followers see how a goal might be attained by following a systematic plan to achieve it. According to Locke and Latham (1990; 2002), goals are the most powerful determinants of task behaviors. Goals serve to direct attention, mobilize effort, help people develop strategies for goal achievement, and help people continue exerting effort until the goal is reached. That leads, in turn, to even higher goals (see Highlight 9.4).

Locke and Latham (1990; 2002) reported that nearly 400 studies and 35 years of research across individuals, groups, and organizations in eight different countries have provided consistent support for several aspects of goal setting. First, this research showed goals that were both *specific* and *difficult* resulted in consistently higher effort and performance when contrasted to "do your best" goals. Second, *goal commitment* is critical. Merely having goals is not enough. Although follower participation in setting goals is one way to increase commitment, goals set either by leaders unilaterally or through participation with followers can lead to necessary levels of commitment. Commitment to assigned goals was often as high as commitment to goals followers helped to set, provided the leader was perceived to have legitimate authority, expressed confidence in followers, and provided clear standards for performance (Locke & Latham, 1990; 2002; Klein, Wesson, Hollenbeck, & Alge, 1999). Third, followers exerted the greatest effort when goals were accompanied by *feedback;* followers getting goals or feedback alone generally exerted less effort.

Several other aspects of goal setting are also worth noting. First, goals can be set for any aspect of performance, be it reducing costs, improving the quality of

The Balanced Scorecard

Highlight 9.4

One technique involving goal setting that has gained popularity over the past 15 years is the Balanced Scorecard (Kaplan & Norton, 1992; 1996; 2001). Kaplan and Norton argue that most of the measures typically used to assess organizational performance are too limited in scope. For example, many organizations set goals and periodically review their financial performance. But financial performance suffers from time lags (it may take a month or longer before the financial results of specific organizational activities are available) and these results also say very little about other key organizational performance indicators, such as customer satisfaction, employee turnover, and key internal operational performance. To get around these problems, Kaplan and Norton advocate creating a set of goals and metrics for customers, employees, internal operations, and finance. Customer and employee goals and metrics make up leading indicators, as problems with customer satisfaction and employee turnover often results in sub-par operational and financial performance.

Curphy (2004 f, g) has developed Balanced Scorecards for rural Minnesota hospitals and school districts. For example, hospitals begin this process by going through a comprehensive review of their market demographics, customer trends, financial performance, internal operations (i.e., pharmacy, surgical use, infection rates, radiology and lab use, etc.), and staffing and facility data. Key community and health care leaders then create a new five-year vision for the hospital, and then set strategic priorities in the customer, financial, internal operations, and workforce and facilities categories. These priorities are refined further to create clear, measurable goals with readily available metrics in order to track monthly progress. These Balanced Scorecard goals are then used to drive specific department goals and track hospital performance and have been very effective in helping all hospital employees understand how their efforts contribute to the hospital's overall performance. In several cases hospital performance has dramatically improved as a result of these Balanced Scorecard efforts. A partial example of a typical Balanced Scorecard for one of these rural hospitals is as follows:

Customer: Improve patient satisfaction ratings from 74 to 86 percent by 1 January 2006.

Customer: Increase the number of live births from 12 to 20 per month by 1 January 2006.

Financial: Reduce average accounts payable from 84 to 53 days by 1 January 2006.

Financial: Increase operating margins from 2 to 6 percent by 1 January 2006.

Internal Operations: Increase orthopedic surgeries from 4 to 8 per day by 1 March 2006.

Internal Operations: Reduce patient infection rates from 1 to .5 percent by 1 March 2006.

Workforce: Reduce days needed to hire nurses from 62 to 22 days by 1 March 2006.

Workforce: Reduce employee turnover rates from 27 to 12 percent by 1 March 2006.

A monthly Balanced Scorecard report is included in all employees' pay statements and is a key topic of discussion in hospital and department staff meetings. Staff members review goal progress and regularly devise strategies for achieving department and hospital goals. One of the nice things about the Balanced Scorecard is that it helps employees to be proactive and gives them permission to win. In all too many organizations employees work hard but never see how their results contribute to team or organizational performance. Adopting Balanced Scorecards is a way to get around these problems.

Sources: G. J. Curphy, *The Blandin Education Leadership Program* (Grand Rapids, MN: The Blandin Foundation, 2004f); G. J. Curphy, *The Blandin Health Care Leadership Program* (Grand Rapids, MN: The Blandin Foundation, 2004g); R. S. Kaplan and D. P. Norton, "The Balanced Scorecard: Measures That Drive Performance," *Harvard Business Review,* January–February, 1992, pp. 71–79; R. S. Kaplan and D. P. Norton, *The Balanced Scorecard* (Boston, MA: Harvard Business School Press, 1996); R. S. Kaplan and D. P. Norton, *The Strategy Focused Organization* (Boston, MA: Harvard Business School Press, 2001).

services and products, increasing voter registra-
tion, or winning a league championship. Nevertheless, leaders need to ensure that they do not set
conflicting goals, as followers can only exert so
much effort over a given period of time (Eddleston, Kidder, & Litzky, 2002). Second, determining
just how challenging to make goals creates a bit of
a dilemma for leaders. Successfully completed
goals provide followers with a sense of job satisfaction, and easy goals are more likely to be com-

*Every substandard organization I
have ever seen had low performance
standards. If you want superior
performance, then you have got to
set high standards for your
employees.*

Norman Schwarzkopf

pleted than difficult goals. However, easily attainable goals result in lower levels
of effort (and, in turn, performance) than do more difficult goals. Locke and
Latham (1990; 2002) suggested that leaders might motivate followers most effectively by setting moderately difficult goals, recognizing partial goal accomplishment, and making use of a continuous-improvement philosophy by making goals
incrementally more difficult (Imai, 1986).

A leader's implicit and explicit expectations about goal accomplishment can
also affect the performance of followers and teams. Research by Dov Eden and his
associates in Israel provided fairly consistent support for the Pygmalion and
Golem effects (Davidson & Eden, 2000; Eden, Geller, Gewirtz, Gordon-Terner, In-
bir, Liberman, Pass, Salomen-Segev, & Shalit, 2000). The **Pygmalion Effect** occurs
when leaders articulate high expectations for followers; in many cases these expectations alone will lead to higher performing followers and teams. Unfortunately, the **Golem Effect** is also true—leaders who have little faith in their
followers' ability to accomplish a goal are rarely disappointed. Thus a leader's expectations for a follower or team have a good chance of becoming a self-fulfilling
prophecy (Chapter 3). These results indicate that leaders wanting to improve team
performance should set high but achievable goals and express confidence and support that the followers can get the job done (White & Locke, 2000; McNatt, 2000).

How could leadership practitioners apply goal setting to Julie and Ling Ling in
order to increase their motivation levels? Given the research findings just described,
Julie and Ling Ling's bosses should work with these two followers to set specific
and moderately difficult goals, express confidence that they can achieve their goals,
and provide regular feedback on goal progress. Julie and her boss could look at
Julie's past performance or other lift operators' performance as a baseline, and then
set specific and measurable goals around the number of hours worked, the number
of people who fall off the lift during a shift, customer satisfaction survey ratings
from skiers, the length of lift lines, or the number of complaints from customers.
Similarly, Ling Ling and her boss could look at some real estate baseline measures
and set goals around the number of apartments rented for the year, the total monetary value of these rentals, the time it takes to close a lease and complete the necessary paperwork, customer complaints, and sales expenses. Note that both Ling Ling
and Julie's bosses would need to take care that they do not set conflicting goals. For
example, if Julie had a goal only for the number of people who fell off the lift, then
she might be more likely to run the lift very slowly, resulting in long lift lines and
numerous customer complaints. In a similar vein, bosses need to ensure that individual goals do not conflict with team or organizational goals. Ling Ling's boss

would need to make sure that Ling Ling's goals did not interfere with those of the other real estate agents in the firm. If Ling Ling's goals did not specify territorial limits, then she might rent properties in other agents' territories, which in turn might cause a high level of interoffice conflict. Both bosses should also take care to set measurable goals; that way they could provide Julie and Ling Ling with the feedback they need to stay on track. More information on the specific steps of goal setting can be found in Part V of this book.

Expectancy Theory

The next cognitive theory is concerned with clarifying the links between what people do and the rewards or outcomes they will obtain. First described by Tolman (1932), **expectancy theory** has been modified for use in work settings (Vroom, 1964; Porter & Lawler, 1968; Lawler, 1973). It involves two fundamental assumptions: (*a*) motivated performance is the result of conscious choice, and (*b*) people will do what they believe will provide them the highest (or surest) rewards. Thus, expectancy theory is a highly *rational* approach to understanding motivation. It assumes that people act in ways that maximize their expectations of attaining valued outcomes, and that reliable predictions of behavior are possible if the factors that influence those expectations can be quantified. In this model, there are three such factors to be quantified. The first two are probability estimates (expectancies), and the third is a vector sum of predicted positive and negative outcomes. Expectancy theory maintains that leadership practitioners will be able to motivate followers if they understand the process followers use to determine whether certain behaviors will lead to valued rewards.

The first probability estimate is the **effort-to-performance expectancy.** Like all probabilities, it ranges from no chance of the event occurring to absolute certainty of its occurring; or, in decimal form, from 0.0 to 1.0. Here, the follower estimates the likelihood of performing the desired behavior adequately, assuming she puts forth the required effort. The second probability estimate is the **performance-to-outcome expectancy.** In this case, our follower estimates the likelihood of receiving a reward, given that she achieves the desired level of performance. This is a necessary step in the sequence since it is not uncommon for people to actually do good work yet not be rewarded for it (e.g., someone else may be the teacher's pet). Finally, the follower must determine the likely outcomes, assuming that the previous conditions have been met, and determine whether their weighted algebraic sum (**valence**) is sufficiently positive to be worth the time and effort. To put it more simply, expectancy theory says that people will be motivated to do a task if three conditions are met: (1) they can perform the task adequately if they put forth enough effort, (2) they will be rewarded if they do it, and (3) they value the reward (see Figure 9.3).

Applying these three concepts to Ling Ling might be helpful here. Since the Chinese government takeover in 1997 and the collapse of the Asian economy, the real estate rental market has been depressed in Hong Kong. Even though Ling Ling has been working three weekday evenings a week and all day Saturday (showing an average of 12 apartments per week), she is 25 percent behind her sales quota. According to expectancy theory, Ling Ling would first determine if working the additional two weekday evenings a week would enable her to rent more apartments—effort-to-performance expectancy. Second, Ling Ling would have to determine if renting these

FIGURE 9.3
An example
of expectancy
theory.

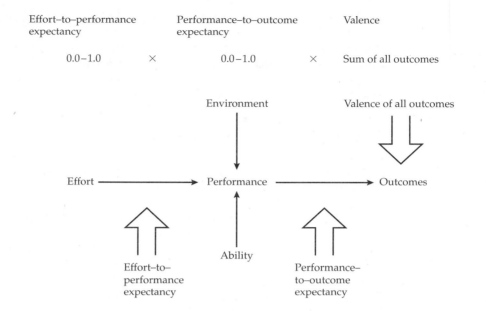

additional apartments would be sufficient to reach her sales quota by the end of the year—performance-to-outcome expectancy. Finally, Ling Ling would have to weigh the advantages of reaching her sales quota (sales bonus, job security) relative to the disadvantages (stress, loss of free time, loss of sleep, etc.)—valences. Notice that if Ling Ling did not believe that (*a*) working additional weekday evenings would help her to rent more apartments, (*b*) renting these additional apartments would be enough to reach her annual sales quota, or (*c*) the benefits of reaching her sales quota outweighed the costs, then Ling Ling would choose not to put forth the effort to rent additional apartments. She may feel that the real estate market is in such bad shape or her bonus so low that even if she were to meet her quota, it would not be worth the additional effort. As seen in Figure 9.3, all three components must have a relatively high probability or be favorably weighted in order for Ling Ling to exert further effort in renting additional apartments.

Leadership practitioners using expectancy theory to motivate a follower to do a work project would need to take three steps. First, the leader would have to increase effort-to-performance expectancy by clarifying the links between the follower's level of effort and project completion. To do this, the leader and follower might discuss what the follower would need to do, and the amount of time and resources it would take to complete the project. Second, the leader would need to increase the performance-to-reward expectancy by discussing the positive outcomes to

A company is always perfectly designed to produce what it is producing. If it has quality problems, cost problems, or productivity problems, then the behaviors associated with these outcomes are being reinforced. This is not conjecture. This is the cold, hard reality of human behavior.

Anonymous

the follower and the organization if the project were completed on time and at cost. This might involve such things as a year-end bonus, increased recognition by upper management, or reduced costs or increased market share for the organization. Finally, the leader would need to clarify all of the potential valences for successfully completing the project. This may not be obvious to the follower, so the leader would need to clearly describe both the pros and the cons but emphasize the positive aspects of the project.

Equity Theory

This cognitive approach assumes that people value fairness in leader–follower exchange relationships (Kanfer, 1990). Followers are said to be most motivated when they believe that what they put into an activity or a job and what they get out of it are roughly equivalent to what others put into and get out of it (Adams, 1963; Vecchio, 1982). **Equity theory** proposes a very rational model for how followers assess these issues. Followers presumably reach decisions about equitable relationships by assigning values to the four elements in Figure 9.4 and then comparing the two ratios (Adams, 1963). Regarding the specific elements in each ratio, personal outcomes refer to what one is receiving for one's efforts, such as pay, recognition, job satisfaction, opportunity for advancement, and personal growth. Personal inputs refer to all those things one contributes to an activity or a job, such as time, effort, knowledge, and skills.

A key aspect of equity theory is that Figure 9.4 contains *two* ratios. Judgments of equity are always based on a comparison to some reference group. It is the *relationship between the two ratios* that is important in equity theory, not the absolute value of either one's own or another's outcomes or inputs, considered by themselves. What matters most is the comparison between one's own ratio and that of a reference group such as one's co-workers or workers holding similar jobs in other organizations. Consider, for example, the story of an investment banker who was making over $400,000 per year but was extremely dissatisfied with her pay. The banker stated that, on the one hand, she got paid a "ridiculously high" amount of money for what she did, but on the other hand, she knew investment bankers who were making considerably more than she was. Similarly, Ling Ling may make more money than her peers, but she may also work longer hours, have more skills, and lease more apartments. In other words, although her outcomes are greater, so are her inputs, and thus the ratios may still be equal; there is equity.

In essence, equity theory does not try to evaluate equality of inputs or equality of outcomes. It is concerned with fairness of inputs relative to outcomes. The perception of inequity creates a state of tension and an inherent pressure for change. As long as there is general equality between the two ratios, there is no motivation (at least based on inequity) to change anything, and people are reasonably satisfied. If, however, the ratios are significantly different, a follower will be motivated to take action likely to restore the balance. Exactly what the follower will be motivated to do de-

FIGURE 9.4
Equity theory ratios.

$$\frac{\text{Personal outcomes}}{\text{Personal inputs}} = \frac{\text{Reference group outcomes}}{\text{Reference group inputs}}$$

pends on the direction of the inequality. Adams (1965) suggested six ways people might restore balance: (*a*) changing their inputs, (*b*) changing their outcomes, (*c*) altering their self-perceptions, (*d*) altering their perceptions of their reference group, (*e*) changing their reference group, or, if all else fails, (*f*) leaving the situation. Thus, if Julie believed her

Capacity is its own motivation.
David Campbell
The Center for
Creative Leadership

ratio was lower than her co-worker's, she might reduce her level of effort or seek higher pay elsewhere. She could also change her reference group to that of ski lift operators at other resorts, or even quit. Research has shown that perceptions of underpayment generally resulted in actions in support of the model, but perceptions of overpayment did not. Instead of working harder in an overpayment condition (to make their own ratio more equitable), subjects often rationalized that they really deserved the higher pay (Campbell & Pritchard, 1976). An example of how equity theory might affect some salary negotiations is presented in Highlight 9.5.

Leadership, Equity Theory, and Professional Athlete Salary Demands

Highlight 9.5

General managers are responsible for the overall performance of their professional sports teams. They help select players and coaches; negotiate media, player, coach, and stadium contracts; keep team morale at a high level; and take action to ensure the team wins the championship and makes money. One of the most difficult issues general managers deal with is negotiating contracts with players. Players look at their own pay and performance and compare them to that of other athletes in the league. If they feel their compensation is not consistent with that of other players, they usually ask to be traded or for a new contract to be negotiated. These comparisons have led to the $100 million-plus salaries now commanded by marquee players in basketball, football, and baseball. But what happens to team morale, the win–loss record, and financial performance when one or two players make substantially more money than the rest of the team? Research on professional baseball teams over an eight-year period indicated that teams with high pay dispersion levels (i.e., large gaps between the highest and lowest paid starting player) did less well financially and were less likely to win division championships. Researchers surmised that this drop in team performance was due to the high levels of pay dispersion which eroded team performance and increased inequity for other players on the team. The trick for general managers seems to be to find enough financial rewards to induce higher levels of performance but not create inequity situations for the rest of the team.

Although the effects of equity theory are readily apparent with professional athletes' pay, the same holds true with top executives. Many Boards of Directors worry that if they do not pay their CEOs and top executives at least on par with those in other companies, they run the risk of executive turnover. But do executives leave simply for more money? In those cases where executives have strong Commercial values, this may be the case. But others more likely leave because their Recognition, Power, or Security needs may not be getting satisfied. This is where the extrinsic motivation bias gets Boards of Directors into trouble, as they pay top dollar to appeal to executives' Commercial values, when many of these executives may be working for more than just money.

Source: M. Bloom, "The Performance Effects of Pay Dispersions on Individuals and Organizations," *Academy of Management Journal* 42, no. 1 (1999), pp. 25–40.

Self-Efficacy

So far in this section we have discussed the importance of goals, linking efforts and rewards to goals, and making sure rewards are commensurate with efforts. But we have yet to discuss whether a person's beliefs about whether he or she can or cannot perform certain tasks have any effect on motivation and performance. The last cognitive theory of motivation is self-efficacy, which concerns one's core beliefs about being able to successfully perform a given task (Bandura & Locke, 2003). **Positive self-efficacy** is used to note beliefs where people feel confident that they have the power to create desired effects; **negative self-efficacy** is used to note self-debilitating beliefs. Research has shown that people who simply believe they can perform a particular task will often exert considerable effort to get the task accomplished. Conversely, people with negative self-efficacy often give up in the face of difficulty.

Although research has shown that self-efficacy is strongly linked to motivation and performance (Bandura & Locke, 2003), it is important to note that self-efficacy varies from one task to the next. A particular follower or team may have positive self-efficacy about one task and negative self-efficacy about others. Because followers' self-efficacy varies from one task to the next, leaders can better motivate followers by finding ways to boost their self-efficacy. Leaders can do this by providing relevant work experience and tying it to training, coaching, encouragement, and support, and ensuring followers get the resources they need to be successful.

So how might we use self-efficacy to increase Julie's level of motivation as a ski lift operator? The first step would be to provide Julie with proper training on how to operate the ski lift equipment. The leader would then want to have Julie practice operating the lift in various emergency situations and give her feedback on how to do it better. Julie will gain positive self-efficacy once she feels comfortable operating the equipment, and the more she operates the equipment the more self-efficacy she will have. This does not mean that Julie will work harder and put in longer hours, but it does mean that she will be much more likely to persist in the face of difficulties than if she did not know how to operate the equipment. Ling Ling's supervisor could use a similar approach to help her rent apartments in Hong Kong. Getting Ling Ling proper training, providing coaching support with her early rentals, and being available to provide help with more difficult rentals will help improve Ling Ling's self-efficacy for renting apartments. But as our flight attendant situation aptly points out, having positive self-efficacy may not be enough to keep people motivated to perform certain activities. Many flight attendants have a number of years of experience and plenty of positive self-efficacy for the job. But many also seem inattentive to customers' needs and unwilling to go the extra mile. Self-efficacy seems very important for understanding why people may be unmotivated to do a task, but having positive self-efficacy may be necessary but insufficient to ensure that people engage in those behaviors that result in higher individual or team performance.

Concluding Thoughts on Cognitive Theories of Motivation

All four of the cognitive theories assume that changing followers' thoughts will help them to engage in particular tasks and activities. Followers will be more inclined to pursue activities that result in the accomplishment of specific goals, that balance perceived inequities, or when they believe they can perform those behaviors needed to accomplish goals. Leaders can influence followers' motivational levels by clearly articulating expected outcomes, clarifying the links between efforts and rewards, and providing training, coaching, and feedback to followers as they go about accomplishing tasks.

Perhaps more than the other theories and approaches described in this section, the cognitive theories place a strong premium on leader–follower communication. It is hard to imagine how goal setting, expectancy theory, equity theory, or self-efficacy would work if the leader did not articulate goals, provide ongoing feedback, and continually clarify motivational links with followers. If leader–follower communication is poor, then it is unlikely that leaders will realize the benefits of these four approaches. The research shows that these theories can effectively increase worker motivation; when they fail it often has more to do with how the theory was implemented than with inadequacy of the theory. Thus, leaders with poor interpersonal communication, feedback, and coaching skills might have a difficult time using these theories to increase follower motivation levels.

Situational Approaches

Assume leaders can change the situation in order to better motivate followers. So far we have discussed how underlying needs, individual differences in achievement orientation, or goals or performance-to-reward links can affect follower motivation levels. However, these motivational techniques are mainly follower- or leader-centric; they pertain to certain follower qualities or leader actions. From Chapter 2 we know that leadership is an interaction between the leader, followers, and the situation, and the theories of motivation can be categorized using the same framework. The two approaches described in this section show how it is possible to change the situation in order to improve followers' motivation levels. In other words, this research shows that some jobs are more motivating than others and that it is possible to reengineer jobs to improve followers' motivation levels. These two situational approaches to motivation include the operant approach and empowerment.

> *You get what you reinforce, but you do not necessarily get what you pay for.*
> Fred Luthans,
> University of Nebraska,
> and Alexander Stajkovic,
> University of California, Irvine

The Operant Approach

One very popular way to change the direction, intensity, or persistence of behavior is through rewards and punishments. It will help at the outset of this discussion of the **operant approach** to define several terms. A **reward** is any consequence that *increases* the likelihood that a particular behavior will be repeated. For example, if Julie gets a cash award for a suggestion to improve customer service at the ski resort, then she will be more likely to forward additional suggestions. **Punishment** is the administration of an aversive stimulus or the withdrawal of something desirable, each of which *decreases* the likelihood a particular behavior will be repeated (Arvey & Ivancevich, 1980). Thus, if Ling Ling loses her bonus for not getting her paperwork in on time, then she will be less likely to do so again in the future. Both rewards and punishments can be administered in a contingent or noncontingent manner. **Contingent** rewards or punishments are administered as *consequences of a particular behavior.* Examples might include giving Julie a medal immediately after she won a skiing race or giving Ling Ling a bonus check for exceeding her sales quota. **Noncontingent** rewards and punishments are not associated with particular behaviors. Monthly paychecks might be examples, if both Julie and Ling Ling receive the same amount of base pay every month whatever their actual effort or output. Finally, behaviors that are not rewarded will eventually be eliminated through the process of **extinction.**

When properly implemented, there is ample evidence to show that the operant approach can be a very effective way to improve follower motivation and performance (Curphy, 2004a; Curphy & Hogan, 2004b; Markham, Scott, & McKee, 2002; Stajkovic & Luthans, 2001; Luthans & Stajkovic, 1999; Bloom & Milkovich, 1998; Jenkins, Mitra, Gupta, & Shaw, 1998; Curphy, 1991a; Komacki, Zlotnick, & Jensen, 1986; Luthans & Kreitner, 1985; Pritchard, Hollenback, & DeLeo, 1976). Some of this research has also shown that rewards work better than punishments, particularly if administered in a contingent manner (Stajkovic & Luthans, 2001; Jenkins, Mitra, Gupta, & Shaw, 1998; Luthans & Kreitner, 1985; Podsakoff & Todor, 1985; Arvey, Davis, & Nelson, 1984; Podsakoff, Todor, & Skov, 1982). When comparing the relative impact of different types of rewards, Stajkovic and Luthans (2001) reported that incentive pay targeted at specific follower behaviors was the most effective, followed by social recognition and performance feedback for improving follower performance in credit card processing centers. Although Kohn (1993) has gained attention by arguing that incentive pay programs do not work, his statements appear to be based on nothing more than his own opinions. The research clearly shows that leaders who properly design and implement contingent reward systems do indeed increase follower productivity and performance.

So how does a leader properly design and implement an operant system for improving followers' motivation and performance levels? Using operant principles properly to improve followers' motivation and hence performance requires several steps. First, *leadership practitioners need to clearly specify what behaviors are important.* This means that Julie's and Ling Ling's leaders will need to specify what they want them to do, how often they should do it, and the level of performance required. Second, *leadership practitioners need to determine if those behaviors are currently being punished, rewarded, or ignored.* Believe it or not, sometimes followers are actually rewarded for behaviors that leaders are trying to extinguish, and punished for behaviors that leaders want to increase. For example, Julie may get considerable positive attention from peers by talking back to her leader or for violating the ski resort dress code. Similarly, Ling Ling may be overly competitive and get promoted ahead of her peers (e.g., by renting apartments in her peers' territories), even when her boss extols the need for cooperation and teamwork. It also may be the case that leaders sometimes just ignore the very behaviors they would like to see strengthened. An example here would be if Julie's boss consistently failed to provide rewards when Julie worked hard to achieve impressive safety and customer service ratings (see Highlight 9.6).

The Folly of Rewarding A While Hoping for B

Highlight 9.6

Steven Kerr has written a compelling article detailing how many of the reward systems found in government, sports, universities, businesses, medicine, and politics often *compel people to act in a manner contrary to that intended.* For example, voters want politicians to provide the specifics of their programs or platform, yet politicians often get punished for doing so. Some constituency is bound to get hurt or offended whenever the specifics of a program are revealed, which in turn will cost the politician votes. If a politician keeps overall goals vague, more voters are likely to agree with the politician and vote for him or her in the next election.

Businesses, like universities and politicians, often utilize inappropriate reward systems. According to Kerr, the following are some of the more common management reward follies:

We hope for . . .	But we often reward . . .
Long-term growth	Quarterly earnings
Teamwork	Individual effort
Commitment to total quality	Shipping on schedule, even with defects
Reporting bad news	Reporting good news, whether it is true or not

Kerr states that managers who complain about unmotivated workers should consider the possibility that their current reward system is incongruent with the performance they desire.

Source: S. Kerr, "On the Folly of Rewarding A, While Hoping for B," *Academy of Management Executive 9*, no. 1 (1995), pp. 7–14.

Third, *leadership practitioners need to find out what followers actually find rewarding and punishing.* Leaders should *not* make the mistake of assuming that followers will find the same things rewarding and punishing as they do, nor should they assume that all followers will find the same things to be rewarding and punishing. What may be one follower's punishment may be another follower's reward. For example, Ling Ling may dislike public attention and actually exert less effort after being publicly recognized, yet some of her peers may find public attention to be extremely rewarding. In all likelihood valued rewards will be related to followers' underlying values. Fourth, *leadership practitioners need to be wary of creating perceptions of inequity when administering individually tailored rewards.* A peer may feel that she got the same results as Ling Ling, yet she received a smaller bonus check for the quarter. Leaders can minimize inequities by being clear and consistent with rewards and punishments. Fifth, *leadership practitioners should not limit themselves to administering organizationally sanctioned rewards and punishments.* Oftentimes leaders are limited in the amount of money they can give followers for good performance. However, research by Stajkovic and Luthans (2001) and Markham, Scott, and McKee (2002) showed that social recognition and performance feedback resulted in significant productivity improvements in followers and these rewards do not cost any money. Using a bit of ingenuity, leaders can often come up with an array of potential rewards and punishments that are effective and inexpensive, and do not violate organizational norms or policies. Julie might find driving the snow cat to be extremely enjoyable, and her boss could use this reward to maintain or increase Julie's motivation levels for operating the ski lift. Finally, because the administration of noncontingent consequences has relatively little impact, *leadership practitioners should administer rewards and punishments in a contingent manner whenever possible.* Highlight 9.7 is an example of the positive results that can come from implementing the operant approach systematically.

Empowerment

Empowerment makes up the other situational approach to motivation. In general, people seem to fall into one of two camps with respect to empowerment. Some people believe empowerment is all about delegation and accountability, a top-down process where senior leaders articulate a vision and specific goals, and hold followers responsible for achieving them. Others believe empowerment is more of a bottom-up approach that focuses on intelligent risk taking, growth, change, trust, and ownership; followers act as entrepreneurs and owners that question rules and make intelligent decisions. Leaders tolerate mistakes and encourage cooperative behavior in this approach to empowerment (Quinn & Spreitzer, 1997; Wagner, Parker, & Christiansen, 2003). Needless to say, these two conceptualizations of empowerment have very different implications for leaders and followers. And it is precisely this conceptual confusion which has caused empowerment programs to fail in many organizations (Quinn & Spreitzer, 1997). Because of the conceptual confusion surrounding empowerment, companies such as Motorola will not use this term to describe programs that push decision making to lower organizational levels. These companies would rather coin their own terms to describe these programs, thus avoiding the confusion surrounding empowerment.

Emery Air Freight

Highlight 9.7

Emery Air Freight is one of the most successful examples of how leaders can change the direction, intensity, and persistence of followers' behaviors through the operant approach. Emery Air Freight discovered that it was using the full capacity of its air freight containers only 45 percent of the time and, because of the highly competitive nature of the air freight shipping business, wanted to reduce costs and increase profits by making better use of its air freight containers. The company initially had given employees detailed instructions on how to better use air freight containers. However, this intervention met with little success, and the senior executives at Emery Air Freight consequently decided to implement an operant motivational strategy.

Emery Air Freight's operant strategy consisted of several different steps. First, checklists for air freight container usage were developed. These checklists consisted of the specific behaviors or actions workers could take when preparing an air container for delivery. Second, workers recorded their performance on the checklists, which provided them with information on their own performance with respect to organizational goals. Third, supervisors were trained to provide positive reinforcement on a contingent basis, and in turn praised and rewarded workers for meeting goals or showing improvement over time. In terms of results, Emery Air Freight credited the operant strategy with $2 million in reduced costs after only three years.

We define empowerment as having two key components. For leaders to truly empower employees, they must delegate leadership and decision making down to the lowest level possible. Employees are often the closest to the problem and have the most information, and as such can often make the best decisions. A classic example was the UPS employee who ordered an extra 737 aircraft to haul presents that had been forgotten in the last-minute Christmas rush. This decision was clearly beyond the employee's level of authority, but UPS praised his initiative for seeing the problem and making the right decision. The second component of empowerment, and the one most often overlooked, is equipping followers with the resources, knowledge, and skills necessary to make good decisions. All too often companies adopt an empowerment program and push decision making down to the employee level, but employees have no experience creating business plans, submitting budgets, dealing with other departments within the company, or directly dealing with customers or vendors. Not surprisingly, ill-equipped employees often make poor, uninformed decisions, and managers in turn are likely to believe that empowerment was not all it was cracked up to be. The same happens with downsizing, as employees are asked to take on additional responsibilities but are provided with little training or support. "Forced" empowerment may lead to some short-term stock gains but tends to be disastrous in the long run. Thus, empowerment has both delegation and developmental components; delegation without development is often perceived as abandonment, and development without delegation can often be perceived as micromanagement. Leaders wishing to empower followers must determine what followers are capable of doing, enhance and broaden these capabilities, and give followers commensurate increases in authority and accountability.

The psychological components of empowerment can be examined at both macro and micro levels. There are three macro psychological components underlying empowerment, and these are motivation, learning, and stress (Howard, 1996). As a concept, empowerment has been around since at least the 1920s, and the vast majority of companies that have implemented empowerment programs have done so to increase employee motivation and, in turn, productivity. As a motivational technique, however, empowerment has not lived up to its promise; empowered workers may not be any more productive than unempowered workers (Howard, 1996). There are several reasons why this may be the case. First, senior leaders tend to see empowerment through rose-colored glasses. They hear about the benefits an empowerment program is having in another company, but do not consider the time, effort, and changes needed to create a truly empowered workforce. Relatedly, many empowerment programs are poorly implemented—the program is announced with great fanfare, but little real guidance, training, or support is provided and managers are quick to pull the plug on the program as soon as followers start making poor decisions. Adopting an effective empowerment program takes training, trust, and time (Offermann, 1996), but companies most likely to implement an empowerment program (as a panacea for their poor financial situation)

> The biggest challenge was really just empowering that incredible group of young New Zealanders. Only a scattering had ever worked on a TV show or film before. Going on a seven-year journey and bringing Tolkien's words to the screen demanded trust, especially given how much doubt there was around the world about whether this project could even be pulled off.
>
> Peter Jackson

often lack these three attributes. Third, worker productivity and job dissatisfaction in the United States are at an all-time high. Many companies are dealing with high levels of employee burnout, and adding additional responsibilities to already over-filled plates is likely to be counterproductive. As reported by Xie and Johns (1995), some empowerment programs create positions that are just too big for a person to handle effectively, and job burnout is usually the result.

Although the motivational benefits of empowerment seem questionable, the learning and stress reduction benefits of empowerment seem more clear-cut. Given that properly designed and implemented empowerment programs include a strong developmental component, one of the key benefits to these programs is that they help employees learn more about their jobs, company, and industry. These knowledge and skill gains increase the intellectual capital of the company and can be a competitive advantage in moving ahead. In addition to the learning benefits, well-designed empowerment programs can actually help to reduce burnout. People can tolerate high levels of stress when they have a high level of control. Given that many employees are putting in longer hours than ever before and work demands are at an all-time high, empowerment can help followers gain some control over their lives and better cope with stress. Although an empowered worker may have the same high work demands as an unempowered worker, the empowered worker will have more choices on how and when to accomplish these demands and as such will suffer from less stress. And because stress is a key component of dysfunctional turnover, giving workers more control over their work demands can reduce turnover and in turn positively impact the company's bottom line (see Highlight 9.8).

There are also four micro components of empowerment. These components can be used to determine whether employees are empowered or unempowered, and include self-determination, meaning, competence, and influence (Quinn & Spreitzer, 1997; Spreitzer, 1995; Wagner, Parker, & Christiansen, 2003). Empowered employees have a sense of self-determination; they can make choices about what they do, how they do it, and when they need to get it done. Empowered employees also have a strong sense of meaning; they believe what they do is important to them and to the company's success. Empowered employees have a high level of competence in that they know what they are doing and are confident they can get the job done. Finally, empowered employees have an impact on others and believe that they can influence their teams or work units and that co-workers and leaders will listen to their ideas. In summary, empowered employees have latitude to make decisions, are comfortable making these decisions, believe what they do is important, and are seen as influential members of their team. Unempowered employees may have little latitude to make decisions, may feel ill equipped and may not want to make decisions, and may have little impact on their work unit, even if they have good ideas. Most employees probably fall somewhere in between the two extremes of the empowerment continuum, depicted in Figure 9.5.

Concluding Thoughts on Situational Approaches to Motivation

Empowerment and the operant approach make an important point that is often overlooked by other theories of motivation: By changing the situation, leaders can enhance followers' motivation, performance, and satisfaction. Unfortu-

Empowerment and Pride

Highlight 9.8

There is far more of a payoff to "working the people side" than most managers think. In a study of 3,000 companies, researchers at the University of Pennsylvania found that spending 10 percent of revenue on capital improvements boosts productivity by 3.9 percent, but a similar investment in developing human capital increased productivity by 8.5 percent—more than twice as much.

John Byrne, Fast Company

Well-designed empowerment programs not only may result in higher productivity, reduced stress, and lower turnover; they can also help to instill a sense of pride in the workforce. It is easy to see that if people are proud of where they work, they will likely be more motivated to do the right things and go the extra mile in order for the team and organization to suc-ceed. The opposite is also true—those who feel no pride or loyalty to their employer will act accordingly. It seems likely that employee pride helps to create a self-fulfilling prophecy at work, so what can a leader do to instill a sense of pride in followers? Author Jon Katzenbach has these suggestions:

Personalize the workplace: Leaders need to get involved with the everyday problems of their people. This may not be in the human resources rules book, but it will help create emotional bonds with employees.

Always have your compass set on pride, not money: It is more important that people feel proud of what they are doing every day than it is for them to be proud of reaching a major goal.

Localize as much as possible: The best efforts at building pride are local—they usually are not part of some corporate-sponsored initiative.

Make your messages simple and direct: Facts tell and stories sell. People seldom tire of good stories that stir up feelings of pride, so leaders should have a set of stories that describe when employees went the extra mile and how it helped the customer and company.

Source: J. A. Katzenbach, *Why Pride Matters More than Money: The Power of the World's Greatest Motivational Force* (New York: Crown, 2003).

FIGURE 9.5
The empowerment continuum.

Empowered Employees ◄――――►	**Unempowered Employees**
• Self-determined	• Other-determined
• Sense of meaning	• Not sure if what they do is important
• High competence	• Low competence
• High influence	• Low influence

nately, many leaders naively assume it is easier to change an *individual* than it is to change the *situation,* but this is often not the case. It is important to remember that the situation is not always fixed, and followers are not the only variable in the performance equation. Leaders can often see positive changes in followers' motivation levels by restructuring work processes and procedures, which in turn can increase their latitude to make decisions and add more meaning to work. Ty-ing these changes with a well-designed and well-implemented reward system can result in further increases in motivation. However, leaders are likely to en-counter some resistance whenever they change the processes, procedures, and rewards for work, even if these changes are for the better. As noted by Peterson and Hicks (1996), doing things the old way is easy, as followers know the expectations for performance and usually have developed the skills needed to achieve results. Followers often find that doing things a new way can be frustrating, as expectations may be unclear and they may not have the requisite skills. Leadership practitioners can help followers work through this initial resistance to new processes and procedures by showing support, providing training and coaching on new skills, and capitalizing on opportunities to reward progress. If the processes, procedures, and rewards are properly designed and administered, then in many cases followers will successfully work through their resistance and, over time, wonder how they ever got work done using the old systems. The successful transition to new work processes and procedures will rest squarely on the shoulders of leaders. So, given the implications of the situational approach to motivation, how could you use empowerment and the operant approach to improve the customer service levels of flight attendants? What information would you need to gather, how would you implement the program, and what would be the potential pitfalls of your program?

Motivation Summary

We hope that, after reading this chapter, you will have a better understanding of how follower characteristics (needs, intrinsic motivation), leader actions (goal setting), and situational factors (contingent rewards) affect how you and your followers are

---

Reducing Risk-Taking Behaviors on Offshore Oil Platforms

Highlight 9.9

One of the most dangerous jobs in the world is that of an offshore oil-rig employee. These employees often work 12–16 hours a day for two- to four-week shifts operating heavy equipment in very confined spaces. Not only is the work long and hard, but many of these platforms face dangers from high seas, cold weather, and even hurricanes. Because of these conditions and the nature of work, many energy companies are very concerned with safety. But what can well managers do to create safe oil platforms? It turns out that using a combination of several motivational techniques may be the best way to reduce oil platform accidents.

To reduce accidents, well managers must first set clear goals and performance expectations for safety. If employees only believe production is important to well managers, then they will do what they think is right to boost productivity and will pay little attention

to safety issues. So managers must set the tone for safety by setting safety goals and constantly reminding employees of safety issues. Second, they must hire employees who are motivated to perform safe work behaviors. Well managers should use personality inventories to hire employees with higher dependability scores, as they tend to be risk-averse and are much more rule abiding than those with lower dependability scores. Third, well managers must ensure that their compensation systems recognize and reward safe behaviors. If the compensation system only rewards productivity, then employees will do what they need to in order to maximize their rewards. The same is true if the compensation system rewards both productivity *and* safety. Using this three-pronged approach will not eliminate all oil-rig accidents, but it will go a long way towards reducing accident rates.

Source: R. Gregory, R. T. Hogan, and G. J. Curphy, "Risk-Taking in the Energy Industry," *Well Connected,* June 2003, 5 (6), pp. 5–7.

motivated (and demotivated). Moreover, you should be able to start recognizing situations where some theories provide better insights about problems in motivation levels than others. For example, if we go back to the survival situation described in Chapter 1, then we can see that the need theories (Maslow and Alderfer) provide better explanations for the behavior of the survivors than the job characteristics model or intrinsic motivation. On the other hand, if we think about the reasons we might not be doing well in a particular class, then we may see that we have not set specific goals for our grades or that the links between our efforts and our grades are not very clear. Or if we are working in a bureaucratic organization, then we may see that there are few consequences for either substandard or superior performance; thus, there is little reason to exert any extra effort. Perhaps the best strategy for leaders is to be flexible in the types of interventions they consider to affect follower motivation. That will require, of course, familiarity with the strengths and weaknesses of the different theories and approaches presented here. Just as a carpenter can more effectively build a house by using a variety of tools, a leader can be more effective by using a variety of motivational interventions to resolve work problems.

At this point it is also important to note that one of the most important tools for motivating followers has not been fully addressed in this chapter. As described in Chapter 13, charismatic or transformational leadership is often associated with extraordinarily high levels of follower motivation, yet none of the theories described in this chapter can adequately explain how these leaders can get their followers to do more than they ever thought possible. Perhaps this is due to the fact that the theories in this chapter take a very rational or logical approach to motivation, yet transformational leadership uses emotion as the fuel to drive followers' heightened motivational levels. Just as our needs, thoughts, personality traits, intrinsic interests, and rewards can motivate us to do something different, so can our emotions drive us to engage in and persist with a particular activity. A good example here may be political campaigns. Do people volunteer to work for these campaigns because of some underlying need, personal goals, or their intrinsic interests in politics? Although these are potential reasons for some followers, the emotions generated by political campaigns, particularly where the two lead candidates represent different value systems, often seem to provide a better explanation for the large amount of time and effort people contribute. Leadership practitioners should not overlook the interplay between emotions and motivation, and the better able they are to address and capitalize on emotions when introducing change, the more successful they are likely to be.

A final point concerns the relationship between motivation and performance. Many leadership practitioners equate the two, but as we pointed out earlier in this chapter, they are not the same concepts. Getting followers to put in more time, energy, and effort on certain behaviors will not help the team to be more successful if they are the wrong behaviors to begin with. Similarly, followers may not know how and when to exhibit those behaviors associated with performance. Leadership practitioners must clearly identify those behaviors related to performance, coach and train their followers on how and when to exhibit these behaviors, and then use one or more of the theories described in this chapter to get followers to exhibit and persist with those behaviors associated with higher performance levels.

Understanding and Influencing Follower Satisfaction

As stated earlier, job satisfaction concerns one's attitudes about work, and there are several practical reasons why job satisfaction is an important concept for leaders to think about. According to Locke and Latham (1990); Ross and Curphy (2000); Sutherland (2000); Armour (2000); Butorac (2001); McElroy, Morrow, and Rude (2001); Rigby (2002); and Krug (2003), satisfied workers are more likely to continue working for an organization. Satisfied workers are also more likely to engage in organizational citizenship behaviors, behaviors that go beyond job descriptions and role requirements and help reduce the workload or stress of others in the organization (Organ & Ryan, 1995; Bettencourt, Gwinner, & Meuter, 2001). Dissatisfied workers are more likely to be adversarial in their relations with leadership (e.g., file grievances) and engage in diverse sorts of counterproductive behaviors (Strauss, 1998; Quigley, 2001). Dissatisfaction is one of the key reasons people leave organizations (Tett & Meyer, 1993; Sutherland, 2000; Armour, 2000; Tepper, 2000; Butorac, 2001; Krug (2003), and many of the reasons people are satisfied or dissatisfied with work are within the leader's control (see Table 9.3). Although the total costs of dissatisfaction are difficult to measure, the direct costs of replacing a first-line supervisor or an executive can range from $5,000 to $200,000 per hire, depending on recruiting, relocation, and training fees, and these costs do not include those associated with the productivity lost as a result of unfilled positions (Curphy, 1998a). Employee dissatisfaction can also affect revenue and capital available for organizational expansion and upgrades. A survey of major corporations showed that 49 percent switched to another vendor because of poor customer service (Peters, 1997). Barry Gibbons, the former CEO of Burger King, stated that "70–90 percent of the decisions not to repeat purchase of anything are not about product or price. They are about dimensions of service" (McKay, 1998). McKay stated that employees are probably not going to provide world-class service if they are unhappy with their job, boss, or company. The inability to retain customers will directly affect revenues and make investors think twice about buying stock in a company. Relatedly, Schellenbarger (1997) reported that 35 percent of investor decisions are driven by nonfinancial factors. Number 5 on a list of 39 factors investors weighed before buying stock was the company's ability to attract and retain talent. These findings imply that a company's stock price is driven not only by market share and profitability, but also by service and bench strength considerations. Thus, employee satisfaction (or dissatisfaction) can have a major impact on the organization's bottom line.

Of these outcomes, perhaps employee turnover has the most immediate impact on leadership practitioners. It would be very hard for Julie's or Ling Ling's bosses to achieve results if ski resort or real estate personnel were constantly having to be replaced, and the leader was spending an inordinate amount of time recruiting, hiring, and training replacements. Although some level of **functional turnover** is

> *One of the symptoms of approaching a nervous breakdown is the belief that one's work is terribly important. If I were a medical man, I would prescribe a holiday to any patient who considered his work important.*
>
> Bertrand Russell

TABLE 9.3
Why People
Leave or
Stay with
Organizations

Sources: Pace
Communication,
Inc., *Hemispheres
Magazine*, November
1994, p. 155; and
"Keeping Workers
Happy," *USA Today*,
February 10, 1998,
p. 1B.

Why Do People Leave Organizations?		Why Do People Stay with Organizations?	
Limited recognition and praise	34%	Promises of long-term employment	82%
Compensation	29%	Supports training and education	78%
Limited authority	13%	Hires/keeps hard-working, smart people	76%
Personality conflicts	8%	Encourages fun, collegial relationships	74%
Other	16%	Bases job evaluation on innovation	72%

healthy for an organization (i.e., these followers are retiring, did not fit into the organization, or were substandard performers), dysfunctional turnover is not. **Dysfunctional turnover** occurs when the "best and brightest" in an organization become dissatisfied and leave it. Bedeian and Armenakis (1998); Hom and Kinicki (2001); McElroy, Morrow, and Rude (2001); Rigby (2002); and Krug (2003) pointed out that dysfunctional turnover is most likely to occur when downsizing is the response to organizational decline (i.e., increased costs or decreased revenues, market web share, or earnings). In these situations, dysfunctional turnover may have several devastating effects. First, those individuals in the best position to turn the company around are no longer there. Second, those who remain are even less capable of successfully dealing with the additional workload associated with the downsizings. Compounding this problem is that training budgets also tend to be slashed during downsizings. Third, organizations that downsize have a very difficult time recruiting people with the skills needed to turn the company around. Either competent candidates avoid applying for jobs within the organization because of the uncertainties of job security, or the less competent managers remaining with the company may decide not to hire anyone who could potentially replace them (Bedeian & Armenakis, 1998). Because leaders can play an important role in followers' satisfaction levels, and because followers' satisfaction levels can have a substantial impact on various organizational outcomes, it is worth going into the topic in greater detail (see Highlights 9.10 and 9.11).

Global, Facet, and Life Satisfaction

There are different ways to look at a person's attitudes about work, but researchers usually collect this data using some type of job satisfaction survey (Bracken, 1992; Butorac, 2001; Curphy, 2001; Morrel-Samuels, 2002). Such surveys typically include items such as those found in Table 9.4, and they are usually sent to a representative sample of employees in the organization. Their responses are collected and tabulated, and the results are usually disseminated throughout the organization. Table 9.4 presents examples of three different types of items typically found on a job satisfaction survey. Item 1 is a **global satisfaction** item, which assesses the overall degree to which employees are satisfied with their organization and their job. Items 2 through 7 are **facet satisfaction** items, which assess the degree to which employees are satisfied with different

A Recipe for Success: The Gallup 12

Highlight 9.10

More and more organizations are beginning to realize that their overall success depends on how they treat their employees. Hiring good people, setting high goals and performance expectations, providing needed resources, developing new skills, and holding people accountable for results seem to be important ingredients in organizational success. Leaders who use these techniques are likely to have more engaged employees, less turnover, and higher team and organizational level performance. The Gallup Organization has surveyed thousands of companies and has identified 12 key questions that assess employee engagement, which are as follows:

1. I know what is expected from me at work.
2. I have the materials and equipment I need to do my job right.
3. At work, I have the opportunity to do what I do best every day.
4. In the last seven days, I have received recognition and praise for doing good work.
5. My supervisor, or someone at work, seems to care about me as a person.
6. There is someone at work who encourages my development.
7. At work, my opinions seem to count.
8. The mission/purpose of my company makes me feel my job is important.
9. My associates (fellow employees) are committed to doing quality work.
10. I have a best friend at work.
11. In the last six months, someone at work has talked to me about my progress.
12. This past year, I have had the opportunities at work to learn and grow.

Leaders with higher scores on these 12 items consistently have more satisfied employees, lower dysfunctional turnover, and higher team performance. Leaders with lower scores generally have just the opposite results. What is interesting about the Gallup 12 is that many of the items are related to the motivational techniques described earlier in this chapter and are under immediate supervisors' direct control. Oftentimes poor leaders blame followers, the organization, or the situation for poor results or high turnover, when the truth of the matter is that they would more likely pinpoint the source of the problem by looking in the mirror.

Sources: M. Buckingham and C. Coffman, *First, Break All The Rules* (New York: Simon & Schuster, 1999); G. J. Curphy and R. T. Hogan. "Managerial Incompetence: Is There a Dead Skunk on the Table?" working paper, 2004a; G. J. Curphy and R. T. Hogan, "What We Really Know about Leadership (But Seem Unwilling to Implement)," working paper, 2004b.

TABLE 9.4

Typical Items on a Satisfaction Questionnaire

1. Overall, I am satisfied with my job.
2. I feel the workload is about equal for everyone in the organization.
3. My supervisor handles conflict well.
4. My pay and benefits are comparable to those in other organizations.
5. There is a real future for people in this organization if they apply themselves.
6. Exceptional performance is rewarded in this organization.
7. We have a good health care plan in this organization.
8. In general, I am satisfied with my life and where it is going.

These items are often rated on a scale ranging from *strongly disagree* (1) to *strongly agree* (5).

A Recipe for Failure: Abusive Bosses Workplace Anger and Violence

Highlight 9.11

What did I tell you the first day? Your thoughts are nothing; you are nothing . . . if you were in my toilet bowl I wouldn't bother flushing it. My bath mat means more to me than you . . . you don't like it here, leave!

George Huang, Swimming with Sharks

Workplace anger and violence seem to be on the rise. A recent Gallup survey showed that 25 percent of employees report themselves as being "somewhat angry" at work. One in 20 employees has been assaulted at work, 1 in 6 has been sexually harassed, and 1 in 3 has been the subject of verbal abuse. Workplace homicides are now the second most prevalent reason for death at work, with 709 homicides occurring in 1998. Unfortunately, poor leadership practices appear to be a leading cause of workplace anger; and workers are four times more likely to leave a company if they have an abusive boss. But what can a leader do to control anger and violence in the workplace? First, given that many people are working longer hours than ever before, leaders need to be especially vigilant of follower stress and strain. Second, leaders must be willing to let people take some time off when things start to get out of hand. The work will still be there tomorrow—few

people have jobs where things really have to be done at a certain time. Third, never, ever abuse followers. There are many more of them than there are of you, and they can make your life miserable with various acts of computer sabotage, work slowdowns, and other passive-aggressive acts. More important, they are the people who are closest to the customer and do most of the work. If you have a performance problem, counsel the individuals in private and if necessary put them on some kind of performance plan. You could also use some of the development planning and coaching techniques described in Part V of this text to turn their performance around.

Sources: A. Quigley, "Organizational Consequences of Workplace Aggression," in R. T. Hogan and D. K. Sheldon (chairs), *Aggression in the Workplace: The Forgotten Problem,* symposium conducted at the 14th Annual Conference of the Society of Industrial & Organizational Psychology, Atlanta, GA, May 1999; B. J. Tepper, "Consequences of Abusive Supervison," *Academy of Management Journal* 43, no. 2 (2000), pp. 178–89; D. Hales and R. E. Hales, "Is Work Driving You Mad?" *Parade Magazine,* March 18, 2001, pp. 8–9; G. Strauss, "Workers Hone the Fine Art of Revenge: Acts of Violence, Harassment toward Boss on Rise in Corporate World," *Denver Post,* August 24, 1998, p. 6E; and K. L. Zellars, B. J. Tepper, & M. K. Duffy, "Abusive Supervisors and Subordinates' Organizational Citizenship Behavior," *Journal of Applied Psychology,* 87 (6), 2002, pp. 1068–1076.

aspects of work, such as pay, benefits, promotion policies, working hours and conditions, and the like. People may be relatively satisfied overall but still dissatisfied with certain aspects of work. For example, a study of junior officers in the Army revealed that overall satisfaction among them has been in decline over the past 10 years, and this decline is beginning to negatively impact reenlistment rates. A higher percentage of junior officers are choosing to leave the Army than ever before; the two primary reasons for this high level of dysfunctional turnover seem to be dissatisfaction with immediate supervisors and top leadership. Many junior officers reported that they were tired of working for career-obsessed supervisors who had a strong tendency to micromanage and would just as soon throw them under a bus if it would advance their career (Stone, 2000). And given the conflict in Iraq one suspects that employee dissatisfaction among National Guard and Reserve units is particularly high, which will in turn drive up turnover and make recruitment that much more difficult. This decline in global satisfaction is not limited only to the Army. Unfortunately, it is happening in many companies today. Much of this decline can be attributed to higher follower expectations, greater follower access to information through technology, economic downturns, organizational downsizings, and incompetent bosses (Curphy, 2001, 2003a, 2004a; Curphy & Hogan, 2004a). The following quote summarizes what many followers are feeling today.

Would life on a slave ship be much better if the galley master first asked the rowers to help write a mission statement? What employers need to come to terms with is the economic, cultural, and societal benefits of being loyal to their employees. If they don't, eventually their abuses will bite them on the ass.

Daniel Levine, Disgruntled: The Darker Side of the World of Work

Leadership practitioners should be aware of several other important findings regarding global and facet satisfaction. The first finding is that people generally tend to be very happy with their vocation or occupation. They may not like the pay, benefits, or their boss, but they do seem to be satisfied with what they do for a living (Campbell & Hyne, 1995). This points out the importance of values and intrinsic motivation, as most people gravitate to tasks or jobs they find interesting and enjoyable. The second finding pertains to the **hierarchy effect.** In general, persons with longer tenure or in higher positions tend to have higher global and facet satisfaction ratings than those new or lower in the organization (Campbell & Hyne, 1995). Because people higher in the organization are happier at work, they may not understand or appreciate why people at lower levels are less satisfied. From below, leaders at the top can appear somewhat naive and out of touch. From above, the complaints about morale, pay, or resources are often perceived as whining. One of the authors once worked with a utilities company that had downsized and was suffering from all of the ill effects associated with high levels of dysfunctional turnover. Unfortunately, the executive vice president responsible for attracting and retaining talent and making the company "an employer of choice" stated that he had no idea why employees were complaining, and that things would be a lot better if they just quit whining. Because the executive did not understand or appreciate the sources of employee complaints, the programs to improve employee morale completely missed the mark, and the high levels of dysfunctional turnover continued. The hierarchy effect also implies that it will take a considerable amount of top leaders' focus and energy to increase the satisfaction levels of nonmanagement employees—lip service alone is never enough.

Compensation is another facet of job satisfaction that can have important implications for leadership practitioners. As you might expect, the hierarchy effect is alive and well with pay: A survey of 3 million employees reported that 71 percent of senior management, 58 percent of middle management, and only 46 percent of nonmanagers rate their pay as "very good." Of nonmanagers, 33 percent rate their pay as "so-so" and 20 percent rate their pay as "very poor" (Kleiman, 1998). Given the wage gap between males and females, it may be correct to assume that a disproportionate amount of females can be found in these less satisfied groups. Many of these females may be the highest performers in their positions; therefore, this wage discrepancy, in combination with relatively small annual pay increases over the past few years, may contribute to disproportionately high levels of dysfunctional turnover among females.

People who are happier with their jobs also tend to have higher life satisfaction ratings (Judge, Boudreau, & Bretz, 1994; Judge & Watanabe, 1993; Hart, 1999). **Life satisfaction** concerns one's attitudes about life in general, and Item 8 in Table 9.4 is an example of a typical life satisfaction question. Since leaders are often some of the most influential people in their followers' lives, they should never underestimate the impact they have on their followers' overall well-being. Unfortunately, at least some of the increasing violence at home and in the workplace may be exacerbated by poor leadership (Ferlise, 1995; Hogan, Curphy, & Hogan, 1994; Curphy, 2001; 2003a; Hales & Hales, 2001; Quigley, 2001; Curphy & Hogan, 2004a, b).

Job satisfaction surveys are used extensively in both public and private institutions. Organizations using these instruments typically administer them every one or two years to assess workers' attitudes about different aspects of work, changes in policies or work procedures, or other initiatives. Such survey results are most useful when they can be compared with those from some **reference group.** The organization's past results can be used as one kind of reference group—are people's ratings of pay, promotion, or overall satisfaction rising or falling over time? Job satisfaction ratings from similar organizations can be another reference group—are satisfaction ratings of leadership and working conditions higher or lower than those in similar organizations?

Figure 9.6 shows the facet and global satisfaction results for approximately 80 employees working at a medium-sized airport in the western United States. Employees completing the survey included the director of aviation and his supervisory staff ($n = 11$), the operations department ($n = 6$), the airfield maintenance department ($n = 15$), the communications department ($n = 6$), the airport facilities staff ($n = 12$), the administration department ($n = 10$), and the custodial staff ($n = 20$). The airport is owned by the city and has seen tremendous growth since the opening of the new terminal in 1995. By 1997 aircraft emplanements had already reached the level projected for the year 2010, and had exceeded the capacity of the new terminal. Unfortunately, staffing had remained at the 1995 levels, and the resulting workload and stress were thought to be adversely affecting morale and job satisfaction. Because of these concerns, the director of aviation decided to do a job satisfaction survey to pinpoint problem areas and develop action plans to resolve them.

Scores above 50 on Figure 9.6 are areas of satisfaction, scores below 50 are areas of dissatisfaction when compared to national norms. Here we see that airport employees are very satisfied with their benefits, are fairly satisfied with the work itself, but are dissatisfied with top leadership, ethics, supervision, feedback,

FIGURE 9.6

Results of a facet satisfaction survey.

Source: D. P. Campbell and S. Hyne, *Manual for the Revised Campbell Organizational Survey* (Minneapolis, MN: National Computing Systems, 1995).

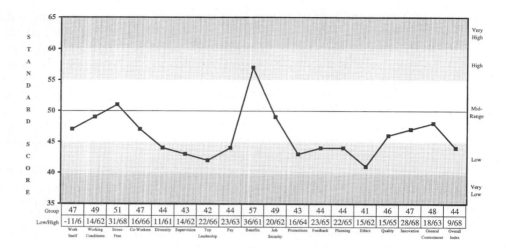

promotion opportunities, and the like. All airport employees got to review these results, and each department discussed the factors underlying the survey results and developed and implemented action plans to address problem areas. Top leadership, in this case the director of aviation, was seen as the biggest source of dissatisfaction by all departments. The director was a genuinely nice person and meant well, but he never articulated his vision for the airport, never explained how employees' actions were related to this mission, failed to set goals for each department, did not provide feedback, never clarified roles or areas of responsibilities for his staff, delegated action items to whomever he happened to see in the hall, often changed his mind with key decisions, and failed to keep his staff informed of airline tenant or city council decisions. When confronted with this information, the director placed the blame on the rapid growth of the airport and the lack of staffing support from the city (the fundamental attribution error in action again). The city manager then gave the director six months to substantially improve employee satisfaction levels. The director did not take the problem very seriously so, not surprisingly, the survey results six months later were no different for top leadership. The director was subsequently removed from his position because of his failure to improve the morale at the airport.

> *Leaders are often the only people surprised by 360-degree feedback or employee satisfaction results. In reality, employees have been talking about the issues identified in these surveys for quite some time.*
>
> Gordy Curphy
> C³

It is important to point out that rarely is it enough to merely administer surveys. Leaders must also be willing to take action on the basis of survey results, or risk losing credibility and actually increasing job dissatisfaction. Upon receiving the results of these surveys, leaders with bad results may feel tempted to not share any results with their followers, but this is almost always a mistake. Although the results may not be flattering, the rumors are likely to be much worse than the results themselves. Also, followers will be less than willing to fill out subsequent satisfaction surveys if they see denial of the results and little if any change to the workplace. Furthermore, leaders feeling defensive about such results and tempted to hide them should remember that the bad results may not be a surprise to anyone but themselves; therefore, what's to hide? On a practical level, leaders should never assess employees' attitudes about work unless they are willing to share the results and take action.

Three Theories of Job Satisfaction

All of the theories of motivation described earlier provide insight into followers' levels of job satisfaction too. For example, it would be difficult for Julie to be satisfied with her job if she was consistently underdressed for weather conditions, or for Ling Ling to be satisfied if her goals were unclear, she was not provided feedback, or she failed to be rewarded for good performance. Nonetheless, several other theories offer even better explanations for job satisfaction.

Affectivity

Affectivity refers to one's tendency to react to stimuli in a consistent emotional manner (Judge & Hulin, 1993; Judge & Locke, 1993; Judge, Locke, Durham, & Kluger, 1998; Ilies & Judge, 2003). People with a disposition for **negative affectivity** consistently react to changes, events, or situations in a negative manner. They tend to be unhappy with themselves and their lives, and are more likely to focus on the downside or disadvantages of a situation. People with a disposition for **positive affectivity** consistently react to changes, events, or situations in a positive manner. They are happy with their lives, and tend to take an upbeat, optimistic approach when faced with new situations. People with a positive affective disposition tend to see a cup as half full; people with a negative affective disposition are more likely to describe a glass as half empty. These two groups of individuals are thought to attend to, process, and recall information differently, and these differences affect both job satisfaction and satisfaction with life itself. Researchers have found that negative affectivity was related to job dissatisfaction, and positive affectivity to job satisfaction (Judge & Hulin, 1993; Judge, Bono, & Locke, 2000; Ilies & Judge, 2003). Of course, such results are hardly surprising—we all know individuals who never seem happy whatever their circumstances, and others who seem to maintain a positive outlook even in the most adverse circumstances.

These findings suggest that leadership initiatives may have little impact on a person's job satisfaction if their affective disposition is either extremely positive or negative. For example, if Ling Ling has a negative affective disposition, she may remain dissatisfied with her pay, working conditions, and so forth, *no matter what her leader does.* This is consistent with the findings of a study of identical twins reared apart and together which discovered that affectivity has a strong genetic component (Arvey, Bouchard, Segal, & Abraham, 1989; Connolly & Viswesvaran, 1998; Ilies & Judge, 2003). Given that leaders can do little to change followers' genetic makeup, these findings again highlight the importance of using good selection procedures when hiring employees. Trying to increase followers' job satisfaction is a reasonable goal, but some followers may be hard (impossible?) to please, no matter what the leader does.

Organizational Fit, Role Ambiguity, and Job Satisfaction

Highlight 9.12

The eleven theories of motivation and three of satisfaction provide useful frameworks for understanding why people may or may not be happy at work. But there are two other key causes of job dissatisfaction that do not fit neatly into one of these frameworks. The first has to do with **organizational fit.** Teams and organizations, like individuals, believe some things are important and others to be relatively unimportant. Teams and organizations reinforce different work values, which can easily be seen in organizational decisions, norms, and climate (see Table 9.2). Leaders and followers are attracted to and are most satisfied when their personal work values align with those of the organization. An example might be when both the individual and the organization believe being around others, abiding by societal norms, and making money are important. But people will experience dissatisfaction when there is a mismatch between their personal values and those of the organization. And the greater the mismatch, the higher the dissatisfaction and the greater the retention risk. According to Curphy (2004a), Curphy and Hogan (2004a), and Hogan and Curphy (2004), the degree of fit between personal and organizational values is a leading cause of employee turnover and satisfaction.

Another major cause of job dissatisfaction is role ambiguity. **Role ambiguity** occurs whenever leaders or followers are unclear about what they need to do and how they should do it. Many people come to work to succeed, but all too many leaders set followers up for failure by not providing them with the direction, training, or resources they need to be successful. In these situations followers may exert a high level of effort, but they often times are not working on the right things and as a result get very little accomplished. This sense of frustration quickly turns to dissatisfaction and eventually causes people to look for someplace else to work. An example here is a Vice President of Human Resources who left a position early in his career after he had only been on the job for two weeks because he had never seen his boss, did not have a desk, and did not even have a phone. The irony of it all was that he was working for a major Canadian phone company. The bottom line is that role ambiguity can have devastating effects but is easily avoidable. Leaders really do not have any good excuses for people leaving because they are uncertain about what they need to do to succeed.

Sources: G. J. Curphy, "What We Really Know about Leadership (But Seem Unwilling to Implement)," presentation given at the Minnesota Professionals for Psychology and Applied Work, Minneapolis, MN, January, 2004a; G. J. Curphy and R. T. Hogan, "Managerial Incompetence: Is There a Dead Skunk on the Table?" working paper, 2004a; R. T. Hogan and G. J. Curphy, "Leadership Matters: Values and Dysfunctional Dispositions," working paper, 2004.

From a leader perspective, affectivity can have several implications in the workplace. First and foremost, one's own affectivity can have a strong influence on followers' morale or satisfaction levels. Say you worked for a leader with negative affectivity. Chances are he or she would find fault in your work, and constantly complain about organizational policies, resources, and so on. The opposite might be true if you worked for someone having positive affectivity. Second, leading a high percentage of followers having either positive or negative affectivity would likely result in very different leadership experiences. The positive group may be much more tolerant and willing to put up with organizational changes; the negative group would likely find fault in any change the leader made. Increasing job satisfaction through affectivity means hiring those with positive affectivity. However, few, if any, selection systems address this important workplace variable. Because negative affectivity may not be assessed or even apparent until a follower has been on the job for a period of time, perhaps the best advice for leadership practitioners is that some followers might well have a permanent chip on their shoulders, and there may be little you can do to change it.

Herzberg's Two-Factor Theory

Herzberg (1964, 1966, 2003) developed the **two-factor theory** from a series of interviews he conducted with accountants and engineers. More specifically, he asked what satisfied them about their work and found that their answers usually could be sorted into five consistent categories. Furthermore, rather than assuming that what dissatisfied people was always just the opposite of what satisfied them, he also specifically asked what *dissatisfied* people about their jobs. Surprisingly, the list of satisfiers and dissatisfiers represented entirely different aspects of work.

Herzberg labeled the factors that led to *satisfaction* at work **motivators,** and he labeled the factors that led to *dissatisfaction* at work **hygiene factors.** The most common motivators and hygiene factors can be found in Table 9.5. According to the two-factor theory, efforts directed toward improving hygiene factors will not increase followers' motivation or satisfaction. No matter how much leaders improve working conditions, pay, or sick-leave policies, for example, followers *will not* exert any additional effort or persist any longer at a task. For example, followers will probably be no more satisfied to do a dull and boring job merely by being given pleasant office furniture. On the other hand, followers may be asked to work in conditions so poor as to create dissatisfaction, which can distract them from constructive work.

Given limited resources on the leader's part, the key to increasing followers' satisfaction levels according to two-factor theory is to just adequately satisfy the hygiene factors while maximizing the motivators for a particular job. It is important for working conditions to be adequate, but it is even more important (for enhancing motivation and satisfaction) to provide plenty of recognition, responsibility, and possibilities for advancement (see Figure 9.7).

Although giving followers meaningful work and then recognizing them for their achievement seems straightforward enough, it is interesting to note that these techniques are tremendously underutilized by leaders (Herzberg, 2003; Curphy, 2004a; Curphy & Hogan, 2004b). Most leaders prefer to give employees a Kick in the Pants (KITA) to get them to do something rather than appealing to their

TABLE 9.5
Motivators and Hygiene Factors of the Two-Factor Theory

Source: Adapted from F. Herzberg, *Work and the Nature of Men* (Cleveland, OH: World Publishing, 1966).

Hygiene Factors	Motivators
Supervision	Achievement
Working conditions	Recognition
Co-workers	The work itself
Pay	Responsibility
Policies/procedures	Advancement and growth
Job security	

FIGURE 9.7
Herzberg's
two-factor
theory.

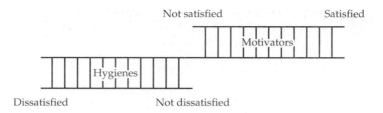

personal values or give them something meaningful to do. Because of the fear of retaliation, most organizations use positive KITAs, such as employee benefits, to keep employees happy and induce them to remain with the company. But Herzberg argues that KITAs do not drive job satisfaction or motivation, and leaders would be better off restructuring work to make it more meaningful and significant than giving out shirts with company logos or increasing medical co-pays. In the words of Fred Herzberg, "If you don't want people to have Mickey Mouse attitudes, then don't give them Mickey Mouse work" (unpublished comments).

The two-factor theory offers leaders ideas about how to, and how not to, bolster followers' satisfaction, but it has received little empirical support beyond Herzberg's (1964; 2003) own results. In other words, it just may not be an accurate explanation for job satisfaction despite its apparent grounding in data. We present it here in part because it has become such a well-known approach to work motivation and job satisfaction that the present account would appear incomplete if we ignore it. The problem with two-factor theory, however, seems to lie in the very aspect that at first seemed its strength: the original data on which it was based. For one thing, as noted earlier, Herzberg developed his theory after interviewing only accountants and engineers, two groups who are hardly representative of workers in other lines of work or activity. Furthermore, his subjects typically attributed job satisfaction to *their* skill or effort, yet blamed their dissatisfaction on circumstances beyond their control. This sounds suspiciously like the fundamental attribution error described earlier in this book. Despite such limitations, however, Landy (1985) concluded that the two-factor theory has provided useful insight into what followers find satisfying and dissatisfying about work.

Organizational Justice

Organizational justice is a cognitive approach based on the premise that people who are treated unfairly are less productive, satisfied, and committed to their organizations. Moreover, these individuals are more likely to initiate collective action and engage in various counterproductive work behaviors (Sheppard, Lewicki, & Minton, 1992). According to Trevino (1992), organizational justice is made up of three related components. **Interactional justice** reflects the degree to which people are given information about different reward procedures and are treated with dignity and respect. **Distributive justice** concerns followers' perceptions of whether the level of reward or punishment is commensurate with an individual's performance or infraction. Dissatisfaction occurs when followers believe someone has received too little or too much reward or punishment. Perceptions of **procedural**

justice involve the process in which rewards or punishments are administered. If someone is to be punished, then followers will be more satisfied if the person being punished has been given adequate warnings and has had the opportunity to explain his or her actions, and if the punishment has been administered in a timely and consistent manner. Research has shown that these different components of organizational justice are related to satisfaction with the leader, pay, promotion, and the job itself (McFarlin & Sweeney, 1992; Sheppard, Lewicki, & Minton, 1992; Trevino, 1992; Moorman, 1991; Brockner & Wisenfeld, 1996; Ployhart & Ryan, 1998; Colquitt, 2001; Colquitt, Conlon, Wesson, Porter, & Ng, 2001; Elovainio, Kjvimaki, & Helkama, 2001; Phillips, Douthitt, & Hyland, 2001; Ambrose & Cropanzano, 2003; Simons & Roberson, 2003; Tepper & Taylor, 2003).

So what would leaders need to do if they wish to improve follower satisfaction and reduce turnover using organizational justice theory? The underlying principle for organizational justice is fairness—going back to our earlier characters, do Ling Ling or Julie feel that the process in which rewards or punishments are administered is fair? Are the potential rewards commensurate with performance? Do Julie and Ling Ling believe the reward system is unbiased? What would the flight attandants have to say about whether they were treated with dignity and respect, whether rewards were commensurate with performance, or the fairness in which rewards were administered? Leaders who want to improve job satisfaction using this approach need to ensure that followers answer yes to these three questions. If followers answer no to any of the questions, then leaders need to change the reward and punishment system if they want to improve job satisfaction using organizational justice theory.

Summary

This chapter has reviewed research concerning motivation, satisfaction, and performance. Motivation was defined as anything that provides direction, intensity, and persistence to behavior. Although motivation is an important aspect of performance, performance and motivation are not the same thing. Performance is a broader concept than motivation, as abilities, skills, group norms, and the availability of resources can all affect followers' levels of performance. Job satisfaction is a set of attitudes that people have about work. Although a majority of people are generally satisfied with their jobs, people often have varying levels of satisfaction for different aspects of their jobs, such as pay, working conditions, supervisors, or co-workers.

Many of the approaches to understanding motivation have distinct implications for increasing performance and satisfaction. Therefore, several different theories of motivation were reviewed in this chapter. The first two theories, Maslow's (1954) hierarchy of needs and Alderfer's (1969) existence-relatedness-growth (ERG) theory, assume that people are motivated to satisfy a universal set of needs. The next three theories examined motivation in terms of individual differences, emphasizing a person's intrinsic motivation to perform a particular task, their personal values, or a person's general level of achievement orientation. The next set of theories, goal setting, equity theory, self-efficacy, and expectancy theory, examined motivation from a cognitive perspective. These theories assume that people make rational, conscious choices about the direction, intensity, and persistence of their behaviors, and generally engage in behaviors that maximize payoffs and minimize costs. The last two theories, empowerment and operant approach, examined motivation from a situational perspective. Leadership practitioners likely will be more effective if they learn to recognize situations where various approaches, or the insights particular to them, may be differentially useful. Just as a carpenter can more effectively build a house by using a variety of tools, a leader can be more effective by using a variety of motivational interventions to enhance work.

Several other theories seem to be more useful for explaining followers' attitudes about work. Some research suggests that individuals vary in the characteristic tenor of their affectivity; some people are generally affectively positive whereas others are generally affectively negative. Such differences may set limits on the extent to which initiatives by leaders will actually impact follower satisfaction. Leaders may also be able to increase satisfaction levels by giving followers more meaningful work and by treating them fairly. Followers (and leaders for that matter) are more likely to have positive attitudes about work if they believe that what they do is important and that the reward and disciplinary systems are fair and just.

Key Terms

motivation, 243
performance, 244
effectiveness, 244
job satisfaction, 244
organizational citizenship behaviors, 244
needs, 250
hierarchy of needs, 250
existence-relatedness-growth (ERG) theory, 251
frustration regression hypothesis, 251
achievement orientation, 253
extrinsic motivational bias, 256
intrinsic motivation, 257
overjustification effect, 258

goal setting, 259
Pygmalion Effect, 261
Golem Effect, 261
expectancy theory, 262
effort-to-performance expectancy, 262
performance-to-outcome expectancy, 262
valence, 262
equity theory, 264
positive self-efficacy, 266
negative-self-efficacy, 266
operant approach, 267
reward, 267
punishment, 267
contingent, 268
noncontingent, 268
extinction, 268
functional turnover, 276

dysfunctional turnover, 277
global satisfaction, 277
facet satisfaction, 277
hierarchy effect, 280
life satisfaction, 281
reference group, 281
negative affectivity, 283
positive affectivity, 283
organizational fit, 284
role ambiguity, 284
two-factor theory, 285
motivators, 285
hygiene factors, 285
organizational justice, 286
interactional justice, 286
distributive justice, 286
procedural justice, 287

Questions

1. Why do you think there are so many different theories or approaches to understanding motivation? Shouldn't it be possible to determine which one is best and just use it? Why or why not?

2. Many good leaders are thought of as good motivators. How would you rate Colin Powell, Peter Jackson, and Aung San Suu Kyi in terms of their ability to motivate others?

3. What is your own view of what motivates people to work hard and perform well?

4. Do you know of any examples where reward systems are inconsistent with desired behavior? How are personal values related to rewards?

5. What do you find personally satisfying or dissatisfying at work or school? For those things you find dissatisfying, how could you make them more satisfying? What theory of job satisfaction best explains your actions?

Skills

Leadership skills relevant to this chapter include:

- Providing constructive feedback
- Setting goals
- Punishment
- Diagnosing performance problems in individuals, groups, and organizations
- Empowerment

Activity

1. Earlier in this chapter you were asked how the four types of motivation theories could be used to improve the customer service levels of flight attendants. Break into four groups, and have each group discuss how they would design and implement a motivation program using either a need, individual difference, cognitive, and situational approach. Each group should then give a 15-minute presentation on their findings. The presentation should include the approach they used, how they would collect any needed additional data, the program design, program implementation, potential barriers to the program, and their evaluation of the effectiveness of their program.

2. Interview someone in a leadership position to determine how he or she motivates employees. Do they use some of the programs outlined in Highlight 9.2? How would you categorize their motivational techniques using the 11 approaches outlined in this chapter?

3. Interview someone in a leadership position on employee satisfaction and retention. Does the organization conduct regular satisfaction surveys? What do the survey results reveal about the organization? Is the organization having any turnover problems? Why or why not?

4. Oftentimes team and organizational values change with changes in leadership, or when an organization is acquired or divested. Interview someone in a leadership position who has been through a merger or a downsizing and determine their level of satisfaction before and after these events.

5. People often leave bosses, not organizations. Interview people with 10–20 years of work experience and ask them to list the reasons why they have left past jobs. How many people left because their bosses demonstrated some of the dark-side personality traits found in Chapter 7?

Minicase

"Initech versus The Coffee Bean"

Consider Peter Gibbons, an employee of the fictional Initech Corporation from the movie *Office Space.* Peter has been asked to meet with efficiency experts (Bob and Bob) to discuss his work environment. One of the Bobs is curious about Peter's tendency toward underperformance and confronts him about his lack of attention to office policies and procedures. It seems Peter has been turning in his TPS reports late and without the company mandated cover sheet:

Peter: You see Bob, it's not that I'm lazy, it's that I just don't care.
Bob: Don't? Don't care?
Peter: It's a problem of motivation, alright? Now if I work my butt off and Initech ships a few extra units, I don't see another dime, so where's the motivation? And here's another thing, I have eight different bosses right now.
Bob: Eight?
Peter: Eight, Bob. So that means when I make a mistake, I have eight different people coming by to tell me about it. That's my only real motivation is not to be hassled, that and the fear of losing my job. But you know, Bob, that will only make someone work just hard enough not to get fired.

The environment at Initech is an all too familiar one to many office workers. It is an environment in which success is directly proportional to how busy you look, where questioning authority is taboo, and where meticulous attention to paperwork is the only way to get promoted.

Contrast Initech to The Coffee Bean—a chain of gourmet coffee shops. In an effort to boost employee morale and increase productivity, the management team at The Coffee Bean decided to pursue the FISH philosophy. FISH is a management training program that stresses fun in the workplace. It espouses four principles:

Play—"Work that is made fun gets done."

Make Their Day—"When you make someone's day through a small act of kindness or unforgettable engagement, you can turn even routine encounters into special memories."

Be There—"Being there is a great way to practice wholeheartedness and fight burnout."

Choose Your Attitude—"When you learn you have the power to choose your response to what life brings, you can look for the best and find opportunities you never imagined possible."

Stores in The Coffee Bean chain were encouraged to use these principles to make the stores a fun place for employees and customers. The stores have created theme days where employees dress up for themes (NFL day, basketball days, pajama day)—and then give discounts to customers who dress the same. There are also trivia games in which customers who can answer trivia questions get discounts on their coffee purchases: Nancy Feilen, a Coffee Bean store manager explains: "We tried to come up with something that would help strike up a conversation with guests and engage fun in the stores for team members and guests." In other stores, customers play Coffee Craps. If a customer rolls a seven or an 11, he gets a free drink.

Some stores have done Fear Factor Fridays—if the store sells a certain number of drinks one of the baristas will agree to some act. In one case a barista ate a cricket.

The results? One store increased the average check by 12 percent in six months, turnover has decreased significantly—general managers typically left after 22 months with the chain but now stay an average of 31 months—and the turnover rate for hourly employees dropped to 69 percent from more than 200 percent over a three-year period.

So, where would you rather work?

1. How would you gauge Peter's achievement orientation? What are some of the needs not being met for Peter Gibbons at Initech? What changes might improve Peter's motivation?
2. Would you judge the leaders at Initech as more likely to invoke the Pygmalion or the Golem Effect?
3. What about the environment at The Coffee Bean? Pygmalion or Golem?
4. Why has The Coffee Bean seen such a significant reduction in its turnover?

Sources: http://www.findarticles.com/p/articles/mi_m3190/is_2_38/ai_112248126; http://www.imdb.com/title/tt0151804/quotes; http://www.charthouse.com/home.asp; http://www.gazettenet.com/business/02242003/3706.htm

10

Groups, Teams, and Their Leadership

Introduction

We are born for cooperation, as are the feet, the hands, the eyelids, and the upper and lower jaws.

Marcus Aurelius

As we have already presented, leaders need to understand some things about themselves. Their skills, abilities, values, motives, and desires are important considerations in determining their leadership style and preferences. Leaders also need to understand, as much as possible, the same characteristics about their followers. But if you could know characteristics about yourself and characteristics about each of your followers, that would still not be enough. This is because groups and teams are different than solely the skills, abilities, values, and motives of those who comprise them. Groups and teams have their own special characteristics.

While much of the leadership literature today is about the individual who fills the leadership role, it is worthwhile noting that a survey of 35 texts on organizational behavior found that in each one, the chapter on leadership is in the section on group behavior (Ginnett 1992). This should not be terribly surprising since groups (even as small as two people) are essential if leaders are to impact anything beyond their own behavior. What may be surprising is that the concept of groups is sometimes omitted entirely from books on leadership. The **group perspective** looks at how different group characteristics can affect relationships both with the leader and among the followers.

With *teams* and *teamwork* being the buzzwords of the new millennium, it is worth clarifying the difference between groups and teams, although the difference is mostly one of degree. We will begin the chapter with that clarification. The larger distinction, as noted above, is between the characteristics of groups and the characteristics of individuals. We will spend the first half of the chapter discussing some of these factors unique to groups. Given the high interest in organizational teamwork, the latter portion of this chapter will present a model developed to help leaders design, diagnose, and leverage high-impact factors to create the conditions that foster team effectiveness. This chapter will conclude with a section on virtual teams, which are becoming ever more present, if not popular.

Individuals versus Groups versus Teams

As noted previously, there is a significant difference between individual work and group work. But what is the difference between group work and teamwork?

You will learn, in the next section of this chapter, two identifying characteristics of groups are mutual interaction and reciprocal influence. Members of teams also have mutual interaction and reciprocal influence, but we generally distinguish teams from groups in four other ways. First, team members usually have a stronger sense of identification among themselves than group members do. Often, both team members and outsiders can readily identify who is and who is not on the team (athletic uniforms are one obvious example); identifying members of a group may be more difficult. Second, teams have common goals or tasks; these may range from the development of a new product to an athletic league championship. Group members, on the other hand, may not have the same degree of consensus about goals as team members do. Group members may belong to the group for a variety of personal reasons, and these may clash with the group's stated objectives. (This phenomenon probably happens with teams, too, although perhaps not to the same extent.)

Third, task interdependence typically is greater with teams than with groups. For example, basketball players usually are unable to take a shot unless other team members set picks or pass the ball to them. On the other hand, group members often can contribute to goal accomplishment by working independently; the successful completion of their assigned tasks may not be contingent on other group members. Of course, task interdependence can vary greatly even across teams. Among athletic teams, for example, softball, football, soccer, and hockey teams have a high level of task interdependence, whereas swimming, cross-country, and track teams have substantially lower levels of task interdependence. Fourth, team members often have more differentiated and specialized roles than group members. In the preceding section, we noted that group members often play a variety

of roles within the group; however, team members often play a single, or primary, role on a team. Finally, it is important to bear in mind that the distinctions we have been highlighting probably reflect only matters of degree. One might consider teams to be highly specialized groups.

The Nature of Groups

Perhaps we should begin by defining what a **group** is. A group can be thought of as "two or more persons who are interacting with one another in such a manner that each person influences and is influenced by each other person" (Shaw, 1981). Three aspects of this definition are particularly important to the study of leadership. First, this definition incorporates the concept of reciprocal influence between leaders and followers, an idea considerably different from the one-way nature of influence implicit in the dictionary's definition of followers. Second, group members interact and influence each other. Thus, people waiting at a bus stop would not constitute a group, as there generally is neither interaction nor influence between the various individuals. On the other hand, eight people meeting to plan a school bond election would constitute a group, as there probably would be a high level of mutual interaction among the attendees. Third, the definition does not constrain individuals to only one group. Everyone belongs to a number of different groups; an individual could be a member of various service, production, sports, religious, parent, and volunteer groups simultaneously.

It is important to realize that though people belong to many groups, just as they do to many organizations, groups and organizations are not the same thing (groups, of course, can exist within organizations). Organizations can be so large that most members do not know most of the other people in the organization. In such cases there is relatively little intermember interaction and reciprocal influence. Similarly, organizations typically are just too large and impersonal to have much effect on anyone's feelings, whereas groups are small and immediate enough to impact both feelings and self-image. People often tend to identify more with the groups they belong to than with the organizations they belong to; they are more psychologically "invested" in their groups. Also, certain important psychological needs (e.g., social contact) are better satisfied by groups than by organizations.

Perhaps an example will clarify the distinction between groups and organizations. Consider a church so large that it may fairly be described as an organization: so large that multiple services must be offered on Sunday mornings; so large that dozens of different study classes are offered each week; so large there are numerous different choirs and musical ensembles. In so large a church, the members hardly could be said to interact with or influence each other except on an occasional basis. Such size often presents both advantages and disadvantages to the membership. On the one hand, it makes possible a rich diversity of activities; on the other hand, such size can make the church itself (i.e., the overall organization) seem relatively impersonal. It may be difficult to identity with a large organization other than in name only (e.g., "I belong to First Presbyterian Church"). In such cases many people identify more with particular groups within the church than with the church itself; it may be easier to *feel* a part of some smaller group such as the high school choir or a weekly study group.

Although groups play a pervasive role in society, in general people spend very little time thinking about the factors that affect group processes and intragroup relationships. Therefore, the rest of this section will describe some group characteristics that can affect both leaders and followers. Much of the research on groups goes well beyond the scope of this chapter (see Gibbard, Hartman, & Mann, 1978; Shaw, 1981; Hackman, 1990), but six concepts are so basic to the group perspective that they deserve our attention. These six concepts are group size, stages of group development, roles, norms, communication, and cohesion. Five of them will be addressed in sections below. The sixth, communication, permeates them all.

Group Size

The size of any group has implications for both leaders and followers. First, leader emergence is partly a function of group size. The greater number of people in a large versus a small group will affect the probability that any individual is likely to emerge as leader. Second, as groups become larger, **cliques** are more likely to develop (Yukl, 1981). Cliques are subgroups of individuals who often share the same goals, values, and expectations. Because cliques generally wield more influence than individual members, they are likely to exert considerable influence—positively or negatively—on the larger group. Leaders need to identify and deal with cliques within their groups, as many intragroup conflicts are the results of cliques having different values, goals, and expectations.

Third, group size also can affect a leader's behavioral style. Leaders with a large **span of control** tend to be more directive, spend less time with individual subordinates, and use more impersonal approaches when influencing followers. Leaders with a small span of control tend to display more consideration and use more personal approaches when influencing followers (Badin, 1974; Goodstadt & Kipnis, 1970; Kipnis, Schmidt, & Wilkinson, 1980; Udell, 1967). Fourth, group size also affects group effectiveness. Whereas some researchers have suggested the optimal number of workers for any task is between five and seven (Bass, 1960; Indik, 1965), it probably is wise to avoid such a simple generalization. The answer to the question of appropriate group size seems to be "just big enough to get the job done." Obviously, the larger the group, the more likely it is that it will involve differentiated skills, values, perceptions, and abilities among its members. Also, there certainly will be more "people power" available to do the work as group size increases.

There are, however, limits to the benefits of size. Consider the question, "If it takes 1 person two minutes to dig a 1-cubic-foot hole, how long will it take 20 people to dig the same size hole?" Actually, it probably will take the larger group considerably *longer,* especially if they all participate at the same time. Beyond the purely physical limitations of certain tasks, there also may be decreasing returns (on a per capita basis) as group size increases. This is true even when the efforts of all group members are combined on what is called an **additive task.** An additive task is one where the

A committee is an animal with four back legs.

Jean le Carre

group's output simply involves the combination of individual outputs (Steiner, 1972). Such a case may be illustrated by the number of individuals needed to push a stalled truck from an intersection. One individual probably would not be enough—maybe not even two or three. At some point, though, as group size increases in this additive task, there will be enough combined force to move the truck. However, as the group size increases beyond that needed to move the truck, the individual contribution of each member will appear to decrease. Steiner (1972) suggested this may be due to **process loss** resulting from factors such as some members not pushing in the right direction. Process losses can be thought of as the inefficiencies created by more and more people working together.

Group size can affect group effectiveness in a number of other ways. As group size increases, the diminishing returns of larger work groups may be due to **social loafing** (Latane, Williams, & Hawkins, 1979). Social loafing refers to the phenomenon of reduced effort by people when they are not individually accountable for their work. Experiments across different sorts of tasks have tended to demonstrate greater effort when every individual's work is monitored than when many individuals' outputs are anonymously pooled into a collective product. Recent evidence, however, suggests the process may be considerably more complicated than initially thought (Porter, Bird, & Wunder, 1991). The performance decrement may be affected more by the level of task complexity or the reward structure (e.g., cooperative versus competitive) than by outcome attribution.

Sometimes, working in the presence of others may actually increase effort or productivity through a phenomenon called **social facilitation.** Social facilitation was first documented in classic experiments at the Hawthorne plant of the Western Electric Company (see Highlight 10.1). However, social facilitation is not limited to research situations. It refers to any time people increase their level of work due to the presence of others. Typically this occurs when the presence of others increases individual accountability for work, in contrast to other occasions when being in a group reinforces individual anonymity and social loafing (Zajonc, 1965).

Developmental Stages of Groups

Just as children go through different stages of development, so do groups. Tuckman's (1965) review of over 60 studies involving leaderless training, experimental, or therapeutic groups revealed that groups generally went through four distinct stages of development. The first stage, **forming,** was characterized by polite conversation, the gathering of superficial information about fellow members, and low trust. The group's rejection of emerging potential leaders with negative characteristics also took place during the forming stage. The second stage, **storming,** usually was marked by intragroup conflict, heightened emotional levels, and status differentiation as remaining contenders struggled to build alliances and fulfill the group's leadership role. The clear emergence of a leader and the development of group norms and cohesiveness were the key indicators of the **norming** stage of group development. Finally, groups reached the **performing** stage when group members played functional, interdependent roles that were focused on the performance of group tasks.

The four stages of group development identified by Tuckman (1965) are important for several reasons. First, people are in many more leaderless groups than they may realize. For example, many sports teams, committees, work groups, and clubs

Social Facilitation and the Hawthorne Effect

Highlight 10.1

Social facilitation was first documented in experiments conducted at the Hawthorne plant of the Western Electric Company during the late 1920s and early 1930s. These classic studies were originally designed to evaluate the impact of different work environments (Mayo, 1933; Roethlisberger & Dickson, 1939). Among other things, researchers varied the levels of illumination in areas where workers were assembling electrical components and found production increased when lighting was increased. When lighting was subsequently decreased, however, production again increased. Faced with these rather confusing data, the researchers turned their attention from physical aspects of the work environment to its social aspects. As it turns out, one reason workers' production increased was simply because someone else (in this case, the researchers) had paid attention to them. The term *Hawthorne effect* is still used today to describe an artificial change in behavior due merely to the fact a person or group is being studied.

start out as leaderless teams. Team or club captains or committee spokespersons are likely to be the emergent leaders from their respective groups. On a larger scale, perhaps even many elected officials initially began their political careers as the emergent leaders of their cliques or groups, and were then able to convince the majority of the remaining members in their constituencies of their viability as candidates.

Another reason it is important to understand stages of group development is the potential relationships between leadership behaviors and group cohesiveness and productivity. Some experts have maintained that leaders need to focus on consideration or group maintenance behaviors during the norming stage to improve group cohesiveness, and on task behaviors during the performing stage in order to improve group productivity (Stogdill, 1972; Terborg, Castore, & DeNinno, 1975). They also have suggested that leaders who reverse these behaviors during the norming and performing stages tend to have less cohesive and less productive groups. Thus, being able to recognize stages of group development may enhance the likelihood that one will emerge as a leader as well as increase the cohesiveness and productivity of the group being led.

> *If you start yelling and becoming obtrusive and beboppin' around, you give the impression of insecurity, and that becomes infectious. It bleeds down into the actors, and they become nervous; then it bleeds down into the crew, and they become nervous, and you don't get much accomplished that way. You have to set a tone and just demand a certain amount of tranquility.*
>
> Clint Eastwood
> on being a film director

While Tuckman's model is widely known if for no other reason than its components rhyme with each other, it is not without criticism. Recall that the subjects for Tuckman's research were training, experimental, or therapy groups. None of these particularly represent teams forming to do work in an organizational context. For example, Ginnett observed many surgical teams and never once saw them engage in storming behaviors as they formed. You wouldn't want to be the patient if there was a formation argument between the surgeon, the anesthesiologist, and the scrub nurse about who was going to get to use the scalpel today.

Gersick (1988, 1989) proposed a better model for teams in organizational settings. In studying **project teams,** she found that teams don't necessarily jump right in and get to work. Rather, they spend most of the first half of the team's life muddling through various ideas and strategies. Then, about midway into the project, the team seems to experience the equivalent of a midlife crisis where there is a flurry of activity and a reexamination of the strategy to see if it will allow them to complete their work. Gersick labeled this process **punctuated equilibrium,** which is obviously quite different from Tuckman's four-stage model.

Group Roles

Group roles are the sets of expected behaviors associated with particular jobs or positions. Most people have multiple roles stemming from the various groups with which they are associated. In addition, it is not uncommon for someone to occupy numerous roles within the same group as situations change. Ginnett (1990) found that members of airline crews have varying roles over the course of a day. Although some behaviors were universally associated with certain roles, effective team members on these airline crews generally were more flexible in changing their behavior as other role demands changed. For example, whereas the captain of an airplane is responsible for the overall operation and decision making during a flight, flight attendants often take over responsibility for planning and carrying out the crew's social activities in the evening (i.e., when the flight is over). One captain in the study, however, continued to make *all* the crew's decisions, including their evening social plans; he was inflexible with regard to the role of decision-maker. Not coincidentally, he was seen as a less-effective leader—even during the actual flights—than more flexible captains.

Some roles, like positions on athletic teams, have meaning only in relatively specific contexts. Generally speaking, for example, one only plays a lineman's role during football games (admittedly, one might argue that at many schools being an intercollegiate athlete is a role that extends to aspects of student life outside sports). Other roles are more general in nature, including certain common ones that play a part in making any group work—or not work—well. Highlight 10.2 presents a vivid example of how powerful roles can be as determinants of behavior.

In Chapter 8, leader behavior was characterized initially in terms of two broad functions. One deals with getting the task done (**task role**), and the other with supporting relationships within the work group (**relationship role**). Similarly, roles in groups can be categorized in terms of task and relationship functions (see Highlight 10.3). Many of the roles in Highlight 10.3 are appropriate for followers, not just the official group leader; all of these different roles are part of the leadership process and all contribute to a group's overall effectiveness. Moreover, it is important to recognize that the very distinction between task and relationship roles is somewhat arbitrary. It is sensible enough when looking at the short-term impact of any given behavior, but in another sense relationship roles are task roles. After all, task-oriented behavior may be adequate for accomplishing short-term objectives, but an appropriately cohesive and supportive group increases the potential for long-term effectiveness at future tasks as well as present tasks.

Although the roles in Highlight 10.3 generally contribute to a group's overall effectiveness, several types of problems can occur with group roles that can impede

The Stanford Prison Experiment

Highlight 10.2

A fascinating demonstration of the power of roles occurred when social psychologist Philip Zimbardo and his colleagues (1973) created a simulated prison environment at Stanford University. From a larger group of volunteers, two dozen male college students were randomly assigned to be either "prisoners" or "guards." The simulation was quite realistic, with actual cells constructed in the basement of one of the university buildings. The guards wore uniforms, and carried nightsticks and whistles; their eyes were covered by sunglasses. The prisoners were "arrested" at their homes by police cars replete with blazing sirens. They were handcuffed, frisked, blindfolded, and brought to the "jail." They were fingerprinted, given prisoner outfits, and assigned numbers by which they would henceforth be addressed.

It did not take long for the students' normal behavior to be overcome by the roles they were playing. The guards became more and more abusive with their power. They held prisoners accountable for strict adherence to arbitrary rules of prison life (which the guards themselves created), and seemed to enjoy punishing them for even minor infractions. They increasingly seemed to think of the prisoners—truly just

other college students—as bad people. The emotional stress on the prisoners became profound, and just six days into the two-week episode the experiment was halted. This unexpected outcome basically occurred because participants' roles had become their reality. They were not just students role-playing guards and prisoners; to a disconcerting degree they became guards and prisoners.

What should people conclude from the Stanford prison study? At an abstract level, the study dramatically points out how behavior is partly determined by social role. Additionally, it is clear how just being in the role of leader, especially to the extent it is attended by tangible and symbolic manifestations of power, can affect how leaders think and act toward followers. Still another lesson people might draw involves remembering the volunteers all had many different roles in life than those assigned to them in the study, though being a guard or a prisoner was certainly the salient one for a period of time. Whereas everyone has many roles, the salience of one or another often depends on the situation, and a person's behavior changes as his or her role changes in a group.

Source: P. Zimbardo, C. Haney, W. Banks, and D. Jaffe, "The Mind Is a Formidable Jailer: A Pirandellian Prison," *New York Times Magazine,* April 8, 1973, pp. 38–60.

group performance. One type of role problem concerns the **dysfunctional roles,** listed in Highlight 10.4. The common denominator among these roles is how the person's behavior primarily serves selfish or egocentric purposes rather than group purposes.

Another role problem is **role conflict.** Role conflict involves receiving contradictory messages about expected behavior and can in turn adversely affect a person's emotional well-being and performance (Jamal, 1984).

Role conflict can occur in several different ways. Perhaps most common is receiving inconsistent signals about expected behavior from the same person. When the same person sends mixed signals, it is called **intrasender role conflict** ("I need this report back in five minutes, and it had better be perfect"). **Intersender role conflict** occurs when someone receives inconsistent signals from several others about expected behavior. Still another kind of role conflict is based on inconsistencies between different roles a person may have. Professional and family demands, for example, often create role conflicts. **Interrole conflict** occurs when someone is unable to perform all of his roles as well as he would like. A final type occurs when role expectations violate a person's values. This is known as **person-role conflict.**

Task and Relationship Roles in Groups

Highlight 10.3

TASK ROLES

Initiating: Defining the problem, suggesting activities, assigning tasks.

Information Seeking: Asking questions, seeking relevant data or views.

Information Sharing: Providing data, offering opinions.

Summarizing: Reviewing and integrating others' points, checking for common understanding and readiness for action.

Evaluating: Assessing validity of assumptions, quality of information, reasonableness of recommendations.

Guiding: Keeping group on track.

RELATIONSHIP ROLES

Harmonizing: Resolving interpersonal conflicts, reducing tension.

Encouraging: Supporting and praising others, showing appreciation for others' contributions, being warm and friendly.

Gatekeeping: Assuring even participation by all group members, making sure that everyone has a chance to be heard and that no individual dominates.

Source: Adapted from K. D. Benne and P. Sheats, "Functional Roles of Group Members," *Journal of Social Issues* 4 (1948), pp. 41–49.

Dysfunctional Roles

Highlight 10.4

Dominating: Monopolizing group time, forcing views on others.

Blocking: Stubbornly obstructing and impeding group work, persistent negativism.

Attacking: Belittling others, creating a hostile or intimidating environment.

Distracting: Engaging in irrelevant behaviors, distracting others' attention.

Source: Adapted from K. D. Benne and P. Sheats, "Functional Roles of Group Members," *Journal of Social Issues* 4 (1948), pp. 41–49.

An example of person-role conflict might be when a store manager encourages a salesperson to mislead customers about the quality of the store's products when this behavior is inconsistent with the salesperson's values and beliefs.

A different sort of role problem is called **role ambiguity.** In role conflict, one receives clear messages about expectations, but the messages are not all congruent. With role ambiguity, the problem is lack of clarity about just what the expectations are (House, Schuler, & Levanoni, 1983; Rizzo, House, & Lirtzman, 1970). There may have been no role expectations established at all, or they may not have been clearly communicated. A person is experiencing role ambiguity if she wonders, "Just what am I supposed to be doing?" It is important for leaders to be able to minimize the degree to which dysfunctional roles, role conflict, and role ambiguity occur in their groups, as these problems have been found to have a negative impact on organizational commitment, job involvement, absenteeism, and satisfaction with co-workers and supervisors (Fisher & Gitelson, 1983).

Group Norms

Norms are the informal rules groups adopt to regulate and regularize group members' behaviors. Although norms are only infrequently written down or openly discussed, they nonetheless often have a powerful and consistent influence on behavior (Hackman, 1976). That is because most people are rather good at reading the social cues that inform them about existing norms. For example, most people easily discern the dress code in any new work environment without needing written guidance. People also are apt to notice when a norm is violated, even though they may have been unable to articulate the norm before its violation was apparent. For example, most students have expectations (norms) about creating extra work for other students. Imagine the reaction if a student in some class complained that not enough reading was being assigned each lesson or that the minimum length requirements for the term paper needed to be substantially raised.

Norms do not govern all behaviors, just those a group feels are important. Norms are more likely to be seen as important and apt to be enforced if they (*a*) facilitate group survival; (*b*) simplify, or make more predictable, what behavior is expected of group members; (*c*) help the group avoid embarrassing interpersonal problems; or (*d*) express the central values of the group and clarify what is distinctive about the group's identity (Feldman, 1984).

The norms that group members import, such as those listed above, are essentially inward looking. They help the team take care of itself and avoid embarrassing situations caused by inappropriate member behaviors. Hackman (2002) recommends that the leader has a responsibility to focus the team outwardly to enhance performance. Specifically, he suggests two core norms be created to enhance performance:

1. Group members should actively scan the environment for opportunities that would require a change in operating strategy to capitalize upon them, and

2. The team should identify the few number of behaviors which team members must always do and those which they should never do to conform to the organization's objectives.

By actively implementing these two norms, the team is forced to examine not only its organizational context but the much larger industry and environmental shells in which it operates.

One irony about norms is that an outsider to a group often is able to learn more about norms than an insider. An outsider, not necessarily subject to the norms himself, is more apt to notice them. In fact, the more "foreign" an observer is, the more likely it is the norms will be perceived. If a man is accustomed to wearing a tie to work, he is less likely to notice that men in another organization also wear ties to work, but is *more* likely to note that the men in a third organization typically wear sweaters and sweatshirts around the office.

Group Cohesion

Group cohesion is the glue that keeps a group together. It is the sum of forces that attract members to a group, provide resistance to leaving it, and motivate them to be active in it. Highly cohesive groups interact with and influence each other more than do less cohesive groups. Furthermore, a highly cohesive group may have lower absenteeism and lower turnover than a less cohesive group, and low absenteeism and turnover often contribute to higher group performance; higher performance can, in turn, contribute to even higher cohesion, thus resulting in an increasingly positive spiral.

However, greater cohesiveness does not always lead to higher performance. A highly cohesive but unskilled team is still an unskilled team, and such teams will often lose to a less cohesive but more skilled one. Additionally, a highly cohesive group may sometimes develop goals that are contrary to the larger organization's goals. For example, members of a highly cohesive research team at a particular college committed themselves to working on a problem that seemed inherently interesting to them. Their nearly zealous commitment to the project, however, effectively kept them from asking, or even allowing others to ask, if the research aligned itself well with the college's stated objectives. Their quite narrow and basic research effort deviated significantly from the college's expressed commitment to emphasize applied research. As a result, the college lost some substantial outside financial support.

Other problems also can occur in highly cohesive groups. Researchers (Alderfer, 1977; Ginnett, 1987) have found that some groups can become so cohesive they erect what amount to fences or boundaries between themselves and others. Such **overbounding** can block the use of outside resources that could make them more effective. Competitive product development teams can become so overbounded (often rationalized by security concerns or inordinate fears of "idea thieves") that they will not ask for help from willing and able staff within their own organizations.

One example of this problem was the failed mission to rescue U.S. embassy personnel held hostage in Iran during the Carter presidency. The rescue itself was a rather complicated mission involving many different sorts of U.S. military forces. Some of these forces included sea-based helicopters. The helicopters and their crews were carried on regular naval vessels, though most sailors on the vessels knew nothing of the secret mission. Senior personnel were so concerned that some sailor might leak information, and thus compromise the mission's secrecy, that maintenance crews aboard the ships were not directed to perform increased levels of maintenance on the helicopters immediately before the critical mission. Even if a helicopter was scheduled for significant maintenance within the next 50 hours of flight time (which would be exceeded in the rescue mission), crews were not told to perform the maintenance. According to knowledgeable sources, this practice did impact the performance of at least one of the failed helicopters, and thus the overall mission.

Janis (1982) discovered still another disadvantage of highly cohesive groups. He found that people in a highly cohesive group often become more concerned with striving for unanimity than in objectively appraising different courses of action. Janis labeled this phenomenon **groupthink** and believed it accounted for a number of historic fiascoes, including Pearl Harbor and the Bay of Pigs invasion. It may have played a role in the *Challenger* disaster, and it also occurs in other cohesive groups ranging from business meetings to air crews, and from therapy groups to school boards.

What is groupthink? Cohesive groups tend to evolve strong informal norms to preserve friendly internal relations. Preserving a comfortable, harmonious group environment becomes a hidden agenda that tends to suppress dissent, conflict, and critical thinking. Unwise decisions may result when concurrence seeking among members overrides their willingness to express or tolerate deviant points of view and think critically. Janis (1982) identified a number of symptoms of groupthink, which can be found in Highlight 10.5.

A policy-making or decision-making group displaying most of the symptoms in Highlight 10.5 runs a big risk of being ineffective. It may do a poor job of clarifying objectives, searching for relevant information, evaluating alternatives, assessing risks, and anticipating the need for contingency plans. Janis (1982) offered the following suggestions as ways of reducing groupthink and thus of improving the quality of a group's input to policies or decisions. First, leaders should encourage all group members to take on the role of critical evaluator. Everyone in the group needs to appreciate the importance of airing doubts and objections. This includes the leader's willingness to listen to criticisms of his or her own ideas. Second, leaders should create a climate of open inquiry through their own impartiality and objectivity. At the outset, leaders should refrain from stating personal preferences or expectations, which may bias group discussion. Third, the risk of groupthink can be reduced if independent groups are established to make recommendations on the same issue. Fourth, at least one member of the group should be assigned the role of devil's advocate, an assignment that should rotate from meeting to meeting.

One final problem with highly cohesive groups may be what Shephard (1991) has called **ollieism.** Ollieism, a variation of groupthink, occurs when illegal actions are taken by overly zealous and loyal subordinates who believe that what

Symptoms of Groupthink

Highlight 10.5

An illusion of invulnerability, which leads to unwarranted optimism and excessive risk taking by the group.

Unquestioned assumption of the group's morality and therefore an absence of reflection on the ethical consequences of group action.

Collective rationalization to discount negative information or warnings.

Stereotypes of the opposition as evil, weak, or stupid.

Self-censorship by group members from expressing ideas that deviate from the group consensus due to doubts about their validity or importance.

An illusion of unanimity such that greater consensus is perceived than really exists.

Direct pressure on dissenting members, which reinforces the norm that disagreement represents disloyalty to the group.

Mindguards, who protect the group from adverse information.

Source: Adapted from I. L. Janis, *Groupthink,* 2nd ed. (Boston: Houghton Mifflin, 1982).

they are doing will please their leaders. It derives its name from the actions of Lieutenant-Colonel Oliver North, who among other things admitted he lied to the U.S. Congress about his actions while working on the White House staff during the Iran-Contra affair. Shephard cited the slaying of Thomas à Becket by four of Henry II's knights and the Watergate break-in as other prime examples of ollieism. We will probably see similar examples in the Enron trials. Ollieism differs from groupthink in that the subordinates' illegal actions usually occur without the explicit knowledge or consent of the leader. Nevertheless, Shephard pointed out that although the examples cited of ollieism were not officially sanctioned, the responsibility for them still falls squarely on the leader. It is the leader's responsibility to create an ethical climate within the group, and leaders who create highly cohesive yet unethical groups must bear the responsibility for the group's actions.

After reading about the uncertain relationships between group cohesion and performance, and the problems with overbounding, groupthink, and ollieism, one might think that cohesiveness should be something to avoid. Nothing, however, could be further from the truth. First of all, problems with overly cohesive groups occur relatively infrequently and, in general, leaders will be better off thinking of ways to create and maintain highly cohesive teams than not developing these teams out of concern for potential groupthink or overbounding situations. Second, perhaps the biggest argument for developing cohesive groups is to consider the alternative—groups with little or no cohesiveness. In the latter groups, followers would generally be dissatisfied with each other and the leader, commitment to accomplishing group and organizational goals may be reduced, intragroup communication may occur less frequently, and interdependent task performance may suffer (Robbins, 1986). Because of the problems associated with groups having low cohesiveness, leadership practitioners need to realize that developing functionally cohesive work groups is a goal they all should strive for.

In summary, the group perspective provides a complementary level of analysis to the individual perspective presented earlier in this chapter. A follower's behavior may be due to his or her values, traits, or experience (i.e., the individual perspective), or this behavior may be due to the followers' roles, the group norms, the group's stage of development, or the group's level of cohesiveness (i.e., the group perspective). Thus, the group perspective can also provide both leaders and followers with a number of explanations of why individuals in groups behave in certain ways. Moreover, the six group characteristics just described can give leaders and followers ideas about (*a*) factors that may be affecting their ability to influence other group members and (*b*) what to do to improve their level of influence in the group.

Teams

With so much attention devoted to teams and teamwork in today's organizations, it is appropriate to spend a fair amount of time examining teams and the factors that impact their effectiveness. After considering some differential measures of team effectiveness, we will look at a comprehensive model of team leadership.

Effective Team Characteristics and Team Building

And yes, teams do vary in their effectiveness. Virtually identical teams can be dramatically different in terms of success or failure (see Highlight 10.6). We must ask, therefore, what makes one team successful and another unsuccessful? Although this is an area only recently studied, exploratory work at the Center for Creative Leadership has tentatively identified several key characteristics for effective team performance (see Highlight 10.7 for an astronaut's perspective on teamwork).

The Center for Creative Leadership's research with teams indicated that successful and unsuccessful teams could be differentiated on the basis of eight key characteristics, the first six of which are primarily concerned with task accomplishment (Hallam & Campbell, 1992). First, effective teams had a *clear mission* and *high performance standards.* Everyone on the team knew what the team was trying to achieve and how well he or she had to perform in order to achieve the team's mission. Second, leaders of successful teams often *took stock* of their equipment, training facilities and opportunities, and outside resources available to help the team. Leaders of effective teams spent a

> *He that would be a leader must be a bridge.*
>
> Welsh proverb

considerable amount of time *assessing the technical skills* of the team members. After taking stock of available resources and skills, good leaders would work to *secure those resources and equipment* necessary for team effectiveness. Moreover, leaders of effective teams would spend a considerable amount of time *planning* and *organizing* in order to make optimal use of available resources, to select new members with needed technical skills, or to improve needed technical skills of existing members.

The last two characteristics of effective teams were concerned with the group maintenance or interpersonal aspects of teams. Hallam and Campbell's (1992) research indicated that *high levels of communication* were often associated with effective

---

Examples of Effective and Ineffective Teams

Highlight 10.6

Most people can readily think up a number of examples of ineffective and effective teamwork. Consider the relative effectiveness of the teams depicted in the following two true stories:

Ineffective Teamwork: After an airline flight crew failed to get a "nose gear down and locked" indicator light to come on while making a landing approach into Miami, all three crew members became involved in trying to change the burned-out indicator bulb in the cockpit. Nobody was flying the airplane and none of them were monitoring the flight of the L-1011 as it descended into the Everglades and crashed.

Effective Teamwork: The crew of a DC-10, after having lost all capability to control the airplane through flight controls as a result of an engine explosion, realized they needed all the help they could get. Captain Al Haynes discovered another experienced captain was traveling in the passenger cabin and invited him to come up to the cabin to help the regular crew out. Miraculously, their combined abilities enabled the crew—using techniques developed on the spot—to control the plane to within a few feet of the ground. Even though there were fatalities, over 100 people survived a nearly hopeless situation.

Women in Leadership: Teamwork from an Astronaut's Perspective

Highlight 10.7

Dr. Bonnie J. Dunbar is an American astronaut. She has flown on four space shuttle missions. We asked her to share a few personal reflections about the meaning of teamwork and followership to her as she was growing up, as well as presently in her role in the space program. She wrote this during preparation for her flight in June 1992. She was payload commander for that space shuttle mission.

Above all, the success of a space flight depends upon teamwork: within the crew and between the ground controllers and the crew. Teamwork is a valued attribute among currently selected astronauts.

I was very fortunate as a young girl to have been exposed to that concept by my family. With four children and a multitude of chores to be performed, my mother and father impressed upon us our responsibilities within the family unit. Success of the farm (and our future) depended upon our contribution. As the oldest, I was expected to participate in all chores, including driving the tractor and "round-up" by horseback. There were no distinctions in these responsibilities between my brothers and me. Group experiences within the 4-H organization (showing steers, etc.) and playing on baseball, volleyball, and basketball teams reinforced the pride of sharing success together and consoling each other in defeat.

When I attended college, some of that team experience was missed. By virtue of my gender, I was considered an unwelcome minority by many in the engineering college. Therefore, I was never invited to the study groups or participated in group solution of the homework problems. Still, I found an outlet in group activities by belonging to Angel Flight (co-ed auxiliary to Air Force ROTC—I was elected Commander of 50 my junior year) and by continuing to play co-ed baseball. Ironically, my engineering classmates needed my athletic ability as first baseman on the playing field.

I was also supported by three very important individuals during this time: my father, my mother, and the chairman of the Ceramic Engineering Department, Dr. James I. Mueller. My parents always encouraged me to pursue my "dreams" and to be the best person I could be. The fact that I was the first in the family to attend college was a source of pride for them. That I subscribed to their principles of hard work, human compassion, and honesty was probably a source of greater pride. They were proud of my selection as an astronaut but my father was more concerned that I not forget how to get manure on my boots.

In my professional life, the closest I have come to real group esprit de corps has come through my association with the Astronaut Office. Perhaps it was due to the concept of "class training," or the similarity of individuals involved, but I consider those I work with as also my closest friends. Our successes are really those of a family team that extends out to the engineers, managers, and administrative support in the Space Shuttle program.

I am now on my third NASA Space Shuttle crew. As Payload Commander I have tried to convey to the noncareer payload specialists on my next flight the importance of being part of the crew . . . that we will share both the successes and the failures of the flight. It has been an interesting experience to assess others' ability to become "part of the team." I have seen what not being part of the team can do, and in a flight environment that can be highly risky. Not being a team member does more than cause internal friction within the crew; it can be hazardous.

So, what does being "part of the team" mean? It doesn't always mean being the smartest or the fastest. It does mean recognizing the big picture goal and the contribution that each individual brings to the whole. It may not mean being the life of the party, but it does mean being able to get along with people and to tread a fine line . . . knowing when to compromise and knowing when to stand firm. And, in an organization such as ours with competitive individuals used to being on top of the hill, it means knowing when to be a Chief and when to be an Indian. In the Astronaut Office, mission specialists rotate through technical jobs and different responsibilities during flights. Sometimes they are Indians instead of Chiefs. Those that perform best and appear to be well-regarded can do each equally well.

teams. These authors believed this level of communication helped team members to stay focused on the mission and to take better advantage of the skills, knowledge, and resources available to the team. High levels of communication also helped to *minimize interpersonal conflicts* on the team, which often drained energy needed for team success and effectiveness. The characteristics of effective teams identified in this research provide leadership practitioners with a number of ideas about how they may be able to increase the effectiveness of their work units or teams.

A different avenue to group and team effectiveness has been to use a normative approach. One example of this technique is described in *Groups That Work (and Those That Don't)* (Hackman, 1990). Ginnett (1993, 1996) has developed an expanded model focusing specifically on team leadership, which we will examine in more detail later in this chapter. For now, our concern is with one of the three major leadership functions in Ginnett's model that focuses on team design. The model suggests four components of design of the team itself that help the team get off to a good start, whatever its task. This is important because it is not uncommon to find that a team's failure can be traced to its being set up inappropriately from the very beginning. If a team is to work effectively, the following four variables need to be in place from the beginning.

1. *Task structure:* Does the team know what its task is? Is the task reasonably unambiguous and consistent with the mission of the team? Does the team have a meaningful piece of work, sufficient autonomy to perform it, and access to knowledge of its results?

2. *Group boundaries:* Is the collective membership of the team appropriate for the task to be performed? Are there too few or too many members? Do the members collectively have sufficient knowledge and skills to perform the work? In addition to task skills, does the team have sufficient maturity and interpersonal skills to be able to work together and resolve conflicts? Is there an appropriate amount of diversity on the team (e.g., members are not so similar that they do not have differing perspectives and experiences, and yet not so diverse that they cannot communicate or relate to one another)?

3. *Norms:* Does the team share an appropriate set of norms for working as a team? Norms can be acquired by the team in three ways: (*a*) They can be imported from the organization existing outside the team, (*b*) they can be instituted and reinforced by the leader or leaders of the team, or (*c*) they can be developed by the team itself as the situation demands. If the team is to have a strategy that works over time, then it must ensure that conflicting norms do not confuse team members. It also needs to regularly scan and review prevailing norms to ensure they support overall objectives.

4. *Authority:* Has the leader established a climate where her authority can be used in a flexible rather than a rigid manner? Has she, at one end of the authority continuum, established sufficient competence to allow the group to comply when conditions demand (such as in emergencies)? Has she also established a climate such that any member of the team feels empowered to provide expert assistance when appropriate? Do team members feel comfortable in questioning the leader on decisions where there are no clear right answers? In short, have conditions been created where authority can shift to appropriately match the demands of the situation?

Many of these team design components may be imported from preexisting conditions in the organization within which the team is forming, from the industry in which the organization operates, or even from the environment in which the industry exists. To help team leaders consider these various levels, Hackman and Ginnett (1986, 1993) developed the concept of **organizational shells** (see Figure 10.1). Notice that the four critical factors for team design (task, boundary, norms, and authority) are necessary for the group to work effectively. In some cases, all the information about one of these critical factors may be input from the industry or organizational shell level. In these cases, the leader need do little else but affirm that condition. In other cases, there may be too little (or even inappropriate) input from the organizational level to allow the team to work effectively. In these cases, the leader needs to modify the factors for team design. Ideally this is done during the formation process—the final shell before the team actually begins work.

These ideas may require a new way of thinking about the relationship between a leader and followers. In many organizational settings, leaders are assigned. Sometimes, however, the people who create conditions for improved group effectiveness are not the designated leaders at all; they may emerge from the ranks of followers. This model has been used to differentiate between effective and ineffective "self-managing work groups"—teams where the followers and leaders were the same people. Moreover, because the model is prescriptive, it also provides a number of suggestions about what ineffective work groups can do to be successful. That same purpose underlies the following model as well.

FIGURE 10.1
Organizational shells.

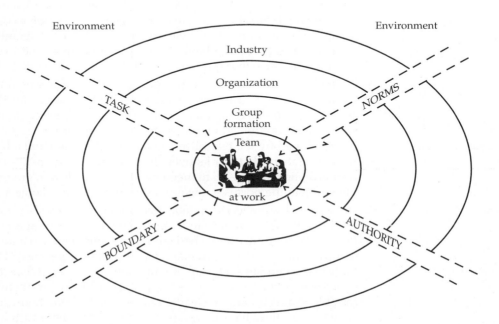

Ginnett's Team Effectiveness Leadership Model

Since we have emphasized that leadership is a group or team function and have suggested that one measure of leadership effectiveness may be whether the team achieves its objectives, it is reasonable to examine a model specifically designed to help teams perform more effectively: the **Team Effectiveness Leadership Model,** or **TELM** (Ginnett, 1993, 1996, 2001.) Another way to think of this model is as a mechanism to first identify what a team needs to be effective, and then to point the leader either toward the roadblocks that are hindering the team or toward ways to make the team even more effective than it already is. This approach is similar to McGrath's (1964) description of leadership, which suggested that the leader's main job is to determine what needs the team is faced with and then take care of them. This approach also will require us to think about leadership not as a function of the leader and his or her characteristics but as a function of the team. As the title of the model suggests, team effectiveness is the underlying driver.

We have mentioned this model of group or team effectiveness briefly before, but now we will explore it in greater detail. The original model for examining the "engine of a group" was developed by Richard Hackman and has been the basis for much research on groups and teams over the last 20 years (Hackman, 1990). The model presented here includes major modifications by Ginnett and represents an example of a leadership model that has been developed primarily using field research. It provides the underlying structure for the "Leadership and High Performance Teams" course offered by the Center for Creative Leadership. While there have been controlled experimental studies validating portions of the model (K. W. Smith, Salas, & Brannick, 1994), the principal development and validation have been completed using actual high-performance teams operating in their own situational context. Examples of the teams studied in this process include commercial and military air crews in actual line flying operations, surgical teams in operating suites, top management teams, product development and manufacturing teams, and teams preparing the Space Shuttle fleet for launch. A complete illustration of the model will be shown later. Because of its complexity, it is easier to understand by starting with a few simpler illustrations.

At the most-basic level, this model (see Figure 10.2) resembles a systems theory approach with inputs on the left (i.e., individual, team, and organizational factors), processes or throughputs in the center (i.e., what one can tell about the team by actually observing team members at work), and outputs on the right (i.e., how well the team did in accomplishing its objectives). We will examine each of these stages. However, we will proceed through the model in reverse order—looking at outputs first, then the process stage, then inputs.

Outputs

What do we mean by outputs? Quite simply, **outputs** (see Figure 10.3) are the results of the team's work. For example, a football team scores 24 points. A production team produces 24 valves in a day. A tank crew hits 24 targets on an artillery range. Such raw data, however, are insufficient for assessing team effectiveness.

FIGURE 10.2
Systems theory
for teams.

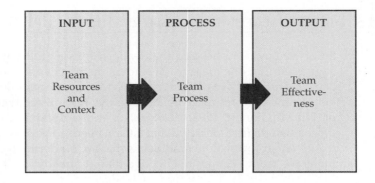

FIGURE 10.3
Basic TELM
components.

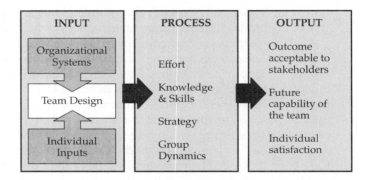

How do we know if a team's output is good? How do we know if a team is effective? Even though it was possible for the three different teams mentioned above to measure some aspect of their work, these measurements are not very helpful in determining their effectiveness, either in an absolute sense or in a relative sense. For comparison and research purposes, it is desirable to have some measures of team effectiveness that can be applied across teams and tasks. Hackman (1990) argued that a group is effective if (*a*) the team's productive output (goods, services, decisions) meets the standards of quantity, quality, and timeliness of the people who use it; (*b*) the group process that occurs while the group is performing its task enhances the ability of the members to work as members of a team (either the one they were on or any new teams they may be assigned to) in the future; and (*c*) the group experience enhances the growth and personal well-being of the individuals who compose the team.

Process

It should be obvious why leaders should be concerned with the outputs listed in the preceding section. After all, if a team does not "produce" (output), then it could not be considered effective. But what is process? And why should a leader care about it? Actually, there are several reasons a leader might want to pay attention to the team's process—how the team goes about its work.

Some teams may have such a limited number of products that the leader can ill afford to wait until the product is delivered to assess its acceptability to the client. For example, a team whose task is to build one (and only one) satellite to be launched into orbit will have no second chances. There may be no opportunity to correct any problem once the satellite is launched (or, as was the case with the flawed Hubble Space Telescope, correction can be made only after great expense). Therefore, it may be desirable for the leader of such a team to assess his team's work while it is working rather than after the satellite is launched. Other kinds of teams have such high standards for routine work that there simply are not enough critical indicators in the end product to determine effectiveness from outcome measures. As an example of this situation, a team operating a nuclear power plant is surrounded by so many technical backup systems that it may be difficult to determine team effectiveness by looking at "safe operation" as a measurement criterion. But we have evidence that not all teams in nuclear power plants operate equally well (Chernobyl and Three Mile Island are but two examples). It would seem helpful to be able to assess real teams "in process" rather than learn of team problems only following disastrous outcomes. Even leaders of noncritical teams might like to be able to routinely monitor their teams for evidence of effective or ineffective processes. So it turns out that the way teams go about their work can provide some very useful information to the leader.

Since process assessment is so important, let us focus for a moment on the block containing the four process measures of effectiveness in Figure 10.4. These four **process measures** of effectiveness provide criteria by which we can examine the ways in which teams work. If a team is to perform effectively, it must (*a*) work hard enough, (*b*) have sufficient knowledge and skills within the team to perform the task, (*c*) have an appropriate strategy to accomplish its work (or ways to approach the task at hand), and (*d*) have constructive and positive group dynamics among its members. The phrase *group dynamics* refers to interactions among team members, including such aspects as how they communicate with others, express feelings toward each other, and deal with conflict with each other, to name but a few of the characteristics. Assessing and improving group process is no trivial matter, as has been documented extensively in a comprehensive view of group process and its assessment by Wheelan (1994).

What should the leader do if she discovers a problem with one of these four process measures? Paradoxically, the answer is not to focus her attention on that process per se. While the four process measures are fairly good diagnostic measures for a team's ultimate effectiveness, they are, unfortunately, not particularly good leverage points for fixing the problem. An analogy from medicine would be a doctor who diagnoses the symptoms of an infection (a fever) but who then treats the symptoms rather than attacking the true underlying cause (a nail in the patient's foot). Similarly at the team level, rather than trying to correct a lack of effort being applied to the task at hand (perhaps a motivation problem), the team leader would be better advised to discover the underlying problem and fix that than to

FIGURE 10.4
Three TELM
leadership
functions.

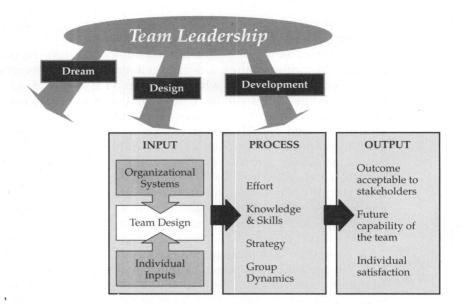

assume that a motivational speech to the team will do the job. This is not to imply that teams cannot benefit from process help. It merely suggests that the leader should ensure that there are no design problems (at the input level) that should be fixed first.

Inputs

In a manufacturing plant, **inputs** are the raw materials that are processed into products for sale. Similarly in team situations, inputs are what is available for teams as they go about their work. However, an important difference between an industrial plant and a team is that for a plant, the inputs are physical resources. Often for team design, we are considering psychological factors. There is a variety of levels of inputs, ranging from the individual level to the environmental level. Some of the inputs provide little opportunity for the leader to have an influence— they are merely givens. Leaders are often put in charge of teams with little or no control over the environment, the industry, or even the organizational conditions. There are other inputs, however, that the leader can directly impact to create the conditions for effective teamwork.

Figure 10.3 shows the multiple levels in the input stage of the model. Note that there are input factors at the individual and organizational levels and that both of these levels affect the team design level, as depicted by the direction of the arrows between these levels.

Ask not what your country can do for you. Ask what you can do for your country.

John F. Kennedy

Leadership Prescriptions of the Model

Creation

Following McGrath's (1964) view of the leader's role (the leader's main job is to identify and help satisfy team needs), and using the TELM, it is possible to identify constructive approaches for the leader to pursue. As described earlier in this chapter, what leaders do depends on where a team is in its development. Ideally, we should build a team like we build a house or an automobile. We should start with a concept, create a design, engineer it to do what we want it to do, and then manufacture it to meet those specifications. The TELM provides the same linear flow for design of a team. The somewhat more complex version of the TELM model is shown in Figure 10.4 and the leader should, as noted above, begin on the left with the Dream, proceed through all of the Design variables and then pay attention to the Development needs of the team. In this way, she can implement the three critical functions for team leadership: **dream, design,** and **development.**

Dream

Obviously, the team needs to have clear vision. In their book *The Wisdom of Teams* (1994) Katzenbach and Smith suggested that this may be the most important single step in teamwork. If the team has a challenging and demanding goal, teamwork may be necessary to accomplish the task. In highly effective work teams, the leader ensures that the team has a clear vision of where they are going. The communication of a vision frequently involves metaphorical language so that team members actually "paint their own picture" of where the team is headed.

Design

The importance of the design function of leadership cannot be overstated. Whether in the startup of a team or in the midstream assignment of leaders, designing the team is critical. It is also often the most frequently omitted step. Managers have long been trained to detect deviations and correct them. But what if the deviations are not detectable until the output stage? At their best, managers often detect deviations at the process stage and attempt to fix them "right where they are seen." Far too often, little time or attention is focused at the input level. Senior-level leaders may resist changing the organizational systems for a number of reasons, including having a vested interest in maintaining the status quo (whatever it is, it at least lets them rise to their current position!). And while individual team leaders may have little control over the organizational context and systems, they always have the opportunity for making an impact in their own team's design.

Development

If the leader finds that the team has a clear sense of direction and vision, and the input variables at the individual, organizational, and team levels are contributing positively to team effectiveness (i.e., the design portion of the leader's job has been taken care of), then she can turn her attention to the development level. Development is the ongoing work done with the team at the process level to continue to find ways to improve an already well-designed team. Given our individualistic culture, we have identified many teams in organizations that are apparently well designed and supported at the input level, but that have had no training or experience in the concept of teamwork. There are times when effective teamwork is based on very different concepts than effective individual work. For example, for a team to do well, the individuals composing the team must sometimes not maximize their individual effort. Referred to as subsystem nonoptimization, this concept is at first not intuitively obvious to many newly assigned team members. Nevertheless, consider the example of a high school football team that has an extremely fast running back and some very good (but considerably slower) blocking linemen as members of the offense. Often, team members are told they all need to do their absolute best if the team is going to do well. If our running back does his absolute best on a sweep around the end, then he will run as fast as he can. By doing so, he will leave his blocking linemen behind. The team is not likely to gain much yardage on such a play, and the linemen and the running back, who have done their individual best, are apt to learn an important experiential lesson about teamwork. Most important, after several such disastrous plays, all of the team members may be inclined to demonstrate poor team process (lower effort, poor strategy, poor use of knowledge, and poor group dynamics represented by intrateam strife). If we assume that all the input stage variables are satisfactorily in place, ongoing coaching may now be appropriate. The coach would get better results if he worked out a better coordination plan between the running back and the linemen. In this case, the fast running back needs to slow down (i.e., not perform maximally) to give the slower but excellent blockers a chance to do their work. After they have been given a chance to contribute to the play, the running back will have a much better chance to then excel individually, and so will the team as a whole.

As straightforward as this seems, very few leaders get the opportunity to build a team from the ground up. More often the leader is placed into a team that already exists, has most, if not all, of its members assigned, and is in a preexisting organizational context that might not be team friendly. While this situation is more difficult, all is not lost. The TELM also provides a method for diagnosis and identification of key **leverage points** for change.

Diagnosis and Leverage Points

Let us assume that you, as a new leader, have been placed in charge of a poorly performing existing team. After a few days of observation, you have discovered that its members are just not working very hard. They seem to be uninterested in the task, frequently wandering off or not even showing up for scheduled teamwork. By focusing on the Process block of the TELM, now shown in its complete form in Figure 10.5, we would diagnose this at the process level as a problem of Effort. Note that preceding the term *Effort* is the label (P-1). Rather than just encouraging them to work harder (or threatening them), we should first look at the Input level to see if there is some underlying problem. But you do not need to examine all 12 Input variables. Since we have already diagnosed a P-1 level process problem, the TELM is designed to focus your attention on the key leverage points to target change. At each of the Input levels (Individual, Team, and Organizational) you will find a 1-level variable identified. These 1-level Input variables are the most likely

FIGURE 10.5

Team effectiveness leadership model, Robert C. Ginnett, Ph.D.

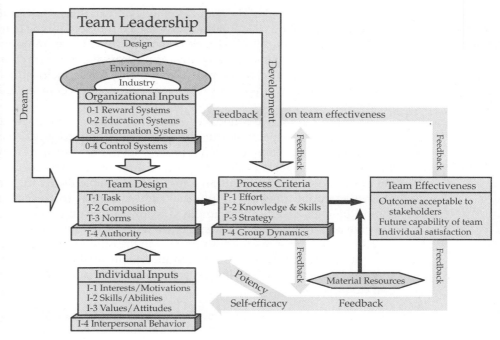

leverage points for impacting (P-1) Effort. The individual level (I-1) suggests that we look at the interests and motivations of the individual team members. These are referred to as **individual factors** in the model. If we have built a team to perform a mechanical assembly task, but the individuals assigned have little or no interest in mechanical work and instead prefer the performing arts, they may have little interest in contributing much effort to the team task. Here, using instruments such as the Campbell Interest and Skills Survey to select personnel may help our team's effort level from an individual perspective (D. P. Campbell, Hyne, & Nilsen, 1992).

While it may seem tempting to move to the team-level inputs next, it is important to remember that this model emphasizes the way teams are influenced by both individual and organizational level inputs. Therefore, we will look at the **organizational level** next. At the organizational level (O-1), the model suggests that we should examine the reward system that may be impacting the team. If the individuals have no incentive provided by the organization for putting forth effort, they might not be inclined to work very hard, or, perhaps, not to work at all. Similarly, the reward system may be solely structured to reward individual performance. Such a reward structure would be inconsistent with designs for a team task where interdependence and cooperation among members is often an underlying premise. If a professional basketball organization provides rewards for players based only on individual points scored, with no bonuses for team performance (games won or making the playoffs), you can expect little passing, setting picks for teammates, and so on.

Both the individual and organizational level variables contribute to the team's ability to perform the task. But there can also be problems at the **team design** level. Here (T-1), a poorly designed task is hypothesized to be unmotivating. (An approach for designing intrinsically rewarding work based on job characteristics will be discussed in the next chapter.) If a job is meaningless, lacks sufficient autonomy, or provides no knowledge of results, we would not expect to see followers putting forth much effort.

Using the model, we found key leverage points at various levels of the input stage that would impact the way the team went about its work (team process). In the example cited, we diagnosed a process-level problem with effort (P-1), so we examined the 1-level variables at the individual, organizational, and team levels as the most likely location for finding input stage problems. By the way, the concept of leverage point does not imply that only factors at corresponding "numbers" should be considered. For example, a team's effort might be affected by an oppressive and authoritarian leader. As we will discuss next, this "foundation-level variable" can have a tremendous impact on the other variables. Indeed, so powerful is this component, we should examine the process measure of group dynamics (P-4) and its corresponding leverage points in more detail. Consider the following two examples:

Surgical team. A surgical team composed of highly experienced members is involved in a surgical procedure that each member has participated in numerous times before. During one portion of the procedure, the surgeon asks for a particular instrument. The scrub nurse looks across the table at the assistant with a questioning gaze and then hands the surgeon the instrument he requested. Recognizing the instrument he has been handed (and asked for) is not correct for the current procedure, he throws it down on the table and curses at the scrub nurse. All members of the surgical team take a half-step back from the table and all casual conversation stops. No one offers any further voluntary assistance to the surgeon.

Commercial airline crew. A commercial airline crew is making a routine approach into an uncrowded airport on a clear day. The captain is flying and has declared a visual approach. His final approach to the runway is not good, which greatly complicates the plane's landing, and the landing is poor. After taxiing to the gate, the captain and his entire crew debrief (discuss) the poor approach, and the team members talk about what they could have done individually and collectively to help the captain avoid or improve a poor approach in the future. The captain thanks the members for their help and encourages them to consider how they could implement their suggestions in other situations.

Obviously, the group dynamics are very different in these two cases. In the first example, the surgeon's behavior, coupled with his status, created a condition inappropriate for effective teamwork. The airline captain in the second example, even though not performing the task well, created a team environment where the team was much more likely to perform well in the future. In both of these cases, we would have observed unusual (one negative and one positive) group dynamics while the team was at work. These are examples of the group dynamics at the P-4 level.

Again returning to the model for determining points of leverage, we would check the I-4 variable at the individual level to determine if the team members involved had adequate interpersonal skills to interact appropriately. At the organizational level, the O-4 variable would suggest we check organizational components to determine if there are organizational control systems that inhibit or overly structure the way in which the team can make decisions or control its own fate. Such factors may include organizational design or structure limitations (a subject we will discuss in more detail in Chapter 11), or it may be a rigid computerized control system that specifies every minute detail of the tasks not only of the teams as a whole but of all the individuals composing the team. These excessive controls at the organizational level can inhibit effective teamwork. Finally, at the team design level, the T-4 variable would have us examine authority dynamics created between the leader and the followers. Authority dynamics describe the various ways the team members, including the leader, relate and respond to authority. It is at the team level that the followers have opportunities to relate directly with the team's authority figure, the team leader. The intricacies of how these various authority dynamics can play themselves out in a team's life are more complex than this chapter warrants. Suffice it to say that there is a range of authority relationships that can be created, from autocratic to laissez-faire. For a more detailed explanation of this concept, see Ginnett (1993). But even without further description, it should be no surprise that the varied group dynamics observed in the previous two examples were leveraged by the leaders' use of authority in very different ways.

It would be simple if leaders could identify and specify in advance the ideal type of authority for themselves and their teams, and then work toward that objective. However, teams seldom can operate effectively under one fixed type of authority over time. The leader might prefer to use his or her favorite style, and the followers might also have an inherent preference for one type of authority or another; but if the team is to be effective, then the authority dynamics they are operating with should complement the demands of the situation. Since situations often change over time, so should the authority dynamics of the team. This idea is very similar to a point made earlier in the book—that effective leaders tend to use all five sources of leader power.

In research on the behavior of leaders in forming their teams, Ginnett (1993) found that highly effective leaders used a variety of authority dynamics in the first few minutes of the team's life. This does not mean that each highly effective leader used a single style that was different from the others (i.e., other leaders). It does mean that each one of the effective leaders used a variety of authority styles. At one point in the first meeting of the team, the leader would behave directively, which enabled him to establish his competence and hence his legitimate authority. At another time, he would engage the team in a very participative process and actively seek participation from each member of the team. By modeling a range of authority behaviors in the early stages of the team's life, the effective leaders laid the groundwork for continuing expectations of shifting authority as the situational demands changed.

Concluding Thoughts about Ginnett's Team Effectiveness Leadership Model

It is helpful to point out the few remaining items depicted in the model which have not been discussed. Note first the box labeled **material resources.** Note that this is a physical requirement, not an issue for the design or coaching of the team itself. Even if a team is well designed, has superior organizational systems supporting its work, and has access to superior-quality ongoing development, without adequate physical resources it is not likely to do well on the output level. Also note that background shells representing the industry and the environment have been included, as discussed earlier in this chapter. While the team leader may have little opportunity to influence these shells, the shells will certainly have an impact on the team.

Finally, there are several feedback loops which provide information to various levels of the organization. Usually, information is available to the organization as a whole (either formally or informally) about which teams are doing well and which are struggling. Whether leaders have access to this information is largely a function of whether they have created or stifled a safe climate. Feedback at the in-

"Well, I guess I did it again guys? Missed a field goal in the final seconds. But hey, we're a team, right? Right, guys? Guys?"

dividual level can influence the perceived efficacy of the individual members of the team (Bandura, 1977; Lindsley, Brass, & Thomas, 1995), while the overall potency of the team is impacted even for tasks that the team has yet to attempt (Guzzo, Yost, Campbell, & Shea, 1993).

Lastly, let us reinforce a limitation noted earlier. For ease of use and guidance, this model has been presented as if it were a machine (e.g., if P-2 breaks, check I-2, O-2, and T-2). As with other models of leadership or other human systems, however, nothing is that simple. There are obviously other variables that impact teams and team effectiveness. There are also complex interactions between the variables described even in this model. But we have considerable evidence that the model can be useful for understanding teams (Hackman, 1990), and, in light of the relationship between teams and leadership, we are now using it as an underlying framework in courses to help leaders more effectively lead their teams.

It has been shown that leaders can influence team effectiveness by (*a*) insuring the team has a clear sense of purpose and performance expectations; (*b*) designing or redesigning input stage variables at the individual, organizational, and team design levels; and (*c*) improving team performance through ongoing coaching at various stages, but particularly while the team is actually performing its task. These "midcourse corrections" should not only improve the team outcomes but also help to avoid many of the team-generated problems that can cause less-than-optimal team performance (Steiner, 1972). Whether the leader gets the luxury of creation or is thrust into the leadership of an existing team, the TELM has been shown to be a useful tool in guiding their behavior. It also is a most effective tool if you believe that the leader's job is to create the conditions for the team to be effective.

Let us integrate the variables from this model into our L-F-S framework (see Figure 10.6). Clearly, there are variables of importance in each of the three arenas. However, in this model the characteristics of the leader play a lesser role because the leader's job is to work on what is not being provided for the team in order for it to perform its task. The focus thus has shifted from the leader to the followers and to the situation.

Virtual Teams

Just as teams and teamwork have become essential to the accomplishment of work in organizations in the present (and as far as we can foresee into the future), so too will be an understanding of teams that are not in a single location. With the movement toward the global marketplace and the resultant globalization of organizations, it is appropriate to briefly consider the difficulties and recommended solutions for leading **[geographically dispersed teams (GDTs),]** or as they are more commonly referred to, virtual teams. There is considerable discussion about the labeling of such teams (Kossler & Prestridge, 1996), but for simplicity we will call them **virtual teams** here.

The marketplace is the globe (see Highlight 10.8). Western corporations are recognizing that growth and development opportunities are often much greater in

FIGURE 10.6

Factors from the normative model of group effectiveness and the interactional framework.

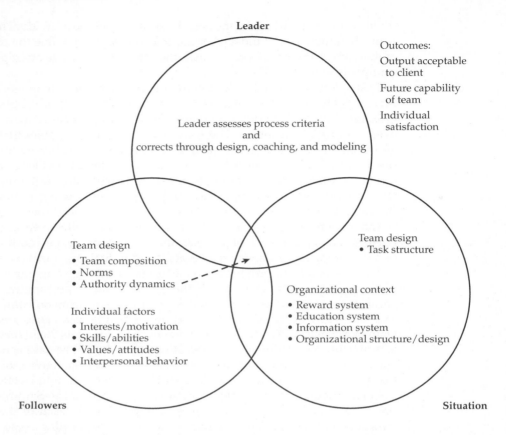

Leader

Leader assesses process criteria and corrects through design, coaching, and modeling

Outcomes:

Output acceptable to client

Future capability of team

Individual satisfaction

Team design
- Team composition
- Norms
- Authority dynamics

Individual factors
- Interests/motivation
- Skills/abilities
- Values/attitudes
- Interpersonal behavior

Team design
- Task structure

Organizational context
- Reward system
- Education system
- Information system
- Organizational structure/design

Followers

Situation

What Is the "Global Population" of Your Classroom?

Highlight 10.8

Your authors attended a training session conducted by a major corporation intended for its newly appointed executives. One session was devoted to demonstrating the need for a global perspective in today's environment. To illustrate the key point, the instructor divided the room into unequal groups representing the geographical distribution of the world's population and had each group stand up in turn. As each group stood, she told them the proportion of the global population they represented. The propor-

tions she used are provided below. You might try it in your classroom—it makes the point dramatically.

Australia and New Zealand	2%
North America	5%
Former Soviet Union	5%
Latin America	7%
Western/Eastern Europe	10%
Africa	12%
Asia	56%

Russia and other nations of the former Soviet Union, China, Latin America, and Africa than they are in their traditional markets of North America and Europe. But with this realization come new challenges for leading teams that are not only dispersed geographically but are often culturally different as well. Fortunately, information and communication technology is offering some new opportunities, if not solutions, for part of these problems. Early in this millennium, personal computer sales should top 100 million annually, or one PC for every 60 people on the planet; more than 60 million people will use cellular phones; and the Internet and World Wide Web are expanding at approximately 100 percent growth annually (Lipnack & Stamps, 1997). But is the mere opportunity to communicate electronically sufficient to ensure teamwork? Apparently not.

Researchers at the Conference Board (1996) reported that there were five major areas that needed to change if global teams were to work. The five listed were senior management leadership, innovative use of communication technology, adoption of an organization design that enhances global operations, the prevalence of trust among team members, and the ability to capture the strengths of diverse cultures, languages, and people.

Armstrong and Cole (1994) did in-depth studies of virtual teams and have reported three conclusions that should be considered by leaders of these teams. First, the distance between members of a virtual team is multidimensional. "Distance" includes not just geographical distance, but also organizational distance (e.g., different group or department cultures), temporal distance (e.g., different time zones), and differences in national culture. Second, the impact of such distances on the performance of a distributed work group is not directly proportional to objective measures of distance. In fact, Armstrong and Cole suggested that a new measure of distance between group members that reflects the degree of group cohesion and identity, a measure of psychological distance between members, would predict group performance better than geographical distance. Finally, the differences in the effects that distance seems to have on work groups is due at least partially to two intervening variables: (1) integrating practices *within* a virtual team, and (2) integrating practices *between* a virtual team and its larger host organization.

Finally, there are a number of frameworks under development to help leaders work with virtual teams, and there may be specific factors that these frameworks provide which can be useful. However, in our admittedly limited exposure to virtual teams in a pure research sense, a number of our clients have reported the TELM (discussed earlier) has been quite useful in considering the process problems that present themselves and in suggesting appropriate leverage points for intervention.

Leading Virtual Teams: Ten Principles

Highlight 10.9

Terence Brake is the President of TMA-Americas and specializes in globalization. He suggests the following guidance for leaders of virtual teams.

Virtual when used in relation to teamwork is an unfortunate term. It implies there is almost teamwork, but not quite. *Virtual* has associations with nearly, close to, and bordering on. As one wit said, "If you want virtual results, create a virtual team." Alternatively, it is a fortunate term if taken it to imply that greater efforts are needed to achieve real teamwork in virtual teams. What principles can help you do this?

1. **Be proactive.** We often talk of 'virtual' teams (VTs) as if they were all of a kind, but each one has its unique challenges. Some have a high level of cultural diversity. Others are more homogeneous. Some use one primary technology for collaboration, while others use a diverse mix. Some are short-lived, targeted on solving an immediate problem. Others are longer-term and strategic. Some cross time zones, and others none. By understanding the most likely challenges to occur, you can take proactive measures and increase team confidence. Confidence is a building block of virtual team performance.

2. **Focus on relationships before tasks.** Early on, team communications should have a significant 'getting to know you' component. They should also demonstrate enthusiasm and optimism. Members need to feel valued for who they are, not just what they do. They need to feel engaged and connected. Trust is usually built early on virtual teams, or not at all. Some observers talk of the 'virtual paradox'—virtual teams being highly dependent on trust, but not operating under conditions supportive of trust-building. Trust is often built on perceived similarities, but distance makes this process difficult. Chances for misunderstanding are also increased. Goodwill and engagement will solve most problems. Isolation and alienation create problems. Connect, and then collaborate.

3. **Seek clarity and focus early on.** Invest upfront time in clarifying the team's purpose and roles and responsibilities. There is enough uncertainty when working at a distance; it doesn't need to be added to by ambiguity and confusion. Clear purpose and accountabilities support cohesion. Translate purpose and overall accountabilities into specific objectives and tasks so that everyone knows what is expected, by whom, and by when. Virtual teams are highly susceptible to 'focus drift' and fragmentation, so keep reminding the team of purpose, objectives, etc.

4. **Create a sense of order and predictability.** In a world wanting us to embrace chaos, 'order' and 'predictability' might appear unfashionable. But they are critical to the success of virtual teams. Uncertainty creates anxiety, fear, and withdrawal. The result is a demotivated and unproductive team. Use common team tools, templates, and processes; have predetermined times for communicating together; check in with team members regularly without trying to micromanage; be accessible and an anchor point for the team. Shared expectations are psychological threads connecting separate minds.

5. **Be a cool-headed, objective problem solver.** Problems on virtual teams can appear larger than they actually are; people feeling isolated can lose perspective. Small issues, quickly resolved when working face-to-face, often fester and spread paranoia and distrust. You should establish yourself as someone who is totally fair; you don't play favorites, and you don't overburden some at the expense of others. You also need to be pragmatic. When there is a problem, you keep calm, you engage the team in finding practical solutions, and you communicate often. Panic is a virus that breeds exceptionally well in silent, isolated spaces.

6. **Develop shared operating agreements.** To reduce threats of uncertainty and ambiguity, common methods and processes—operating agreements—need to be established quickly. These agreements provide the team with shared mental models for working together. Typically, operating agreements need to be created in

(continued)

Leading Virtual Teams: Ten Principles *(continued)*

areas such as: planning, decision making, communicating, and coordination. A Team Charter acts as a common reference point, and can help orient new team members. Take time during team 'meetings' to review how well the operating agreements are working.

7. **Give team members personal attention.** Just as you would on a face-to-face team, allocate time to 'meet' with individuals. Find out how he or she is feeling about things. Give each person an opportunity to share personal successes, challenges, needs, and wants. It can be difficult to do this in team 'meetings' where the emphasis is on shared tasks and problem solving. Empathize with that person who is on the road, working at home, or in a remote office. Listening, caring, sympathizing, recognizing—they cost little, but benefit everyone.

8. **Respect the challenges of the virtual environment.** I once lived on a boat, and I soon learned to respect the power of nature—the winds, tides, swells, rain, ice, and drought. I had to pay very close attention to these elements or they could sink me, swamp me, or ground me. There is always the temptation to carry over habits from one environment (e.g., land, face-to-face teamwork) into another (e.g., river, working at a distance). We must recognize the differences and adapt. Listening, empathizing, communicating, coordinating, engaging, energizing, and enabling all need to be enhanced.

9. **Recognize the limits of available technologies.** Unless you really have to, don't try and do everything via a virtual team. Sometimes teams are working on projects so complex that no matter how much video or teleconferencing time they have, it will not be enough. Sometimes it pays dividends to bring people together for a few days. Never assume that because you have been designated a 'virtual' team, you must always work in that mode. Focus on cost/benefit over the life of the project. Technology is a tool, and all tools are good for some tasks and not others.

10. **Stay people-focused.** Distance can make faceless abstractions of us all. Never lose site of the fact that your virtual team members are people, with all that that entails—needs for belonging, meaning, accomplishment, and recognition; feelings of frustration, anger, excitement, boredom, and alienation; political pressures and personal pressures. Think about those features of your physical workplace that enable teams to work well together, e.g., formal meeting rooms, informal spaces, the coffee area, and see what you can do to humanize your virtual workplace, e.g., team pictures and bio's, bulletin boards, chat areas.

Applying these virtual team leadership principles will help you avoid *almost* and *close to* teamwork. Virtual teamwork is only going to increase, so many of us need to re-skill ourselves for leading at a distance.

Summary

The group perspective showed that followers' behaviors can be the result of factors somewhat independent of the individual characteristics of followers. Group factors that can affect followers' behaviors include group size, stages of group development, roles, norms, and cohesion. Leadership practitioners should use these concepts to better understand followers' behaviors. Leaders should also use a team perspective for understanding follower behavior and group performance. Leadership practitioners need to bear in mind how a team's sense of identity, common goals or tasks, level of task interdependence, and differentiated roles affect functional and dysfunctional follower behavior. Additionally, because effective teams have several readily identifiable characteristics, leadership practitioners may want to use the suggestions provided by Hackman (1990), Ginnett (1992), or Hallam and Campbell (1992) to develop more effective teams.

The Team Effectiveness Leadership Model posited that team effectiveness can best be understood in terms of inputs, processes, and outcomes. The input level consists of the individual characteristics of the followers; the design of the team itself; and various organizational systems that create the context in which the teams will operate. The process level concerns the way in which teams behave while going about their tasks, and the output level concerns whether customers and clients are satisfied with the team's product, whether the team improves and develops as a performing unit, and whether followers are satisfied to be members of the team. By identifying certain process problems in teams, leaders can use the model to diagnose appropriate leverage points for action at the individual, team design, or organizational levels, or for ongoing development at the process level. Leaders concerned with teamwork in organizational settings have found this framework useful in helping them conceptualize factors affecting team effectiveness and identifying targets for change.

Key Terms

group perspective, *292*
group, *294*
cliques, *295*
span of control, *295*
additive task, *295*
process loss, *296*
social loafing, *296*
social facilitation, *296*
forming, *296*
storming, *296*
norming, *296*
performing, *296*
project teams, *298*
punctuated
equilibrium, *298*
group roles, *298*
task role, *298*

relationship role, *298*
dysfunctional roles, *299*
role conflict, *299*
intrasender role
conflict, *299*
intersender role
conflict, *299*
interrole conflict, *299*
person-role conflict, *299*
role ambiguity, *300*
norms, *301*
group cohesion, *302*
overbounding, *302*
groupthink, *302*
ollieism, *303*
organizational shells, *308*

Team Effectiveness
Leadership Model
(TELM), *309*
outputs, *309*
process measures, *311*
inputs, *312*
dream, *313*
design, *313*
development, *313*
leverage point, *314*
individual factors, *315*
organizational level, *315*
team design, *316*
material resources, *318*
geographically dispersed
teams (GDTs), *319*
virtual teams, *319*

Questions

1. How do the tenets of Ginnett's Team Effectiveness Leadership Model compare with the components of team performance described earlier?

2. Not all group norms are positive or constructive from the leader's perspective. If a group holds counterproductive norms, what should the leader do?

3. On the basis of what you know about U.S., Asian, and New Zealand cultures, which of our three leaders (Powell, Suu Kyi, and Jackson) would be more comfortable with a group or team-based approach to work?

Skills

Leadership skills relevant to this chapter include:

- Diagnosing performance problems in individuals, groups, and organizations
- Team building for work teams
- Team building at the top.

Activity

NASA Exercise: Lost on the Moon

Your spaceship has crash-landed on the dark side of the moon and you are scheduled to rendezvous with the mother ship, which is 200 miles away on the lighted side of the moon. The crash has ruined the ship and destroyed all the equipment except for the 15 items listed below. Your crew's survival depends on reaching the mother ship, so you must choose the most critical items available to take on the 200-mile trip. Your task is to rank-order the 15 items in the order of their importance for your survival. Place a "1" beside the most important item, a "2" beside the second most important item, and so on until you have ranked all 15 items.

_____ Box of matches
_____ Food concentrate
_____ 50 feet of nylon rope
_____ Parachute silk
_____ Solar-powered portable heating unit
_____ Two .45 caliber pistols
_____ One case of dehydrated milk
_____ Two 100-pound tanks of oxygen
_____ Stellar map
_____ Self-inflating life raft
_____ Magnetic compass
_____ Five gallons of water
_____ Signal flares
_____ First-aid kit with hypodermic syringes
_____ Solar-powered FM transmitter/receiver

Your instructor has the "NASA Expert" answers and the instructions for completing the exercise.

Minicase

"Integrating Teams at Hernandez & Associates"

Marco Hernandez is president of Hernandez & Associates Inc., a full-service advertising agency with clients across North America. The company provides a variety of marketing services to support its diverse group of clients. Whether called on to generate a strategic plan, create interactive websites, or put together a full-blown media campaign, the team at Hernandez & Associates prides itself on creative solutions to its clients' marketing challenges.

The firm was founded in 1990 with an emphasis in the real estate industry. It quickly expanded its client base to include health care, as well as food and consumer products. Like many small firms, the company grew quickly in the "high-flying" 1990s, but its administrative costs to obtain and service businesses also skyrocketed. And, like many businesses, the terrorist attacks of September 11 and the economic downturn that followed greatly affected business. Clients' shrinking budgets forced them to scale back their business with Hernandez & Associates and cutbacks in staffing meant clients needed more marketing support services as opposed to full-scale campaigns.

Hernandez & Associates now faced a challenge—to adapt its business to focus on what the clients were asking for. Specifically, clients, with their reduced staffs, were looking for help responding to their customers' requests and looking for ways to make the most of their more limited marketing budgets. Its small, cohesive staff of 20 employees needed to make some changes, and quickly.

As president of Hernandez & Associates, Marco Hernandez knew his team was up for the challenge. He had worked hard to create an environment to support a successful team—he recruited people who had solid agency experience and he consistently communicated the firm's mission to his team. He made sure the team had all the resources it needed to succeed and constantly took stock of these resources. He had built his team as he built his business and knew the group would respond to his leadership. But where to start? Getting the team to understand that growth depended on a shift in how it serviced its clients was not difficult—each of the employees of the small firm had enough contact with the clients that they knew their needs were changing. But making significant changes to the status quo at Hernandez and Associates would be difficult. Group roles had to change—creative folks had to think about how to increase a client's phone inquiries and website visits; account people needed a better understanding of the client's desire for more agency leadership. And everyone had to have a better sense of the costs involved. The company as a whole needed a more integrated approach to servicing their clients if they hoped to survive. Marco needed a plan.

1. Like many leaders, Marco has a team in place and does not have the luxury of building a new team from the ground up to adapt to the changing business environment his firm is faced with. Use the TELM to help Marco diagnose the problems faced by the firm and identify leverage points for change.
   a. Consider the major functions of the TELM—input, process, and output. Where do most of the firm's challenges fall?
   b. What are the team's goals for outputs?
2. Identify potential resources for Marco and his team in implementing a strategy to change the way they do business at Hernandez & Associates.

Focus on the Situation

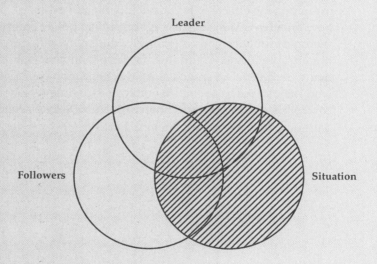

In previous chapters we noted that understanding leaders and followers is much more complicated than many people first think. For example, we examined how leaders' personality characteristics, behaviors, and attitudes affect the leadership process. Similarly, followers' attitudes, experience, personality characteristics, and behaviors, as well as group norms and cohesiveness, also affect the leadership process. Despite the complexities of leaders and followers, however, perhaps no factor in the interactional framework is as complex as the situation. Not only do a variety of task, organizational, and environmental factors affect behavior, but the relative salience or strength of these factors varies dramatically across people. What one person perceives to be the key situational factor affecting his or her behavior may be relatively unimportant to another person.

Moreover, the relative importance of the situational factors also varies over time. Even in the course of a single soccer game, for example, the situation changes constantly: The lead changes, the time remaining in the game changes, weather conditions change, injuries occur, and so on. Given the dynamic nature of situations, it may be a misnomer to speak of "the" situation in reference to leadership.

Because of the complex and dynamic nature of situations and the substantial role perceptions play in the interpretation of situations, no one has been able to develop a comprehensive taxonomy describing all of the situational variables affecting a person's behavior. In all likelihood, no one ever will. Nevertheless, considerable research about situational influences on leadership has been accomplished. Leadership researchers have examined how different task, organizational, and environmental factors affect both leaders' and followers' behavior, though most have examined only the effects of one or two situational variables on leaders' and followers' behavior. For example, a study might have examined the effects of task difficulty on subordinates' performance yet ignored how broader issues, such as organizational policy or structure, might also affect their performance. This is primarily due to the difficulty of studying the effects of organizational and environmental factors on behavior. As you might imagine, many of these factors, such as market conditions or crisis situations, do not easily lend themselves to realistic laboratory experiments where conditions can be controlled and interactions analyzed. Nonetheless, several consistent findings have emerged. We review them in Part IV.

11

Characteristics of the Situation

Introduction

In a book designed to introduce students to the subject of leadership, a chapter about "the situation" poses some challenging obstacles and dilemmas. The very breadth of the topic is daunting; it could include almost everything else in the world that has not been covered in the previous chapters! To the typical student who has not yet begun a professional career, pondering the magnitude of variables making up the situation is a formidable request. For one thing, the situation you find yourself in is often seen as completely beyond your control. For example, how many times have you heard someone say, "Hey, I don't make the rules around here. I just follow them." Furthermore, the subject is made more difficult by the fact that most students have limited organizational experience as a frame of reference. So why bother to introduce the material in this chapter? Because the situation we are in often explains far more about what is going on and what kinds of leadership behaviors will be best than any other single variable we have discussed so far!

> *When you've exhausted all possibilities, remember this: You haven't!*
>
> Robert H. Schuller

In this chapter we will try to sort out some of the complexity and magnitude of this admittedly large topic. First, we will review some of the research which has led us to consider these issues. Then, after considering a huge situational change that is now occurring, we will present a model to help in considering key situational variables. Finally, we will take a look forward through one interesting lens. Throughout the chapter, though, our objective will be primarily to increase awareness rather than to prescribe specific courses of leader action.

Background

The appropriateness of a leader's behavior with a group of followers often makes sense only when you look at the situational context in which the behavior occurs. Whereas severely disciplining a follower might seem a poor way to lead, if the follower in question had just committed a safety violation endangering the lives of hundreds of people, then the leader's actions may be exactly right. In a similar fashion, the situation may be the primary reason personality traits, experience, or cognitive abilities are related less consistently to leadership effectiveness than to leadership emergence (R. T. Hogan, J. Hogan, & Curphy, 1992; Yukl, 1989). Most leadership emergence studies have involved leaderless discussion groups, and for the most part the situation is quite similar across such studies. In studies of leadership effectiveness, however, the situation can and does vary dramatically. The personal attributes needed to be an effective leader of a combat unit, chemical research-and-development division, community service organization, or fast-food restaurant may change considerably. Because the situations facing leaders of such groups may be so variable, it is hardly surprising that studies of leader characteristics have yielded inconsistent results when looking at leadership effectiveness across jobs or situations. Thus, the importance of the situation in the leadership process should not be overlooked.

Trying to change individual and/or corporate behavior without addressing the larger organizational context is bound to disappoint. Sooner or later bureaucratic structures will consume even the most determined of collaborative processes. As Woody Allen once said, "The lion and the lamb may lie down together, but the lamb won't get much sleep." What to do? Work on the lion as well as the lamb designing teamwork into the organization . . . Although the Boston Celtics have won 16 championships, they have never had the league's leading scorer and never paid a player based on his individual statistics. The Celtics understand that virtually every aspect of basketball requires collaboration.

Robert W. Keidel

Historically, some leadership researchers emphasized the importance of the situation in the leadership process in response to the Great Man theory of leadership. These researchers maintained that the situation, not someone's traits or abilities, plays the most important role in determining who emerges as a leader (Murphy, 1941; Person, 1928; Spiller, 1929). As support for the situational viewpoint, these researchers noted that great leaders typically emerged during economic crises, social upheavals, or revolutions; great leaders were generally not associated with periods of relative calm or quiet. For example, Schneider (1937) noted that the number of individuals identified as great military leaders in the British armed forces during any time period depended on how many conflicts the country was engaged in; the greater the number of conflicts, the greater the number of great military leaders. Moreover, researchers advocating the situational viewpoint believed leaders were made, not born, and that prior leadership experience helped forge effective leaders (Person, 1928). These early situational theories of leadership tended to be very popular in the United States, as they fit more closely with American ideals of equality and meritocracy, and ran counter to the genetic views of leadership that were more popular among European researchers at the time (Bass, 1990). (The fact that many of these European researchers had aristocratic backgrounds probably had something to do with the popularity of the Great Man theory in Europe.)

More recent leadership theories have explored how situational factors affect leaders' behaviors. In **role theory,** for example, a leader's behavior was said to depend on a leader's perceptions of several critical aspects of the situation: rules and regulations governing the job; role expectations of subordinates, peers, and superiors; the nature of the task; and feedback about subordinates' performance (Merton, 1957; Pfeffer & Salancik, 1975). Role theory clarified how these situational demands and constraints could cause role conflict and role ambiguity. Leaders may experience role conflict when subordinates and superiors have conflicting expectations about a leader's behavior or when company policies contradict how superiors expect tasks to be performed. A leader's ability to successfully resolve such conflicts may well determine leadership effectiveness (Tsui, 1984).

The way of the superior is threefold, but I am not equal to it. Virtuous, he is free from anxieties; wise, he is free from perplexities; bold, he is free from fear.

Confucius

Another effort to incorporate situational variables into leadership theory was Hunt and Osborn's (1982) **multiple-influence model.** Hunt and Osborn distinguished between microvariables (e.g., task characteristics) and macrovariables (e.g., the external environment) in the situation. Although most researchers looked at the effects tasks had on leader behaviors, Hunt and Osborn believed macrovariables had a pervasive influence on the ways leaders act. Both role theory and the multiple-influence model highlight a major problem in addressing situational factors, which was noted previously: that situations can vary in countless ways. Because situations can vary in so many ways, it is helpful for leaders to have an abstract scheme for conceptualizing situations. This would be a step in knowing how to identify what may be most salient or critical to pay attention to in any particular instance.

One of the most basic abstractions is **situational levels.** The idea behind situational levels may best be conveyed with an example. Suppose someone asked you, "How are things going at work?" You might respond by commenting on the specific tasks you perform (e.g., "It is still pretty tough. I am under the gun for getting next year's budget prepared, and I have never done that before."). Or, you might respond by commenting on aspects of the overall organization (e.g., "It is really different. There are so many rules you have to follow. My old company was not like that at all."). Or, you might comment on factors affecting the organization itself (e.g., "I've been real worried about keeping my job—you know how many cutbacks there have been in our whole industry recently."). Each response deals with the situation, but each refers to a very different level of abstraction: the task level, the organizational level, and the environmental level. Each of these three levels provides a different perspective with which to examine the leadership process (see Figure 11.1).

These three levels certainly do not exhaust all the ways situations vary. Situations also differ in terms of physical variables like noise and temperature levels, workload demands, and the extent to which work groups interact with other groups. Organizations also have unique "corporate cultures," which define a context for leadership. And there are always even broader economic, social, legal, and technological aspects

FIGURE 11.1
An expanded
leader-
follower-
situation
model.

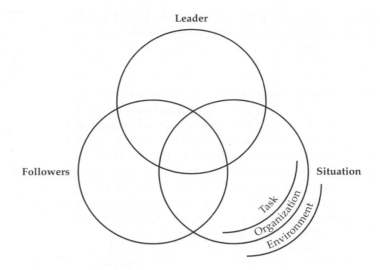

of situations within which the leadership process occurs. What, amid all this situational complexity, should leaders pay attention to? We will try to provide some insights into this question by presenting a model which considers many of these factors. But first, let us consider an environmental aspect of the situation that is changing for virtually all of us as we move into the new millennium.

From the Industrial Age to the Information Age

All of us have grown up in the age of industry, but perhaps in its waning years. Starting just before the American Civil War and continuing up through the last quarter of the 20th century, the industrial age supplanted the age of agriculture. During the industrial age, companies succeeded according to how well they could capture the benefits from "economies of scale and scope" (Chandler, 1990). Technology mattered, but mostly to the extent that companies could increase the efficiencies of mass production. Now a new age is emerging, and in this information age many of the fundamental assumptions of the industrial age are becoming obsolete.

Kaplan and Norton (1996) described a new set of operating assumptions underlying the information age and contrasted them with their predecessors in the industrial age. They described changes in the following ways companies operate:

> **Cross Functions.** Industrial age organizations gained competitive advantage through specialization of functional skills in areas like manufacturing, distribution, marketing, and technology. This specialization yielded substantial benefits, but over time, also led to enormous inefficiencies, and slow response processes. The information age organization operates with integrated business processes that cut across traditional business functions.
>
> **Links to Customers and Suppliers.** Industrial age companies worked with customers and suppliers via arm's-length transactions. Information technology enables today's organizations to integrate supply, production, and delivery processes and to realize enormous improvements in cost, quality, and response time.

Growing Up with The Gap

Highlight 11.1

Gap, Inc. is growing up in the information age. The retail company got its start in 1969 when Don and Doris Fisher opened the first Gap store in San Francisco. The Fishers' goal was to appeal to young consumers and bridge "the generation gap" they saw in most retail stores. Their first store sold jeans only and targeted customers mainly in their 20s. As Gap customers have grown up so has the brand. In 1983 The Gap acquired Banana Republic mainly for its thriving catalog business and evolved the company from its original travel theme to an upscale alternative to the more casual Gap stores. In 1990 Baby Gap was born, appealing to young parents looking for stylish alternatives for their children. In 1994 Old Navy stores were introduced as the Gap looked for ways to appeal to value-oriented shoppers. Recently, The Gap has announced plans to test a specialty women's retail apparel brand in the United States in the second half of 2005, opening up to 10 stores in two geographic regions. The brand will target women over age 35, offering apparel for a range of occasions in a new specialty retail store environment. From young adult, to career professional, to parent, to cost-conscious family, to aging baby boomer, The Gap has stuck close to its customers and evolved to offer products that would appeal to their changing needs.

Sources: http://www.sfgate.com/cgi-bin/article.cgi?file=/c/a/2004/08/20/BUG8288V9244.DTL&type=printable; http://www.gapinc.com/financmedia/press_releases.htm; http://www.gapinc.com/about/ataglance/milestones.htm.

Customer Segmentation. Industrial age companies prospered by offering low-cost but standardized products and services (remember Henry Ford's comment that his customers "can have whatever color they want as long as it is black." Information age companies must learn to offer customized products and services to diverse customer segments.

Global Scale. Information age companies compete against the best companies throughout the entire world. In fact, the large investments required for new products and services may require customers worldwide to provide adequate returns on those costs.

Innovation. Product life cycles continue to shrink. Competitive advantage in one generation of a product's life is no guarantee of success for future generations of that product. Companies operating in an environment of rapid technological innovation must be masters at anticipating customers' future needs, innovating new products and services, and rapidly deploying new technologies into efficient delivery processes.

Knowledge Workers. Industrial companies created sharp distinctions between an intellectual elite on the one hand (especially managers and engineers), and a direct labor workforce on the other. The latter group performed tasks and processes under direct supervision of white-collar engineers and managers. This typically involved physical rather than mental capabilities. Now, all employees must contribute value by what they know and by the information they can provide.

One needs only to reflect upon Kaplan and Norton's list of changing operating assumptions to recognize that the situation leaders find themselves in today is different from the situation of 20 years ago. What's more, it is probably changing at an ever increasing rate. In a very real sense, the pace of change today is like trying to navigate white-water rapids; things are changing so rapidly it can be difficult to get one's bearings. Therefore, we believe it is helpful to use a model that identifies some of the key elements of the situation in an organizational setting.

The Congruence Model

Like Ginnett's Team Effectiveness Leadership Model (TELM) described in the previous chapter, the Congruence Model, presented most recently by Nadler and Tushman (1997), is a systems model with *inputs, processes,* and *outputs.* We will focus on the four factors making up the organizational processes in this chapter, but we should briefly discuss the inputs and outputs first. As can be seen in Figure 11.2, there are three components under inputs: the environment, the resources, and the history. Attention to these components must be kept to a minimum here, but their importance in impacting leaders and followers is nonetheless significant. We already have noted the magnitude of changes resulting from the shift in environment from the industrial age to the information age. Beyond that, *environment* also includes market changes, governmental regulations and laws, competitors, financial institutions, and even changes in weather patterns (consider the impact of *El Niño* in 1998 or the drought in the western United States since 2002). We will return to examine some further ways to specify environmental factors later in the chapter. *Resources* are anything which the organization can use to its benefit, and may include not only material components such as capital or information, but also less tangible components such as perceptions of quality (e.g., Nikkon cameras or Mercedes automobiles). *History of the organization* includes not only the recent past that bears upon today's work but also myths about the organization's origin. For example, when taking important visitors on tours of the facilities at a large manufacturing plant, the guides would always stop and point out a series of visitor parking spots located near the executive wing of the building. The guides explained that the first plant manager and his team had decided to do away with executive parking slots by consensus, and that "consensus decision making was still the way everyone worked here"—25 years later.

Outputs are evaluated by the impact on the system as a whole, the unit, and the individual (again, very much like the TELM). At each of these levels, it is appropriate to ask how well the organization met its objectives, how efficient it was at achieving those outcomes, and how well the organization has scanned the horizon

FIGURE 11.2

A congruence model.

Source: *Competing by Design: The Power of Organizational Architecture,* by David Nadler and Michael Tushman. Copyright © 1997 Oxford University Press. Used by permission of Oxford University Press, Inc.

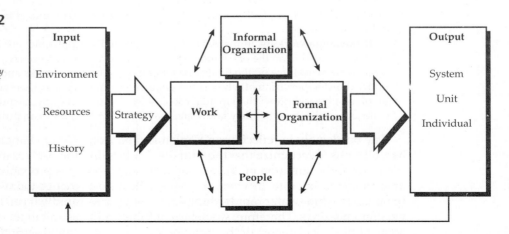

for new opportunities and threats. Before moving to the core process variables of the situation in this model, it is necessary to note that strategy is the collective set of business decisions about how to allocate scarce resources to maximize the strengths of the organization, given the external opportunities, while minimizing the organizational weaknesses, given the external threats.

The core of the Congruence Model has four components: the work, the people, the formal organization, and the informal organization. Note that each component relates to the other three. This is a key component of this model and is the basis of its name. Based upon a tenet of systems theory, the components of the model attempt to stay in balance or homeostasis. The better the fit of all the components, the more "congruence" there is between its various elements. Just one implication of this idea is that if a leader wanted to make changes in the outputs of his or her team, the model suggests it would be better to make small but equal changes in all the subsystems than it would be to make a substantial change in only one component. If only one element is changed, the other major components in the model, in trying to achieve homeostasis, would tend to resist and react to pull the "out-of-balance" element back in line.

The Work

At the most fundamental level, the work is "what is to be done" by the organization and its component parts. Given the variety of tasks people perform, it is natural for people to try to order and make sense of them. In thinking back across the many different tasks you have performed, you might categorize them as boring, challenging, dangerous, fun, interesting, and so on. However, labeling tasks is just a reaction to them and does not foster understanding about what aspects of any task may have caused a particular reaction. In looking at tasks, therefore, we want to get beyond subjective reactions to more objective ways of analyzing them.

> *The brain is a wonderful organ; it begins working the moment you get up in the morning and does not stop until you get to the office.*
>
> Robert Frost

There are several objective ways to categorize tasks performed by leaders and followers. Tasks can be categorized according to their function, the skills or abilities needed to perform them, the equipment needed to perform them, and so on. As seen in an earlier chapter, tasks also can be described in terms of the characteristics of the job itself: skill variety, task identity, task significance, autonomy, and feedback from the job. We will add to those characteristics two other dimensions: task structure and task interdependence.

Job Characteristics

Skill variety and the next four dimensions of tasks are all components of the job characteristics model (Hackman & Oldham, 1976, 1980) described in Chapter 9. Skill variety refers to the degree to which a job involves performing a variety of different activities or skills. For example, if an individual attaches the left taillight to a car on an automobile assembly line by mechanically screwing in the fasteners, there would be increased work but no increased skill variety if he subsequently stepped over the line to the other side to install the right taillight. Skill variety involves using different skills, whether mechanical, cognitive, or physical. We might also add that there is a qualitative dimension to skill variety. In general, jobs requiring greater skill variety are more enjoyable than those requiring lesser skill variety, but it also matters whether any particular individual personally values the skills she performs.

Although satisfaction may also depend on growth-need strength (the individual's psychological need for personal accomplishment, for learning, and for personal development), typically jobs that require a low variety of skills are repetitive, monotonous, boring, and dissatisfying (Bass, 1990; Hackman & Oldham, 1980; House & Dressler, 1974). And like structured tasks, tasks with low levels of skill variety make it easier for leaders to use directive behaviors but, because followers already know how to do the job, also make directive leadership behavior somewhat redundant (Howell & Dorfman, 1981, 1986; Kerr & Jermier, 1978; Kipnis, 1984). In such situations, leaders might try to restructure a subordinate's job in order to increase the number of (valued) skills needed. If that is not possible, then high levels of support and consideration for followers are helpful (Hackman & Oldham, 1980; House & Dressler, 1974).

Task identity refers to the degree to which a situation or task requires completion of a whole unit of work from beginning to end with a visible outcome. For example, if one works on an assembly line where circuit boards for compact disc (CD) players are being produced, and the task is to solder one wire to one electronic component and then pass the circuit board on to the next assembly worker, then this job would lack task identity. At the other extreme, if one assembled an entire CD player, perhaps involving 30 or 40 different tasks, then the perception of task identity would increase dramatically as one could readily see the final results of one's efforts. Furthermore, the job's skill variety (as discussed above) would increase as well.

Task significance is the degree to which a job substantially impacts others' lives. Consider an individual whose task is to insert a bolt into a nut and tighten it down to a certain specification using a torque wrench. If that bolt is one of several that fasten a fender to other parts of an automobile body on an assembly line, then both skill variety and task identity would probably be very low. Moreover, if the assembly person leaves the entire bolt off, it may cause a squeak or a rattle, but probably would not cause the fender to fall off. In such a job, task significance would be quite low as well. However, if the worker tightens the only bolt securing a critical component of a brake assembly on the space shuttle, then skill variety and task identity would be exactly the same as for our fender installer. However, task significance would be substantially higher.

Autonomy is the degree to which a job provides an individual with some control over what he does and how he does it. Someone with considerable autonomy would have discretion in scheduling work and deciding the procedures used in accomplishing it. Autonomy often covaries with technical expertise, as workers with considerable expertise will be given more latitude, and those with few skills will be given more instruction and coaching when accomplishing tasks (Hersey &

Blanchard, 1977, 1984). Moreover, responsibility and job satisfaction often increase when autonomy increases (Hackman & Oldham, 1980).

The last task component in the job characteristics model is **feedback,** which refers to the degree to which a person accomplishing a task receives information about performance *from performing the task itself.* In this context feedback does not refer to feedback received from supervisors but rather to what is intrinsic to the work activity itself. Driving a car is one example of feedback intrinsic to a task. If you are a skilled driver on a road with a number of twists and turns, then you get all the feedback you need about how well you are accomplishing the task merely by observing how the car responds to the inputs you make. This is feedback from the job itself as opposed to feedback from another person

> *If you want to give a man credit, put it in writing. If you want to give him hell, do it on the phone.*
>
> Charles Beacham

(who in this example would be a classic backseat driver). Extending this example to work or team settings, leaders sometimes may want to redesign tasks so that they (the tasks) provide more intrinsic feedback. Although this does not absolve the leader from giving periodic feedback about performance, it can help to free up some of the leader's time for other work-related activities. Additionally, leaders should understand that followers may eventually become dissatisfied if leaders provide high levels of feedback for tasks that already provide intrinsic feedback (House & Dressler, 1974; Howell & Dorfman, 1981; Kerr & Jermier, 1978).

Task Structure

Perhaps the easiest way to explain **task structure** is by using an example demonstrating the difference between a structured and an unstructured task. Assume the task to be accomplished is solving for x given the formula $3x + 2x = 15$. If that problem were given to a group of people who knew the fundamental rules of algebra, then everyone would arrive at the same answer. In this example there is a known procedure for accomplishing the task; there are rules governing how one goes about it; and if people follow those rules, there is one result. These features characterize a *structured task.*

On the other hand, if the task is to resolve a morale problem on a team, committee, or work group, then there may be no clear-cut method for solving it. There are many different ways, perhaps none of which is obvious or necessarily best for approaching a solution. It may even be that different observers would not see the problem in the same way; they may even have quite different ideas of *what morale is.* Solving a morale problem, therefore, exemplifies an *unstructured task.*

People vary in their preferences for, or ability to handle, structured versus unstructured tasks. With the Myers-Briggs Type Indicator (MBTI), for example, perceivers are believed to prefer unstructured situations, whereas judgers prefer activities that are planned and organized (Myers & McCaulley, 1985). Individuals with high tolerance for stress may handle ambiguous and unstructured tasks more easily than people with low tolerance for stress (Bass, 1990). Aside from these differences, however, we might ask whether there are any general rules for how leaders should interact with followers as a function of task structure. One consideration here is that while it is *easier* for a leader or coach to give instruction in structured tasks, it is not necessarily the most helpful thing to do.

We can see that by returning to the algebra problem described earlier. If a student had never seen such an algebra problem before, then it would be relatively easy for the teacher to teach the student the rules needed to solve the problem. Once any student has learned the procedure, however, he can solve similar problems on his own. Extending this to other situations, once a subordinate knows or understands a task, a supervisor's continuing instruction (i.e., initiating structure or directive behavior) may provide superfluous information and eventually become irritating (Ford, 1981; House & Dressler, 1974; Kerr & Jermier, 1978; Yukl, 1989). Subordinates *need* help when a task is unstructured, when they do not know what the desired outcome looks like, and when they do not know how to achieve it. Anything a supervisor or leader can do to increase subordinates' ability to perform unstructured tasks is likely to increase their performance and job satisfaction (Siegall & Cummings, 1986). Paradoxically, though, unstructured tasks are by nature somewhat ill defined. Thus, they often are more difficult for leaders themselves to analyze and provide direction in accomplishing. Nonetheless, reducing the degree of ambiguity inherent in an unstructured situation is a leadership behavior usually appreciated by followers.

Task Interdependence

Task interdependence concerns the degree to which tasks require coordination and synchronization in order for work groups or teams to accomplish desired goals. Task interdependence differs from autonomy in that workers or team members may be able to accomplish their tasks in an autonomous fashion, but the products of their efforts must be coordinated in order for the group or team to be successful. Tasks with high levels of interdependence place a premium on leaders' organizing and planning, directing, and communication skills (Curphy, 1991a, 1992; Galbraith, 1973). In one study, for example, coaches exhibiting high levels of initiating-structure behaviors had better-performing teams for sports requiring relatively interdependent effort, such as football, hockey, lacrosse, rugby, basketball, and volleyball; the same leader behaviors were unrelated to team performance for sports requiring relatively independent effort, such as swimming, track, cross-country, golf, and baseball (Fry, Kerr, & Lee, 1986). Like task structure and skill variety, task interdependence can also dictate which leader behaviors will be effective in a particular situation.

In summary, these seven task dimensions provide a variety of ways in which to categorize or describe tasks. For example, ironing a shirt would probably have high task structure, autonomy, task identification, and feedback, and low skill variety, task significance, and task interdependence. On the other hand, building your own home may garner high ratings on all seven dimensions. Still another familiar activity is evaluated on these dimensions in Highlight 11.2. These seven dimensions can provide leaders with insight about how their behavior and work assignments may either help or hinder followers' satisfaction and performance. At the same time, leaders should remember that these dimensions exist somewhat in

Golf and the Task Factors of the Situation

Highlight 11.2

Golf provides a convenient skill for illustrating the seven task factors described in this chapter. Golf provides a reasonable amount of *task structure,* as there are basic rules and procedures for properly hitting woods, long irons, and short irons, and for putting.

Skill variety comes into play because golfers use a variety of skills and talents. These include deciding on a club, the method used to swing the club, how hard to swing it, what kind of equipment to use, where to target the ball, how to compensate for wind, when to putt, and so on.

Because one person does all of the driving, pitching, and putting and is solely responsible for his or her score, a round of golf has a high level of *task identity.*

Task significance may be a little more difficult to appreciate in this example. It may not be there at all unless one is a particularly poor golfer (where he or she endangers the lives of other people) or, in the case of the professional golfer, has a family who depends on his or her performance.

Autonomy is certainly present when playing golf. The golfer gets to decide when to do the "work," how to do it, which clubs to use, and what strategies and tactics to use.

Feedback from the job is also apparent. Shortly after a golfer strikes the ball, she receives feedback on how well her swing worked. Whether it slices, hooks, or goes straight down the fairway is a bit of information that tells the golfer immediately how well her work is being accomplished.

Finally, golf generally lacks *task interdependence.* Golfers are not dependent on the other members in their foursome for their own score.

the eye of the beholder. What one follower perceives as an unstructured task might be seen by another as fairly structured. Finally, as we have emphasized before, leaders should use their communication and listening skills to assure that they understand subordinates' feelings and beliefs about the work they perform.

The People

We can afford to be very brief here since much of the rest of the book has focused on this topic. Still, it is worth repeating that leaders should look at the followers in terms of skills, knowledge, experience, expectations, needs, and preferences. In an increasingly global society, leaders can no longer afford to be parochial in their selection of followers. Compounding the global nature of work is, as noted earlier, the increasing rate of change in the environment. In a stable environment, any species can select a niche and survive for eons. But in a rapidly changing environment, diversity allows the species to sense and adapt more quickly. The same is true in the leadership world as well. Diversity is no longer merely the politically correct facade of leadership—it is essential to quality and survival in a rapidly changing world.

The Formal Organization

As with tasks, there also are a variety of dimensions for conceptualizing the organizational level of situations. This section will address how level of authority, organizational structure, organizational design, lateral interdependence, and organizational culture affect leaders' and followers' behavior.

A man may speak very well in the House of Commons, and fail very complete in the House of Lords. There are two distinct styles requisite.

Benjamin Disraeli

Level of Authority

Level of authority concerns one's hierarchical level in an organization. The types of behaviors most critical to leadership effectiveness can change substantially as one moves up an organizational ladder. First-line supervisors, lower-level leaders, and coaches spend a considerable amount of time training followers, resolving work-unit or team-performance problems, scheduling practices or arranging work schedules, and implementing policies. Leaders at higher organizational levels have more autonomy and spend relatively more time setting policies, coordinating activities, and making staffing decisions (Blankenship & Miles, 1968; Luthans, Rosenkrantz, & Hennessey, 1985; Mintzberg, 1973; Page & Tornow, 1987). Moreover, leaders at higher organizational levels often perform a greater variety of activities and are more apt to use participation and delegation (Chitayat & Venezia, 1984; Kurke & Aldrich, 1983). A quite different aspect of how level of authority affects leadership is presented in Highlight 11.3.

The Glass Ceiling and the Wall

Highlight 11.3

While the past 15 years have been marked by increasing movement of women into leadership positions, women still occupy only a tiny percentage of the highest leadership positions. In Fortune 500 companies, for example, less than 5 percent of the corporate officers are women. Researchers at the Center for Creative Leadership embarked on the Executive Woman Project to understand why (Morrison, White, & Van Velsor, 1987).

They studied 76 women executives in 25 companies who had reached the general-management level or the one just below it. The average woman executive in the sample was 41 and married. More than half had at least one child, and the vast majority were white.

The researchers expected to find evidence of a "glass ceiling," an invisible barrier that keeps women from progressing higher than a certain level in their organizations *because they are women.* One reason the women in this particular sample were interesting was precisely because they had apparently "broken" the glass ceiling, thus entering the top 1 percent of the workforce. These women had successfully confronted three different sorts of pressure throughout their careers, a greater challenge than their male counterparts faced. One pressure was that from the job itself, and this was no different for women than for men. A second level of pressure, however, involved being a female executive, with attendant stresses such as being particularly visible, excessively scrutinized, and a role model for other women. A third level of pressure involved the demands of coordinating personal and professional life. It is still most people's expectation that women will take the greater responsibility in a family for managing the household and raising children. And beyond the sheer size of such demands, the roles of women in these two spheres of life are often at odds (e.g., being businesslike and efficient, maybe even tough, at work yet intimate and nurturing at home).

The Center for Creative Leadership researchers described the "lessons for success" of this group of women who had broken through the glass ceiling. They also reported, however, a somewhat unexpected finding. Breaking through the glass ceiling presented women executives with an even tougher obstacle. They "hit a wall" that kept them out of the very top positions. The researchers estimated that only a handful of the women executives in their sample would enter the topmost echelon, called senior management, and that none would become president of their corporation.

Organizational Structure

Organizational structure refers to the way an organization's activities are coordinated and controlled, and represents another level of the situation in which leaders and followers must operate. Organizational structure is a conceptual or procedural reality, however, not a physical or tangible one. Typically, it is depicted in the form of a chart that clarifies formal authority relationships and patterns of communication within the organization. Most people take organizational structure for granted and fail to realize that structure is really just a tool for getting things done in organizations. Structure is not an end in itself, and different structures might exist for organizations performing similar work, each having unique advantages and disadvantages. There is nothing sacrosanct or permanent about any structure, and leaders may find that having a basic understanding of organizational structure is not only useful but imperative. Leaders may wish to design a structure to enhance the likelihood of attaining a desired outcome, or they may wish to change structure to meet future demands. There are a number of ways to describe organizational structures, but perhaps the simplest way is to think of structure in terms of complexity, formalization, and centralization.

Complexity   Horizontal, vertical, and spatial elements make up organizational complexity. Concerning an organizational chart, **horizontal complexity** refers to the number of "boxes" at any particular organizational level. The greater the number of boxes at a given level, the greater the horizontal complexity. Typically, greater horizontal complexity is associated with more specialization within subunits and an increased likelihood for communication breakdowns between subunits. **Vertical complexity** refers to the number of hierarchical levels appearing on an organization chart. A vertically simple organization may have only two or three levels from the highest person to the lowest. A vertically complex organization, on the other hand, may have 10 or more. Vertical complexity can affect leadership by impacting other factors such as authority dynamics and communication networks. **Spatial complexity** describes geographical dispersion. An organization that has all of its people in one location is typically less spatially complex than an organization that is dispersed around the country or around the world. Obviously, spatial complexity makes it more difficult for leaders to have face-to-face communication with subordinates in geographically separated locations, and to personally administer rewards or provide support and encouragement. Generally, all three of these elements are partly a function of organizational size. Bigger organizations are more likely to have more specialized subunits (horizontal complexity) and a greater number of hierarchical levels (vertical complexity), and to have subunits that are geographically dispersed (spatial complexity).

Formalization   **Formalization** describes the degree of standardization in an organization. Organizations having written job descriptions and standardized operating procedures for each position have a high degree of formalization. The degree of formalization in an organization tends to vary with its size, just as complexity generally increases with size (Robbins, 1986). Formalization also varies with the nature of work performed. Manufacturing organizations, for example, tend to have fairly formalized structures, whereas research-and-development organizations tend to be less formalized. After all, how could there be a detailed job description for developing a nonexistent product or making a scientific discovery?

The degree of formalization in an organization poses both advantages and disadvantages for leaders and followers. Whereas formalizing procedures clarifies methods of operating and interacting, it also may constitute demands and constraints on leaders and followers. Leaders may be constrained in the ways they communicate requests, order supplies, or reward or discipline subordinates (Hammer & Turk, 1987; Podsaskoff, 1982). If followers belong to a union, then union rules may dictate work hours, the amount of work accomplished per day, or who will be the first to be laid off (Hammer & Turk, 1987). Other aspects of the impact of formalization and other situational variables on leadership are presented in Highlight 11.4.

Centralization   **Centralization** refers to the diffusion of decision making throughout an organization. An organization that allows decisions to be made by only one person is highly centralized. When decision making is dispersed to the lowest levels in the organization, the organization is very decentralized. Advantages of decentralized organizations include increased participation in the decision process and, consequently, greater acceptance and ownership of decision outcomes. These are both desirable outcomes. There are also, however, advantages to centralization, such as uniform policies and procedures (which can increase feel-

Are There Substitutes for Leadership?

Highlight 11.4

Are leaders always necessary? Or are certain kinds of leader behaviors, at least, sometimes unnecessary? Kerr and Jermier (1978) proposed that certain situational or follower characteristics may well effectively neutralize or substitute for leaders' task or relationship behaviors. *Neutralizers* are characteristics that reduce or limit the effectiveness of a leader's behaviors. *Substitutes* are characteristics that make a leader's behaviors redundant or unnecessary.

Kerr and Jermier (1978) developed the idea of **substitutes for leadership** after comparing the correlations between leadership behaviors and follower performance and satisfaction with correlations between various situational factors and follower performance and satisfaction. Those subordinate, task, and organizational characteristics having higher correlations with follower performance and satisfaction than the two leadership behaviors were subsequently identified as substitutes or neutralizers. The following are a few examples of the situational factors Kerr and

Jermier found to substitute for or neutralize leaders' task or relationship behaviors:

- A subordinate's ability and experience may well substitute for task-oriented leader behavior. A subordinate's indifference toward rewards overall may neutralize a leader's task and relationship behavior.

- Tasks that are routine or structured may substitute for task-oriented leader behavior, as can tasks that provide intrinsic feedback or are intrinsically satisfying.

- High levels of formalization in organizations may substitute for task-oriented leader behavior, and unbending rules and procedures may even neutralize the leader's task behavior. A cohesive work group may provide a substitute for the leader's task and relationship behavior.

Source: S. Kerr and J. M. Jermier, "Substitutes for Leadership: Their Meaning and Measurement," *Organizational Behavior and Human Performance* 22 (1978), pp. 375–403.

ings of equity), and clearer coordination procedures (Bass, 1990). The task of balancing the degree of centralization necessary to achieve coordination and control, on the one hand, and gaining desirable participation and acceptance, on the other, is an ongoing challenge for the leader.

Organizational Design

In addition to being classified by their degree of complexity, formalization, and centralization, organizations can also be classified into several different kinds of organizational design. Organizational design can be thought of most easily in the following two questions: (1) How do I want to divide up the work? (2) How do I want the divisions to coordinate their work? Three of the most common kinds of **organizational designs** in the traditional (or industrial age) format include functional, product, and matrix organizations.

Functional Some organizations have their structures designed around certain important and continuing functions. For example, a manufacturing company with a **functional design** might have its organizational chart include one block for manufacturing, one for sales or marketing, one for research and development, and so on (see Figure 11.3). Advantages of functional organizations include efficient use of scarce resources, skill development for technical personnel, centralized decision making and control, and excellent coordination within each functional department. Disadvantages of functional organizations can include poor coordination across departments, slow responses to change, a piling up of decisions at the top of the hierarchy, and narrow or limited views by employees of overall organizational goals

FIGURE 11.3 A manufacturing company with a functional design.

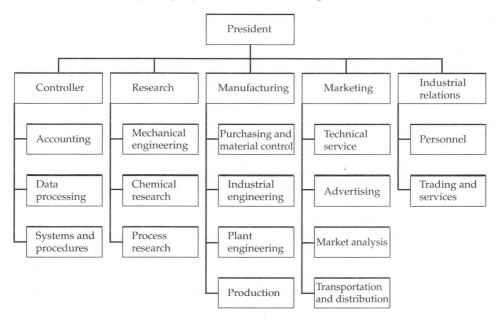

(Austin, Conlon, & Daft, 1986). In other words, in organizations structured functionally the very commonality within the various functional units can create problems. Functional groups can become so cohesive that they create rigid boundaries and dysfunctional competitiveness between themselves and other groups within the same organization.

Product In an organization with a **product design,** the blocks on the organization chart define the various products or services that are delivered ultimately to the consumer. One might consider an automobile organization such as General Motors, where there are the Buick, Chevrolet, Cadillac, Saturn, and Pontiac divisions. These are identifiable products, and employees are assigned to these product groupings. A different product design is represented in Figure 11.4. A product organization design overcomes some of the problems associated with functional organizations, as a product organization has better coordination across functional skills, places a premium on organizational goals rather than functional goals, and has better control over diverse products or services. The disadvantages of product organizations include duplication of resources, less in-depth technical expertise, and weak coordination across different product groupings.

Matrix The **matrix design** is a combination of the product and functional designs. In this design, both product orientation and functional specialties are maintained (see Figure 11.5). In a matrix organization, there is a product manager for each product and one of his or her tasks is to obtain the resources necessary from the functional specialties as requirements demand. If the product will require the services of a computer software engineer, for example, then the product manager must acquire those services from the manager of the engineering function.

FIGURE 11.4 A petroleum company with a product design.

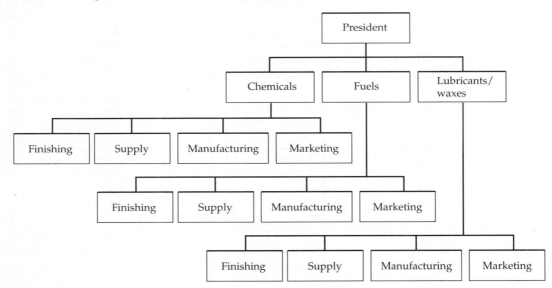

FIGURE 11.5   A manufacturing company with a matrix design.

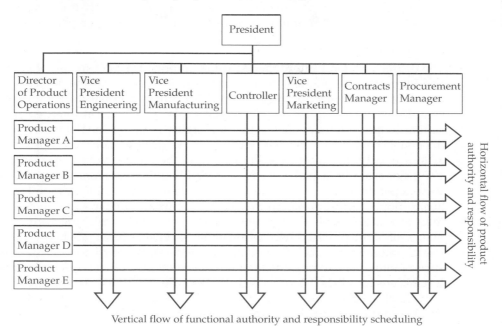

The greatest advantage of the matrix is efficient utilization of human resources. Imagine putting together a team to design a new product, and further suppose that a chemical engineer's services are among the team's needs. Also imagine, however, that the chemical engineer is required for only one month's work whereas the total product design phase encompasses a whole year. If our imaginary organization were designed according to a product orientation, the product manager would have to hire a full-time chemical engineer despite needing his or her services for only one month. In a matrix organization, on the other hand, the chemical engineer could be assigned to the engineering division, and the various product managers could arrange to acquire the engineer's time on an as-needed basis. Such an arrangement can create scheduling nightmares, but it also results in more efficient utilization of unusual or scarce resources. Another advantage of the matrix design includes increased lateral communication and coordination.

The greatest disadvantage of the matrix design is that employees end up working for two bosses. Such a dual-authority structure can create confusion and frustration. In the case above, the chemical engineer may have "professional loyalty" to the engineering group (which would dictate the highest-quality engineering possible) and "profitability loyalty" to the product group (which would dictate the most cost-effective engineering). Our chemical engineer might very well experience conflict over which loyalty to serve first. Additionally, matrix designs can lead to conflict and disagreements over the use of shared resources, and time is lost through frequent meetings to resolve such issues. Thus, administrative costs are high in matrix organizations. Finally, matrix designs can work well only if managers see the big picture and do not adopt narrow functional or product perspectives.

Lateral Interdependence

The degree of **lateral interdependence** in an organization can also affect leaders' and followers' behaviors. Lateral interdependence concerns the degree of coordination or synchronization required between organizational units in order to accomplish work-group or organizational goals. Thus, lateral interdependence is similar to task interdependence but at a higher organizational level; lateral interdependence represents the degree to which a leader's work group is affected by the actions or activities of other subunits within the organization (Bass, 1990; Sayles, 1979). For example, a leader of a final assembly unit for personal computers will be very dependent on the activities of the power supply, cabinet, monitor, mother board, floppy drive, and hard drive manufacturing units in order to successfully meet production goals. On the other hand, the leader of a manufacturing unit that makes all of the products used to assemble backpacks has a much lower degree of lateral interdependence. As lateral interdependence increases, leaders usually spend more time building and maintaining contacts in other work units or on public relations activities (Hammer & Turk, 1987; Kaplan, 1986). Moreover, leaders are more likely to use rational persuasion as an influence tactic when the level of lateral interdependence is high (Kanter, 1982; Kaplan, 1986).

The Informal Organization

One word which sums up the informal organization better than any other is its culture. Although most people probably think of culture in terms of very large social groups, the concept also applies to organizations. **Organizational culture** has been defined as a system of shared backgrounds, norms, values, or beliefs among members of a group (Schein, 1985), and **organizational climate** concerns members' subjective reactions about the organization (Bass, 1990; Kozlowski & Doherty, 1989). These two concepts are distinct in that organizational climate is partly a function of, or reaction to, organizational culture; one's feelings or emotional reactions about an organization are probably affected by the degree to which a person shares the prevailing values, beliefs, and backgrounds of organizational members (Schneider, 1983). If a person does not share the values or beliefs of the majority of members, then in all likelihood this person would have a fairly negative reaction about the organization overall. Thus, organizational climate (and indirectly organizational culture) is related to how well organizational members get along with each other (Bass, 1990; Kozlowski & Doherty, 1989). It is also important to note that organizational climate is narrower in scope but highly related to job satisfaction. Generally, organizational climate has more to do with nontask perceptions of work, such as feelings about co-workers or company policies, whereas job satisfaction usually also includes perceptions of workload and the nature of the tasks performed.

Just as there are many cultures across the world, there are a great number of different cultures across organizations. Members of many military organizations have different norms, background experiences, values, and beliefs, for example, from those of the faculty at many colleges. Similarly, the culture of an investment firm is very different from the culture of a research-and-development firm, a freight hauling company, or a college rugby team. Cultural differences can even exist between different organizations within any of these sectors. The culture of the U.S. Air Force is different from the culture of the U.S. Marine Corps, and Yale University has a different culture than the University of Colorado even though they are both fine institutions of higher learning.

One of the more fascinating aspects of organizational culture is that it often takes an outsider to recognize it; organizational culture becomes so second nature to many organizational members that they are unaware of how it affects their behaviors and perceptions (Bass, 1990). Despite this transparency to organizational members, a fairly consistent set of dimensions can be used to differentiate between organizational cultures. For example, Kilmann and Saxton (1983) stated that organizational cultures can be differentiated based on members' responses to questions like those found in Table 11.1. Another way to understand an organization's culture is in terms of myths and stories, symbols, rituals, and language (Schein, 1985). A more detailed description of the four key factors identified by Schein can be found in Highlight 11.5.

Here is an example of how stories contribute to organizational culture. A consultant was asked to help a plant that had been having morale and production problems for years. After talking with several individuals at the plant, the consultant believed he had located the problem. It seems everyone he talked to told him about Sam, the plant manager. He was a giant of a man with a terrible temper. He had demolished unacceptable products with a sledgehammer, stood on the plant roof screaming at workers, and done countless other things sure to intimidate everyone around. The consultant decided he needed to talk to this plant manager. When he did so, however, he met a very agreeable person named Paul. Sam, it seems, had been dead for nearly a decade, but his legacy lived on (Dumaine, 1990).

It is important for leaders to realize that they can play an active role in changing an organization's culture, not just be influenced by it (Bass, 1985; Kouzes & Posner, 1987; Schein, 1985; Tichy & Devanna, 1986). Leaders can change culture by attending to or ignoring particular issues, problems, or projects. They can modify culture

TABLE 11.1 Some Questions That Define Organizational Culture	• What can be talked about or not talked about? • How do people wield power? • How does one get ahead or stay out of trouble? • What are the unwritten rules of the game? • What are the organization's morality and ethics? • What stories are told about the organization?

Source: Adapted from R. H. Kilmann and M. J. Saxton, *Organizational Cultures: Their Assessment and Change* (San Francisco: Jossey-Bass, 1983).

Schein's Four Key Organizational Culture Factors

Highlight 11.5

Myths and stories are the tales about the organization that are passed down over time and communicate a story of the organization's underlying values. Virtually any employee of Wal-Mart can tell you stories about Sam Walton and his behavior—how he rode around in his pickup truck, how he greeted people in the stores, and how he tended to "just show up" at different times. The Center for Creative Leadership has stories about its founder, H. Smith Richardson, who as a young man creatively used the mail to sell products. Sometimes stories and myths are transferred between organizations even though the truth may not lie wholly in either one. A story is told in AT&T about one of its founders and how he trudged miles and miles through a blizzard to repair a faulty component so that a woman living by herself in a rural community could get phone service. Interestingly enough, this same story is also told in MCI.

Symbols and artifacts are objects that can be seen and noticed and that describe various aspects of the culture. In almost any building, for example, symbols and artifacts provide information about the organization's culture. For example, an organization may believe in egalitarian principles, and that might be reflected in virtually everyone having the same-size office. Or there can be indications of opulence, which convey a very different message. Even signs might act as symbols or artifacts of underlying cultural values. At one university that believed students should have first priority for facilities, an interesting sign showed up occasionally to reinforce this value. It was not a road sign, but a sign appearing on computer monitors. When the university's main computer was being overused, the computer was programmed to identify nonstudent users, note the overload, and issue a warning to nonstudent users to sign off. This was a clear artifact, or symbol, underlying the priority placed on students at that school.

Rituals are recurring events or activities that reflect important aspects of the underlying culture. An organization may have spectacular sales meetings for its top performers and spouses every two years. This ritual would be an indication of the value placed on high sales and meeting high quotas. Another kind of ritual is the retirement ceremony. Elaborate or modest retirement ceremonies may signal the importance an organization places on its people.

Language concerns the jargon, or idiosyncratic terms, of an organization and can serve several different purposes relevant to culture. First, the mere fact that some know the language and some do not indicates who is in the culture and who is not. Second, language can also provide information about how people within a culture view others. Third, language can be used to help create a culture. A good example of the power of language in creating culture is in the words employees at Disneyland or Walt Disney World use in referring to themselves and park visitors. Employees—all employees, from the costumed Disney characters to popcorn vendors—are told to think of themselves as members of a cast, and never to be out of character. Everything happening at the park is part of the "show," and those who paid admission to enter the park are not mere tourists, but rather "the audience." Virtually everyone who visits the Disney parks is impressed with the consistently friendly behavior of its staff, a reflection of the power of words in creating culture. (Of course, a strict and strongly enforced policy concerning courtesy toward park guests also helps.)

through their reactions to crises, by rewarding new or different kinds of behavior, or by eliminating previous punishments or negative consequences for certain behaviors. Their general personnel policies send messages about the value of employees to the organization (e.g., cutting wages to avoid layoffs). They can use role modeling and self-sacrifice as a way to inspire or motivate others to work more vigorously or interact with each other differently. Finally, leaders can also change culture by the criteria they use to select or dismiss followers.

John DeLorean and Counterculture at GM

Highlight 11.6

One of the more interesting stories about organizational culture and the actions taken to change a culture concerns John DeLorean (Martin & Siehl, 1983). DeLorean was a senior executive at GM, an institution with a well-established culture. One of GM's key cultural values was showing deference and respect to authority. For example, subordinates were expected to meet out-of-town superiors at the airport, carry their bags, pay their hotel and meal bills, and chauffeur them around day and night. Additionally, the more senior the executive, the bigger the traveling party would be. Some employees were so eager to please their boss that a group of Chevrolet sales people had a refrigerator put in the hotel room of a visiting senior executive after they had learned he liked to have a few cold beers and to make a sandwich before going to bed. Unfortunately, the door to the suite was too small to accommodate the refrigerator, so the Chevrolet sales personnel went so far as to hire a crane to bring in and later remove the refrigerator through the windows of the suite. A second core value at GM was communicating invisibility by visible cues. Ideal GM employees dressed identically, had the same office decor and layout, were "team players," and could easily fit in without drawing attention to themselves. The last key cultural value at GM was loyalty to one's boss. Loyalty to one's boss was clearly

evident in the ritual of the retirement dinner, where a loyal subordinate was given the task of providing a detailed account of the retiree's steady rise through the corporation, counterpointed with allusions to the retiree's charming wife and family.

DeLorean took a number of actions to change the dominant culture at GM. First, DeLorean liked independence and dissent, and he modeled the behavior he wished others to emulate. He wore suits that stood out, and when appointed to head the Chevrolet division, he immediately changed the office furniture, carpeting, and decor and allowed executives to decorate their offices any way they wanted to "within reasonable limits." Second, because DeLorean believed that subordinates were more productive doing work than catering to superiors, he traveled by himself and did not greet his superiors at the airport, nor did he have his subordinates pick him up. Third, he changed the performance appraisal system within his division. Subordinates were to be rewarded on the basis of objective performance data, not subjective data that indicated a willingness to fit in. Although for a time DeLorean managed to maintain a delicate balance between culture and counterculture, his dissent was eventually met with disfavor, and he left GM to form a company of his own. Nevertheless, DeLorean's story provides several insights about the pervasiveness of organizational culture and the actions a leader might take to change culture.

Changing an organization's culture, of course, takes time and effort, and sometimes it may be extremely difficult. This is especially true in very large organizations or those with strong cultures (see, for example, Highlight 11.6). New organizations, on the other hand, do not have the traditions, stories or myths, or established rites to the same extent that older companies do, and it may be easier for leaders to change culture in these organizations.

Why would a leader *want* to change an organization's culture? It all should depend on whether the culture is having a positive or a negative impact on various desirable outcomes. We remember one organization with a very "polite" culture, an aspect that seemed very positive at first. There were never any potentially destructive emotional outbursts in the organization, and there was an apparent concern for other individuals' feelings in all interactions. However, a darker side of that culture gradually became apparent. When it was appropriate to give feedback for performance appraisals or employee development, supervisors were hesitant to raise negative aspects of behavior; they interpreted doing so as not being polite. And so the organization continued to be puzzled by employee behavior that tended not to improve; the organization was a victim of its own culture.

Leaders especially need to be sensitive to how their own "brilliant ideas" may adversely impact subtle but important aspects of organizational culture. What may appear to be a major technical innovation (and therefore seemingly desirable) may also be devastating to organizational culture. For example, for hundreds of years in England, coal was mined by teams of three persons each. In England, coal is layered in very narrow seams, most only a few feet high. In the past, the only practical means to get the coal out was to send the three-person teams of miners down into the mines to dig coal from the seam and then haul it to the surface on a tram. These mining teams had extremely high levels of group cohesiveness. A technological development called the long-wall method of coal extraction was to upset these close relationships, however. In the long-wall method, workers were arrayed all along an entire seam of coal rather than in distinct teams, and the method should have resulted in higher productivity among the miners. However, the breakdown of the work teams led to unexpected decreases in productivity, much higher levels of worker dissatisfaction, and even disruption of social life among the miners' families. Although the long-wall method was technically superior to the three-person mining team, the leaders of the coal-mining companies failed to consider the cultural consequences of this technological advancement (Emery & Trist, 1965).

After reading these examples, you may be asking whether it is better for leaders to create cultures that emphasize interpersonal relationships or organizational productivity. We can glean some insights into this question by looking at Mitchell's (1985) study of two groups of successful organizations. Mitchell compared two different groups of organizational cultures: those of organizations considered well managed, and those of organizations considered well liked by people working in the organization. The former group consisted of the 62 organizations identified in *In Search of Excellence* (Peters & Waterman, 1982), and the latter group included firms identified in *The One Hundred Best Companies to Work for in America* (Levering, Moskowitz, & Katz, 1984).

Interestingly, there was relatively little overlap between the two lists. According to Mitchell, this lack of overlap was due primarily to differences between task- and relationship-oriented organizational cultures. Cultures in the well-liked organizations emphasized making employees feel they were part of a family, reducing social distance, and making the organization a pleasant one to work in. Cultures in the well-managed organizations, on the other hand, were much more manipulative. Those firms had cultures that valued people not for themselves but as instruments of productivity. Although which type of culture is best for an organization is still under debate, it is important to note that the 62 companies deemed excellently managed by Peters and Waterman did not provide any higher returns on investments than less well managed firms (Simpson & Ireland, 1987), and many of these 62 companies and cultures look considerably less excellent today.

An Afterthought on Organizational Issues for Students and Young Leaders

Let us conclude this section by adding an afterthought about what relevance organizational issues may have for students or others at the early stages of their careers, or at lower levels of leadership within their organizations. It is unlikely that such individuals will be asked soon to redesign their organization's structure or change its culture. As noted earlier, this chapter is not intended as a how-to manual for changing culture. On the other hand, it has been our experience that younger colleagues sometimes develop biased impressions of leaders or have unrealistic expectations about decision making in organizations, based on their lack of familiarity with, and appreciation for, the sorts of organizational dynamics discussed in this section. In other words, one of the primary reasons for being familiar with such organizational variables is the context they provide for understanding the leadership process at your own level in the organization. Finally, we have worked with some senior leaders of huge organizations who have been with their company for their entire career. They have often been unable to identify *any* of the dimensions of their culture because they have never seen anything else. In these cases we were amazed by how junior managers were far better at describing the culture of the large organization. While these junior people may have had only five to eight years of total work experience, if that experience had been obtained in several different organizations, they were much better prepared to describe the characteristics of their new large organization's culture than were the senior executives.

Environmental Characteristics

We mentioned the environment earlier in the chapter as an input variable in the Congruence Model. We now return to a slightly more in-depth analysis of environmental characteristics since not attending to environmental characteristics is the root of extinction, both for the organization and for the population at large. Environmental characteristics concern situational factors outside the task or organization that still affect the leadership process. These include technological, economic, political, social, and legal forces. For example, imagine how changing economic conditions, such as threats of layoffs from a recession, a hostile takeover, or global "off-shoring" would affect leaders' and followers' behavior. These factors often create anxiety, and therefore cause an increase in employees' security needs. They also tend to result in decreased training budgets for workers (Bass, 1990). Recent changes in the valuation of high-technology and telecommunication stocks cannot be ignored. Political changes also can have substantial impacts on leaders and followers. Just imagine, for example, how leaders' and followers' behaviors are changing in Eastern Europe as the various countries move from communist systems to private ownership of companies even though the changes have not gone smoothly or uniformly. Legal forces affecting Western organizations include those contributing to the growth of new industries (e.g., industrial waste disposal) or to personnel reductions in other industries due to changes in governmental

Workplace Trends

Highlight 11.7

1. *Employment Market Turbulence.* More secure employees will stimulate unprecedented churning in the labor marketplace. This turbulence will threaten corporate stability and capacity to serve customers, particularly for employers who took employees for granted in recent years.

2. *Shift to Sellers' Market in Labor.* Employers will face the most severe shortage of skilled labor in history. Corporations will become more aggressive to attract and hold top talent. People will change jobs to find their personal Employer of Choice®.

3. *Fluid International Job Movement.* Economic issues and skilled labor shortages in the United States will move even more jobs to other countries. However, employers will discover that some situations are unsatisfactory and jobs will be returned.

4. *Retirement Will Evaporate.* Traditional retirement will continue its metamorphosis. Retirees will move into jobs in other fields, start their own businesses, and engage in other activities to remain active and productive.

5. *Training and Education Will Accelerate.* Corporate development programs will reach out to new employees and existing staff. Demand for vocational education will grow. Educators will be challenged to make major changes to produce graduates ready to be productive in a faster-moving world.

6. *Leadership Deficit Will Be Crippling.* As employers discover serious inadequacies, leadership development will take on new importance. Up and coming managers will be expected to learn and practice leadership skills before assuming new positions.

7. *Flexible Employment Will Gain Popularity.* As more people work flexible hours, work from home, and use technology to work for employers in distant locations, traditional work arrangements will further erode.

8. *Casual Is Here to Stay.* Despite some movement to return to more formality in the workplace, informality will dominate in clothing, culture, office décor, and workplace structural design.

9. *Advantage of Agility.* Companies will re-create themselves to be more agile, nimble, and responsive to customers and employees. Relationships, resources, knowledge, and speed will become strategic weapons.

10. *Workers Becoming Independent.* More people will become independent contractors, selling their services on a project, contract, or set-term basis. This movement will stimulate emergence of specialized staffing firms and electronic communities to connect workers with employers.

Source: © Copyright 1998–2004 by The Herman Group, Inc.—reproduction for publication is encouraged, with the following attribution: From "The Herman Trend Alert," by Roger Herman and Joyce Gioia, Strategic Business Futurists. (800) 227–3566 or http://www.hermangroup.com. The Herman Trend Alert is a trademark of The Herman Group, Inc.

rules and regulations (Ungson, James, & Spicer, 1985). Finally, technological advances are changing leader-follower relationships. For example, the advent of personal computers, fax machines, and high-speed access lines allows people to work at geographically dispersed locations.

Technology and Uncertainty

Technology affects the leadership process in other ways as well. For example, it might determine what design is best for an organization (Woodward, 1965). In environments of low **technological complexity,** workers play a large role and are able to modify their behavior depending on the situation. In environments of high technological complexity, there is a highly predictable work flow.

Examples of organizations in environments of low technological complexity are printing shops, tailor shops, and cabinetmakers. In each case, the organization is well suited to meeting specific customer orders. One of the authors of this book encountered an organization fitting this mold in trying to find an oak wall unit that would meet his requirements for a stereo system. After much frustrating shopping and finding a number of mass-produced units that would not work, he found a shop that had a variety of different units. Some of these came close to what he needed, but even the closest was not quite right. After listening in detail to the requirements, the owner agreed he didn't have anything on the floor that would work. In the next breath, however, he said, "But if you can draw it, we can build it."

A higher level of technological complexity occurs when mass production is the focus and orders are filled from inventory. An example would be furniture purchased from large warehouse stores. As opposed to the individually crafted wall unit described above, most furniture is not specifically designed and built precisely to meet special customer needs. Instead, manufacturers produce large quantities of various pieces of furniture likely to adequately meet the tastes and needs of most customers.

The highest level of technological complexity occurs when a continuous process is mechanized from beginning to end. People don't play much of a role in such organizations at all except to monitor the process flow and detect problems. Oil refining operations, chemical production plants, and nuclear power plants are all examples of continuous-process organizations. In such plants, people are merely observing and monitoring the processes and detecting anomalies that need to be corrected.

The significance of such a range of technological complexity is that different kinds of organizational structures or designs are best suited for different technological environments. An organization is most likely to be successful if the structure fits the technology. If the technological environment is one of moderately high complexity (like large furniture-manufacturing companies), a mechanistic or bureaucratic structure to the organization may be most appropriate. On the other hand, if the technological environment is one of low complexity (like the custom cabinetmaker or printer), setting up a rigid, bureaucratic structure will make it difficult for your organization to produce and "flex" as required by the different specific orders.

In addition to technology, the degree of **environmental uncertainty** also affects optimal organizational design. In stable environments where there is little change, a relatively formalized, centralized, and bureaucratic structure may be desirable. In turbulent environments, on the other hand, structures should be flexible enough to adapt to changing conditions (Burns & Stalker, 1961). In a similar fashion, flat, highly differentiated, and organic structures are most appropriate for very uncertain environments (Lawrence & Lorsch, 1967a, 1967b).

Crises

Another environmental variable that affects the leadership process is the presence or absence of **crises.** Some researchers believe crises play such an important part in charismatic leadership that certain leaders will purposely create crises in order to be perceived as being charismatic (Bass, 1985; Curphy, 1991; Roberts & Bradley, 1988). Furthermore, the behaviors associated with effective leadership during crises differ from those associated with noncrisis situations. During crises, followers are more likely to look to leaders to identify the problem as well as develop and implement a solution. Thus, work groups facing strong deadlines or crises generally expect their leaders to be more assertive, directive, and decisive (Mulder & Stemerding, 1963). Moreover, leaders are less apt to use participation or consultation during crises (Mulder, de Jong, Koppelaar, & Verhage, 1986; Pfeffer & Salancik, 1975). These findings make sense when contrasting emergency and nonemergency situations. For example, surgeons spend considerable time consulting with colleagues prior to conducting a difficult surgery. However, surgeons do not have time to consult with other specialists when a patient's heart has just stopped during surgery; the doctor must quickly diagnose the reason for the heart failure and coordinate the efforts of the surgical team for the patient to live. Similarly, coaches often spend considerable time consulting with other coaches and staff members when preparing for games, but during particularly close games they may consult with relatively few members of even their own staffs.

Situational Engineering

One of the most important points this chapter can make concerns the idea of **situational engineering.** Although leaders' and followers' behaviors are affected by a variety of situational factors, all too often leaders and followers completely overlook how changing the situation can help them to change their behavior. Just as a dieter can better stick to a diet by identifying bad eating habits and limiting food cues, so can a leader or follower become more effective by identifying problem areas and restructuring the situation so that these problems become easier to overcome.

Say, for example, a leader attended a leadership development program and received feedback that he did not interact enough with his subordinates. This leader might set a goal and may genuinely make an attempt to increase the level of interaction with his followers. Because his typical day is hectic and he manages a work group with a high level of lateral interdependence, however, situational demands may more or less force him to revert to his old behaviors. This leader would be likely to realize more success if he also restructured the situation in order to facilitate the accomplishment of this goal.

He could, for example, delegate more activities to subordinates. This would give the leader more opportunities to interact with followers (by mutually setting performance goals and monitoring progress), and it would give the leader more time to engage in other activities. Moreover, the leader could project a more approachable and friendly attitude by rearranging office furniture, keeping his door open as much as possible, and building specific times into his daily schedule to "manage by wandering around" (Peters & Waterman, 1982).

There are a variety of ways in which leaders and followers can change the task, organizational, and environmental factors affecting their behaviors and attitudes. By asking questions and listening effectively, leaders may be able to redesign work using the suggestions from Hackman and Oldham's (1980) job characteristics model or Herzberg's (1966) two-factor theory in order to improve followers' satisfaction and productivity levels. Similarly, leaders might discover ways to adjust followers' work-

". . . Then it's agreed. As a crowd, we'll be subdued in innings one through seven, then suddenly become a factor in innings eight and nine . . ."

loads, responsibilities, or levels of task interdependence; rearrange office layouts; establish new or different policies or procedures; or modify reporting relationships and appraisal systems (Yukl, 1989). More senior leaders might be able to change the organization itself or work to influence changes in the environment. Perhaps the most important point regarding situational engineering is to get leaders and followers to understand that the situation is not set in concrete, and to think about how they can change the situation in order for everyone to be more satisfied and productive.

One final example may be useful not only to illustrate the powerful impact of the situational variables but also to link this section to our previous discussion of Ginnett's Team Effectiveness Leadership Model, introduced in Chapter 10. You may recall that one of the important inputs in the TELM was the organizational level where we identified four types of systems impacting team process. These systems involved rewards, information, education, and control. In one of our research projects, we were observing a series of work processes performed by teams in a highly centralized and controlled organization. No work was ever performed without specific directions which were generated by a complex computer

Taking Charge

Highlight 11.8

A critical period for any leader often involves those first few moments and days of assuming command. It is a time when first impressions are formed and expectations are set. It is a crucial time for any leader in any situation, but can be a matter of life or death for a young leader in a combat situation. Here are one young officer's first reactions upon arriving in Southeast Asia to command a platoon.

I was alone. That was my first sensation as a leader. The men were going about the morning's business—breaking out C rations, relieving themselves, shaving, brushing their teeth. They moved among each other comfortably, a word here, a smile there. I could hear snatches of conversation: "A good night's sleep. . ." "Only ninety days left." Occasionally a man would nod in my direction, or glance at me for a fleeting moment.

I gathered up my belongings—weapon, web gear, and rucksack—and moved toward the command post. I needed a few minutes to gather my thoughts before I made my debut as a platoon leader. I knew it was going to be a tricky business.

I had assumed that I would have a company commander nearby to give me my orders. But I had not even met him yet; I would not meet him for weeks. The fact was, I was totally on my own. What should I do? Whose advice could I ask? The platoon sergeant's? The squad leaders'? In time I would listen to their ideas and incorporate them with my own, but I could hardly begin my tour with "Well what do you think we ought to do, men?" No, I knew that the basic decisions were mine to make.

The first few moments would be crucial. Obviously, I was the object of interest that morning. Everyone was wondering what the new lieutenant would be like, and I would be telling them with my first words, my gestures, my demeanor, my eyes. I would have no grace period in which to learn my way around. This was a life and death environment. If I began with a blunder, my credibility as a leader would be shot, and so might some of the men.

I decided to begin by giving my attention to tactics. In a military environment, everything is determined by tactical considerations. Where you sleep, when you sleep, where you go, what you do, and in whose company you do it—all are dictated by underlying tactical necessities. I would communicate my style of leadership through my tactical instructions.

As I surveyed the soldiers, the nearby village, the distant rice paddies, the heavy undergrowth, the varied terrain, my mind raced back over the years of tactical training I had received. Conscious of the stares of the men, I hoped to appear composed as I fought back the panic of having to decide, both quickly and correctly.

Source: J. M. McDonough, *Platoon Leader* (San Francisco: Presidio Press, 1985), pp. 30–31. Reprinted with permission.

---

program. Engineers, who were not in the buildings where the work was performed, would prepare the working procedures, which were then integrated in the computer system and finally printed out for each task. While engineers could change the procedures, the perception of the workers in the processing facility was that the procedures were "like the bible—and equally difficult to change." In one series of work sequences, a team would prepare a sheet of flexible insulation (according to the printed instructions) for installation by the next team. However, when we followed the insulation, we found that the first thing the installation team would do was to unfold the flexible sheet and refold it in exactly the opposite manner so that it could be installed. When we asked the preparation team if they were aware that the installation team was having to redo their work, they had no idea that was happening. Even more surprising was that when they did learn of this, both teams decided it was easier to continue their work as described on the computer task sheets than to try to change it! Using the TELM model, we were able to identify at least two systems that were creating problems. First, the interteam information system was inadequate; it should have allowed them to correct inappropriate strategies (e.g., folding it one way only to have that work undone and redone), but it didn't. Of equal impact was the teams' perception of powerlessness because of the oppressive control system in which they operated. Even after problems were discovered, the situation in which the teams operated created conditions that reduced the creative potential of those with direct knowledge of the work flow. Leadership could have changed the way work was done by these teams by improving the information system and modifying the control system. Highlight 11.8 describes one final example of dealing with situations. In this case, a young leader dealt with the stress of being in a new and dangerous situation with a team he'd only just met.

Summary

The situation may well be the most complex factor in the leader-follower-situation framework. Moreover, situations vary not only in complexity but also in strength. Situational factors can play such a pervasive role that they can effectively minimize the effects of personality traits, intelligence, values, and preferences on leaders' and followers' behaviors, attitudes, and relationships. Given the dynamic nature of leadership situations, finding fairly consistent results is a highly encouraging accomplishment for leadership researchers.

As an organizing framework, this chapter introduced the Congruence Model as a way to consider many of the situational factors leaders should consider. In terms of work factors, leaders need to be aware of how task interdependence, task structure, and job characteristics can affect both their own and their followers' behaviors, and how they might change these factors in order to improve followers' satisfaction and performance. Research also has shown that organizational factors, such as lateral interdependence, structure, design, and culture, play major roles in determining why certain communication problems and conflicts might exist, how work is accomplished, and why some people may be more satisfied in the organization than others. The informal organization or the organizational culture can have a profound impact on the way both leaders and followers behave—and may be the least recognizable since it is the water in the bowl where all the fish are swimming. Factors in the environment, such as legal, political, or economic forces, can also affect leaders' and followers' behaviors. Sometimes these may effectively wipe out any changes a leader may make to improve productivity or satisfaction among work-group members.

Finally, let's look back one more time at our three outstanding leaders: Colin Powell, Aung San Suu Kyi, and Peter Jackson. Except this time, change the situation they find themselves in. Imagine instead Colin Powell as a filmographer and producer, Aung San Suu Kyi as the U.S. Secretary of State, and Peter Jackson as the nonviolent leader of human rights in Myanmar. Consider the implications of how their personalities would impact their work in these situations and what would still make them effective. These are the kinds of questions we are continuing to ask and research in the 21st century.

Key Terms   role theory, *331*
multiple-influence
model, *331*
situational levels, *331*
cross functions, *332*
links to customers and
suppliers, *332*
customer
segmentation, *333*
global scale, *333*
innovation, *333*
knowledge workers, *333*
skill variety, *335*
task identity, *336*
task significance, *336*
autonomy, *336*
feedback, *337*
task structure, *337*

task
interdependence, *338*
level of authority, *340*
organizational
structure, *341*
horizontal
complexity, *341*
vertical complexity, *341*
spatial complexity, *341*
formalization, *341*
centralization, *342*
substitutes for
leadership, *342*
organizational
designs, *343*
functional design, *343*
product design, *344*
matrix design, *344*

lateral
interdependence, *346*
organizational
culture, *346*
organizational
climate, *346*
myths and stories, *348*
symbols and artifacts, *348*
rituals, *348*
language, *348*
technological
complexity, *352*
environmental
uncertainty, *353*
crises, *353*
situational
engineering, *354*

Questions   1. The term *bureaucratic* has a pejorative connotation to most people. Can you think of any positive aspects of a bureaucracy?

2. Think of a crisis situation you are familiar with involving a group, team, organization, or country, and analyze it in terms of the leader-follower-situation framework. For example, were the followers looking for a certain kind of behavior from the leader? Did the situation demand it? Did the situation, in fact, contribute to a particular leader's emergence?

3. Can you identify reward systems that impact the level of effort students are likely to put forth in team or group projects? Should these reward systems be different than for individual effort projects?

Skills   Leadership skills relevant to this chapter include:

- Problem solving
- Diagnosing performance problems in individuals, groups, and organizations
- Development planning

Activity   Your instructor has several exercises available which demonstrate the impact of situational factors on behavior. They are not described here since identifying the situational factors being manipulated in an exercise undercuts the purpose of that exercise.

Minicase

"Innovation at IKEA"

Redecorating and renovating have become *the* international pasttime. In a post 9/11 world facing persistent terrorist alerts, more and more people are opting to stay home and make their homes safe havens. This phenomenon, coupled with lagging economies worldwide, has contributed tremendously to the success of IKEA—the Swedish home furniture giant. In the past 10 years sales for IKEA have tripled, growing from over $4 billion in 1993 to over $12 billion in 2003.

Much of IKEA's success can be attributed to its founder, Ingvar Kamprad. Kamprad used graduation money to start IKEA in the small Swedish village where he was born. He started off selling belt buckles, pens, and watches, whatever residents in the small local village of Agunnaryd needed. Eventually, Kamprad moved on to selling furniture. One day in 1952, while struggling to fit a large table in a small car, one of Kamprad's employees came up with the idea that changed the furniture industry forever—he decided to remove the legs. IKEA's flat-pack and self-assembly methodology was born. It rocketed the company past the competition. "After that [table] followed a whole series of other self-assembled furniture, and by 1956 the concept was more or less systematized," writes Kamprad.

Kamprad is dedicated to maintaining the corporate culture he has helped define over the past 50 years. He is a simple man—his idea of a luxury vacation is riding his bike. He is fiercely cost-conscious and, even though his personal wealth has been estimated in the billions, he refuses to fly first class. He values human interaction above all, and, even though retired, he still visits IKEA stores regularly to keep tabs on what is going on where the business really happens.

The culture at IKEA is a culture closely connected with Kamprad's simple, farm-raised, Swedish roots. It is a culture that strives "to create a better everyday for the many people." IKEA supports this culture by

- hiring coworkers (IKEA prefers the word *coworkers* to "employees") who are supportive and work well in teams;
- expecting coworkers to look for innovative, better ways of doing things in every aspect of their work;
- respecting coworkers and their views;
- establishing mutual objectives and working tirelessly to realize them;
- making cost-consciousness part of everything they do from improving processes for production to purchasing wisely to traveling cost-effectively;
- avoiding complicated solutions—simplicity is a strong part of the IKEA culture;
- leading by example, so IKEA leaders are expected to pitch in when needed and create a good working environment; and
- believing that a diverse workforce strengthens the company overall.

The IKEA culture is one that resonates for many. The buildings are easy to identify—the giant blue and gold warehouses that resemble oversized Swedish flags are hard to miss. Millions of customers browse through the Klippan sofas and Palbo footstools (Nordic names are given to all IKEA products) in the stark, dimly lit warehouses. The surroundings may not be lavish and the service may be mostly self-service, but customers keep going back not just for the bargains, but to experience the IKEA culture as well.

1. Discuss the three input components of the Congruence Model as they apply to the success of IKEA.
2. Consider Schein's Four Key Organizational Culture Factors as described in Highlight 11.5. What examples can you identify within the IKEA organization that contribute to the company's strong corporate culture?
3. Based on the level of technological complexity and the degree of environmental uncertainty present at IKEA, what type of organizational structure would you expect?

Sources: http://archive.cinweekly.com/content/2004/03/24/0324travelikea.asp; http://www.azcentral.com/home/design/articles/0812ikea12.html; http://strategis.ic.gc.ca/epic/internet/inimr-ri.nsf/en/gr-76894e.html; http://www.geocities.com/TimesSquare/1848/ikea.html; http://www.sustainability.com/news/press-room/JE-teflon-shield-Mar01.asp?popup=1; http://www.benefitnews.com/retire/detail.cfm?id=345

12

Contingency Theories of Leadership

Introduction

If we were to provide an extremely short summary of the book to this point, we would say leadership is a process that involves aspects, of the leader, the followers, and the situation. In Part I we discussed the process aspects, while Part II was devoted exclusively to the leader. Part III focused on the followers, and in the previous chapter we discussed the situational components of leadership. You may have also noted that as much as we attempted to focus exclusively on the component of interest for the section, there were often overlapping areas in our leader-follower-situation (L-F-S) model. The overlap is true, and our attempts to segregate the concepts were done merely for simplicity. The world of leadership is really a rather complex one where multiple aspects of the L-F-S model will come into play. Leadership is contingent upon the interplay of all three aspects of our model, and these contingencies are the focus of this chapter.

> It is a capital mistake to theorize before one has data.
>
> Sir Arthur Conan Doyle

This chapter reviews four of the more well-known contingency theories of leadership. All four address certain aspects of the leader, the followers, and the situation. These four theories also share several other similarities. First, because they are theories rather than someone's personal opinions, these four models have been the focus of a considerable amount of empirical research over the years. Second, these theories implicitly assume that leaders are able to accurately diagnose or assess key aspects of the followers and the leadership situation. Third, with the exception of the contingency model (Fiedler, 1967), leaders are assumed to be able to act in a flexible manner. In other words, leaders can and should change their behaviors as situational and follower characteristics change. Fourth, a correct match between situational and follower characteristics and leaders' behaviors is assumed to have a positive effect on group or organizational outcomes. Thus, these theories maintain that leadership effectiveness is maximized when leaders correctly make their behaviors *contingent* on certain situational and follower characteristics. Because of these similarities, Chemers (1984) argued that these four theories were more similar than they were different. He said they differed primarily in terms of the types of situational and follower characteristics upon which various leader behaviors should be contingent.

The Normative Decision Model

Obviously, in some situations leaders can delegate decisions to subordinates or should ask subordinates for relevant information before making a decision. In other situations, such as emergencies or crises, leaders may need to make a decision with little, if any, input from subordinates. The level of input subordinates have in the decision-making process can and does vary substantially depending on the issue at hand, followers' level of technical expertise, or the presence or absence of a crisis. Although the level of participation varies due to various leader, follower, and situational factors, Vroom and Yetton (1973) maintained that leaders could often improve group performance by using an optimal amount of participation in the decision-making process. Thus, the normative decision model is directed solely at determining how much input subordinates should have in the decision-making process. Precisely because the normative decision model is limited only to decision making and is not a grand, all-encompassing theory, it is a good model with which to begin the chapter.

Levels of Participation

Like the other theories in this chapter, the **normative decision model** (Vroom & Yetton, 1973) was designed to improve some aspects of leadership effectiveness. In this case, Vroom and Yetton explored how various leader, follower, and situational factors affect the degree of subordinates' participation in the decision-making process and, in turn, group performance. To determine which situational and follower factors affect the level of participation and group performance, Vroom and Yetton first investigated the decision-making processes leaders use in group settings. They discovered a continuum of decision-making processes ranging from completely autocratic (labeled "AI") to completely democratic, where all members of the group have equal participation (labeled "GII"). These processes are listed in Highlight 12.1.

Decision Quality and Acceptance

After establishing a continuum of decision processes, Vroom and Yetton (1973) established criteria to evaluate the adequacy of the decisions made—criteria they believed would be credible to leaders and equally applicable across the five levels of participation. Although a wide variety of criteria could be used, Vroom and Yetton believed decision quality and decision acceptance were the two most important criteria for judging the adequacy of a decision.

Decision quality means simply that if the decision has a rational or objectively determinable "better or worse" alternative, the leader should select the better alternative. Vroom and Yetton (1973) intended quality in their model to apply when

Levels of Participation in the Normative Decision Model

Highlight 12.1

AUTOCRATIC PROCESSES

AI: The leader solves the problem or makes the decision by him- or herself using the information available at the time.

AII: The leader obtains any necessary information from followers, then decides on a solution to the problem herself. She may or may not tell followers the purpose of her questions or give information about the problem or decision she is working on. The input provided by them is clearly in response to her request for specific information. They do not play a role in the definition of the problem or in generating or evaluating alternative solutions.

CONSULTATIVE PROCESSES

CI: The leader shares the problem with the relevant followers individually, getting their ideas and suggestions without bringing them together as a group. Then he makes a decision. This decision may or may not reflect the followers' influence.

CII: The leader shares the problem with her followers in a group meeting. In this meeting, she obtains their ideas and suggestions. Then she makes the decision, which may or may not reflect the followers' influence.

GROUP PROCESS

GII: The leader shares the problem with his followers as a group. Together they generate and evaluate alternatives and attempt to reach agreement (consensus) on a solution. The leader's role is much like that of a chairman, coordinating the discussion, keeping it focused on the problem, and making sure that the critical issues are discussed. He can provide the group with information or ideas that he has, but he does not try to "press" them to adopt "his" solution. Moreover, leaders adopting this level of participation are willing to accept and implement any solution that has the support of the entire group.

Source: Adapted from V. H. Vroom and P. W. Yetton, *Leadership and Decision Making* (Pittsburgh: University of Pittsburgh Press, 1973).

the decision could result in an objectively or measurably better outcome for the group or organization. In the for-profit sector, this criterion can be assessed in several ways, but perhaps the easiest to understand is, Would the decision show up on the balance sheet? In this case, a high-quality (or, conversely, low-quality) decision would have a direct and measurable impact on the organization's bottom line. In the public sector, one might determine if there was a quality component to a decision by asking, "Will one alternative have a greater cost saving than the other?" or "Does this decision improve services to the client?" Although it may seem that leaders should always choose the alternative with the highest decision quality, this is not always the case. Often, leaders are confronted with equally good (or bad) alternatives. At other times, the issue in question is fairly trivial, rendering the quality of the decision relatively unimportant.

Decision acceptance implies that followers accept the decision as if it were their own and do not merely comply with the decision. Acceptance of the decision outcome by the followers may be critical, particularly if it is the followers who will bear principal responsibility for implementing the decision. With such acceptance, there will be no need for superiors to monitor compliance, which can be a continuing and time-consuming activity (and virtually impossible in some circumstances, such as with a geographically dispersed sales staff).

As with quality, acceptance of a decision is not always critical for implementation. For example, most organizations have an accounting form that employees use to obtain reimbursement for travel expenses. Suppose a company's chief financial officer (CFO) has decided to change the format of the form for reimbursing travel expenses and has had the new forms printed and distributed throughout the company. Further, she has sent out a notice that effective June 1, the old forms will no longer be accepted for reimbursement—only claims made using the new forms will be processed and paid. Assuming the new form has no gross errors, problems, or omissions, our CFO really has no concern with acceptance as defined here. If people want to be reimbursed for their travel expenses, then they will use the new form. This decision, in essence, implements itself.

On the other hand, leaders sometimes assume that they do not need to worry about acceptance because they have so much power over their followers that overt rejection of a decision is not likely to occur. A corporate CEO is not apt to see a junior accountant stand up and openly challenge the CEO's decision to implement a new policy, even though the young accountant may not "buy into" the new policy at all. Because followers generally do not openly object to the decisions made by leaders with this much power, these leaders often mistakenly assume that their decisions have been accepted and will be fully implemented. This is a rather naive view of what really goes on in organizations. Just because the junior subordinate does not publicly voice his opposition does not mean he will rush right out and wholeheartedly implement the decision. In fact, the junior accountant has a lot more time to destructively undermine the policy than the CEO does to check to ensure it is being carried out to the letter.

The Decision Tree

Having settled on quality and acceptance as the two principal criteria for effective decisions, Vroom and Yetton then developed a normative decision model. (A normative model is one based on what ought to happen rather than describing what does happen.) They also developed a set of questions to protect quality and acceptance by eliminating decision processes that would be wrong or inappropriate. Generally, these questions concern the problem itself, the amount of pertinent information possessed by the leader and followers, and various situational factors.

In order to make it easier for leaders to determine how much participation subordinates should have to optimize decision quality and acceptance, Vroom and Yetton (1973) incorporated these questions into a decision tree (see Figure 12.1). To use the decision tree, one starts at the left by stating the problem and then proceeds through the model from left to right. Every time a box is encountered, the question associated with that box must be answered with either a yes or a no response. Eventually, all paths lead to a set of decision processes that, if used, will lead to a decision that protects both quality and acceptance.

Having reached a set of feasible alternatives that meet the desirable criteria for quality and acceptance among followers, the leader may then wish to consider additional criteria. One very practical consideration is the amount of time available. If time is critical, then the leader should select the alternative in the feasible set that is farthest to the *left,* again noting that the feasible set is arranged from AI through

FIGURE 12.1

Vroom and Yetton's leadership decision tree.

Source: Reprinted from *Leadership and Decision Making*, by Victor H. Vroom and Philip W. Yetton, by permission of the University of Pittsburgh Press, © 1973 by the University of Pittsburgh Press.

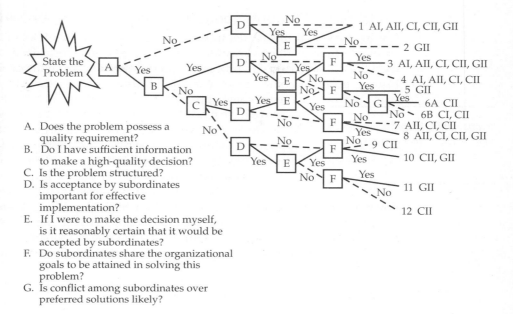

A. Does the problem possess a quality requirement?
B. Do I have sufficient information to make a high-quality decision?
C. Is the problem structured?
D. Is acceptance by subordinates important for effective implementation?
E. If I were to make the decision myself, is it reasonably certain that it would be accepted by subordinates?
F. Do subordinates share the organizational goals to be attained in solving this problem?
G. Is conflict among subordinates over preferred solutions likely?

GII. It generally takes less time to make and implement autocratic decisions than it does to make consultative or group decisions. Nevertheless, it is important to note that the first step is to protect quality and acceptance (by using the model). Only *after* arriving at an appropriate set of outcomes should leaders consider time in the decision-making process. This tenet is sometimes neglected in the workplace by leaders who overemphasize time as a criterion. Obviously, there are some situations where time is absolutely critical, as in life-or-death emergencies. But too often, leaders ask for a decision to be made as if the situation were an emergency when, in reality, they (the leaders, not the situation) are creating the time pressure. Despite such behavior, it is difficult to imagine a leader who would knowingly prefer a fast decision that lacks both quality and acceptance among the implementers to one that is of high quality and acceptable to followers but that takes more time.

Another important consideration is follower development. Again, after quality and acceptance have been considered using the decision tree, and if the leader has determined that time is not a critical element, she may wish to follow a decision process more apt to allow followers to develop their own decision-making skills. This can be achieved by using the decision tree and then selecting the alternative within the feasible set that is farthest to the *right*. As was the case above, the arrangement of processes from AI to GII provides an increasing amount of follower development by moving from autocratic to group decisions.

Finally, if neither time nor follower development is a concern and multiple options are available in the feasible set of alternatives, the leader may select a style that best meets his or her needs. This may be the process with which the leader is most comfortable ("I'm a CII kind of guy"), or it may be a process in which he or she would like to develop more skill.

Concluding Thoughts about the Normative Decision Model

Having looked at this model in some detail, we will now look at it from the perspective of the leader-follower-situation (L-F-S) framework. To do this, we have used the different decision processes and the questions from the decision tree to illustrate different components in the L-F-S framework (see Figure 12.2). Several issues become apparent in this depiction. First, for ease of presentation we have placed each question or factor solely within one circle or another. Nevertheless, one could argue that some of the questions could or should be placed in another part of the model. For example, the question "Do I have sufficient information to make a high-quality decision?" is placed in the leader block. It might be argued, however, that no leader could answer this question without some knowledge of the situation. Strictly speaking, therefore, perhaps this question should be placed in the intersection between the leader and the situation. Nonetheless, in keeping with our theme that leadership involves interactions among all three elements, it seems sufficient at this point to illustrate them in their simplest state.

> *Irrationally held truths may be more harmful than reasoned errors.*
>
> Thomas Huxley

FIGURE 12.2
Factors from the normative decision model and the interactional framework.

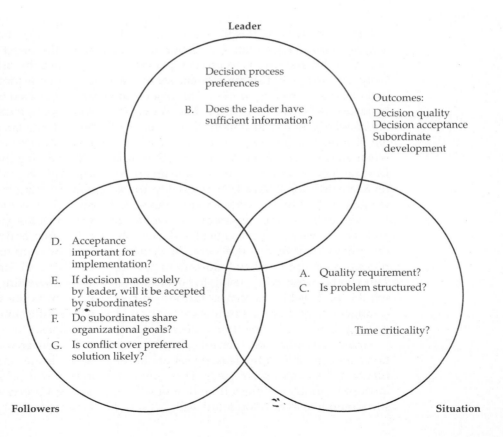

How Much Time Do I Have?

Highlight 12.2

In a world of instant messages that require lightning-fast responses, Steven B. Sample, president of the University of Southern California, is touting the benefits of "artful procrastination." In his course on leadership and his book, *The Contrarian's Guide to Leadership,* a key lesson is never make a decision today that can reasonably be put off to tomorrow:

"With respect to timing, almost all great leaders have understood that making quick decisions is typically counterproductive. I'm not talking about what to have for breakfast or what tie to wear today. President Harry Truman almost personified this concept. When anyone told him they needed a decision, the first thing he would ask is 'how much time do I have—a week, 10 seconds, six months?' What he understood was that the nature of the decision that a leader makes depends to a large extent on how much time he has in which to make it. He also understood that delaying a decision as long as reasonably possible generally leads to the best decisions being made."

Other lessons from Sample include:

- Think gray. Don't form opinions if you don't have to.
- Think free. Move several steps beyond traditional brainstorming.
- Listen first, talk later. And when you listen, do so artfully.
- You can't copy your way to the top.

Sources: http://www.usc.edu/president/book/; http://www.refresher.com/!enescontrarian.html; http://bottomlinesecrets.com/blpnet/article.html?article_id=33302

A second issue also becomes apparent when the normative decision model is viewed through the L-F-S framework. Notice how the Vroom and Yetton (1973) model shifts focus away from the leader toward both the situation and, to an even greater degree, the followers. There are no questions about the leader's personality, motivations, values, or attitudes. In fact, the leader's preference is considered only after higher-priority factors have been considered. The only underlying assumption is that the leader is interested in implementing a high-quality decision (when quality is an issue) that is acceptable to followers (when acceptance is critical to implementation). Given that assumption and a willingness to consider aspects of the situation and aspects of the followers, the leader's behavior can be channeled into more effective decision-making processes.

A third issue is that the L-F-S framework organizes concepts in a familiar conceptual structure. This is an advantage even for a theory with as limited a focus as the normative decision model (i.e., decision making); it will be even more helpful later as we consider more complex theories.

Finally, because the normative decision model is a *leadership theory* rather than Vroom and Yetton's personal opinions, a number of empirical studies have investigated the model's efficacy. Research conducted by Field (1982) and Vroom and Jago (1974, 1988) provided strong support for the model, as these studies showed that leaders were much more likely to make effective or successful decisions when they followed its tenets than when they ignored them. Nevertheless, although leaders may be more apt to make more effective decisions when using the model, there is no evidence to show that these leaders are more effective overall than leaders not using the model (Miner, 1975). The latter findings again point out that both the leadership process and leadership effectiveness are complex phenomema; being a good decision-maker is not enough to be a good leader (although it certainly helps). Other problems with the model are that it views decision making as taking place at a single point in time (Yukl, 1989), assumes that leaders are equally skilled at using all five decision procedures (Yukl & Van Fleet, 1992), and assumes that some of the prescriptions of the model may not be the best for a given situation. For example, the normative decision model prescribes that leaders use a GII decision process if conflict may occur over a decision, but leaders may be more effective if they instead make an AI decision and avoid intragroup conflict (Couch & Yetton, 1987). Despite these problems, the normative model is one of the best supported of the four major contingency theories of leadership, and leaders would be wise to consider using the model when making decisions.

The Situational Leadership® Model

It seems fairly obvious that leaders do not interact with all followers in the same manner. For example, a leader may give general guidelines or goals to her highly competent and motivated followers but spend considerable time coaching, directing, and training her unskilled and unmotivated followers. Or leaders may provide relatively little praise and assurances to followers with high self-confidence but high amounts of support to followers with low self-confidence. Although leaders often have different interactional styles when dealing with individual followers, is there an optimum way for leaders to adjust their behavior with different followers and thereby increase their likelihood of success? And if there is, then what factors should the leader base his behavior on—the follower's intelligence? Personality traits? Values? Preferences? Technical competence? A model called **Situational Leadership**® offers answers to these two important leadership questions.

Leader Behaviors

The Situational Leadership® model has evolved over time. Its essential elements first appeared in 1969 (Hersey & Blanchard), with roots in the Ohio State studies, in which the two broad categories of leader behaviors, initiating structure and consideration, were initially identified (see Chapter 8). As Situational Leadership® evolved, so did the labels (but not the content) for the two leadership behavior categories. Initiating structure changed to **task behaviors,** which were defined as the extent to which the leader spells out the responsibilities of an individual or group. Task behaviors include telling people what to do, how to do it, when to do it, and who is to do it. Similarly, consideration changed to **relationship behaviors,** or how much the leader engages in two-way communication. Relationship behaviors include listening, encouraging, facilitating, clarifying, explaining why the task is important, and giving support.

When the behavior of actual leaders was studied, there was little evidence to show these two categories of leader behavior were consistently related to leadership success; the relative effectiveness of these two behavior dimensions often depended on the situation. Hersey's Situational Leadership® model explains why leadership effectiveness varies across these two behavior dimensions and situations. It arrays the two orthogonal dimensions as in the Ohio State studies and then divides each of them into high and low segments (see Figure 12.3). According to the model, depicting the two leadership dimensions this way is useful because certain combinations of task and relationship behaviors may be more effective in some situations than in others. For example, in some situations high levels of task but low levels of relationship behaviors are effective; in other situations, just the opposite is true. So far, however, we have not considered the key follower or situational characteristics with which these combinations of task and relationship behaviors were most effective. Hersey says that these four combinations of task and relationship behaviors would increase leadership effectiveness if they were made contingent on the readiness level of the individual follower to perform a given task.

The real world is a messy place— yet, even a messy place can (should?) be attacked systematically.

Alex Cornell

FIGURE 12.3

Situational Leadership.®

Source: Paul Hersey, Kenneth Blanchard, and Dewey Johnson, *Management of Organizational Behavior: Utilizing Human Resources*, 7th ed. (Englewood Cliffs, NJ: Prentice Hall, 1996), p. 200. Used with permission.

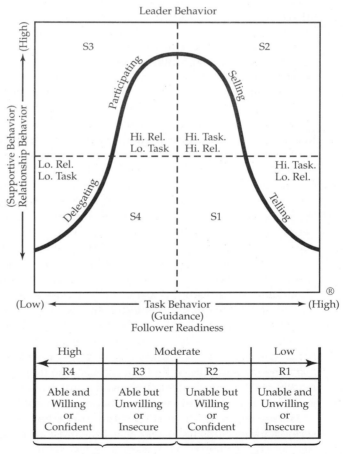

Follower Readiness

In Situational Leadership®, **follower readiness** refers to a follower's ability and willingness to accomplish a particular task. Readiness is not an assessment of an individual's personality, traits, values, age, etc. It's not a personal characteristic, but rather how ready an individual is to perform a particular task. Any given follower could be low on readiness to perform one task but high on readiness to perform a different task. An experienced emergency room physician would be high in readiness on tasks like assessing a patient's medical status, but could be relatively low on readiness for facilitating an interdepartmental team meeting to solve an ambiguous and complex problem like developing hospital practices to encourage collaboration across departments.

Prescriptions of the Model

Now that the key contingency factor, follower readiness, has been identified, let us move on to another aspect of the figure—combining follower readiness levels with the four combinations of leader behaviors described earlier. The horizontal bar or arrow in Figure 12.3 depicts follower readiness as increasing from right to left (not in the direction we are used to seeing). There are four segments along this continuum, ranging from R1 (the lowest) to R4 (the highest). Along this continuum, however, the assessment of follower readiness can be fairly subjective. A follower who possesses high levels of readiness would clearly fall in the R4 category, just as a follower unable and unwilling (or insecure) to perform a task would fall in R1.

To complete the model, a curved line is added that represents the leadership behavior that will most likely be effective given a particular level of follower readiness. In order to apply the model, leaders should first assess the readiness level (R1-R4) of the follower relative to the task to be accomplished. Next, a vertical line should be drawn from the center of the readiness level up to the point where it intersects with the curved line in Figure 12.3. The quadrant in which this intersection occurs represents the level of task and relationship behavior that has the best chance of producing successful outcomes. For example, imagine you are a fire chief and have under your command a search-and-rescue team. One of the team members is needed to rescue a backpacker who has fallen in the mountains, and you have selected a particular follower to accomplish the task. What leadership behavior should you exhibit? If this follower has both substantial training and experience in this type of rescue, you would assess his readiness level as R4. A vertical line from R4 would intersect the curved line in the quadrant where both low task and low relationship behaviors by the leader are most apt to be successful. As the leader, you should exhibit a low level of task and relationship behaviors and delegate this task to the follower. On the other hand, you may have a brand-new member of the fire department who still has to learn the ins and outs of firefighting. Because this particular follower has low task readiness (R1), the model maintains that the leader should use a high level of task and a low level of relationship behaviors when initially dealing with this follower.

Hersey suggests one further step leaders may wish to consider. The model described above helps the leader select the most appropriate behavior given the current level of follower readinesss. However, there may be cases when the leader would like to see the followers increase their level of readiness for particular tasks

A Developmental Intervention Using SLT

Highlight 12.3

Dianne is a resident assistant in charge of a number of students in a university dorm. One particular sophomore, Michael, has volunteered to work on projects in the past but never seems to take the initiative to get started on his own. Michael seems to wait until Dianne gives him explicit direction, approval, and encouragement before he will get started. Michael can do a good job, but he seems to be unwilling to start without some convincing that it is all right, and unless Dianne makes explicit what steps are to be taken. Dianne has assessed Michael's readiness level as R2, but she would like to see him develop, both in task readiness and in psychological maturity. The behavior most likely to fit

Michael's current readiness level is selling, or high task, high relationship. But Dianne has decided to implement a developmental intervention to help Michael raise his readiness level. Dianne can be most helpful in this intervention by moving up one level to participating, or low task, high relationship. By reducing the amount of task instructions and direction while encouraging Michael to lay out a plan on his own and supporting his steps in the right direction, Dianne is most apt to help Michael become an R3 follower. This does not mean the work will get done most efficiently, however. Just as we saw in the Vroom and Yetton model earlier, if part of the leader's job is development of followers, then time may be a reasonable and necessary trade-off for short-term efficiency.

by implementing a series of **developmental interventions** to help boost follower readiness levels. The process would begin by first assessing the follower's current level of readiness and then determining the leader behavior that best suits that follower in that task. Instead of using the behavior prescribed by the model, however, the leader would select the next higher leadership behavior. Another way of thinking about this would be for the leader to select the behavior pattern that would fit the follower if that follower were one level higher in readiness. This intervention is designed to help followers in their development, hence its name (see Highlight 12.3, on developmental interventions).

Concluding Thoughts about the Situational Leadership® Model

In Figure 12.4, we can see how the factors in Situational Leadership® fit within the L-F-S framework. In comparison to the Vroom and Yetton model, there are fewer factors to be considered in each of the three elements. The only situational consideration is knowledge of the task, and the only follower factor is readiness. On the other hand, the theory goes well beyond decision making, which was the sole domain of the normative decision model.

Situational Leadership® is usually appealing to students and practitioners because of its commonsense approach as well as its ease of understanding. Unfortunately, there is little published research to support the predictions of Situational Leadership® in the workplace (Vecchio, 1987; Yukl & Van Fleet, 1992). A great deal of research has been done within organizations that have implemented Situational Leadership®, but most of those findings are not available for public dissemination. Nevertheless, even with these shortcomings, Situational Leadership® is a useful way to get leaders to think about how leadership effectiveness may depend somewhat on being flexible with different subordinates, not on acting the same way toward them all.

FIGURE 12.4

Factors from the Situational Leadership® model and the interactional framework.

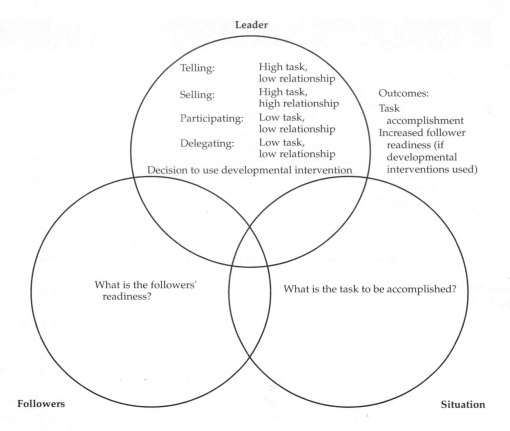

Leader

Telling: High task, low relationship
Selling: High task, high relationship
Participating: Low task, low relationship
Delegating: Low task, low relationship

Decision to use developmental intervention

Outcomes:

Task accomplishment
Increased follower readiness (if developmental interventions used)

What is the followers' readiness?

What is the task to be accomplished?

Followers

Situation

The Contingency Model

Although leaders may be able to change their behaviors toward individual subordinates, leaders also have dominant behavioral tendencies. Some leaders may be generally more supportive and relationship-oriented, whereas others may be more concerned with task or goal accomplishment. The contingency model (Fiedler, 1967) recognizes that leaders have these general behavioral tendencies and specifies situations where certain leaders (or behavioral dispositions) may be more effective than others.

Fiedler's (1967) **contingency model** of leadership is probably the earliest and most well-known contingency theory, and is often perceived by students to be almost the opposite of SLT. Compared to the contingency model, SLT emphasizes flexibility in leader behaviors, whereas the contingency model maintains that leaders are much more consistent (and consequently less flexible) in their behavior. Situational leadership theory maintains that leaders who *correctly base their behaviors* on follower maturity will be more effective, whereas the contingency model suggests that leader effectiveness is primarily determined by *selecting the right kind of leader for a certain situation or changing the situation* to fit the particular leader's style. Another way to say this is that leadership effectiveness depends on both the leader's style and the favorableness of the leadership situation. Some leaders are better than others in some situations but less effective in other situations. To understand contingency theory, therefore, we need to look first at the critical characteristics of the leader and then at the critical aspects of the situation.

The Least-Preferred-Coworker Scale

In order to determine a leader's general style or tendency, Fiedler developed an instrument called the **least-preferred-coworker (LPC) scale.** The scale instructs a leader to think of the single individual with whom he has had the greatest difficulty working (i.e., the least-preferred coworker) and then to describe that individual in terms of a series of bipolar adjectives (e.g., friendly-unfriendly, boring-interesting, sincere-insincere). Those ratings are then converted into a numerical score.

In thinking about such a procedure, many people assume that the score is determined primarily by the characteristics of whatever particular individual the leader happened to identify as his least-preferred coworker. In the context of contingency theory, however, it is important to understand that the score is thought to *represent something about the leader, not the specific individual the leader evaluated.*

The current interpretation of these scores is that they identify a leader's motivation hierarchy (Fiedler, 1978). Based on their LPC scores, leaders are categorized into two groups: **low-LPC leaders** and **high-LPC leaders.** In terms of their motivation hierarchy, low-LPC leaders are primarily motivated by the task, which means that these leaders primarily gain satisfaction from task accomplishment. Thus, their dominant behavioral tendencies are similar to the initiating structure behavior described in the Ohio State research or the task behavior of SLT. However, if tasks are being accomplished in an acceptable manner, then low-LPC leaders will move to their secondary level of motivation, which is forming and maintaining relationships with followers. Thus, low-LPC leaders will focus on improving their relationships with followers *after* they are assured that assigned tasks are being satisfactorily accomplished. As soon as tasks are no longer being accomplished in an acceptable manner, however, low-LPC leaders will refocus their efforts on task accomplishment and persist with these efforts until task accomplishment is back on track.

In terms of motivation hierarchy, high-LPC leaders are primarily motivated by relationships, which means that these leaders are primarily satisfied by establishing and maintaining close interpersonal relationships. Thus, their dominant behavioral tendencies are similar to the consideration behaviors described in the Ohio State research or the relationship behaviors in SLT. If high-LPC leaders have established good relationships with their followers, then they will move to their secondary level of motivation, which is task accomplishment. As soon as leader-follower relations are jeopardized, however, high-LPC leaders will cease working on tasks and refocus their efforts on improving relationships with followers.

You can think of the LPC scale as identifying two different sorts of leaders with their respective motivational hierarchies depicted in Figure 12.5. Lower-level needs must be satisfied first. Low-LPC leaders will move "up" to satisfying relationship needs when they are assured the task is being satisfactorily accomplished. High-LPC leaders will move "up" to emphasizing task accomplishment when they have established good relationships with their followers.

Because all tests have some level of imprecision, Fiedler (1978) suggested that the LPC scale cannot accurately identify the motivation hierarchy for those individuals with certain intermediate scores. Research by Kennedy (1982) suggested an alternative view. Kennedy has shown that individuals within the intermediate range of LPC scale scores may more easily or readily switch between being task- or relationship-oriented leaders than those individuals with more extreme scale scores. They may be equally satisfied by working on the task or establishing relationships with followers.

Situational Favorability

The other critical variable in the contingency model is **situational favorability,** which is the amount of control the leader has over the followers. Presumably, the more control a leader has over followers, the more favorable the situation is, at least from the leader's perspective. Fiedler included three subelements in situation favorability. These were leader-member relations, task structure, and position power.

Leader-member relations is the most powerful of the three subelements in determining overall situation favorability. It involves the extent to which relationships between the leader and followers are generally cooperative and friendly or antagonistic and difficult. Leaders who rate leader-member relations as high would feel they had the support of their followers and could rely on their loyalty.

Task structure is second in potency in determining overall situation favorability. Here the leader would objectively determine task structure by assessing whether there were detailed descriptions of work products, standard operating procedures, or objective indicators of how well the task is being accomplished. The more one could answer these questions affirmatively, the higher the structure of the task.

FIGURE 12.5
Motivational hierarchies for low- and high-LPC leaders.

Low-LPC leader motivational hierarchy

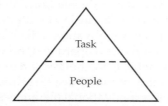

High-LPC leader motivational hierarchy

Position power is the weakest of the three elements of situational favorability. Leaders who have titles of authority or rank, the authority to administer rewards and punishments, and the legitimacy to conduct follower performance appraisals have greater position power than leaders who lack them.

The relative weights of these three components, taken together, can be used to create a continuum of situational favorability. When using the contingency model, leaders are first asked to rate items that measure the strength of leader-member relations, the degree of task structure, and their level of position power. These ratings are then weighted and combined to determine an overall level of situational favorability facing the leader (Fiedler & Chemers, 1982). Any particular situation's favorability can then be plotted on a continuum Fiedler divided into octants representing distinctly different levels of situational favorability. The relative weighting scheme for the subelements and how they make up each of the eight octants can be seen in Figure 12.6.

You can see that the octants of situational favorability range from 1 (highly favorable) to 8 (very unfavorable). The highest levels of situational favorability occur when leader-member relations are good, the task is structured, and position power is high. The lowest levels of situational favorability occur when there are high levels of leader-member conflict, the task is unstructured or unclear, and the leader does not have the power to reward or punish subordinates. Moreover, the relative weighting of the three subelements can easily be seen by their order of precedence in Figure 12.6, with leader-member relations appearing first, followed by task structure and then position power. For example, because leader-member relations carry so much weight, it is impossible for leaders with good leader-member relations to have anything worse than moderate situational favorability, regardless of their task structure or position power. In other words, leaders with good leader-member relations will be in a situation that has situational favorability no worse than octant 4; leaders with poor leader-member relations will be facing a leadership situation with situational favorability no better than octant 5.

Prescriptions of the Model

Fiedler and his associates have conducted numerous studies to determine how different leaders (as described by their LPC scores) have performed in different situations (as described in terms of situational favorability). Figure 12.7 describes

FIGURE 12.6
Contingency model octant structure for determining situational favorability.

	High ⟵ Overall situation favorability							Low
Leader-member relations	Good				Poor			
Task structure	Structured		Unstructured		Structured		Unstructured	
Position power	High	Low	High	Low	High	Low	High	Low
Octant	1	2	3	4	5	6	7	8

which type of leader (high or low LPC) Fiedler found to be most effective, given different levels of situation favorability. The solid dark line represents the relative effectiveness of a low-LPC leader, and the dashed line represents the relative effectiveness of a high-LPC leader. It is obvious from the way the two lines cross and recross that there is some interaction between the leader's style and the overall situation favorability. If the situational favorability is moderate (octants 4, 5, 6, or 7), then those groups led by leaders concerned with establishing and maintaining relationships (high-LPC leaders) seem to do best. However, if the situation is either very unfavorable (octant 8) or highly favorable (octants 1, 2, or 3), then those groups led by the task-motivated (low-LPC) leaders seem to do best.

Fiedler suggested that leaders will try to satisfy their primary motivation when faced with unfavorable or moderately favorable situations. This means that low-LPC leaders will concentrate on the task and high-LPC leaders will concentrate on relationships when faced with these two levels of situational favorability. Nevertheless, leaders facing highly favorable situations know that their primary motivations will be satisfied and thus will move to their secondary motivational state. This means that *leaders will behave according to their secondary motivational state only when faced with highly favorable situations* (see Highlight 12.4).

There are several interesting implications of Fiedler's (1967) model worthy of additional comment. Because leaders develop their distinctive motivation hierarchies and dominant behavior tendencies through a lifetime of experiences, Fiedler believed these hierarchies and tendencies would be difficult to change through training. Fiedler maintained it was naive to believe that sending someone to a relatively brief leadership training program could substantially alter any leader's personality or typical way of acting in leadership situations; after all, such tendencies had been developed over many years of experience. Instead of trying to change the leader, Fiedler concluded, training would be more effective if it showed leaders how to recognize and change key situational characteristics to better fit their personal motivational hierachies and behavioral tendencies. Thus, according to Fiedler, the

FIGURE 12.7
Leader
effectiveness
based on the
contingency
between leader
LPC score and
situation
favorability.

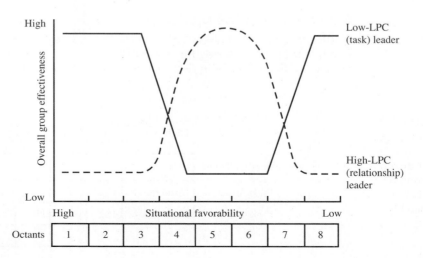

High- and Low-LPC Leaders and the Contingency Model

Highlight 12.4

Suppose we had two leaders, Tom Low (a low-LPC or task-motivated leader) and Brenda High (a high-LPC or relationship-motivated leader). In unfavorable situations, Tom will be motivated by his primary level and will thus exhibit task behaviors. In similar situations, Brenda will also be motivated by her primary level and as a result will exhibit relationship behaviors. Fiedler found that in unfavorable situations, task behavior will help the group to be more effective, so Tom's behavior would better match the requirements of the situation. Group effectiveness would not be aided by Brenda's relationship behavior in this situation.

In situations with moderate favorability, both Tom and Brenda are still motivated by their primary motivations, so their behaviors will be precisely the same as described: Tom will exhibit task behaviors and Brenda will exhibit relationship behaviors. Because the situation has changed, however, group effectiveness no longer requires task behavior. Instead, the combination of situational variables leads to a condition where a leader's relationship behaviors will make the greatest contribution to group effectiveness. Hence, Brenda will be the most effective leader in situations of moderate favorability.

In highly favorable situations, the explanation provided by Fiedler gets more complex. When leaders find themselves in highly favorable situations, they no longer have to be concerned about satisfying their primary motivations. In highly favorable situations, leaders switch to satisfying their secondary motivations. Because Tom's secondary motivation is to establish and maintain relationships, in highly favorable situations he will exhibit relationship behaviors. Similarly, Brenda will also be motivated by her secondary motivation, so she would manifest task behaviors in highly favorable situations. Fiedler believed that leaders who manifested relationship behaviors in highly favorable situations helped groups to be more effective. In this case, Tom is giving the group what they need to be more effective.

content of leadership training should emphasize situational engineering rather than behavioral flexibility in leaders. Relatedly, organizations could become more effective if they matched the characteristics of the leader (in this case LPC scores) with the demands of the situation (i.e., situational favorability) than if they tried to change the leader to fit the situation. These suggestions imply that high- or low-LPC leaders in mismatched situations should either change the situation or move to jobs that better match their motivational hierachies and behavorial patterns.

Concluding Thoughts about the Contingency Model

Before reviewing the empirical evidence, perhaps we can attain a clearer understanding of the contingency model by examining it through the L-F-S framework. As seen in Figure 12.8, task structure is a function of the situation and LPC scores are a function of the leader. Because position power is not a characteristic of the leader but of the situation the leader finds him- or herself in, it is included in the situational circle. Leader-member relations is a joint function of the leader and the followers; thus, it best belongs in the overlapping intersection of the leader and follower circles.

As opposed to the dearth of evidence for Hersey and Blanchard's (1969, 1982) situational theory, Fiedler and his fellow researchers have provided considerable evidence that the predictions of the model are empirically valid, particularly in

FIGURE 12.8
Factors from
Fiedler's
contingency
theory and the
interactional
framework.

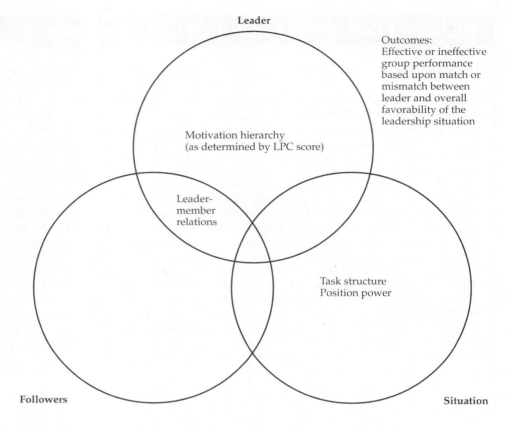

laboratory settings (Fiedler, 1978, 1995; Fiedler & Chemers, 1982; Peters, Hartke, & Pohlmann, 1985; Strube & Garcia, 1981). However, a review of the studies conducted in field settings yielded only mixed support for the model (Peters, Hartke, & Pohlmann, 1985). Moreover, researchers have criticized the model for the uncertainties surrounding the meaning of LPC scores (Kennedy, 1982; Rice, 1978; Schriesheim & Kerr, 1977), the interpretation of situational favorability (Jago & Ragan, 1986a, 1986b), and the relationships between LPC scores and situational favorability (Jago & Ragan, 1986a, 1986b, Vecchio, 1983). Despite such questions, however, the contingency model has stimulated considerable research and is the most validated of all leadership theories.

The Path-Goal Theory

Perhaps the most sophisticated (and comprehensive) of the four contingency models is path-goal theory. The underlying mechanism of **path-goal theory** deals with expectancy, a cognitive approach to understanding motivation where people calculate effort-to-performance probabilities (If I study for 12 hours what is the probability I will get an A on the final exam?), performance-to-outcome probabilities (If I get an A on the final what is the probability of getting an A in the course?), and assigned valences or values to outcome (How much do I value a higher GPA?). Theoretically at least, people were assumed to make these calculations on a rational basis, and the theory could be used to predict what tasks people will put their energies into, given some finite number of options.

Path-goal theory uses the same basic assumptions as expectancy theory. At the most fundamental level, the effective leader will provide or ensure the availability of valued rewards for followers (the "goal") and then help them find the best way of getting there (the "path"). Along the way, the effective leader will help the followers identify and remove roadblocks, and avoid dead ends; the leader will also provide emotional support as needed. These "task" and "relationship" leadership actions essentially involve increasing followers' probability estimates for effort-to-performance and performance-to-reward expectancies. In other words, the leader's actions should strengthen followers' beliefs that if they exert a certain level of effort, then they will be more likely to accomplish a task, and if they accomplish the task, then they will be more likely to achieve some valued outcome.

Although not very complicated in its basic concept, the model added more variables and interactions over time. Evans (1970) is credited with the first version of path-goal theory, but we will focus on a later version developed by House and Dressler (1974). Their conceptual scheme is ideally suited to the L-F-S framework because they described three classes of variables, which include leader behaviors, followers, and the situation. We will examine each of these in turn.

Leader Behaviors

The four types of leader behavior in path-goal theory can be seen in Table 12.1 (see page 381). Like SLT, path-goal theory assumes that leaders not only may use varying styles with different subordinates but might very well use differing styles with the same subordinates in different situations. Path-goal theory suggests that depending on the followers and the situation, these different leader behaviors can increase followers' acceptance of the leader, enhance their level of satisfaction, and raise their expectations that effort will result in effective performance, which in turn will lead to valued rewards (see Highlight 12.5).

The Followers

Path-goal theory contains two groups of follower variables. The first relates to the *satisfaction of followers,* and the second relates to the *followers' perception of their own abilities* relative to the task to be accomplished. In terms of followers' satisfaction, path-goal theory suggests that leader behaviors will be acceptable to the followers to the degree followers see the leader's behavior either as an immediate source of satisfaction or as directly instrumental in achieving future satisfaction. In other words, followers will actively support a leader as long as they view the leader's actions as a means for increasing their own levels of satisfaction. However, there is only so much a leader can do to increase followers' satisfaction levels, as satisfaction also depends on characteristics of the followers themselves.

Shifting Behaviors at Caterpillar

Highlight 12.5

James Despain was a leader with a very directive leadership style. He began his career at Caterpillar, Inc., as a young man, sweeping up the factory floor. He followed the lead of others of his generation—the 1950s was a time when leaders were the ultimate authority and words like *participative* and *consultative* were unheard of. Despain worked his way into supervisory positions and finally was named vice president of the track-type tractor division. Despain claims he "spent much of (his) career as a manager focusing on what employees were doing wrong." He focused on the tasks at hand and little else. But in the early 1990s Despain had to face some hard facts: his $1.2 billion dollar division was losing millions of dollars per year, his management team was getting hundreds of grievances from their employees, and morale at the Caterpillar plant was extremely low.

Despain and his leadership group identified the need for a strategic plan to transform the working culture. Key to the plan was to determine a strategy for dealing with employee attitudes and behavior. Despain and his transformation team identified nine behaviors or "Common Values" that they wanted every employee to emulate every day—trust, mutual respect, customer satisfaction, a sense of urgency, teamwork, empowerment, risk taking, continuous improvement, and com-

mitment. Employee evaluations were then based on the manifestation of these behaviors. Above and beyond those behaviors, top executives and management were expected to lead by example and commit themselves to practice 100 positive leadership traits. Statements such as "I will know every one of my employees by name . . . will recognize their accomplishments with praise . . . will trust my employees to do their work" became the new mantra for those in charge.

Through this process, Despain came to understand that "the most important thing for employees in the workplace is to achieve self-worth." The principal change he was striving to achieve was to make employees accountable for how their jobs got done—for workers that meant stretching a little more every day, to achieve their full potential: For managers it meant shifting away from achieving traditional metrics and toward drawing desired behavior from workers. "And we found that the more we focused on behavior, the better the metrics got." The result: Despain's division cut its break-even point in half within five years of launching the transformation.

Sources: http://www.tribuneindia.com/2004/20040509/spectrum/book2.htm; http://www.sodexho-usa.com/printer_friendly.htm; http://www.stchas.edu/press/despain.shtml

A frequently cited example of how followers' characteristics influence the impact of leader behaviors on followers' levels of satisfaction involves the trait of locus of control. People who believe they are "masters of their own ship" are said to have an internal locus of control; people who believe they are (relatively speaking) "pawns of fate" are said to have an external locus of control. Mitchell, Smyser, and Weed (1975) found that follower satisfaction was not directly related to the degree of participative behaviors manifested by the leader (i.e., followers with highly participative leaders were not any more satisfied than followers with more autocratic leaders). However, when followers' locus-of-control scores were taken into account, a contingency relationship was discovered. As can be seen in Figure 12.9, internal-locus-of-control followers, who believed outcomes were a result of their own decisions, were much more satisfied with leaders who exhibited participative behaviors than they were with leaders who were directive. Conversely, external-locus-of-control followers were more satisfied with directive leader behaviors than they were with participative leader behaviors.

TABLE 12.1
The Four
Leader
Behaviors of
Path-Goal
Theory

Directive leadership. These leader behaviors are very similar to the task behaviors from SLT. They include telling the followers what they are expected to do, how to do it, when it is to be done, and how their work fits in with the work of others. This behavior would also include setting schedules, establishing norms, and providing expectations that followers will adhere to established procedure and regulations.

Supportive leadership. Supportive leadership behaviors include having courteous and friendly interactions, expressing genuine concern for the followers' well-being and individual needs, and remaining open and approachable to followers. These behaviors, which are very similar to the relationship behaviors in SLT, also are marked by attention to the competing demands of treating followers equally while recognizing status differentials between the leader and the followers.

Participative leadership. Participative leaders engage in the behaviors that mark the consultative and group behaviors described by Vroom and Yetton (1973). As such, they tend to share work problems with followers; solicit their suggestions, concerns, and recommendations; and weigh these inputs in the decision-making process.

Achievement-oriented leadership. Leaders exhibiting these would be seen as both demanding and supporting in interactions with their followers. In the first place, they would set very challenging goals for group and follower behavior, continually seek ways to improve performance en route, and expect the followers to always perform at their highest levels. But they would support these behaviors by exhibiting a high degree of ongoing confidence that subordinates can put forth the necessary effort; will achieve the desired results; and, even further, will assume even more responsibility in the future.

FIGURE 12.9
Interaction
between
followers'
locus of control
scores and
leader behavior
in decision
making.

Source: Adapted
from T. R. Mitchell,
C. M. Smyser, and S.
E. Weed, "Locus of
Control: Supervision
and Work
Satisfaction,"
*Academy of
Management Journal*
18 (1975), pp. 623–30.

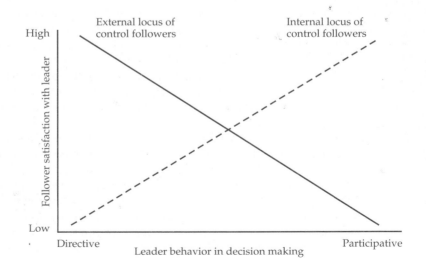

Followers' perceptions of their own skills and abilities to perform particular tasks can also affect the impact of certain leader behaviors. Followers who believe they are perfectly capable of performing a task are not as apt to be motivated by, or as willing to accept, a directive leader as they would a leader who exhibits participative behaviors. Using the same rationale as for locus of control, one can predict the opposite relationship for followers who do not perceive they have sufficient abilities to perform the task. Once again, the acceptability of the leader and the motivation to perform are in part determined by followers' characteristics. Thus, path-goal theory suggests that both leader behaviors and follower characteristics are important in determining outcomes.

The Situation

Path-goal theory considers three situational factors that impact or moderate the effects of leader behavior on follower attitudes and behaviors. These include the *task, the formal authority system, and the primary work group.* Each of these three factors can influence the leadership situation in one of three ways. These three factors can serve as an independent motivational factor, as a constraint on the behavior of followers (which may be either positive or negative in outcome), or as a reward.

However, it should also be increasingly apparent that these variables can often affect the impact of various leader behaviors. For example, if the task is very structured and routine, the formal authority system has constrained followers' behaviors, and the work group has established clear norms for performance, then leaders would be serving a redundant purpose by manifesting directive or achievement-oriented behaviors. These prescriptions are similar to some of those noted in substitutes for leadership theory (Kerr & Jermier, 1978), as everything the follower needs to understand the effort-to-performance and performance-to-reward links is provided by the situation. Thus, redundant leader behaviors might be interpreted by followers as either a complete lack of understanding or empathy by the leader, or an attempt by the leader to exert excessive control. Neither of these interpretations is likely to enhance the leader's acceptance by followers or increase their motivation.

Although people object when a scientific analysis traces their behavior to external conditions and thus deprives them of credit and the chance to be admired, they seldom object when the same analysis absolves them of blame.

B. F. Skinner

Although we have already described how follower characteristics and situational characteristics can impact leader behaviors, path-goal theory also maintains that follower and situational variables can impact each other. In other words, situational variables, such as the task performed, can also impact the influence of followers' skills, abilities, or personality traits on followers' satisfaction. Although this seems to make perfect sense, hopefully you are beginning to see how complicated path-goal theory can be when one starts considering how situational variables, follower characteristics, and leader behaviors interact in the leadership process.

Prescriptions of the Theory

In general, path-goal theory maintains that leaders should first assess the situation and select a leadership behavior appropriate to situational demands. By manifesting the appropriate behaviors, leaders can increase followers' effort-to-performance

FIGURE 12.10
Examples of
applying path-
goal theory.

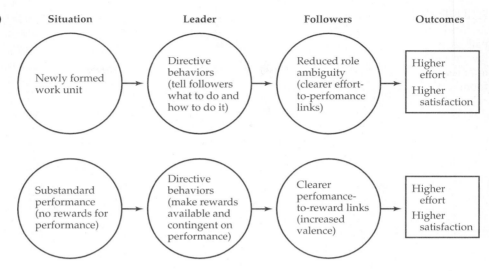

expectancies, performance-to-reward expectancies, or valences of the outcomes. These increased expectancies and valences will improve subordinates' effort levels and the rewards attained, which in turn will increase subordinates' satisfaction and performance levels and the acceptance of their leaders. Perhaps the easiest way to explain this fairly complicated process is through the use of an example. Suppose we have a set of followers who are in a newly created work unit and do not have a clear understanding of the requirements of their positions. In other words, the followers have a reasonably high level of role ambiguity. According to path-goal theory, leaders should exhibit a high degree of directive behaviors in order to reduce the role ambiguity of their followers. The effort-to-performance link will become clearer when leaders tell followers what to do and how to do it in ambiguous situations, which in turn will cause followers to exert higher effort levels. Because role ambiguity is assumed to be unpleasant, these directive leader behaviors and higher effort levels should eventually result in higher satisfaction levels among followers. Figure 12.10 illustrates this process. Similarly, leaders may look at the leadership situation and note that followers' performance levels are not acceptable. The leader may also conclude that the current situation offers few, if any, incentives for increased performance. In this case, the leader may use directive behaviors to increase the value of the rewards (or valence), which in turn will increase followers' effort levels and performance.

Concluding Thoughts about the Path-Goal Theory

Before getting into the research surrounding path-goal theory, you may wish to examine the theory using the L-F-S framework. As seen in Figure 12.11, the components of path-goal theory fit quite nicely into the L-F-S model. The four leader behaviors fit nicely in the leader circle, the characteristics of the followers fit into

FIGURE 12.11

Factors from
path-goal
theory and the
interactional
framework.

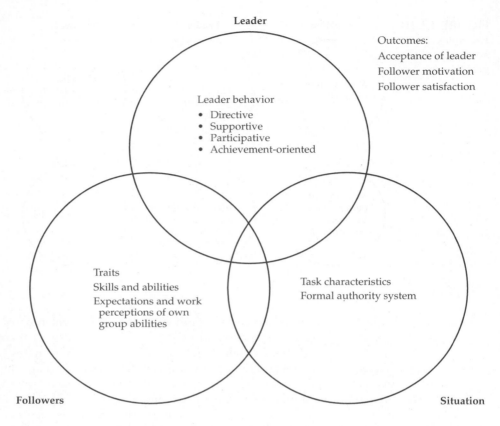

Leader

Leader behavior
• Directive
• Supportive
• Participative
• Achievement-oriented

Outcomes:
Acceptance of leader
Follower motivation
Follower satisfaction

Traits
Skills and abilities
Expectations and work
    perceptions of own
    group abilities

Task characteristics
Formal authority system

Followers

Situation

the follower circle, and the task and the formal authority system fit into the situation circle. Of all the components of path-goal theory, the only "mismatch" with the L-F-S model deals with the primary work group. The norms, cohesiveness, size, and stage of development of groups is considered to be part of the follower function in the L-F-S model but is part of the situation function in path-goal theory. In that regard, we hasten to note we use the L-F-S framework primarily for heuristic purposes. Ultimately, the concepts described in these four theories are sufficiently complex and ambiguous that there probably is no right answer to any single depiction.

In terms of research, the path-goal theory has received only mixed support to date (Schriesheim & DeNisi, 1981; Schriesheim & Kerr, 1977; Yukl, 1989). Although many of these mixed findings may be due to the fact that the path-goal theory excludes many of the variables found to impact the leadership process, that may also be due to problems with the theory. Yukl (1989) maintained that most of these criticisms deal with the methodology used to study path-goal theory and the limitations of expectancy theory. Moreover, the path-goal theory assumes that the only way to increase performance is to increase followers' motivation levels. The theory ignores the roles leaders play in selecting talented followers, building their skill levels through training, and redesigning their work (Yukl & Van Fleet, 1992).

Nonetheless, path-goal theory is useful for illustrating two points. First, as noted by Yukl (1989), "path-goal theory has already made a contribution to the study of leadership by providing a conceptual framework to guide researchers in identifying potentially relevant situational moderator variables" (p. 104). Path-goal theory also illustrates that as models become more complicated, they may be more useful to researchers and less appealing to practitioners. Our experience is that pragmatically oriented students and in-place leaders want to take something from a model that is understandable and can be applied in their work situation right away. This does not mean they prefer simplicity to validity—they generally appreciate the complexity of the leadership process. But neither do they want a model that is so complex as to be indecipherable.

> *To act is easy; to think is hard.*
>
> Goethe

Summary

This chapter is designed to provide an overview of four of the more well-known contingency theories of leadership, which include the normative decision model (Vroom & Yetton, 1973), the Situational Leadership® model, the contingency model (Fiedler, 1967), and the path-goal theory (House & Dessler, 1974). All four models are fairly similar in that they specify that leaders should make their behaviors contingent on certain aspects of the followers or the situation in order to improve leadership effectiveness. In addition, all four theories implicitly assume that leaders can accurately assess key follower and situational factors. However, as the material regarding perception in Chapter 3 shows, it is entirely possible that two leaders in the same situation may reach very different conclusions about followers' level of knowledge, the strength of leader-follower relationships, the degree of task structure, or the level of role ambiguity being experienced by followers. These differences in perception could lead these two leaders to reach different conclusions about the situation, which may in turn cause them to take very different actions in response to the situation. Furthermore, these actions may be in accordance or in conflict with the prescriptions of any of these four theories. Also, the fact that leaders' perceptions may have caused them to act in a manner not prescribed by a particular model may be an underlying reason why these four theories have reported conflicting findings, particularly in field settings.

Another reason these theories have generally found mixed support in field settings concerns the fact that they are all fairly limited in scope. Many of the factors that affect leader and follower behaviors in work group, team, or volunteer committee settings are not present in laboratory studies but often play a substantial role in field studies. For example, none of the models take into account how levels of stress, organizational culture and climate, working conditions, technology, economic conditions, or type of organizational design affect the leadership process. Nevertheless, the four contingency theories have been the subject of considerable research, and even if only mixed support for the models has been found, this research has succeeded in adding to our body of knowledge about leadership and has given us a more sophisticated understanding of the leadership process.

Key Terms

normative decision model, *362*
decision quality, *362*
autocratic processes, *363*
consultative processes, *363*
group process, *363*
decision acceptance, *363*
Situational Leadership®, *368*
task behaviors, *368*

relationship behaviors, *368*
follower readiness, *370*
developmental interventions, *371*
contingency model, *372*
least-preferred-coworker (LPC) scale, *373*
low-LPC leaders, *373*
high-LPC leaders, *373*

situational favorability, *374*
path-goal theory, *378*
directive leadership, *381*
supportive leadership, *381*
participative leadership, *381*
achievement-oriented leadership, *381*

Questions

1. Given the description of the leadership situation facing the airplane crash survivors described in Chapter 1, how would the normative decision model, the situational leadership theory, the contingency model, and path-goal theory prescribe that a leader should act?

2. Can leaders be flexible in how they interact with others? Do you believe leaders can change their behavior? Their personalities?

3. Think of a leadership situation you are fairly familiar with. Apply each of the theories in this chapter to the situations; which theory best fits the interaction of the leader, followers, and situation in your example? Does any theory allow you to predict a likely or preferred outcome for a current challenge?

Skills

Leadership skills relevant to this chapter include:

- Diagnosing performance problems in individuals, groups, and organizations
- Development planning

Activity

Tower Building

Purpose:
Observe decision-making skills in a leaderless group challenged to build a freestanding tower out of Tinker-Toys. Process how situational leadership theory was applied—how the group reacted to a skilled worker. Have the group determine the situational favorability for the task.

Summary:
Divide the class into small groups of approximately 8 to 10 students each. Each group will need its own container of Tinker-Toys. Additionally, it is especially worthwhile in this exercise to appoint at least one observer for each group.

Each group receives identical instructions:
Your task is to build the tallest freestanding tower you can, using the materials in this container (i.e., the Tinker-Toys). You will have 20 minutes to plan your tower and 40 seconds to actually build it. During the planning phase, you may examine your materials but you may not connect any pieces. If you do so, those pieces will be removed and you will not be allowed to use them to construct your tower. The

instructor will announce when the planning phase begins and when it ends. At the end of the planning phase, all of the pieces must be returned to the container; the pieces must be in the container when the building phase begins. As with the planning phase, the instructor will announce when the building period starts and when it ends. When the instructor says "Stop" you must cease all construction. (If there are any questions, reread the relevant portion of the instructions.)

Minicase

"Big Changes for a Small Hospital"

As F. Nicholas Jacobs toured Windber Medical facility he was dismayed by the industrial pink painted walls, the circa 1970 furniture, and the snow leaking through the windows of the conference room. Employees earned 30 percent less than their counterparts in the area, and turnover was steep. As Windber's newest president, Jacobs knew he was the facility's last hope—if he couldn't successfully turn around the aging facility, it would mean closing the doors forever.

Coming to Windber Medical Center in 1997, Jacobs was keenly aware that the hospital could be the next in a series of small hospitals that had fallen victim to a struggling economy. Determined not to see that happen, he began by making connections with the employees of the hospital and the community at large. Jacobs's first step was to interview each of the employees to find out firsthand what they wanted for the Windber community and the medical center. He also looked to members of local community groups like the local library, the Agency on Aging, and local politicians and asked these groups what they wanted from their local medical facility. When Jacobs realized that octogenarians make up a larger percent of the population in Windber, Pennsylvania, than in all of Dade County, Florida, he made it a priority to provide more options to seniors for improving their health and quality of life. He set forth a vision of a medical center that was more of a community center—a center that would allow members of the community to exercise in a state-of-the-art facility while having access to professionals to answer health-related questions. Jacobs realized that keeping people in the community both physically and mentally healthy also meant keeping the hospital financially healthy. He made the center's new preventative-care philosophy clear to the public: "Work out at our hospital so you can stay out of our hospital."

Jacobs's efforts have paid off—in an era when small hospitals are closing left and right, Windber Medical Center is thriving. Under Jacobs's leadership Windber has established an affiliation with the Planetree treatment system, which integrates meditation, massage, music, and other holistic methods into traditional health care. Windber's wellness center, which offers fitness training, yoga, and acupuncture, among other treatments, opened in January 2000 and now generates over $500,000 annually. Gone are the pink walls and dated furniture—replaced with fountains, plants, and modern artwork. Jacobs recruited a former hotel manager to oversee food service. And, despite the dismissal of about 32 employees (those used to a more traditional hospital setting had a tough time in the new environment), the staff has nearly doubled to 450 employees, and pay has improved. Windber has raised more than $50 million in public and private funding and has forged research partnerships with the Walter Reed Army Health System and the University of Pittsburgh, among others. The Windber Research Institute, Windber's heart-disease-reversal program, has treated about 250 patients.

1. Consider the factors from the situational leadership theory outlined in Figure 12.4. Apply these factors to Jacobs and Windber.
2. How do you think Jacobs would score on the least-preferred-coworker (LPC) scale? Why?
3. Based on the success of Windber, in what range would you guess the overall situational favorability might fall for Jacobs on the continuum illustrated in Figure 12.6?

Sources: http://www.careerjournaleurope.com/columnists/inthelead/20030827-inthelead.html; http://www.haponline.org/ihc/hospitalshealthsystems/models2.asp; http://www.post-gazette.com/pg/04013/260747.stm

Chapter

13

Leadership and Change

Old is easy, new is hard.

David B. Peterson and Mary Dee Hicks, Personnel Decisions International

Introduction

Organizations today face a myriad of potential challenges. To be successful they must cope effectively with the implications of new technology, globalization, changing social and political climates, new competitive threats, shifting economic conditions, industry consolidation, swings in consumer preferences, and new performance and legal standards. Think how technology affected Peter Jackson's ability to make the *Lord of the Rings* trilogy, or the changes Colin Powell had to make as the Chairman of the Joint Chiefs of Staff as the U.S. military shifted from stemming the tide of communism to fighting more regionalized conflicts. And how the events of 9/11, the wars in Iraq and Afghanistan, the threats of global terrorism, the emergence of the European Union, and the growth of the Chinese and Indian economies have affected how Colin Powell leads the State Department and influences other world leaders. Likewise, the ability of Aung San Suu Kyi to influence others was dramatically affected by the military takeover of Burma. Her long bouts of house arrest and constant surveillance by the military authorities have changed the way she leads others to create a democratic Burma. These three leaders had to change the organizations they led, and leading change is perhaps the most difficult challenge facing any leader. Yet it may be that this skill is the best differentiator of managers from leaders, and of mediocre from exceptional leaders. The best leaders are those who recognize the situational and follower factors inhibiting or facilitating change, paint a compelling vision of the future, and formulate and execute a plan that moves their vision from a dream to reality.

The scope of any change initiative varies dramatically. Leaders can use goal setting, coaching, mentoring, delegation, or empowerment skills to effectively change the behaviors and skills of individual direct reports. But what would you need to do if you led a pharmaceutical company of 5,000 employees, and you had just

389

received FDA approval to introduce a revolutionary new drug into the marketplace? How would you get the research and development, marketing, sales, manufacturing, quality, shipping, customer service, accounting, and information technology departments to work together to ensure a profitable product launch? Or what would you do if you had to reduce company expenses by 40 percent for the next two years, or deal with a recent acquisition of a competitor? Obviously, change on this scale involves more than individual coaching and mentoring. Because this chapter builds on much of the content of the previous chapters, it is fitting that it appears at the end of the text. To successfully lead larger-scale change initiatives, leaders need to attend to the situational and follower factors affecting their group or organization (Chapters 10–12). They then must use their intelligence, problem-solving skills, creativity, and values to sort out what is important and formulate solutions to the challenges facing their group (Chapters 6–8). But solutions in and of themselves are no guarantee for change; leaders must use their power and influence, personality traits, coaching and planning skills, and knowledge of motivational techniques and group dynamics in order to drive change (Chapters 5, 7–10). Finally, leaders can use some of the measures described in Chapter 4 to monitor the progress of their change initiatives (see Highlight 13.1).

Change in the Waste Industry

Highlight 13.1

Even something as mundane as trash disposal can present some significant leadership challenges. One company, Waste Management, has acquired over 1,600 smaller waste disposal companies since the late 1990s. All of the acquired companies had their own financial systems, pay scales and benefits, trucks and equipment, and operating procedures. None of the IT or financial systems could "talk" to each other, drivers followed very different operating procedures and had different performance standards and compensation packages, many of the companies were former competitors that now had to collaborate in order to achieve overall company goals, and few if any supervisors had been through any type of leadership training. The Board of Directors brought in an outsider, Maury Myers from Yellow Freight, to integrate all these acquisitions into a single company. As CEO, Maury's first task was to create a common financial system so that all the company's revenues and expenses could be consolidated into a single financial statement. And given the large number of acquired companies, this in itself was no small task. He also created a system that allowed supervisors and drivers to set goals and measure daily productivity and customer satisfaction rates and introduced other major organizational change initiatives to improve safety and vehicle maintenance, optimize vehicle use, and reduce operating expenses.

The results of these change initiatives have been nothing short of spectacular. Waste Management is now the industry leader in the waste industry, consisting of approximately 50,000 employees that create $1.5 billion in profits on a $12 billion annual revenue stream. Driver productivity, customer satisfaction, and driver safety have improved over 50 percent, and operating expenses have been dramatically reduced. Maury Myers retired from the CEO role in November 2004 and has been replaced by David Steiner, the former CFO. Moving ahead, David Steiner plans to focus on execution, people development, and capital allocation in order for the company to reach the next level of performance.

As an overview, this chapter begins by revisiting the leadership versus management discussion from Chapters 1 and 2. We then describe a rational approach to organizational change and spell out what leaders can do if they are to be successful with their change efforts. This model also provides a good diagnostic framework for understanding why many change efforts fail. We conclude the chapter with a discussion of an alternative approach to change—charismatic and transformational leadership. The personal magnetism, heroic qualities, and spellbinding powers of these leaders can have unusually strong effects on followers, which often leads to dramatic organizational, political, or societal change. Unlike the rational approach to change, the charismatic and transformational leadership framework places considerable weight on followers' heightened emotional levels to drive organizational change. Much of the leadership research over the past 20 years has helped us to better understand the situational, follower, and leader characteristics needed for charismatic or transformational leadership to occur. The chapter concludes with an overview of these factors and a review of the predominant theory in the field, Bass's (1985) theory of transformational and transactional leadership.

Leadership and Management: Revisited Again

Earlier in this text we described leadership as "the process of influencing an organized group toward accomplishing its goals" (Roach & Behling, 1984). We also differentiated leadership from management, with leadership being more concerned with doing the right thing and management more concerned with doing things right. Bennis (1989) stated that leaders inspire and develop others, challenge the status quo, ask what and why questions, and are more apt to take a long-term view. Managers administer programs, control budgets and costs, maintain the status quo, and are more likely to take a short-term view. Building on Bennis's distinctions, one could say that leadership involves changing the way things are, whereas management involves maintaining the current state of affairs. This distinction between leadership and management is more clearly depicted in Table 13.1. Much like a driver uses the gas, brakes, clutch, gears, and steering wheel to control the speed and direction of a car, a manager uses various accounting, information, hiring, performance management, compensation, training, planning, quality, and inventory systems to align the behavior of followers toward the accomplishment of team or organizational goals. If followers are over budget on travel expenses or fail to come to work on time, then managers use various levers in the accounting or performance management system to correct the situation. These systems help followers to behave in both a consistent and an efficient manner. Organizations tend to be more successful when followers exhibit those behaviors most closely aligned with organizational goals. And organizations that need

> *A manager is a person who directs the work of employees and is responsible for results. An effective manager brings a degree of order and consistency to tasks. A leader, by contrast, inspires employees with a vision and helps them cope with change.*
>
> D. Hellriegel, J. Slocum Jr., and R. Woodman,
> *Organizational Behavior* (7th ed.)

TABLE 13.1
Leadership
versus
Management

Leadership = Change	Management = Control
Vision	Plan
Inspire	Reward
Empower	Direct
Coach	Train
Revenues	Expenses
Forecasts	Budgets
Possibilities	Systems and procedures
Opportunity	Schedule
Synergy	Coordinate

fewer resources to deliver goods and services tend to be more profitable (i.e., efficient) than those needing more resources to do the same thing. There is nothing inherently good or bad with organizational systems, but to some degree the quality of these systems dictates the ease with which a manager can do his or her job.

Although there are several benefits to organizational systems, one of their inherent problems is that they are fairly resistant to change. And well they should be, as they are specifically designed to minimize variability in the way expenses are paid, how software packages are used, the quality of goods and services provided, and so forth. Adding to this resistance is that many people have high security values and have a tendency to fall in love with their systems. Whole bureaucracies and departments are designed to do nothing but support organizational systems.

The definition of neurotic management is to continue to do the same thing but expect a different result.

Anonymous

Oftentimes the people working in the accounting, information technology, or quality departments invented the relevant systems used throughout the organization, and pride of ownership may get in the way of needed changes. Likewise, the users of these systems may not want to learn new graphics programs, accounting procedures, sales models, or six sigma quality processes. Even if current systems are inefficient and dysfunctional, people know how to use them, and with this knowledge comes a certain degree of stability and predictability. Learning new systems and behaviors requires some tolerance for ambiguity and can take a considerable amount of patience, persistence, and hard work. All things being equal, many followers may prefer to have a predictable path rather than risk their success on some uncharted course for the future (O'Toole, 1995; Pritchett, 2001; McNulty, 2002; Heifetz & Linsky, 2000d; Moss Kanter, 2003; Curphy, 2003; Krile, Lund & Curphy, 2005).

So where does leadership come into play in the car analogy? A leader is a person who takes the car down a different road, has a different final destination, or determines whether a car is even the right vehicle. Because technology, globalization, market conditions, consumer preferences, and demographic changes can have big impact on any team or organization, leadership is the key to aligning organizational systems and follower behaviors around a new organizational vision. Whereas managers focus on compliance with existing procedures, leaders take a step back and ask why a system even exists. They create and align systems around a new set of goals for the organization, rather than having existing systems dictate what the organization can and cannot do. Successful leaders are also able to align followers' behaviors with this new vision and systems. But changing followers' behaviors and organizational systems, structure, and goals takes a tremendous amount of skill and effort. You will see that it takes a combination of both leadership and management skills to successfully implement any team or organizational change effort. One of the main reasons for the high base rate of managerial incompetence is that many people in positions of authority struggle with leadership, management, or both sets of skills (see Highlight 13.2). The rest of this chapter describes some of the pertinent research and the steps leadership practitioners must take if they wish to use either the rational or the emotional approach to drive organizational change.

Change in a Rural Community

Highlight 13.2

There is no limit to what an organized group can do if it wants to.

George McLean, the father of the Tupelo Model

Change does not just happen in organizations, it also occurs in communities. Whereas many suburbs are experiencing dramatic growth, most urban and rural communities are experiencing declines in population and business. Some communities are working hard to attract new businesses and build new schools or new community centers; others are organizing to prevent Wal-Mart or other large retailers from building stores in their communities. One of the real success stories of how a community transformed itself is Tupelo, Mississippi. Tupelo is famous for being the birth place of Elvis Presley; in 1940 it also had the distinction of being the county seat of the poorest county in the poorest state in the country. But Lee County now has a medical center with over 6,000 employees, boasts 18 *Fortune* 500 manufacturing plants, and has added 1,000 new manufacturing jobs in each of the past 13 years. Tupelo now has a symphony, an art museum, a theater group, an 8,000-seat coliseum, and an outstanding recreational program. Its public schools have won national academic honors and its athletic programs have won several state championships.

So how was Tupelo able to transform from a poor to a vibrant rural community? The town had no natural advantages, such as harbor or natural resources, which would give it a competitive advantage. It also had no interstate highways and the closest metropolitan centers were over 100 miles away. The key to Tu-

pelo's success was the ability of the town's citizens to work together. More specifically, the citizens of Tupelo were able to: (1) collaborate effectively in identifying the problems and needs of the community; (2) achieve a working consensus on goals and priorities; (3) agree on ways and means to implement goals and priorities; and (4) collaborate effectively in the agreed actions.

Tupelo's success started when local community members pooled resources to acquire a siring bull. The bull's offspring were used to start local ranches. Farmers shifted from planting cotton to those crops needed to support the ranchers and local populace, and farming and ranching equipment distributors started up local operations. George McLean, the local newspaper publisher, kept the community focused on economic development and helped local entrepreneurs by subsidizing office and warehouse space. With various tax breaks and incentives from local bankers, furniture manufacturers started moving to town. A number of other businesses then sprang up to support the manufacturers, and community leaders made a concerted effort to expand and improve local health care and educational facilities to support the new workforce. Despite the successes to date, Tupelo is now facing even bigger challenges, as many of the local furniture manufacturers are being threatened by low-cost manufacturers in China. But if any community were to succeed in the face of challenge, it would likely be Tupelo. The community seems to have the leaders needed to help citizens fully understand these new challenges and what to do to meet them.

Source: V. L. Grisham, Jr., *Tupelo: The Evolution of a Community* (Dayton, OH: Kettering Foundation Press, 1999).

The Rational Approach to Organizational Change

A number of authors have written about organizational change, including Burns (1978), Kanter (1983), Bennis and Nanus (1985), Tichy and Devanna (1986), Bridges (1991), O'Toole (1995), Kotter (1996), Collins and Porras (1997), Treacy and Wiersma (1997), Beer (1988, 1999), Fryer (2001), Huy (2001), Pritchett (2001, 2002), Heifetz and Laurie (2001), Collins (2001), Hirschhorn (2002), McNulty (2002), Heifetz and Linsky (2002), Moss Kanter (2003), Ruvolo and Bullis (2003), and Curphy (2003d, 2004). All of these authors have unique perspectives on leadership and change, but they also share a number of common characteristics. Beer (1988, 1999) has offered a rational and straightforward approach to organizational change that addresses many of the issues raised by the other authors. Beer's model also provides a road map for leadership practitioners wanting to implement an organizational change initiative, as well as a diagnostic tool for understanding why change initiatives fail. According to Beer:

Seventy percent of TQM and reengineering initiatives fail to live up to the expectations of senior management.

Michael Beer,
Harvard Business School

$$C = D \times M \times P > R$$

The D in this formula represents followers' **dissatisfaction** with the current status quo. M symbolizes the **model** for change, and includes the leader's vision of the future as well as the goals and systems that need to change to support the new vision. P represents **process:** This is concerned with developing and implementing a plan that articulates the who, what, when, where, and how of the change initiative. R stands for **resistance;** people resist change because they fear a loss of identity or social contacts, and good change plans address these sources of resistance. Finally the C corresponds to the **amount of change.** Notice that leaders can increase the amount of change by increasing the level of dissatisfaction, increasing the clarity of vision, developing a well-thought-out change plan, or decreasing the amount of resistance in followers. You should also note that the $D \times M \times P$ is a multiplicative function—increasing dissatisfaction but having no plan will result in little change. Likewise, if followers are content with the status quo, then it may be very difficult for leaders to get followers to change, no matter how compelling their vision or change plan may be. This model maintains that organizational change is a very systematic process, and large-scale changes can take months if not years to implement (Beer, 1988, 1999). Leadership practitioners who possess a good understanding of the model should be able to do a better job developing change initiatives and diagnosing where their initiatives may be getting stuck. Because change is an important component of leadership, we will go into more detail on each of the components of Beer's model.

Dissatisfaction

Followers' level of satisfaction is an important ingredient in a leader's ability to drive change. Followers who are relatively content are not apt to change; malcontents are much more likely to do something to change the situation. Although employee satisfaction is an important outcome of leadership, leaders who want to change the status quo may need to take action to *decrease* employee satisfaction levels. Follower's emotions are the fuel for organizational change, and change often requires a considerable amount of fuel. The key for leadership practitioners is to increase dissatisfaction (D) to the point where followers are inclined to take action, but not so much that they decide to leave the organization. So what can leaders do to increase follower dissatisfaction levels? Probably the first step is to determine just how satisfied followers are with the current situation. This information can be gleaned from employee satisfaction surveys, grievance records, customer complaints, or conversations with followers. To increase dissatisfaction, leaders can talk about potential competitive, technology, or legal threats or employee concerns about the status quo. They can also capitalize on or even create some type of financial or political crisis, benchmark against other organizations, or substantially increase performance standards. All of these actions can potentially heighten followers' emotional levels; however, leaders must ensure that these emotions are channeled toward the leader's vision for the organization.

> *The ultimate curse is to be a passenger on a large ship, to know that the ship is going to sink, to know precisely what to do to prevent it, and to realize that no one will listen.*
>
> Myron Tribus, Massachusetts Institute of Technology

Model

There are four key components to the model (M) variable in the change formula, and these include environmental scanning, a vision, setting new goals to support the vision, and identifying needed system changes. As discussed earlier, organizations are constantly bombarded with economic, technological, competitive, legal, and social challenges. Good leaders are constantly scanning the external environment to assess the seriousness of these threats. They are also adept at internal scanning; they understand where the organization is doing well and falling short. Thus, keeping up to date on current events, spending time reviewing organizational reports, and taking time to listen to followers' concerns are some of the techniques leaders use to conduct external and internal scans (O'Toole, 1995; Kotter, 1996; Beer, 1999; Curphy, 2002, 2003c, 2004b, c, f, g; Krile, Lund, & Curphy, 2005). This information in turn is used to formulate a vision for the change initiative. What would a new organization look like if it were to successfully counter the gravest external threats, take advantage of new market opportunities, and overcome organizational shortcomings? What would be the purpose of the new organization and why would people want to work in it? A good vision statement should answer these questions. The good news about a vision statement is that it does not have to be a solo effort on the part of the leader. Oftentimes leaders will either solicit followers for ideas or work with a team of followers to craft a vision statement (Bennis & Nanus, 1985; Tichy & Devanna, 1996; Curphy, 2004b, c, f, g; Krile, Lund, & Curphy, 2005). Both of these actions can help to increase followers' commitment to the new vision.

> *A vision is only a dream if it does not have the commitment and support of the people involved.*
>
> David Lee and Lou Quast, Personnel Decisions International

It is important to understand the difference between an organization's vision and goals. Just as the ancient mariners used the stars to navigate, so too should a vision provide guidance for an organization's actions. A vision helps the organization make choices about what it should and should not do, the kind of people it should hire and retain, the rules by which it should operate, and so on (Treacy & Wiersma, 1997; Curphy, 2004b, c, f, g). But just as the stars were not the final destination for the ancient mariners, so too is a vision not the final destination for an organization. An organization's goals are the equivalent of the ancient mariner's final destination, and they should spell out specifically what the organization is trying to accomplish and when they will get done (Collins & Porras, 1997; O'Toole, 1995; Curphy, 2004b, c, f, g; Krile, Lund, & Curphy, 2005). Depending on the organization, these goals might concern market share, profitability, revenue or customer growth, quality, the implementation of new customer service or information technology systems, the number of patents awarded, school test scores, fundraising targets, or the reduction of crime rates. Thus, an organization's goals can be externally or internally focused or both, depending on the results of the environmental scan and the vision of the organization. Highlight 13.3 provides an example of a vision statement and organizational goals for a hospital in rural Minnesota.

After determining its goals, the leader will need to determine which systems need to change in order for the organization to fulfill its vision and accomplish its goals. In other words, how do the marketing, sales, manufacturing, quality, human resource, shipping, accounting, or customer service systems need to change if the organization is to succeed? And does the current organizational structure or culture support or interfere with the new vision? Leaders wanting their organizational change initiatives to succeed will need to take a systems thinking approach (Senge, 1994; Curphy, 2004f, g, i) after setting organizational goals. A **systems thinking approach** asks leaders to think about the organization as a set of interlocking systems, and explains how changes in

An Example of a Vision Statement and Organizational Goals

Highlight 13.3

VISION STATEMENT
The mission of this organization is to improve and enhance the well-being of individuals and our communities through education, prevention, treatment, and intervention.

SELECTED ORGANIZATIONAL GOALS

- Improve local market share from 28 to 45 percent.
- Achieve 4.5 out of 5.0 physician satisfaction ratings.
- Improve net revenues from 18 to 20.4 million dollars.

- Improve operating margins from $-.2$ to 5.0 percent.
- Improve operating room utilization from 49 to 55 percent.
- Increase the number of births from 8 to 12 per month.
- Reduce employee turnover from 18 to 10 percent.
- Reduce time to hire from 62 to 25 days.

Source: G. J. Curphy, *The Blandin Health Care Leadership Program* (Grand Rapids, MN: The Blandin Foundation, 2004f).

one system can have intended and unintended consequences for other parts of the organization. For example, if a company wanted to grow market share and revenues, then it might change the compensation system to motivate salespeople to go after new customers. However, this approach could also cause a number of problems in the manufacturing, quality, shipping, accounting, and customer service departments. Leaders who anticipate these problems make all of the necessary systems changes in order to increase the odds of organizational success. Leaders may need to set goals and put action plans in place for each of these system changes. These actions can be contrasted to **siloed thinking,** where leaders act to optimize their part of the organization at the expense of suboptimizing the organization's overall effectiveness (Senge, 1994; Curphy, 2004f, g, i). For example, the vice president of sales could change the sales compensation plan if she believed her sole concern was annual revenues. This belief could be reinforced if her compensation was primarily based on hitting certain revenue targets. If she is a siloed thinker, she would also believe that profitability, quality, or customer service were not her concern. However, this mode of thinking could ultimately lead to her downfall, as quality and order fulfillment problems may cause customers to leave at a faster rate than new customers are buying products.

> *The most important component of organizational change is not the seed—it's the soil.*
>
> Michael Beer,
> Harvard Business School

Figure 13.1 is a graphic depiction of a systems model for leadership practitioners. All of the components of this model interact with and affect all the other components of the model. Therefore, leaders changing organizational vision or goals will need to think through the commensurate changes in the organization's structure, culture, systems, and leader and follower capabilities. Similarly, changes in the information or hiring systems can affect the organization's capabilities, culture, structure, or ability to meet its goals. One of the keys to successful organizational change is ensuring that all components in Figure 13.1 are in alignment. A common mistake for many leaders is to change the organization's vision, structure, and systems and overlook the organization's culture and leader and follower capabilities. This makes sense in that it is relatively easy to create a new vision statement, organization chart, or compensation plan. Leaders either discount the importance of organizational culture and capabilities, falsely believe they are easy to change, or believe they are a given because they are so difficult to change. It is possible to change the culture and capabilities of an organization, but it takes considerable time and focused effort (Dickson, Smith, Grojean, & Ehrhart, 2001). Unfortunately, about 70 percent of change initiatives fail, and the underlying cause for many of these failures is the leader's inability or unwillingness to address these culture and capabilities issues (Beer, 1999; Marks & Mirvis, 2001; Pritchett & Pound, 2001; Heifetz & Laurie, 2001; Huy, 2001; Heifetz & Linsky, 2002; Moss Kanter, 2003; Ruvolo & Bullis, 2003; Krile, Lund, & Curphy, 2005).

Process

At this point in the change process, the leader may have taken certain steps to increase follower dissatisfaction. She may also have worked with followers to craft a new vision statement, set new team or organizational goals, and determined what

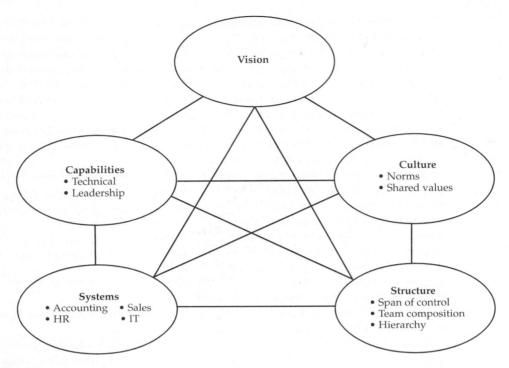

FIGURE 13.1 The components of organizational alignment.

organizational systems, capabilities, or structures need to change. In many ways, the D and M components of the change model are the easiest for leadership practitioners to accomplish. The process (P) component of the change model is where the change initiative becomes tangible and actionable because it consists of the development and execution of the **change plan** (Bossidy & Charan, 2002; Curphy, 2004f, g; Krile, Lund, & Curphy, 2005). Good change plans outline the sequence of events, key deliverables, timelines, responsible parties, metrics, and feedback mechanisms needed to achieve the new organizational goals. It may also include the steps needed to increase dissatisfaction and deal with anticipated resistance, an outline of training and resource needs, and a comprehensive communication plan to keep all relevant parties informed.

Depending on the depth and breadth of change, change plans can be fairly detailed and complicated. For example, the hospital discussed earlier could no longer do what it had always done if it were to reach its goals outlined in Highlight 13.3. The hospital needed new behaviors, metrics, and feedback systems to achieve these goals. The hospital's change plan was quite extensive, and consisted of an overall plan for the hospital as well as department specific goals and change plans. Each of these plans outlined the action steps, responsible parties, metrics, and due dates; progress against the plans was regularly reviewed in hospital and depart-

Organizational change initiatives will only succeed when the changes are specified down to the individual employee level. Employees need to understand which old attitudes and behaviors are to be discarded and which new ones are to be acquired.

Jerry Jellison,
University of Southern California

ment meetings. The goals and change plans were constantly adjusted in these meetings to take into account unforeseen barriers, sooner than expected progress, etc.

Of course the plan itself is only a road map for change. Change will only occur when the action steps outlined in the plan are actually carried out. This is another area where leadership practitioners can run into trouble. One of the reasons why CEOs fail is an inability to execute (Charan & Colvin, 1999; Hirschhorn, 2002; Bossidy & Charan, 2002; Hogan & Curphy 2004; Curphy & Hogan, 2004a), and it is also one of the reasons why first-line supervisors through executives derail. Perhaps the best way to get followers committed to a change plan is to have them create it. This way followers become early adopters and know what, why, when, where, who, and how things are to be done. Nevertheless, many times it is impossible for all the followers affected by the change to be involved with the creation of the plan. In these cases follower commitment can be increased if the new expectations for behavior and performance are explicit, the personal benefits of the change initiative are made clear, and followers already have a strong and trusting relationship with their leader (Curphy, 2004b, c). Even after taking all of these steps, leadership practitioners will still need to spend considerable time holding people accountable for their roles and responsibilities in the change plan. Followers face competing demands for the time and effort, and a lack of follow-through will cause many followers to drop the change initiative off of their radar screens. Leaders should also anticipate shifts in followership styles once the change plan is implemented. Exemplary followers may shift to become alienated followers, conformist to passive followers, or passive to alienated followers. Leaders who address these shifts in styles and inappropriate follower behaviors in a swift and consistent manner are more likely to succeed with their change initiatives.

> *Without a clear vision and an explicit set of goals, all decisions are based on politics.*
>
> Pete Ramstad,
> Personnel Decisions International

Resistance

So why would followership styles shift as a result of a change initiative? One reason is that it may take some time before the benefits of change are realized. Many times leaders, followers, and other stakeholders assume that performance, productivity, or customer service will immediately improve upon the acquisition of new equipment, systems, behaviors, and so on. However, there is often a temporary drop in performance or productivity as followers learn new systems and skills (Jellison, 2000; Curphy 2004b, c, f, g). This difference between initial expectations and reality can be the source of considerable frustration (see Figure 13.2). If not managed properly, it can spark resistance (R), causing followers to revert back to old behaviors and systems to get things done. Leadership practitioners can help followers deal with their frustration by setting realistic expectations, demonstrating a high degree of patience, and ensuring followers gain proficiency with the new systems and skills as quickly as possible.

> *In terms of barriers to change, there is not a single rural community that wouldn't benefit from a few timely deaths.*
>
> Jim Krile,
> The Blandin Foundation

Saving Continental Airlines

Highlight 13.4

By all accounts, Continental Airlines was ready to go under in 1993. The company ranked last in customer service of the 10 major airlines, it lost $600 million in 1994, and employees were so disgrunted that they tore the Continental Airlines logos off their uniforms. The company had gone through 10 CEOs in as many years, and had no vision or strategy in place to pull out of its nosedive. Because of the crisis facing the company, Gordon Berthune from Boeing and Greg Brenneman from Bain & Company were asked in early 1994 to be the next in line to turn Continental Airlines around. Fortunately for the customers, employees, and shareholders, these two leaders have been remarkably successful with their change efforts. But how were they able to turn around such a company facing such a crisis? They did so through a combination of rational and emotional change approaches. They started with a thorough assessment of the situation facing the company. They then built a vision and im-

plemented a set of strategies to improve financial and customer service results. Some of these strategies included changing the Continental Airlines brand, eliminating nonprofitable routes, improving maintenance and operational performance, tracking cash flow, building employee trust and morale through constant communication and numerous "town hall" meetings, eliminating 7,000 positions (of 50,000 employees), and aligning the compensation system around desired employee behaviors. None of these changes were easy—Brenneman likened them to having a 12-hour surgery without anesthesia. However, during the time that these two leaders were on board, Continental Airlines' revenues doubled, the company made a profit every year from 1995 to 2000, stock prices increased fivefold, employee morale soared, and customer satisfaction ratings placed the airline among the best in the industry.

Source: G. Brenneman, *Right Away and All at Once: How We Saved Continental.* Reprint No. 98503 (Boston: Harvard Business School Publishing Division, 1998).

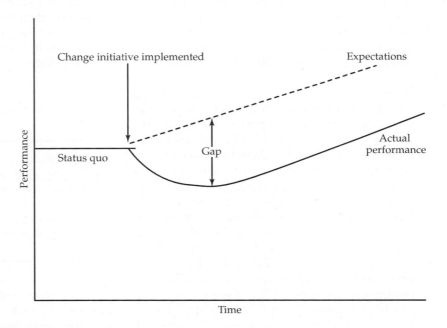

FIGURE 13.2 The expectation-performance gap.

Good change plans address the expectation-performance gap by building in training and coaching programs to improve follower skill levels.

Another reason why followers resist change is a fear of loss (Beer, 1988; Pritchett, 2001, 2002; Pritchett & Pound, 2001; Heifetz & Laurie, 2001; Heifetz & Linsky, 2002; McNulty, 2002; Hirschhorn, 2002; Ruvolo & Bullis, 2003; Curphy, 2004f, g; Krile, Lund, & Curphy, 2005). Because of the change, followers are afraid of losing power, close relationships with others, valued rewards, and their sense of identity or, on the other hand, being seen as in-

> *Everybody resists change, particularly those who have to change the most.*
>
> James O'Toole,
> Aspen Institute

competent. According to Beer (1999), the fear of loss is a predictable and legitimate response to any change initiative, and some of a leader's responses to these fears can be found in Table 13.2. Change initiatives are more likely to be successfully adopted if their change plans identify potential and address these areas of resistance. People also seem to go through some very predictable reactions when confronted with change. An example might help to clarify the typical stages people go through when coping with change. Suppose you were working for a large company that needed to lay off 30 percent of the workforce due to a slowdown in the economy and declining profits. If you were one of the people asked to leave, your first reaction might be shock or surprise. You may not have been aware that market conditions were so soft, or that you would be among those affected by the layoff. Next you would go through an anger stage. You may be angry that you had dedicated many long evenings and weekends to the company, and now the company no longer wanted your services. After anger comes the rejection stage. In this stage, you start to question whether the company really knew what it was doing by letting you go, and perhaps rationalize that they will probably be calling you back. In the final stage, acceptance, you realize that the company is not going to ask you back and you start to explore other career options. These four reactions to change—shock, anger, rejection, and acceptance—make up what is known as the **SARA model** (Kubler-Ross, 1981). It is important to note that most people go through these four stages whenever they get passed over for a promotion, receive negative feedback on a 360-degree report, get criticized by their boss, and so on.

But what should a leadership practitioner do with the SARA model? Perhaps the first step is to simply recognize the four reactions to change. Second, leaders

TABLE 13.2
Common Losses with Change

Source: M. Beer, *Leading Change* (Boston: Harvard Business School Press, 1988).

Loss of:	Possible Leader Actions
Power	Demonstrate empathy, good listening skills, and new ways to build power.
Competence	Coaching, mentoring, training, peer coaching, job aids, and so forth.
Relationships	Help employees build new relationships before change occurs, or soon thereafter.
Rewards	Design and implement new reward system to support change initiative.
Identity	Demonstrate empathy; emphasize value of new roles.

need to understand that individual followers can take more or less time to work through the four stages. Leaders can, however, accelerate the pace in which followers work though the four stages by maintaining an open door policy, demonstrating empathy, and listening to concerns. Third, it is important to note that people are not likely to take any positive action toward a change initiative until they reach the acceptance stage. This does not mean they are happy with the change; only that they accept the inevitability of the change. Fourth, they also need to understand that where people are in the SARA model often varies according to organization level. Usually the first people to realize that a change initiative needs to be implemented are the organization's top leaders. Like everyone else, they go through the four stages, but they are the first to do so. The next people to hear the news are middle managers, followed by first-line supervisors and individual contributors. These three groups also go through the emotional stages of the SARA model, but do so at different times. These differences in emotional reactions by organizational level are depicted in Figure 13.3. What is interesting in Figure 13.3 is that just when top executives have reached the acceptance stage, first-line supervisors and individual contributors are in the shock or anger stages. By this time top

FIGURE 13.3
Reactions
to change.

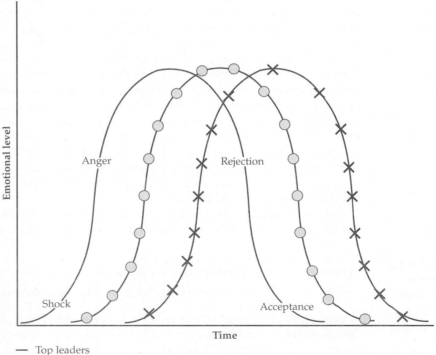

leaders are ready to get on with the implementation of the change initiative and may not understand why the rest of the organization is still struggling. Because they are already at the acceptance stage, top leaders may fail to demonstrate empathy and listening skills, and this may be another reason for the depressed performance depicted in Figure 13.2.

Concluding Comments about the Rational Approach to Organizational Change

The situational, follower, and leader components of the rational approach to organizational change are shown in Figure 13.4. Although organizational vision, goals, and change plans are often a collaborative effort between the leader and followers, they are the primary responsibility of the leader. Leaders also need to think about the importance of critical mass for driving change (Huy, 2001; Curphy, 2004f, g; Krile, Lund, & Curphy, 2005). They may be more successful by initially focusing their change efforts on early adopters and those on the fence rather than on those followers who are the most adamant about maintaining the status quo. Once critical mass is reached, the adopters can then exert peer

> *Commitment is nice, but doses of compliance may be necessary.*
>
> Michael Beer,
> Harvard Business School

FIGURE 13.4
The rational approach to organization change and the interactional framwork.

pressure on those followers reluctant to change (Beer, 1999; Curphy, 2004f, g; Krile, Lund, & Curphy, 2005). This approach also maintains that the leader needs both good leadership and good management skills if a change initiative is to be successful over the long term. Leadership skills are important for determining a new vision for the organization, increasing dissatisfaction, coaching followers on how to do things differently, and overcoming resistance. Management skills are important when setting new goals and creating and implementing change plans. Both sets of skills not only are important components in organizational change but also may play a key role in determining whether a new company will succeed or fail. Because of their strong leadership skills, entrepreneurs are often very good at starting up new organizations, such as dot-coms. Many of these leaders can get followers excited about the leader's vision for the new company. However, if entrepreneurial leaders fail to possess or appreciate the importance of management skills, they may not create the systems, policies, and procedures necessary to keep track of shifting consumer preferences, revenues, customer satisfaction, quality, and costs. As a result, these leaders may not have the information needed to make good operational and financial decisions, and their companies may eventually have to file for bankruptcy. On the other hand, it is hard to see how planning and execution skills alone will result in the formation of a new company or drive organizational change. It is almost impossible to start up a new company—or an organization to successfully change—if the person in charge does not have a compelling vision or fails to motivate others to do something different. As seen in Table 13.3, many of the other reasons why organizational change initiatives succeed or fail also have their roots in underdeveloped leadership or management skills.

Although both sets of skills are important, leadership practitioners should recognize that there is a natural tension between leadership and management skills. In many ways management skills help to maintain the status quo; they help to ensure consistency in behaviors and results. Leadership skills are often used to change the status quo; they help to change the purpose and processes by which an organization gets things done. Leaders who overuse or overemphasize either set of skills are likely to suboptimize team or organizational performance. The first part of this chapter was designed to help leadership practitioners better under-

| **TABLE 13.3**
Eight Reasons
Why Change
Efforts
Succeed or Fail

Source: J. P. Kotter,
Leading Change
(Boston: Harvard
Business School
Press, 1996). | 1. Demonstrate a sense of urgency.
2. Form a strong change coalition.
3. Envision the future and build strategy.
4. Constantly communicate the vision.

5. Remove barriers and align the organization.
6. Build on early successes.
7. Maintain (or increase) the pace of change.
8. Put systems in place to reinforce change. | 1. Allow too much complacency.
2. Fail to create a strong change coalition.
3. Underestimate the power of vision.
4. Undercommunicate the vision by a factor of 10.
5. Permit obstacles to block the vision.

6. Fail to create short-term wins.
7. Declaring victory too soon.

8. Neglect to anchor changes in the culture. |

stand when to use these skills in the change process, and education and experience can help leadership practitioners to improve both sets of skills.

Finally, it is worth noting that the rational approach provides leaders with a systematic process on how to drive change and increased understanding on why change initiatives succeed or fail in their respective organizations. Leadership practitioners can use the C = D × M × P > R model as a roadmap for creating a new vision and goals, changing the products and services their organizations provide, or changing the IT, financial, operations, maintenance, or human resource systems used to support organizational goals. Likewise, leadership practitioners can also use this model as diagnostic to determine where their change initiatives have fallen short—perhaps followers were reasonably satisfied with the status quo, did not buy-in to the new vision and goals, critical systems changes were not adequately identified, or change plans were incomplete or were not properly implemented. Given the explanatory power of the model, the rational approach to change provides leaders and leaders-to-be with a useful heuristic for driving organizational and community change.

The Emotional Approach to Organizational Change: Charismatic and Transformational Leadership

Although the rational approach provides a straightforward model for organizational change, it seems like many of the large-scale political, societal, or organizational changes were not this formulaic. For example, it is doubtful that Jesus Christ, Muhammad, Joan of Arc, Vladimir Lenin, Adolf Hitler, Mahatma Gandhi, Mao Zedong, Martin Luther King, Jr., the Ayatollah Khomeini, Nelson Mandela, Charles Taylor, Foday Sankoh, or Muhammad Omar followed some change formula or plan, yet these individuals were able to fundamentally change their respective societies. Although these leaders differ in a number of important ways, one distinct characteristic they all share is charisma. Charismatic

> *Leadership is the art of getting someone else to do something you want done because he wants to do it.*
>
> Dwight D. Eisenhower

leaders are passionate, driven individuals who are able to paint a compelling vision of the future. Through this vision they are able to generate high levels of excitement among followers and build particularly strong emotional attachments with them. The combination of a compelling vision, heightened emotional levels, and strong personal attachments often compels followers to put forth greater effort to meet organizational or societal challenges. The enthusiasm and passion generated by charismatic leaders seems to be a dual-edged sword, however. Some charismatic movements can result in positive and relatively peaceful organizational or societal changes; some more recent examples might include the Falun Gong movement in China, Louis Farrakhan's Million Man March, or Aung San Suu Kyi's democracy movement in Burma. On the downside, when this passion is used for selfish or personal gains, history mournfully suggests it can have an equally devastating effect on society. Examples here might include David Koresh of Waco infamy, Adolf Hitler, the Serbian leader Slobodan Milosevic, Foday Sankoh of Sierra Leore, or Muhammad Omar, the leader of the Taliban movement in Afghanistan.

So what is it about charismatic leadership that causes followers to get so excited about future possibilities that they may willingly give up their lives for a cause? Even though many people conjure up images of charismatic individuals when thinking about leadership, the systematic investigation of charismatic leadership is relatively recent. The remainder of this chapter begins with a historical review of the research on charismatic leadership and the leader-follower-situation components of charismatic leadership. We will then review the most popular conceptualization of charisma, Bass's (1985) theory of transformational and transactional leadership. We conclude this chapter by comparing and contrasting the rational and emotional approaches to organizational change.

Charismatic Leadership: A Historical Review

Prior to the mid-1970s charismatic leadership was studied primarily by historians, political scientists, and sociologists. Of this early research, Max Weber (1947) arguably wrote the single most important work. Weber was a sociologist interested primarily in how authority, religious, and economic forces affected societies over time. Weber maintained that societies could be categorized into one of three types of authority systems: traditional, legal-rational, and charismatic.

In the **traditional authority system,** the traditions or unwritten laws of the society dictate who has authority and how this authority can be used. The transfer of authority in such systems is based on traditions such as passing power to the first-born son of a king after the king dies. Historical examples would include the monarchies of England from the 1400s to 1600s or the dynasties of China from 3000 B.C. to the 1700s. Some of the modern-day examples of the traditional authority system include Saudi Arabia, Kuwait, Syria, North Korea, Brunei, and Libya. But these examples should not be limited to countries, as many of the CEOs in privately held companies or publicly traded companies that are controlled by a majority shareholder are often the children or relatives of the previous CEO. Examples include Ford, Anheuser-Busch, Cargill, Coors, Amway, and Carlson Companies (owners of T.G.I.F. restaurants and Radisson Hotels). In the **legal-rational authority system** a person possesses authority not because of tradition or birthright, but because of the laws that govern the position occupied. For example, elected officials and most leaders in nonprofit or publicly traded companies are authorized to take certain actions because of the position they occupy. The power is in the position itself, rather than in the person who occupies the position. Thus, Colin Powell can take certain actions not because of who he is or is related to, but because of his role as secretary of state.

It's better to burn out than it is to rust.

Neil Young, songwriter

These two authority systems can be contrasted to the **charismatic authority system,** in which persons derive authority because of their exemplary characteristics. Charismatic leaders are thought to possess superhuman qualities or powers of divine origin that set them apart from ordinary mortals. The locus of authority in this system rests with the individual possessing these unusual qualities; it is not derived from birthright or laws. According to Weber, charismatic leaders come from the margins of society and emerge as leaders in times of great social crisis. These leaders serve to focus society both on the problem it faces and on the revolutionary solutions proposed by the leader. Thus, charismatic authority systems are usually the result of a revolution against the traditional and legal-rational authority systems. Examples of these revolutions might be the overthrow of the shah of Iran by the Ayatollah Khomeini, the ousting of the British in India by Mahatma Gandhi, the success of Martin Luther King, Jr., in changing the civil rights laws in the United States, or the democracy movement led by Aung San Suu Kyi in Burma. Unlike traditional or legal-rational authority systems, charismatic authority systems tend to be short-lived. Charismatic leaders must project an image of success in order for followers to believe they possess superhuman qualities; any failures will cause followers to question the divine qualities of the leader and in turn erode the leader's authority.

A number of historians, political scientists, and sociologists have commented on various aspects of Weber's conceptualization of charismatic authority systems. Of all these comments, however, probably the biggest controversy surrounding Weber's theory concerns the locus of charismatic leadership. Is charisma primarily the result of the situation or social context facing the leader, the leader's extraordinary qualities, or the strong relationships between charismatic leaders and followers? A number of authors argued that charismatic movements could not take place unless the society was in a crisis (Blau, 1963; Chinoy, 1961; Wolpe, 1968). Along these lines, Friedland (1964), Gerth and Mills (1946), and Kanter (1972) argued that before a leader with extraordinary qualities would be perceived as charismatic, the social situation must be such that followers recognize the relevance of the leader's qualities. Others have argued that charismatic leadership is primarily a function of the leader's extraordinary qualities, not the situation (Tucker, 1968; Dow, 1969). These qualities include having extraordinary powers of vision, the rhetorical skills to communicate this vision, a sense of mission, high self-confidence and intelligence, and setting high expectations for followers. Finally, several authors have argued that the litmus test for charismatic leadership does not depend on the leader's qualities or the presence of a crisis, but rather on followers' reactions to their leader (Clark, 1972; Deveraux, 1955; Downton, 1973; Marcus, 1961; Shils, 1965). According to this argument, charisma is attributed only to those leaders who can develop particularly strong emotional attachments with followers.

The debate surrounding charismatic leadership shifted dramatically with the publication of James MacGregor Burns's *Leadership* (1978). Burns was a prominent political scientist who had spent a career studying leadership in the national political arena. He believed that leadership could take one of two forms. **Transactional leadership** occurred when leaders and followers were in some type of exchange relationship in order to get needs met. The exchange could be economic, political, or psychological in nature, and examples might include exchanging money for work, votes for political favors, loyalty for consideration, and so forth. Transactional leadership is very common

> *Some men see things as they are and ask why? I dream things that never were and ask, why not?*
>
> Edward Kennedy,
> U.S. Senator, in the eulogy to his brother, Robert F. Kennedy

but tends to be transitory, in that there may be no enduring purpose to hold parties together once a transaction is made. Burns also noted that while this type of leadership could be quite effective, it did not result in organizational or societal change and instead tended to perpetuate and legitimize the status quo.

The second form of leadership is **transformational leadership,** which serves to change the status quo by appealing to followers' values and their sense of higher purpose. Transformational leaders articulate the problems in the current system and have a compelling vision of what a new society or organization could be. This new vision of society is intimately linked to the values of both the leader and the followers; it represents an ideal that is congruent with their value systems. According to Burns, transformational leadership is ultimately a moral exercise in that it serves to raise the standard of human conduct. This implies that the acid test for transformational leadership might be the answer to the question, "Do the changes advocated by the leader advance or hinder the development of the organization or society?" Transformational leaders are also adept at **reframing** issues; they point out how the problems or issues facing followers can be resolved if they fulfill the leader's vision of the future. These leaders also teach followers how to become leaders in their own right and incite them to play active roles in the change movement (see Highlight 13.5).

It is important to note that all transformational leaders are charismatic, but not all charismatic leaders are transformational. Transformational leaders are charis-

An Example of a Transformational Leader: Nelson Mandela

Highlight 13.5

South Africa was ruled by a white minority government for much of the past 200 years. Although blacks made up over 75 percent of the populace, whites owned most of the property, ran most of the businesses, and controlled virtually all of the country's resources. Moreover, blacks did not have the right to vote and often worked under horrible conditions for little or no wages. Seeing the frustration of his people, Nelson Mandela spent 50 years working to overturn white-minority rule. He started by organizing the African National Congress, a nonviolent organization that protested white rule through work stoppages, strikes, and riots. Several whites were killed in the early riots, and in 1960 the police killed or injured over 250 blacks in Sharpeville. Unrest over the Sharpeville incident caused 95 percent of the black workforce to go on strike for two weeks, and the country declared a state of emergency. Mandela then orchestrated acts of sabotage to further pressure the South African government to change. The organiza-

tion targeted installations and took special care to ensure no lives were lost in the bombing campaign. Mandela was arrested in 1962 and spent the next 27 years in prison. While in prison he continued to promote civil unrest and majority rule, and his cause eventually gained international recognition. He was offered but turned down a conditional release from prison in 1985. After enormous international and internal pressure, South African President F. W. de Klerk "unbanned" the ANC and unconditionally released Nelson Mandela from prison. Nonetheless, South Africa remained in turmoil, and in 1992 four million workers went on strike to protest white rule. Because of this pressure, Mandela forced de Klerk to sign a document outlining multiparty elections. Mandela won the 1994 national election and was the first truly democratically elected leader of the country.

Sources: M. Fatima, *Higher than Hope: The Authorized Biography of Nelson Mandela* (New York: Harper & Row, 1990); S. Clark, *Nelson Mandela Speaks: Forming a Democratic, Nonracist South Africa* (New York: Pathfinder Press, 1993).

matic because they are able to articulate a compelling vision of the future and form strong emotional attachments with followers. However, this vision and these relationships are aligned with followers' value systems and help them get their needs met (Turner, Barling, Epitropaki, Butcher, & Milner, 2002; Price, 2003). Charismatic leaders who are *not* transformational can convey a vision and form strong emotional bonds with followers, but they do so in order to get their own (i.e., the leader's) needs met. Both charismatic and transformational leaders strive for organizational or societal change; the difference is whether the changes are for the benefit of the leader or the followers. This distinction can be appreciated more fully by reading Highlight 13.6. Finally, transformational leaders are always controversial. Charismatic leadership almost inherently raises conflicts over values or definitions of the social "good." Controversy also arises because the people with the most to lose in any existing system will put up the most resistance to a transformational change initiative. The emotional levels of those resisting the transformational leadership movement are often just as great as those who embrace it, and this may be the underlying cause for the violent ends to Martin Luther King, Jr., John F. Kennedy, Mahatma Gandhi, Joan of Arc, or Jesus Christ. Burns stated that transformational leadership always involves conflict and change, and transformational leaders must be willing to embrace conflict, make enemies, exhibit a high level of self-sacrifice, and be thick-skinned and focused in order to perpetuate the cause.

An Example of a Charismatic Leader: David Koresh

Highlight 13.6

In April 1993 approximately 85 people died at a religious compound outside Waco, Texas. Many of them died from the fire that consumed the compound, but a single shot in the head had killed others. Twenty-five of the deceased were children. How did this happen? The story of David Koresh is a classic example of what can go wrong when the situational, follower, and leadership elements necessary for charismatic leadership are in place but the leader exploits followers for his own selfish purposes. As a child, David's nickname was Sputnik—he was smart, inquisitive, energetic, but also had a strong need for security. When David turned nine his mother decided to attend the local Seventh-day Adventist church. Apparently David loved church and religion—he would be spellbound during sermons and spend hours listening to religious programs on the radio. David had a strong need to be the center of attention and spent time convincing others that he was special and worthwhile (i.e., color-

ful, bold, mischievous, imaginative, and skeptical—dark-side personality traits from Chapter 7). He did so by reciting long passages of Scripture during church meetings and by telling others that God was talking to him. He eventually joined the Branch Davidians, a splinter group of the Seventh-day Adventists. Over the next four years David consolidated his hold on leadership, and convinced his fellow sect members that he was a living prophet and that Armageddon was at hand. To meet the challenge of Armageddon, he and fellow Branch members acquired a large cache of handguns, assault weapons, and explosives. During this time David's behavior became increasingly temperamental and violent. He made fellow members watch violent war movies, listen to his rock and roll sessions, and put them through long fasts and strange diets. This bizarre behavior continued until the Alcohol, Tobacco, and Firearms raid in February 1993.

Source: K. R. Samples; E. M. deCastro; R. Abanes; and R. J. Lyle, *Prophets of the Apocalypse: David Koresh and Other American Messiahs* (Grand Rapids, MI: Baker Books, 1994).

Yukl (1999), Hunt (1999) and Conger and Hunt (1999) all maintained that the publication of *Leadership* (Burns, 1978) played a key role in renewing interest in the topic of leadership. As a result, research over the past 25 years has explored cross-cultural, gender, succession, leader, follower, situational, and performance issues in charismatic or transformational leadership. From these efforts we now know that charismatic or transformational leadership is both common and rare. It is common because it can occur in almost every social stratum across every culture. For example, a high school student leader in France, a military cadet leader at the United States Air Force Academy, a Kenyan community leader, an Indonesian hospital leader, or a Russian business executive could all be perceived as charismatic or transformational leaders (Bass, 1999; Den Hartog, Hanges, Dorfman, Ruitz-Quintana & Associates, 1999). But it is also rare because most people in positions of authority are not perceived to be charismatic or transformational leaders. We also know that females such as Margaret Thatcher, Mary Kay Ash, or Anita Roddick tend to be perceived as more charismatic than their male counterparts, and that transformational leadership results in higher group performance than transactional leadership (Eagly, 1987; Rosener, 1990; Druskat, 1994; Bass, Avolio, & Atwater, 1996; Ross & Offermann, 1991; Avolio & Bass, 2000; Bass, 1999, 2000; Waldman, Ramirez, House, & Puranam, 2001; Barling, Laughlin, & Kelloway, 2002; Dvir, Eden, Avolio, & Shamir, 2002; Bono, 2002; Bass, Avolio, Jung, & Berson, 2003; Towler, 2003; Waldman, Javidan, & Varella, 2004). Although charismatic or transformational leadership often results in large-scale organizational change and higher organizational performance, there is little evidence that these changes remain permanent in business settings after the leader moves on (Conger, 1999). In addition, some researchers have found that charismatic or transformational leaders did not result in higher organizational performance, but they did earn higher paychecks for themselves (Khurana, 2002; Tosi, Misangyi, Fanelli, Waldman, & Yammarino, 2004). In other words, these leaders were very good at calling attention to themselves and changing their respective organizations, but many of these changes did not result in higher organizational performance.

As a result of this research, we also have three newer theories of charismatic or transformational leadership. Conger and Kanungo (1998) used a stage model to differentiate charismatic from noncharismatic leaders. Charismatic leaders begin by thoroughly assessing the current situation and pinpointing problems with the status quo. They then articulate a vision that represents a change from the status quo. This vision represents a challenge to and is a motivating force for change for followers. The vision must be articulated in such a way that increases dissatisfaction with the status quo and compels followers to take action. In the final stage, leaders build trust in their vision and goals by personal example, risk taking, and their total commitment to the vision. The theory developed by House and his colleagues (House, 1977; House & Shamir, 1993; Shamir, House, & Arthur, 1993) describes how charismatic leaders achieve higher performance by changing followers' self-concepts. Charismatic leaders are believed to motivate followers by changing their perceptions of work itself, offering an appealing vision of the future, developing a collective identity among followers, and increasing their confidence in getting the job done. Avolio and Bass's (2000) theory of transactional and transformational leadership is essentially an extension of Burns's theory. Unlike Burns, who viewed transactional and transformational leadership as the extremes of a single continuum, Avolio and Bass viewed these two concepts as independent leadership dimensions. Thus, leaders can be transformational and transactional, transactional but not transformational, and so on. Transformational leaders are believed to achieve stronger results because they heighten followers' awareness of goals and the means to achieve them, they convince followers to take action for the collective good of the group, and their vision of the future helps followers satisfy higher-order needs. Because Avolio and Bass created a questionnaire to assess a leader's standing on transactional and transformational leadership, this theory is by far the most thoroughly researched and will be discussed in more detail later in this chapter.

What Are the Common Characteristics of Charismatic and Transformational Leadership?

Although there are some important differences in the theories offered by Conger and Kanungo (1998), House (1977), and Avolio and Bass (2000), in reality they are far more similar than different. It is also important to note that these researchers either do not differentiate charismatic from transformational leadership, or see charisma as a component of transformational leadership. Therefore, we will use the terms somewhat interchangeably in the next section, although we acknowledge the fundamental difference between these two types of leadership. A review of the common leader, follower, and situational factors from Burns and the three more recent theories can be found in Figure 13.5. Like the past debates surrounding charismatic leadership, modern researchers are divided on whether charismatic leadership is due to the leader's superhuman qualities, a special relationship between leaders and followers, the situation, or some combination of these factors. Irrespective of the locus of charismatic leadership, the research does provide overwhelming support for the notion that transformational leaders are effective at large-scale societal or organizational change.

> *We've long believed that when the rate of change inside an institution becomes slower than the rate of change outside, the end is in sight. The only question is when.*
>
> Jack Welch,
> former CEO of General Electric

Leader Characteristics

Leadership researchers have spent considerably more time and effort trying to identify the unique characteristics of charismatic leaders than they have exploring follower or situational factors (Conger, 1999). This is partly because some researchers believe that it is possible to drive higher levels of organizational change or performance through the selection or training of charismatic leaders (Avolio & Bass, 1998, 2000; Bass, 1999; Hooijberg & Choi, 2000; Ross & Offermann, 1997; Zacharatos, Barling, & Kelloway, 2000; Bono, 2002; Bass, Avolio, Jung, & Berson, 2003; Towler, 2003; Frese, Beimel, & Schoenborn, 2003). Although some scholars have argued that the

FIGURE 13.5

Factors pertaining to charismatic leadership and the interactional framework.

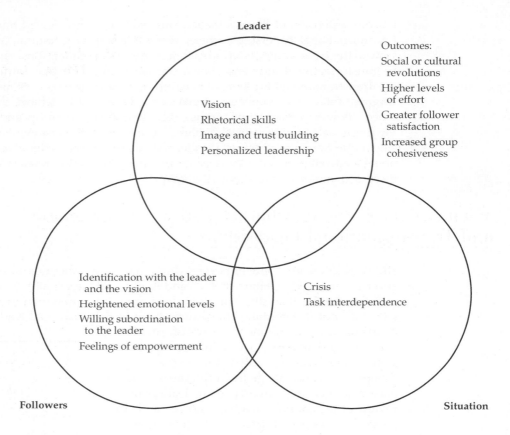

Charismatic leaders are meaning makers. They pick and choose from the rough materials of reality and construct pictures of great possibilities. Their persuasion then is of the subtlest kind, for they interpret reality to offer us images of the future that are irresistible.

Jay Conger,
University of Southern California

leader's personal qualities are the key to charismatic or transformational leadership (Boal & Bryson, 1987; C. W. Hill; 1984; Kets de Vries, 1977, 1993; Sashkin, 1988; Zeleznik, 1974), we do not believe the leader's qualities alone result in charismatic leadership. We do, however, acknowledge several common threads in the behavior and style of both charismatic and transformational leaders, and these include their vision and values, rhetorical skills, ability to build a particular kind of image in the hearts and minds of their followers, and personalized style of leadership.

Vision

Both transformational and charismatic leaders are inherently future-oriented. They involve helping a group move "from here to there." Charismatic leaders perceive fundamental discrepancies between the way things are and the way things can (or should) be. They recognize the shortcomings of a present order and offer an imaginative **vision** to overcome them. Several aspects of vision are worth elaboration. First, vision is not limited to grand social movements; leaders can use vision to help drive organizational change and performance in any kind or level of organization. Second, both Bennis and Nanus (1985) and Tichy and Devanna (1986) reported that the leader's vision of the future is often a collaborative effort; the genius of the leader is his or her ability to synthesize seemingly disparate issues and problems and develop a vision that ties all of these concerns together. Paradoxically, the magic of a leader's vision is often that the more complicated the problem, the more people may be drawn to simplistic solutions. Third, values play a key role in the leader's vision, and serve as a moral compass for aligning the actions of leaders and followers with change initiatives (Ket de Vries, 1993; Shamir, Arthur, & House, 1994; Shamir, House, & Arthur, 1993; Bass, 1999; Bass & Steidlmeier, 1999; Turner, Barling, Eptiropaki, Butcher, & Milner, 2002; Strange & Mumford, 2002; Popper & Mayseless, 2003; Price, 2003). As noted previously, this is one way transformational leaders differ from "mere" charismatic leaders: the former builds a vision based on *followers'* values whereas the latter's vision is based solely on their *own* values. Fourth, the leader's vision helps followers interpret events and actions in terms of a common perceptual framework (Wofford & Goodwin, 1994; Fairhurst & Sarr, 1996; Gardner & Avolio, 1998; McKee, 2003; Palus, Horth, Selvin, & Pulley, 2003). Fifth, Berlew (1974, 1992) maintained that the vision of the charismatic leader had both a stimulating and a unifying effect on the efforts of followers. As seen in Figure 13.6, these effects can help drive greater organizational change and higher performance levels by followers.

> *Win or lose, hit the booze.*
>
> Gordy Curphy
> C^3

FIGURE 13.6
A leader's vision of the future can align efforts and help groups accomplish more.

Source: Adapted from P. M. Senge, *The Fifth Discipline* (New York: Doubleday, 1990).

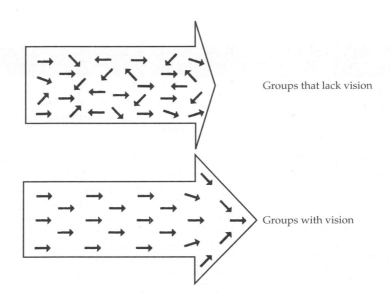

Groups that lack vision

Groups with vision

Image and Trust Building

As seen in Highlight 13.8, transformational leaders build trust in their leadership and the attainability of their goals through an **image** of seemingly unshakable self-confidence, strength of moral conviction, personal example and self-sacrifice, and unconventional tactics or behavior (House, 1977; Conger, 1989; Bass & Avolio, 1994; Bass, 1997; Gardner & Avolio, 1998; Bass & Steidlmeier, 1999; Conger, 1999; Yorges, Weiss, & Strickland, 1999; Choi & Mai-Dalton, 1999; Sosik, Avolio, & Jung, 2002; Pillai, Williams, Lowe, & Jung, 2003). They are perceived to have unusual insight and ability and act in a manner consistent with their vision and values. Some charismatic leaders even seem to place more importance on creating the *appearance* of success than on success per se (House, 1977; Khurana, 2002; Tosi, Misangyi, Fanelli, Waldman, & Yammarino, 2004). Whereas transformational leaders **build trust** by showing commitment to followers' needs over self-interest, some charismatic leaders are not beyond taking credit for others' accomplishments or exaggerating their expertise (Conger, 1989).

> *Setting an example is not the main means of influencing another; it is the only means.*
>
> Albert Einstein

Personalized Leadership

One of the most important aspects of charismatic and transformational leadership is the personal nature of the leader's power. These leaders share strong, personal bonds with followers, even when the leader occupies a formal organizational role (Yagil, 1998; Conger, 1999; Avolio & Bass, 2000). It is this **personalized leadership** style that seems to be responsible for the feelings of empowerment notable among followers of charismatic or transformational leaders, and it has three important components. First, charismatic leaders are more sensitive to the emotional states of followers (Judge & Bono, 2000). They seem to be more adept at picking up social cues and tailoring their messages accordingly. Second, they also tend to be emotionally expressive, especially through such nonverbal channels as their eye contact,

---

Image and Trust Building of Aung San Suu Kyi

Highlight 13.8

Aung San Suu Kyi was involved in a dramatic incident on the evening of April 5, 1989. As they were returning home, she and a group of pro-democracy organizers were stopped and ordered off the road by government soldiers. Rather than having everyone get out of the car, Aung San Suu Kyi told everyone to remain in the car and then got out to approach the soldiers. "It seemed so much simpler," she later explained, "to provide them with a single target." The captain of the soldiers ordered his troops to raise their rifles and shoot, but Aung San Suu Kyi continued to advance. At the last second, a major ran forward and overruled the captain. Later that year at her mother's funeral, she stated that she would serve the Burmese people without fear of personal cost, and she eventually was placed under house arrest for "endangering the state."

posture, movement, gestures, tone of voice, and facial expressions (Bass, 1990; Den Hartog & Verburg, 1997). It is partly through their ability to pick up on emotional cues and their nonverbal behaviors that some people are perceived to have a "magnetic" personality. Third, transformational leaders empower followers by building their self-efficacy. They do this by giving followers tasks that lead to successively greater success experiences and heightened self-confidence, encouraging followers to continually upgrade their skills, and creating an environment of heightened expectations and positive emotions (Larmore & Ayman, 1998; Bass, 1997; Bass & Avolio, 1994; Conger & Kanungo, 1998; Rost, 1991; Bono & Judge, 2003). In all likelihood, charismatic leaders possess more surgency; agreeableness, and adjustment (see Chapter 7) than noncharismatic leaders (Curphy, 2003a; Antonakis & House, 2004).

Follower Characteristics

If charismatic leadership were defined solely by a leader's characteristics, then it would be relatively easy to identify those individuals with good visioning, rhetorical, and impression management skills, and place them in leadership positions. Over time we would expect that a high percentage of followers would embrace and act on the leader's vision. However, a number of leaders appear to possess these attributes, yet are not seen as charismatic. They may be good, competent leaders in their own right, but they seem unable to evoke strong feelings in followers or to get followers to do more than they thought possible. In reality, charisma is probably more a function of the followers' reactions to a leader than of the leader's personal characteristics. If followers do not accept the leader's vision or become emotionally attached to the leader, then the leader simply will not be perceived to be either charismatic or transformational. Thus, **charisma** is in the eyes and heart of the beholder; it is a particularly strong emotional reaction to, identification with, and belief in some leaders by some followers. It is important to note that this definition is value-free—leaders seen as charismatic may or may not share the same values as their followers or meet Burns's criteria for transformational leadership. A recent example of followers' divergent reactions can be seen in President George W. Bush. Some followers, particularly those in the Republican party, perceive President Bush to be a very charismatic leader. Most Democrats believe he lacks charisma and does not share the same values as the American people, yet he is clearly the same person. Many of the more popular conceptualizations of charisma and charismatic leadership today also define charisma in terms of followers' reactions to the leader (Bass, 1985, 1997; Avolio & Bass, 2000; Conger & Kanungo, 1998; Shamir, House, & Arthur, 1993; Howell, 1988; Willner, 1984). Defining charisma as a reaction that followers have toward leaders makes it reasonable to turn our attention to the four unique characteristics of these reactions.

I am much more electable than I am qualified.

Martin Sheen,
Actor

To be an effective leader, one must become a leader of leaders . . . The ultimate measure of Christ's leadership is that the movement he founded continued to spread after his death. In fact, from the moment of his first conversions, Christianity belonged not to Christ but to the Christians.

James O'Toole,
The Aspen Institute

Identification with the Leader and the Vision

Two of the effects associated with charismatic leadership include a strong affection for the leader and a similarity of follower beliefs with those of the leader. These effects describe a sort of bonding or **identification with the leader** personally, and a parallel psychological investment to a goal or activity (a "cause") bigger than oneself. Followers bond with a leader because they see the implementation of the vision as a solution to all of their problems. Followers may be intensely dissatisfied with the status quo but unsuccessful in developing a satisfactory solution on their own. Charismatic leaders capitalize on this dissatisfaction and on the belief that most people want to make a difference in their organizations or society. Followers' identities or self-concepts also become defined in terms of the leader. Being like the leader, or approved by the leader, becomes an important part of one's self-worth (Ehrhart & Klein, 2001; Lord & Brown, 2001; Kark, Shamir, & Chen, 2003). Effects like these go well beyond what might be expected from the typical contractual or exchange relationships between most supervisors and subordinates.

Heightened Emotional Levels

Charismatic leaders are able to stir followers' feelings, and this **heightened emotional level** results in increased levels of effort and performance (Fox & Amichai-Hamburger, 2001; Bono & Judge, 2003). Emotions are often the fuel driving large-scale initiatives for change, and charismatic leaders will often do all they can to maintain them,

> *We're not worthy; we're not worthy!*
> Wayne and Garth,
> *Wayne's World*

including getting followers to think about their dissatisfaction with the status quo or making impassioned appeals directly to followers. There are several dangers with increasing followers' emotional levels, however. The leader must ensure that followers' emotions are channeled toward the change initiative, otherwise followers will find some other outlet for their feelings and efforts (see Table 13.4). In addition, the people alienated by a charismatic leader and the movement can have emotions just as intense as those of the followers of the vision. This polarizing effect of charismatic leaders may be one reason why they tend to have violent deaths, as those alienated by a charismatic leader are just as likely to act on their emotions as followers within the movement (House, Woycke, & Fodor, 1988).

TABLE 13.4
Followers'
Responses to
Change

Source: B. Yager
(Boise, ID: The
Bryan Yager Group,
2003).

Malicious Compliance: This occurs when followers either ignore or actively sabotage change requests.
Compliance: This takes place when followers do no more than abide by the policies and procedures surrounding change requests.
Cooperation: Followers willingly engage in those activities needed to make the change request become reality.
Commitment: Followers embrace change requests as their own and often go the extra mile to make sure work gets done. Charismatic and transformational leaders are very adept at getting followers committed to their vision of the future.

Willing Subordination to the Leader

Whereas the preceding factor dealt with followers' emotional and psychological closeness to the leader, **willing subordination to the leader** involves their deference to his or her authority (Kark, Shamir, & Chen, 2003). Charismatic leaders often seem imbued with superhuman qualities. As a result, followers often naturally and willingly submit to the leader's apparent authority and superiority. Followers seem to suspend their critical thinking skills; they have few if any doubts about the intentions or skills of the leader, the correctness of the vision or change initiative, or the actions they need to take in order to achieve the vision.

> *Never tell people how to do things. Tell them what to do, and they will surprise you with their ingenuity.*
>
> George Patton,
> U.S. Army

Feelings of Empowerment

Followers of charismatic leaders are moved to expect more of themselves, and they work harder to achieve these higher goals. Charismatic leaders capitalize on the Pygmalion Effect: They set high expectations while boosting the self-confidence of followers by expressing confidence in their abilities and providing ongoing encouragement and support (Dvir, Eden, Avolio, & Shamir, 1999, 2000; Larmore & Ayman, 1998; Bass & Avolio, 1994; Bono & Judge, 2003; Popper & Mayseless, 2003). Somewhat paradoxically, followers feel stronger and more powerful at the same time they willingly subordinate themselves to the charismatic leader. Charismatic leaders are able to make their followers feel more powerful without any diminution or threat to their own status. These **feelings of empowerment,** when combined with heightened emotional levels and a leader's vision of the future, often result in increases in organizational, group, or team performance or significant social change.

Situational Characteristics

Most of the research up to now has focused on identifying the leader attributes associated with charismatic leadership. There is considerably more to learn about the underlying attributes of followers and the situational characteristics of charismatic or transformational leadership (Beyer, 1999; Conger, 1999). Despite this gap in knowledge, some researchers believe that situational factors do play an important role in determining whether a leader will be perceived as charismatic (Bradley, 1987; Roberts & Bradley, 1988; Westley & Mintzberg, 1988; Gardner & Avolio, 1998; Conger, 1999; Hunt, Boal, & Dodge, 1999; Shamir & Howell, 1999; Waldman, Ramirez, House, & Puranam, 2001; Bono, 2002; Tosi, Misangyi, Fanelli, Waldman, & Yammarino, 2004). It may be that individuals possessing the qualities of charismatic leaders will be perceived as charismatic *only when confronting certain types of situations.* It may also be that the more favorable the situation is for charismatic leadership, the fewer qualities leaders will need before they are perceived to be charismatic (Conger, 1999). Because the situation may play an important role in the attribution of charisma, it will be useful to review some of the situational factors believed to affect charismatic leadership (see also Highlight 13.9).

Force Field Analysis

Highlight 13.9

One way to better understand organizational change is through the use of a technique called **Force Field Analysis (FFA).** An FFA uses vectors to graphically depict the driving forces and the barriers to an orga-

nizational change. Stronger forces and barriers are represented by larger vectors; weaker forces and barriers are represented by smaller vectors. An example of an FFA for a rural school district trying to improve third grade student achievement test scores in math can be found below:

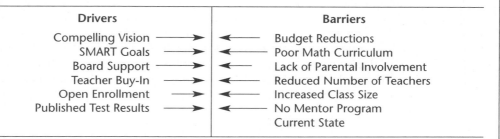

Drivers		Barriers
Compelling Vision ⟶	⟵	Budget Reductions
SMART Goals ⟶	⟵	Poor Math Curriculum
Board Support ⟶	⟵	Lack of Parental Involvement
Teacher Buy-In ⟶	⟵	Reduced Number of Teachers
Open Enrollment ⟶	⟵	Increased Class Size
Published Test Results ⟶	⟵	No Mentor Program
		Current State

The first step in an FFA is to graphically depict the current state such as shown above. In many cases the drivers and barriers to change in the current state should more or less balance out, as they represent the current status quo. The second step in an FFA is to formulate strategies to increase the drivers or reduce the barriers to organizational change. (Leaders will often get better results if they focus on reducing barriers rather than increasing the number or size of the drivers for change.) The third and final step in an FFA is to create and implement change plans that outline the steps, accountable parties, and timelines for increasing drivers and reducing the barriers to change.

Source: K. Lewin, "Field Theory and Experiment in Social Psychology: Concepts and Methods," *American Journal of Sociology,* 44, 1939, pp. 868–896.

Crises

Perhaps the most important situational factor associated with charismatic leadership is the presence or absence of a **crisis.** Followers who are content with the status quo are relatively unlikely to perceive a need for a charismatic leader or be willing to devote great effort to fundamentally change an organization or society. On the other hand, a crisis—whether reflected by the failure of traditional social institutions or a corporation's imminent financial failure—often creates a "charisma hunger" in followers; they are looking for a leader to alleviate or resolve their crisis (Madsen & Snow, 1983; Trice & Beyer, 1986). Leaders are given considerably more latitude and autonomy and may temporarily (or sometimes permanently) suspend accepted rules, policies, and procedures in order to pull the organization out of the crisis. Some researchers even believe that some leaders purposely create or manufacture crises to increase followers' acceptance of their vision, the range of actions they can take, and followers' level of effort (Pawar & Eastman, 1997; Avolio & Bass, 1988; Boal & Bryson, 1987; Kets de Vries, 1977). Although a crisis situation does not necessarily make every leader look charismatic, such a situation may "set the stage" for particular kinds of leader behaviors to be effective (Hunt, Boal, & Dodge, 1999; Waldman, Ramirez, House, & Puranam, 2001; Bono, 2002; Tosi, Misangyi, Fanelli, Waldman, & Yammarino, 2004).

Task Interdependence and Social Networks

It may be easier for leaders to be seen as charismatic when the tasks performed by their followers require a high level of interdependent rather than independent effort (Curphy, 1991a, 1992a). With **task interdependence,** for example, it may be easier for leaders to be perceived as charismatic when they are leading a software design team rather than a sales team because each individual programmer's code could be affected by the code developed by the other programmers. However, a sales representative with a defined territory will probably not be affected by efforts of the other sales representatives on the team. In addition to task interdependence, **social networks** can also affect the attribution of charisma. Attributions of charisma will spread more quickly in organizations having well-established social networks, where everybody tends to know everyone else (Pastor, Meindl, & Mayo, 2002).

Other Situational Characteristics

Several other situational characteristics may help or hinder the emergence of a charismatic leader. Howell and Avolio (1993) found that organizations placing a premium on innovation were much more supportive of transformational leadership than those less committed to innovation. Another situational factor that may affect charismatic leadership is outsourcing and organizational downsizing. In the minds of many peoples, downsizing has destroyed the implicit contract between employer and employee, and left many employees disillusioned with corporate life (Church, 1994). On the one hand, because charismatic or transformational leadership is intensely relational in nature, destroying the implicit contract between leaders and followers could greatly diminish the odds of charismatic leadership emergence. On the other hand, this disillusionment has caused many talented managers to leave large organizations to form their own companies. Employees are drawn to these start-up organizations precisely because the company's vision is consistent with their own personal values. But of all the situational variables affecting charismatic leadership, perhaps the most important and overlooked variable is **time.** Charismatic or transformational leadership does not happen overnight. It takes time for leaders to develop and articulate their vision, heighten followers' emotional levels, build trusting relationships with followers, and direct and empower followers to fulfill the vision. It may be that a crisis compresses the amount of time while relatively stable situations lengthen the amount of time needed for charismatic leadership to emerge.

Concluding Thoughts about the Characteristics of Charismatic and Transformational Leadership

Several final points about the characteristics of charismatic leadership need to be made. First, although we defined charisma as a quality attributed to certain leaders based on the relationships they share with followers, charismatic leadership is most fully understood when we also consider how leader and situational factors affect this attribution process. The special relationships charismatic leaders share with followers do not happen by accident; rather, they are often the result of interaction between the leader's qualities, leader and follower values, and the presence of certain situational factors. Second, it seems unlikely that all the characteristics of charismatic

Communication is the currency of leadership.

David Lee,
Personal Decisions International

leadership need to be present before charisma is attributed to a leader. The bottom line for charisma seems to be the relationships certain leaders share with followers, and there may be a variety of ways in which these relationships can develop. This also implies that charisma may be more of a continuum than an all-or-nothing phenomenon. Some leaders may be able to form particularly strong bonds with a majority of followers, others with a few followers, and still others may get along with most but not form particularly strong bonds with any followers. Third, it does seem that charismatic leadership can happen anywhere—schools, churches, communities, businesses, government organizations, and nations—and does not happen only on the world stage.

Fourth, given that there are a number of ways to develop strong emotional attachments with followers, one important question is whether it is possible to attribute charisma to an individual based solely on his or her position or celebrity status (Etzioni, 1961; Hollander, 1978; Bass, 1990). Some individuals in positions of high public visibility and esteem (e.g., film stars, musicians, athletes, television evangelists, and politicians) can develop (even cultivate) charismatic images among their fans and admirers. In these cases, it is helpful to recognize that charismatic leadership is a two-way street. Not only do followers develop strong emotional bonds with leaders, but leaders also develop strong emotional bonds with followers and are concerned with follower development (Burns, 1978; Dvir, Eden, Avolio, & Shamir, 1999, 2002, Popper & Mayseless, 2003). It is difficult to see how the one-way communication channels of radio and television can foster these two-way relationships or enhance follower growth. Thus, although we sometimes view certain individuals as charismatic based on media manipulation and hype, this is not transformational leadership in the truest sense.

So what can leadership practitioners take from this research if they want to use an emotional approach to drive organizational change? They will probably be more successful at driving organizational change if they capitalize on or create a crisis. They also need to be close enough to their followers to determine the sources of discontent and ensure their vision is aligned with followers' values and paints a compelling picture of the future. Leaders must passionately articulate their vision of the future; it is difficult to imagine followers being motivated toward a vision that is unclear or presented by a leader who does not seem to really care about it. Leadership practitioners also need to understand that they alone cannot make the vision a reality; they need their followers' help and support to create organizational or societal changes. Along these lines, they will need to be a role model and coach followers on what they should (and should not) be doing, provide feedback and encouragement, and persuade followers to take on more responsibilities as their skills and self-confidence grow. Finally, leadership practitioners using this approach to organizational change also need to be thick skinned, resilient, and patient (see Highlight 13.10). They will need to cope with the polarization effects of charismatic leadership and understand that it takes time for the effects of this type of leadership to yield results. However, the rewards appear to be well worth the efforts. There appears to be overwhelming evidence that charismatic or transformational leaders are more effective than their noncharismatic counterparts, whether they be presidents of the United States (Deluga, 1998), CEOs (Waldman, Ramirez, House, & Puranam, 2001; Waldman, Javidan, & Varella, 2004), military cadets and officers (Bass, 2000; Curphy, 1991a;

Good to Great: An Alternative Framework to the Rational and Emotional Approaches to Organizational Change

Highlight 13.10

An alternative conceptualization of organizational change worth noting comes from the book *Good to Great* (Collins, 2001). Collins and his research team reviewed the financial performance of 1,435 companies that appeared on the *Fortune* 500 list from 1965–1995. From this list, 11 companies made the leap from being a good to a truly great company—a company that yielded financial returns much higher than those for the overall stock market or industry competitors for at least 15 consecutive years. For example, a dollar invested in these 11 companies in 1965 would have yielded $471 in January 2000, whereas the same dollar invested in the stock market would have returned $56. Collins's research indicates that these 11 companies all followed the same six rules:

1. **Level 5 Leadership:** The *Good to Great* companies were not led by high profile celebrity leaders, but rather by humble, self-effacing and reserved individuals who also possessed an incredibly strong drive to succeed.

2. **First Who, Then What:** Before developing a future vision or goals, these leaders first made sure they had the right people with the right skills in the right jobs. Leadership talent management was a key focus of these top companies.

3. **Confront the Brutal Facts (Yet Never Lose Faith):** These leaders met reality head-on—they did not sugarcoat organizational challenges or difficulties. But they also had an unshakable faith in their organizations' ability to meet these challenges.

4. **The Hedgehog Concept:** These companies all focused on being the best in the world at what they did, were deeply passionate about their business, and identified one or two key financial or operational metrics to guide their decision making and day-to-day activities.

5. **A Culture of Discipline:** Companies that had disciplined people did not need hierarchies, bureaucracies, or excessive controls, as the people out in the field knew what they needed to do and made sure it happened.

6. **Technology Accelerators:** All these companies selectively used technology as a means for enhancing business operations, but they were not necessarily leaders in technical innovation.

There were several other surprising findings in Collins's research. First, none of these top performing companies was led by transformational or charismatic leaders. Second, because these top companies were constantly undergoing small but noticeable changes, they did not need to launch major change initiatives or organizational restructuring programs. Third, companies need to abide by all six of these rules to go from good to great; three or four of the six rules were not enough for companies to make the leap to becoming a top performer.

Source: J. Collins, *Good to Great* (New York: HarperCollins, 2001).

Clover, 1990; Adams, Price, Instone, & Rice, 1984), college professors (Labak, 1973), or first-line supervisors and middle-level managers in a variety of public and private sector companies (Avolio & Bass, 2000; Bono, 2002; Barling, Loughlin, & Kelloway, 2002; Bono & Judge, 2003; Shin & Zhou, 2003).

Bass's Theory of Transformational and Transactional Leadership

Much of what we know about the leader, follower, and situational characteristics associated with charismatic or transformational leaders comes from research on Bass's (1985, 1997) **Theory of Transformational and Transactional Leadership.** Bass believed that transformational leaders possessed those leader characteristics described earlier; he used perceptions or reactions of subordinates' to determine whether or not a leader was transformational. Thus, transformational leaders possess good visioning, rhetorical, and impression management skills, and they use these skills to develop strong emotional bonds with followers. Transformational leaders are believed to be more successful at driving organizational change because of followers' heightened emotional levels and their willingness to work toward the accomplishment of the leader's vision (Antonakis & House, 2004; Bono & Judge, 2003; Avolio & Bass, 2000; Bass, 1997; Bass & Avolio, 1996). In contrast, transactional leaders do not possess these leader characteristics, nor are they able to develop strong emotional bonds with followers or inspire followers to do more than followers thought they could. Instead, transactional leaders were believed to motivate followers by setting goals and promising rewards for desired performance. Avolio and Bass (1987, 1988) maintained that transactional leadership could have positive effects on follower satisfaction and performance levels, but they also stated that these behaviors were often underutilized because of time constraints, a lack of leader skills, and a disbelief among leaders that rewards could boost performance. Bass (1997) also maintained that transactional leadership only perpetuates the status quo; a leader's use of rewards does not result in the long-term changes associated with transformational leadership.

> *Rules are good servants, but not always good masters.*
>
> Russell Page,
> Master Landscaper

Like the "initiating structure" and "consideration" behaviors described in Chapter 8, Bass hypothesized that transformational and transactional leadership comprised two independent leadership dimensions. Thus, individuals could be high transformational but low transactional leaders, low transformational and low transactional leaders, and so on. Bass developed a questionnaire, known as the **Multifactor Leadership Questionnaire (MLQ),** to assess the extent to which leaders exhibited transformational or transactional leadership and the extent to which followers were satisfied with their leader and believed their leader was effective. The MLQ is a 360-degree feedback instrument that assesses five transformational and three transactional factors and a nonleadership factor (Rafferty & Griffen, 2004; Antonakis, Avolio, & Sivasubramaniam, 2003; Bass & Avolio, 2000; Bass, 1997). The transformational leadership factors assess the degree to which the leader instills pride in others, displays power and confidence, makes personal sacrifices or champions new possibilities, considers the ethical or moral consequences of decisions, articulates a compelling vision of the future, sets challenging standards, treats followers as individuals, and helps followers understand the problems they face. The three transactional leadership factors assess the extent to which leaders set goals, make rewards contingent on performance, obtain necessary resources, provide rewards when performance goals have been met, monitor followers' performance levels, and intervene when problems occur. The MLQ also assesses another factor called laissez-faire leadership, which assesses the extent to which leaders avoid responsibilities, fail to make decisions, are absent when needed, or fail to follow up on requests.

Research Results of Transformational and Transactional Leadership

To date, over 200 studies have used the MLQ to investigate transformational and transactional leadership across a wide variety of situations. These results indicated that transformational leadership can be observed in all countries, institutions, and organizational levels, but it was more prevalent in public institutions and at lower organizational levels (Bono, 2002; Sosik, Avolio & Jung, 2002; Avolio & Bass, 2000; Bass, 1999, 2000; Lowe, Kroeck, & Sivasubramaniam, 1996). In other words, there seemed to be more transformational leaders in the lower levels of the military or other public sector organizations than anywhere else. Second, there is overwhelming evidence that transformational leadership is a significantly better predictor of organizational effectiveness than transactional or laissez-faire leadership. Transformational leaders, whether they are U.S. presidents, CEOs, school administrators, or plant managers, seem to be more effective at driving organizational change and getting results than transactional leaders (see Highlight 13.11). Avolio and Bass (2000) also believed that transformational leadership augments performance above and beyond what is associated with transactional leadership. Third, as expected, laissez-faire leadership was negatively correlated with effectiveness.

Given that the MLQ can reliably identify transformational leaders and that these leaders can drive higher levels of organizational change and effectiveness than their transactional counterparts, it seems reasonable to ask whether it is possible to train or select charismatic leaders. Fortunately, Bono (2002), Bass, Avolio, Jung & Berson (2003), Towler, (2003), Frese, Beimel & Schoenborn (2003), Avolio (1999), Avolio and Bass (1998; 2000), Bass (1999), and Barling, Weber, and Kelloway (1996) have all looked at the effects of transformational leadership training on the performance of military, public sector, and private industry leaders in the United States, Canada, and Israel. Usually these training programs consisted of a one- to five-day initial training session where participants learned about the Theory of Transformational and Transactional Leadership; received MLQ feedback on the extent to which they exhibit transformational, transactional, and laissez-faire leadership; and then went through a series of skill-building exercises and activities to improve their leadership effectiveness. At the end of the initial session, participants were asked to create a development plan to improve specific transformational or transactional leadership skills. Approximately 6 to 24 months after the initial program, participants attended a second training session that also provided a second round

Duane Lund: A Rural Transformational Leader

Highlight 13.11

Although transformational leaders come from all walks of life, one common characteristic they share is their ability to drive change and get things done. One of the best examples of a rural transformational leader is Duane Lund, a retired school superintendent in Staples, MN. In his first year as Superintendent of the Staples-Motley school district, Duane lobbied the state legislature and Department of Education to build a new vocational school in the community. Although no new vocational schools had been built in the previous several years, Duane was able to convince key state officials to provide the funding necessary to make this happen. He also helped secure the equipment needed for what would soon be one of the largest machine and allied trades programs in the country. Duane then worked closely with the local Chamber of Commerce and other economic development groups to attract manufacturers that would employ vocational school graduates, and through his efforts more than a dozen such plants sprang up around town.

A tireless promoter of the community, Duane convinced the local railroad to give up some land on a lake just outside of town in order to develop a city park, swimming beach, campground, and athletic fields. An avid writer, Duane has written 36 books and started up and was President of the Community Arts Council for a number of years.

Duane also played a key role in changing the school district–community relationships. He helped pass a bond issue in order to build a new high school auditorium and pool, both of which were made available to community members. He assembled a team of grant writers and secured enough additional funding to keep his class sizes small, his student achievement scores were among the best in the state, and his athletic teams won a number of state championships.

Some of the keys to Duane's success are his ability to create a compelling vision of the future, ability to tell jokes and stories, his unbridled optimism and enthusiasm, and genuine down-to-earth charm. All of these qualities help him to get diverse groups working together to get things done. Because of his positive impact on the community, a local foundation has decided to create the "Duane Lund Lifetime Achievement Community Service Award" in his honor, and awards the prize to one person every other year or so for outstanding community service.

of MLQ feedback. The time 1 and time 2 MLQ results allowed researchers to determine quantitatively whether the training program improved the transformational and transactional leadership skills of the participants. These results indicated that improving transactional leadership skills is fairly easy; participants who targeted these skills for improvement reported higher time 2 MLQ scores on the transactional leadership factor. There were also modest gains in the time 2 MLQ transformational leadership factor scores for those participants who targeted these skills in their development plan. Moreover, those areas that were not targeted for improvement saw no commensurate increase in time 2 MLQ scores. Thus, the higher time 2 scores were not due to some general effect, but rather were limited only to those skills that were part of a participant's development plan. These results provided strong evidence that it is possible for leaders to systematically develop their transformational and transactional leadership skills.

An alternative to training leaders to be more transformational is to select leaders with the propensity to be transformational or charismatic in the first place. Several researchers have looked at the importance of childhood experiences, leadership traits, and even genetics in transformational leadership. Zacharatos, Barling, and

TABLE 13.5

Correlations between Five Factor Model Dimensions and Charismatic Leadership Characteristics for 125 Corporate CEOs and Presidents

Personality Dimension	Transformational Leadership Characteristics			
	Visionary Thinking	Empowering Others	Inspiring Trust	High Impact Delivery
Surgency	.32	.33	.16	.47
Dependability	−.08	−.01	.06	−.04
Agreeableness	.02	.52	.48	.35
Adjustment	−.03	.29	.38	.22
Intellectance	.47	.30	.14	.40

Source: D. Nilsen, "Using Self and Observers' Ratings for Personality to Predict Leadership Performance." Unpublished doctoral dissertation, University of Minnesota, Minneapolis, 1995.

Kelloway (2000) reported that adolescents who were rated by coaches and peers to be more transformational were also more likely to have parents who were transformational leaders. There is also evidence that certain leadership traits differentiate transformational from transactional leaders. Antonakis and House, (2004), Hogan, Curphy, and Hogan (1994), Curphy and Nilsen (1995), Nilsen (1995), House, Spangler, and Woycke (1991), House, Woycke, and Fodor (1988), Ross and Offermann (1991), and Judge and Bono (2000) all showed that certain Five Factor Model (FFM) leadership traits (Chapter 7) could be reliably used to identify transformational leaders. Some of the most compelling evidence comes from Nilsen (1995), who looked at the relationships between FFM personality traits and 125 CEOs. As seen in Table 13.5, not only are the FFM personality dimensions strongly correlated with certain components of transformational leadership, but the pattern of high and low correlations seems to make sense. Given that certain leadership traits are related to transformational leadership, and that leadership traits have a genetic component, then it is not surprising that some researchers also believe that some aspect of transformational leadership is also heritable (Hooijberg & Choi, 2000).

Despite this evidence that it may be possible to select and train transformational leaders, the fact remains that charisma ultimately exists in the eyes of the beholder. Thus, there never could be any guarantee that leaders who had the right stuff and were schooled in the appropriate techniques will be seen as charismatic by followers. As discussed earlier, follower and situational variables will play a key role in determining whether leaders are perceived to be transformational and drive organizational change. Certain leaders may get higher transformational leadership scores as a result of a training program, but do they actually heighten followers' emotional levels, get followers to exert extra effort, and as a result achieve greater organizational change or performance after the program? Furthermore, while it may be possible to train some leaders to improve their visioning, impression management, and rhetorical skills, leaders who have relatively low scores on certain personality traits or other individual differences (e.g., intelligence, creativity, surgency, agreeableness, adjustment, and intellectance) may not benefit much from transformational leadership training. Bass (1985), Curphy (1991a; 2002; 2003c), Judge and Bono (2000), and Segal (1985) have all stated that personality is going to have a big effect on whether a leader will be seen as charismatic. Given what we know about individual differences and leadership skills training, it seems likely that a leader's personality will also play a major role in determining whether he or she will benefit from such training.

Finally, several other important comments about the Theory of Transformational and Transactional Leadership are worth noting. First, and perhaps most important, this theory has generated a considerable amount of interest among leadership researchers. This research has helped leadership practitioners to better understand the leader, follower, and situational components of charismatic or transformational leadership, whether transformational leaders are born or made, and so forth. Nevertheless, much of the research is based on surveys and correlational studies; the handful of experiments exploring the effects of transformational and transactional leadership have involved college students, not leadership practitioners (Hunt, 1999; Yukl, 1999). Third, this approach to leadership seems to have a strong bias toward people, in that measures such as the MLQ may be more a reflection of socially desirable leadership behaviors than the full range of skills needed by leaders (Beyer, 1999; Antonakis & House, 2004). For example, it seems likely that business leaders wanting to drive organizational change or performance need to have a good understanding of the industry, business operations, market trends, finance, strategy, and technical/functional knowledge; they also need to effectively cope with stress, negotiate contracts with vendors, demonstrate good planning skills, and develop and monitor key metrics. Yet none of these attributes and skills are directly measured by the MLQ. Relatedly, Beyer (1999), Yukl (1999), and Antonakis and House (2004) pointed out that the primary problem with this theory is that there is only one way to be an effective leader, and that is by demonstrating transformational leadership skills. The contingency theories of leadership no longer matter, and situational or follower factors have little impact on leadership effectiveness. In this regard Beyer, Yukl, and Antonakis and House may be right; leaders probably need to do more than exhibit only transformational leadership skills if they wish to achieve greater organizational change and performance.

Summary

This chapter began by revisiting the topic of leadership and management. Management skills are important to ensure compliance with existing systems, processes, and procedures; they are used to help preserve the status quo, improve consistency and efficiency, and maintain control. Leadership skills are needed when changes need to be made to existing systems and processes; they are used to create new systems and drive organizational change. The chapter then reviewed two major approaches to organizational change. Although independent lines of research were used to develop the rational and emotional approaches to change, in reality these approaches have several important similarities. With the rational approach, leaders increase follower dissatisfaction by pointing out problems with the status quo, systematically identifying areas of needed change, developing a vision of the future, and developing and implementing a change plan. In the emotional approach, leaders develop and articulate a vision of the future, heighten the emotions of followers, and empower followers to act on their vision. Charismatic leaders are also more likely to emerge during times of uncertainty or crisis, and may actually manufacture a crisis to improve the odds that followers will become committed to their vision of the future. The rational approach puts more emphasis on analytic, planning, and management skills whereas the emotional approach puts more emphasis on leadership skills, leader–follower relationships, and the presence of a crisis to drive organizational change. This chapter described the steps leadership practitioners must take if they wish to drive organizational change. There is ample evidence to suggest that either the rational or the emotional approach can result in organizational change, but the effectiveness of the change may depend on which approach leadership practitioners are most comfortable with and the skill with which they can carry it out.

Key Terms

$C = D \times M \times P > R$, *394*
dissatisfaction, *394*
model, *394*
process, *394*
resistance, *394*
amount of change, *394*
systems thinking approach, *396*
siloed thinking, *397*
change plan, *398*
SARA model, *401*
traditional authority system, *406*
legal-rational authority system, *406*
charismatic authority system, *406*

transactional leadership, *407*
transformational leadership, *408*
reframing, *408*
vision, *412*
rhetorical skills, *414*
image, *415*
build trust, *415*
personalized leadership, *415*
charisma, *416*
identification with the leader, *417*
heightened emotional level, *417*
willing subordination to the leader, *418*

feelings of empowerment, *418*
force field analysis (FFA), *419*
crisis, *419*
task interdependence, *420*
social networks, *420*
time, *420*
Theory of Transformational and Transactional Leadership, *423*
Multifactor Leadership Questionnaire (MLQ), *423*

Questions

1. Are Colin Powell, Peter Jackson, or Aung San Suu Kyi transformational or charismatic leaders? What data would you need to gather to answer this question?

2. Is Osama bin Laden a charismatic or transformational leader? Would your answer differ if you were sympathetic to his cause?

3. Research shows that females are seen as more transformational leaders, yet hold relatively few top leadership positions compared to men. Why do you think this is the case? What, if anything, could you do to change this situation?

4. How does the model of community leadership (Chapter 8) compare to the rational and emotional approaches to organizational change?

5. Research shows that charismatic and transformational leaders need to project an image of success, but muckraking and negativity in political campaigns are at an all-time high. Which leader, follower, or situational components of

charismatic leadership do political advertisements attempt to undermine? Given these ads, is it even possible for a political leader today to be seen as charismatic?

6. Can leaders possess the dark-side personality traits described in Chapter 7 and still be seen as charismatic?

7. Suppose you wanted to build a new student union at your school. What would you need to do to make this happen it you used a rational versus emotional approach to organizational change?

Skills

Leadership skills relevant to this chapter include:

- Communication
- Setting goals
- Credibility
- Coaching
- Empowerment

Activity

1. Break up into teams and identify something that needs to change at your school or at work. Use the rational approach to change (C=D×M×P) to develop a plan for your change initiative.

2. Interview a mid-level leader or executive and ask him or her about the biggest change initiative they were ever a part of. Did they use more of a rational or emotional approach to organizational change, and was the change initiative successful? Why or why not?

3. Create a force field analysis diagram for a change you would like to see happen at your work or school.

Minicase

"Keeping Up with Bill Gates"

Bill Gates inherited intelligence, ambition, and a competitive spirit from his father, a successful Seattle attorney. After graduating from a private prep school in Seattle, he enrolled in Harvard but dropped out to pursue his passion—computer programming. Paul Allen, a friend from prep school, presented Gates with the idea of writing a version of the BASIC computer language for the Altair 8800, one of the first personal computers on the market. Driven by his competitive nature, Gates decided he wanted to be the first to develop a language to make the personal computer accessible for the general public. He and Allen established the Microsoft Corporation in 1975. Gates's passion and skill were programming—he would work night and day to meet the extremely aggressive deadlines he set for himself and his company. Eventually Gates had to bring in other programmers—he focused on recent college graduates. "We decided that we wanted them to come with clear minds, not polluted by some other approach, to learn the way that we liked to develop software, and to put the kind of energy into it that we thought was key."

In the early days of Microsoft, Gates was in charge of product planning and programming while Allen was in charge of the business side. He motivated his programmers with the claim that whatever deadline was looming, no matter how tight, he could beat it personally if he had to. What eventually developed at Microsoft was a culture in which Gates was king. Everyone working under Gates was made to feel they were lesser programmers who couldn't compete with his skill or drive, so they competed with each other. They worked long hours and tried their best to mirror Gates—his drive, his ambition, his skill. This internal competition motivated the programmers and made Microsoft one of the most successful companies in the computer industry, and one of the most profitable. The corporation has created a tremendous amount of wealth—many of its employees have become millionaires while working at Microsoft, including, of course, Bill Gates, currently one of the richest men in the world. During the 1990s, Bill Gates's net worth grew at an average rate of $34 million per day; that's $200 million per week!

Gates needed a castle for his kingdom and so he built a much-talked-about house on Lake Washington. The house lies mainly underground and looks like a set of separate buildings when viewed from above. The house was conceived as a showcase for Microsoft technology—it took $60 million dollars, seven years of planning and construction, and three generations of computer hardware before it was finally finished. A feature of the house that reveals a lot about its owner is the house's system of electronic badges. These badges let the house computers know where each resident and visitor is in the house. The purpose of the badges is to allow the computer to adjust the climate and music and to match the preferences of people in the house as they move from room to room. What happens when more than one person is in a room? The computer defaults to Gates's personal preferences.

1. Would you classify Bill Gates as a charismatic or transformational leader? Why?
2. Consider followers/employees of Gates. What are some of the unique characteristics of Gates's followers that might identify him as charismatic or transformational?

Sources: http://www.microsoft.com/; http://news.bbc.co.uk/1/hi/programmes/words_most_powerful/3284811.stm; http://ei.cs.vt.edu/ ~history/Gates.Mirick.html; http://www.time.com/time/time100/builder/profile/gates3.html; http://www.pbs.org/cringely/pulpit/pulpit20001123.html

Leadership Skills

One reason any person can improve his or her leadership effectiveness is that part of leadership involves skills, and skills can be practiced and developed. A further advantage of looking at leadership skills is that most people are less defensive about deficits in skills (which can be improved) than about suggested deficits in, say, personality. Our rationale for this final portion of the book is that (1) certain skills do contribute to leadership effectiveness, and (2) they can be learned.

Presenting the skills in this final section does not, however, indicate we believe they should not be covered until the preceding material in the book has been completed. Quite the contrary. We believe it will be most useful to intersperse work on these skills with the other chapters. We also trust that professors and students in a particular course will know better for themselves what order of coverage of the various skills will work best in their unique circumstances. We have taken the liberty, however, of categorizing the skills into two broad groups of basic and more advanced leadership skills. While even this categorization is inherently somewhat arbitrary, it may provide a useful starting point for the reader. Furthermore, as you have seen throughout the text, the end of each chapter contains a list of skills which we believe relate directly to the content of that chapter.

List of Skills in Part V

Basic Leadership Skills

Advanced Leadership Skills

Basic Leadership Skills

Learning from Experience

Creating Opportunities to Get Feedback
Taking a 10 Percent Stretch
Learning from Others
Keeping a Journal
Having a Developmental Plan

Leadership practitioners can enhance the learning value of their experiences by (*a*) creating opportunities to get feedback, (*b*) taking a 10 percent stretch, (*c*) learning from others, (*d*) keeping a journal of daily leadership events, and (*e*) having a developmental plan.

Creating Opportunities to Get Feedback

It may be difficult for leaders to get relevant feedback, particularly if they occupy powerful positions in an organization. Yet leaders often need feedback more than subordinates do. Leaders may not learn much from their leadership experiences if they get no feedback about how they are doing. Therefore, they may need to create opportunities to get feedback, especially with regard to feedback from those working for them.

First of all, leaders should not assume they have invited feedback merely by saying that they have an open-door policy. A mistake some bosses make is presuming that others perceive them as open to discussing things just because they say they are open to discussing things. How truly open a door is, clearly, is in the eye of the beholder. In that sense, the key to constructive dialogue (i.e., feedback) is not just expressing a policy but also being perceived as approachable and sincere in the offer.

Some of the most helpful information for developing your own leadership can come from asking for feedback from others about their perceptions of your behavior and its impact on your group's overall effectiveness. Leaders who take psychological tests and use periodic surveys or questionnaires will have greater access to feedback than leaders who fail to systematically solicit feedback from their followers. Unless leaders ask for feedback, they may not get it.

Taking a 10 Percent Stretch

Learning always involves stretching. Learning involves taking risks and reaching beyond one's comfort zone. This is true of a toddler's first unsteady steps, a student's first serious confrontation with divergent worlds of thought, and leadership development. The phrase *10 percent stretch* conveys the idea of voluntary but determined efforts to improve leadership skills. It is analogous to physical exercise, though in this context stretching implies extending one's behavior, not muscles, just a bit beyond the comfort zone. Examples could include making a point to converse informally with everyone in the office at least once each day, seeking an opportunity to be chairman of a committee, or being quieter than usual at meetings (or more assertive, as the case may be). There is much to be gained from a commitment to such ongoing "exercise" for personal and leadership development.

Several positive outcomes are associated with leaders who regularly practice the 10 percent stretch. First, their apprehension about doing something new or different gradually decreases. Second, leaders will broaden their repertoire of leadership skills. Third, because of this increased repertoire, their effectiveness will likely increase. And finally, leaders regularly taking a 10 percent stretch will model something very valuable to others. Few things will send a better message to others about the importance of their own development than the example of how sincerely a leader takes his or her own development.

One final aspect of the 10 percent stretch is worth mentioning. One reason the phrase is so appealing is that it sounds like a measurable yet manageable change. Many people will not offer serious objection to trying a 10 percent change in some behavior, whereas they might well be resistant (and unsuccessful) if they construe a developmental goal as requiring fundamental change in their personality or interpersonal style. Despite its nonthreatening connotation, though, an actual 10 percent change in behavior can make an enormous difference in effectiveness. In many kinds of endeavor the difference between average performers and exceptional performers is 10 percent. In baseball, for example, many players hit .275, but only the best hit over .300—a difference of about 10 percent.

Learning from Others

Leaders learn from others, first of all, by recognizing they *can* learn from others and, importantly, from *any* others. That may seem self-evident, but in fact people often limit what and whom they pay attention to, and thus what they may learn from. For example, athletes may pay a lot of attention to how coaches handle leadership situations. However, they may fail to realize they could also learn a lot by watching the director of the school play and the band conductor. Leaders should not limit their learning by narrowly defining the sorts of people they pay attention to.

Similarly, leaders also can learn by asking questions and paying attention to everyday situations. An especially important time to ask questions is when leaders are new to a group or activity and have some responsibility for it. When possible, leaders should talk to the person who previously had the position to benefit from his or her insights, experience, and assessment of the situation. In addition, observant leaders are able to extract meaningful leadership lessons from everyday situations. Something as plain and ordinary as a high school car wash or the activities at a fast-food restaurant may offer an interesting leadership lesson. Leaders can learn a lot by actively observing how others react to and handle different challenges and situations, even very common ones.

Keeping a Journal

Another way leaders can mine experiences for their richness and preserve their learning is by keeping a journal (Csikszentmihalyi, 1990). Journals are similar to diaries, but they are not just accounts of a day's events. A journal should include entries that address some aspect of leaders or leadership. Journal entries may include comments about insightful or interesting quotes, anecdotes, newspaper articles, or even humorous cartoons about leadership. They may also include reflections on personal events, such as interactions with bosses, coaches, teachers, students, employees, players, teammates, roommates, and so on. Such entries can emphasize a good (or bad) way somebody handled something, a problem in the making, the differences between people in their reactions to situations, or people in the news, a book, or a film. Leaders should also use their journals to "think on paper" about leadership readings from textbooks or formal leadership programs or to describe examples from their own experience of a concept presented in a reading.

There are at least three good reasons for keeping a journal. First, the very process of writing increases the likelihood that leaders will be able to look at an event from a different perspective or feel differently about it. Putting an experience into words can be a step toward taking a more objective look at it. Second, leaders can (and should) reread earlier entries. Earlier entries provide an interesting and valuable autobiography of a leader's evolving thinking about leadership and about particular events in his or her life. Third, journal entries provide a repository of ideas that leaders may later want to use more formally for papers, pep talks, or speeches. As seen in Highlight LFE.1, good journal entries provide leaders with a wealth of examples that they may use in speeches, presentations, and so on.

Having a Developmental Plan

Leadership development almost certainly occurs in ways and on paths that are not completely anticipated or controlled. That is no reason, however, for leaders to avoid actively directing some aspects of their own development. A systematic plan outlining self-improvement goals and strategies will help leaders take advantage of opportunities they otherwise might overlook. Developing a systematic plan also will help leaders prioritize the importance of different goals so that their efforts can be put into areas with the greatest relative payoffs. Leaders who carefully choose which seminars and conferences to attend may help themselves maximize their contribution to their personal developmental goals. Leaders should look for opportunities on the job or in volunteer work for responsibilities that may further their growth. Leaders should recognize, however, that they may experience conflict—both internal and external—between doing more of what they already do well and stretching developmentally.

The following is an example of such a conflict. Suppose Sheila is an accountant who has just joined the board of a local charity. Because handling financial records is something many people do not enjoy, and because Sheila has a demonstrable knack for and interest in it, others on the board may well ask her to become the treasurer. Almost certainly Sheila would do as good a job as anyone else on the board. But suppose Sheila's personal goals included developing her public speaking skills. In such a case, doing what she does best (and what others want her to do) might stand in the way of growth in another area.

Sheila has several alternatives. She could refuse the job of treasurer because she has had her fill of accounting. Alternatively, she could accept the job of treasurer and look for yet another activity in which to develop her public speaking skills.

Sample Journal Entries

Highlight LFE.1

I went skiing this weekend and saw the perfect example of a leader adapting her leadership style to her followers and situation. While putting on my skis I saw a ski instructor teaching little kids to ski. She did it using the game "red light, green light." The kids loved it and seemed to be doing very well. Later that same day, as I was going to the lodge for lunch, she was teaching adults, and she did more demonstrating than talking. But when she talked she was always sure to encourage them so they did not feel intimidated when some little kid whizzed by. She would say to the adults that it's easier for children, or that smaller skis are easier. She made the children laugh and learn, and made the adults less self-conscious to help them learn too . . .

Today may not exactly be a topic on leadership, but I thought it would be interesting to discuss. I attended the football game this afternoon and could not help but notice our cheerleaders. I was just thinking of their name in general, and found them to be a good example (of leadership). Everyone gets rowdy at a football game, but without the direction of the cheerleaders there would be mayhem. They do a good job of getting the crowd organized and the adrenaline pumping (though of course the game is most important in that too!). It's just amazing to see them generate so much interest that all of the crowd gets into the cheering. We even chant their stupid-sounding cheers! You might not know any of them personally, but their enthusiasm invites you to try to be even louder than them. I must give the cheerleaders a round of applause . . .

I've been thinking about how I used to view/ understand leadership, trying to find out how my present attitudes were developed. It's hard to remember past freshman year, even harder to go past high school. Overall, I think my father has been the single most important influence on my leadership development—long before I even realized it. Dad is a strong "Type A" person. He drives himself hard and demands a great deal from everyone around him, especially his family and especially his only son and oldest child. He was always pushing me to study, practice whatever sport I was involved in at the time, get ahead of everybody else in every way possible.

Unfortunately, both of these options may present their own problems. Still another alternative would be to negotiate to expand the role of treasurer to allow greater opportunity to blend the role with her own developmental goals. For example, Sheila might choose to make regular oral reports to the board instead of submitting solely written reports. Additionally, she might take on a larger share of speaking at local service clubs for the purpose of public education about the charity and her own expert view of its needs with regard to fund-raising and financial support. The point here is that leaders simply need to be deliberate in seeking opportunities to put their personal development plans into action. Leaders should exercise control over events to the extent they can; they should not let events exercise a counterproductive control over them.

A leader's first step in exercising control over his personal development is to identify what his goals actually are. The example above presumed Sheila already had identified public speaking as a skill she wanted to improve. But what if a leader is uncertain about what he or she needs to improve? As described earlier, leaders should systematically collect information from a number of different sources. One place a leader can get information about where to improve is through a review of current job performance, if that is applicable. Ideally, leaders will have had feedback sessions with their own superiors, which should help them identify areas of relative strength and weakness. Leaders should treat this feedback as a helpful perspective on their developmental needs. Leaders also should look at their interactions with peers as a source of ideas about what they might work on. Leaders should especially take notice if the same kind of problem comes up in their interactions with different individuals in separate situations. Leaders need to look at their own role in such instances as objectively as they can; there might be clues about what behavioral changes might facilitate better working relationships with others. Still another way to identify developmental objectives is to look ahead to what new skills are needed to function effectively at a higher level in the organization, or in a different role than the leader now has. Finally, leaders can use formal psychological tests and questionnaires to determine what their relative strengths and weaknesses as a leader may be.

On a concluding note, there is one activity leaders should put in their developmental plans whatever else might be included in them: a program of personal reading to broaden their perspectives on leadership. This reading can include the classics as well as contemporary fiction, biographies and autobiographies of successful leaders, essays on ethics and social responsibility, and assorted self-improvement books on various leadership and management issues. A vital part of leadership development is intellectual stimulation and reflection, and an active reading program is indispensable to that. Leaders might even want to join (or form) a discussion group that regularly meets to exchange ideas about a book everyone has read.

Communication

Know What Your Purpose Is

Choose an Appropriate Context and Medium

Send Clear Signals

Actively Ensure That Others Understand the Message

Bass (1990) defined communication effectiveness as the degree to which someone tells others something and ensures they understand what was said. In an even more general sense, **effective communication** involves the ability to transmit and receive information with a high probability that the intended message is passed from sender to receiver. Few skills are more vital to leadership. Studies show that good leaders communicate feelings and ideas, actively solicit new ideas from others, and effectively articulate arguments, advocate positions, and persuade others (Bennis & Nanus, 1985; Kanter, 1983; Parks, 1985). It seems likely the same can be said of good followers, though far less study has gone into that question. Moreover, the quality of a leader's communication is positively correlated with subordinate satisfaction (Klimoski & Haynes, 1980) as well as with productivity and quality of services rendered (Snyder & Morris, 1984). Effective communication skills are also important because they provide leaders and followers with greater access to information relevant to important organizational decisions (Fiechtner & Krayer, 1986).

A systems view of communication is depicted in Figure C.1. Communication is best understood as a process beginning with an intention to exchange certain information with others. That intention eventually takes form in some particular expression, which may or may not adequately convey what was intended. The next stage is reception. Just as with a weak or garbled radio signal or malfunctioning antenna, what is received is not always what was sent. Reception is followed by interpretation. If a driver asks, "Do I turn here?" and a passenger answers, "Right," did the passenger mean *yes* or *turn right*? Finally, it is not enough merely to receive

FIGURE C.1
A systems view of communication.

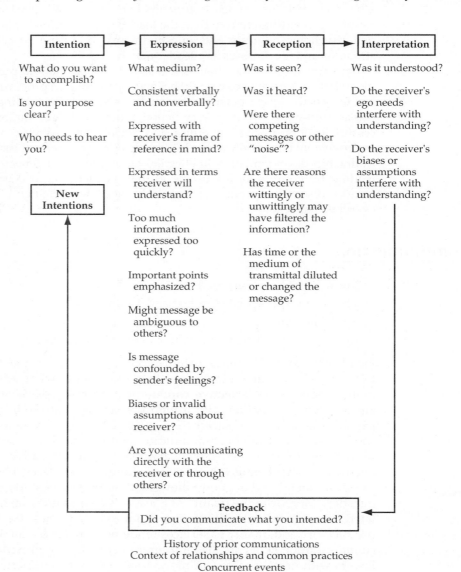

Intention	Expression	Reception	Interpretation
What do you want to accomplish?	What medium?	Was it seen?	Was it understood?
Is your purpose clear?	Consistent verbally and nonverbally?	Was it heard?	Do the receiver's ego needs interfere with understanding?
Who needs to hear you?	Expressed with receiver's frame of reference in mind?	Were there competing messages or other "noise"?	Do the receiver's biases or assumptions interfere with understanding?
	Expressed in terms receiver will understand?	Are there reasons the receiver wittingly or unwittingly may have filtered the information?	
	Too much information expressed too quickly?	Has time or the medium of transmittal diluted or changed the message?	
	Important points emphasized?		
	Might message be ambiguous to others?		
	Is message confounded by sender's feelings?		
	Biases or invalid assumptions about receiver?		
	Are you communicating directly with the receiver or through others?		

New Intentions

Feedback
Did you communicate what you intended?

History of prior communications
Context of relationships and common practices
Concurrent events

and interpret information; others' interpretations may or may not be consistent with what was intended at the outset. Therefore, it always helps to have a feedback loop to assess any communication's overall effectiveness.

We also can use the scheme in Figure C.1 to think about the knowledge, behaviors, and criteria used to evaluate communication skills. According to this model, the knowledge component of communication skills concerns the intentions of the leader, knowing what medium is most effective, and knowing whether the message was heard and understood. The behavioral component of communication skills concerns the behaviors associated with communicating verbally and nonverbally. Feedback concerning whether or not the message was understood by the receiver constitutes the evaluative component of communication skills. An important aspect regarding feedback is that it is an outcome of the previous steps in the communication process. In reality, the effectiveness of the communication process depends on the successful integration of all of the steps in the communication process. Effectiveness in just one step (e.g., speaking ability) is not enough. Successful communication needs to be judged in terms of the effective operation of the whole system.

The model also suggests a number of reasons why communication breakdowns might occur. For example, communication breakdowns can occur because the purpose of the message was unclear, the leader's or follower's verbal and nonverbal behaviors were inconsistent, the message was not heard by the receiver, or because someone may have misinterpreted another's message. Most people see themselves as effective communicators, and senders and receivers of messages often seem disposed to believe communication breakdowns are the other person's fault. Communication breakdowns often lead to blaming someone else for the problem, or "finger pointing" (see Figure C.2). One way to avoid the finger pointing associated with communication breakdowns is to think of communication as a process, not as a set of discrete individual acts (i.e., giving instructions to someone). By using the communication model, leadership practitioners can minimize the conflict typically associated with communication breakdowns.

The model in Figure C.1 can provide leadership practitioners with many ideas about how to improve communication skills. They can do so by (*a*) determining the purpose of their communication before speaking, (*b*) choosing an appropriate context and medium for the message, (*c*) sending clear signals, and (*d*) actively ensuring that others understand the message. The following is a more detailed discussion of some of the different ways in which leaders can improve their communication skills.

FIGURE C.2
Breakdowns in communication sometimes lead to finger pointing.

Person A

"You weren't listening!"
"That isn't what I said."
"You didn't follow directions."
"That isn't what you were supposed to do."

Person B

"I only did what you told me to."
"Why didn't you say so?"
"But you didn't seem serious."

Know What Your Purpose Is

One will communicate more effectively with others if one is clear about what one intends to communicate. By knowing purpose, a leader or follower can better decide whether to communicate publicly or privately, orally or in writing, and so on. These decisions may seem trivial, but often the specific content of a message will be enhanced or diminished by how and where it is communicated.

Choose an Appropriate Context and Medium

There is a rule of thumb that says leaders should praise followers in public and punish them in private. It points out the importance of selecting physical and social settings that will enhance the effectiveness of any communication. If the leader has an office, for example, then how much communication with subordinates should occur in her office and how much in the followers' workplace?

Sometimes, of course, an office is the best place to talk. Even that decision, however, is not all a leader needs to consider. The arrangement of office furniture can enhance or interfere with effective communication. Informal, personal communications are enhanced when two people sit at a 90-degree angle and are relatively close to each other; more formal communication is enhanced when the follower remains standing when the leader is sitting or if the leader communicates across his desk to followers.

Additionally, a leader's communications often take place in a whole organizational context involving broader existing practices, policies, and procedures. Leaders need to take care that their words and deeds do not inadvertently undercut or contradict such broader organizational communications, including their own bosses. Organizational factors also help determine whether any particular communication is most appropriately expressed orally or in writing. Oral communication is the most immediate, the most personal, the most dynamic, and often the most impactive; it is ideal when communication needs to be two-way or when the personalized aspect is especially important. At the other extreme, a more permanent modality is probably most appropriate when the leader needs a record of the communication or when something needs to be expressed in a particular way to different people, at different times, in different settings.

Send Clear Signals

Leaders and followers can enhance the clarity of their communications in several ways. First, it is helpful to be mindful of others' level of expertise, values, experiences, and expectations and how these characteristics affect their **frames of reference.** For example, the leader may brief a new organizational policy to followers, and they may come up with different interpretations of this policy based on different values and expectations. By being sensitive to followers' frames of reference and modifying messages accordingly, leaders can minimize communication breakdowns. Another way to clarify messages is to create a common frame of reference for followers before communicating a message. For example, consider the following passage:

> With hocked gems financing him, our hero bravely defied all scornful laughter that tried to prevent his scheme. "Your eyes deceive," he had said. "An egg, not a table, correctly typifies this unexplored planet." Now, three sisters sought sturdy proof.

Forging along, sometimes through calm vastness, yet more often over turbulent peaks and valleys, days became weeks as many doubters spread fearful rumors about the edge. At last, welcome winged creatures appeared signifying momentous success. (Sanford & Garrod, 1981)

Many are slow to recognize that the passage is about Christopher Columbus. Once the correct frame of reference is known, however, the previously confusing elements become sensible. Followers more readily understand new or ambiguous material when leaders paint a common frame of reference prior to introducing new material.

Another way to send clear signals is to use familiar terms, jargon, and concepts. This can serve to clarify and abbreviate messages when receivers are familiar with the terms. However, messages containing jargon can also be confusing to receivers unfamiliar with those terms. For example, a freshman cadet at the United States Air Force Academy might say to another, "I hope we get an ONP this weekend, because after three GRs, a PCE, and a SAMI, I'll need it." Because the second cadet understands this organizational jargon, he or she would have no difficulty understanding what was said. However, a person unfamiliar with the Air Force Academy would not have the slightest idea what this conversation meant. Leaders should make sure followers understand any jargon they use—especially if the followers are relatively inexperienced. (In case you were wondering, the cadet said, "I hope we get a pass to go downtown this weekend, because after three academic tests, a military test, and a room inspection, I'll need it.")

Two other ways to improve the clarity of messages are to use unambiguous, concrete terms and to send congruent verbal and nonverbal signals. For example, a leader who tells a follower, "Your monthly sales were down 22 percent last month" will more effectively communicate her concerns and cause less follower defensiveness than a leader who states, "Your performance has been poor." Thus, the more specific the message, the less likely receivers will be confused over what it means. In addition, leaders will be more effective communicators if their nonverbal signals match the content of the message. Followers, like everyone, can get confused, and tend to believe nonverbal signals when leaders send mixed verbal and nonverbal messages (Remland, 1981). Similarly, followers may send mixed messages to leaders; communication goes both ways.

One particularly destructive form of incongruent verbal and nonverbal signals is sarcasm. It is not the anger of the message per se but rather the implicit message conveyed by dishonest words that drives a wedge in the trust between leaders and followers. It is not a wise idea for leaders to always share their transitory feelings with subordinates, but if the leader is going to share his or her feelings, it is important to do so in a congruent manner. Similarly, it can be just as unwise for followers to share transitory feelings with leaders; but if it's done, it's important for verbal and nonverbal behaviors to be congruent.

Actively Ensure That Others Understand the Message

Leaders and followers can ensure that others understand their messages by practicing two-way communication and by paying attention to the others' emotional responses. Effective leaders and followers tend to actively engage in two-way communication (though this usually is more under the control of the leader than the follower). They can do so in many ways: by seeking feedback, by mingling in each other's work areas, and, in the case of leaders, by being sincere about having an open-door policy (Luthans & Larsen, 1986).

Although such steps appear to be straightforward, leaders typically believe they utilize two-way communication more frequently than their followers perceive them to be using it (Sadler & Hofstede, 1972). Leaders can get clues about the clarity of their messages by paying attention to the nonverbal signals sent by their followers. When followers' verbal and nonverbal messages seem to be incongruent, it may be because the message sent to them was unclear. For example, followers may look confused when they verbally acknowledge that they understand a particular task. In this case, leaders may find it useful to address the mixed signals directly in order to clear up such confusion.

Listening

> Demonstrate Nonverbally That You Are Listening
> Actively Interpret the Sender's Message
> Attend to the Sender's Nonverbal Behavior
> Avoid Becoming Defensive

Our systems view of communication emphasized that effectiveness depends upon both *transmitting and receiving* information. It may seem inconsistent, therefore, to distinguish the topic of listening from the more general topic of communication. Isn't listening *part* of communication, you may ask? Of course, and we do not intend to imply it's not. Our separate treatment of listening is simply for emphasis. It seems to us most discussions of communication emphasize the transmission side and neglect the receiving side. Good leaders and followers recognize the value of two-way communication. Listening to others is just as important as expressing oneself clearly to them. People in leadership roles are only as good as the information they have, and much of their information comes from watching and listening to what goes on around them.

At first, it may seem strange to describe listening as a skill. Listening may seem like an automatic response to things being said, not something one practices to improve, like free throws. However, the best listeners are **active listeners,** not passive listeners (Davis, Hellervik, & Sheard, 1989). In passive listening, someone may be speaking but the receiver is not focused on understanding the speaker. Instead, the receiver may be thinking about the next thing he will say or how bored he is in listening to the speaker. In either case, the receiver is not paying attention to what the sender is saying. To truly get the fullest meaning out of what someone else says, one needs to practice active listening. Individuals who are listening actively exhibit a certain pattern of nonverbal behaviors, do not disrupt the sender's message, try to put the sender's message into their own words, and scan the sender for various nonverbal signals. Knowing what nonverbal signals to send and correctly interpreting the sender's nonverbal signals are the knowledge component of listening skills. One's nonverbal signals are the behavioral component, and how well one can paraphrase a sender's message makes up the evaluative component of listening skills.

In addition to helping one understand others better, active listening is a way to visibly demonstrate that one respects others. People, particularly those with high self-monitoring scores, can often sense when others are not truly paying attention to what they are saying. Followers will quickly decide it is not worth their time to give their leader information if they perceive they are not being listened to. Leaders may do the same. To avoid turning off others, leaders and followers can improve their active listening skills in a number of ways. Some of these tips include learning to (*a*) model nonverbal signals associated with active listening, (*b*) actively interpret the sender's message, (*c*) be aware of the sender's nonverbal behaviors, and (*d*) avoid becoming defensive. The following is a more detailed discussion of these four ways to improve active listening skills.

Demonstrate Nonverbally That You Are Listening

Make sure your nonverbal behaviors show that you have turned your attention entirely to the speaker. Many people mistakenly assume that listening is a one-way process. Although it seems plausible to think of information flowing only from the sender to the receiver, the essence of active listening is to see all communication, even listening, as a two-way process. Listeners show they are paying attention to the speaker with their own body movements. They put aside, both mentally and physically, other work they may have been engaged in. Individuals who are actively listening establish eye contact with the speaker, and they do not doodle, shoot rubber bands, or look away at other things. They show they are genuinely interested in what the speaker has to say.

Actively Interpret the Sender's Message

The essence of active listening is trying to understand what the sender truly means. It is not enough merely to be (even if you could) a perfect human tape recorder. One must look for the meaning behind someone else's words. In the first place, this means one needs to keep one's mind open to the sender's ideas. This, in turn, implies not interrupting the speaker and not planning what to say while the speaker is delivering the message. In addition, good listeners withhold judgment about the sender's ideas until they have heard the entire message. This way, they avoid sending the message that their mind is made up and avoid jumping to conclusions about what the sender is going to say. Another reason to avoid sending a closed-minded message is that it may lead others to *not* bring up things one definitely needs to hear.

Another valuable way to actively interpret what the sender is saying is to **paraphrase** the sender's message. By putting the speaker's thoughts into their own words, leaders can better ensure that they fully understand what their followers are saying, and vice versa. The value of paraphrasing even a simple idea is apparent in the following dialogue:

> **Sarah:** "Jim should never have become a teacher."
>
> **Fred:** "You mean he doesn't like working with kids? Do you think he's too impatient?"
>
> **Sarah:** "No, neither of those things. I just think his tastes are so expensive he's frustrated with a teacher's salary."

In this example, Fred indicated what he thought Sarah meant, which prompted her to clarify her meaning. If he had merely said, "I know what you mean," Fred and Sarah mistakenly would have concluded they agreed when their ideas were really far apart. Paraphrasing also actively communicates your interest in what the other person is saying. Highlight L.1 offers various "communication leads" that may help in paraphrasing others' messages to improve your listening skills.

Attend to the Sender's Nonverbal Behavior

People should use all the tools at their disposal to understand what someone else is saying. This includes paraphrasing senders' messages, and being astute at picking up on senders' nonverbal signals. Much of the social meaning in messages is conveyed nonverbally, and when verbal and nonverbal signals conflict, people often tend to trust the nonverbal signals. Thus, no one can be an effective listener without paying attention to nonverbal signals. This requires listening to more than just the speaker's words themselves; it requires listening for feelings expressed via the speaker's loudness, tone of voice, and pace of speech as well as watching the speaker's facial expressions, posture, gestures, and so on. These behaviors convey a wealth of information that is immensely richer in meaning than the purely verbal content of a message, just as it is richer to watch actors in a stage play rather than merely read their script (Robbins, 1989). Although there may not be any simple codebook of nonverbal cues with which one can decipher what a sender "really" feels, listeners should explore what a sender is trying to say whenever they sense mixed signals between the sender's verbal and nonverbal behaviors.

Communication Leads for Paraphrasing and Assuring Mutual Understanding

Highlight L.1

From your point of view . . .

It seems you . . .

As you see it . . .

You think . . .

What I hear you saying is . . .

Do you mean . . . ?

I'm not sure I understand what you mean; is it . . . ?

I get the impression . . .

You appear to be feeling . . .

Correct me if I'm wrong, but . . .

Avoid Becoming Defensive

Defensive behavior is most likely to occur when someone feels threatened (Gibb, 1961). Although it may seem natural to become defensive when criticized, defensiveness lessens a person's ability to constructively make use of the information. Acting defensively may also decrease followers' subsequent willingness to pass additional unpleasant information on to the leader or other followers, or even the leader's willingness to give feedback to followers. Defensiveness on the part of the leader can also hurt the entire team or organization, as it includes a tendency to place blame, categorize others as morally good or bad, and generally question others' motives. Such behaviors on a leader's part hardly build a positive work or team climate.

Leaders can reduce their defensiveness when listening to complaints by trying to put themselves in the other person's shoes. Leaders have an advantage if they can empathize with how they and their policies are seen by others; they can better change their behaviors and policies if they know how others perceive them. Leaders need to avoid the temptation to explain how the other person is wrong and should instead just try to understand how he perceives things. A useful warning sign that a leader may be behaving defensively (or perhaps closed-mindedly) is if he begins a conversation saying, "Yes, but . . ."

Assertiveness

Use "I" Statements

Speak Up for What You Need

Learn to Say No

Monitor Your Inner Dialogue

Be Persistent

What is **assertive behavior,** and what are assertiveness skills? Basically, individuals exhibiting assertive behavior are able to stand up for their own rights (or their group's rights) in a way that also recognizes the concurrent right of others to do the same (see Highlight A.1). Like the skills already discussed, assertiveness skills also have knowledge, behavioral, and evaluative components. The behavioral component of assertiveness skills was mentioned already—it involves standing up for one's own or the group's rights in a constructive, nonhostile way. The knowledge component of assertiveness skills concerns knowing where and when not to behave assertively. People who are overly assertive may be perceived as aggressive and often may "win the battle but lose the war." Finally, the evaluative component comes into play when individuals are successful (or unsuccessful) in standing up for their own or their group's rights and continually working in an effective manner with others.

Perhaps the best way to understand assertiveness is to distinguish it from two other styles people have for dealing with conflict: acquiescence (nonassertiveness) and aggression (Alberti & Emmons, 1974). **Acquiescence** is avoiding interpersonal conflict entirely either by giving up and giving in or by expressing one's needs in

Assertiveness Questionnaire

Highlight A.1

Do you let someone know when you think he or she is being unfair to you?

Can you criticize someone else's ideas openly?

Are you able to speak up in a meeting?

Can you ask others for small favors or help?

Is it easy for you to compliment others?

Can you tell someone else you don't like what he or she is doing?

When you are complimented, do you really accept the compliment without inwardly discounting it in your own mind?

Can you look others in the eye when you talk to them?

If you could answer most of these questions affirmatively for most situations, then you do behave assertively.

Source: Adapted from R. E. Alberti and M. L. Emmons, *Your Perfect Right* (San Luis Obispo, CA: Impact, 1974).

an apologetic, self-effacing way. Acquiescence is *not* synonymous with politeness or helpfulness, though it is sometimes rationalized as such. People who are acquiescent, or nonassertive, back down easily when challenged. By not speaking up for themselves, they abdicate power to others and, in the process, get trampled on. Besides the practical outcome of not attaining one's goals, an acquiescent style typically leads to many negative feelings such as guilt, resentment, and self-blame, as well as a low self-image. Sometimes people justify their nonassertiveness to themselves with the idea that acquiescing to others is being polite or helpful, but this often is just a rationalization.

Aggression, on the other hand, is an effort to attain objectives by attacking or hurting others. Aggressive people trample on others, and their aggressiveness can take such direct forms as threats, verbal attacks, physical intimidation, emotional outbursts, explosiveness, bullying, and hostility—and such indirect forms as nagging, passive-aggressive uncooperativeness, guilt arousal, and other behaviors that undermine an adversary's autonomy. It is important to understand that aggressiveness is not just an emotionally strong form of assertiveness. Aggressiveness tends to be reactive, and it tends to spring from feelings of vulnerability and a lack of self-confidence. Aggressive people inwardly doubt their ability to resolve issues constructively through the give-and-take of direct confrontation between mutually respecting equals. Aggressiveness is a form of interpersonal manipulation in which one tries to put oneself in a "top dog" role and others in a "bottom dog" role (Shostrom, 1967). Additionally, aggressive people have difficulty expressing positive feelings.

Assertiveness is different from both acquiescence and aggression; it is not merely a compromise between them or a midpoint on a continuum. Assertiveness involves direct and frank statements of one's own goals and feelings, and a willingness to address the interests of others in the spirit of mutual problem solving and a belief that openness is preferable to secretiveness and hidden agendas. Assertiveness is the behavioral opposite of both acquiescence and aggression, as depicted in Figure A.1. The qualitative differences between these three styles are like

FIGURE A.1
Relationships
between
assertiveness,
acquiescence,
and aggression.

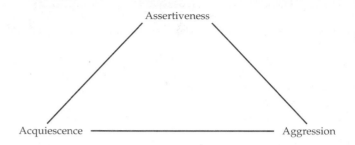

the differences between fleeing (acquiescence), fighting (aggression), and problem solving (assertiveness).

It may seem axiomatic that leaders need to behave assertively with subordinates. Sometimes, however, leaders also need to be assertive with their own bosses. Followers often need to be assertive with other followers and even with their leaders sometimes. For example, middle-level supervisors need to communicate performance expectations clearly and directly to subordinates, and they need to be strong advocates for their subordinates' interests with senior supervisors. Likewise, leaders sometimes need to give their own superiors bad news, and it is best to do so directly rather than hesitantly and guardedly. Followers may sometimes need to be assertive with a peer whose poor work habits are adversely impacting the work group. In addition, leaders sometimes need to be assertive with representatives of other power-holding or special-interest groups. For example, the leader of a community group seeking a new elementary school in a residential area may need to take a very assertive stand with local school board officials.

It is important to note that sometimes the hardest people to be assertive with are friends, family, and peers. Leaders who fail to be assertive with friends and peers run the risk of becoming victims of the Abilene paradox (see Highlight A.2).

The **Abilene paradox** (Harvey, 1974) occurs when someone suggests that the group engage in a particular activity or course of action, and no one in the group really wants to do the activity (including the person who made the suggestion). However, because of the false belief that everyone else in the group wants to do the activity, no one behaves assertively and voices an honest opinion about it. Only after the activity is over does anyone voice an opinion (and it is usually negative). For example, someone in your group of friends may suggest that the group go to a particular movie on a Friday night. No one in the group really wants to go, yet because of the false belief everyone else is interested, no one points out the movie is not supposed to be very good and the group should do something else instead. If group members' true opinions surface only *after* the movie, then the group has fallen victim to the Abilene paradox. Leaders can avoid the Abilene paradox by being assertive when suggestions about group decisions and activities are first made.

There are several things everyone can do to help themselves behave more assertively. These things include (*a*) using "I" statements, (*b*) speaking up for what you need, (*c*) learning to say no, (*d*) monitoring your inner dialogue, and (*e*) being persistent. The following is a more detailed discussion of these assertiveness tips.

The Abilene Paradox

Highlight A.2

That July afternoon in Coleman, Texas (population 5,607), was particularly hot—104 degrees according to the Rexall's thermometer. In addition, the wind was blowing fine-grained West Texas topsoil through the house. But the afternoon was still tolerable—even potentially enjoyable. A fan was stirring the air on the back porch; there was cold lemonade; and finally, there was entertainment. Dominoes. Perfect for the conditions. The game requires little more physical exertion than an occasional mumbled comment, "Shuffle 'em," and an unhurried movement of the arm to place the tiles in their appropriate positions on the table. All in all, it had the makings of an agreeable Sunday afternoon in Coleman. That is, until my father-in-law suddenly said, "Let's get in the car and go to Abilene and have dinner at the cafeteria."

I thought, "What, go to Abilene? Fifty-three miles? In this dust storm and heat? And in an unairconditioned 1958 Buick?"

But my wife chimed in with, "Sounds like a great idea. I'd like to go. How about you, Jerry?" Since my own preferences were obviously out of step with the rest, I replied, "Sounds good to me," and added, "I just hope your mother wants to go."

"Of course I want to go," said my mother-in-law. "I haven't been to Abilene in a long time."

So into the car and off to Abilene we went. My predictions were fulfilled. The heat was brutal. Perspiration had cemented a fine layer of dust to our skin by the time we arrived. The cafeteria's food could serve as a first-rate prop in an antacid commercial.

Some four hours and 106 miles later, we returned to Coleman, hot and exhausted. We silently sat in front of the fan for a long time. Then, to be sociable and to break the silence, I dishonestly said, "It was a great trip, wasn't it?"

No one spoke.

Finally, my mother-in-law said, with some irritation, "Well, to tell the truth, I really didn't enjoy it much and would rather have stayed here. I just went along because the three of you were so enthusiastic about going. I wouldn't have gone if you all hadn't pressured me into it."

I couldn't believe it. "What do you mean 'you all'?" I said. "Don't put me in the 'you all' group. I was delighted to be doing what we were doing. I didn't want to go. I only went to satisfy the rest of you. You're the culprits."

My wife looked shocked. "Don't call me a culprit. You and Daddy and Mama were the ones who wanted to go. I just went along to keep you happy. I would have had to be crazy to want to go out in heat like that."

Her father entered the conversation with one word. "Shee-it." He then expanded on what was already absolutely clear: "Listen, I never wanted to go to Abilene. I just thought you might be bored. You visit so seldom I wanted to be sure you enjoyed it. I would have preferred to play another game of dominoes and eat the leftovers in the icebox."

After the outburst of recrimination, we all sat back in silence. Here we were, four reasonably sensible people who—of our own volition—had just taken a 106-mile trip across a godforsaken desert in furnace-like heat and a dust storm to eat unpalatable food at a hole-in-the-wall cafeteria in Abilene, when none of us had really wanted to go. To be concise, we'd done just the opposite of what we wanted to do. The whole situation simply didn't make sense.

At least it didn't make sense at the time. But since that day in Coleman, I have observed, consulted with, and been a part of more than one organization that has been caught in the same situation. As a result, the organizations have either taken side trips or, occasionally, terminal journeys to Abilene, when Dallas or Houston or Tokyo was where they really wanted to go. And for most of those organizations, the negative consequences of such trips, measured in terms of both human misery and economic loss, have been much greater than for our little Abilene group.

I now call the tendency for groups to embark on excursions that no group member wants "the Abilene paradox." Stated simply, when organizations blunder into the Abilene paradox, they take actions in contradiction to what they really want to do and therefore defeat the very purpose they are trying to achieve. Business theorists typically believe that managing conflict is one of the greatest challenges faced by an organization, but a corollary of the Abilene paradox states that the inability to manage agreement may be the major source of organization dysfunction.

Source: Jerry B. Harvey, "The Abilene Paradox: The Management of Agreement," *Organizational Dynamics,* Summer 1974. Reprinted by permission of the publisher. American Management Association New York. http:www.amanet.org. All rights reserved.

Use "I" Statements

Assertive people take responsibility for what they say. They are clear in their own minds and with others about what they believe and what they want. One of the easiest ways to do this is to use first-person pronouns when you speak. Highlight A.3 provides examples of how to be more assertive by using first-person pronouns.

Speak Up for What You Need

No one has all of the skills, knowledge, time, or resources needed to do all of the taskings assigned to their work group. Virtually everyone will need to ask superiors, peers, or subordinates for help at some time. Both effective leaders and effective followers ask for help from others when they need it. Highlight A.3 also provides guidelines when making requests for help.

Learn to Say No

No one can be all things to all people, but it takes assertiveness to say no to others. Leaders, for example, may need to say no to their own superiors at times to stand up for their subordinates' or organization's rights and to keep from spreading themselves too thin and detracting from other priorities. Additionally, people who cannot (i.e., who *do not*) say no often build up a reservoir of negative emotions, such as those associated with the feeling of being taken advantage of. Tips for assertively refusing to do something also can be found in Highlight A.3.

Tips for Being Assertive

Highlight A.3

EXAMPLES OF GOOD AND BAD "I" STATEMENTS

Bad: Some people may not like having to maintain those new forms.

Good: I don't think these new forms are any good. I don't think they're worth the effort.

Bad: Maybe that candidate doesn't have all the qualifications we're looking for.

Good: I think his academic record looks fine, but we agreed only to consider candidates with at least five years' experience. I think we should keep looking.

TIPS FOR SPEAKING UP FOR WHAT YOU NEED

Do not apologize too much or justify yourself for needing help or assistance (e.g., "I just hate to ask you, and I normally wouldn't need to, but . . .").

At the same time, giving a brief reason for your request often helps.

Be direct. Do not beat around the bush, hinting at what you need and hoping others get the message.

Do not play on someone's friendship.

Do not take a refusal personally.

TIPS FOR SAYING NO

Keep your reply short and polite. Avoid a long, rambling justification.

Do not invent excuses.

Do not go overboard in apologizing because you cannot do it.

Be up-front about your limitations and about options you could support.

Ask for time to consider it if you need to.

Source: Adapted from K. Back and K. Back, *Assertiveness at Work* (New York: McGraw-Hill, 1982).

Monitor Your Inner Dialogue

Most of us talk to ourselves, though not out loud. Such self-talk is natural and common, though not everyone is aware of how much it occurs or how powerful an influence on behavior it can be. Assertive people have self-talk that is positive and affirming. Nonassertive people have self-talk that is negative, doubtful, and questioning. Learning to say no is a good example of the role self-talk plays in assertiveness. Suppose that someone was asked to serve on a volunteer committee he simply does not have time for and that he *wants* to say no. In order to behave assertively, the person would need to talk to himself positively. He would need to ensure that he is not defeated by his own self-talk. It would hardly help the person's resolve, for example, to have an inner dialogue that says, "They'll think I'm selfish if I don't say yes," or "If they can make time for this committee, I should be able to make time for it, too." In learning to behave more assertively, therefore, it is necessary for leaders to become more aware of their own counterproductive self-talk, confront it, and change it.

Be Persistent

Assertive individuals stick to their guns without becoming irritated, angry, or loud. They persistently seek their objectives, even in the face of another person's excuses or objections. Exchanging merchandise can provide a good occasion for assertive persistence. Suppose someone had purchased a shirt at a department store, had worn it once, and then noticed the seam was poorly sewn. A person acting assertively might have an exchange much like that found in Highlight A.4. An assertive person is similarly persistent in standing up for his own or his group's rights.

Example Exchange between a Buyer and a Clerk

Highlight A.4

Buyer: "I bought this shirt last week, and it's poorly made."

Clerk: "It looks like you've worn it. We don't exchange garments that already have been worn."

Buyer: "I understand that is your policy, but it's not that I don't like the shirt. It is obviously defective. I didn't know it had these defects when I wore it."

Clerk: "Maybe this seam came loose because of the way you wore it."

Buyer: "I didn't do anything unusual. It is defective. I want it exchanged."

Clerk: "I'm sorry, but you should have returned it earlier. We can't take it back now."

Buyer: "I understand your point, but I didn't get what I paid for. You need to return my money or give me a new shirt."

Clerk: "It's beyond my authority to do that. I don't make the policies. I just have to follow them."

Buyer: "I understand you don't think you have the authority to change the policy. But your boss does. Please tell her I'd like to see her right now."

Providing Constructive Feedback

Make It Helpful
Be Specific
Be Descriptive
Be Timely
Be Flexible
Give Positive as Well as Negative Feedback
Avoid Blame or Embarrassment

Giving constructive feedback involves sharing information or perceptions with another about the nature, quality, or impact of that person's behavior. It can range from giving feedback pertaining specifically to a person's work (i.e., performance feedback) to impressions of how aspects of that person's interpersonal behavior may be pervasively affecting relationships with others. Our use of the term *feedback* here is somewhat different from its use in the systems view of communication (Figure C.1). In the communication model, the feedback loop begins with actively checking the receiver's *interpretation* of one's own message, and then initiating or modifying subsequent communications as necessary. A simple example of that meaning of feedback might be noting another person's quizzical expression when you try to explain a complicated point, thereby realizing that you'd better say it differently. The skill of giving constructive feedback, however, inherently involves *actively giving feedback to someone else.*

Getting helpful feedback is essential to a subordinate's performance and development. Without feedback, a subordinate will not be able to tell whether she's doing a good job or whether or not her abrasiveness is turning people off and hurting her chances for promotion. And it's not just subordinates who need constructive feedback to learn and grow. Peers may seek feedback from peers, and leaders may seek feedback from subordinates. Besides fostering growth, effective supervisory feedback also plays a major role in building morale.

In many ways, the development of good feedback skills is an outgrowth of developing good communication, listening, and assertiveness skills. Giving good feedback depends on being clear about the purpose of the feedback and on choosing an appropriate context and medium for giving it. Giving good feedback also depends on sending the proper nonverbal signals and trying to detect emotional signals from whoever may be receiving the feedback. In addition, giving good feedback depends on being somewhat assertive in providing it, even when it may be critical of a person's performance or behavior. Although feedback skills are related to communication, listening, and assertiveness skills, they are not the same thing. Someone may have good communication, listening, and assertiveness skills but poor feedback skills. Perhaps this distinction can be made clearer by examining the knowledge, behavior, and evaluative components of feedback skills.

The knowledge component of feedback concerns knowing when, where, and what feedback is to be given. For example, knowing when, where, and how to give positive feedback may be very different from knowing when, where, and how to give negative feedback. The behavioral component of feedback concerns how feedback actually is delivered (as contrasted with knowing how it should be delivered). Good feedback is specific, descriptive, direct, and helpful; poor feedback is often too watered down to be useful to the recipient. Finally, one way to evaluate feedback is to examine whether recipients actually modify their behavior accordingly after receiving it. Of course, this should not be the only way to evaluate feedback skills. Even when feedback is accurate in content and delivered skillfully, a recipient may fail to acknowledge it or do anything about it.

Although most leaders probably believe that feedback is an important skill, research has shown that leaders also believe they give more feedback than their subordinates think they do (Greller, 1980). There are many reasons leaders may be reluctant to give feedback. Leaders may be reluctant to give positive feedback because of time pressures, doubts about the efficacy of feedback, or lack of feedback skills (Komacki, 1982). Sometimes supervisors are hesitant to use positive feedback because they believe subordinates may see it as politically manipulative, ingratiating, or insincere (Bass, 1990). Leaders also may give positive feedback infrequently if they rarely leave their desks, if their personal standards are too high, or if they believe good performance is expected and should not be recognized at all (Deep & Sussman, 1990). Other reasons may explain the failure to give negative feedback (Larson, 1986), such as fears of disrupting leader–follower relations (Harrison, 1982) or fear of employee retaliation (Parsons, Herold, & Leatherwood, 1985).

Although there are a number of reasons why leaders are hesitant to provide both positive and negative feedback, leaders need to keep in mind that followers, committee members, or team members will perform at a higher level if they are given accurate and frequent feedback. It is difficult to imagine how work-group or team performance could improve without feedback. Positive feedback is necessary to tell followers they should keep doing what they are doing well, and negative feedback is needed to give followers or team members ideas on how to change other behavior to improve their performance. Although accurate and frequent feedback is necessary, there are several other aspects of feedback that everyone can work on to improve their feedback skills, including (*a*) making sure it's helpful, (*b*) being direct, (*c*) being specific, (*d*) being descriptive, (*e*) being timely, (*f*) being flexible, (*g*) giving both positive and negative feedback, and (*h*) avoiding blame and embarrassment when giving feedback. Highlight F.1 gives examples of each of these different aspects of feedback, and the following is a more complete description of ways leaders can improve their feedback skills.

Make It Helpful

The purpose of feedback is to provide others with information they can use to change their behavior. Being clear about the intent and purpose is important because giving feedback sometimes can become emotional for both the person giving it and the person receiving it. If the person giving feedback is in an emotional state (e.g., angry), she may say things that make her temporarily feel better but that only alienate the receiver. In order to be helpful, individuals need to be clear and unemotional when giving feedback, and should give feedback only about behaviors actually under the other person's control.

Tips for Improving Feedback Skills

Highlight F.1

BEING HELPFUL

Do not: "I got better scores when I was going through this program than you just did."

Do: "This seems to be a difficult area for you. What can I do to help you master it better?"

BEING DIRECT

Do not: "It's important that we all speak loud enough to be heard in meetings."

Do: "I had a difficult time hearing you in the meeting because you were speaking in such a soft voice."

BEING SPECIFIC

Do not: "Since you came to work for us, your work has been good."

Do: "I really like the initiative and resourcefulness you showed in solving our scheduling problem."

BEING DESCRIPTIVE

Do not: "I'm getting tired of your rudeness and disinterest when others are talking."

Do: "You weren't looking at anyone else when they were talking, which gave the impression you were bored. Is that how you were feeling?"

BEING TIMELY

Do not: "Joe, I think I need to tell you about an impression you made on me in the staff meeting last month."

Do: "Joe, do you have a minute? I was confused by something you said in the meeting this morning."

BEING FLEXIBLE

Do not (while a person is crying, or while they are turning beet-red with clenched teeth in apparent anger): "There's another thing I want to tell you about your presentation yesterday . . ."

Do: When a person's rising defenses or emotionality gets in the way of their really listening, deal with those feelings first, or wait until later to finish your feedback. Do not continue giving information.

People can improve the impact of the feedback they give when it is addressed to a specific individual. A common mistake in giving feedback is addressing it to "people at large" rather than to a specific individual. In this case, the individuals for whom the feedback was intended may not believe the feedback pertained to them. In order to maximize the impact of the feedback, people should try to provide it to specific individuals, not large groups.

Be Specific

Feedback is most helpful when it specifies particular behaviors that are positive or negative. One of the best illustrations of the value of specific feedback is in compositions or term papers written for school. If someone turned in a draft of a paper to the instructor for constructive comments and the instructor's comments about the paper were "Good start, but needs work in several areas," then the person would have a difficult time knowing just what to change or correct. More helpful feedback from the instructor would be specific comments like "This paragraph does not logically follow the preceding one" or "Cite an example here." The same is true of feedback in work situations. The more specifically leaders can point out which behaviors to change, the more clearly they let the other person know what to do.

Be Descriptive

In giving feedback, it is good to stick to the facts as much as possible, being sure to distinguish them from inferences or attributions. A behavior description reports actions that others can see, about which there could be little question or disagreement. Such descriptions must be distinguished from inferences about someone else's feelings, attitudes, character, motives, or traits. It is a behavior description, for example, to say that Sally stood up and walked out of a meeting while someone else was talking. It is an inference, though, to say she walked out because she was angry. However, sometimes it is helpful to describe both the behavior itself and the corresponding impressions when giving feedback. This is particularly true if the feedback giver believes that the other person does not realize how the behavior negatively affects others' impressions.

Another reason to make feedback descriptive is to distinguish it from evaluation. When a person gives feedback based mostly on inferences, he often conveys evaluations of the "goodness" or "badness" of behavior as well. For example, saying "You were too shy" has a more negative connotation than saying "You had little to say." In the former case, the person's behavior was evaluated unfavorably, and by apparently subjective criteria. Yet evaluation is often an intrinsic part of a supervisor's responsibilities, and good performance feedback may necessitate conveying evaluative information to a subordinate. In such cases, leaders are better off providing evaluative feedback when clear criteria for performance have been established. Filley and Pace (1976) described criteria that can be used to provide evaluative feedback; some are listed in Highlight F.2.

An issue related to impressions and evaluative feedback concerns the distinction between job-related (i.e., performance feedback) and more personal or discretionary feedback. Although leaders have a right to expect followers to listen to their performance feedback, that is not necessarily true concerning feedback about

Types of Criteria to Use for Evaluative Feedback

Highlight F.2

1. Compare behavior with others' measured performance. With this method, the subordinate's behavior is compared with that of her peers or co-workers; also called norm-referenced appraisal. For example, a subordinate may be told her counseling load is the lightest of all 10 counselors working at the center.

2. Compare behavior with an accepted standard. An example of this method would be where a counselor was told her workload was substantially below the standard of acceptable performance set at 30 cases per week. This is known as criterion-referenced appraisal.

3. Compare behavior with an a priori goal. With this method, the subordinate must participate in and agree with a goal. This is a form of criterion-referenced appraisal, with the subordinate's "ownership" and acceptance of the goal before the fact critical to the feedback procedure.

4. Compare behavior with past performance.

Source: Adapted from A. C. Filley and L. A. Pace, "Making Judgments Descriptive," in J. E. Jones and J. W. Pfeiffer, eds, *The 1976 Annual Handbook for Group Facilitators* (La Jolla, CA: University Associates Press, 1976), pp. 128–31.

other behaviors. It may well be that sharing perceptions of the person's behavior could be very helpful to that person even when the behavior doesn't pertain specifically to his formal responsibilities; in such cases, however, it is the follower's choice whether to hear it or, if he hears it, whether to act on it or not.

Be Timely

Feedback usually is most effective when it is given soon after the behavior occurs. The context and relevant details of more recent events or behaviors are more readily available to everyone involved, thus facilitating more descriptive and helpful feedback.

Be Flexible

Although feedback is best when it is timely, sometimes waiting is preferable to giving feedback at the very earliest opportunity. In general, everyone should remember that the primary purpose of feedback is to be helpful. Feedback sessions should be scheduled with that in mind. For example, a subordinate's schedule may preclude conveniently giving him feedback right away, and it may not be appropriate to give him feedback when it will distract him from another more immediate and pressing task. Furthermore, it may not be constructive to give someone else feedback when the person receiving it is in a very emotional state (whether about the behavior in question or other matters entirely). Moreover, it is important to be attentive to the other person's emotional responses while giving feedback and to be ready to adjust one's own behavior accordingly.

A final important part of being flexible is to give feedback in manageable amounts. In giving feedback, one does not need to cover every single point at one time, as doing so would only overload the other person with information. Instead, anyone who needs to give a lot of feedback to someone else may want to spread out the feedback sessions and focus on covering only one or two points in each session.

Give Positive as Well as Negative Feedback

Giving both positive and negative feedback is more helpful than giving only positive or negative feedback alone. Positive feedback tells the other person or the group only what they are doing right, and negative feedback tells the other person or group only what they are doing wrong. Providing both kinds of feedback is best.

Avoid Blame or Embarrassment

Because the purpose of feedback is to give useful information to other people to help them develop, talking to them in a way merely intended (or likely) to demean or make them feel bad is not a helpful part of the development process. Followers tend to be more likely to believe feedback if it comes from leaders who have had the opportunity to observe the behavior and are perceived to be credible, competent, and trustworthy (Coye, 1982; Quaglieri & Carnazza, 1985; Stone, Guetal, & MacIntosh, 1984). Bass (1990) pointed out that followers will continue to seek feedback even if their leaders are not competent or trustworthy—though they will not seek it from their leaders. They will seek it from others they do trust, such as peers or other superiors.

Guidelines for Effective Stress Management

Monitor Your Own and Your Followers' Stress Levels
Identify What Is Causing the Stress
Practice a Healthy Lifestyle
Learn How to Relax
Develop Supportive Relationships
Keep Things in Perspective
The A-B-C Model

People use the term *stress* in a number of different ways. Sometimes people use the term to describe particular sorts of events or *environmental conditions*. For example, fans might speculate that a professional football coach's heart attack was caused by the *pressures* of his profession. Other examples might include receiving a failing grade on a physics exam, or arriving noticeably late to an important meeting, or playing a sudden-death overtime in hockey. We would acknowledge, for example, that walking in late to a meeting could be very embarrassing (i.e., stressful). Likewise for working at the service counter of a major department store on the day after Christmas; it's a *stressful job*. In each of these instances, stress refers to *characteristics of the environment*. But people also use the term in a quite different way. Sometimes it refers to the *effects* of those environments. The phrase "I'm feeling a lot of stress" might refer to various *symptoms* a person is experiencing, such as muscular tension or difficulty concentrating. Before we proceed further, therefore, it will be useful to agree upon some conventions of terminology.

We will define stress as the whole process by which we appraise and respond to events that challenge or threaten us (Myers, 1989). These responses usually include increased levels of emotional arousal and changes in physiological symptoms, such as increases in perspiration and heart rates, cholesterol levels, or blood pressure. Stress often occurs in situations that are overly complex, demanding, or unclear. Stressors are those specific characteristics in individuals, tasks, organizations, or the environment that pose some degree of threat or challenge to people (see Highlight S.1). Although all the factors in Highlight S.1 probably have an adverse impact on people, the degree of stress associated with each of them depends on one's overall level of stress tolerance and previous experience with the stressor in question (Benner, 1984). Similarly, it is important to realize that stress is in the eye of the beholder—what one person may see as challenging and potentially rewarding, another may see as threatening and distressful (McCauley, 1987; Staw, 1984).

Who do you think typically experiences greater stress—leaders or followers? In one sense, the answer is the same as that for much psychological research: it depends. The role of leader certainly can be quite stressful. Leaders face at least one major stressful event at least once a month (Ivancevich, Schweiger, & Ragan, 1986). Followers' stress levels, on the other hand, often depend on their leaders. Leaders can help followers cope with stress or, alternatively, actually increase their followers' stress levels. Many leaders recognize when followers are under a lot of stress

Stress Symptoms

Highlight S.1

Are you behaving "unlike" yourself?

Has your mood become negative, hostile, or depressed?

Do you have difficulty sleeping?

Are you defensive or touchy?

Are your relationships suffering?

Have you made more mistakes or bad decisions lately?

Have you lost interest in normally enjoyable activities?

Are you using alcohol or other drugs?

Do you seem to have little energy?

Do you worry a lot?

Are you nervous much of the time?

Have you been undereating or overeating?

Have you had an increase in headaches or back pains?

This checklist can also be used to help determine the level of stress in followers.

and will give them time off, try to reduce their workload, or take other actions to help followers cope. On the other hand, about two out of three workers say their bosses play a bigger part in creating their stress than any other personal, organizational, or environmental factor (R. T. Hogan & Morrison, 1991; Shipper & Wilson, 1992). Similarly, McCormick and Powell (1988) reported that working for a tyrannical boss was the most frequently cited source of stress among workers. It is clear that leaders play a substantial role in how stressful their followers' work experience is, for good or ill.

Stress can either facilitate or inhibit performance, depending on the situation. Too much stress can take a toll on individuals and organizations that includes decreased health and emotional well-being, reduced job performance, and decreased organizational effectiveness (see Highlight S.2 for an example of how too much stress impaired one person's performance).

In order to understand the effects of stress, an analogy might be helpful. Kites need an optimal amount of wind to fly; they will not fly on windless days, and the string may break on a day that is too windy. You can think of stress as like the wind for a kite: There is a certain level that is optimal, neither too little nor too much. Another analogy is your car. Just as an automobile engine operates optimally within a certain range of revolutions per minute (RPM), most people function best at certain levels of stress. A certain amount of stress or arousal is helpful in increasing motivation and performance, but too much stress can be counterproductive. For example, it is common and probably helpful to feel a little anxiety before giving a speech, but being too nervous can destroy one's effectiveness.

The optimal level of stress depends on a number of factors. One is the level of physical activity actually demanded by the task. Another is the perceived difficulty of the task. Performance often suffers when difficult tasks are performed under stressful situations. For example, think how one's performance might differ when

Stress on a TV Game Show

Highlight S.2

The television game show *Wheel of Fortune* pits contestants against each other in trying to identify common sayings. By spinning a wheel, contestants determine varying dollar amounts to be added to their potential winnings.

The game is similar to the game of "Hangman" you may have played as a child. It begins with spaces indicating the number of words in a saying and the number of letters in each word. One player spins the wheel, which determines prize money, and then guesses a letter. If the letter appears somewhere in the saying, then the player spins the wheel again, guesses another letter, and so on. The letters are "filled in" as they are correctly identified. A player may try to guess the saying after naming a correct letter.

If a player names a letter which does not appear in the saying, then that prize money is not added to the contestant's potential winnings and play moves on to another contestant.

One day a contestant was playing for over $50,000 to solve the puzzle below. Perhaps because of the stress of being on television and playing for so much money, the contestant could not accurately name a letter for one of the four remaining spaces. Most people, not experiencing such stress, easily solve the problem. Can you? For the answer, see the bottom of the box.

```
T  H  E      T  H  R  I  __  __  __
O  F      __  I  __  T  O  R  Y
   A  N  D      T  H  E
A  G  O  N  Y      O  F
   D  E  F  E  A  T
```

Answer: The Thrill of Victory and the Agony of Defeat

learning to first drive a car with an instructor who is quiet and reserved rather than one who yells a lot. Chances are, performance will be much better with the first instructor than with the second.

It is important to note that task difficulty is generally a function of experience; the more experience one has with a task, the less difficult it becomes. Thus, the more driving experience one has, the easier the task becomes. Moreover, not only do people cope with stress more readily when performing easier tasks; people often need higher levels of stress for performing them optimally. One underlying purpose behind any type of practice, be it football, marching band, soccer, or drama, is to reduce task difficulty and help members or players to perform at an even higher level when faced with the stress of key performances and games.

Although stress can have positive effects, research has focused on the negative implications of too much stress on health and work. In terms of health, stress has been linked to heart disease (Friedman & Ulmer, 1984), immune system deficiencies (Pomerleau & Rodin, 1986), and the growth rates of tumors (Justice, 1985). In terms of work behaviors, both Latack (1986) and Quayle (1983) reported that work-related stress has caused a dramatic increase in drug and alcohol use in the workplace, and Jamal (1984) found that stress was positively related to absenteeism, intentions to quit, and turnover. Relatedly, Quayle (1983) and Albrecht (1979) estimated the economic impact of stress to companies in the Unites States to be somewhere between $70 billion and $150 billion annually. Stress can also affect the decision-making process. Although leaders need to act decisively in stressful situations (i.e., crises), they may not make good decisions under stress (Fiedler, 1992; Gibson, 1992; Mulder, de Jong, Koppelaar, & Verhage, 1986). According to Weschler (1955) and Tjosvold (1985), people make poor decisions when under stress because they revert to their intuition rather than think rationally about problems.

As we have noted, too much stress can take a toll on individuals and their organizations. For individuals, the toll can be in terms of their health, mental and emotional well-being, job performance, or interpersonal relationships. For organizations, the toll includes decreased productivity and increased employee absenteeism, turnover, and medical costs. It stands to reason, then, that leaders in any activity should know something about stress. Leaders should understand the nature of stress because the leadership role itself can be stressful and because leaders' stress can impair the performance and well-being of followers. To prevent stress from becoming so excessive that it takes a toll in some important dimension of your own or your followers' lives, the following guidelines for effective stress management are provided.

Monitor Your Own and Your Followers' Stress Levels

One of the most important steps in managing stress is to *monitor your own and your followers' stress levels.* Although this seems straightforward, a seemingly paradoxical fact about stress is that it often takes a toll without one's conscious awareness. A person experiencing excessive stress might manifest various symptoms apparent to everyone but him or her. For that reason, it is useful to develop the habit of regularly attending to some of the warning signs that your stress level may be getting too high. Some of the warning signs of stress are in Highlight S.1. If you answered yes to any of these questions, then your own or your followers' stress levels may be getting too high and it would probably be a good idea to put some of the following stress management strategies into practice right away. On the other hand, answering some of the questions affirmatively does not necessarily mean your stress level is too high. There could, for example, be some other physiological explanation.

Identify What Is Causing the Stress

Monitoring your stress will reduce the chances that it will build to an unhealthy level before you take action, but monitoring is not enough. Leaders also need to *identify what is causing the stress.* It may seem at first that the causes of stress always will be obvious, but that is not true. Sometimes the problems are clear enough even if the solutions are not (e.g., family finances or working in a job with a high workload and lots of deadlines). At other times, however, it may be difficult to identify the root problem. For example, a coach may attribute his anger to the losing record of his team, not recognizing that a bigger cause of his emotional distress may be the problems he is having at home with his teenage son. A worker may feel frustrated because her boss overloads her with work, not realizing that her own unassertiveness keeps her from expressing her feelings to her boss. Problem solving can be applied constructively to managing stress, but only if the problem is identified properly in the first place. Once the problem is identified, then a plan for minimizing stress or the effects of the stressor can be developed.

Practice a Healthy Lifestyle

Practicing a healthy lifestyle is one of the best ways to minimize stress. There are no substitutes for balanced nutrition, regular exercise, adequate sleep, abstention from tobacco products, and drinking only moderate amounts of alcohol (if at all) as keys to a healthy life. A long-term study of the lifestyles of nearly 7,000 adults confirmed these as independent factors contributing to wellness and the absence of stress symptoms (Wiley & Camacho, 1980). Insufficient sleep saps energy, interferes with alertness and judgment, increases irritability, and lowers resistance to illness. Exercise, besides being a valuable part of any long-term health strategy, is also an excellent way to reduce tension.

Learn How to Relax

Believe it or not, some people just do not know how to relax. Although physical exercise is a good relaxation technique, sometimes you will need to relax but not have an opportunity to get a workout. Having practiced other relaxation techniques will come in handy when the situation prevents strenuous exercise. Also, of course, some people simply prefer alternative relaxation techniques to exercise. *Deep-breathing techniques, progressive muscle relaxation, and thinking of calming words and images* can be powerful on-the-spot calming techniques to reduce arousal level. They are applicable in stressful situations ranging from job interviews to sports. The effectiveness of these techniques is somewhat a matter of personal preference, and no single one is best for all purposes or all people.

Develop Supportive Relationships

Another powerful antidote to stress is having a *network of close and supportive relationships* with others (Berkman & Syme, 1979). People who have close ties to others through marriage, church membership, or other groups tend to be healthier than those with weaker social ties. Also, social supports of various kinds (e.g., the supportiveness of one's spouse, co-workers, or boss) can buffer the impact of job stress (Cummings, 1990; Jayaratne, Himle, & Chess, 1988), and unit cohesion is believed to be a critical element of soldiers' ability to withstand even the extreme physical and psychological stresses of combat (West Point Associates, 1988). Leaders can play a constructive role in developing mutual supportiveness and cohesiveness among subordinates, and their own open and frank communication with subordinates is especially important when a situation is ambiguous as well as stressful.

Keep Things in Perspective

As we noted earlier, the stressfulness of any event depends partly on the way one interprets it, not just on the event itself. For example, a poor grade on an examination may be more stressful for one student than for another, just as a rebuke from a boss may be more stressful for one worker than for another. This is partly due, of course, to the fact individuals invest themselves in activities to different degrees because they value different things. A problem in an area of heavy personal investment is more stressful than one in an area of little personal investment. It goes deeper than that, however. Managing stress effectively depends on *keeping things in perspective.* This is difficult for some people because they have a style of interpreting events that aggravates their felt stress.

Individuals who have relatively complex self-concepts, as measured by the number of different ways they describe or see themselves, are less susceptible to common stress-related complaints than are people with lesser degrees of "self-complexity" (Linville, 1987). Take, for example, someone who has suffered a setback at work, such as having lost out to a colleague for a desired promotion. Someone low in self-complexity (e.g., a person whose self-concept is defined solely in terms of professional success) could be devastated by the event. Low self-complexity implies a lack of resilience to threats to one's ego. Consider, on the other hand, someone with high self-complexity facing the same setback. The person could understandably feel disappointed and perhaps dejected about work, but if she were high in self-complexity, then the event's impact would be buffered by the existence of relatively uncontaminated areas of positive self-image. For example, she might base her feelings of professional success on more criteria than just getting (or not getting) a promotion. Other criteria, such as being highly respected by peers, may be even more important bases for her feelings of professional success. Furthermore, other dimensions of her life (e.g., her leadership in the local Democratic Party, support to her family) may provide more areas of positive self-image.

The A-B-C Model

Unfortunately, because there are no shortcuts to developing self-complexity, it is not really a viable stress management strategy. There are other cognitive approaches to stress management, however, that can produce more immediate results. These approaches have the common goal of changing a person's self-talk about stressful events. One of the simplest of these to apply is called the A-B-C model (Ellis & Harper, 1975; Steinmetz, Blankenship, Brown, Hall, & Miller, 1980).

To appreciate the usefulness of the A-B-C model, it is helpful to consider the chain of events that precedes feelings of stress. Sometimes people think of this as a two-step sequence. Something external happens (i.e., a stressful event), and then something *internal* follows (i.e., symptoms of stress). We can depict the sequence like this:

A. Triggering Event (e.g., knocking your boss's coffee onto his lap)
C. Feelings and Behaviors (e.g., anxiety, fear, embarrassment, perspiration)

In other words, many people think their feelings and behaviors result directly from external events. Such a view, however, leaves out the critical role played by our thoughts, or self-talk. The actual sequence looks like this:

A. Triggering Event (knocking your boss's coffee onto his lap)
B. Your Thinking ("He must think I'm a real jerk.")
C. Feelings and Behaviors (anxiety, fear, embarrassment, perspiration)

From this perspective you can see the causal role played by inner dialogue, or self-talk, in contributing to feelings of stress. Such inner dialogue can be rational or irrational, constructive or destructive—and which it will be is under the individual's control. People gain considerable freedom from stress when they realize that by changing their own self-talk, they can control their emotional responses to events around them. Consider a different sequence for our scenario:

A. Triggering Event (knocking your boss's coffee onto his lap)
B. Your Thinking ("Darn it! But it was just an accident.")
C. Feelings and Behavior (apologizing and helping clean up)

Thus, a particular incident can be interpreted in several different ways, some likely to increase feelings of stress and distress, and others likely to maintain self-esteem and positive coping. You will become better at coping with stress as you practice listening to your inner dialogue and changing destructive self-talk to constructive self-talk. Even this is not a simple change to make, however. Changing self-talk is more difficult than you might think, especially in emotionalized situations. Because self-talk is covert, spontaneous, fleeting, and reflexive (McKay, Davis, & Fanning, 1981), it, like any bad habit, can be difficult to change. Nevertheless, precisely because self-talk is just a habit, you can change it.

Finally, leaders need to recognize their role in their followers' stress levels. A leader in a stressful situation who is visibly manifesting some of the symptoms found in Highlight S.1 is not going to set much of an example for followers. On the contrary, because followers look to leaders for guidance and support, these behaviors and symptoms could become contagious and may serve to increase followers' stress levels. Leaders need to recognize the importance of role modeling in reducing (or increasing) followers' stress levels. Leaders also need to make sure their style of interacting with subordinates does not make the leaders "stress carriers."

Building Technical Competence

Determining How the Job Contributes to the Overall Mission
Becoming an Expert in the Job
Seeking Opportunities to Broaden Experiences

Technical competence concerns the knowledge and repertoire of behaviors one can bring to bear to successfully complete a task. For example, a highly skilled surgeon possesses vast knowledge of human anatomy and surgical techniques and can perform an extensive set of highly practiced surgical procedures; a highly skilled volleyball player has a thorough understanding of the rules, tactics, and strategies of volleyball and can set, block, and serve effectively. Individuals usually acquire technical competence through formal education or training in specialized topics (i.e., law, medicine, accounting, welding, carpentry), on-the-job training, or experience (Yukl, 1989), and many studies have documented the importance of technical competence to a person's success and effectiveness as both a leader and a follower. This section describes why technical competence is important to followers and leaders; it also provides readers with ideas about how to increase their own technical competence.

There are many reasons why followers need to have a high level of technical competence. First, performance is often a function of technical competence (Borman, Hanson, Oppler, & Pulakos, 1993; Schmidt & Hunter, 1992). Relatedly, research has shown that technical expertise plays a key role in supervisors' performance appraisal ratings of subordinates (Borman, White, Pulakos, & Oppler, 1991; J. Hogan, 1992b). Second, followers with high levels of technical competence have a lot of expert power, and at times can wield more influence in their groups than the leader does (Bugental, 1964; Farris, 1971). Third, individuals with high levels of technical competence may be more likely to be a member of a leader's in-group (Duchon, Green, & Taber, 1986). Relatedly, followers with high levels of technical competence are more likely to be delegated tasks and asked to participate in the decision-making process. Conversely, supervisors are more likely to use a close, directive leadership style when interacting with subordinates with poor technical skills (Dewhirst, Metts, & Ladd, 1987; Leana, 1987; Lowin & Craig, 1968; Rosen & Jerdee, 1977). Similarly, Blau (1968) noted that organizations with relatively high numbers of technically competent members tended to have a flatter organizational structure; organizations with relatively fewer qualified members tended to be more centralized and autocratic. Thus, if followers wish to earn greater rewards, exert more influence in their groups, and have greater say in the decision-making process, then they should do all they can to enhance their technical competence.

There are also many reasons why it benefits leaders to have high levels of technical competence. First, technical competence has been found to be consistently related to managerial promotion rates. Managers having higher levels of technical competence were much more likely to rise to the top managerial levels at AT&T than managers with lower levels of technical competence (Howard, 1986; Howard & Bray, 1989). Second, having a high level of technical competence is important because many leaders, particularly first-line supervisors, often spend considerable time training followers (Wexley & Latham, 1981). Perhaps nowhere is the importance of technical competence in training more readily apparent than in coaching; little is as frustrating as having a coach who knows less about the game than the team members. Third, leaders with high levels of technical competence seem to be able to reduce the level of role ambiguity and conflict in their groups (Podsakoff, Todor, & Schuler, 1983; Walker, 1976), and followers are generally more satisfied with leaders who have high rather than average levels of technical competence (Bass, 1985; Penner, Malone, Coughlin, & Herz, 1973). Finally, leaders who have a high level of technical competence may be able to stimulate followers to think about problems and issues in new ways, which in turn has been found to be strongly related to organizational climate ratings and followers' motivation to succeed (Avolio & Bass, 1988; Curphy, 1991a). Given these findings for both leaders and followers, below is some practical advice for improving technical competence.

Determining How the Job Contributes to the Overall Mission

The first step in building technical competence is to determine how one's job contributes to the overall success of the organization. By taking this step, individuals can better determine what technical knowledge and which behaviors are most strongly related to job and organizational success. Next, people should evaluate their current level of technical skills by seeking verbal feedback from peers and superiors, reviewing past performance appraisal results, or reviewing objective performance data (e.g., golf scores, team statistics, the number of products rejected for poor quality). These actions will help individuals get a better handle on their own strengths and weaknesses, and in turn can help people be certain that any formal education or training program they pursue is best suited to meet their needs.

Becoming an Expert in the Job

Becoming an expert in one's primary field is often the springboard for further developmental opportunities. There are a number of ways in which individuals can become experts in their field, and these include enrolling in formalized education and training programs, watching others, asking questions, and teaching others. Attending pertinent education and training courses is one way to acquire technical skills, and many companies often pay the tuition and fees associated with these courses. Another way to increase expertise in one's field is by being a keen observer of human behavior. Individuals can learn a lot by observing how others handle work-coordination problems, achieve production goals, discipline team members, or develop team members with poor skills. However, merely observing how others do things is not nearly as effective as observing and reflecting about how others do things. One method of reflection is trying to explain others' behaviors in terms of the concepts or theories described in this book. Observers should look for concepts that cast light on both variations and regularities in how others act and think about the reasons why a person might have acted a certain way. Additionally, observers can develop by trying to think of as many different criteria as possible for evaluating another person's actions.

It is also important to ask questions. Because everyone makes inferences regarding the motives, expectations, values, or rationale underlying another person's actions, it is vital to ask questions and seek information likely to verify the accuracy of one's inferences. By asking questions, observers can better understand why team practices are conducted in a particular way, what work procedures have been implemented in the past, or what really caused someone to quit a volunteer organization. Finally, perhaps nothing can help a person become a technical expert more than having to teach someone else about the equipment, procedures, strategies, problems, resources, and contacts associated with a job, club, sport, or activity. Teachers must have a thorough understanding of the job or position in order to effectively teach someone else. By seeking opportunities to teach others, individuals enhance their own technical expertise as well as that of others.

Seeking Opportunities to Broaden Experiences

Individuals can improve their technical competence by seeking opportunities to broaden their experiences. Just as a person should try to play a variety of positions in order to better appreciate the contributions of other team members, so should a person try to perform the tasks associated with the other positions in his or her work group in order to better appreciate how the work contributes to organizational success. Similarly, people should visit other parts of the organization in order to gain an understanding of its whole operation. Moreover, by working on team projects, people get a chance to interact with members of other work units and often get the opportunity to develop new skills. Additionally, volunteering to support school, political, or community activities is another way to increase one's organization and planning, public speaking, fund-raising, and public relations skills, all of which may be important aspects of technical competence for certain jobs.

Building Effective Relationships with Superiors

Understanding the Superior's World
Adapting to the Superior's Style

As defined here, superiors are those individuals with relatively more power and authority than the other members of the group. Thus, superiors could be teachers, band directors, coaches, team captains, heads of committees, or first-line supervisors. Needless to say, there are a number of advantages to having a good working relationship with superiors. First, superiors and followers sharing the same values, approaches, and attitudes will experience less conflict, provide higher levels of mutual support, and be more satisfied with superior–follower relationships than superiors and followers having poor working relationships (Duchon, Green, & Taber, 1986; Porter, 1992). Relatedly, individuals having good superior–follower relationships are often in the superior's in-group and thus are more likely to have a say in the decision-making process, be delegated interesting tasks, and have the superior's support for career advancement (Yukl, 1989). Second, followers are often less satisfied with their supervisor and receive lower performance appraisal ratings when superior–follower relationships are poor (Pulakos & Wexley, 1983; Weiss, 1977).

Although the advantages of having a good working relationship with superiors seem clear, one might mistakenly think that followers have little, if any, say in the quality of the relationship. In other words, followers might believe their relationships with superiors are a matter of luck; either the follower has a good superior or a bad one, or the superior just happens to like or dislike the follower, and there is little if anything the follower can do about it. However, the quality of a working relationship is not determined solely by the superior, and effective subordinates do not limit themselves to a passive stance toward superiors. Effective subordinates have learned how to take active steps to strengthen the relationship and enhance the support they provide their superior and the organization (Gabarro & Kotter, 1980; Kelley, 1988).

Wherever a person is positioned in an organization, an important aspect of that person's work is to help his superior be successful, just as an important part of the superior's work is to help followers be successful. This does not mean that followers should become apple-polishers, play politics, or distort information just to make superiors look good. It does mean, however, that followers should think of their own and their superior's success as interdependent. It means that followers are players on their superior's team and should be evaluated on the basis of the team's success, not just their own. If the team succeeds, then both the coach and the team members should benefit; if the team fails, then the blame should fall on both the coach and the team members. Because team, club, or organizational outcomes depend to some extent on good superior–follower relationships, understanding how superiors view the world and adapting to superiors' styles are two things followers can do to increase the likelihood their actions will have positive results for themselves, their superiors, and their organizations (Gabarro & Kotter, 1980).

Understanding the Superior's World

There are a number of things followers can do to better understand their superior's world. First, they should try to get a handle on their superior's personal and organizational objectives. Loyalty and support are a two-way street, and just as a superior can help subordinates attain their personal goals most readily by knowing what they are, so can subordinates support their superior if they understand the superior's goals and objectives. Relatedly, knowing a superior's values, preferences, and personality can help followers better understand why superiors act the way they do and can give followers insights into how they might strengthen relationships with superiors.

Second, followers need to realize that superiors are not supermen or superwomen; superiors do not have all the answers, and they have both strengths and weaknesses. Subordinates can make a great contribution to the overall success of a team by recognizing and complementing a superior's weaknesses, and understanding his constraints and limitations. For example, a highly successful management consultant might spend over 200 days a year conducting executive development workshops, providing organizational feedback to clients, or giving speeches at various public events. This same consultant, however, might not be skilled in designing and making effective visual aids for presentations, or she might dislike having to make her own travel and accommodation arrangements. A follower could make both the consultant and the consulting firm more successful through his own good organization and planning, attention to detail, computer graphics skills, and understanding that the consultant is most effective when she has at least a one-day break between engagements. A similar process can take place in other contexts, as when subordinates help orient and educate a newly assigned superior whose expertise and prior experience may have been in a different field or activity.

In an even more general sense, subordinates can enhance superior–follower relationships by keeping superiors informed about various activities in the work group or new developments or opportunities in the field. Few superiors like surprises, and any news should come from the person with responsibility for a particular area—especially if the news is potentially bad or concerns unfavorable developments. Followers wishing to develop good superior–follower relationships should never put their superior in the embarrassing situation of having someone else know more about her terrain than she does (her own boss, for instance). As Kelley (1988) maintained, the best followers think critically and play an active role in their organizations, which means that followers should keep their superiors informed about critical information and pertinent opinions concerning organizational issues.

Adapting to the Superior's Style

Research has shown that some executives fail to get promoted (i.e., are derailed) because they are unable or unwilling to adapt to superiors with leadership styles different from their own (McCall & Lombardo, 1983). Followers need to keep in mind that it is their responsibility to adapt to their superior's style, not vice versa. For example, followers might prefer to interact with superiors face-to-face, but if their superior appreciates written memos, then written memos it should be. Similarly, a follower might be accustomed to informal interactions with superiors, but a new superior might prefer a more businesslike and formal style. Followers need to be flexible in adapting to their superiors' decision-making styles, problem-solving strategies, modes of communication, styles of interaction, and so on.

One way followers can better adapt to a superior's style is to clarify expectations about their role on the team, committee, or work group. Young workers often do not appreciate the difference between a job description and one's role in a job. A job description is a formalized statement of tasks and activities; a role describes the personal signature an incumbent gives to a job. For example, the job description of a high school athletic coach might specify such responsibilities as selecting and training a team or making decisions about lineups. Two different coaches, however, might accomplish those basic responsibilities in quite different ways. One might emphasize player development in the broadest sense, getting to know her players personally and using sports as a vehicle for their individual growth; another might see his role simply to produce the most winning team possible. Therefore, just because followers know what their job is does not mean their role is clear.

Although some superiors take the initiative to explicitly spell out the roles they expect subordinates to play, most do not. Usually it is the subordinate's task to discern his or her role. One way followers can do this is to make a list of major responsibilities and use it to guide a discussion with the superior about different ways the tasks might be accomplished and the relative priorities of the tasks. Relatedly, followers will also find it helpful to talk to others who have worked with a particular superior before.

Finally, followers interested in developing effective relationships with superiors need to be honest and dependable. Whatever other qualities or talents a subordinate might have, a lack of integrity is an absolutely fatal flaw. No one—superior, peer, or subordinate—wants to work with someone who is untrustworthy. After integrity, superiors value dependability. Superiors value workers who have reliable work habits, accomplish assigned tasks at the right time in the right order, and do what they promise (Kouzes & Posner, 1987).

Building Effective Relationships with Peers

Recognizing Common Interests and Goals
Understanding Peers' Tasks, Problems, and Rewards
Practicing a Theory Y Attitude

The phrase *influence without authority* (Cohen & Bradford, 1990) captures a key element of the work life of increasing numbers of individuals. More and more people are finding that their jobs require them to influence others despite having no formal authority over them. No man is an island, it is said, and perhaps no worker in today's organizations can survive alone. Virtually everyone needs a co-worker's assistance or resources at one time or another. Along these lines, some researchers have maintained that one of the fundamental requirements of leadership effectiveness is the ability to build strong alliances with others, and groups of peers generally wield more influence (and can get more things done) than individuals working separately (R. T. Hogan, J. Hogan, & Curphy, 1992). Similarly, investing the time and effort to develop effective relationships with peers not only has immediate dividends but also can have long-term benefits if a peer ends up in a position of power in the future. Many times, leaders are selected from among the members of a group, committee, club, or team and, having previously spent time developing a friendly rather than an antagonistic relationship with other work group members, will lay the groundwork for building effective relationships with superiors and becoming a member of superiors' in-groups. Given the benefits of strong relationships with peers, the following are a few ideas about how to establish and maintain good peer relationships.

Recognizing Common Interests and Goals

Although Chapters 5 through 8 described a variety of ways people vary, one of the best ways to establish effective working relationships with peers is to acknowledge shared interests, values, goals, and expectations (Cohen & Bradford, 1990). In order to acknowledge shared aspirations and interests, however, one must know what peers' goals, values, and interests actually are. Establishing informal communication links is one of the best ways to discover common interests and values. To do so, one needs to be open and honest in communicating one's own needs, values, and goals, as well as being willing to acknowledge others' needs, aspirations, and interests. Little can destroy a relationship with peers more quickly than a person who is overly willing to share his own problems and beliefs but unwilling to listen to others' ideas about the same issues. Moreover, although some people believe that participating in social gatherings, parties, committee meetings, lunches, company sport teams, or community activities can be a waste of time, peers with considerable referent power often see such activities as opportunities to establish and improve relationships with others. Thus, an effective way to establish relationships with other members of a team, committee, or organization is to meet with them in contexts outside of normal working relationships.

Understanding Peers' Tasks, Problems, and Rewards

Few things reinforce respect between co-workers better than understanding the nature of each other's work. Building a cooperative relationship with others depends, therefore, on knowing the sorts of tasks others perform in the organization. It also depends on understanding what their problems and rewards are. With the former, one of the best ways to establish strong relationships is by lending a hand whenever peers face personal or organizational problems. With the latter, it is especially important to remember that people tend to repeat those behaviors that are rewarded and are less likely to repeat behaviors that go unrewarded. A person's counterproductive or negative behaviors may be due less to his personal characteristics (e.g., "He is just uncooperative") than to the way his rewards are structured. For example, a teacher may be less likely to share successful classroom exercises with others if teachers are awarded merit pay on the basis of classroom effectiveness. To secure cooperation from others, it helps to know which situational factors reinforce both positive and negative behaviors in others (Cohen & Bradford, 1990). By better understanding the situation facing others, people can determine whether their own positive feedback (or lack thereof) is contributing to, or hindering the establishment of, effective relationships with peers. People should not underestimate the power of their own sincere encouragement, thanks, and compliments in positively influencing the behavior of their colleagues.

Practicing a Theory Y Attitude

Another way to build effective working relationships with peers is to view them from a Theory Y perspective (see Chapter 6). When a person assumes that others are competent, trustworthy, willing to cooperate if they can, and proud of their work, peers will look on that person in the same light. Even if one practices a Theory Y attitude, however, it may still be difficult to get along with a few co-workers. In such cases, it is easy to become preoccupied with the qualities one dislikes. This should be resisted as much as possible. A vicious cycle can develop in which people become enemies, putting more and more energy into criticizing each other or making the other person look bad than into doing constructive work on the task at hand. The costs of severely strained relationships also can extend beyond the individual parties involved. Cliques, or sides, can develop among other co-workers as well, which can impair the larger group's effectiveness. The point here is not to overlook interpersonal problems, but rather to not let the problems get out of hand.

Practicing Theory Y does *not* mean looking at the world through rose-colored glasses, but it *does* mean recognizing someone else's strengths as well as weaknesses. Nevertheless, sometimes peers will be assigned to work on a task together when they don't get along with each other, and the advice "Practice a Theory Y attitude" may seem too idealistic. At such times, it is important to decide whether to focus energy first on improving the relationship (before addressing the task) or to focus it solely on the task (essentially ignoring the problem in the relationship).

Cohen and Bradford (1990) suggested several guidelines for resolving this problem. They said it is best to work on the task if there is little animosity between the parties, if success can be achieved despite existing animosities, if group norms inhibit openness, if success on the task will improve the feelings between the parties, if the other person handles directness poorly, or if you handle directness poorly. Conversely, they said it is best to work on the relationship if there is great animosity between the parties, if negative feelings make task success unlikely, if group norms favor openness, if feelings between the parties are not likely to improve even with success on the task, if the other person handles directness well, *and* if you handle directness well.

Setting Goals

Goals Should Be Specific and Observable

Goals Should Be Attainable but Challenging

Goals Require Commitment

Goals Require Feedback

The Roman philosopher Seneca wrote, "When a man does not know what harbor he is making for, no wind is the right wind." Setting goals and developing plans of action to attain them are important for individuals and for groups. For example, the purpose or goal is often the predominant norm in any group. Once group goals are agreed on, they serve to induce member compliance, act as a criterion for evaluating the leadership potential of group members, and become the criteria for evaluating group performance (Bass, 1990).

Perhaps the most important step in accomplishing a personal or group goal is stating it right in the first place. The reason many people become frustrated with the outcomes of their New Year's resolutions is not any character flaw on their part (e.g., "I don't have any willpower"), but that their resolutions are so vague or unrealistic they are unlikely to ever lead to demonstrable results. It is possible to keep New Year's resolutions, but one must set them intelligently. In a more general sense, some ways of writing goal statements increase the likelihood that someone will successfully achieve the desired goals. Goals should be specific and observable, attainable and challenging, based on top-to-bottom commitment, and designed to provide feedback to personnel about their progress toward them. The following is a more detailed discussion of each of these points.

Goals Should Be Specific and Observable

As described in Chapter 9, research provides strong support for the idea that specific goals lead to higher levels of effort and performance than general goals. General goals do not work as well because they often do not provide enough information regarding which particular behaviors are to be changed or when a clear end-state has been attained. This may be easiest to see with a personal example.

Assume that a student is not satisfied with her academic performance and wants to do something about it. She might set a very general goal, such as "I will do my best next year" or "I will do better in school next year." At first, such a goal may seem fine; after all, as long as she is motivated to do well, what more would be needed? However, on further thought you can see that "do my best" or "do better" are so ambiguous as to be unhelpful in directing her behavior and ultimately assessing her success. General goals have relatively little impact on energizing and directing immediate behavior, and they make it difficult to assess, in the end, whether someone has attained them or not. A better goal statement for this student would be, for example, to attain a B average or to get no deficient grades this semester. Specific goals like these make it easier to chart one's progress. A more business-oriented example might deal with improving productivity at work. Specific goal statements in this case might include a 20 percent increase in the number of products being produced by the work unit over the next three months or a 40 percent decrease in the number of products being returned by quality control next year.

The idea of having specific goals is closely related to that of having observable goals. It should be clear to everyone when the goal has or has not been reached. It is easy to say your goal is to go on a diet, but a much better goal is "to lose 10 pounds by March." Similarly, it is easy to say the team should do better next season, but a better goal is to say the team will win more than half of next season's games. It is important to note that specific, observable goals are also time limited. Without time limits for accomplishing goals, there would be little urgency associated with them. Neither would there be a finite point at which it is clear a person or group has or has not accomplished the goals. For example, it is better to set a goal of improving the next quarter's sales figures than just improving sales.

Goals Should Be Attainable but Challenging

Some people seem to treat goals as a sort of loyalty oath they must pass, as if it would be a break with one's ideals or be a reflection of insufficient motivation if any but the loftiest goals were set for oneself or one's organization. Yet to be useful, goals must be realistic. The struggling high school student who sets a goal of getting into Harvard may be unrealistic; but it may be realistic to set a goal of getting into the local state university. A civil rights activist may wish to eliminate prejudice completely, but a more attainable goal might be to eliminate racial discrimination in the local housing project over the next five years. A track team is not likely to win every race, but it may be realistic to aim to win the league championship.

The corollary to the preceding point is that goals should also be challenging. If goals merely needed to be attainable, then there would be nothing wrong with setting goals so easy that accomplishing them would be virtually guaranteed. As we have seen previously, setting easy goals does not result in high levels of performance; higher levels of performance come about when goals stretch and inspire people toward doing more than they thought they could. Goals need to be challenging but attainable to get the best out of oneself and others.

Goals Require Commitment

There is nothing magical about having goals; having goals per se does not guarantee success. Unless supported by real human commitment, goal statements are mere words. Organizational goals are most likely to be achieved if there is commitment to them at both the top and the bottom of the organization. Top leadership needs to make clear that it is willing to put its money where its mouth is. When top leadership sets goals, it should provide the resources workers need to achieve the goals and then should reward those who do. Subordinates often become committed to goals simply by seeing the sincere and enthusiastic commitment of top leadership to them. Another way to build subordinate acceptance and commitment to goals is to have subordinates participate in setting the goals in the first place. Research on the effects of goal setting demonstrates that worker acceptance and satisfaction tend to increase when workers are allowed to participate in setting goals (Erez, Earley, & Hulin, 1985; Locke, Latham, & Erez, 1987).

On the other hand, research is less conclusive about whether participation in goal setting actually increases performance or productivity. These mixed findings about participation and performance may be due to various qualities of the group and the leader. In terms of the group, groupthink may cause highly cohesive groups to commit to goals that are unrealistic and unachievable. Group members may not have realistically considered equipment or resource constraints, nor have the technical skills needed to successfully accomplish the goal. In addition, group members may not have any special enthusiasm for accomplishing a goal if the leader is perceived to have little expert power or is unsupportive, curt, or inept (House, 1984; Latham & Lee, 1986; Locke, Latham, & Erez, 1987). However, if leaders are perceived to be competent and supportive, then followers may have as much goal commitment as they would if they had participated in setting the goal. Thus, participation in goal setting often leads to higher levels of commitment and performance if the leader is perceived to be incompetent, but it will not necessarily lead to greater commitment and performance than is achieved when a competent leader assigns a goal. Again, these findings lend credence to the importance of technical competence in leadership effectiveness.

Goals Require Feedback

One of the most effective ways to improve any kind of performance is to provide feedback about how closely a person's behavior matches some criterion, and research shows that performance was much higher when goals were accompanied by feedback than when either goals or feedback were used alone. Goals that are specific, observable, and time limited are conducive to ongoing assessment and performance-based feedback, and leaders and followers should strive to provide and/or seek feedback on a fairly regular basis. Moreover, people should seek feedback from a variety of sources or provide feedback using a variety of criteria. Often, different sources and criteria can paint very different pictures about goal progress, and people can get a better idea of the true level of their progress by examining the information provided and integrating it across the different sources and criteria.

Punishment

Myths Surrounding the Use of Punishment

Punishment, Satisfaction, and Performance

Administering Punishment

In an ideal world, perhaps everyone would be dependable, achievement oriented, and committed to the organization's goals. The fact is, however, that leaders sometimes will need to deal with followers who are openly hostile or insubordinate, create conflicts among co-workers, do not work up to standards, or openly violate important rules or policies. In such cases leaders may need to administer punishment to change the follower's behavior.

Of all of the different aspects of leadership, few are as controversial as punishment. Some of the primary reasons for this controversy stem from myths surrounding the use of punishment, as well as the lack of knowledge regarding the effects of punishment on followers' motivation, satisfaction, and performance. This section is designed to shed light on the punishment controversy by (*a*) addressing several myths about the use of punishment, (*b*) reviewing research findings concerning the relationships between punishment and various organizational variables, and (*c*) providing leadership practitioners with advice on how to properly administer punishment.

Myths Surrounding the Use of Punishment

We should begin by repeating the definition of punishment stated earlier in the book. Punishment is the administration of an aversive event or the withdrawal of a positive event or stimulus, which in turn *decreases* the likelihood a particular behavior will be repeated (Arvey & Ivancevich, 1980). Examples of punishment might include verbal reprimands, being moved to a less prestigious office, having pay docked, being fired, being made to run several laps around the athletic field, or losing eligibility for a sport entirely. We should note that according to this definition, only those aversive events administered on a contingent basis are considered to be forms of punishment; aversive events administered on a noncontingent basis may constitute harsh and abusive treatment but are not punishment. Additionally, punishment appears to be in the eye of the beholder; aversive events that effectively change the direction, intensity, or persistence of one follower's behavior may have no effect on another's (Curphy, Gibson, Asiu, McCown, & Brown, 1992). It is even possible that some followers may find the administration of a noxious event or the removal of a positive event to be reinforcing. For example, it is not uncommon for some children to misbehave if that increases the attention they receive from parents, even if the latter's behavior outwardly may seem punishing to others. (To the children, some parental attention of any kind may be preferable to no attention.) Similarly, some followers may see the verbal reprimands and notoriety they receive by being insubordinate or violating company policies as forms of attention. Because these followers enjoy being the center of attention, they may find this notoriety rewarding. From an operant perspective, they may be even more likely to be insubordinate in the future.

We will examine four myths surrounding the use of punishment. Three of these myths were reviewed by Arvey and Ivancevich (1980) and included beliefs that the use of punishment resulted in undesirable emotional side effects on the part of the recipient, was unethical and inhumane, and rarely worked anyway (i.e., seldom eliminated the undesirable behavior).

B. F. Skinner's (1938) work in behavioral psychology lent support to the idea that punishment was ineffective and caused undesirable side effects. He based his conclusions on the unnatural behaviors manifested by rats and pigeons punished in various conditioning experiments. Despite the dangers of generalizing from the behavior of rats to humans, many people accepted Skinner's contention that punishment was a futile and typically counterproductive tool for controlling human behavior. This was so despite the fact that considerable research regarding the emotional effects of punishment on humans did not support Skinner's claim (Kazdin, 1975; Johnston, 1972; Solomon, 1964). Parke (1972), for example, suggested that undesirable emotional side effects of punishment might occur only when punishment was administered indiscriminately or was particularly harsh.

With respect to the myth that punishment is unethical or inhumane, Arvey and Ivancevich (1980) maintained there is an ethical distinction between "future-oriented" and "past-oriented" punishment. Future-oriented punishment, intended to help improve behavior, may be effective in diminishing or eliminating undesirable behavior. Past-oriented punishment, or what we commonly think of as retribution, on the other hand, is simply a payback for past misdeeds. This sort of punishment may be more questionable ethically, especially when it is intended *only* as payback and not, say, as deterrent to others. Moreover, when considering the ethics of administering punishment, one must also consider the ethics of *failing* to administer punishment. The costs of *failing* to punish a potentially harmful behavior, such as unsafe workplace practices, may far outweigh those associated with the punishment itself (Arvey & Ivancevich, 1980).

A third myth concerns the efficacy of punishment. Skinner (1938, 1985), and more recently Campbell (1977) and Luthans (1989), claimed that punishment did not result in a permanent behavior change but instead only temporarily suppressed behavior. Evidence to support this claim was found by Huberman (1964), who reported that incarcerated prisoners had a recidivism rate of 85 percent. However, this high recidivism rate may be due to the fact that criminals may have received punishment primarily for retribution rather than for corrective purposes. Judicious administration of sanctions, combined with advice about how to avoid punishment in the future, may successfully eliminate undesirable behaviors on a more permanent basis (Arvey & Ivancevich, 1980). Furthermore, it may be a moot point to argue (as Skinner did) that punishment only temporarily suppresses behavior; so long as sanctions for misdeeds remain in place, their impact on behavior should continue. In that regard, it's relevant to note that the "temporary" effects of punishment on behavior are no different from the "temporary" effects of reinforcement on behavior.

Punishment, Satisfaction, and Performance

It appears that properly administered punishment does not cause undesirable emotional side effects, is not unethical, and may effectively suppress undesirable behavior. However, we also should ask what effect punishment has on followers' satisfaction and performance. Most people probably would predict that leaders who use punishment more frequently will probably have less-satisfied and lower-performing followers. Interestingly, this does not appear to be the case—at least when punishment is used appropriately. Let us look a little more closely at this issue.

Several researchers have looked at whether leaders who administer punishment on a contingent basis also administered rewards on a contingent basis. Generally, researchers have found that there is a moderate positive relationship between leaders' contingent reward behaviors and contingent punishment behaviors (Arvey, Davis, & Nelson, 1984; Podsakoff & Todor, 1985; Strasser, Dailey, & Bateman, 1981). There also are consistently strong negative correlations found between leaders' contingent reward and noncontingent punishment behaviors. Thus, leaders meting out rewards on a contingent basis were also more likely to administer punishment only when followers behaved inappropriately or were not performing up to standards.

Keller and Szilagyi (1976, 1978) maintained that punishment can serve several constructive organizational purposes. They said it can help clarify roles and expectations, as well as reduce role ambiguity. Several other authors have found contingent punishment either was unrelated to followers' satisfaction with their supervisor ratings or had a low positive relationship with it (Arvey, Davis, & Nelson, 1984; Podsakoff, Todor, Grover, & Huber, 1984). In other words, leaders who follow certain rules in administering punishment need not have dissatisfied subordinates. As a matter of fact, judicious and appropriate use of punishment by leaders may result in somewhat *higher* satisfaction of followers overall. These findings make sense when the entire work unit is considered; failing to use punishment when it seems called for in most followers' eyes may lead to perceptions of inequity, which may in turn lead to lower group cohesiveness and satisfaction (Curphy et al., 1992; Dobbins & Russell, 1986).

With respect to followers' work behaviors, Arvey and Jones (1985) reported that punishment has generally been found to reduce absenteeism and tardiness rates. Nevertheless, the evidence about punishment's impact on performance appears mixed. Some authors report a strong positive relationship between punishment and performance (Beyer & Trice, 1984; Katz, Maccoby, Gurin, & Floor, 1951; Podsakoff & Todor, 1985; Schnake, 1986), whereas others found either no relationship between punishment and performance or a negative one (Curphy et al., 1992; Curtis, Smith, & Smoll, 1979).

Despite such mixed findings, there are several points about the relationship between punishment and performance findings still worth noting. First, the level of punishment as well as the manner in which it was administered across studies could have differed dramatically, and these factors could have affected the results. Second, of the studies reporting positive results, Schnake's (1986) experiment of the vicarious effects of punishment is by far the most provocative. Schnake hired college students for a temporary job, and after several hours at work, publicly reduced the pay or threatened to reduce the pay of a confederate in the work group. As predicted, the more severe the punishment witnessed (either the threat of reduced pay or the reduction of pay), the higher the subsequent performance of other work-group members.

Although these findings demonstrated that merely witnessing rather than receiving punishment could result in increased performance, these results should be interpreted with some caution. Because most of the individuals in the experiment did not know each other and had only been working together for several hours, there was probably not enough time for group cohesiveness or norms to develop. It is not at all clear whether members of cohesive groups or groups with strong norms would react in the same way if they had observed another group member being punished (Curphy et al., 1992).

Third, of the studies reporting less favorable punishment-performance results, the Curtis, Smith, and Smoll (1979) study made an important point about the opportunities to punish. Curtis, Smith, and Smoll examined the relationships between Little League coaches' behaviors and their teams' win–loss records. They found coaches who punished more often had less-successful teams. These coaches also, however, had less-talented players and therefore had many more opportunities to use punishment. Coaches of successful teams had little if any reason to use punishment. Fourth, many behaviors that do get punished may not have a direct link to job performance. For example, being insubordinate, violating company dress codes, and arriving late to meetings are all punishable behaviors that may not be directly linked to solving work-related problems or producing goods or services.

Finally, almost all these studies implicitly assumed punishment enhanced performance (by correcting problem behaviors), but Curphy and his associates (1992) were the only researchers who actually tested this assumption. They collected over 4,500 incidents of documented punishment and performance data from 40 identical organizations over a three-month period. (The punishment and performance data were collected monthly.) They found that low performance led to higher levels of punishment. Moreover, they found that inexperienced leaders administered almost twice as much punishment as experienced leaders. The authors hypothesized that inexperienced leaders used punishment (i.e., relied on their coercive power) more frequently because by being the newest arrivals to the organization, they lacked knowledge of the organizational norms, rules, and policies (i.e., expert power); had not yet established relationships with followers (i.e., referent power); and were severely limited in the rewards they could provide to followers (i.e., reward power).

In summary, the research evidence shows that punishment can lead to positive organizational outcomes if administered properly. When administered on a contingent basis, it may help increase job satisfaction; may decrease role ambiguity and absenteeism rates; and depending on the behaviors being punished, may have a positive effect on performance. However, administering intense levels of punishment in a noncontingent or capricious manner can have a devastating effect on the work unit. Group cohesiveness may suffer, followers are likely to become more dissatisfied and less apt to come to work, and they may perform at a lower level in the long term. Thus, learning how to properly administer punishment may be the key to maximizing the benefits associated with its use.

Administering Punishment

Usually, leaders administer punishment in order to rectify some type of behavioral or performance problem at work. However, not every behavior or performance problem is punished, and leaders probably weigh several different factors before deciding whether or not to administer punishment. Green and Mitchell (1979) maintained that leaders' decisions concerning punishment depended on whether leaders made internal or external attributions about a subordinate's substandard performance. Leaders making internal attributions were more likely to administer punishment; leaders making external attributions were more likely to blame the substandard performance on situational factors beyond the follower's control.

Attribution theory (Mitchell, Green, & Wood, 1981; Mitchell & Wood, 1980) maintains that leaders weigh three factors when making internal or external attributions about a follower's substandard performance. More specifically, leaders would be more likely to make an internal attribution about a follower's substandard performance (and administer punishment) if the follower had previously completed the task before, if other followers had successfully completed the task, and if the follower had successfully completed other tasks in the past. Moreover,

Mitchell, Green, and Wood (1981) and Mitchell and Wood (1980) reported that leaders were biased toward making internal attributions about followers' poor performance (i.e., the fundamental attribution error) and thus more likely to use punishment to modify a follower's behavior.

Because leaders are biased toward making internal attributions about followers' substandard performance, leaders can administer punishment more effectively by being aware of this bias and getting as many facts as possible *before* deciding whether or not to administer punishment. Leaders also can improve the manner or skill with which they administer punishment by using tips provided by Arvey and Ivancevich (1980), who said punishment is administered most effectively when it focuses on the act, not the person. Followers probably cannot change their personalities, values, or preferences, but they can change their behaviors. By focusing on specific behaviors, leaders minimize the threat to followers' self-concepts. Also, punishment needs to be consistent across *both* behaviors and leaders; the same actions need to have the same consequences across work groups, or feelings of inequity and favoritism will pervade the organization. One way to increase the consistency in punishment is through the establishment of clearly specified organizational policies and procedures.

Administering punishment properly depends on effective two-way communication between the leader and follower. Leaders need to provide a clear rationale for punishment and indicate the consequences for unacceptable behavior in the future. Finally, leaders need to provide followers with guidance about how to improve. This guidance may entail role-modeling proper behaviors for followers, suggesting followers take additional training courses, or just giving followers accurate feedback about their behavior at work (Arvey & Ivancevich, 1980).

Overall, it may be the manner in which punishment is administered, rather than the level of punishment, that has the greatest effect on followers' satisfaction and performance. Leaders need to realize that they may be biased toward administering punishment to rectify followers' substandard performance, and the best way to get around this bias is to collect as much information as possible before deciding whether or not to punish. By collecting the facts, leaders will be better able to focus on the act, not the person; be able to administer a punishment consistent with company policy; provide the rationale for the punishment; and give guidance to followers on how to improve.

A final caution which leaders need to be aware of concerns the reinforcing or rewarding nature of punishment. As stated earlier in the discussion of the operant approach to motivation, behaviors that are rewarded are likely to be repeated. When leaders administer punishment and subsequently see improvement in a follower's behavior, the leader will be rewarded and be more apt to use punishment in the future. Over time, this may lead to an overreliance on punishment and an underemphasis of the other motivational strategies as the means for correcting performance problems. Again, by collecting as much information as possible and by carefully considering the applicability of goal setting, the operant approach, job characteristics theory, and so on, to the problem, leaders may be able to successfully avoid having only one tool in their motivational tool kit.

Conducting Meetings

Determine Whether It Is Necessary
List the Objectives
Stick to the Agenda
Provide Pertinent Materials in Advance
Make It Convenient
Encourage Participation
Keep a Record

Meetings are a fact of organizational life. It is difficult to imagine a leader who could (or should) avoid them, particularly when groups, committees, or teams have high levels of task or lateral interdependence. Well-planned and well-led meetings are a valuable mechanism for accomplishing diverse goals and are an important way of exchanging information and keeping open lines of communication within and between work groups or volunteer organizations (Bass, 1990; O'Reilly, 1977). Although meetings have many advantages, they also cost time and money. The annual cost of meetings in the corporate sector alone may well be in the billions of dollars. Furthermore, unnecessary or inefficient meetings can be frustrating and are often a source of dissatisfaction for participants. Given the investment of time and energy meetings require, leaders have a responsibility to make them as productive as possible. Guth and Shaw (1980) provided seven helpful tips for running meetings, which are discussed in the following paragraphs.

Determine Whether It Is Necessary

Perhaps the most important step in conducting a meeting is to take the time to *determine whether or not a meeting is really necessary.* If you are evaluating whether or not to have a meeting, assess what it can accomplish. Have a meeting only if the potential benefits outweigh the costs. As part of this process, get the opinions of the other participants beforehand if that is possible. Moreover, if meetings are regularly scheduled, then you should have significant business to conduct in each meeting. If not, then these meetings should probably be scheduled less frequently.

List the Objectives

Once you have decided that a meeting is necessary, you should then *list your objectives for the meeting and develop a plan for attaining them* in an orderly manner. Prioritize what you hope to accomplish at the meeting. It is often helpful to indicate approximately how much time will be spent on each agenda item. Finally, get the agenda and issues to be covered to the participants well in advance; also let them know who else will be attending.

Stick to the Agenda

Once the meeting gets started, is it important for leaders to *stick to the agenda*. It is easy for groups to get sidetracked by tangential issues or good-natured story-telling. Although you should try to keep a cooperative and comfortable climate in the meeting, it is better to err on the side of being organized and businesslike than being lax and laissez-faire. If items were important enough to put on the agenda, they are important enough to get to in the time allotted for the meeting.

Provide Pertinent Materials in Advance

Besides having an agenda, a meeting is often more effective if leaders also provide the other participants with *pertinent reports or support materials well in advance.* Passing out materials and waiting for people to read them at the meeting itself wastes valuable time. Most people will come prepared, having read relevant material beforehand, if you have given it to them, and almost everyone will resent making a meeting longer than necessary doing work that could and should have been done earlier. In a similar vein, prepare well in advance for any presentations you will make. If you did not provide reports before the meeting, then it is often helpful to provide an outline of your presentation for others to take notes on. Finally, of course, be sure the information you pass out is accurate.

Make It Convenient

Another way to maximize the benefits of meetings is to *pick a time and place as convenient as possible for all participants.* Besides maximizing attendance, this will also keep key participants from being distracted with thoughts of other pressing issues. Similarly, choose a place that is convenient for the participants and suitable for the nature of the meeting. Be sure to consider whether you need such things as a table for the meeting (with seating around it for all participants); a blackboard, an overhead projector, or similar audiovisual aids; coffee or other refreshments; and directions on how to find the meeting place. And start on time; waiting for stragglers is unfair to those who were punctual, and it sends the wrong signal about the seriousness of the meeting. Also plan and announce a time limit on the meeting beforehand and stick to it.

Encourage Participation

Leaders have a responsibility to *encourage participation;* everyone at the meeting should have an opportunity to be heard and should feel some ownership in the meeting's outcome. In some cases, you may need to solicit participation from quieter participants at the meeting, as these members often make valuable contributions to the group when given the chance. Furthermore, ensuring that the quieter members participate will also help you to avoid interpreting someone's quietness as implied consent or agreement. By the same token, you sometimes may need to curtail the participation of more verbal and outspoken participants. You can do this respectfully by merely indicating that the group has a good idea of their position and that it would be useful also to hear from some others. You also help encourage relevant participation by providing interim summaries of the group's discussion.

Keep a Record

During a meeting, the points of discussion and various decisions or actions taken may seem clear to you. However, do not trust your memory to preserve them all. *Take minutes for the record* so you and others can reconstruct what the participants were thinking and why you did or did not take some action. Record decisions and actions to be taken, including *who* will be responsible for doing it and *when* it is supposed to be accomplished. Such records are also very useful for preparing future meeting agendas.

By following the preceding simple steps, both leaders and followers are likely to get much more out of their meetings, as well as appear well organized and effective.

Advanced Leadership Skills

Delegating

Why Delegating Is Important
Common Reasons for Avoiding Delegation
Principles of Effective Delegation

Although delegation is a relatively simple way for leaders to free themselves of time-consuming chores; provide followers with developmental opportunities; and increase the number of tasks accomplished by the work group, team, or committee, delegation is often an overlooked and underused management option (Bass, 1990; Leana, 1986). Delegation implies that one has been empowered by one's leader, boss, or coach to take responsibility for completing certain tasks or engaging in certain activities (Bass, 1990). Delegation gives the responsibility for decisions to those individuals most likely to be affected by or to implement the decision, and delegation is more concerned with autonomy, responsibility, and follower development than with participation (Leana, 1987).

Research has shown that leaders who delegate authority more frequently often have higher-performing businesses (Miller & Toulouse, 1986), but followers are not necessarily happier when their leaders frequently delegate tasks (Stogdill & Shartle, 1955). Bass (1990) maintained that the latter findings were due to subordinates who felt they were (*a*) not delegated the authority needed to accomplish delegated tasks, (*b*) monitored too closely, or (*c*) only delegated tasks leaders did not want to do. Nevertheless, Wilcox (1982) showed that leaders who delegated skillfully had more satisfied followers than leaders who did not delegate well. Because leaders who delegate skillfully often have more satisfied and higher-performing work groups, teams, or committees, the following suggestions from Taylor (1989) are provided to help leadership practitioners delegate more effectively and successfully. Taylor provided useful ideas about why delegating is important, common reasons for avoiding delegation, and principles of effective delegation.

Why Delegating Is Important

Delegation Frees Time for Other Activities

The essence of leadership is achieving goals through others, not trying to accomplish them by oneself. Learning to think like a leader partly involves developing a frame of mind wherein one thinks in terms of the whole group's or organization's capabilities and not just one's own. This requires a new frame of reference for many individuals, especially those whose past successes resulted primarily from personal achievement in interpersonally competitive situations. Still, leaders typically have so many different responsibilities they invariably must delegate some of them to others.

It is not just the mere quantity of work that makes delegation necessary. There is a qualitative aspect, too. Because leaders determine what responsibilities will be delegated, the process is one by which leaders can ensure that their time is allocated most judiciously to meet group needs. The leader's time is a precious commodity that should be invested wisely in those activities for which the leader is uniquely suited or situated to accomplish and that will provide the greatest long-term benefits to the group. What the leader *can* delegate, the leader *should* delegate.

Delegation Develops Followers

Developing subordinates is one of the most important responsibilities any leader has, and delegating significant tasks to them is one of the best ways to support their growth. It does so by providing opportunities for initiative, problem solving, innovation, administration, and decision making. By providing practical experience in a controlled fashion, delegation allows subordinates the best training experience of all: learning by doing.

Delegation Strengthens the Organization

Delegation is an important way to develop individual subordinates, but doing so also strengthens the entire organization. For one thing, an organization that uses delegation skillfully will be a motivating one to work in. Delegation sends an organizational signal that subordinates are trusted and their development is important. Moreover, skillful delegation inherently tends to increase the significance and satisfaction levels of most jobs, thus making subordinates' jobs better. Delegation also can be seen as a way of developing the entire organization, not just the individuals within it. To the extent that a whole organization systematically develops its personnel using delegation, its overall experience level, capability, and vitality increase. Finally, delegation stimulates innovation and generates fresh ideas and new approaches throughout the whole organization.

Common Reasons for Avoiding Delegation

Delegation Takes Too Much Time

Delegation saves time for the leader in the long run, but it costs time for the leader in the short run. It takes time to train a subordinate to perform any new task, so it often really does take less time for a leader to do the task herself than to put in the effort to train someone else to do it. When a task is a recurring or repetitive one, however, the long-term savings will make the additional effort in initial training worth it—both for the leader and for the subordinate.

Delegation Is Risky

It can feel threatening to delegate a significant responsibility to another person because doing so reduces direct personal control over the work one will be judged by (Dewhirst, Metts, & Ladd, 1987). Delegation may be perceived as a career risk by staking one's own reputation on the motivation, skill, and performance of others. It is the essence of leadership, though, that the leader will be evaluated in part by the success of the entire team. Furthermore, delegation need not and should not involve a complete loss of control by the leader over work delegated to others. The leader has a responsibility to set performance expectations, ensure that the task is understood and accepted, provide training, and regularly monitor the status of all delegated tasks and responsibilities (Bass, 1990).

The Job Will Not Be Done as Well

Often the leader can do many specific tasks or jobs better than anyone else. That is not surprising, as the leader is often the most experienced person in the group. This fact, however, can become an obstacle to delegation. The leader may rationalize not delegating a task to someone else because the follower lacks technical competence and the job would subsequently suffer (Dewhirst, Metts, & Ladd, 1987). However, this may be true only in the short term, and letting subordinates make a few mistakes is a necessary part of their development, just as it was for the leader at an earlier stage in her own development. Few things are likely to be so stifling to an organization as a leader's perfectionistic fear of mistakes. When thinking about delegating tasks to others, leaders should remember what their own skill levels used to be, not what they are now. Leaders should assess subordinates' readiness to handle new responsibilities in terms of the former, not the latter.

The Task Is a Desirable One

A leader may resist delegating tasks that are a source of power or prestige. He may be quite willing to delegate relatively unimportant responsibilities but may balk at the prospect of delegating a significant one having high visibility (Bass, 1990; Dewhirst, Metts, & Ladd, 1987). The greater the importance and visibility of the delegated task, though, the greater will be the potential developmental gains for the subordinate. Furthermore, actions always speak louder than words, and nothing conveys trust more genuinely than a leader's willingness to delegate major responsibilities to subordinates.

Others Are Already Too Busy

A leader may feel guilty about increasing a subordinate's already full workload. It is the leader's responsibility, though, to continually review the relative priority of all the tasks performed across the organization. Such a review might identify existing activities that could be eliminated, modified, or reassigned. A discussion with the subordinate about her workload and career goals would be a better basis for a decision than an arbitrary and unilateral determination by the leader that the subordinate could not handle more work. The new responsibility could well be something the subordinate wants and needs, and she might also have some helpful ideas about alternative ways to manage her present duties.

Principles of Effective Delegation

Decide What to Delegate

The first step leaders should take when deciding what to delegate is to identify all of their present activities. This should include those functions regularly performed and decisions regularly made. Next, leaders should estimate the actual time spent on these activities. This can be done fairly easily by developing and maintaining a temporary log. After collecting this information, leaders need to assess whether each activity justifies the time they are spending on it. In all likelihood, at least some of the most time-consuming recurring activities should be delegated to others. This process will probably also identify some activities that could be done more efficiently (either by the leader or someone else) and other activities that provide so little benefit they could be eliminated completely.

Decide Whom to Delegate To

There might be one individual whose talent and experience makes her the logical best choice for any assignment. However, leaders must be careful not to overburden someone merely because that individual always happens to be the best worker. Additionally, leaders have a responsibility to balance developmental opportunities among all their followers. Leaders should look for ways to optimize, over a series of assignments, the growth of all subordinates by matching particular opportunities to their respective individual needs, skills, and goals.

Make the Assignment Clear and Specific

As with setting goals, leaders delegating an assignment must be sure the subordinate understands just what the task involves and what is expected of him. Nevertheless, at times leaders provide too brief an explanation of the task to be delegated. A common communication error is overestimating one's own clarity, and in the case of delegation this can happen when the leader already knows the ins and outs of the particular task. Some of the essential steps or potential pitfalls in an assignment that seem self-evident to the leader may not be as obvious to someone who has never done the assignment before. Leaders should welcome questions and provide a complete explanation of the task. The time leaders invest during this initial training will pay dividends later on. When giving an assignment, leaders should ensure that they cover all of the points listed in Highlight D.1.

Points to Cover When Delegating a Task

Highlight D.1

How does the task relate to organizational goals?

When does the subordinate's responsibility for the task begin?

How has the task been accomplished in the past?

What problems were encountered with the task in the past?

What sources of help are available?

What unusual situations might arise in the future?

What are the limits of the subordinate's authority?

How will the leader monitor the task (e.g., provide feedback)?

Finally, in covering the above points, always convey high confidence and expectations.

Assign an Objective, Not a Procedure

Indicate what is to be accomplished, not *how* the task is to be accomplished. End results are usually more important than the methods. It is helpful to demonstrate procedures that have worked before, but not to specify rigid methods to follow in the future. Leaders should not assume their ways always were and always will be best. Leaders need to be clear about the criteria by which success will be measured, but allowing subordinates to achieve it in their own ways will increase their satisfaction and encourage fresh ideas.

Allow Autonomy, but Monitor Performance

Effective delegation is neither micromanagement of everything the subordinate does nor laissez-faire indifference toward the subordinate's performance. Leaders need to give subordinates a degree of autonomy (as well as time, resources, and authority) in carrying out their new responsibilities, and this includes the freedom to make certain kinds of mistakes. An organizational climate where mistakes are punished suppresses initiative and innovation. Furthermore, mistakes are important sources of development. Knowing this, one wise executive reassured a subordinate who expected to be fired for a gigantic mistake by saying, "Why should I fire you when I've just invested $100,000 in your development?" (McCall, Lombardo, & Morrison, 1988, p. 154).

Once a task has been delegated, even though the subordinate's training and development are continuing, the leader should be cautious about providing too much unsolicited advice or engaging in "rescue" activities. An exception would be when a subordinate's mistake would put significant organizational assets at risk. On the other hand, the leader needs to establish specific procedures for periodically reviewing the subordinate's performance of the delegated task. Leaders need to maintain good records of all the assignments they have delegated, including appropriate milestone and completion dates for each one.

Give Credit, Not Blame

Whenever leaders delegate, they must give subordinates *authority* along with responsibility. In the final analysis, however, leaders always remain fully responsible and accountable for any delegated task. If things should go wrong, then *leaders* should accept responsibility for failure fully and completely and never try to pass blame on to subordinates. On the other hand, if things go well, as they usually will, then leaders should give all the public credit to the subordinates. Also, when providing performance feedback privately to a subordinate, emphasize what went right rather than what went wrong. Leaders should not ignore errors in judgment or implementation, but they need not dwell on them, either. One helpful approach to performance feedback is called the sandwich technique. With this technique, negative feedback is placed in between two "pieces" of positive feedback. It affirms the subordinate's good work, puts the subordinate at least somewhat at ease, and keeps the ratio of positive and negative comments in balance. The idea of a sandwich, however, should not be taken too literally. There is nothing magical about two pieces of positive feedback for one piece of negative feedback. In fact, from the receiver's point of view the balance between positive and negative feedback may seem "about right" when the ratio is considerably higher than 2:1.

In summary, Taylor (1989) has provided useful insight about the importance of delegation as well as specific and helpful suggestions for delegating more effectively.

Managing Conflict

What Is Conflict?

Is Conflict Always Bad?

Conflict Resolution Strategies

We read or hear every day in the news about various types of negotiations. Nations often negotiate with each other over land or fishing rights, trade agreements, or diplomatic relations. Land developers often negotiate with city councils for variances on local zoning laws for their projects. Businesses often spend considerable time negotiating employee salaries and fringe benefits with labor unions. In a similar fashion, negotiations go on every day about matters ranging from high school athletic schedules to where a new office copying machine will be located. In one sense, all these negotiations, big or small, are similar. In every case, representatives from different groups meet to resolve some sort of conflict. Conflict is an inevitable fact of life and an inevitable fact of leadership. Researchers have found that first-line supervisors and middle-level managers can spend more than 25 percent of their time dealing with conflict (Thomas & Schmidt, 1976), and resolving conflicts has been found to be an important factor in leadership effectiveness (Morse & Wagner, 1978). In fact, successfully resolving conflicts is so important that it is a central theme in some of the literature about organizations (Brown, 1983; Ouchi, 1981; Peters & Waterman, 1982). Moreover, successfully resolving conflicts will become an increasingly important skill as leadership and management practice moves away from authoritarian directives and toward cooperative approaches emphasizing rational persuasion, collaboration, compromise, and solutions of mutual gain.

What Is Conflict?

Conflict occurs when two opposing parties have interests or goals that appear to be incompatible (Robbins, 1986). There are a variety of sources of conflict in team, committee, work-group, and organizational settings. For example, conflict can occur when group or team members (a) have strong differences in values, beliefs, or goals; (b) have high levels of task or lateral interdependence; (c) are competing for scarce resources or rewards; (d) are under high levels of stress; or (e) face uncertain or incompatible demands—that is, role ambiguity and role conflict (Yukl, 1989). Conflict can also occur when leaders act in a manner inconsistent with the vision and goals they have articulated for the organization (Kets de Vries & Miller, 1984). Of these factors contributing to the level of conflict within or between groups, teams, or committees, probably the most important source of conflict is the lack of communication between parties (Thomas & Schmidt, 1976). Because many conflicts are the result of misunderstandings and communication breakdowns, leaders can minimize the level of conflict within and between groups by improving their communication and listening skills, as well as spending time networking with others (Yukl, 1989).

Before reviewing specific negotiation tips and conflict resolution strategies, it is necessary to describe several aspects of conflict that can have an impact on the resolution process. First, the size of an issue (bigger issues are more difficult to resolve), the extent to which parties define the problem egocentrically (how much they have personally invested in the problem), and the existence of hidden agendas (unstated but important concerns or objectives) can all affect the conflict resolution process. Second, seeing a conflict situation in win–lose or either/or terms restricts the (perceived) possible outcomes to either total satisfaction or total frustration. A similar but less-extreme variant is to see a situation in zero-sum terms. A zero-sum situation is one in which intermediate degrees of satisfaction are possible (i.e., not either/or), but increases in one party's satisfaction inherently decrease the other party's satisfaction, and vice versa. Still another variant can be when parties perceive a conflict as unresolvable. In such cases neither party gains at the expense of the other, but each continues to perceive the other as an obstacle to satisfaction (Thomas, 1976).

Is Conflict Always Bad?

So far, we have described conflict as an inherently negative aspect of any group, team, committee, or organization. This certainly was the prevailing view of conflict among researchers during the 1930s and 1940s, and it probably also represents the way many people are raised today (i.e., most people have a strong value of minimizing or avoiding conflict). Today, researchers studying group effectiveness have come to a different conclusion. Some level of conflict may be helpful in order to bolster innovation and performance (Robbins, 1986). Conflict that enhances group productivity is viewed as useful, and conflict that hinders group performance is viewed as counterproductive (Robbins, 1986). Various possible positive and negative effects of conflict are listed in Highlight MC.1.

Possible Effects of Conflict

Highlight MC.1

Possible Positive Effects of Conflict	Possible Negative Effects of Conflict
Increased effort	Reduced productivity
Feelings get aired	Decreased communication
Better understanding of others	Negative feelings
Impetus for change	Stress
Better decision making	Poorer decision making
Key issues surfaced	Decreased cooperation
Critical thinking stimulated	Political backstabbing

Along these lines, researchers have found that conflict can cause a radical change in political power (Bass, 1985; Weber, 1947; Willner, 1984), as well as dramatic changes in organizational structure and design, group cohesiveness, and group or organizational effectiveness (Roberts & Bradley, 1988; Kanter, 1983). Nevertheless, it is important to realize that this current conceptualization of conflict is still somewhat limited in scope. For example, increasing the level of conflict within a group or team may enhance immediate performance but may also have a disastrous effect on organizational climate and turnover. As we noted in Chapter 4, however, leaders may be evaluated in terms of many criteria, only one of which is group performance. Thus, leaders should probably use criteria such as turnover and absenteeism rates and followers' satisfaction or organizational climate ratings in addition to measures of group performance when trying to determine whether conflict is good or bad. Leaders are cautioned against using group performance alone, as these indices may not reveal the overall effects of conflict on the group or team.

Conflict Resolution Strategies

In addition to spending time understanding and clarifying positions, separating people from the problem, and focusing on interests, there are five strategies or approaches leaders can use to resolve conflicts. Perhaps the best way to differentiate between these five strategies is to think of conflict resolution in terms of two independent dimensions: cooperativeness/uncooperativeness and assertiveness/unassertiveness (see Figure MC.1). Parties in conflict do vary in their commitment to satisfy the other's concerns, but they also vary in the extent to which they assertively stand up for their own concerns (Thomas, 1976). Thus, conflict resolution can be understood in terms of how cooperative or uncooperative the parties are and how assertive or unassertive they are.

Using this two-dimension scheme, Thomas (1976) described five general approaches to managing conflict:

1. **Competition** reflects a desire to achieve one's own ends at the expense of someone else. This is domination, also known as a win–lose orientation.
2. **Accommodation** reflects a mirror image of competition, entirely giving in to someone else's concerns without making any effort to achieve one's own ends. This is a tactic of appeasement.
3. **Sharing** is an approach that represents a compromise between domination and appeasement. Both parties give up something, yet both parties get something. Both parties are moderately, but incompletely, satisfied.
4. **Collaboration** reflects an effort to fully satisfy both parties. This is a problem-solving approach that requires the integration of each party's concerns.
5. **Avoidance** involves indifference to the concerns of both parties. It reflects a withdrawal from or neglect of any party's interests.

Does one of these approaches seem clearly a better method than the other to you? Each of them does, at least, reflect certain culturally valued modes of behavior (Thomas, 1977). For example, the esteem many people hold for athletic, business, and military heroes reflects our cultural valuation of competition. Valuation of a pragmatic approach to settling problems is reflected in the compromising ap-

FIGURE MC.1

Five conflict-handling orientations, plotted according to party's desire to satisfy own and other's concerns.

Source: K. W. Thomas, "Conflict and Conflict Management," in *Handbook of Industrial and Organizational Psychology*, ed. M. D. Dunnette (Chicago: Rand McNally, 1976). Used by permission of Marvin D. Dunnette.

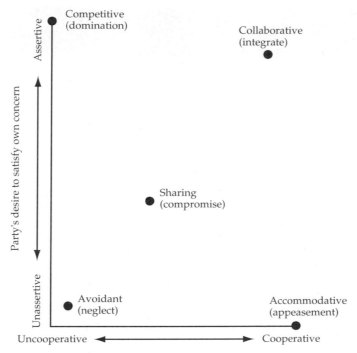

proach. Cultural values of unselfishness, kindness, and generosity are reflected in accommodation, and even avoidance has roots in philosophies that emphasize caution, diplomacy, and turning away from worldly concerns. These cultural roots to each of the approaches to managing conflict suggest that no single one is likely to be the right one all the time. There probably are circumstances when each of the modes of conflict resolution can be appropriate. Rather than seeking to find some single best approach to managing conflict, it may be wisest to appreciate the relative advantages and disadvantages of all approaches, and the circumstances when each may be most appropriate. A summary of experienced leaders' recommendations for when to use each strategy is presented in Highlight MC.2 (Thomas, 1977).

Negotiation

Prepare for the Negotiation
Separate the People from the Problem
Focus on Interests, Not Positions

Negotiation is an approach that may help resolve some conflicts. The following negotiating tips, from Fisher and Ury (1981), include taking the time to prepare for a negotiating session; keeping the people and problems separate; focusing on issues, not positions; and seeking win–win outcomes.

Situations in Which to Use the Five Approaches to Conflict Management

Highlight MC.2

COMPETING

1. When quick, decisive action is vital—e.g., emergencies.
2. On important issues where unpopular actions need implementing—e.g., cost cutting, enforcing unpopular rules, discipline.
3. On issues vital to company welfare when you know you're right.
4. Against people who take advantage of noncompetitive behavior.

COLLABORATING

1. To find an integrative solution when both sets of concerns are too important to be compromised.
2. When your objective is to learn.
3. To merge insights from people with different perspectives.
4. To gain commitment by incorporating concerns into a consensus.
5. To work through feelings which have interfered with a relationship.

COMPROMISING

1. When goals are important, but not worth the effort or potential disruption of more assertive modes.
2. When opponents with equal power are committed to mutually exclusive goals.
3. To achieve temporary settlements of complex issues.
4. To arrive at expedient solutions under time pressure.
5. As a backup when collaboration or competition is unsuccessful.

AVOIDING

1. When an issue is trivial or more important issues are pressing.
2. When you perceive no chance of satisfying your concerns.
3. When potential disruption outweighs the benefits of resolution.
4. To let people cool down and regain perspective.
5. When gathering information supersedes immediate decision.
6. When others can resolve the conflict more effectively.
7. When issues seem tangential to or symptomatic of other issues.

ACCOMMODATING

1. When you find you are wrong—to allow a better position to be heard, to learn, and to show your reasonableness.
2. When issues are more important to others than yourself—to satisfy others and maintain cooperation.
3. To build social credits for later issues.
4. To minimize loss when you are outmatched and losing.
5. When harmony and stability are especially important.
6. To allow subordinates to develop by learning from mistakes.

Source: K. W. Thomas, "Toward Multidimensional Values in Teaching: The Example of Conflict Management," *Academy of Management Review* 2, no. 3 (1977), pp. 484–90. Used with permission.

Prepare for the Negotiation

To successfully resolve conflicts, leaders may need to *spend considerable time preparing for a negotiating session.* Leaders should anticipate each side's key concerns and issues, attitudes, possible negotiating strategies, and goals.

Separate the People from the Problem

Fisher and Ury (1981) also advised negotiators to *separate the people from the problem.* Because all negotiations involve substantive issues and relationships between negotiators, it is easy for these parts to become entangled. When that happens, parties may inadvertently treat the people *and* the problem as though they were the same. For example, a group of teachers angry that their salary has not been raised for the fourth year in a row may direct their personal bitterness toward the school board president. However, reactions such as these are usually a mistake, as the decision may be out of the other party's hands, and personally attacking the other party often only serves to make the conflict even more difficult to resolve.

There are several things leaders can do to separate the people from the problem. First, leaders should not let their fears color their perceptions of each side's intentions. It is easy to attribute negative qualities to others when one feels threatened. Similarly, it does no good to blame the other side for one's own problems (Blake, Shepard, & Mouton, 1964). Even if it is justified, it is still usually counterproductive. Another thing leaders can do to separate the people from the problem is to communicate clearly. Earlier in this text, we suggested techniques for active listening. Those guidelines are especially helpful in negotiating and resolving conflicts.

Focus on Interests, Not Positions

Another of Fisher and Ury's (1981) main points is to *focus on interests, not positions.* Focusing on interests depends on understanding the difference between interests and positions. Here is one example. Say Raoul has had the same reserved seats to the local symphony every season for several years and he was just notified he will no longer get his usual tickets. Feeling irate, he goes to the ticket office to complain. One approach he could take would be to demand the same seats he has always had; this would be his *position.* A different approach would be to find alternative seats that are just as satisfactory as his old seats had been; this would be his *interest.* In negotiating, it is much more constructive to satisfy interests than to fight over positions. Furthermore, it is important to focus both on your counterpart's interests (not position) and on your own interests (not position).

Finally, winning a negotiation at your counterpart's expense is likely to be only a short-term gain. Leaders should attempt to work out a resolution by looking at long-term rather than short-term goals, and they should try to build a working relationship that will endure and be mutually trusting and beneficial beyond the present negotiation. Along these lines, leaders should always seek win–win outcomes, which try to satisfy both sides' needs and continuing interests. It often takes creative problem solving to find new options that provide gains for both sides. Realistically, however, not all situations may be conducive to seeking win–win outcomes (see Highlight N.1).

Problem Solving

Identifying Problems or Opportunities for Improvement

Analyzing the Causes

Developing Alternative Solutions

Selecting and Implementing the Best Solution

Assessing the Impact of the Solution

How to Swim with Sharks

Highlight N.1

It is dangerous to swim with sharks, but not all sharks are found in the water. Some people may behave like sharks, and a best-selling book for executives written a few years ago took its title from that theme. However, an article appeared in the journal *Perspectives in Biology and Medicine* nearly three decades ago claiming to be a translated version of an essay written in France more than a century earlier for sponge divers (Cousteau, 1973). The essay notes that while no one wants to swim with sharks, it is an occupational hazard for certain people. For those who must swim with sharks, it can be essential to follow certain rules. See if you think the following rules for interacting with the sharks of the sea serve as useful analogies for interacting with the sharks of everyday life.

Rule 1: Assume any unidentified fish is a shark. Just because a fish may be acting in a docile manner does not mean it is not a shark. The real test is how it will act when blood is in the water.

Rule 2: Don't bleed. Bleeding will prompt even more aggressive behavior and the involvement of even more sharks. Of course, it is not easy to keep from bleeding when injured. Those who cannot do so are advised not to swim with sharks at all.

Rule 3: Confront aggression quickly. Sharks usually give warning before attacking a swimmer. Swim-

mers should watch for indications an attack is imminent and take prompt counteraction. A blow to the nose is often appropriate since it shows you understand the shark's intentions and will respond in kind. It is particularly dangerous to behave in an ingratiating manner toward sharks. People who once held this erroneous view often can be identified by a missing limb.

Rule 4: Get out of the water if anyone starts bleeding. Previously docile sharks may begin attacking if blood is in the water. Their behavior can become so irrational, even including attacking themselves, that it is safest to remove yourself entirely from the situation.

Rule 5: Create dissension among the attackers. Sharks are self-centered and rarely act in an organized fashion with other sharks. This significantly reduces the risk of swimming with sharks. Every now and then, however, sharks may launch a coordinated attack. The best strategy then is to create internal dissension among them since they already are quite prone to it; often sharks will fight among themselves over trivial or minor things. By the time their internal conflict is settled, sharks often have forgotten about their organized attack.

Rule 6: Never divert a shark attack toward another swimmer. Please observe this final item of swimming etiquette.

Identifying Problems or Opportunities for Improvement

The first step in problem solving is to state the problem so that everyone involved in developing a solution has an informed and common appreciation and understanding of the task. This is a critical stage in problem solving and will take time and probably group discussion. It is dangerous to assume that everyone (or anyone!) knows at the outset what the problem is. A hurried or premature definition of the problem (e.g., as a result of groupthink) may lead to considerable frustration and wasted effort. In counseling and advising, for example, a significant portion of the work with a client is devoted to clarifying the problem. A student may seek help at the school counseling center to improve his study skills because he is spending what seems to be plenty of time studying yet is still doing poorly on examinations. A little discussion, however, may reveal that he is having difficulty concentrating on schoolwork because of problems at home. If the counselor had moved immediately to develop the client's study skills, the real cause of his difficulties would have gone untreated, and the client might have become even more pessimistic about his abilities and the possibility that others can help him. Or consider the case of a police chief who is concerned about the few volunteers willing to serve on a citizen's advisory committee to her department. There are many problems she might identify here, such as citizen apathy or poor publicity concerning the need and importance of the committee. The real problem, however, might be her own reputation for rarely listening to or heeding recommendations made by similar advisory committees in the past. If the chief were to take the time to explore and clarify the problem at the outset, then she *could* discover this important fact and take steps to solve the *real* problem (her own behavior). If, on the other hand, she pressed ahead aggressively, trusting her own appraisal of the problem, then nothing likely would change.

The reason it helps to take time to define a problem carefully is that sometimes people mistake symptoms for causes. In the case of the student, his poor studying was a symptom of another cause (family difficulties), not the cause of his poor grades. In the case of the police chief, lack of citizen participation on the advisory committee was a symptom of a problem, not the problem itself. If a plan addresses a symptom rather than the causes of a problem, the desired results will not be attained. It also is important during this stage to avoid scapegoating or blaming individuals or groups for the problem, which may just engender defensiveness and reduce creative thinking. This is a stage where conflict resolution techniques and negotiating skills can be very important. Finally, the statement of a problem should not imply that any particular solution is the correct one.

As an application of these considerations, let us consider two pairs of problem statements that a teacher might present to his class as a first step in addressing what he considers to be an unsatisfactory situation. These samples of dialogue touch on many aspects of communication, listening, and feedback skills addressed earlier in this book. Here, however, our focus is on differences in defining problems. In each case, the second statement is the one more likely to lead to constructive problem solving.

A: I don't think you care enough about this course. No one is ever prepared. What do I have to do to get you to put in more time on your homework?

B: What things are interfering with your doing well in this course?

A: Your test grades are too low. I'm going to cancel the field trip unless they improve. Do you have any questions?

B: I'm concerned about your test scores. They're lower than I expected them to be, and I'm not sure what's going on. What do you think the problem is?

Another aspect of this first stage of problem solving involves identifying those factors that, when corrected, are likely to have the greatest impact on improving an unsatisfactory situation. Since there are almost always more problems or opportunities for improvement than time or energy to devote to them all, it is crucial to identify those whose solutions offer the greatest potential payoff. A useful concept here is known as the Pareto principle. It states that about 80 percent of the

FIGURE PS.1
A cause-and-
effect diagram.

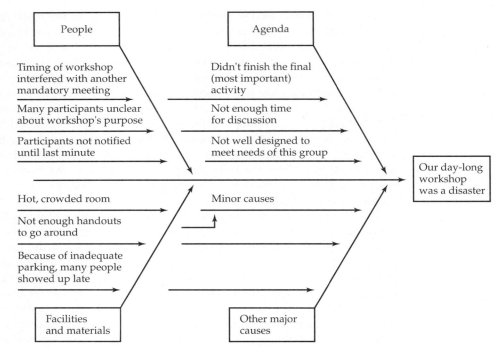

problems in any system are the result of about 20 percent of the causes. In school, for example, most of the discipline problems are caused by a minority of the students. Of all the errors people make on income tax returns, just a few kinds of errors (e.g., forgetting to sign them) account for a disproportionately high percentage of returned forms. We would expect about 20 percent of the total mechanical problems in a city bus fleet to account for about 80 percent of the fleet's downtime. The Pareto principle can be used to focus problem-solving efforts on those causes that have the greatest overall impact.

Analyzing the Causes

Once a problem is identified, the next step is to analyze its causes. Analysis of a problem's causes should precede a search for its solutions. Two helpful tools for identifying the key elements affecting a problem situation are the cause-and-effect diagram (also called the "fishbone" diagram because of its shape, or the Ishikawa diagram after the person who developed it) and force field analysis. The cause-and-effect diagram uses a graphic approach to depict systematically the root causes of a problem, the relationships between different causes, and potentially a prioritization of which causes are most important (see Figure PS.1).

Force field analysis (see Figure PS.2) also uses a graphic approach, this time to depict the opposing forces that tend to perpetuate a present state of affairs. It is a way of depicting any stable situation in terms of dynamic balance, or equilibrium,

FIGURE PS.2
Force field
analysis
example:
Starting
personal
exercise
program.

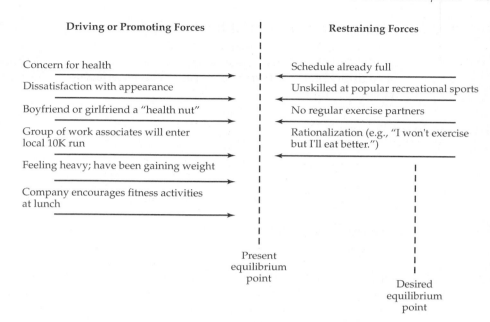

Driving or Promoting Forces	Restraining Forces
Concern for health	Schedule already full
Dissatisfaction with appearance	Unskilled at popular recreational sports
Boyfriend or girlfriend a "health nut"	No regular exercise partners
Group of work associates will enter local 10K run	Rationalization (e.g., "I won't exercise but I'll eat better.")
Feeling heavy; have been gaining weight	
Company encourages fitness activities at lunch	

Present
equilibrium
point

Desired
equilibrium
point

between those forces that tend to press toward movement in one direction and those other forces that tend to restrain movement in that direction. So long as the net sum of all those forces is zero, no movement occurs. When a change is desirable, force field analysis can be used to identify the best way to upset the balance between positive and negative forces so that a different equilibrium can be reached.

Developing Alternative Solutions

Several ideas we've examined previously are relevant here (e.g., brainstorming), as is the importance of solutions meeting criteria for quality and acceptance. A procedure called Nominal Group Technique (NGT) is another way to generate a lot of ideas pertinent to a problem (Delbecq, Van de Ven, & Gustafson, 1975). This procedure is similar to brainstorming in that it is an idea-generating activity conducted in a group setting. With NGT, however, group members write down ideas on individual slips of paper, which are later transferred to a blackboard or flipchart for the entire group to work with.

Selecting and Implementing the Best Solution

The first solution one thinks of is not necessarily the best solution, even if everyone involved finds it acceptable. It is better to select a solution on the basis of established criteria. These include such questions as the following: Have the advantages and disadvantages of all possible solutions been considered? Have all the possible solutions been evaluated in terms of their respective impacts on the whole organization, not just a particular team or department? Is the information needed to make a good decision among the alternatives available?

Assessing the Impact of the Solution

One should not assume that just by going through the preceding steps the actions implemented will solve the problem. The solution's continuing impact must be assessed, preferably in terms of measurable criteria of success that all parties involved can agree on.

Improving Creativity

> Seeing Things in New Ways
> Using Power Constructively
> Forming Diverse Problem-Solving Groups

Seeing Things in New Ways

There are several things leaders can do to increase their own and their followers' creativity. Some of these facilitating factors have already been discussed and include assuring adequate levels of technical expertise, delaying and minimizing the evaluation or judgment of solutions, focusing on the intrinsic motivation of the task, removing unnecessary constraints on followers, and giving followers more latitude in making decisions. One popular technique for stimulating creative thinking in groups is called brainstorming (see Highlight IC.1).

An additional thing leaders can do to enhance creativity is to *see things in new ways,* or to look at problems from as many perspectives as possible. This is, though, easier said than done. It can be difficult to see novel uses for things we are very familiar with, or to see such in novel ways. Psychologists call this kind of mental block functional fixedness (Duncker, 1945). Creative thinking depends on overcoming the functional fixedness associated with the rigid and stereotyped perceptions we have of the things around us.

One way to see things differently is to think in terms of analogies. Thinking in terms of analogies is a practical extension of Cronbach's (1984) definition of creativity—making fresh observations, or seeing one thing as something else. In this case, the active search for analogies is the essence of the problem-solving method. In fact, finding analogies is the foundation of a commercial creative-problem-solving approach called Synectics (W. J. J. Gordon, 1961). An actual example of use of analogies in a Synectics problem-solving group concerned designing a new roofing material that would adjust its color to the season, turning white in the summer to reflect heat and black in the winter to absorb heat. The group's first task was to find an analogy in nature, and it thought of fishes whose colors change to match their surroundings. The mechanism for such changes in fish is the movement of tiny compartments of pigments closer to or farther away from the skin's surface, thus changing its color. After some discussion, the group designed a black roof impregnated with little white plastic balls which would expand when it is hot, making the roof lighter, and contract when it is cold, making the roof darker (W. J. J. Gordon, 1961).

Another way to see things differently is to try putting an idea or problem into a picture rather than into words. Feelings or relationships that have eluded verbal description may come out in a drawing, bringing fresh insights to an issue.

Steps for Enhancing Creativity through Brainstorming

Highlight IC.1

Brainstorming is a technique designed to enhance the creative potential of any group trying to solve a problem. Leaders should use the following rules when conducting a brainstorming session:

1. Groups should consist of five to seven people: Fewer than five limits the number of ideas generated, but more than seven often can make the session unwieldy. It may be more important to carefully decide who should attend a session than how many people should attend.

2. Everybody should be given the chance to contribute. The first phase of brainstorming is idea generation, and members should be encouraged to spontaneously contribute ideas as soon as they get them. The objective in the first phase is quantity, not quality.

3. No criticism is allowed during the idea generation phase. This helps to clearly separate the activities of imaginative thinking and idea production from idea evaluation.

4. Freewheeling and outlandish ideas should be encouraged. With some modification, these ideas may be eventually adopted.

5. "Piggybacking" off others' ideas should be encouraged. Combining ideas or extending others' ideas often results in better solutions.

6. The greater the quantity and variety of ideas, the better. The more ideas generated, the greater the probability a good solution will be found.

7. Ideas should be recorded. Ideally, ideas should be recorded on a blackboard or butcher paper so that members can review all of the ideas generated.

8. After all of the ideas have been generated, each idea should be evaluated in terms of pros and cons, costs and benefits, feasibility, and so on. Choosing the final solution often depends on the results of these analyses.

Source: A. F. Osborn, *Applied Imagination* (New York: Scribner's, 1963).

Using Power Constructively

In addition to getting followers to see problems from as many perspectives as possible, a leader can also *use her power constructively to enhance creativity.* As noted earlier, groups may suppress creative thinking by being overly critical or by passing judgment during the solution generation stage. This effect may be even more pronounced when strong authority relationships and status differences are present. Group members may be reluctant to take the risk of raising a "crazy" idea when superiors are present, especially if the leader is generally perceived as unreceptive to new ideas, or they may be reluctant to offer the idea if they believe others in the group will take potshots at it in front of the leader. Leaders who wish to create a favorable climate for fostering creativity need to use their power to encourage the open expression of ideas and to suppress uncooperative or aggressive reactions (overt or covert) between group members. Further, leaders can use their power to encourage creativity by rewarding successes and by not punishing mistakes. Leaders can also use their power to delegate authority and responsibility, relax followers' constraints, and empower followers to take risks. By taking these steps, leaders can help followers to build idiosyncratic credits, which in turn will encourage them to take risks and to be more creative. Along these same lines, the entire climate of an organization can be either more or less conducive to creative thinking, differences that may be due to the use of power within the organization. In an insightful turn of the familiar adage, "Power corrupts," Kanter (1982) noted how powerlessness also corrupts. She pointed out how managers who feel powerless in an organization may spend more energy guarding their territory than collaborating with others in productive action. The need to actively support followers' creativity may be especially important for leaders in bureaucratic organizations, as such organizations tend to be so inflexible, formalized, and centralized as to make many people in them feel relatively powerless.

Forming Diverse Problem-Solving Groups

Leaders can enhance creativity by *forming diverse problem-solving groups.* Group members with similar experiences, values, and preferences will be less likely to create a wide variety of solutions and more apt to agree on a solution prematurely than more diverse groups. Thus, selecting people for a group or committee with a variety of experiences, values, and preferences should increase the creativity of the group, although these differences may also increase the level of conflict within the group and make it more difficult for the leader to get consensus on a final solution. One technique for increasing group diversity and, in turn, creativity in problem-solving groups involves the use of the four preference dimensions of the Myers-Briggs Type Indicator (MBTI). Actual evidence to support this specific approach appears scanty (Thayer, 1988), but perhaps preferences only assume significance after certain other conditions for group creativity already have been met. For example, diversity cannot make up for an absence of technical expertise. Although the MBTI dimensions may be useful in selecting diverse groups, this instrument should only be used after ensuring that all potential members have high levels of technical expertise. Choosing members based solely on MBTI preferences ignores the crucial role that technical expertise and intrinsic motivation play in creativity. Another aspect of the relationship between creativity and leadership is described in Highlight IC.2.

Diagnosing Performance Problems in Individuals, Groups, and Organizations

Expectations
Capabilities
Opportunities
Motivation

In many ways leaders will only be as effective as the followers and teams they lead. Along these lines, one of the more difficult issues leaders must deal with is managing individuals or teams that are not performing up to expectations. What makes this issue even more difficult is that although the lack of performance may be obvious, the reasons for it may not. Leaders who correctly determine why a follower or team is exhibiting suboptimal performance are much more likely to implement an appropriate intervention to fix the problem. Unfortunately, many leaders do not have a model or framework for diagnosing performance problems at work, and as

Managing Creativity

Highlight IC.2

T. Hogan and Morrison (1993) maintained that people who are seen as more creative tend to have several distinguishing personality characteristics. In general, creative people are open to information and experience, have high energy, can be personally assertive and even domineering, react emotionally to events, are impulsive, are more interested in music and art than in hunting and sports, and finally are very motivated to prove themselves (i.e., are concerned with personal adequacy). Thus, creative people tend to be independent, willful, impractical, unconcerned with money, idealistic, and nonconforming. Given that these tendencies may not make them ideal followers, the interesting question raised by Hogan and Morrison is: How does one lead or manage creative individuals? This question becomes even more interesting when considering the qualities of successful leaders or managers. As discussed earlier, successful leaders tend to be intelligent, dominant, conscientious, stable, calm, goal-oriented, outgoing, and somewhat conventional. Thus, one might think that the personalities of creative followers and successful leaders might be the source of considerable conflict and make them natural enemies in organizational settings. Because many organizations depend on creativity to grow and prosper, being able to successfully lead creative individuals may be a crucial aspect of success for these organizations. Given that creative people already possess technical expertise, imaginative thinking skills, and intrinsic motivation, Hogan and Morrison suggested that leaders take the following steps to successfully lead creative followers:

1. Set goals. Because creative people value freedom and independence, this step will be best accomplished if leaders use a high level of participation in the goal-setting process. Leaders should ask followers what they can accomplish in a particular time frame.

2. Provide adequate resources. Followers will be much more creative if they have the proper equipment to work with, as they can devote their time to resolving the problem rather than spending time finding the equipment to get the job done.

3. Reduce time pressures, but keep followers on track. Try to set realistic milestones when setting goals, and make organizational rewards contingent on reaching these milestones. Moreover, leaders need to be well organized to acquire necessary resources and to keep the project on track.

4. Consider nonmonetary as well as monetary rewards. Creative people often gain satisfaction from resolving the problem at hand, not from monetary rewards. Thus, feedback should be aimed at enhancing their feelings of personal adequacy. Monetary rewards perceived to be controlling may decrease rather than increase motivation toward the task.

5. Recognize that creativity is evolutionary, not revolutionary. Although followers can create truly novel products (such as the Xerox machine), often the key to creativity is continuous product improvement. Making next year's product faster, lighter, cheaper, or more efficient requires minor modifications that can, over time, culminate in major revolutions. Thus, it may be helpful if leaders think of creativity more in terms of small innovations than major breakthroughs.

Source: R. T. Hogan and J. Morrison, "Managing Creativity," in *Create & Be Free: Essays in Honor of Frank Barron,* ed. A. Montouri (Amsterdam: J. C. Gieben, 1993).

a result many do a poor job of dealing with problem performers. The model in Figure DPP.1 provides leaders with a pragmatic framework for understanding why a follower or team may not be performing up to expectations and what the leader can do to improve the situation. This model maintains that performance is a function of expectations, capabilities, opportunities, and motivation and integrates concepts discussed in more detail earlier in this book.

FIGURE DPP.1
A model of performance.

Performance = f (Expectations × Capabilities × Opportunities × Motivation)

The model is also a modification of earlier models developed by J. P. Campbell (1977), Campbell, McCloy, Oppler, and Sager (1993), and Ramstad and Boudreau (2000). As a multiplicative rather than a compensatory model, a deficit in any one component should result in a substantial decrement in performance that cannot be easily made up by increasing the other components. An example might help to illuminate this point. Recently one of the authors was asked to help the manager of a nuclear power plant fix several safety and operational issues affecting the plant. Apparently many plant personnel did not feel they had to comply with governmental regulations regarding the proper use of safety equipment. An investigation into the problem revealed that the expectations for compliance were clear, everyone had been trained on the proper use of safety equipment, and the equipment was readily available. However, many personnel felt the equipment and procedures were a nuisance and unnecessary. The plant manager's initial attempt to rectify this problem was to run all plant personnel through a three-day nuclear safety training program. Much to the manager's surprise, the training program actually appeared to have a negative impact on safety compliance! This was due to the fact that the underlying issue was not expectations, capabilities, or opportunities but rather motivation. Even if the staff had 30 days of training it still would not have positively affected motivation, which was the underlying barrier to performance. Because there were few if any positive or negative consequences for the staff for properly using the equipment, the problem did not improve until the manager implemented a system of rewards and punishments for safety compliance. A more thorough explanation of the components of the model and what leaders can do to improve performance can be found below.

Expectations

Performance problems often occur because individuals or groups do not understand what they are supposed to do. There are many instances where talented, skilled groups accomplished the wrong objective because of miscommunication or sat idly by while waiting for instructions that never arrived. It is the leader's responsibility for ensuring that followers understand their roles, goals, performance standards, and the key metrics for determining success. More information about goal setting and clarifying team goals and roles can be found in the "Setting Goals" and "The Building Blocks of Team Building" sections in Part V of this text.

Capabilities

Just because followers understand what they are supposed to do does not necessarily mean they can do it. Sometimes followers and teams lack the capabilities needed to achieve a goal or perform above expectations. Abilities and skills are the two components that make up capabilities. Ability is really another name for raw talent, and includes such individual difference variables as athleticism, intelligence, creativity, and personality traits. As such, abilities are characteristics that are relatively difficult to change with training. Because abilities are relatively insensitive to training interventions, sending people who lack the required abilities to more training or motivating them to work harder will have relatively little impact on performance. Instead, the best remedy for this situation is to select those individuals with the abilities needed for performance.

Although followers may have the raw talent needed to perform a task, they still may lack the skills needed to perform at a high level. Such is the case with many athletic teams or musical groups at the beginning of the season or when a work group gets a new set of equipment or responsibility for tasks they have no previous experience with. As discussed in the "Leadership Behavior" chapter (8), skills consist of a well-defined body of knowledge and a set of related behaviors. Unlike abilities, skills are very amenable to training, and leaders with high levels of relevant expertise may coach others in the development of skills, see that they are obtained in other ways on the job, or send their followers to training programs in order to improve followers' skill levels. More information about selecting people with the right abilities can be found in Chapter 4. See Chapters 3 and 9 and the sections on "Building Technical Competence," "Coaching," and "Development Planning" in Part V for more information on building skills.

Opportunities

Performance can also be limited when followers lack the resources needed to get the job done. At other times followers may lack the opportunity to demonstrate acquired skills. Such is the case when passengers are hungry but flight attendants do not have any meals to pass out during the flight. In this situation the flight attendants could have very high levels of customer service goals, capabilities, and motivation but will still not be able to satisfy customer needs. Leaders must ensure that followers and teams have the needed equipment, financial resources, and the opportunities to exhibit their skills if they want to eliminate this constraint on performance. More about opportunities can be found in "The Building Blocks of Team Building" section in Part V of this text.

Motivation

Many performance problems can be attributed to a lack of motivation. The two critical issues here are whether followers or groups choose to perform or exhibit the level of effort necessary to accomplish a task. If this does not occur, then the leader should first try to learn why people are unmotivated. Sometimes the task may involve risks the leader is not aware of. At other times individuals or groups may simply run out of steam to perform the task or there are few consequences for superior or unsatisfactory performance. Leaders have several options to resolve motivation problems in followers and teams. First, they can select followers who have higher levels of achievement or intrinsic motivation for the task. Second, they can set clear goals or do a better job providing feedback about performance. Third, they can reallocate work across the team or redesign the task to improve skill variety, task significance, and task identity. Fourth, they can restructure rewards and punishments so they are more closely linked to performance levels. See the "Motivation, Satisfaction, and Performance" chapter (9) for more information about motivating followers.

Concluding Comments on the Diagnostic Model

In summary, this model provides an integrative framework for many of the topics affecting performance previously reviewed in this text. It reviews some of the factors that affect performance and suggests ideas for rectifying performance problems. It should be emphasized, however, that this model only addresses follower, group, and organizational performance. Leaders need to be mindful that there are other desirable outcomes, too, such as organizational climate and job satisfaction, and that actions to increase performance (especially just in the short term) may adversely impact these other desirable outcomes.

Team Building for Work Teams

Team-Building Interventions
What Does a Team-Building Workshop Involve?
Examples of Interventions

Few activities have become more commonplace in organizations these days than "team-building workshops." One reason for this level of activity is the powerful shift that has occurred in the workplace from a focus primarily on individual work to team-centered work. Unfortunately, however, they do not always achieve their objectives. As noted earlier in this text, it doesn't make sense to hold teams responsible for work if nothing else in the organizational environment changes. Team-building interventions, at the team level, may help team members understand why they are having so much difficulty in achieving team objectives, and even suggest coping strategies for an intolerable situation. They are not, however, very likely to remove root causes of the problem. In order to better understand the importance of looking at teams this way, let's use an example of this kind of erroneous thinking from a quite different context.

Team-Building Interventions

Suppose you have decided that the next car you drive must have outstanding ride and handling characteristics. Some cars you test, such as some huge American-made automobiles, have outstanding ride characteristics, but you are not happy with their handling. They sway and "float" in tight slalom courses. Other cars you test have just the opposite characteristics. They are as tight and as stable as you could hope for in turns and stops, but their ride is so hard that your dental work is in serious jeopardy. But you do find one car that seems to meet your requirements. In fact, a Mercedes-Benz does provide both an extremely comfortable ride and tremendous road handling characteristics in high-performance situations. There is, however, one small problem. The Mercedes costs a lot of money up front—more than you are willing to put into this project. So you arrive at an alternative solution. You find a used Yugo, a little car built in Yugoslavia and no longer imported into the United States, largely because of inferior quality. But it is really cheap, and after purchasing it, you know you will have lots of money left over to beef up the suspension, steering, and braking systems to provide you with the Mercedes-Benz ride you really want.

FIGURE TW.1

A rationale for individual, interpersonal, team, and organizational training.

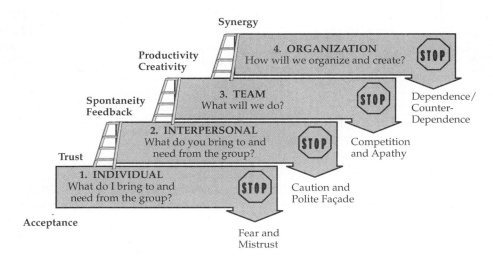

Ludicrous! Obviously, you are never going to get a Mercedes-Benz ride unless you are willing to put in considerable money and effort *up front* rather than doing little up front and putting all your money into repair work. But that is precisely what many organizations are attempting to do with teams. They do not seem willing to create the conditions necessary for teamwork to occur naturally (a point we will discuss in the section "Team Building at the Top"), but when the teams struggle in a hostile environment, as they invariably will, the leaders seem more than willing to pour tremendous amounts of money into team-building interventions to fix the problem. (And there are lots of team-building consultants out there willing to take their money.) These types of team-building problems are those we would categorize as "top-down."

An equally vexing problem occurs when organizations are committed to teamwork, are willing to change structures and systems to support it, but are not committed to the "bottom-up" work that will be required. This is best illustrated in the rationale for team training shown in Figure TW.1. In our work with organizations, we are frequently asked to help teams that are struggling. In Figure TW.1 we would place these requests at the "TEAM" level, which is the third platform up from the bottom. We believe this type of intervention will work only if the team members have achieved a stable platform from which to work. In this case, that would include the two previous platforms in Figure TW.1. If the foundation is not well established, the solely team-based intervention often leads to intrateam competition or apathy and withdrawal.

As a basis for any work at the team level, individual team members must first be comfortable with themselves. They must be able to answer the questions, "What do I bring to the team?" and "What do *I* need from the team?" Not to answer these questions breeds inherent fear and mistrust. When these questions have been answered, team members are then in a position to begin dealing at the interpersonal level, where they may now comfortably ask, "What do *you* bring to the team and what do *you* need from the team?" Not to resolve these issues results in caution in dealing with other members, and interactions at the "polite-façade" level rather than at the level of truth and understanding. If the first- and second-level platforms are in place, a true team-building intervention can be useful. (Incidentally, just because team members have not stabilized themselves at levels 1 and 2 does not mean an intervention can not be conducted. Rather, it means a more extensive intervention will be required than a solely team-based effort.)

What Does a Team-Building Workshop Involve?

There are literally hundreds, if not thousands, of team-building interventions that are being conducted today. There are many good sources, such as the *Team and Organization Development Sourcebook,* which contain team-based activities such as conflict resolution, problem solving, development of norms, building trust, or goal setting, to name but a few. Rather than trying to describe all of these suggestions, however, we will give you a few recommendations that we have found to be useful and then share a few examples of interventions we have used.

At the Center for Creative Leadership, staff are frequently asked to design custom team interventions for mid- to upper-level teams. While we enter these design meetings with no agenda of activities, neither do we enter with a completely blank slate. We believe an intervention at the team level must meet three general requirements to be successful, and at least one activity must be included in the intervention pertaining to each of those three requirements.

The first requirement involves awareness raising. As we noted in our previous chapters, not all cultures are equally prepared or nurtured in the concepts of teamwork. In fact, many of the lessons we think we have learned about teams are incorrect. So we believe we need to dispel such myths and include a healthy dose of team-based research findings about how teams *really* work as a critical element of a workshop. Second, we need some diagnostic, instrument-based feedback so team members can have a reasonably valid map of where they and their teammates now are located. Finally, each intervention must include a practice field, to use Senge's (1990) term. Practice is necessary for athletic success, and it is necessary in organizations too. It would be foolish to design a whole new series of plays for a hockey team to implement, talk about them in the locker room, but never actually practice any of them before expecting the team to implement them in a game. Similarly, if you are asking people to change their behaviors in the way they interact to improve teamwork, then it is only fair to provide them with a practice field upon which they can test their new behaviors in a reasonably risk-free, protected environment. This is where experiential exercises can be extremely useful. And it is here that the quality of the team-building facilitator is most critical. Conducting a pencil-and-paper exercise in the classroom does not require the same facilitator skill set as that required to conduct, say, a team-rappelling exercise off the face of a cliff—few facilitators get those requirements wrong and we have seldom discovered problems here. Where we have seen a significant breakdown in facilitator skills is in being able to make the link between the exercise that is conducted and the real world in which the team will be asked to perform. Here facilitators must have not only a good sense of real-time team dynamics, but also a sense of the business in which the team operates. They must help the participants make the links back to team dynamics that occur on the manufacturing floor or in the boardroom, and this seems to be the skill that separates highly effective facilitators from the pack.

Examples of Interventions

Now let us provide a few examples of the range of interventions that can be included in team building. Ginnett (1984) conducted an intervention with three interdependent teams from a state youth psychiatric hospital. The teams included members of the administrative services, the professional staff, and the direct care providers. The members of each team were dedicated to their roles in providing high-quality service to the youths under their care, but the three groups experienced great difficulty in working with each other. Extensive diagnosis of the groups revealed two underlying problems. First, each group had a very different vision of what the hospital was or should be. Second, each of the groups defined themselves as "care givers," thus making it very difficult for them to ask others for help since, in their minds, asking for help tended to put them in the role of their patients. We conducted a series of workshops to arrive at a common vision for the hospital, but the second problem required considerably more work. Since the staff members needed to experientially understand that asking for help did not place them in an inherently inferior position, a "Wilderness Experience" was designed where the entire staff was asked to spend four days together in a primitive wilderness environment with difficult hiking, climbing, and mountaineering requirements. By the end of the experience, everyone had found an occasion to ask someone else for help. Even more important, everyone found that actually asking others for help—something they had previously resisted—moved the overall team much higher in its ability to perform. Considerable time was spent each evening linking the lessons of the day with the work in the hospital.

In one of the more interesting programs we've conducted, a team of senior executives spent a week together at a ranch in Colorado. Each morning, the team met for a series of awareness sessions and data feedback sessions. Afternoons were reserved by the chief operating officer for fun and relaxation, with the only requirement being that attendees participate in them as a team or subteams. As facilitators, we actively participated with the teams, and related their team experiences each day to the lessons of the next morning, and to challenges facing the team in its normal work. In interventions like this we have learned that team building can be fun, and that the venues for it are almost limitless. Second, we have learned that being able to observe and process team activity in a real-time mode is critical for team-building facilitators. There is no substitute for first-hand observation as a basis for discerning group dynamics and noting the variety of revealing behaviors that emerge in unstructured team activities.

Building High Performance Teams: The Rocket Model

> Mission
>
> Talent
>
> Norms
>
> Buy-In
>
> Power
>
> Morale
>
> Results
>
> Implications of the Rocket Model

As stated throughout this text, leadership is not an individual process. Rather, it involves influencing a group to pursue some type of overarching goal. From Chapter 10 we know that teams vary on a number of important factors, such as group size, norms, development stages, and cohesion. We also know that leaders need to take these factors into consideration when creating and leading teams. The Team Effectiveness Leadership Model in Chapter 10 provides a very comprehensive description of team dynamics and what leaders must do if they want to create high performing teams. What follows is a much simpler and more pragmatic model of team effectiveness. **The Rocket Model of Team Effectiveness** (Curphy, 1999, 2000, 2004a, b, c; Curphy & Hogan, 2004; Krile, Curphy, & Lund, in press) is both a prescriptive and diagnostic model of team building. The model is prescriptive in that it tells leaders what steps to take and when to take them when building new teams. The model can also be used as a diagnostic tool for understanding where existing teams are falling short and what leaders need to do to get them back on track.

The Rocket Model is based on extensive research on and experience with teams in the health care, education, retail, manufacturing, service, software, telecommunications, energy, and financial service industries. The model has been used with executive teams at The Home Depot, Waste Management, and the Strategic Health Authority in the United Kingdom; midmanagement teams at Waste Management, Pfizer, and a number of rural hospitals and school districts; and project teams at Qwest Communications and Hewlett-Packard. The model seems to work equally well with different types of teams at different organizational levels in different industries. Leaders in particular like the Rocket Model because of its straightforward and practical approach to team building.

A graphic of the Rocket Model can be found in Figure BHPT.1. As depicted in the graphic, building a team can be analogous to building a house. Just as the booster stage is critical for getting a rocket off the ground, so are the Mission and Talent stages critical for starting a team. Once the Mission and Talent issues have been addressed, leaders will then need to work with team members to sort out team Norms and Buy-In, and so on. Research shows that the teams with the best Results are usually those who report a high level of team functioning on the six other components of the Rocket Model. Teams reporting a high level of functioning in only some of the components usually report mediocre Results, and those with low functioning on all six components usually achieve few if any Results. The following is a more in-depth description of the seven components of the Rocket Model.

**FIGURE
BHPT.1**
The Rocket
Model.

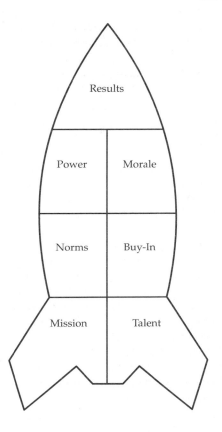

Results

Power

Morale

Norms

Buy-In

Mission

Talent

Mission

When building a new team, the first thing a leader must do is clarify the team's purpose and goals, set team performance standards, and ensure individual team member goals are aligned with the team's goals. Thus, the **Mission** component of the Rocket Model is concerned with setting a common direction for the team. In some cases the leader works closely with team members to sort out these issues; in other cases the leader makes these determinations; and in other cases the organization may make these decisions. For this component of the model, who makes these decisions is not as important as ensuring that everyone on the team understands what the team is trying to accomplish and how they personally contribute to team success. Teams with this common understanding often experience much lower levels of role ambiguity and conflict.

Of all the components in the Rocket Model, Mission may be the most important component. This is the case because it drives all the other components of the model. The Mission of the team will play a big role in determining the number and skills of people needed to achieve results (Talent), the rules by which the team operates (Norms), and the equipment and budget needed (Power). Because Mission plays such a critical role in team building, leaders of underperforming teams often find it worthwhile to first review the team's purpose, goals, and performance standards when striving to improve team performance.

If we were to apply the Rocket Model to a learning team in a college Leadership course, then the first thing the team should do is clarify what the team wants to accomplish. This might include such things as everyone on the team getting an A on the midterm, final exam, and overall course. Once the overall Mission and team goals are determined, the learning team would then need to decide who would do what and what the performance standards would be for each team member.

Talent

Teams with too many or too few people or with team members lacking the skills needed to achieve team goals often will report lower Talent scores than teams having the right number of people with the right skills. Selecting the right kind of people and continuously developing those skills needed to achieve team goals are two key leadership activities in this component of the Rocket Model. And the selection and development of Talent is precisely where many teams fall short. Professional athletic and elite military combat teams obsess over hiring decisions and spend countless hours practicing; they actually spend very little time performing. Most other teams seem to do just the opposite in that they do nothing more than throw a group of available people together and expect them to produce. These latter teams do not think through who needs to be on the team, spend little if any time developing needed skills, and never practice.

In the learning team example, Talent would come into play if team leaders selected their teammates on the basis of GPA and how well potential team members got along with others. Once the team was assembled, team leaders would then determine what skills they still needed to develop and work to ensure the team improved in these areas. Team skills could be developed through coaching, training programs, practice test sessions, and so on. Of course, this scenario assumes the leader gets to pick team members. Many times leaders do not have this luxury. If leaders do not get to pick team members, then it is imperative that they assess and develop those skills needed to accomplish team goals.

Norms

Once team members are selected and have a clear understanding of the team's purpose and goals, leaders then need to address the Norms component of the Rocket Model. Norms are the rules that govern how teams make decisions, conduct meetings, get work done, hold team members accountable for results, and share information. There are several important aspects of norms that are worth noting. First, the decisions the team makes, the way in which it makes decisions, how often and how long the team meets, and so forth, should all be driven by the team's purpose and goals. Second, Norms happen. If the team or team leader is not explicit about setting the rules that govern team behavior, they will simply evolve over time. And when they are not explicitly set, these rules may run counter to the team's purpose and goals. For example, one of the authors was working with a software development team that was responsible for delivering several new products in a six-month time period. The time frame was very aggressive, but one of the team Norms that had evolved was that it was okay for team members to show up late to team meetings, if they even bothered to show up. But the team meetings were very important to the success of the team, as they were the only time the team could discuss problems and coordinate its software development efforts. Team member behavior did not change until an explicit norm was set for team-meeting participation.

Third, there are many team Norms. These Norms might include where people sit in meetings, what time team members come in to work, what team members wear, the acronyms and terms they use, and so on. But of domain of possible Norms, those involving decision making, communication, meetings, and accountability seem to be the most important to team functioning. High performance teams are very explicit about what decisions the team makes and how it makes those decisions. These teams have also set rules about the confidentiality of team meetings, when team members speak for themselves or speak for the team, and how difficult or controversial topics get raised in team meetings. High performance teams also have explicit rules about team meetings and team member accountability. In our learning team example, the team would need to decide how it would prepare for the midterm exam, what the format and quality of the prep material would be, how often and where they would meet to prepare for the exam, what they would do both in and outside of the preparation meetings, and how they would use the results of the midterm exams to adjust their preparations for the final exam. Corporate teams often fail because they do not explicitly set decision-making, communication, meeting, and accountability Norms or ask themselves if the rules they have adopted are still working or need to be improved.

Buy-In

Just because team members understand the team's purpose and goals and the rules by which the team operates does not necessarily mean they will automatically be committed to them. Many times team members will do north to south head nods on the team's goals, rules, and action steps in team meetings, but then turn around and do something entirely different after the meetings. This is an example of a team that lacks Buy-In. Teams with high levels of Buy-In have team members who believe in what the team is trying to accomplish and will enthusiastically put forth the effort needed to make the team successful.

There are three basic ways team leaders can build Buy-In. One way to build Buy-In is to develop a compelling team vision or purpose. Many times team members want to be part of something bigger than themselves, and a team can be one venue for fulfilling this need. Whether or not team members will perceive the team to have a compelling vision will depend to a large extent on the degree to which the team's purpose and goals matches up to their personal values. Charismatic or transformational leaders (Chapter 13) are particularly adept at creating visions aligned with followers' personal values. A second way to create Buy-In is for the team leader to have a high level of credibility. Leaders with high levels of relevant expertise who share trusting relationships with team members often enjoy high levels of Buy-In. Team members often question the judgment of team leaders who lack relevant expertise, and they question the agendas of team leaders they do not trust. And because people prefer to make choices as opposed to being told what to do, a third way to enhance team Buy-In is to involve team members in the goal, standard, and rule-setting process.

In our learning team example, team Buy-In would likely be enhanced if the team got together and jointly determined their purpose, goals, roles, and rules. Alternatively, the team leader could assemble a group of students who wanted to achieve the same means and believed being part of a team would be the best way to make an A in the class. Team Buy-In might be somewhat lower if the instructor determined the learning team's Mission and Norms. Many teams in the public and private sector world fail because team members do not trust the team leader, believe the team leader to be incompetent, do not see how they personally benefit for being on the team, or were not involved with setting the team's goals.

Power

The Power component of the Rocket Model concerns the decision-making latitude and resources the team has in order to accomplish its goals. Teams reporting high levels of Power have considerable decision-making authority and all of the equipment, time, facilities, and funds needed to accomplish team goals. Teams with low Power often lack the necessary decision-making authority or resources needed to get things done. One of the authors was working with a group of public school administrators who felt they had very little Power to make decisions affecting the school district. The district had had three Superintendents over the past four years, and as a result the school board had stepped in to take over the day-to-day operation of the school district.

To improve the Power component of the Rocket Model, team leaders will first need to determine if they have all the decision-making latitude and resources they need to accomplish group goals. If they do not have enough Power, then they will either need to lobby higher ups to get what they need, devise ways to get team goals accomplished with limited resources, or revise team goals in light of the resource shortfalls. Most teams do not believe they have all the time, resources, or decision-making latitude they need to succeed, but more often than not they have enough of these things to successfully accomplish their goals. Good teams figure out ways to make do with what they have or devise ways to get what they need; dysfunctional teams spend all their time and energy complaining about a perceived lack of resources rather than figuring out ways to achieve team goals. Along these lines, many poor performing teams often make false assumptions or erect barriers that do not really exist. Team leaders will need to challenge these assumptions and break barriers if they are to help the team succeed.

Team Power will play a role in our learning team. In this case, the team leader may need to secure a room or facility to conduct the study sessions, obtain computer resources for team members, or even work with the instructor to see if the members could take group rather than individual exams. They will also need to determine how much time will be needed to adequately prepare for the examinations and whether all the team members can devote the time needed for the team to succeed. If the team does not have all the resources or time it believes it needs, then the team will either have to find ways to make do with what it has or make a downward revision of the team's goals.

Morale

Just because individual team members understand what the team is trying to accomplish, are committed to achieving team objectives, and understand the rules by which the team gets work done does not necessarily mean team members will all get along with each other. Teams that report high levels of Morale tend to effectively deal with interpersonal conflict and have high levels of morale and cohesion. This does not mean that highly cohesive teams do not experience interpersonal conflict. Instead, teams with high Morale scores have learned how to get conflict out in the open and deal with it in an effective manner. One way leaders can improve Morale is to work with team members to determine the rules for addressing team conflict. On the other hand, some of the best techniques for destroying team Morale are for leaders to either ignore interpersonal conflict or to tell team members to "quit fighting and just get along."

Because of values differences, work load inequities, miscommunication, and differing levels of commitment, it is likely that our learning team will experience some level of interpersonal conflict. If the learning team wanted to improve cohesiveness, then it would have to discuss how members were going to address conflict in the group. These discussions should happen relatively early in the group's formation and team conflict should be a regular topic in team meetings. Interestingly enough, many public and private sector teams report low Morale scores and often take some kind of action to improve team cohesiveness. Usually these actions include sending the team to some sort of team-building program, such as an outdoor learning or high ropes course. In almost all these cases, these interventions have little if any long-term effect on team cohesiveness, the reason being the Morale component of the Rocket Model is often a symptom of a deeper team problem. More often than not, the reason team members are not getting along is due to unclear goals and roles, ill-defined performance standards or accountability norms, a lack of commitment or resources, and so forth. In other words, the reason why team members are fighting has to do with a problem in one or more of the other components of the Rocket Model. Successfully addressing these problem components will not only improve results; they will also have a positive impact on team Morale.

Results

The Mission through Morale components of the Rocket Model describe the "how" of team building. In other words, these components tell team leaders what they specifically need to do if they need to improve team Mission, Norms, and so forth. The Results component of the Rocket model describes the "what" of team building—what did the team actually accomplish? Like Morale, Results are a symptom or an outcome of the other components of the Rocket Model. High performing teams get superior results because they have attended to the other six components of the Rocket Model. Those teams achieving less than optimal results can improve team performance by focusing on those problematic components of the Rocket Model. In our learning team example, if the team received a B on the midterm exam, the team could reexamine its purpose and goals, determine if it had some talent gaps, review its rules to see if they were spending enough time practicing the right things, find another venue or time to study, and so on.

FIGURE BHPT.2

Team assessment results for a dysfunctional health care team.

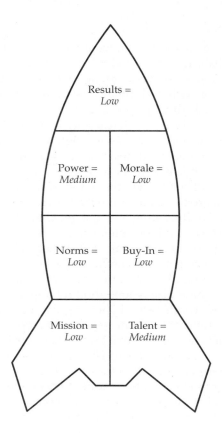

One thing we do know about high performing teams is that they often build executable action plans with clear timelines and accountable parties in order to achieve results. These plans include key milestones and metrics, and good teams regularly review team progress and revise their plans accordingly. Many times these plans include specific action steps to improve team functioning as well as the actions specific team members need to take for the team to achieve results.

Implications of the Rocket Model

As stated at the beginning of this section, the Rocket Model is both prescriptive and diagnostic, and the model works equally well with student- through executive-level teams. When building a new team or determining where an existing team is falling short, leaders should always start with the Mission and Talent components before moving to other parts of the model. Just as a rocket needs a large booster to get off the ground, so do teams need a clear purpose and the right players in order to be successful. Along these lines, the Team Assessment Survey (Curphy, 2004c) was designed to provide teams with feedback on where they stand with respect to the seven components of the Rocket Model. Figures BHPT.2 and BHPT.3 show the

FIGURE BHPT.3

Team assessment results for a high performing retail team.

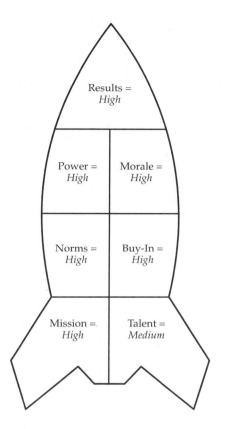

results of two executive level teams. Figure BHPT.2 is a highly dysfunctional group of executives who led a billion dollar health care organization. Because these executives never learned how to work together as a team, many were let go less than six months after their Team Assessment Survey was completed. Figure BHPT.3 shows the results for a top executive running a six billion dollar retail organization. This team was more or less hitting on all cylinders; its only real issue was grooming a successor for the soon to retire Division President.

Second, the components of the Rocket Model roughly correspond to Tuckman's (1965) four development stages of groups. According to Tuckman, forming is the first stage teams go through. Team leaders can help teams to successfully work through this stage by focusing on the Mission and Talent components of the Rocket Model. Tuckman maintained that teams then go into the storming stage, during which team leaders should concentrate on the Norms and Buy-In components of the model. Team leaders should focus on Power and Morale in Tuckman's norming phase and the Results component of the Rocket Model in Tuckman's performing stage.

Team Building at the Top

Executive Teams Are Different
Applying Individual Skills and Team Skills
Tripwise Lessons

In certain ways, executive teams are similar to any other teams. For example, just about any group of senior executives that has faced a dire crisis and survived will note that teamwork was essential for their survival. In a nutshell, then, *when teamwork is critical,* all the lessons of the previous section apply. More specifically, to really be able to benefit from a team-building intervention, individual members must be comfortable with their own strengths and weaknesses and the strengths and weaknesses of their peers. But this raises a question: If all this is true, why do we include a separate section on team building for top teams? Because there are two critical differences between most teams and "teams at the top" that should be addressed.

Executive Teams Are Different

As opposed to other kinds of work teams, not all the work at the executive level requires all (or even any) of the team to be present. An example might help. In our research on teams we studied the air crews who fly the B-1 bomber. These are four-person teams comprising an aircraft commander, a copilot, an offensive systems officer, and a defensive systems officer. While each has individual responsibilities, in every single bombing run we observed, it was absolutely essential that the team work together to accomplish the mission. They had all of the components of a true team (complex and common goal, differentiated skills, interdependence), and no individual acting alone could have achieved success. But this is not always the case for executive teams.

As Katzenbach (1998) has observed, many top leadership challenges do not really require teamwork at all. Furthermore, many top leadership challenges that do constitute real team opportunities do not require or warrant full involvement by everyone who is officially on the team. In fact, an official "team at the top" rarely functions as a collective whole involving all the formal members. Thus, the real trick for executive teams is to be able to apply both the technical individual skills that probably got the individuals to the team in the first place and the skills required for high-performance teamwork when a team situation presents itself.

Applying Individual Skills and Team Skills

There are two critical requirements if this is to work. First, one must have the diagnostic skills to discern whether the challenge presenting itself involves an individual situation or a team situation. Then, it requires that leaders "stay the course" when a team situation is present. This means, for example, when pressure for results intensifies, not slipping back into the traditional modes of assigning work to an individual (e.g., one member of that top team), but rather allowing the team to complete the work *as a team.* Again, Katzenbach (1998) stated this clearly:

Some leadership groups, of course, err in the opposite way, by attempting to forge a team around performance opportunities that do not call for a team approach. In fact, the increasing emphasis that team proponents place on "team-based organizations" creates real frustrations as top leadership groups try to rationalize good executive leadership instincts into time-consuming team building that has no performance purpose. Catalyzing real team performances at the top does not mean replacing executive leadership with executive teams; it means being rigorous about the distinction between opportunities that require single-leader efforts and those that require team efforts—and applying the discipline that fits.

To summarize this point, executives do not always need to perform as a team to be effective. But when they do need to perform as a team, the same lessons of team building discussed earlier can be very useful in helping them to enhance their team performance.

The second difference with executive teams is that they have an opportunity to enhance teamwork throughout their organization that few others have. It is our experience that *only the executive team can change organizational systems.* Recall from a chapter earlier in the book that we described the Team Effectiveness Leadership Model and mentioned there were four system issues critical to team performance. These systems were all located at the organizational level and consisted of reward systems, education systems, information systems, and control systems. The impact of these systems can be so pervasive across the entire organization that a small change in a system can have monumental impact in the organization. In a sense, then, the executive team has within its control the power to do widespread "team building" in a very different manner than we have discussed to this point. Just consider the impact of changing a compensation system (one element of a reward system) from an individual-based bonus plan to a team-based bonus plan!

Tripwire Lessons

Finally, our experience in working with executives has taught us that leaders at this level have some important lessons to learn about team building at the top. Richard Hackman, in preparing the huge editorial task of having many people produce one coherent book (by his own admission, not necessarily the best of team tasks), assembled the various authors at a conference center. As one of the contributors, one of this text's authors (RCG) recalls a most frustrating task of attempting to put together the simple checklist of steps to ensure a team developed properly. As this arduous process dragged on and tempers flared, it became obvious that "Teamwork for Dummies" was never going to emerge. But something else did start to emerge. It became clear *that some behaviors leaders engaged in could virtually guarantee failure for their teams.* While not our intent, this experience yielded a worthwhile set of lessons. A condensed version of those lessons, labeled "tripwires" by Hackman (1990), concludes our discussion of team building at the top.

Trip Wire 1: Call the Performing Unit a Team but Really Manage Members as Individuals

One way to set up work is to assign specific responsibilities to specific individuals and then choreograph individuals' activities so their products coalesce into a team product. A contrasting strategy is to assign a team responsibility and accountability for an entire piece of work and let members decide among themselves how they will proceed to accomplish the work. While either of these strategies can be effective, a choice must be made between them. A mixed model, in which people are told they are a team but are treated as individual performers with their own specific jobs to do, sends mixed signals to members, is likely to confuse everyone, and in the long run is probably untenable.

To reap the benefits of teamwork, one must actually build a team. Calling a set of people a team or exhorting them to work together is insufficient. Instead, explicit action must be taken to establish the team's boundaries, to define the task as one for which members are collectively responsible and accountable, and to give members the authority to manage both their internal processes and the team's relations with external entities such as clients and co-workers. Once this is done, management behavior and organizational systems gradually can be changed as necessary to support teamwork.

Trip Wire 2: Create an Inappropriate Authority Balance

The exercise of authority creates anxiety, especially when one must balance between assigning a team authority for some parts of the work and withholding it for other parts. Because both managers and team members tend to be uncomfortable in such situations, they may collude to "clarify" them. Sometimes the result is the assignment of virtually all authority to the team—which can result in anarchy or a team that heads off in an inappropriate direction. At other times, managers retain virtually all authority, dictating work procedures in detail to team members and, in the process, losing many of the advantages that can accrue from teamwork. In both cases, the anxieties that accompany a mixed model are reduced, but at significant cost to team effectiveness.

To achieve a good balance of managerial and team authority is difficult. Moreover, merely deciding how much authority will be assigned to the group and how much will be retained by management are insufficient. Equally important are the domains of authority that are assigned and retained. Our findings suggest that managers should be unapologetic and insistent about exercising their authority about *direction*—the end states the team is to pursue—and about *outer-limit constraints* on team behavior—the things the team must always do or never do. At the same time, managers should assign to the team full authority for the means by which it accomplishes its work—and then do whatever they can to ensure that team members understand and accept their responsibility and accountability for deciding how they will execute the work.

Few managerial behaviors are more consequential for the long-term being of teams than those that address the partitioning of authority between managers and teams. It takes skill to accomplish this well, and it is a skill that has emotional and behavioral as well as cognitive components. Just knowing the rules for partitioning authority is insufficient; one also needs some practice in applying those rules in situations where anxieties, including one's own, are likely to be high. Especially challenging for managers are the early stages in the life of a team (when managers often are tempted to give away too much authority) and when the going gets rough (when the temptation is to take authority back too soon). The management of authority relations with task-performing teams is indeed much like walking a balance beam, and our evidence suggests that it takes a good measure of knowledge, skill, and perseverance to keep from falling off.

Trip Wire 3: Assemble a Large Group of People, Tell Them in General Terms What Needs to Be Accomplished, and Let Them "Work Out the Details"

Traditionally, individually focused designs for work are plagued by constraining structures that have built up over the years to monitor and control employee behavior. When groups are used to perform work, such structures tend to be viewed as unnecessary bureaucratic impediments to team functioning. Thus, just as managers sometimes (and mistakenly) attempt to empower teams by relinquishing all authority to them, so do some attempt to get rid of the dysfunctional features of existing organizational structures simply by taking down all the structures they can. Apparently, the hope is that removing structures will release teams and enable members to work together creatively and effectively.

Managers who hold this view often wind up providing teams with less structure than they actually need. Tasks are defined only in vague, general terms. Group composition is unclear or fluid. The limits of the team's authority are kept deliberately fuzzy. The unstated assumption is that there is some magic in the group interaction process and that, by working together, members will evolve any structures that the team actually needs.

It is a false hope; there is no such magic. Indeed, our findings suggest the opposite: groups that have appropriate structures tend to develop healthy internal processes, whereas groups with insufficient or inappropriate structures tend to have process problems. Worse, coaching and process consultation are unlikely to resolve these problems, precisely because they are rooted in the team structure. For members to learn how to interact well within a flawed or underspecified structure is to swim upstream against a very strong current.

Trip Wire 4: Specify Challenging Team Objectives, but Skimp on Organizational Supports

Even if a work team has clear, engaging direction and an enabling structure, its performance can go sour—or, at least, it can fall below the group's potential—if the team is not well supported. Teams in high-commitment organizations (Walton, 1985) fall victim to this trip wire when given "stretch" objectives but not the wherewithal to accomplish them; high initial enthusiasm soon changes into disillusionment.

It is no small undertaking to provide these supports to teams, especially in organizations designed to support work by individuals. Corporate compensation policy, for example, may make no provision for team bonuses and, indeed, may explicitly prohibit them. Human resource departments may be primed to identify individuals' training needs and provide first-rate courses to fill those needs, but training in team skills may not be available at all. Existing performance appraisal systems, which may be state-of-the-art for measuring individual contributions, are likely to be wholly inappropriate for assessing and rewarding work done by teams. Information systems and control systems may provide managers with the data they need to monitor and control work processes, but they may be neither available nor appropriate for use by work teams. Finally, the material resources required for the work may have been prespecified by those who originally designed it, and there may be no procedure in place for a team to secure the special configuration of resources it needs to execute the particular performance strategy it has developed.

To align existing organizational systems with the needs of teams often requires managers to exercise power and influence upward and laterally in the organization.

An organization set up to provide teams with full support for their work is noticeably different from one whose systems and policies are intended to support and control individual work, and many managers may find the prospect of changing to a group-oriented organization both unsettling and perhaps even vaguely revolutionary.

It is hard to provide good organizational support for task-performing teams, but generally it is worth the trouble. The potential of a well-directed, well-structured, well-supported team is tremendous. Moreover, to stumble over the organizational support trip wire is, perhaps, the saddest of all team failures. When a group is both excited about its work and all set up to execute it superbly, it is especially shattering to fail merely because the organizational supports required cannot be obtained. It is like being all dressed up and ready to go to the prom only to have the car break down en route.

Trip Wire 5: Assume That Members Already Have All the Competence They Need to Work Well as a Team

Once a team is launched and operating under its own steam, managers sometimes assume their work is done. As we have seen, there are indeed some good reasons for giving a team ample room to go about its business in its own way: inappropriate or poorly timed managerial interventions impaired the work of more than one group in our research. However, a strict, hands-off managerial stance also can limit a team's effectiveness, particularly when members are not already skilled and experienced in teamwork.

Development Planning

Conducting a GAPS Analysis

Identifying and Prioritizing Development Needs: Gaps of GAPS

Bridging the Gaps: Building a Development Plan

Reflecting on Learnings: Modifying Development Plans

Transfer Learnings to New Environments

Change before you have to.

Jack Welch, General Electric CEO

Development planning is the systematic process of building knowledge and experience or changing behavior. Two people who have done a considerable amount of cutting-edge research in the development-planning process are Peterson and

Hicks (1995). These two researchers believe development planning consists of five interrelated phases. The first phase of development planning is identifying development needs. Here leadership practitioners identify career goals, assess their abilities in light of career goals, seek feedback about how their behaviors are affecting others, and review the organizational standards pertaining to their career goals. Once this information has been gathered, the second phase consists of analyzing this data to identify and prioritize development needs. The prioritized development needs in turn are used to create a highly focused and achievable development plan, the third phase of this process. To help ensure permanent behavioral change takes place, the plan itself must utilize many of the best-practices techniques described in Chapter 8. Some of these best practices include having a plan that is limited to no more than two or three objectives, that capitalizes on on-the-job activities, and that incorporates multiple sources of feedback. The fourth phase in development planning is periodically reviewing the plan, reflecting on learnings, and modifying or updating the plan as appropriate. As you might expect, the Action-Observation-Reflection (AOR) model, described in Chapter 3, is a key component during this phase of the development planning process. The last phase in development planning is transferring learnings to new environments. Just because a leadership practitioner can successfully delegate activities to his 3-person team may not mean he will effectively delegate tasks or utilize his staff efficiently when he is leading a group of 25 people. In that case, the leader will need to build and expand on the delegation skills he learned when leading a much smaller team. These five phases are well grounded in research—Hazucha, Hezlett, and Schneider (1993), Peterson (1993b), and Hezlett and Koonce (1995) show that approximately 75 percent of the leadership practitioners adopting these phases were successful in either changing their behaviors permanently or developing new skills. Because these five phases are so important to the development planning process, the remainder of this section will describe each phase in more detail.

Conducting a GAPS Analysis

The first phase in the development-planning process is to conduct a GAPS (Goals, Abilities, Perceptions, Standards) analysis. A GAPS analysis helps leadership practitioners to gather and categorize all pertinent development planning information. A sample GAPS analysis for an engineer working in a manufacturing company can be found in Figure DP.1. This individual wants to get promoted to a first-line supervisor position within the next year, and all of the information pertinent to this promotion can be found in her GAPS analysis. The specific steps for conducting a GAPS analysis are as follows:

- *Step 1: Goals.* The first step in a GAPS analysis is to clearly identify what you want to do or where you want to go with your career over the next year or so. This does not necessarily mean moving up or getting promoted to the next level. An alternative career objective might be to master one's current job, as you may have just gotten promoted and advancing to the next level is not as important at the moment. Other career objectives might include taking on more responsibilities in your current position, taking a

FIGURE DP.1

A sample GAPS analysis.

Sources: D. B. Peterson and M. D. Hicks, *Leader as Coach* (Minneapolis: Personnel Decisions International, 1996); and G. J. Curphy, *Career and Development Planning Workshop: Planning for Individual Development* (Minneapolis: Personnel Decisions International, 1998).

Goals: Where do you want to go?	Abilities: What can you do now?
Step 1: Career objectives: Career strategies:	*Step 2:* What strengths do you have for your career objectives? *Step 3:* What development needs will you have to overcome?
Standards: What does your boss or the organization expect?	Perceptions: How do others see you?
Step 5: Expectations:	*Step 4:* 360 and Performance Review Results, and feedback from others: • *Boss* • *Peers* • *Direct Reports*

lateral assignment in another part of the company, taking an overseas assignment, or even cutting back on job responsibilities to gain more work-life balance. This latter career objective may be very appropriate for leaders who are just starting a family or are taking care of loved ones who are suffering from poor health. The two most important aspects of this step in the GAPS analysis are that leadership practitioners will have a lot more energy to work on development needs that are aligned with career goals, and in many cases advancing to the next level may not be a viable or particularly energizing career goal. This latter point may be especially true with organizations that have been recently downsized. Management positions often bear the brunt of downsizing initiatives, resulting in fewer available positions for those wishing to advance.

- *Step 2: Abilities.* People bring a number of strengths and development needs to their career goals. Over the years, you may have developed specialized knowledge or a number of skills that have helped you to be successful in your current and previous jobs. Similarly, you may also have received feedback over the years that there are certain skills you need to develop or behaviors you need to change. Good leaders know themselves—over the years they know which strengths they need to leverage and which skills they need to develop.
- *Step 3: Perceptions.* The perceptions component of the GAPS model concerns how your abilities, skills, and behaviors impact others. What are others saying about your various attributes? What are their reactions to both your strengths and your development needs? A great way of obtaining this information is by asking others for feedback or through performance reviews or 360-degree feedback instruments.
- *Step 4: Standards.* The last step in a GAPS analysis concerns the standards your boss or the organization has for your career objectives. For example, your boss may say that you may need to develop better public speaking, delegation, or coaching skills before you can get promoted. Similarly, the organization may have policies stating that people in certain overseas positions must be proficient in the country's native language, or it may have educational or experience requirements for various jobs.

When completing a GAPS analysis you may discover that you do not have all the information you need. If you do not, then you need to get it before you complete the next step of the development-planning process. Only you can decide upon your career objectives, but you can solicit advice from others on whether these objectives are realistic given your abilities, the perceptions of others, and organizational standards. You may find that your one-year objectives are unrealistic given your development needs, organizational standards, or job opportunities. In this case, you may need to either reassess your career goals or consider taking a number of smaller career steps that will ultimately help you achieve your career goal. If you are lacking information about the other quadrants, then you can ask your boss or others whose opinions you value about your abilities, perceptions, or organizational standards. Getting as much up-to-date and pertinent information for your GAPS analysis will help ensure that your development plan is focusing on high-priority objectives.

Identifying and Prioritizing Development Needs: Gaps of GAPS

As seen in Figure DP.2, the Goals and Standards quadrants are future oriented; these quadrants ask where you want to go and what your boss or your organization expects of people in these positions. The Abilities and Perceptions quadrants are focused on the present; what strengths and development needs do you currently have and how are these attributes affecting others? Given what you currently have and where you want to go, what are the gaps in your GAPS? In other words, after looking at all of the information in your GAPS analysis, what are your biggest development needs? And how should these development needs be prioritized? You need to

FIGURE DP.2

A gaps-of-the-GAPS analysis.

Sources: D. B. Peterson and M. D. Hicks, *Leader as Coach* (Minneapolis, Personnel Decisions International, 1996); and G. J. Curphy, *The Leadership Development Process Manual* (Minneapolis, Personnel Decisions International, 1998).

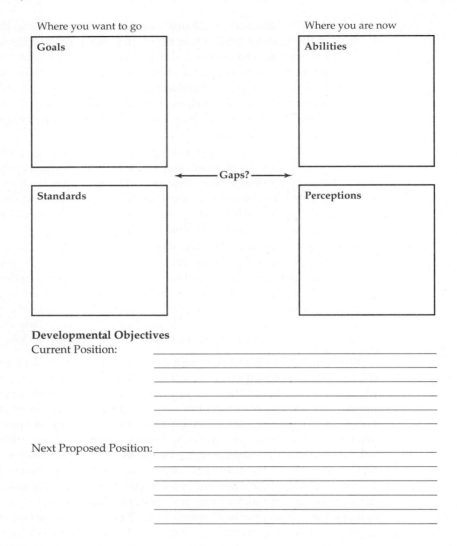

Where you want to go

Goals

Where you are now

Abilities

◄──── Gaps? ────►

Standards

Perceptions

Developmental Objectives

Current Position: _____

_____
_____
_____
_____
_____
_____

Next Proposed Position:_____

_____
_____
_____
_____
_____

review the information from the GAPS model, look for underlying themes and patterns, and determine what behaviors, knowledge, experiences, or skills will be the most important to change or develop if you are to accomplish your career goals.

Bridging the Gaps: Building a Development Plan

A gaps-of-the-GAPS analysis helps leadership practitioners identify high-priority development needs, but does not spell out what leaders need to do to overcome these needs. A good development plan is like a road map; it clearly describes the final destination, lays out the steps or interim checkpoints, builds in regular feedback to keep people on track, identifies where additional resources are needed, and builds in reflection time so that people can periodically review progress and determine whether an alternative route is needed. (See page 000 for a sample development plan.) The specific steps for creating a high-impact development plan are as follows:

- *Step 1: Career and Development Objectives.* Your career objective comes directly from the Goals quadrant of the GAPS analysis; it is where you want to be or what you want to be doing in your career a year or so in the future. The development objective comes from your gaps-of-the-GAPS analysis; it should be a high-priority development need pertaining to your career objective. People should be working on no more than two to three development needs at any one time.

- *Step 2: Criteria for Success.* What would it look like if you developed a particular skill, acquired technical expertise, or changed the behavior outlined in your development objective? This can be a difficult step in development planning, particularly with "softer" skills, such as listening, managing conflict, or building relationships with others.

- *Step 3: Action Steps.* The focus in the development plan should be on the specific, on-the-job action steps leadership practitioners will take in order to overcome their development need. However, sometimes it is difficult for leaders to think of the on-the-job action steps to overcome their development needs. Three excellent resources that provide on-the-job action steps for overcoming a variety of development needs are two books, *The Successful Manager's Handbook* (Davis, Skube, Hellervik, Gebelein, & Sheard, 1996) and *For Your Improvement* (Lombardo & Eichinger, 1996), and the development planning and coaching software *DevelopMentor* (PDI, 1995). These three resources can be likened to restaurant menus in that they provide leadership practitioners with a wide variety of action steps to overcome just about any development need.

- *Step 4: Whom to Involve and Reassess Dates.* This step in a development plan involves feedback—whom do you need to get it from and how often do you need to get it? This step in the development plan is important as it helps to keep you on track. Are your efforts being noticed? Do people see any improvement? Are there things you need to do differently? Do you need to refocus your efforts?

- *Step 5: Stretch Assignments.* When people reflect on when they have learned the most, they often talk about situations where they felt they were in over their heads. These situations stretched their knowledge and skills and often are seen as extremely beneficial to learning. If you know of a potential assignment, such as a task force, a project management team, or a rotational assignment, that would emphasize the knowledge and skills you need to develop and accelerate your learning, you should include it in your development plan.

- *Step 6: Resources.* Oftentimes people find it useful to read a book, attend a course, or watch a videotaped program to gain foundational knowledge about a particular development need. These methods generally describe the how-to steps for a particular skill or behavior.

- *Step 7: Reflect with a Partner.* In accordance with the Action-Observation-Reflection model of Chapter 3, people should periodically review their learnings and progress with a partner. The identity of the partner is not particularly important, as long as you trust his or her opinion and the partner is familiar with your work situation and development plan.

Reflecting on Learnings: Modifying Development Plans

Just as the development plan is a road map, this phase of development planning helps leaders to see whether the final destination is still the right one, if an alternative route might be better, and whether there is need for more resources or equipment. Reflecting on your learnings with a partner is also a form of public commitment, and people who make public commitments are much more likely to fulfill them. All things considered, in most cases it is probably better to periodically review your progress with your boss. Your boss should not be left in the dark with respect to your development, and periodically reviewing progress with your boss will help ensure there are no surprises at your performance appraisal.

Transfer Learnings to New Environments

The last phase in development planning concerns ongoing development. Your development plan should be a "live" document; it should be changed, modified, or updated as you learn from your experiences, receive feedback, acquire new skills, and overcome targeted development needs. There are basically three ways to transfer learnings to new environments. The first way is to constantly update your development plan. Another way to enhance your learning is to practice your newly acquired skills to a new environment. A final way to hone and refine your skills is to coach others in the development of your newly acquired skills. Moving from the student role to that of a master is an excellent way to reinforce your learnings.

Credibility

The Two Components of Credibility
Building Expertise
Building Trust
Expertise × Trust

Leaders know that while their position may give them authority, their behavior earns them respect. Leaders go first. They set an example and build commitment through simple, daily acts that create progress and momentum.

Jim Kouzes and Barry Posner

Interviews with thousands of followers as well as the results of over half a million 360-degree feedback reports indicate that credibility may be one of the most important components of leadership success and effectiveness (Kouzes & Posner, 1987, 1996; PDI, 1992). Employees working for leaders they thought were credible were willing to work longer hours, felt more of a sense of ownership in the company, felt more personally involved in work, and were less likely to leave the company over the next two years (Kouzes & Posner, 1996). Given the difficulties companies are having finding and retaining talented leaders and workers and the role intellectual capital and bench strength play in organizational success, it would appear that credibility could have a strong bottom-line impact on many organizations. Credibility is a little like leadership in that many people have ideas of what credibility is (or is not), but there may not be a lot of consensus on one "true" definition of credibility. This section will define what we believe credibility is, present the two components of credibility, and explore what leadership practitioners can do (and avoid doing) if they want to build their credibility.

The Two Components of Credibility

Credibility can be defined as the ability to engender trust in others. Leaders with high levels of credibility are seen as trustworthy; they have a strong sense of right and wrong, stand up and speak up for what they believe in, protect confidential information, encourage ethical discussions of business or work issues, and follow through with commitments. Sometimes dishonest leaders, personalized charismatic leaders, or power wielders can initially be seen by followers to be credible, but their selfish and self-serving interests usually come to light over time. Credibility is made up of two components, which include expertise and trust. Followers will not trust leaders if they feel their leaders do not know what they are talking about. Similarly, followers will not trust leaders if they feel confidential information will be leaked, if their leaders are unwilling to take stands on moral issues, or if their leaders do not follow through with their promises. Much about these two components of credibility have already been discussed in the sections on "Building Technical Competence," "Building Effective Relationships with Superiors," and "Building Effective Relationships with Peers." What follows is a brief overview of these three skills as well as some additional considerations that can help leadership practitioners build their credibility.

Building Expertise

Expertise consists of technical competence as well as organizational and industry knowledge, so building expertise means increasing your knowledge and skills in these three areas. Building technical competence, described earlier in Part V, concerns increasing the knowledge and repertoire of behaviors one can bring to bear to successfully complete a task. To build technical competence, leadership practitioners must determine how their job contributes to the overall mission of the company or organization, become an expert in the job through formal training or teaching others, and seek opportunities to broaden their technical expertise.

Nonetheless, building expertise takes more than just technical competence. Leaders also need to understand the company and the industry they are in. Many followers are not only looking for leaders to coach them on their skills, they are also looking to their leaders to provide some context for organizational, industry, and market events. Building one's organizational or industry knowledge may be just as important as building technical competence. However, the ways in which leadership practitioners build these two knowledge bases is somewhat different from building technical competence. Building technical competence often takes more of a hands-on approach to development, but it is hard to do this when building organizational or industry knowledge. One way to build your organizational or industry knowledge is by regularly reading industry-related journals, annual reports, *The Wall Street Journal, Fortune, Inc.,* or various websites. Many leaders spend 5–10 hours a week building their industry and organizational knowledge bases using this approach. Getting a mentor or being coached by your boss is another way to build these knowledge bases. Other leadership practitioners have taken stretch assignments where they work on special projects with senior executives. Often these assignments allow them to work closely with executives, and through this contact they better understand the competitive landscape, the organization's history and business strategies, and organizational politics. The bottom line is that your learning is not over once you have obtained your degree. In many ways, it will have just started.

Finally, it is important to remember that expertise is more than experience. As noted previously, some leaders get one year's worth of experience out of five years' work, whereas others get five years' worth of experience after one year's work. Leaders who get the most from their experience regularly discuss what they have been learning with a partner, and they frequently update their development plans as a result of these discussions.

Building Trust

The second component of credibility is building trust, which can be broken down into clarifying and communicating your values, and building relationships with others. In many ways leadership is a moral exercise. For example, one of the key differences between charismatic and transformational leaders is that the latter base their vision on their own and their followers' values, whereas the former base their vision on their own possibly selfish needs. Having a strong values system is an important component both in the Building Blocks Model of Skills and in leadership success. Because of the importance of values and relationships in building trust, the remainder of this section explores these two topics in more depth.

Chapter 6 defined values as generalized behaviors or states of affairs that an individual considers to be important. Provided that leaders make ethical decisions and abide by organizational rules, however, differences in values among leaders and followers may be difficult to discern. Since people do not come to work with their values tattooed to their foreheads, others typically make inferences about a leader's values based on their day-to-day behaviors (or just as importantly, their absence of certain day-to-day behaviors). Unfortunately, in many cases leaders' day-to-day behaviors are misaligned with their personal values; they are not living their life (at work, at least) in a manner consistent with their values.

An example of a leader not living life according to his values might be illustrative. An executive with an oil and gas firm was responsible for all exploration (i.e., drilling) operations in western Canada. Because he felt the discovery of new oil and gas fields was the key to the company's long-term success, he worked up to 18 hours a day, pushed his followers to work similar sorts of hours, had little patience for and would publicly disparage those oil rig operators who were behind schedule, and almost fired a manager who gave one of his followers a week off to see the birth of his son back in the United States. As these behaviors continued over time, more and more of his followers either requested transfers or quit to join other companies. Because of these problems with turnover and morale, he was asked to participate in a formal coaching program. Not surprisingly, his 360-degree feedback showed that his boss, peers, and followers found him very difficult to work with or for. These results indicated that he put a premium on getting results, getting ahead, and economic rewards, yet when he was asked to name the things he felt were most important to him as a leader, his priorities were his family, his religion, getting along with others, and developing his followers (altruism). Obviously, there was a huge gap between what he truly believed in and how he behaved. He felt the company expected him to hold people's feet to the fire and get results no matter what the cost, yet neither the boss nor his peers felt that this was the case. The executive had misconstrued the situation and was exhibiting behaviors that were misaligned with his values.

Although the case above was somewhat extreme, it is not unusual to find leaders acting in ways that are misaligned with their personal values. One way to assess the degree to which leaders are living their lives according to their personal values is by asking what they truly believe in and what they spend their time and money on. For example, you could write down the five things you believe most strongly in (i.e., your top five values), and then review your calendar, daytimer, checkbook, and credit card statements to determine where you spend your time and money. If the two lists are aligned, then you are likely to be living your life according to your values. If not, then you may be living your life according to how others think you should act. And if there is some level of discrepancy between the two lists, what should you do? Of course, some level of discrepancy is likely to occur, as situational demands and constraints can often influence the way leaders behave. On the other hand, large discrepancies between the lists may indicate that you are not living life consistently with your values, and those you interact with may infer that you have a very different set of values than those you personally believe in. A good first step in clarifying this discrepancy is to craft a personal mission statement or a leadership credo, a statement that describes what you truly believe in as a leader.

Examples of different leadership credos for managers across corporate America can be found in Highlight CR.1. There are several aspects of leadership credos worth additional comment. First, leadership credos are personal and are closely linked with a leader's values—a credo should describe what the leader believes in and will (or will not) stand for. Second, it should also describe an ideal state. A leader's behavior may never be perfectly aligned with his or her personal mission statement, but it should be a set of day-to-day behaviors that he or she will strive to achieve. Third, leadership credos should be motivating; leaders should be passionate and enthusiastic about the kind of leader they aspire to be. If the leader does not find his or her personal mission statement to be particularly inspiring, then it is hard to see how followers will be motivated by it. Much of the inspiration of a leadership credo stems from its being personal and values-based. Fourth, personal mission statements should be made public. Leaders need

Sample Leadership Credos

Highlight CR.1

As a leader, I . . .

. . . believe in the concept of whole persons and will seek to use the full range of talents and abilities of colleagues whenever possible.

. . . will seek to keep people fully informed.

. . . will more consistently express appreciation to others for a job well done.

. . . will take risks in challenging policies or protocol when they do not permit us to effectively serve our customers.

. . . will selectively choose battles to fight—rather than trying to fight all of the possible battles.

. . . will actively support those providing the most effective direction for our company.

. . . will seek to change the things I can in a positive direction and accept those things I have no chance or opportunity to change.

Source: *Impact Leadership* (Minneapolis: Personnel Decisions International, 1995).

to communicate their values to others, and a good way to do this is to display their leadership credos prominently in their offices. This not only lets others know what you as a leader think is important, it also is a form of public commitment to your leadership credo.

Another key way to build trust is to form strong relationships with others. There is apt to be a high level of mutual trust if leaders and followers share strong relationships; if these relationships are weak, then the level of mutual trust is apt to be low. Techniques for building relationships with peers and superiors have already been described in this section of the text. Perhaps the best way to build relationships with followers is to spend time listening to what they have to say. Because many leaders tend to be action oriented and get paid to solve (rather than listen to) problems, some leaders overlook the importance of spending time with followers. Yet leaders who take the time to build relationships with followers are much more likely to understand their followers' perspectives of organizational issues, intrinsic motivators, values, level of competence for different tasks, or career aspirations. Leaders armed with this knowledge may be better able to influence and get work done through others. More on building relationships with followers can be found in the "Coaching" section of Part V.

Expertise × Trust

Leaders vary tremendously in their levels of both expertise and trust, and these differences have distinct implications for leaders wanting to improve their credibility. Take leaders who fall into the first quadrant of Figure CR.1. These individuals have a high level of trust and a high level of expertise; they would likely be seen by others as highly credible. Individuals falling into the second quadrant might include leaders who have spent little time with followers, who do not follow through with commitments, or who are new to the organization and have had little time to build relationships with co-workers. In all three cases, leaders wanting to improve their

FIGURE CR.1
The credibility matrix.

Source: G. J. Curphy, *Credibility: Building Your Reputation throughout the Organization* (Minneapolis: Personnel Decisions International, 1997).

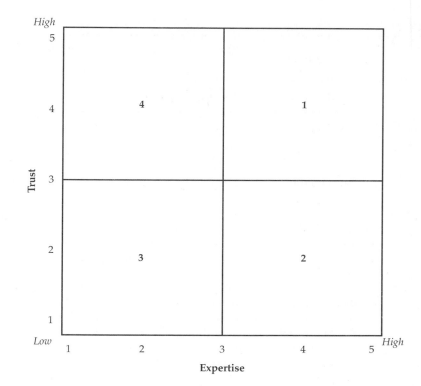

credibility should include building relationships with co-workers as key development objectives. Leaders falling into the third quadrant may be new college hires or people joining the company from an entirely different industry. It is unlikely that either type of leader would have the technical competence, organizational or industry knowledge, or time to build relationships with co-workers. These leaders may be in touch with their values and have a personal mission statement, but they will need to share their statement with others and act in a manner consistent with this statement in order to build their credibility. Other development objectives could include building expertise and strong relationships with others. Leaders falling into the fourth quadrant might include those promoted from among peers or transferring from another department within the company. Both sets of leaders may be in touch with their values, have a leadership credo, share strong relationships with co-workers, and have organizational and industry knowledge, but the former may need to develop leadership knowledge or skills and the latter technical competence if they wish to increase their credibility. Finally, it is important to note that leadership credos and development plans also have credibility implications because leaders who do not strive to live up to their ideals or fail to follow through with their developmental commitments are likely to be seen as less trustworthy than those who do.

Coaching

People who are coaches will be the norm. Other people won't get promoted.

Jack Welch, General Electric CEO

A key success factor in most organizations today is having leaders and followers with the right knowledge and skills. More and more, companies are looking at "bench strength" as a competitive advantage moving into the next century. There are essentially two ways to acquire bench strength; employers can either buy (i.e., hire) the talent they need, or they can build their existing talent through development and coaching programs. Given that many employers face a labor shortage in certain critical positions, many are looking to build their own internal talent (Tichy & Cohen, 1997). Much of this talent is being developed through informal coaching. As we noted in Chapter 8, most leaders engage in some form of informal coaching. But how good of a coach are they? The authors' conversations with a multitude of leaders indicate that almost every single one was unsure what to do as a coach. Some thought it involved directing their employees on how to do tasks. Others thought it involved counseling employees on personal problems. One stated that his only example of coaching came from his high school football coach, and he wouldn't want to wish that on anyone.

Two thought leaders in this area are Peterson and Hicks (1996), who described coaching as the "process of equipping people with the tools, knowledge, and opportunities they need to develop themselves and become more successful" (p. 14). According to Peterson and Hicks, good coaches orchestrate rather than dictate development. Good coaches help followers clarify career goals, identify and prioritize development needs, create and stick to development plans, and create environments that support learning and coaching. To some extent, many of the steps to coaching have been described under some of the other skills in Part V. Thus, coaching is really a blend of several different leadership skills. Being a good coach means having well-developed skills, determining where a follower is in the coaching process, and intervening as appropriate. The five steps of coaching provide leaders with both a good road map and a diagnostic model for improving the bench strength of their followers.

Peterson and Hicks (1996) pointed out that this model works particularly well for high performers—individuals who tend to benefit the most from, but are often overlooked by, leaders when coaching. We noted in Chapter 9 that high performers produce 20–50 percent more than average employees (Hunter, Schmidt, & Judiesch, 1990), so coaching can have a considerable impact on the bottom line if it is targeted at high performers. Further support for the idea that top performers may benefit the most from coaching comes from athletics. If you watched any of the Sydney Olympics in 2000, then you would have seen that many of the world's top athletes had at least one and sometimes two or three coaches. If these world-class athletes feel that coaching can enhance their performance, then it is likely that good coaches can also enhance the performance of any organization's top employees. Although the five-step model also works with poorly performing employees, more appropriate interventions might also include diagnosing performance problems, goal setting, providing rewards and constructive feedback, and punishing these individuals, particularly if informal coaching is not achieving desired results.

Forging a Partnership

The first step in informal coaching involves establishing a relationship built on mutual trust and respect with a follower. If a follower does not trust or respect her leader, then it will be very unlikely that she will pay much attention to his ideas for her development. There are several things leaders can do to forge a partnership with coachees. First, it will be much easier for leaders with high credibility to build strong partnerships with followers than for leaders with low credibility. Therefore, leaders need to determine where they are on the credibility matrix (Figure CR.1), and they may need to take appropriate developmental steps to improve their credibility before their coaching suggestions will have much impact. These developmental steps may include building technical and organizational knowledge as well as building strong relationships with the individuals they want to coach. Having an understanding of the context in which the employee operates can be as important as the relationship the leader shares with the employee. In the "Credibility" section, we noted that leaders will also need to spend time listening to their coachees; they need to understand coachees' career aspirations, values, intrinsic motivators, view of the organization, and current work situation. Good coaches can put themselves in their coachees' shoes, and can understand how coachees may view issues or opportunities differently from themselves. While forging a partnership, leaders can also provide coachees with realistic career advice, as sometimes coachees have unrealistic estimations of their skills and opportunities. For example, a new graduate from a top MBA program might want to be a partner at a consulting firm after two years with the company, but company policy may dictate that this decision will not be made until she has been with the firm for at least eight years. Her coach should inform her of this policy, and then work with her to map out a series of shorter-term career objectives that would help her become a partner in eight years. If coaches do not know what drives their coachees' behaviors, then another step to forging a partnership is to start asking a lot of questions. This is an excellent opportunity for leaders to practice their listening skills so as to better understand their coachees' career aspirations and intrinsic motivators.

Inspiring Commitment: Conducting a GAPS Analysis

This step in the coaching process is very similar to the GAPS analysis and the gaps-of-the-GAPS analysis, discussed in "Development Planning." The only difference is that these two analyses are now done from the coachee's perspective. Figure CH.1

FIGURE CH.1
A GAPS
analysis for an
employee.

Source: D. B. Peterson,
and M. D. Hicks,
Leader as Coach
(Minneapolis:
Personnel Decisions
International, 1996);
and G. J. Curphy, *The
Leadership Development
Process Manual*
(Minneapolis:
Personnel Decisions
International, 1998).

Goals: What does the employee want to do?	Abilities: What can the employee do now?
Step 1: Career objectives: —To become an Engineering Supervisor	*Step 2:* What strengths does the employee have for his or her career objectives? — Understand operational side of the business — Good planning skills — Good job function definition skills — Set clear individual and team goals *Step 3:* What development needs will he or she have to overcome? — Multidirection communication; may need to improve listening skills — May need to improve conflict resolution skills
Standards: What do you or the organization expect?	Perceptions: How do others see the employee?
Step 5: Expectations: • *Boss:* To be promoted, will need to: — Get along better with peers — Develop stronger listening skills	*Step 4:* PPRP and feedback from others: • *Boss* — Good technician — Develops good plans and holds people accountable — More interested in own rather than others' ideas • *Peers* — Can be counted on to get the job done — Can be too set in ways; too argumentative • *Direct Reports* — Has clear goals — Understands technical side of business — Doesn't value our ideas and opinions

might help to clarify this difference in perspective. Thus, in the Goals quadrant of the GAPS analysis the leader should write down the coachee's career objectives, and in the Perceptions quadrant the leader would write down how the coachee's behavior is impacting others. It is entirely possible that the leader may not be able to complete all of the quadrants of the GAPS for a coachee. If so, then the leader will need to gather more information before going any further. This information gathering may include discussing career goals and abilities with the coachee, reviewing the coachee's 360-degree feedback results, asking peers about how the coachee comes across or impacts others, or asking human resources about the educational or experience standards relevant to the coachee's career goals. One way to gather additional information is to have both the leader and the coach complete a GAPS analysis independently, and then get together and discuss areas of agreement and disagreement. This can help ensure that the best information is available for the GAPS analysis and also help to build the partnership between the leader and

TABLE CH.1
Development
Plan Checklist

Source: G. J.
Curphy, *The
Leadership
Development Process
Manual*
(Minneapolis:
Personnel Decisions
International, 1998).

Objectives:
❑ One-year career objective identified?
❑ No more than a total of two or three development goals?
❑ Areas in which the employee is motivated and committed to change and develop?

Criteria for Success:
❑ Is the new behavior clearly described?
❑ Can the behavior be measured or observed?

Action Steps:
❑ Specific, attainable, and measurable steps?
❑ Mostly on-the-job activities?
❑ Includes a variety of types of activities?
❑ Are activities divided into small, doable steps?

Seek Feedback and Support:
❑ Involvement of a variety of others?
❑ Includes requests for management support?
❑ Are reassess dates realistic?

Stretch Assignments:
❑ Do the stretch assignments relate to the employee's career objectives?

Resources:
❑ Uses a variety of books, seminars, and other resources?

Reflect with a Partner:
❑ Includes periodic reviews of learnings?

coachee. During this discussion the leader and coachee should also do a gaps-of-the-GAPS analysis to identify and prioritize development needs. Usually leaders will get more commitment to development needs if coachees feel they had an important role in determining these needs, and a gaps-of-the-GAPS discussion is a way to build buy-in. This discussion can also help ensure that development needs are aligned with career goals.

Growing Skills: Creating Development and Coaching Plans

Once the coachee's development needs are identified and prioritized, coachees will need to build development plans to overcome targeted needs. These plans are identical to those described in the "Development Planning" section. Leaders generally do not build development plans for their coachees. Instead, they may want to go over a sample (or their own) development plan and coach their coachees on the seven steps in building a plan. They can then either jointly build a plan or have the coachee individually build a plan for the leader to review. Providing coachees with an important role in development planning should increase their level of commitment to the plan. Once a draft development plan is created, the leader and coach can then use the development planning checklist in Table CH.1 to review the plan.

In addition to the development plan, leaders will need to build a coaching plan that outlines the actions they will take to support their coachees' development. Some of these actions might include meeting with the coachees on a regular basis to provide developmental feedback, identifying developmental resources or opportunities, or helping the coachee reflect on what they have learned. As with development plans, leaders should share their coaching plans so that coachees know what kind of support they will be getting. This will also publicly commit the leaders to the coachees' development, which will make it more likely that they will follow through with the coaching plan.

Promoting Persistence: Helping Followers Stick to Their Plans

Just because development and coaching plans are in place is no guarantee that development will occur. Sometimes coachees build development plans with great enthusiasm, but then never take any further action. This step in the coaching process is designed to help coachees "manage the mundane." An example of managing the mundane might be illustrative. One of the authors successfully completed a triathlon. The most difficult part of this accomplishment was not the event itself, but rather doing all of the training needed to successfully complete the event. Similarly, the inability to stick to a diet or keep a New Year's resolution is primarily due to an inability to manage the mundane; people are initially committed to these goals but have a difficult time sticking to them. The same is true with development planning. Conducting a GAPS analysis and creating a development plan are relatively easy; sticking to the plan is much more difficult. From the leader's perspective, a large part of coaching is helping followers stick to their development plan.

Several development-planning steps were specifically designed to promote persistence. For example, ensuring alignment between career and development objectives, getting feedback from multiple sources on a regular basis, and reflecting with a partner can help keep coachees focused on their development. If the leader is a coachee's developmental partner, then reflection sessions can help followers persist with their development. If leaders are not designated as partners in the development plan, then they should commit to meeting regularly with the coachees to discuss progress, what the leaders can do to support development, developmental opportunities, developmental feedback, and so forth.

Leaders can also help to promote persistence by capitalizing on coachable moments. Say a coachee was working on listening skills, and the leader and coach were in a staff meeting together. If the leader provides feedback to the coachee about her listening skills immediately after the staff meeting, then the leader has capitalized on a coachable moment. To capitalize on a coachable moment, leaders must know the followers' developmental objectives, be in situations where they can observe followers practicing their objectives, and then provide immediate feedback on their observations. Few coaches capitalize on coachable moments, but they can go a long way toward promoting persistence in coachees. It is important to note that capitalizing on coachable moments should take little time, often less than two minutes. In the example above, the leader could provide feedback to the coachee during their walk back to the office after the staff meeting.

Transferring Skills: Creating a Learning Environment

To build bench strength, leaders need to create a learning environment so that personal development becomes an ongoing process rather than a one-time event. As Tichy and Cohen (1997) aptly point out, the most successful organizations are those that emphasize the learning and teaching process—they focus on constantly creating leaders throughout the company. In reality, leaders have quite a bit of control over the kind of learning environments they want to create for their followers, and there are several interventions they can take to ensure that development becomes an ongoing process. Perhaps the most important intervention is for leaders to role-model development. In that regard, if leaders are not getting regular feedback from followers, then they are probably not doing a good job of role-modeling development. By regularly soliciting feedback from followers, leaders are also likely to create a feedback-rich work environment. Once feedback becomes a group norm, people will be much more willing to help build team member skills, which in turn can have a catalytic effect on group performance. It is important to note that the leader will play a large role in this group norm, because if the leader is feedback averse, it will be difficult to see how this norm will be adopted by followers.

Leaders can also create learning environments by regularly reviewing their followers' development. Perhaps the easiest way to do this is by making leaders and followers development partners; then both parties can provide regular feedback and on-going support. During these discussions leaders and followers should review and update their development plans to capitalize on new development opportunities or acquire new skills. Leaders and followers can also review coaching plans to see what is and is not working and make the necessary adjustments.

Concluding Comments

Perhaps one of the greatest misperceptions of coaching, and the primary reason why leaders state they do not coach others, is that it takes a lot of time. In reality, nothing could be further from the truth. Leaders are working to build credibility, build relationships with followers, and understand followers' career aspirations and view of the world. Although these do take time, they are also activities leaders should be engaged in even if they are not coaching followers. Doing a GAPS analysis, identifying and prioritizing development needs, helping followers create development plans, and creating coaching plans often takes less than four hours. Although leaders will need to take these steps with all their followers, these four hours can be spread out over a four- to six-week period. As stated earlier, meeting with followers on a regular basis to review development (perhaps monthly) and capitalizing on coachable moments also take little time. Finally, many of the actions outlined in "Create a Learning Environment" either take little time or are extensions of actions outlined earlier. The bottom line is that coaching really can take little additional time; it is really more a function of changing how you spend time with followers so that you can maximize their development.

Another note about the coaching model is that good coaches are equally versatile at all five steps of coaching. Some leaders are very good at forging a partnership, but then fail to carry development to the next level by conducting a GAPS analysis or helping followers build a development plan. Other leaders may help followers build a development plan but do not do anything to promote persistence or create a learning environment. Just as leaders need to develop their technical skills, so might they need to assess and in turn develop certain coaching skills. It is also important to remember that coaching is a very dynamic process—good coaches assess where followers are in the coaching process and intervene appropriately. By regularly assessing where they are with followers, they may determine that the relationship with a particular follower is not as strong as they thought, and this lack of relationship is why followers are not sticking to their development plan. In this case, a good coach would go back to forging a partnership with the follower and, once a trusting relationship had been created, go through another GAPS analysis, and so forth.

Finally, it is important to note that people can and do develop skills on their own. Nevertheless, leaders who commit to the five steps of informal coaching outlined above will both create learning organizations and help to raise development to a new level. Given the competitive advantage of companies that have a well-developed and capable workforce, in the future it will be hard to imagine leadership excellence without coaching. Good leaders are those who create successors, and coaching may be the best way to make this happen.

Empowerment

What Is Empowerment?
The Psychological Components of Empowerment
Six Best Practices of Empowerment

Do what you can, where you are at, with what you have.

Teddy Roosevelt

Inside every old company is a new company waiting to be born.

Alvin Toffler

Empowerment has become a very popular concept over the past 10 years. Many companies have embarked on various types of empowerment programs to improve results, yet the success of these programs has been mixed at best (Howard, 1996). One of the reasons for the mixed results is that empowerment often means different things to different people. This section describes what empowerment is (and is not), as well as some of the psychological constructs underlying empowerment and some of the best practices of empowering others.

What Is Empowerment?

In general, people seem to fall into one of two camps with respect to empowerment. Some people believe empowerment is all about delegation and accountability, a top-down process where senior leaders articulate a vision and specific goals, and hold followers responsible for achieving them. Others believe empowerment is more of a bottom-up approach that focuses on intelligent risk taking, growth, change, trust, and ownership; followers act as entrepreneurs and owners that question rules and make intelligent decisions. Leaders tolerate mistakes and encourage cooperative behavior in this approach to empowerment (Quinn & Spreitzer, 1997). Needless to say, these two conceptualizations of empowerment have very different implications for leaders and followers. And it is precisely this conceptual confusion which has caused empowerment programs to fail in many organizations (Quinn & Spreitzer, 1997). Because of the conceptual confusion surrounding empowerment, companies such as Motorola will not use this term to describe programs that push decision making to lower organizational levels. These companies would rather coin their own terms to describe these programs, thus avoiding the confusion surrounding empowerment.

We define empowerment as having two key components. For leaders to truly empower employees, they must delegate leadership and decision making down to the lowest level possible. Employees are often the closest to the problem and have the most information, and as such can often make the best decisions. A classic example was the UPS employee who ordered an extra 737 aircraft to haul presents that had been forgotten in the last-minute Christmas rush. This decision was clearly beyond the employee's level of authority, but UPS praised his initiative for seeing the problem and making the right decision. The second component of empowerment, and the one most often overlooked, is equipping followers with the resources, knowledge, and skills necessary to make good decisions. All too often companies adopt an empowerment program and push decision making down to the employee level, but employees have no experience creating business plans, submitting budgets, dealing with other departments within the company, or directly dealing with customers or vendors. Not surprisingly, ill-equipped employees often make poor, uninformed decisions, and managers in turn are likely to believe that empowerment was not all it was cracked up to be. The same happens with downsizing, as employees are asked to take on additional responsibilities but are provided with little training or support. As we stated in Chapter 9, this "forced" empowerment may lead to some short-term stock gains but tends to be disastrous in the long run. Thus, empowerment has both delegation and developmental components; delegation without development is often perceived as abandonment, and development without delegation can often be perceived as micromanagement. Leaders wishing to empower followers must determine what followers are capable of doing, enhance and broaden these capabilities, and give followers commensurate increases in authority and accountability.

The Psychological Components of Empowerment

The psychological components of empowerment can be examined at both macro and micro levels. There are three macro psychological components underlying empowerment, and these are motivation, learning, and stress (Howard, 1996). As a concept, empowerment has been around since at least the 1920s, and the vast majority of companies that have implemented empowerment programs have done so to increase employee motivation and, in turn, productivity. As a motivational technique, however, empowerment has not lived up to its promise; empowered workers may not be any more productive than unempowered workers (Howard, 1996). There are several reasons why this may be the case. First, senior leaders tend to see empowerment through rose-colored glasses. They hear about the benefits an empowerment program is having in another company, but do not consider the time, effort, and changes needed to create a truly empowered workforce. Relatedly, many empowerment programs are poorly implemented—the program is announced with great fanfare, but little real guidance, training, or support is provided and managers are quick to pull the plug on the program as soon as followers start making poor decisions. Adopting an effective empowerment program takes training, trust, and time (Offermann, 1996), but companies most likely to implement an empowerment program (as a panacea for their poor financial situation) often lack these three attributes. Third, as described in Chapter 9, worker productivity and job dissatisfaction in the United States are at an all-time high. Many companies are dealing with high levels of employee burnout, and adding additional responsibilities to already overfilled plates is likely to be counterproductive. As reported by Xie and Johns (1995), some empowerment programs create positions that are just too big for a person to handle effectively, and job burnout is usually the result.

Although the motivational benefits of empowerment seem questionable, the learning and stress reduction benefits of empowerment seem more clear-cut. Given that properly designed and implemented empowerment programs include a strong developmental component, one of the key benefits to these programs is that they help employees learn more about their jobs, company, and industry. These knowledge and skill gains increase the intellectual capital of the company and can be a competitive advantage in moving ahead. In addition to the learning benefits, well-designed empowerment programs can actually help to reduce burnout. People can tolerate high levels of stress when they have a high level of control. Given that many employees are putting in longer hours than ever before and work demands are at an all-time high, empowerment can help followers gain some control over their lives and better cope with stress. Although an empowered worker may have the same high work demands as an unempowered worker, the empowered worker will have more choices on how and when to accomplish these demands and as such will suffer from less stress. And because stress is a key component of dysfunctional turnover, giving workers more control over their work demands can reduce turnover and in turn positively impact the company's bottom line.

There are also four micro components of empowerment. These components can be used to determine whether employees are empowered or unempowered, and include self-determination, meaning, competence, and influence (Quinn & Spreitzer, 1997; Spreitzer, 1995). Empowered employees have a sense of self-determination; they can make choices about what they do, how they do it, and when they need to get it done. Empowered employees also have a strong sense of meaning; they be-

FIGURE EM.1
The empowerment continuum.

Empowered Employee	← →	Unempowered Employees
• Self-determined		• Other-determined
• Sense of meaning		• Not sure if what they do is important
• High competence		• Low competence
• High influence		• Low influence

lieve what they do is important to them and to the company's success. Empowered employees have a high level of competence in that they know what they are doing and are confident they can get the job done. Finally, empowered employees have an impact on others and believe that they can influence their teams or work units and that co-workers and leaders will listen to their ideas. In summary, empowered employees have latitude to make decisions, are comfortable making these decisions, believe what they do is important, and are seen as influential members of their team. Unempowered employees may have little latitude to make decisions, may feel ill equipped and may not want to make decisions, and may have little impact on their work unit, even if they have good ideas. Most employees probably fall somewhere in between the two extremes of the empowerment continuum, depicted in Figure EM.1. Leaders wanting to create more empowered followers may want to adopt some of the best practices techniques outlined below.

Six Best Practices of Empowerment

Do We Really Want or Need Empowerment?

Perhaps the first question leaders should ask before adopting an empowerment program is whether the company wants or needs empowerment. Leaders may agree that empowerment is important but may have fundamental differences as to the actions leaders need to take to create an empowered organization. Having a clear initial understanding of just what empowerment is will make the implementation of the program that much easier.

Leaders wanting to adopt an empowerment program must also consider how their own jobs and roles will be affected. They may need to fundamentally change their leadership style to better tolerate employee mistakes, play more of a coaching than directing role, and be willing to be challenged on a regular basis. Because empowered employees have access to considerably more information, they will be much more likely to question past or current decisions, and leaders will need to exert more personal power in order to get decisions adopted. Leaders feeling that this role transition is too much of a stretch will not enthusiastically embrace an empowerment program, making companywide adoption of the program difficult.

Creating a Clear Vision, Goals, and Accountabilities

Once a decision is made to develop and implement an empowerment program, top management must ensure that the company's vision, business strategies, and operational goals are clear and are understood by everyone in the company. It is difficult to ask employees to make wise decisions if they do not know where the company is headed. Employees should know what the company and work unit are trying to accomplish and how these accomplishments will be measured, and they should be given regular feedback on progress. In addition, employees will need to understand how their own goals are related to work unit and company goals.

Developing Others

Just because employees have a clear understanding of their work goals does not mean they have the knowledge, skills, and resources necessary to get them accomplished. Leaders will need to determine what employees can currently do, what they need to be able to do, and how they will help employees bridge the gaps between current and future capabilities. Perhaps the best way to do this is for leaders to adopt the five steps described in the "Coaching" section of Part V. A key component of empowerment is trust, and leaders can build trust by taking the actions prescribed in "Forging a Partnership." Leaders can identify and prioritize development needs through a GAPS analysis, and can work to increase knowledge and skills through development plans, coaching plans, and the actions outlined under "Promote Persistence" and "Transferring Skills." The five steps of informal coaching give leaders a road map for improving the bench strength of their followers and systematically equipping them to meet the increased challenges of empowerment. Taking these development steps helps with the competence component of empowerment.

Delegating Decision Making to Followers

Once followers are starting to develop the skills, knowledge, and experience necessary to make wise decisions, leaders must systematically increase the degree of latitude and autonomy employees are given to make decisions. Although this sounds fairly straightforward, in practice it can be fairly difficult. Some of the typical mistakes leaders make in this area are pushing followers into decision making too quickly, holding on to decision-making power too long, or taking decision-making power away from followers during a crisis. Other difficulties include the fact that many leaders associate decision making with leadership and may feel personally threatened by delegating decision-making authority to others. This may be particularly true when organizations have recently gone through a downsizing or when the level of trust between leaders and followers is low. Some followers may also feel reluctant to take on increased decision-making responsibility, as their level of skill may be exposed in ways it never had before (Offermann, 1996). Another complication is that some employees may feel that because they are taking on additional responsibilities, they should be paid more. This is particularly true when empowerment programs are introduced in union environments.

One way to determine how much latitude and authority to provide followers is to use the Situational Leadership® Theory, described in Chapter 12. This model provides a useful heuristic for developing employees and determining when they

References

Aberman, R. "Emotional Intelligence." Paper presented at the Quarterly Meeting of the Minnesota Human Resource Planning Society, Minneapolis, MN, November 29, 2000.

Adams, J.; H. T. Prince; D. Instone; and R. W. Rice. "West Point: Critical Incidents of Leadership." *Armed Forces and Society* 10 (1984), pp. 597–611.

Adams, J. S. "Inequity in Social Exchange." In *Advances in Experimental Social Psychology*. Ed. L. Berkowitz. Vol. 2. New York: Academic Press, 1965, pp. 267–96.

———. "Toward an Understanding of Inequity." *Journal of Abnormal and Social Psychology* 67 (1963), pp. 422–36.

Adler, N. J. "Global leaders: Women of influence." In *Handbook of Gender & Work*. Ed. G. N. Powell. Thousand Oaks, CA: Sage, 1999.

Alberti, R. E., and M. L. Emmons. *Your Perfect Right*. San Luis Obispo, CA: Impact, 1974.

Albrecht, K. *Stress and the Manager*. Englewood Cliffs, NJ: Prentice Hall, 1979.

Alderfer, C. P. "An Empirical Test of a New Theory of Human Needs." *Organizational Behavior and Human Performance* 4 (1969), pp. 142–75.

———. "Group and Intergroup Relations." In *Improving Life at Work*. Ed. J. R. Hackman and J. L. Suttle, Santa Monica, CA: Goodyear, 1977.

Allen, T. D., L. T. Eby, M. L. Poteet, E. Lentz, and L. Lima. "Career Benefits Associated with Mentoring for Proteges: A Meta-Analysis." *Journal of Applied Psychology*, 89 (1) (2004), pp. 127–36.

Amabile, T. M. "Beyond Talent: John Irving and the Passionate Craft of Creativity." *American Psychologist* 56, no. 4 (2001), pp. 333–36.

Amabile, T. M. "Motivation and Creativity: Effects of Motivation Orientation on Creative Writers." *Journal of Personal and Social Psychology* 48 (1985), pp. 393–99.

———. "The Motivation to Be Creative." In *Frontiers in Creativity: Beyond the Basics*. Ed. S. Isaksen. Buffalo, NY: Bearly, 1987.

———. *The Social Psychology of Creativity*. New York: Springer-Verlag, 1983.

Amabile, T. M., and R. Conti. "What Downsizing Does to Creativity." *Issues & Observations* 15, no. 3 (1995), pp. 1–6.

Amabile, T. M., and S. S. Gryskiewicz. "Creativity in the R&D Laboratory." (Tech Report No. 30). Greensboro, N.C.: Center for Creative Leadership, 1987.

Amabile, T. M., and B. A. Hennessey. "The Motivation for Creativity in Children." In *Achievement and Motivation: A Social-Developmental Perspective*. Ed. A. K. Boggiano and T. Pittman. New York: Cambridge University Press, 1988.

Amabile, T. M.; E. A. Schatzel; G. B. Moneta; and S. J. Kramer. "Leader Behaviors and the Work Environment for Creativity: Perceived Leader Support." *The Leadership Quarterly*, 15 (1) (2004), pp. 5–32.

Ambrose, M. L., and R. Cropanzano. "A Longitudinal Analysis of Organizational Fairness: An Examination of Reactions to Tenure and Promotion Decisions." *Journal of Applied Psychology*, 88 (2), 2003, pp. 266–75.

Antonakis, J.; B. J. Avolio; and N. Sivasubramainiam. "Context and Leadership: An Examination of the Nine Factor Full Range Leadership Theory Using the Multifactor Leadership Questionnaire. *The Leadership Quarterly*, 15 (2) (2003), pp. 261–95.

Antonakis, J., and R. J. House. "On Instrumental Leadership: Beyond Transactions and Transformations." Presentation delivered at the UNL Gallup Leadership Summit, June 2004, Lincoln, Nebraska.

Argyris, C. *Increasing Leadership Effectiveness*. New York: John Wiley, 1976.

Armour, S. "Bosses Held Liable for Keeping Workers." *USA Today*, April 12, 2000, p. 1B.

Arthur, W., Jr.; W. Bennett Jr.; P. S. Edens; and S. T. Bell. "Effectiveness of Training in Organizations: A Meta-Analysis of Design and Evaluation Features." *Journal of Applied Psychology*, 88 (2) (2003), pp. 234–45.

Arthur, W. Jr.; E. A. Day; T. L. McNelly; and P. S. Edens. "A Meta-Analysis of the Criterion-Related Validity of Assessment Center Dimensions." *Personnel Psychology*, 56 (1) (2003), pp. 125–54.

Arvey, R. D., et al. "Mainstream Science on Intelligence." *The Wall Street Journal,* December 13, 1994.

Arvey, R. D.; T. J. Bouchard, Jr.; N. L. Segal; and L. M. Abraham. "Job Satisfaction: Environmental and Genetic Components." *Journal of Applied Psychology* 74 (1989), pp. 187–92.

Arvey, R. D.; G. A. Davis; and S. M. Nelson. "Use of Discipline in an Organization: A Field Study." *Journal of Applied Psychology* 69 (1984), pp. 448–60.

Arvey, R. D., and J. M. Ivancevich. "Punishment in Organizations: A Review, Propositions, and Research Suggestions." *Academy of Management Review* 5 (1980), pp. 123–32.

Arvey, R. D., and A. P. Jones. "The Use of Discipline in Organizational Settings; A Framework for Future Research." In *Research in Organizational Behavior.* Ed. L. L. Cummings and B. M. Staw. Vol. 7. Greenwich, CT: JAI, 1985, pp. 367–408.

Arvey, R. D., and K. R. Murphy. "Performance Evaluation in Work Settings." *Annual Review of Psychology* 49 (1998), pp. 141–68.

Astin, A. W., Parrrott, S. A., Korn, W. S., and Sax, L. J. *The American Freshman: Thirsty Year Trends.* Los Angeles: Higher Education Research Institute, University of California, 1997.

Astin, H. S., and C. Leland. *Women of Influence, Women of Vision.* San Francisco: Jossey-Bass, 1991.

Atkins, P. W. B., and R. E. Wood. "Self- Versus Others' Ratings as Predictors of Assessment Center Ratings: Validation Evidence for 360-Degree Feedback Programs." *Personnel Psychology,* 55 (2002), pp. 871–84.

Atkinson, J. W. "Motivational Determinants of Risk Taking Behavior." *Psychological Review* 64 (1957), pp. 359–72.

Atwater, L. E; C. Ostroff; F. J. Yammarino; and J. W. Fleenor. "Self-Other Agreement: Does It Really Matter?" *Personnel Psychology* 51, no. 3 (1998), pp. 577–98.

Atwater, L. E; D. Waldman; D. Atwater; and P. Cartier. "An Upward Feedback Field Experiment: Supervisors' Cynicism, Reactions, and Commitment to Subordinates." *Personnel Psychology* 53, no. 2 (2000), pp. 275–97.

Austin, J. S.; E. J. Conlon; and R. L. Daft. "Organizing for Effectiveness: A Guide to Using Structural Design for Mission Accomplishment." LMDC-TR-84-3-0. Maxwell AFB, AL: Leadership and Management Development Center, Air University, 1986.

Avolio, B. J., and B. M. Bass. *Developing a Full Range of Leadership Potential: Cases on Transactional and Transformational Leadership.* Binghamton: State University of New York at Binghamton, 2000.

———. "Transformational Leadership, Charisma, and Beyond." In *Emerging Leadership Vista.* Ed. J. G. Hunt, B. R. Baliga, and C. A. Schriesheim. Lexington, MA: D. C. Heath, 1988.

———. "You Can Drag a Horse to Water but You Can't Make It Drink Unless It Is Thirsty." *Journal of Leadership Studies* 5, no. 1 (1998), pp. 1–17.

Awamleh, R., and W. L. Gardner. "Perceptions of Leader Charisma and Effectiveness: The Effects of Vision Content, Delivery, and Organizational Performance." *Leadership Quarterly* 10, no. 3 (1998), pp. 245–374.

Azar, B. "Searching for Intelligence Beyond G." *APA Monitor* 26, no. 1 (1995), p. 1.

———. "Which Traits Predict Job Performance?" *APA Monitor,* July 1995, pp. 30–31.

Back, K., and K. Back. *Assertiveness at Work.* New York: McGraw-Hill, 1982.

Badin, I. J. "Some Moderator Influences on Relationships between Consideration, Initiating Structure, and Organizational Criteria." *Journal of Applied Psychology* 59 (1974), pp. 380–82.

Baldwin, B., and S. Trovas. *Leadership in Action,* 21 (6), January/February 2002, p. 17.

Baltzell, E. D. *Puritan Boston and Quaker Philadelphia.* New York: Free Press, 1980.

Bandura, A. "Self-Efficacy: Toward a Unifying Theory of Behavioral Change." *Psychological Review* 84 (1977), pp. 191–215.

Bandura, A., and E. A. Locke. "Negative Self-Efficacy and Goal Effects Revisited." *Journal of Applied Psychology,* 88 (1) (2003), pp. 87–99.

Bar-On, R. *The Emotional Quotient Inventory (EQi).* Toronto, Canada: Multi-Health Systems, 1996.

Barling, J., C. Loughlin, and E. K. Kelloway. "Development and Test of a Model Linking Safety-Specific Transformational Leadership and Occupational Safety." *Journal of Applied Psychology,* 87 (3) (2002), pp. 488–96.

Barnes, F. "Mistakes New Presidents Make." *Reader's Digest,* January 1989, p. 43.

Barnum, D. F. "Effective Membership in the Global Business Community." In *New Traditions in Business.* Ed. J. Renesch. San Francisco: Berrett-Koehler, 1992.

Barrett, A., and J. Beeson. "Developing Business Leaders for 2010." *The Conference Board,* New York (2002).

Barrick, M. R. "Answers to Lingering Questions about Personality Research." Paper presented at the 14th Annual Conference of the Society of Industrial and Organizational Psychology, Atlanta, GA, 1999.

Barrick, M. R., and M. K. Mount. "The Big Five Personality Dimensions and Job Performance: A Meta-analysis." *Personal Psychology* 44 (1991), pp. 1–26.

———. "Effects of Impression Management and Self-Deception on the Predictive Validity of Personality Constructs." *Journal of Applied Psychology* 81, no. 3 (1996), pp. 261–72.

Basadur, M. "Leading Others to Think Innovatively Together: Creative Leadership." *The Leadership Quarterly,* 15 (1) (2004), pp. 103–21.

Bass, B. M. *Bass and Stogdill's Handbook of Leadership.* 3rd ed. New York: Free Press, 1990.

———. "Does the Transactional-Transformational Leadership Paradigm Transcend Organizational and National Boundaries?" *American Psychologist* 52, no. 3 (1997), pp. 130–39.

———. *Leadership, Psychology, and Organizational Behavior.* New York: Harper, 1960.

———. *Leadership and Performance beyond Expectations.* New York: Free Press, 1985.

———. "Thoughts and Plans." In *Cutting Edge: Leadership 2000.* Eds. B. Kellerman and L. R. Matusak. Carbondale: Southern Illinois University Press, 2000, pp. 5–9.

———. "Two Decades of Research and Development in Transformational Leadership." *European Journal of Work and Organizational Psychology* 8, no. 1 (1999), pp. 9–32.

Bass, B. M., and B. J. Avolio, eds. *Increasing Organizational Effectiveness through Transformational Leadership.* Thousand Oaks, CA: Sage, 1994.

———. *The Multifactor Leadership Questionnaire Report.* Palo Alto, CA: Mind Garden, 1996.

Bass, B. M., B. J. Avolio, D. I. Jung, and Y. Berson. "Predicting Unit Performance by Assessing Transformational and Transactional Leadership." *Journal of Applied Psychology,* 88 (2) (2003), pp. 207–18.

Bass, B. M., and P. Steidlmeier. "Ethics, Character, and Authentic Transformational Leadership Behavior." *Leadership Quarterly* 10, no. 2 (1999), pp. 181–218.

Bass, B. M., and F. J. Yammarino. *Long-term Forecasting of Transformational Leadership and Its Effects among Naval Officers: Some Preliminary Findings.* Technical Report No. ONR-TR-2. Arlington, VA: Office of Naval Research, 1988.

Bedeian, A. G., and A. A. Armenakis. "The Cesspool Syndrome: How Dreck Floats to the Top of Declining Organizations." *Academy of Management Executive* 12, no. 1 (1998), pp. 58–63.

Beer, M. "Developing Organizational Fitness: Towards a Theory and Practice of Organizational Alignment." Paper presented at the 14th Annual Conference of the Society of Industrial and Organizational Psychology, Atlanta, GA, 1999.

———. *Leading Change.* Reprint No. 9-488-037. Boston: Harvard Business School Publishing Division, 1988.

Behar, K; D. Arvidson; W. Omilusik; B. Ellsworth; and B. Morrow. *Developing Husky Oil Leaders: A Strategic Investment,* Calgary, Canada: Husky Energy, 2000.

Benner, P. E. *Stress and Satisfaction on the Job.* New York: Praeger, 1984.

Bennis, W., and J. Goldsmith. *Learning to Lead.* Reading, MA: Perseus Books, 1997.

Bennis, W. G. "Leadership Theory and Administrative Behavior: The Problem of Authority." *Administrative Science Quarterly* 4 (1959), pp. 259–260.

———. *On Becoming a Leader.* Reading, MA: Addison-Wesley, 1989.

Bennis, W. G., and B. Nanos. *Leaders: The Strategies for Taking Charge.* New York: Harper & Row, 1985.

Bennis, W. G., and R. J. Thomas. "Crucibles of Leadership." *Harvard Business Review,* September (2002), pp. 39–45.

Berglas, S. "The Very Real Dangers of Executive Coaching." *Harvard Business Review,* June 2002, pp. 86–93.

Berkman, L., and S. L. Syme. "Social Networks, Host Resistance, and Mortality: A Nine-Year Follow-up Study of Alameda County Residents." *American Journal of Epidemiology* 109 (1979), pp. 186–204.

Bernardin, H. J., and R. W. Beatty. *Performance Appraisal: Assessing Human Behavior at Work.* Boston: Kent, 1984.

Berry, J. K. "Linking Management Development to Business Strategies." *Training and Development Journal*, August 1990, pp. 20–22.

Berson, Y.; B. Shamir; B. J. Avolio; and M. Popper. "The Relationship between Vision Strength, Leaders Style, and Context." *Leadership Quarterly* 12, no. 1 (2001), pp. 53–74.

Bettencourt, L. A.; K. P. Gwinner; and M. L. Meuter. "A Comparison of Attitude, Personality, and Knowledge Predictors of Service-Oriented Organizational Citizenship Behaviors." *Journal of Applied Psychology*, 86, no. 1 (2001), pp. 29–41.

Betz, E. L. "Two Tests of Maslow's Theory of Need Fulfillment." *Journal of Vocational Behavior* 24 (1984), pp. 204–20.

Beyer, J. M. "Training and Promoting Charisma to Change Organizations." *Leadership Quarterly* 10, no. 2 (1999), pp. 307–30.

Beyer, J. M., and H. M. Trice. "A Field Study in the Use and Perceived Effects of Discipline in Controlling Work Performance." *Academy of Management Journal* 27 (1984), pp. 743–64.

Bickman, L. "The Social Power of a Uniform." *Journal of Applied Social Psychology* (1974), pp. 47–61.

Blake, P. "Walt Disney World: No Mere Amusement Park." *Architectural Forum* 136, no. 5 (1972), pp. 24–40.

———. "The Lessons of the Parks." In *The Art of Walt Disney: From Mickey Mouse to the Magic Kingdom.* Ed. C. Finch. New York: Harry N. Abrams, 1973, pp. 423–49.

Blake, R. J. "Relations between Worker Satisfactories and Personality." In R. T. Hogan (chair), *Personality and Organizational Behavior.* Symposium presented at the 104th Annual Meeting of the American Psychological Association, Toronto, Canada, 1996.

Blake, R. R., and A. A. McCanse. *Leadership Dilemmas—Grid Solutions.* Houston, TX: Gulf, 1991.

Blake, R. R., and J. S. Mouton. *The Managerial Grid.* Houston, TX: Gulf, 1964.

Blake, R. R.; H. A. Shepard; and J. S. Mouton. *Managing Intergroup Conflict in Industry.* Houston, TX: Gulf, 1964.

Blankenship, L. V., and R. E. Miles. "Organizational Structure and Managerial Decision Behavior." *Administrative Science Quarterly* 13 (1968), pp. 106–20.

Blau, P. M. "Critical Remarks on Weber's Theory of Authority." *American Political Science Review* 57, no. 2 (1963), pp. 305–15.

———. "The Hierarchy of Authority in Organizations." *American Journal of Sociology* 73 (1968), pp. 453–67.

Block, P. *Stewardship.* San Francisco: Berrett-Koehler, 1992.

Bloom, M. "The Performance Effects of Pay Dispersions on Individuals and Organizations." *Academy of Management Journal* 42, no. 1 (1999), pp. 25–40.

Bloom, M., and G. T. Milkovich. "Relationships among Risk, Incentive Pay, and Organizational Performance." *Academy of Management Journal* 41, no. 3 (1998), pp. 283–97.

Bolino, M. C., and W. H. Turnley. "Going the Extra Mile: Cultivating and Managing Employee Citizenship Behavior." *Academy of Management Executive,* 17 (3) (2003), pp. 60–71.

Bolino, M. C., W. H. Turnley, and J. M. Bloodgood. "Citizenship Behavior and the Creation of Social Capital." *Academy of Management Review,* 27 (4) (2002), pp. 505–22.

Bolman, L. G., and T. E. Deal. *Leading with Soul.* San Francisco: Jossey-Bass, 1995.

Bono, J. E. "Transformational Leadership: What We Know and Why You Should Care!" Presentation delivered to the Minnesota Professionals for Psychology Applied to Work, Minneapolis, MN, September 2002.

Bono, J. E., and T. A. Judge. "Self-Concordance at Work: Toward Understanding the Motivational Effects of Transformational Leaders." *Academy of Management Journal,* 46(5) (2003), pp. 554–71.

Borman, W. C.; L. A. White; E. D. Pulakos; and S. A. Oppler. "Models Evaluating the Effects of Rated Ability, Knowledge, Proficiency, Temperament, Awards, and Problem Behavior on Supervisor Ratings." *Journal of Applied Psychology* 76 (1991), pp. 863–72.

Bossidy, L., and R. Charan. *Execution: The Discipline of Getting Things Done.* New York: Crown Business Publishing, 2002.

Boudreau, J. W.; W. R. Boswell; T. A. Judge; and R. D. Bretz, Jr. "Personality and Cognitive Ability as Predictors of Job Search among Employed Managers." *Personnel Psychology* 54, no. 1 (2001), pp. 25–50.

Bowers, D. G., and S. E. Seashore. "Predicting Organizational Effectiveness with a Four Factor Theory of Leadership." *Administrative Science Quarterly* 11 (1966), pp. 238–63.

Boyatzis, R., A. McKee, and D. Goleman. "Reawakening Your Passion for Work." *Harvard Business Review,* April 2002, pp. 86–96.

Boyatzis, R. E., E. C. Stubbs, and S. N. Taylor. "Learning Cognitive and Emotional Intelligence Competencies through Graduate Management Education." *Academy of Management Learning and Education,* 1 (2) (2002), 150–62.

Bracken, D. W. "Straight Talk about Multi-rater Feedback." *Training & Development,* September 1994.

Bracken, D. W.; C. W. Timmreck; and A. H. Church. *The Handbook of Multisource Feedback.* San Francisco: Jossey-Bass, 2000.

Bradley, R. T. *Charisma and Social Power: A Study of Love and Power, Wholeness and Transformation.* New York: Paragon, 1987.

Bray, D. W.; R. J. Campbell; and D. L. Grant. *Formative Years in Business: A Long-term AT&T Study of Managerial Lives.* New York: Wiley-Interscience, 1974.

Bray, D. W., and A. Howard. "The AT&T Longitudinal Study of Managers." In *Longitudinal Studies of Adult Psychological Development.* Ed. K. W. Schaiel. New York: Guilford, 1983.

Brenner, O. C.; J. Tomkiewicz; and V. E. Schein. "The Relationship between Sex Role Stereotypes and Requisite Management Characteristics Revisited." *Academy of Management Journal* 32 (1989), pp. 662–69.

Brett, J. F., and L. E. Atwater. "360° Feedback: Accuracy, Reactions, and Perceptions of Usefulness." *Journal of Applied Psychology,* 86 (5) (2001), pp. 930–42.

Brett, J. M., and L. K. Stroh. "Working 61 Plus Hours a Week: Why Do Managers Do It?" *Journal of Applied Psychology,* 88 (1) (2003), pp. 67–78.

Bridges, W. *Managing Transitions: Making the Most of Change.* Reading, MA: Addison-Wesley, 1991.

Brinkmeyer, K. R., and R. T. Hogan. "An Exploration of the Structure of Individual Differences." In R. T. Hogan (chair), *Personality Applications in the Workplace: Thinking Outside the Dots.* Symposium presented at the 12th Annual Conference of the Society of Industrial and Organizational Psychology, St. Louis, MO, 1997.

Britt, T. W. "Black Hawk Down at Work." *Harvard Business Review,* January 2003, pp. 16–17.

Brockner, J., and L. Adsit. "The Moderating Impact of Sex on the Equity-Satisfaction Relationship." *Journal of Applied Psychology* 71 (1986), pp. 585–90.

Brody, N. *Intelligence.* San Diego: Academic Press, 1992.

———. "Intelligence, Schooling, and Society." *American Psychologist* 52, no. 10 (1997), pp. 1046–50.

Brown, A. D. "Narcissism, Identity, and Legitimacy." *Academy of Management Review* 22, no. 3 (1997), pp. 643–86.

Brown, L. D. *Managing Conflict at Organizational Interfaces.* Reading, MA: Addison-Wesley, 1983.

Brumback, G. "Institutionalizing Ethics in Government." *Public Personnel Management* 20, no. 3 (1991), pp. 353–64.

Brungardt, C. "Benchmarking Employee Attitudes." *Training and Development,* June 1992, pp. 49–53.

———. "The Making of Leaders: A Review of the Research in Leadership Development and Education." *Journal of Leadership Studies* 3, no. 3. (1996), pp. 81–95.

Buckingham, M., and C. Coffman. *First, Break All The Rules.* New York: Simon & Schuster, 1999.

Bugental, D. E. "A Study of Attempted and Successful Social Influence in Small Groups as a Function of Goal-Relevant Skills." *Dissertation Abstracts* 25 (1964), p. 660.

Bunker, K. A., and A. Webb. *Learning How to Learn from Experience: Impact of Stress and Coping.* Report No. 154. Greensboro, NC: Center for Creative Leadership, 1992.

Bunker, K. A., K. E. Kram, and S. Ting. "The Young and the Clueless." *Harvard Business Review,* December 2002, pp. 80–88.

Burke, M. J., and R. R. Day. " A Cumulative Study of the Effectiveness of Managerial Training." *Journal of Applied Psychology* 71 (1986), pp. 242–45.

Burns, J. M. *Leadership.* New York: Harper & Row, 1978.

Burns, T., and G. M. Stalker. *The Management of Innovation.* London: Tavistock, 1961.

Butorac, T. "Recruitment and Retention: The Keys to Profitability at Carlson Companies." Presentation given at Personnel Decisions International, Minneapolis, MN, June 11, 2001.

Byham, B. C., A. B. Smith, and M. J. Pease. *Grow Your Own Leaders: How to Identify, Develop, and Retain Leadership Talent.* New York: Financial Times/Prentice Hall, 2002.

Calder, B. J., and B. M. Staw. "Self-Perception of Intrinsic and Extrinsic Motivation." *Journal of Personality and Social Psychology* 31 (1975), pp. 599–605.

Caldwell, D. F., and J. M. Burger. "Personality Characteristics of Job Applicants and Success in Screening Interviews." *Personnel Psychology* 51, no. 1 (1998), pp. 119–36.

Caliguiri, P. M. "The Big Five Personality Characteristics as Predictors of Expatriot's Desire to Terminate the Assignment and Supervisor-Rated Performance." *Personnel Psychology* 53, no. 1 (2000), pp. 67–88.

Campbell, D. P. *Campbell Leadership Index Manual.* Minneapolis, MN: National Computer Systems, 1991.

Campbell, D. P.; G. J. Curphy; and T. Tuggle. *360 Degree Feedback Instruments: Beyond Theory.* Workshop presented at the Tenth Annual Conference of the Society for Industrial and Organizational Psychology. Orlando, FL, May 1995.

Campbell, D. P., and S. Hyne. *Manual for the Revised Campbell Organizational Survey.* Minneapolis, MN: National Computer Systems, 1995.

Campbell, D. P.; S. Hyne; and D. L. Nilsen. *Campbell Interests and Skill Survey Manual.* Minneapolis, MN: National Computer Systems, 1992.

Campbell, J. P. "The Cutting Edge of Leadership: An Overview." In *Leadership: The Cutting Edge.* Ed. J. G. Hunt and L. L. Larson. Carbondale: Southern Illinois University Press, 1977.

———. "Training Design for Performance Improvement." In *Productivity in Organizations: New Perspectives from Industrial and Organizational Psychology.* Ed. J. P. Campbell; R. J. Campbell; and associates. San Francisco: Jossey-Bass, 1988, pp. 177–216.

Campbell, J. P.; R. A. McCloy; S. H. Oppler; and C. E. Sager. "A Theory of Performance." In *Frontiers in Industrial/Organizational Psychology and Personnel Selection.* Ed. N. Schmitt and W. C. Borman. San Francisco: Jossey-Bass, 1993, pp. 35–70.

Campbell, J. P., and R. D. Pritchard. "Motivation Theory in Industrial and Organizational Psychology." In *Handbook for Industrial and Organizational Psychology.* Ed. M. D. Dunnette. Chicago: Rand McNally, 1976, pp. 60–130.

Carr, J. Z.; A. M. Schmidt; J. K. Ford; and R. P. DeShon. "Climate Perceptions Matter: A Meta-Analytic Path Analysis Relating Molar Climate, Cognitive and Affective States, and Individual Level Work Outcomes." *Journal of Applied Psychology,* 89 (4) (2004), pp. 605–19.

Caruso, D. R.; J. D. Mayer; and P. Salovey. "Emotional Intelligence and Emotional Leadership." In *Multiple Intelligences and Leadership.* R. E. Riggio, S. E. Murphy, and F. J. Pirozzolo (Eds.). Mahwah, NJ: Lawrence Erlbaum Associates, 2002, pp. 55–74.

Cascio, W. F. *A Guide to Responsible Restructuring.* Washington, DC: U.S. Government Printing Office, 1995.

Case, T.; L. Dosier; G. Murkison; and B. Keys. "How Managers Influence Superiors: A Study of Upward Influence Tactics." *Leadership and Organization Development Journal* 9, no. 4 (1988), pp. 4, 25–31.

Cashman, K., and J. Forem. *Awakening the Leader Within.* Hoboken, NJ: John Wiley & Sons, 2003.

Chandler, A. D. *Scale and Scope: The Dynamics of Industrial Capitalism.* Cambridge: Harvard University Press, 1990.

Charan, R. *What the CEO Wants You to Know.* New York: Random House. 2001.

Charan, R., and G. Colvin. "Why CEOs Fail." *Fortune,* June 21, 1999, pp. 69–82.

Charan, R.; S. Drotter; and J. Noel. *The Leadership Pipeline: How to Build the Leadership-Powered Company.* San Francisco: Jossey-Bass, 2001.

Chemers, M. M. "The Social, Organizational, and Cultural Contest of Effective Leadership." In *Leadership: Multidisciplinary Perspectives.* Ed. B. Kellerman. Englewood Cliffs, NJ: Prentice Hall, 1984.

Chen, X. P.; C. Hui; and D. J. Sego. "The Role of Organizational Citizenship Behavior in Turnover: Conceptualization and Preliminary Tests of Key Hypotheses." *Journal of Applied Psychology* 83, no. 6 (1998), pp. 922–31.

Chinoy, E. *Society.* New York: Random House, 1961.

Chitayat, G., and I. Venezia. "Determinates of Management Styles in Business and Nonbusiness Organizations." *Journal of Applied Psychology* 69 (1984), pp. 437–47.

Choi, Y., and R. R. Mai-Dalton. "The Model of Followers' Responses to Self-Sacrificial Leadership: An Empirical Test." *Leadership Quarterly* 10, no. 3 (1999), pp. 397–422.

Chueng, G. W. "Multifaceted Conceptions of Self-Other Ratings Disagreement." *Personnel Psychology* 52, no. 1 (1999), pp. 1–36.

Church, A. H. "Do Higher Performing Managers Actually Receive Better Ratings?" *Consulting Psychology Journal* 52, no. 2 (2000), pp. 99–116.

———. "From Both Sides Now: The Utility of Individual Personality Theory in I/O Psychology." *Industrial-Organizational Psychologist* 31, no. 3 (1994), pp. 108–16.

———. "Managerial Self-Awareness in High-Performing Individuals in Organizations." *Journal of Applied Psychology* 82, no. 2 (1997) pp. 281–92.

Church, A. H., and J. Waclawski. "A Five-Phase Framework for Designing a Successful Multisource Feedback System." *Consulting Psychology Journal* 53, no. 2 (2001), pp. 82–95.

Cialdini, R. B. *Influence.* New York: William Morrow, 1984.

Clark, B. R. "The Organizational Saga in Higher Education." *Administrative Science Quarterly* 17 (1972), pp. 178–84.

Clover, W. H. "Transformational Leaders: Team Performance Leadership Ratings and Firsthand Impressions." In *Measures of Leadership.* Ed. K. E. Clark and M. B. Clark. West Orange, NJ: Leadership Library of America, 1990.

———. "At TRW, Executive Training Contributes to Quality." *Human Resources Professional,* Winter 1991, pp. 16–20.

Clutterbuck, D. "How Much Does Success Depend upon a Helping Hand from Above?" *International Management* 37 (1982), pp. 17–19.

Cohen, A. R., and D. L. Bradford. *Influence without Authority.* New York: John Wiley, 1990.

Collins, J. *Good to Great.* New York: HarperCollins. 2001.

Collins, J. C., and J. I. Porras. *Built to Last: Successful Habits of Visionary Companies.* Reading, MA: Perseus Books, 1997.

Colquitt, J. A. "On the Dimensionality of Organizational Justice: A Construct Validation of a Measure." *Journal of Applied Psychology* 86, no. 2 (2001), pp. 386–400.

Colquitt, J. A.; D. E. Conlon; M. J. Wesson; C. O. L. H. Porter; and K. Y. Ng. "Justice at the Millennium: A Meta-Analytic Review of 25 Years of Organizational Justice Research." *Journal of Applied Psychology* 86, no. 2 (2001), pp. 425–45.

Conference Board. "Global Management Teams: A Perspective." *HR Executive Review* 4 (1996).

Conger, J. "Can We Really Train Leadership?" *Strategy, Management, Competition,* Winter 1996, pp. 52–65.

Conger, J. A. "Charismatic and Transformational Leadership in Organizations: An Insider's Perspective on These Developing Streams of Research." *Leadership Quarterly* 10, no. 2 (1999), pp. 145–80.

Conger, J. A. *The Charismatic Leader.* San Francisco: Jossey-Bass, 1989.

Conger, J. A. "Qualitative Research as the Cornerstone Methodology for Understanding Leadership. *Leadership Quarterly* 9, no. 1 (1998), pp. 107–22.

Conger, J. A., and J. G. Hunt. "Charismatic and Transformational Leadership: Taking Stock of the Present and Future." *Leadership Quarterly* 10, no. 2 (1999), pp. 121–28.

Conger, J. A., and R. M. Fulmer. "Developing Your Leadership Pipeline." *Harvard Business Review,* December 2003, pp. 76–85.

Conger, J. A., and R. N. Kanungo. *Charismatic Leadership in Organizations.* Thousand Oaks, CA: Sage, 1998.

Conlin, M. "The New Gender Gap. From Kindergarten to Grad School, Boys Are Becoming the Second Sex." *Business Week,* May 26, 2003.

Connelly, M. S.; J. A. Gilbert; S. J. Zaccaro; K. V. Threlfell; M. A. Marks; and M. D. Mumford. "Exploring the Relationship of Leadership Skills and Knowledge to Leader Performance." *The Leadership Quality,* 11(1), 2000, pp. 65–80.

Connolly, J. J., and C. Viswesvaran. *Affectivity and Job Satisfaction: A Meta-Analysis.* Presentation given at the 13th Annual Conference of the Society of Industrial and Organizational Psychology, Dallas, TX, April 1998.

Cornwell, J. M. "A Meta-Analysis of Selected Trait Research in the Leadership Literature." Paper presented at the Southeastern Psychological Association, Atlanta, GA, 1983.

Costa, P. T. Jr., and R. R. McCrae. *Revised NEO-PI Personality Inventory (NEO-PI-R) and NEO Five Factor Inventory (NEO-FFI) Professional Manual.* Odessa, FL: Psychological Assessment Resources, 1992.

Costa, P. T. Jr., and R. R. McCrae. "Domains and Facets: Hierarchical Personality Assessment Using the Revised NEO Personality Inventory." *Journal of Personality Assessment,* 64 (1995), pp. 21–50.

Couch, A., and P. W. Yetton. "Manager Behavior, Leadership Style, and Subordinate Performance: An Empirical Extension of the Broom-Yetton Conflict Rule." *Organizational Behavior and Human Decision Processes* 39 (1987), pp. 384–96.

Cousteau, V. "How to Swim with Sharks: A Primer." *Perspectives in Biology and Medicine,* Summer 1973, pp. 525–28.

Coye, R. W. "Subordinate Responses to Ineffective Leadership." *Dissertation Abstracts International* 43, 6A (1982), p. 2070.

Cronbach, L. J. *Essentials of Psychological Testing.* 4th ed. San Francisco: Harper & Row, 1984.

Cropanzano, R., D. E. Rupp, and Z. S. Byrne. "The Relationship of Emotional Exhaustion to Work Attitudes, Job Performance, and Organizational Citizenship Behaviors." *Journal of Applied Psychology,* 88 (1) (2003), pp. 160–69.

Csikszentmihalyi, M. *Flow: The Psychology of Optimal Experience.* New York: Harper & Row, 1990.

Cudney, M. R., and R. E. Hardy. *Self-Defeating Behaviors.* San Francisco: HarperCollins, 1993.

Cummings, R. C. "Job Stress and the Buffering Effect of Supervisory Support." *Group and Organizational Studies* 15, no. 1 (1990), pp. 92–104.

Cummings, W. H. "Age Group Differences and Estimated Frequencies of the MBTI Types: Proposed Changes." *Proceedings of the Psychology in the Department of Defense Thirteenth Symposium.* Colorado Springs, CO: U. S. Air Force Academy, April 1992.

Curphy, G. J. *The Blandin Education Leadership Program.* Grand Rapids, MN: The Blandin Foundation, 2004f.

Curphy, G. J. The *Blandin Health Care Leadership Program.* Grand Rapids, MN: The Blandin Foundation, 2004g.

Curphy, G. J. "The Consequences of Managerial Incompetence." Presentation given at the 3rd Hogan Assessment Systems International Users Conference, Prague, The Czech Republic, September 2004h.

Curphy, G. J. "A Commentary on Moral Character Screening." In W. Sellman (chair), *Moral Character Screening: Sorting Good and Bad Apples.* Symposium presented at the 105th Annual Meeting of the American Psychological Association, Chicago, 1997d.

Curphy, G. J. "Early Leadership Talent Identification and Development." Paper presented at the Conference for Executives of Saudi Aramco, Dhahran, Saudi Arabia, October 2001.

Curphy, G. J. "Concluding Remarks on Executive Assessment and Development." In *The Role of I/O Psychology in Executive Assessment and Development,* G. J. Curphy (chair). Symposium presented at the 15th Annual Conference of the Society for Industrial and Organizational Psychology, New Orleans, LA, 2000.

Curphy, G. J. "A Roadmap for Creating High Performing Teams." Presentation given at the Strategic Staff Meeting of the Mid-Atlantic Division of the Home Depot, Atlantic City, NJ, September 2000.

———. "The Effects of Transformational and Transactional Leadership on Organizational Climate, Attrition, and Performance." In *Impact of Leadership.* Ed. K. E. Clark, M. B. Clark, and D. P. Campbell. Greensboro, NC: Center for Creative Leadership, 1992a.

———. "An empirical investigation of Bass' (1985) theory of transformational and transactional leadership." Ph.D. dissertation, University of Minnesota, 1991a.

———. "Executive Integrity and 360-Degree Feedback." In R. T. Hogan (chair), *Assessing Executive Failure: The Underside of Performance.* Symposium presented at the 18th Annual Conference of the Society of Industrial and Organizational Psychology, Orlando, FL, 2003.

———. *Hogan Assessment Systems Certification Workshop Training Manuals.* Tulsa, OK: Hogan Assessment Systems, 2003c.

———. "In-Depth Assessments, 360-Degree Feedback, and Development: Key Research Results and Recommended Next Steps." Presentation at the Annual Conference for HR Managers at U S WEST Communications, Denver, CO, January 1998a.

———. "Leadership Transitions and Succession Planning." In J. Lock (chair), *Developing and Implementing Succession Planning Programs.* Symposium conducted at the 19th Annual Conference for the Society of Industrial and Organizational Psychology, Chicago, April, 2004e.

———. "Leadership Transitions and Teams." Presentation given at the Hogan Assessment Systems International Users Conference, Istanbul, September 2003b.

———. "New Directions in Personality." In R. T. Hogan (chair), *Personality and Organizational Behavior.* Symposium presented at the 104th Annual Meeting of the American Psychological Association, Toronto, Canada, 1996b.

———. "Personality and Work: Some Food for Thought." In R. T. Hogan (chair), *Personality Applications in the Workplace: Thinking outside the Dots.* Symposium presented at the 12th Annual Conference of the Society of Industrial and Organizational Psychology, St. Louis, MO, 1997c.

———. "Personality, Intelligence, and Leadership." Presentation given to the Pioneer Leadership Program at Denver University, Denver, CO, 1997a.

———. "Some Closing Remarks about the Use of Self- and Other-Ratings of Personality and Behaviors." In *Multirater Assessment Systems: What We've Learned.* M. D. Dunnette, chair. Symposium conducted at the 99th American Psychological Association Convention, San Francisco, August 1991b.

———. The Team Assessment Survey. Minneapolis, MN. Personnel Decisions International, 1999.

———. *Users Guide and Interpretive Report for the Leadership Personality Survey.* Minneapolis, MN: Personnel Decisions International, 1998b.

———. "What Role Should I/O Psychologists Play in Executive Education?" Presentation given in R. T. Hogan (chair), *Models of Executive Education* at the 17th Annual Society for Industrial and Organizational Psychology, Toronto, Canada, April 2002.

———. "What We Really Know about Leadership." Presentation Given at the Hogan Assessment Systems International Users Conference, Istanbul, Turkey, September 2003b.

———. "What We Really Know about Leadership (But Seem Unwilling to Implement)." Presentation given at the Minnesota Professionals for Psychology and Applied Work, Minneapolis, MN, January, 2004a.

Curphy, G. J., F. W. Gibson; B. Asiu; J. Horn; and G. Macomber. *The Attaché & Selection Project.* Technical Report No. 94-2. Colorado Springs, CO: U.S. Air Force Academy, 1994.

Curphy, G. J.; F. W. Gibson; B. W. Asiu; C. P. McCown; and C. Brown. "A Field Study of the Causal Relationships between Organizational Performance, Punishment, and Justice," working paper, 1992.

Curphy, G. J.; F. W. Gibson; G. Macomber; C. J. Calhoun; L. A. Wilbanks; and M. J. Burger. "Situational Factors Affecting Peer Reporting Intentions at the United States Air Force Academy: A Scenario-Based Investigation." *Military Psychology,* 10 no. 1 (1998), pp. 27–43.

Curphy, G. J., and R. T. Hogan. "Managerial Incompetence: Is There a Dead Skunk on the Table?" working paper, 2004a.

———. "What We Really Know about Leadership (But Seem Unwilling to Implement)." Working paper, 2004b.

Curphy, G. J., and K. D. Osten. *Technical Manual for the Leadership Development Survey.* Technical Report No. 93-14. Colorado Springs, CO: U.S. Air Force Academy, 1993.

Curtis, B.; R. E. Smith; and F. L. Smoll. "Scrutinizing the Skipper: A Study of Behaviors in the Dugout." *Journal of Applied Psychology* 64 (1979), pp. 391–400.

Dalton, M. A. "Using 360-Degree Feedback Successfully." *Leadership in Action* 18, no. 1 (1998), pp. 2–11.

Davidson, O. B., and D. Eden. "Remedial Self-Fulfilling Prophecy: Two Field Experiments to Prevent Golem Effects among Disadvantaged Women." *Journal of Applied Psychology* 83, no. 3 (2000), pp. 386–98.

Davis, B. L.; L. W. Hellervik; and J. L. Sheard. *The Successful Manager's Handbook.* 3rd ed. Minneapolis, MN: Personnel Decisions, 1989.

Davis, B. L.; C. J. Skube; L. W. Hellervik; S. H. Gelelein; and J. L. Sheard. *The Successful Manager's Handbook.* Minneapolis, MN: Personnel Decisions, 1992.

Davis, R. C. *The Fundamentals of Top Management.* New York: Harper, 1942.

Deary, J. J. "A (Latent) Big-Five Personality Model in 1915? A Reanalysis of Webb's Data." *Journal of Applied Psychology* 71, no. 5 (1996), pp. 992–1005.

Deci, E. L. "Effects of Contingent and Noncontingent Rewards and Controls on Intrinsic Motivation." *Organizational Behavior and Human Performance* 22 (1972), pp. 113–20.

———. *Intrinsic Motivation.* New York: Plenum, 1975.

Deep, S., and L. Sussman. *Smart Moves.* Reading MA: Addison-Wesley, 1990.

De Janasz, S. C.; S. E. Sullivan, and V. Whiting. "Mentor Networks and Career Success: Lessons for Turbulent Times." *Academy of Management Executive,* 17 (3) (2003), pp. 78–88.

Delbecq, A. L.; A. H. Van de Ven; and D. H. Gustafson. *Group Techniques for Program Planning: A Guide to Nominal and Delphi Processes.* Glenview, IL: Scott, Foresman, 1975.

Deluga, R. J. "American Presidential Proactivity, Charismatic Leadership and Rated Performance." *Leadership Quarterly* 9, no. 2 (1998), 265–92.

Den Hartog, D. N., and R. M. Verburg. Charisma and Rhetoric: Communicative Techniques of International Business Leaders." *Leadership Quarterly* 8, no. 4 (1997), pp. 355–92.

Den Hartog, D. N.; R. J. House; P. J. Hanges; S. A. Ruiz-Quintanilla; P. W. Dorfman; and Associates. "Culture Specific and Cross-Culturally Generalizable Implicit Leadership Theories: Are Attributes of Charismatic/Transformational Leadership Universally Endorsed?" *Leadership Quarterly* 10, no. 2 (1999), pp. 219–56.

DeNisi, A. S., and A. N. Kluger. "Feedback Effectiveness: Can 360-Degree Appraisals Be Improved?" *Academy of Management Executive* 14, no. 1 (2000), pp. 129–39.

Deveraux, G. "Charismatic Leadership and Crisis." In *Psychoanalysis and the Social Sciences*. Ed. W. Muensterberger and S. Axelrod. New York: International University Press, 1955.

Dewhirst, H. D.; V. Metts; and R. T. Ladd. "Exploring the Delegation Decision: Managerial Responses to Multiple Contingencies." Paper presented at the Academy of Management Convention, New Orleans, LA, 1987.

De Zarate, R. O. "Women World Leaders: 1945–2003." (2003) retrieved from http://www.terra.es/personal2/monolith/00women.htm.

Dickson, M. W.; D. B. Smith; M. W. Grojean; and M. G. Ehrhart. "An Organizational Climate regarding Ethics: The Outcome of Leader Values and the Practices That Reflect Them." *Leadership Quarterly* 12, no. 2 (2001), pp. 197–218.

Diedrich, R. C. "Lessons Learned in—and Guidelines for—Coaching Executive Teams." *Consulting Psychology Journal*, 53 (4) (2001), pp. 238–39.

Dingfelder, S. F. "Creativity on the Clock." *Monitor on Psychology*, November 2003, p. 58.

Dobbins, G. H., and J. M. Russell. "The Biasing Effects of Subordinate Likeableness on Leaders' Responses to Poor Performance." *Personnel Psychology* 39 (1986), pp. 759–77.

Donno, D. "Introduction." In *The Prince and Selected Discourses: Machiavelli*. Ed. and trans., D. Dunno. New York: Bantam, 1966.

Dosier, L.; T. Case; and B. Keys. "How Managers Influence Subordinates: An Empirical Study of Downward Influence Tactics." *Leadership and Organization Development Journal* 9, no. 5 (1988), pp. 22–31.

Dotlich, D. L., and P. E. Cairo. *Why CEOs Fail: The 11 Behaviors That Can Derail Your Climb to the Top and How to Manage Them*. New York: Wiley, 2001.

Dow, T. E. "The Theory of Charisma." *Sociological Quarterly* 10 (1969), pp. 306–18.

Downton, J. V. *Rebel Leadership: Commitment and Charisma in the Revolutionary Process*. New York: Free Press, 1973.

Druskat, V. U. "Gender and Leadership Style: Transformational and Transactional Leadership in the Roman Catholic Church." *Leadership Quarterly* 5, no. 1 (1994), pp. 99–120.

Druskat, V. U., and S. B. Wolff. "Building the Emotional Intelligence of Groups." *Harvard Business Review*, March 2001, pp. 80–91.

Dubois, P. H. "A Test Dominated Society: China 1115 BC–1905." In *Testing Problems in Perspective*. Ed. A. Anastasi. American Council on Education, 1964.

Duchon, D.; S. G. Green; and T. D. Taber. "Vertical Dyad Linkage: A Longitudinal Assessment of Antecedents, Measures, and Consequences." *Journal of Applied Psychology* 71 (1986), pp. 56–60.

Dukerich, J. M.; M. L. Nichols; D. R. Elm; and D. A. Vollrath. "Moral Reasoning in Groups: Leaders Make a Difference," *Human Relations* 43 (1990), pp. 473–93.

Dumaine, B. "Creating a New Company Culture." *Fortune*, 1990, pp. 127–131.

Duncker, K. "On Problem Solving." *Psychological Monographs* 58, no. 5, 1945.

Dvir, T.; D. Eden; B. J. Avolio; and B. Shamir. "Impact of Transformational Leadership Training on Follower Development and Performance: A Field Experiment." Paper presented at 14th Annual Conference of the Society for Industrial and Organizational Psychology, Atlanta, GA, 1999.

Dvir, T.; D. Eden; B. J. Avolio; and B. Shamir. "Impact of Transformational Leadership on Follower Development and Performance: A Field Experiment." *Academy of Management Journal*, 45 (4) (2002), pp. 735–44.

Eagly, A. H. *Sex Differences in Social Behavior: A Social Role Interpretation*. Hillsdale, NJ: Erlbaum. 1987.

Eagly, A. H., and Carli, L. L. "The Female Leadership Advantage: An Evaluation of the Evidence." *The Leadership Quarterly* 14 (2003), 807–834.

Eddleston, K. A.; D. L. Kidder; and B. E. Litzky. "Who's the Boss? Contending with Competing Expectations from Customers and Management." *Academy of Management Executive*, 16 (4) (2002), pp. 85–94.

Eden, D., and A. B. Shani. "Pygmalion Goes to Boot Camp: Expectancy, Leadership, and Trainee Performance." *Journal of Applied Psychology* 67 (1982), pp. 194–99.

Eden, D.; D. Geller; A. Gewirtz; R. Gordon-Terner; I. Inbar; M. Liberman; Y. Pass; I. Salomon-Segev; and M. Shalit. "Implanting Pygmalion Leadership Style through Workshop Training: Seven Field Experiments." *Leadership Quarterly* 11, no. 2 (2000), pp. 171–210.

Edmondson, A. C., and S. E. Cha. "When Company Values Backfire." *Harvard Business Review,* November 2002, pp. 18–19.

Edwards, M. R., and A. J. Ewen. *360 Degree Feedback: The Powerful New Model for Employee Assessment and Performance Improvement.* New York. American Management Association, 1996.

Ehrhart, M. G., and K. J. Klein. "Predicting Followers' Preferences for Charismatic Leadership: The Influence of Followers Values and Personality." *Leadership Quarterly* 12, no. 2 (2001), pp. 153–80.

Ehrlichman, J. *Witness to Power.* New York: Simon & Schuster, 1982.

Eisenberger, R., and J. Cameron. "Detrimental Effects of Reward: Reality or Myth?" *American Psychologist* 51, no. 11 (1996), pp. 1153–66.

Eisenberger, R.; F. Stinglhamber; C. Vandenberghe; I. L. Sucharski; and L. Rhoades. "Perceived Supervisor Support: Contributions to Perceived Organizational Support and Employee Retention." *Journal of Applied Psychology,* 87 (3) (2002), pp. 565–73.

Ellis, A., and R. Harper. *A New Guide to Rational Living.* Englewood Cliffs, NJ: Prentice Hall, 1975.

Elovainio, M.; M. Kivimaki; and K. Helkama. "Organizational Justice Evaluations, Job Control, and Occupational Strain." *Journal of Applied Psychology* 86, no. 2 (2001), pp. 418–24.

Emery, F. E., and E. L. Trist. "The Causal Texture of Organizational Environments." *Human Relations* 18 (1965), pp. 21–32.

England, G. W., and R. Lee. "The Relationship between Managerial Values and Managerial Success in the United States, Japan, India, and Australia." *Journal of Applied Psychology* 59 (1974), 411–19.

Erez, M.; P. C. Earley; and C. L. Hulin. "The Impact of Participation on Goal Acceptance and Performance: A Two-Step Model." *Academy of Management Journal* (1985), pp. 359–72.

Etzioni, A. *A Comparative Analysis of Complex Organizations.* New York: Free Press, 1961.

Evans, M. G. "The Effects of Supervisory Behavior on the Path-Goal Relationship." *Organizational Behavior and Human Performance* 5 (1970), pp. 277–98.

Fairholm, G. W. *Values Leadership.* Praeger: New York, 1991.

Fairhurst, G. T., and R. A. Sarr. *The Art of Framing: Managing the Language of Leadership.* San Francisco, CA: Jossey-Bass, 1996.

Farmer, S. M.; P. Tierney; and K. Kung-McIntyre. "Employee Creativity in Taiwan: An Application of Role Identity Theory." *Academy of Management Journal,* 46 (5) (2003), pp. 618–30.

Farris, G. F. "Colleagues' Roles and Innovation in Scientific Teams." Working paper No. 552-71. Cambridge, MA: Alfred P. Sloan School of Management, MIT., 1971.

Farson, R., and R. Keyes. "The Failure-Tolerant Leader." *Harvard Business Review,* August 2002, pp. 64–75.

Feldman, D. C. "The Development and Enforcement of Group Norms," *Academy of Management Review,* January 1984, pp. 47–53.

Ferlise, W. G. "Violence in the Workplace." *Labor and Employment Newsletter,* Washington, DC: Semmes, Bowen, & Semmes, Winter 1995.

Ferris, G. R.; L. A. Witt; and W. A. Hochwarter. "Interaction of Social Skill and General Mental Ability on Job Performance and Salary." *Journal of Applied Psychology,* 86 (6) (2001), pp. 1075–82.

Fiechtner, B., and J. J. Krayer, "Variations in Dogmatism and Leader-Supplied Information: Determinants of Perceived Behavior in Task-Oriented Groups." *Group and Organizational Studies* 11 (1986), 403–18.

Fiedler, F. E. "Cognitive Resources and Leadership Performance." *Applied Psychology: An International Review* 44, no. 1 (1995), pp. 5–28.

———. "The Contingency Model and the Dynamics of the Leadership Process." In *Advances in Experimental Social Psychology.* Ed. L. Berkowitz. New York: Academic Press, 1978.

———. "The Curious Role of Cognitive Resources in Leadership." In R. E. Riggio, S. E. Murphy, and F. J. Pirozzolo (Eds.). *Multiple Intelligences and Leadership.* Mahwah, NJ: Lawrence Erlbaum Associates, 2002, pp. 91–104.

———. "The Effect and Meaning of Leadership Experience: A Review of Research and a Preliminary Model." In *Impact of Leadership.* Ed. K. E. Clark, M. B. Clark, and D. P. Campbell. Greensboro, NC: Center for Creative Leadership, 1992.

———. "Reflections by an Accidental Theorist." *Leadership Quarterly* 6, no. 4 (1995), pp. 453–61.

———. *A Theory of Leadership Effectiveness.* New York: McGraw-Hill, 1967.

Fiedler, F. E., and M. M. Chemers. *Improving Leadership Effectiveness: The Leader Match Concept,* 2nd ed. New York: John Wiley, 1982.

Fiedler, F. E., and J. E. Garcia. *New Approaches to Leadership: Cognitive Resources and Organizational Performance.* New York: John Wiley, 1987.

Field, R. H. G. "A Test of the Vroom-Yetton Normative Model of Leadership." *Journal of Applied Psychology* 67 (1982), pp. 523–32.

Filley, A. C., and L. A. Pace. "Making Judgments Descriptive." In *The 1976 Annual Handbook for Group Facilitators.* Ed. J. E. Jones and J. W. Pfeiffer. La Jolla, CA: University Associates Press, 1976.

Fisher, C. D., and R. Gitleson. "A Meta-Analysis of the Correlates of Role Conflict and Ambiguity." *Journal of Applied Psychology* 68 (1983), pp. 320–33.

Fisher, R., and W. Ury. *Getting to Yes.* Boston: Houghton Mifflin, 1981.

Flanagan, J. C. "Defining the Requirements of the Executive's Job." *Personnel* 28, no. 1 (1951), pp. 28–35.

Fleenor, J. W.; C. D. McCauley; and S. Brutus. "Self-Other Rating Agreement and Leader Effectiveness." *Leadership Quarterly* 7, no. 4 (1996), pp. 487–506.

Fleishman, E. A. *Examiner's Manual for the Leadership Opinion Questionnaire.* Rev. ed. Chicago: Science Research Associates, 1989.

———. *Examiner's Manual for the Supervisory Behavior Description Questionnaire.* Washington, DC: Management Research Institute, 1972.

———. "Twenty Years of Consideration and Structure." In *Current Developments in the Study of Leadership.* Ed. E. A. Fleishman and J. G. Hunt. Carbondale: Southern Illinois University Press, 1973.

Florida, R.; R. Cushing; and G. Gates. "When Social Capital Stifles Innovation." *Harvard Business Review,* August 2002, p. 20.

Fodor, E. "Motive Pattern as an Influence on Leadership in Small Groups." Paper presented at the meeting of the American Psychological Association, New York, August 1987.

Foley, E., and A. LeFevre. *Understanding Generation X.* Zagnoli McEvoy Foley LLC. www.zmf.com. (2001).

Ford, J. D. "Department Context and Formal Structure as Constraints on Leader Behavior." *Academy of Management Journal* 24 (1981), pp. 274–88.

Fox, S., and Y. Amichai-Hamburger. "The Power of Emotional Appeals in Promoting Organizational Change Programs." *The Academy of Management Executive,* 15 (4) (2001), pp. 84–94.

French, J., and B. H. Raven. "The Bases of Social Power." In *Studies of Social Power.* ed. D. Cartwright. Ann Arbor, MI: Institute for Social Research, 1959.

Frese, M.; S. Beimel; and S. Schoenborn. "Action Training for Charismatic Leadership: Two Evaluations of Studies of a Commercial Training Module on Inspirational Communication of a Vision." *Personnel Psychology,* 56 (3) (2003), pp. 671–97.

Friedland, W. H. "For a Sociological Concept of Charisma." *Social Forces,* no. 1 (1964), pp. 18–26.

Friedman, M., and D. Ulmer. *Treating Type A Behavior—and Your Heart.* New York: Knopf, 1984.

Frisch, M. H. "The Emerging Role of the Internal Coach." *Consulting Psychology Journal,* 53 (4) (2001), pp. 240–50.

Fry, L.; W. Kerr; and C. Lee. "Effects of Different Leader Behaviors under Different Levels of Task Interdependence." *Human Relations* 39 (1986), pp. 1067–82.

Fryer, B. "Tom Seibel of Seibel Systems: High-Tech the Old-Fashioned Way." *Harvard Business Review,* March 2001, pp. 118–30.

Gabarro, J. J., and J. P. Kotter. "Managing Your Boss." *Harvard Business Review* 58, no. 1 (1980), pp. 92–100.

Galbraith, J. *Designing Complex Organizations.* Menlo Park, CA: Addison-Wesley, 1973.

Ganzach, Y. "Intelligence and Job-Satisfaction." *Academy of Management Journal,* 41(5), pp. 526–39.

Ganzach, Y.; A. N. Kluger; and N. Klayman. "Making Decisions from an Interview: Expert Measurement and Mechanical Combination. *Personnel Psychology* 53 no. 1 (2000), pp. 1–20.

Gardner, H. *Frames of Mind: The Theory of Multiple Intelligences.* New York: Basic Books, 1983.

Gardner, J. W. "The Antileadership Vaccine." Essay in the Carnegie Corporation of New York annual report, 1965.

———. *On Leadership.* New York: Free Press, 1990.

———. The Tasks of Leadership. Leadership paper No. 2. Washington, DC: Independent Sector, 1986.

Gardner, W. L., and B. J. Avolio. "The Charismatic Relationship: A Dramaturgical Perspective." *Academy of Management Review* 23, no. 1 (1998), pp. 32–58.

Garforth, F. I. De la P. "War Office Selection Boards." *Occupational Psychology* 19 (1945), pp. 97–108.

Gargiulo, T. F. *Making Stories: A Practical Guide for Organizational Leaders and Human Resource Specialists.* Westport, CT: Greenwood Publishing, 2001.

Gebelein, S. H. "Multi-rater Performance Appraisal: The Promise, the Pitfalls, and the Steps." Paper presented at the American Society of Training and Development Convention. Anaheim, CA, May 1994.

———. "360-Degree Feedback Goes Strategic." *PDI Portfolio,* Summer 1996, pp. 1–3.

Gelade, G. A., and M. Ivery. "The Impact of Human Resource Management and Work Climate on Organizational Performance." *Personnel Psychology,* 56 (2) (2003), pp. 383–404.

Gerth, H. H., and C. W. Mills. *Max Weber: Essays in Sociology.* New York: Oxford University Press, 1946.

Ghiselli, E. E. "Intelligence and Managerial Success." *Psychological Reports* 12 (1963), p. 89.

Ghorpade, J. "Managing Six Paradoxes of 360-Degree Feedback." *Academy of Management Executive* 14, no. 1 (2000), pp. 140–150.

Gibb, C. A. "Leadership." In *The Handbook of Social Psychology.* Ed. G. Lindzey and E. Aronson. Vol. 4. 2nd ed. Reading, MA: Addison-Wesley, 1968, pp. 205–82.

Gibb, J. R. "Defensive Communication." *Journal of Communication* 13, no. 3 (1961), pp. 141–48.

Gibbard, G. S.; J. J. Hartman; and R. D. Mann. *Analysis of Groups: Contribution to the Theory, Research, and Practice.* San Francisco: Jossey-Bass, 1974.

Gibble, J. L., and J. D. Lawrence. "Peer Coaching for Principals." *Educational Leadership* 45 (1987), pp. 72–73.

Gibson, F. W. "A Taxonomy of Leader Abilities and Their Influence on Group Performance as a Function of Interpersonal Stress." In *Impact of Leadership.* Ed. K. E. Clark, M. B. Clark, and D. P. Campbell. Greensboro, NC: Center for Creative Leadership, 1992.

Gibson, F. W., and G. J. Curphy. "The MBTI: Skewering A Sacred Cow." Presentation given to the Colorado Organizational Development Network, Denver, CO, 1996.

Ginnett, R. C. "Airline Cockpit Crew." In *Groups That Work (and Those That Don't).* Ed. J. Richard Hackman. San Francisco: Jossey-Bass, 1990.

———. "Cockpit Crew Effectiveness from the Inside Out: A Micro-Analysis Leading to Macro Considerations." *Proceedings of the Eleventh Psychology in the Department of Defense Symposium.* Colorado Springs, CO, 1988.

———. "Crews as Groups: Their Formation and Their Leadership." In *Cockpit Resource Management.* Ed. E. Wiener, B. Banki, and R. Helmreich. Orlando, FL: Academic Press, 1993.

———. "Effectiveness Begins Early: The Leadership Role in the Formation of Intra-Organizational Task Groups." (unpublished manuscript, 1992).

———. "The Formation Process of Airline Flight Crews." *Proceedings of the Fourth International Symposium on Aviation Psychology.* Columbus, OH, 1987.

———. "Team Effectiveness Leadership Model: Identifying Leverage Points for Change." *Proceedings of the 1996 National Leadership Institute Conference.* College Park, MD: National Leadership Institute, 1996.

———. "To the Wilderness and Beyond: The Application of a Model for Transformal Change." *Proceedings of the 9th Psychology in the Department of Defense Symposium.* Colorado Springs, CO, 1984.

Gilligan, C. *In a Different Voice.* Cambridge: Harvard University Press, 1982.

Goff, M. *Critical Leadership Skills Valued by Every Organization.* Minneapolis, MN: Personnel Decisions International, 2000.

Goleman, D. *Emotional Intelligence.* New York: Bantam Doubleday Dell, 1995.

———. *Working with Emotional Intelligence.* New York: Bantam Doubleday Dell, 1998.

———. *Working with Emotional Intelligence.* New York: Bantam Books. 1998.

Goleman, D.; R. Boyatzis; and A. McKee. "Primal Leadership: The Hidden Driver of Great Performance." *Harvard Business Review,* December, 2001, pp. 42–53.

Goleman, D.; R. Boyatzis; and A. McKee. *Primal Leadership: Realizing the Power of Emotional Intelligence.* Boston: Harvard Business School Press, 2002.

Goodstadt, B. E., and D. Kipnis. "Situational Influences on the Use of Power." *Journal of Applied Psychology* 54 (1970), pp. 201–7.

Gordon, L. V. *Measurement of Interpersonal Values.* Chicago: Science Research Associates, 1975.

Gordon, W. J. J. *Synectics*. New York: Harper & Row, 1961.

Gowing, M., and B. O'Leary. Demystifying Emotional Intelligence: Psychometric Answers and Practical Applications. Presentation given at the Personnel Testing Council of Metropolitan Washington D.C., Washington, DC., August 2003.

Graeff, C. L. "The Situational Judgement Theory: A Critical Review." *Academy of Management Journal* 8 (1983), pp. 285–96.

Graen, G. B., and J. F. Cashman. "A Role-Making Model of Leadership in Formal Organizations: A Developmental Approach." In *Leadership Frontiers*. Ed. J. G. Hunt and L. L. Larson. Kent, OH: Kent State University Press, 1975.

Grant, L. "Happy Workers, High Returns." *Fortune*, January 12, 1998, p. 81.

Green, S. G.; G. T. Fairhurst; and B. K. Snavely. "Chains of Poor Performance and Supervisory Control." *Organizational Behavior and Human Decision Processes* 38 (1986), pp. 7–27.

Green, S. G., and T. R. Mitchell. "Attributional Processes of Leaders in Leader-Member Interactions." *Organizational Behavior and Human Performances* 23 (1979), pp. 429–58.

Greguras, G. J., and C. Robie. "A New Look at Within-Source Interrater Reliability of 360-Degree Feedback Ratings." *Journal of Applied Psychology* 83, no. 6 (1998), pp. 960–68.

Greguras, G. J.; C. Robie; D. J. Schleicher; and M. Goff III. "A Field Study of the Effects of Rating Purpose on the Quality of Multisource Ratings." *Personnel Psychology*, 56 (1) (2003), pp. 1–22.

Greller, M. M. "Evaluation of Feedback Sources as a Function of Role and Organizational Development." *Journal of Applied Psychology* 65 (1980), pp. 24–27.

Grey, R. J. and G. G. Gordon. "Risk-Taking Managers: Who Gets the Top Jobs?" *Management Review* 67 (1978), pp. 8–13.

Griffin, R. W.; A. Welsh; and G. Moorehead. "Perceived Task Characteristics and Employee Performance: A Literature Review." *Academy of Management Review* 6 (1981), pp. 655–64.

Guilford, J. P. *The Nature of Human Intelligence*. New York: McGraw-Hill, 1967.

Guth, C. K., and S. S. Shaw. *How to Put on Dynamic Meetings*. Reston, VA: Reston, 1980.

Guzzo, R. A.; P. R. Yost; R. J. Campbell; and G. P. Shea. "Potency in Teams: Articulating a Construct." *British Journal of Social Psychology* 32 (1993), pp. 87–106.

Hackman, J. R. "Group Influences on Individuals." In *Handbook of Industrial and Organizational Psychology*. Ed. M. D. Dunnette. Chicago: Rand McNally, 1976.

———. "Group Level Issues in the Design and Training of Cockpit Crews." In *Proceedings of the NASA/MAC Workshop on Cockpit Resource Management*. Ed. H. H. Orlady and H. C. Foushee. Moffett Field, CA: NASA Ames Research Center, 1986.

———. *Groups That Work (and Those That Don't)*. San Francisco: Jossey-Bass, 1990.

Hackman, J. Richard. *Leading Teams—Setting the Stage for Great Performances*. 2002.

Hackman, J. R., and G. R. Oldham. "Motivation through the Design of Work: Test of a Theory." *Organizational Behavior and Human Performance* 16 (1976), pp. 250–79.

———. *Work Redesign*. Reading, MA: Addison-Wesley, 1980.

Hales, D., and R. E. Hales. "Is Work Driving You Mad?" *Parade Magazine*, March 18, 2001, pp. 8–9.

Hallam, G. L., and D. P. Campbell. "Selecting Team Members? Start with a Theory of Team Effectiveness." Paper presented at the Seventh Annual Meeting of the Society of Industrial/Organizational Psychologists, Montreal, Canada, May 1992.

Hallam, S. *Leadership Matters: Research about Leadership Is Important*. Akron, OH: University of Akron, 2001.

Halpin, A. W., and B. J. Winer. "A Factorial Study of the Leader Behavior Descriptions." In *Leader Behavior: Its Descriptions and Measurement*. Ed. R. M. Stogdill and A. E. Coons. Columbus: Ohio State University, Bureau of Business Research, 1957.

Hambrick, D. C. "Environment, Strategy and Power within Top Management Teams." *Administrative Science Quarterly* 26 (1981), pp. 253–75.

Hammer, T. H., and J. Turk. "Organizational Determinants of Leader Behavior and Authority." *Journal of Applied Psychology* 71 (1987), pp. 674–82.

Harrison, E. L. "Training Supervisors to Discipline Effectively." *Training and Development Journal* 36, no. 11 (1982), pp. 111–13.

Harter, J. K.; F. L. Schmidt; and T. L. Hayes. "Business-Unit-Level Relationship between Employee Satisfaction, Employee Engagement, and Business Outcomes: A Meta-Analysis." *Journal of Applied Psychology,* 87 (2) (2002), pp. 268–79.

Harvey, J. B. "The Abilene Paradox: The Management of Agreement." *Organizational Dynamics* 3 (1974), pp. 63–80.

Hazucha, J. F. *PDI Indicator: Competence, Potential, and Jeopardy. What Gets Managers Ahead May Not Keep Them out of Trouble.* Minneapolis, MN: Personnel Decisions, September 1992.

Hazucha, J. F.; S. A. Hezlett; and R. J. Schneider. "The Impact of 360-Degree Feedback on Management Skills Development." *Human Resource Management* 32 (1993), pp. 325–51.

Health, Education, and Welfare Task Force. *Work in America.* Cambridge, MA: MIT Press, 1973.

Heckman, R. J., and B. W. Roberts. "Personality Profiles of Effective Managers across Functions: A Person-Centered Approach." In R. T. Hogan (chair), *Personality Applications in the Workplace: Thinking outside the Dots.* Symposium presented at the 12th Annual Conference of the Society of Industrial and Organizational Psychology, St. Louis, MO, 1997.

———. "Some Determinants of Unethical Decision Behavior: An Experiment." *Journal of Applied Psychology* 63 (1978), pp. 451–57.

Hedlund, J.; G. B. Forsythe; J. A. Horvath; W. M. Williams; S. Snook; and R. J. Sternberg. "Identifying and Assessing Tacit Knowledge: Understanding the Practical Intelligence of Military Leaders." *The Leadership Quarterly,* 14 (2) (2003), pp. 117–40.

Heifetz, R. A., and D. L. Laurie. "The Work of Leadership." *Harvard Business Review,* December 2001, pp. 131–40.

Heifetz, R. A., and M. Linsky. "A Survival Guide for Leaders." *Harvard Business Review,* June 2002, pp. 65–75.

Heine, D. "Using I/O Psychology to Turn Around a Business." In *The Role of I/O Psychology in Executive Assessment and Development,* G. J. Curphy (chair). Symposium presented at the 15th Annual Conference of the Society for Industrial and Organizational Psychology, New Orleans, LA, 2000.

Hemphill, J. K. "The Leader and His Group." *Journal of Educational Research* 28 (1949), pp. 225–29, 245–46.

Hemphill, J. K., and A. E. Coons. "Development of the Leader Behavior Description Questionnaire." In *Leader Behavior: Its Description and Measurement.* Ed. R. M. Stogdill and A. E. Coons. Columbus: Ohio State University, Bureau of Business Research, 1957.

Hernez-Broome, G., and Hughes, R. L. "Leadership Development: Past, Present and Future." *Human Resource Planning,* 27 (1) (2004), 24–32.

Herrnstein, R. J., and C. Murray. *The Bell Curve: Intelligence and Class Structure in American Life.* New York: Free Press, 1994.

Hersey, P., and K. H. Blanchard. "Life Cycle Theory of Leadership." *Training and Development Journal* 23 (1969), pp. 26–34.

———. *Management of Organizational Behavior: Utilizing Human Resources.* 3rd ed. Englewood Cliffs, NJ: Prentice Hall, 1977.

———. *Management of Organizational Behavior: Utilizing Human Resources.* 4th ed. Englewood Cliffs, NJ: Prentice Hall, 1984.

Herzberg, F. "The Motivation-Hygiene Concept and Problems of Manpower." *Personnel Administrator* 27 (1964), pp. 3–7.

———. *Work and the Nature of Man.* Cleveland, OH: World Publishing, 1966.

———. "One More Time: How Do You Motivate Employees?" *Harvard Business Review,* January 2003, pp. 87–96.

Hewlett, S. A. "Executive Women and the Myth of Having it All." *Harvard Business Review,* April 2002, pp. 66–67.

Hezlett, S. A., and B. A. Koonce. "Now That I've Been Assessed, What Do I Do? Facilitating Development after Individual Assessments." Paper presented at the IPMA Assessment Council Conference on Public Personnel Assessment, New Orleans, LA, June 1995.

Highhouse, S. "Assessing the Candidate as a Whole: A Historical and Critical Analysis of Individual Psychological Assessment for Personnel Decision Making." *Personnel Psychology,* 55 (2) (2002), pp. 363–96.

Hill, C. W. "Leadership and Symbolic Authority in Psychoanalysis." In *Multidisciplinary Perspectives.* Ed. B. Kellerman. Englewood Cliffs, NJ: Prentice Hall, 1984.

Hill, N. "Self-Esteem: The Key to Effective Leadership." *Administrative Management* 40, no. 9, (1985), pp. 71–76.

Hinkin, T. R., and C. A. Schriesheim. "Development and Application of New Scales to Measure the French and Raven (1959) Bases of Social Power." *Journal of Applied Psychology* 74 (1989), pp. 561–67.

Hirsh, S. K., and J. M. Kummerow. *Introduction to Type in Organizations.* Palo Alto, CA: Consulting Psychologists Press, 1990.

Hirschhorn, L. "Campaigning for Change." *Harvard Business Review,* July 2002, pp. 98–106.

Hogan, R. H., and J. Hogan. "Assessing Leadership: A View from the Dark Side." *International Journal of Selection and Assessment,* 9 (1/2) (2001), pp. 40–51.

———. *The Leadership Potential Report.* Tulsa, OK: Hogan Assessment Systems, 2002.

Hogan, R. T. "Leadership and Values." In R. T. Hogan (chair), *Assessing Executive Failure: The Underside of Performance.* Symposium presented at the 18th Annual Conference of the Society of Industrial and Organizational Psychology, Orlando, FL, 2003.

———. "Personality and Personality Measurement." In *Handbook of Industrial and Organizational Psychology.* Vol. 2. Ed. M. D. Dunnette and L. M. Hough. Palo Alto, CA: Consulting Psychologists Press, 1991, pp. 873–919.

Hogan, R. T. "The View from Below." In *The Future of Leadership Selection.* R. T. Hogan (chair). Symposium conducted at the 13th Biennial Psychology in the Department of Defense Conference, United States Air Force Academy, Colorado Springs, CO, 1992b.

Hogan, J., and B. Holland. "Using Theory to Evaluate Personality and Job-Performance Relations: A Socioanalytic Perspective." *Journal of Applied Psychology,* 88 (1) (2003), pp. 100–12.

Hogan, J., and R. T. Hogan. *Motives, Values and Preferences Inventory.* Tulsa, OK: Hogan Assessment Systems, 1996.

Hogan, R. T. "The Role of Big Five Personality Traits in Executive Selection." In G. J. Curphy (chair). *The Role of I/O Psychology in Executive Assessment and Development.* Paper presented at the 15th Annual Conference of the Society of Industrial and Organizational Psychology, New Orleans, LA, 2000.

Hogan, R. T., and G. J. Curphy. "Leadership Matters: Values and Dysfunctional Dispositions," working paper, 2004.

Hogan, R. T.; G. J. Curphy; and J. Hogan. "What Do We Know about Personality: Leadership and Effectiveness?" *American Psychologist* 49 (1994), pp. 493–504.

Hogan, R. T., and J. Hogan. *Manual for the Hogan Personality Inventory.* Tulsa, OK: Hogan Assessment Systems, 1992.

Hogan, R. T.; J. Hogan; and B. W. Roberts. "Personality Measurement and Employment Decisions: Questions and Answers." *American Psychologist* 51, no. 5 (1996), pp. 469–77.

Hogan, R. T., and A. M. Morrison. "The Psychology of Managerial Incompetence." Paper presented at a joint conference of the American Psychological Association–National Institute of Occupational Safety and Health. Washington, DC, October 1991.

Hogan, R. T., and R. Warrenfelz. "Educating the Modern Manager." *Academy of Management Learning and Education,* 2 (1), 2003, pp. 74–84.

Hogan, R. T., and J. Morrison. "Managing Creativity," In *Create to Be Free: Essays in Honor of Frank Barron.* Ed. A. Montouri. Amsterdam: J. C. Gieben, 1993.

Holladay, S. J., and W. T. Coombs. "Speaking of Visions and Visions Being Spoken: An Exploration of the Effects of Content and Delivery on Perceptions of Leader Charisma." *Management Communication Quarterly* 7 (1994), pp. 165–89.

Hollander, E. P. *Leadership Dynamics: A Practical Guide to Effective Relationships.* New York: Free Press, 1978.

Hollander, E. P., and J. W. Julian. "Contemporary Trends in the Analysis of Leadership Processes." *Psychological Bulletin* 71 (1969), pp. 387–91.

Hollander, E. P., and L. R. Offermann. "Power and Leadership in Organizations." *American Psychologist* 45 (1990), pp. 179–89.

Hom, P. W., and A. J. Kinicki. "Towards a Greater Understanding of How Dissatisfaction Drives Employee Turnover." *Academy of Management Journal,* 44 (5) (2001), pp. 975–87.

Hooijberg, R., and J. Choi. "Which Leadership Roles Matter to Whom? An Examination of Rater Effects on Perceptions of Effectiveness." *Leadership Quarterly* 11, no. 3 (2000), pp. 341–64.

———. "From Selling Peanuts and Beer in Yankee Stadium to Creating a Theory of Transformational Leadership: An Interview with Bernie Bass." *Leadership Quarterly* 11, no. 2 (2000), pp. 291–300.

Hoppock, R. *Job Satisfaction.* New York: Harper, 1935.

Hough, L. M. "The Big Five Personality Variables—Construct Confusion: Description Versus Prediction." *Human Performance* 5 (1992), pp. 139–55.

House, R. J. "A 1976 Theory of Charismatic Leadership." In *Leadership: The Cutting Edge*. Ed. J. G. Hunt and L. L. Larson. Carbondale: Southern Illinois University Press, 1977.

———. "Power in Organizations: A Social Psychological Perspective." Unpublished manuscript, University of Toronto, 1984.

House, R. J., and G. Dressler. "The Path-Goal Theory of Leadership: Some Posthoc and A Priori Tests." In *Contingency Approaches to Leadership*. Ed. J. G. Hunt and L. L. Larson. Carbondale: Southern Illinois University Press, 1974.

House, R. J.; R. S. Schuler; and E. Levanoni. "Role Conflict and Ambiguity Scales: Reality or Artifact?" *Journal of Applied Psychology* 68 (1983), pp. 334–37.

House, R. J., and B. Shamir. "Toward an Integration of Transformational, Charismatic, and Visionary Theories." In *Leadership Theory and Research Perspective and Directions*. Ed. M. Chemers and R. Ayman. Orlando, FL: Academic Press, 1993, pp. 577–94.

House, R. J.; J. Woycke; and E. M. Fodor. "Charismatic and Noncharismatic Leaders: Differences in Behavior and Effectiveness." In *Charismatic Leadership: The Elusive Factor in Organizational Effectiveness*. Ed. J. A. Conger and R. N. Kanungo. San Francisco: Jossey-Bass, 1988, pp. 98–121.

Howard, A. "College Experiences and Managerial Performance." *Journal of Applied Psychology* 71 (1986), pp. 530–52.

Howard, A., and D. W. Bray. "Predictors of Managerial Success over Long Periods of Time." In *Measures of Leadership*. Ed. M. B. Clark and K. E. Clark. West Orange, NJ: Leadership Library of America, 1989.

Howard, P. J., and J. M. Howard. "Buddy, Can You Paradigm?" *Training & Development*, September 1995, pp. 28–34.

Howell, J. M., and P. Frost. "A Laboratory Study of Charismatic Leadership." *Organizational Behavior and Human Decision Processes* 43 (1988), pp. 243–69.

Howell, J. P., and P. W. Dorfman. "Leadership and Substitutes for Leadership among Professional and Nonprofessional Workers." *Journal of Applied Behavioral Science* 22 (1986), pp. 29–46.

———. "Substitute for Leadership: Test of a Construct." *Academy of Management Journal* 24 (1981), pp. 714–28.

Huberman, J. "Discipline without Punishment." *Harvard Business Review*, July–August 1964, p. 62.

Humphreys, L. G. "General Intelligence." In *Perspectives on Bias in Mental Testing*. Ed. C. R. Reynolds and R. T. Brown. New York: Plenum, 1984, pp. 221–47.

———. "Intelligence: Three Kinds of Instability and Their Consequences for Policy." In *Intelligence: Measurement, Theory, and Public Policy*. Ed. R. L. Linn. Chicago: University of Illinois Press, 1989, pp. 193–216.

Hunt, J. G. "Transformational/Charismatic Leadership's Transformation of the Field: An Historical Essay." *Leadership Quarterly*, 10, no. 2 (1999), pp. 129–44.

Hunt, J. G.; K. B. Boal; and G. E. Dodge. "The Effects of Visionary and Crisis-Responsive Charisma on Followers: An Experimental Examination of Two Kinds of Charismatic Leadership." *Leadership Quarterly* 10, no. 3 (1999), pp. 423–48.

Hunt, J. G., and R. N. Osborn. "Toward a Macro-oriented Model of Leadership: An Odyssey." In *Leadership: Beyond Establishment Views*. Ed. J. G. Hunt, U. Sekaran, and C. A. Schriesheim. Carbondale: Southern Illinois University Press, 1982, pp. 196–221.

Hunter, J. E.; F. L. Schmidt; and M. K. Judiesch. "Individual Differences in Output Variability as a Function of Job Complexity." *Journal of Applied Psychology* 74 (1990), pp. 28–42.

Hurtz, G. M., and J. J. Donovan. "Personality and Job Performance: The Big Five Revisited." *Journal of Applied Psychology* 85, no. 6 (2000), pp. 869–79.

Huselid, M. A. "The Impact of Human Resource Practices on Turnover, Productivity, and Corporate Financial Performance." *Academy of Management Journal* 38, no. 4 (1995), pp. 635–72.

Huy, Q. N. "In Praise of Middle Managers." *Harvard Business Review*, September, 2001, pp. 72–81.

Iacocca, L., with W. Novack. *Iacocca: An Autobiography*. New York: Bantam, 1984.

Iaffaldano, M. T., and P. M. Muchinsky. "Job Satisfaction and Job Performance: A Meta-Analysis." *Psychological Bulletin* 97 (1985), pp. 251–73.

Ilies, R., and Judge, T. A. "On the Heritability of Job Satisfaction: The Mediating Role of Personality." *Journal of Applied Psychology*, 88 (4) (2003), pp. 750–59.

Imai, M. *Kaizen: The Key to Japan's Competitive Success*. New York: Random House, 1986.

Indik, B. P. "Organizational Size and Member Participation: Some Empirical Tests of Alternative Explanations." *Human Relations* 18 (1965), pp. 339–50.

Ittner, C. D., and D. F. Larcker. "Coming Up Short on Nonfinancial Performance Measurement." *Harvard Business Review,* November 2003, pp. 88–95.

Ivancevich, J. M.; D. M. Schweiger; and J. W. Ragan. "Employee Stress, Health, and Attitudes: A Comparison of American, Indian, and Japanese Managers." Paper presented at the Academy of Management convention, Chicago, 1986.

Jackman, J. M., and M. H. Strober. "Fear of Feedback." *Harvard Business Review,* April 2003, pp. 101–8.

Jago, A. G., and J. W. Ragan. "The Trouble with LEADER MATCH Is That It Doesn't Match Fiedler's Contingency Model." *Journal of Applied Psychology* 71 (1986a), pp. 555–59.

————. "Some Assumptions Are More Troubling than Others: Rejoinder to Chemers and Fiedler." *Journal of Applied Psychology* 71 (1986b), pp. 564–65.

Jamal, M. "Job Stress and Job Performance Controversy: An Empirical Assessment." *Organizational Behavior and Human Performance* 33 (1984), pp. 1–21.

Janis, I. L. *Groupthink.* 2nd ed. Boston: Houghton Mifflin, 1982.

————. *Stress and Frustration.* New York: Harcourt Brace Jovanovich, 1971.

Jansen, P. G. W., and B. A. M. Stoop. "The Dynamics of Assessment Center Validity: Results of a 7-Year Study." *Journal of Applied Psychology,* 86 (4) (2001), pp. 741–53.

Jayaratne, S.; D. Himle; and W. A. Chess. "Dealing with Work Stress and Strain: Is the Perception of Support More Important than Its Use?" *Journal of Applied Behavioral Science* 24, no. 2 (1988), pp. 34–45.

Jellison, J. "Leading Agile Organizations in Turbulent Times." Presentation given at The Saint Paul Companies, St. Paul, MN, October 2000.

Jenkins, G. D.; A. Mitra; N. Gupta; and J. D. Shaw. "Are Financial Incentives Related to Performance? A Meta-Analytic Review of Empirical Research." *Journal of Applied Psychology* 83, no. 5 (1998), pp. 777–87.

Jennings, G. *The Mobile Manager.* New York: McGraw-Hill, 1971.

Jones, D. "Firms Spend Billions to Fire Up Workers—With Little Luck." *USA Today,* May 10, 2001, pp. 1–2A.

Johnson, K., and J. Johnson. *Economic Value of Performance Change after 360 Degree Feedback.* Minneapolis, MN: Personnel Decisions International, 2001.

Johnson, S. *Who Moved My Cheese?* New York: Putnam, 1999.

Johnston, J. M. "Punishment of Human Behavior." *American Psychologist* 27 (1972), pp. 1033–54.

Jones, E. E., and R. E. Nisbett. "The Actor and the Observer: Divergent Perceptions of the Causes of Behavior." In *Attribution: Perceiving the Causes of Behavior.* Ed. E. E. Jones, D. E. Kanouse, H. H. Kelley, R. E. Nisbett, S. Valins, and B. Weiner. Morristown, NJ: General Learning Press, 1972.

Jordan, P. J.; N. M. Ashkanasy; and C. E. J. Hartel. "Emotional Intelligence as a Moderator of Emotional and Behavioral Reactions to Job Security." *Academy of Management Review,* 27 (3) (2002), pp. 361–72.

Judge, T. A., and J. E. Bono. "Five-Factor Model of Personality and Transformational Leadership." *Journal of Applied Psychology,* 85, no. 5 (2000), pp. 751–65.

Judge, T.A, J. E. Bono, R. Ilies, and M. W. Gerhardt. "Leadership and Personality: A Qualitative and Quantitative Review." *Journal of Applied Psychology,* 87 (4) (2002), pp. 765–80.

Judge, T. A.; J. E. Bono; and E. A. Locke. "Personality and Job Satisfaction: The Mediating Role of Job Characteristics." *Journal of Applied Psychology* 85, no. 2 (2000), pp. 237–49.

Judge, T. A.; D. Heller; and M. K. Mount. "Five-Factor Model of Personality and Job Satisfaction." *Journal of Applied Psychology,* 87 (2) (2002), pp. 530–41.

Judge, T. A.; C. A. Higgins; C. J. Thoresen; and M. R. Barrick. "The Big Five Personality Traits, General Mental Ability, and Career Success across the Life Span." *Personnel Psychology* 52, no. 3 (1999), pp. 621–52.

Judge, T. A., and C. L. Hulin. "Job Satisfaction as a Reflection of Disposition: A Multiple Source Causal Analysis." *Organizational Behavior and Human Decision Processes* 56 (1993), pp. 388–421.

Judge, T. A.; C. J. Thoresen; J. E. Bono; and G. K. Patton. "The Job Satisfaction–Job Performance Relationship: A Qualitative and Quantitative Review." *Psychological Bulletin,* 127 (2001), pp. 376–407.

Judge, T. A.; C. J. Thoresen; V. Pucik; and T. W. Welbourne. "Managerial Coping with Change: A Dispositional Perspective." *Journal of Applied Psychology* 84, no. 1 (1999), pp. 107–22.

Judge, T. A., and E. A. Locke. "Effect of Dysfunctional Thought Processes on Subjective Well-Being and Job Satisfaction." *Journal of Applied Psychology* 78 (1993), pp. 475–490.

Judge, T. A.; R. F. Piccolo; and R. Ilies. "The Forgotten Ones? The Validity of Consideration and Initiating Structure in Leadership Research." *Journal of Applied Psychology,* 89 (1) (2004), pp. 36–51.

Judge, T. A., and R. Ilies. "Relationship of Personality to Performance Motivation: A Meta-Analytic Review." *Journal of Applied Psychology,* 87 (4) (2002), pp. 797–807.

Justice, A. "Review of the Effects of Stress on Cancer in Laboratory Animals: Importance of Time of Stress Application and Type of Tumor." *Psychological Bulletin* 98 (1985), pp. 108–38.

Kampa-Kokesch, S., and M. Z. Anderson. "Executive Coaching: A Comprehensive Review of the Literature." *Consulting Psychology Journal,* 53 (4) (2001), pp. 205–28.

Kanfer, R. "Motivation Theory in Industrial and Organizational Psychology." In *Handbook of Industrial and Organizational Psychology.* Vol. 1. Ed. M. D. Dunnette and L. M. Hough. Palo Alto, CA: Consulting Psychologists Press, 1990, pp. 75–170.

Kanter, R. M. *The Change Masters.* New York: Simon & Schuster, 1983.

———. *Commitment and Community.* Cambridge: Harvard University Press, 1972.

Kaplan, R. E. "The Warp and Woof of the General Manager's Jobs." In *Facilitating Work Effectiveness.* Ed. B. Schneider and D. Schoorman. Lexington, MA: Lexington Books, 1986.

Kaplan, R. S., and D. P. Norton. *The Balanced Scorecard: Translating Strategy into Action.* Boston: Harvard Business School Press, 1996.

Kark, R.; B. Shamir; and G. Chen. "The Two Faces of Transformational Leadership: Empowerment and Dependency." *Journal of Applied Psychology,* 88 (2) (2003), pp. 246–55.

Karp, D. A., and W. C. Yoels. *Symbols, Selves, and Society.* New York: Lippincott, 1979.

Katz, D.; N. Maccoby; G. Gurin; and L. G. Floor. *Productivity, Supervision, and Morale Among Railroad Workers.* Ann Arbor: University of Michigan, Survey Research Center, Institute of Social Research, 1951.

Katzell, R. A., and R. A. Guzzo. *Teams at the Top.* Boston: Harvard Business School Press, 1998.

Katzenbach, J. R., and B. K. Smith. *The Wisdom of Teams.* Boston: HarperBusiness, 1994.

Kazdin, A. E. *Behavior Modification in Applied Settings.* Homewood, IL: Dorsey, 1975.

Kegan, R., and L. Laskow Lahey. "The Real Reason People Won't Change." *Harvard Business Review,* November 2001, pp. 84–93.

Keller, R. T., and A. D. Szilagyi. "Employee Reactions for Leader Reward Behavior." *Academy of Management Journal* 19 (1976), pp. 619–27.

———. "A Longitudinal Study of Leader Reward Behavior, Subordinate Expectancies, and Satisfaction." *Personnel Psychology* 11 (1978), pp. 119–29.

Kelley, R. *The Power of Followership.* New York: Doubleday Currency, 1992.

Kelley, R. E. "In Praise of Followers." *Harvard Business Review* 66, no. 6 (1988), pp. 142–48.

Kelly, G. *The Psychology of Personal Constructs.* New York: W. W. Norton, 1955.

Kennedy, J. K. "Middle LPC Leaders and the Contingency Model of Leader Effectiveness." *Organizational Behavior and Human Performance* 30 (1982), pp. 1–14.

Kerr, S., and J. M. Jermier. "Substitutes for Leadership: Their Meaning and Measurement." *Organizational Behavior and Human Performance* 22 (1978), pp. 375–403.

Kersting, "What Exactly Is Creativity?" *Monitor on Psychology,* November 2003, pp. 40–41.

Kets de Vries, M. F. R. "Crises Leadership and the Paranoid Potential: An Organizational Perspective." *Bulletin of the Menninger Clinic* 41 (1977), pp. 349–65.

Kets de Vries, M. F. R., and D. Miller. "Managers Can Drive Their Subordinates Mad." In *The Irrational Executive: Psychoanalytic Explorations in Management.* Ed. M. F. R. Kets de Vries. New York: International Universities Press, 1984.

Keys, B.; T. Case; T. Miller; K. E. Curran; and C. Jones. "Lateral Influence Tactics in Organizations." *International Journal of Management* 4 (1987), pp. 425–37.

Khurana, R. "The Curse of the Superstar CEO." *Harvard Business Review,* September 2002, pp. 60–67.

Kiewitz, C. "Happy Employees and Firm Performance: Have We Been Putting the Cart before the Horse?" *Academy of Management Executive,* 18 (2) (2004), pp. 127–29.

Kilmann, R. H., and M. J. Saxton. *Organizational Cultures: Their Assessment and Change.* San Francisco: Jossey-Bass, 1983.

King, A. W.; S. W. Fowler; and C. P. Zeithaml. "Managing Organizational Competencies for Competitive Advantage: The Middle-Management Edge." *Academy of Management Executive* 15, no. 2 (2001), pp. 95–106.

Kinni, T. B. "The Empowered Workforce." *Industry Week,* September 19, 1994, pp. 37–41.

Kipnis, D. "Technology, Power, and Control." *Research in the Sociology of Organizations* 3 (1984a), pp. 125–56.

Kipnis, D., and S. M. Schmidt. "The Language of Persuasion." *Psychology Today* 19, no. 4 (1985), pp. 40–46.

———. *Profiles of Organizational Strategies.* Form M. San Diego, CA: University Associates, 1982.

Kipnis, D.; S. M. Schmidt; and I. Wilkinson. "Intraorganizational Influence Tactics: Explorations in Getting One's Way." *Journal of Applied Psychology* 65 (1980), pp. 440–52.

Kirkpatrick, D. L. "Evaluation of Training." In *Training and Development Handbook.* Ed. R. L. Craig and L. R. Bittel. New York: McGraw-Hill, 1967.

Kirton, M. J. *Test Manual for the Kirton Adaptation-Innovation Inventory.* Hatfield, U.K.: Occupational Research Centre, 1987.

Kleiman, C. "Survey: Job Satisfaction Can Be Costly to Employers." *Denver Post,* June 22, 1997, p. J-4.

Klein, H. J.; M. J. Wesson; J. R. Hollenbeck; and B. J. Alge. "Goal Commitment and the Goal-Setting Process: Conceptual Clarification and Empirical Synthesis." *Journal of Applied Psychology* 84, no. 6 (1999), pp. 885–96.

Klein, S. B. *Learning.* 2nd ed. New York: McGraw-Hill, 1991.

Klimoski, R. J., and N. J. Hayes. "Leader Behavior and Subordinate Motivation." *Personnel Psychology* 33 (1980), pp. 543–55.

Koene, B. A. S.; A. L. W. Vogelaar; and J. L. Soeters. "Leadership Effects on Organizational Climate and Financial Performance: Local Leadership Effect in Chain Organizations." *The Leadership Quarterly,* 13 (3) (2002), pp. 193–216.

Kohlberg, L. *The Psychology of Moral Development: Essays on Moral Development.* Vol. 2. San Francisco: Harper & Row, 1984.

Kohn, A. "It's Hard to Get Left Out of a Pair." *Psychology Today,* October 1987, pp. 53–57.

———. "Why Incentive Plans Cannot Work." *Harvard Business Review,* September–October 1993, pp. 54–63.

Komacki, J. L. "Why We Don't Reinforce: The Issues." *Journal of Organizational Behavior Management* 4, nos. 3–4 (1982), pp. 97–100.

Komacki, J. L.; S. Zlotnick; and M. Jensen. "Development of an Operant-based Taxonomy and Observational Index on Supervisory Behavior." *Journal of Applied Psychology* 71 (1986), pp. 260–69.

Konrad, A. M.; J. E. Ritchie Jr.; P. Lieb; and E. Corrigall. "Sex Differences and Similarities in Job Attribute Preferences: A Meta-analysis." *Psychological Bulletin,* 126, pp. 593–641 (2000).

Kossler, M., and S. Prestridge. "Geographically Dispersed Teams." *Issues and Observations* 16 (1996), pp. 2–3.

Kotter, J. *Matsushista Leadership.* New York: Free Press, 1997.

Kotter, J. P. *Leading Change.* Boston: Harvard Business School Press, 1996.

Kotter, J. R. "Power and Influence: Beyond Formal Authority. *Macmillan Executive Summary Program,* September 1985, pp. 1–8.

———. "What Leaders Really Do." *Harvard Business Review,* May–June 1990, pp. 103–111.

Kouzes, J. M., and B. Z. Posner. *The Credibility Factor.* San Francisco: Jossey-Bass, 1996.

———. *The Leadership Challenge: How to Get Extraordinary Things Done in Organizations.* San Francisco: Jossey-Bass, 1987.

Koys, D. J. "The Effects of Employee Satisfaction, Organizational Citizenship Behavior, and Turnover on Organizational Effectiveness: A Unit-Level, Longitudinal Study." *Personnel Psychology* 54, no. 1 (2001), pp. 101–14.

Kozlowski, S. W. J., and M. L. Doherty. "Integration of Climate and Leadership: Examination of a Neglected Issue." *Journal of Applied Psychology* 74 (1989), pp. 546–53.

Kramer, R. M. "The Harder They Fall." *Harvard Business Review,* October 2003, p. 68.

Kroeger, O., and J. M. Thuesen. *Type Talk.* New York: Delacourt, 1988.

Krug, J. A. "Why Do They Keep Leaving?" *Harvard Business Review,* February 2003, pp. 14–15.

Kubler-Ross, E. *Living with Death and Dying.* New York: Macmillan, 1981.

Kurke, L. B., and H. E. Aldrich. "Mintzberg Was Right! A Replication and Extension of The Nature of Managerial Work.'" *Management Science* 29 (1983), pp. 975–84.

Labak, A. S. "The Study of Charismatic College Teachers." *Dissertation Abstracts International* 34 (1973), pp. 1258B.

LaBarre, P. "Marcus Buckingham Thinks Your Boss Has an Attitude Problem." *Fast Company*, August 2001, pp. 88–98.

Lall, R. "Mentoring Experiences of Retired Navy Admirals." Paper presented at Personnel Decisions International, Denver, CO, May 6, 1999.

Landy, F. J. *Psychology of Work Behavior*. 3rd ed. Homewood, IL: Dorsey, 1985.

Lankau, M. J., and Scandura, T. A. "An Investigation of Personal Learning and Mentoring Relationships: Content, Antecedents, and Consequences." *Academy of Management Journal*, 45 (4) (2002), pp. 779–90.

LaPine, J. A.; A. Erez; and D. E. Johnson. "The Nature and Dimensionality of Organizational Citizenship Behavior: A Critical Review and Meta-Analysis." *Journal of Applied Psychology*, 87 (1) (2002), pp. 52–65.

Larmore, A., and R. Ayman. "Empowering Leadership, Transformational Leadership, and Feelings of Empowerment: A Multi-Level Analysis." Paper presented at the 13th Annual Conference of the Society of Industrial and Organizational Psychology, Dallas, TX, 1998.

Larson, J. R., Jr. "Supervisors' Performance Feedback to Subordinates: The Impact of Subordinate Performance Valence and Outcome Dependence." *Organizational Behavior and Human Decision Processes* 37 (1986), pp. 391–408.

Latack, J. C. "Coping with Job Stress: Measures and Future Decisions for Scale Development." *Journal of Applied Psychology* 71 (1986), pp. 377–85.

Latane, B.; K. Williams; and S. Harkins. "Social Loafing." *Psychology Today* (1979), p. 104.

Latham, G. P., and T. W. Lee. "Goal Setting." In *Generalizing from Laboratory to Field Settings*. Ed. E. A. Locke. Lexington, MA: Lexington Books, 1986.

Lawler, E. E. III. *Motivation in Work Organizations*. Pacific Grove, CA: Brooks/Cole, 1973.

Lawrence, P. R., and J. W. Lorsch. "Differentiation and Integration in Complex Organizations." *Administrative Science Quarterly* 12 (1967a), pp. 1–47.

———. *Organization and Environment*. Boston: Harvard University Press, 1967b.

Leana, C. R. "Power Relinquishment vs. Power Sharing: Theoretical Clarification and Empirical Comparison of Delegation and Participation." *Journal of Applied Psychology* 72 (1987), pp. 228–33.

Lee, K., and N. J. Allen. "Organizational Citizenship Behavior and Workplace Deviance: The Role of Affect and Cognitions." *Journal of Applied Psychology*, 87 (1) (2002), pp. 131–42.

Leib, J. "Poor Management Blamed on Most New-Airline Failures." *Denver Post*, July 1, 1998, p. 10C.

Lepper, M. R.; D. Greene; and R. E. Nisbett. "Undermining Children's Intrinsic Interests with Extrinsic Rewards: A Test of the 'Overjustification' Hypothesis." *Journal of Personality and Social Psychology* 28 (1973), pp. 128–37.

Lepsinger, R., and A. D. Lucia. *The Art and Science of 360° Feedback*. San Francisco: Pfeiffer, 1997.

Levering, R.; M. Moskowitz; and M. Katz. *The 100 Best Companies to Work for in America*. Reading, MA: Addison-Wesley, 1984.

Levinson, H. "Management by Whose Objectives?" *Harvard Business Review*, January 2003, pp. 107–16.

Levy-Leboyer, C. "Leadership Performance: Towards a More Complex Model." *Applied Psychology: An International Review* 44, no. 1 (1995), pp. 43–44.

Lievens, F.; M. H. Harris; E. Van Keer; and C. Bisqueret. "Predicting Cross-Cultural Training Performance: The Validity of Personality, Cognitive Ability, and Dimensions Measures by an Assessment Center and a Behavior Description Interview." *Journal of Applied Psychology*, 88 (3), 2003, pp. 476–89.

Likert, R. *New Patterns of Management*. New York: McGraw-Hill, 1961.

Lindsley, D. H.; D. J. Brass.; and J. B. Thomas. " Efficacy-Performance Spirals: A Multilevel Perspective." *Academy of Management Review* 20 (1995), pp. 645–78.

Linn, R. L., Ed. *Intelligence: Measurement, Theory, and Public Policy*. Chicago: University of Illinois Press, 1989.

Linville, P. W. "Self-Complexity as a Cognitive Buffer against Stress-Related Illness and Depression." *Journal of Personality and Social Psychology* 52, no. 4 (1987), pp. 663–76.

Lipnack, J., and J. Stamps. *Virtual Teams: Reaching across Space, Time and Organizations with Technology*. New York: John Wiley, 1997.

Lippitt, R. "The Changing Leader-Follower Relationships of the 1980s." *Journal of Applied Behavioral Science* 18 (1982), pp. 395–403.

Locke, E. A., and G. P. Latham. "Building a Practically Useful Theory of Goal Setting and Task Motivation: A 35–Year Odyssey." *American Psychologist,* 57 (9) (2002), pp. 705–18.

———. *Goal Setting: A Motivational Technique That Works.* Englewood Cliffs, NJ: Prentice Hall, 1984.

———. "Work Motivation and Satisfaction: Light at the End of the Tunnel." *Psychological Science* 1 (1990), pp. 240–46.

Locke, E. A.; G. P. Latham; and M. Erez. "Three-way Interactive Presentation and Discussion; A Unique Approach to Resolving Scientific Disputes; Designing Crucial Experiments." Papers presented at the Society of Industrial and Organizational Psychology Convention, Atlanta, GA, 1987.

Lombardo, M. M., and R. W. Eichinger. *Eighty-eight Assignments for Development in Place: Enhancing the Developmental Challenge of Existing Jobs.* Greensboro, NC: Center for Creative Leadership, 1990.

———. *For Your Improvement: A Development and Coaching Guide.* Minneapolis, MN: Lominger, 1996.

Lombardo, M. M., M. N. Ruderman; and C. D. McCauley. "Explorations of Success and Derailment in Upper-Level Management Positions." Paper presented at meeting of the Academy of Management, New York, 1987.

Lord, R. G., and D. J. Brown. "Leadership, Values, and Subordinate Self-Concepts." *Leadership Quarterly* 12, no. 2 (2001), pp. 133–52.

Lord, R. G.; C. L. DeVader; G. M. Allinger. "A Meta-Analysis of the Relationship between Personality Traits and Leadership Perceptions: An Application of Validity Generalization Procedures." *Journal of Applied Psychology* 71 (1986), pp. 402–10.

Louiselle, K.; S. Bridges; and G. J. Curphy. "Talent Assessment Overview." Working paper, 2003.

Lowe, K. B.; K. G. Kroeck; and N. Sivasubramaniam. "Effectiveness Correlates of Transformational and Transactional Leadership: A Meta-Analytic Review of the MLQ Literature." *Leadership Quarterly* 7, no. 3 (1996), pp. 385–425.

Lowin, A., and J. R. Craig. "The Influence of Level of Performance on Managerial Style: An Experimental Object-Lesson in the Ambiguity of Correlational Data." *Organizational Behavior and Human Performance* 3 (1968), pp. 68–106.

Lubit, R. "The Long-Term Impact of Destructively Narcissistic Managers." *Academy of Management Executive,* 16 (1) (2002), pp. 127–38.

Luthans, F. 1989. *Organizational Behavior.* 5th ed. New York: McGraw-Hill, 1992.

Luthans, F., and R. Kreitner. *Organizational Behavior Modification and Beyond: An Operant and Social Learning Approach.* Glenview, IL: Scott, Foresman, 1985.

Luthans, F., and J. K. Larsen. "How Managers Really Communicate." *Human Relations* 39 (1986), pp. 161–78.

Luthans, F.; S. A. Rosenkrantz; and H. W. Hennessey. "What Do Successful Managers Really Do? An Observational Study of Managerial Activities." *Journal of Applied Behavioral Science* 21 (1985), pp. 255–70.

Luthans, F., and A. D. Stajkovic. "Reinforce for Performance: The Need to Go Beyond Pay and Even Rewards." *Academy of Management Executive* 13, no. 2 (1999), pp. 49–57.

Maccoby, M. "Management: Leadership and the Work Ethic." *Modern Office Procedures* 28, no. 5 (1983), pp. 14, 16, 18.

Macrorie, K. *Twenty Teachers.* Oxford: Oxford University Press, 1984.

Madjar, N.; G. R. Oldham; and M. G. Pratt. "There's No Place Like Home? The Contributions of Work and Nonwork Creativity Support to Employees' Creative Performance." *Academy of Management Journal,* 45 (4) (2002), pp. 757–68.

Madsen, D., and P. G. Snow. "The Dispersion of Charisma." *Comparative Political Studies* 16, no. 3 (1983), pp. 337–62.

Malinkowski, C. I., and C. P. Smith. "Moral Reasoning and Moral Conduct: An Investigation Prompted by Kohlberg's Theory." *Journal of Personality and Social Psychology* 49 (1985), pp. 1016–27.

Mann, R. D. "A Review of the Relationships between Personality and Performance in Small Groups." *Psychological Bulletin* 56 (1959), pp. 241–70.

Marcus, J. T. "Transcendence and Charisma." *Western Political Quarterly* 16 (1961), pp. 236–41.

Marentette, D. *SHRM/PD1 2000 Performance Management Survey.* Minneapolis, MN: Personnel Decisions International, 2000.

Markham, S. E.; K. D. Scott; and G. H. McKee. "Recognizing Good Attendance: A Longitudinal Quasi-Experimental Field Study." *Personnel Psychology,* 55 (3) (2002), pp. 639–60.

Marks, M. L., and P. H. Mirvis. "Making Mergers and Acquisitions Work." *Academy of Management Executive* 15, no. 2 (2001), pp. 80–94.

Maslow, A. H. *Motivation and Personality.* New York: Harper & Row, 1954.

Massey, M. *The People Puzzle: Understanding Yourself and Others.* Reston: VA: Reston, 1979.

Mayo, E. *The Human Problems of an Industrial Civilization.* New York: Macmillan, 1933.

McCall, M. W., Jr., and M. M. Lombardo. "Off the Track: Why and How Successful Executives Get Derailed." Technical Report No. 21. Greensboro, NC: Center for Creative Leadership, 1983.

———. "Using Simulation for Leadership and Management Research: Through the Looking Glass." *Management Science* 28 (1982), pp. 533–49.

McCall, M. W., Jr.; M. M. Lombardo; and A. M. Morrison. *The Lessons of Experience: How Successful Executives Develop on the Job.* Lexington, MA: Lexington Books, 1988.

McCarley, N., and T. G. Carskadon. "Test-Retest Reliabilities of Scales and Subscales of the Myers-Briggs Type Indicator and of Criteria for Clinical Interpretive Hypothesis Involving Them." *Research in Psychological Type* 6 (1983), pp. 24–36.

McCauley, C. D.; "Stress and the Eye of the Beholder." *Issues & Observations* 7, no. 3 (1987), pp. 1–16.

McCauley, C. D.; Ruderman, M. N.; Ohlott, P. J.; and J. E. Morrow "Assessing the Developmental Components of Managerial Jobs." *Journal of Applied Psychology* 79, no. 4 (1994), pp. 544–60.

McCaulley, M. H. "The Myers-Briggs Type Indicator and Leadership." In *Measures of Leadership.* Ed. K. E. Clark and M. B. Clark. Greensboro, NC: Center for Creative Leadership, 1988.

McClelland, D. C. *Human Motivation.* Glenview, IL: Scott Foresman, 1985.

———. *Power: The Inner Experience.* New York: Irvington, 1975.

McClelland, D. C., and R. E. Boyatzis. "Leadership Motive Pattern and Long-Term Success in Management." *Journal of Applied Psychology* 67 (1982), pp. 737–43.

McCormick, J., and B. Powell. "Management for the 1990s" *Newsweek,* April 1988, pp. 47–48.

McDaniel, S. L. "The Dark Side of the Big Five: New Perspectives for Personnel Selection." Paper presented at the 14th Annual Conference of the Society of Industrial and Organizational Psychology, Atlanta, GA, 1999.

McElreath, J., and A. R. Bass. *Development of a Biodata Measure of Leadership Effectiveness: A Life History Essay Approach.* Paper Presented at the 14th Annual Conference of the Society for Industrial and Organizational Psychology, Atlanta, GA, May 1999.

McElroy, J. C.; P. C. Morrow; and S. N. Rude. "Turnover and Organizational Performance: A Comparative Analysis of the Effects of Voluntary, Involuntary, and Reduction-in-Force Turnover." *Journal of Applied Psychology,* 86 (6) (2001), pp. 1294–99.

McFarlin, D. B., and P. D. Sweeney. "Distributive and Procedural Justice as Predictors of Satisfaction with Personal and Organizational Outcomes." *Academy of Management Journal* 35 (1992), pp. 626–37.

McGrath, J. E. *Leadership Behavior: Some Requirements for Leadership Training.* Washington, DC: Office of Career Development, U.S. Civil Service Commission, 1964.

McGregor, D. *Leadership and Motivation.* Cambridge, MA: MIT Press, 1966.

McGue, M., and T. J. Bouchard, Jr. "Genetic and Environmental Determinants of Information Processing and Special Mental Abilities: A Twin Analysis." In *Advances in the Psychology of Human Intelligence.* Ed. R. J. Sternberg. Hillsdale, NJ: Erlbaum, 1989, pp. 7–45.

McKay, M.; M. Davis; and P. Fanning. *Thoughts and Feelings: The Art of Cognitive Stress Intervention.* Richmond, CA: New Harbinger, 1981.

McKee, R. "Storytelling That Moves People: A Conversation with Screenwriting Coach Robert McKee." *Harvard Business Review,* June 2003, pp. 51–57.

McNatt, D. B. "Ancient Pygmalion Joins Contemporary Management: A Meta-Analysis of the Result." *Journal of Applied Psychology* 83, no. 2 (2000), pp. 314–21.

McNulty, E. "Welcome Aboard (But Don't Change a Thing)." *Harvard Business Review,* October 2002, pp. 32–41.

Meindl, J. R., and S. B. Ehrlich. "The Romance of Leadership and the Evaluation of Organizational Performance." *Academy of Management Journal* 30 (1987), pp. 90–109.

Menttium. *Menttium 100: Cross-Company Mentoring for High Potential Women.* Minneapolis, MN: The Menttium Corporation, 2004.

Merton, R. K. *Social Theory and Social Structure.* New York: Free Press, 1957.

Michel, R., and R. T. Hogan. "Personality and Organizational Behavior." In R. T. Hogan (chair), *Personality and Organizational Behavior.* Symposium presented at the 104th Annual Meeting of the American Psychological Association, Toronto, Canada, 1996.

Milgram, S. "Behavioral Study of Obedience." *Journal of Personality and Social Psychology* 67 (1963), pp. 371–78.

Miller, D. D. *The Story of Walt Disney.* New York: Henry Holt, 1956.

Miller, D. T., and M. Ross. "Self-Serving Biases in the Attribution of Causality: Fact or Fiction?" *Psychological Bulletin* 82 (1975), pp. 213–25.

Miller, W. R., and S. Rollnick. *Motivational Interviewing: Preparing People to Change Addictive Behavior.* New York: Guilford Press, 1991.

Mills, V. "Longer Hours, Extra Work." *Orlando Sentinel,* June 16, 1999, p. 3C.

Miner, J. B. "Student Attitudes toward Bureaucratic Role Prescriptions and the Prospects for Managerial Shortages." *Personnel Psychology* 27 (1974), pp. 605–13.

———. "Twenty Years of Research on Role Motivation Theory of Managerial Effectiveness." *Personnel Psychology* 31 (1978), pp. 739–60.

———. "The Uncertain Future of the Leadership Concept: An Overview." In *Leadership Frontiers.* Ed. J. G. Hunt and L. L. Larson. Kent, OH: Kent State University, 1975.

Mitchell, R. R.; C. M. Smyser; and S. E. Weed. "Locus of Control: Supervision and Work Satisfaction." *Academy of Management Journal.* 18 (1975), pp. 623–30.

Mitchell, T. R. "Review of *In Search of Excellence* versus *The 100 Best Companies to Work for in America:* A Question of Perspective and Values." *Academy of Management Review* 10 (1985), pp. 350–55.

Mitchell, T. R.; S. G. Green; and R. E. Wood. "An Attributional Model of Leadership and the Poor Performing Subordinate: Development and Validation." In *Research in Organizational Behavior.* Ed. B. M. Staw and L. L. Cummings. Greenwich, CN: JAI 1981, pp. 197–234.

Mitchell, T. R., and R. E. Wood. "Supervisors' Responses to Subordinate Poor Performance: A Test of an Attributional Model." *Organizational Behavior and Human Performance* 25 (1980), pp. 123–38.

Moore, L. I. "The FMI: Dimensions of Follower Maturity." *Group and Organizational Studies* 1 (1976), pp. 203–22.

Moore, M. *Downsize This! Random Threats from an Unarmed American.* New York: Perennial, 1997.

Moorman, R. H. "Relationships between Organizational Justice and Organizational Citizenship Behaviors: Do Fairness Perceptions Influence Employee Citizenship?" *Journal of Applied Psychology* 76 (1991), pp. 845–55.

Morical, K. E. "A Product Review: 360 Assessments." *Training & Development,* April 1999, pp. 43–47.

Morrel-Samuels, P. "Getting the Truth into Workplace Surveys." *Harvard Business Review,* February 2002, pp. 111–20.

Morrison, A. M.; R. P. White; and E. Van Velsor. *Breaking the Glass Ceiling.* Reading, MA: Addison-Wesley, 1987.

Morse, G. "Why We Misread Motives." *Harvard Business Review,* January 2003, p. 18.

Morse, J. J., and F. R. Wagner. "Measuring the Process of Managerial Effectiveness." *Academy of Management Journal* 21 (1978), pp. 23–35.

Moss Kanter, E. "Leadership and the Psychology of Turnarounds." *Harvard Business Review,* June 2003, pp. 58–64.

Motowidlo, S. J.; M. D. Dunnette; and G. W. Carter. "An Alternative Selection Procedure: The Low-Fidelity Simulation." *Journal of Applied Psychology* 75 (1990), pp. 640–47.

Mount, M. K.; M. R. Barrick; and J. K. Strauss. "Validity of Observers Ratings of the Big Five Personality Factors." *Journal of Applied Psychology* 79 (1994), pp. 272–80.

Mount, M. K.; T. A. Judge; S. E. Scullen; M. R. Sytsma; and S. A. Hezlett. "Trait, Rater, and Level Effects in 360-Degree Performance Ratings." *Personnel Psychology* 51, no.3 (1998), pp. 557–77.

Mount, M. K.; M. R. Sytsma; J. F. Hazucha; and K. E. Holt. "Rater-Ratee Effects in Development Performance Ratings of Managers." *Personnel Psychology* 50, no. 1, pp. 51–70. 1997.

Mowday, R. T. "Leader Characteristics, Self-Confidence, and Methods of Upward Influence in Organizational Decision Situations." *Academy of Management Journal* 22, no. 4 (1979), pp. 709–25.

Mulder, M., R. D. de Jong; L. Koppelar; and J. Verhage. "Power, Situation, and Leaders' Effectiveness: An Organizational Study." *Journal of Applied Psychology* 71 (1986), pp. 566–70.

Mulder, M. and A. Stemerding. "Threat, Attraction to Group, and Need for Strong Leadership." *Human Relations* 16 (1963), pp. 317–34.

Mumford, M. D.; G. M. Scott; B. Gaddis; and J. M. Strange. "Leading Creative People: Orchestrating Expertise and Relationships." *The Leadership Quarterly,* 13 (6) (2002), pp. 705–50.

Mumford, M. D.; S. J. Zaccaro; J. F. Johnson; M. Diana; J. A. Gilbert; and K. V. Threlfall. "Patterns of Leader Characteristics: Implications for Performance and Development." *Leadership Quarterly* 11, no. 1 (2000), pp. 115–36.

Murphy, A. J. "A Study of the Leadership Process." *American Sociological Review* 6 (1941), pp. 674–87.

Murray, H. A., and D. W. MacKinnon. "Assessment of OSS Personnel." *Journal of Consulting Psychology* 10 (1946), pp. 76–80.

Murray, M., and M. A. Owen. *Beyond the Myths and Magic of Mentoring.* San Francisco: Jossey-Bass, 1991.

Myers, D. G. *Psychology.* 2nd ed. New York: Worth, 1989.

Myers, I. *Gifts Differing.* Palo Alto, CA: Consulting Psychologists Press, 1980.

Myers, I. B. *Introduction to Type.* Palo Alto, CA: Consulting Psychologists Press, 1976.

———. *The Myers-Briggs Type Indicator: Supplementary Manual.* Palo Alto, CA: Consulting Psychologists Press, 1977.

Myers, I. B., and K. C. Briggs. *The Myers-Briggs Type Indicator.* Palo Alto, CA: Consulting Psychologists Press, 1943/1962.

Myers, I. B., and B. H. McCaulley. *Manual: A Guide to the Development and Use of the Myers-Briggs Type Indicator.* Palo Alto, Calif.: Consulting Psychologists Press, 1985.

Naglieri, J. A.; F. Drasgow; M. Schmitt; L. Handler; A. Prifitera; A. Margolis; and R. Velasquez. "Psychological Testing on the Internet: New Problems, Old Issues." *American Psychologist,* 59 (3), 2004, pp. 150–62.

Nevins, M., and S. Stumpf. "21st-Century Leadership: Redefining Management Education. *Strategy, Management, Competition,* 3rd quarter 1999, pp. 41–51.

Nilsen, D. L. *Using Self and Observers' Rating of Personality to Predict Leadership Performance.* Unpublished doctoral dissertation, University of Minnesota, 1995.

Nixon, R. M. *Leaders.* New York: Warner Books, 1982.

Nutt, P. C. "Surprising but True: Half the Decisions in Organizations Fail." *Academy of Management Executive* 13, no. 4 (1999), pp. 75–90.

Nystrom, P. C. "Comparing Beliefs of Line and Technostructure Managers." *Academy of Management Journal* 29 (1986), pp. 812–19.

O'Brien, B. "Designing an Organization's Governing Ideas." In *The Fifth Discipline Fieldbook.* Ed. P. Senge, A. Kleiner, C. Roberts, R. Ross, and B. Smith. New York: Doubleday, 1994.

O'Connor, J.; M. D. Mumford; T. C. Clifton; T. L. Gessner; and M. S. Connelly. "Charismatic Leaders and Destructiveness: An Historiometric Study." *Leadership Quarterly* 6, no. 4 (1995), pp. 529–40.

Offermann, L. R. "Leading and Empowering Diverse Followers." In *The Balance of Leadership and Followership.* Ed. E. P. Hollander and L. R. Offerman. Kellogg Leadership Studies Project. College Park: University of Maryland Press, 1997, pp. 31–46.

Ohlott, P. "Change and Leadership Development: The Experience of Executive Women." *Leadership in Action* 19, no. 5 (1999), pp. 8–12.

Oldham, G. R., and A. Cummings. "Employee Creativity: Personal and Contextual Factors at Work." *Academy of Management Journal* 39 (1996), pp. 607–34.

Ones, D. S.; M. K. Mount; M. R. Barrick; and J. E. Hunter. "Personality and Job Performance: A Critique of Tett, Jackson, and Rothstein (1991) Meta-Analysis." *Personnel Psychology* 47 (1994), pp. 147–56.

Ones, D. S.; C. Viswesvaran; and A. D. Reiss. "Role of Social Desirability in Personality Testing for Personnel Selection: The Red Herring." *Journal of Applied Psychology* 81, no. 6 (1996), pp. 660–79.

O'Reilly, B. "360-Degree Feedback Can Change Your Life." *Fortune,* October 17, 1994.

O'Reilly, C. A. "Supervisors and Peers as Informative Sources, Group Supportiveness, and Individual Decision-Making Performance." *Journal of Applied Psychology* 62 (1977), pp. 632–35.

Organ, D. W., and K. Ryan. "A Meta-Analytic Review of Attitudinal and Dispositional Predictors of Organizational Citizenship Behavior." *Personnel Psychology* 48 (1995), pp. 775–802.

Oswald, F. L.; N. Schmitt; B. H. Kim; L. J. Ramsay; and M. A. Gillespie. "Developing a Biodata Measure and Situational Judgment Inventory as Predictors of College Student Performance." *Journal of Applied Psychology,* 89 (2), 2004, pp. 187–207.

O'Toole, J. *Leading Change.* San Francisco: Jossey-Bass, 1995.

Ouchi, W. G. *How American Business Can Meet the Japanese Challenge.* Reading, MA: Addison-Wesley, 1981.

Paajanen, G. E.; T. L. Hansen; and R. A. McLellan. *PDI Employment Inventory and PDI Customer Service Inventory Manual.* Minneapolis, MN: Personnel Decisions, 1993.

Page, R. C., and W. W. Tornow. "Managerial Job Analysis: Are We Any Further Along?" Paper presented at a meeting of the Society of Industrial Organizational Psychology, Atlanta, GA, 1987.

Palus, C. J.; D. M. Horth; A. M. Selvin; and M. L. Pulley. "Exploration for Development: Developing Leaders by Making Shared Sense of Complex Challenges." *Consulting Psychology Journal*, 55 (1) (2003), pp. 26–40.

Parke, R. D. "Some Effects of Punishment on Children's Behavior." In *The Young Child: Reviews of Research.* Vol. 2. Ed. W. W. Hartup. Washington, DC: National Association for the Education of Young Children, 1972.

Parks, M. R. "Interpersonal Communication and the Quest for Personal Competence." In *Handbook of Interpersonal Communication.* Ed. M. L. Knapp and G. R. Miller. Beverly Hills, CA: Sage, 1985.

Parsons, C. K.; D. M. Herold; and M. L. Leatherwood. "Turnover during Initial Employment: A Longitudinal Study of the Role of Causal Attributions." *Journal of Applied Psychology* 70 (1985), pp. 337–41.

Pastor, J. C.; J. R. Meindl; and M. C. Mayo. "A Network Effects Model of Charismatic Attributions." *The Academy of Management Journal*, 45 (2) (2002), pp. 410–20.

Pawar, B. S., and K. K. Eastman. "The Nature and Implications of Contextual Influences on Transformational Leadership: A Conceptual Examination." *Academy of Management Review* 22, no. 1 (1997), pp. 80–109.

Peiperl, M. A. "Getting 360-Degree Feedback Right." *Harvard Business Review,* January 2001, pp. 142–48

Penner, D. D.; D. M. Malone; T. M. Coughlin; and J. A. Herz. *Satisfaction with U.S. Army Leadership.* Leadership Monograph Series, no. 2. U.S. Army War College, 1973.

Perkins, D. N. "Thinking Frames." *Educational Leadership* 43 (1986), pp. 4–10.

Perry-Smith, J. E., and C. E. Shalley. "The Social Side of Creativity: A Static and Dynamic Social Network Perspective." *Academy of Management Review,* 28 (1) (2003), pp. 89–106.

Person, H. S. "Leadership as a Response to Environment." *Educational Record Supplement* no. 6 (1928), pp. 9–21.

Personnel Decisions International. *PROFILOR® Certification Workshop Manual.* Minneapolis, MN: Author, 1992.

———. *Develop Mentor: Assessment, Development, and Coaching Software.* Minneapolis, MN: Personnel Decisions International, 1995.

———. *The Evolution of Assessment over the Past Three Decades.* Minneapolis, MN: Author, 2001.

———. *The Successful Manager's Handbook.* Minneapolis, MN: Author, 2000.

Peters, L. H.; D. D. Hartke; and J. T. Pohlmann. "Fielder's Contingency Theory of Leadership: An Application of the Meta-Analytic Procedures of Schmidt and Hunter." *Psychological Bulletin* 97 (1985), pp. 274–85.

Peters, T. *The Circle of Innovation: You Can't Shrink Your Way to Greatness.* New York: Random House. 1997.

Peters, T. J., and R. H. Waterman. *In Search of Excellence.* New York: Harper & Row, 1982.

Peterson, D. B. "Executive Coaching at Work: The Art of One-on-One Change." *Consulting Psychology Journal* 48 no. 2 (1996), pp. 78–86.

———. *Individual Coaching Services: Coaching That Makes a Business Difference.* Minneapolis, MN: Personnel Decisions International, 1999.

———. "Making the Break from Middle Manager to a Seat at the Top." *The Wall Street Journal,* July 7, 1998, p. B16.

———. *A Psychometric Approach to Evaluating Individual Training Outcomes.* Paper presented at the Eighth Annual Conference of the Society of Industrial and Organizational Psychology. San Francisco, April, 1993a.

———. *The Science and Art of Self-Development.* Paper presented at the Arabian States Human Resource Management Society Annual Conference, Bahrain, October 2001.

———. "Skill Learning and Behavioral Change in an Individually Tailored Management Coaching and Training Program." Unpublished doctoral dissertation. University of Minnesota, 1993b.

Peterson, D. B., and M. D. Hicks. "Coaching across Borders: It's Probably a Long Distance Call." *Development Matters* no. 9, (1997), pp. 1–4.

———. *Development FIRST: Strategies for Self-Development.* Minneapolis, MN: Personnel Decisions International, 1995.

Peterson, D. B., and M. D. Hicks. *Leader as Coach: Strategies for Coaching and Developing Others.* Minneapolis, MN: Personnel Decisions International, 1996.

Peterson, D. B., and M. D. Hicks. *Professional Coaching: State of the Art, State of the Practice.* Minneapolis, MN: Personnel Decisions International, 1998.

Peterson, R. S.; D. B. Smith; P. V. Martorana; and P. D. Owens. "The Impact of Chief Executive Officer Personality on Top Management Team Dynamics: One Mechanism by Which Leadership Affects Organizational Performance." *Journal of Applied Psychology,* 88 (5) (2003), pp. 795–808.

Petrick, J. A., and G. E. Manning. "Developing an Ethical Climate for Excellence." *Journal of Quality and Participation,* March 1990, pp. 13–18.

Pfau, B., and I. Kay. "Does 360-Degree Feedback Negatively Affect Company Performance?" *HR Magazine,* June 2002, pp. 55–59.

Pfau, B. N., and S. A. Cohen. "Aligning Human Capital Practices and Employee Behavior with Shareholder Value." *Consulting Psychology Journal,* 55 (3), 2003, pp. 169–78.

Pfeffer, J. "The Ambiguity of Leadership." In *Leadership: Where Else Can We Go?,* Ed. M. W. McCall, Jr., and M. M. Lombardo. Durham, NC: Duke University Press, 1977.

Pfeffer, J., and G. R. Salancik. "Determinants of Supervisory Behavior: A Role Set Analysis." *Human Relations* 28 (1975), pp. 139–54.

Phelps, J. L., and M. F. Addonizio. *How Much Do Schools and Districts Matter? A Production Function Approach to School Accountability.* Working paper, Wayne State University, 2002.

Phillips, J. M.; E. A. Douthitt; and M. M. Hyland. "The Role of Justice in Team Member Satisfaction with the Leader and Attachment to the Team." *Journal of Applied Psychology* 86, no. 2 (2001), pp. 316–25.

Pillai, R.; E. A. Williams; K. B. Lowe; and D. I. Jung. "Personality, Transformational Leadership, Trust, and the 2000 Presidential Vote." *The Leadership Quarterly,* 14 (2) (2003), pp. 161–92.

Pitt, L. F. "Managerial Attitudes Towards Corruption: A Pilot Study." *South African Journal of Business Management* 16 (1985), pp. 27–30.

Ployhart, R. E., and A. M. Ryan. "Applicants' Reactions to the Fairness of Selection Procedures: The Effects of Positive Rule Violations and Time of Measurement." *Journal of Applied Psychology* 83, no. 1 (1998), pp. 3–16.

Podsakoff, P. M. "Determinants of a Supervisor's Use of Rewards and Punishments: A Literature Review and Suggestions for Future Research." *Organizational Behavior and Human Performance* 29 (1982), pp. 58–83.

Podsakoff, P. M., and C. A. Schriesheim. "Field Studies of French and Raven's Bases of Power: Critique, Reanalysis, and Suggestions for Future Research." *Psychological Bulletin* 97 (1985), pp. 387–411.

Podsakoff, P. M., and W. D. Todor. "Relationships between Leader Reward and Punishment Behavior and Group Process and Productivity." *Journal of Management* 11 (1985), pp. 55–73.

Podsakoff, P. M.; W. D. Todor; R. A. Grover; and V. L. Huber. "Situational Moderators of Leader Reward and Punishment Behaviors: Fact or Fiction?" *Organizational Behavior and Human Performance* 34 (1984), pp. 21–63.

Podsakoff, P. M.; W. D. Todor; and R. S. Schuler. "Leadership Expertise as a Moderator of the Effects of Instrumental and Supportive Leader Behaviors." *Journal of Management* 9 (1983), pp. 173–85.

Podsakoff, P. M.; W. D. Todor; and R. Skov. "Effects of Leader Contingent and Noncontigent Reward and Punishment Behaviors on Subordinate Performance and Satisfaction." *Academy of Management Journal* 25 (1982), pp. 810–25.

Podsakoff, P. M., and L. J. Williams. "The Relationship between Job Performance and Job Satisfaction." In *Generalizing from Laboratory to Field Setting.* Ed. E. A. Locke. Lexington, MA: Lexington, 1986.

Polivy, J., and C. P. Herman. "If at First You Don't Succeed: False Hopes of Self-Change." *American Psychologist,* 57 (9) (2002), pp. 677–89.

Pomerleau, O. F., and J. Rodin. "Behavioral Medicine and Health Psychology." In *Handbook of Psychotherapy and Behavior Change.* 3rd ed. Ed. S. L. Garfield and A. E. Bergin. New York: John Wiley, 1986.

Popper, M., and O. Mayseless. "Back to Basics: Applying a Parenting Perspective to Transformational Leadership." *The Leadership Quarterly,* 14 (1) (2003), pp. 41–66.

Porter, D. A. "Student Course Critiques: A Case Study in Total Quality in the Classroom." In *Proceedings of the 13th Biennial Psychology in Department of Defense Conference.* Colorado Springs, CO: U.S. Air Force Academy, 1992, pp. 26–30.

Porter, D. B.; M. Bird; and A. Wunder. "Competition, Cooperation, Satisfaction, and the Performance of Complex Tasks among Air Force Cadets." *Current Psychology Research and Reviews* 9, no. 4 (1991), pp. 347–54.

Porter, L. W., and E. E. Lawler, III. *Managerial Attitudes and Performance.* Homewood, IL: Dorsey, 1968.

Posthuma, R. A.; F. P. Morgeson; and M. A. Campion. "Beyond Employment Interview Validity: A Comprehensive Narrative Review of Recent Research and Trends over Time." *Personnel Psychology,* 55 (1) (2002), pp. 1–82.

Poundstone, W. "Beware the Interview Inquistion." *Harvard Business Review,* May 2003, pp. 18–19.

Powell, C., with Joe Pirsico. *My American Journey.* New York: Random House, 1995.

Price, T. L. "The Ethics of Authentic Transformational Leadership." *The Leadership Quarterly,* 14 (1) (2003), pp. 67–82.

Prince, G. M. "Creative Meetings through Power Sharing." *Harvard Business Review* 50, no. 4 (1972), pp. 47–54.

Pritchard, R. D.; J. Hollenback; P. J. DeLeo. "The Effects of Continuous and Partial Schedules of Reinforcement of Effort, Performance, and Satisfaction." *Organizational Behavior and Human Performance* 16 (1976), pp. 205–30.

Pritchard, R. D.; S. D. Jones; P. L. Roth; K. K. Stuebing; and S. E. Ekeberg. "Effects of Group Feedback, Goal Setting, and Incentives on Organizational Productivity." *Journal of Applied Psychology* 73, no. 2 (1988), pp. 337–58.

Pritchett, P. *The Employee Guide to Mergers and Acquisitions.* Dallas, TX: Pritchett Rummler-Brache, 2002.

Pritchett, P. *Firing up Commitment During Organizational Change.* Dallas, TX: Pritchett and Associates, 2001.

Pritchett, P., and R. Pound. *Smart Moves: A Crash Course on Merger Integration Management.* Pritchett and Associates, 2001.

Pugh, S. D.; J. Dietz; J. W. Wiley; and S. M. Brooks. "Driving Service Effectiveness Through Employee-Customer Linkages." *Academy of Management Executive,* 16 (4) (2002), pp. 73–81.

Pulakos, E. D., and K. N. Wexley. "The Relationship among Perceptual Similarity, Sex, and Performance Ratings in Manager-Subordinate Dyads." *Academy of Management Journal* 26 (1983), pp. 129–39.

Quaglieri, P. L., and J. P. Carnazza. "Critical Inferences and the Multidimensionality of Feedback." *Canadian Journal of Behavioral Science* 17 (1985), pp. 284–93.

Quast, L. N., and T. L. Hansen. *The Relationship between MBTI Expanded Analysis Report (EAR) Scores and Leaders' Management Behaviors.* Minneapolis, MN: Personnel Decisions International, 1996.

Quast, L. N., Hazucha, J. F., and Johnson, C. *The Leadership Effect.* Minneapolis, MN: Personnel Decisions International, 1993.

Quayle, D. "American Productivity: The Devastating Effect of Alcoholism and Drug Use." *American Psychologist* 38 (1983), pp. 454–58.

Quinn, R. E., and G. M. Spreitzer. "The Road to Empowerment: Seven Questions Every Leader Should Consider." *Organizational Dynamics,* Autumn 1997, pp. 37–49.

Quirk, M. P., and P. M. Fandt. *The Second Language of Leadership.* Mahwah, NJ: Erlbaum, 2000.

Rafferty, A. E., and M. A. Griffen. "Dimensions of Transformational Leadership: Conceptual and Empirical Extensions." *The Leadership Quarterly,* 15 (3) (2004), pp. 329–54.

Ragins, B. R., and J. L. Cotton. "Mentoring Functions and Outcomes: A Comparison of Men and Women in Formal and Informal Mentoring Relationships." *Journal of Applied Psychology* 84, no. 4 (1999), pp. 529–500.

Ragins, B. R.; J. L. Cotton; and J. S. Miller. "Marginal Mentoring: The Effects of Types of Mentor, Quality of Relationship, and Program Design of Work and Career Attitudes." *Academy of Management Journal,* 43, no. 6 (2000), pp. 1177–94.

Read, P. P. *Alive.* New York: J. B. Lippincott, 1974.

Ree, M. J., and J. A. Earles. "G Is to Psychology What Carbon Is to Chemistry: A Reply to Sternberg and Wagner, McClelland, and Calfee." *Current Directions in Psychological Science* 2, no. 1 (1993), pp. 11–12.

———. "Intelligence Is the Best Predictor of Job Performance." *Current Directions in Psychological Science* 1, no. 3 (1992), pp. 86–89.

Reiter-Palmon, R., and J. J. Illies. "Leadership and Creativity: Understanding Leadership from a Creative Problem Solving Perspective." *The Leadership Quarterly,* 15 (1) (2004), pp. 55–77.

Remland, M. S. "Developing Leadership Skills in Nonverbal Communication: A Situation Perspective." *Journal of Business Communication* 18, no. 3 (1981), pp. 17–29.

Rest, J. "Research on Moral Judgment in College Students." In *Approaches to Moral Development, New Research and Emerging Themes.* Ed. A. Garrod. New York: Teachers College Press, Columbia University, 1993, pp. 201–13.

Rice, R. W. "Construct Validity of the Least Preferred Co-Worker Score." *Psychological Bulletin* 85 (1978), pp. 1199–1237.

Rigby, D. "Look before You Lay Off." *Harvard Business Review,* April 2002, pp. 20–21.

Riggio, R. E. "Multiple Intelligences and Leadership: An Overview." In R. E. Riggio, S. E. Murphy, and F. J. Pirozzolo (Eds.). *Multiple Intelligences and Leadership.* Mahwah, NJ: Lawrence Erlbaum Associates, 2002, pp. 1–7.

Rizzo, J. R.; R. J. House; and S. I. Lirtzman. "Role Conflict and Ambiguity in Complex Organizations." *Administrative Science Quarterly* 15 (1970), pp. 150–63.

Roach, C. F., and O. Behling. "Functionalism: Basis for an Alternate Approach to the Study of Leadership." In *Leaders and Managers: International Perspectives on Managerial Behavior and Leadership.* Ed. J. G. Hunt, D. M. Hosking, C. A. Schriesheim, and R. Stewar. Elmsford, NY: Pergamon, 1984.

Robbins, S. P. *Organizational Behavior: Concepts, Controversies, and Applications.* Englewood Cliffs, NJ: Prentice Hall, 1986.

———. *Training in Interpersonal Skills.* Englewood Cliffs, NJ: Prentice Hall, 1989.

Roberts, N. C., and R. T. Bradley. "Limits of Charisma." In *Charismatic Leadership: The Elusive Factor in Organizational Effectiveness.* Ed. J. A. Conger and R. N. Kanungo. San Francisco: Jossey-Bass, 1988, pp. 253–75.

Robie, C.; K. Kanter; D. L. Nilsen; and J. Hazucha. *The Right Stuff: Understanding Cultural Differences in Leadership Performance.* Minneapolis, MN: Personnel Decisions International, 2001.

Roethlisberger, F. J.; and W. J. Dickson. *Management and the Worker: An Account of a Research Program Conducted by the Western Electric Company, Hawthorne Works, Chicago.* Cambridge: Harvard University Press, 1939.

Rokeach, M. *The Nature of Human Values.* New York: Free Press, 1973.

Rosen, B., and T. H. Jerdee. "Influence of Subordinate Characteristics on Trust and Use of Participative Decision Strategies in a Management Simulation." *Journal of Applied Psychology* 59 (1977), pp. 9–14.

Rosenbach, W. E. "Mentoring: A Gateway to Leader Development." In *Contemporary Issues in Leadership.* 2nd ed. Ed. W. E. Rosenbach and R. L. Taylor. Boulder, CO: Westview, 1989, pp. 139–48.

Rosener, J. B. "Ways Women Lead." *Harvard Business Review* 68 (1990), pp. 119–25.

Ross, S., and G. J. Curphy. *Foundations of Leadership Executive Overview.* Presentation given to executives at Williams-Sonoma Inc., San Francisco, April 24, 2000.

Ross, S. M., and L. R. Offermann. "Transformational Leaders: Measurement of Personality Attributes and Work Group Performance." Paper presented at the Sixth Annual Society of Industrial and Organizational Psychologists Convention, St. Louis, MO, April 1991.

Rost, J. C. *Leadership in the 21st Century.* New York; Praeger, 1991.

Rushton, J. P. "Race, IQ, and the APA Report on the Bell Curve." *American Psychologist* 52, no. 1 (1997), pp. 69–70.

Ruvolo, C. M., and R. C. Bullis. "Essentials of Cultural Change: Lessons Learned the Hard Way." *Consulting Psychology Journal,* 55 (3) (2003), pp. 155–68.

Ryan, E. M.; V. Mims; and R. Koestner. "Relation of Reward Contingency and Interpersonal Context to Intrinsic Motivation: A Review and Test Using Cognitive Evaluation Theory." *Journal of Personality and Social Psychology* 45 (1983), pp. 736–50.

Rybicki, S. L., and D. D. Klippel. "Exploring the Impact of Personality Syndromes on Job Performance." In R. T. Hogan (chair). *Personality Applications in the Workplace: Thinking outside the Dots.* Symposium presented at the 12th Annual Conference of the Society of Industrial and Organizational Psychology, St. Louis, MO, 1997.

Rynes, S. L.; J. M. Bartunek; and R. L. Daft. "Across the Great Divide: Knowledge Creation and Transfer between Practitioners and Academics." *Academy of Management Journal* 44, no. 2 (2001), pp. 340–55.

Saal, F. E., and P. A. Knight. *Industrial Organizational Psychology: Science and Practice.* Belmont, CA: Brooks/Cole, 1988.

Sadler, P. J., and G. H. Hofstede. "Leadership Styles: Preferences and Perceptions of Employees of an International Company in Different Countries." *Mens en Onderneming* 26 (1972), pp. 43–63.

Sala, F. "Executive Blind Spots: Discrepancies Between Self- and Other-Ratings." *Consulting Psychology Journal,* 55 (4) (2003), pp. 222–29.

Sala, F., and S. A. Dwight. "Predicting Executive Performance with Multirater Surveys: Whom You Ask Makes a Difference." *Consulting Psychology Journal,* 55 (3) (2003), pp. 166–72.

Sales, C. A.; E. Levanoni; and D. H. Saleh. "Satisfaction and Stress as a Function of Job Orientation, Style of Supervision, and the Nature of the Task." *Engineering Management International* 2 (1984), pp. 145–53.

Salgado, J. F. "The Five-Factor Model of Personality and Job Performance in the European Community." *Journal of Applied Psychology* 82, no. 1 (1997), pp. 30–43.

Salgado, J. F. "Predicting Job Performance Using FFM and non-FFM Personality Measures." *Journal of Occupational and Organizational Psychology*, 76 (3) (2003), pp. 323–46.

Salgado, J. F.; N. Anderson; S. Moscoso; C. Bertua; F. de Fruyt; and J. P. Rolland. "A Meta-Analytic Study of General Mental Ability Validity for Different Occupations in the European Community." *Journal of Applied Psychology*, 88 (6) (2003), pp. 1068–81.

Salovey, P., and J. D. Mayer. "Emotional Intelligence." *Imagination, Cognition, and Personality* 9 (1990), pp. 185–211.

Sandal, G. M.; I. M. Endresen; R. Vaernes; and H. Ursin. "Personality and Coping Strategies during Submarine Missions." *Military Psychology* 11, no. 4 (1999), pp. 381–404.

Sanford, A., and S. Garrod. *Understanding Written Language*. New York: John Wiley, 1981.

Sarason, I. "Stress, Anxiety, and Cognitive Interference: Reactions to Stress." *Journal of Personality and Social Psychology* 46 (1986), pp. 929–39.

Sarchione, C. D.; M. J. Cuttler; P. M. Muchinsky; and R. O. Nelson-Grey. "Prediction of Dysfunctional Job Behaviors among Law Enforcement Officers." *Journal of Applied Psychology* 83, no. 6 (1998), pp. 904–12.

Sashkin, M. "The Visionary Leader." In *Charismatic Leadership: The Elusive Factor in Organizational Effectiveness*. Ed. J. A. Conger and R. N. Kanungo. San Francisco: Jossey-Bass, 1988.

Sayles, L. *Leadership: What Effective Managers Really Do . . . and How They Do It*. New York: McGraw-Hill, 1979.

Scandura, T. A; G. B. Graen; and M. A. Novak. "When Managers Decide Not to Decide Autocratically: An Investigation of Leader-Member Exchange and Decision Influence." *Journal of Applied Psychology* 52 (1986), pp. 135–47.

Scarr, S. "Protecting General Intelligence: Constructs and Consequences for Interventions." In *Intelligence: Measurement, Theory, and Public Policy*. Ed. R. L. Linn. Chicago: University of Illinois Press, 1989.

Schein, E. *Career Dynamics: Matching Individual and Organizational Needs*. Reading, MA: Addison-Wesley, 1978.

Schein, E. H. *Organizational Culture and Leadership: A Dynamic View*. San Francisco: Jossey-Bass, 1985.

Schellenbarger, S. "Investors Seem Attracted to Firms with Happy Employees." *The Wall Street Journal*, March 19, 1997, p. I2.

Schlesinger, L. "Building a Family." Presentation given at The Limited Brands Leadership Meeting, Columbus, OH, May 20, 2002.

Schmidt, F. L., and J. E. Hunter. "Development of a Causal Model of Job Performance." *Current Directions in Psychological Science* 1, no. 3 (1992), pp. 89–92.

Schmidt, M. J.; J. A. Kihm; and C. Robie. "Development of a Global Measure of Personality." *Personnel Psychology* 53, no. 1 (2000), pp. 153–92.

Schmidt, W. H., and B. Z. Posner. "Values and Expectations of Federal Service Executives." *Public Administrative Review* 46 (1986), pp. 447–54.

Schnake, M. E. "Vicarious Punishment in a Work Setting." *Journal of Applied Psychology* 71 (1986), pp. 343–45.

Schneider, B.; P. J. Hanges; D. B. Smith; and A. N. Salvaggio. " Which Comes First: Employee Attitudes or Organizational Financial and Market Performance?" *Journal of Applied Psychology*, 88 (5) (2003), pp. 836–51.

Schneider, J. "The Cultural Situation as a Condition for the Condition of Fame." *American Sociology Review* 2 (1937), pp. 480–91.

Schonpflug, W. "The Noncharismatic Leader-Vulnerable." *Applied Psychology: An International Review* 44, no. 1 (1995), pp. 39–42.

Schriesheim, C. A., and A. S. DeNisi. "Task Dimensions as Moderators of the Effects of Instrumental Leadership: A Two Sample Replicated Test of Path-Goal Leadership Theory." *Journal of Applied Psychology* 66 (1981), pp. 589–97.

Schriesheim, C. A., and T. R. Hinkin. "Influence Tactics Used by Subordinates: A Theoretical and Empirical Analysis and Refinement of the Kipnis, Schmidt, and Wilkinson Subscales." *Journal of Applied Psychology* 75 (1990), pp. 246–57.

Schriesheim, C. A., and S. Kerr. "Theories and Measures of Leadership: A Critical Appraisal of Current and Future Directions." In *Leadership: The Cutting Edge*. Ed. J. G. Hunt and L. L. Larson. Carbondale: Southern Illinois University Press, 1977.

Schwartz, T. "How Do You Feel?" *Fast Company*, June 2000, pp. 297–312.

Schwarzkopf, N. *It Doesn't Take a Hero: The Autobiography of General H. Norman Schwarzkopf*. New York: Bantam Books, 1993.

Senge, P. M. *The Fifth Discipline: The Art and Practice of the Learning Organization.* New York: Doubleday/Currency, 1994.

Shalley, C. E., and L. L. Gilson. "What Leaders Need to Know: A Review of the Social and Contextual Factors That Can Foster or Hinder Creativity." *The Leadership Quarterly,* 15 (1), 2004, pp. 33–53.

Shamir, B.; M. B. Arthur; and R. J. House. "The Rhetoric of Charismatic Leadership: A Theoretical Extension, a Case Study, and Implications for Research." *Leadership Quarterly* 5 (1994), pp. 25–42.

Shamir, B.; R. J. House; and M. B. Arthur. "The Motivation Effects of Charismatic Leadership: A Self-Concept Based Theory." *Organizational Science* 4 (1993), pp. 577–94.

Shamir, B., and J. M. Howell. "Organizational and Contextual Influences on the Emergence and Effectiveness of Charismatic Leadership." *Leadership Quarterly,* 10, no. 2 (1999), pp. 257–84.

Shaw, M. *Group Dynamics: The Psychology of Small Group Dynamics.* 3rd ed. New York: McGraw-Hill, 1981.

Shephard, J. E. "Thomas Becket, Ollie North, and You." *Military Review* 71, no. 5 (1991), pp. 20–33.

Sheppard, B. H.; R. J. Lewicki; and J. W. Minton. *Organizational Justice: The Search for Fairness in the Workplace.* New York: Lexington Books, 1972.

Shils, E. "Charisma, Order, and Status." *American Sociological Review* 30 (1965), pp. 199–213.

Shin, S. J., and J. Zhou. "Transformational Leadership, Conservation, and Creativity: Evidence from Korea." *Academy of Management Journal,* 46 (6), pp. 703–14.

Shipper, F., and C. L. Wilson. "The Impact of Managerial Behaviors on Group Performance, Stress, and Commitment." In *Impact of Leadership.* Ed. K. E. Clark, M. B. Clark, D. P. Campbell. Greensboro, NC: Center for Creative Leadership, 1992.

Shippmann, J. S.; R. A. Ash; M. Battista; L. Carr; L. D. Eyde; B. Hesketh; J. Kehoe; K. Pearlman; E. P. Prien; and J. I. Sanchez. "The Practice of Competency Modeling." *Personnel Psychology* 53, no. 3 (2000), pp. 703–40.

Shostrom, E. L. *Man, the Manipulator.* New York: Bantam, 1967.

Siegall, M., and L. L. Cummings. "Task Role Ambiguity, Satisfaction, and the Moderating Effect of Task Instruction Source." *Human Relations* 39 (1986), pp. 1017–32.

Simoneit, M. *Grundris de Charakterologischen Diagnostik.* Leipzig: Teubner, 1944.

Simons, T., and Q. Roberson. "Why Managers Should Care about Fairness: The Effects of Aggregate Justice Perceptions on Organizational Outcomes." *Journal of Applied Psychology,* 88 (3) (2003), pp. 432–43.

Simpson, W. G., and T. C. Ireland. "Managerial Excellence and Shareholder Returns." *American Association of Individual Investors Journal* 9 (1987), pp. 4–8.

Sirota Consulting. *Establishing the Linkages between Employee Attitudes, Customer Attitudes, and Bottom-Line Results.* Chicago: Author, 1998.

Skinner, B. F. *The Behavior of Organisms.* New York: Appleton-Century-Crofts, 1938.

Slater, R. *Jack Welch and the GE Way.* New York: McGraw-Hill Professional Publishing, 1998.

Sloane, E. B.; S. A. Hezlett; N. R. Kuncel; and M. R. Systma. "Performance, Potential, and Peril: What It Takes to Succeed at the Top." Paper presented at the 11th Annual Conference of the Society for Industrial and Organizational Psychology, San Diego, CA, April 1996.

Slovic, P., and B. Fischoff. "On the Psychology of Experimental Surprises." *Journal of Experimental Social Psychology* 22 (1977), pp. 544–51.

Smith, F. J.; K. D. Scott; and C. L. Hulin. "Trends in Job-Related Attitudes in Managerial and Professional Employees." *Academy of Management Journal* 20 (1977), pp. 454–60.

Smith, K. W.; E. Salas; and M. T. Brannick. "Leadership Style as a Predictor of Teamwork Behavior: Setting the Stage by Managing Team Climate." Paper presented at the Ninth Annual Conference of the Society for Industrial and Organizational Psychology, Nashville, TN, 1994.

Smith, L. "The Executive's New Coach." *Fortune,* December 27, 1993.

Smither, J. W.; M. London; R. Flautt; Y. Vargas; and I. Kucine. "Can Working with an Executive Coach Improve Multisource Feedback Ratings over Time? A Quasi-Experimental Field Study." *Personnel Psychology,* 56 (1) (2003), pp. 23–44.

Smithey-Fulmer, I.; B. Gerhart; and K. S. Scott. "Are the 100 Best Better? An Empirical Investigation of the Relationship between Being a "Great Place to Work" and Firm Performance." *Personnel Psychology,* 56 (4) (2003), pp. 965–93.

Snyder, N. H.; J. J. Dowd; and D. M. Houghton. *Vision, Values, and Courage.* New York: Free Press, 1994.

Snyder, R. A., and J. H. Morris. "Organizational Communication and Performance." *Journal of Applied Psychology* 69 (1984), pp. 461–65.

Solomon, R. L. "Punishment." *American Psychologist* 19 (1964), pp. 239–53.

Sorcher, M., and J. Brant. "Are You Picking the Right Leaders?" *Harvard Business Review,* February 2002, pp. 78–86.

Sosik, J. J.; B. J. Avolio; and D. I. Jung. "Beneath the Mask: Examining the Relationship of Self-Presentation and Impression Management to Charismatic Leadership." *The Leadership Quarterly,* 13 (3) (2002), pp. 217–42

Spiller, G. "The Dynamics of Greatness." *Sociological Review* 21 (1929), pp. 218–32.

Spitzberg, I. J. "Paths of Inquiry into Leadership." *Liberal Education* 73, no. 2 (1987), pp. 24–28.

Spreitzer, G. M. "Psychological Empowerment in the Workplace: Dimensions, Measurement, and Validation." *Academy of Management Journal* 38, no. 5 (1995), pp. 1442–65.

Stahl, M. J. "Achievement, Power, and Managerial Motivation: Selecting Managerial Talent with the Job Choice Exercise." *Personnel Psychology* 36 (1983), pp. 775–89.

Staines, G. L., and R. P. Quinn. "American Workers Evaluate the Quality of Their Jobs." *Monthly Labor Review* 102, no. 1 (1979), pp. 3–12.

Stajkovic, A. D., and F. Luthans. "Differential Effects of Incentive Motivators on Performance." *Academy of Management Journal* 44, no. 3 (2001), 580–90.

Stamps, D. "Are We Smart for Our Jobs?" *Training,* April 1996, pp. 44–50.

Staw, B. M. "Organizational Behavior: A Review and Reformulation of the Field's Outcome Variables." *Annual Review of Psychology* 35 (1984), pp. 627–66.

Steinberg, A. G., and D. M. Foley. "Mentoring in the Army: From Buzzword to Practice." *Military Psychology* 11, no. 4 (1999), pp. 365–380.

Steiner, I. D. *Group Process and Productivity.* New York: Academic Press, 1972.

Steinmetz, J.; J. Blankenship; L. Brown; D. Hall; and G. Miller. *Managing Stress Before It Manages You.* Palo Alto, CA: Bull, 1980.

Sternberg, R. J. *Beyond IQ: A Triarchic Theory of Human Intelligence.* New York: Cambridge University Press, 1985.

———. "A Broad View of Intelligence: The Theory of Successful Intelligence." *Journal of Consulting Psychology,* 55 (3) (2003b), pp. 139–54.

———. "Creativity as a Decision." *American Psychologist,* May 2002, p. 376.

———. "The Concept of Intelligence: Its Role in Lifelong Learning and Success." *American Psychologist* 52, no. 10 (1997), pp. 1030–37.

———. "What Is the Common Thread of Creativity? Its Dialectical Relationship to Intelligence and Wisdom." *American Psychologist* 56, no. 4 (2001), pp. 360–62.

———. "WICS: A Model of Leadership in Organizations." *Academy of Management: Learning and Education,* 2 (4) (2003a), pp. 386–401.

Sternberg, R. J., and N. K. Dees. "Creativity for the New Millenium." *American Psychologist* 56, no. 4 (2001), p. 332.

Sternberg, R. J., and E. L. Grigorenko. "Are Cognitive Styles Still in Style?" *American Psychologist* 51, no. 7 (1996), pp. 677–88.

Sternberg, R. J., and T. I. Lubart. "Investing in Creativity." *American Psychologist* 52, no. 10 (1997), pp. 1046–50.

Sternberg, R. J.; R. K. Wagner; W. M. Williams; and J. A. Horvath. "Testing Common Sense." *American Psychologist* 50, no. 11 (1995), pp. 912–927.

Stock, G. *The Book of Questions: Business, Politics, and Ethics.* New York: Workman Publishing, 1991.

Stogdill, R. M. "Group Productivity, Drive, and Cohesiveness." *Organizational Behavior and Human Performance* 8 (1972), pp. 26–43.

———. *Handbook of Leadership.* New York: Free Press, 1974.

———. *Individual Behavior and Group Achievement.* New York: Oxford University Press, 1959.

———. "Personal Factors Associated with Leadership: A Review of the Literature." *Journal of Psychology* 25 (1948), pp. 35–71.

Stone, A. "Army Sees Leaders of the Future Leaving Today." *USA Today,* April 18, 2000, p. 10A.

Stone, D. L.; H. G. Gueutal; and B. MacIntosh. "The Effects of Feedback Sequence and Expertise of Rater of Perceived Feedback Accuracy." *Personal Psychology* 37 (1984), pp. 487–506.

Strange, J. M., and M. D. Mumford. "The Origins of Vision: Charismatic versus Ideological Leadership." *The Leadership Quarterly,* 13 (4) (2002), pp. 343–78.

Strasser, S.; R. C. Dailey; and T. S. Bateman. "Attitudinal Moderators and Effects of Leaders' Punitive Behavior." *Psychological Reports* 49 (1981), pp. 695–98.

Strauss, G. "Workers Hone the Fine Art of Revenge: Acts of Violence, Harassment toward Boss on Rise in Corporate World." *Denver Post,* August 24, 1998, p. 6E.

Strube, M. J., and J. E. Garcia. "A Meta-Analytic Investigation of Fielder's Contingency Model of Leadership Effectiveness." *Psychological Bulletin* 90 (1981), pp. 307–21.

Sutherland, E. *Bosses Encouraged to Play Nice.* Minneapolis, MN: Personnel Decisions International, 2000.

Sutton, C. D., and R. W. Woodman. "Pygmalion Goes to Work: The Effects of Supervisor Expectations in the Retail Setting." *Journal of Applied Psychology* 74 (1989), pp. 943–50.

Swan, M., and V. Mills. "Building Impact and Influence Through a Client-Centered Approach." Presentation given at the Society of Consulting Psychology Mid-Winter Conference, Pasedena, CA, February 2004.

Tanoff, G. F., and Barlow, C. B. "Leadership and Followership: Same Animal, Different Spots?" *Consulting Psychology Journal: Practice and Research,* Summer 2002, 157–65.

Taylor, H. L. *Delegate: The Key to Successful Management.* New York: Warner Books, 1989.

Tellegen, A.; D. T. Lykken; T. J. Bouchard; K. J. Wilcox; N. L. Segal; and S. Rich. "Personality Similarity in Twins Reared Apart and Together." *Journal of Personality and Social Psychology* 54 (1988), pp. 1031–39.

Tepper, B. J. "Consequences of Abusive Supervision." *Academy of Management Journal* 43, no. 2 (2000), pp. 178–90.

Tepper, B. J., and E. C. Taylor. "Relationships among Supervisors' and Subordinates' Procedural Justice Perceptions and Organizational Citizenship Behaviors." *Academy of Management Journal,* 46 (1) (2003), pp. 97–105.

Tepper, B. J.; M. K. Duffy; J. Hoobler; and M. D. Ensley. "Moderators of the Relationships between Coworkers' Organizational Citizenship Behaviors and Fellow Employees' Attitudes." *Journal of Applied Psychology,* 89 (3) (2004), pp. 455–65.

Terborg, J. R.; C. H. Castore; and J. A. DeNinno. "A Longitudinal Field Investigation of the Impact of Group Composition on Group Performance and Cohesion." Paper presented at the annual meeting of the Midwestern Psychological Association, Chicago, 1975.

Tett, R. P., and D. D. Burnett. "A Personality Trait-Based Interactionalist Model of Job Performance." *Journal of Applied Psychology,* 88 (3) (2003), pp. 500–17.

Tett, R. P.; H. A. Guterman; A. Bleier; and P. J. Murphy. "Development and Content Validation of a 'Hyperdimensional' Taxonomy of Managerial Competence." *Human Performance* (in press).

Tett, R. P.; D. N. Jackson; M. Rothstein; J. R. Reddon. "Meta-Analysis of Personality-Job Performance Relations: A Reply on Ones, Mount, Barrick, and Hunter, 1994" *Personnel Psychology* 47 (1994), pp. 157–79.

Thayer, P. W. "The Myers-Briggs Type Indicator and Enhancing Human Performance." Report prepared for the Committee on Techniques for the Enhancement of Human Performance of the National Academy of Sciences, 1988.

Thomas, D. A. "The Truth about Mentoring Minorities: Race Matters." *Harvard Business Review,* April 2001, pp. 98–111.

Thomas, K. W. "Conflict and Conflict Management." In *Handbook of Industrial and Organizational Psychology.* Ed. M. D. Dunnette. Chicago: Rand McNally, 1976.

———. "Toward Multidimensional Values in Teaching: The Example of Conflict Management." *Academy of Management Review* 2, no. 3 (1977), pp. 484–90.

Thomas, K. W.; and W. H. Schmidt. "A Survey of Managerial Interests with Respect to Conflict." *Academy of Management Journal* 19 (1976), pp. 315–18.

Thurstone, L. L. "The Factors of the Mind." *Psychological Review* 41 (1934), pp. 1–32.

Tichy, N. M., and E. Cohen. *The Leadership Engine: How Winning Companies Build Leaders at Every Level.* New York: HarperCollins, 1997.

Tichy, N. M., and M. A. Devanna. *The Transformational Leader.* New York: John Wiley, 1986.

Tierney, P., and S. M. Farmer. "Creative Self-Efficacy: Potential Antecedents and Relationship to Creative Performance." *Academy of Management Journal,* 45 (6) (2002), pp. 1137–48.

Tierney, P.; S. M. Farmer; and G. B. Graen. "An Examination of Leadership and Employee Creativity: The Relevance of Traits and Relationships." *Personnel Psychology* 52, no. 3 (1999), pp. 591–620.

Tjosvold, D. "Stress Dosage for Problem Solvers." *Working Smart,* August 1995, p. 5.

Toegel, G., and J. A. Conger. "360–Degree Assessment: Time for Reinvention." *Academy of Management Learning and Education,* 2 (3), pp. 297–311.

Tolman, E. C. *Purposeful Behavior in Animals and Men.* New York: Appleton-Century-Crofts, 1932.

Tornow, W. W., and M. London. *Maximizing the Value of 360-Degree Feedback.* San Francisco, CA: Jossey-Bass, 1998.

Tosi, H. L.; V. F. Misangyi; A. Fanelli; D. A. Waldman; and F. J. Yammarino. "CEO Charisma, Compensation, and Firm Performance." *The Leadership Quarterly,* 15 (3) (2004), pp. 405–20.

Towler, A. J. "Effects of Charismatic Influence Training on Attitudes, Behavior, and Performance." *Personnel Psychology,* 56 (2), pp. 363–82.

Trautman, N. *Integrity Leadership.* Longwood FL: National Institute of Ethics, 1998.

Treacy, M., and F. Wiersma. *The Discipline of Market Leaders.* Reading, MA: Perseus Books, 1997.

Trevino, L. K. "The Social Effects of Punishment in Organizations: A Justice Perspective." *Academy of Management Review* 17 (1992), pp. 647–76.

Trevino, L. K., and S. A. Youngblood. "Bad Apples in Bad Barrels: A Causal Analysis of Ethical Decision-Making Behavior." *Journal of Applied Psychology* 75 (1990), pp. 378–85.

Trice, H. M., and J. M. Beyer. "Charisma and Its Routinization in Two Social Movement Organizations." In *Research in Organizational Behavior.* Vol. 8. Ed. B. M. Staw and L. L. Cummings. Greenwich, CN: JAI Press, 1986.

Tsui, A. "A Role Set Analysis of Managerial Reputation." *Organizational Behavior and Human Performance* 34 (1984), pp. 64–96.

Tucker, R. C. "The Theory of Charismatic Leadership." *Daedalus* 97 (1968), pp. 731–56.

Tuckman, B. W. "Developmental Sequence in Small Groups." *Psychological Bulletin* 63 (1965), pp. 384–99.

Turner, N.; J. Barling; O. Eptiropaki; V. Butcher; and C. Milner. "Transformational Leadership and Moral Reasoning." *Journal of Applied Psychology,* 87 (2) (2002), pp. 304–11.

Twenge, J. M. "Changes in Masculine and Feminine Traits over Time: A Meta-analysis." *Sex Roles,* 36 (1997), 305–25.

Twenge, J. M. "Changes in Women's Assertiveness in Response to Status and Roles: A Cross-Temporal Meta-analysis," 1931–1993. *Journal of Personality and Social Psychology,* 81, 133–145 (2001).

Udell, J. G. "An Empirical Test of Hypotheses Relating to Span of Control." *Administrative Science Quarterly* 12 (1967), pp. 420–39.

Uecker, M. E., and B. L. Dilla. "Mentoring as a Leadership Development Tool in the United States Air Force." *Proceedings of the 26th Annual Meeting of the Military Testing Association,* Munich, Germany, 1985, pp. 423–28.

Ulrich, D.; J. Zenger; and N. Smallwood. *Results-Based Leadership.* Boston: Harvard Business School Press, 1999.

Ungson, G. R.; C. James; and B. H. Spicer. "The Effects of Regulatory Agencies on Organizations in Wood Products and High Technology/Electronics Organizations." *Academy of Management Journal* 28 (1985), pp. 426–45.

U.S. Bureau of Labor Statistics. *Labor force statistics derived from the current population survey: A databook* (Vol. 1: Bulletin 2096). Washington, DC: U.S. Department of Labor, 1982.

U.S. Bureau of Labor Statistics. "Household data: Monthly household data (Table A-19: Employed persons by occupation, sex and age)" (2002). Retrieved November 24, 2002 from ftp://ftp.bls.gov/pub/auppl/empsit.cpseea19.txt.

Van der Zee, K. I.; A. B. Bakker; and P. Bakker. "Why Are Structured Interviews So Rarely Used in Personnel Selection?" *Journal of Applied Psychology,* 87 (1), 2002, pp. 176–84.

Van Velsor, E., and J. B. Leslie. "Why Executives Derail: Perspectives across Time and Cultures." *Academy of Management Executive* 9, no. 4 (1995), pp. 62–71.

Vecchio, R. P. "Assessing the Validity of Fiedler's Contingency Model of Leadership Effectiveness: A Closer Look at Strube and Garcia." *Psychological Bulletin* 93 (1983), pp. 404–08.

———. "Predicting Worker Performance in Inequitable Settings." *Academy of Management Review* 7 (1982), pp. 103–10.

———. "Situational Leadership Theory: An Examination of a Prescriptive Theory." *Journal of Applied Psychology* 72 (1987), pp. 444–51.

Vroom, V. H. *Work and Motivation.* New York: John Wiley, 1964.

Vroom, V. H., and A. G. Jago. "Leadership and Decision Making: A Revised Normative Model." Paper presented at the Academy of Management Convention, Boston, MA, 1974.

———. *The New Theory of Leadership: Managing Participation in Organizations.* Englewood Cliffs, NJ: Prentice Hall, 1988.

Vroom, V. H., and P. W. Yetton. *Leadership and Decision Making.* Pittsburgh, PA: University of Pittsburgh Press, 1973.

Wagner, S. H.; C. P. Parker; and N. D. Christiansen. "Employees That Think and Act like Owners: Effects of Ownership Beliefs and Behaviors on Organizational Effectiveness." *Personnel Psychology,* 56 (4) (2003), pp. 847–71.

Wakin, M. M. "Ethics of Leadership." In *Military Leadership.* Ed. J. H. Buck and L. J. Korb. Beverly Hills, CA: Sage, 1981.

Waldman, D. A. "Does Working with an Executive Coach Enhance the Value of Multisource Performance Feedback?" *Academy of Management Executive,* 17 (3) (2003), pp. 146–48.

Waldman, D. A.; M. Javidan; and P. Varella. "Charismatic Leadership at the Strategic Level: A New Application of Upper Echelons Theory." *The Leadership Quarterly,* 15 (3) (2004), pp. 355–80.

Waldman, D. A.; G. G. Ramirez; R. J. House; and P. Puranam. "Does Leadership Matter? CEO Leadership Attributes and Profitability under Conditions of Perceived Environmental Uncertainty." *Academy of Management Journal,* 44, no. 1 (2001), pp. 134–43.

Walker, A. and J. W. Smither. "A Five-Year Study of Upward Feedback: What Managers Do with Their Results Matters." *Personnel Psychology* 52, no. 2 (1999), pp. 395–423.

Walker, T. G. "Leader Selection and Behavior in Small Political Groups." *Small Group Behavior* 7 (1976), pp. 363–68.

Wasylyshyn, K. M. "Executive Coaching: An Outcome Study." *Consulting Psychology Journal,* 55 (2) (2003), pp. 94–106.

Weber, J. "Managers' Moral Meaning: An Exploratory Look at Managers' Responses to the Moral Dilemmas." *Proceedings of the Academy of Management Convention,* Washington, DC, 1989, pp. 333–37.

Weber, M. *The Theory of Social and Economic Organization.* Ed. Talcott Parsons; trans. A. M. Henderson and T. Parsons. New York: Free Press, 1964.

Weiss, H. M. "Subordinate Imitation of Supervisor Behavior: The Role of Modeling in Organizational Socialization." *Organizational Behavior and Human Performance* 19 (1977), pp. 89–105.

Welbourne, T. M., and L. A. Cyr. "The Human Resource Executive Effect in Initial Public Offering Firms." *Academy of Management Journal* 42, no. 6 (1999), pp. 616–29.

Welch, J., and J. A. Byrne. *Jack: Straight from the Gut.* New York: Warner Books, 2001.

Wenzel, L. H. "Understanding Managerial Coaching: The Role of Manager Attributes and Skills in Effective Coaching." Unpublished doctoral dissertation, Colorado State University, 2000.

Weschler, D. *Weschler Adult Intelligence Scale: Manual.* New York: Psychological Corporation, 1955.

West, M. A., and N. R. Anderson. "Innovation in Top Management Teams." *Journal of Applied Psychology* 81, no. 6, (1996), pp. 680–93.

West Point Associates, the Department of Behavior Sciences and Leadership, United States Military Academy. *Leadership in Organizations.* Garden City Park, NY: Avery, 1988.

Westley, F. R., and H. Mintzberg. "Profiles of Strategic Vision: Levesque and Iacocca." In *Charismatic Leadership: The Elusive Factor in Organizational Effectiveness.* Ed. J. A. Conger and R. N. Kanungo. San Francisco: Jossey-Bass, 1988.

Wexley, K. N., and G. P. Latham. *Developing and Training Human Resources in Organizations.* Glenview, IL: Scott, Foresman, 1981.

Wheelan, S. A. *Group Processes.* Needham Heights, MA: Allyn & Bacon, 1994.

White, S. S., and E. A. Locke. "Problems with the Pygmalion Effect and Some Proposed Solutions." *Leadership Quarterly* 11, no. 3 (2000), pp. 389–416.

Whitely, W.; T. W. Dougherty; and G. F. Dreher. "The Relationship of Mentoring and Socioeconomic Origin to Managers' and Professionals' Early Career Progress." *Proceedings of the Academy of Management.* Anaheim, CA: 1988, pp. 58–62.

Wilcox, W. H. "Assistant Superintendents' Perceptions of the Effectiveness of the Superintendent, Job Satisfaction, and Satisfaction with the Superintendent's Supervisory Skills." Ph.D. dissertation, University of Missouri, Columbia, 1982.

Wiley, J., and T. Comacho. "Life-Style and Future Health: Evidence from the Alameda County Study." *Preventive Medicine* 9 (1980), pp. 1–21.

Willner, A. R. *The Spellbinders: Charismatic Political Leadership.* New Haven: Yale University Press, 1984.

Wilson, J. A., and N. S. Elman. "Organizational Benefits of Mentoring." *Academy of Management Executive* 4 (1990), pp. 88–93.

Wilson, P. R. "The Perceptual Distortion of Height as a Function of Ascribed Academic Status." *Journal of Social Psychology* 74 (1968), pp. 97–102.

Wiseman, R. *The Luck Factor.* Miramax Books (2003).

Wofford, J. C., and V. L. Goodwin. "A Cognitive Interpretation of Transformational and Transactional Leadership Theories." *Leadership Quarterly* 5 (1994), pp. 161–86.

Wolpe, H. "A Critical Analysis of Some Aspects of Charisma." *Sociological Review* 16 (1968), pp. 305–18.

Wong, C. S., and K. S. Law. "The Effects of Leader and Follower Emotional Intelligence on Performance and Attitude: An Exploratory Study." *The Leadership Quarterly,* 13 (3) (2002), pp. 243–74.

Wood, G. "The Knew-It-All-Along Effect." *Journal of Experimental Psychology: Human Perception and Performance* 4 (1979), pp. 345–53.

Woodward, J. *Industrial Organization.* London: Oxford University Press, 1965.

Xie, J. L., and G. Johns. "Job Scope and Stress: Can Job Scope Be Too High?" *Academy of Management Journal* 38, no. 5 (1995), pp. 1288–1309.

Yagil, D. "Charismatic Leadership and Organizational Hierarchy: Attribution of Charisma to Close and Distance Leaders." *Leadership Quarterly* 9, no. 2 (1998), pp. 161–76.

Yorges, S. L.; H. M. Weiss; and O. J. Strickland. "The Effect of Leader Outcomes on Influence, Attributions, and Perceptions of Charisma." *Journal of Applied Psychology,* 84, no. 3 (1999), pp. 428–36.

Yukl, G. "An Evaluation of Conceptual Weaknesses in Transformational and Charismatic Leadership Theories." *Leadership Quarterly* 10, no. 2 (1999), pp. 285–306.

———. *Leadership in Organizations.* 2nd ed. Englewood Cliffs, NJ: Prentice Hall, 1989.

———. "Reflections and Directions in Leadership Research." Paper presented at the 14th Annual Conference of the Society of Industrial and Organizational Psychologists, Atlanta, GA, May 1999.

Yukl, G. A., and D. D. Van Fleet. "Cross-Situational Multi-Method Research on Military Leader Effectiveness." *Organizational Behavior and Human Performance* 30 (1982), pp. 87–108.

———. "Theory and Research on Leadership in Organizations." In *Handbook of Industrial & Organizational Psychology.* Vol. 3. Ed. M. D. Dunnette and L. M. Hough. Palo Alto, CA: Consulting Psychologists Press, 1992, pp. 1–51.

Yukl, G. A.; R. Lepsinger; and T. Lucia. "Preliminary Report on the Development and Validation of the Influence Behavior Questionnaire." In *Impact of Leadership.* Ed. K. E. Clark, M. B. Clark, and D. P. Campbell. Greensboro, NC: Center for Creative Leadership, 1992.

Yukl, G. A.; S. Wall; and R. Lepsinger. "Preliminary Report on Validation of the Managerial Practices Survey." In *Measures of Leadership.* Ed. K. E. Clark and M. B. Clark. Greensboro, NC: Center for Creative Leadership, 1989.

Zaccaro, S. J. "Leader Resources and the Nature of Organizational Problems." *Applied Psychology: An International Review* 44, no. 1 (1995), pp. 32–36.

Zacharatos, A.; J. Barling; and E. K. Kelloway. "Development and Effects of Transformational Leadership in Adolescents." *Leadership Quarterly* 11, no. 2 (2000), pp. 211–26.

Zajonc, R. "Social Facilitation." *Science* 149 (1965), pp. 269–74.

Zaleznik, A. "Charismatic and Consensus Leaders: A Psychological Comparison." *Bulletin of the Menninger Clinic* 38 (1974), pp. 22–38.

———. "The Leadership Gap." *Washington Quarterly* 6, no. 1 (1983), pp. 32–39.

Zey, M. G. *The Mentor Connection.* Homewood, IL: Dow Jones-Irwin, 1984.

Zhou, J. "Feedback Valence, Feedback Style, Task Autonomy, and Achievement Orientation: Interactive Effects on Creative Performance." *Journal of Applied Psychology* 83, no. 2 (1998), pp. 261–76.

Zhou, J. "When the Presence of Creative Co-Workers is Related to Creativity: Role of Supervisor Close Monitoring, Developmental Feedback, and Creative Personality." *Journal of Applied Psychology,* 88 (3) (2003), pp. 413–22.

Zimbardo, P.; C. Haney; W. Banks; and D. Jafe. "The Mind Is a Formidable Jailer: A Pirandellian Prison." *New York Times Magazine,* April 8, 1973, pp. 38–60.

Name Index

Subject Index